Alphabetical Listing of Readings in *Transnational Management*, 4/e

TransnationalManagement

TEXT, CASES, AND READINGS IN CROSS-BORDER MANAGEMENT

FOURTH EDITION

Christopher A. Bartlett
Harvard Business School

Sumantra Ghoshal
London Business School

Julian Birkinshaw
London Business School

Boston   Burr Ridge, IL   Dubuque, IA   Madison, WI   New York   San Francisco   St. Louis
Bangkok   Bogotá   Caracas   Kuala Lumpur   Lisbon   London   Madrid   Mexico City
Milan   Montreal   New Delhi   Santiago   Seoul   Singapore   Sydney   Taipei   Toronto

The McGraw-Hill Companies

TRANSNATIONAL MANAGEMENT:
TEXT, CASES, AND READINGS IN CROSS-BORDER MANAGEMENT
Published by McGraw-Hill/Irwin, a business unit of The McGraw-Hill Companies, Inc., 1221 Avenue of the Americas, New York, NY, 10020. Copyright © 2004, 2000, 1995, 1992 by The McGraw-Hill Companies, Inc. All rights reserved. No part of this publication may be reproduced or distributed in any form or by any means, or stored in a database or retrieval system, without the prior written consent of The McGraw-Hill Companies, Inc., including, but not limited to, in any network or other electronic storage or transmission, or broadcast for distance learning.
Some ancillaries, including electronic and print components, may not be available to customers outside the United States.

This book is printed on acid-free paper.

The copyright on each case in this book unless otherwise noted is held by the President and Fellows of Harvard College and they are published herein by express permission. Permission requests to use individual Harvard copyrighted cases should be directed to the Permissions Editor, Harvard Business School Publishing, Boston, MA 02163.

Case material of the Harvard Graduate School of Business Administration is made possible by the cooperation of business firms and other organizations which may wish to remain anonymous by having names, quantities, and other identifying details disguised while maintaining basic relationships. Cases are prepared as the basis for class discussion rather than to illustrate either effective or ineffective handling of an administrative situation.

With respect to Ivey cases (Cases 5-4a, 5-4b, 5-4c, 5-4d, 7-3), Ivey Management Services prohibits any form of reproduction, storage or transmittal without its written permission. This material is not covered under authorization from CanCopy or any reproduction rights organization. To order copies or request permission to reproduce materials, contact Ivey Publishing, Ivey Management Services, c/o Richard Ivey School of Business, The University of Western Ontario, London, Ontario, Canada, N6A 3K7; phone (519) 661-3208, fax (519) 661-3882, email cases@ivey.uwo.ca.
One-time permission to reproduce Ivey cases granted by Ivey Management Services on February 6, 2003.

1 2 3 4 5 6 7 8 9 0 DOC/DOC 0 9 8 7 6 5 4 3

ISBN   0-07-248276-1

Publisher: *John E. Biernat*
Sponsoring editor: *Ryan Blankenship*
Developmental editor: *Tammy Higham*
Editorial coordinator: *Lindsay Harmon*
Marketing manager: *Lisa Nicks*
Project manager: *Susanne Riedell*
Production supervisor: *Gina Hangos*
Lead designer: *Pam Verros*

Supplement producer: *Vicki Laird*
Senior digital content specialist: *Brian Nacik*
Cover design: *Jenny El-Shamy*
Interior design: *© Digital Vision*
Typeface: *10/12 Times New Roman*
Compositor: *Interactive Composition Corporation*
Printer: *R. R. Donnelley*

Library of Congress Cataloging-in-Publication Data

Bartlett, Christopher A., 1943–
    Transnational management : text, cases, and readings in cross-border management /
Christopher A. Bartlett, Sumantra Ghoshal, Julian Birkinshaw.—4th ed.
        p. cm.
    Includes bibliographical references and index.
    ISBN 0–07–248276–1 (alk. paper)
    1. International business enterprises—Management   I. Ghoshal, Sumantra.   II.
Birkinshaw, Julian M.   III. Title.
HD62.4.B365 2004
658'.049—dc21

                                            2003052671

www.mhhe.com

About the Authors

Christopher Bartlett is the Thomas D. Casserly, Jr., Professor of Business Administration at Harvard Graduate School of Business Administration. He received an economics degree from the University of Queensland, Australia (1964), and both masters and doctorate degrees in business administration from Harvard University (1971 and 1979). Prior to joining the faculty of Harvard Business School, he was a marketing manager with Alcoa in Australia, a management consultant in McKinsey and Company's London office, and general manager at Baxter Laboratories' subsidiary company in France.

Since joining the faculty of Harvard Business School in 1979, his interests have focused on strategic and organizational challenges confronting managers in multinational corporations and on the organizational and managerial impact of transformational change. He served as faculty chair of the International Senior Management Program from 1990 through 1993, and as area head of the School's General Management Unit from 1995 to 1997. He was faculty chairman of HBS's international executive program, Program for Global Leadership, from 1998 to 2002.

He has published eight books, including (coauthored with Sumantra Ghoshal) *Managing Across Borders: The Transnational Solution,* reissued by Harvard Business School Press in a new edition in 1998 and named by the *Financial Times* as one of the 50 most influential business books of the century; and *The Individualized Corporation,* published by HarperBusiness in 1997, winner of the Igor Ansoff Award for the best new work in strategic management and named one of the Best Business Books for the Millennium by *Strategy + Business* magazine. Both books have been translated into multiple foreign languages. He has authored or coauthored over 50 chapters or articles which have appeared in journals such as *Harvard Business Review, Sloan Management Review, Strategic Management Journal, Academy of Management Review,* and *Journal of International Business Studies.* He has also researched and written over 100 case studies and teaching notes.

Sumantra Ghoshal is Professor of Strategic and International Management at the London Business School. He also serves as the Founding Dean of the Indian School of Business in Hyderabad, of which LBS is a partner, and as a member of The Committee of Overseers of the Harvard Business School. *Managing Across Borders: The Transnational Solution,* a book he coauthored with Christopher Bartlett, has been listed in the *Financial Times* as one of the 50 most influential management books and has been translated into nine languages. *The Differentiated Network: Organizing the Multinational Corporation for Value Creation,* a book he coauthored with Nitin Nohria, won the George Terry Book Award in 1997. *The Individualized Corporation,* coauthored with Christopher Bartlett, won the Igor Ansoff Award in 1997, and has been translated into multiple foreign languages. His last book, *Managing Radical Change,* won the Management Book of the Year award in India. With doctoral degrees from both the MIT

School of Management and Harvard Business School, Sumantra serves on the editorial boards of several academic journals and has been nominated to fellowships at the Academy of Management, the Academy of International Business, and the World Economic Forum.

Julian Birkinshaw   is Cochair and Associate Professor in the Department of Strategic and International Management at the London Business School. He received his Ph.D. from the Ivey School of Business, University of Western Ontario, and he has also worked at the University of Toronto and the Stockholm School of Economics. Professor Birkinshaw is the author of 7 books and over 40 articles in leading journals such as *Harvard Business Review, Strategic Management Journal,* and *Academy of Management Review.*

Preface

In writing this introduction to the fourth edition, it came as quite a shock to realize that it is now well over a decade ago that the first edition of *Transnational Management* was published. Over that intervening period, the challenges facing managers of large multinational corporations (MNCs) have continued to evolve. Today, for example, MNCs are making their operations in large emerging economies like China and India central to their global strategies; they are coming to grips with social responsibility questions and challenges raised by the antiglobalization movement; and they are dealing with widespread excess capacity worldwide and the threat of a prolonged period of economic slowdown in the global economy.

Although each of these challenges requires its own dedicated response, MNC managers must still understand them within a broader context of global strategy and cross-border management. The purpose of this book is to provide such a context—a conceptual framing of the interplay between the MNC, the countries in which it does business, and the competitive environment in which it operates. And even though many of the specific challenges will continue to evolve, we believe that the conceptual framework—the powerful lens through which the changes can be viewed—should be robust enough to endure. The aim of this textbook is to provide such a lens.

When we first put this book together, we wanted to present a strong point of view that would frame vigorous and engaged discussion about transnational management. The ideas and frameworks we presented were built on a combination of our own experience as MNC managers, findings from our own research on the topic, and the writings of many of our respected colleagues working in the same area. Over the next decade and three editions, the book evolved with the times. New cases, readings, and even whole chapters were added to capture some of the important emerging trends and to reflect our own evolving research interests.

As the first edition in the new Millennium, the fourth edition of *Transnational Management* gave us the opportunity to step back and review the book's overall content, framing, and structure—indeed, its entire intellectual architecture. To help with this task, it seemed like an ideal time to bring a new voice and a fresh perspective to the book, and we are delighted to welcome our good friend and colleague, Julian Birkinshaw as a coauthor. Even though the text's original point of view and conceptual framework has survived the review, Julian's insights and perspectives will be clearly seen in many of the new ideas, structure, and materials in this edition. In the remainder of this introduction, our objective is to guide the reader through the logic of the book's structural outline, and to make its point of view explicit.

■ Distinguishing Characteristics of the MNC

What makes the study of the MNC unique? The most fundamental distinction between a domestic company and an MNC derives from the social, political, and economic context in which each exists. The former operates in a single national environment where social and cultural norms, government regulations, customer tastes and preferences, and the economic and competitive context of a business tend to be fairly consistent. Although within-country local variations do exist for most of these factors, they are nowhere near as diverse or as conflicting as the differences in demands and pressures the MNC faces in its multiple host countries.

The one feature that categorically distinguishes these intercountry differences from the intracountry ones, however, is that of *sovereignty.*[1] Unlike the local or regional bodies, the nation-state generally represents the ultimate rule-making authority against whom no appeal is feasible. Consequently, the MNC faces an additional and unique element of risk: the political risk of operating in countries with different political philosophies, legal systems, and social attitudes toward private property, corporate responsibility, and free enterprise.

A second major difference relates to competitive strategy. The purely domestic company can respond to competitive challenges only within the context of its single market; the MNC can, and often must, play a much more complex competitive game. Global-scale or low-cost sourcing may be necessary to achieve competitive position, implying the need for complex cross-border logistical coordination. Furthermore, on the global chessboard, effective competitive strategy might require that the response to an attack in one country be directed to a different country—perhaps the competitor's home market. These are options and complexities a purely domestic company does not face.

Third, a purely domestic company can measure its performance in a single comparable unit—the local currency. Because the currency values fluctuate against each other, however, the MNC is required to measure results with a flexible measuring stick. In addition, it is exposed to the economic risks associated with shifts in both nominal and real exchange rates.

Finally, the purely domestic company must manage an organizational structure and management systems that reflect its product and functional variety; the MNC organization is intrinsically more complex because it must provide for management control over its product, functional, *and* geographic diversity. Furthermore, the resolution of this three-way tension must be accomplished in an organization that is divided by barriers of distance and time, and impeded by differences in language and culture.

The Management Challenge

Historically, the study of international business focused on the environmental forces, structures, and institutions that provided the context within which MNC managers had to operate. In such a macro approach, countries or industries rather than companies were the primary units of analysis. Reflecting the environment of its time, this traditional approach directed most attention to trade flows and the capital flows that defined the foreign investment patterns.

---

[1] This difference is elaborated in J. N. Behrman and R. E. Gross, *International Business and Governments: Issues and Institutions* (Columbia: University of South Carolina Press, 1990). See also J. J. Boddewyn, "Political Aspects of MNE Theory," *Journal of International Business Studies* 19, no. 3 (1988), pp. 341–63.

During the 1970s and 1980s, a new perspective on the study of international management began to emerge, with a far greater emphasis on the MNC and management behavior, rather than on global economic forces and international institutions. With the firms as the primary unit of analysis and management decisions as the key variables, these studies both highlighted and provided new insights on the management challenges associated with international operations.

This book builds on the company- and management-level perspective. More specifically, we adopt what is often called the *administrative point of view.* In other words, in order to make sense of the practice of managing the MNC, it is necessary to see the world through the eyes of the executive who is in the thick of it—whether that is the CEO of the corporation, the global account manager, the country subsidiary manager, or the frontline business manager. The most powerful way to do this is to employ cases that require decisions to be made, and most provide the reader not only with data on the business context, but also with detailed information about the characters involved, their roles, responsibilities, and personal motivations. In many instances, videos and follow-up cases lead to further insight.

We have also chosen to focus on *managerial processes* such as the entrepreneurial process (identifying and acting on new opportunities), the integrative learning process (linking and leveraging those pockets of entrepreneurial initiative), or the leadership process (articulating a vision and inspiring others to follow). It would be easy to build our structure around the traditional functions of the company—R&D, manufacturing, marketing, etc.—and many texts have done so. But we find such an approach limiting because almost all real-world problems cut across these functional boundaries. They require executives to understand all the disparate parts of the organization, and they demand integrative solutions that bring together, rather than divide, the people working in their traditional functional silos. (This is a reality reflected in the multidimensional organizations most MNCs have developed.) A process perspective is more difficult to grasp than a functional one, but ultimately it provides a more fulfilling and realistic approach to management of today's MNC.

By adopting the perspective of the MNC manager, however, we do not ignore the important and legitimate perspectives, interests, and influences of other key actors in the international operating environment. However, we do view the effects of these other key actors from the perspective of the company, and focus on understanding how the various forces they influence shape the strategic, organizational, and operational tasks of MNC managers.

▪ The Structure of the Book

The book is divided into three parts (see figure on page x). **Part One** consists of three chapters that examine the development of strategy in the MNC. In Chapter 1, we focus on the motivations that draw—or drive—companies abroad, the means by which they expand across borders, and the mind-sets of those who built the worldwide operations. Understanding what we call a company's "administrative heritage" is important because it shapes both the current configuration of assets and capabilities and the cognitive orientations of managers toward future growth—attitudes that can either enable or constrain future growth.

In Chapter 2, we examine the political, economic, and social forces that shape the business environment in which the MNC operates. In particular, the chapter explores the tension created by political demands to be responsive to national differences, economic pressures to be globally integrated, and the growing competitive need to develop and diffuse worldwide innovation and learning.

In Chapter 3, the focus shifts from the global business environment to MNCs' competitive responses to those external pressures. Building on the themes developed in Chapter 2, we examine the various approaches an MNC can use to generate competitive advantage in its international context. We identify three traditional strategic approaches—global, international and multinational—each of which focuses on a different source of competitive advantage. We then go on to describe the transnational strategy, which combines the benefits of the other three models.

Part Two changes the focus from the MNC's strategic imperatives to the organizational capabilities required to deliver them. Chapter 4 examines the organizational structures and systems that need to be put in place to be effective in a complex and dynamic world. Mirroring the three traditional strategic approaches, we explore three organizational models that all appear to be evolving toward the integrated network form required to manage transnational strategies.

Chapter 5 focuses on one of the most important processes to be developed in a transnational organization. The need to manage effective cross-border knowledge transfer and worldwide learning is creating new organizational demands, and in this chapter, we explore how such processes are built and managed.

Then, in Chapter 6 we lift our organizational analysis up a level to examine the boundary-spanning structures and processes needed to create alliances and interfirm networks in a global context. In this chapter, we explore how such partnerships can be built and managed to develop strategic capabilities that may not be available inside any single MNC.

Part Three focuses on the management challenges of operating a successful MNC. In Chapter 7, the focus is on those who must implement the transnational strategies, operate within the integrated network organizations, and above all, deliver the results. This chapter allows us to look at the world through the eyes of frontline country subsidiary managers, and shows how their actions can have important implications for the competitiveness of the entire corporation.

Finally, in Chapter 8, we address the broad themes of renewal and change in the MNC, focusing in particular on how the roles and responsibilities of key managers continue to evolve. Based on our current research interests, this chapter is positioned in terms of emerging challenges facing large MNCs. But rather than presenting a rigid set of predictions, we present this concluding section as a point of departure for provocative discussions about future directions of MNCs and the management challenges that might be implied. After all, it is the current generation of students who will shape the future of the transnational company.

In order to keep this book current, we have added a large number of new case studies, some written by ourselves and some by colleagues (see below). However, it is worth noting that we have retained a few older cases, notably Caterpillar Tractor and Komatsu. Despite their age, these two cases continue to be very widely used, and the issues they raise continue to be important. So we have kept them in the collection as "classic" cases.

Acknowledgments

Once again, the book has benefited from the insights and comments of many people. First, we would like to thank our faculty colleagues at hundreds of institutions around the world who have adopted this book, and particularly those who have taken the trouble to provide use with specific feedback and suggestions for its improvement.

Next, we owe an enormous debt of gratitude to the researchers and authors who have contributed new cases and/or articles to this edition. New cases were provided by Debora Spar, Tarun Khanna, Joe DiStefano, Tima Bansal, Harry Korine, George Yip, and Mike Yoshino. Similarly, new articles incorporate the interesting and important recent research of C. K. Prahalad, Kenneth Lieberthal, David Arnold, Omar Toulan, Neil Hood, Lynda Gratton, Yves Doz, Jose Santos, and Peter Williamson. To all of them we offer our sincere thanks.

We must also acknowledge the coordination task undertaken by our respective administrative assistants who worked over many months to coordinate the flow of manuscript documents back and forth between London, Boston, and Sydney. To Andrea Truax and Sharon Wilson, we give our heartfelt thanks for helping us through the long and arduous revision process. To Ryan Blankenship, our sponsoring editor, and Tammy Higham and Lindsay Harmon, our editorial coordinators, at McGraw-Hill, we thank you for your patience and tolerance through this long process, and look forward to a long a productive working relationship. And to Jennifer Roche and Craig Beytien, our previous sponsoring editors at McGraw-Hill, we owe the greatest vote of thanks for their continued support of this book.

Despite the best efforts of all the contributors, however, we must accept responsibility for the shortcomings of the book that remain. Our only hope is that they are outweighed by the value you find in these pages and the exciting challenges they represent in the constantly changing field of transnational management.

Christopher A. Bartlett
Sumantra Ghoshal
Julian Birkinshaw

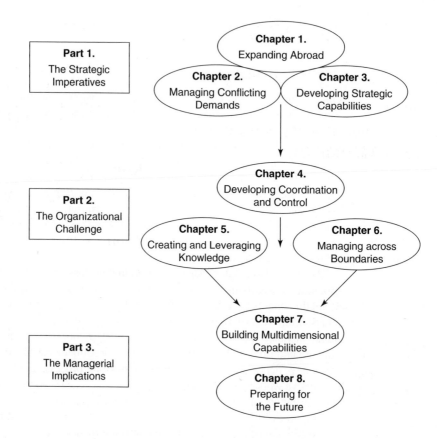

Contents

Chapter 5

*Creating and Leveraging Knowledge:
The Worldwide Learning Challenge*   456

Chapter 6

*Managing across Boundaries: The
Collaborative Challenge*   556

Part 3   The Managerial Implications

Chapter 7

*Building Multidimensional
Capabilities: The Management
Challenge*   666

Chapter 8

Preparing for the Future: Evolution of the Transnational   756

Cases

Readings

Index   840

CHAPTER 1

Expanding Abroad:
Motivations, Means, and Mentalities

This book focuses on the management challenges associated with developing strategies and managing the operations of companies whose activities stretch across national boundaries. Clearly, operating in an international rather than a domestic arena presents the manager with many new opportunities. Having worldwide operations not only gives a company access to new markets and specialized resources, it also opens up new sources of information and knowledge and broadens the options of strategic moves the company might make in competing with its domestic and international rivals. However, with all these new opportunities come the challenges of managing strategy, organization, and operations that are innately more complex, diverse, and uncertain.

In this introductory chapter, we provide a conceptual baseline and a historical backdrop for the more detailed discussions of these management opportunities and challenges that run through the rest of the book. Our starting point is to focus on the dominant vehicle of internationalization, the multinational corporation (MNC), and briefly review its role and influence in the global economy.[1] Next, we examine the motivations that led such companies to expand abroad, and the process of internationalization that they followed. We are then ready to review some of the typical attitudes and mentalities that shape the actions of managers in MNCs and suggest how these attitudes and mentalities evolve as their offshore operations progress from the state of initial investments to a fully integrated worldwide network of affiliates.

The MNC: Definition, Scope, and Influence

An economic historian could trace the origins of international business back to the seafaring traders of Greece and Egypt, through the merchant traders of medieval Venice and the great British and Dutch trading companies of the 17th and 18th centuries. By the 19th century, the newly emerged capitalists in industrialized Europe began investing in the less-developed areas of the world (including the United States), but particularly within the vast empires held by Britain, France, Holland, and Germany.

---

[1]Such companies are referred to variously—and often interchangeably—as *multinational, international,* and *global corporations.* In later chapters, we want to give each of those terms specific different meanings, but will adopt the widely used MNC abbreviation in the broader, more general sense in referring to all companies whose operations extend across national borders.

Definition

In terms of the working definition we use, few if any of these entities through history could be called true MNCs. Most of the traders would be excluded by our first qualification, which requires that an MNC have *substantial direct investment* in foreign countries, not just an export business. And most of the companies with international operations in the 19th century would be excluded by our second criterion, which requires that they be engaged in the *active management* of these offshore assets rather than simply holding them in a passive financial portfolio.

Thus, although companies that source their raw materials offshore, license their technologies abroad, export their products into foreign markets, or even hold minority equity positions in overseas ventures without any management involvement may regard themselves as "international," by our definition they are not true MNCs unless they have substantial direct investment in foreign countries *and* actively manage those operations and regard those operations as integral parts of the company both strategically and organizationally.

Scope

Under our definition, the MNC is a very recent phenomenon, with the vast majority developing only in the post–World War II years. However, their motivations for international expansion and the nature of their offshore activities have evolved significantly over this relatively short period, and we explore some of these changes later in this chapter.

It is interesting to observe how the United Nations has changed its definition of the MNC as these companies grew in size and importance.[2] In 1973, it defined such an enterprise as one "which controls assets, factories, mines, sales offices, and the like in two or more countries." By 1984, it had changed the definition to

> An enterprise (a) comprising entities in two or more countries, regardless of the legal form and fields of activity of those entities, (b) which operates under a system of decision-making permitting coherent policies and a common strategy through one or more decision-making centers, (c) in which the entities are so linked, by ownership or otherwise, that one or more of them may be able to exercise a significant influence over the activities of the others, and, in particular, to share knowledge, resources, and responsibilities with others.

In essence, the changing definition highlights the importance of strategic and organizational integration and, thereby, *management integration* of operations located in different countries as the key differentiating characteristics of an MNC. The resources committed to those units can just as well take the form of skilled people or research equipment as plant and machinery or computer hardware. What really differentiates the MNC is that it creates an internal organization to carry out key cross-border tasks and transactions internally rather than depending on trade through the open markets. This

---

[2]The generic term for companies operating across national borders in most UN studies is the *transnational corporation* (TNC). Because we will use that term very specifically, we will continue to define the general form of organizations with international operations as MNCs.

new definition also moves away from traditional ownership patterns between the parent company and its worldwide operations to a new and varied set of financial, legal, and contractual relationships with different foreign affiliates. With this understanding, our definition of MNCs includes American Express, McKinsey and Company, and Fuji Bank just as well as IBM, Unilever, and Hitachi.

MNC Influence in the Global Economy

Most frequent international business travelers have had an experience like the following. She arrives on her British Airways flight, rents a Toyota at Hertz, and drives to the downtown Hilton hotel. In her room, she flips on the Sony TV, and absent-mindedly gazes out at the neon signs flashing "Coca-Cola," and "Canon," and "BMW." The latest episode of *Friends* is flickering on the screen when room service delivers dinner along with the bottle of Perrier she ordered. All of a sudden, a feeling of disorientation engulfs her. Is she in Sydney, Singapore, Stockholm, or Seattle? Her surroundings and points of reference over the past few hours have provided few clues.

Such experiences, more than any data, provide the best indication of the enormous influence of MNCs in the global economy. As the cases and articles in this book will show, few sectors of the economy and few firms—not even those that are purely domestic in their operations—are free from this pervasive influence. Collectively, MNCs account for over 40 percent of the world's manufacturing output and almost a quarter of world trade. About 85 percent of the world's automobiles, 70 percent of computers, 35 percent of toothpaste, and 65 percent of soft drinks are produced and marketed by MNCs.

Not all MNCs are large, but most large companies in the world are MNCs. In fact, about 450 companies with annual revenues in excess of $1 billion account for over 80 percent of the total investment made by all companies outside their home countries. A different perspective on their size and potential impact is provided by Table 1-1, which

Table 1-1   Comparison of Top 10 MNCs and Selected Countries: 2000

Company	Value-Added 2000	Country	Value-Added 2000
Exxon Mobil	$63 billion	United States	$9,810 billion
General Motors	$56 billion	Japan	$4,765 billion
Ford Motor	$44 billion	Germany	$1,866 billion
DaimlerChrysler	$42 billion	Chile	$71 billion
General Electric	$39 billion	Pakistan	$62 billion
Toyota Motor	$38 billion	New Zealand	$51 billion
Royal Dutch/Shell	$36 billion	Hungary	$46 billion
Siemens	$32 billion	Romania	$37 billion
BP	$30 billion	Morocco	$32 billion
Wal-Mart	$30 billion	Vietnam	$31 billion

Note: "Value-added" refers to GDP for countries, and to the sum of salaries, pretax profits, and depreciation and amortization for companies.
Source: World Development Report published by The United Nations Conference on Trade and Development.

compares the overall value-added of the largest 10 MNCs with the GDPs of selected countries. According to the 2002 World Investment Report, the measure of company value-added (which is the sum of salaries, pretax profits, amortization, and depreciation) provides a more meaningful comparison with country GDP than simply looking at a company's gross revenues. By using this measure, it is clear that the world's largest MNCs are equivalent in their economic importance to such medium-sized economies as Chile, Pakistan, and New Zealand. They have considerable influence on the global economy, employ a high percentage of business graduates, and pose the most complex strategic and organizational challenges for their managers. For the same reasons, they will provide the focus for much of our attention in this book.

■ The Motivations: Pushes and Pulls to Internationalize

What motivates companies to expand their operations internationally? Although occasionally the motives may be entirely idiosyncratic, such as the desire of the CEO to spend time in Mexico or in Europe, an extensive body of research suggests some more-systematic patterns.

Traditional Motivations

Among the earliest motivations that drove companies to invest abroad was the need to *secure key supplies.* Aluminum producers needed to ensure their supply of bauxite, tire companies went abroad to develop rubber plantations, and oil companies wanted to open up new fields in Canada, the Middle East, and Venezuela. By the early part of this century, Standard Oil, Alcoa, Goodyear, Anaconda Copper, and International Nickel were among the largest of the emerging MNCs.

Another strong trigger for internationalization could be described as *market-seeking* behavior. This motivation was particularly strong in companies that had some intrinsic advantage, typically related to their technology or their brand recognition, that gave them some competitive advantage in offshore markets. Although their initial moves were often opportunistic, many companies eventually realized that additional sales allowed them to exploit economies of scale and scope, thereby providing a source of competitive advantage over their domestic rivals. This was a particularly strong motive for some of the European multinationals whose small home markets were insufficient to support the volume-intensive manufacturing processes that were sweeping through industries from food and tobacco to chemicals and automobiles. Companies like Nestlé, Bayer, and Ford expanded internationally primarily in search of new markets.

Another traditional and important trigger of internationalization was the desire to *access low-cost factors* of production. Particularly as tariff barriers declined in the 1960s, many U.S. and European countries for whom labor represented a major cost found that their products were at a competitive disadvantage compared to imports. In response, a number of companies in clothing, electronics, household appliances, watch-making, and other such industries established offshore sourcing locations for producing components or even complete product lines. Soon it became clear that labor was not the only productive factor that could be sourced more economically overseas. For example, the availability of lower-cost capital (perhaps through a government investment subsidy) also became a strong force for internationalization.

These three motives (or two, if we ignore the historical differences and combine securing supplies and accessing low-cost factors into a single resource-seeking motive) were the main traditional driving force behind the overseas expansion of MNCs. The ways in which these motives interacted to push companies—particularly those from the United States—to become MNCs are captured in the well-known product cycle theory developed by Professor Raymond Vernon.[3]

This theory suggests that the starting point for the internationalization process is typically an innovation that a company creates in its home country. In the first phase of exploiting the development, the company—let's assume it is in the United States—will build production facilities in its home market not only because this is where its main customer base is located, but also because of the need to maintain close linkages between research and production in this phase of the development cycle. In this early stage, some demand may also be created in other developed countries—in European countries, for example—where consumer needs and market development are similar to the United States. These requirements normally would be met out of home production, thereby generating exports for the United States.

As the product matures and production processes become standardized, the company enters a new stage. By this time, demand in the European countries may have become quite sizable and export sales, from being a marginal side benefit, are now an important part of the revenues from the new business. Furthermore, competitors will probably begin to see the growing demand for the new product as a potential opportunity to establish themselves in markets served by exports. To prevent or counteract such competition and also to meet the foreign demand more effectively, the innovating company typically sets up production facilities in the importing countries, thereby making the transition from being an exporter to becoming a true MNC.

Finally, in the third stage, the product becomes highly standardized and many competitors enter the business. Competition now focuses on price and, therefore, on cost. This activates the resource-seeking motive, and the company moves production to low-wage developing countries to meet the demands of its customers in the developed markets at a lower cost. In this final phase, the developing countries may become net exporters of the product while the developed countries become net importers.

Although the product cycle theory provided a useful way to describe much of the internationalization of the postwar decades,[4] by the 1980s its explanatory power was beginning to wane, as Professor Vernon was quick to point out. As the international business environment became increasingly complex and sophisticated, companies developed a much richer rationale for their worldwide operations.

---

[3] Raymond Vernon, "International Investment and International Trade in the Product Cycle," *Quarterly Journal of Economics,* May 1966, pp. 190–207.

[4] The record of international expansion of countries in the post–World War II era is quite consistent with the pattern suggested by the product cycle theory. For example, between 1950 and 1980, U.S. firms' direct foreign investment (DFI) increased from $11.8 billion to $200 billion. In the 1950s, much of this investment focused on the neighboring countries in Latin America and Canada. By the early 1960s, attention had shifted to Europe and the EEC's share of U.S. firms' DFI increased from 16 percent in 1957 to 32 percent by 1966. Finally, in the 1970s, attention shifted to developing countries, whose share of U.S. firms' DFI grew from 18 percent in 1974 to 25 percent in 1980.

Emerging Motivations

Once MNCs had established international sales and production operations, their perceptions and strategic motivations gradually changed. Initially, the typical attitude was that the foreign operations were strategic and organizational appendages to the domestic business, and should be managed opportunistically. Gradually, however, managers began to think about their strategy in a more integrated worldwide sense. In this process, the forces that originally triggered their expansion overseas often became secondary to a new set of motivations that underlay their emerging global strategies.

The first such set of forces were the increasing *scale economies, ballooning R&D investments,* and *shortening product life cycles* that transformed many industries into global rather than national structures, and made worldwide scope of activities not a matter of choice but an essential prerequisite for companies to survive in those businesses. These forces are described in detail in the next chapter.

A second factor that often became critical to a company's international strategy—though it was rarely the original motivating trigger—was its global *scanning and learning* capability.[5] A company drawn offshore to secure supplies of raw materials was more likely to become aware of alternative low-cost production sources around the globe; a company tempted abroad by market opportunities was often exposed to new technologies or market needs that stimulated innovative product development. The very nature of an MNC's worldwide presence gave it a huge informational advantage that could result in locating more-efficient sources or more-advanced product and process technologies. Thus, a company whose international strategy was triggered by a technological or marketing advantage could enhance that advantage through the scanning and learning potential inherent in its worldwide network of operations.

A third benefit that soon became evident was that being a multinational rather than a national company brought important advantages of *competitive positioning.* Certainly, the most controversial of the many global competitive strategic actions taken by MNCs in recent years have been those based on cross-subsidization of markets. For example, a Korean TV producer could challenge a national company in the United States by subsidizing its U.S. losses with funds from its profitable Asian or South American operations. If the U.S. company depended entirely on its home market, its competitive response could only be to defend its positions—typically by seeking government intervention or by matching or offsetting the competitive price reductions. Recognition of these competitive implications of multicountry operations led some companies to change the criteria for their international investment decisions so as to reflect not only market attractiveness or factor cost-efficiency choices, but also to reflect the leverage such investments provided over competitors.[6]

Although for purposes of analysis—and also to reflect some sense of historical development—the motives behind the expansion of MNCs have been reduced to a few distinct categories, it should be clear that companies were rarely driven by a single

---

[5]This motivation was highlighted by Raymond Vernon in "Gone Are the Cash Cows of Yesteryear," *Harvard Business Review,* November–December 1980, pp. 150–55.

[6]These competitive aspects of global operations are discussed in detail in Chapter 3.

motivating force. The more-adaptable companies soon learned how to capitalize on all of the potential advantages available from their international operations—ensuring critical supplies, entering new markets, tapping low-cost factors of production, leveraging their global information access, and capitalizing on the competitive advantage of their multiple market positions—and began to use these strengths to play a new strategic game that we will describe in later chapters as *global chess*.

The Means of Internationalization: Prerequisites and Processes

Having explored *why* the aspiring MNC wants to expand abroad—its motivation—we must now understand *how* it does so by exploring the means of internationalization. Beyond the desire to expand offshore, a company must posses certain competencies—attributes we describe as prerequisites—if it is to succeed in overseas markets. It must then be able to implement its desire to expand abroad through a series of decisions and commitments that define the internationalization process.

Prerequisites for Internationalization

In each national market, a foreign company suffers from some disadvantages vis-à-vis local competitors, at least initially. Being more familiar with the national culture, industry structure, government requirements, and other aspects of doing business in that country, domestic companies have a huge natural advantage. Their existing relationships with relevant customers, suppliers, regulators, and so on provide additional advantages that the foreign company must either match or counteract with some unique strategic capability.

Most often, this countervailing strategic advantage is found in the MNC's superior knowledge or skills that typically take the form of advanced technological expertise or specific marketing competencies. At other times, scale economies in R&D, production, or some other part of the value chain become the main source of the MNC's advantage over the domestic firm. It is important to note, however, that the MNC cannot expect to succeed in the international environment unless it has some such distinctive competency so as to overcome the liability of its foreignness.[7]

But even such knowledge or scale-based strategic advantages are, by themselves, insufficient to justify the internationalization of operations. A company can, as we have seen, sell or license its technology to foreign producers, franchise its brand name internationally, or sell its products abroad through general trading companies or local distributors, without having to set up its own offshore operations. This was the approach explicitly adopted by General Sarnoff, who decided that RCA should aggressively license its extensive television and other patents to European or Japanese companies rather than setting up its own international operations. He argued that the safe return from license fees were preferable to the uncertainties and complexities of multinational management.

The other precondition for a company to become an MNC, therefore, is that it must have the organizational capability to leverage its strategic assets more effectively

---

[7]The need for such strategic advantages for a company to become an MNC is highlighted in what is referred to as the *market imperfections theory of MNCs*. For a comprehensive review of this theory, see Richard E. Caves, *Multinational Enterprise and Economic Analysis* (Cambridge, England: Cambridge University Press, 1982).

through its own subsidiaries than through contractual relations with outside parties. If superior knowledge is the main source of an MNC's competitive advantage, for example, it must have an organizational system that allows better returns from extending and exploiting its knowledge through direct foreign operations than the return it could get by selling or licensing that knowledge.[8]

To summarize, three conditions must be met for the existence of an MNC. First, some foreign countries must offer certain location-specific advantages so as to provide requisite *motivation* for the company to invest there. Second, the company must have some *strategic competencies* or ownership-specific advantages to counteract the disadvantages of its relative unfamiliarity with foreign markets. Third, it must also have some *organizational capabilities* so as to get better returns from leveraging its strategic strengths internally rather than through external market mechanisms such as contracts or licenses.[9] Understanding these prerequisites is important not only because they explain why MNCs exist but also, as we show in Chapter 3, because they help define the strategic options for competing in worldwide businesses.

The Process of Internationalization

The process of developing these strategic and organizational attributes is at the heart of the internationalization process through which a company builds its position in world markets. This process is rarely well thought out in advance, and it typically builds on a combination of rational analysis, opportunism, and pure luck. Nonetheless, it is still possible to make out some general patterns of behavior that firms typically follow.

The most well-known model for internationalization was developed during the 1970s by two Swedish academics based in Uppsala.[10] It described foreign-market entry as a learning process. The company makes an initial commitment of resources to the foreign market, and through this investment it gains local market knowledge—about customers, competitors, and regulatory conditions. On the basis of this market knowledge, the company is able to evaluate its current activities, the extent of its commitment to the market, and thus the opportunities for additional investment. It then makes a subsequent resource commitment, perhaps buying out its local distributor or investing in a local manufacturing plant, which allows it to develop additional market knowledge. Gradually, and through several cycles of investment, the company develops the necessary levels of local capability and market knowledge to become an effective competitor in the foreign country (see Figure 1-1).

Whereas many companies internationalize in the manner depicted by the so-called Uppsala model, there are also a great many that do not. Some companies invest in or acquire local partners to shortcut the process of building up local market knowledge. For

---

[8]This issue of organization capability is the focus of what has come to be known as the *internalization theory of MNCs.* See Alan N. Rugman, "A New Theory of the Multinational Enterprise: Internationalization versus Internalization," *Columbia Journal of World Business,* Spring 1982, pp. 54–61. For a more detailed exposition, see Peter J. Buckley and Mark Casson, *The Future of Multinational Enterprise* (London: MacMillan, 1976).

[9]These three conditions are highlighted in John Dunning's eclectic theory. See John H. Dunning, *International Production and the Multinational Enterprise* (Winchester, Mass.: Allen & Unwin, 1981).

[10]Jan Johanson and Jan-Erik Vahlne, "The Internationalization Process of the Firm—a Model of Knowledge Development and Increasing Foreign Market Commitments," *Journal of International Business Studies* 88 (1977), pp. 23–32.

Figure 1-1   A Learning Model of Internationalization

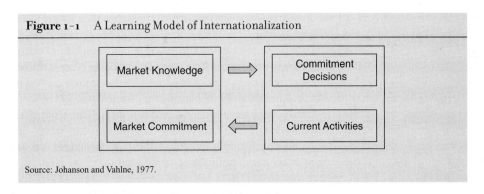

Source: Johanson and Vahlne, 1977.

Figure 1-2   Approaches to Foreign Market Entry

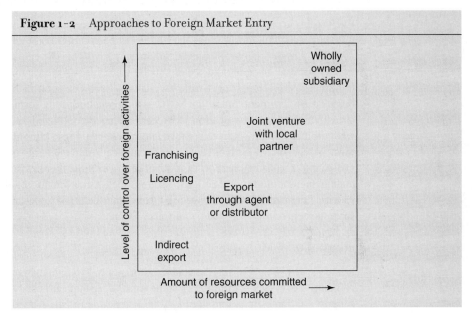

example, Wal-Mart entered the United Kingdom by buying supermarket chain Asda, rather than by developing its own stores. Others prefer to minimize their local presence by subcontracting to local partners. Amazon.com, for example, has a business in Canada without a single Canadian employee—it manages its website from the United States, and it fulfils orders through the Canadian postal service. Cases such as these highlight the complexity of the decisions the MNC faces in entering a foreign market. One important set of factors is the assimilation of local market knowledge by the subsidiary unit, as suggested by the Uppsala model. But other equally important factors to the MNC are its overall level of commitment to the foreign market in question, the required level of control of foreign operations, and the timing of its entry. To help make sense of these different factors, it is useful to think of the different modes of operating overseas in terms of two factors: the level of market commitment and the level of control (see Figure 1-2).

Some companies internationalize by gradually moving up the scale, from exporting through joint venturing to direct foreign investment. Some, like Wal-Mart, prefer to move straight to the high-commitment–high-control mode of operating, in part because they are entering mature markets where it would be very difficult to build a business from nothing. And others choose to adopt a low-commitment–low-control mode such as exporting or subcontracting. Amazon.com, for example, is able to make this approach work in Canada because it retains control of its website from the United States, and it has secured a reliable local partner for order fulfillment. To be clear, none of these approaches is necessarily right or wrong, but they should be consistent with the overall strategic intentions and motivations of the MNC.

The Evolving Mentality: International to Transnational

Even from this brief description of the changing motivations for and means of internationalization, it should be clear that there has been a gradual evolution in the strategic role that foreign operations played in emerging MNCs. We can categorize this evolutionary pattern into four stages that may be visualized as the way in which management thinking has developed over time as changes have occurred in both the international business environment and in the MNC as a unique corporate form.

Although such classification is necessarily overgeneralized and undoubtedly somewhat arbitrary, it allows us to achieve two objectives. First, it highlights the fact that for most MNCs the objectives that initially induced management to go overseas usually evolve into a very different set of motivations over time, thereby progressively changing management attitudes and actions. Second, such a classification allows us to develop a specific language system that we use throughout the book to describe the very different strategic approaches adopted by various MNCs.[11]

International Mentality

In the earliest stages of internationalization, many MNC managers tend to think of the company's overseas operations as some kind of distant outposts whose main role is to support the domestic parent company in different ways such as contributing incremental sales of the domestic manufacturing operations. This is what we label as the *international* strategic mentality.

The *international* terminology derives directly from the international product cycle theory that reflects many of the assumptions implicit in this approach. Products are developed for the domestic market, and only subsequently sold abroad; technology and other knowledge are transferred from the parent company to the overseas operators; and offshore manufacturing is seen as a means to protect the company's home market.

Companies with this mentality regard themselves fundamentally as a domestic company with some foreign appendages. Managers assigned to overseas operations are often the domestic misfits who happen to know a foreign language or who have previously

---

[11]It should be noted that the terms *international, multinational, global,* and *transnational* have been used very differently—and sometimes interchangeably—by various writers. We want to give each term *specific* and *different* meaning, and ask that you put aside your previous usage of the terms—at least for the duration of our exposition.

lived abroad. Decisions related to the foreign operations tend to be made in an opportunistic or ad hoc manner.

Multinational Mentality

The exposure of the organization to foreign environments and the growing importance of sales and profits from these sources gradually convince managers that the international activities can provide opportunities of more than marginal significance. Increasingly, they also realize that to leverage those opportunities, they have to do more than ship out old equipment, technology, or product lines that had been developed for the home market. Local competitors in the foreign markets and the host governments often accelerate the learning of companies that retain an unresponsive international mentality for too long.

A *multinational* strategic mentality develops as managers begin to recognize and emphasize the differences among national markets and operating environments. Companies with this mentality adopt a more flexible approach to their international operations by modifying their products, strategies, and even management practices country by country. As they develop national companies that are increasingly sensitive and responsive to their local environments, these companies develop a strategic approach that is literally multinational: Their worldwide strategy is built on the foundation of the multiple, nationally responsive strategies of the company's worldwide subsidiaries.

In companies operating with such a multinational mentality, managers of foreign operations tend to be highly independent entrepreneurs, often nationals of the host country. Using their local market knowledge and the parent company's willingness to invest in these growing opportunities, these entrepreneurial country managers are often able to build up significant local growth and considerable independence from headquarters.

Global Mentality

Although the multinational mentality typically results in very responsive marketing approaches in the different national markets, it also gives rise to an inefficient manufacturing infrastructure within the company. Plants are often built more to provide local marketing advantages or to improve political relations than to maximize production efficiency. Similarly, the proliferation of products designed to meet local needs also contributes to a general loss of efficiency in design, production, logistics, distribution, and other functional tasks.

In an operating environment of improving transportation and communication facilities and falling trade barriers, some companies adopted a very different strategic approach in their international operations. These companies, many of them of Japanese origin, think in terms of creating products for a world market and manufacturing them on a global scale in a few highly efficient plants, often at the corporate center.

We define this as a classic *global* strategic mentality because it views the world as its unit of analysis. The underlying assumption is that national tastes and preferences are more similar than different, or that they can be made similar by providing customers with standardized products with adequate cost and quality advantages over those national varieties that they have been used to. Managers with this global strategic approach subscribe to Professor Levitt's argument that the future belongs to those companies that make and sell "the same thing, the same way, everywhere."[12]

This strategic approach requires considerably more central coordination and control than the other and is typically associated with an organization structure in which various product or business managers have worldwide responsibility. In such companies, research and development and manufacturing activities are typically managed from the headquarters, and most strategic decisions are also taken at the center.

Transnational Mentality

Throughout the 1980s, many of these global companies seemed invincible. In a rapidly globalizing environment, they chalked up overwhelming victories, not only over local companies, but over international and multinational competitors as well. Their success, however, created and strengthened a set of countervailing forces of localization.

To many host governments, for example, these global companies appeared to be a more powerful and thus more threatening version of the earlier unresponsive companies with their unsophisticated international strategic mentality. Many host governments increased both the restrictions and the demands they placed on global companies, requiring them to invest, transfer technology, meet local content requirements, and so forth.

Customers also contributed to this strengthening of localizing forces by rejecting homogenized global products and reasserting their national preferences—albeit without relaxing their expectations of the high-quality levels and low costs that global products had offered. Finally, the increasing volatility in the international economic and political environments, especially the rapid changes in currency exchange rates, also undermined the efficiency of such a centralized global approach.

As a result of these developments, many worldwide companies recognized that the demands to be responsive to local market and political needs and the pressures to develop global-scale competitive efficiency were simultaneous, if sometimes conflicting. Under these conditions, the either/or attitude reflected in both the multinational and the global strategic mentalities were increasingly inappropriate. The emerging requirement was for companies to become more responsive to local needs while retaining their global efficiency—an emerging approach to worldwide management that we call the *transnational* strategic mentality.

In such companies, key activities and resources are neither centralized in the parent company, nor decentralized so that each subsidiary can carry out its own tasks on a local-for-local basis. Instead, the resources and activities are dispersed but specialized, so as to achieve efficiency and flexibility at the same time. Furthermore, these dispersed resources are integrated into an interdependent network of worldwide operations.

In contrast to the global model, the transnational mentality recognizes the importance of flexible and responsive country-level operations—hence the return of *national* into the terminology. And compared to the multinational approach, it provides for linking

---

[12]See Theodore Levitt, "The Globalization of Markets," *Harvard Business Review,* May–June 1983, pp. 92–102, reproduced in the readings section of the next chapter.

and coordinating those operations to retain competitive effectiveness and economic efficiency—as indicated by the prefix *trans*. The resulting need for intensive organizationwide coordination and shared decision making implies that this is a much more sophisticated and subtle approach to MNC management. In future chapters, we will explore its strategic, organizational, and managerial implications.

It should be clear, however, that there is no inevitability in either the direction or the end point of this evolving strategic mentality in worldwide companies. Depending on the industry, the individual company's strategic position, the host countries' diverse needs, and a variety of other factors, a company might reasonably operate with any one of these strategic mentalities. More likely, bearing in mind that this is an arbitrary classification, most companies will probably exhibit some attributes of each of these different strategic approaches.[13]

Concluding Comments

This chapter has provided the historical context on the nature of the MNC, and it has introduced a number of important concepts on which subsequent chapters will build. In particular, we described the motivations that led companies to expand abroad in the first place, the processes of internationalization they followed, and the typical mentalities that they developed. Collectively, these motivations, means, and mentalities are the prime drivers of a company's *administrative heritage,* which in turn plays an important part in shaping the company's strategic and organizational capabilities.

[13]Professor Howard Perlmutter was perhaps the first to highlight the different strategic mentalities. See his article, "The Tortuous Evolution of the Multinational Corporation," *Columbia Journal of World Business,* January–February 1969, pp. 9–18, reproduced in the readings section of this chapter.

Case 1-1   Jollibee Foods Corporation (A): International Expansion

Protected by his office air conditioner from Manila's humid August air, in mid-1997, Manolo P. ("Noli") Tingzon pondered an analysis of demographic trends in California. As the new head of Jollibee's International Division, he wondered if a Philippine hamburger chain could appeal to mainstream American consumers or whether the chain's proposed US operations could succeed by focusing on recent immigrants and Philippine expatriates. On the other side of the Pacific, a possible store opening in the Kowloon district of Hong Kong raised other issues for Tingzon. While Jollibee was established in the region, local managers were urging the company to adjust its menu, change its operations, and refocus its marketing on ethnic Chinese customers. Finally, he wondered whether

Professor Christopher A. Bartlett and Research Associate Jamie O'Connell prepared this case. HBS cases are developed solely as the basis for class discussion. Cases are not intended to serve as endorsements, sources of primary data, or illustrations of effective or ineffective management.
Copyright © 1998 President and Fellows of Harvard College. Harvard Business School case 398-007.

entering the nearly virgin fast food territory of Papua New Guinea would position Jollibee to dominate an emerging market—or simply stretch his recently-slimmed division's resources too far.

With only a few weeks of experience in his new company, Noli Tingzon knew that he would have to weigh these decisions carefully. Not only would they shape the direction of Jollibee's future internalization strategy, they would also help him establish his own authority and credibility within the organization.

Company History

Started in 1975 as an ice cream parlor owned and run by the Chinese-Filipino Tan family, Jollibee had diversified into sandwiches after company President Tony Tan Caktiong (better known as TTC) realized that events triggered by the 1977 oil crisis would double the price of ice cream. The Tans' hamburger, made to a home-style Philippine recipe developed by Tony's chef father, quickly became a customer favorite. A year later, with five stores in metropolitan Manila, the family incorporated as Jollibee Foods Corporation.

The company's name came from TTC's vision of employees working happily and efficiently, like bees in a hive. Reflecting a pervasive courtesy in the company, everyone addressed each other by first names prefaced by the honorific "Sir" or "Ma'am," whether addressing a superior or subordinate. Friendliness pervaded the organization and become one of the "Five Fs" that summed up Jollibee's philosophy. The others were flavorful food, a fun atmosphere, flexibility in catering to customer needs, and a focus on families (children flocked to the company's bee mascot whenever it appeared in public). Key to Jollibee's ability to offer all of these to customers at an affordable price was a well developed operations management capability. A senior manager explained:

> It is not easy to deliver quality food and service consistently and efficiently. Behind all that fun and friendly environment that the customer experiences is a well oiled machine that keeps close tabs on our day-to-day operations. It's one of our key success factors.

Jollibee expanded quickly throughout the Philippines, financing all growth internally until 1993. (Exhibit 1 shows growth in sales and outlets.) Tan family members occupied several key positions particularly in the vital operations functions, but brought in professional managers to supplement their expertise. "The heads of marketing and finance have always been outsiders," TTC noted. (Exhibit 2 shows a 1997 organization chart.) Many

Year	Total Sales (millions of pesos)	Total Stores at End of Year	Company-Owned Stores	Franchises
1975	NA	2	2	0
1980	NA	7	4	3
1985	174	28	10	18
1990	1,229	65	12	54
1991	1,744	99	21	80
1992	2,644	112	25	89
1993	3,386	124	30	96
1994	4,044	148	44	106
1995	5,118	166	55	113
1996	6,588	205	84	124
1997 (projected)	7,778	223	96	134

Exhibit 1   Jollibee Philippines Growth, 1975–1997

NA = Not available.

Exhibit 2 Jollibee Corporation Organization Chart, 1997 (members of Tan family shaded)

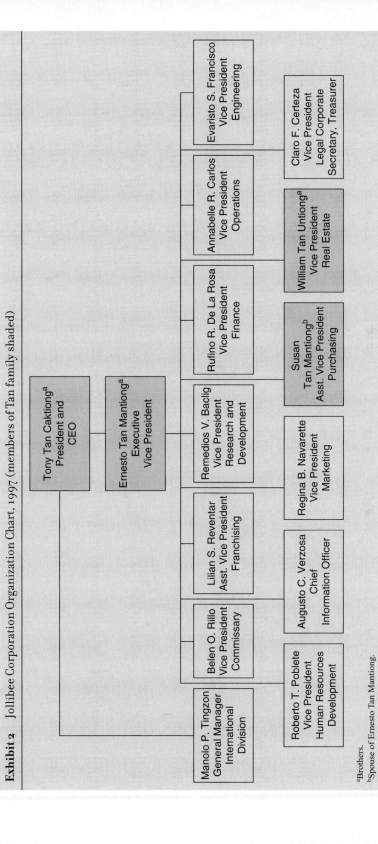

[a]Brothers.

[b]Spouse of Ernesto Tan Mantiong.

franchisees were also members or friends of the Tan family.

In 1993, Jollibee went public and in an initial public offering raised 216 million pesos (approximately US $8 million). The Tan family, however, retained the majority ownership and clearly controlled Jollibee. Although the acquisition of Greenwich Pizza Corporation in 1994 and the formation of a joint venture with Deli France in 1995 diversified the company's fast food offerings, in 1996 the chain of Jollibee stores still generated about 85% of the parent company's revenues. (Exhibits 3 and 4 present Jollibee's consolidated financial statements from 1992 through 1996.)

McDonald's: Going Burger to Burger   The company's first serious challenge arose in 1981, when McDonald's entered the Philippines. Although Jollibee already had 11 stores, many saw McDonald's as a juggernaut and urged TTC to concentrate on building a strong second-place position in the market. A special meeting of senior management concluded that although McDonald's had more money and highly developed operating systems, Jollibee had one major asset: Philippine consumers preferred the taste of Jollibee's hamburger by a wide margin. The group decided to go head to head with McDonald's. "Maybe we were very young, but we felt we could do anything," TTC recalled. "We felt no fear."

McDonald's moved briskly at first, opening six restaurants within two years and spending large sums on advertising. Per store sales quickly surpassed Jollibee's and, by 1983, McDonald's had grabbed a 27% share of the fast food market, within striking range of Jollibee's 32%. The impressive performance of the Big Mac, McDonald's largest and best-known sandwich, led Jollibee to respond with a large hamburger of its own, called the Champ. Jollibee executives bet that the Champ's one wide hamburger patty, rather than the Big Mac's smaller two, would appeal more to Filipinos' large appetites. Market research indicated that Filipinos still preferred Jollibee burgers' spicy taste to McDonald's plain beef patty, so the Champ's promotions focused on its taste, as well as its size.

But the Champ's intended knockout punch was eclipsed by larger events. In August 1983, political opposition leader Benigno Aquino was assassinated as he returned from exile. The economic and political crisis that followed led most foreign investors, including McDonald's, to slow their investment in the Philippines. Riding a wave of national pride, Jollibee pressed ahead, broadening its core menu with taste-tested offerings of chicken, spaghetti and a unique peach-mango dessert pie, all developed to local consumer tastes. By 1984, McDonald's foreign brand appeal was fading.

In 1986, dictator Ferdinand Marcos fled the Philippines in the face of mass demonstrations of "people power" led by Aquino's widow, Corazon. After she took office as president, optimism returned to the country, encouraging foreign companies to reinvest. As the local McDonald's franchisee once again moved to expand, however, its management found that Jollibee now had 31 stores and was clearly the dominant presence in the market.

Industry Background

In the 1960s, fast food industry pioneers, such as Ray Kroc of McDonald's and Colonel Sanders of Kentucky Fried Chicken, had developed a value proposition that became the standard for the industry in the United States and abroad. Major fast food outlets in the United States, which provided a model for the rest of the world, aimed to serve time-constrained customers by providing good-quality food in a clean dining environment and at a low price.

Managing a Store   At the store level, profitability in the fast food business depended on high customer traffic and tight operations management. Opening an outlet required large investments in equipment and store fittings, and keeping it open imposed high fixed costs for rent, utilities, and labor. This meant attracting large numbers of customers ("traffic") and, when possible, increasing the size of the average order (or "ticket"). The need for high volume put a premium on convenience and made store location critical. In choosing a site, attention had to be paid not only to the potential of a city or neighborhood

Exhibit 3 Jollibee Foods Corporation Consolidated Balance Sheets (in Philippine pesos)

Years Ended December 31

	1996	1995	1994	1993	1992
Assets					
Current assets					
Cash and cash equivalents	480,822,919	355,577,847	474,480,298	327,298,749	116,716,643
Accounts receivable:					
Trade	579,089,680	206,045,303	135,663,597	107,680,327	86,885,668
Advances and others	105,836,646	70,731,546	66,224,534	35,838,295	15,091,648
Inventories	323,019,198	201,239,667	183,154,582	135,263,988	116,828,086
Prepaid expenses and other current assets	223,680,221	132,077,935	88,995,824	41,462,780	66,028,987
Total current assets	1,712,448,664	965,672,298	948,518,835	647,544,139	401,551,032
Investments and advances	283,758,590	274,878,713	132,277,028	67,000,362	60,780,936
Property and equipment	2,177,944,193	1,181,184,783	753,876,765	568,904,831	478,857,474
Refundable deposits and other assets—net	363,648,234	224,052,247	91,575,543	92,035,464	72,310,079
Total assets	4,537,799,681	2,645,788,041	1,926,248,171	1,375,484,796	1,013,499,521
Liabilities and Stockholders' Equity					
Current liabilities:					
Bank loans	771,690,724	—	—	—	—
Accounts payable and accrued expenses	1,274,801,219	715,474,384	497,238,433	323,029,967	297,029,436
Income tax payable	58,803,916	28,103,867	17,205,603	23,206,109	19,851,315
Notes payable	—	—	—	—	133,000,000
Current portion of long-term debt	6,707,027	7,524,098	—	—	22,034,635
Dividends payable	16,810,812	—	—	—	—
Total current liabilities	2,128,813,698	751,102,349	514,444,036	346,236,076	471,915,386
Long-term debt	28,936,769	33,725,902	—	—	—
Minority interest	45,204,131	1,479,723	1,331,529	—	21,127,827
Stockholders' equity					
Capital stock—par value	880,781,250	704,625,000	563,315,000	372,000,000	66,000,000
Additional paid-in capital	190,503,244	190,503,244	190,503,244	190,503,244	—
Retained earnings	1,263,560,589	964,351,823	656,654,362	466,745,476	454,456,308
Total stockholders' equity	2,334,845,083	1,859,480,067	1,410,472,606	1,029,248,720	520,456,308
Total liabilities	4,537,799,681	2,645,788,041	1,926,248,171	1,375,484,796	1,013,499,521
Average exchange rate during year: pesos per US$	26.22	25.71	26.42	27.12	25.51

17

Exhibit 4 Jollibee Foods Corporation Consolidated Statements of Income and Retained Earnings (in Philippine pesos)

	Years Ended December 31				
	1996	1995	1994	1993	1992
Systemwide Sales (incl. franchisees)	8,577,067,000	6,894,670,000	5,277,640,000	4,102,270,000	NA
Company sales	6,393,092,135	4,403,272,755	3,277,383,084	2,446,866,690	2,074,153,386
Royalties and franchise fees	511,510,191	448,200,271	328,824,566	255,325,825	221,884,104
	6,904,602,326	4,851,473,026	3,606,207,650	2,702,192,515	2,296,037,490
Cost and Expenses					
Cost of sales	4,180,809,230	2,858,056,701	2,133,240,206	1,663,600,632	1,469,449,458
Operating expenses	1,943,536,384	1,403,151,840	1,013,999,640	674,288,268	545,749,275
Operating income	780,256,712	590,264,485	458,967,804	364,303,615	280,838,757
Interest and other income—net	44,670,811	102,134,296	83,342,805	32,716,223	(13,599,219)
Minority share in net earnings of a subsidiary			499,770		
Provision for income tax	219,900,353	168,589,520	138,001,953	104,230,670	66,172,056
Income before minority interest and cumulative effect of accounting change	605,027,170	523,809,261	403,808,886	292,789,168	201,067,482
Minority interest	2,829,654	137,694			
Cumulative effect of accounting change		13,733,644			
Net income	602,197,516	537,405,211	403,808,886	292,789,168	201,067,482
Earnings per share	0.68	0.61	0.81	0.59	0.58
Average exchange rate (pesos per $US)	26.22	25.71	26.42	27.12	25.51

but also to the traffic patterns and competition on particular streets or even blocks.

Yet even an excellent location could not make a store viable in the absence of good operations management, the critical ingredient in reducing waste, ensuring quality service and increasing staff productivity. Store managers were the key to motivating and controlling crew members responsible for taking orders, preparing food, and keeping the restaurant clean. Efficient use of their time—preparing raw materials and ingredients in advance, for example—not only enabled faster service, but could also reduce the number of crew members needed.

Managing a Chain   The high capital investment required to open new stores led to the growth of franchising which enabled chains to stake out new territory by rapidly acquiring market share and building brand recognition in an area. Such expansion created the critical mass needed to achieve economies of scale in both advertising and purchasing.

Fast food executives generally believed that chain-wide consistency and reliability was a key driver of success. Customers patronized chains because they knew, after eating at one restaurant in a chain, what they could expect at any other restaurant. This not only required standardization of the menu, raw material quality, and food preparation, but also the assurance of uniform standards of cleanliness and service. Particularly among the U.S. chains that dominated the industry, there also was agreement that uniformity of image also differentiated the chain from competitors: beyond selling hamburger or chicken, they believed they were selling an image of American pop culture. Consequently, most major fast food chains pushed their international subsidiaries to maintain or impose standardized menus, recipes, advertising themes, and store designs.

▋ Moving Offshore: 1986–1997

Jollibee's success in the Philippines brought opportunities in other Asian countries. Foreign business-people, some of them friends of the Tan family, heard about the chain's success against McDonald's and began approaching TTC for franchise rights in their countries. While most of his family and other executives were caught up in the thriving Philippine business, TTC was curious to see how Jollibee would fare abroad.

Early Forays: Early Lessons

Singapore   Jollibee's first venture abroad began in 1985, when a friend of a Philippine franchisee persuaded TTC to let him open and manage Jollibee stores in Singapore. The franchise was owned by a partnership consisting of Jollibee, the local manager, and five Philippine-Chinese investors, each with a one-seventh stake. Soon after the first store opened, however, relations between Jollibee and the local manager began to deteriorate. When corporate inspectors visited to check quality, cleanliness, and efficiency in operations, the franchisee would not let them into his offices to verify the local records. In 1986, Jollibee revoked the franchise agreement and shut down the Singapore store. "When we were closing down the store, we found that all the local company funds were gone, but some suppliers had not been paid," said TTC. "We had no hard evidence that something was wrong, but we had lost each other's trust."

Taiwan   Soon after the closure in Singapore, Jollibee formed a 50/50 joint venture with a Tan family friend in Taiwan. Although sales boomed immediately after opening, low pedestrian traffic by the site eventually led to disappointing revenues. Over time, conflict arose over day-to-day management issues between the Jollibee operations staff assigned to maintain local oversight and the Taiwanese partner. "Because the business demands excellent operations, we felt we had to back our experienced Jollibee operations guy, but the partner was saying, 'I'm your partner, I've put in equity. Who do you trust?'" When the property market in Taiwan took off and store rent increased dramatically, Jollibee decided to dissolve the joint venture and pulled out of Taiwan in 1988.

Brunei   Meanwhile, another joint venture opened in August 1987 in the small sultanate of Brunei, located on the northern side of the island of Borneo. (Exhibit 5 shows the locations of Jollibee International stores as of mid-1997.) The CEO of Shoemart, one of the Philippines' largest department stores, proposed that Jollibee form a joint-venture with a Shoemart partner in Brunei. By the end of 1993, with four successful stores in Brunei, TTC identified a key difference in the Brunei entry strategy: "In Singapore and Taiwan, the local partners ran the operation, and resented our operating control. In Brunei, the local investor was a silent partner. We sent managers from the Philippines to run the operations and the local partner supported us."

Indonesia An opportunity to enter southeast Asia's largest market came through a family friend. In 1989, Jollibee opened its first store, in Jakarta. Initially, the operation struggled, facing competition from street vendors and cheap local fast food chains. When conflict between the local partners and the manager they had hired paralyzed the operation, in late 1994, Jollibee dissolved the partnership and sold the operation to a new franchisee. Nevertheless, the company viewed the market as promising.

TTC summed up the lessons Jollibee had learned from its first international ventures:

> McDonald's succeeded everywhere because they were very good at selecting the right partners. They can get 100 candidates and choose the best—we don't have the name to generate that choice yet.
>
> Another key factor in this business is location. If you're an unknown brand entering a new country or city, you have trouble getting access to prime locations. McDonald's name gets it the best sites. People were telling us not to go international until we had solved these two issues: location and partner.

Building an Organization In 1993, TTC decided that Jollibee's international operations required greater structure and more resources. Because most of his management team was more interested in the fast-growing domestic side of the business, in January 1994, he decided to hire an experienced outsider as Vice President for International Operations. He selected Tony Kitchner, a native of

Australia, who had spent 14 years in Pizza Hut's Asia-Pacific regional office in Hong Kong. Reporting directly to TTC, Kitchner asked for the resources and autonomy to create an International Division.

Kitchner felt that his new division needed to be separate from Jollibee's Philippine side, with a different identity and capabilities. He agreed with TTC that attracting partners with good connections in their markets should be a priority, but worried that Jollibee's simple image and basic management approach would hamper these efforts. To project an image of a world-class company, he remodeled his division's offices on the seventh floor of Jollibee's Manila headquarters and instituted the company's first dress code, requiring his managers to wear ties. As one manager explained, "We had to look and act like a multinational, not like a local chain. You can't have someone in a short-sleeved open-neck shirt asking a wealthy businessman to invest millions."

Within weeks of his arrival, Kitchner began recruiting experienced internationalists from inside and outside Jollibee. To his inherited three-person staff, he quickly added seven more professionals, including new managers of marketing, finance, and quality control and product development that he brought in from outside Jollibee. The addition of two secretaries rounded out his staff. He claimed that greater internal recruiting had been constrained by two factors—Philippine management's resistance to having their staff "poached," and employees' lack of interest in joining this upstart division.

Strategic Thrust While endeavoring to improve the performance of existing stores in Indonesia and Brunei, Kitchner decided to increase the pace of international expansion with the objective of making Jollibee one of the world's top ten fast food brands by 2000. Kitchner's strategy rested on two main themes formulated during a planning session in the fall of 1994—"targeting expats" and "planting the flag."

The Division's new chief saw the hundreds of thousands of expatriate Filipinos working in the Middle East, Hong Kong, Guam, and other Asian territories as a latent market for Jollibee and as a

Exhibit 5 Locations of Jollibee International Division Stores, mid-1997 (locations with Jollibee outlets are underlined)

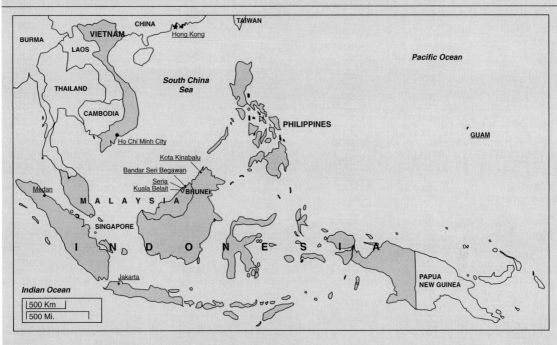

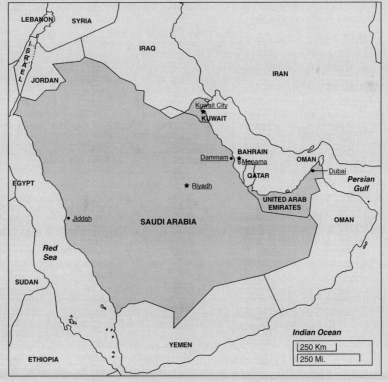

good initial base to support entry. Looking for a new market to test this concept, he focused on the concentrations of Filipino guest-workers in the Middle East. After opening stores in Dubai, Kuwait, and Dammam, however, he found that this market was limited on the lower end by restrictions on poorer workers' freedom of movement, and on the upper end by wealthier expatriates' preference for hotel dining, where they could consume alcohol. Not all overseas Filipinos were potential customers, it seemed.

The other strategic criterion for choosing markets rested on Kitchner's belief in first-mover advantages in the fast food industry. Jay Visco, International's Marketing manager, explained:

> We saw that in Brunei, where we were the pioneers in fast food, we were able to set the pace and standards. Now, we have six stores there, while McDonald's has only one and KFC has three. . . . That was a key learning: even if your foreign counterparts come in later, you already have set the pace and are at top of the heap.

The International Division therefore began to "plant the Jollibee flag" in countries where competitors had little or no presence. The expectation was that by expanding the number of stores, the franchise could build brand awareness which in turn would positively impact sales. One problem with this approach proved to be its circularity: only after achieving a certain level of sales could most franchisees afford the advertising and promotion needed to build brand awareness. The other challenge was that rapid expansion led to resource constraints—especially in the availability of International Division staff to support multiple simultaneous startups.

Nonetheless, Kitchner expanded rapidly. Due to Jollibee's success in the Philippines and the Tan family's network of contacts, he found he could choose from many franchising inquiries from various countries. Some were far from Jollibee's home base—like the subsequently abandoned plan to enter Romania ("our gateway to Europe" according to one manager). In an enormous burst of energy, between November 1994 and December 1996, the company entered 8 new national markets and opened 18 new stores. The flag was being planted. (See Exhibit 6.)

Operational Management

Market Entry Once Jollibee had decided to enter a new market, Tony Kitchner negotiated the franchise agreement, often with an investment by the parent company, to create a partnership with the franchisee. At that point he handed responsibility for the opening to one of the division's Franchise Services Managers (FSM). These were the key contacts between the company and its franchisees, and Kitchner was rapidly building a substantial support group in Manila to provide them with the resources and expertise they needed to start up and manage an offshore franchise. (See Exhibit 7.)

About a month before the opening, the FSM hired a project manager, typically a native of the new market who normally would go on to manage the first store. The FSM and project manager made most of the important decisions during the startup process, with the franchisees' level of involvement varying from country to country. However, one responsibility in which franchisee was deeply involved was the key first step of selecting and securing the site of the first store, often with advice from International Division staff, who visited the country several times to direct market research. (Sometimes the franchisee had been chosen partly for access to particularly good sites.) Once the franchisee had negotiated the lease or purchase, the project manager began recruiting local store managers.

The FSM was responsible for engaging local architects to plan the store. The kitchen followed a standard Jollibee design that ensured proper production flow, but Kitchner encouraged FSMs to adapt the counter and dining areas to the demands of the space and the preferences of the franchisee. A design manager in the International Division provided support.

During the planning phase, the project manager worked with International Division finance staff to develop a budget for raw materials, labor, and other major items in the operation's cost structure. He or

Exhibit 6   Jollibee International Store Openings

Location	Date Opened	
Bandar Seri Begawan, *Brunei*	August 1987	
Bandar Seri Begawan, *Brunei* (second store)	June 1989	
Seria, Brunei	August 1992	
Jakarta, *Indonesia*	August 1992	
Jakarta, Indonesia (second store)	March 1993	
Bandar Seri Begawan, Brunei (third store)	November 1993	International Division created
Kuala Belait, Brunei	November 1994	
Dubai, *United Arab Emirates*	April 1995	
Kuwait City, *Kuwait*	December 1995	
Dammam, *Saudi Arabia*	December 1995	
Guam	December 1995	
Jiddah, Saudi Arabia	January 1996	
Bahrain	January 1996	
Kota Kinabalu, *Malaysia*	February 1996	
Dubai (second store)	June 1996	
Riyadh, Saudi Arabia	July 1996	
Kuwait City, Kuwait (second store)	August 1996	
Kuwait City, Kuwait (third store)	August 1996	
Jiddah, Saudi Arabia (second store)	August 1996	
Hong Kong	September 1996	
Bandar Seri Begawan, Brunei (fourth store)	October 1996	
Ho Chi Minh City, *Vietnam*	October 1996	
Medan, Indonesia	December 1996	
Hong Kong (second store)	December 1996	
Dammam, Saudi Arabia	April 1997	
Hong Kong (third store)	June 1997	
Jakarta, Indonesia (third store)	July 1997	
Jakarta, Indonesia (fourth store)	September 1997	

Italics represent new market entry.

she also identified local suppliers, and—once International Division quality assurance staff had accredited their standards—negotiated prices. (Some raw materials and paper goods were sourced centrally and distributed to franchisees throughout Asia.)

Once architectural and engineering plans were approved, construction began. As it often did in other offshore activities, the International Division staff had to develop skills very different from those of their Jollibee colleagues working in the Philippines. For example, high rents in Hong Kong forced them to learn how to manage highly com-

pacted construction schedules: construction there could take one-third to one-half the time required for similar work in the Philippines.

Under FSM leadership, the International Division staff prepared marketing plans for the opening and first year's operation. They included positioning and communications strategies and were based on their advance consumer surveys, aggregate market data, and analysis of major competitors. Division staff also trained the local marketing manager and the local store manager and assistant managers who typically spent three months in Philippine

Exhibit 7 International Division Organization Chart, Late 1996 (pre-restructuring)

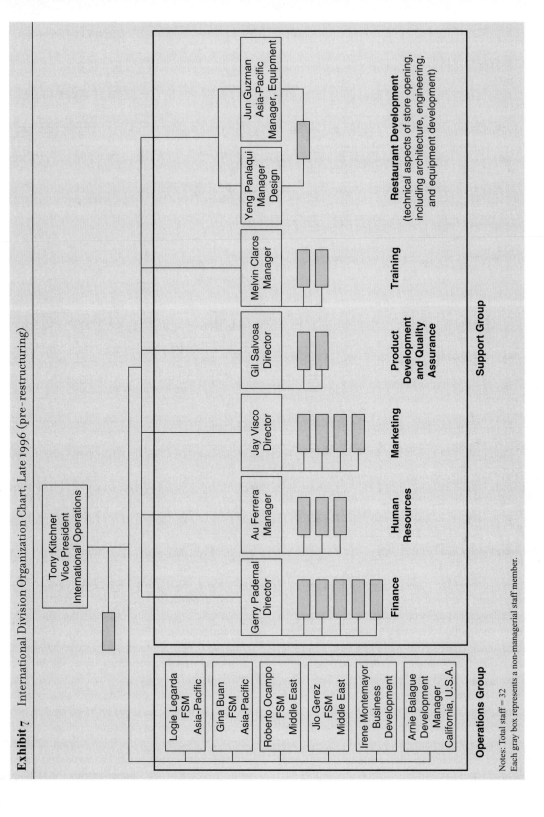

Notes: Total staff = 32
Each gray box represents a non-managerial staff member.

Exhibit 8 Organization of Typical Jollibee International Franchise

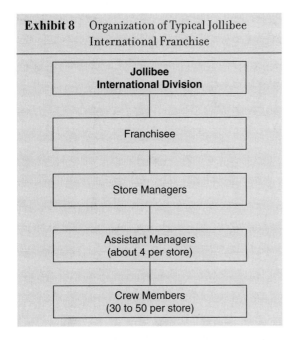

```
┌─────────────────────────┐
│        Jollibee         │
│ International Division   │
└─────────────────────────┘
            │
┌─────────────────────────┐
│       Franchisee        │
└─────────────────────────┘
            │
┌─────────────────────────┐
│     Store Managers      │
└─────────────────────────┘
            │
┌─────────────────────────┐
│   Assistant Managers    │
│   (about 4 per store)   │
└─────────────────────────┘
            │
┌─────────────────────────┐
│      Crew Members       │
│   (30 to 50 per store)  │
└─────────────────────────┘
```

stores. (Where appropriate local managers had not been found, the store managers were sometimes drawn from Jollibee's Philippine operations.) Just before opening, the project manager hired crew members, and International Division trainers from Manila instructed them for two weeks on cooking, serving customers, and maintaining the store. (See Exhibit 8 for a typical franchise's organization.)

Oversight and Continuing Support   After a store opened, the FSM remained its key contact with Jollibee, monitoring financial and operational performance and working to support and develop the store manager. For approximately two months after opening, FSMs required stores in their jurisdictions to fax them every day their figures for sales by product, customer traffic, and average ticket. As operations stabilized and the store manager started to see patterns in sales and operational needs, FSMs allowed stores to report the same data weekly and provide a monthly summary.

FSMs used this information not only to project and track royalty income for corporate purposes, but also to identify ways they could support the local franchisee. When the data suggested problems, the FSM would contact the store manager, highlight the issue, and ask for an appropriate plan of action. For example, if FSM Gina Buan saw a decline in sales for two consecutive weeks, she demanded specific plans within 24 hours of her call. If managers could not come up with solutions themselves, she would coach them to help them generate answers. "My aim," she remarked with a smile, "is to turn them into clones of me—or at least teach them my expertise."

In addition to the required sales reports, many stores voluntarily reported on their costs, because they found their FSM's analysis so helpful. This open partnership fit with TTC's view of franchise relations. "We get data from franchisees more to help us provide consulting assistance than for control," he said. Ernesto Tan, TTC's brother, explained that although Jollibee's royalty was a percentage of franchisees' sales, and local operations were focused more on profits, both interests were similar: "We want sales to grow, so that our royalty grows. But this will not happen if stores are not profitable, because our franchisees will not push to expand."

As well as support, however, the International Division was also concerned with control—especially in quality. Unannounced on-site inspections every quarter were Jollibee's primary tool. Over two days, the FSM evaluated every aspect of operations in detail, including product quality and preparation (taste, temperature, freshness, availability, and appearance), cleanliness, restaurant appearance, service speed, and friendliness. The manual for intensive checks was several inches thick. All international staff had been trained in Jollibee's quality standards and conducted less detailed "quick checks" whenever they traveled. Based on a 15-page questionnaire, a quick check took roughly two hours to complete and covered all of the areas that intensive ones did, although with less rigor and detail. Each store received an average of two quick checks per quarter.

In addition to FSMs' own rich industry experiences—Gina Buan, for example, had managed stores, districts, and countries for Jollibee and another chain—these field managers engaged the expertise of International Division functional staff. While they tried to shift responsibility gradually to the franchisee, division support staff often bore much of the responsibility long after startup. For example, the marketing staff tried to limit their franchise support role to creating initial marketing plans for new openings and reviewing new store plans. However, often they were drawn into the planning of more routine campaigns for particular stores, work they felt should be handled by the franchisee and store managers.

International vs. Domestic Practice   As operations grew, Kitchner and his staff discovered that international expansion was not quite as simple as the metaphor of "planting flags" might suggest. It sometimes felt more like struggling up an unconquered, hostile mountain. After numerous market entry battles, the international team decided that a number of elements of Jollibee's Philippine business model needed to be modified overseas. For example, the company's experience in Indonesia led Visco to criticize the transplantation of Jollibee's "mass-based positioning":

> When Jollibee arrived in Indonesia, they assumed that the market would be similar to the Philippines. But the Indonesian masses are not willing to spend as much on fast food as the Philippine working and lower-middle class consumers, and there were lots of cheap alternatives available. We decided that we needed to reposition ourselves to target a more up-market clientele.

Kitchner and Visco also felt that Jollibee needed to present itself as "world class," not "local" or "regional." In particular, they disliked the Philippine store design—a "trellis" theme with a garden motif—which had been transferred unchanged as Jollibee exported internationally. Working with an outside architect, a five-person panel from the International Division developed three new store decors, with better lighting and higher quality furniture. After Kitchner got TTC's approval, the Division remodeled the Indonesian stores and used the designs for all subsequent openings.

International also redesigned the Jollibee logo. While retaining the bee mascot, it changed the red background to orange and added the slogan, "great burgers, great chicken." Visco pointed out that the orange background differentiated the chain's logo from those of other major brands, such as KFC, Coca-Cola, and Marlboro, which all had red-and-white logos. The slogan was added to link the Jollibee name and logo with its products in people's minds. Visco also noted that, unlike Wendy's Old Fashioned Hamburgers, Kentucky Fried Chicken, and Pizza Hut, Jollibee did not incorporate its product in its name and market tests had found that consumers outside the Philippines guessed the logo signified a toy chain or candy store.

Kitchner and his staff made numerous other changes to Jollibee's Philippine business operating model. For example, rather than preparing new advertising materials for each new promotion as they did in the Philippines, the international marketing group created a library of promotional photographs of each food product that could be assembled, in-house, into collages illustrating new promotions (e.g., a discounted price for buying a burger, fries, and soda). And purchasing changed from styrofoam to paper packaging to appeal to foreign consumers' greater environmental consciousness.

Customizing for Local Tastes   While such changes provoked grumbling from many in the large domestic business who saw the upstart international group as newcomers fiddling with proven concepts, nothing triggered more controversy than the experiments with menu items. Arguing that the "flexibility" aspect of Jollibee's "Five Fs" corporate creed stood for a willingness to accommodate differences in customer tastes, managers in the International Division believed that menus should be adjusted to local preferences.

The practice had started in 1992 when a manager was dispatched from the Philippines to respond to the Indonesian franchisee's request to create a fast food version of the local favorite *nasi lema,* a mixture of rice and coconut milk. Building on this precedent, Kitchner's team created an international menu item they called the Jollimeal. This was typically a rice-based meal with a topping that could vary by country—in Hong Kong, for example, the rice was covered with hot and sour chicken, while in Vietnam it was chicken curry. Although it accounted for only 5% of international sales, Kitchner saw Jollimeals as an important way to "localize" the Jollibee image.

But the International Division expanded beyond the Jollimeal concept. On a trip to Dubai, in response to the local franchisee's request to create a salad for the menu, product development manager Gil Salvosa spent a night chopping vegetables in his hotel room to create a standard recipe. That same trip, he acquired a recipe for chicken masala from the franchisee's cook, later adapting it to fast food production methods for the Dubai store. The International Division also added idiosyncratic items to menus, such as dried fish, a Malaysian favorite. Since other menu items were seldom removed, these additions generally increased the size of menus abroad.

Although increased menu diversity almost always came at the cost of some operating efficiency (and, by implication, complicated the task of store level operating control), Kitchner was convinced that such concessions to local tastes were necessary. In Guam, for example, to accommodate extralarge local appetites, division staff added a fried egg and two strips of bacon to the Champ's standard large beef patty. And franchisees in the Middle East asked the Division's R&D staff to come up with a spicier version of Jollibee's fried chicken. Although Kentucky Fried Chicken (KFC) was captivating customers with their spicy recipe, R&D staff on the Philippine side objected strenuously. As a compromise, International developed a spicy sauce that customers could add to the standard Jollibee chicken.

Overall, the International Division's modification of menus and products caused considerable tension with the Philippine side of Jollibee. While there was no controversy about reformulating hamburgers for Muslim countries to eliminate traces of pork, for example, adding new products or changing existing ones led to major arguments. As a result, International received little cooperation from the larger Philippine research and development staff and customization remained a source of disagreement and friction.

Strained International–Domestic Relations   As the International Division expanded, its relations with the Philippine-based operations seemed to deteriorate. Tensions over menu modifications reflected more serious issues that had surfaced soon after Kitchner began building his international group. Philippine staff saw International as newcomers who, despite their lack of experience in Jollibee, "discarded practices built over 16 years." On the other side, International Division staff reported that they found the Philippine organization bureaucratic and slow-moving. They felt stymied by requirements to follow certain procedures and go through proper channels to obtain assistance.

The two parts of Jollibee continued to operate largely independently, but strained relations gradually eroded any sense of cooperation and reduced already limited exchanges to a minimum. Some International Division staff felt that the Philippine side, which controlled most of Jollibee's resources, should do more to help their efforts to improve and adapt existing products and practices. Visco recalled that when he wanted assistance designing new packaging, the Philippine marketing manager took the attitude that international could fend for itself. Similarly, Salvosa wanted more cooperation on product development from Philippine R&D, but was frustrated by the lengthy discussions and approvals that seemed to be required.

However, the domestic side viewed things differently. Executive Vice President Ernesto Tan, who was in charge of Jollibee in the Philippines, recalled:

> The strains came from several things. It started when International tried to recruit people directly from the Philippine side, without consulting with their superiors. There also was some jealousy on a personal level because the people recruited were immediately promoted to the next level, with better pay and benefits.
>
> The international people also seemed to develop a superiority complex. They wanted to do everything

Exhibit 9 International Division Organization Chart, March 1997 (post-restructuring)

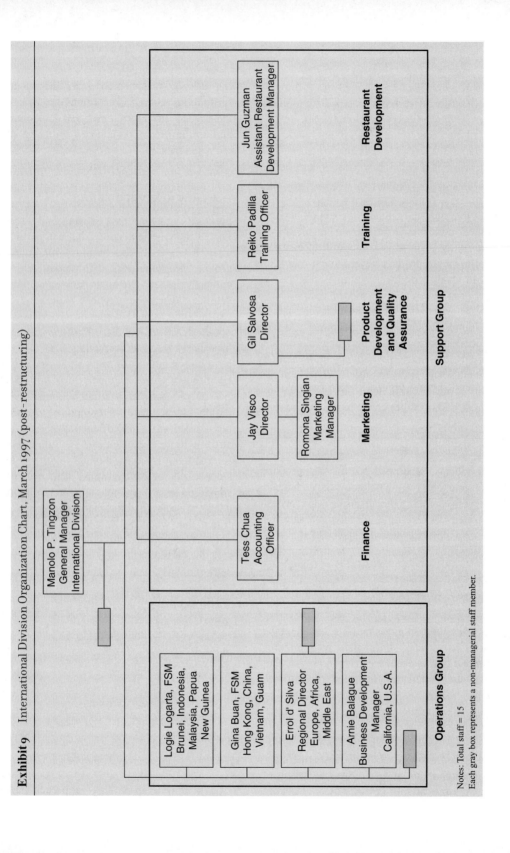

Notes: Total staff = 15
Each gray box represents a non-managerial staff member.

differently, so that if their stores did well, they could take all the credit. At one point, they proposed running a store in the Philippines as a training facility, but we thought they also wanted to show us that they could do it better than us. We saw them as lavish spenders while we paid very close attention to costs. Our people were saying, "We are earning the money, and they are spending it!" There was essentially no communication to work out these problems. So we spoke to TTC, because Kitchner reported to him.

Matters grew worse throughout 1996. One of the first signs of serious trouble came during a project to redesign the Jollibee logo, which TTC initiated in mid-1995. Triggered by International's modification of the old logo, the redesign project committee had representatives from across the company. Having overseen International's redesign, Kitchner was included. During the committee's deliberations, some domestic managers felt that the International vice-president's strong opinions were obstructive, and early in 1996 Kitchner stopped attending the meetings.

During this time, TTC was growing increasingly concerned about the International Division's continuing struggles. Around November 1996, he decided that he could no longer support Kitchner's strategy of rapid expansion due to the financial problems it was creating. Many of the International stores were losing money, but the cost of supporting these widespread unprofitable activities was increasing. Despite the fact that even unprofitable stores generated franchise fees calculated as a percentage of sales, TTC was uncomfortable:

> Kitchner wanted to put up lots of stores, maximizing revenue for Jollibee. Initially, I had supported this approach, thinking we could learn from an experienced outsider, but I came to believe that was not viable in the long term. We preferred to go slower, making sure that each store was profitable so that it would generate money for the franchisee, as well as for us. In general, we believe that whoever we do business with— suppliers and especially franchisees—should make money. This creates a good, long-term relationship.

In February 1997, Kitchner left Jollibee to return to Australia. A restructuring supervised

directly by TTC shrank the International Division's staff from 32 to 14, merging the finance, MIS and human resources functions with their bigger Philippine counterparts. (See Exhibit 9.) Jay Visco became interim head of International while TTC searched for a new Division leader.

■ A New International Era: 1997

In the wake of Kitchner's departure, TTC consulted intensively with Jollibee's suppliers and other contacts in fast food in the Philippines regarding a replacement. The name that kept recurring was Manolo P. ("Noli") Tingzon, one of the industry's most experienced managers. Although based in the Philippines his entire career, Tingzon had spent much of this time helping foreign chains crack the Philippine market. In 1981 he joined McDonald's as a management trainee and spent the next 10 years in frustrating combat with Jollibee. After a brief experience with a food packaging company, in 1994 he took on the challenge to launch Texas Chicken, another U.S. fast food chain, in its Philippines entry. When TTC contacted him in late 1996, he was intrigued by the opportunity offered by his old nemesis and joined the company in July 1997 as general manager, International Division.

A Fresh Look at Strategy   Upon his arrival, Tingzon reviewed International's current and historical performance. (See Exhibit 10.) He concluded that because of the scale economies of fast food franchising, an "acceptable" return on investment in international operations would require 60 Jollibee restaurants abroad with annual sales of US$800,000 each, the approximate store level sales at McDonald's smaller Asian outlets. Feeling that Jollibee's international expansion had sometimes been driven less by business considerations than by a pride in developing overseas operations, Tingzon thought that a fresh examination of existing international strategies might reveal opportunities for improvement. As he consulted colleagues at Jollibee, however, he heard differing opinions.

Many of his own staff felt that the rapid expansion of the "plant-the-flag" approach had served

Exhibit 10   International Store Sales by Country: 1996 (in U.S. dollars at contemporary exchange rates)

		1996	
		Sales	**Number of Stores**
Bahrain		262,361	1
Brunei		2,439,538	6
Guam		1,771,202	1
Hong Kong		1,142,240	2
Indonesia		854,259	3
Kuwait		864,531	3
Malaysia		391,328	1
Saudi Arabia		976,748	4
United Arab Emirates		487,438	2
Vietnam		112,578	1
Total	US$	9,302,223	24

Jollibee well and should be continued. For example, Visco argued that establishing a presence in each market before competitors conferred important first-mover advantages in setting customer expectations, influencing tastes and building brand. He and others felt that Jollibee's success in the Philippines and Brunei illustrated this point especially well.

Others, particularly on Jollibee's domestic side, felt the flag-planting strategy was ill-conceived, leading the company into what they saw as rash market choices such as the Middle East, where outlets continued to have difficulty attracting either expatriates or locals. For example, Ernesto Tan advised Tingzon to "focus on expanding share in a few countries while making sure each store does well." He urged Tingzon to consolidate and build on existing Jollibee markets that had either high profit potential, such as Hong Kong, or relatively mild competition, such as Malaysia and Indonesia.

With respect to the strategy of initially focusing on Filipino expatriates in new markets, Tingzon appreciated that this approach had eased Jollibee's entry into Guam and Hong Kong, but wondered whether it might trap the chain. "Might we risk boxing ourselves into a Filipino niche that prevents us from growing enough to support operations in each country?" he asked. Again opinion was divided between those favoring the expatriate-led strategy and those who felt it was time for Jollibee to shake its Philippine identity and target the mainstream market wherever it went.

Strategy in Action: Three Decisions   Although he eventually wanted to resolve these issues at the level of policy, Tingzon faced three immediate growth opportunities that he knew would shape the emergence of the future strategy.

Papua New Guinea: Raising the Standard   In early 1996, at the recommendation of Quality Assurance Manager Gil Salvosa, a local New Guinea entrepreneur in the poultry business approached Tony Kitchner about a Jollibee franchise. He described a country of five million people served by only one poorly managed, 3-store fast-food chain that had recently broken ties with its Australian chicken restaurant franchise. "Port Moresby does not have a single decent place to eat," he told Kitchner. He believed Jollibee could raise the quality of service and food enough to take much of the Australian chain's market share while discouraging further entrants.

Although the original plan had been to open just one store in the foreseeable future—in the capital, Port Moresby—Tingzon was certain that the franchisee could only cover the costs of developing the market if he put in at least three or four stores soon after. But he was uncertain whether Papua New Guinea could support the 20 stores that he saw as the target critical mass for new markets. (For comparison, in the Philippines, approximately 1,200 fast food outlets competed for the business of 75 million people. GNP per capita in both countries was almost at US$2,500.)

When Tingzon explained his concerns, the would-be franchisee's response was that he would negotiate with a major petroleum retailer and try to open stores in five of their service stations around the country. Furthermore, he emphasized that he was willing to build more stores if necessary and would put up all the capital so that Jollibee would risk no equity in the venture.

Hong Kong: Expanding the Base   Also on Tingzon's plate was a proposal to expand to a fourth store in Hong Kong. The franchise, owned by Jollibee in partnership with local businessmen and managed by Tommy King, TTC's brother-in-law, opened its first store in September 1996 to instant, overwhelming success. Located near a major transit hub in the Central district, it became a gathering place for Filipino expatriates, primarily domestic workers. However, appealing to the locals had proven more difficult. While volume was high on weekends, when the Filipinos came to Central to socialize, it fell off during the week, when business was primarily from local office workers.

Although two more stores in Central had attracted many Filipinos, they both relied extensively on Chinese customers and generated sales of only about one-third of the first outlet. One problem was that, despite strenuous efforts, Jollibee had been unable to hire many local Chinese as crew members. According to one manager, Chinese customers who did not speak English well were worried that they would be embarrassed if they were not understood by the predominantly Philippine and Nepalese counter staff. Another problem was that in a city dominated by McDonald's, Jollibee's brand recognition among locals was weak. Working with Henry Shih, the sub-franchisee who owned the second store, Jollibee staff were trying to help

launch a thematic advertising campaign, but due to the Hong Kong operation's small size, the franchise could not inject sufficient funds.

Shih also blamed rigidity over menu offerings for Jollibee's difficulties appealing to Chinese customers. In early 1997, his Chinese managers had suggested serving tea the Hong Kong way—using tea dust (powdered tea leaves) rather than tea bags and adding evaporated milk. More than six months later, he had still not received a go-ahead. His proposal to develop a less-fatty recipe for Chicken Joy, one of Jollibee's core menu items, had met more direct resistance. "The Chinese say that if you eat lots of deep-fried food you become hot inside and will develop health problems," said Shih who believed that the domestic side had pressured the International Division to reject any experimentation with this "core" menu item.

Meanwhile, staffing problems were worsening. The four locally-recruited Chinese managers clashed with the five Filipinos imported from Tommy King's Philippine franchise, with the Chinese calling the Filipinos' discipline lax and their style arrogant, while the Filipinos saw the Chinese managers as uncommitted. By August 1997, all of the Chinese managers had resigned, leaving Jollibee with only Filipinos in store-level management positions. Shih was afraid this would further undermine Jollibee's ability to hire local crews, as Chinese preferred to work for Chinese.

Partly due to staff turnover, store managers were focused on dealing with day-to-day operations issues such as uneven product quality and had little time to design even short-term marketing strategies. King's focus on his Philippine stores slowed decision-making. And while Gina Buan, the FSM, had visited Hong Kong more often than any other markets she supervised (including for an extraordinary month-long stay), she had been unable to resolve the management problems. In June, King appointed Shih General Manager to oversee the entire Hong Kong venture.

In this context, Shih and King proposed to open a fourth store. The site in the Kowloon district was one of the busiest in Hong Kong, located at one of just two intersections of the subway and the rail line that was the only public transport from the New Territories, where much of the city's workforce resided. However, the area saw far fewer Filipinos than Central and the store would have to depend on locals. Acknowledging that the fourth store would test Jollibee's ability to appeal to Hong Kong people, Shih argued that the menu would have to be customized more radically. However, Tingzon wondered whether expansion was even viable at this time, given the Hong Kong venture's managerial problems. Even if he were to approve the store, he wondered if he should support the menu variations that might complicate quality control. On the other hand, expansion into such a busy site might enhance Jollibee's visibility and brand recognition among locals, helping increase business even without changing the menu. It was another tough call.

California: Supporting the Settlers   Soon after signing his contract, Tingzon had learned of a year-old plan to open one Jollibee store per quarter in California starting in the first quarter of 1998. Supporting TTC's long-held belief that Jollibee could win enormous prestige and publicity by gaining a foothold in the birthplace of fast food, Kitchner had drawn up plans with a group of Manila-based businessmen as 40% partners in the venture. Once the company stores were established, they hoped to franchise in California and beyond in 1999.

Much of the confidence for this bold expansion plan came from Jollibee's success in Guam, a territory of the U.S. Although they initially targeted the 25% of the population of Filipino extraction, management discovered that their menu appealed to other groups of Americans based there. They also found they could adapt the labor-intensive Philippine operating methods by developing different equipment and cooking processes more in keeping with a high labor cost environment. In the words of one International Division veteran, "In Guam, we learned how to do business in the United States. After succeeding there, we felt we were ready for the mainland."

The plan called for the first store to be located in Daly City, a community with a large Filipino population but relatively low concentration of fast-food competitors in the San Francisco area. (With more than a million immigrants from the Philippines living in California, most relatively affluent, this state had one of the highest concentrations of Filipino expatriates in the world.) The menu would be transplanted from the Philippines without changes. After initially targeting Filipinos, the plan was to branch out geographically to the San Francisco and San Diego regions, and demographically to appeal to other Asian-American and, eventually, Hispanic-American consumers. The hope was that Jollibee would then expand to all consumers throughout the U.S.

Like the expansion strategies in PNG and Hong Kong, this project had momentum behind it, including visible support from Filipino-Americans, strong interest of local investors, and, not least, TTC's great interest in succeeding in McDonald's back-yard. Yet Tingzon realized that he would be the one held accountable for its final success and wanted to bring an objective outsider's perspective to this plan before it became accepted wisdom. Could Jollibee hope to succeed in the world's most competitive fast-food market? Could they provide the necessary support and control to operations located 12 hours by plane and eight time zones away? And was the Filipino-to-Asian-to-Hispanic-to-mainstream entry strategy viable or did it risk boxing them into an economically unviable niche?

Looking Forward   Noli Tingzon had only been in his job a few weeks, but already it was clear that his predecessor's plan to open 1000 Jollibee stores abroad before the turn of the century was a pipe dream. "It took McDonald's 20 years for its international operations to count for more than 50% of total sales," he said. "I'll be happy if I can do it in 10." But even this was an ambitious goal. And the decisions he made on the three entry options would have a significant impact on the strategic direction his international division took and on the organizational capabilities it needed to get there.

Case 1-2   Acer, Inc: Taiwan's Rampaging Dragon

With a sense of real excitement, Stan Shih, CEO of Acer, Inc., boarded a plane for San Francisco in early February 1995. The founder of the Taiwanese personal computer (PC) company was on his way to see the Aspire, a new home PC being developed by Acer America Corporation (AAC) Acer's North American subsidiary. Although Shih had heard that a young American team was working on a truly innovative product, featuring a unique design, voice recognition, ease-of-use, and cutting-edge multimedia capabilities, he knew little of the project until Ronald Chwang, President of AAC, had invited him to the upcoming product presentation. From Chwang's description, Shih thought that Aspire could have the potential to become a blockbuster product worldwide. But he was equally excited that this was the first Acer product conceived, designed, and championed by a sales-and-marketing-oriented regional business unit (RBU) rather than one of Acer's production-and-engineering-focused strategic business units (SBUs) in Taiwan.

Somewhere in mid-flight, however, Shih's characteristic enthusiasm was tempered by his equally well-known pragmatism. Recently, AAC had been one of the company's more problematic overseas units, and had been losing money for five years. Was this the group on whom he should pin his hopes for Acer's next important growth initiative? Could such a radical new product succeed in the highly competitive American PC market? And if so, did this unit—one of the company's sales-and-marketing-oriented RBUs—have the resources and capabilities to lead the development of this important new product, and, perhaps, even its global rollout?

Professor Christopher A. Bartlett and Research Associate Anthony St. George prepared this case as the basis for class discussion rather than to illustrate either effective or ineffective handling of an administrative situation. Some historical information was drawn from Robert H. Chen, "Made in Taiwan: The Story of Acer Computers," Linking Publishing Co., Taiwan, 1996, and Stan Shih, "Me-too is Not My Style," Acer Foundation, Taiwan, 1996. We would like to thank Eugene Hwang and Professor Robert H. Hayes for their help and advice.

Copyright © 1998 by the President and Fellows of Harvard College. Harvard Business School case 399-010.

Birth of the Company

Originally known as Multitech, the company was founded in Taiwan in 1976 by Shih, his wife, and three friends. From the beginning, Shih served as CEO and Chairman, his wife as company accountant. With $25,000 of capital and 11 employees, Multitech's grand mission was "to promote the application of the emerging microprocessor technology." It grew by grasping every opportunity available—providing engineering and product design advice to local companies, importing electronic components, offering technological training courses, and publishing trade journals. "We will sell anything except our wives," joked Shih. Little did the founders realize that they were laying the foundations for one of Taiwan's great entrepreneurial success stories. (See Exhibit 1.)

Laying the Foundations   Because Multitech was capital constrained, the new CEO instituted a strong norm of frugality. Acting on what he described as "a poor man's philosophy," he leased just enough space for current needs (leading to 28 office relocations over the next 20 years) and, in the early years, encouraged employees to supplement their income by "moonlighting" at second jobs. Yet while Multitech paid modest salaries, it offered key employees equity, often giving them substantial ownership positions in subsidiary companies.

Frugality was one of many business principles Shih had learned while growing up in his mother's tiny store. He told employees that high-tech products, like his mother's duck eggs, had to be priced with a low margin to ensure turnover. He preached the importance of receiving cash payment quickly and avoiding the use of debt. But above all, he told them that customers came first, employees second, and shareholders third, a principle later referred to as "Acer 1-2-3."

Shih's early experience biased him against the patriarch-dominated, family-run company model that was common in Taiwan. "It tends to generate

Exhibit 1   Selected Financials: Sales, Net Income, and Headcount, 1976–1994

	1976	1977	1978	1979	1980	1981	1982	1983	1984
Sales ($M)	0.003	0.311	0.80	0.77	3.83	7.08	18.1	28.3	51.6
Net income ($M)	N/A	N/A	N/A	N/A	N/A	N/A	N/A	1.4	0.4
Employees	11	12	18	46	104	175	306	592	1,130

opinions which are neither balanced nor objective," he said. He delegated substantial decision-making responsibility to his employees to harness "the natural entrepreneurial spirit of the Taiwanese." With his informal manner, bias for delegation, and "hands-off" style, Shih trusted employees to act in the best interests of the firm. "We don't believe in control in the normal sense. . . . We rely on people and build our business around them," he said. It was an approach many saw as the polar opposite of the classic Chinese entrepreneur's tight personal control. As a result, the young company soon developed a reputation as a very attractive place for bright young engineers.

Shih's philosophy was reflected in his commitment to employee education and his belief that he could create a company where employees would constantly be challenged to "think and learn." In the early years, superiors were referred to as "shifu," a title usually reserved for teachers and masters of the martial arts. The development of strong teaching relationships between manager and subordinate was encouraged by making the cultivation and grooming of one's staff a primary criterion for promotion. The slogan, "Tutors conceal nothing from their pupils" emphasized the open nature of the relationship and reminded managers of their responsibility.

This created a close-knit culture, where coworkers treated each other like family, and the norm was to do whatever was necessary for the greater good of the company. But is was a very demanding "family," and as the patriarch, Stan Shih worked hard to combat complacency—what he called "the big rice bowl" sense of entitlement—by creating a constant sense of crisis and showering subordinates

with ideas and challenges for their examination and follow-up. As long as the managers took responsibility for their actions—acted as responsible older sons or daughters—they had the freedom to make decisions in the intense, chaotic, yet laissez-faire organization. Besides his constant flow of new ideas, Shih's guidance came mainly in the form of the slogans, stories, and concepts he constantly communicated.

This philosophy of delegation extended to organizational units, which, to the extent possible, Shih forced to operate as independent entities and to compete with outside companies. Extending the model externally, Shih began experimenting with joint ventures as a way of expanding sales. The first such arrangement was struck with a couple of entrepreneurs in central and southern Taiwan. While capturing the partners' knowledge of those regional markets, this approach allowed Multitech to expand its sales without the risk of hiring more people or raising more capital.

Early successes through employee ownership, delegated accountability, management frugality, and joint ventures led to what Shih called a "commoner's culture." This reflected his belief that the way to succeed against wealthy multinationals—"the nobility"—was to join forces with other "commoners"—mass-market customers, local distributors, owner-employees, small investors and supplier-partners, for example. The "poor man's" values supported this culture and guided early expansion. As early as 1978, Shih targeted smaller neighboring markets that were of lesser interest to the global giants. At first, response to Multitech's promotional letters was poor since few foreign distributors believed that a Taiwanese company

1985	1986	1987	1988	1989	1990	1991	1992	1993	1994
94.8	165.3	331.2	530.9	688.9	949.5	985.2	1,259.8	1,883	3,220
5.1	3.9	15.3	26.5	5.8	(0.7)	(26.0)	(2.8)	85.6	205
1,632	2,188	3,639	5,072	5,540	5,711	5,216	5,352	7,200	5,825

could supply quality hi-tech products. Through persistence, however, Multitech established partnerships with dealers and distributors in Indonesia, Malaysia, Singapore, and Thailand. Shih described this early expansion strategy:

> It is like the strategy in the Japanese game *Go*—one plays from the corner, because you need fewer resources to occupy the corner. Without the kind of resources that Japanese and American companies had, we started in smaller markets. That gives us the advantage because these smaller markets are becoming bigger and bigger and the combination of many small markets is not small.

Expansion abroad—primarily through Asia, Middle East and Latin America—was greatly helped by a growing number of new products. In 1981, Multitech introduced its first mainstream commercial product, the "Microprofessor" computer. Following the success of this inexpensive, simple computer (little more than an elaborate scientific calculator), Shih and his colleagues began to recognize the enormous potential of the developing PC market. In 1983, Multitech began to manufacture IBM-compatible PCs—primarily as an original equipment manufacturer (OEM) for major brands but also under its own Multitech brand. In 1984 sales reached $51 million, representing a sevenfold increase on revenues three years earlier.

By 1986, the company felt it was ready to stake a claim in Europe, establishing a marketing office in Dusseldorf and a warehouse in Amsterdam. Multitech also supplemented the commission-based purchasing unit it had previously opened in the United States with a fully fledged sales office.

Birth of the Dragon Dream   By the mid-1980s, Multitech's sales were doubling each year and confidence was high. As the company approached its tenth anniversary, Shih announced a plan for the next ten years that he described as "Dragon Dreams." With expected 1986 revenues of $150 million, employees and outsiders alike gasped at his projected sales of $5 billion by 1996. Critics soon began quoting the old Chinese aphorism, "To allay your hunger, draw a picture of a big cake." But Shih saw huge potential in overseas expansion. After only a few years of international experience, the company's overseas sales already accounted for half the total. In several Asian countries Multitech was already a major player: in Singapore, for example, it had a 25% market share by 1986. To build on this Asian base and the new offices in Europe and the United States, Shih created the slogan, "The Rampaging Dragon Goes International." To implement the initiative, he emphasized the need to identify potential overseas acquisitions, set up offshore companies, and seek foreign partners and distributors.

When the number of Acer employees exceeded 2000 during the tenth year anniversary, Shih held a "Renewal of Company Culture Seminar" at which he invited his board and vice presidents to identify and evaluate the philosophies that had guided Multitech in its first ten years. Middle-level managers were then asked to participate in the process, reviewing, debating, and eventually voting on the key principles that would carry the company forward. The outcome was a statement of four values that captured the essence of their shared beliefs: an assumption that human nature is essentially good; a commitment to maintaining a fundamental pragmatism and accountability in all business affairs; a belief in placing the customer first; and a norm of pooling effort and sharing knowledge. (A decade later, these principles could still be found on office walls worldwide.)

Finally, the anniversary year was capped by another major achievement: Acer became the second company in the world to develop and launch a 32-bit PC, even beating IBM to market. Not only did the product win Taiwan's Outstanding Product Design Award—Acer's fifth such award in seven years—it also attracted the attention of such major overseas high-tech companies as Unisys, ICL and ITT, who began negotiations for OEM supply, and even technology licensing agreements.

Rebirth as Acer: Going Public Unfortunately, Multitech's growing visibility also led to a major problem. A U.S. company with the registered name "Multitech" informed its Taiwanese namesake that they were infringing its trademark. After ten years of building a corporate reputation and brand identity, Shih conceded he had to start over. He chose the name "Acer" because its Latin root meant "sharp" or "clever," because "Ace" implied first or highest value in cards—but mostly because it would be first in alphabetical listings. Despite advice to focus on the profitable OEM business and avoid the huge costs of creating a new global brand, Shih was determined to make Acer a globally recognized name.

Beyond branding, the success of the 32-bit PC convinced Shih that Acer would also have to maintain its rapid design, development and manufacturing capability as a continuing source of competitive advantage. Together with the planned aggressive international expansion, these new strategic imperatives—to build a brand and maintain its technological edge—created investment needs that exceeded Acer's internal financing capability. When officials from Taiwan's Securities and Exchange Commission approached Shih about a public offering, he agreed to study the possibility although he knew that many Taiwanese were suspicious of private companies that went public.

A program that allowed any employee with one year of company service to purchase shares had already diluted the Shihs' original 50% equity to about 35%, but in 1987 they felt it may be time to go further. (Shih had long preached that it was "better to lose control but make money" and that "real control came through ensuring common interest.") An internal committee asked to study the issue of going public concluded that the company would not only raise needed funds for expansion but also would provide a market for employee-owned shares. In 1988, Acer negotiated a complex multi-tiered financing involving investments by companies (such as Prudential, Chase Manhattan, China Development Corporation, and Sumitomo), additional sales to employees and, finally, a public offering. In total, Acer raised NT $2.2 billion (US $88 million). Issued at NT $27.5, the stock opened trading at NT $47 and soon rose to well over NT $100. After the IPO, Acer employees held about 65% of the equity including the Shihs' share, which had fallen to less than 25%.

The Professionalization of Acer

While the public offering had taken care of Acer's capital shortage, Shih worried about the company's acute shortage of management caused by its rapid growth. In early 1985, when the number of employees first exceeded 1,000, he began to look outside for new recruits "to take charge and stir things up with new ideas." Over the next few years, he brought in about a dozen top-level executives and 100 middle managers. To many of the self-styled "ground troops" (the old-timers), these "paratroopers" were intruders who didn't understand Acer's culture or values but were attracted by the soaring stock. For the first time, Acer experienced significant turnover.

Paratroopers and Price Pressures Because internally grown managers lacked international experience, one of the key tasks assigned to the "paratroopers" was to implement the company's ambitious offshore expansion plans. In late 1987, Acer acquired Counterpoint, the U.S.-based manufacturer of low-end minicomputers—a business with significantly higher margins than PCs. To support this new business entry, Acer then acquired and expanded the operations of Service Intelligence, a computer service and support organization. Subsequently, a dramatic decline in the market for minicomputers led to Acer's first new product for this segment, the Concer, being a dismal disappointment. Worse still, the substantial infrastructure installed to support it began generating huge losses.

Meanwhile, the competitive dynamics in the PC market were changing. In the closing years of the 1980s, Packard Bell made department and discount stores into major computer retailers, while Dell established its direct sales model. Both moves led to dramatic PC price reductions, and Acer's historic gross margin of about 35% began eroding rapidly, eventually dropping ten percentage points. Yet despite these problems, spirits were high in Acer, and in mid-1989 the company shipped its one millionth PC. Flush with new capital, the company purchased properties and companies within Taiwan worth $150 million. However, Acer's drift from its "commoner's culture" worried Shih, who felt he needed help to restore discipline to the "rampaging dragon." The ambition to grow had to be reconciled with the reality of Acer's financial situation.

Enter Leonard Liu   Projected 1989 results indicated that the overextended company was in a tailspin. Earnings per share were expected to fall from NT $5 to NT $1.42. The share price, which had been as high as NT $150, fell to under NT $20. (See Exhibit 2.) Concerned by the growing problems, Shih decided to bring in an experienced top-level executive. After more than a year of courting, in late 1989, he signed Leonard Liu, Taiwan-born, U.S.-based, senior IBM executive with a reputation for a no-nonsense professional management style. In an announcement that caught many by surprise, Shih stepped down as president of the Acer Group, handing over that day-to-day management role to Liu. In addition, Liu was named CEO and Chairman of AAC, the company's North American subsidiary.

Exhibit 2   Acer Share Price History, November 1988–January 1995

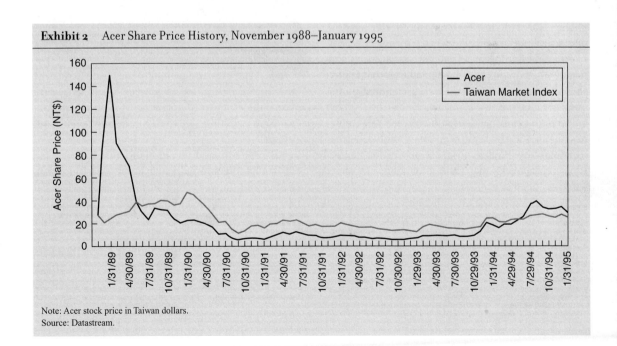

Note: Acer stock price in Taiwan dollars.
Source: Datastream.

Given Shih's desire to generate $5 billion in sales by 1996, Liu began to focus on opportunities in the networking market in the United States. Despite the continuing problems at Counterpoint and Service Intelligence, he agreed with those who argued that Acer could exploit this market by building on its position in high-end products, particularly in the advanced markets of the United States and Europe. In particular, Liu became interested in the highly regarded multi-user minicomputer specialist, Altos. Founded in 1977, this Silicon Valley networking company had 700 employees, worldwide distribution in 60 countries, and projected sales of $170 million for 1990. Although it had generated losses of $3 million and $5 million in the previous two years, Liu felt that Altos's $30 million in cash reserves and $20 million in real estate made it an attractive acquisition. In August 1990, Acer paid $94 million to acquire the respected Altos brand, its technology and its distribution network.[1] Almost immediately, however, powerful new PCs began to offer an alternative means of multi-user networking, and, as if to remind management of the eclipse of Counterpoint's minicomputers, within a year of its purchase, Altos was losing $20 million. Through the 1990s, AAC's losses increased.

In addition to this strategic thrust, Liu also began working on Acer's established organization and management approaches. For example, under Shih's leadership, while managers had been given considerable independence to oversee their business units, they had not been given profit and loss responsibility. Furthermore, because of the family-style relationship that existed among long-time company members, inter-company transfers were often priced to do friends a favor and ensure that a buyer did not "lose face" on a transaction. Even outsourced products were often bought at prices negotiated to make long-term suppliers look good. With no accountability for the profits of their business units, managers had little incentive to ensure quality or price, and would let the group absorb the loss. As one Acer observer noted, the company was "frugal and hard-working, but with little organizational structure or procedure-based administration."

As Shih had hoped, Liu brought to Acer some of IBM's professional management structures, practices and systems. To increase accountability at Acer, the new president reduced management layers, established standards for intra-company communications, and introduced productivity and performance evaluations. Most significantly, he introduced the Regional Business Unit/Strategic Business Unit (RBU/SBU) organization. Acer's long-established product divisions became SBUs responsible for the design, development, and production of PC components and system products, including OEM product sales. Simultaneously, the company's major overseas subsidiaries and marketing companies became RBUs responsible for developing distribution channels, providing support for dealers, distributor networks, and customers, and working to establish JVs in neighboring markets. All SBUs and RBUs had full profit responsibility. "The pressure definitely increased. I was eating fourteen rice boxes a week," said one RBU head, referring to the practice of ordering in food to allow meetings to continue through lunch and dinner.

By 1992, in addition to the four core SBUs, five RBUs had been established: Acer Sertek covering China and Taiwan; Acer Europe headquartered in the Netherlands; Acer America (AAC) responsible for North America; and Acer Computer International (ACI), headquartered in Singapore and responsible for Asia, Africa, and Latin America. (See Exhibits 3a and 3b.) One of the immediate effects of the new structures and systems was to highlight the considerable losses being generated by AAC, for which Liu was directly responsible. While no

---

[1]Because this was a much larger deal than either Counterpoint (acquired for $1 million plus a stock swap) or Service Intelligence (a $500,000 transaction), Shih suggested the deal be structured as a joint venture to maintain the Altos managers' stake in the business. However, Liu insisted on an outright acquisition to ensure control, and Shih deferred to his new president's judgment.

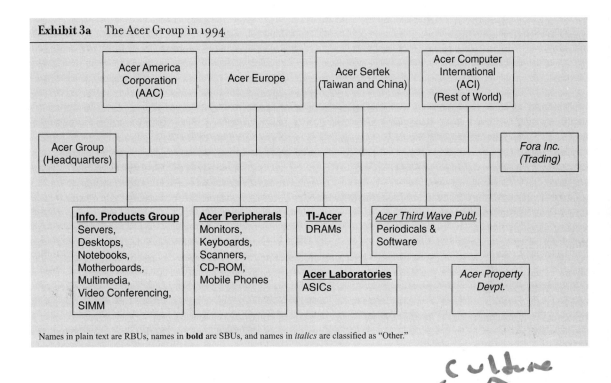

Exhibit 3a   The Acer Group in 1994

Names in plain text are RBUs, names in **bold** are SBUs, and names in *italics* are classified as "Other."

longer formally engaged in operations, Shih was urging the free-spending Altos management to adopt the more frugal Acer norms, and even began preaching his "duck egg" pricing theory. But demand was dropping precipitously and Liu decided stronger measures were required. He implemented tight controls and began layoffs.

Meanwhile, the company's overall profitability was plummeting. (See Exhibits 4 and 5.) A year earlier, Shih had introduced an austerity campaign that had focused on turning lights off, using both sides of paper, and traveling economy class. By 1990, however, Liu felt sterner measures were called for, particularly to deal with a payroll that had ballooned to 5,700 employees. Under an initiative dubbed Metamorphosis, managers were asked to rank employee performance, identifying the top 15% and lowest 30%. In January 1991, 300 of the Taiwan-based "thirty percenters" were terminated—Acer's first major layoffs.

The cumulative effect of declining profits, layoffs, more "paratroopers," and particularly the new iron-fisted management style challenged Acer's traditional culture. In contrast to Shih's supportive, family-oriented approach, Liu's "by-the-numbers" management model proved grating. There was also growing resentment of his tendency to spend lavishly on top accounting and law firms and hire people who stayed at first-class hotels, all of which seemed out of step with Acer's "commoner's culture." Soon, his credibility as a highly respected world-class executive was eroding and Acer managers began questioning his judgement and implementing his directives half-heartedly.

In January 1992, when Shih realized that Acer's 1991 results would be disastrous, he offered his resignation. The board unanimously rejected the offer, suggesting instead that he resume his old role as CEO. In May 1992, Leonard Liu resigned.

Exhibit 3b Acer's Geographical Distribution in 1994

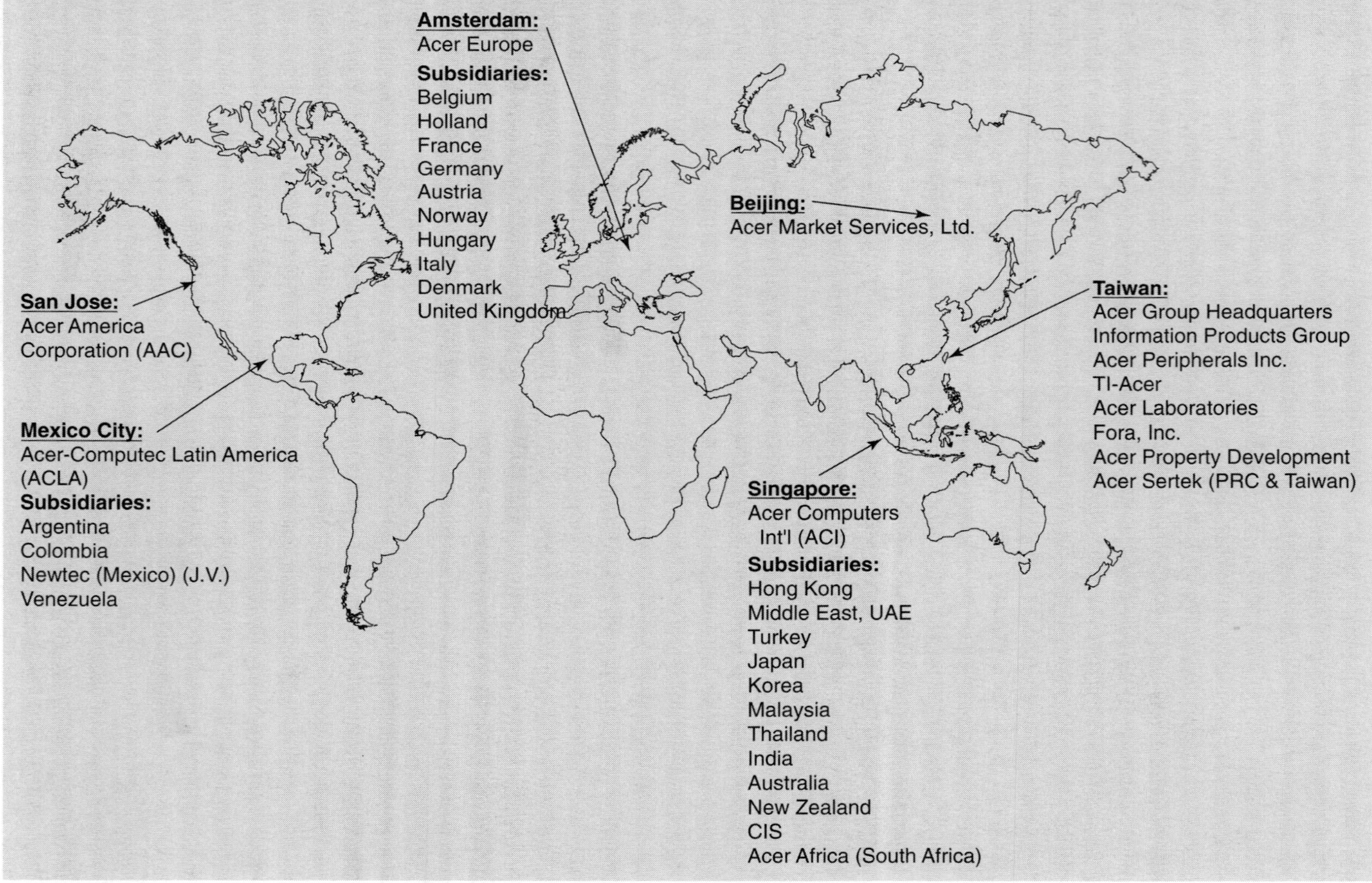

Amsterdam:
Acer Europe
Subsidiaries:
Belgium
Holland
France
Germany
Austria
Norway
Hungary
Italy
Denmark
United Kingdom

San Jose:
Acer America
Corporation (AAC)

Mexico City:
Acer-Computec Latin America
(ACLA)
Subsidiaries:
Argentina
Colombia
Newtec (Mexico) (J.V.)
Venezuela

Beijing:
Acer Market Services, Ltd.

Taiwan:
Acer Group Headquarters
Information Products Group
Acer Peripherals Inc.
TI-Acer
Acer Laboratories
Fora, Inc.
Acer Property Development
Acer Sertek (PRC & Taiwan)

Singapore:
Acer Computers
Int'l (ACI)
Subsidiaries:
Hong Kong
Middle East, UAE
Turkey
Japan
Korea
Malaysia
Thailand
India
Australia
New Zealand
CIS
Acer Africa (South Africa)

Exhibit 4 Acer Combination Income Statement, 1988–1994

	1988	1989	1990	1991	1992	1993	1994
Income Statement ($ millions)							
Turnover	530.9	688.9	949.5	985.2	1,260	1,883	3,220
Cost of sales	(389.4)	(532.7)	(716.7)	(737.7)	(1,000)	(1,498)	(2,615)
Gross profit	141.6	156.3	232.8	247.5	260	385	605
SG&A expenses	(88.2)	(118.2)	(192.2)	(217.2)	(217)	(237)	(316)
R&D and other expenses	(17.9)	(25.4)	(47.7)	(42.3)	(38)	(48)	(59)
Operating profit/(loss)	35.6	12.7	(7.1)	(12.0)	5	100	230
Non-operating profit/(loss)	(8)	(6.3)	(1.5)	(15)	(4)	(11)	(19)
Profit before tax	27.6	6.4	(8.6)	(27.0)	1	89	212
Tax	(1.2)	(1)	(1.2)	1	(3)	(3)	(7)
Profit (loss) after tax	26.4	5.4	(9.8)	(26.0)	(3)	86	205
Sales by Region (%)							
North America	NA	31	31	31	38	44	39
Europe	NA	32	28	28	22	23	17
Rest of world	NA	37	41	41	40	33	44
Combination Revenue by Product (%)							
Portables	NA	NA	3.2	2.9	7.9	18 ⎫	60%
Desktops and motherboards	NA	NA	60.9	56.3	54.9	47 ⎬	
Minicomputers	NA	NA	13.9	11.3	6.6	⎭	
Peripherals and other	NA	NA	22	29.5	30.6	35	40%
Combination Revenue by Business (%)							
Brand	NA	53	47	NA	58	68	56%
OEM	NA	34	22	NA	18	32	36%
Trading	NA	13	31	NA	24	NA	7%

Source: Company Annual Reports year ending December 31.

Exhibit 5   Consolidated Balance Sheet, 1988–1994

Acer Group Balance Sheet ($ millions)	1988	1989	1990	1991	1992	1993	1994
Current Assets	277.30	448.80	579.50	600.90	700.20	925.00	1355.00
Fixed Assets							
Land, plant, and equipment (after depreciation)	53.10	126.90	191.10	161.50	179.60	590.00	645.00
Deferred charges and other assets	11.50	22.90	60.90	239.50	212.30	69.00	82.00
Total assets	341.90	598.60	831.50	1001.90	1092.10	1584.00	2082.00
Total current liabilities	189.40	248.60	464.60	505.80	504.20	752.00	1067.00
Long-term liabilities	11.20	16.60	43.70	168.50	214.30	342.00	312.00
Total liabilities	200.60	265.20	508.40	674.30	718.50	1094.00	1379.00
Stockholders equity and minority interest (including new capital infusions)	141.30	333.40	323.10	327.60	373.60	490.00	703.00

Source: Company documents.

Rebuilding the Base

Shih had long regarded mistakes and their resulting losses as "tuition" for Acer employees' growth—the price paid for a system based on delegation. He saw the losses generated in the early 1990s as part of his personal learning, considering it an investment rather than a waste. ("To make Acer an organization that can think and learn," he said, "we must continue to pay tuition as long as mistakes are unintentional and long-term profits exceed the cost of the education.") As he reclaimed the CEO role, Shih saw the need to fundamentally rethink Acer's management philosophy, the organizational model that reflected it, and even the underlying basic business concept.

"Global Brand, Local Touch" Philosophy   At Acer's 1992 International Distributors Meeting in Cancun, Mexico, Shih articulated a commitment to linking the company more closely to its national markets, describing his vision as "Global Brand, Local Touch." Under this vision, he wanted Acer to evolve from a Taiwanese company with offshore sales to a truly global organization with deeply planted local roots.

Building on the company's long tradition of taking minority positions in expansionary ventures, Shih began to offer established Acer distributors equity partnerships in the RBU they served. Four months after the Cancun meeting, Acer acquired a 19% interest in Computec, its Mexican distributor. Because of its role in building Acer into Mexico's leading PC brand, Shih invited Computec to form a joint venture company responsible for all Latin America. The result was Acer Computec Latin America (ACLA), a company subsequently floated on the Mexican stock exchange. Similarly, Acer Computers International (ACI), the company responsible for sales in Southeast Asia, planned an initial public offering in Singapore in mid-1995. And in Taiwan, Shih was even considering taking some of Acer's core SBUs public.

As these events unfolded, Shih began to articulate an objective of "21 in 21," a vision of the Acer Group as a federation of 21 public companies, each with significant local ownership, by the 21st century. It was what he described as "the fourth way," a strategy of globalization radically different from the control-based European, American or Japanese models, relying instead on mutual interest and voluntary cooperation of a network of interdependent companies.

Client Server Organization Model   To reinforce the more networked approach of this new management philosophy, in 1993, Shih unveiled his client-server organization model. Using the metaphor of the network computer, he described the role of the Taiwan headquarters as a "server" that used its resources (finance, people, intellectual property) to support "client" business units, which controlled key operating activities. Under this concept of a company as a network, business units could leverage their own ideas or initiatives directly through other RBUs or SBUs without having to go through the corporate center which was there to help and mediate, not dictate or control. Shih believed that this model would allow Acer to develop speed and flexibility as competitive weapons.

While the concept was intriguing, it was a long way from Acer's operating reality. Despite the long-established philosophy of decentralization and the introduction of independent profit-responsible business units in 1992, even the largest RBUs were still viewed as little more than the sales and distribution arms of the Taiwan-based SBUs. To operationalize the client server concept, Shih began to emphasize several key principles. "Every man is lord of his castle," became his battle cry to confirm the independence of SBU and RBU heads. Thus, when two SBUs—Acer Peripherals (API) and Information Products (IPG)—both decided to produce CD-ROM drives, Shih did not intervene to provide a top-down decision, opting instead to let the market decide. The result was that both units succeeded, eventually supplying CD-ROMs to almost 70% of PCs made in Taiwan, by far the world's leading source of OEM and branded PCs.

In another initiative, Shih began urging that at least half of all Acer products and components be sold outside the Group, hoping to ensure internal sources were competitive. Then, introducing the principle, "If it doesn't hurt, help," he spread a doctrine that favored internal suppliers. However, under the "lord of the castle" principle, if an RBU

decided to improve its bottom line by sourcing externally, it could do so. But it was equally clear that the affected SBU could then find an alternative distributor for its output in that RBU's region. In practice, this mutual deterrence—referred to as the "nuclear option"—was recognized as a strategy of last resort that was rarely exercised. Despite Shih's communication of these new operating principles, the roles and relationships between SBU and RBUs remained in flux over several years as managers worked to understand the full implications of the client server model on their day-to-day responsibilities.

The Fast-Food Business Concept   But the biggest challenges Shih faced on his return were strategic. Even during the two and a half years he had stepped back to allow Liu to lead Acer, competition in the PC business had escalated significantly, with the product cycle shortening to 6 to 9 months and prices dropping. As if to highlight this new reality, in May 1992, the month Liu left, Compaq announced a 30% across-the-board price reduction on its PCs. Industry expectations were for a major shakeout of marginal players. Given Acer's financial plight, some insiders urged the chairman to focus on OEM sales only, while others suggested a retreat from the difficult U.S. market. But Shih believed that crisis was a normal condition in business and that persistence usually paid off. His immediate priority was to halve Acer's five months of inventory—two months being inventory "in transit."

Under Shih's stimulus, various parts of the organization began to create new back-to-basics initiatives. For example, the System PC unit developed the "ChipUp" concept. This patented technology allowed a motherboard to accept different types of CPU chips—various versions of Intel's 386 and 486 chips, for example—drastically reducing inventory of both chips and motherboards. Another unit, Home Office Automation, developed the "2-3-1 System" to reduce the new product introduction process to two months for development, three months for selling and one month for phase-out. And about the same time, a cross-unit initiative to

Exhibit 6   Stan Shih's PC Industry Conceptualization

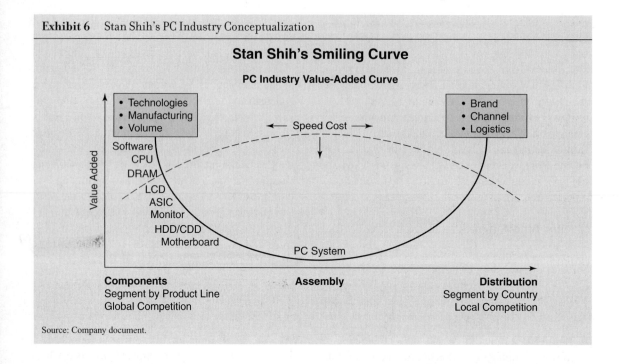

Source: Company document.

support the launch of Acer's home PC, Acros, developed a screwless assembly process, allowing an entire computer to be assembled by snapping together components, motherboard, power source, etc.[2] Integrating all these initiatives and several others, a team of engineers developed Uniload, a production concept that configured components in a standard parts palette for easy unpacking, assembly, and testing, facilitating the transfer of final assembly to RBU operations abroad. The underlying objective was to increase flexibility and responsiveness by moving more assembly offshore.

Uniload's ability to assemble products close to the customer led the CEO to articulate what he termed his "fast-food" business model. Under this approach, small, expensive components with fast-changing technology that represented 50%–80% of total cost (e.g., motherboards, CPUs, hard disc

drives) were airshipped "hot and fresh" from SBU sources in Taiwan to RBUs in key markets, while less-volatile items (e.g., casings, monitors, power supplies) were shipped by sea. Savings in logistics, inventories and import duties on assembled products easily offset higher local labor assembly cost, which typically represented less than 1% of product cost.

As Shih began promoting his fast-food business concept, he met with some internal opposition, particularly from SBUs concerned that giving up systems assembly would mean losing power and control. To convince them that they could increase competitiveness more by focusing on component development, he created a presentation on the value-added elements in the PC industry. "Assembly means you are making money from manual labor," he said. "In components and marketing you add value with your brains." To illustrate the point, Shih developed a disintegrated value-added chart that was soon dubbed "Stan's Smiling Curve." (See Exhibit 6.)

---

[2] To promote the innovative idea, Shih sponsored internal contests to see who could assemble a computer the fastest. Although his personal best time was more than a minute, experts accomplished the task in 30 seconds.

The Turnaround   Describing his role as "to pro-vide innovative stimulus, to recognize the new strat-egy which first emerges in vague ideas, then to com-municate it, form consensus, and agree on action," Shih traveled constantly for two years, taking his message to the organization. Through 1993, the im-pact of the changes began to appear. Most dramati-cally, the fast-food business concept (supported by Liu's systems) caused inventory turnover to double by late 1993, reducing carrying costs, while lower-ing the obsolescence risk. In early 1994, the Group reported a return to profit after three years of losses.

Acer America and the Aspire

After Liu's resignation in April 1992, Shih named Ronald Chwang to head AAC. With a Ph.D. in Electrical Engineering, Chwang joined Acer in 1986 in technical development. After overseeing the start-up of Acer's peripherals business, in 1991

he was given the responsibility for integrating the newly acquired Altos into AAC as president of the Acer/Altos Business Unit.

Because AAC had been losing money since 1987, Chwang's first actions as CEO focused on stemming further losses. As part of that effort, he embraced the dramatic changes being initiated in Taiwan, making AAC's Palo Alto plant the first test assembly site of the Uniload system. Under the new system, manufacture and delivery time was cut from 80 days to 45 days, reducing inventory levels by almost 45%. To support its Uniload site, AAC established a department of approximately 20 engi-neers, primarily to manage component testing, but also to adapt software design to local market needs. By 1994, AAC was breaking even. (See Exhibit 7.)

Birth of Aspire   Despite these improvements, AAC and other RBUs still felt that Acer's Taiwan-based SBUs were too distant to develop product

Exhibit 7	AAC Selected Financials (1990–1994)				
AAC Results ($ millions)	**1990**	**1991**	**1992**	**1993**	**1994**
Revenue	161	235	304	434	858
Cost of sales	133	190	283	399	764
Selling and marketing	27	61	25	23	55
General administration	20	16	17	19	20
Research and development	5	8	6	4	4
Operating profit/(loss)	(24)	(40)	(26)	(11)	15
Non-operating profit/(loss)	(1)	(7)	(3)	(5)	(3)
Profit/(loss) before tax	(25)	(47)	(29)	(16)	12
Tax	1	(2)	0	0	1
Net income/(loss)	(26)	(45)	(29)	(16)	11
Current assets	155	153	123	144	242
Fixed assets (net)	39	43	28	25	25
Other assets (net)	37	37	31	19	11
Total assets	231	233	182	188	278
Current liabilities	155	169	154	136	218
Long-term debt	17	15	18	58	47
Stockholder equity (including additional capital)	58	50	10	(6)	12
Total liabilities	231	233	182	188	278

Note: Totals may not add due to rounding.
Source: Company documents.

configurations that would appeal to diverse consumer and competitive situations around the globe. What might sell well in Southeast Asia could be a year out of date in the United States, for example. However, the emerging "global brand, local touch" philosophy and the client-server organization model supporting it gave them hope that they could change the situation.

In January 1994, Mike Culver was promoted to become AAC's Director of Product Management, a role that gave him responsibility for the product development mandate he felt RBUs could assume under the new client-server model. The 29-year-old engineer and recent MBA graduate had joined Acer America just $2\frac{1}{2}$ years earlier as AAC's product manager for notebook computers. Recently, however, he had become aware of new opportunities in home computing.

Several factors caught Culver's attention. First, data showed an increasing trend to working at home—from 26 million people in 1993 to a projected 29 million in 1994. In addition, there was a rapidly growing interest in the Internet. And finally, developments in audio, telecom, video, and computing technologies were leading to industry rumblings of a new kind of multimedia home PC. Indeed, rumor had it that competitors like Hewlett Packard were already racing to develop new multimedia systems. Sharing this vision, Culver believed the time was right to create "the first Wintel-based PC that could compete with Apple in design, ease-of-use, and multimedia capabilities."

In October of 1994, Culver commissioned a series of focus groups to explore the emerging opportunity. In one of the groups, a consumer made a comment that had a profound impact on him. She said she wanted a computer that wouldn't remind her of work. At that moment, Culver decided that Acer's new home PC would incorporate radically new design aesthetics to differentiate it from the standard putty-colored, boxy PCs that sat in offices throughout the world.

By November, Culver was convinced of the potential for an innovative multimedia consumer PC,

and began assembling a project team to develop the concept. While the team believed the Acer Group probably had the engineering capability to develop the product's new technical features, they were equally sure they would have to go outside to get the kind of innovative design they envisioned. After an exhaustive review, the team selected Frog Design, a leading Silicon Valley design firm that had a reputation for "thinking outside of the box." Up to this point, Culver had been using internal resources and operating within his normal budget. The selection of Frog Design, however, meant that he had to go to Chwang for additional support. "The approval was incredibly informal," related Culver, "it literally took place in one 20 minute discussion in the hallway in late November. I told Ronald we would need $200,000 for outside consulting to create the cosmetic prototype." Chwang agreed on the spot, and the design process began.

In 1994, Acer was in ninth place in the U.S. market, with 2.4% market share, largely from sales of the Acros, Acer's initial PC product, which was an adaptation of its commercial product, the Acer Power. (See Exhibit 8 for 1994 market shares.) Culver and Chwang were convinced they could not only substantially improve Acer's U.S. share, but

Exhibit 8   Top Ten PC Manufacturers in the U.S. and Worldwide in 1994

Company	U.S. Market Share	Worldwide Market Share
Compaq	12.6%	9.8%
Apple	11.5%	8.1%
Packard Bell	11.4%	5.1%
IBM	9.0%	8.5%
Gateway 2000	5.2%	2.3%
Dell	4.2%	2.6%
AST	3.9%	2.7%
Toshiba	3.6%	2.4%
Acer	2.4%	2.6%
Hewlett Packard	2.4%	2.5%

Source: *Los Angeles Times,* January 31, 1996.

also create a product with potential to take a larger share of the global multimedia desktop market estimated at 10.4 million units and growing at more than 20% annually, primarily in Europe and Asia.

Working jointly with designers from Frog Design, the project team talked to consumers, visited computer retail stores and held discussions to brainstorm the new product's form. After almost two months, Frog Design developed six foam models of possible designs. In January 1995, the Acer team chose a striking and sleek profile that bore little resemblance to the traditional PC. Market research also indicated that customers wanted a choice of colors, so the team decided that the newly named Aspire PC would be offered in charcoal grey and emerald green. (See Exhibit 9.)

Meanwhile, the team had been working with AAC software engineers and a development group in Taiwan to incorporate the new multimedia capabilities into the computer. One significant introduction was voice-recognition software that enabled users to open, close, and save documents by

voice commands. However, such enhancements also required new hardware design: to accommodate the voice-recognition feature, for example, a microphone had to be built in, and to properly exploit the machine's enhanced audio capabilities, speakers had to be integrated into the monitor. The multimedia concept also required the integration of CD-ROM capabilities, and a built-in modem and answering machine incorporating fax and telephone capabilities. This type of configuration was a radical innovation for Acer, requiring significant design and tooling changes.

In early 1995 the price differential between upper-tier PCs (IBM, for example) and lower-end products (represented by Packard Bell) was about 20%. Culver's team felt the Aspire could be positioned between these two segments offering a high-quality innovative product at a less-than-premium price. They felt they could gain a strong foothold by offering a product range priced from $1,199 for the basic product to $2,999 for the highest-end system with monitor. With a September launch, they budgeted US sales of $570 million and profits of $17 million for 1995. A global rollout would be even more attractive with an expectation of breakeven within the first few months.

Stan Shih's Decisions

On his way to San Jose in February 1995, Stan Shih pondered the significance of the Aspire project. Clearly, it represented the client-server system at work: this could become the first product designed and developed by an RBU, in response to a locally sensed market opportunity. Beyond that, he had the feeling it might have the potential to become Acer's first global blockbuster product.

Despite its promise, however, Shih wanted to listen to the views of the project's critics. Some pointed out that AAC had just begun to generate profits in the first quarter of 1994, largely on the basis of its solid OEM sales, which accounted for almost 50% of revenues. Given its delicate profit position, they argued that AAC should not be staking its future on the extremely expensive and highly

Exhibit 9 First Generation Aspire Prototype Design

competitive branded consumer products business. Established competitors were likely to launch their own multimedia home PCs—perhaps even before Acer. Building a new brand in this crowded, competitive market was extremely difficult as proven by many failed attempts, including the costly failure of Taiwan-based Mitac, launched as a branded PC in the early 1990s.

Even among those who saw potential in the product, there were several who expressed concern about the project's implementation. With all the company's engineering and production expertise located in Taiwan, these critics argued that the task of coordinating the development and delivery of such an innovative new product was just too risky to leave to an inexperienced group in an RBU with limited development resources. If the project were to be approved, they suggested it be transferred back to the SBUs in Taiwan for implementation.

Finally, some wondered whether Acer's client-server organization model and "local touch" management would support Aspire becoming a viable global product. With the growing independence of the RBUs worldwide, they were concerned that each one would want to redesign the product and marketing strategy for its local market, thereby negating any potential scale economies.

As his plane touched down in San Francisco, Shih tried to resolve his feelings of excitement and concern. Should he support the Aspire project, change it, or put it on hold? And what implications would his decisions have for the new corporate model he had been building?

Case 1-3   Icon Medialab International A.B.

Introduction

In October 2001, as Jesper Jos Olsson, Magnus Bergman, and Rens Buchwaldt, three members of the board of Icon Medialab International AB (Icon), took in the sweeping view of downtown Stockholm from the 16th floor of the firm's Swedish offices, they knew that they and the rest of Icon's board of directors were about to make the most pivotal decision in the life of the company. After five years of spectacular growth that had seen Icon grow from one office in Sweden in 1996 to 32 offices in 19 countries in 2001 (see Exhibit 1 for a list of offices), the company was facing rapidly mounting losses and a dramatic downturn in its business. Revenues had decreased from 427.8 million Swedish kroner[1] (SEK) in the first quarter to SEK 233.5 million in the third quarter while operating losses had increased from SEK 81.6 million in the first quarter to SEK 146.9 million in the third quarter (see Exhibit 2 for financial statements). The board had to decide the best course of action to stem Icon's losses while maintaining its vision of being a global provider of integrated digital solutions. Rens Buchwaldt, interim CEO, summed up the challenges facing Icon:

> We are at a critical juncture in the life of Icon. Our industry is in a turbulent period—we are facing an economic downturn and the industry is consolidating fast. Icon needs to come up with a strategy that will help us survive in the short term and position us for growth in the long term.

This case was written by Ph.D. Candidate Niels Billou (London Business School) under the supervision of Associate Professor Julian Birkinshaw (London Business School) and Ph.D. Candidate Robin Teigland (Stockholm School of Economics). The authors are extremely grateful to Björn Westerberg, Vice President of Strategy at Icon Medialab International, for his generous assistance in making this case study possible. Certain information in this case study has been disguised to protect confidentiality.
© London Business School, 11 December 2001, Regent's Park, London NW1 4SA, United Kingdom.

[1]At the time of case 1EUR = 9.4 SEK and $1 US = 10.4 SEK.

Exhibit 1   Icon Medialab Offices

Region	Country	City	Profit/Loss	Number of Employees
North America	U.S.	New York	+	150
		San Francisco	−	40
		St. Louis,	−	100
		Washington, D.C.	+	50
Europe	Austria	Vienna	+	10
	Belgium	Brussels	+	50
	Denmark	Arhus	+	15
		Copenhagen	−	60
	Finland	Helsinki	+	40
		Tampere	+	60
	France	Paris	=	60
	Germany	Berlin	−	30
		Frankfurt	−	20
		Hamburg	+	80
		Munich	+	30
	Italy	Milan	=	60
	The Netherlands	Amsterdam	−	20
	Norway	Oslo	+	80
	Portugal	Lisbon	=	20
	Spain	Barcelona	+	60
		Madrid	−	120
	Sweden	Gothenburg	−	50
		Malmö	−	30
		Stockholm	=	250
	Switzerland	Basel,	−	20
		Lausanne	−	30
	UK	London	=	50
Australasia	China	Hong Kong	−	70
	Malaysia	Kuala Lumpur	=	20
	Singapore	Singapore	−	60
	Australia	Melbourne	=	50
		Sydney	+	50

Legend: = Breakeven, + Profitable, − Losing money

Company Background

The Founding Years 1996–1998   Icon Medialab was the brainchild of four friends all in their twenties: Johan Staël von Holstein, Jesper Jos Olsson, Erik Wickström, and Magnus Lindahl. Having gained experience in the IT, media, and finance in-dustries by working at the Kinnevik group, a media and financial conglomerate known as a training ground for young Swedish entrepreneurs, the four-some founded Icon around von Holstein's kitchen table in March 1996 in Stockholm, Sweden. Led by the brash von Holstein, the founders forged ahead

Exhibit 2   Icon Medialab Financial Statements

	2001		
	Q3 SEK Millions	Q2 SEK Millions	Q1 SEK Millions
Net sales	233.5	318	427.8
Change % from same Q prior year	−52%	−26%	−54%
Change% sequential Q	−27%	−26%	−16%
Operating earnings	−233.7	−97.9	−178.4
Operating margin	−100%	−31%	−42%
One time items	86.8		96.8
Operating earnings excluding one time changes	**−146.9**	**−97.9**	**−81.6**

Profit and Loss Account

Consolidated Accounts	31/12/2000 12 Months SEK Thousands	31/12/1999 12 Months SEK Thousands	31/12/1998 12 Months SEK Thousands	31/12/1997 12 Months SEK Thousands	31/12/1996 10 Months SEK Thousands
Operating revenue/turnover	1,700,183	416,607	131,611	39,831	7,722
Costs of goods sold	−3,208,409	−479,167	−102,054	−45,899	−9,215
Gross profit	−1,508,226	−62,560	29,557	−6,068	−1,493
Other operating expenses	−919,188	−230,568	−64,170	−19,469	−7,722
Operating P/L	**−2,427,414**	**−293,128**	**−34,613**	**−25,537**	**−9,215**
Financial revenue	−98,306	−1,738	8,030	786	n.a.
Financial expenses	63,292	4,220	998	1,472	n.a.
Financial P/L	−161,598	−5,958	7,032	−686	n.a.
P/L before tax	−2,589,012	−295,700	−27,581	−26,223	−9,386
Taxation	20,893	2,240	18	11	0
P/L after tax	−2,609,905	−297,940	−27,599	−26,234	−9,386
Extraordinary P/L	0	−805	−7	9	0
P/L for period	**−2,609,905**	**−298,745**	**−27,606**	**−26,225**	**−9,386**

Balance Sheet

Consolidated Accounts	31/12/2000 12 Months SEK Thousands	31/12/1999 12 Months SEK Thousands	31/12/1998 12 Months SEK Thousands	30/04/1998 12 Months SEK Thousands	30/04/1997 10 Months SEK Thousands
Intangible fixed assets	466,477	1,160,428	9,501	7,939	0
Tangible fixed assets	195,840	70,607	24,064	9,960	2,848
Other fixed assets	155,588	10,647	4,571	736	285
Stocks	0	10,875	1,017	402	3,255
Debtors	471,539	189,673	38,074	12,946	7,168
Other current assets	173,331	48,640	11,217	11,524	2,881
Cash and cash equivalent	267,068	253,694	51,756	2,446	16
Total assets	**1,729,843**	**1,744,564**	**140,200**	**45,953**	**16,453**

Exhibit 2   *(Continued)*

Consolidated Accounts	31/12/2000 12 Months SEK Thousands	31/12/1999 12 Months SEK Thousands	31/12/1998 12 Months SEK Thousands	30/04/1998 12 Months SEK Thousands	30/04/1997 10 Months SEK Thousands
Restricted equity	3,918,869	1,741,670	165,841	37,539	7,978
Loss brought forward	−324,648	−75,874	−36,429	−2,811	−5
Net loss for the year	−2,609,905	−298,745	−36,827	−31,825	−2,606
Minority interests	0	0	91	82	0
Provisions	145,059	108,323	0	0	0
Long-term liabilities	53,162	15,249	12,564	19,838	3,549
Advance payments from customers	9,141	20,024	985	427	4,208
Other short term liabilities	538,165	233,917	33,975	22,703	3,329
Total equity and liabilities	**1,729,843**	**1,744,564**	**140,200**	**45,953**	**16,453**
Number of employees	1,990	1,056	300	141	62

with their idea to rapidly create a global, world-class e-business professional service firm. The firm would provide a one-stop shop for its clients' Internet development needs, bringing together strategy, design and technology skills under one roof.

The company's first office was in a garment warehouse in one of Stockholm's harbours, but it had grand ambitions of going global and pursing large multinational clients from the beginning. Initially, however, they had a difficult time finding funding for their plans, as Swedish venture capitalists were scarce and reluctant to invest in what they perceived to be a high-risk venture. Despite this, the founders managed to convince enough investors to begin realising their international growth plans. By December 1996 Icon had established its first office outside of Sweden, in Madrid, Spain, and in January 1997, a second one was opened in San Francisco. The company also quickly signed up its first high-profile client, The Swedish Post.

The picture, however, was not all that rosy: the company's rapid international expansion had stretched its resources and the firm was nearly out of cash when it was rescued by two entrepreneurs from Gothenburg. This new round of financing helped put Icon back on track. By the end of 1997

Icon had established offices, or *Labs,* in Denmark, Finland, Spain, the UK, and the US, and had over 100 employees. By the time of its initial public offering (IPO) in June 1998, which was fourteenfold oversubscribed, Icon had around 200 employees and seven Labs in Europe and the USA, with plans underway to open Labs in Asia.

The Golden Years 1998–2000   After the IPO, armed with a soaring stock price and a healthy war chest, Icon began to aggressively pursue its goal to become a globally networked company providing digital solutions to local clients and start-ups as well as large multinational firms. Icon's growth strategy followed two paths. The primary growth strategy was to build relationships with leading local Internet consultancies and then acquire and enlarge their operations. The owners were usually asked to remain in charge, and their company adopted the Icon Medialab moniker followed by the city in which it was located, e.g., Icon Medialab Berlin. The secondary strategy was to build greenfield operations, which were set up by Icon managers and staffed locally. Icon's growth strategy gave the firm the advantage of being perceived as an international company with a global reach but with in-depth local market knowledge. This strategy, dubbed "going glocal" by Icon, paid off handsomely. At the end of 1999, the company had over 1000 employees, revenues of SEK 400 million, and an enviable client list that included blue-chip multinationals such as Ericsson, Hewlett-Packard, Siemens, and Sony. The company won a string of awards for its interactive websites and was featured in numerous articles in the international business press, including being chosen as one of the top 250 small-to-medium firms by *Fortune* magazine in 1998.

As Icon continued to grow, it realized it needed to make the transition from a brash start-up to a more mature multinational. In September of 1999, Icon signed on as CEO Ulf Dahlsten, former head of Sweden Post. Mr. Dahlsten was credited with transforming the Swedish Post from a stodgy mail service into an efficient and Internet savvy business-to-business firm. Under Dahlsten, Icon moved its headquarters to Brussels to be more centrally located in its far-flung network of Medialabs and recruited more seasoned managers to lead the firm. The firm entered into a strategic investment relationship with the Interpublic Group of Companies (IPG), a global holding company that consisted of advertising agencies and marketing services in over 100 countries. Icon continued to aggressively expand, increasing the size of current labs and adding new labs. A separate company, Icon Medialab Asia, led by von Holstein was formed in 2000 and Labs were established in Hong Kong, Kuala Lumpur, Melbourne, Singapore and Sydney. By the end of the second quarter 2000, the firm had 1700 employees in 16 countries, was on target to make sales of SEK 1.5 billion for the year, and had reached operating profitability.

The Icon Medialab Business Model

As Icon strove to achieve its dream of becoming a global provider of digital solutions, its executives realised they would have to create a unique organization model.

Management and Organisation   Icon's organisation was a decentralised regional structure with six regions, United States, Sweden, United Kingdom,

Northern Europe, Central Europe, and Southern Europe. The managers of these six regions, along with the CEO, and two other managers, one in charge of offerings and alliances, and the other in charge of industry verticals, comprised the executive team.

The company was also organised along global industry verticals. Icon segmented their clients and clients-to-be into six verticals: Pharma/Health, Financial Services, Media/Telecom, Retail, Manufacturing, and Travel.

Culture   Central to the organization model was the intention to build an ethos that was very different from the traditional, reserved Swedish business culture. The founders set about to create a high-energy, high-performance culture by offering what they called the "3M's," Money, Meaning, and Magic. For example, Icon's focus on Money led it to be one of the first Swedish companies to offer stock options to all employees and to use performance bonuses as a significant part of an employee's pay. To create Meaning, Icon pursued market leaders as clients, used multidisciplinary teams to deliver projects, and allowed 20% of employees' time to be spent on training and development. To create Magic, the founders promoted a fast-paced, flexible, flat and close-knit organisation culture, located their offices in prime locations, and kept the media spotlight on the firm's achievements. Employees were encouraged to be creative, go beyond acceptable solutions and try ideas that were new and innovative. With the 3M's in place, Icon strived to achieve its internal slogan of becoming a "Kick Ass!" company.

Systems and Processes   In step with the culture, Icon instituted systems and processes that would help deliver superior value to its customers. A cornerstone of this was the use of multidisciplinary teams, each possessing skills across the business, user, and technology competencies (see Exhibit 3 for team structure). Referred to as the Cube, the idea was that each side of the cube represents a fundamental skillset or competency needed for implementing world-class e-business. The six competencies, represented by the sides of the cube, were

Exhibit 3   Team Structure

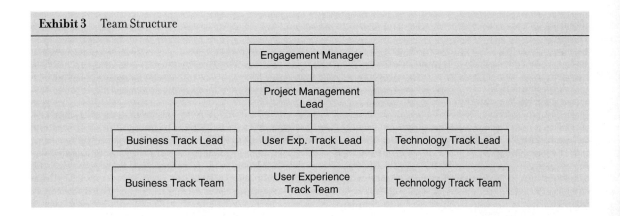

Management Consulting, Technology, Design and Communication, Branding, Human Computer Interaction (HCI—optimising the design of an application for users) and Statistics and Analysis (analysis of web traffic and user statistics). The assigned Icon expert, known as a competency coach, would be responsible for maintaining and developing that particular skill set throughout the entire Icon Medialab group of companies. A final competency that functioned as the glue that held the cube together was Project Management.

The close coordination of the team members allowed Icon to offer a well-integrated solution that delivered on all the requirements of the client. However, this approach came at a cost. Coordination was difficult to achieve, especially if multiple sites were involved. For example, on a large-scale project that involved seven countries, one project manager would have to fly around to various locations, attempting to balance the needs of each client in each region, while coordinating different competencies in different offices.

▎ The Icon Process™

The firm had developed the Icon Process™ (see Exhibit 4 for diagram and Exhibit 5 for account of an actual project), a four-phase iterative project management process that aimed to achieve specific pre-determined milestones and produce actionable plans that would lead to the timely completion of each phase of development.

As a result, Icon had the capability to deliver a range of products from small, 500 man-hour web design projects for a local company to large, 50,000 man-hour, global projects that involved business strategy, web design, and system integration. The average project typically involved 2,000–3,000 man-hours. The following outlines each step of the Icon Process™.

Phase 1: Inception   In the first phase, the requirements of the client were assessed in order to determine the scope, timing and costs of the project. Depending on the project's needs, a series of analyses (e.g., competitive analysis, enterprise analysis, user research, usability benchmarks) was undertaken to develop a "concept book," Icon's vision for a new e-business, Intranet, extranet, or other web-based application.

Phase 2: Elaboration   In this stage, the team began to focus more deeply on the user experience and technical software architecture. The key task at this stage was to build a user interface prototype based on the information architecture and the creative concept.

Phase 3: Construction   In this phase, the prototype was refined in an iterative process that increased the functionality and quality until reaching the agreed scope.

Phase 4: Transition   In this last phase, the clients performed the final acceptance testing and the

Exhibit 4   The Icon Process

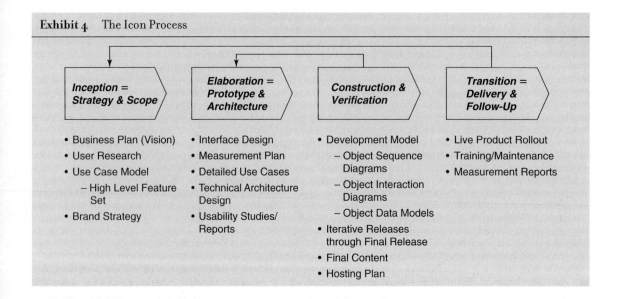

application went live. This phase included monitoring and evaluating the live site, and fine-tuning for optimum performance and results. A senior project manager commented on the process:

> The Icon Process allows us to focus on the client's requirements and make sure that we are meeting them every step of the way. Combined with our Cube approach of pulling people with the right mix of skills and competencies together, we are able to deliver a better value proposition than our competitors. For example, we recently won a bid against some large rivals by doing a great deal of up-front work in the inception phase to uncover the real needs of the client's business, not just what they told us they needed, and then by offering them a concept that included not only a technical perspective, but also strategic and user perspectives.

Knowledge Management at Icon

As a professional service firm, Icon knew that its key task was to leverage the knowledge resources of the firm. Consequently, Icon instituted a set of activities and structures that would help with the creation of new knowledge and the dissemination and leveraging of existing knowledge throughout

the company. In early 2000, Icon hired Ulf Tingström as the Chief Knowledge Officer (CKO) to head a group called Knowledge Management International (KMI). KMI's objectives were to drive the overall knowledge management (KM) strategy, projects and implementation for the firm.

The cornerstone of Icon's KM activities was to establish communities of practice, called Knowledge Communities (KCs). These KCs were networks of individuals connected across Labs with the same experiences and interests. These communities were organised by knowledge area, e.g., competencies such as branding and industries such as automotive. Several key roles were created to organize the knowledge communities, as described and shown in the Exhibit 6. However, with the exception of the CKO, there were no dedicated knowledge management positions. Individuals were assigned to roles and responsibilities on a rotating basis according to volunteer participation and interest and were expected to spend 5–40% of their time on knowledge management activities, depending on their role.

To facilitate the flow of knowledge, Icon installed an intranet, where community members could

Exhibit 5   Project Management

A project manager described the process on a project completed for Ericsson's Radio Systems Division:

"For this project, Ericsson was interested in creating an online version of their monthly magazine for their global sales force, called *In Brief*. The engagement manager and I met with the editor of the newsletter to discuss her vision for the newsletter, her requirements, the main starting areas and the length of the project. This meeting determined which competencies to bring together and who would be on the team. In this case, the team consisted of an art director, an HCI specialist, a web designer, a systems architect and three programmers.

I then wrote a project definition document that detailed the deliverables, people involved, and the cost. Once the client agreed to this, we did a series of workshops, involving the clients and the team members. For example, the HCI specialist would meet with users to see how they would interact with application, the art director would meet with editors to produce design sketches for the web pages, and the system architects would meet with technical people to understand the system requirements. The team would meet as a group daily for 30 min to share information and discuss the evolving requirements of the project.

When we had gathered enough information, all members of the team worked together to build a prototype. The HCI specialist fed information from the users to the art director, web designer, and technical people, who fed back information to each other to come up with a prototype that was visually appealing, easy to navigate, and reliable. Once the prototype was built, it was tested with 15 users in four countries, England, Holland, Norway, and Sweden. The Labs outside of Sweden helped to facilitate these tests by serving as contact points for the users in those countries.

After the testing was complete, a usability report was written that outlined the performance of the prototype and issues that needed to be resolved. This led to a refining of the project definition document as some requirements were dropped and others were added. The group was still meeting every day, and I was filing weekly status reports to document the progress of the project over the course of the week.

We were now into the construction phase on this project. The programmers and the web designer did the bulk of the remaining work. The programmers were building the 'back end'—the databases, content management systems and integrating the system with the current Ericsson architecture, while the web designer was working on the 'front end,' writing the HTML code for the web pages. There needed to be close cooperation between the two groups as there were usually incompatibilities between what was desired on the front end and what could be delivered at the back end.

As the magazine came closer to completion, it was tested within Icon by an HCI specialist, a senior programmer, and myself. A fault report was generated for identifying and addressing key problems and a timeline given for correcting them.

The entire group was no longer meeting on a daily basis. The HCI specialist and art director had started to take on other projects although they were still kept involved in this project and kept appraised of the project via the weekly status reports.

With the testing complete, we moved into the final phase of project. We staged a live run for one week as a final acceptance test. A few small bugs were identified and corrected. I then wrote a final report and made a presentation to the editor of the magazine. She was very satisfied with the project, which is just they way I like to end a project! To make sure they remained satisfied, three months after the launch, we contacted a small sample of users to receive feedback on the site. As well, we monitored the site traffic to see if the site had been popular."

Exhibit 6   Knowledge Communities Structure

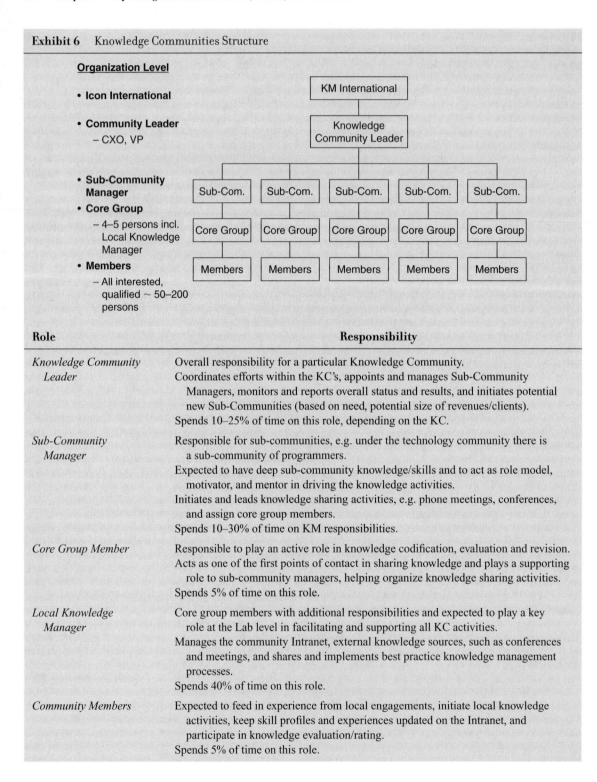

Role	Responsibility
Knowledge Community Leader	Overall responsibility for a particular Knowledge Community. Coordinates efforts within the KC's, appoints and manages Sub-Community Managers, monitors and reports overall status and results, and initiates potential new Sub-Communities (based on need, potential size of revenues/clients). Spends 10–25% of time on this role, depending on the KC.
Sub-Community Manager	Responsible for sub-communities, e.g. under the technology community there is a sub-community of programmers. Expected to have deep sub-community knowledge/skills and to act as role model, motivator, and mentor in driving the knowledge activities. Initiates and leads knowledge sharing activities, e.g. phone meetings, conferences, and assign core group members. Spends 10–30% of time on KM responsibilities.
Core Group Member	Responsible to play an active role in knowledge codification, evaluation and revision. Acts as one of the first points of contact in sharing knowledge and plays a supporting role to sub-community managers, helping organize knowledge sharing activities. Spends 5% of time on this role.
Local Knowledge Manager	Core group members with additional responsibilities and expected to play a key role at the Lab level in facilitating and supporting all KC activities. Manages the community Intranet, external knowledge sources, such as conferences and meetings, and shares and implements best practice knowledge management processes. Spends 40% of time on this role.
Community Members	Expected to feed in experience from local engagements, initiate local knowledge activities, keep skill profiles and experiences updated on the Intranet, and participate in knowledge evaluation/rating. Spends 5% of time on this role.

read daily news alerts, weekly newsletters, and monthly status reports. They could also post any documents or information, input their timesheets, and update their personal homepage, which detailed their competencies, experiences and interests. In April 2001, Icon installed a sophisticated knowledge management software system, called Service-Sphere. Labs in various cities and countries were connected via a virtual private network (VPN) that allowed them to log onto desktops in their home lab and access a host of services, such as acquiring information on a project at any point in its development or working on a live project in real time with any other lab in the Icon network. For example, two technology team leaders who were working on a rollout for Siemens in Germany and Sweden could work on a project-progress update together in real time. The software also had specific discussion areas for different competencies and functional areas such as sales and human resources. The ServiceSphere software was not only a knowledge management tool but also a powerful management information system. It could forecast resource needs, calculate utilisation per consultant, be used to assign consultants to various jobs, give performance feedback, and track the selling cycle of a project.

In addition to the IT systems, Icon facilitated knowledge sharing by encouraging semiannual face-to-face meetings amongst community members from across labs as well as monthly phone meetings between the community and sub community leaders. Within Labs, open workspaces and ample conference rooms and social spaces, such as lounges, were provided to ensure that knowledge flowed unfettered by physical constraints.

The results of these initiatives and practices, however, were mixed. A study by an outside consultant showed that a significant number of Icon employees primarily relied on external sources of knowledge. According to the report:

> A C++ programmer who had a particularly difficult issue to resolve would first ask his neighbour, and if he could not get a satisfactory answer would then access an external mailing list for those in his profession or go to an external website, before going to another programmer in the same Lab or another Icon Lab.

While knowledge at some Labs was leading edge, knowledge sharing between Labs was found to be weak. When asked why they did not use internal sources more regularly, some complained that the intranet was not updated regularly and the information that was posted was not very helpful. Ulf Tingström, CKO, added his perspective to the issue.

> We have several challenges to knowledge management at Icon. First, we have a diverse set of Labs, many with systems, procedures, and cultures that were already set before they joined Icon. Second, as we grew, we added many young and inexperienced employees who were working in a knowledge intensive business for the first time. Third, we haven't quite put the incentives in place to get people to really use our systems. We have an incredibly powerful tool for communicating and knowledge sharing. The challenge is to get everyone to buy into using it. People are used to using their informal channels of communication—both internal and external to the firm. Until that changes, the full benefits of the system won't be realised. But, if we can get everyone on board and create a knowledge management culture, we will have a real advantage over our competitors, because most of them either don't do it or do it badly.

Industry Overview

The rapid proliferation of Internet technology and its rising popularity as a medium for conducting commerce helped fuel an explosive growth in the e-consulting[2] industry. From 1998 to 2000 the industry grew from USD 2.6 billion to USD 11.7 billion, and it was expected to grow to USD 30 billion by 2003. The bulk of the market was forecast to be concentrated in North America, followed by Europe and then select Asian countries. However, the highest growth rates were expected to occur in European, and selected Asian and Latin American countries.

The enormous potential of the e-consulting industry attracted a large number of new entrants,

---

[2]E-consulting is defined as "the services of consulting companies in helping firms conceive and launch an e-commerce business model and integrate it, if necessary, with an existing business . . . e-consulting is not one but a range of services that includes strategy, implementation, and outsourcing" (Agan et al. 2000:1).

backed by venture capitalists eager to cash in on the stratospheric price-to-earnings multiples afforded to "new economy" companies and the seemingly insatiable demand for their services. At the same time, established companies were creating their own e-commerce programmes to increase the value of their businesses by exploiting the premium placed by equity markets in e-commerce business models and to reduce costs and drive efficiencies.

Competitive Landscape 1995–2000

Players in the e-consulting space competed in three broad segments: business strategy, creative, and technology. They could be divided into two categories, incumbents and new entrants, and grouped along two dimensions, the globalisation of their operations and extent to which they offered "end-to-end" solutions, i.e., provided all the services required by a business to achieve its e-commerce strategy.

Incumbents　These firms included established IT consultancies such as IBM, Ernst and Young, Accenture (formerly Anderson Consulting), EDS, and management consultancies such as McKinsey, Boston Consulting Group, and Bain & Company. The incumbents benefited from a global scope, deeper pockets, extensive industry knowledge, and more project management expertise. They suffered, however, from a reputation for having less knowledge of Internet technologies, being less creative, and being much slower to deliver solutions on "internet time," the accelerated pace at which events occurred in a new economy firm compared to a traditional firm. Due to the unprecedented boom for their traditional services in the mid-1990's, these companies were slow to get into the e-consulting game. However, as the e-consulting sector continued to expand, they began to pay attention to the opportunities in the sector and the threats posed by the new entrants, especially the poaching of their senior managers that led to a "brain drain" from the incumbent firms. Incumbents, flush with cash from the prosperous times, entered the fray with massive

investments and in some cases wholesale changes to their business practices. McKinsey for example, not only started a new practice, @McKinsey, and an e-business incubator, but also altered one of its core tenets, independence from its clients, by accepting equity from start-up firms for its services. IBM spent $200 million USD marketing its e-business solutions and repositioned almost all its services under the e-business umbrella. Accenture launched a $1 billion USD venture capital fund and established 22 dot-com launch centres around the world to initiate e-commerce efforts at traditional companies.

These large investments were aimed at improving their market perception as Internet savvy, new economy firms. Coupled with their extensive networks of contacts at all levels within major corporations, incumbent firms were becoming formidable competitors in the e-consulting space.

New Entrants　New entrants began to appear in earnest in the mid-1990s. From the thousands of ventures that were started, a cadre of a two dozen or so grew rapidly to challenge the incumbents. Firms like Razorfish, Scient, Sapient, Viant, FramFab, Pixelpark, AGENCY.COM, and Icon were referred to as "pure plays" for their focus solely on e-consulting. These companies used their deeper knowledge of Internet technologies, a creative and young workforce, a faster delivery schedule, and lower costs to win new clients. The incredible demand for their services, combined with an initially lacklustre response by the incumbents, allowed new entrants to increasingly feature Fortune 1000 firms on their roster of clients, in addition to their existing list of emerging companies. At the same time, the high stock valuations allowed them to lure away talent from incumbent firms and make acquisitions[3] that increased the breadth and depth of their competencies, as well as increase their international reach. In early 2000, there were 21 US plus 5 Euro-

---

[3]The exception to the grow-by-acquisition route was Viant, which has increased its size entirely through organic growth.

pean companies that were considered pure play e-consulting firms. With the exception of Icon, most of these companies generated most of their revenues in their home country.

Despite their rapid rise, the new entrants faced formidable challenges. They still remained very small relative to the incumbents, which hindered their efforts to win large projects from global corporations. Their small size and young workforce was perceived as lacking the insight and experience needed to develop detailed strategies, especially those that were appropriate for a particular industry, and needed to manage large projects. Furthermore, few boasted any profits since they strived to build their businesses, making large companies wary of their financial stability.

By early 2000, the demand for e-consulting services continued to remain strong, and the battle to become a top-tier player intensified. Mergers and acquisitions continued at a frantic pace. In March 2000, Whittman-Hart, a 4000-person systems integrator firm with strong technical skills and USWeb/CKS, a 4500-person firm with strong web design skills, combined their operations and renamed the new firm MarchFirst. New entrants continued to expand to add competencies and industries to their portfolio of skills as well as pushing to have a global footprint, while incumbents stepped up there efforts to be seen as a new economy firm.

The Internet Bubble Bursts

On April 14, 2000, the longest running bull market in history came crashing down as Internet stocks saw their values fall by 50–70%. By December 2000 some USD 1 trillion in value had been lost and the shakeout of Internet-related companies had begun. By the latter half of 2000, e-consulting businesses were reeling from the effects of a sharp decline in the valuation of shares in the high technology sector. A large portion of their dot-com clients, unable to raise further financing, went bankrupt, leaving hefty debts that widened the losses of e-consultants. At the same time, the massive devaluation of shares in the high technology sector led to further losses as firms wrote down the goodwill on their acquisitions. The e-consultancies continued to lose sales as their large clients reduced their spending on e-business and Internet operations and the general global downturn continued.

The reaction of the e-consulting firms to the downturn was an attempt to reduce costs, refocus their operations, and secure financing. In Europe, Stockholm-based Framfab decreased its headcount by 40%, divested numerous subsidiaries, closed down others, and raised SEK 175 through a rights issue. Similarly, Cell Network, divested its media and communication division as well as its web-oriented companies, reduced its headcount by 35%, and carried out a rights issue for SEK 256 million. German-based, Pixelpark, actually made an acquisition in its Swiss market, but reduced its total headcount by 10%. Stockholm-based Adcore, took the most radical restructuring steps by divesting or liquidating 24 enterprises, in 11 countries with 1200 staff to concentrate solely on stabilising its one office in Stockholm, with a staff of 600. In US, MarchFirst, who one year ago had been hailed as one of the top players in the industry with a market capitalisation of nearly USD 14 billion, shed 50% of its workforce before declaring bankruptcy. Other firms such as Scient, Viant, and Razorfish, took similar actions: reduction in the headcount, closing of offices, and refocusing of services (see Exhibit 7 for list of current competitors).

As the conditions in the industry worsened during the first three quarters of 2001, firms looked at other strategic options that would help ensure their survival. One such option was merging with another player. Scient and iXL merged their operations and continued under the Scient name. Another option was to be acquired by one of the deep-pocketed incumbent firms. IBM Global services bought Mainspring, an e-business strategy firm. With valuations of the e-consulting firms up to 99% off their highs, they could be attractive to incumbents looking to pick up a complementary competency for a pittance.

Exhibit 7   Competitors

Company	Revenues Millions USD Fiscal Year 2000	Offices
AGENCY.COM	202.1	US, Holland, Denmark, UK, France
Cambridge Technology Partners	586.6	20 Countries
Cap Gemini	6,520	30 Countries
Cell Network	122.9	Europe
DiamondCluster International	259.3	North America, Latin America, Europe, US
IBM	88,396	150+ Countries
FramFab	179	Europe, US
Luminant Worldwide	134.6	US
Organic	128.6	Asia, Europe, Latin America, North America
Pixel Park	49.2	Austria, France, Germany, UK
Proxicom	207.1	South Africa, Italy, Spain, UK
Razorfish	267.9	US, Asia, Europe
Sapient	503.3	North America, Europe, Asia
Scient	300	North America, Europe, Asia
Viant	127.2	US

Icon's Troubles Begin: Q3 2000–Q3 2001

By the third quarter of 2000, the technology industry's downturn had begun to affect Icon's performance. Although the company continued to grow through acquisitions, its losses begin to widen as some of its dot-com clients began to default on their payments. At the same time, the massive devaluation of shares in the high technology sector led to a SEK 1.6 billion write down of goodwill on its acquisitions. Icon ended 2000 with losses of SEK 199 million on sales of SEK1.7 billion. In January 2001, CEO Dalhsten departed from the company. Rens Buchwald, the current CFO, stepped in as interim CEO until a suitable CEO could be found. In 2001, the company continued to lose sales as its large clients reduced their spending on e-business and Internet operations and the general global downturn continued. By the third quarter 2001, the crisis in the industry had deepened, further exacerbated by the terrorist attacks of September 11, 2001, in New York. Icon responded to the downturn by cutting almost 600 staff, but did not close any offices.

Current Situation

By October 2001, Icon was facing an extremely challenging situation. In nine months the firm's revenues per quarter had almost halved, while its losses had almost doubled. After the meltdown in the share valuations of the high technology sector, the reputation of the e-consulting sector was in tatters, scaring off investors and large clients.

The board knew they had to do something to stop the losses. While some of the labs were profitable, several were not profitable (see Exhibit 1). One option was to close down a few of the money-losing operations. The board members wondered how this would appear to investors who had bought into Icon's vision of a global firm.

Another option was to try to merge with one of the remaining e-consultancies. The new entrants such as Icon were mostly in the same situation—the board wondered to what extent it would make sense to team up with another player that was struggling.

Similarly, Icon could try to attract an incumbent firm like CapGemini or IBM as a potential buyer.

However, this option was not without drawbacks— the board wondered what would happen to Icon's unique culture if it became part of a mammoth, more traditional organisation.

Another option that the board was considering was to find a buyer to take the firm private. With the stock trading at SEK 4, the market cap of Icon was only SEK 260 million. Magnus Bergman, board member commented:

> Icon is lucky in that it has some patient investors. If we could find another patient investor or two, we could then focus on building the business and wait for market conditions to get better before listing again on the exchange.

A final option was to try to capitalise on the tax losses that Icon had accumulated over the years, approximately SEK 2.5 billion. Jesper Jos Olsson, board member and one of the founders, explained:

> These losses are actually quite valuable. We can sell them by incorporating another company and transferring all assets and liabilities to the new Icon. Then we can sell the shares in the old Icon, along with the tax losses, to a willing buyer. The buyer would get a huge tax savings at an attractive price, and we would get the money we need to weather the storm, become healthy and then start growing again.

The board was not sure, however, how much the firm could get for selling these losses and who might be a willing buyer.

At the same time, the board knew that raising financing and reducing costs was not going to help Icon without an increase in sales. Icon's sales force was for the first time in its history actively having to chase sales—in the boom years, Icon's sales people only had to make a mild effort, if at all, to win new business. Rens Buchwaldt, CFO and interim CEO, commented:

> In the past, Icon never had to worry about getting sales—we just waited for the clients to come to us. We are in a very different environment now. We need to have a shift in mindset if we are going to raise our sales levels, and that is tough to do in an organisation that is spread out over 19 countries.

Whatever the company decided to do, the board knew that it had to be done fast—Icon could not withstand these losses for much longer—it needed a strategy now to survive in the short-term and the long-term.

Reading 1-1   The Tortuous Evolution of the Multinational Corporation

Howard V. Perlmutter

Four senior executives of the world's largest firms with extensive holdings outside the home country

▌ Trained as an engineer and a psychologist, Howard V. Perlmutter spent eight years at M.I.T.'s Center for International Studies and five years at the Institut pour l'Etude des Methodes de Direction de l'Enterprise (IMEDE) in Lausanne, Switzerland. His main interests are in the theory and practice of institution building, particularly the international corporation. He has recently been appointed Director for Research and Development of Worldwide Institutions in association with the Management Science Center at the University of Pennsylvania, as well as a member of the faculty at the Wharton School.

speak:

Company A: "We are a multinational firm. We distribute our products in about 100 countries. We manufacture in over 17 countries and do research and development in three countries. We look at all new investment projects—both domestic and overseas—using exactly the same criteria."

Company B: "We are a multinational firm. Only 1% of the personnel in our affiliate companies are non-nationals. Most of these are U.S. executives on temporary assignments. In all major markets, the affiliate's managing director is of the local nationality."

Company C: "We are a multinational firm. Our product division executives have worldwide profit responsibility. As our organizational chart shows, the United States is just one region on a par with Europe, Latin America, Africa, etc., in each product division."

Company D (non-American): "We are a multinational firm. We have at least 18 nationalities represented at our headquarters. Most senior executives speak at least two languages. About 30% of our staff at headquarters are foreigners."

While a claim to multinationality based on their years of experience and the significant proportion of sales generated overseas is justified in each of these four companies, a more penetrating analysis changes the image.

The executive from Company A tells us that most of the key posts in Company A's subsidiaries are held by home-country nationals. Whenever replacements for these men are sought, it is the practice, if not the policy, to "look next to you at the head office" and "pick someone (usually a home-country national) you know and trust."

The executive from Company B does not hide the fact that there are very few non-Americans in the key posts at headquarters. The few who are there are "so Americanized" that their foreign nationality literally has no meaning. His explanation for this paucity of non-Americans seems reasonable enough: "You can't find good foreigners who are willing to live in the United States, where our headquarters is located. American executives are more mobile. In addition, Americans have the drive and initiative we like. In fact, the European nationals would prefer to report to an American rather than to some other European."

The executive from Company C goes on to explain that the worldwide product division concept is rather difficult to implement. The senior executives in charge of these divisions have little overseas experience. They have been promoted from domestic posts and tend to view foreign consumer needs "as really basically the same as ours." Also, product

division executives tend to focus on the domestic market because the domestic market is larger and generates more revenue than the fragmented European markets. The rewards are for global performance, but the strategy is to focus on domestic. His colleagues say "one pays attention to what one understands—and our senior executives simply do not understand what happens overseas and really do not trust foreign executives in key positions here or overseas."

The executive from the European Company D begins by explaining that since the voting shareholders must by law come from the home country, the home country's interest must be given careful consideration. In the final analysis he insists: "We are proud of our nationality; we shouldn't be ashamed of it." He cites examples of the previous reluctance of headquarters to use home-country ideas overseas, to their detriment, especially in their U.S. subsidiary. "Our country produces good executives, who tend to stay with us a long time. It is harder to keep executives from the United States."

◼ A Rose by Any Other Name . . .

Why quibble about how multinational a firm is? To these executives, apparently being multinational is prestigious. They know that multinational firms tend to be regarded as more progressive, dynamic, geared to the future than provincial companies which avoid foreign frontiers and their attendant risks and opportunities.

It is natural that these senior executives would want to justify the multinationality of their enterprise, even if they use different yardsticks: ownership criteria, organizational structure, nationality of senior executives, percent of investment overseas, etc.

Two hypotheses seem to be forming in the minds of executives from international firms that make the extent of their firm's multinationality of real interest. The first hypothesis is that the degree of multinationality of an enterprise is positively related to the firm's long-term viability. The "multinational" category makes sense for executives if it means a quality of decision making which leads to survival, growth and profitability in our evolving world economy.

The second hypothesis stems from the proposition that the multinational corporation is a new kind of institution—a new type of industrial social architecture particularly suitable for the latter third of the twentieth century. This type of institution could make a valuable contribution to world order and conceivably exercise a constructive impact on the nation-state. Some executives want to understand how to create an institution whose presence is considered legitimate and valuable in each nation-state. They want to prove that the greater the degree of multinationality of a firm, the greater its total constructive impact will be on host and home nation-states as well as other institutions. Since multinational firms may produce a significant proportion of the world's GNP, both hypotheses justify a more precise analysis of the varieties and degrees of multinationality.[1] However, the confirming evidence is limited.

State of Mind

Part of the difficulty in defining the degree of multinationality comes from the variety of parameters along which a firm doing business overseas can be described. The examples from the four companies argue that (1) no single criterion of multinationality such as ownership or the number of nationals overseas is sufficient, and that (2) external and quantifiable measures such as the percentage of investment overseas or the distribution of equity by nationality are useful but not enough. The more one penetrates into the living reality of an international firm, the more one finds it is necessary to give serious weight to the way executives think about doing business around the world. The orientation toward "foreign people, ideas, resources," in headquarters and subsidiaries, and in host and home environments, becomes crucial in estimating the multinationality of a firm. To be sure, such external indices as the proportion of nationals in different countries

holding equity and the number of foreign nationals who have reached top positions, including president, are good indices of multinationality. But one can still behave with a home-country orientation despite foreign shareholders, and one can have a few home-country nationals overseas but still pick those local executives who are home-country oriented or who are provincial and chauvinistic. The attitudes men hold are clearly more relevant than their passports.

Three primary attitudes among international executives toward building a multinational enterprise are identifiable. These attitudes can be inferred from the assumptions upon which key product, functional and geographical decisions were made.

These states of mind or attitudes may be described as ethnocentric (or home-country oriented), polycentric (or host-country oriented) and geocentric (or world-oriented).[2] While they never appear in pure form, they are clearly distinguishable. There is some degree of ethnocentricity, polycentricity or geocentricity in all firms, but management's analysis does not usually correlate with public pronouncements about the firm's multinationality.

Home-Country Attitudes

The ethnocentric attitude can be found in companies of any nationality with extensive overseas holdings. The attitude, revealed in executive actions and experienced by foreign subsidiary managers, is: "We, the home nationals of X company, are superior to, more trustworthy and more reliable than any foreigners in headquarters or subsidiaries. We will be willing to build facilities in your country if you acknowledge our inherent superiority and accept our methods and conditions for doing the job."

Of course, such attitudes are never so crudely expressed, but they often determine how a certain type of "multinational" firm is designed. Table 1 illustrates how ethnocentric attitudes are expressed

---

[1] H. V. Perlmutter, "Super-Giant Firms in the Future," *Wharton Quarterly,* Winter 1968.

[2] H. V. Perlmutter, "Three Conceptions of a World Enterprise," *Revue Economique et Sociale,* May 1965.

Table 1   Three Types of Headquarters Orientation toward Subsidiaries in an International Enterprise

Organization Design	Ethnocentric	Polycentric	Geocentric
Complexity of organization	Complex in home country, simple in subsidiaries	Varied and independent	Increasingly complex and interdependent
Authority; decision making	High in headquarters	Relatively low in headquarters	Aim for a collaborative approach between headquarters and subsidiaries
Evaluation and control	Home standards applied for persons and performance	Determined locally	Find standards which are universal and local
Rewards and punishments; incentives	High in headquarters, low in subsidiaries	Wide variation; can be high or low rewards for subsidiary performance	International and local executives rewarded for reaching local and worldwide objectives
Communication; information flow	High volume to subsidiaries; orders, commands, advice	Little to and from headquarters; little between subsidiaries	Both ways and between subsidiaries; heads of subsidiaries part of management team
Identification	Nationality of owner	Nationality of host country	Truly international company but identifying with national interests
Perpetuation (recruiting, staffing, development)	Recruit and develop people of home country for key positions everywhere in the world	Develop people of local nationality for key positions in their own country	Develop best men everywhere in the world for key positions everywhere in the world

in determining the managerial process at home and overseas. For example, the ethnocentric executive is more apt to say: "Let us manufacture the simple products overseas. Those foreign nationals are not yet ready or reliable. We should manufacture the complex products in our country and keep the secrets among our trusted home-country nationals."

In a firm where ethnocentric attitudes prevailed, the performance criteria for men and products are "home-made." "We have found that a salesman should make 12 calls per day in Hoboken, New Jersey (the headquarters location), and therefore we apply these criteria everywhere in the world. The salesman in Brazzaville is naturally lazy, unmotivated. He shows little drive because he makes only two calls per day (despite the Congolese salesman's explanation that it takes time to reach customers by boat)."

Ethnocentric attitudes are revealed in the communication process where "advice," "counsel," and directives flow from headquarters to the subsidiary in a steady stream, bearing this message: "This works at home; therefore, it must work in your country."

Executives in both headquarters and affiliates express the national identity of the firm by associating the company with the nationality of the headquarters: this is "a Swedish company," "a Swiss company," "an American company," depending on the location of headquarters. "You have to accept the fact that the only way to reach a senior post in our firm," an English executive in a U.S. firm said, "is to take out an American passport."

Crucial to the ethnocentric concept is the current policy that men of the home nationality are recruited and trained for key positions everywhere in the world. Foreigners feel like "second-class" citizens.

There is no international firm today whose executives will say that ethnocentrism is absent in their company. In the firms whose multinational investment began a decade ago, one is more likely to hear, "We are still in a transitional stage from our ethnocentric era. The traces are still around! But we are making progress."

Host-Country Orientation

Polycentric firms are those which, by experience or by the inclination of a top executive (usually one of the founders), begin with the assumption that host-country cultures are different and that foreigners are difficult to understand. Local people know what is best for them, and the part of the firm which is located in the host country should be as "local in identity" as possible. The senior executives at headquarters believe that their multinational enterprise can be held together by good financial controls. A polycentric firm, literally, is a loosely connected group with quasi-independent subsidiaries as centers—more akin to a confederation.

European multinational firms tend to follow this pattern, using a top local executive who is strong and trustworthy, of the "right" family and who has an intimate understanding of the workings of the host government. This policy seems to have worked until the advent of the Common Market.

Executives in the headquarters of such a company are apt to say: "Let the Romans do it their way. We really don't understand what is going on there, but we have to have confidence in them. As long as they earn a profit, we want to remain in the

background." They assume that since people are different in each country, standards for performance, incentives and training methods must be different. Local environmental factors are given greater weight (see Table 1).

Many executives mistakenly equate polycentrism with multinationalism. This is evidenced in the legalistic definition of a multinational enterprise as a cluster of corporations of diverse nationality joined together by ties of common ownership. It is no accident that many senior executives in headquarters take pride in the absence of nonnationals in their subsidiaries, especially people from the head office. The implication is clearly that each subsidiary is a distinct national entity, since it is incorporated in a different sovereign state. Lonely senior executives in the subsidiaries of polycentric companies complain that: "The home office never tells us anything."

Polycentrism is not the ultimate form of multinationalism. It is a landmark on a highway. Polycentrism is encouraged by local marketing managers who contend that: "Headquarters will never understand us, our people, our consumer needs, our laws, our distribution, etc. . . ."

Headquarters takes pride in the fact that few outsiders know that the firm is foreign-owned. "We want to be a good local company. How many Americans know that Shell and Lever Brothers are foreign-owned?"

But the polycentric personnel policy is also revealed in the fact that no local manager can seriously aspire to a senior position at headquarters. "You know the French are so provincial; it is better to keep them in France. Uproot them and you are in trouble," a senior executive says to justify the paucity of non-Americans at headquarters.

One consequence (and perhaps cause) of polycentrism is a virulent ethnocentrism among the country managers.

A World-Oriented Concept

The third attitude which is beginning to emerge at an accelerating rate is geocentrism. Senior executives with this orientation do not equate superiority with nationality. Within legal and political limits, they seek the best men, regardless of nationality, to solve the company's problems anywhere in the world. The senior executives attempt to build an organization in which the subsidiary is not only a good citizen of the host nation but is a leading exporter from this nation in the international community and contributes such benefits as (1) an increasing supply of hard currency, (2) new skills and (3) a knowledge of advanced technology. Geocentrism is summed up in a Unilever board chairman's statement of objectives: "We want to Unileverize our Indians and Indianize our Unileverans."

The ultimate goal of geocentrism is a worldwide approach in both headquarters and subsidiaries. The firm's subsidiaries are thus neither satellites nor independent city states, but parts of a whole whose focus is on worldwide objectives as well as local objectives, each part making its unique contribution with its unique competence. Geocentrism is expressed by function, product and geography. The question asked in headquarters and the subsidiaries is: "Where in the world shall we raise money, build our plant, conduct R&D, get and launch new ideas to serve our present and future customers?"

This conception of geocentrism involves a collaborative effort between subsidiaries and headquarters to establish universal standards and permissible local variations, to make key allocational decisions on new products, new plants, new laboratories. The international management team includes the affiliate heads.

Subsidiary managers must ask: "Where in the world can I get the help to serve my customers best in this country?" "Where in the world can I export products developed in this country—products which meet worldwide standards as opposed to purely local standards?"

Geocentrism, furthermore, requires a reward system for subsidiary managers which motivates them to work for worldwide objectives, not just to defend country objectives. In firms where geocentrism prevails, it is not uncommon to hear a subsidiary manager say, "While I am paid to defend our interests in this country and to get the best resources for this affiliate, I must still ask myself the question 'Where in the world (instead of where in my country) should we build this plant?' " This approach is still rare today.

In contrast to the ethnocentric and polycentric patterns, communication is encouraged among subsidiaries in geocentric-oriented firms. "It is your duty to help us solve problems anywhere in the world," one chief executive continually reminds the heads of his company's affiliates. (See Table 1.)

The geocentric firm identifies with local company needs. "We aim not to be just a good local company but the best local company in terms of the quality of management and the worldwide (not local) standards we establish in domestic and export production." "If we were only as good as local companies, we would deserve to be nationalized."

The geocentric personnel policy is based on the belief that we should bring in the best man in the world regardless of his nationality. His passport should not be the criterion for promotion.

■ The EPG Profile

Executives can draw their firm's profile in ethnocentric (E), polycentric (P) and geocentric (G) dimensions. They are called EPG profiles. The degree of ethnocentrism, polycentrism and geocentrism by product, function and geography can be established. Typically R&D often turns out to be more geocentric (truth is universal, perhaps) and less ethnocentric than finance. Financial managers are likely to see their decisions as ethnocentric. The marketing function is more polycentric, particularly in the advanced economies and in the larger affiliate markets.

The tendency toward ethnocentrism in relations with subsidiaries in the developing countries is marked. Polycentric attitudes develop in consumer goods divisions, and ethnocentrism appears to be greater in industrial product divisions. The agreement is almost unanimous in both U.S.- and European-based international firms that their companies are at various stages on a route toward geocentrism but none has reached this state of affairs. Their executives would agree, however, that:

1. A description of their firms as multinational obscures more than it illuminates the state of affairs;
2. The EPG mix, once defined, is a more precise way to describe the point they have reached;
3. The present profile is not static but a landmark along a difficult road to genuine geocentrism;
4. There are forces both to change and to maintain the present attitudinal "mix," some of which are under their control.

Forces Toward and Against

What are the forces that determine the EPG mix of a firm? "You must think of the struggle toward functioning as a worldwide firm as just a beginning—a few steps forward and a step backward," a chief executive puts it. "It is a painful process, and every firm is different."

Executives of some of the world's largest multinational firms have been able to identify a series of external and internal factors that contribute to or hinder the growth of geocentric attitudes and decisions. Table 2 summarizes the factors most frequently mentioned by over 500 executives from at least 17 countries and 20 firms.

From the external environmental side, the growing world markets, the increase in availability of managerial and technological know-how in different countries, global competition and international customers' advances in telecommunications, regional political and economic communities are positive factors, as is the host country's desire to increase its balance-of-payments surplus through the location of export-oriented subsidiaries of international firms within its borders.

In different firms, senior executives see in various degrees these positive factors toward geocentrism: top management's increasing desire to use human and material resources optimally, the observed lowering of morale after decades of ethnocentric practices, the evidence of waste and duplication under polycentric thinking, the increased awareness and

respect for good men of other than the home nationality, and, most importantly, top management's own commitment to building a geocentric firm as evidenced in policies, practices and procedures.

The obstacles toward geocentrism from the environment stem largely from the rising political and economic nationalism in the world today, the suspicions of political leaders of the aims and increasing power of the multinational firm. On the internal side, the obstacles cited most frequently in U.S.-based multinational firms were management's inexperience in overseas markets, mutual distrust between home-country people and foreign executives, the resistance to participation by foreigners in the power structure at headquarters, the increasing difficulty of getting good men overseas to move, nationalistic tendencies in staff, and linguistic and other communication difficulties of a cultural nature.

Any given firm is seen as moving toward geocentrism at a rate determined by its capacities to build on the positive internal factors over which it has control and to change the negative internal factors which are controllable. In some firms the geocentric goal is openly discussed among executives of different nationalities and from different subsidiaries as well as headquarters. There is a consequent improvement in the climate of trust and acceptance of each other's views.

Programs are instituted to assure greater experience in foreign markets, task forces of executives are upgraded, and international careers for executives of all nationalities are being designed.

But the seriousness of the obstacles cannot be underestimated. A world of rising nationalism is hardly a precondition for geocentrism; and overcoming distrust of foreigners even within one's own firm is not accomplished in a short span of time. The route to pervasive geocentric thinking is long and tortuous.

Costs, Risks, Payoffs

What conclusions will executives from multinational firms draw from the balance sheet of advantages

Table 2   International Executives' View of Forces and Obstacles toward Geocentrism in Their Firms

Forces toward Geocentrism		Obstacles toward Geocentrism	
Environmental	**Intra-Organizational**	**Environmental**	**Intra-Organizational**
1. Technological and managerial know-how increasing in availability in different countries	1. Desire to use human versus material resources optimally	1. Economic nationalism in host and home countries	1. Management inexperience in overseas markets
2. International customers	2. Observed lowering of morale in affiliates of an ethnocentric company	2. Political nationalism in host and home countries	2. Nation-centered reward and punishment structure
3. Local customers' demand for best product at fair price	3. Evidence of waste and duplication in polycentrism	3. Military secrecy associated with research in home country	3. Mutual distrust between home-country people and foreign executives
4. Host country's desire to increase balance of payments	4. Increasing awareness and respect for good people of other than home nationality	4. Distrust of big international firms by host-country political leaders	4. Resistance to letting foreigners into the power structure
5. Growing world markets	5. Risk diversification in having a worldwide production and distribution system	5. Lack of international monetary system	5. Anticipated costs and risks of geocentrism
6. Global competition among international firms for scarce human and material resources	6. Need for recruitment of good people on a worldwide basis	6. Growing differences between the rich and poor countries	6. Nationalistic tendencies in staff
7. Major advances in integration of international transport and telecommunications	7. Need for worldwide information system	7. Host-country belief that home countries get disproportionate benefits of international firms' profits	7. Increasing immobility of staff
8. Regional supranational economic and political communities	8. Worldwide appeal products	8. Home-country political leaders' attempts to control firm's policy	8. Linguistic problems and different cultural backgrounds
	9. Senior management's long-term commitment to geocentrism as related to survival and growth		9. Centralization tendencies in headquarters

and disadvantages of maintaining one's present state of ethnocentrism, polycentrism or geocentrism? Not too surprisingly, the costs and risks of ethnocentrism are seen to out-balance the payoffs in the long run. The costs of ethnocentrism are ineffective planning because of a lack of good feedback, the departure of the best men in the subsidiaries, fewer innovations, and an inability to build a high calibre local organization. The risks are political and social repercussions and a less flexible response to local changes.

The payoffs of ethnocentrism are real enough in the short term, they say. Organization is simpler. There is a higher rate of communication of know-how from headquarters to new markets. There is more control over appointments to senior posts in subsidiaries.

Polycentrism's costs are waste due to duplication, to decisions to make products for local use but which could be universal, and to inefficient use of home-country experience. The risks include an excessive regard for local traditions and local growth at the expense of global growth. The main advantages are an intense exploitation of local markets, better sales since local management is often better informed, more local initiative for new products, more host-government support, and good local managers with high morale.

Geocentrism's costs are largely related to communication and travel expenses, educational costs at all levels, time spent in decision making because consensus seeking among more people is required, and an international headquarters bureaucracy. Risks include those due to too wide a distribution of power, personnel problems and those of reentry of international executives. The payoffs are a more powerful total company throughout, a better quality of products and service, worldwide utilization of best resources, improvement of local company management, a greater sense of commitment to worldwide objectives, and last, but not least, more profit.

Jacques Maisonrouge, the French-born president of IBM World Trade, understands the geocentric concept and its benefits. He wrote recently:

"The first step to a geocentric organization is when a corporation, faced with the choice of whether to grow and expand or decline, realizes the need to mobilize its resources on a world scale. It will sooner or later have to face the issue that the home country does not have a monopoly of either men or ideas. . . .

"I strongly believe that the future belongs to geocentric companies. . . . What is of fundamental importance is the attitude of the company's top management. If it is dedicated to 'geocentrism,' good international management will be possible. If not, the best men of different nations will soon understand that they do not belong to the 'race des seigneurs' and will leave the business."[3]

Geocentrism is not inevitable in any given firm. Some companies have experienced a "regression" to ethnocentrism after trying a long period of polycentrism, of letting subsidiaries do it "their way." The local directors built little empires and did not train successors from their own country. Headquarters had to send home-country nationals to take over. A period of home-country thinking took over.

There appears to be evidence of a need for evolutionary movement from ethnocentrism to polycentrism to geocentrism. The polycentric stage is likened to an adolescent protest period during which subsidiary managers gain their confidence as equals by fighting headquarters and proving "their manhood," after a long period of being under headquarters' ethnocentric thumb.

"It is hard to move from a period of headquarters domination to a worldwide management team quickly. A period of letting affiliates make mistakes may be necessary," said one executive.

Window Dressing

In the rush toward appearing geocentric, many U.S. firms have found it necessary to emphasize progress by appointing one or two non-nationals to senior posts—even on occasion to headquarters.

[3]Jacques Maisonrouge, "The Education of International Managers," *Quarterly Journal of AIESEC International,* February 1967.

The foreigner is often effectively counteracted by the number of nationals around him, and his influence is really small. Tokenism does have some positive effects, but it does not mean geocentrism has arrived.

Window dressing is also a temptation. Here an attempt is made to demonstrate influence by appointing a number of incompetent "foreigners" to key positions. The results are not impressive for either the individuals or the company.

Too often what is called "the multinational view" is really a screen for ethnocentrism. Foreign affiliate managers must, in order to succeed, take on the traits and behavior of the ruling nationality. In short, in a U.S.-owned firm the foreigner must "Americanize"—not only in attitude but in dress and speech—in order to be accepted.

Tokenism and window dressing are transitional episodes where aspirations toward multinationalism outstrip present attitudes and resources. The fault does not lie only with the enterprise. The human demands of ethnocentrism are great.

▮ A Geocentric Man—?

The geocentric enterprise depends on having an adequate supply of men who are geocentrically oriented. It would be a mistake to underestimate the human stresses which a geocentric career creates. Moving where the company needs an executive involves major adjustments for families, wives and children. The sacrifices are often great and, for some families, outweigh the rewards forthcoming—at least in personal terms. Many executives find it difficult to learn new languages and overcome their cultural superiority complexes, national pride and discomfort with foreigners. Furthermore, international careers can be hazardous when ethnocentrism prevails at headquarters. "It is easy to get lost in the world of the subsidiaries and to be 'out of sight, out of mind' when promotions come up at headquarters," as one executive expressed it following a visit to headquarters after five years overseas. To his disappointment, he knew few senior executives. And fewer knew him!

The economic rewards, the challenge of new countries, the personal and professional development that comes from working in a variety of countries and cultures are surely incentives, but companies have not solved by any means the human costs of international mobility to executives and their families.

A firm's multinationality may be judged by the pervasiveness with which executives think geocentrically—by function, marketing, finance, production, R&D, etc., by product division and by country. The takeoff to geocentrism may begin with executives in one function, say marketing, seeking to find a truly worldwide product line. Only when this worldwide attitude extends throughout the firm, in headquarters and subsidiaries, can executives feel that it is becoming genuinely geocentric.

But no single yardstick, such as the number of foreign nationals in key positions, is sufficient to establish a firm's multinationality. The multinational firm's route to geocentrism is still long because political and economic nationalism is on the rise, and, more importantly, since within the firm ethnocentrism and polycentrism are not easy to overcome. Building trust between persons of different nationality is a central obstacle. Indeed, if we are to judge men, as Paul Weiss put it, "by the kind of world they are trying to build," the senior executives engaged in building the geocentric enterprise could well be the most important social architects of the last third of the twentieth century. For the institution they are trying to erect promises a greater universal sharing of wealth and a consequent control of the explosive centrifugal tendencies of our evolving world community.

The geocentric enterprise offers an institutional and supranational framework which could conceivably make war less likely, on the assumption that bombing customers, suppliers and employees is in nobody's interest. The difficulty of the task is thus matched by its worthwhileness. A clearer image of the features of genuine geocentricity is thus indispensable both as a guideline and as an inviting prospect.

Reading 1-2   Managing in a Borderless World

Kenichi Ohmae

Most managers are nearsighted. Even though today's competitive landscape often stretches to a global horizon, they see best what they know best: the customers geographically closest to home. These managers may have factories or laboratories in a dozen countries. They may have joint ventures in a dozen more. They may source materials and sell in markets all over the world. But when push comes to shove, their field of vision is dominated by home-country customers and the organizational units that serve them. Everyone—and everything—else is simply part of "the rest of the world."

This nearsightedness is not intentional. No responsible manager purposefully devises or implements an astigmatic strategy. But by the same token, too few managers consciously try to set plans and build organizations as if they saw all key customers equidistant from the corporate center. Whatever the trade figures show, home markets are usually in focus; overseas markets are not.

Effective global operations require a genuine equidistance of perspective. But even with the best will in the world, managers find that kind of vision hard to develop—and harder to maintain. Not long ago, the CEO of a major Japanese capital-goods producer canceled several important meetings to attend the funeral of one of his company's local dealers. When I asked him if he would have done the same for a Belgian dealer, one who did a larger volume of business each year than his late counterpart in Japan, the unequivocal answer was no. Perhaps headquarters would have had the relevant European manager send a letter of condolence. No more than that. In Japan, however, tradition dictated the CEO's presence. But Japanese tradition isn't everything, I reminded him. After all, he was the head of

a global, not just a Japanese organization. By violating the principle of equidistance, his attendance underscored distinctions among dealers. He was sending the wrong signals and reinforcing the wrong values. Poor vision has consequences.

It may be unfamiliar and awkward, but the primary rule of equidistance is to see—and to think—global first. Honda, for example, has manufacturing divisions in Japan, North America, and Europe—all three legs of the Triad—but its managers do not think or act as if the company were divided between Japanese and overseas operations. Indeed, the very word *overseas* has no place in Honda's vocabulary because the corporation sees itself as equidistant from all its key customers. At Casio, the top managers gather information directly from each of their primary markets and then sit down together once a month to lay out revised plans for global product development.

There is no single best way to avoid or overcome nearsightedness. An equidistant perspective can take many forms. However managers do it, however they get there, building a value system that emphasizes seeing and thinking globally is the bottom-line price of admission to today's borderless economy.

A Geography without Borders

On a political map, the boundaries between countries are as clear as ever. But on a competitive map, a map showing the real flows of financial and industrial activity, those boundaries have largely disappeared. What has eaten them away is the persistent, ever speedier flow of information—information that governments previously monopolized, cooking it up as they saw fit and redistributing in forms of their own devising. Their monopoly of knowledge about things happening around the world enabled them to fool, mislead, or control the people because only the governments possessed real facts in anything like real time.

Reprinted by permission of *Harvard Business Review.* "Managing in a Borderless World" by Kenichi Ohmae (May/June 1989). Copyright © 1989 by the President and Fellows of Harvard College; all rights reserved.

Today, of course, people everywhere are more and more able to get the information they want directly from all corners of the world. They can see for themselves what the tastes and preferences are in other countries, the styles of clothing now in fashion, the sports, the lifestyles. In Japan, for example, our leaders can no longer keep the people in substandard housing because we now know—directly—how people elsewhere live. We now travel abroad. In fact, ten million Japanese travel abroad annually these days. Or we can sit in our living rooms at home, watch CNN, and know instantaneously what is happening in the United States. During 1988, nearly 90% of all Japanese honeymooners went abroad. This kind of fact is hard to ignore. The government now seriously recognizes that it has built plants and offices but has failed to meet the needs of its young people for relaxation and recreation. So, for the first time in 2,000 years, our people are revolting against their government and telling it what it must do for them. This would have been unthinkable when only a small, official elite controlled access to all information.

In the past, there were gross inefficiencies—some purposeful, some not—in the flow of information around the world. New technologies are eliminating those inefficiencies, and, with them, the opportunity for a kind of top-down information arbitrage—that is, the ability of a government to benefit itself or powerful special interests at the expense of its people by following policies that would never win their support if they had unfettered access to all relevant information. A government could, for example, protect weak industries for fear of provoking social unrest over unemployment. That is less easy to do now, for more of its people have become cosmopolitan and have their own sources of information. They know what such a policy would cost them.

In Korea, students demonstrate in front of the American embassy because the government allows the United States to export cigarettes to Korea and thus threaten local farmers. That's what happens when per capita GNP runs in the neighborhood of $5,000 a year and governments can still control the flow of information and mislead their people. When GNP gets up to around $10,000 a year, religion becomes a declining industry. So does government.

At $26,000 a year, where Japan is now, things are really different. People want to buy the best and the cheapest products—no matter where in the world they are produced. People become genuinely global consumers. We import beef and oranges from the United States, and everyone thinks it's great. Ten years ago, however, our students would have been the ones throwing stones at the American embassy. Our leaders used to tell us American and Australian beef was too lean and too tough to chew. But we've been there and tasted it and know for ourselves that it is cheap and good.

Through this flow of information, we've become global citizens, and so must the companies that want to sell us things. Black-and-white television sets extensively penetrated households in the United States nearly a dozen years before they reached comparable numbers of viewers in Europe and Japan. With color television, the time lag fell to about five or six years for Japan and a few more for Europe. With videocassette recorders, the difference was only three or four years—but this time, Europe and Japan led the way; the United States, with its focus on cable TV, followed. With the compact disc, household penetration rates evened up after only one year. Now, with MTV available by satellite across Europe, there is no lag at all. New music, styles, and fashion reach all European youngsters almost at the same time they are reaching their counterparts in America. We all share the same information.

More than that, we are all coming to share it in a common language. Ten years ago when I would speak in English to students at Bocconi, an Italian university, most of them would listen to me through a translator. Last year, they listened to me directly in English and asked me questions in English. (They even laughed when they should at what I said, although my jokes have not improved.) This is a momentous change. The preparation for 1992 has taken place in language much sooner than it has in politics. We can all talk to each other now, understand each other, and governments cannot stop us. "Global citizenship" is no longer just a nice phrase in the lexicon of rosy futurologists. It is every bit as real and concrete as measurable changes in GNP or trade flows. It is actually coming to pass.

The same is true for corporations. In the pharmaceutical industry, for example, the critical activities of drug discovery, screening, and testing are now virtually the same among the best companies everywhere in the world. Scientists can move from one laboratory to another and start working the next day with few hesitations or problems. They will find equipment with which they are familiar, equipment they have used before, equipment that comes from the same manufacturers.

The drug companies are not alone in this. Most people, for example, believed that it would be a very long time before Korean companies could produce state-of-the-art semiconductor chips—things like 256K NMOS DRAMs. Not so. They caught up with the rest of the Triad in only a few short years. In Japan, not that long ago, a common joke among the chip-making fraternity had to do with the "Friday Express." The Japanese engineers working for different companies on Kyūshū, Japan's southwestern "Silicon Island" only 100 km or so away from Korea, would catch a late flight to Korea on Friday evenings. During the weekend, they would work privately for Korean semiconductor companies. This was illegal, of course, and violated the engineers' employment agreements in Japan. Nonetheless, so many took the flight that they had a tacit gentleman's agreement not to greet or openly recognize each other on the plane. Their trip would have made no sense, however, if semiconductor-related machines, methods, software, and workstations had not already become quite similar throughout the developed world.

Walk into a capital-goods factory anywhere in the developed world, and you will find the same welding machines, the same robots, the same machine tools. When information flows with relative freedom, the old geographic barriers become irrelevant. Global needs lead to global products. For managers, this universal flow of information puts a high premium on learning how to build the strategies and the organizations capable of meeting the requirements of a borderless world.

What Is a Universal Product?

Imagine that you are the CEO of a major automobile company reviewing your product plans for the years ahead. Your market data tell you that you will have to develop four dozen different models if you want to design separate cars for each distinct segment of the Triad market. But you don't have enough world-class engineers to design so many models. You don't have enough managerial talent or enough money. No one does. Worse, there is no single "global" car that will solve your problems for you. America, Europe, and Japan are quite different markets with quite different mixes of needs and preferences. Worse still, as head of a worldwide company, you cannot write off any of these Triad markets. You simply have to be in each of them—and with first-rate successful products. What do you do?

If you are the CEO of Nissan, you first look at the Triad region by region and identify each market's dominant requirements. In the United Kingdom, for example, tax policies make it essential that you develop a car suitable for corporate fleet sales. In the United States, you need a sporty "Z" model as well as a four-wheel-drive family vehicle. Each of these categories is what Nissan's president, Yutaka Kume, calls a "lead country" model—a product carefully tailored to the dominant and distinct needs of individual national markets. Once you have your short list of "lead-country" models in hand, you can ask your top managers in other parts of the Triad whether minor changes can make any of them suitable for local sales. But you start with the lead-country models.

"With this kind of thinking," says Mr. Kume, "we have been able to halve the number of basic models needed to cover the global markets and, at the same time, to cover 80% of our sales with cars designed for specific national markets. Not to miss the remaining 20%, however, we also provided each country manager with a range of additional model types that could be adapted to the needs of local segments. This approach," Mr. Kume reports, "allowed us to focus our resources on each of our largest core markets and, at the same time, provide a pool of supplemental designs that could be adapted to local preferences. We told our engineers to 'be American,' 'be European,' or 'be Japanese.' If the Japanese happened to like something we tailored for the American market, so much the better. Low-cost, incremental sales never hurt. Our main challenge, however, was to avoid the trap of pleasing no one well by trying to please everyone halfway."

Imagine, instead, if Nissan had taken its core team of engineers and designers in Japan and asked them to design only global cars, cars that would sell all over the world. Their only possible response would have been to add up all the various national preferences and divide by the number of countries. They would have had to optimize across markets by a kind of rough averaging. But when it comes to questions of taste and, especially, aesthetic preference, consumers do not like averages. They like what they like, not some mathematical compromise. Kume is emphatic about this particular point. "Our success in the U.S. with Maxima, 240 SX, and Pathfinder—all designed for the American market—shows our approach to be right."

In high school physics, I remember learning about a phenomenon called diminishing primaries. If you mix together the primary colors of red, blue, and yellow, what you get is black. If Europe says its consumers want a product in green, let them have it. If Japan says red, let them have red. No one wants the average. No one wants the colors all mixed together. Of course it makes sense to take advantage of, say, any technological commonalities in creating the paint. But local managers close to local customers have to be able to pick the color.

When it comes to product strategy, managing in a borderless world doesn't mean managing by aver-

ages. It doesn't mean that all tastes run together into one amorphous mass of universal appeal. And it doesn't mean that the appeal of operating globally removes the obligation to localize products. The lure of a universal product is a false allure. The truth is a bit more subtle.

Although the needs and tastes of the Triad markets vary considerably, there may well be market segments of different sizes in each part of the Triad that share many of the same preferences. In the hair-care market, for instance, Japanese companies know a lot more about certain kinds of black hair, which is hard and thick, than about blond or brown hair, which is often soft and thin. As a result, they have been able to capture a few segments of the U.S. market in, say, shampoos. That makes a nice addition to their sales, of course. But it does not position them to make inroads into the mainstream segments of that market.

Back to the automobile example: there is a small but identifiable group of Japanese consumers who want a "Z" model car like the one much in demand in the United States. Fair enough. During the peak season, Nissan sells about 5,000 "Z" cars a month in the United States and only 500 in Japan. Those 500 cars make a nice addition, of course, generating additional revenue and expanding the perceived richness of a local dealer's portfolio. But they are not—and cannot be—the mainstay of such portfolios.

There is no universal "montage" car—a rear axle from Japan, a braking system from Italy, a drive train from the United States—that will quicken pulses on all continents. Remember the way the tabloids used to cover major beauty contests? They would create a composite picture using the best features from all of the most beautiful entrants—this one's nose, that one's mouth, the other one's forehead. Ironically, the portrait that emerged was never very appealing. It always seemed odd, a bit off, lacking in distinctive character. But there will always be beauty judges—and car buyers—in, say, Europe, who, though more used to continental standards, find a special attractiveness in the features of a Japanese or a Latin American. Again, so much the better.

For some kinds of products, however, the kind of globalization that Ted Levitt talks about makes excellent sense. One of the most obvious is, oddly enough, battery-powered products like cameras, watches, and pocket calculators. These are all part of the "Japan game"—that is, they come from industries dominated by Japanese electronics companies. What makes these products successful across the Triad? Popular prices, for one thing, based on aggressive cost reduction and global economies of scale. Also important, however, is the fact that many general design choices reflect an in-depth understanding of the preferences of leading consumer segments in key markets throughout the Triad. Rigid model changes during the past decade have helped educate consumers about the "fashion" aspects of these products and have led them to base their buying decisions in large measure on such fashion-related criteria.

With other products, the same electronics companies use quite different approaches. Those that make stereophonic equipment, for example, offer products based on aesthetics and product concepts that vary by region. Europeans tend to want physically small, high-performance equipment that can be hidden in a closet; Americans prefer large speakers that rise from the floor of living rooms and dens like the structural columns of ancient temples. Companies that have been globally successful in white goods like kitchen appliances focus on close interaction with individual users; those that have prospered with equipment that requires installation (air conditioners, say, or elevators) focus on interactions with designers, engineers, and trade unions. To repeat: approaches to global products vary.

Another important cluster of these global products is made up of fashion-oriented, premium-priced branded goods. Gucci bags are sold around the world, unchanged from one place to another. They are marketed in virtually the same way. They appeal to an upper bracket market segment that shares a consistent set of tastes and preferences. By definition, not everyone in the United States or Europe or Japan belongs to that segment. But for those who do, the growing commonality of their tastes qualifies them as members of a genuinely cross-Triad, global segment. There is even such a segment for top-of-the-line automobiles like the Rolls-Royce and the Mercedes-Benz. You can—in fact, should—design such cars for select buyers around the globe. But you cannot do that with Nissans or Toyotas or Hondas. Truly universal products are few and far between.

Insiderization

Some may argue that my definition of universal products is unnecessarily narrow, that many such products exist that do not fit neatly into top-bracket segments: Coca-Cola, Levi's, things like that. On closer examination, however, these turn out to be very different sorts of things. Think about Coca-Cola for a moment. Before it got established in each of its markets, the company had to build up a fairly complete local infrastructure and do the groundwork to establish local demand.

Access to markets was by no means assured from day one; consumer preference was not assured from day one. In Japan, the long-established preference was for carbonated lemon drinks known as saida. Unlike Gucci bags, consumer demand did not "pull" Coke into these markets; the company had to establish the infrastructure to "push" it. Today, because the company has done its homework and done it well, Coke is a universally desired brand. But it got there by a different route: local replication of an entire business system in every important market over a long period of time.

For Gucci-like products, the ready flow of information around the world stimulates consistent primary demand in top-bracket segments. For relatively undifferentiated, commodity-like products, demand expands only when corporate muscle pushes hard. If Coke is to establish a preference, it has to build it, piece by piece.

Perhaps the best way to distinguish these two kinds of global products is to think of yourself browsing in a duty-free shop. Here you are in something of an oasis. National barriers to entry do not apply. Products from all over the world lie available to you on the shelves. What do you reach for? Do you think about climbing on board your jetliner with a newly purchased six-pack of Coke? Hardly. But what about a Gucci bag? Yes, of course. In a sense, duty-free shops are the precursor to what life will be like in a genuinely borderless environment. Customer pull, shaped by images and information from around the world, determine your product choices. You want the designer handbag or the sneakers by Reebok, which are made in Korea and sold at three times the price of equivalent no-brand sneakers. And there are others like you in every corner of the Triad.

At bottom, the choice to buy Gucci or Reebok is a choice about fashion. And the information that shapes fashion-driven choices is different in kind from the information that shapes choices about commodity products. When you walk into the 7-Elevens of the world and look for a bottle of cola, the one you pick depends on its location on the shelf, its price, or perhaps the special in-store promotion going on at the moment. In other words, your preference is shaped by the effects of the cola company's complete business system in that country.

Now, to be sure, the quality of that business system will depend to some extent on the company's ability to leverage skills developed elsewhere or to exploit synergies with other parts of its operations—marketing competence, for example, or economies of scale in the production of concentrates. Even so, your choice as a consumer rests on the power with which all such functional strengths have been brought to bear in your particular local market—that is, on the company's ability to become a full-fledged insider in that local market.

With fashion-based items, where the price is relatively high and the purchase frequency low, insiderization does not matter all that much. With commodity items, however, where the price is low and the frequency of purchase high, the insiderization of functional skills is all-important. There is simply no way to be successful around the world with this latter category of products without replicating your business system in each key market.

Coke has 70% of the Japanese market for soft drinks. The reason is that Coke took the time and made the investments to build up a full range of local functional strengths, particularly in its route sales force and franchised vending machines. It is, after all, the Coke van or truck that replaces empty bottles with new ones, not the trucks of independent wholesalers or distributors. When Coke first moved into Japan, it did not understand the complex, many-layered distribution system for such products. So it used the capital of local bottlers to re-create the kind of sales force it has used so well in the United States. This represented a heavy, front-end, fixed investment, but it has paid off handsomely. Coke redefined the domestic game in Japan—and it did so, not from a distance, but with a deliberate "insiderization" of functional strengths. Once this sales force is in place, for example, once the company has become a full-fledged insider, it can move not only soft drinks but also fruit juice, sport drinks, vitamin drinks, and canned coffee through the same sales network. It can sell pretty much whatever it wants to. For Coke's competitors, foreign and domestic, the millions of dollars they are spending on advertising are like little droplets of water sprinkled over a desert. Nothing is going to bloom—at least, not if that is all they do. Not if they fail to build up their own distinctive "insider" strengths.

When global success rests on market-by-market functional strength, you have to play a series of domestic games against well-defined competitors. If the market requires a first-class sales force, you simply have to have one. If competition turns on dealer support programs, that's where you have to excel. Some occasions *do* exist when doing more better is the right, the necessary, course to follow. Still, there are usually opportunities to redefine these domestic games to your own advantage. Companies that fail to establish a strong insider position tend to mix up the strategies followed by the Cokes and the Guccis. The managers of many leading branded-goods companies are often loud in their complaints about how the Japanese market is closed to their products. Or, more mysteriously, about the inexplicable refusal of Japanese consumers to buy their products when they are obviously better than those of any competitor anywhere in the world. Instead of making the effort to understand Japanese distribution and Japanese consumers, they assume that something is wrong with the Japanese market. Instead of spending time in their plants and offices or on the ground in Japan, they spend time in Washington.

Not everyone, of course. There are plenty of branded-goods companies that *are* very well represented on the Japanese retailing scene—Coke, to be sure, but also Nestlé, Schick, Wella, Vicks, Scott, Del Monte, Kraft, Campbell, Unilever (its Timotei shampoo is number one in Japan), Twinings, Kellogg, Borden, Ragú, Oscar Mayer, Hershey, and a host of others. These have all become household names in Japan. They have all become insiders.

For industrial products companies, becoming an insider often poses a different set of challenges. Because these products are chosen largely on the basis of their performance characteristics, if they cut costs or boost productivity, they stand a fair chance of being accepted anywhere in the world. Even so, however, these machines do not operate in a vacuum. Their success may have to wait until the companies that make them have developed a full range of insider functions—engineering, sales, installation, finance, service, and so on. So, as these factors become more critical, it often makes sense for the companies to link up with local operations that already have these functions in place.

Financial services have their own special characteristics. Product globalization already takes place at the institutional investor level but much less so at the retail level. Still, many retail products now originate overseas, and the money collected from them is often invested across national borders. Indeed, foreign exchange, stock markets, and other trading facilities have already made money a legitimately global product.

In all these categories, then, as distinct from premium fashion-driven products like Gucci bags, insiderization in key markets is the route to global success. Yes, some top-of-the-line tastes and preferences have become common across the Triad. In many other cases, however, creating a global product means building the capability to understand and respond to customer needs and business system requirements in each critical market.

The Headquarters Mentality

By all reasonable measures, Coke's experience in Japan has been a happy one. More often than not, however, the path it took to insiderization—replicating a home-country business system in a new national market—creates many more problems than it solves. Managers back at headquarters, who have had experience with only one way to succeed, are commonly inclined to force that model on each new opportunity that arises. Of course, sometimes it will work. Sometimes it will be exactly the right answer. But chances are that the home-country reflex, the impulse to generalize globally from a sample of one, will lead efforts astray.

In the pharmaceutical industry, for example, Coke's approach would not work. Foreign entrants simply have to find ways to adapt to the Japanese distribution system. Local doctors will not accept or respond favorably to an American-style sales force. When the doctor asks a local detail man to take a moment and photocopy some articles for him, he has to be willing to run the errands. No ifs, ands, or buts.

One common problem with insiderization, then, is a misplaced home-country reflex. Another, perhaps more subtle, problem is what happens back at headquarters after initial operations in another market really start paying off. When this happens, in most companies everyone at home starts to pay close attention. Without really understanding why things have turned out as well as they have, managers at headquarters take an increasing interest in what is going on in Japan or wherever it happens to be.

Functionaries of all stripes itch to intervene. Corporate heavyweights decide they had better get into the act, monitor key decisions, ask for timely reports, take extensive tours of local activities.

Every power-that-be wants a say in what has become a critical portion of the overall company's operations. When minor difficulties arise, no one is willing to let local managers continue to handle things themselves. Corporate jets fill the skies with impatient satraps eager to set things right.

We know perfectly well where all this is likely to lead. A cosmetics company, with a once enviable position in Japan, went through a series of management shake-ups at home. As a result, the Japanese operation, which had grown progressively more important, was no longer able to enjoy the rough autonomy that made its success possible. Several times, eager U.S. hands reached in to change the head of activities in Japan, and crisp memos and phone calls kept up a steady barrage of challenges to the unlucky soul who happened to be in the hot seat at the moment. Relations became antagonistic, profits fell, the intervention grew worse, and the whole thing just fell apart. Overeager and overanxious managers back at headquarters did not have the patience to learn what really worked in the Japanese market. By trying to supervise things in the regular "corporate" fashion, they destroyed a very profitable business.

This is an all-too-familiar pattern. With dizzying regularity, the local top manager changes from a Japanese national to a foreigner, to a Japanese, to a foreigner. Impatient, headquarters keeps fitfully searching for a never-never ideal "person on the spot." Persistence and perseverance are the keys to long-term survival and success. Everyone knows it. But headquarters is just not able to wait for a few years until local managers—of whatever nationality—build up the needed rapport with vendors, employees, distributors, and customers. And if, by a miracle, they do, then headquarters is likely to see them as having become too "Japanized" to represent their interests abroad. They are no longer "one of us." If they do not, then obviously they have failed to win local acceptance.

This headquarters mentality is not just a problem of bad attitude or misguided enthusiasm. Too bad, because these would be relatively easy to fix. Instead, it rests on—and is reinforced by—a company's entrenched systems, structures, and behaviors. Dividend payout ratios, for example, vary from country to country. But most global companies find it hard to accept low or no payout from investment in Japan, medium returns from Germany, and larger returns from the United States. The usual wish is to get comparable levels of return from all activities, and internal benchmarks of performance reflect that wish. This is trouble waiting to happen. Looking for 15% ROI a year from new commitments in Japan is going to sour a company on Japan very quickly. The companies that have done the best there—the Coca-Colas and the IBMs—were willing to adjust their conventional expectations and settle in for the long term.

Or, for example, when top managers rely heavily on financial statements, they can easily lose sight of the value of operating globally—because these statements usually mask the performance of activities outside the home country. Accounting and reporting systems that are parent-company dominated—and remember, genuinely consolidated statements are still the exception, not the rule—merely confirm the lukewarm commitment of many managers to global competition. They may talk a lot about doing business globally, but it is just lip service. It sounds nice, and it may convince the business press to write glowing stories, but when things get tough, most of the talk turns out to be only talk.

Take a closer look at what actually happens. If a divisionalized Japanese company like Matsushita or Toshiba wants to build a plant to make widgets in Tennessee, the home-country division manager responsible for widgets often finds himself in a tough position. No doubt, the CEO will tell him to get that Tennessee facility up and running as soon as possible. But the division manager knows that, when the plant does come on-stream, his own operations are going to look worse on paper. At a minimum, his division is not going to get credit for American sales that he used to make by export from Japan. Those are now going to come out of Tennessee. The CEO tells him to collaborate, to help out, but he is afraid that the better the job he does, the worse it will be for him—and with good reason!

This is crazy. Why not change company systems? Have the Tennessee plant report directly to him, and consolidate all widget-making activities at the divisional level. Easier said than done. Most companies use accounting systems that consolidate at the corporate, not the divisional, level. That's traditional corporate practice. And every staff person since the time of Homer comes fully equipped with a thousand reasons not to make exceptions to time-honored institutional procedures. As a result, the division manager is going to drag his feet. The moment Tennessee comes on-line, he sees his numbers go down, he has to lay off people, and he has to worry about excess capacity. Who is going to remember his fine efforts in getting Tennessee started up? More to the point, who is going to care—when his Japanese numbers look so bad?

If you want to operate globally, you have to think and act globally, and that means challenging entrenched systems that work against collaborative efforts. Say our widget maker has a change of heart and goes to a division-level consolidation of accounts. This helps, but the problems are just beginning. The American managers of a sister division that uses these widgets look at the Tennessee plant as just another vendor, perhaps even a troublesome one because it is new and not entirely reliable. Their inclination is to treat the new plant as a problem, ignore it if possible, and to continue to buy from Japan where quality is high and delivery guaranteed. They are not going to do anything to help the new plant come on-stream or to plan for long-term capital investment. They are not going to supply technical assistance or design help or anything. All it represents is fairly unattractive marginal capacity.

If we solve this problem by having the plant head report to the division manager, then we are back where we started. If we do nothing, then this new plant is just going to struggle along. Clearly, what we need is to move toward a system of double counting of credits—so that both the American manager *and* the division head in Japan have strong reasons to make the new facility work. But this runs afoul of our entrenched systems, and they are very hard to change. If our commitment to acting globally is not terribly strong, we are not going to be inclined to make the painful efforts needed to make it work.

Under normal circumstances, these kinds of entrepreneurial decisions are hard enough to reach anyway. It is no surprise that many of the most globally successful Japanese companies—Honda, Sony, Matsushita, Canon, and the like—have been led by a strong owner-founder for at least a decade. They can override bureaucratic inertia; they can tear down institutional barriers. In practice, the managerial decision to tackle wrenching organizational and systems changes is made even more difficult by the way in which problems become visible. Usually, a global systems problem first comes into view in the form of explicitly local symptoms. Rarely do global problems show up where the real underlying causes are.

Troubled CEOs may say that their Japanese operations are not doing well, that the money being spent on advertising is just not paying off as expected. They will not say that their problems are really back at headquarters with its superficial understanding of what it takes to market effectively in Japan. They will not say that it lies in the design of their financial reporting systems. They will not say that it is part and parcel of their own reluctance to make long-term, front-end capital investments in new markets. They will not say that it lies in their failure to do well the central job of any headquarters operation: the development of good people at the local level. Or at least they are not likely to. They will diagnose the problems as local problems and try to fix them.

Thinking Global

Top managers are always slow to point the finger of responsibility at headquarters or at themselves. When global faults have local symptoms, they will be slower still. When taking corrective action means a full, zero-based review of all systems, skills, and structures, their speed will decrease even further. And when their commitment to acting globally is itself far from complete, it is a wonder there is any motion at all. Headquarters mentality is the prime expression of managerial nearsightedness, the sworn enemy of a genuinely equidistant perspective on global markets.

In the early days of global business, experts like Raymond Vernon of the Harvard Business School proposed, in effect, a United Nations model of globalization. Companies with aspirations to diversify and expand throughout the Triad were to do so by cloning the parent company in each new country of operation. If successful, they would create a mini-U.N. of clonelike subsidiaries repatriating profits to the parent company, which remained the dominant force at the center. We know that successful companies enter fewer countries but penetrate each of them more deeply. That is why this model gave way by the early 1980s to a competitor-focused approach to globalization. By this logic, if we were a European producer of medical electronics equipment, we had to take on General Electric in the United States so that it would not come over here and attack us on our home ground. Today, however, the pressure for globalization is driven not so much by diversification or competition as by the needs and preferences of customers. Their needs have globalized, and the fixed costs of meeting them have soared. That is why we must globalize.

Managing effectively in this new borderless environment does not mean building pyramids of cash flow by focusing on the discovery of new places to invest. Nor does it mean tracking your competitors to their lair and preemptively undercutting them in their own home market. Nor does it mean blindly trying to replicate home-country business systems in new colonial territories. Instead, it means paying central attention to delivering value to customers—and to developing an equidistant view of who they are and what they want. Before everything else comes the need to see your customers clearly. They—and only they—can provide legitimate reasons for thinking global.

Reading 1-3   Going Global: Lessons from Late Movers

Christopher A. Bartlett and Sumantra Ghoshal

In his autobiography, former South African president Nelson Mandela recalls his dismay when he boarded an airplane and found that the pilot was African. With shock, he realized his reaction was exactly what he had been fighting against all his life. Mandela was discussing racism, but the same involuntary reactions surface in commerce.

▌ **Christopher A. Bartlett** is the Daewoo Professor of Business Administration at Harvard Business School in Boston.
▌ **Sumantra Ghoshal** is the Robert P. Bauman Professor of Strategic Leadership at London Business School.
▌ Reprinted by permission of Harvard Business Review. "Going Global: Lessons from Late Movers" by Christopher A. Bartlett and Sumantra Ghoshal (March–April 2000). Harvard Business Review 78(2): 132–142.
▌ Copyright © 2000 by the President and Fellows of Harvard College. All rights reserved.

Consider labels such as "Made in Brazil" and "Made in Thailand." Someday they may be symbols of high quality and value, but today many consumers expect products from those countries to be inferior. Unfortunately, that perception is often shared by managers of the local companies that are striving to become global players.

That's just one reason why companies from peripheral countries find it so difficult to compete against established global giants from Europe, Japan, and the United States—the triad that dominates global commerce. And when they do compete, the experience of emerging multinationals often reinforces their self-doubt. Consider Arvind Mills, an Indian garment manufacturer that in the mid-1990s found a niche supplying denim to leading Western apparel companies. As Arvind's overseas sales grew, its stock soared on the Bombay Stock Exchange, and the company's CEO confidently declared that the company was well on its way to becoming a powerful global player. But within a couple of years, Arvind had become a victim of the fickle demands of the fashion business and the cutthroat competition among offshore apparel makers battling for the shrinking U.S. jeans market.

Stories such as Arvind's are told and retold in management circles. The moral is consistently negative. Companies from developing countries have entered the game too late. They don't have the resources. They can't hope to compete against giants. Yet despite the plausibility of such stories, we believe they are condescending and represent the counsel of despair. Indeed, there is plenty of evidence of an altogether different story. After all, companies like Sony, Toyota, and NEC transformed the cheap, low-quality image of Japanese products in little more than a decade. Is that type of turnaround still possible? To find out, we looked at

companies that, unlike Arvind, have successfully built a lasting and profitable international business from home countries far from the heart of the global economy.

We studied 12 emerging multinationals in depth. They operate in a wide range of businesses, but they are all based in countries that have not produced many successful multinationals—from large emerging markets like Brazil to relatively more prosperous yet still peripheral nations such as Australia to small developing countries like the Philippines. And while these companies are distinguished by strategic, organizational, and management diversity, they share some common traits. Most notably, each used foreign ventures in order to build capabilities to compete in more-profitable segments of their industry.

The evolution into more-profitable product segments can be clearly tracked on what we call the value curve. All industries can be seen as a collection of product market segments; the value curve is a tool used to differentiate the various segments. (For an example, see Figure 1 "The Pharmaceutical

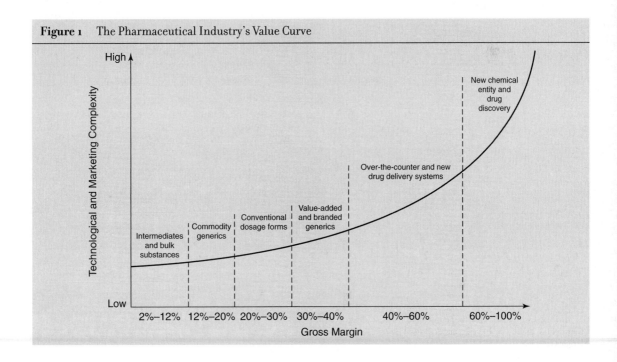

Figure 1   The Pharmaceutical Industry's Value Curve

Industry's Value Curve.") The more profitable a segment, the more sophisticated are the capabilities needed to compete in it—in R&D, distribution, or marketing. The problem for most aspiring multinationals from peripheral countries is that they typically enter the global marketplace at the bottom of the value curve—and they stay there. This is true even when a company's internal capabilities exceed the demands of a particular segment. Arvind Mills, for example, expanded abroad with commodity-like products even though it competed successfully in higher-value segments at home. And it's not that companies don't see the profitability of value-added products; the performance of companies above them on the value curve is usually quite evident. Basically, their failure is due to a paralysis of will. Managers either lack confidence in their organization's ability to climb the value curve or they lack the courage to commit resources to mounting that challenge. Often, as Nelson Mandela's memoir illustrates, they are crippled by a vision of themselves as second-class citizens.

A Model of Success

The Indian pharmaceutical company Ranbaxy is one of the success stories. For 18 years after it launched its export business in 1975, Ranbaxy was trapped at the bottom of the pharmaceutical value curve. Even though it had developed advanced product and process capabilities in its home market, when Ranbaxy decided to go overseas it opted to produce and sell bulk substances and intermediates in relatively unsophisticated markets. Because gross margins were between 5% and 10%, the additional revenue generated by the foreign business did not even offset the added costs of international sales and distribution. Management justified the negative returns by celebrating the prestige associated with being a multinational and making vague promises about using overseas contacts and experience to upgrade the business.

In 1993, Ranbaxy's approach to internationalization changed fundamentally. Parvinder Singh, the chairman and CEO from then until his death in 1999, challenged the top management team with his dream of transforming Ranbaxy into "an international, research-based pharmaceutical company." When his colleagues questioned how a small Indian company could compete with the rich giants from the West, he responded, "Ranbaxy cannot change India. What it can do is to create a pocket of excellence. Ranbaxy must be an island within India."

Once there was a shift in mind-set, the strategy was straightforward. The company moved into the higher-margin business of selling branded generics in large markets like Russia and China—a change that required building new customer relationships, a strong brand image, and different distribution channels. Ranbaxy then entered the U.S. and European markets, in which the company needed to meet much more stringent regulatory requirements. But by using its growing international knowledge and experience to develop new resources and capabilities, Ranbaxy established a profitable international business that accounted for more than half of its $250 million in revenue in 1996.

Not content with that, Ranbaxy has already begun the long, slow climb to the upper regions of the pharmaceutical value curve. Thanks to consistently investing 4% to 6% of its revenue in R&D, the company has built a world-class laboratory staffed by 250 scientists. Pushed by Singh's persistent question—Why do we say that new drug discovery is the exclusive preserve of the United States and Europe?—these scientists are committed to developing a $500 million drug before 2003. They cannot spend $300 million in R&D to develop the drug, the average expense in the West, but they believe they can cut that figure by a factor of four or five. "We have significant cost advantages in R&D, and we are prepared to invest $100 million," says J.M. Khanna, Ranbaxy's head of R&D.

Ranbaxy's growth path is shared by the other companies in our study. They all faced and overcame the same core challenges as they attempted to go global. Their immediate challenge was to break out of the mind-set that they couldn't compete successfully on the global stage. Once freed of that burden, they had to find strategies in which being a

Navigating the PC Industry's Value Curve

The drive up the value curve sometimes requires a company not just to shift product market segments but also to migrate to different points in the supply chain. Consider Acer, the Taiwanese company that started in 1976 as an electronic components importer and became the world's number three manufacturer of personal computers in just two decades.

As the PC market matured, Acer used its growing global presence to build capabilities at both ends of the supply chain, where the margins are higher than in the assembly business, which was its early focus. Acer learned from its exposure to global technology and best manufacturing practices, which helped the company move upstream into manufacturing motherboards, peripherals, and central processing units. In 1989, Acer partnered with Texas Instruments to produce semiconductors. Nine years later, it bought out TI's share.

Downstream, Acer's regional business units took over local assembly, started sourcing locally, opened new channels, and invested in the global brand that the company felt was key to freeing it from the low-margin OEM business. CEO Stan Shih calls this reorientation his "smiling curve." "Assembly means you are making money from manual labor. In components and marketing, you add value with your brains."

Shih's commitment to push his company to add value through the "smiling curve" saved Acer from the fate of dozens of other Taiwanese electronics suppliers that became captive suppliers of OEM goods to major computer companies. More than that, it has led Acer's continuing evolution in the global market. The company is now developing software and Internet businesses, which it believes will be the high-end value-added segments that will drive the next stage of Acer's global expansion.

Figure 2   Stan Shih's Smiling Curve

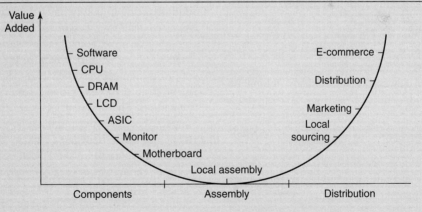

Recognizing that Acer's focus on assembling PCs was keeping the company in the least profitable segment of the market, CEO Stan Shih decided to move up the value curve by developing capabilities in components and distribution. Succeeding in components required strong technology and enough manufacturing skill to produce economies of scale. Succeeding in distribution required a solid brand, established channels, and effective logistics. Acer has built both.

late mover was a source of competitive advantage rather than a disadvantage. Finally, they had to develop a culture of continual cross-border learning. Winning companies enjoyed global success because they learned how to learn from the constant flow of new demands, opportunities, and challenges that international competition brings. This is quite a leap for most emerging multinationals; the ability to see globalization as more than a path to new markets or resources is rare in all but the most sophisticated global companies.

Breaking out of the Marginal Mind-Set

Let's take a closer look at the psychological factors that hold back most companies and the ways our emerging multinationals dealt with them. Companies from peripheral countries can fall into several traps, which we call liabilities of origin. First, some companies feel as though they are locked in a prison of local standards because of the gap between technical requirements and design norms at home and world-class standards abroad. If demand at home is strong, managers then can reasonably postpone the investments needed to comply with international standards. This insidious situation causes potential multinationals to duck the challenge of going abroad.

Some companies fall into a second trap. Even though their products and services are already up to snuff, because of the peripheral location, management is either unaware of the company's global potential or too debilitated by self-doubt to capitalize on it.

Finally, there are a few companies for which the liability of origin derives from a limited exposure to global competition, leaving them overconfident in their abilities or blind to potential dangers. Unfortunately, there are no quick solutions to any of these psychological barriers. But our emerging multinationals started to overcome them by creating a push from home and a pull from abroad.

Push from Home   There are basically two ways for a company to create a push from home. In the first, a moment of truth stimulates the initial steps down the long path toward internationalization. This

is particularly the case for companies that are so blinded by their domestic success that they fail to see that their origins present a liability. Therefore, management's greatest challenge is to shock or challenge the company to push it from its nest. It was just such a moment of truth that enabled the Korean giant Samsung to turn around its international sales of consumer electronics. Less than a decade ago, Samsung was struggling to expand into overseas markets, even though its products were technologically equal to its competitors' offerings. The problem was that most of Samsung's managers were unaware of or denied the existence of negative consumer perceptions abroad, largely because Samsung's products were so well regarded at home.

To force the company to deal with the problem, chairman Kun-Hee Lee flew 100 senior managers to the United States to show them how Samsung's products were treated. The visit was traumatic. Prominently displayed in storefronts were Sony, Bang & Olufsen, and the products of other prestigious companies. Lined up behind them were brands such as Philips, Panasonic, Toshiba, and Hitachi. In the back of the stores, frequently with big "bargain sale" stickers on them, were the Samsung TVs and VCRs, often with a layer of dust dulling the high-quality finish that the company had invested trillions of *won* to achieve. As the distraught executives joined their chairman in dusting their products with their handkerchiefs, he spelled out what all of them could clearly see: they had a lot of work to do to change overseas consumers' expectations. That moment of truth had an enduring impact. The executives initiated a series of actions that eventually led to a major turnaround of Samsung's global consumer electronics business.

The second way to create a push from home requires a leap of faith more than a shock of recognition. These leaps can be dramatic, and they are always risky, like performing on a trapeze without a net. Some CEOs, for example, demonstrate their commitment to globalization by investing far ahead of demand, even if doing so reduces the company's responsiveness to its successful home market.

Consider Thermax, a domestic Indian manufacturer of small boilers. Thermax had developed a radically different design for its boilers, which reduced their size by a third. Clearly, the new product could be a winner in the Indian market, where demand for such products was strong. But designing this new boiler to Indian specifications would make it virtually unsellable overseas. To succeed globally, the company not only had to meet the highest international technical standards but also had to develop a fundamentally different design concept. Overseas markets demanded sophisticated, and more expensive, integrated systems that enabled quick on-site installation, whereas India's lower labor costs allowed domestic contractors to take on more of the installation task themselves. Although the Indian market accounted for almost 80% of Thermax sales and 100% of profits, managing director Abhay Nalwade nonetheless decided to design the boiler for international markets. He believed the innovation gave the company one good shot at breaking into the European and North American markets. He was right. Today Thermax is the sixth-largest producer of small boilers in the world.

Pull from Abroad   Pushes from home are indispensable, but if companies are to use international expansion to move up the value curve, they also need to invest in the management capabilities of their overseas units to provide pull from abroad. Simply sending home-office managers with a vague charge to explore opportunities and open the market rarely achieves the objective; organizations need an engaged trading post, not just a passive listening post. Companies need offshore champions—often senior executives from the target market—who can provide the young, overseas organization with credibility and confidence, both internally and externally. Strong and credible voices from abroad can greatly increase the likelihood that emerging multinationals will have the courage to transfer organizational assets, resources, and influence outside their home country.

Natura, a direct-sales cosmetics company that has been named Brazil's most admired company for three consecutive years, learned that lesson the hard way. Although Natura has defended its strong market position in Brazil against international giants like Revlon, Estée Lauder, P&G, and Shiseido, it has failed to leverage its enormous product development and marketing strengths abroad—even in nearby markets like Argentina, Chile, and Peru. Absorbed by 40% to 50% growth at home, the company was unwilling to assign heavyweight managers to the new market opportunities. Abroad, it relied on unsupported midlevel expatriates and hastily hired outsiders who failed one by one. They didn't have the credibility needed to win top management's attention or the clout required to get the resources and the support vital to building a viable business abroad.

By contrast, Ranbaxy's Singh was committed to investing in overseas markets well ahead of demand. He realized that to do this he would have to create an organization in which managers from other parts of the world had a seat at the table on key corporate decisions. He divided the world into four regions, of which India was just one, even though its sales and profits were four times larger than the other three combined. Equally strong managers were assigned to each region. For example, although the size of Ranbaxy's European operation could not justify it, Singh hired a senior British executive from a leading pharmaceutical multinational to head the region. This executive's clear and unwavering belief in Ranbaxy and his commitment to building its European business became a powerful pull from abroad, helping the Indian-based pharmaceutical company believe it could compete in developed Western markets.

Devising Strategies for Late Movers

Once freed from the gravitational pull of its domestic market, the next major challenge for the emergent multinational is to choose a strategy to enter the global marketplace. On the face of it, the disadvantages of being a late entrant seem overwhelming. Management thinkers concluded long ago that the dominance of today's global giants is rooted in their first-mover status. Coca-Cola, for example, was the first soft-drink company to build a recognizably global brand. Moving first allowed Caterpillar to get a lock on overseas sales channels and service capabilities. Being a first mover enabled Matsushita to establish VHS as the global technical standard for videocassette recorders.

There are, however, some distinct advantages to turning up late for the global party. The emerging multinationals we observed typically exploited late-mover advantages in one of two ways. Some started by benchmarking the established global players and then maneuvered around them, often by exploiting niches that the larger companies had overlooked. Other companies adopted an alternative, though riskier, strategy. They used their newcomer status to challenge the rules of the game, capitalizing on the inflexibilities in the existing players' business models.

Benchmark and Sidestep Managers of small companies with limited international exposure fear that they will be ill equipped to face established global competitors in unfamiliar foreign environments. Yet in today's global market, you don't have to go abroad to experience international competition. Sooner or later the world comes to you. As a result, emerging multinationals can learn how to compete against the players in foreign markets simply by adapting and responding to those players as they enter the home market. That's exactly what the Philippines-based, fast-food chain Jollibee did. When the U.S. giant McDonald's began opening stores in Manila in 1981, few people believed Jollibee's tiny 11-store chain would survive. But CEO Tony Tan Caktiong and his management team decided to use the entry of McDonald's as a training ground to bring their young chain up to world class.

Going head-to-head against the experienced global company gave Jollibee's managers a first-hand view of the sophisticated operating systems that allowed McDonald's to control its quality, costs, and service at the store level. The lesson came at an ideal stage in the small chain's development, when the need for robust operating controls was the major constraint to further expansion. And what better model to learn from than a company whose refined systems control the day-to-day operations of thousands of stores worldwide? Indeed, it

was on the strength of its improved operating systems that Jollibee established a network of 65 domestic stores by 1990—far outdistancing the expansion of McDonald's in the Philippines.

But Jollibee's management did not just copy McDonald's; it also looked for ways to innovate. As it gained a better understanding of McDonald's business model, Jollibee started to recognize the gaps in its strategy. The U.S. company's standard product line and its U.S.-dominated decision processes did not easily incorporate local taste preferences. Jollibee offered a more tailored menu—a slightly sweeter hamburger, an innovative chicken product, a kid-oriented spaghetti plate—to differentiate itself from the U.S. giant. The combination of Jollibee's new, efficient stores and consumer-sensitive menu earned the loyalty of existing customers and allowed Jollibee to expand the fast-food market to new consumers.

The insights born of having survived McDonald's arrival in the Philippines taught Jollibee how it could move abroad. Knowing that it needed to provide for local tastes, the company developed the Jollimeal, a rice-based dish that could be adapted to the dominant local cuisine of the nearby markets that Jollibee began to enter in 1986. Jollibee respected McDonald's enough that it did not want to take on the global giant head-to-head in its first overseas forays. Instead, it started with the smaller markets where fast food was not yet well established, such as Brunei, Guam, and Vietnam. These early ventures helped Jollibee refine its strategy and learn about the problems of managing offshore franchises.

As Jollibee grew, it recognized that there was plenty of space for its differentiated products and that it had the capabilities to survive in larger and more competitive markets such as Indonesia and Hong Kong. Its niche products such as the *nasi lema,* a rice and coconut milk dish sold in Indonesia, and the chicken-mushroom rice offered in Hong Kong moved Jollibee beyond the increasingly commoditized product segments of hamburgers and fried chicken. By the early 1990s, Jollibee had established 24 overseas stores in ten countries, mostly in Southeast Asia and the Middle East. Though hardly on the scale of McDonald's network of more than 3,000 overseas outlets in almost 100 countries, Jollibee's operations nonetheless formed a sound basis for building a global franchise. In 1998, the company felt ready to take on the most demanding fast-food market in the world. Today, its first San Francisco store is performing at almost 50% above forecast levels, and two new stores have just opened. And Jollibee plans to roll out new stores in 17 other locations in California over the next 18 months.

Confront and Challenge   Jollibee's success illustrates how a late entrant can benchmark and adapt the business models of its competitors. A more radical strategy is to introduce new business models that challenge the industry's established rules of competition. Though risky, this approach can be very effective in industries deeply embedded with tradition or comfortably divided among an established oligopoly. The typical business model in these industries has become inflexible. Among the companies we studied, the one that took advantage of others' inflexibilities the best was BRL Hardy, an Australian wine company that defied many of the well-entrenched traditions of international wine production, trading, and distribution—despite the fact that its home country produces only 2% of the world's wine.

From a 1991 base of $31 million in export sales—much of it bulk for private labels and the rest a potpourri of bottled products sold through distributors—Hardy built its foreign sales to $178 million in 1998, almost all of it directly marketed as branded products. Managing director Steve Millar describes the insight that triggered this turnaround: "We began to realize that for a lot of historical reasons, the wine business—unlike the soft-drinks or packaged-foods industries—had very few true multinational companies and therefore very few true global brands. There was a great opportunity, and we were as well placed as anyone to grab it."

Millar was alluding to the inflexibility of the European practice of labeling wines by region, sub-region, and even village—the French *appellation* or the Italian *dominazione* systems are classic examples. A vineyard could be further categorized according to its historical quality classification such as the French premier grand cru, the grand cru, and so on. The resulting complexity not only confuses consumers but also fragments producers, whose small scale prevents them from building brand strength or distribution capability. This created an opportunity for major retailers, such as Sainsbury's in the United Kingdom, to overcome consumers' confusion—and capture more value themselves—by buying in bulk and selling under the store's own label.

For decades, BRL Hardy's international business was caught in this trap. It distributed its Hardy label wines to retailers through local agents and sold bulk wine directly for private labels. But Millar's insight gave the company a way out, if it was willing to change the rules of the game on both the demand and supply sides. First, new staff was appointed and new resources allocated to upgrade overseas sales offices. Instead of simply supporting the sales activities of distributing agents, they took direct control of the full sales, distribution, and marketing. Their primary objective was to establish Hardy as a viable global brand. The company's supply-side decision was even more significant. In order to exploit the growing marketing expertise of these overseas units, Hardy encouraged them to supplement their Australian product line by sourcing wine from around the world. Not only did Hardy offset the vintage uncertainties and currency risks of sourcing from a single country, it also gained clout in its dealings with retailers. By breaking the tradition of selling only its own wine, Hardy was able to build the scale necessary for creating strong brands and negotiating with retail stores.

The advantages have been clear and powerful. The company's range of wines—from Australia as well as France, Italy, and Chile—responds to supermarkets' needs to deal with a few broad line suppliers. At the same time, the scale of operation has supported the brand development so vital to pulling products out of the commodity range. Results have been outstanding. In Europe, the volume of Hardy's brands has increased 12-fold in seven years, making it the leading Australian wine brand in the huge UK market, and number two overall to Gallo in the United Kingdom. And branded products from other countries have grown to represent about a quarter of its European volume. Hardy has evolved from an Australian wine exporter to a truly global wine company.

The company's new strategy and capabilities are visible in its recent introduction of a branded wine from Sicily called D'istinto. Under a supply agreement and marketing program initiated by BRL Hardy Europe, in its first year this product has sold 200,000 cases in the United Kingdom alone—an exceptional performance. As the brand is introduced to the rest of Europe, North America, and Australia, Hardy expects sales to top a million cases by 2003.

■ Learning How to Learn

Ask most managers why they are steering their companies into international expansion and they will talk about increasing sales or securing low-cost labor and raw materials. Important as those objectives are, they do not ensure a company's success abroad. The global marketplace is information based and knowledge intensive. To survive in this environment, you must know how to learn: it is the central skill that allows a company to move up the value curve. Yet all learning requires tuition, and every company faces the risk that the effort involved in acquiring new capabilities may draw off too many vital resources and threaten the domestic business. The trick is to protect the past while building the future.

Protect the Past   The first rule of companies that want to learn is to fully exploit the resources and capabilities that have provided competitive advantage to date. This is a simple notion, yet in the quest for global position, too many companies become so focused on where they are going that they forget where they are coming from. In the early stages of Jollibee's expansion, for example, an aggressive international division manager fell into the trap of trying to reinvent the company's business. By constantly

emphasizing the differences of overseas markets, he deliberately isolated his overseas managers from the highly successful Philippines fast-food organization. Then he systematically differentiated his operating systems, store design, menus, advertising themes, and even the company's logo and slogan. Despite his enthusiasm and energy, Jollibee's international sales struggled and losses mounted. Eventually that manager was replaced with someone more willing to build on existing expertise.

The new manager took a few simple steps that were crucial to the company's subsequent international growth. First, he broke down the barriers between the international and domestic organizations and began building relationships that acknowledged his respect for their success and dependence on the home country's expertise. For example, international managers now train in the Philippines operations, learning from that organization's experience and making useful support contacts as they do. They also have given up trying to manage all their own financial and operations reporting systems, relying instead on the efficient home market staff. And when major overseas appointments come up—as one did to manage the key China and Hong Kong operations—the international group now feels comfortable drawing on the best and brightest from the Philippines—in this case the domestic VP of operations—rather than trying to staff from international ranks.

This sort of close cooperation between the parent company and its overseas subsidiaries establishes a dynamic of mutual learning. In Jollibee's case, the domestic organization's openness and exposure to international developments has allowed it to benefit from some of the adaptations and adjustments made to accommodate different situations abroad. For example, even through it is only a year old, the U.S. operations have already located chicken and beef suppliers for its restaurants in Southeast Asia, and the Philippines stores have just launched a cheesy bacon-mushroom sandwich originally developed for the U.S. market. So the operation that started by teaching its international managers has ended up learning from them. Such cross-pollination of ideas is key if emerging multinationals are to compete successfully with the giants they take on.

Build the Future   Entering a new market successfully usually requires considerably more than simply tweaking the home-market formula. Often companies lack the expertise needed to tailor the product or strategy to the new environment. So many emerging multinationals try to take a shortcut to learning by entering into a partnership with a foreign company. But while some of these international partnerships become successful long-term ventures, more fall apart due to an asymmetry of interests or a shift in the partners' power balance. When that happens, the emergent multinational as a new and small player is often left at a serious disadvantage.

Consider the situation faced by VIP Industries, India's largest luggage company and the world's second-largest producer after Samsonite of molded luggage. When it entered the UK market, VIP formed a marketing partnership with a local distributor that promised access to the country's largest retailers. A breakthrough came when the distributor, with VIP's help, won the franchise to establish a specialty luggage department in each of Debenham's 75 stores nationwide. VIP invested heavily in staff training for the specialty departments, and it was rewarded with a 60% share of Debenham's hard luggage sales. Yet when Samsonite offered VIP's distributor exclusive rights to its revolutionary Oyster II model, the local agent switched allegiances with hardly a thought. With no direct investment in its own local sales and marketing capabilities, VIP was powerless to respond.

In theory, companies can sidestep the disadvantages of partnering by buying the necessary capabilities. But that can create problems of its own. That was the mistake that Hardy made when it committed to international expansion. In the course of just two business trips to Europe, the company's management had snapped up two established London wine merchants, a large French winery and estate, and a historic Italian vineyard. Hardy believed the acquisitions would provide an asset base and knowledge pool to broaden its product sources and increase its marketing clout. But the challenge of simultaneously developing expertise in Italian and French wine making as well as English marketing proved overwhelming and soon placed huge financial and management strains on the company.

After that false start, Hardy realized that in international business new capabilities cannot simply be installed; they must be developed and internalized. That's why, despite acute financial pressures, the company rejected a tempting opportunity to rapidly expand its UK market volume by supplying wine for a leading grocery chain's private label. Instead, it opted for the more difficult task of building Hardy's own brand image and the marketing and distribution capabilities to support it. That has required considerable investment in new personnel and training, as well as a major reorientation of internal culture.

In 1991, Christopher Carson, an experienced international wine marketer, was appointed managing director of the company's UK operations. Over the next 18 months, Carson pruned three-quarters of the items in the fragmented product line, replaced half his management team, and began building a culture around creativity and disciplined execution. Within three years, he had not only quadrupled sales of Hardy brands but also developed one of his imported wines from Chile into the biggest-selling Chilean brand in the United Kingdom. Hardy's revenues and profits have amply rewarded this investment, and the organization has developed a worldwide pool of knowledge and expertise that benefits the entire company. Carson, for example, has become the company's acknowledged expert in structuring sourcing partnerships and marketing outsourced wine brands. After building experience negotiating the Chilean partnership, he led the company's efforts on the Italian joint venture that sourced and marketed the successful D'istinto brand. Leveraging this expertise, he is now leading a new Spanish project.

Having the Right Stuff

As we examined the activities of this handful of companies that overcame their liabilities of origin, exploited their late-mover advantages, and captured and leveraged learning in global markets, we were struck by one commonality. From fast food to pharmaceuticals, from Brazil to Thailand, moving from the periphery into the mainstream of global competition is such a big leap that it was always led from the top. In each and every case, the emerging multinationals had leaders who drove them relentlessly up the value curve. These leaders shared two characteristics. First, their commitment to global entrepreneurialism was rooted in an unshakable belief that their company would succeed internationally. Second, as their operations expanded, they all exhibited a remarkable openness to new ideas that would facilitate internationalism—even when those ideas challenged established practice and core capabilities.

With a PhD in pharmacology from the University of Michigan, Ranbaxy's Parvinder Singh was always a scientist-entrepreneur at heart. It was Singh who envisioned Ranbaxy as an international, research-based pharmaceutical company. Every time urgent domestic needs appeared to overwhelm R&D priorities, he protected the programs that would support foreign markets and those that searched for either new drugs or new drug-delivery systems. Whenever the well-established intermediates business appeared to monopolize international managers's time and energy, he reminded them that their ultimate purpose was to move up the value curve and that the intermediates business was a means, not the end. Beyond specific actions, Singh protected the faith. Just like the ancient priests in rural India who seldom intervene in the community but who nonetheless exert a constant influence over the lives and behaviors of the villagers, Singh was always there, standing up for internationalization. Respecting him meant respecting his dream, and that perhaps more than anything else pushed senior managers to persist with international initiatives, even when the costs appeared too high.

The second quality of global leadership—openness to new ideas—was most clearly and forcibly displayed by Dr. Peter Farrell, CEO of ResMed. ResMed is an Australia-based medical equipment company that specializes in the treatment of a breathing disorder known as obstructive sleep apnea (OSA). Spun off in 1989 by U.S. giant Baxter International, ResMed was a struggling start-up with a crude early product generating just $1 million in annual revenue. By 1999, it was the world's number two competitor in the fast-growing market for OSA treatment devices, and its products were generating sales of some $90 million a year.

Farrell's receptivity to new ideas was responsible for this dramatic change in fortune. Although the company's cofounder, Dr. Colin Sullivan, the inventor of ResMed's product, was acknowledged as one of the industry's most knowledgeable experts, Farrell pushed ResMed's researchers to build strong networks with other leaders in the international medical community. He led a team on a worldwide fact-finding tour of leading researchers and physicians, for example, and he put together a medical advisory board to help ResMed develop its products to be the industry standard. To help shape the medical debate, the company also organized annual global medical conferences on OSA, distributing the proceedings in ResMed-sponsored CD-ROMs. More recently, Farrell launched a campaign to have the medical profession recognize the strong links between sleep-disordered breathing and the incidence of strokes and congestive heart failure. It is a bold initiative and requires substantial investment, but it has the potential to raise the medical profile of OSA dramatically, and in doing so, multiply ResMed's target market substantially. Farrell has also moved the company's center of operations in order to be closer to his largest and most sophisticated markets. In these and other ways, Farrell pushed the company to act like a leading global player long before that was an operating reality.

Strong leaders changed the fates of ResMed and Ranbaxy, Hardy and Jollibee, and the other companies discussed here. These leaders are models for the heads of thousands of marginal companies in peripheral economies that have the potential to become legitimate global players. Like Nelson Mandela, they can lead their followers out of the isolationism and parochialism that constrains them. They can do so by climbing up the value curve into the mainstream of the global economy.

CHAPTER 2

Managing Conflicting Demands:
Global Integration, Local Responsiveness, and Worldwide Learning

Recent changes in the international business environment have revolutionized the task facing MNC managers. Important shifts in political, social, economic, and technological forces have combined to create management challenges for today's MNCs that are fundamentally different from those facing companies just 20 years ago. Yet despite intense study by academics, consultants, and practicing managers, both the nature of the various external forces and their strategic and organizational implications are still widely disputed.

Twenty years ago when Professor Theodore Levitt's classic *Harvard Business Review* article, "The Globalization of Markets," was published, the ideas provoked widespread debate (see the readings in Chapter 3). In Levitt's view, technological, social, and economic trends were combining to create a unified world marketplace that was driving companies to develop globally standard products that enabled them to capture global economies. His critics, however, claimed that Levitt presented only one side of the story. They suggested that, like many managers, he had become so focused on the forces for globalization that he was blind to their limitations and to equally powerful countervailing forces.

The ensuing debate helped better define the diverse, changeable, and often contradictory forces that were reshaping so many industries in the 1980s and 1990s. In this chapter, we summarize a few of the most powerful of these environmental forces and suggest how they have collectively led to a new and complex set of challenges that require managers of MNCs to respond to three simultaneous yet often conflicting sets of external demands—the need for cross-market integration, national responsiveness, and worldwide learning.

Forces for Global Integration and Coordination

The phenomenon of globalization of certain industries described by Levitt was not a sudden or discontinuous development. It was simply the latest round of change brought about by economic, technological, and competitive factors that, a hundred years earlier, had transformed the structures of many industries from regional to national scope. Economies of scale, economies of scope, and national differences in the availability and cost of productive resources were the three principal economic forces that had driven this process of structural transformation of businesses of which globalization was perhaps the final stage.[1] And the impact of these forces on MNC strategy was facilitated by the increasingly liberal trading environment of the 1980s and 1990s.

Economies of Scale

The Industrial Revolution created pressure for much larger plants that could capture the benefits of the economies of scale offered by the new technologies it had spawned. Cheap and abundant energy combined with good transportation networks and new production technologies to restructure capital-incentive industries. For the first time, companies combined intermediate processes into single plants and developed large-batch or continuous-process technologies to achieve low-cost volume production.

However, in many industries, like fine chemicals, automobiles, airframes, and oil refining, production at scale economy volumes exceeded the sales levels individual companies could achieve in all but the largest nations, pushing them to seek markets abroad. Even in industries where the largest companies retained a large enough share of their domestic markets to achieve scale economies without exports, those on the next rung were often forced to seek markets outside their home countries if they were to remain competitive.

Economies of Scope

In less-capital-intensive industries, even companies that were largely unaffected by scale economies were transformed by opportunities for economies of scope that were opened up by more-efficient worldwide communication and transportation networks. One classic example of how such economies could be exploited internationally was provided by trading companies handling consumer goods. By exporting the products of many companies, they achieved a greater volume and lower per unit cost than any narrow-line manufacturer could in marketing and distributing its products abroad.

In many industries there were opportunities for both economies of scale and scope. Consumer electronics companies such as Matsushita, for example, derived scale advantages from their standardized TV and VCR plants, and scope advantages through their marketing and sales network that offered service, repair, and credit for a broad range of home electronics.

Factor Costs

With changes in technology and markets came the requirement for access to new resources at the lowest possible cost. Often there were no home-country sources of supply for companies wishing to expand into new industry segments. European petroleum companies, for example, explored the Middle East because they had limited domestic crude oil sources. Others went overseas in search of bauxite from which to produce aluminum, rubber to produce tires for a growing automobile industry, and tea to be consumed by an expanding middle class.

---

[1]For a more detailed analysis of these environmental forces, read Alfred D. Chandler, Jr., "The Evolution of the Modern Global Corporation," in *Competition in Global Industries,* ed. Michael Porter (Boston: Harvard Business School Press, 1986) pp. 405–48. For those interested in an even more detailed exposition, Chandler's book, *Scale and Scope* (Cambridge, Mass.: Harvard University Press, 1990) will prove to be compelling reading.

Less-capital-intensive industries like textiles, apparel, and shoes turned to international markets as a source of cheap labor. The increased costs of transportation and logistics management were more than paid for by much lower production costs. However, many companies found that, once educated, the cheap labor rapidly became expensive. Indeed, the typical life cycle of a country as a source of cheap labor for an industry is now only about five years. This forced companies to chase cheap labor from southern Europe, to Central America, to the Far East and later to eastern Europe.

The Liberalizing Environment for Trade

Whereas the economics of scale and scope and the differences in factor costs between countries provided the underlying motivation for global coordination, it was the increasingly liberal environment for world trade that facilitated the broad transition we have seen. Beginning with the formation of the General Agreement on Tariffs and Trade (GATT) in 1945, and moving through various rounds of trade talks, the creation of regional free trade agreements such as the EU and NAFTA, and the formation of the World Treaty Organization (WTO), the dominant trend has been toward the reduction of barriers to international trade. The result is that at the beginning of the 21st century, the international trading environment is probably less restricted than ever before, and this has enabled MNCs to realize most of the potential economic benefits that arise from global coordination.

The Expanding Spiral of Globalization

During the 1970s and 1980s, these forces began to globalize the structure and competitive characteristics of a variety of industries. In some, the change was driven by a major technological innovation that forced a fundamental realignment of industry economics. The impact of transistors and integrated circuits on the design and production of radios, televisions, and other consumer electronics represents a classic example of new technologies driving minimum efficient scale of production beyond the demand of most single markets. More recently, advances in semiconductor technology led to the boom in the PC industry, and innovations in wireless technology led to the creation of the mobile phone industry.

Many other industries lacked strong external forces for change, but transformed themselves through internal restructuring efforts, such as rationalizing their product lines, standardizing parts design, and specializing their manufacturing operations. This led to a further wave of globalization, with companies in industries as diverse as automobiles, office equipment, industrial bearings, construction equipment, and machine tools all seeking to gain competitive advantage by capturing scale economies that extended beyond national markets.

More recently, even some companies in classically local rather than global businesses have begun to examine the opportunities for capturing economies beyond their national borders. Rather than responding to the enduring differences in consumer tastes and market structures across European countries, many of the large branded packaged goods companies such as Procter & Gamble and Unilever have transformed traditionally national businesses like soap and detergent manufacturing. By standardizing product formulations, rationalizing pack sizes, and printing multilingual labels, they have been able to restructure and specialize their nationally dominated plant configurations and achieve substantial scale economies, gaining significant advantage over purely local competitors. Even labor-intensive local industries such as office cleaning and catering are not immune from the forces of globalization. For example, ISS, the Danish cleaning services company, has been able to build a successful international business through the transfer of practices and know-how across countries, and by offering a consistent and high-quality service across countries to its international customers. Sodexho, a French company, has adopted a similar approach in the catering and food services industry, and has become highly successful on an international basis.

In market terms also, the spread of global forces expanded from businesses in which the global standardization of products was relatively easy (calculators and cameras, for example) to others in which consumers' preferences and habits were only slowly converging (automobiles and appliances, for instance). Again, major external discontinuities greatly facilitated the change process as in the case of the oil shocks of the 1970s, which triggered a worldwide demand for smaller, more fuel-efficient cars.

Even in markets where national tastes or behaviors varied widely, however, globalizing forces could be activated if one or more competitors in a business chose to activate and influence changes in consumer preference. Food tastes and eating habits were long thought to be the most culture-bound of all consumer behaviors. Yet, as companies like McDonald's, Coca-Cola, and Starbucks have shown, in Eastern and Western countries alike, even these culturally linked preferences can be changed.

Global Competitors as Change Agents

As the forces driving companies to coordinate their worldwide operations spread from industries where such changes were triggered by some external structural discontinuity to others where managers had to create the opportunity themselves, there emerged a new globalization force that spread rapidly across a large number of businesses. It was a competitive strategy that some called *global chess* and that could only be played by companies that managed their worldwide operations as interdependent units implementing a coordinated global strategy. Unlike the traditional multinational strategic approach that was based on an assumption that each national market was unique and independent of others, these global competitive games assumed that a company's competitive position in all markets was linked by financial and strategic interdependence. Regardless of consumer tastes or manufacturing scale economies, it was suggested that the corporation with worldwide operations had a great advantage over the national company in that it could use funds generated in one market to subsidize its position in another.

For example, British Airways became one of the most profitable airlines in the world during the late 1980s because its dominant position at Heathrow Airport allowed it to make large profits on its long-haul routes (particularly to New York), and essentially subsidize its lower margin U.K. and European business. This allowed it to fend off new entrants in Europe by pushing its prices down there, while not putting its most profitable routes at risk. And existing competitors such as British Midland suffered because they lacked access to the lucrative Heathrow–U.S. routes.

By the 1980s, there was little argument that all these diverse globalizing forces were transforming the nature of competition worldwide. But although few challenged the existence or widespread influence of such forces, some did question the unidimensionality of their influence and the universality of their strategic implications. They took issue, for example, with Levitt's suggestions that "the world's needs and desires have been irrevocably homogenized," that "no one is exempt and nothing can stop the process," and that "the commonality of preference leads inescapably to the standardization of products, manufacturing, and the institution of trade and commerce." The critics argued that, although these might indeed be long-term trends in many industries, there were important short- and medium-term impediments and countertrends that had to be taken into account if companies were to operate successfully in an international economy that jolts along—*perhaps* eventually toward Levitt's "global village."

Forces for Local Differentiation and Responsiveness

There are many different stories of multinational companies making major blunders in transferring successful products or ideas from their home countries to foreign markets. General Motors is believed to have faced difficulties in selling the popular Chevrolet Nova in Mexico where the product name sounded like "no va" meaning "it does not go" in Spanish.[2] Similarly, when managers began investigating why its advertising campaign built around the highly successful "come alive with Pepsi" theme was not having the expected impact in Thailand, they discovered that the Thai copy translation read more like "come out of the grave with Pepsi." Although these and other such cases are widely cited, they represent the most extreme and simple-minded examples of an important strategic task facing managers of all MNCs: how to sense, respond to, and even exploit the differences in the environments of the many different countries in which their company operates.

National environments are different on many dimensions. For example, there are clear differences in the per capita GNP or the industry-specific technological capabilities in Japan, Australia, Brazil, and Poland. They also differ in terms of political systems, government regulation, social norms, and cultural values of their people. It is these national differences that force managers to be sensitive and responsive to national social, economic, and political differences in the host countries in which they operate around the globe.

Far from being overshadowed by the forces of globalization, the impact of these localizing forces was being felt with increasing intensity and urgency throughout the 1980s and 1990s. First, many Japanese companies that had so successfully ridden the wave of globalization began to feel the strong need to become much more sensitive to host-country economic and political forces. This led to a wave of investment abroad, as Japanese companies sought to become closer to their export markets and more responsive to host governments.

Then throughout the 1990s, many North American and European companies also realized that they had pushed the logic of globalization too far, and that a reconnection with the local environments in which they were doing business was necessary. For

---

[2]For this many other such examples of international marketing problems, see David A Ricks, *Big Business Blunders* (Homewood, Ill.: Richard D. Irwin, 1983).

example, in March 2000, Coca Cola's incoming CEO, Douglas Daft, explained his company's shift in policy in the March 27, 2000, *Financial Times* newspaper: "As the 1990s were drawing to a close, the world had changed course, and Coca-Cola had not," said Daft. "We were operating as a big, slow, insulated, sometimes even insensitive 'global' company; and we were doing it in an era when nimbleness, speed, transparency and local sensitivity had become absolutely essential."

Cultural Differences

A large body of academic research provides strong evidence that nationality plays an important and enduring role in shaping the assumptions, beliefs, and values of individuals. Perhaps the most celebrated effort to date to describe and categorize these differences in the orientations and values of people in different countries is Geert Hofstede's study that described national cultural differences along four key dimensions: power distance, uncertainty avoidance, individualism, and "masculinity."[3] This study demonstrates how distinct cultural differences across countries result in wide variations in social norms and individual behavior (for example, the Japanese respect for their elders, or the culturally embedded American response to time pressure) and is reflected in the effectiveness of different organizational forms (for example, the widespread French difficulty with the dual reporting relationships of the matrix organization) and management systems (the Swedes, egalitarian culture leads them to prefer flatter organizations and smaller wage differentials).

However, cultural differences are also reflected in nationally differentiated consumption patterns: the way people dress or the foods they prefer. Take the single example of tea as a beverage consumed around the globe. The British drink their tea as a light brew further diluted with milk, whereas Americans consume it primarily as a summer drink served over ice and Saudi Arabians drink theirs as a thick, hot brew heavily sweetened. To succeed in a world of such diversity, companies often had to modify their quest for global efficiency through standardization and find ways to respond to the needs and opportunities created by cultural differences.

Government Demands

Inasmuch as cultural differences among countries have been an important localizing force, diverse demands and expectations of their home and host governments have perhaps been the most severe constraint to the global strategies of many companies. Traditionally, the interactions between MNCs and the host governments have had many attributes of a classic love–hate relationship.

The "love" of the equation was built on the benefits each could bring to the other. To the host government, the MNC represented an important source of funds, technology, and expertise that could help further national priorities such as regional development,

---

[3]For a more detailed exposition see Hofstede's book *Culture's Consequences* (Beverly Hills, Calif.: Sage Publications, 1984). A brief overview of the four different aspects of national culture are presented in the reading "Culture and Organization" at the end of this chapter. For managerial implications of such differences in national culture, see also Nancy J. Alder, *International Dimensions of Organisational Behavior* (Boston: Kent Publishing 1986), and Fons Trompenaars and Charles Hampden-Turner, *Riding the Waves of Culture* (London: Nicholas Brealey Publishing 1997).

employment, import substitution, and export promotion. To the MNC, the host government represented the key to local-market or resource access, which provided new opportunities for profit, growth, and improvement of its competitive position.

The "hate" side of the relationship—though more often frustration than outright antagonism—arose from the differences in the motivations and objectives of the two partners. To be effective global competitors, MNCs sought three important operating objectives: unrestricted access to resources and markets throughout the world; the freedom to integrate manufacturing and other operations across national boundaries; and the unimpeded right to coordinate and control all aspects of the company on a worldwide basis. The host government, on the other hand, sought to develop an economy that could survive and prosper in a competitive international environment. At times, this objective led to the designation of another company—perhaps a "national champion"—as its standard bearer in the specific industry, bringing it into direct conflict with the MNC. This is particularly visible in the international airline business where flag-carrying companies such as Air France or Malaysia Airlines compete only after receiving substantial government subsidies.

Even when the host government did not have such a national champion and was willing to permit and even support an MNC's operations within its boundaries, it would usually do so only at a price. Although both parties might be partners in search for global competitiveness, the MNC typically tried to achieve that objective within its global system, while the host government strove to capture it within its national boundaries, thereby leading to conflict and mutual resentment.

The potential for conflict between the host government and the MNC arose not only from economic, but also from social, political, and cultural issues. MNC operations often cause social disruption in the host country through rural exodus, rising consumerism, rejection of indigenous values, or breakdown of traditional community structures. Similarly, even without the maliciousness of MNCs that in earlier decades blatantly tried to manipulate host-government structures or policies (for example, ITT's attempt to overthrow the Allende government in Chile), MNCs can still represent a political threat because of their size, power, and influence, particularly in developing economies.

Because of these differences in objectives and motivations, MNC–host-government relationships are often seen as a zero-sum game in which the outcome depends on the balance between the government's power (arising from its control over local-market access and from competition among different MNCs for that access) and the MNC's power (arising from its financial, technological, and managerial resources and the competition among national governments for those resources). If, in the 1960s, the multinational companies had been able to hold "sovereignty at bay" as one respected international researcher concluded,[4] by the 1980s, the balance had tipped in the other direction. The rapidly growing power of the global companies was perceived as a threat by various national governments that saw their social and economic policies being upset by the rising import penetration.

In an effort to stem the flood of imports, many countries began bending or sidestepping trade agreements signed in earlier years. By the early 1980s, even the U.S. government, traditionally one of the strongest advocates of free trade, began to negotiate a

---

[4]Raymond Vernon, *Sovereignty at Bay* (New York: Basic Books, 1971).

series of orderly marketing agreements and voluntary restraints on Japanese exports, while threats of sanctions were debated with increasing emotion in legislative chambers around the globe. And countries became more sophisticated in the demands they placed on inward-investing MNCs. Rather than allowing superficial investment in so-called screwdriver plants that provided only limited low-skill employment, governments began to specify levels of local content, technology transfer, and a variety of other conditions from reexport commitment to plant location requirements.

Moving into the 1990s, however, the power of national governments was once again on the wane. The success of countries such as Ireland and Singapore in driving their economic development through foreign investment led many other countries—both developed and developing—to launch aggressive inward investment policies of their own. And this increased demand for investment allowed MNCs to play countries off against each other, and in many cases to extract a high price from the host country. For example, according to *The Economist,* the incentives paid by Alabama to Mercedes for its 1993 auto plant cost $167,000 per direct employee.

In the first years of the new millenium, the once-troublesome issue of MNC–country bargaining power has evolved into a relatively efficient market system for inward investment, at least in the developed world. However, the developing world was a rather different story, with MNCs continuing to be embroiled in political disputes, such as the 1995 hanging of environmental activist Ken Saro-Wiwa by the Nigerian government because of his opposition to Shell's exploitation of his people's land. MNCs have also attracted the brunt of the criticism from so-called antiglobalization protestors during WTO meetings in Seattle, Genoa, and elsewhere. The antiglobalization movement is a diverse mix of groups with different agendas, but united in their concern that the increasing liberalization of trade through the WTO is being pursued for the benefit of MNCs, and at the expense of people and companies in less-developed parts of the world. Although this movement does not have a coherent set of policy proposals of its own, it provides a salutary reminder to policymakers and to the executives managing MNCs that the globalization of business is a contentious issue. The rewards are not spread evenly, and for many people in many parts of the world, the process of globalization makes things worse before making them better. The movement has forced MNCs to rethink their more contentious policies, and it has encouraged them to better articulate the benefits they bring to less-developed countries. For example, oil majors Shell and BP now actively promote polices for sustainable development—including research into renewable sources of energy, and investments in the local communities in which they operate around the world.

Growing Pressures for Localization

Although there is no doubt that the increasing frequency of world travel and the ease with which communication linkages occur across the globe have lately done a great deal toward reducing the effect of national consumer differences, it would be naïve to believe that worldwide tastes, habits, and preferences have become anywhere near homogenous.

Furthermore, even though many companies have succeeded in appealing to—and accelerating—such convergence worldwide, even this trend toward standardized products designed to appeal to a lowest common denominator of consumer demand has a flip side. In industry after industry, a large group of consumers emerged that rejected the homogenized product design and performance on standardized global products. By reasserting traditional preferences for more differentiated products, they created openings—often very profitable ones—for companies that were willing to respond to, and even expand, the need for products and services that were more responsive to those needs.

The success of U.K. electronics company Amstrad is a good example of the phenomenon. In the 1980s, Alan Sugar, the company's entrepreneurial founder, correctly perceived that many English consumers were unhappy about the transformation of traditional hi-fi equipment into globally standardized, sleek, and simple metal boxes that became known as "music centers." Amstrad sensed this consumer preference and responded by designing a product line that put back a technical feel into the hi-fi control panel, reintroduced the component elements to the system, and enclosed it in teak cases. Locking in with the country's largest discount retailers, it was able to capture market leadership from its larger global competitors. Amstrad subsequently expanded by applying the same market-sensitive logic to other consumer electronic products, including receiver dishes for satellite TV and a combination web browser–telephone.

Other consumer and market trends are emerging to counterbalance the forces of global standardization of products. In an increasing number of markets from telecommunications to office equipment to consumer electronics, consumers are not so much buying individual products as selecting systems. With advances in wireless and Internet technology, for example, the TV set is now becoming part of a home entertainment and information system, connected to the VCR, the hi-fi system, the home computer, and an online databank and information network. This transformation is forcing companies to adapt their standard hardware-oriented products to more-flexible and locally differentiated systems consisting of hardware plus software services. In such an environment, the competitive edge lies less with the company with the most scale-efficient global production capability and more with the one that is sensitive and responsive to local requirements and able to develop the software and services to meet it.

In addition to such barriers, there are other important impediments. Although it is obvious that the benefits of scale economies must outweigh the additional costs of supplying markets from a central point, companies often ignore the fact that those costs consist of more than just freight charges. In particular, the administrative costs of coordination and scheduling worldwide demand through global-scale plants is normally quite significant and must be taken into account. For some products, lead times are so short or market service requirements so high that these scale economies may well be offset by other costs.

More significantly, developments in computer-aided design and manufacturing, robotics, and other advanced production technologies have made the concept of flexible manufacturing a viable reality. Companies that previously had to produce tens or hundreds of thousands of standardized printed circuit boards (PCBs) in a central global-scale plant now find they can achieve minimum efficient scale in smaller distributed national plants closer to their customers. Flexible manufacturing technologies mean that there is little difference in unit costs between making 1,000 or 100,000 PCBs. When linked to the consumer's growing disenchantment with homogenized global products, this technology appears to offer multinational companies an important tool that will enable them to respond to localized consumer preferences and national political constraints without compromising their economic efficiency.

Forces for Worldwide Innovation and Learning

The trends we have described have created an extremely difficult competitive environment in a large number of industries, and only those firms that have been able to adapt to the often conflicting forces for global coordination and national differentiation have been able to survive and prosper. But on top of these forces, another set of competitive demands is taking shape around the need for rapid and globally coordinated innovation. Indeed, in the emerging competitive game, victory most often goes to the company that can most effectively harness its access to worldwide information and expertise to develop and diffuse innovative products and processes on a worldwide basis.

The trends that are driving this shift in the competitive game in many ways derive from the globalizing and localizing forces we described earlier. The increasing cost of R&D, coupled with shortening life cycles for new technologies and the products that they spawn, have combined to reinforce the need for companies to seek global volume in order to amortize the heavy investment as quickly as possible. At the same time, even the most advanced technology has diffused rapidly around the globe, particularly over the past few decades. In part, this trend has been in response to the demands, pressures, and coaxing of host governments as they bargain for increasing levels of national production and high levels of local content in the leading-edge products being sold in their markets. But the high cost of product and process development has also encouraged companies to transfer new technologies voluntarily, with licensing becoming an important source of funding, cross-licensing a means to fill technology gaps for many MNCs, and joint development programs and strategic alliances a strategy for rapidly building global competitive advantage.

When coupled with converging consumer preferences worldwide, this diffusion of technology has had an important effect on both the pace and locus of innovation. No longer can U.S.–based companies assume, as they often did in the immediate postwar decades, that their domestic environment provided them with the most sophisticated consumer needs and the most advanced technological capabilities, and thus the most innovative environment in the world. Today, the newest consumer trend or market need can emerge in Australia or Italy, and the latest technologies to respond to new needs may be located in Japan or Sweden. Innovations are springing up worldwide, and companies are recognizing that they can gain competitive advantage by sensing needs in one country, responding with capabilities located in a second, and diffusing the resulting innovation to markets around the globe.

A related trend is the increasing importance of global standards in such industries as computer software, telecommunications, consumer electronics, and even consumer goods. The winners in the battle for a new standard—from software platforms to razor blade cartridges—can build and defend dominant competitive positions around the world that can endure for decades. First-mover advantages have increased substantially and have provided strong incentives for companies to focus attention not only on the internal task of rapidly creating and diffusing innovations within their own worldwide operations, but also on the external task of establishing the new product as an industry standard.

Responding to the Diverse Forces Simultaneously

Trying to distill the key environmental demands in large and complex industries is a hazardous venture but, at the risk of oversimplification, one can make the case that until the late 1980s most worldwide industries presented relatively unidimensional environmental requirements. But, although this led to the development of industries with very different characteristics—those we distinguish as global, multinational, and international industries—more recently this differentiation has been eroding with important consequences for companies' strategies.

Global, Multinational, and International Industries

In some businesses, the economic forces of globalization were historically especially strong and dominated the other environmental demands. For example, in the consumer electronics industry, the invention of the transistor led to decades of inexorable expansion in the benefits of scale economics: Successive rounds of technological change such as introduction of integrated circuits and microprocessors have led to an increase of the minimum efficient scale of operations from about 50,000 sets per annum to over 3 million television sets per annum. In an environment of falling transportation costs, relatively low tariffs, and increasing homogenization of national markets, these huge-scale economics dominated the strategic tasks for managers of consumer electronics companies in the closing decades of the last century.

Such industries, in which the economic forces of globalization are dominant, we designate as *global industries*. In such businesses, success typically belonged to companies that adopted classic *global strategies* of capitalizing on highly centralized scale-intensive manufacturing and R&D operations, and leveraging them through worldwide exports of standardized global products.

In some other businesses, the localizing forces of national, cultural, social, and political differences dominated the development of industry characteristics. In laundry detergents, for example, R&D and manufacturing costs were relatively small parts of a company's total expenses, and all but the smallest markets could justify the investment in a detergent tower and benefit from its scale economies. At the same time, sharp differences in laundry practices, perfume preferences, phosphate legislation, distribution channels, and other such attributes of different national markets led to significant benefits from differentiating products and strategies on a country-by-country basis.

This is typical of what we call *multinational industries*—worldwide businesses in which the dominance of national differences in cultural, social, and political environments made multiple national industry structures flourish. Success in such businesses typically belonged to companies that followed *multinational strategies* of building strong and resourceful national subsidiaries that were sensitive to local-market needs and opportunities, and allowing them to manage their local businesses by developing or adapting products and strategies to respond to the powerful localizing forces.

Finally, in some other industries, technological forces were central, and the need for companies to develop and diffuse innovations was the dominant source of competitive advantage. For example, the most critical task for manufacturers of telecommunications switching equipment was the ability to develop and harness new technologies and to exploit them worldwide. In these *international industries,* it was the ability to innovate and to appropriate the benefits of those innovations in multiple national markets that differentiated the winners from the losers in this highly complex business.

In such industries, the key to success lay in a company's ability to exploit the technological forces by creating new products and to leverage the international life cycles of the product by effectively transferring the technologies to overseas units. We describe this as an *international strategy*—the ability to effectively manage the creation of new products and processes in one's home market, and sequentially diffuse those innovations to their foreign affiliates.

Transition to Transnationality

Our portrayal of the traditional demands in some major worldwide industries is clearly oversimplified. Different tasks in the value-added chains of the different businesses were subject to different levels of the economic, political, cultural, and technological forces. We have described what can be called the *center of gravity* of these activities— the environmental forces that had the most significant impact on the industry's strategic task demands.

By the early 1990s, however, these external demands were undergoing some important changes. In many industries, the earlier dominance of a single set of environmental forces was replaced by a much more complex environmental demand in which each of the different sets of forces were becoming strong simultaneously. For example, new economies of scale and scope and intensifying competition among a few competitors were enhancing the economic forces for increased global integration in many multinational and international industries. In the detergent business, for example, product standardization has become more feasible because the growing penetration and standardization of washing machines has narrowed the differences in washing practices across countries. Companies have leveraged this potential for product standardization by developing global or regional brands, uniform multilingual packaging, and common advertising themes, all of which have led to additional economies.

Similarly, localizing forces are growing in strength in global industries such as consumer electronics. While the strengths of the economic forces of scale and scope have continued to increase, host government pressures and renewed customer demand for differentiated products are forcing companies with global strategies to reverse their earlier strategies, which were based on exporting standard products. To protect their competitive positions, they have begun to give more emphasis to local design and production of differentiated product ranges in different countries and for different international segments.

Finally, in the emerging competitive battle among a few large firms with comparable capabilities in global-scale efficiency and nationally responsive strategies, the ability to innovate and to exploit the resulting developments globally is becoming more and more important for building durable comparative advantage even in industries where global economic forces or local political and cultural influences had earlier been dominant.

In the emerging international environment, therefore, there are fewer and fewer examples of pure global, textbook multinational, or classic international industries. Instead, more and more businesses are driven by *simultaneous* demands for global efficiency, national responsiveness, and worldwide innovation. These are the characteristics of what we call a *transnational industry*. In such industries, companies will find it increasingly difficult to defend a competitive position on the basis of only one dominant capability. They will need to develop their ability to respond effectively to all the diverse and conflicting forces at one and the same time so as to manage efficiency, responsiveness, and innovation without trading off any one for the other.

The emergence of the transnational industry has not only made the needs for efficiency, responsiveness, and innovation simultaneous, but it has also led to the tasks for achieving each of these capabilities becoming more demanding and complex. Rather than achieve world-scale economies through centralized and standardized production, companies must instead build global efficiency through a worldwide infrastructure of distributed but specialized assets and capabilities that exploit comparative advantages, scale economies, and scope economies simultaneously. In most industries, a few global competitors now compete head-to-head in almost all major markets.

To succeed in such an environment, companies need to understand the logic of global chess: building and defending profit sanctuaries that are impenetrable to competitors, leveraging existing strengths to build new advantages through cross-subsidizing weaker products and market positions; making high-risk preemptive investments that raise the stakes and force out rivals with weaker stomachs and purse strings; and forming alliances and coalitions to isolate and outflank competitors. These and other similar maneuvers must now be combined with world-scale economies to develop and maintain global competitive efficiency.

Similarly, responsiveness through differentiated and tailor-made local-for-local products and strategies in each host environment is neither necessary nor feasible anymore. National customers no longer demand differentiation: They demand differentiation along with the level of cost and quality standard global products that they have become used to. At the same time, host governments' desire to build their national competitiveness dominates economic policy in many countries, and MNCs are frequently viewed as key instruments in the implementation of national competitive strategies. Changes in regulations, tastes, exchange rates, and related factors have become less predictable and more frequent. In such an environment, more responsiveness has become inadequate. The flexibility to continuously change product design, sourcing patterns, and pricing policies in order to remain responsive to continually changing national environments has become essential for survival.

And, finally, exploiting centrally developed products and technologies is also no longer enough. MNCs must now build the capability to learn from the many environments to which they are exposed and to appropriate the benefits of such learning throughout their global operations. Although some products and processes must still be developed centrally for worldwide use and others must be created locally in each environment to meet purely local demands, MNCs must increasingly use their access to multiple centers of technologies and familiarity with diverse customer preferences in different countries to create truly transnational innovations. Similarly, environmental and competitive information acquired in different parts of the world must be collated and interpreted so as to become a part of the company's shared knowledge base, and be input to future strategy.

▪ Concluding Comments: The Strategic and Organizational Challenge

The increasing complexity of forces in the global environment and the need to respond simultaneously to their diverse and often conflicting demands have created some major new challenges for many multinational companies. The classic global companies, such as many highly successful Japanese MNCs, with their competitive advantage rooted in a highly efficient and centralized system, have been forced to respond more effectively to the demands for national responsiveness and worldwide innovation. The traditional multinational companies—many of them European—had the advantage of national responsiveness but faced the challenge of exploiting global-scale economic and technological forces more effectively. And U.S. companies, with their more international approach of leveraging home-country innovations abroad, struggled to build more understanding of the cultural and political forces and to respond to national differences more effectively while simultaneously enhancing global-scale efficiency through improved scale economies.

For most MNCs, the challenge of the 2000s is both strategic and organizational. On the one hand, they are now forced to develop a more complex array of strategic capabilities that allow them to capture the competitive advantages that accrue to efficiency, responsiveness, and learning. At the same time, the traditional organizational approaches of these companies, developed to support their earlier global, multinational, or international approaches, have become inadequate for the more complex strategic tasks they now have to accomplish. In the following chapters, we discuss some of the ways in which companies can respond to these new strategic and organizational challenges.

Case 2-1   Toys "R" Us Japan

I do not believe the Japanese have chosen freely to have these limitations. All we would have to do is open a large retail store where prices were 40% less and choices were very broad. If the Japanese consumer didn't like products offered in that fashion, then the store would not be a success. . . .

Carla Hills, *United States Trade Representative, February 1990*

In early 1991, Toys "R" Us seemed poised on the brink of a high-profile entry into the world's second largest toy market. A "category killer" that enjoyed

▪ This case was prepared by Professor Debora Spar with the assistance of Jacqueline MacKenzie and Research Associate Laura Bures.
▪ Copyright © 1995 by the President and Fellows of Harvard College. Harvard Business School case 796-077.

phenomenal success in the United States and Europe, Toys "R" Us had tried for several years to crack the lucrative but forbidding Japanese market. At every step, the U.S. company had faced difficulty and opposition. Japanese retailers had tried repeatedly to block the chain's entrance, as had small shopkeepers from the area around Niigata, site of the first Toys "R" Us store. The Japanese media had loudly denounced Toys "R" Us as the "black ship of Kawasaki," and a host of Japanese toy manufacturers, including Nintendo, had refused to deal directly with the U.S. retailer.[1] The very structure of Japan's multilayered distribution system also seemed to conspire against Toys "R" Us, thwarting the company's attempts and perpetuating Japan's infamously high consumer prices.

Despite this litany of problems, though, success seemed finally within reach. Toys "R" Us had found an influential local partner, Den Fujita, and won approval from Japan's powerful Ministry of International Trade and Investment (MITI). Management also felt confident that some of the more restrictive aspects of Japanese retail regulation were about to change. But still some basic questions remained: Would Japanese customers, accustomed to small shops and personal service, ever accept a self-service discount warehouse? Would Japanese manufacturers risk damaging long-standing relationships with wholesalers and retailers by dealing directly with Toys "R" Us? And how quickly and efficiently could the chain hope to expand in the face of protracted local opposition?

■ The Toys "R" Us Company

Toys "R" Us was the brainchild of Charles Lazarus, a shop owner who founded the chain in 1957. Born in Washington, D.C., in 1923, Lazarus had learned about the retail business from his father, who rebuilt bicycles and sold them at the family store. When Lazarus asked why the store did not sell new bicycles, his father explained that the big chain stores could sell them much cheaper—a comment Lazarus would clearly recall later in his career.[2]

After a wartime career as a cryptographer, Lazarus inherited the family shop and turned to selling children's furniture in a market boosted by the post-war baby boom. Over time, he began to realize that because baby furniture did not wear out, repeat purchases of items such as cribs were rare.[3] Toys, by contrast, were frequently requested. Toys, he therefore decided, created a far superior business opportunity. After studying the U.S. discounter Korvettes, Lazarus decided to experiment with a self-service, supermarket-style format. In his new Children's Supermarket, he vowed to undercut competition and have a bigger, better selection than any single toy store. Discounting had arrived in the toy business.

Children's Supermarket quickly grew into a thriving chain of four stores, renamed Toys "R" Us after Lazarus decided he needed better signs with "shorter words, bigger letters."[4] He sold the chain to Interstate Stores in 1966 for $7.5 million, retaining a seat on the company's Board. When Interstate folded in 1978, Lazarus rescued his company, determined to build it into a nationwide chain. Over the next decade, Toys "R" Us sales compounded by 26% per year, with sales productivity per square foot double that of the retailer's nearest competitor.[5] By 1988, Toys "R" Us had captured 20% of the U.S. toy market, with sales surpassing the $4 billion mark.[6] Sourcing directly from manufacturers, the chain used its huge buying clout to offer goods at 10–20% discounts compared to smaller toy retailers. Year-round advertising campaigns encouraged consumers to buy toys at any time, instead of just at Christmas.

A typical Toys "R" Us store brought together 8–15,000 SKUs (stockkeeping units) of toys and children's products in a warehouse-sized (54,000 sq. ft.) self-service outlet. The presentation was simple and colorful, based on a "cookie cutter conformity" where stores resembled each other down to the layout of each aisle. Central control was a key feature of the organization, and extensive computer networks

■ [1]The epithet referred to Commodore Matthew C. Perry's four black warships that sailed into the harbor at Edo (now Tokyo) in 1854, forcing the Shogun's government to end three centuries of self-imposed Japanese isolation. "Black ships" thus became symbolic of the opening of Japanese culture to Western influence. *Reuters,* December 19, 1991, and *The Toronto Star,* December 23, 1991.
■ [2]David Owen, *The Man Who Invented Saturday Morning,* Villard, 1988.

■ [3]Ibid.
■ [4]*Newsmakers,* October 1992.
■ [5]*Business Quarterly,* June 22, 1989, and *Newsmakers,* October 1992.
■ [6]*Tokyo Business Today,* February 1990.

ensured almost automatic replacement of every toy sold once inventories dropped below pre-determined levels. The key to the sales and inventory formula, according to Lazarus, was that "No decisions are made in the field."[7]

In 1984, the company took its retailing concept global, opening its first international outlet in Canada and then moving quickly into Europe, Hong Kong, and Singapore. As it had in the United States, the discount formula quickly proved popular with customers who flocked to the new Toys "R" Us outlets. Whenever the chain expanded abroad, however, it drew the ire of local retailers, who feared (correctly in many cases) that the giant discount stores would drive them out of business. German manufacturers, for example, refused to sell to Toys "R" Us in 1987 for fear of damaging their relationships with the thousands of small retailers and wholesalers who dominated toy distribution. And in the United Kingdom, retailers also protested, noting that the number of British toy stores had declined from 3,500 to 2,000 in the five years after Toys "R" Us first arrived.[8]

But Toys "R" Us regularly overcame the protests and its foreign outlets flourished. By 1991, the chain operated 97 stores abroad, with international operations accounting for 14% of the chain's total sales. Commenting on this spectacular growth, Larry Bouts, president of the chain's international division since 1991, suggested that the expansion of Toys "R" Us actually benefited foreign retailers as well as consumers. "Initially I think there was a fair amount of consternation from competitors," he acknowledged, "but now the industry has grown so much, there's really a lot warmer feeling. From the consumer's point of view, they're very happy . . . coming to us in droves. . . . People said it wouldn't work, but consumers want value today."[9] Confident that this formula applied broadly, Toys "R" Us management began to contemplate an entry into one of the world's toughest retail markets: Japan.

The Japanese Market for Toys

By any measure, Japan was an extremely attractive market for toys. Throughout the 1980s, the entire retail market in Japan had expanded dramatically, propelled by the economy's continued strength and a long-awaited increase in consumer spending. According to the Bank of Japan, annual retail sales grew 94% during the 1980s, while Japan's GDP grew at an average annual rate of 7%.[10] Japan's children were particularly strong beneficiaries of this boom. Despite a rigorous education system that left children with little time for play, children's products accounted for a significant proportion of consumer spending in Japan. Perhaps to compensate for the constant pressure to excel in school, parents lavished expensive toys and clothes on their offspring.[11] Japan's falling birthrate also allowed parents and grandparents to focus their spending on fewer children; and fewer mouths to feed enabled families to spend less money on food and more on toys.[12]

Thus Japan's toy market had become the second largest in the world, lagging only behind the United States'. In 1991, the Japanese toy market was worth Y932 billion ($7.1 billion), up Y26 billion from the previous year. Responding to this boom, large retailers designed special formats to appeal to children. In October of 1990, Isetan opened a special section called "Dr. Kids Town" within one of its Tokyo department stores, while Seibu's flagship store opened a "Kids Farm," complete with a hollow miniature mountain amidst clothing racks and toy shelves.[13] A Sesame Street theme park was opened outside of Tokyo in 1990.

On the surface, these developments suggested that the Japanese toy market was ripe for Toys "R" Us. But as the chain's management quickly

---

[7]*Newsweek,* November 11, 1991.

[8]*Wall Street Journal,* September 10, 1990.

[9]*Europe,* September 1992.

[10]*Business Tokyo,* May 1992, and *International Marketing Data and Statistics 1995,* p. 183.

[11]*The Washington Post,* February 11, 1991.

[12]The average number of children per family had fallen from four in the early post-war years to just two by the early 1990s. *Washington Post,* February 11, 1991.

[13]Ibid.

discovered, the structure of Japan's retail industry made it very difficult for new retailers—particularly foreign discount retailers—to establish a market position. Despite the rapid growth it had experienced, Japan's toy industry remained highly fragmented and locally focused. Though some estimates claimed that the number of toy stores had fallen from 8,000 in 1980, at least 6,000 remained in 1990.[14] A typical toy store was less than 3,200 square feet in area and sold 1–2,000 SKUs. Display areas were customarily cramped, inventories turned slowly, and most stores stocked very similar merchandise. Nearly all retail shops were domestically owned and bought their toys from local wholesalers, usually for 75–80% of the manufacturer's "suggested price."[15] Retailers then sold the toys for the "suggested price," deviating from it only rarely.[16] In exchange for maintaining prices, retailers were able to return their unsold goods to the wholesaler or manufacturer for full credit. In this tightly-knit system, only two national players existed: Chiyoda, which sold through the Hello Mac and Ace formats; and Marutomi, which operated a traditional toy chain, Banban, as well as a discount format, Toy Ryutsu Center. With a combined 700–800 stores, the two chains accounted for over Y100 billion in annual sales.[17]

At the wholesale level, the Japanese toy industry was again marked by its characteristic pattern of fragmentation and long-standing relationships. Even such giants as Nintendo, the Kyoto-based maker of Gameboy and other popular electronic games, distributed its products through a sprawling network of 70 affiliated distributors.[18] These distributors served as the key link between manufacturers and retailers, cementing long-term relationships based on personal commitments rather than competitive terms. They also served as a barrier to foreign firms, making it difficult for foreigners to

achieve sufficient scale in either manufacturing or retailing to cover the costs of their investment. As a result, foreign firms were almost entirely absent from the Japanese domestic toy industry, and even imports accounted for only 9.2% of sales.[19]

Potentially, Toys "R" Us had the ability to change the Japanese toy industry and profit handsomely in the process. Merely by undercutting the "suggested price" it could capture the entire discount market. All it needed to do was to mimic precisely what it had done elsewhere: establish large-scale stores and use the buying power created by these stores to negotiate lower prices from toy manufacturers. Since 1987, the chain's management had been trying to implement this strategy. But in Japan, they came to realize, the very structure of the retail sector made their customary strategy almost inconceivable.

The Structure of Japanese Retail

A "Nation of Shops"   For years, Japan had been aptly described as a nation of small shopkeepers. Though the population of the four islands was approximately half that of the United States, the number of retail outlets in Japan was almost the same, resulting in twice as many outlets per capita.[20] Many of these outlets were the country's famous "mom and pop" stores. In 1988, over half of all retail outlets in Japan employed just one or two people; less than 15% of outlets employed more than five people.[21] In the early 1980s, such small stores accounted for a full 75% of retail spending. Nearly half of these outlets sold food, compared with 20% in the United States.[22]

The fragmentation of the retailers was matched by the fragmentation of the wholesalers who served them. Of the 436,421 wholesalers operating in 1988, less than half employed more than five people, and nearly all sold their products through a complex

---

[14]*Nihon Keizai Shimbun,* February 10, 1990.
[15]*Nikkei Weekly,* February 22, 1993.
[16]In 1989, 70% of toy retailers priced at the manufacturer's "suggested price," according to figures from Japan's Fair Trade Commission.
[17]*Nikkei Weekly,* February 22, 1993.
[18]*Nikkei Weekly,* June 29, 1991.

[19]*Nikkei Weekly,* June 20, 1992.
[20]Jack G. Kaikati, "Don't crack the Japanese distribution system—just circumvent it," *Columbia Journal of Business,* Summer 1993.
[21]MITI survey.
[22]*The Economist,* September 19, 1981.

distribution system that typically involved between three and five layers of intermediaries. The primary wholesaler was often a subsidiary, or close affiliate, of the manufacturer. The secondary wholesaler was a regional distributor, while the tertiary wholesaler operated on the local level. As in the toy industry, prices of goods were effectively controlled by the manufacturers, who sold to wholesalers at a pre-arranged discount of the "manufacturers' suggested price." With the added inducements of credit and generous payment terms, manufacturers throughout the Japanese system gained guaranteed distribution of their products, while wholesalers and retailers gained some measure of protection against economic swings and fluctuations in demand.

While Western observers tended to mock the Japanese retail system as cumbersome and archaic, most Japanese consumers genuinely seemed to enjoy and appreciate its benefits. As an article in *The Economist* explained, "The Japanese are as sentimental about their tiny shops as the French are about their peasants and the British about their old industries. Small Japanese shops are the centers of village neighborhoods in big cities. Small stores flourished before the rest of Japan modernized because merchants were restricted by law to their local patch, and retailers were encouraged to mop up labor from the land."[23]

In addition to its commercial function, small store retailing thus served a valuable social purpose. Described directly by some as a "social service," the retail sector was "filled with under-employed workers who in other societies might well be unemployed."[24] All together, the Japanese distribution system accounted for 18% of the nation's employees and 13% of its GNP.[25] In a 1980s survey, 26% of shopkeepers reported "security in old age" as a reason for opening a shop, and 10% said they opened a shop because their husbands would soon retire.[26]

One quarter of owner-operators of stores were over 60. In a country with few pension provisions, small-scale retailing offered a safety net for retirement.

Supporters of the Japanese system further argued that small stores were a natural reflection of the Japanese way of life, that Japanese consumers preferred to shop every day for small quantities of fresh goods.[27] Small homes and kitchens allowed no space for storing large amounts of goods, and use of automobiles was impractical in Japan's congested streets.[28] High quality and personalized service, many claimed, were expected by Japanese consumers, who were willing to pay for the privilege.

Detractors, though, argued that small stores continued to exist simply because they were protected from more efficient competitors by laws restricting the construction of large stores and by tacit non-competition arrangements. Japanese consumers *would* accept less service in exchange for lower prices, they asserted, but by 1991, they had rarely been offered the choice.

Keiretsu Stores   In fact, choice of retail goods in some sectors was actively restricted by the activities of diversified conglomerates such as Matsushita and Toshiba. Working through their own distribution keiretsu (related groups of companies), these giant firms supported tens of thousands of small affiliate stores that stocked only "their" manufacturer's brand at manufacturer-specified prices. Where these stores prevailed, customers found no benefit in comparison-shopping, since price uniformity was nearly absolute. What they did get however, and what many Japanese reportedly preferred over low prices, was personal attention from the shop-owner and guaranteed repair or replacement service for the life of their purchase.

The operators of the small keiretsu stores also effectively made a trade-off between prices and personal loyalty. Simply by becoming a store owner, one gained a position of some visibility in

[23]Ibid.

[24]Ibid, and Hugh T. Patrick and Thomas P. Rohlen, "Small-Scale Family Enterprises," *The Political Economy of Japan: The Domestic Transformation,* Vol. 1, Stanford University Press, 1987, p. 350.

[25]*Business Asia,* January 4, 1993.

[26]Patrick and Rohlen, "Small-Scale Family Enterprises," p. 350.

[27]Takatoshi Ito, *The Japanese Economy,* MIT Press, 1992, p. 392.

[28]Japanese typically had 60% of the living space enjoyed by their U.S. counterparts. *Business Review Weekly,* January 12, 1990.

the community, a position symbolized by the storefront pairing of the proprietor's name with that of a well-known manufacturer. Through the manufacturers' many affiliates, store operators also received financial and marketing advice and even information about their competitors' activities. In exchange for this assistance, they implicitly agreed to tie themselves closely to the keiretsu's lead manufacturer. Storekeepers who dared to meddle with the manufacturer's "suggested price" faced expulsion from the network and blacklisting by other manufacturers. In 1979, Yoshio Terada, a National (Matsushita) retailer in Tokyo, incurred the wrath of his supplier by discounting batteries by 20%. When he refused to remove the discount, a truck arrived instead to remove the National sign from his store and with it, his entire business.[29] Terada subsequently set up a no-service discount electrical appliance business called STEP and, despite Japanese consumers' alleged preferences for full-service stores, built a $100 million business in ten years. Yet, few keiretsu retailers at the time would have dared to defy the might of Matsushita. In 1991, over 20,000 keiretsu stores still existed, and the principle of loyalty to manufacturers remained strong in both retailing and wholesaling.

The Role of Regulation   In addition to customers' habits and personal loyalties, Japan's retail structure was also bolstered by a series of laws restricting the spread of larger retail stores. By sheer force of numbers, the country's 1.4 million store owners wielded considerable voting power. For decades, they had used this power to extract concessions and explicit protection from Japan's reigning political party, the Liberal Democratic Party (LDP). In 1990, the Chairman of the National Shopkeepers Promotion Association described the political situation succinctly: "The big stores stuff the politicians with money, but we have the power of 20 million votes."[30]

The small store owners won their first victory in 1956, just after the LDP came to power. The 1956 Department Store Law required that a permit be obtained for each new department store, effectively allowing department store construction to be blocked by smaller retailers. By 1990, there were still only about 1,600 department stores in Japan—one for every 75,000 people. With the growth of department stores so severely limited, most innovation in Japanese retailing came through the emerging supermarkets—large, non-specialized, low-price stores with large grocery sections. But just as the supermarkets were starting to gain ground, they, too, encountered the shopkeepers' force.

In 1973, Japan's Ministry of International Trade and Investment (MITI) responded to the small retailers' demands by introducing the Large Scale Retail Law, legislation that subjected all would-be large retailers to a rigorous screening process. Before building any stores over 1,500 sq. m. (16,000 sq. ft.), retailers had to submit detailed plans to MITI and then allow these plans to be passed on to a local review board composed of consumers and retailers. In 1982, the law was made even more stringent, requiring large store operators to "explain" their plans to local retailers directly, even before notifying MITI. With this provision in place, small store owners could effectively delay the construction of large stores for years, simply by boycotting "explanation meetings" or raising objections to a myriad of small details. As a result, even powerful supermarket chains such as Daiei found themselves entangled for years in local negotiations.[31]

Innovations

If Japan's fragmented and hierarchical retail sector had remained unchanged in the 1980s, it is unlikely that even so powerful a force as Toys "R" Us would have dared enter the market. But as the Japanese economy expanded and developed in the late 1980s, several cracks in the retail structure began to appear.

[29]Kenichi Miyashita and David W. Russell, *Keiretsu,* McGraw-Hill, 1994, pp. 203–4.
[30]*East Asian Executive Reports,* May 15, 1990.

[31]*Business Week,* December 9, 1991.

The Rise of Convenience Stores   The first major change in Japan's retail structure came from a quiet and unlikely source: convenience stores. Usually occupying no more than 1100 sq. ft., convenience stores were small enough to slip past restrictive laws and establish themselves in the very heart of Japan's towns and villages. By 1982, Japan had 23,235 convenience stores, accounting for 2.3% of total retail sales.[32] Between 1982 and 1985, convenience store sales rose faster than any other form of retailing sales;[33] and by 1992, they accounted for nearly 8% of Japan's total retail sales.[34]

The most successful convenience store was the 7-Eleven chain, licensed from its U.S. parent Southland in 1974 by Ito-Yokado. At first glance a 7-Eleven Japan store fit the profile of many Japanese stores: small, locally focused, and "open all hours." At the core of this business, however, was an information-oriented strategy unlike anything dreamed of by its "mom and pop" competitors. The key to 7-Eleven's strategy was close inventory control facilitated by early and comprehensive adoption of information technology. In the late 1970s, 7-Eleven cut its wholesale suppliers from 80 to 40 by closely supervising their inventory and eliminating goods which did not generate adequate sales. From 1985 onwards, the chain used point of sales equipment to track sales of each item and ensure timely replenishment. Employees also entered specific information about shoppers with each sale to predict product-specific shopping habits. Ito-Yokado used this information to refine product offerings and inventory replacement schedules to the point of providing fresh *o nigiri* (rice balls popular as lunch snacks) at lunch time in every store as well as adequate supplies of soft drinks for children on their way home from school in the afternoon. The information was also used as a bargaining chip with manufacturers, who could be persuaded to deliver according to 7-Eleven's precise requirements.

By 1990, almost 85% of goods in the chain's 94 wholly owned and 4,140 franchised stores throughout Japan were distributed through the chain's own elaborate regional distribution system, and 7-Eleven Japan had been described as one of the most efficient retailers in the world. As 7-Eleven grew, it also spawned a series of imitators, stores hoping to make similar use of information technologies and catering to the demands of Japan's aging population and increasing numbers of women in the workforce.

MITI's "Vision for the 1990s"   Just as the convenience stores were demonstrating the commercial potential of new retailing formats, the established format was also coming under pressure from Japan's changing demographics. Increasingly, young Japanese balked at the idea of taking over their parents' small shops and wanted instead to experiment with bolder ventures. With significantly greater international exposure than their parents, the younger generation also realized that they were paying highly inflated prices for many consumer goods. Slowly, their demands for fewer commercial restrictions and lower prices began to influence the political process.

In 1989, MITI quietly advocated reform of Japan's retailing sector. In a public document on Japan's distribution system, it first defended the existing retail structure, arguing that:

1. It cannot necessarily be said that our distribution system is inefficient; however, there is room for further rationalization as respects costs.

2. Though our country's distribution system is as a whole highly competitive, there are some factors which mitigate competition.

3. Due to unfamiliarity with commercial customs in Japan, foreign firms may feel difficulty attempting to gain access to the Japanese distribution sector; however, this system does not

---

[32]*The Economist*, January 31, 1987.

[33]Frank Upsham, "Privatizing Regulation: The Implementation of the Large-Scale Retail Stores Law," in Gary D. Allison and Yasunori Sone, eds., *Political Dynamics in Contemporary Japan*, Ithaca, 1993, p. 265. Cited in Jeff Bernstein and Thomas K. McCraw, "Convenience-Store Retailing in Two Countries: Southland and Seven-Eleven Japan," HBS Case Number N9-395-092.

[34]Cited in Jeffrey Rayport, "Japanese Retailing System: Tokugawa Period to the Present," HBS Industry Note prepared for Professor Thomas K. McCraw, April 1991.

fundamentally discriminate against either domestic or foreign firms, and there are a large variety of distribution channels available to importing firms.

4. There are a variety of reasons for the gap in domestic and foreign prices, and some of them lie in the nature of the distribution system.[35]

MITI's document proceeded, though, to propose significant changes to the Large Scale Retail Stores Law, including limits on the amount of time each stage in the notification process could take. The law would remain in force, MITI explained, "since Japan still has a large number of retail stores and a limited amount of land, [and] giving large stores free rein to set up business would cause serious problems for regional communities."[36] Yet MITI did commit to "amending the system . . . to reflect recent changes in socio-economic circumstances" and to removing "all practices which deviate from the original intent of the system," noting in particular that "the purpose of [the "explanation" of store plans to relevant constituencies] is not to obtain the approval of local retailers."[37]

Accordingly, MITI proposed reducing the permissible time between pre-notification and approval to as little as 18 months. It even promised to re-examine restrictions on opening hours, which required large stores to close at 6 pm and for at least one full day per month. If MITI succeeded in implementing these proposed changes, small store owners would at last lose their power to hold back a tidal wave of space-hungry domestic retailers.

The Structural Impediments Initiative[38]   At the same time that MITI launched its re-evaluation of the retail system, it also began to respond to demands that Japan open its market to foreign investors. Even after half a decade of dramatically increased global investment flows, Japan's stock of foreign direct investment remained low. In manufacturing, for example, which attracted 65% of total foreign investment flows, foreign affiliated companies accounted for 2.1% of total capitalization and 2.3% of sales in 1988. By comparison, FDI in the United States at the same time accounted for 14.7% of capitalization and 12.2% of sales.[39] In 1990, Japan was host to less accumulated U.S. direct investment than Canada, the UK, Germany, Switzerland, or the Netherlands.[40]

For many in the United States, the imbalance in investment levels was evidence that the Japanese market remained unfairly closed to U.S. investors. Consequently, in the fall of 1989, U.S. negotiators launched a series of discussions with their Japanese counterparts "to identify and solve structural problems in both countries that stand as impediments to trade and to balance of payments adjustment with the goal of contributing to the reduction of payments imbalances."[41] Dubbed the Structural Impediments Initiative, the talks theoretically covered "structural impediments" in both countries. The bulk of the negotiation, however, was devoted to the perennial problem of perceived trade barriers to U.S. imports and investment in Japan. In particular, U.S. negotiators pushed their Japanese counterparts to address the prevalence of keiretsu structures and other interlocked relationships which, they argued, prevented foreign firms from competing on equal terms. The U.S. team also suggested that consumer prices in Japan were higher than they should be, compared with prices in other markets, and that Japan's distribution system remained a major impediment to U.S. export sales.[42]

---

[35]*News from MITI,* September 1989.

[36]Ibid.

[37]Ibid.

[38]This section draws heavily on Ito, *The Japanese Economy,* Chapter 12.

[39]The retail sector was host to a tiny but growing fraction of foreign direct investment in Japan. Between 1985 and 1990 U.S. investment in Japanese retailing quadrupled to reach $340m. *Business Tokyo,* May 1992.

[40]Mark Mason, "United States Direct Investment in Japan: Trends and Prospects," *California Management Review,* Fall 1992.

[41]*Final Report of Structural Impediments Initiative.*

[42]The Large Scale Retail Law, for example, impeded the distribution of foreign goods by supporting the 1.6 million small family-run stores which were less likely to carry imported goods than were large stores.

Toys "R" Us: The Move into Japan

For Toys "R" Us, both the Structural Impediments Initiative and MITI's changes to the Large Scale Retail Store Law came at a propitious time. Together with domestic developments in the retail sector, they seemed to indicate that the largest barriers to the chain's entry—the distribution sector and the legal restrictions on establishment—were at last about to change. And so long as they changed, Toys "R" Us felt confident that the chain could succeed in the Japanese market.

Because the Japanese market retained so many idiosyncrasies, however, Toys "R" Us management decided to seek an alliance with a strong local partner. Initially, the chain followed the same strategy that most foreign retailers had adopted and launched negotiations with a major Japanese retailer. But once the negotiations were underway, the Toys "R" Us representatives realized that the two sides had fundamentally different assumptions of how to run a business. According to one Toys "R" Us executive, "they pushed traditional business practices on us, like using wholesalers. That would distort the basic principle of our business."[43] And so Toys "R" Us broke off the first round of talks and began to search for someone in Japan with a better grasp of U.S. retailing practices.

Den Fujita   In 1989, Joseph Baczko, then head of Toys "R" Us International, met Den Fujita, president of McDonald's Japan. Fujita, the son of an engineer, had grown up in Osaka, a city famous for its merchant tradition. He graduated from the Law Department of Tokyo University, the most prestigious university in Japan and traditional training ground for the country's political elite.[44] During the U.S. occupation of Japan, he had worked as a translator at McArthur's Headquarters in Tokyo, despite having lost his father and two sisters in U.S. bombing raids.

In 1950, he took the unusual step (for a Tokyo Law graduate) of starting his own trading venture, Fujita & Company, to import a range of items, such as Dior handbags, to a luxury-starved Japan.[45] Since post-war rationing and restrictions on imports had eliminated most other luxury goods, Fujita prospered, building one of Japan's strongest import businesses over the next two decades.

In 1971, McDonald's approached Fujita and asked him to join them in introducing U.S.-style fast food to Japan. Fujita agreed, arguing in public that McDonald's-style food would be good for Japan. As he later explained, "the Japanese are very hardworking, but very weak, very small . . . we had to strengthen ourselves."[46] Fellow retailers, though, were not amused—the Ginza Street Association was still attempting to evict the first McDonald's from its prestigious location more than 10 years after its establishment.[47] Fujita, undaunted, told Japanese teenagers that eating beef might give them the blond hair of their American counterparts.[48] Whatever the rationale, McDonald's sales in Japan had topped Y50 billion by 1980 and reached Y208 billion ($1.6 billion) by 1991.

What Fujita had brought to McDonald's—retail experience, political influence, vision, and a unique understanding of both Japanese and American cultures—was equally attractive to Toys "R" Us. With strong links to influential government figures, Fujita also had unrivaled knowledge of real estate in Japan, boasting that "If you name a city, I can see the post office, the train station, everything."[49] Fujita's flamboyant style and frequent new ventures guaranteed publicity for each business. Often described as a heretic, he was quoted as wishing to "blow a hole in the under-developed structure of the Japanese retail industry."[50]

So impressed was Toys "R" Us with Fujita that Robert Nakasone, the American-born Vice Chairman of Toys "R" Us, described him as not only the first choice as a partner, but "our second, third, fourth, fifth, and so on. . . . We could see he was a bit of a maverick. He was not only bilingual, but

---

[43]*Nikkei Weekly,* May 16, 1992.
[44]*New York Times,* March 22, 1992.

[45]Ibid.
[46]Ibid.
[47]*Nihon Keizai Shimbun,* October 11, 1983.
[48]*Reuters,* February 1, 1986.
[49]*Business Week,* December 9, 1991.
[50]*Nikkei Weekly,* May 16, 1992.

bicultural."[51] Likewise Fujita regarded Toys "R" Us as a natural partner due to the similarities in the two companies' target markets. Soon after hearing of Toys "R" Us' plans, in fact, he began to think of ways to combine Toys "R" Us, McDonald's, and Blockbuster Entertainment, another foreign business seeking his help, in specially developed family shopping malls. In the spring of 1989, Toys "R" Us formally asked Fujita to cooperate with the company in a Japanese joint venture. McDonald's Japan took a 20% stake in the new subsidiary: Toys "R" Us Japan.

Criticism and Opposition   Almost as soon as plans for the new venture were announced, other retailers and manufacturers claimed that Toys "R" Us Japan was doomed to failure. Consumers would check out the stores initially, they elaborated, but Japanese consumers would not like warehouse stores, and it was "unrealistic" to consider bypassing wholesalers.[52]

Explicit opposition to Toys "R" Us emerged rapidly from those most threatened by the chain's expansion. In January 1990, Toys "R" Us applied to the municipal government of Niigata, a city of 500,000 on the Japan Sea coast, for permission to open the first of its Japanese superstores. Local toy sellers were horrified. At 5,000 sq. m. (54,000 sq. ft.), the proposed store would be over 50 times larger than the average Niigata toy shop; projected first year revenues of Y2 billion represented half the combined sales of the city's existing toy merchants.[53] Mobilizing quickly, the Niigata toy sellers warned publicly that, "If Toys "R" Us comes in, Japanese toy shops will be wiped out."[54] The group's spokesman, owner of eight Niigata toy shops, further argued that, "Toys "R" Us is making this a political problem. But toys are more than that. Toys are culture."[55]

The Niigata application was just one of ten applications that Toys "R" Us filed across Japan, many of which sparked opposition of some kind.

[51]*New York Times,* March 22, 1992.
[52]Ibid.
[53]*The Economist,* June 16, 1990.
[54]*Wall Street Journal,* February 7, 1990.
[55]Ibid.

Exhibit 1   Toys "R" Us Inc. Balance Sheet (millions of U.S.$)

	January 1990	January 1991
Assets		
Cash and cash equivalents	40.9	35.0
Net receivables	53.1	73.2
Inventories	1,230.4	1,275.2
Prepaid expenses	14.0	21.0
Current assets—total	1,338.4	1,404.3
Net property, plant, and equipment	1,703.0	2,141.3
Other assets	33.4	36.8
Total assets	3,074.7	3,582.4
Liabilities		
Long-term debt due within year	1.4	1.6
Notes payable	205.5	386.5
Accounts payable	517.9	483.9
Taxes payable	96.0	81.6
Other current liabilities	279.1	274.0
Total current liabilities	1,100.0	1,227.6
Long-term debt	173.0	195.2
Deferred taxes	96.4	113.4
Equity		
Common stock	19.8	29.8
Capital surplus	322.7	352.6
Retained earnings	1,459.9	1,793.2
Less: treasury stock	97.0	129.3
Total equity	1,705.3	2,046.3
Total liabilities and equity	3,074.7	3,582.4

Note: Numbers may not add due to rounding.
Source: *Standard & Poor's Compustat, Compustat PC Plus.*

Toy retailers and wholesalers in Fukuoka submitted a petition to their local government demanding a one-year delay to the opening of a proposed Toys "R" Us. The toy industry in Sagamihara (near Tokyo) reacted with similar defensiveness. After

Exhibit 2   Toys "R" Us Inc. Income Statement (millions of U.S.$)

	January 1990	January 1991
Sales	4,787.8	5,510.0
Cost of goods sold	3,309.7	3,820.8
Gross profit	1,478.2	1,689.2
Selling, general, and administrative expense	866.4	1,024.8
Operating income before depreciation	611.8	664.4
Depreciation, depletion, and amortization	65.8	79.1
Operating profit	545.9	585.3
Interest expense	52.8	82.7
Non-operating income/expense	20.5	19.7
Special items	0.0	1.0
Pretax income	513.7	523.2
Total income taxes	192.6	197.2
Net income	321.1	326.0

Note: Numbers may not add due to rounding.
Source: *Standard & Poor's Compustat, Compustat PC Plus.*

Toys "R" Us announced its intentions to open seven stores by 1993, with an eventual target as high as 100, a group of 520 small toy retailers formed the Japan Association of Specialty Toy Shops to help small retailers develop ways to compete with Toys "R" Us and other foreign retailers.

Central to this concern was the effect Toys "R" Us would have on the long-standing ties between Japan's toy manufacturers and toy wholesalers. To leverage the economies of scale inherent in their large stores, Toys "R" Us would have to replicate in Japan the same buying structure that had worked so effectively elsewhere. That is, the chain would have to buy directly from the manufacturers, using the sheer size of its outlets to circumvent the wholesalers and win price concessions from the toy makers. If Toys "R" Us had to rely on Japan's cumbersome system of wholesale distribution, it would inevitably have to charge much higher retail prices, undermining its whole competitive strategy. If the chain did not use the wholesalers, though, it risked raising the ire of the manufacturers, who were tied so tightly to both the wholesalers and the small retail outlets. As one newspaper explained, "Japanese toy

Exhibit 3   Toys "R" Stock Price (U.S.$), 1979–1992

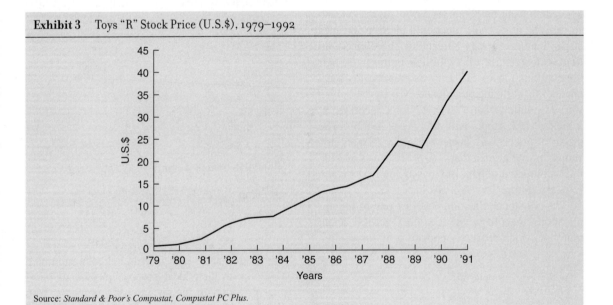

Source: *Standard & Poor's Compustat, Compustat PC Plus.*

Exhibit 4   Distribution of Toys "R" Us Stores, 1991

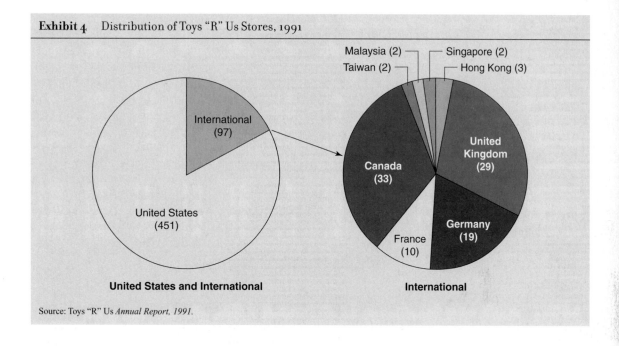

Source: Toys "R" Us *Annual Report, 1991.*

Exhibit 5   Total Retail Sales of Toys and Games, Selected Countries, 1992

Country	Sales of Toys and Games (millions of U.S.$)	Country	Sales of Toys and Games (millions of U.S.$)
Canada	1,033.0	Mexico	220.0
China	140.0	Philippines	32.0
Hong Kong	200.0	Singapore	55.0
India	260.0	South Korea	425.0
Japan	7,884.0	Taiwan	375.0
Malaysia	20.0	United States	20,684.0

Source: *International Marketing Data and Statistics 1994.*

makers drool at the prospect of supplying Toys "R" Us, but worry they'll be locked out of their current distribution channels if they play ball with the U.S. company."[56] Accordingly, there were indications that toy manufacturers would resist, if not actually oppose, the U.S. discounter. Top toy manufacturers such as Bandai Co. refused to comment on whether they would deal directly with Toys "R" Us, insisting

that anything they (Bandai) said could "have a great influence on toy wholesalers. . . . [E]ven the smallest comments cause concern."[57]

Meanwhile, like all foreign retailers hoping to invest in Japan, Toys "R" Us still faced major problems in obtaining suitable real estate. With a population density of 322 people per square kilometer and a land-mass filled 80% with mountains,

[56] *Japan Economic Journal,* February 16, 1991.

[57] *Wall Street Journal,* September 10, 1990.

Exhibit 6   Index of Urban Land Prices in Japan, 1982–1991 (end of March 1990 = 100)

	1982	1983	1984	1985	1986	1987	1988	1989	1990	1991
All Urban Land										
Total average	61.5	64.4	66.5	68.3	70.2	74.1	81.5	87.6	100.0	110.4
Commercial	55.6	58.0	59.8	61.7	64.2	69.2	78.4	86.3	100.0	111.5
Residential	64.6	68.3	70.7	72.7	74.2	77.6	84.0	88.7	100.0	109.7
Industrial	66.2	68.8	70.7	72.4	73.9	76.4	82.3	88.2	100.0	109.8
Six Major Cities										
Total average	28.4	29.7	31.3	33.6	38.4	48.3	61.8	76.9	100.0	103.0
Commercial	19.5	20.8	22.7	25.6	33.0	44.2	62.6	78.3	100.0	103.3
Residential	33.5	34.8	36.0	38.0	41.7	52.9	65.2	75.1	100.0	102.1
Industrial	35.7	37.0	38.2	39.6	41.6	48.7	58.1	77.2	100.0	103.8

Source: *Japan Statistical Yearbook 1995.*

Exhibit 7   Monthly Living Expenditure per Average Household in Japan, 1980–1991 (value in Yen)

	1980	1985	1990	1991
Food	66,923	73,735	78,956	82,130
Medical care	5,865	6,931	8,866	9,016
Transportation/communication	18,416	24,754	29,469	30,533
Education	8,325	10,853	14,471	14,211
Reading/recreation	19,620	24,191	30,122	31,442
Housing	10,682	12,686	14,814	16,712
Fuel/light/water	13,225	17,724	17,147	17,981
Furniture/household items	9,875	11,665	12,396	13,401
Clothes/footwear	18,163	19,606	22,967	23,814
Miscellaneous/personal	12,411	15,589	17,207	19,173
Pocket money	21,002	24,345	27,569	28,502
Social expenses	21,504	25,573	29,830	32,543
Annual rate of inflation (percent growth)	7.7	2.0	3.1	3.3

Note: Numbers may not add due to rounding.
Source: *Japan Statistical Yearbook 1995, International Marketing Data and Statistics 1995.*

Japan had very limited amounts of land suitable or desirable for retailing.[58] In the late 1980s, land prices around Tokyo were at an all time high, with a 540 sq. ft. shop in the exclusive Ginza area renting for about $11,500 per month.[59] Finding local workers also presented a serious and potentially expensive challenge. With the Japanese economy in a state of virtual full employment, competition for

[58]The U.S. population density was only 26 people per square kilometer.

[59]*Business Tokyo,* May 1992.

Exhibit 8   Employees and Establishments in Japan, 1970–1991

Year	Retail Establishments	Employees (ooos)	Average/ Outlet	Wholesale Establishments	Employees (ooos)	Average/ Business
1970	1,471,297	4926	3.35	255,974	2861	11.18
1972	1,495,510	5141	3.44	259,163	3008	11.61
1974	1,548,184	5303	3.43	292,155	3290	11.26
1976	1,614,067	5580	3.46	340,249	3513	10.32
1979	1,673,667	5960	3.56	368,608	3673	9.96
1982	1,721,465	6369	3.70	428,858	4091	9.54
1985	1,628,644	6329	3.89	413,016	3998	9.68
1988	1,619,752	6851	4.23	436,421	4332	9.93
1991	1,591,223	6937	4.36	475,983	4773	10.03

Source: Census of Commerce, MITI.

Exhibit 9   Number of Outlets in Japan by Format, 1988 and 1991

Outlet Format	1988	1991
Department store	433	455
General supermarket	1,478	1,549
Other general supermarket	373	375
Specialty supermarket	6,397	7,130
Convenience store	34,550	41,847
Other supermarket	53,834	67,473
Specialty store	1,007,756	1,000,166
Miscellaneous retail stores	513,338	470,289
Others	1,593	1,939
Total	1,619,752	1,591,223

Source: *Retail Trade International,* Euromonitor 1995.

top male graduates was intense, particularly for foreign firms, which remained less prestigious employers than their Japanese counterparts.[60] Searching for something positive to say on the labor front, one report could only comment that "for flexible firms willing to hunt around, there is a strong supply of bright, well-educated women."[61]

A final set of concerns centered on the company's choice of partner: the maverick Fujita had his detractors. In a letter to *The New York Times,* he was accused of anti-Semitism and of supporting Communism to provoke the Americans.[62] These criticisms stemmed from Fujita's well-known claim that Osaka-born Japanese (like himself) were more business-oriented than their Tokyo cousins because Jews had settled in Osaka hundreds of years ago. He had also written several books on "the Jewish way of doing business" and described himself as "the Ginza Jew."

As a result of all the resistance that Toys "R" Us Japan faced, the schedule of store openings began to slip steadily. Though initial publicity had suggested six stores by the end of 1991, subsequent plans slated only the first store to open in December 1991.[63] Without direct distribution deals, the high land prices and labor costs would render the cost structure of the superstores almost insurmountable.

[60]*Business Asia,* April 16, 1990.

[61]Ibid.

[62]Harold Solomon, "To the Editor: Beware the Agenda of Den Fujita," *New York Times,* April 12, 1992.

[63]*The Daily Yomiuri,* November 12, 1991.

Exhibit 10   Number of Outlets in Japan by Size, 1988 and 1991

Outlet Size (sq. m.)	1988	1991
Under 10	83,510	72,387
10–19	280,761	246,657
20–29	267,077	239,425
30–49	367,266	360,059
50–99	271,227	282,388
100–199	96,260	109,050
200–499	48,423	56,490
500–999	8,408	8,799
1,000–1,499	3,888	4,358
1,500–2,999	2,047	2,269
Over 3,000	2,107	2,371
Not reported	188,778	206,970
Total	1,619,752	1,591,223

Note: 1 sq. m. = 0.092 sq. ft.
Source: *Retail Trade International*, Euromonitor 1995.

Exhibit 11   Comparison of Price Levels by Store Type in Japan (manufacturer's suggested retail price = 100)

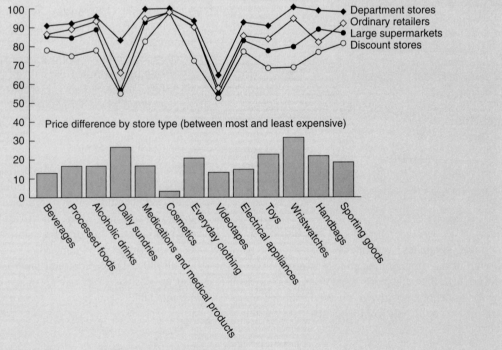

Notes 1: Prices of specific brands were surveyed. Does not include private brands.
    2: 'Electrical appliances' is the average for TVs and air conditioners, and includes delivery, piping and installation charges.
Source: Adapted from the Japanese Economic Planning Agency, *Price Survey by Store Type,* July 1994.

Exhibit 12   Leading Foreign Retailers in Japan, 1991

Company	Year Opened	Number of Stores	Owners
Clothing/Accessories			
Brooks Brothers (Japan)	1979	3	Brooks Brothers Inc. (51%) Daidoh Ltd. (49%)
Hermes Japan Co.	1979	1	Hermes S.A. (50%) Seibu Department Stores Ltd. (50%)
Laura Ashley Japan	1986	12	Aeon Group (40%) Laura Ashley Group Plc. (40%)
Louis Vuitton Japan	1981	1	Louis Vuitton Malletier (99%)
Audio/Visual			
Blockbuster Japan	1990	1	Blockbuster Entertainment (50%) Fujita & Co. (50%)
HMV Japan	1990	3	HMV Group Ltd. (100%)
Tower Records	1980	14	MTS Inc. (100%)
Virgin Mega Stores Japan	1990	1	Virgin Group Ltd. (50%) Marui Co. (50%)
Others			
Tireplus	1990	3	Sears, Roebuck & Co. (50%) Saison Group (50%)
Toys "R" Us	1991	0	Toys "R" Us Inc. (80%) McDonald's Co. (Japan) (20%)

Note: The first Toys "R" Us store in Japan opened on December 20, 1991.
Source: *Nikkei Weekly,* November 16, 1991.

Exhibit 13   Foreign Direct Investment in the United States and Japan, 1985 and 1991 (millions of U.S.$)

| Year | United States | | Japan | |
	Total Stock of Foreign Investment	Stock of Japanese-owned Foreign Investment	Total Stock of Foreign Investment	Stock of U.S.-owned Foreign Investment
1985	184,615	19,313	6,397	3,067
1991	414,358	92,896	22,771	9,907

Source: *International Direct Investment Statistics Yearbook 1994.*

Case 2-2   Global Wine Wars: New World Challenges Old

It's an art, not a science. We're creating products that are crafted literally, just as an artist or a chef would create.

Jean-Claude Boisset, *CEO of a French Wine Company*

Total commitment to innovation and style from vine to palate.

Mission Statement, *Australia Wine Foundation*

These different views on the purpose of the wine industry entering the new millennium frame the evolving competitive battle between traditional winemakers and new entrants in the global wine industry. Many companies from the old world wine producers—France, Italy, Germany and Spain, for example—found themselves constrained by embedded traditions and practices, restrictive industry regulations and complex national and European Community legislation. This provided opportunities for new-world wine companies—from Australia, United States, Chile and South Africa, for example—to challenge the more established, old-world producers.

After decades of being dismissed and even ridiculed for their attempts to compete with exports from traditional wine countries, in the 1980s and 1990s the new world companies began winning international respect, and with it global market share. At the November 2000 annual charity wine auction in Beaune, Louis Trébuchet, head of the Burgundy Growers Association, told his French colleagues that they needed to be on guard against increasing challenges from Australian, South African, and South American wines.[1] The warning was underscored by a market forecast that in 2002 Australia would overtake France as the leading wine exporter to the United Kingdom, a prize market and a bellwether for trends in other import markets.

▌ In the Beginning[2]

Grape growing and winemaking have been human preoccupations for many thousands of years. Early archeological evidence of winemaking has been found in Mesopotamia, and ancient Egyptians and Greeks offered wine as tributes to dead Pharaohs and tempestuous gods. Under the Roman Empire, viticulture spread throughout the Mediterranean region, where almost every town had its local vineyards and winemaker.

In the Christian era, wine became part of liturgical services and monasteries planted vines and built wineries. While today wine is often considered a sophisticated drink, during most of European history it was a peasant's beverage to accompany everyday meals. Eventually, the Benedictine monks raised viticulture to a new high level, making wine not only for religious use, but also to show hospitality to travelers requiring lodging. By the Middle Ages, the European nobility began planting vineyards as a mark of prestige, competing with each other in the quality of wine served at their tables. A niche market for premium wine was born.

▌[1]"Le success des vins du nouveau monde inquite la filiere viticole [Burgundy Winegrowers Worried about Success of New World Wines]." *La Tribune* (Oct. 24, 2000): 25.

▌ Professor Christopher A. Bartlett prepared this case with the research assistance of Janet Cornebise and Andrew N. McLean. This case was developed from published sources. HBS cases are developed solely as the basis for class discussion. Cases are not intended to serve as endorsements, sources of primary data, or illustrations of effective or ineffective management.

▌ Copyright © 2002 President and Fellows of Harvard College.

▌[2]Historical discussions are indebted to Harry W. Paul, *Science, Vine and Wine in Modern France* (Cambridge University Press, 1996), pp. 2–15; to Jancis Robinson, ed., *The Oxford Companion to Wine,* 2nd ed. (Oxford University Press, 1999); and to James Wilson, *Terroir* (Berkeley: University of California Press, 1998), pp. 10–45.

Wine Production   Tending and harvesting grapes has always been labor-intensive, and one worker could typically look after only a three-hectare lot (1 hectare = approx. 2.5 acres)—less for hillside vineyards where yields were also lower. The introduction of horses to vineyards in the early nineteenth century led to vines being planted in rows and to more efficient tending and harvesting. One person could now work a seven-hectare plot.

Yet despite these efficiencies, vineyards became smaller, not larger, over time. Over many centuries, small agricultural holdings were continually fragmented as land was parceled out by kings and emperors, taken through war, or broken up through inheritance. During the French Revolution, for example, the government seized many large estates, broke them up, and sold them at auction. After 1815, the Napoleonic inheritance code prescribed how land had to be divided among all rightful heirs. As a result, some vineyards had as many as 90 owners, with a single proprietor controlling a few rows of vines. By the mid-nineteenth century, the average holding in France was 5.5 hectares, and still being subdivided. (In Italy, similar historical events left the average vineyard holding at 0.8 hectares.)

Few farmers had either the volume of grapes or the time available to make wine, a specialist task typically undertaken by the local vintner or winemaker. Since most sold their grapes by weight, the growers' emphasis was often on maximizing yield. (The large estates that made their own wine were more willing to sacrifice quantity for quality.) To gain more control and compete with the larger estates, some small growers formed cooperatives. By sharing communal winemaking, and bottling equipment and sometimes pooling resources to distribute the finished product, they were able to participate in winemaking's downstream profit.

Distribution and Marketing   Traditionally, wine was sold in bulk to merchant traders—"négociants" in France—who often blended and bottled the product before distributing it. As roads and shipping links improved, some négociants expanded beyond their local distribution role and began shipping the product abroad. But wine often did not travel well

and much of it spoiled on long journeys. Furthermore, poor roads and complex toll and tax systems made transportation extremely expensive. For example, in the early nineteenth century, shipments of wine from Strasbourg to the Dutch border had to pass through 31 toll stations.[3] As a result, only the most sophisticated négociants could handle exports, and only the rich could afford the imported luxury.

In the late eighteenth and early nineteenth centuries, however, a few innovations revolutionized the industry. Mass production of glass bottles, the introduction of the cork stopper, and the development of the pasteurization process all contributed to wine stability and longevity in the bottle. This not only allowed distribution to more distant markets, it also allowed bottlings of the best vintages to age to maturity, greatly enhancing their quality. Together, these factors led to increased vine plantings, expanded production, and the expansion of the market for fine wines.

Regulation and Classification   As it developed, the industry became increasingly important to the cultural and economic life of the traditional producing countries. In France, for example, not only was wine a staple item on every table, but in the mid-eighteenth century it also supported 1.5 million grower families and an equal number of workers in related businesses. It was the country's second largest export, growing to represent about one sixth of the country's total trading revenue.

Not surprisingly, the industry's cultural and economic importance attracted a great deal of political attention, and over the years laws, regulations, and policies increasingly controlled almost every aspect of winemaking. Germany was typical, introducing a wine classification scheme in 1644. By the 1830s, these regulations had expanded to encompass 65 classes of quality, with legislation prescribing ripeness required for harvesting, definitions of minimum sugar content, and penalties for those who added sugar. (Even as late as 1971, laws were passed in Germany requiring the registration of

[3]Jancis Robinson, *Oxford Companion to Wine*, p. 308.

each vineyard and the appointment of a government panel to taste each vineyard's annual vintage and assign it a quality level.)[4] Similar laws and regulations prescribing winemaking practices also developed in France and Italy.

These trends were reinforced within the industry, as regional producers added to the classification schemes and regulatory controls as a way of differentiating their product in an increasingly complex market for wine. The venerable French classification system was created by the Bordeaux event committee preparing for the 1855 Exposition in Paris. To help consumers recognize their finest wines—and to help distinguish Bordeaux as the region most notable for fine wines—they classified vineyards on one of five levels, from *premier cru* (first growth) to *cinquième cru* (fifth growth).

Because it helped consumers sort through the complexity of a highly fragmented market, this marketing tool immediately gained wide recognition. As a result, the government codified much of the 1855 classification in the *Appellation d'Origin Controllée* (AOC) laws that extended the original Bordeaux concept by defining the boundaries and setting the standards for vineyards and winemakers in France's other major wine-growing regions.[5] A similar classification scheme was later introduced in Italy defining 213 *denominazione di origne controllate* (or DOC) regions, each with regulations prescribing area, grape varieties permitted, yields, etc. These laws also prescribed almost all aspects of production, from the permissible types of grape to the alcohol content of the wine.[6]

Later, other wine regions of France were given official recognition with the classification of *Vins Delimités de Qualite Superieure* (VDQS), but these were usually regarded as of lower rank that AOC wines. Below VDQS were *Vins de Pays,* or country wine, primarily producing "*vins ordinaries.*" There was almost no movement across the

categories or within the hierarchies created by these classifications, since the French nurtured the concept of *terroir,* the almost mystical combination of soil, aspect, microclimate, rainfall, and cultivation and they passionately believed was at the heart of the unique taste of each region's—and indeed, each vineyard's—grapes and wine.

But *terroir* could not always guarantee quality. As an agricultural product, wine was always subject to the vagaries of weather and disease. In the last quarter of the nineteenth century, a deadly new world insect, phylloxera, devastated the French vine stock. From production of over 5 million hectoliters (hls) in 1876, output dropped to just 2 million hls by 1885. (A hectoliter is 100 liters, or about 25 gallons.) Government and industry mobilized, eventually finding a solution in an unexpected quarter. French vines were successfully grafted onto phylloxera-resistant vine roots native to the eastern United States and imported from the upstart Californian wine industry. It was the first time many in the Old World acknowledged the existence of a wine industry outside Europe. It would not be the last.

Stirrings in the New World

Although insignificant in both size and reputation compared to the well-established industry in traditional wine producing countries, vineyards and winemakers had been set up in many "new world" countries since the eighteenth century. In the United States, for example, Thomas Jefferson, an enthusiastic oenologist, became a leading voice for establishing vineyards in Virginia. And in Australia, vines were brought over along with the first fleet carrying convicts and settlers in 1788. At the same time, nascent wine industries were developing in Argentina, Chile, and South Africa, usually under the influence of immigrants from the old world wine countries.

Opening New Markets   While climate and soil allowed grape growing to flourish in each of these new environments, the penetration of wine into local markets varied widely. In Argentina and

---

[4]Ibid., p. 312.

[5]Dewey Markham, *1855: A History of the Bordeaux Classification* (New York: Wiley, 1998), p. 177.

[6]Jancis Robinson, *Oxford Companion to Wine*, p. 235.

Chile, wine eventually became as central a part of their national cultures as in Europe. By the mid-1960s, per capita consumption was about 80 liters per annum in Argentina and 50 liters in Chile. While such rates were comparable to the 60 liter p.a. level in Spain, they were in a second tier behind France and Italy with consumption rates of 110–120 liters per person annually. (See Exhibit 1 for wine consumption figures over time.)

Other new world cultures were not so quick to embrace the new industry for a variety of reasons. In Australia, the hot climate and a dominant British heritage made beer the alcoholic beverage of preference, with wine being consumed mostly by old world immigrants. The U.S. market developed in an even more complex, schizophrenic nature. Born of the country's role as a key player in the rum trade,

one segment of the population followed a tradition of distilling and drinking hard liquor, while another group espoused temperance, perhaps inherited from a strong Puritan culture. (As late as 1994, a Gallup survey found that 45% of U.S. respondents did not drink at all, and that 21% would favor a total ban on the sale of alcohol.) As a result, until the post–World War II era, wine was largely made by and sold to European immigrant communities. In the post-war era, however, demand for wine began to increase quite dramatically in the United States and Australia, as well as in other new world producers such as South Africa and New Zealand. In the United States, for example, consumption grew from a post-prohibition per capita level of 1 liter per annum to 8 liters by 1976, while in Australia, the increase was even more dramatic from less that

Exhibit 1   Wine Consumption per Capita, Selected Countries, 1966–1998

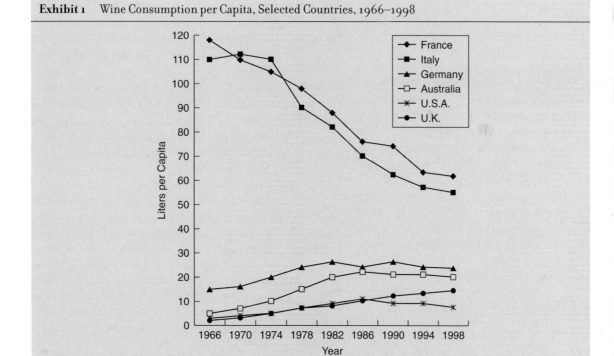

Source: 1966 through 1994 figures adapted by casewriters from Annemiek Geene, Arend Heijbroek, Anne Lagerwerf, and Rafi Wazir, "The World Wine Business," Market Study, May 1999, available from Rabobank International. 1998 figures from Wine Institute, "Wine Institute, the Voice for California Wine" Web site, <http://www.wineinstitute.org/communications/statistics/index.htm> (accessed September 10, 2002).

2 liters in 1960 to 22 liters by 1986. Equally important, this growth in total consumption was coupled with a growing demand for higher quality wines. It was this boom in domestic demand for both quality and quantity that firmly established the young wine industry in these new world countries.

Challenging Production Norms   Expanding on the back of the post-war economic boom, new world wine production regimes developed in a very different economic context and business environment than most of their European counterparts. First, suitable land was widely available and thus less expensive, allowing the growth of much more extensive vineyards. In the early 1990s, the average holding for a vineyard among "new world" wine producers was 158 hectares compared to less than 1 hectare in the old world countries.[7]

Unconstrained by either small size or tradition, producers in the United States and Australia in particular began to experiment with new technology in both grape growing and winemaking. In Australia, controlled drip irrigation reduced vintage variability and allowed expansion into new growing regions. Larger vineyards also favored new developments in specialized equipment. Mechanical harvesters, then mechanical pruners, became the industry standard. Trellis systems developed in Australia permitted vineyard planting at twice the traditional density, while other experiments with everything from fertilizers to pruning increased yield and improved grape flavor. These bold experiments, when coupled with the sunny climates of the new growing regions, allowed the new world producers to make remarkably consistent wines year to year. In contrast, the rainy maritime climate in Bordeaux made late autumn harvests risky and held producers hostage to year-to-year vintage variations.

Experimentation also extended to winemaking, where the new world companies were more willing to break with centuries-old traditions. Large estates usually had on-site labs to run tests and provide

data helpful in making growing and harvest decisions. [More controversially, by the 1990s many new world winemakers had employed some form of a reverse osmosis technology to concentrate the juice (or *must*), thus ensuring a deeper-colored, richer-tasting wine. Ironically, the technique was developed by a couple of French desalination equipment makers, but most French producers publicly deplored the practice as "removing the poetry of wine."] The newer winemakers also developed processes that allowed much of the fermentation and even the aging to occur in huge computer-controlled stainless steel tanks rather than in the traditional small oak barrels.

Reinventing the Marketing Model   Beyond their experiments in growing and winemaking, new world producers also innovated packaging and marketing. While following the European example of targeting the huge market for basic bulk wines, the Americans and Australians did so in their own way. In the United States, the old world standard liter bottle of "*vin de table*" was replaced by the half-gallon flagon with a screw cap closure, while the Australians developed the innovative "wine-in-a-box" package, featuring a collapsible plastic bag in a compact box with a dispensing spigot. Not only did this design economize on shipping costs due to the lighter weight and packing efficiency of the box, it also made storage in the consumer's refrigerator more convenient.

In both countries, producers also began differentiating their products to make them more appealing to palates unaccustomed to wine. This also allowed forays into branding and marketing, skills that were rare in this industry prior to the 1970s. Several products were wildly successful commercially—Ripple and Thunderbird in the United States or Barossa Pearl in Australia, for example—but held in great disdain by wine connoisseurs.

When Coca-Cola acquired Taylor California Cellars in 1977—and was followed by other experienced consumer marketers such as Nestlé, Pillsbury, and Seagram's—the conventional wisdom was that the application of sophisticated branding

Exhibit 2   Wine Industry Value Chain

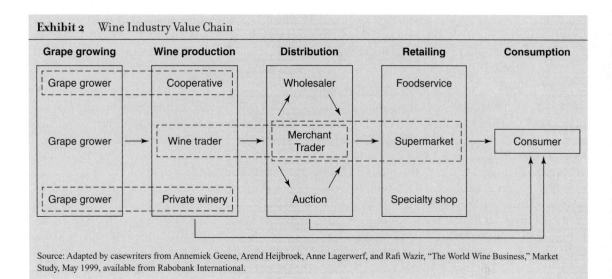

Source: Adapted by casewriters from Annemiek Geene, Arend Heijbroek, Anne Lagerwerf, and Rafi Wazir, "The World Wine Business," Market Study, May 1999, available from Rabobank International.

and marketing techniques would finally crack this resistant market. But forecasts of 25% annual demand growth proved wildly optimistic, and within a few years almost all the outsiders had sold out. Yet their influence endured, and experimentation with branding, labeling, and other market innovations continued.

The other major change driven by new world companies occurred in distribution. Historically, the fragmented nature of the traditional producers and the constellation of government regulations had resulted in a long, multi-level value chain from grape grower to consumer. (See Exhibit 2 for a diagram of the wine industry value chain.) In the old world, the tasks of grape growing, winemaking, distribution, and marketing were typically handled by different entities, with many of them lacking either the scale or the expertise to operate efficiently.

Recognizing this long, compartmentalized chain as a major competitive disadvantage, some small grape growers had formed cooperatives that allowed them to integrate forward into winemaking, most relied on nécociants who had moved upstream into winemaking and downstream into marketing and distribution. In contrast, the large fully integrated wine companies from the new world typically controlled the full value chain, extracting margins at every level and retaining critical bargaining power with increasingly concentrated retailers.

To traditionalists, these breaks with the old grape-growing and winemaking ways were sacrilege. They argued that in their drive for efficiency and consistency, new world producers had lost the depth, character, and unpredictable differences that came with more variable vintages made in traditional ways. What piqued them even more was that, as part of their marketing approach, these upstart new wineries were selling their more engineered products using the appellation names—burgundy, chablis, champagne, etc.—they had proudly promoted. In the 1960s, the European Economic Community passed regulations making it illegal to use such names on wines other than those produced in the region.

While some new world producers continued unauthorized labeling for decades after these regulations, their enforcement outside Europe was difficult. Others responded by labeling their wine with the grape variety being used. Eventually consumers recognized and developed preferences defined by varietal type—cabernet sauvignon or chardonnay, for example. Indeed, many seemed to find it an easier way to understand the product they were buying rather than trying to penetrate the different regional designations in various traditional wine-producing countries.

The Judgment of Paris: 1976   In 1976, the dismissive attitude of some old world producers and the inferiority complex of many new world wineries were radically changed by a widely publicized event. A British wine merchant set up a blind tasting panel to rate top wines from France and California and determine how far the new world challengers had come to meeting the quality set by the old world standard bearers. Against all odds—the French had an enormous "home field advantage" in an event held in Paris with a judging panel of 15 French wine critics—the American entries took top honors in what became known as "The Judgment of Paris." Chagrined French producers complained that the test was rigged, but when a similar judging was held two years later, the California wines triumphed again.[8]

The event was a watershed in the industry for several reasons. First, publicity surrounding the event raised public awareness of quality wines from new world sources and severely undermined the views of "wine snobs" who regularly dismissed innovative approaches to winemaking. Second, it was a wake-up call to traditional producers, many of whom began taking their new challengers seriously for the first time. And finally, it gave confidence to new world producers that they had the quality to compete against the best on global markets. In short, it was the bell for the opening round in a fight for export sales.

Maturing Markets, Changing Demand

The "Judgment of Paris" was only one element of a series of disruptive changes the wine industry faced in the last quarter of the twentieth century. More immediately alarming for most traditional producers was a pattern of declining demand that saw a 25% drop in worldwide consumption from 1976 to 1990, coupled with some radical changes in consumer tastes and preferences, these trends presented industry participants with an important new set of opportunities and threats.

Country Demand Patterns   The most dramatic decline in demand occurred in the highest consumption countries: France and Italy. In the mid-1960s, per capita consumption in both countries was around 120 liters p.a.; by the late 1980s it had fallen to half that level. Among factors in the decline were a younger generation's different drinking preferences, an older generation's concern about health issues, and stricter drunk-driving penalties. Similar steep declines occurred in other high consumption countries during the same two decades—Spain dropped from 60 liters to 30, Argentina declined from 80 to 40, and Chile plummeted from 50 to 15.

In contrast, demand was growing in the last two decades of the century in most wine-importing countries, although not fast enough to offset the losses in the traditional producing countries. However these changing demand patterns served to escalate competition for export sales. (See Exhibit 3 for data on key countries' consumption, production, and trade.) From 1966 to 1998, per capita consumption in the United Kingdom rose from 3 liters to 14 liters, in Belgium from 10 liters to 25 liters, in Sweden from 5 liters to 15 liters, and in Canada from 3 liters to 8 liters. Even more promising was the more recent growth of new markets, particularly in Asia. Although starting from a low per capita consumption base—from less than 1 liter p.a.—Asia's largest wine importing countries (China, Japan, Taiwan, Singapore, South Korea, and Thailand) grew at an average of 12% annually through the 1990s. The growth potential could be seen in Japan where wine emerged as the fashionable drink of the late 1990s. In just three years, per capita consumption jumped from 1.5 liters in 1996 to 3 liters in 1999.[9]

[8]Gideon Rachman, "The Globe in a Glass," *The Economist* (December 18, 1999): 91.

[9]All statistics from Wine Institute, "Wine Institute, the Voice for California Wine" Web site, <http://www.wineinstitute.org/communications/statistics/index.htm> (accessed September 10, 2002).

Exhibit 3   Consumption, Production, Export and Import Figures for Selected Old World and New World Wine Producing and Consuming Countries, 1999

Country	Consumption Liters per Capita	Consumption Total hls ooos	Production Total hls (ooos)	Exports Total hls (ooos)	Exports Value ($ooos)	Imports Total hls (ooos)	Imports Value ($ooo)
France	60	35,000	54,000	15,924	$22,357,296	6,101	$8,565,804
Italy	58	34,000	51,000	14,516	20,380,464	1,530	2,148,120
Argentina	39	13,500	14,000	1,300	1,825,200	n/a	n/a
Spain	37	14,500	34,000	10,499	14,740,596	664	932,256
Germany	23	18,500	8,300	2,598	3,647,592	12,478	17,519,112
Australia	19	3,500	6,000	2,400	3,369,600	141	197,964
United Kingdom	14	8,100	—[a]	343	481,572	8,876	12,461,904
United States	7	20,000	20,000	2,850	4,001,400	2,743	3,851,172

[a]Nominal United Kingdom wine production was 27 hectoliters.

Sources: Eurostat. *Yearbook* (Luxembourg: Office for Official Publications of the European Communities, 1999) for European production, export and import data. United Nations. *International Trade Statistics Yearbook* (New York: United Nations, 1997) for export and import data for Argentine and Australia. Wine Institute, "Wine Institute, the Voice for California Wine" Web site, <http://www.wineinstitute.org/communications/statistics/index.htm> (accessed September 10, 2002) for all others.

Shift to Quality   Another trend partly offsetting the overall volume decline was a growing demand for higher quality wines. In terms of the fine consumer segments defined by industry analyst Rabobank (see Exhibit 4), the major shift was from the basic segment to premium and super-premium wines. While the basic segment (less that $5 a bottle) still accounted for half the world market in volume, the premium ($5 to $7) and the super-premium ($7 to $14) now represented 40% of the total—and closer to 50% in younger markets like the United States and Australia.

The trend was worldwide. Even in the 12 EU countries, where overall demand was declining, consumption of premium wine kept rising. Despite government subsidies, per capita consumption of basic wine in the EU fell from 31 liters in 1985 to 20 liters in 1997 even as demand for quality wine increased from 10 to 14 liters. In less regulated markets the rate of substitution was even more rapid. In the same 12-year period jug wine sales in the United States declined from 800 million to 650 million liters while consumption of premium wines increased from 150 million to 550 million liters.

Fluctuations in Fashion   With the declining importance of working families consuming locally produced table wine, the market was increasingly driven by upscale urban consumers. The whole buying process changed dramatically, as educated consumers chose bottles on the basis of grape variety, vintage, and source. With the shift to quality came a greater fashion element that caused wider fluctuations in demand that put new pressures on grape producers and winemakers.

At the most basic level, there were increasingly wide swings in the consumption of red versus white wine. In the 1980s, an emphasis on light foods resulted in an increase in demand for white wines. In the U.S. market, the trend led to white wine spritzers (diluting the wine with soda water and a lime) becoming a fashionable drink. White wine represented over 75% of U.S. sales by the late 1980s. In the 1990s, however, the trend began to reverse itself. Demand for red wine began surging in 1991 following the publication of a medical report identifying red wine consumption as the major reason for the so-called "French paradox"—the curious fact that the French enjoyed very low rates

Exhibit 4   Quality Segments in the Wine Industry

	Icon	Ultra-Premium	Super-Premium	Premium	Basic
Price range	More than $50	$14–50	$7–14	$5–7	Less than $5
Consumer profile	Connoisseur	Wine lover	Experimenting consumer	Experimenting consumer	Price-focused consumer
Purchase driver	Image, style	Quality, image	Brand, quality	Price, brand	Price
Retail outlets	Winery, boutique, food service	Specialty shop, food service	Better supermarket, specialty shop	Supermarket	Supermarket, discounter
Market trend	Little growth	Little growth	Growing	Growing	Decreasing
Competition	Limited, "closed" segment	Gradually increasing	Increasing, based on brand and quality/price ratio	Fierce, based on brand, price	Based on price
Volume market share	1%	5%	10%	34%	50%
Availability	Scarce	Scarce	Sufficient, year round	Large quantities, year round	Surplus

Source: Adapted by casewriters from Annemiek Geene, Arend Heijbroek, Anne Lagerwerf, and Rafi Wazir, "The World Wine Business," Market Study, May 1999, available from Rabobank International.

of heart disease, despite their well known love for rich food. The report, widely reported in the press and featured on the television program *60 Minutes,* gave a huge and immediate boost to red wine sales. In the United States, market share for red wine went from 27% in 1991 to 43% five years later, while in fashion-conscious Japan, red's share jumped from 25% to 65% in just two years.[10]

Even within this broad trend of red versus white preference, wine made from different grape varieties also moved with the fashions. The white wine boom made chardonnay the grape of choice with other white varietals falling in relative popularity. In red wine, a love affair with cabernet sauvignon was followed by a boom in demand for merlot, particularly in the United States.

Such swings in fashion posed a problem for most producers, who could not easily or quickly adjust supply to changing demand. Although vines

had a productive life of 60 to 70 years, they typically took 3 to 4 years to produce their first harvest, 5 to 7 years to reach full productive capacity, and up to 35 years to produce the best quality grapes for wine. It was a life cycle that did not respond well to rapid changes in demand. Nonetheless, new world wine regions still had capacity to plant new vineyards. For example, the California acreage planted with chardonnay grapes increased 36% in the 1990s and merlot plantings increased 31%. Australia's new planting in newly opened areas was even more dramatic, driven by the five major wine-producing companies that controlled 85% of the market.

For producers in many old world regions, however, shifting demand was more challenging. First, there was often no new land available to plant, particularly in controlled regions such as AOC. Equally restrictive were the numerous regulations prescribing grape varieties for a region's wines, affording no flexibility when consumer preferences shifted. One of the biggest victims of the fashion

[10]Gideon Rachman, "The Globe in a Glass," *The Economist* (December 18, 1999): 100.

switch from sweeter white wines to drier reds was the German wine industry. Constrained by tight regulations on sugar content, the German winemakers watched their exports drop from over 3 million hectoliters in 1992 to under 2 million just five years later.

As these trends continued, the league table of the world's top wine companies underwent some radical change. Despite their relative newness and the comparative smallness of their home market, U.S. and Australian wine companies had taken nine slots on the list of the world's top 20, which until recently, had been dominated by French, German, and other old world companies (see Exhibit 5).

The Battle for Britain

In the turmoil occurring in markets worldwide, nowhere were the stakes more important than in the bellwether United Kingdom wine market. It became the front line in the battle between old world and new world producers, with France acting as the standard bearer of the traditional producers, and Australia as the leader among the challengers.

The Prize: The Huge U.K. Market Long before Napoleon derided the English as a nation of shopkeepers, England was a nation of importers. Table wine tastes of the traditional upper crust were satisfied with French, German and Italian wines, while the drinking habits of the rest of the nation ran to pub fare. But by 2000, the burnished image of the upper class importing claret by the case was a thing of the past, as the British middle classes increasingly turned to wine as a mealtime beverage of choice. As the second richest import market in the world after Germany, the United Kingdom was not only a rich market opportunity, but also crucial territory in any quest for world wine domination.

The U.K. market was large and showed both increased consumption trends and a capacity for further growth. As their domestic markets shrank, many traditional European wine producers began looking at the U.K. market as more than a source of opportunistic or incremental sales. At the same time, however, as newly confident companies from the emerging wine countries began to see the possibility of selling their products abroad, the United Kingdom became a prime target—particularly for countries with old British Commonwealth ties. The stage was set for a serious competitive battle in which many of the contestants not only brought different weapons to the field, they came with an entirely different understanding of the rules.

Ascendancy of Brand Power Historically, the extreme fragmentation of European producers gave few of them the volume to develop branding economies. As a result, only the handful of producers whose wines achieved icon status—Lafite, Margaux, Veuve Cliquot, Chateau d'Yquem—became recognized brands, but these appealed to the elite who were the target of their historic export efforts. Government efforts to compensate for lack of branding through regional and vineyard classifications such as France's AOC or Italy's DOC had only been partially successful in ensuring consumer confidence due to the complexity of the classifications and the recognition that most of them had become compromised. For example, Burgundy's most famous vineyard, Chambertin, had its 32 acres divided among 23 different proprietors. While many produced the high quality wine that has earned *grand cru* status, others rode on that reputation to sell—at $150 a bottle—a legitimately labeled Chambertin that wine critic Robert Parker describes as "thin, watery, and a complete rip-off."[11]

As wine consumption broadened well beyond educated connoisseurs, new consumers in the fast-growing premium wine segment were faced with hundreds of options on the shelf and insufficient knowledge to make an informed—or even a comfortable—choice. To make a good choice, they felt they had to learn the intricacies of region,

[11]The same problem plagued wines from Italy where DOC regulations were so often violated that the government introduced a DOCG classification in 1980 (the G stood for *guarantita*) to restore consumer confidence in notable wine regions. And in Germany, government standards were so diluted that, even in mediocre years, over 75% of wine produced was labeled *Qualitatswein,* while less that 5% earned the more modest *Tatelwein* (table wine) designation.

Exhibit 5   World's 20 Largest Wine Companies, 1998

Company	Country	Wine Sales ($ooos)	Major Brands
LVMH[a]	France	$1,462,000	Moet & Chandon, Krug, Dom Perignon, Veuve Cliquot, Pommery, Green Point (Australia), Domaine Chandon (Napa and Argentina). Stakes in Chateau d'Yquem and Cloudy Bay (New Zealand)
E&J Gallo[b]	USA	1,428,000	Livingston Cellars, Carlo Rossi, Turning Leaf, Garnet Point, Ecco Domani (Italy), E&J Gallo
Seagram[c]	Canada	800,000	Wineries in 12 countries, including Sterling, Monterey and Mumm Cuvee (United States)
Castel Frères[d]	France	700,000	Castelvins, Nicolas, Vieux Papes
Canandaigua[e]	USA	614,000	Inglenook, Almaden, Paul Masson, Arbor Mist, Franciscan Estate
Hengell & Sohnein Group[f]	Germany	521,000	Henkell Trocken (sparkling wine), Dienhard, Schloss Johannisberg
Reh Gruppe[f]	Germany	500,000	Kenderman, Black Tower
Diageo	U.K.	500,000	Le Piat d'Or (France), Blossom Hill, Glen Ellen, Beaulieu (United States), Croft Port, Navarro (Argentina)
Wein International Verw.[f]	Germany	480,000	Mainly generic wines for supermarkets
The Wine Group	USA	426,000	Franzia
Val d'Orbieu[g]	France	400,000	
Grands Chais de France[d]	France	390,000	Supermarket label wines in France
Southcorp[c]	Australia	376,000	Penfolds, Lindemans, Seppelt, Coldstream Hills, Rouge Homme (Australia), Lames Herrick (France), Seven Peaks (United States)
R. Mondavi[h]	USA	325,000	Woodbridge, Mondavi Coastal, Opus One (with Rothschild), Vichon (France), ventures in Chile and Italy
Freixenet[j]	Spain	318,000	Own-label sparkling wine
BRL Hardy Ltd.	Australia	292,000	Nottage Hill, Hardy's Stamp, Banrock Station, D'Istinto (Italy)
Beringer Wine Estates	USA	279,000	Own-label varieties, Stag's Leap, Meridian
Mildara Blass	Australia	260,000	Wolf Blass, Rothbury, Mildara
Brown-Foreman Beverage	USA	260,000	Fetzer
Pernod Ricard[e]	France	250,000	Jacob's Creek (Australia), Long Mountain (South Africa), Terra Andina (Chile), Alexis Lichine (France), Etechart (Argentina), Dragon Seal (China)

Notes: [a]Mainly champagne. [b]Largest wine company in volume. [c]Diversified company. [d]Négociant. [e]Beverage company. [f]Includes *sekt,* a sparkling wine. [g]Co-operative in Corbiéres and Minervois. [h]All wine. [j]World's largest sparkling wine producer.
Source: Adapted by casewriters from Gideon Rachman, "The Globe in a Glass," *The Economist* (December 18, 1999): 102, and from Annemiek Geene, Arend Heijbroek, Anne Lagerwerf, and Rafi Wazir, "The World Wine Business," Market Study, May 1999, available from Rabobank International.

Exhibit 6   Ten Largest Wine Brands in the U.K., 1998

Brand	Company and Country of Origin	Sales ($000s)
E&J Gallo	Gallo (USA)	$55,600
Hardy's	BRL Hardy (Australia)	38,500
Jacob's Creek	Orlando (Australia)	38,400
Moet et Chandon	LVMH (France)	28,500
Le Piat[a]	Le Piat (France)	27,200
Sowells of Chelsea	Matthew Clark (U.K.)	26,400
Penfolds	Southcorp (Australia)	19,200
Lindemans	Southcorp (Australia)	15,200
Rosemount	Rosemount Estate (Australia)	13,000
Lanson	Lanson (France)	12,300

[a] Négociant.

Source: Adapted by casewriter from Annemiek Geene, Arend Heijbroek, Anne Lagerwerf, and Rafi Wazir, "The World Wine Business," Market Study, May 1999, available from Rabobank International.

vintage, and vineyard reputation. And even when they found a wine they liked, chances were that by their next purchase, the same producer was not stocked or the new vintage was much less appealing. Unsurprisingly, survey data showed 65% of shoppers had no idea of what they would choose when they entered a wine store.

For years, the wine industry appeared ripe for branding. Compared to soft drinks, beer, and liquor, where top brands dominate market share, in 1990 no wine brand had even 1% of the global wine market. Although European producers—and more often, their importing agents—had succeeded in promoting a handful of brands on the basic segment in the 1960s and 1970s (e.g., Blue Nun, Mateus, Liebfraumilch, Hirondelle), it was the new world producers who made branding and labeling a routine part of wine marketing. After experimenting with these techniques in the 1960s and 1970s, producers in both the United States and Australia dominated their home markets with strong brands by the 1980s. By the mid 1990s, for example, 75% of sales on the Australian market accounted for by 6% of the brands. But, with a small home market, beginning in the 1980s and particularly through the 1990s, these producers became very aggressive in taking those brands abroad. The results were dramatic. By

2000, the Australians claimed 6 of the top 10 wine brands sold in the U.K. (See Exhibit 6 for top wine brands in the U.K.)

European winemakers' response to the growing success of Australian brands was slow and limited. Most had become accustomed to competing at the low end on price, the middle level on the umbrella reassurance of appellation reputation, and at the top end on the reflected image of the icon brands. As a result, they lacked the skills, the resources, and even the interest to enter the battle developing for the increasingly branded middle market. (As Exhibit 6 shows, apart from the high value champagnes Moet et Chandon and Lanson, the French only had one wine brand—LePiat, a négociant's label—among the top 10 brands in the U.K. No other traditional producing country made the list.) There were a few exceptions, however, that some felt could serve as inspirations and role models. As early as the 1930s, Baron Philipe de Rothschild had created a second label for "output deemed unworthy" of the icon level Mouton-Rothschild brand. Mouton Cadet grew to be a significant mid-price brand, and more recently Baron Philipe's daughter, Baroness Philippine, had begun sourcing wines from the south of France and marketing them as Cadet Chardonnay, Cadet Merlot, etc.

Exhibit 7   U.K. Off-License Wine Sales by Outlet, 1989–1995

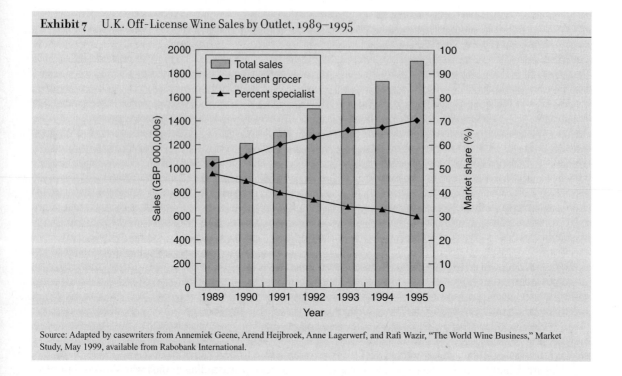

Source: Adapted by casewriters from Annemiek Geene, Arend Heijbroek, Anne Lagerwerf, and Rafi Wazir, "The World Wine Business," Market Study, May 1999, available from Rabobank International.

Increasingly, intermediaries started filling the need for consistent quality and supply that branding ensured. Indeed, the names of negotiants like Georges Deboeuf and Louis Jardot became more well known than the vast majority of Beaujolais and Burgundy producers they represented. And UK wine merchants like Sowells of Chelsea or Oddbins developed their own brands to minimize buyer confusion while also capturing some of the value in the fast-growing premium market segment.

A different approach was being followed by other traditional producers who felt they were too small and unskilled to mount their own marketing plans. They saw their best hope in linking up with the established marketing and distribution powerhouses—like the Australians or the Americans. For example, in 1997, Vinicola Caltrasi, a family-owned Sicilian company linked to local growers' cooperatives entered into a joint venture with Australian producer BRL Hardy, a company that had already used its experience in branding and marketing to make a wine it imported

from Chile the leading brand in its segment. Hardy developed the brand, label design, and marketing strategy for a line of Italian wines it called *D'istinto* ("instinctively") that was launched on the U.K. market at prices from £3.49 to £6.99 per bottle (roughly $2.25 to $4.50).[12]

Increasing Distribution Power Because their branding and marketing had typically been handled by their négociant or their cooperative, most European producers were still very isolated from increasingly fast-changing consumer tastes and preferences—particularly in export markets like the United Kingdom. Equally problematic was their lack of bargaining power when dealing with the rapidly concentrating retailers, and particularly the growing buying power of the supermarket chains. (See Exhibit 7.)

---

[12]For a full account of BRL Hardy's global strategy, including its Italian sourcing and branding decisions, see Christopher A. Bartlett, "BRL Hardy: Globalizing an Australian Wine Company," HBS Case No. 300-018 (Boston: Harvard Business School Publishing, 1999).

In contrast, new world wine companies tended to be larger and more integrated, with major players controlling operations from the vineyard to the retailer. They used their scale and integration to achieve market power in their domestic markets. (In Australia, the largest five companies accounted for 85% market share), thereby generating the resources and expertise to attack export markets. In contrast, the largest five French wine companies (excluding champagne specialists) accounted for only 8% of their market. (The comparable number in Italy was 4%.)

Consumers were even more sensitive to pricing than brand, however, and retailers reported that their sales trends followed whatever was offered with the highest perceived quality to value ratio. The larger size new world producers developed significant distribution advantages from their scale and scope. Without multiple intermediaries, they added even more cost advantages to their lower production costs by avoiding more handling stages, more inventory in the chain, and more stages adding their markup. Even transport and trade economics, which once favored European suppliers selling into the United Kingdom, had changed in the last decades of the century. Tariff barriers dropped under successive WTO negotiations, and transportation differentials shifted as trucking costs rose while container-ship costs fell. As a result, the cost of shipping wine from Australia to the U.K. was now about the same as trucking it from the south of France.

Size had also given the new world companies bargaining power in their dealings with the concentrating retail sector. As a result, Australian wines enjoyed a strong ongoing position in the U.K.'s fastest growing wine retail channel: the multi-outlet supermarket. Supermarket retailers preferred branded products that translated into high-volume sales and consistent delivery from suppliers.[13] As U.K. consumers became willing to spend more per bottle of wine, new world imports offering competitive pricing, strong branding, and consistent quality took the lion's share of the growth. In the face of this distribution-driven growth, French market share was maintained only with the aid of large-scale promotions.[14] Even so, market share continued to slip.

Reports from the Front: Victories, Defeats, and Responses   Results in the wine companies' Battle for Britain—and particularly in the contest between Australia and France for dominance in the U.K. market—were dramatic. During the 1990s French wine exports to the U.K. increased approximately 5%, while Australian imports grew seven times faster. So while French market share eroded from 39% in 1994 to 26% in 2000, the Australians' share of the U.K. increased from 8% to 17%. But of greater concern to the French was the forecast that the Australians would overtake them as market leaders by 2002. (See Exhibit 8 for source country market share in the U.K.)

The Australian claim for dominance was even stronger that simple market share indicated. The bulk of French wine sales were in the less expensive (and less profitable) categories, which also were the market segments that expected little or no growth. Australian wines were largely positioned in the premium and super-premium segments, where trends indicated the greatest potential for growth. (See Exhibit 9 for distributions of price points of U.K. imports.)

By the summer of 2001, many in the French wine industry were becoming concerned. To evaluate the threat, the French minister of agriculture appointed his general controller, Jacques Berthomeau, as wine crisis manager and asked him to prepare a report on the French industry. Released on July 31st, the report was frank in its evaluation and strong in its recommendations. "[The French wine industry] has lived too long on its past good name," it concluded. "It needs to come out of its haughty elitism and take the threat of the new world

---

[13]Gideon Rachman, "The Globe in a Glass," *The Economist* (December 18, 1999): 99.

[14]Annemiek Geene, Arend Heijbroek, Anne Lagerwerf, and Rafi Wazir, "The World Wine Business," Market Study, May 1999, available from Rabobank International.

Exhibit 8   U.K. Retail Wine Sales: Market Share by Source, 1988–2002E

	1988	1994	2000	2002E
France	43%	39%	26%	22%
Germany	30	19	11	9
Italy	10	10	13	12
Other (including Chile and South Africa)	15	23	27	25
USA	1	2	7	10
Australia	2	8	17	22
	100%	100%	100%	100%

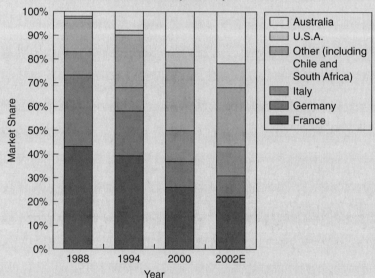

Source: Adapted by casewriters from Sheryle Bagwell, "The French Correction," *Business Review Weekly* (August 29, 2002): 34; and Paul Tranter and Christian van Tienhoven "Why the New World Is Winning in the Wine Industry," unpublished ms, May 3, 2002.

challenge seriously."[15] One of the report's main recommendations was that the French industry had to adopt some of the technical and marketing advances that had allowed the Australians and Americans to succeed. In particular, it proposed developing a much stronger commitment to branding.

Said Berthomeau:

> The French . . . have marketed wine based on heritage of growing regions, down to the fields of the chateaus where the vines are planted. France's rivals, by contrast, address the consumer the way you would with beer. . . . The question for us French is, can we do the same thing? The answer is yes.[16]

[15]Jacques Berthomeau, "Comment mieux positionner les vins français sur les marchés d'exportation?" Report to Jean Glavany, ministre de l'agriculture [French Minister of Agriculture] (July 31, 2001).

[16]John Tagliabue, "For French Vintners, Lessons in Mass Marketing," *New York Times* (April 14, 2002): Section 3, p. 4.

Exhibit 9   Price Point Breakdown of Volume of U.K. Imports by Country of Origin, 2001

Price Range (£)	Australia	USA	France	Germany
>£4.51	41%	31%	18%	2%
£4.01–£4.50	16	22	7	2
£3.01–£4.00	41	44	43	28
£2.06–£3.00	2	3	29	47
<£2.05	—	—	3	21
	100%	100%	100%	100%

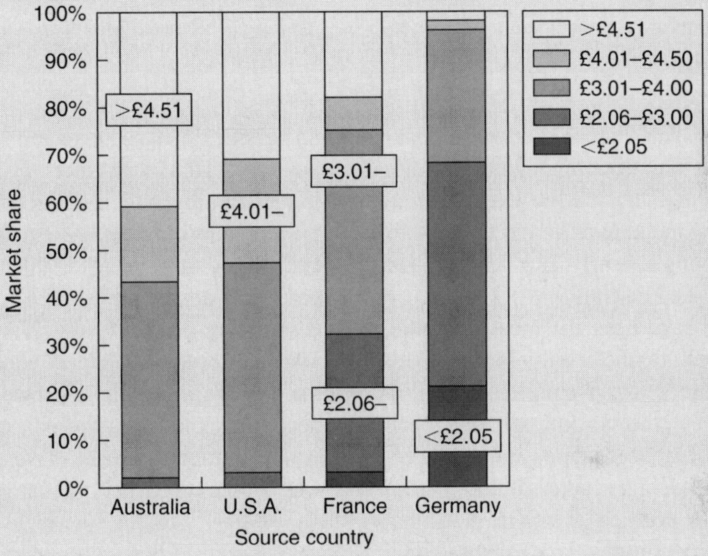

Source: Adapted by casewriters from Mike Gibbs, Steve Branley-Jackson, Claire Ross, Mark Lynch, Stephen Potter, Lisa Heffernan and Girish Pamnani, "Beverages: Wines" Europe, February 11, 2002, available from Goldman Sachs Global Equity Research.

Others were not so sure. Jean-Luc Darien, director of Onivins, the French wine industry association, worried that such an approach was too radical and risked simplifying the product to such a degree it would "toss the baby out with the bath water." After all, French wine still had 40% of the global market, and was still the standard by which most consumers gauged other countries' wines. Rather than seeing the great fragmentation and diversity of French wine markets as a liability, he felt they should work to make an asset.[17] It was a point of view that had many supporters and was helping to fuel a healthy debate amongst growers, winemakers, merchants, and policy makers as they debated how best to respond to the ongoing challenge.

[17]Ibid.

Case 2-3   Hitting the Wall: Nike and International Labor Practices

Moore: Twelve year olds working in [Indonesian] factories? That's O.K. with you?
Knight: They're not 12-year-olds working in factories . . . the minimum age is 14.
Moore: How about 14 then? Does that bother you?
Knight: No.

Phil Knight, *Nike CEO, talking to Director Michael Moore in a scene from documentary film* The Big One, 1997.

Nike is raising the minimum age of footwear factory workers to 18 . . . Nike has zero tolerance for underage workers.[1]

Phil Knight, 1998

In 1997, Nguyen Thi Thu Phuong died while making sneakers. As she was trimming synthetic soles in a Nike contracting factory, a co-worker's machine broke, spraying metal parts across the factory floor and into Phuong's heart. The 23 year-old Vietnamese woman died instantly.[2]

Although it may have been the most dramatic, Phuong's death was hardly the first misfortune to hit Nike's far-flung manufacturing empire. Indeed, in the 1980s and 1990s, the corporation had been plagued by a series of labor incidents and public relations nightmares: underage workers in Indonesian plants, allegations of coerced overtime in China, dangerous working conditions in Vietnam. For a while, the stories had been largely confined to labor circles and activist publications. By the time of Phuong's death, however, labor conditions at Nike had hit the mainstream. Stories of reported abuse at Nike plants had been carried in publications such as *Time* and *Business Week* and students from major

universities such as Duke and Brown had organized boycotts of Nike products. Even Doonesbury had joined the fray, with a series of cartoons that linked the company to underage and exploited Asian workers. Before these attacks, Nike had been widely regarded as one of the world's coolest and most successful companies. Now Nike, the company of Michael Jordan and Tiger Woods; Nike, the sign of the swoosh and athletic prowess, was increasingly becoming known as the company of labor abuse. And its initial response—"We don't make shoes"— was becoming harder and harder to sustain.[3]

Nike, Inc.

Based in Beaverton, Oregon, Nike had been a corporate success story for more than three decades. It was a sneaker company, but one armed with an inimitable attitude, phenomenal growth, and the apparent ability to dictate fashion trends to some of the world's most influential consumers. In the 1970s, Nike had first begun to capture the attention of both trend-setting teenagers and financial observers. Selling a combination of basic footwear and street-smart athleticism, Nike pushed its revenues from a 1972 level of $60,000 to a startling

[1]"Nike CEO Phil Knight Announces New Labor Initiatives," *PR Newswire*, May 12, 1998.
[2]Tim Larimer, "Sneaker Gulag: Are Asian Workers Really Exploited?" *Time International*, May 11, 1998, p. 30.
Research Associate Jennifer L. Burns prepared this case under the supervision of Professor Debora L. Spar. This case was developed from published sources. HBS cases are developed solely as the basis for class discussion. Cases are not intended to serve as endorsements, sources of primary data, or illustrations of effective or ineffective management.
Copyright © 2000 President and Fellows of Harvard College. Harvard Business School case 700-047.

[3]The quote is from Martha Benson, Nike's regional spokeswoman in Asia. See Larimer, p. 30.

$49 million in just ten years.[4] It went public in 1980 and then astounded Wall Street in the mid-1990s as annual growth stayed resolutely in the double digits and revenues soared to over $9 billion. By 1998, Nike controlled over 40% of the $14.7 billion U.S. athletic footwear market. It was also a growing force in the $64 billion sports apparel market, selling a wide range of sport-inspired gear to consumers around the globe.[5]

What differentiated Nike from its competitors was not so much its shoes as its strategy. Like Reebok and Adidas and New Balance, Nike sold a fairly wide range of athletic footwear to a fairly wide range of consumers: men and women, athletes and non-athletes, in markets around the world. Its strategy, though, was path breaking, the product of a relatively simple idea that CEO Phil Knight had first concocted in 1962 while still a student at Stanford Business School. The formula had two main prongs. First, the company would shave costs by outsourcing *all* manufacturing. There would be no in-house production, no dedicated manufacturing lines. Rather all product would be made by independent contracting factories, creating one of the world's first "virtual" corporations—a manufacturing firm with no physical assets. Then, the money saved through outsourcing would be poured into marketing. In particular, Knight focussed from the start on celebrity endorsements, using high-profile athletes to establish an invincible brand identity around the Nike name. While other firms had used celebrity endorsements in the past, Nike took the practice to new heights, emblazoning the Nike logo across athletes such as Michael Jordan and Tiger Woods, and letting their very celebrity represent the Nike image. "To see name athletes wearing Nike shoes," Knight insisted, "was more convincing than anything we could say about them."[6] With the help of the "swoosh," a distinctive and instantly recognizable logo, Nike became by the 1990s one of the world's best known brands, as well as a global symbol of athleticism and urban cool.

But within this success story lay a central irony that would only become apparent in the late 1990s. While the *marketing* of Nike's products was based on selling a high-profile fashion item to affluent Americans who only wished they could "Just Do It" as well as Woods or Jordan, the *manufacture* of these sneakers was based on an arms-length and often uneasy relationship with low-paid, non-American workers. For according to Knight's original plan, not only would Nike outsource, but it would outsource specifically to low-cost parts of the world.

Nike signed its first contracts with Japanese manufacturers but eventually shifted its supply base to firms in South Korea and Taiwan, where costs were lower and production reliable. In 1982, 86% of Nike sneakers came from one of these two countries and Nike had established a large network of suppliers in both nations. But as South Korea and Taiwan grew richer, costs rose and Nike began to urge its suppliers to move their operations to new, lower cost regions. Eager to remain in the company's good graces, most manufacturers rapidly complied, moving their relatively inexpensive plants to China or Indonesia. By 1990, these countries had largely replaced South Korea and Taiwan as the core of Nike's global network. Indonesia, in particular, had become a critical location, with six factories that supplied Nike and a booming, enthusiastic footwear industry.[7]

Taking Care of Business

At first, Indonesia seemed an ideal location for Nike. Wages were low, the workforce was docile, and an authoritarian government was yearning for foreign direct investment. There were unions in the country and occasional hints of activism, but the

[4]David B. Yoffie, *Nike: A (Condensed),* HBS Case 391-238 (Boston: HBS Press, 1991), p. 1.

[5]Both figures are for retail sales. *Footwear 1999* (North Palm Beach; Athletic Footwear Association, 1999), introduction; Dana Eisman Cohen and Sabina McBride, *Athletic Footwear Outlook 1999* (New York: Donaldson, Lufkin & Jenrette, 1998), p. 3.

[6]Yoffie, p. 6.

[7]Philip M. Rosenzweig and Pam Woo, *International Sourcing in Footwear: Nike and Reebok,* HBS Case 394-189 (Boston: HBS Press, 1994), pp. 2–5.

Suharto government clearly was more interested in wooing investors than in acceding to any union demands. So wages stayed low and labor demands were minimal. In 1991, the daily minimum wage in Indonesia's capital city was barely $1, compared to a typical daily wage of $24.40 in South Korea[8] and a U.S. hourly wage in athletic shoe manufacturing of about $8.[9] For firms like Nike, this differential was key: according to a reporter for the *Far Eastern Economic Review,* shoes coming out of China and Indonesia cost roughly 50% less than those sourced from Taiwan and South Korea.[10]

Just as Nike was settling into its Indonesian operations, though, a rare wave of labor unrest swept across the country. Strikes, which had been virtually nonexistent in the 1980s, began to occur with increasing frequency; according to government figures, there were 112 strikes in 1991,[11] a sharp increase from the 19 reported in 1989.[12] A series of polemical articles about foreign companies' labor abuses also appeared in Indonesian newspapers, triggering unprecedented demands from factory workers and empowering a small but potent band of labor organizers.

The source of these strikes and articles was mysterious. Some claimed that the Indonesian government was itself behind the movement, trying to convince an increasingly suspicious international community of the country's commitment to freedom of speech and labor rights. Others saw the hand of outside organizers, who had come to Indonesia solely to unionize its work force and embarrass its foreign investors. And still others saw the outbursts as random eruptions, cracks in the authoritarian veneer which quickly took on a life of their own. In any case, though, the unrest occurred just around the time of Nike's expansion into Indonesia. In 1991 the Asian-American Free Labor Association (AAFLI, a branch of the AFL-CIO) published a highly critical report on foreign companies in Indonesia. Later that year, a group of Indonesian labor economists at the Institut Teknology Bandung (ITB), issued a similar report, documenting abusive practices in Indonesian factories and tracing them to foreign owners. In the midst of this stream of criticism was a labor organizer with a deep-seated dislike for Nike and a determination to shape its global practices. His name was Jeff Ballinger.

The Role of Jeff Ballinger   A labor activist since high school, Ballinger felt passionately that any company had a significant obligation towards even its lowliest workers. He was particularly concerned about the stubborn gap between wage rates in developed and developing worlds, and about the opportunities this gap created for rich Western companies to exploit low-wage, politically repressed labor pools. In 1988, Ballinger was assigned to run the AAFLI office in Indonesia, and was charged with investigating labor conditions in Indonesian plants and studying minimum wage compliance by overseas American companies. In the course of his research Ballinger interviewed workers at hundreds of factories and documented widespread worker dissatisfaction with labor conditions.

Before long, Nike emerged as a key target. Ballinger believed that Nike's policy of competing on the basis of cost fostered and even encouraged contractors to mistreat their workers in pursuit of unrealistic production quotas. Although Indonesia had worker protection legislation in place, widespread corruption made the laws essentially useless. While the government employed 700 labor inspectors, Ballinger found that out of 17,000 violations reported in 1988, only 12 prosecutions were ever made. Bribery took care of the rest.[13] Nike contractors, in particular, he believed, were regularly flouting Indonesian labor laws and paying

[8]Elliot B. Smith, "K-Swiss in Korea," *California Business,* October 1991, p. 77.

[9]Rosenzweig and Woo, p. 3.

[10]Mark Clifford, "Pain in Pusan," *Far Eastern Economic Review,* November 5, 1992, p. 59.

[11]Suhaini Aznam, "The Toll of Low Wages," *Far Eastern Economic Review,* April 2, 1992, p. 50.

[12]Margot Cohen, "Union of Problems: Government Faces Growing Criticism on Labour Relations," *Far Eastern Economic Review,* August 26, 1993, p. 23.

[13]Interview with casewriter, Cambridge, MA, July 6, 1999.

below-subsistence wages that did not enable workers to meet their daily requirements for food and other necessities. And to top matters off, he found Nike's attitude in the face of these labor practices galling: "It was right around the time that the swoosh started appearing on everything and everyone," Ballinger remembered. "Maybe it was the swagger that did it."[14]

What also "did it," though, was Ballinger's own strategic calculation—a carefully crafted policy of "one country-one company." Ballinger knew that his work would be effective only if it was carefully focused. And if his goal was to draw worldwide attention to the exploitation of third-world factory workers by rich U.S. companies, then Nike made a nearly ideal target. The arithmetic was simple. The same marketing and branding power that drove Nike's bottom line could also be used to drive moral outrage against the exploitation of Asian workers. After the publication of his AAFLI report, Ballinger set out to transform Nike's competitive strength into a strategic vulnerability.

For several years he worked at the fringes of the activist world, operating out of his in-laws' basement and publishing his own newsletter on Nike's practices. For the most part, no one really noticed. But then, in the early 1990s Ballinger's arguments coincided with the strikes that swept across Indonesia and the newfound interest of media groups. Suddenly his stories were big news and both the Indonesian government and U.S. firms had begun to pay attention.

Early Changes   The first party to respond to criticism from Ballinger and other activists was the government itself. In January 1992 Indonesia raised the official minimum daily wage from 2100 rupiah to 2500 rupiah (US$1.24). According to outside observers, the new wage still was not nearly enough: it only provided 70% of a worker's required minimal physical need (as determined by the Indonesian government) and was further diluted by the way in which many factories distributed wages and

benefits.[15] The increased wage also had no impact on "training wages," which were lower than the minimum wage and often paid long after the training period had expired. Many factories, moreover, either ignored the new wage regulations or successfully petitioned the government for exemption. Still, the government's actions at least demonstrated some willingness to respond. The critics took note of this movement and continued their strikes and media attacks.

Despite the criticism, Nike insisted that labor conditions in its contractors' factories were not— could not—be Nike's concern or its responsibility. And even if labor violations did exist in Nike's contracting factories, stated the company's general manager in Jakarta, "I don't know that I need to know."[16] Nike's company line on the issue was clear and stubborn: without an inhouse manufacturing facility, the company simply could not be held responsible for the actions of independent contractors.

Realizing the severity of the labor issue, though, Nike did ask Dusty Kidd, a newly hired member of its public relations department, to draft a series of regulations for its contractors. In 1992, these regulations were composed into a Code of Conduct and Memorandum of Understanding and attached to the new contracts sent to Nike contractors. In the Memorandum, Nike addressed seven different aspects of working conditions, including safety standards, environmental regulation and worker insurance. It required its suppliers to certify they were following all applicable rules and regulations and outlined general principles of honesty, respect, and non-discrimination.

Meanwhile, other shoe companies had been facing similar problems. Reebok, a chief competitor of Nike, also sourced heavily from Indonesia and South Korea. Like Nike, it too had been the subject of activist pressure and unflattering media. But

---

[14]Ibid.

[15]A factory, for example, could pay a base wage lower than 2500 rupiah, but bring total compensation up to legal levels by the addition of a food allowance and incentive payments (see Aznam, p. 50).

[16]Adam Schwarz, "Running a Business," *Far Eastern Economic Review,* June 20, 1991, p. 16.

unlike Nike, Reebok had moved aggressively into the human rights arena. In 1988, it created the Reebok Human Rights Award, bestowed each year on youthful contributors to the cause of human rights, and in 1990 it adopted a formal human rights policy.[17] When activists accused the company of violating workers' rights in Indonesia, Reebok responded with a far-reaching set of guidelines, one that spoke the explicit language of human rights, set forth specific standards for the company's contractors and promised to audit these contractors to ensure their compliance.[18] It was a big step for an American manufacturer and considerably farther than Nike had been willing to go.

Into the Spotlight

By 1992, criticism of Nike's labor practices had begun to seep outside of Indonesia. In the August issue of *Harper's* magazine, Ballinger published an annotated pay stub from an Indonesian factory, making the soon-to-be famous comparison between workers' wages and Michael Jordan's endorsement contract. He noted that at the wage rates shown on the pay stub, it would take an Indonesian worker 44,492 years to make the equivalent of Jordan's endorsement contract.[19] Then the Portland *Oregonian,* Nike's hometown newspaper, ran a series of critical articles during the course of the 1992 Barcelona Olympics. Also at the Olympics, a small band of protestors materialized and handed out leaflets that charged Nike with exploitation of factory workers. The first mainstream coverage of the issue came in July 1993, when CBS interviewed Indonesian workers who revealed that they were paid just 19¢ an hour. Women workers could only leave the company barracks on Sunday, and needed a special letter of permission from management to do so. Nike responded somewhat more forcefully to this next round of allegations, hiring accounting firm Ernst & Young to conduct formal audits of

its overseas factories. However, because Ernst & Young was paid by Nike to perform these audits, activists questioned their objectivity from the start. Public criticism of Nike's labor practices continued to mount.

Then suddenly, in 1996, the issue of foreign labor abuse acquired a name and a face: it was Kathie Lee Gifford, a popular daytime talk show host. In April human rights activists revealed that a line of clothing endorsed by Gifford had been manufactured by child labor in Honduras. Rather than denying the connection Gifford instantly rallied to the cause. When she appeared on television, crying and apologetic, a wave of media coverage erupted. Or as Ballinger recalls, "That's when my phone really started ringing."[20] Although Nike was not directly involved in the Gifford scandal, it quickly emerged as a symbol of worker exploitation and a high-profile media scapegoat.

Child labor was the first area of concern. In July, *Life* magazine ran a story about child labor in Pakistan, and published a photo of a 12-year-old boy stitching a Nike soccer ball.[21] Then Gifford herself publicly called upon fellow celebrities such as Michael Jordan to investigate the conditions under which their endorsed products were made and to take action if need be. Jordan brushed away suggestions that he was personally responsible for conditions in Nike factories, leaving responsibility to the company itself. When Nike refused to let Reverend Jesse Jackson tour one of its Indonesian factories the media jumped all over the story, noting by contrast that Reebok had recently flown an executive to Indonesia just to give Jackson a tour.

At this point, even some pro-business observers began to jump on the bandwagon. As an editorial in *Business Week* cautioned: "Too few executives understand that the clamor for ethical sourcing isn't

▌ [17]Rosenzweig and Woo, p. 7.
▌ [18]Ibid., pp. 16–17.
▌ [19]Jeff Ballinger, "The New Free-Trade Heel," *Harper's Magazine,* August 1992, p. 64.

▌ [20]Casewriter interview.
▌ [21]Nike's vigorous protests stopped the magazine from running the photo on its cover. Nike convincingly argued that the photo was staged, because the ball was inflated so that the Nike "swoosh" was clearly visible. In fact, soccer balls are stitched while deflated. However, the company did admit it had inadvertently relied on child labor during its first months of production in Pakistan.

going to disappear with the wave of a magic press release. They have protested, disingenuously, that conditions at factories run by subcontractors are beyond their control. . . . Such attitudes won't wash anymore. As the industry gropes for solutions," the editorial concluded, "Nike will be a key company to watch."[22]

The View from Washington   Before long, the spotlight on the labor issue extended all the way to Washington. Sensing a hot issue, several senators and representatives jumped into the action and began to suggest legislative solutions to the issue of overseas labor abuse. Representative George Miller (D-CA) launched a campaign aimed at retailers that would mandate the use of "No Sweat" labels to guarantee that no exploited or child labor had been employed in the production of a garment. "Parents," he proclaimed, "have a right to know that the toys and clothes they buy for their children are not made by exploited children." To enforce such guarantees, Miller added, "I think Congress is going to have to step in."[23]

On the heels of this public outcry, President Clinton convened a Presidential task force to study the issue, calling on leaders in the apparel and footwear industries to join and help develop acceptable labor standards for foreign factories. Known as the Apparel Industry Partnership (AIP), the coalition, which also included members of the activist, labor, and religious communities, was meant to be a model collaboration between industry and its most outspoken critics, brokered by the U.S. government. Nike was the first company to join.

In order to supplement its hiring of Ernst & Young, in October 1996 Nike also established a Labor Practices Department, headed by former public relations executive Dusty Kidd. In a press release, Knight announced the formation of the new department and praised Nike's recent initiatives regarding fair labor practices, such as participation in

Clinton's AIP, membership in the organization Business for Social Responsibility, and an ongoing dialogue with concerned non-governmental organizations (NGOs). "Every year we continue to raise the bar," said Knight. "First by having Ernst & Young audits, and now with a group of Nike employees whose sole focus will be to help make things better for workers who make Nike products. In labor practices as in sport, we at Nike believe 'There is No Finish Line.' "[24] And indeed he was right, for the anti-Nike campaign was just getting started.

The Hotseat   As far as public relations were concerned, 1997 was even worse for Nike than 1996. Much as Ballinger had anticipated, Nike's giant marketing machine was easily turned against itself and in a climate awash with anti-Nike sentiment, any of Nike's attempts at self promotion became easy targets. In 1997 the company began expanding its chain of giant retail stores, only to find that each newly opened Niketown came with an instant protest rally, complete with shouting spectators, sign-waving picketers, and police barricades. Knowing a good story when they saw it, reporters eagerly dragged Nike's celebrity endorsers into the fracas. Michael Jordan was pelted with questions about Nike at press conferences intended to celebrate his athletic performance, and football great Jerry Rice was hounded to the point of visible agitation when he arrived at the grand opening of a new Niketown in San Francisco.[25]

Perhaps one of the clearest indicators that Nike was in trouble came in May 1997, when Doonesbury, the popular comic strip, devoted a full week to Nike's labor issues. In 1,500 newspapers, millions of readers watched as Kim, Mike Doonesbury's wife, returned to Vietnam and found a long-lost cousin laboring in dismal conditions at a Nike factory. The strips traced Kim's growing involvement in the activist movement and the corrupt

[22]Mark L. Clifford, "Commentary: Keep the Heat on Sweatshops," *Business Week,* December 23, 1996, p. 90.

[23]"Honduran Child Labor Described," *The Boston Globe,* May 30, 1996, p. 13.

[24]"Nike Establishes Labor Practices Department," *PR Newswire,* October 2, 1996.

[25]"Protestors Swipe at the Swoosh, Catch Nike's Jerry Rice Off Guard," *The Portland Oregonian,* February 21, 1997, p. C1.

factory manager's attempts to deceive her about true working conditions in Nike contracting factories. In Doonesbury, Nike had reached an unfortunate cultural milestone. As one media critic noted: "It's sort of like getting in Jay Leno's monologue. It means your perceived flaws have reached a critical mass, and everyone feels free to pick on you."[26] The appearance of the Doonesbury strips also marked the movement of anti-Nike sentiment from the fringes of American life to the mainstream. Once the pet cause of leftist activists, Nike bashing had become America's newest spectator sport.

Even some of the company's natural friends took a dim view of its actions. The *Wall Street Journal* ran an opinion piece alleging that "Nike Lets Critics Kick It Around." The writer argued that Nike had been "its own worst enemy" and that its public relations efforts had only made the problem worse. According to the writer, had Nike acknowledged its wrongdoing early on and then presented economic facts that showed the true situation of the workers, the crisis would have fizzled.[27] Instead it had simply gathered steam. Even more trouble loomed ahead with the anticipated release of *The Big One,* a documentary film by Michael Moore that was widely expected to be highly critical of Nike's labor practices.

▌ Damage Control

Late in 1996 the company decided to turn to outside sources, hiring Andrew Young, the respected civil rights leader and former mayor of Atlanta, to conduct an independent evaluation of its Code of Conduct. In January 1997, Knight granted Young's newly formed GoodWorks International firm "blanket authority . . . to go anywhere, see anything, and talk with anybody in the Nike family about this issue."[28]

Shortly thereafter Young went to Asia, visited Nike suppliers and returned to issue a formal report. On the day the report was released, Nike took out full-page advertisements in major newspapers that highlighted one of Young's main conclusions: "It is my sincere belief that Nike is doing a good job. . . . But Nike can and should do better."[29] Young did not give Nike carte blanche with regard to labor practices. Indeed, he made a number of recommendations, urging Nike to improve their systems for reporting workers' grievances, to publicize their Code more widely and explain it more clearly, and to implement cultural awareness and language training programs for expatriate managers. Young also stated that third party monitoring of factories was necessary, but agreed that it was not appropriate for Nike's NGO critics to fulfill that function.

Rather than calming Nike's critics, though, Young's report had precisely the opposite effect. Critics were outraged by the report's research methodology and conclusions, and unimpressed by Young's participation. They argued that Young had failed to address the issue of factory wages, which was for many observers the crux of the issue, and had spent only 10 days interviewing workers. During these interviews, moreover, Young had relied on translators provided by Nike, a major lapse in accepted human rights research technique. Finally, critics also noted that the report was filled with photos and used a large, showy typeface, an unusual format for a research report.

From the start, Nike executives had argued in vain that they were the target of an uninformed media campaign, pointing out that although Nike was being vigorously monitored by activists and the media, no one was monitoring the monitors. This point was forcefully made by the publication of a five page *New Republic* article in which writer Stephen Glass blasted the Young report for factual inaccuracies and deception, and summed up: "This was a public relations problem, and the world's largest sneaker company did what it does best: it purchased a celebrity endorsement."[30] Glass's

---

[26]Jeff Manning, "Doonesbury Could Put Legs on Nike Controversy," *The Portland Oregonian,* May 25, 1997, p. D01.

[27]Greg Rushford, "Nike Lets Critics Kick it Around," *The Wall Street Journal,* May 12, 1997, p. A14.

[28]Andrew Young, *Report: The Nike Code of Conduct* (GoodWorks International, LLC, 1997) p. 27.

[29]Young, p. 59.

[30]Stephen Glass, "The Young and the Feckless," *The New Republic,* September 8, 1997, p. 22.

claims were echoed by several other media outlets that also decried Nike's disingenuousness and Young's ineptitude. However, within months a major scandal erupted at the *New Republic* when it was discovered that most of Glass's articles were nearly fictional. Apparently, Glass routinely quoted individuals with whom he had never spoken or who did not even exist, and relied upon statistics and information from organizations he invented himself.

The Issue of Wages

In the public debate, the question of labor conditions was largely couched in the language of human rights. It was about child labor, or slave labor, or workers who toiled in unsafe or inhumane environments. Buried beneath these already contentious issues, though, was an even more contentious one: wages. According to many labor activists, workers in the developing world were simply being paid too little—too little to compensate for their efforts, too little compared to the final price of the good they produced, too little, even, to live on. To many business economists, though, such arguments were moot at best and veiled protectionism at worst. Wages, they maintained, were simply set by market forces: by definition, wages could not be too low, and there was nothing firms could or should do to affect wage rates. As the debate over labor conditions evolved, the argument over wages had become progressively more heated.

Initially, Nike sought to defuse the wage issue simply by ignoring it, or by reiterating the argument that this piece of the labor situation was too far beyond their control. In the Young Report, therefore, the issue of wages was explicitly set aside. As Young explained in his introduction: "I was not asked by Nike to address compensation and 'cost of living' issues which some in the human rights and NGO community had hoped would be a part of this report." Then he went on: "Are workers in developing countries paid far less than U.S. workers? Of course they are. Are their standards of living painfully low by U.S. standards? Of course they are. This is a blanket criticism that can be leveled at almost every U.S. company that manufactures

abroad. . . . But it is not reasonable to argue that any one particular U.S. company should be forced to pay U.S. wages abroad while its direct competitors do not."[31] It was a standard argument, and one that found strong support even among many pro-labor economists. In the heat of public debate, however, it registered only as self-serving.

The issue of wages emerged again in the spring of 1997, when Nike arranged for students at Dartmouth's Amos Tuck School of Business to conduct a detailed survey on "the suitability of wages and benefits paid to its Vietnamese and Indonesian contract factory workers."[32] Completed in November 1997, the students' *Survey of Vietnamese and Indonesian Domestic Expenditure Levels* was a 45-page written study with approximately 50 pages of attached data. The authors surveyed both workers and residents of the areas in which the factories were located to determine typical spending patterns and the cost of basic necessities.

In Vietnam, the students found that "The factory workers, after incurring essential expenditures, can generate a significant amount of discretionary income."[33] This discretionary income was often used by workers to purchase special items such as bicycles or wedding gifts for family members. In Indonesia, results varied with worker demographics. While 91% of workers reported being able to support themselves individually, only 49% reported being able to also support their dependents. Regardless of demographic status, 82% of workers surveyed in Indonesia either saved wages or contributed each month to their families.[34]

Additionally, the survey found that most workers were not the primary wage earners in their households. Rather, in Vietnam at least, factory wages were generally earned by young men or women and served "to *augment* aggregate household income,

[31]Young, pp. 9–11.
[32]Derek Calzini, Shawna Huffman, Jake Odden, Steve Tran, and Jean Tsai, *Nike, Inc: Survey of Vietnamese and Indonesian Domestic Expenditure Levels,* November 3, 1997, Field Study in International Business (Dartmouth, NH: The Amos Tuck School, 1997), p. 5.
[33]Ibid., p. 8.
[34]Ibid., p. 9.

with the primary occupation of the household parents being farming or shopkeeping."[35] The same was often true in Indonesia. For instance, in one Indonesian household the students visited, a family of six had used one daughter's minimum wage from a Nike factory to purchase luxury items such as leather couches and a king sized bed.[36] While workers in both countries managed to save wages for future expenditure, the authors found that Indonesians typically put their wages in a bank, while Vietnamese workers were more likely to hold their savings in the form of rice or cows.

Economically, data such as these supported the view that companies such as Nike were actually furthering progress in the developing countries, providing jobs and wages to people who formerly had neither. In the public view, however, the social comparison was unavoidable. According to the Tuck study, the average worker in a Vietnamese Nike factory made about $1.67 per day. A pair of Penny Hardaway basketball sneakers retailed at $150. The criticism continued to mount.

In November there was even more bad news. A disgruntled Nike employee leaked excerpts of an internal Ernst & Young report that uncovered serious health and safety issues in a factory outside of Ho Chi Minh City. According to the Ernst & Young report, a majority of workers suffered from a respiratory ailment caused by poor ventilation and exposure to toxic chemicals. The plant did not have proper safety equipment and training, and workers were forced to work 15 more hours than allowed by law. But according to spokesman Vada Manager the problems no longer existed: "This shows our system of monitoring works. We have uncovered these issues clearly before anyone else, and we have moved fairly expeditiously to correct them."[37] Once again, the denial only made the criticism worse.

Hitting the Wall

Fiscal Year 1998   Until the spring of 1997, Nike sneakers were still selling like hotcakes. The company's stock price had hit $76 and futures orders reached a record high. Despite the storm of criticism lobbied against it, Nike seemed invincible.

Just a year later, however, the situation was drastically different. As Knight admitted to stockholders, Nike's fiscal year 1998 "produced considerable pain." In the third quarter 1998, the company was beset by weak demand and retail oversupply, triggered in part by the Asian currency crisis. Earnings fell 69%, the company's first loss in 13 years. In response, Knight announced significant restructuring charges and the layoff of 1,600 workers.[38]

Much the same dynamic that drove labor criticism drove the 1998 downturn: Nike became a victim of its own popularity. Remarked one analyst: "When I was growing up, we used to say that rooting for the Yankees is like rooting for U.S. Steel. Today, rooting for Nike is like rooting for Microsoft."[39] The company asserted that criticism of Nike's labor practices had nothing to do with the downturn. But it was clear that Nike was suffering from a serious image problem. For whatever reasons, Americans were sick of the swoosh. Although Nike billed its shoes as high-performance athletic gear, it was well known that 80% of its shoes were sold for fashion purposes. And fashion was a notoriously fickle patron. Competing sneaker manufacturers, particularly Adidas, were quick to take advantage of the giant's woes. Adidas' three-stripe logo fast replaced Nike's swoosh among the teen trendsetter crowd; rival brands New Balance and Airwalk tripled their advertising budgets and saw sales surge.

To make matters worse, the anti-Nike headlines had trickled down to the nation's campuses, where a

[35]Ibid., p. 31.
[36]Ibid., p. 44.
[37]Tunku Varadarajan, "Nike Audit Uncovers Health Hazards at Factory," *The Times of London,* November 10, 1997, p. 52.

[38]Nike Corporation, *Annual Report 1998* (Nike, Inc.: Beaverton, OR) p. 1, 17–30.
[39]Quoted in Patricia Sellers, "Four Reasons Nike's Not Cool," *Fortune,* March 30, 1998, p. 26.

Exhibit 1 Nike Inc. Financial History, 1989–1999 (in millions of dollars)

Year Ended May 31	1999	1998	1997	1996	1995	1994	1993	1992	1991	1990	1989
Revenues	$8,776.9	$9,553.1	$9,186.5	$6,470.6	$4,760.8	$3,789.7	$3,931.0	$3,405.2	$3,003.6	$2,235.2	$1,710.8
Gross margin	3,283.4	3,487.6	3,683.5	2,563.9	1,895.6	1,488.2	1,544.0	1,316.1	1,153.1	851.1	636.0
Gross margin %	37.4	36.5	40.1	39.6	39.8	39.3	39.3	38.7	38.4	38.1	37.2
Restructuring charge, net	45.1	129.9	—	—	—	—	—	—	—	—	—
Net income	451.4	399.6	795.8	553.2	399.7	298.8	365.0	329.2	287.0	243.0	167.0
Cash flow from operations	961.0	517.5	323.1	339.7	254.9	576.5	265.3	435.8	11.1	127.1	169.4
Price range of common stock											
High	65.500	64.125	76.375	52.063	20.156	18.688	22.563	19.344	13.625	10.375	4.969
Low	31.750	37.750	47.875	19.531	14.063	10.781	13.750	8.781	6.500	4.750	2.891
Cash and equivalents	$198.1	$108.6	$445.4	$262.1	$216.1	$518.8	$291.3	$260.1	$119.8	$90.4	$85.7
Inventories	1,199.3	1,396.6	1,338.6	931.2	629.7	470.0	593.0	471.2	586.6	309.5	222.9
Working capital	1,818.0	1,828.8	1,964.0	1,259.9	938.4	1,208.4	1,165.2	964.3	662.6	561.6	419.6
Total assets	5,247.7	5,397.4	5,361.2	3,951.6	3,142.7	2,373.8	2,186.3	1,871.7	1,707.2	1,093.4	824.2
Long-term debt	386.1	379.4	296.0	9.6	10.6	12.4	15.0	69.5	30.0	25.9	34.1
Shareholders' equity	3,334.6	3,261.6	3,155.9	2,431.4	1,964.7	1,740.9	1,642.8	1,328.5	1,029.6	781.0	558.6
Year-end stock price	60.938	46.000	57.500	50.188	19.719	14.750	18.125	14.500	9.938	9.813	4.750
Market capitalization	17,202.2	13,201.1	16,633.0	14,416.8	5,635.2	4,318.8	5,499.3	4,379.6	2,993.0	2,942.7	1,417.4
Geographic Revenues:											
United States	$5,042.6	$5,460.0	$5,538.2	$3,964.7	$2,997.9	$2,432.7	$2,528.8	$2,270.9	$2,141.5	$1,755.5	$1,362.2
Europe	2,255.8	2,096.1	1,789.8	1,334.3	980.4	927.3	1,085.7	919.8	664.7	334.3	241.4
Asia/Pacific	844.5	1,253.9	1,241.9	735.1	515.6	283.4	178.2	75.7	56.2	29.3	32.0
Americas (exclusive of U.S.)	634.0	743.1	616.6	436.5	266.9	146.3	138.3	138.8	141.2	116.1	75.2
Total revenues	$8,776.9	$9,553.1	$9,186.5	$6,470.6	$4,760.8	$3,789.7	$3,931.0	$3,405.2	$3,003.6	$2,235.2	$1,710.8

All per common share data has been adjusted to reflect the 2-for-1 stock splits paid October 23, 1996, October 30, 1995 and October 5, 1990. The Company's Class B Common Stock is listed on the New York and Pacific Exchanges and traded under the symbol NKE. At May 31, 1999, there were approximately 170,000 shareholders.
Source: Nike, Inc., *Annual Report 1999.*

Exhibit 2	Estimated Cost Breakdown of an Average Nike Shoe, 1999
$ 3.37	Labor costs
$ 3.41	Manufacturer's overhead
$14.60	Materials
$ 1.12	Profit to factory
$22.50	Factory price to Nike
$45	Wholesale price
$90	Retail price

Source: Jennifer Lin, "Vietnam Gives Nike a Run for Its Money," *The Philadelphia Enquirer,* March 23, 1998, p. 1.

newly invigorated activist movement cast Nike as a symbol of corporate greed and exploitation. With its roots deep in the University of Oregon track team (Knight had been a long-distance runner for the school), Nike had long treasured its position as supplier to the top athletic universities. Now, just as young consumers were choosing Adidas over Nike at the cash register, campus activists rejected Nike's contracts with their schools and demanded all contracts cease until labor practices were rectified. In late 1997, Nike's $7.2 million endorsement deal with the University of North Carolina sparked protests and controversy on campus; in early 1998 an assistant soccer coach at St. John's University, James Keady, publicly quit his job rather than wear the swoosh. "I don't want to be a billboard for a company that would do these things," said Keady.[40]

Before long, the student protests spread to campuses where Nike had no merchandising contracts. Organized and trained by unions such as UNITE! and the AFL-CIO, previously apathetic college students stormed university buildings to protest sweatshop labor and the exploitation of foreign workers. In 1999, activists took over buildings at Duke, Georgetown, the University of Michigan and the University of Wisconsin, and staged sit-ins at countless other colleges and universities. The protests focused mostly on the conditions under which collegiate logo gear was manufactured. Declared Tom Wheatley, a Wisconsin student and national movement leader: "It really is quite sick. Fourteen-year-old girls are working 100-hour weeks and earning poverty-level wages to make my college T-shirts. That's unconscionable."[41] University administrators heeded the student protests, and many began to consider codes of conduct for contract manufacturers.

Saving the Swoosh   Nike's fiscal woes did what hundreds of harsh articles had failed to do: they took some of the bravado out of Phil Knight. In a May 1998 speech to the National Press Club, a humbled Knight admitted that "the Nike product has become synonymous with slave wages, forced overtime, and arbitrary abuse."[42] Knight announced a series of sweeping reforms, including raising the minimum age of all sneaker workers to 18 and apparel workers to 16; adopting U.S. OSHA clean air standards in all its factories; expanding its monitoring program; expanding educational programs for workers; and making micro loans available to workers. Although Nike had been formally addressing labor issues since 1992, Knight's confession marked a turning point in Nike's stance towards its critics. For the first time, he and his company appeared ready to shed their defensive stance, admit labor violations did occur in Nike factories, and refashion themselves as leaders in the effort to reform third world working conditions.

Nike's second step was to get more involved with Washington-based reform efforts. In the summer of 1998, President Clinton's initial task force on labor, the Apparel Industry Partnership (AIP), lay deadlocked over the ever-delicate issues of factory monitoring and wages. Although the AIP had a tentative proposal, discussion ground to a halt when the task force's union, religious, and corporate members clashed.

---

[40]William McCall, "Nike's Image Under Attack: Sweatshop Charges Begin to Take a Toll on the Brand's Cachet," *The Buffalo News,* October 23, 1998, p. 5E.

[41]Nancy Cleeland, "Students Give Sweatshop Fight the College Try," *Los Angeles Times,* April 22, 1999, p. C1.

[42]John H. Cushman Jr., "Nike to Step Forward on Plant Conditions," *The San-Diego Union-Tribune,* May 13, 1998, p. Al.

Exhibit 3   Prices of Some Popular Running Shoe Styles in New York City, 1996

	Nike Air Max		New Balance 999		Saucony Grid Shadow	
	Men's	Women's	Men's	Women's	Men's	Women's
Foot Locker	$140	$135	$124	$105	$85	$85
Paragon Sports	140	135	135	109	70	70
Sports Authority	140	140	101	101	78	78
Super Runners Shop	140	130	125	110	85	85

Source: "Feet Don't Fail . . . ," *The New York Times,* November 3, 1996, Section 13, p. 12.

Exhibit 4   Summary Revenue and Expense Profile of Minimum Wage Workers by Demographic Type (in Indonesian Rupiah)

	SH	SO	Dorm	MH	MO	Total (weighted)
Number of respondents	67	161	33	21	32	314
Base wages	172,812	172,071	172,197	173,905	172,650	172,424
Total wages	**225,378**	**238,656**	**239,071**	**248,794**	**244,458**	**236,893**
Rent	14,677	40,955	12,121[a]	24,775	56,050	32,838
Food	84,774	95,744	90,455	103,421	128,793	103,020
Transportation	48,984	24,189	7,219	17,471	38,200	28,560
Savings	38,369	41,783	70,303	29,412	49,185	44,154
Contribution to home	22,175	37,594	57,644	25,222	25,089	34,441
Total uses	**208,980**	**240,266**	**237,741**	**200,301**	**297,318**	**243,013**

[a]17 of the 33 respondents were provided free housing by the factory. The remaining 16 paid a subsidized monthly rent of Rp 25,000.
Note: Monthly wages and total uses of wages may not match due to averaging.

Key to demographic type:

SH—Single workers living at home
SO—Single workers living away from home and paying rent
Dorm—Single workers living away from home and living in factory subsidized housing
MH—Married workers living at home
MO—Married workers living away from home

Source: Derek Calzini, Shawna Huffman, Jake Odden, Steve Tran, and Jean Tsai, *Nike, Inc: Survey of Vietnamese and Indonesian Domestic Expenditure Levels,* November 3, 1997, Field Study in International Business (Dartmouth, NH: The Amos Tuck School, 1997), pp. 9–10.

While the AIP proclaimed itself as an exemplar of cooperative solution making, it soon became apparent that its members had very different views. One key concept—"independent monitoring"—was highly contentious. To Nike, the hiring of a separate and unrelated multinational firm like Ernst & Young fulfilled any call for independent monitoring. But activists and other critics alleged that if an independent monitor, such as an accounting firm, was hired by a corporation, it thereby automatically lost autonomy and independence. According to such critics, independent monitoring could only be done by an organization that was not on a corporate payroll, such as an NGO or a

Exhibit 5   Typical "Basket" of Basic Food Expenditures for Indonesian Workers (in rupiah)

Rice	800–1,300	Per 5 servings
Instant noodles	300–500	Per serving
Eggs	2,800–3,000	Per 18 eggs
Tofu	1,500	Per 15 servings
Tempe	1,500	Per 15 servings
Kancang pangung	1,500	Per 15 servings
Peanuts	2,600	Per kilogram
Oil	2,300	Per liter
Other "luxury" foods		
Fish	6,000	Per kilogram
Chicken	4,500–5,000	Per chicken

Source: Derek Calzini, Shawna Huffman, Jake Odden, Steve Tran, and Jean Tsai, *Nike, Inc.: Survey of Vietnamese and Indonesian Domestic Expenditure Levels,* November 3, 1997, Field Study in International Business (Dartmouth, NH: The Amos Tuck School, 1997), p. 45.

Exhibit 6   Strikes and Lockouts in Indonesia, 1988–1997

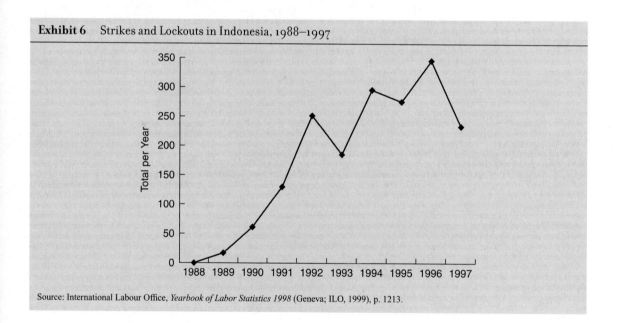

Source: International Labour Office, *Yearbook of Labor Statistics 1998* (Geneva; ILO, 1999), p. 1213.

religious group. The corporations, by contrast, insisted that a combination of internal monitoring and audits by accounting firms was sufficient. Upset at what they saw as corporate intransigence, the task force's union and religious membership abruptly exited the coalition.

The remaining corporate members of the AIP were soon able to cobble together a more definitive agreement, complete with an oversight organization known as the Fair Labor Association (FLA). The FLA was to be a private entity controlled evenly by corporate members and human rights or

Exhibit 7   Wages and Productivity in Industrialized and Developing Nations (figures in $ per year)

	Average Hours Worked per Week		Yearly Minimum Wage		Labor Cost per Worker in Manufacturing		Value Added per Worker in Manufacturing	
	1980–84	1990–94	1980–84	1990–94	1980–84	1990–94	1980–84	1990–94
North America								
United States	35	34	6,006	8,056[b]	19,103	32,013[b]	47,276	81,353
Canada	32	33	4,974	7,897[b]	17,710	28,346[b]	36,903	60,712
Mexico	—	34	1,002	843	3,772	6,138	17,448	25,991
Europe								
Denmark	—	37	9,170	19,933[b]	16,169	35,615[b]	27,919	49,273
France	39	39	10,815	22,955[b]	16,060	38,900[b]	26,751	61,019[e]
Germany	41	40	[a]	[a]	21,846[d]	63,956[b,d]	—	—
Greece	—	41	—	5,246	6,461	15,899[b]	14,561	30,429
Ireland	41[c]	41[c]	—	—	10,190	25,414[b]	26,510	86,036
Netherlands	40	39	9,074	15,170[b]	18,891	39,865[b]	27,491	56,801
Asia								
China (PRC)	—	—	—	—	472	434[d]	3,061	2,885
Hong Kong	48	46	—	—	4,127	13,539[b]	7,886	19,533
India	48	48	—	408	1,035	1,192	2,108	3,118
Indonesia	—	—	—	241	898	1,008	3,807	5,139
Japan	47	46	3,920	8,327[b]	12,306	40,104[b]	34,456	92,582
South Korea	52	48	—	3,903[b]	3,153	15,819[b]	11,617	40,916
Malaysia	—	—	—	[a]	2,519	3,429	8,454	12,661
Philippines	—	43	—	1,067	1,240	2,459	5,266	9,339
Singapore	—	46	—	—	5,576	21,534[b]	16,442	40,674
Thailand	48	—	—	1,083	2,305	2,705	11,072	19,946

[a]Country has sectoral minimum wage but no minimum wage policy. [b]Data refer to 1995–1999. [c]Data refer to hours worked per week in manufacturing. [d]Data refer to wage per worker in manufacturing. [e]International Labor Organisation data.
Source: World Bank, *World Development Indicators 1999* (Washington, D.C.; World Bank, 1999), pp. 62–64.

labor representatives (if they chose to rejoin the coalition). It would support a code of conduct that required its members to pay workers the legal minimum wage or the prevailing local standard, whichever was higher. The minimum age of workers was set at 15, and employees could not be required to work more than 60 hours per week. Companies that joined the Association would be required to comply with these guidelines and to establish internal monitoring systems to enforce them; they would then be audited by certified independent inspectors, such as accounting firms. In the first three years after a company joined, auditors would inspect 30% of a company's factories; later they would inspect 10%. All audits would be confidential.

Nike worked tirelessly to bring other manufacturers into the FLA, but the going was tough. As of August 1999, the only other corporate members were Adidas, Liz Claiborne, Reebok, Levi's, L.L. Bean, and Phillips Van Heusen. However, Nike's efforts to foster the FLA hit pay dirt with U.S.

Exhibit 8   Indonesia: Wages and Inflation, 1993–1997

	1993		1994		1995		1996		1997	
	Mini-mum	Maxi-mum	Mini-mum	Maxi-mum	Mini-mum	Maxi-mum	Mini-mum	Maxi-mum	Mini-mum	Maxi-mum
Monthly wages in manufacturing industry (thousands of rupiah)	196	2,920	207	3,112	238	3,453	241	3,453	439	6,050
Minimum wage regional average[a] (thousands of rupiah)	72		94		112		118		130	
Annual percent change	17.7		30.8		19.5		5.4		10.2	
Consumer price inflation	8.5		9.4		8.0		6.7		57.6	
Exchange rates (average Rp:$)	2,161		2,249		2,342		2,909		10,014	

Figures are based on periodic surveys of primarily urban-based business establishments and include transportation, meal, and attendance allowances.
[a]Calculated from minimum daily figure for 30 days per month. Increased by 9% to Rp122,000 in 1996 and by 10% to Rp135,000 in 1997.
Source: International Monetary Fund, Economist Intelligence Unit.

colleges and universities. The vocal student anti-sweatshop movement had many administrators scrambling to find a solution, and over 100 colleges and universities eventually signed on. Participants ranged from the large state universities that held Nike contracts to the eight Ivy League schools. The FLA was scheduled to be fully operational by the fall of 2000.

Meanwhile, by 1999 Nike was running extensive training programs for its contractors' factory managers. All managers and supervisors were required to learn the native language of their workers, and received training in cultural differences and acceptable management styles. In addition to 25 employees who would focus solely on corporate responsibility, Nike's 1,000 production employees were explicitly required to devote part of their job to maintaining labor standards. In Vietnam, the company partnered with the National University of Vietnam in a program designed to identify and meet worker needs. It also helped found the Global Alliance, a partnership between the International Youth Foundation, the MacArthur Foundation, the World Bank, and Mattel, that was dedicated to improving the lives of workers in the developing world.

Although Nike's various concessions and new programs were welcomed as a victory by several human rights groups, other observers argued that Nike still failed to deal with the biggest problem, namely wages.[43] Wrote *New York Times* columnist Bob Herbert: "Mr. Knight is like a three-card monte player. You have to keep a close eye on him at all times. The biggest problem with Nike is that its overseas workers make wretched, below-subsistence wages. It's not the minimum age that needs raising,

[43]John H. Cushman, Jr., "Nike Pledges to End Child Labor and Apply U.S. Rules Abroad," *The New York Times,* May 13, 1998, p. D1.

Exhibit 9   *Life* Magazine Photo of Pakistani Child Worker

Source: *Life* magazine, June 1996, p. 39.

Exhibit 10   Doonesbury Cartoons about Nike

Copyright: Doonesbury © 1997 G. B. Trudeau. Reprinted with Permission of Universal Press Syndicate. All rights reserved.

Exhibit 11   Anti-Nike Activist Materials

Nike, Inc. in Indonesia I

JUST DO IT!

"You know when you need a break. And you know when it's time to take care of yourself, for yourself. Because you know it's never too late to have a life. " (Nike advertisement)

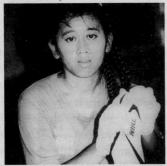

Twelve thousand Indonesian woman work 60 hours a week making Nike shoes. Many earn less than their government's minimum wage of $1.80 a day. Numerous strikes and protests have been broken up by security forces eager to placate foreign capital; labor activists have even been murdered. Factories producing Nike shoes have been cited in the State Department's Human Rights Report to Congress. Asked about local labor practices, Nike VP David Taylor said: "I don't feel bad about it. I don't think we are doing anything wrong."

One percent of Nike's advertising budget would double the wages of the women making the company's shoes and raise them above the poverty line.

Nike, Inc. in Indonesia newsletter: *$20 for six months, teachers free*
Press for Change, Inc. PO Box 230, Bayonne, New Jersey, 07002-9998

Source: Jeff Ballinger; http://www.nikeworkers.org [10/29/99]; http://www.corpwatch.org/nike/ [10/29/99].

it's the minimum wage."[44] Similarly, while some labor leaders accepted the FLA as the best compromise possible, others decried it as sham agreement that simply provided cover for U.S. corporations. A main objection of these critics was that the FLA standards included notification of factories that were to be inspected, a move criticized by some as equivalent to notifying a restaurant when a critic was coming to dine. According to Jeff Ballinger, Nike's original critic, the company's reform record was mixed. Ballinger was confident that Nike had at least removed dangerous chemicals from factories, but otherwise he remained skeptical: "If you present yourself as a fitness company you can't very well go around the globe poisoning people. But on wages, they're still lying through their teeth."[45]

[44]Bob Herbert, "Nike Blinks," *The New York Times,* May 21, 1998, p. A33.

[45]Casewriter interview.

Reading 2-1   Culture and Organization

Susan Schneider and Jean-Louis Barsoux

Intuitively, people have always assumed that bureaucratic structures and patterns of action differ in the different countries of the Western world and even more markedly between East and West. Practitioners know it and never fail to take it into account. But contemporary social scientists . . . have not been concerned with such comparisons.

Michel Crozier[1]

Just how does culture influence organization structure and process? To what extent do organizational structures and processes have an inherent logic which overrides cultural considerations? Given the nature of today's business demands, do we find convergence in the ways of organizing? To what extent will popular techniques such as team management and empowerment be adopted across cultures? With what speed and with what possible (re) interpretation? What cultural dimensions need to be recognized which may facilitate or hinder organizational change efforts?

In order to demonstrate the impact of culture on organizational structure, systems, and processes, we present the evidence for national differences and consider the cultural reasons for these differences. Examining the degree to which organizations have centralized power, specialized jobs and roles, and formalized rules and procedures, we find distinct patterns of organizing which prevail despite pressures for convergence. This raises concerns regarding the transferability of organizational forms across borders and questions the logic of universal "best practices."

▇ Different Schools, Different Cultures

While many managers are ready to accept that national culture may influence the way people relate to each other, or the "soft stuff," they are less convinced that it can really affect the nuts and bolts of organization: structure, systems, and processes. The culture-free (or *emic*) argument is that structure is determined by *organizational* features such as size and technology. For example, the famous Aston studies,[2] conducted in the late 1960s in the United Kingdom and widely replicated, point to size as the most important factor influencing structure: larger firms tend to have greater division of labor (specialized) and more formal policies and procedures (formalized) but are not necessarily more centralized. Furthermore, the nature of technology, such as mass production, is considered to favor a more centralized and formal (mechanistic) rather than decentralized and informal (organic) approach.[3]

Other management scholars argue that the *societal* context creates differences in structure in different countries (*etic*).[4] In effect, the "structuralists" argue that structure creates culture, while the "culturalists" argue that culture creates structure. The debate continues, with each side arming up with more sophisticated weapons: measurements and methodologies.

▇ [2]Pugh, D.S., Hickson, D.J., Hinings, C.R., and Turner, C. (1969) "The context of organization structure," *Administrative Science Quarterly*, 14, 91–114; Miller, G.A. (1987) "Meta-analysis and the culture-free hypothesis," *Organization Studies*, 8(4), 309–25; Hickson, D.J. and McMillan, I. (eds) (1981) *Organization and Nation: The Aston Programme IV*, Farnborough: Gower.

▇ [3]Burns, T. and Stalker, G.M. (1961) *The Management of Innovation*, London: Tavistock.

▇ [4]Child, J. (1981) "Culture, contingency and capitalism in the cross-national study of organizations" in L.L. Cummings and B.M. Staw (eds) *Research in Organizational Behavior*, Vol 3, 303–56, Greenwich, CT: JAI Press; Scott, W.R. (1987) "The adolescence of institutional theory," *Administrative Science Quarterly*, 32, 493–511; Lincoln, J. R., Hanada, M. and McBride, K. (1986) "Organizational structures in Japanese and US manufacturing," *Administrative Science Quarterly*, 31, 338–64.

▇ [1]Crozier, M. (1964) *The Bureaucratic Phenomenon*, Chicago: University of Chicago Press, p. 210.

▇ Excerpted from *Managing Across Cultures*, by Susan Schneider and Jean-Louis Barsoux. London: Prentice-Hall, 1997.

Taking an historical perspective, theories about how best to organize—Max Weber's (German) bureaucracy, Henri Fayol's (French) administrative model, and Frederick Taylor's (American) scientific management—all reflect societal concerns of the times as well as the cultural backgrounds of the individuals.[5] Today, their legacies can be seen in the German emphasis on structure and competence, the French emphasis on social systems, roles and relationships (unity of command), and the American emphasis on the task system or machine model of organization, now popularized in the form of re-engineering.

Indeed, many of the techniques of modern management—performance management, participative management, team approach, and job enrichment all have their roots firmly embedded in a particular historical and societal context: *scientific management* in the United States at the turn of the century; *human relations,* brought about by Hawthorne studies (1930s) in the United States; *socio-technical* brought by the Tavistock studies of the coal mines in the United Kingdom (1930s); and *human resources* brought about in Sweden (1970s) with Saab Scania's and Volvo's redesign of auto assembly into autonomous teams.

These approaches reflect different cultural assumptions regarding, for example, human nature and the importance of task and relationships. While the scientific management approach focused on how best to accomplish the task, the human relations approach focused on how best to establish relationships with employees. The human resources approach assumed that workers were self-motivated, while earlier schools assumed that workers needed to be motivated by more or less benevolent management.

These models of management have diffused across countries at different rates and in different ways. For example, mass-production techniques promoted by scientific management were quickly adopted in Germany, while practices associated with the human relations school transferred more readily to Spain.[6] For this reason the historical and societal context needs to be considered to understand the adoption and diffusion of different forms of organization across countries. While some theorists focus on the *institutional arrangements,*[7] such as the nature of markets, the educational system, or the relationships between business and government, to explain these differences, we focus here, more specifically, on the cultural reasons.

This does not mean that institutional factors are irrelevant. In effect, it is quite difficult to separate out the influence of institutions from culture as they have both evolved together over time and are thus intricately linked. For example, the strong role of the state and the cultural emphasis on power and hierarchy often go hand in hand, as in the case of France. Or in the words of the French *roi soleil* Louis XIV, *L'état, c'est moi* ("The state is me"). Our argument (the culturalist perspective) is that different forms of organization emerge which reflect underlying cultural dimensions.

Culture and Structure

Hofstede's Findings   One of the most important studies which attempted to establish the impact of culture differences on management was conducted by Geert Hofstede, first in the late 1960s, and continuing through the next three decades.[8] The original study, now considered a classic, was based on an employee opinion survey involving 116,000 IBM employees in 40 different countries. From the

[5]Weber, M. (1947) *The Theory of Social and Economic Organization,* New York: Free Press; Fayol, H. (1949) *General Industrial Management,* London: Pitman; Taylor, F. (1947, first published 1912) *Scientific Management,* New York: Harper & Row.

[6]Kogut, B. (1991) "Country capabilities and the permeability of borders," *Strategic Management Journal,* 12, 33–47; Kogut, B. and Parkinson, D. (1993) "The diffusion of American organizing principles to Europe" in B. Kogut (ed.) *Country Competitiveness: Technology and the Organizing of Work,* Ch. 10, New York: Oxford University Press, 179–202; Guillen, M. (1994) "The age of eclecticism: Current organizational trends and the evolution of managerial models," *Sloan Management Review,* Fall, 75–86.

[7]Westney, D.E. (1987) *Imitation and Innovation,* Cambridge, MA: Harvard University Press.

[8]Hofstede, G. (1980) *Cultures Consequences,* Beverly Hills, CA: Sage; Hofstede, G. (1991) *Cultures and Organizations: Software of the Mind,* London: McGraw-Hill.

results of this survey, which asked people for their preferences in terms of management style and work environment, Hofstede identified four "value" dimensions on which countries differed: power distance, uncertainty avoidance, individualism/collectivism, and masculinity/femininity.

Power distance indicates the extent to which a society accepts the unequal distribution of power in institutions and organizations. **Uncertainty avoidance** refers to a society's discomfort with uncertainty, preferring predictability and stability. **Individualism/collectivism** reflects the extent to which people prefer to take care of themselves and their immediate families, remaining emotionally independent from groups, organizations, and other collectivities. And the **masculinity/femininity** dimension reveals the bias towards either "masculine" values of assertiveness, competitiveness, and materialism, or towards "feminine" values of nurturing, and the quality of life and relationships. Country rankings on each dimension are provided in Table 1.

Given the differences in value orientations, Hofstede questioned whether American theories could be applied abroad and discussed the consequences of cultural differences in terms of motivation, leadership, and organization.[9] He argued, for example, that organizations in countries with high power distance would tend to have more levels of hierarchy (vertical differentiation), a higher proportion of supervisory personnel (narrow span of control), and more centralized decision-making. Status and power would serve as motivators, and leaders would be revered or obeyed as authorities.

In countries with high uncertainty avoidance, organizations would tend to have more formalization evident in greater amount of written rules and procedures. Also there would be greater specialization evident in the importance attached to technical competence in the role of staff and in defining jobs and functions. Managers would avoid taking risks and would be motivated by stability and security.

The role of leadership would be more one of planning, organizing, coordinating, and controlling.

In countries with a high collectivist orientation, there would be a preference for group as opposed to individual decision-making. Consensus and cooperation would be more valued than individual initiative and effort. Motivation derives from a sense of belonging, and rewards are based on being part of the group (loyalty and tenure). The role of leadership in such cultures is to facilitate team effort and integration, to foster a supportive atmosphere, and to create the necessary context or group culture.

In countries ranked high on masculinity, the management style is likely to be more concerned with task accomplishment than nurturing social relationships. Motivation will be based on the acquisition of money and things rather than quality of life. In such cultures, the role of leadership is to ensure bottom-line profits in order to satisfy shareholders, and to set demanding targets. In more feminine cultures, the role of the leader would be to safeguard employee well-being, and to demonstrate concern for social responsibility.

Having ranked countries on each dimension, Hofstede then positioned them along two dimensions at a time, creating a series of cultural maps. He too found country clusters—Anglo, Nordic, Latin, and Asian—similar to those reported in the previous chapter.[10] While some concern has been voiced that the country differences found in Hofstede's research are not representative due to the single company sample, further research by him and others supports these dimensions and the preferences for different profiles of organization.

One such cultural map, as shown in Figure 1 (see also Table 2), is particularly relevant to structure in that it simultaneously considers power distance (acceptance of hierarchy) and uncertainty avoidance (the desire for formalized rules and procedures). Countries which ranked high both on power distance and uncertainty avoidance would be

[9]Hofstede, G. (1980) "Motivation, leadership, and organization: Do American theories apply abroad?" *Organizational Dynamics,* Summer, 42–63.

[10]Ronen, S. and Shenekar, O. (1985) "Clustering countries on attitudinal dimensions: A review and synthesis," *Academy of Management Review,* 10(3), 435–54.

Table 1   Hofstede's Rankings

Country	Power Distance Index	Power Distance Rank	Individualism Index	Individualism Rank	Masculinity Index	Masculinity Rank	Uncertainty Avoidance Index	Uncertainty Avoidance Rank
Argentina	49	35–6	46	22–3	56	20–1	86	10–15
Australia	36	41	90	2	61	16	51	37
Austria	11	53	55	18	79	2	70	24–5
Belgium	65	20	75	8	54	22	94	5–6
Brazil	69	14	38	26–7	49	27	76	21–2
Canada	39	39	80	4–5	52	24	48	41–2
Chile	63	24–5	23	38	28	46	86	10–15
Colombia	67	17	13	49	64	11–12	80	20
Costa Rica	35	42–4	15	46	21	48–9	86	10–15
Denmark	18	51	74	9	16	50	23	51
Equador	78	8–9	8	52	63	13–14	67	28
Finland	33	46	63	17	26	47	59	31–2
France	68	15–16	71	10–11	43	35–6	86	10–15
Germany (F.R.)	35	42–4	67	15	66	9–10	65	29
Great Britain	35	42–4	89	3	66	9–10	35	47–8
Greece	60	27–8	35	30	57	18–19	112	1
Guatemala	95	2–3	6	53	37	43	101	3
Hong Kong	68	15–16	25	37	57	18–19	29	49–50
Indonesia	78	8–9	14	47–8	46	30–1	48	41–2
India	77	10–11	48	21	56	20–1	40	45
Iran	58	19–20	41	24	43	35–6	59	31–2
Ireland	28	49	70	12	68	7–8	35	47–8
Israel	13	52	54	19	47	29	81	19
Italy	50	34	76	7	70	4–5	75	23
Jamaica	45	37	39	25	68	7–8	13	52
Japan	54	33	46	22–3	95	1	92	7
Korea (S)	60	27–8	187	43	39	41	85	16–17
Malaysia	104	1	26	36	50	25–6	36	46
Mexico	81	5–6	30	32	69	6	82	18
Netherlands	38	40	80	4–5	14	51	53	35
Norway	31	47–8	69	13	8	52	50	38
New Zealand	22	50	79	6	58	17	49	39–40
Pakistan	55	32	14	47–8	50	25–6	70	24–5
Panama	95	2–3	11	51	44	34	86	10–15
Peru	64	21–3	16	45	42	37–8	87	9
Philippines	94	4	32	31	64	11–12	44	44
Portugal	63	24–5	27	33–5	31	45	104	2
South Africa	49	36–7	65	16	63	13–14	49	39–40
Salvador	66	18–19	19	42	40	40	94	5–6
Singapore	74	13	20	39–41	48	28	8	53
Spain	57	31	51	20	42	37–8	86	10–15
Sweden	31	47–8	71	10–11	5	52	29	49–50

(continued)

Table 1   *(concluded)*

Country	Power Distance		Individualism		Masculinity		Uncertainty Avoidance	
	Index	Rank	Index	Rank	Index	Rank	Index	Rank
Switzerland	34	45	68	14	70	4–5	58	33
Taiwan	58	29–30	17	44	45	32–3	69	26
Thailand	64	21–3	20	39–41	34	44	64	30
Turkey	66	18–19	37	28	45	31–3	85	16–17
Uruguay	61	26	36	29	38	42	100	4
United States	40	38	91	1	62	15	46	43
Venezuela	81	5–6	12	50	73	3	76	21–2
Yugoslavia	76	12	27	33–5	21	48–9	88	8
Regions:								
East Africa	64	21–3	27	33–5	41	39	52	36
West Africa	77	10–11	20	39–41	46	30–1	54	34
Arab countries	80	7	38	26–7	53	23	68	27

Rank numbers: 1—Highest; 53—Lowest.
Source: G. Hofstede (1991) *Cultures and Organizations: Software of the Mind,* McGraw-Hill, Maidenhead.

expected to be more "mechanistic"[11] or what is commonly known as bureaucratic. In this corner we find the Latin countries.

In the opposite quadrant, countries which rank low both on power distance and uncertainty avoidance are expected to be more "organic"[12]—less hierarchic, more decentralized, having less formalized rules and procedures. Here we find the Nordic countries clustered and to a lesser extent, the Anglo countries.

In societies where power distance is low but uncertainty avoidance is high, we expect to find organizations where hierarchy is downplayed, decisions are decentralized, but where rules and regulations are more formal, and task roles and responsibilities are more clearly defined. Thus there is no need for a boss, as the organization runs by routines. This is characteristic of the Germanic cluster.

In societies where power distance is high but uncertainty avoidance is low, organizations resemble families or tribes. Here, "the boss is the boss", and the organization may be described as paternalistic. Subordinates do not have clearly defined task roles and responsibilities (formalization), but instead social roles. Here we find the Asian countries where business enterprise is often characterized by centralized power and personalized relationships.

Emerging Cultural Profiles: Converging Evidence
These differences in structural preferences also emerged in a study conducted by Stevens[13] at INSEAD. When presented with an organizational problem, a conflict between two department heads within a company, MBA students from Britain, France, and Germany proposed markedly different solutions. The majority of French students referred the problem to the next level up, the president. The Germans argued that the major problem was a lack of structure; the expertise, roles, and responsibilities of the two conflicting department heads had never been clearly defined. Their suggested solution involved establishing procedures for better coordination. The British saw it as an interpersonal

[11]Burns and Stalker, *Op. cit.*
[12]*Ibid.*

[13]Stevens, O.J., cited in Hofstede, G. (1991) *Cultures and Organizations,* London: McGraw-Hill, 140–2.

Figure 1 Hofstede's Maps

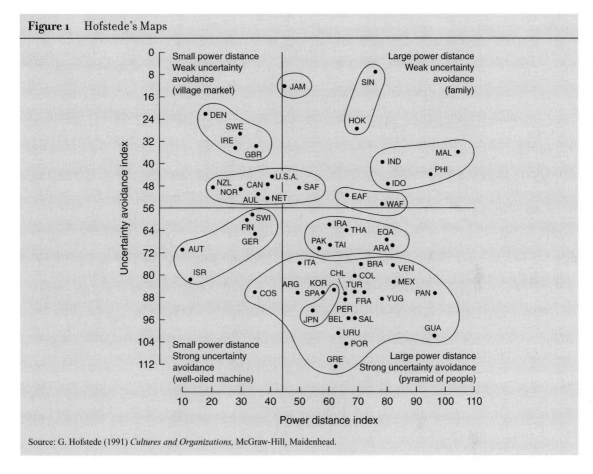

Source: G. Hofstede (1991) *Cultures and Organizations,* McGraw-Hill, Maidenhead.

communication problem between the two department heads which could be solved by sending them for interpersonal skills training, preferably together.

On the basis of these findings, Stevens described the "implicit model" of the organization held by each culture. For the French, the organization represents a "pyramid of people" (formalized and centralized). For the Germans, the organization is like a "well-oiled machine" (formalized but not centralized), in which management intervention is limited to exceptional cases because the rules resolve problems. And for the British, it was more like a "village market" (neither formalized nor centralized) in which neither the hierarchy nor the rules, but rather the demands of the situation determine structure.

Going beyond questionnaires by observing the actual behavior of managers and company practices, further research reveals such cultural profiles as shown in Figure 2. Indeed, in studies comparing firms in France, Germany, and the United Kingdom,[14] French firms were found to be more centralized and formalized with less delegation when compared with either German or British firms. The role of the PDG (French CEO) was to provide coordination at the top and to make key

[14]Brossard, A. and Maurice, M. (1976) "Is there a universal model of organization structure?" *International Studies of Management and Organizations,* 6, 11–45; Horovitz, J. (1980) *Top Management Control in Europe,* London: Macmillan; Stewart, R., Barsoux, J.-L., Kieser, A., Ganter, D. and Walgenbach, P. (1994) *Managing in Britain and Germany,* London: Macmillan.

Table 2   Abbreviations for the Countries and Regions Studied

Abbreviation	Country or Region	Abbreviation	Country or Region
ARA	Arab-speaking countries (Egypt, Iraq, Kuwait, Lebanon, Libya, Saudi Arabia, United Arab Emirates)	ITA	Italy
		JAM	Jamaica
		JPN	Japan
		KOR	South Korea
ARG	Argentina	MAL	Malaysia
AUL	Australia	MEX	Mexico
AUT	Austria	NET	Netherlands
BEL	Belgium	NOR	Norway
BRA	Brazil	NZL	New Zealand
CAN	Canada	PAK	Pakistan
CHL	Chile	PAN	Panama
COL	Colombia	PER	Peru
COS	Costa Rica	PHI	Philippines
DEN	Denmark	POR	Portugal
EAF	East Africa (Ethiopia, Kenya, Tanzania, Zambia)	SAF	South Africa
		SAL	Salvador
EQA	Equador	SIN	Singapore
FIN	Finland	SPA	Spain
FRA	France	SWE	Sweden
GBR	Great Britain	SWI	Switzerland
GER	Germany F.R.	TAI	Taiwan
GRE	Greece	THA	Thailand
GUA	Guatemala	TUR	Turkey
HOK	Hong Kong	URU	Uruguay
IDO	Indonesia	USA	United States
IND	India	VEN	Venezuela
IRA	Iran	WAF	West Africa (Ghana, Nigeria, Sierra Leone)
IRE	Ireland (Republic of)		
ISR	Israel	YUG	Yugoslavia

Source: G. Hofstede (1991) *Cultures and Organizations,* McGraw-Hill, Maidenhead.

decisions, which demands a high level of analytical and conceptual ability that need not be industry- or company-specific. The staff function plays an important role in providing analytic expertise. These capabilities are developed in the elite *grandes écoles* of engineering and administration.

The research findings confirmed the image of German firms as "well-oiled machines" as they were more likely to be decentralized, specialized, and formalized. In fact, German managers were more likely to cite structure as a key success factor, having a

logic of its own, apart from people. German firms were more likely to be organized by function (sometimes to the extent that they are referred to as "chimney" organizations) with coordination achieved through routines and procedures.

Although German organizations tended to be flatter and to have a broader span of control when compared with the French, middle managers had less discretion than their British counterparts as they were limited to their specific technical competence. The premium placed on competence was expressed

Figure 2   Emerging Cultural Profiles

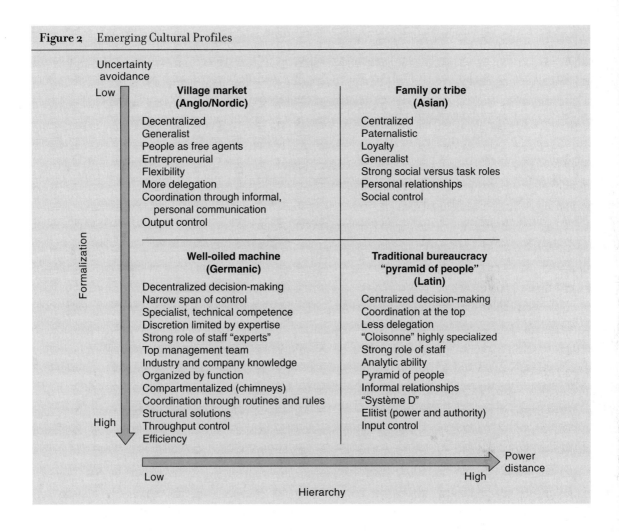

in the concern to find competent people to perform specialized tasks, the strong role of staff to provide technical expertise, and expectations that top management not only has specific technical competence, but also in-depth company knowledge. Furthermore, top management typically consists of a managing board, *Vorstand,* which integrates the specialized knowledge of the various top managers (rather than in the head of a lone individual as in the case of France, Britain, or the United States).

In contrast to the well-oiled machine model with its greater concern for efficiency, the "village market" model reflects a greater concern for flexibility.

Indeed, structure in British firms was found to be far more flexible, more decentralized and less formalized, when compared with the French and German firms. Organized by divisions, there is greater decentralization and delegation in the company and the role of central staff is far less important. Here, the burden of coordinating functions was placed on individual managers requiring a constant need for persuasion and negotiation to achieve cooperation.[15]

British managers, compared with Germans, were more ready to adapt the structure to the people

[15]Stewart *et al., Op. cit.*

working in it. Changes in personnel were often used as opportunities to reshuffle the jobs and responsibilities in order to accommodate available talent, and to create opportunities for personal development (free agents). Top management's role was to identify market opportunities and convince others to pursue them, underlining the importance of taking a more strategic view and of being able to communicate it persuasively.[16]

Studies in Asia have also found companies to fit the "family model," being more hierarchic and less formalized, with the exception of Japan. When compared with the Japanese, Hong Kong Chinese firms were less likely to have written manuals and Hong Kong Chinese bosses were also found to be more autocratic and paternalistic.[17] Another study of thirty-nine multinational commercial banks from fourteen different countries operating in Hong Kong found the Hong Kong banks to have the greatest number of hierarchical levels (eleven); the banks from Singapore, the Philippines, and India were also among those most centralized.[18]

A recent study of Chinese entrepreneurs found the Confucian tradition of patriarchal authority to be remarkably persistent. Being part of the family is seen as a way of achieving security. Social roles are clearly spelled out in line with Confucian precepts, which designate the responsibilities for the roles of father, son, brothers, and so on. Control is exerted through authority, which is not questioned. In 70 percent of the entrepreneurial firms studied, even large ones, the structure of Chinese organizations was found to resemble a hub with spokes

around a powerful founder, or a management structure with only two layers.[19]

What begins to emerge from these various research studies is a converging and coherent picture of different management structures when comparing countries within Europe, as well as when comparing countries in Europe, the United States, and Asia. The primary cultural determinants appear to be those related to relationships between people in terms of power and status and relationship with nature, for example how uncertainty is managed and how control is exercised.

These underlying cultural assumptions are expressed in beliefs (and their subsequent importance, or value) regarding the need for hierarchy, for formal rules and procedures, specialized jobs and functions. These beliefs and values, in turn, are observable in behavior and artifacts, such as deference to the boss, the presence of executive parking and dining facilities ("perks"), and the existence of written policies and procedures, specific job descriptions, or manuals outlining standard operating procedures.

The research findings in the above-mentioned studies were based on observations as well as questionnaires and interviews of managers and companies in different countries. The same, of course, can be done comparing companies in different industries or within the same industry, and managers in different functions providing corresponding models of industry, corporate and/or functional cultures. From these findings, management scholars interpret underlying meaning.

The Meaning of Organizations: Task versus Social System   André Laurent argues that the country differences in structure described above reflect different conceptions (or understandings) of what is an organization.[20] These different conceptions were discovered in surveys which asked managers to

‖ [16]*Ibid.*
‖ [17]Redding, S.G. and Pugh, D.S. (1986) "The formal and the informal: Japanese and Chinese organization structures" in S. Clegg, D. Dunphy, and S.G. Redding (eds) *The Enterprise and Management in East Asia,* Hong Kong: Center of Asian Studies, University of Hong Kong, 153–68; Vertinsky, I., Tse, D.K., Wehrung, D.A. and Lee, K. (1990) "Organization design and management norms: A comparative study of managers' perceptions in the People's Republic of China, Hong Kong and Canada," *Journal of Management,* 16(4), 853–67.
‖ [18]Wong, G.Y.Y. and Birnbaum-More, P.H. (1994) "Culture, context and structure: A test on Hong Kong banks," *Organization Studies,* 15(l), 99–23.

‖ [19]Kao, J. (1993) "The worldwide web of Chinese business," *Harvard Business Review,* March–April, 24–35.
‖ [20]Laurent, A. (1983) "The cultural diversity of western conception of management," *International Studies of Management and Organization,* 13(l–2), 75–96.

Table 3   Management Questionnaire

A = Strongly agree
B = Tend to agree
C = Neither agree, nor disagree
D = Tend to disagree
E = Strongly disagree

1. When the respective roles of the members of a department become complex, detailed job descriptions are a useful way of clarifying.	A	B	C	D	E
2. In order to have efficient work relationships, it is often necessary to bypass the hierarchical line.	A	B	C	D	E
8. An organizational structure in which certain subordinates have two direct bosses should be avoided at all costs.	A	B	C	D	E
13. The more complex a department's activities, the more important it is for each individual's functions to be well-defined.	A	B	C	D	E
14. The main reason for having a hierarchical structure is so that everyone knows who has authority over whom.	A	B	C	D	E
19. Most organizations would be better off if conflict could be eliminated forever.	A	B	C	D	E
24. It is important for a manager to have at hand precise answers to most of the questions that his/her subordinates may raise about their work.	A	B	C	D	E
33. Most managers have a clear notion of what we call an organizational structure.	A	B	C	D	E
38. Most managers would achieve better results if their roles were less precisely defined.	A	B	C	D	E
40. Through their professional activity, managers play an important role in society.	A	B	C	D	E
43. The manager of tomorrow will be, primarily, a negotiator.	A	B	C	D	E
49. Most managers seem to be more motivated by obtaining power than by achieving objectives.	A	B	C	D	E
52. Today there seems to be an authority crisis in organizations.	A	B	C	D	E

Source: A. Laurent. Reproduced by permission.

agree or disagree with statements regarding beliefs about organization and management. A sample of the questions are shown in Table 3.

The results of this survey are very much in line with the discussion above in that they show similar cultural differences regarding power and uncertainty in views of organizations as systems of hierarchy, authority, politics, and role formalization. What would these different views of organization actually look like, were we to observe managers at

work and even to question them? What arguments would managers from different countries put forth to support their responses?

Having a view of organizations as **hierarchical systems** would make it difficult, for example, to tolerate having to report to two bosses, as required in a matrix organization, and it would make it difficult to accept bypassing or going over or around the boss. The boss would also be expected to have precise answers to most of the questions that subordinates have about their work. Asian and Latin managers argue that in order for bosses to be respected, or to have power and authority, they must demonstrate expert knowledge. And if the most efficient way to get things done is to bypass the hierarchical line they would consider that there was something wrong with the hierarchy.

Scandinavian and Anglo managers, on the other hand, argue that it is perfectly normal to go directly to anyone in the organization in order to accomplish the task. It would seem intolerable, for example, to have to go through one's own boss, who would contact his or her counterpart in a neighboring department before making contact with someone in that other department.

Furthermore, they argue that it is impossible to have precise answers, since the world is far too complex and ambiguous, and even if you could provide precise answers, this would not develop the capability of your subordinates to solve problems. Thus a Swedish boss with a French subordinate can anticipate some problems: the French subordinate is likely to think that the boss, not knowing the answers, is incompetent, while the Swedish boss may think that the French subordinate does not know what to do and is therefore incompetent.

Those who view the organization as a **political system** consider managers to play an important political role in society, and to negotiate within the organization. Thus obtaining power is seen as more important than achieving specific objectives. Here again, Latin European managers are more likely to adhere to this view than their Nordic and Anglo counterparts.

In France, for example, executives have often played important roles in the French administration before assuming top positions in companies. Furthermore, Latin managers are acutely aware that it is necessary to have power in order to get things done in the organization. Nordic and Anglo managers, however, tend to downplay the importance of power and therefore reject the need for political maneuvering.

When organizations are viewed as systems of **role formalization,** managers prefer detailed job

descriptions, and well-defined roles and functions. These serve to clarify complex situations and tasks. Otherwise it is difficult to know who is responsible for what and to hold people accountable. In addition they argue that lack of clear job descriptions or role definitions creates overlap and inefficiency. Nordic and Anglo managers, on the other hand, argue that the world is too complex to be able to clearly define roles and functions. Furthermore they say that detailed descriptions interfere with maintaining flexibility and achieving coordination.

From his research, Laurent concluded that underlying these arguments managers had different conceptions of organization: one which focused on the task, called **instrumental,** and one which focused on relationships, called **social.** For Latin European managers, organizations are considered as **social systems,** or systems of relationships, where personal networks and social positioning are important. The organization achieves its goals through relationships and how they are managed (as prescribed by Fayol). Roles and relationships are defined formally (by the hierarchy) and informally, based on authority, power, and status which are seen as attributes of the person, not the task or function. Personal loyalty and deference to the boss are expected.

However, getting things done means working around the system—using informal, personal networks to circumvent the hierarchy as well as the rules and regulations—what the French call, *Système D.* According to sociologist Michel Crozier, it is this informal system that gives the French "bureaucratic model" its flexibility.[21] Organizations are thus considered to be necessarily political in nature. When asked to diagnose organizational problems, French social scientists and consultants typically start by analyzing the power relationships and power games (*les enjeux*).[22]

In contrast, for Anglo-Saxon, and northern European managers, the organization is a system of

---

[21]Crozier, M. (1964) *The Bureaucratic Phenomenon,* Chicago: University of Chicago Press.

[22]Crozier, M. and Friedberg, E. (1977) *L'Acteur et le système: Les contraintes de l'action collective,* Paris: Seuil.

tasks where it is important to know what has to be done, rather than who has power and authority to do so (as in the socio/political view). This instrumental or functionalist view of organizations (very much in keeping with Taylor's scientific management) focuses on what is to be achieved and whether objectives are met (achievement orientation). Structure is defined by activities—what has to be done—and the hierarchy exists only to assign responsibility. It follows that authority is defined by function and is limited, specific to the job not the person.

Here, coordination and control are impersonal, decentralized, and reside in the structure and systems. Rules and regulations are applied universally. If the rules and regulations are dysfunctional, then they are changed rather than circumvented or broken. Management consultants are called in to figure out the best way to devise strategy, design structure, classify jobs and set salary scales, and develop concrete programs such as "total quality" or "performance management."

These different conceptions of organization were confirmed recently when Trompenaars[23] asked 15,000 managers to choose between the following statements:

> A company is a system designed to perform functions and tasks in an efficient way. People are hired to fulfill these functions with the help of machines and other equipment. They are paid for the tasks they perform.
>
> A company is a group of people working together. The people have social relations with other people and with the organization. The functioning is dependent upon these relations.

He too found large differences between Anglo and Nordic managers compared with Latin and Asian managers, as shown in Figure 3. These different beliefs reveal the underlying cultural meaning of organizations as task versus social systems.

As We See Us . . . (Revisited)   These findings can be further corroborated by asking managers to describe the approach to management in their coun-

tries, or "how we see us," . . . For example, many of the research results discussed above place Scandinavian managers at one end of a continuum, with Latin and Asian managers at the other. Jan Selmer,[24] a Swedish management professor, proposed the following profile of "Viking Management." Compare this with the self-descriptions of Brazilian[25] and Indonesian managers in Table 4.

According to self-reports, clear differences and similarities emerge in terms of the nature of relationships (hierarchy) and the relationship with nature (uncertainty and control). For example, in keeping with the findings discussed above, Viking Management is characterized as decentralized (less hierarchy) when compared with the Brazilian and Indonesian views, which emphasize status and power or respect for elders.

On the other hand, in each case there is a strong emphasis on the importance of relationships: family (mother–daughter) and friends, avoiding conflict, being tolerant, seeking consensus, and "keeping everyone happy." For the Swedes, this corresponds to their keen concern for social well-being and quality of relationships, reflected in their number one ranking on Hofstede's femininity dimension.

In all three self-descriptions there is less emphasis placed on formalization. For the Swedes, organization goals and structures are experienced as vague and ambiguous. Uncertainty is managed with a "case by case" (and *not* a universal) approach, through informal communication channels, and "through values not rules." For the Indonesians, it is the "Five principles" established by President Suharto that provide the rules, rather than organizational ones. In comparison with the Swedes, however, the Indonesians perceive little control over their environment, *Insh'allah* (if God wills . . .)." Thus the Swedish approach to getting things done may be frustrated by the Indonesian sense of letting things happen.

[23]Trompenaars, F. (1993) *Riding the Waves of Culture,* London: Nicholas Brealey.

[24]Selmer, J. (1988) Presentation, International Conference on Personnel and Human Resource Management Conference, Singapore.
[25]Amado, G. and Brasil, H.V. (1991) "Organizational behaviors and cultural context: The Brazilian 'Jeitiñho,' " *International Studies of Management and Organization,* 21(3), 38–61.

Figure 3 Organizations as Task versus Social Systems

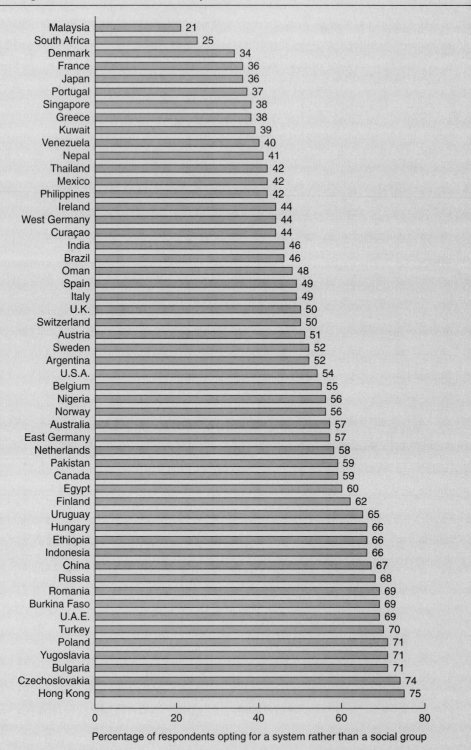

Percentage of respondents opting for a system rather than a social group

Source: F. Trompenaars (1993) *Riding the Waves of Culture: Understanding Cultural Diversity in Business,* Nicholas Brealey, London.

Table 4   As We See Us . . .

Viking Management

Decentralized decision-making
Organization structure is often ambiguous
Perceived by others to be indecisive
Goal formulation, long-range objectives, and performance evaluation criteria are vague and implicit
informal channels of communication
Coordinate by values not rules (normative versus coercive)
Case by case approach versus standard procedures
Consensus-oriented
Avoid conflict
Informal relationships between foreign subsidiaries and headquarters (mother–daughter relationships)

Brazilian Management

Hierarchy and authority; status and power are important
Centralized decision-making
Personal relationships are more important than the task
Rules and regulations are for enemies
Flexible and adaptable (too much?) *Jeitiñho*
Anything is possible
Short-term oriented—immediatism
Avoid conflict—seen as win/lose
Rely on magic—low control over environment
Decisions based on intuition and feeling

Indonesian Management

Respect for hierarchy and elders
Family-oriented
Group- versus individual-oriented
Friendly and helpful, hospitable
Tolerant
Decisions based on compromise—"keep everyone happy"
Importance of religion—(Islam)
Five principles
Bhinneka Tunggal lka (unity through diversity)

Brazilian managers, faced with great uncertainty in the day-to-day business environment over which they feel they have little control, say that they have developed a finely tuned sense of intuition, having learned to trust their "gut" feel, as previ-

ously mentioned. For the Brazilians, the notion of *Jeitiñho* is similar to that of the French *Système D,* going around the system in order to get things done. This assures flexibility and adaptability such that anything is possible (although perhaps too much so as Brazilian managers themselves acknowledge).

Now imagine a Brazil–Sweden–Indonesia joint venture. This raises the possibility that three firms would have to resolve their differences on several fronts while using their similarities to create a shared sense of purpose. In particular, there would probably be a clash between the cultural assumptions underlying Swedish management—little concern with power and status and high perceived control over the environment—with those of Brazilian and Indonesian management—more emphasis on power and authority and less perceived control.

This would probably cause the biggest headaches for the Swedes when it came to efforts to delegate decision-making and to encourage individual responsibility and accountability. For the Indonesian and Brazilian managers, the frustration would come from confusion as to "who is the boss?" and "why isn't he/she making decisions?," and "how can I be held responsible when I have no control over what happens?" In decision-making, the Brazilians would find the Indonesians and Swedes interminably slow, seeking consensus or democratic compromise, while they in turn would see the Brazilians as impetuous, and too individualistic. On the other hand, the similarity in importance placed on relationships, on informal communication, and on avoiding conflict can help to work through these difficulties together, on a personal basis.

Although there are variations within countries, due to industry and corporate culture, as well as individual styles of key managers, the above research findings and self-descriptions point to different cultural profiles of organization. The underlying assumptions can be interpreted to reveal the nature of relationships, as seen in the importance of hierarchy, and control over nature, as seen in the need for formal or social rules and procedures. The underlying cultural meaning of the organization can then be interpreted as systems of tasks versus systems of relationships. These cultural profiles provide a starting point to explore different structural preferences and to begin to anticipate potential problems when transferring practices from one country to another or in forming joint ventures and strategic alliances.

On a less serious note, these differences have been caricatured in the organizational charts shown in Figure 4. Using these caricatures can provoke discussion of structural differences across countries in a humorous mode while allowing us to discover the grain of truth within and to imagine how our own organization chart might seem to others. Constructing cultural profiles enables us to appreciate the impact of culture on management as multidimensional. It would therefore be a mistake to base a prediction regarding structure or process on a single cultural dimension.

In addition, managers need to recognize that the relationships between cultural dimensions and structure (or processes) are not simple cause–effect links, but instead, are multidetermined. Similar approaches may exist for different cultural reasons, and different approaches may exist for the same reason. Thus formalized rules and procedures or participative management approaches may have a different *raison d'être* on different sides of the national border.

Having considered cultural differences in organization and structure, we can now turn our attention to organizational processes. In addition to cultural preferences regarding hierarchy and formalization, other cultural dimensions are considered to explain the reasons for some of the country differences that may seem contradictory. And to show why similar business practices may have different underlying cultural roots, or meaning.

Culture and Processes

The characterization of organizations as pyramids, well-oiled machines, village markets, and family tribes, and the structural correlates are further reflected in the organizational processes. In effect, structures are similar to fossils, as they bear the traces of organizational processes over time. Thus

the influence of culture can also be seen in organizational processes such as the nature of policies and procedures, planning and control, information processing and communication, and decision-making.

Policies and Procedures   The formalization and standardization of policies and procedures may reflect low tolerance for uncertainty, as they can be clearly spelled out, leaving little room for doubt. Other cultural dimensions may also have a hand in explaining differences found between cultures. For instance, although the United States ranks low on uncertainty avoidance, European managers working for U.S. multinationals often complain about the formal reporting systems, and volume of written policies and procedures that come down from headquarters.

This is perhaps more understandable given the contractual view of employment in the United States, an instrumental view of the firm, and low-context communication. All of these dimensions encourage a high level of explicitness which is evident in the ubiquitous standard operating procedures. Policies and job descriptions are thus written down and standardized so that anyone can perform them. Information is embedded in the system not in the person, as the organization is thought to exist independently from its members. This might seem contrary to the primacy of the individual, but in fact it is this standardization which allows individuals to move easily in and out of jobs/organizations and guarantees their career mobility in the village market. Also, given U.S. commitment to universalism, rules and procedures are necessary to assure that all people are treated equally.[26]

A comparison of British and German firms[27] showed that all the British firms had detailed job descriptions while only one of the German firms did. This seems contrary to expectations, given the respective attitudes to uncertainty avoidance in the two countries (Germany high, Britain low). However, as German managers are specialists and tend

[26]Hampden-Turner, C. and Trompenaars, F. (1994) *Seven Cultures of Capitalism*, London: Piatkus.
[27]Stewart *et al., Op. cit.*

Figure 4   The Organization Chart

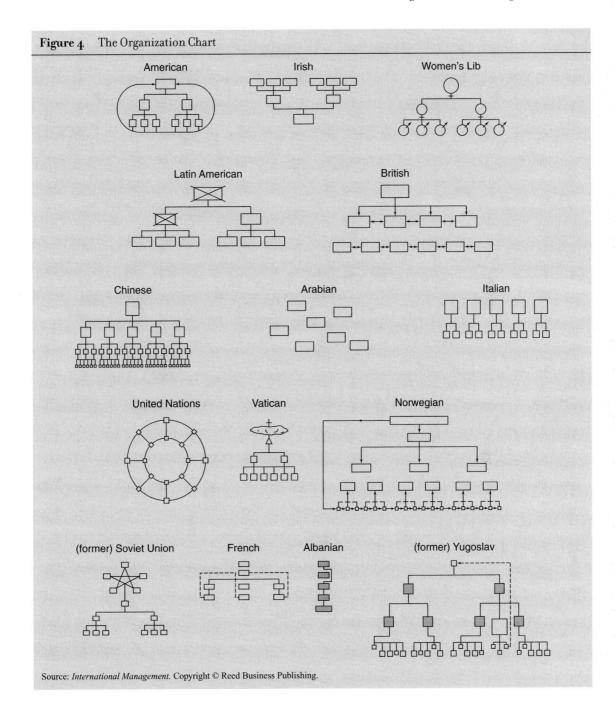

Source: *International Management.* Copyright © Reed Business Publishing.

to stay longer in one job, job descriptions are well-internalized, and there is less of a need to formalize them.

On the other hand, British managers are generalists, and tend to rotate jobs more often. One study found that in matched companies twenty-five out of thirty British managers had changed jobs within four years, compared with ten out of thirty German managers.[28] Therefore job descriptions are formalized to provide general guidelines to new incumbents.

Furthermore, British managers had a higher tolerance for mismatch between written expectations and actual responsibilities and thus did not feel constrained to follow the job descriptions. German resistance to written descriptions stemmed from the desire to preserve flexibility. Unlike the British managers, the German managers would have felt uncomfortable with any divergence between written procedures and practice (uncertainty).

Procedures or job descriptions are less likely to be made explicit where communication is more embedded in relationships and in situations (high context). Japanese managers tend to have broader general knowledge of the company, which is often tacit, having been gained through observation and on-the-job experience, like a craft.[29] In addition, tasks are assigned to groups not individuals, and individual accountability remains vague. This creates a stronger link between people, the group, and the organization, making knowledge company-specific, thereby reducing career mobility outside the organization, keeping it all in the family.

Systems and Controls   Control systems also reflect different cultural assumptions regarding relationships with people (in terms of power and human nature) and relationship with nature (uncertainty and control). For example, French managers indicate that the most important function for a manager is to control, while British managers say it is to coordinate.[30] This reflects different attitudes towards

power. For the French, control derives from the hierarchy; for the British, coordination is achieved through persuasion and negotiation, since the boss is not seen as all-powerful.

Furthermore, the nature of control depends on assumptions regarding human nature. When employees are seen as capable and self-directed (Theory Y),[31] there is more reliance on communication, rather than direct supervision. When managers assume that workers are basically lazy and need to be directed by others (Theory X), they are more likely to set up tight control processes.

Different types of control—input, throughout, and output—are also evident across cultures. The French are particularly careful about recruiting future senior managers from the top schools. This reflects input control—choosing the best and the brightest—and then assuming that they will manage and produce results. German companies are less concerned with hiring elites than with developing managers through rigorous apprenticeships and in-depth job-specific experience. The focus on detailed plans and operational controls also reflects the importance of throughput controls. In the United States and Britain, the emphasis is on budgets, financial controls, and reporting procedures, which reflects more output control.

This can be seen in different ideas regarding the purpose of budgets. One comparative study[32] of managers in U.S. and French subsidiaries of the same firm found that for the American managers, budgets were treated as useful tools which provided concrete objectives against which performance could be measured. French managers, on the other hand, were more concerned with the overall logic and perfection of the budgeting system. These differences reflect American managers' confidence in their ability to control events by being pragmatic (instrumental) and results (achievement)-oriented, while French managers rely more on their analytic (Cartesian) capability, or the quality of thinking.

---

[28]*Ibid.*

[29]Nonaka, I. (1991) "The knowledge-creating company," *Harvard Business Review,* November–December, 96–104.

[30]Laurent, A. (1986) "The cross-cultural puzzle of global human resource management," *Human Resource Management,* 25(1), 91–102.

[31]McGregor, D. (1960) *The Nature of Human Enterprise,* New York: McGraw-Hill.

[32]Perret, M.S. (1988) "The impact of cultural differences in budgeting," unpublished Ph.D. dissertation, University of Western Ontario.

Planning practices also reflect underlying cultural assumptions. A study by Horovitz[33] comparing planning practices in the United Kingdom, Germany and France found that planning practices in the United Kingdom were more strategic in focus, more long term (six year horizon), with more participation in the process. In Germany, planning was more operational (including stringent, detailed one year plans), more short term (three year horizon), with little participation from the ranks. In France, planning was also more short term (less than half of the firms had long-range planning), more administrative (three year financial forecasts), and also less participative. The shorter term and the more operational/administrative orientation reflects the need to limit uncertainty to more manageable time frames and with more concrete outcomes. Thus the need to reduce uncertainty and to impose controls will result in planning that is more operational than strategic, more short term, and less participative.

Information and Communication   Organizations must process information in order to make decisions, to communicate policies and procedures, and to coordinate across units. Yet what kind of information is sought or heeded, how information circulates, and what information is shared with whom, are likely to reflect cultural preferences for hierarchy, formalization, and participation.

For example, French companies are often characterized by French managers as *cloisonné* (compartmentalized), very clearly structured vertically as well as horizontally. This makes very clear the personal roles and responsibility, privileges and obligations, and hence the degree of discretion in performing one's job.[34] Thus the flow of information between groups is limited.

Furthermore, given the view of organization as a social system based on relationships, information may not be readily shared as it is viewed as personal, not public. Information is passed through personal connections. According to one French manager, "Information which is widely distributed is obviously useless."[35] In addition, the political nature of French organizations encourages information to be seen as a source of power, and therefore not easily given away.

For these reasons, it is not surprising that informal communication assumes considerable importance in French companies. A survey in the *Nouvel Economiste*[36] found that information was more likely obtained from rumours than from one's immediate boss. Informal channels compensate for the centralized, formalized, and limited participative nature of information flows.

In contrast, managers in Sweden, which is more egalitarian and more tolerant of uncertainty, pay very little attention to formal structure or hierarchy. Communication patterns are much more open and informal. This is supported in the research findings of André Laurent that Swedish managers were far less inhibited than their French counterparts about bypassing the hierarchical line.[37] Given the Swedish view of organizations as instrumental rather than socio-political, there is a greater willingness to share information with anyone who has an interest in it. Information can be put to use; its value is instrumental, not social.

The Swedish insistence on transparency, or the open sharing of information, created initial difficulties for Electrolux when they acquired Italian company, Zanussi.[38] The Italian managers and labor unions, although first surprised by this transparency, came to respect and trust the "Viking" acquirers because of it. Nevertheless, Zanussi managers had trouble unlearning the previous habit of keeping information to themselves as a way of preserving power.[39]

In Japanese companies, intensive and extensive discussion is encouraged at all levels both within (among employees) and outside (with suppliers

---

[33]Horovitz, *Op. cit.*

[34]D'Iribarne, P. (1989) *La logique de l'honneur,* Paris: Seuil.

[35]Orleman, P.A. (1992) "The global corporation: Managing across cultures," Masters thesis, University of Pennsylvania.

[36]"La communication dans l'entreprise," *Nouvel Economiste,* May 12, 1980, 42–7.

[37]Laurent, *Op. cit.*

[38]Haspeslagh, P. and Ghoshal, S. (1992) *Electrolux Zanussi,* INSEAD case.

[39]Lorenz, C. (1989) "The Italian connection—a stark contrast in corporate manners," *Financial Times,* June 23, 20.

and customers) the organization. The adaptability of Japanese companies is often attributed to this cross-boundary, open flow of information. By maximizing the informal exchange of information, Japanese firms are able to generate and leverage knowledge, to create a "learning company."[40]

Consider the special case of Kao, the Japanese competitor of Proctor & Gamble and Unilever.[41] CEO Dr. Maruta strongly believes that,

> If everyone discusses on an equal footing, there is nothing that cannot be resolved . . . [As such,] the organization was designed to "run as a flowing system" which would stimulate interaction and the spread of ideas in every direction and at every level . . . [Thus] organizational boundaries and titles were abolished.

Kao's head office is indeed designed in such a way as to encourage the cross-fertilization of ideas.

> On the 10th floor, known as the top management floor, sat the Chairman, the President, four executive vice presidents, and a pool of secretaries. A large part of the floor was open space, with one large conference table and two smaller ones, and chairs, blackboards and overhead projectors strewn around; this was known as the Decision Space, where all discussions with and among the top management took place. Anyone passing, including the President, could sit down and join in any discussion on any topic . . . This layout was duplicated on the other floors . . . Workplaces looked like large rooms; there were no partitions, but again tables and chairs for spontaneous or planned discussions at which everyone contributed as equals. Access was free to all, and any manager could thus find himself sitting round the table next to the President, who was often seen waiting in line in Kao's Tokyo cafateria.

Furthermore, any employee can retrieve data on sales or product development, the latest findings from R&D, details of yesterday's production and inventory at every plant, and can even check up on the President's expense account.

Thus office design, building layout, and information technology can encourage managers to share information or to keep it to themselves, and can facilitate whether communication channels are open and multiple, or limited to a one-to-one basis, serial, and secretive. The Japanese scientists from Toshiba, assigned to a joint venture with IBM and Siemens, found it unproductive to be in separate little rooms. So they spent most of their time standing in the halls discussing ideas.[42] The German scientists preferred privacy.

This use of physical space and the consequent patterns of interaction are cultural artifacts which reveal different beliefs regarding the optimal degree of hierarchy, formalization, and level of participation. These beliefs influence the flow of information and communication within companies in different countries. Digging deeper, we find differences in the assumptions regarding the use of information under conditions of uncertainty, whether people are seen as trustworthy and capable, and whether information is used to preserve power or to be shared. In addition we find the underlying cultural meaning of information as serving instrumental versus political purposes.

Decision-Making   The nature of decision-making is also culturally rooted. Who makes the decision, who is involved in the process, and where decisions are made (in formal committees or more informally in the hallways and corridors, or on the golf course) reflect different cultural assumptions. In turn, the very nature of the decision-making processes as well as different time horizons influences the speed with which decisions are taken.

It is perhaps not surprising that in countries such as Sweden and Germany, where power and hierarchy are played down, there is the greatest evidence of participation in decision-making. In Sweden, perhaps furthest along on the road of industrial democracy, union leaders often sit on the management board and are involved in making major strategic

[40]Nonaka, *Op. cit.;* Schütte, H. (1993) "Competing and cooperating with Japanese firms," Euro–Asia Center, INSEAD.
[41]Ghoshal, S. and Butler, C. (1991) KAO Corporation, INSEAD case.

[42]Browning, E.S. (1994) "Computer chip project brings rivals together, but the cultures clash," *Wall Street Journal,* May 3, A7.

decisions, including decisions to relocate factories abroad. Everyone has the right to contribute to a decision. Decision-making means seeking consensus.

In The Netherlands and Germany, the works council, or labor representation, also plays an important role in deciding business affairs. The strong commitment to consensus, social equality, and human welfare reveals assumptions regarding collectivism and the importance of the quality of working life.[43]

In contrast, companies in cultures which emphasize power and hierarchy are more likely to centralize decision-making. In France, for example, the government plays an important role in determining company strategy and policy, often choosing top management. This has earned France the reputation of being "the father of industrial policy."[44] The PDG (CEO) may well have more experience in government than in business. Furthermore, he (in rare cases she) is expected to make decisions and is respected for it. Power is jealously guarded by each actor, such that management and unions often end up in violent confrontation, neither willing to concede to the other party. While industry is currently being privatized, and employees have become more involved through participation and through quality circles, French management is criticized for remaining centralized and elitist.[45]

The difference in decision-making between Nordic and Latin European firms was sharply illustrated when Sweden's Electrolux acquired Italy's Zanussi. The Swedish top management was often frustrated in its efforts to get Italian managers to arrive at a consensus among themselves in solving problems. The Italian managers, in turn, expected the senior management to settle problems such as transfer pricing between Italian product lines and

the UK sales offices. According to one senior Italian manager, ". . . the key in this complex international organization is to have active mechanisms in place to create—and force—the necessary integration." However, the Swedish CEO preferred to let them solve their own problems; "Force is a word that is rarely heard in the Electrolux culture."[46]

Japanese firms, with their collectivist orientation, take yet another approach to decision-making. In the Japanese *Ringi* system, petitions (decision proposals) are circulated requiring individuals to "sign on." Signing, however, does not necessarily mean approval, but means that if the decision is taken, the person agrees to support it. While the opinions of superiors are sought, these opinions tend to be more implicit than explicit. Therefore, Japanese managers devote extra time in trying to "read their boss" to find out what is actually desired. In this way, Japanese firms reconcile the importance placed on both collectivism and the hierarchy.

Northern European and American managers often complain about the "slowness" with which Japanese companies *make* decisions. Japanese managers, on the other hand, often complain about the time it takes American and European companies to *implement* decisions. Although in Japan more time is taken to reach decisions, once the decision is taken it can be implemented more quickly as everyone has been involved and understands why the decision has been taken, what has been decided, and what needs to be done. Americans may pride themselves on being "decisive," making decisions quickly on their own. However, they then have to spend more time back at the office selling these decisions, explaining why, what, and how, and gathering support. Inevitably, implementation takes longer.

These different approaches to decision-making therefore have repercussions on the time taken to reach decisions, even in countries that appear to share cultural assumptions. For example, one study comparing strategic decision-making in Sweden and Britain demonstrated that it took twice as long in Sweden, not just to identify strategic issues

---

[43]Fry, J.A. (ed.) (1979) *Limits of the Welfare State: Critical Views on Post-war Sweden,* Farnborough: Saxon House.

[44]Aubert, N., Ramantsoa, B. and Reitter, R. (1984) "Nationalizations, managerial power, and societal change," Working paper Harvard Business School.

[45]Schmidt, V.A. (1993) "An end to French economic exceptionalism: The transformation of business under Mitterand," *California Management Review,* Fall, 75–98.

[46]Lorenz, *Op. cit.*

(37 months versus 17 months), but also to decide what to do about those issues (23 months versus 13 months).[47]

These differences in the amount of time for reaching decisions was explained by the degree of involvement of others in the process and desire for consensus. In Sweden, more participants are involved in contributing information and more time is taken to collect information and compare alternatives. Also, strategic decisions were more often taken by the management board (a collective) in Sweden rather than, as in Britain, by the Managing Director (CEO), an individual. The Swedish consensus-driven approach (which includes government and union officials) results in the tendency to appoint commissions or special working groups which are often time-consuming.

The speed of decision-making reflects not just the process, but also the prevailing attitude towards time. Many Western managers complain that their sense of urgency is not shared in other parts of the world where the attitude seems to be "what's the big hurry?" Yet in Asia and the Middle East, a decision made quickly may indicate that it has little importance. Otherwise, more time for consideration, reflection, and discussion would be warranted. Thus taking quick decisions is not universally admired as a sign of determination and strong leadership but can be regarded as a sign of immaturity and irresponsibility, or even stupidity.

Furthermore, in cultures where the past plays an important role, traditions cannot be dismissed so quickly. Therefore, decisions need to be taken and implemented more slowly. While this may be more obvious in Asian cultures, important differences exist between countries with otherwise similar cultural profiles. American managers, who are less tradition-bound, may perceive European managers as rather slow in making decisions.

British society, for example, has been described as conservative and tradition-bound, with a marked reluctance to change.[48] The slower speed of decision-making in British firms is also attributed to its being more decentralized (assigned to standing committees) and more informal (guided by unwritten rules and procedures which are maintained through personal connections).[49]

A study comparing strategic decision-making in British and Brazilian firms found that Brazilian executives tend to take decisions more quickly.[50] This was attributed to their centralized power which enables them to take decisions individually. Also according to Brazilian managers, the greater perceived uncertainty and lack of control over the environment contributes to a strong sense of urgency (or as referred to in Table 4 "immediatism") and need for change.

Thus differences in approaches to decision-making can be attributed to multiple, interacting cultural dimensions. In addition to cultural preferences for hierarchy, and formalization, assumptions regarding time and change are important considerations in *how* and *how quickly* decisions will be made. In addition, the level of participation in decision-making may be similar but for different reasons. In some countries, such as the United States, participation may be seen as a way of integrating different individual perspectives and preserving everyone's right to decide. In other cultures, such as Japan, it is a way to preserve group harmony and relationships, while in The Netherlands and Sweden it serves to promote social welfare. This results in different underlying cultural reasons for empowerment.

In Sweden where interested parties have the "right to negotiate" (*forhandlingsratt*), and in Germany where they have the "right to decide" (*Mitbestimmung*),[51] "empowerment" signifies power sharing in

[47]Axelsson, R., Cray, D., Mallory, G.R. and Wilson, D.C. (1991) "Decision style in British and Swedish organizations: A comparative examination of strategic decision making," *British Journal of Management*, 2, 67–79.

[48]Tayeb, M.H. (1988) *Organizations and National Culture: A Comparative Analysis*, London: Sage.

[49]Mallory, G.R., Butler, R.J., Cray, D., Hickson, D.J. and Wilson, D.C. (1983) "Implanted decision making: American owned firms in Britain," *Journal of Management Studies*, 20, 191–211; Fry, *Op. cit.*

[50]Oliveira, B. and Hickson, D.J. (1991) "Cultural bases of strategic decision making: A Brazilian and English comparison," presented at EGOS conference, Vienna.

[51]Lawrence, P. and Spybey, T. (1986) *Management and Society in Sweden*, London: Routledge and Kegan Paul.

order to arrive at a consensus regarding collective well-being. In countries such as the United States, where you are supposed to be self-sufficient and take care of yourself (high degree of individualism), labor and management relationships are more characterized by distributive bargaining. Each actor insists on safeguarding their own interests at the expense of the others and having the resources, support, and authority to pursue individual well-being independently.[52]

Transferability of Best Practice? Alternative Approaches

By pulling together the various experiences of managers and more systematic research studies, we have demonstrated how culture affects organization structure and process. We have proposed different profiles or models of organizing which evolve from different underlying cultural assumptions. This raises questions about what is considered to be "universal wisdom" and the transferability of "best practice." For the most part, arguments for transferability are in line with convergence notions which claim universality; "Management is management and best practice can be transferred anywhere." This was the rationale behind the 1980s rush to copy Japanese management practice and current rash of American-style restructuring and re-engineering.

Those that question transferability point to differences in the cultural or national (institutional) context. The culturalists question the effectiveness with which Japanese quality circles, say, can be transferred to individualist countries, such as the United States and France. The institutionalists stress the nature of ownership, and the role of government, and of labour unions in promoting such practices. Whether the success of Japanese management practices is due to cultural or institutional factors remains a matter of ongoing debate.[53]

The transfer of best practice nevertheless assumes, to some extent, universality. For example, matrix structures were heralded in the 1970s as a means of combining the benefits of product, geographic, and functional structures. In theory, decentralized decision-making, overlapping roles and responsibilities, and multiple information channels were all supposed to enable the organization to capture and analyze external complexity, to overcome internal parochialism, and to enhance response time and flexibility.[54]

While matrix management may have promised more than it could deliver, Laurent found deep resistance to matrix structures among both French and German managers, but for different reasons.[55] For the French, matrix structures violated the principle of "unity of command" and clear hierarchical reporting relationships. The idea of having two bosses was undesirable, as it created divided loyalties and caused unwelcome conflict. On the other hand, German managers resisted matrix structures, as they frustrated the need for clear-cut structure, information channels, roles and responsibilities. Again, the principles underlying matrix management ran counter to the German need to reduce uncertainty.

Thus cultural differences often undermine the best intentions and the assumed rationality of best practices. Different logics of organization exist in different countries, which can be equally effective, if not more so, given different societal contexts. In fact, there seems to be little doubt that some contexts are more favorable to the success of certain management practices, and it need not always be the country where that practice originated. Japanese quality-control methods originally came from the American gurus, Demming and Juran. Quality circles were the Japanese value-added.

Effectively transferring management structures and processes relies on the ability to recognize their inherent assumptions and to compare them with the

---

[52]Irene Rodgers, Cross-cultural consultant, personal communication.
[53]See Whitley, R.D. (ed.) (1992) *Business Systems in East Asia: Firms, Markets and Societies,* London: Sage.

[54]Davis, S. and Lawrence, P.R. (1977) *Matrix,* Reading, MA: Addison-Wesley.
[55]Laurent, A. (1981) "Matrix organization and Latin cultures," *International Studies of Management and Organization,* 10(4), 101–14.

cultural assumptions of the potential host country recipient. Countries also differ in their readiness to adopt or adapt foreign models, or to manifest a NIH (not invented here) syndrome. Throughout their history, the Japanese have borrowed models from China and then Europe. Other countries, such as Germany, may be more resistant to importing alien management practices. In eastern European countries, such as Poland, and in the developing Asian countries, such as Thailand, the eagerness to adopt foreign models is tempered by the desire to develop their own models which are more culturally appropriate.

For example, managers in eastern Europe may reject "team" approaches looking for strong leadership and a sense of clear direction in an effort to break with the more collective approach of the past.[56] Despite the prevailing wisdom that organizations need to be less hierarchical and more flexible, some managers argue that faced with competitive threats and conditions of economic decline or instability, greater centralization and stronger controls are needed.

Indeed, companies in Hong Kong, Japan, and Singapore, where the hierarchy remains firmly in place, have performed well in industries, such as banking, which are facing turbulent environments. Here, other value orientations, not readily apparent in Western business, may be at work. For example, when trying to replicate Hofstede's original study in China, another dimension was discovered— "Confucian dynamism," thrift, persistence and a long-term perspective. This added dimension was considered to account for the competitiveness of the "Five Asian Dragons": China, Hong Kong, Taiwan, Japan, and South Korea.[57]

Consider this testimony regarding the entrepreneurial, family model characteristic of the overseas Chinese business community which has been quite

successful whether transplanted to Malaysia or Canada.

> . . . The Confucian tradition of hard work, thrift and respect for one's social network may provide continuity with the right twist for today's fast-changing markets. And the central strategic question for all current multinationals—be they Chinese, Japanese or Western—is how to gather and integrate power through many small units. The evolution of a worldwide web of relatively small Chinese businesses, bound by undeniable strong cultural links, offers a working model for the future.[58]

Whatever the model of the future, be it team management or network organizations, we need to consider how culture may facilitate or hinder their diffusion. Will the more collective culture of Russia facilitate the team approach, while the greater relationship orientation of Chinese culture facilitates creating networks? Could it be that the greater emphasis on the task and the individual, which prevails in the performance management approach, will actually hinder American firms in their attempts to become more team- and network-oriented?

Given recent trends in the United States and Europe towards participative management and empowerment, the role of the leadership is changing. Rather than the more authoritarian notion of being the "boss," the role model is that of the "coach." Rather than directing and controlling, the new role calls for facilitating and developing. Notions of empowerment and the leader as coach, however, may not readily transfer.

Take, for example, two items from the Management Questionnaire designed by Laurent regarding the role of the boss (hierarchy) and of power as shown in Figure 5. Comparing the responses of managers attending training seminars from 1990 to 1994 with the results reported in 1980, we find some signs of convergence. According to self-reports, managers are becoming less authoritarian and more concerned with achieving objectives than obtaining power. Nevertheless, while country

[56]Cyr, D.J. and Schneider, S.C. (1996) "Implications for learning: human resources management in east-west joint ventures," *Organization Studies*, 17(2), 207–226.

[57]Hofstede, G. and Bond, M.H. (1988) "The Confucius connection: From cultural roots to economic growth," *Organizational Dynamics*, 16, 4–21; see also Hofstede, G. (1991) *Cultures and Organizations: Software of the Mind*, London: McGraw-Hill.

[58]Kao, *Op. cit.*, p. 36.

Figure 5   Convergence?

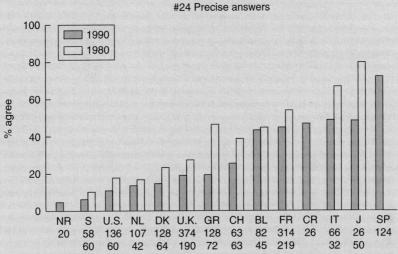

It is important for a manager to have at hand precise answers to most of the questions his/her subordinates may raise about their work.

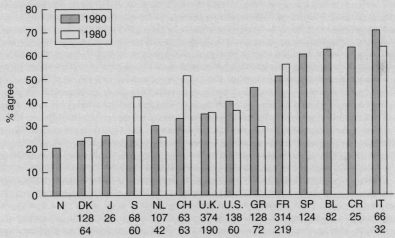

Most managers seem to be more motivated by obtaining power than by achieving objectives.

Source: Reproduced by permission of A. Laurent.

differences may have eroded, the different country rankings remain in place.

Even in countries which supposedly do not put much stock in hierarchy, such as The Netherlands and the United Kingdom, this new leadership behavior may be difficult to achieve. Therefore, what will that mean for countries in Asia where the hierarchy is still revered? What would the Asian version of empowerment look like? Perhaps there are different means of achieving this end. In the case of Japanese firms, the hierarchy is clearly, albeit implicitly, present. Nevertheless, there are apparently high levels of participation.

And as hierarchies collapse and as cooperation between units becomes more of a necessity, there is a greater need for negotiation and persuasion.

Managers will increasingly have to elicit the cooperation of people over whom they have no formal authority. In fact this may demand a more political view of organizations to which Latin firms may be more attuned.

These are the challenges facing many companies as they remodel their corporate structures. They must not lose sight of the impact of national culture in their search for a model of organization that can respond best to the demands of the rapidly changing business context, and the pressures for internationalization. They must also recognize that the "best models" are not necessarily "home grown," but that other ways of organizing may be equally, if not more, effective.

Reading 2-2   Clusters and the New Economics of Competition

Michael E. Porter

Now that companies can source capital, goods, information, and technology from around the world, often with the click of a mouse, much of the conventional wisdom about how companies and nations compete needs to be overhauled. In theory, more open global markets and faster transportation and communication should diminish the role of

▌**Michael E. Porter** is the C. Roland Christensen Professor of Business Administration at the Harvard Business School in Boston, Massachusetts. Further discussion of clusters can be found in two new essays—"Clusters and Competition" and "Competing Across Locations"—in his new collection titled *On Competition* (Harvard Business School Press, 1998).
▌ Reprinted by permission of *Harvard Business Review*. "Clusters and the New Economics of Competition" by Michael E. Porter (November–December 1998).
▌ Copyright © 1998 by the President and Fellows of Harvard College. All rights reserved.

location in competition. After all, anything that can be efficiently sourced from a distance through global markets and corporate networks is available to any company and therefore is essentially nullified as a source of competitive advantage.

But if location matters less, why, then, is it true that the odds of finding a world-class mutual-fund company in Boston are much higher than in most any other place? Why could the same be said of textile-related companies in North Carolina and South Carolina, of high-performance auto companies in southern Germany, or of fashion shoe companies in northern Italy?

Today's economic map of the world is dominated by what I call *clusters:* critical masses—in one place—of unusual competitive success in particular fields. Clusters are a striking feature of virtually every national, regional, state, and even metropolitan economy, especially in more economically advanced nations. Silicon Valley and Hollywood may be the world's best-known clusters. Clusters are not unique, however; they are highly typical—and therein lies a paradox: the enduring competitive advantages in a global economy lie increasingly in local things—knowledge, relationships, motivation—that distant rivals cannot match.

Although location remains fundamental to competition, its role today differs vastly from a generation ago. In an era when competition was driven heavily by input costs, locations with some important endowment—a natural harbor, for example, or a supply of cheap labor—often enjoyed a *comparative advantage* that was both competitively decisive and persistent over time.

Competition in today's economy is far more dynamic. Companies can mitigate many input-cost disadvantages through global sourcing, rendering the old notion of comparative advantage less relevant. Instead, competitive advantage rests on making more productive use of inputs, which requires continual innovation.

Untangling the paradox of location in a global economy reveals a number of key insights about how companies continually create competitive advantage. What happens *inside* companies is important, but clusters reveal that the immediate business environment *outside* companies plays a vital role as well. This role of locations has been long overlooked, despite striking evidence that innovation and competitive success in so many fields are geographically concentrated—whether it's entertainment in Hollywood, finance on Wall Street, or consumer electronics in Japan.

Clusters affect competitiveness within countries as well as across national borders. Therefore, they lead to new agendas for all business executives—not just those who compete globally. More broadly, clusters represent a new way of thinking about location, challenging much of the conventional wisdom about how companies should be configured, how institutions such as universities can contribute to competitive success, and how governments can promote economic development and prosperity.

What Is a Cluster?

Clusters are geographic concentrations of interconnected companies and institutions in a particular field. Clusters encompass an array of linked industries and other entities important to competition. They include, for example, suppliers of specialized inputs such as components, machinery, and services, and providers of specialized infrastructure. Clusters also often extend downstream to channels and customers and laterally to manufacturers of complementary products and to companies in industries related by skills, technologies, or common inputs. Finally, many clusters include governmental and other institutions—such as universities, standards-setting agencies, think tanks, vocational training providers, and trade associations—that provide specialized training, education, information, research, and technical support.

The California wine cluster is a good example. It includes 680 commercial wineries as well as several thousand independent wine grape growers. (See the Figure 1 "Anatomy of the California Wine Cluster.") An extensive complement of industries supporting both wine making and grape growing exists, including suppliers of grape stock, irrigation and harvesting equipment, barrels, and labels; specialized public relations and advertising firms; and numerous wine publications aimed at consumer and trade audiences. A host of local institutions is involved with wine, such as the world-renowned viticulture and enology program at the University of California at Davis, the Wine Institute, and special committees of the California senate and assembly. The cluster also enjoys weaker linkages to other California clusters in agriculture, food and restaurants, and wine-country tourism.

Consider also the Italian leather fashion cluster, which contains well-known shoe companies such as Ferragamo and Gucci as well as a host of specialized suppliers of footwear components, machinery, molds, design services, and tanned leather. (See the Figure 2 "Mapping the Italian Leather Fashion Cluster.") It also consists of several chains of related industries, including those producing different types of leather goods (linked by common inputs and

Figure 1   Anatomy of the California Wine Cluster

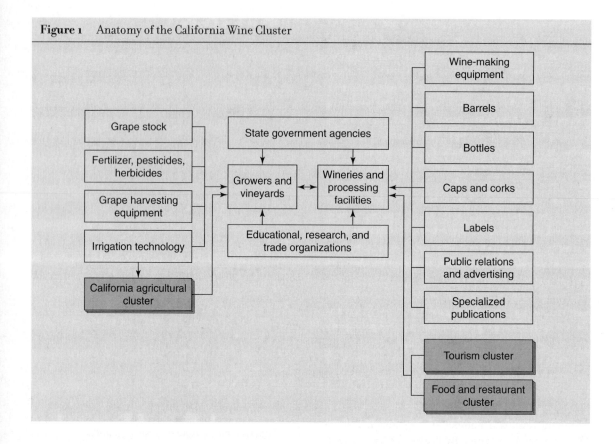

technologies) and different types of footwear (linked by overlapping channels and technologies). These industries employ common marketing media and compete with similar images in similar customer segments. A related Italian cluster in textile fashion, including clothing, scarves, and accessories, produces complementary products that often employ common channels. The extraordinary strength of the Italian leather fashion cluster can be attributed, at least in part, to the multiple linkages and synergies that participating Italian businesses enjoy.

A cluster's boundaries are defined by the linkages and complementarities across industries and institutions that are most important to competition. Although clusters often fit within political boundaries, they may cross state or even national borders. In the United States, for example, a pharmaceuticals cluster straddles New Jersey and Pennsylvania near Philadelphia. Similarly, a chemicals cluster in Germany crosses over into German-speaking Switzerland.

Clusters rarely conform to standard industrial classification systems, which fail to capture many important actors and relationships in competition. Thus significant clusters may be obscured or even go unrecognized. In Massachusetts, for example, more than 400 companies, representing at least 39,000 high-paying jobs, are involved in medical devices in some way. The cluster long remained all but invisible, however, buried within larger and overlapping industry categories such as electronic equipment and plastic products. Executives in the medical devices cluster have only recently come together to work on issues that will benefit them all.

Clusters promote both competition and cooperation. Rivals compete intensely to win and retain customers. Without vigorous competition, a cluster

Figure 2   Mapping the Italian Leather Fashion Cluster

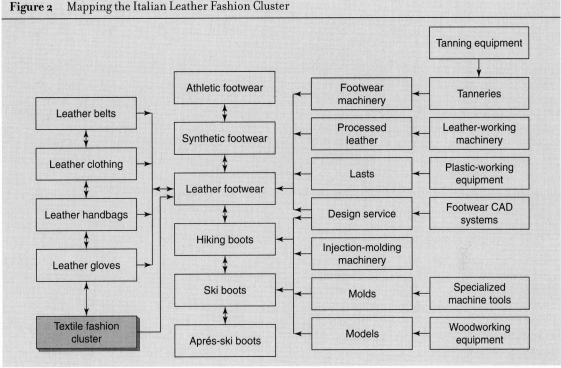

will fail. Yet there is also cooperation, much of it vertical, involving companies in related industries and local institutions. Competition can coexist with cooperation because they occur on different dimensions and among different players.

Clusters represent a kind of new spatial organizational form in between arm's-length markets on the one hand and hierarchies, or vertical integration, on the other. A cluster, then, is an alternative way of organizing the value chain. Compared with market transactions among dispersed and random buyers and sellers, the proximity of companies and institutions in one location—and the repeated exchanges among them—fosters better coordination and trust. Thus clusters mitigate the problems inherent in arm's-length relationships without imposing the inflexibilities of vertical integration or the management challenges of creating and maintaining formal linkages such as networks, alliances, and partnerships. A cluster of independent and informally linked companies and institutions represents a robust organizational form that offers advantages in efficiency, effectiveness, and flexibility.

Why Clusters Are Critical to Competition

Modern competition depends on productivity, not on access to inputs or the scale of individual enterprises. Productivity rests on *how* companies compete, not on the particular fields they compete in. Companies can be highly productive in any industry—shoes, agriculture, or semiconductors— if they employ sophisticated methods, use advanced technology, and offer unique products and services. All industries can employ advanced technology; all industries can be knowledge intensive.

The sophistication with which companies compete in a particular location, however, is strongly influenced by the quality of the local business environment.[1] Companies cannot employ advanced logistical techniques, for example, without a high-quality transportation infrastructure. Nor can companies effectively compete on sophisticated service without well-educated employees. Businesses cannot operate efficiently under onerous regulatory red tape or under a court system that fails to resolve disputes quickly and fairly. Some aspects of the business environment, such as the legal system, for example, or corporate tax rates, affect all industries. In advanced economies, however, the more decisive aspects of the business environment are often cluster specific; these constitute some of the most important microeconomic foundations for competition.

Clusters affect competition in three broad ways: first, by increasing the productivity of companies based in the area; second, by driving the direction and pace of innovation, which underpins future productivity growth; and third, by stimulating the formation of new businesses, which expands and strengthens the cluster itself. A cluster allows each member to benefit *as if* it had greater scale or *as if* it had joined with others formally—without requiring it to sacrifice its flexibility.

Clusters and Productivity   Being part of a cluster allows companies to operate more productively in sourcing inputs; accessing information, technology, and needed institutions; coordinating with related companies; and measuring and motivating improvement.

Better Access to Employees and Suppliers Companies in vibrant clusters can tap into an existing pool of specialized and experienced em-ployees, thereby lowering their search and transaction costs in recruiting. Because a cluster signals opportunity and reduces the risk of relocation for employees, it can also be easier to attract talented people from other locations, a decisive advantage in some industries.

A well-developed cluster also provides an efficient means of obtaining other important inputs. Such a cluster offers a deep and specialized supplier base. Sourcing locally instead of from distant suppliers lowers transaction costs. It minimizes the need for inventory, eliminates importing costs and delays, and—because local reputation is important—lowers the risk that suppliers will overprice or renege on commitments. Proximity improves communications and makes it easier for suppliers to provide ancillary or support services such as installation and debugging. Other things being equal, then, local outsourcing is a better solution than distant outsourcing, especially for advanced and specialized inputs involving embedded technology, information, and service content.

Formal alliances with distant suppliers can mitigate some of the disadvantages of distant outsourcing. But all formal alliances involve their own complex bargaining and governance problems and can inhibit a company's flexibility. The close, informal relationships possible among companies in a cluster are often a superior arrangement.

In many cases, clusters are also a better alternative to vertical integration. Compared with in-house units, outside specialists are often more cost effective and responsive, not only in component production but also in services such as training. Although extensive vertical integration may have once been the norm, a fast-changing environment can render vertical integration inefficient, ineffective, and inflexible.

Even when some inputs are best sourced from a distance, clusters offer advantages. Suppliers trying to penetrate a large, concentrated market will price more aggressively, knowing that as they do so they can realize efficiencies in marketing and in service.

Working against a cluster's advantages in assembling resources is the possibility that competition will render them more expensive and scarce. But

[1] I first made this argument in *The Competitive Advantage of Nations* (New York: Free Press, 1990). I modeled the effect of the local business environment on competition in terms of four interrelated influences, graphically depicted in a diamond: factor conditions (the cost and quality of inputs); demand conditions (the sophistication of local customers); the context for firm strategy and rivalry (the nature and intensity of local competition); and related and supporting industries (the local extent and sophistication of suppliers and related industries). Diamond theory stresses how these elements combine to produce a dynamic, stimulating, and intensely competitive business environment.

A cluster is the manifestation of the diamond at work. Proximity—the colocation of companies, customers, and suppliers—amplifies all of the pressures to innovate and upgrade.

companies do have the alternative of outsourcing many inputs from other locations, which tends to limit potential cost penalties. More important, clusters increase not only the demand for specialized inputs but also their supply.

Access to Specialized Information Extensive market, technical, and competitive information accumulates within a cluster, and members have preferred access to it. In addition, personal relationships and community ties foster trust and facilitate the flow of information. These conditions make information more transferable.

Complementarities A host of linkages among cluster members results in a whole greater than the sum of its parts. In a typical tourism cluster, for example, the quality of a visitor's experience depends not only on the appeal of the primary attraction but also on the quality and efficiency of complementary businesses such as hotels, restaurants, shopping outlets, and transportation facilities. Because members of the cluster are mutually dependent, good performance by one can boost the success of the others.

Complementarities come in many forms. The most obvious is when products complement one another in meeting customers' needs, as the tourism example illustrates. Another form is the coordination of activities across companies to optimize their collective productivity. In wood products, for instance, the efficiency of sawmills depends on a reliable supply of high-quality timber and the ability to put all the timber to use—in furniture (highest quality), pallets and boxes (lower quality), or wood chips (lowest quality). In the early 1990s, Portuguese sawmills suffered from poor timber quality because local landowners did not invest in timber management. Hence most timber was processed for use in pallets and boxes, a lower-value use that limited the price paid to landowners. Substantial improvement in productivity was possible, but only if several parts of the cluster changed simultaneously. Logging operations, for example, had to modify cutting and sorting procedures, while sawmills had to develop the capacity to process wood in more sophisticated ways. Coordination to develop standard wood classifications and measures was an important enabling step. Geographically dispersed companies are less likely to recognize and capture such linkages.

Other complementarities arise in marketing. A cluster frequently enhances the reputation of a location in a particular field, making it more likely that buyers will turn to a vendor based there. Italy's strong reputation for fashion and design, for example, benefits companies involved in leather goods, footwear, apparel, and accessories. Beyond reputation, cluster members often profit from a variety of joint marketing mechanisms, such as company referrals, trade fairs, trade magazines, and marketing delegations.

Finally, complementarities can make buying from a cluster more attractive for customers. Visiting buyers can see many vendors in a single trip. They also may perceive their buying risk to be lower because one location provides alternative suppliers. That allows them to multisource or to switch vendors if the need arises. Hong Kong thrives as a source of fashion apparel in part for this reason.

Access to Institutions and Public Goods Investments made by government or other public institutions—such as public spending for specialized infrastructure or educational programs—can enhance a company's productivity. The ability to recruit employees trained at local programs, for example, lowers the cost of internal training. Other quasi-public goods, such as the cluster's information and technology pools and its reputation, arise as natural by-products of competition.

It is not just governments that create public goods that enhance productivity in the private sector. Investments by companies—in training programs, infrastructure, quality centers, testing laboratories, and so on—also contribute to increased productivity. Such private investments are often made collectively because cluster participants recognize the potential for collective benefits.

Better Motivation and Measurement Local rivalry is highly motivating. Peer pressure amplifies competitive pressure within a cluster, even among noncompeting or indirectly competing companies.

Figure 3   Mapping Selected U.S. Clusters

Here are just some of the clusters in the United States. A few—Hollywood's entertainment cluster and High Point, North Carolina's household-furniture cluster—are well known. Others are less familiar, such as golf equipment in Carlsbad, California, and optics in Phoenix, Arizona. A relatively small number of clusters usually account for a major share of the economy within a geographic area as well as for an overwhelming share of its economic activity that is "exported" to other locations. *Exporting clusters*—those that export products or make investments to compete outside the local area—are the primary source of an area's economic growth and prosperity over the long run. The demand for local industries is inherently limited by the size of the local market, but exporting clusters can grow far beyond that limit.

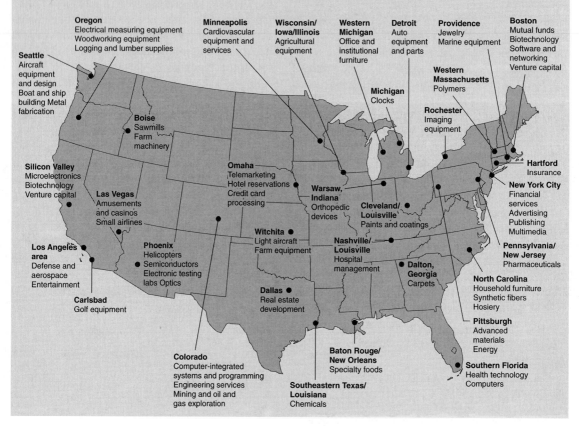

Pride and the desire to look good in the local community spur executives to attempt to outdo one another.

Clusters also often make it easier to measure and compare performances because local rivals share general circumstances—for example, labor costs and local market access—and they perform similar activities. Companies within clusters typically have intimate knowledge of their suppliers' costs. Managers are able to compare costs and employees' performance with other local companies. Additionally, financial institutions can accumulate knowledge about the cluster that can be used to monitor performance.

Clusters and Innovation   In addition to enhancing productivity, clusters play a vital role in a company's ongoing ability to innovate. Some of the same characteristics that enhance current productivity have an even more dramatic effect on innovation and productivity growth.

Because sophisticated buyers are often part of a cluster, companies inside clusters usually have a better window on the market than isolated competitors do. Computer companies based in Silicon Valley and Austin, Texas, for example, plug into customer needs and trends with a speed difficult to match by companies located elsewhere. The ongoing relationships with other entities within the cluster also help companies to learn early about evolving technology, component and machinery availability, service and marketing concepts, and so on. Such learning is facilitated by the ease of making site visits and frequent face-to-face contact.

Clusters do more than make opportunities for innovation more visible. They also provide the capacity and the flexibility to act rapidly. A company within a cluster often can source what it needs to implement innovations more quickly. Local suppliers and partners can and do get closely involved in the innovation process, thus ensuring a better match with customers' requirements.

Companies within a cluster can experiment at lower cost and can delay large commitments until they are more assured that a given innovation will pan out. In contrast, a company relying on distant suppliers faces greater challenges in every activity it coordinates with other organizations—in contracting, for example, or securing delivery or obtaining associated technical and service support. Innovation can be even harder in vertically integrated companies, especially in those that face difficult trade-offs if the innovation erodes the value of in-house assets or if current products or processes must be maintained while new ones are developed.

Reinforcing the other advantages for innovation is the sheer pressure—competitive pressure, peer pressure, constant comparison—that occurs in a cluster. Executives vie with one another to set their

companies apart. For all these reasons, clusters can remain centers of innovation for decades.

Clusters and New Business Formation   It is not surprising, then, that many new companies grow up within an existing cluster rather than at isolated locations. New suppliers, for example, proliferate within a cluster because a concentrated customer base lowers their risks and makes it easier for them to spot market opportunities. Moreover, because developed clusters comprise related industries that normally draw on common or very similar inputs, suppliers enjoy expanded opportunities.

Clusters are conducive to new business formation for a variety of reasons. Individuals working within a cluster can more easily perceive gaps in products or services around which they can build businesses. Beyond that, barriers to entry are lower than elsewhere. Needed assets, skills, inputs, and staff are often readily available at the cluster location, waiting to be assembled into a new enterprise. Local financial institutions and investors, already familiar with the cluster, may require a lower risk premium on capital. In addition, the cluster often presents a significant local market, and an entrepreneur may benefit from established relationships. All of these factors reduce the perceived risks of entry—and of exit, should the enterprise fail.

The formation of new businesses within a cluster is part of a positive feedback loop. An expanded cluster amplifies all the benefits I have described— it increases the collective pool of competitive resources, which benefits all the cluster's members. The net result is that companies in the cluster advance relative to rivals at other locations.

Birth, Evolution, and Decline

A cluster's roots can often be traced to historical circumstances. In Massachusetts, for example, several clusters had their beginnings in research done at MIT or Harvard. The Dutch transportation cluster owes much to Holland's central location within Europe, an extensive network of waterways, the efficiency of the port of Rotterdam, and the skills accumulated by the Dutch through Holland's long maritime history.

Clusters may also arise from unusual, sophisticated, or stringent local demand. Israel's cluster in irrigation equipment and other advanced agricultural technologies reflects that nation's strong desire for self-sufficiency in food together with a scarcity of water and hot, arid growing conditions. The environmental cluster in Finland emerged as a result of pollution problems created by local process industries such as metals, forestry, chemicals, and energy.

Prior existence of supplier industries, related industries, or even entire related clusters provides yet another seed for new clusters. The golf equipment cluster near San Diego, for example, has its roots in southern California's aerospace cluster. That cluster created a pool of suppliers for castings and advanced materials as well as engineers with the requisite experience in those technologies.

New clusters may also arise from one or two innovative companies that stimulate the growth of many others. Medtronic played this role in helping to create the Minneapolis medical-device cluster. Similarly, MCI and America Online have been hubs for growing new businesses in the telecommunications cluster in the Washington, D.C., metropolitan area.

Sometimes a chance event creates some advantageous factor that, in turn, fosters cluster development—although chance rarely provides the sole explanation for a cluster's success in a location. The telemarketing cluster in Omaha, Nebraska, for example, owes much to the decision by the United States Air Force to locate the Strategic Air Command (SAC) there. Charged with a key role in the country's nuclear deterrence strategy, SAC was the site of the first installation of fiber-optic telecommunications cables in the United States. The local Bell operating company (now U.S. West) developed unusual capabilities through its dealings with such a demanding customer. The extraordinary telecommunications capability and infrastructure that consequently developed in Omaha, coupled with less unique attributes such as its central-time-zone location and easily understandable

local accent, provided the underpinnings of the area's telemarketing cluster.

Once a cluster begins to form, a self-reinforcing cycle promotes its growth, especially when local institutions are supportive and local competition is vigorous. As the cluster expands, so does its influence with government and with public and private institutions.

A growing cluster signals opportunity, and its success stories help attract the best talent. Entrepreneurs take notice, and individuals with ideas or relevant skills migrate in from other locations. Specialized suppliers emerge; information accumulates; local institutions develop specialized training, research, and infrastructure; and the cluster's strength and visibility grow. Eventually, the cluster broadens to encompass related industries. Numerous case studies suggest that clusters require a decade or more to develop depth and real competitive advantage.[2]

Cluster development is often particularly vibrant at the intersection of clusters, where insights, skills, and technologies from various fields merge, sparking innovation and new businesses. An example from Germany illustrates this point. The country has distinct clusters in both home appliances and household furniture, each based on different technologies and inputs. At the intersection of the two, though, is a cluster of built-in kitchens and appliances, an area in which Germany commands a higher share of world exports than in either appliances or furniture.

Clusters continually evolve as new companies and industries emerge or decline and as local institutions develop and change. They can maintain vibrancy as competitive locations for centuries; most successful clusters prosper for decades at least. However, they can and do lose their competitive edge due to both external and internal forces.

---

[2]Selected case studies are described in "Clusters and Competition" in my book *On Competition* (Boston: Harvard Business School Press, 1998), which also includes citations of the published output of a number of cluster initiatives. Readers can also find a full treatment of the intellectual roots of cluster thinking, along with an extensive bibliography.

Technological discontinuities are perhaps the most significant of the external threats because they can neutralize many advantages simultaneously. A cluster's assets—market information, employees' skills, scientific and technical expertise, and supplier bases—may all become irrelevant. New England's loss of market share in golf equipment is a good example. The New England cluster was based on steel shafts, steel irons, and wooden-headed woods. When companies in California began making golf clubs with advanced materials, East Coast producers had difficulty competing. A number of them were acquired or went out of business.

A shift in buyers' needs, creating a divergence between local needs and needs elsewhere, constitutes another external threat. U.S. companies in a variety of clusters, for example, suffered when energy efficiency grew in importance in most parts of the world while the United States maintained low energy prices. Lacking both pressure to improve and insight into customer needs, U.S. companies were slow to innovate, and they lost ground to European and Japanese competitors.

Clusters are at least as vulnerable to internal rigidities as they are to external threats. Overconsolidation, mutual understandings, cartels, and other restraints to competition undermine local rivalry. Regulatory inflexibility or the introduction of restrictive union rules slows productivity improvement. The quality of institutions such as schools and universities can stagnate.

Groupthink among cluster participants— Detroit's attachment to gas-guzzling autos in the 1970s is one example—can be another powerful form of rigidity. If companies in a cluster are too inward looking, the whole cluster suffers from a collective inertia, making it harder for individual companies to embrace new ideas, much less perceive the need for radical innovation.

Such rigidities tend to arise when government suspends or intervenes in competition or when companies persist in old behaviors and relationships that no longer contribute to competitive advantage. Increases in the cost of doing business begin to outrun the ability to upgrade. Rigidities of this nature currently work against a variety of clusters in Switzerland and Germany.

As long as rivalry remains sufficiently vigorous, companies can partially compensate for some decline in the cluster's competitiveness by outsourcing to distant suppliers or moving part or all of production elsewhere to offset local wages that rise ahead of productivity. German companies in the 1990s, for example, have been doing just that. Technology can be licensed or sourced from other locations, and product development can be moved. Over time, however, a location will decline if it fails to build capabilities in major new technologies or needed supporting firms and institutions.

Implications for Companies

In the new economics of competition, what matters most is not inputs and scale, but productivity—and that is true in all industries. The term *high tech,* normally used to refer to fields such as information technology and biotechnology, has distorted thinking about competition, creating the misconception that only a handful of businesses compete in sophisticated ways.

In fact, there is no such thing as a low-tech industry. There are only low-tech companies—that is, companies that fail to use world-class technology and practices to enhance productivity and innovation. A vibrant cluster can help any company in any industry compete in the most sophisticated ways, using the most advanced, relevant skills and technologies.

Thus executives must extend their thinking beyond what goes on inside their own organizations and within their own industries. Strategy must also address what goes on outside. Extensive vertical integration may once have been appropriate, but companies today must forge close linkages with buyers, suppliers, and other institutions.

Specifically, understanding clusters adds the following four issues to the strategic agenda.

1. Choosing locations. Globalization and the ease of transportation and communication have led many companies to move some or all of their operations to locations with low wages, taxes, and utility

Clusters, Geography, and Economic Development

Poor countries lack well-developed clusters; they compete in the world market with cheap labor and natural resources. To move beyond this stage, the development of well-functioning clusters is essential. Clusters become an especially controlling factor for countries moving from a middle-income to an advanced economy. Even in high-wage economies, however, the need for cluster upgrading is constant. The wealthier the economy, the more it will require innovation to support rising wages and to replace jobs eliminated by improvements in efficiency and the migration of standard production to low-cost areas.

Promoting cluster formation in developing economies means starting at the most basic level. Policymakers must first address the foundations: improving education and skill levels, building capacity in technology, opening access to capital markets, and improving institutions. Over time, additional investment in more cluster-specific assets is necessary.

Government policies in developing economies often unwittingly work against cluster formation. Restrictions on industrial location and subsidies to invest in distressed areas, for example, can disperse companies artificially. Protecting local companies from competition leads to excessive vertical integration and blunted pressure for innovation, retarding cluster development.

In the early stages of economic development, countries should expand internal trade among cities and states and trade with neighboring countries as important stepping stones to building the skills to compete globally. Such trade greatly enhances cluster development. Instead, attention is typically riveted on the large, advanced markets, an orientation that has often been reinforced by protectionist policies restricting trade with nearby markets. However, the kinds of goods developing countries can trade with advanced economies are limited to commodities and to activities sensitive to labor costs.

While it is essential that clusters form, *where* they form also matters. In developing economies, a large proportion of economic activity tends to concentrate around capital cities such as Bangkok and Bogotá. That is usually because outlying areas lack infrastructure, institutions, and suppliers. It may also reflect an intrusive role by the central government in controlling competition, leading companies to locate near the seat of power and the agencies whose approval they require to do business.

This pattern of economic geography inflicts high costs on productivity. Congestion, bottlenecks, and inflexibility lead to high administrative costs and major inefficiencies, not to mention a diminished quality of life. Companies cannot easily move out from the center, however, because neither infrastructure nor rudimentary clusters exist in the smaller cities and towns. (The building of a tourism cluster in developing economies can be a positive force in improving the outlying infrastructure and in dispersing economic activity.)

Even in advanced economies, however, economic activity may be geographically concentrated. Japan offers a particularly striking case, with nearly 50% of total manufacturing shipments located around Tokyo and Osaka. This is due less to inadequacies in infrastructure in outlying areas than to a powerful and intrusive central government, with its centralizing bias in policies and institutions. The Japanese case vividly illustrates the major inefficiencies and productivity costs resulting from such a pattern of economic geography, even for advanced nations. It is a major policy issue facing Japan.

An economic geography characterized by specialization and dispersion—that is, a number of metropolitan areas, each specializing in an array of clusters—appears to be a far more productive industrial organization than one based on one or two huge, diversified cities. In nations such as Germany, Italy, Switzerland, and the United States, this kind of internal specialization and trade—and internal competition among locations—fuels productivity growth and hones the ability of companies to compete effectively in the global arena.

Figure 4   Mapping Portugal's Clusters

In a middle-income economy like Portugal, exporting clusters tend to be more natural-resource labor intensive.

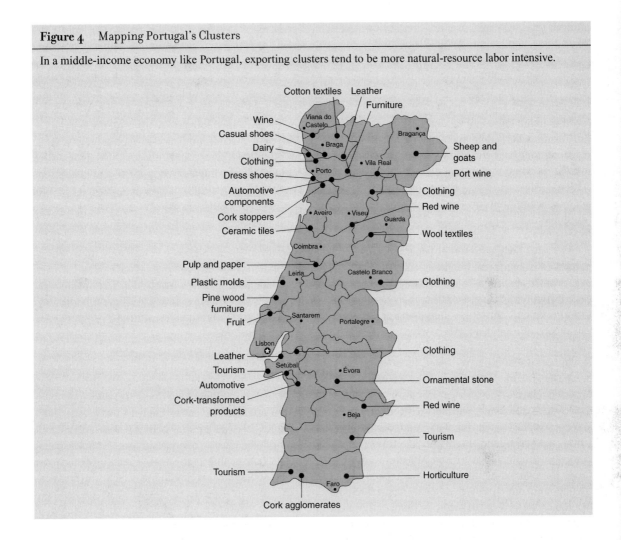

costs. What we know about clusters suggests, first, that some of those cost advantages may well turn out to be illusory. Locations with those advantages often lack efficient infrastructure, sophisticated suppliers, and other cluster benefits that can more than offset any savings from lower input costs. Savings in wages, utilities, and taxes may be highly visible and easy to measure up front, but productivity penalties remain hidden and unanticipated.

More important to ongoing competitiveness is the role of location in innovation. Yes, companies have to spread activities globally to source inputs and gain access to markets. Failure to do so will lead to a competitive *disadvantage*. And for stable, labor-intensive activities such as assembly and software translation, low factor costs are often decisive in driving locational choices.

For a company's "home base" for each product line, however, clusters are critical. Home base activities—strategy development, core product and process R&D, a critical mass of the most sophisticated production or service provision—create and renew the company's product, processes, and services. Therefore locational decisions must be based on both total systems costs and innovation potential, not on input costs alone. Cluster thinking suggests that every product line needs a home base, and the most vibrant cluster will offer the best location. Within the United States, for example, Hewlett-Packard has chosen cluster locations for the home bases of its major product lines: California, where almost all of the world's leading personal computer and workstation businesses are located, is home to personal computers and workstations; Massachusetts, which has an extraordinary concentration of world-renowned research hospitals and leading medical instrument companies, is home to medical instruments.

As global competition nullifies traditional comparative advantages and exposes companies to the best rivals from around the world, a growing number of multinationals are shifting their home bases to more vibrant clusters—often using acquisitions as a means of establishing themselves as insiders in a new location. Nestlé for example, after acquiring Rowntree Mackintosh, relocated its confectionary business to York, England, where Rowntree was originally based, because a vibrant food cluster thrives there. England, with its sweet-toothed consumers, sophisticated retailers, advanced advertising agencies, and highly competitive media companies, constitutes a more dynamic environment for competing in mass-market candy than Switzerland did. Similarly, Nestlé has moved its headquarters for bottled water to France, the most competitive location in that industry. Northern Telecom has relocated its home base for central office switching from Canada to the United States—drawn by the vibrancy of the U.S. telecommunications-equipment cluster.

Cluster thinking also suggests that it is better to move groups of linked activities to the same place than to spread them across numerous locations. Colocating R&D, component fabrication, assembly, marketing, customer support, and even related businesses can facilitate internal efficiencies in sourcing and in sharing technology and information. Grouping activities into campuses also allows

companies to extend deeper roots into local clusters, improving their ability to capture potential benefits.

2. Engaging locally. The social glue that binds clusters together also facilitates access to important resources and information. Tapping into the competitively valuable assets within a cluster requires personal relationships, face-to-face contact, a sense of common interest, and "insider" status. The mere colocation of companies, suppliers, and institutions creates the *potential* for economic value; it does not necessarily ensure its realization.

To maximize the benefits of cluster involvement, companies must participate actively and establish a significant local presence. They must have a substantial local investment even if the parent company is headquartered elsewhere. And they must foster ongoing relationships with government bodies and local institutions such as utilities, schools, and research groups.

Companies have much to gain by engaging beyond their narrow confines as single entities. Yet managers tend to be wary, at least initially. They fear that a growing cluster will attract competition, drive up costs, or cause them to lose valued employees to rivals or spin-offs. As their understanding of the cluster concept grows, however, managers realize that many participants in the cluster do not compete directly and that the offsetting benefits, such as a greater supply of better trained people, for example, can outweigh any increase in competition.

3. Upgrading the cluster. Because the health of the local business environment is important to the health of the company, upgrading the cluster should be part of management's agenda. Companies upgrade their clusters in a variety of ways.

Consider Genzyme. Massachusetts is home to a vibrant biotechnology cluster, which draws on the region's strong universities, medical centers, and venture capital firms. Once Genzyme reached the stage in its development when it needed a manufacturing facility, CEO Henri Termeer initially considered the pharmaceuticals cluster in the New

Jersey and Philadelphia area because it had what Massachusetts lacked: established expertise in drug manufacturing. Upon further reflection, however, Termeer decided to influence the process of creating a manufacturing capability in Genzyme's home base, reasoning that if his plans were successful, the company could become more competitive.

Thus Genzyme deliberately chose to work with contractors committed to the Boston area, bypassing the many specialized engineering firms located near Philadelphia. In addition, it undertook a number of initiatives, with the help of city and state government, to improve the labor force, such as offering scholarships and internships to local youth. More broadly, Genzyme has worked to build critical mass for its cluster. Termeer believes that Genzyme's success is linked to the cluster's—and that all members will benefit from a strong base of supporting functions and institutions.

4. Working collectively. The way clusters operate suggests a new agenda of collective action in the private sector. Investing in public goods is normally seen as a function of government, yet cluster thinking clearly demonstrates how companies benefit from local assets and institutions.

In the past, collective action in the private sector has focused on seeking government subsidies and special favors that often distort competition. But executives' long-term interests would be better served by working to promote a higher plane of competition. They can begin by rethinking the role of trade associations, which often do little more than lobby government, compile some statistics, and host social functions. The associations are missing an important opportunity.

Trade associations can provide a forum for the exchange of ideas and a focal point for collective action in overcoming obstacles to productivity and growth. Associations can take the lead in such activities as establishing university-based testing facilities and training or research programs; collecting cluster-related information; offering forums on common managerial problems; investigating

solutions to environmental issues; organizing trade fairs and delegations; and managing purchasing consortia.

For clusters consisting of many small and midsize companies—such as tourism, apparel, and agriculture—the need is particularly great for collective bodies to assume scale-sensitive functions. In the Netherlands, for instance, grower cooperatives built the specialized auction and handling facilities that constitute one of the Dutch flower cluster's greatest competitive advantages. The Dutch Flower Council and the Association of Dutch Flower Growers Research Groups, in which most growers participate, have taken on other functions as well, such as applied research and marketing.

Most existing trade associations are too narrow; they represent industries, not clusters. In addition, because their role is defined as lobbying the federal government, their scope is national rather than local. National associations, however, are rarely sufficient to address the local issues that are most important to cluster productivity.

By revealing how business and government together create the conditions that promote growth, clusters offer a constructive way to change the nature of the dialogue between the public and private sectors. With a better understanding of what fosters true competitiveness, executives can start asking government for the right things. The example of MassMEDIC, an association formed in 1996 by the Massachusetts medical-devices cluster, illustrates this point. It recently worked successfully with the U.S. Food and Drug Administration to streamline the approval process for medical devices. Such a step clearly benefits cluster members and enhances competition at the same time.

What's Wrong with Industrial Policy

Productivity, not exports or natural resources, determines the prosperity of any state or nation. Recognizing this, governments should strive to create an environment that supports rising productivity. Sound macroeconomic policy is necessary but not sufficient. The microeconomic foundations for competition will ultimately determine productivity and competitiveness.

Governments—both national and local—have new roles to play. They must ensure the supply of high-quality inputs such as educated citizens and physical infrastructure. They must set the rules of competition—by protecting intellectual property and enforcing antitrust laws, for example—so that productivity and innovation will govern success in the economy. Finally, governments should promote cluster formation and upgrading and the buildup of public or quasi-public goods that have a significant impact on many linked businesses.

This sort of role for government is a far cry from industrial policy. In industrial policy, governments target "desirable" industries and intervene—through subsidies or restrictions on investments by foreign companies, for example—to favor local companies. In contrast, the aim of cluster policy is to reinforce the development of *all* clusters. This means that a traditional cluster such as agriculture should not be abandoned; it should be upgraded. Governments should not choose among clusters, because each one offers opportunities to improve productivity and support rising wages. Every cluster not only contributes directly to national productivity but also affects the productivity of *other* clusters. Not all clusters will succeed, of course, but market forces—not government decisions—should determine the outcomes.

Government, working with the private sector, should reinforce and build on existing and emerging clusters rather than attempt to create entirely new ones. Successful new industries and clusters often grow out of established ones. Businesses involving advanced technology succeed not in a vacuum but where there is already a base of related activities in the field. In fact, most clusters form independently of government action—and sometimes in spite of it. They form where a foundation of locational advantages exists. To justify cluster development efforts, some seeds of a cluster should have already passed a market test.

Cluster development initiatives should embrace the pursuit of competitive advantage and specialization rather than simply imitate successful clusters in other locations. This requires building on local sources of uniqueness. Finding areas of specialization normally proves more effective than head-on competition with well-established rival locations.

New Public-Private Responsibilities

Economic geography in an era of global competition, then, poses a paradox. In a global economy—which boasts rapid transportation, high-speed communication, and accessible markets—one would expect location to diminish in importance. But the opposite is true. The enduring competitive advantages in a global economy are often heavily local, arising from concentrations of highly specialized skills and knowledge, institutions, rivals, related businesses, and sophisticated customers. Geographic, cultural, and institutional proximity leads to special access, closer relationships, better information, powerful incentives, and other advantages in productivity and innovation that are difficult to tap from a distance. The more the world economy becomes complex, knowledge based, and dynamic, the more this is true.

Leaders of businesses, government, and institutions all have a stake—and a role to play—in the new economics of competition. Clusters reveal the mutual dependence and collective responsibility of all these entities for creating the conditions for productive competition. This task will require fresh thinking on the part of leaders and the willingness to abandon the traditional categories that drive our thinking about who does what in the economy. The lines between public and private investment blur. Companies, no less than governments and universities, have a stake in education. Universities have a stake in the competitiveness of local businesses. By revealing the process by which wealth is actually created in an economy, clusters open new public–private avenues for constructive action.

Reading 2-3   The End of Corporate Imperialism

C.K. Prahalad and Kenneth Lieberthal

As they search for growth, multinational corporations will have to compete in the big emerging markets of China, India, Indonesia, and Brazil. The operative word is *emerging*. A vast consumer base of hundreds of millions of people is developing rapidly. Despite the uncertainty and the difficulty of doing business in markets that remain opaque to outsiders, Western MNCs will have no choice but to enter them. (See Table 1 "Market Size: Emerging Markets versus the United States.")

During the first wave of market entry in the 1980s, MNCs operated with what might be termed an imperialist mind-set. They assumed that the big emerging markets were new markets for their old products. They foresaw a bonanza in incremental sales for their existing products or the chance to squeeze profits out of their sunset technologies. Further, the corporate center was seen as the sole locus of product and process innovation. Many multinationals did not consciously look at emerging markets as sources of technical and managerial talent for their global operations. As a result of this imperialist mind-set, multinationals have achieved only limited success in those markets.

Many corporations, however, are beginning to see that the opportunity that big emerging markets represent will demand a new way of thinking. Success will require more than simply developing greater cultural sensitivity. The more we understand the nature of these markets, the more we believe that multinationals will have to rethink and reconfigure every element of their business models.

So while it is still common today to question how corporations like General Motors and McDonald's will change life in the big emerging markets, Western executives would be smart to turn the question around. Success in the emerging markets will require innovation and resource shifts on such a scale that life within the multinationals themselves will inevitably be transformed. In short, as MNCs achieve success in those markets, they will also bring corporate imperialism to an end.

We would not like to give the impression that we think markets such as China, India, Brazil, and Indonesia will enjoy clear sailing. As Indonesia is showing, these markets face major obstacles to continued high growth; political disruptions, for example, can slow down and even reverse trends toward more open markets. But given the long-term growth prospects, MNCs will have to compete in those markets. Having studied in-depth the evolution of India and China over the past 20 years, and having worked extensively with MNCs competing in these and other countries, we believe that there are five basic questions that MNCs must answer to compete in the big emerging markets:

- Who is the emerging middle-class market in these countries, and what kind of business model will effectively serve their needs?
- What are the key characteristics of the distribution networks in these markets, and how are the networks evolving?
- What mix of local and global leadership is required to foster business opportunities?
- Should the MNC adopt a consistent strategy for all its business units within one country?

▌ **C.K. Prahalad** is the Harvey C. Fruehauf Professor of Business Administration and professor of corporate strategy and international business at the University of Michigan Business School in Ann Arbor. **Kenneth Lieberthal** is the William Davidson Professor of Business Administration, professor of international business, and the Arthur F. Thurnau Professor of Political Science at the University of Michigan.
▌ Reprinted by permission of *Harvard Business Review*. "The End of Corporate Imperialism" by C. K. Prahalad and Kenneth Lieberthal (July–August 1998).
▌ Copyright © 1998 by the President and Fellows of Harvard College. All rights reserved.

Table 1   Market Size: Emerging Markets versus the United States

Product	China	India	Brazil	United States
Televisions (million units)	13.6	5.2	7.8	23.0
Detergent (kilograms per person)	2.5	2.7	7.3	14.4
(million tons)	3.5	2.3	1.1	3.9
Shampoo (in billions of dollars)	1.0	0.8	1.0	1.5
Pharmaceuticals (in billions of dollars)	5.0	2.8	8.0	60.6
Automotive (million units)	1.6	0.7	2.1	15.5
Power (megawatt capacity)	236,542	81,736	59,950	810,964

- Will local partners accelerate the multinational's ability to learn about the market?

What Is the Business Model for the Emerging Middle Class?

What is big and emerging in countries like China and India is a new consumer base consisting of hundreds of millions of people. Starved of choice for over 40 years, the rising middle class is hungry for consumer goods and a better quality of life and is ready to spend. The emerging markets have entered a new era of product availability and choice. In India alone, there are 50 brands of toothpaste available today and more than 250 brands of shoes.

Consumers are experimenting and changing their choice of products rapidly. Indians, for example, will buy any product once, but brand switching is common. One survey found that Indian consumers tried on average 6.2 brands of the same packaged-goods product in one year, compared with 2.0 for American consumers. But does this growth of consumer demand add up to a wealth of opportunity for the MNCs?

The answer is yes . . . but. Consider the constitution of the middle class itself. When managers in the West hear about the emerging middle class of India or China, they tend to think in terms of the middle class in Europe or the United States. This is one sign of an imperialist mind-set—the assumption that everyone must be just like "us." True, consumers in the emerging markets today are much

more affluent than they were before their countries liberalized trade, but they are not affluent by Western standards. This is usually the first big miscalculation that MNCs make.

When these markets are analyzed, moreover, they turn out to have a structure very unlike that of the West. Income levels that characterize the Western middle class would represent a tiny upper class of consumers in any of the emerging markets. Today the active consumer market in the big emerging markets has a three-tiered pyramid structure. (See Figure 1 "The Market Pyramid in China, India, and Brazil.")

Consider India. At the top of the pyramid, in tier one, is a relatively small number of consumers who are responsive to international brands and have the income to afford them. Next comes tier two, a much larger group of people who are less attracted to international brands. Finally, at the bottom of the pyramid of consumers is tier three—a massive group that is loyal to local customs, habits, and often to local brands. Below that is another huge group made up of people who are unlikely to become active consumers anytime soon.

MNCs have tended to bring their existing products and marketing strategies to the emerging markets without properly accounting for these market pyramids. They end up, therefore, becoming high-end niche players. That's what happened to Revlon, for example, when it introduced its Western beauty products to China in 1976 and to India in 1994. Only the top tier valued and could afford the cachet

Figure 1   The Market Pyramid in China, India, and Brazil

Purchasing Power Parity in U.S. Dollars		Population in Millions		
		China	India	Brazil
Tier 1	Greater than $20,000	2	7	9
Tier 2	$10,000 to $20,000	60	63	15
Tier 3	$5,000 to $10,000	330	125	27
	Less than $5,000	800	700	105

of Revlon's brand. And consider Ford's recent foray into India with its Escort, which Ford priced at more than $21,000. In India, anything over $20,000 falls into the luxury segment. The most popular car, the Maruti-Suzuki, sells for $10,000 or less. Fiat learned to serve that tier of the market in Brazil, designing a new model called the Palio specifically for Brazilians. Fiat is now poised to transfer that success from Brazil to India.

While it is seductive for companies like Ford to think of big emerging markets as new outlets for old products, a mind-set focused on incremental volume misses the real opportunity. To date, MNCs like Ford and Revlon have either ignored tier two of the pyramid or conceded it to local competitors. But if Ford wants to be more than a small, high-end player, it will have to design a robust and roomy $9,000 car to compete with Fiat's Palio or with a locally produced car.

Tailoring products to the big emerging markets is not a trivial task. Minor cultural adaptations or marginal cost reductions will not do the job. Instead, to overcome an implicit imperialism, companies must undergo a fundamental rethinking of every element of their business model.

Rethinking the Price-Performance Equation
Consumers in big emerging markets are getting a fast education in global standards, but they often are unwilling to pay global prices. In India, an executive in a multinational food-processing company told us the story of a man in Delhi who went to McDonald's for a hamburger. He didn't like the food or the prices, but he liked the ambience. Then he went to Nirula's, a successful Delhi food chain. He liked the food and the prices there, but he complained to the manager because Nirula's did not have the same pleasant atmosphere as McDonald's. The moral of the story? Price-performance expectations are changing, often to the consternation of both the multinationals and the locals. McDonald's has been forced to adapt its menu to local tastes by adding vegetable burgers. Local chains like Nirula's have been pushed to meet global standards for cleanliness and ambience.

Consumers in the big emerging markets are far more focused than their Western counterparts on the price-performance equation. That focus tends to give low-cost local competitors the edge in hotly contested markets. MNCs can, however, learn to turn this price sensitivity to their advantage.

Philips Electronics, for example, introduced a combination video-CD player in China in 1994. Although there is virtually no market for this product in Europe or the United States, the Chinese quickly embraced it as a great two-for-one bargain. More than 15 million units have been sold in China, and the product seems likely to catch on in Indonesia and India. Consumers in those countries see the player as good value for the money.

Rethinking Brand Management   Armed with powerful, established brands, multinationals are likely to overestimate the extent of Westernization in the emerging markets and the value of using a consistent approach to brand management around the world.

In India, Coca-Cola overvalued the pull of its brand among the tier-two consumers. Coke based its advertising strategy on its worldwide image and then watched the advantage slip to Pepsi, which had adopted a campaign that was oriented toward the Indian market. As one of Coke's senior executives recently put it in the *Wall Street Journal,* "We're so successful in international business that we applied a tried and true formula . . . and it was the wrong formula to apply in India."

It took Coke more than two years to get the message, but it is now repositioning itself by using local heroes, such as popular cricket players, in its advertising. Perhaps more important, it is heavily promoting a popular Indian brand of cola—Thums Up—which Coke bought from a local bottler in 1993, only to scorn it for several years as a poor substitute for the Real Thing.

Rethinking the Costs of Market Building   For many MNCs, entering an emerging market means introducing a new product or service category. But Kellogg, for example, found that introducing breakfast cereals to India was a slow process because it meant creating new eating habits. Once the company had persuaded Indians to eat cereal, at great expense, local competitors were able to ride on Kellogg's coattails by introducing breakfast cereals with local flavors. As a result, Kellogg may discover in the long run that they paid too high a price for too small a market. Sampling, celebrity endorsements, and other forms of consumer education are expensive: regional tastes vary and language barriers can create difficulties. India, for example, has 13 major languages and pronounced cultural differences across regions.

Multinationals would do well to rethink the costs of building markets. Changing developed habits

is difficult and expensive. Providing consumers with a new product that requires no reeducation can be much easier. For example, consider the rapid adoption of pagers in China. Because telephones are not widely available there, pagers have helped fill the void as a means of one-way communication.

Rethinking Product Design   Even when consumers in emerging markets appear to want the same products as are sold elsewhere, some redesign is often necessary to reflect differences in use, distribution, or selling. Because the Chinese use pagers to send entire messages—which is not how they were intended to be used—Motorola developed pagers capable of displaying more lines of information. The result: Motorola encountered the enviable problem of having to scramble to keep up with exploding demand for its product.

In the mid-1980s, a leading MNC in telecommunications began exporting its electronic switching systems to China for use in the phone system. The switching systems had been designed for the company's home market, where there were many customers but substantial periods when the phones were not in use. In China, on the other hand, there were very few phones, but they were in almost constant use. The switching system, which worked flawlessly in the West, simply couldn't handle the load in China. Ultimately, the company had to redesign its software.

Distribution can also have a huge impact on product design. A Western maker of frozen desserts, for example, had to reformulate one of its products not because of differences in consumers' tastes, but because the refrigerators in most retail outlets in India weren't cold enough to store the product properly. The product had been designed for storage at minus 15 degrees centigrade, but the typical retailer's refrigerator operates at minus 4 degrees. Moreover, power interruptions frequently shut down the refrigerators.

Rethinking Packaging   Whether the problem is dust, heat, or bumpy roads, the distribution infrastructure in emerging markets places special strains on packaging. One glass manufacturer, for example, was stunned at the breakage it sustained as a result of poor roads and trucks in India.

And consumers in tiers two and three are likely to have packaging preferences that are different from consumers in the West. Single-serve packets, or sachets, are enormously popular in India. They allow consumers to buy only what they need, experiment with new products, and conserve cash at the same time. Products as varied as detergents, shampoos, pickles, cough syrup, and oil are sold in sachets in India, and it is estimated that they make up 20% to 30% of the total sold in their categories. Sachets are spreading as a marketing device for such items as shampoos in China as well.

Rethinking Capital Efficiency   The common wisdom is that the infrastructure problems in emerging markets—inefficient distribution systems, poor banking facilities, and inadequate logistics—will require companies to use more capital than in Western markets, not less. But that is the wrong mindset. Hindustan Lever, a subsidiary of Unilever in India, saw a low-cost Indian detergent maker, Nirma, become the largest branded detergent maker in the world over a seven-year period by courting the tier-two and tier-three markets. Realizing that it could not compete by making marginal changes, Hindustan Lever rethought every aspect of its business, including production, distribution, marketing, and capital efficiency.

Today Hindustan Lever operates a $2 billion business with effectively zero working capital. Consider just one of the practices that makes this possible. The company keeps a supply of signed checks from its dealers. When it ships an order, it simply writes in the correct amount for the order. This practice is not uncommon in India. The Indian agribusiness company, Rallis, uses it with its 20,000 dealers in rural India. But this way of doing things is unheard of in Unilever's home countries, the United Kingdom and the Netherlands.

Hindustan Lever also manages to operate with minimal fixed capital. It does so in part through an active program of supplier management; the company works with local entrepreneurs who own and manage plants whose capacity is dedicated to Hindustan Lever's products. Other MNCs will find that there is less need for vertical integration in emerging markets than they might think. Quality suppliers can be located and developed. Their lower overhead structure can help the MNCs gain a competitive cost position. Supply chain management is an important tool for changing the capital efficiency of a multinational's operations.

Rather than concede the market, Hindustan Lever radically changed itself and is today successfully competing against Nirma with a low-cost detergent called Wheel. The lesson learned in India has not been lost on Unilever. It is unlikely to concede tier-two and tier-three markets in China, Indonesia, or Brazil without a fight.

How Does the Distribution System Work?

One of the greatest regrets of multinational executives, especially those we spoke with in China, was that they had not invested more in distribution before launching their products. Access to distribution is often critical to success in emerging markets, and it cannot be taken for granted. There is no substitute for a detailed understanding of the unique characteristics of a market's distribution system and how that system is likely to evolve.

Consider the differences between China and India. Distribution in China is primarily local and provincial. Under the former planned economy, most distribution networks were confined to political units, such as counties, cities, or provinces. Even at present, there is no real national distribution network for most products. Many MNCs have gained access to provincial networks by creating joint ventures. But these JVs are now impediments to the creation of the badly needed national network. Chinese JV partners protect their turf. This gap between the MNCs' need for a national, cost-effective distribution system and the more locally oriented goals of their partners is creating serious tensions. We expect that many JVs formed originally to allow multinationals market and distribution access will be restructured because of this very issue during the next five to seven years.

In India, on the other hand, individual entrepreneurs have already put together a national distribution system in a wide variety of businesses. Established companies such as Colgate-Palmolive and Godrej in personal care, Hindustan Lever in packaged goods, Tatas in trucks, Bajaj in scooters—the list is long—control their own distribution systems. Those systems take the form of long-standing arrangements with networks of small-scale distributors throughout the country, and the banking network is part of those relationships. Many of the established packaged-goods companies reach more than 3 million retail outlets—using trains, trucks, bullock-drawn carts, camels, and bicycles. And many companies claim to service each one of those outlets once a week.

Any MNC that wants to establish its own distribution system in India inevitably runs up against significant obstacles and costs. Ford, for example, is trying to establish a new, high-quality dealer network to sell cars in India. To obtain a dealership, each prospective dealer is expected to invest a large amount of his own money and must undergo special training. In the long haul, Ford's approach may prove to be a major source of advantage to the company, but the cost in cash and managerial attention of building the dealers' network will be substantial.

Ironically, the lack of a national distribution system in China may be an advantage. MNCs with patience and ingenuity can more easily build distribution systems to suit their needs, and doing so might confer competitive advantages. As one manager we talked to put it, "The trick to sustained, long-term profitability in China lies not in technology or in savvy advertising or even in low pricing, but rather in building a modern distribution system." Conceivably, China may see consolidation of the retail market earlier than India.

The Chinese and Indian cases signal the need for MNCs to develop a market-specific distribution strategy. In India, MNCs will have to determine who controls national distribution in order to distinguish likely partners from probable competitors. In China, multinationals seeking national distribution of their products must consider the motivations of potential partners before entering relationships that may frustrate their intentions.

Will Local or Expatriate Leadership Be More Effective?

Leadership of a multinational's venture in an emerging market requires a complex blend of local sensitivity and global knowledge. Getting the balance right is critical but never easy. MNCs frequently lack the cultural understanding to get the mix of expatriate and local leaders right.

Expatriates from the MNCs' host country play multiple roles. They transfer technology and management practices. They ensure that local employees understand and practice the corporate culture. In the early stages of market development, expatriates are the conduits for information flow between the multinational's corporate office and the local operation. But while headquarters staff usually recognizes the importance of sending information to the local operation, they tend to be less aware that information must also be received from the other direction. Expatriates provide credibility at headquarters when they convey information, especially information concerning the adaptations the corporation must make in order to be successful in the emerging market. Given these important roles, the large number of expatriates in China—170,000 by one count—is understandable.

Every multinational operation we observed in China had several expatriates in management positions. In India, by contrast, we rarely saw expatriate managers, and the few that we did see were usually of Indian origin. That's because among the big emerging markets, India is unique in that it has developed, over time, a cadre of engineers and managers. The Indian institutes of technology and institutes of management turn out graduates with a high degree of technical competence.

Perhaps more important from the perspective of a multinational, Indian managers speak English fluently and seem adept at learning a new corporate culture. At the same time, they have a much better appreciation of local nuances and a deeper commitment to the Indian market than any expatriate could have.

Those seeming advantages may be offset, however, by two disadvantages. First, a management team of native-born managers may not have the same "share of voice" at corporate headquarters that expatriate managers have. Yet maintaining a strong voice is essential, given the difficulty most managers at corporate headquarters have in understanding the dynamics and peculiar requirements of operating in emerging markets. Second, the "soft technology" that is central to Western competitive advantage—the bundle of elements that creates a dynamic, cost-effective, market-sensitive organization—is hard to develop when the management team consists of people who have worked only briefly, if at all, in such an organization.

Several multinationals have sent expatriates of Chinese or Indian origin from their U.S. or European base back to their Chinese or Indian operations in order to convey the company's soft technology in a culturally sensitive way. But that strategy has not, in general, been successful. As one manager we spoke to noted, "Indians from the United States who are sent back as expatriates are frozen in time. They remember the India they left 20 years ago. They are totally out of sync. But they do not have the humility to accept that they have to learn." We heard the same sentiment echoed in China, both for Chinese-Americans and, less frequently, for Chinese who had obtained a higher education in the United States and then returned as a part of a multinational management team.

Using American or West European expatriates during the early years of market entry can make sense, but this approach has its own set of problems. Cultural and language difficulties in countries like China and India typically limit expats' interaction with the locals as well as their effectiveness. In addition, the need to understand how to deal with the local political system, especially in China, makes long-term assignments desirable. It often takes an expatriate manager two years to get fully up to speed. From the company's perspective, it makes sense to keep that manager in place for another three years to take full advantage of what he or she has learned. But few Western expatriates are willing to stay in China that long; many feel that a long assignment keeps them out of the loop and may impose a high career cost. Multinationals, therefore, need to think about how to attract and retain high-quality expatriate talent, how to maintain expats' links to the parent company, and how to use and pass along expats' competencies once they move on to another post.

Is It Necessary to "Present One Face"?

Beyond the normal organizational questions that would exist wherever a company does business, there is a question of special importance in emerging markets: Do local political considerations require the multinational to adopt a uniform strategy for each of its business units operating in the country, or can it permit each unit to act on its own?

As with the issue of distribution, the contrasts between China and India make clear why there is no one right answer to this question. In China, massive governmental interference in the economy makes a uniform country strategy necessary. The Chinese government tends to view the activities of individual business units as part of a single company's effort, and therefore concessions made by any one unit—such as an agreement to achieve a certain level of local sourcing—may well become requirements for the others. An MNC in China must be able to articulate a set of principles that conforms to China's announced priorities, and it should coordinate the activities of its various business units so that they resonate with those priorities.

Given the way most multinationals operate, "presenting one face" to China is very difficult. Business units have their own P&L responsibilities and are reluctant to lose their autonomy. Reporting lines can become overly complex. Although we observed many organizational approaches, not a single MNC we looked at is completely satisfied with its approach to this difficult issue.

Is it any wonder? Consider the life of one MNC executive we visited in China. As the head of his company's China effort, he has to coordinate with the company's regional headquarters in Japan, report to international headquarters in Europe, and maintain close contact with corporate headquarters in North America. He also has to meet with members of the Chinese government, with the MNC's business-unit executives in China, and with the leaders of the business units' Chinese partners. Simply maintaining all of these contacts is extraordinarily taxing and time consuming.

There is somewhat less need to present one face to India. Since 1991, the Indian government has scaled back its efforts to shape what MNCs do in the country. Business units may therefore act more independently than would be appropriate in China. The strategy for India can be developed on a business-by-business basis. Nonetheless, the market is large and complex. National regulations are onerous, and state-level governments are still so different from one another that MNCs are well advised to develop knowledge that they can share with all their business units in India.

Do Partners Foster Valuable Learning?

In the first wave of market entry, multinationals used joint ventures extensively as a way not only to navigate through bureaucratic processes but also to learn about new markets. With few exceptions, however, JVs in emerging markets have been problematic. In some cases, executives of the multinationals mistakenly thought the JVs would do their strategic thinking for them. In most cases, tensions in JV relationships have diverted management attention away from learning about the market.

One consistent problem is that companies enter joint ventures with very different expectations. One Chinese manager described the situation in terms of an old saying: We are sleeping in the same bed, with different dreams. The local partner sees the MNC as a source of technology and investment, and the multinational sees the partner as a means to participate in the domestic market.

When they come to an emerging market, multinationals usually are still building their manufacturing and marketing infrastructures, and they don't expect immediate returns. Local partners, however, often want to see short-term profit. This disparity of aims leads to enormous strain in the relationship. The costs associated with expatriate managers also become a bone of contention. Who controls what can be yet another source of trouble—especially when the domestic partner has experience in the business. And when new investment is needed to grow the business, local partners often are unable to bring in the matching funds, yet they resent the dilution of their holding and the ensuing loss of control.

MNCs are finally learning that their local partners often do not have adequate market knowledge. The experience of most local partners predates the emergence of real consumer markets, and their business practices can be archaic. But as markets evolve toward greater transparency, as MNCs develop senior managers who understand how "the system" works, and as the availability of local talent increases, multinationals have less to gain by using intermediaries as a vehicle for learning.

The MNCs' need for local partners clearly is diminishing. In 1997, a consulting firm surveyed 67 companies invested in China and found that the percentage of their projects that became wholly foreign-owned enterprises grew steadily from 18% in 1992 to 37% in 1996. A *passive* partner that can provide a local face may still be important in some industries, but this is a very different matter from the JV.

Success Will Transform the Multinationals

As executives look for growth in the big emerging markets, they tend quite naturally to focus on the size of the opportunity and the challenges that lie ahead. Few, however, stop to think about how success will transform their companies. But consider the magnitude of the changes we have been describing and the sheer size of the markets in question. Success in the big emerging markets will surely change the shape of the modern multinational as we know it today.

For years, executives have assumed they could export their current business models around the globe. That assumption has to change. Citicorp, for example, aims to serve a billion banking customers by 2010. There is no way Citicorp, given its current cost structure, can profitably serve someone in Beijing or Delhi whose net wealth is less than $5,000. But if Citicorp creates a new business model—rethinking every element of its cost structure—it will be able to serve not only average Chinese people but also inner-city residents in New York. In short, companies must realize that the innovation required to serve the large tier-two and tier-three segments in emerging markets has the potential to make them more competitive in their traditional markets—and therefore in *all* markets.

Over time, the imperialist assumption that innovation comes from the center will gradually fade away and die. Increasingly, as multinationals develop products better adapted to the emerging markets, they are finding that those markets are becoming an important source of innovation. Telecommunications companies, for example, are discovering that people in markets with no old technology to "forget" may accept technological changes faster. MNCs such as Texas Instruments and Motorola are assigning responsibility for software-oriented business development to their Indian operations. China has become such a significant market for video-CD players that the Chinese are likely to be major players in introducing the next round of video-CD standards around the world.

The big emerging markets will also have a significant influence on the product development philosophy of the MNCs. One major multinational recognized to its surprise that the Chinese have found a way of producing high-quality detergents with equipment and processes that cost about one-fifth of what the MNC spends. Stories like that get repeated in a wide variety of businesses, including fine chemicals, cement, textile machinery, trucks, and television sets.

As product development becomes decentralized, collaboration between labs in Bangalore, London, and Dallas, for example, will gradually become the rule, not the exception. New-product introductions will have to take into consideration nontraditional centers of influence. Thus in the CD business at Philips, new-product introductions, which previously occurred almost exclusively in Europe, now also take place in Shanghai and California.

As corporate imperialism draws to a close, multinationals will increasingly look to emerging markets for talent. India is already recognized as a source of technical talent in engineering, sciences, and software, as well as in some aspects of management. All high-tech companies recruit in India not only for the Indian market but also for the global market. China, given its growth and its technical and managerial-training infrastructure, has not yet reached that stage, but it may well reach it in the not-too-distant future.

A major shift in geographical resources will take place within the next five years. Philips is already downsizing in Europe and reportedly employs more Chinese than Dutch workers. Over 40% of the market for Coke, Gillette, Lucent, Boeing, and GE power systems is in Asia. And in the last two years, ABB has shrunk its European head count by more than 40,000 while adding 45,000 people in Asia.

In addition to these changes, an increasing percentage of the investment in plant and equipment and marketing will go to the emerging markets. As those markets grow to account for 30% to 40% of capital invested—and even a larger percentage of market share and profits—they will attract much more attention from top management.

The importance of these markets will inevitably be reflected in the ethnic and national origin of senior management. At present, with a few exceptions such as Citicorp and Unilever, senior management ranks are filled with nationals from the company's home country. By the year 2010, however, the top 200 managers from around the world for any multinational will have a much greater cultural and ethnic mix.

How many of today's multinationals are prepared to accommodate 30% to 40% of their top team of 200 coming from China, India, and Brazil? How will that cultural mix influence decision making, risk taking, and team building? Diversity will put an enormous burden on top-level managers to articulate clearly the values and behaviors expected of senior managers, and it will demand large investments in training and socialization. The need for a single company culture will also become more critical as people from different cultures begin to work together. Providing the right glue to hold companies together will be a big challenge.

That challenge will be intensified by an impending power shift within multinationals. The end of corporate imperialism suggests more than a new relationship between the developed and the emerging economies. It also suggests an end to the era of centralized corporate power—embodied in the attitude that "headquarters knows best"—and a shift to a much more dispersed base of power and influence.

Consider the new patterns of knowledge transfer we are beginning to see. Unilever, for example, is transferring Indian managers with experience in low-cost distribution to China, where they will build a national distribution system and train Chinese managers. And it has transferred Indian managers with knowledge of tier-two markets to Brazil. The phenomenon of using managers from outside the home country to transfer knowledge is relatively new. It will grow over time to the point where the multinational becomes an organization with several centers of expertise and excellence.

Multinationals will be shaped by a wide variety of forces in the coming decades. The big emerging markets will be one of the major forces they come up against. And the effect will be nothing short of dramatic change on both sides. Together, they will challenge each other to change for the better as a truly global twenty-first century economy takes shape. The MNCs will create a higher standard of products, quality, technology, and management practices. Large, opaque markets will gradually become more transparent. The process of transition to market economies will be evolutionary, uneven, and fraught with uncertainties. But the direction is no longer in question.

In order to participate effectively in the big emerging markets, multinationals will increasingly have to reconfigure their resource base, rethink their cost structure, redesign their product development process, and challenge their assumptions about the cultural mix of their top managers. In short, they will have to develop a new mind-set and adopt new business models to achieve global competitiveness in the postimperialist age.

CHAPTER 3

Developing Strategic Capabilities:
Building Layers of Competitive Advantage

As the turbulent international environment reshaped global competition in the closing decades of the 20th century, a number of different perspectives and prescriptions emerged on how companies could create strategic advantage in their worldwide businesses. Consider, for example, three of the most influential articles on global strategy published during the 1980s—the decade in which many of the new trends first emerged.[1] Each is reasonable and intuitively appealing. What soon becomes clear, however, is that their prescriptions are very different and, at times, contradictory:

- Theodore Levitt argued that effective global strategy was not a bag of many tricks but the successful practice of just one: product standardization. According to him, the core of a global strategy lay in developing a standardized product to be produced and sold the same way throughout the world.
- An article by Thomas Hout, Michael Porter, and Eileen Rudden, on the other hand, suggested that effective global strategy required the approach not of a hedgehog, who knows only one trick, but that of a fox, who knows many. These include exploiting economies of scale through global volume, taking preemptive positions through quick and large investments, and managing interdependently to achieve synergies across different activities.
- Gary Hamel and C. K. Prahalad's prescription for a global strategy contradicted that of Levitt even more sharply. Instead of a single standardized product, they recommended a broad product portfolio, with many product varieties, so that investments in technologies and distribution channels could be shared. Cross-subsidization across products and markets and the development of a strong worldwide distribution system were at the center of these authors' views on how to succeed in the game of global chess.

These different analyses and prescriptions not only highlight the complexity of the strategic challenge that faced managers in large, worldwide companies, but also the confusion of advice being offered to them. As we described in the preceding chapter, to achieve sustainable competitive advantage, these companies need to develop layers of competitive advantage—global-scale efficiency, multinational flexibility, and the ability to develop innovations and leverage knowledge on a worldwide basis. Each of the

---

[1]Levitt's article is included in Reading 3-1. References for the other two: T. Hout, M. E. Porter, E. Rudden, "How Global Companies Win Out," *Harvard Business Review* 60, no. 5 (1982), pp. 98–109. G. Hamel and C. K. Prahalad, "Do you Really Have a Global Strategy?" *Harvard Business Review* 63, no. 4 (1985), pp. 139–149.

different prescriptions highlighted above focuses on one or the other of these different strategic objectives: The challenge for most companies, however, is to achieve all of them simultaneously.

In this chapter, we first present a broad framework that relates the different strategic objectives and the different means available to a company for achieving these objectives. From this, we highlight some specific issues that managers must consider for developing worldwide competitive advantage. We then use this framework to describe some of the key characteristics of multinational, international, and global strategies—the three traditional approaches to worldwide management we introduced in the previous two chapters—and to highlight the respective strengths and vulnerabilities of each of these approaches.

We conclude by showing how the framework helps us understand some of the requirements for developing a transnational strategy—the approach companies need to respond to the new challenges in the global environment. And we highlight some of the ways companies can build such transnational strategies—or if they are either unable or unwilling to develop such a comprehensive strategic approach and infrastructure, how they might defend themselves against the transnational's onslaughts.

Worldwide Competitive Advantage: Goals and Means

To develop worldwide advantage, a company must achieve three strategic objectives. It must build global-scale efficiency in its existing activities, it must develop multinational flexibility so as to manage diverse country-specific risks and opportunities, and it must create the ability to learn from its international exposure and opportunities and to exploit that learning on a worldwide basis. Competitive advantage is developed by taking strategic actions that optimize a company's achievement of these different and, at times, conflicting goals.

In developing each of these capabilities, the MNC can utilize three very different tools and approaches, which we also described briefly in Chapter 1 as the main forces motivating companies to internationalize. It can exploit the differences in sourcing and market opportunities among the many countries in which it operates; it can capitalize on the diversity of its activities and operations to create synergies or develop economies of scope; and it can leverage the scale economies that are potentially available in its different worldwide activities.

The MNC's strategic challenge, then, is to exploit all three sources of global competitive advantage—national differences, scope economies, and scale economies—in order to optimize global efficiencies, multinational flexibility, and worldwide learning. And this means that the key to worldwide competitive advantage lies in managing the interactions between the different goals and the different means.

The Goals: Efficiency, Flexibility, and Learning

In Chapter 2, we argued that to respond effectively to the new international challenges a company must develop its competitiveness on platforms of global efficiency, multinational flexibility, and the capability of worldwide learning. Let us now consider each of these strategic goals in a little more detail.

Figure 3-1   The Integration–Responsiveness Framework

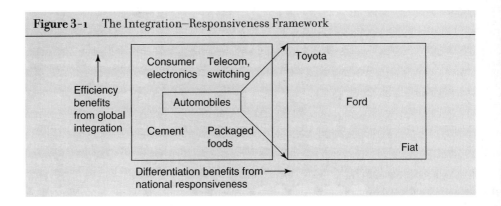

Global Efficiency   Viewing an MNC as an input–output system, we can think of its overall efficiency as the ratio of the value of its outputs to the value of its inputs. In this simplified view of the firm, its efficiency could be enhanced by increasing the value of outputs (i.e., by securing higher revenues), by lowering the value of its inputs (i.e., by lowering its costs), or by doing both. This is a simple point, but one that is often overlooked: Efficiency improvement is not just cost reduction, but also revenue enhancement.

To help understand the concept of global efficiency, we will use the global integration–national responsiveness framework first developed by C. K. Prahalad (see Figure 3-1).[2] The vertical axis represents the potential benefits from global integration of activities—benefits that largely translate into lower costs through scale and scope economies. The horizontal axis represents the benefits of national responsiveness—those that result from country-by-country differentiation of product, strategies, and the way activities are carried out. These benefits essentially translate into better revenues from more-effective differentiation to respond to national differences in tastes, industry structures, distribution systems, and government regulations.

As illustrated in Figure 3-1, the framework can be used to understand differences in the benefits of integration and responsiveness at the aggregate level of industries, as well as to identify and describe differences in the strategic approaches of companies competing in the same industry. As the figure indicates, industry characteristics alone do not determine company strategies. In automobiles, for example, Fiat has long pursued a classical multinational strategy, helping establish national auto industries through its joint venture partnerships and host government support in Spain, Yugoslavia, Poland, and many other locations. Toyota, by contrast, succeeded by developing products and manufacturing them in centralized globally scaled facilities in Japan. While Toyota appears on current evidence to have produced the more sustainable position, it is important to clarify that it made a strategic choice to focus on the objective of global efficiency (rather than local responsiveness), and that this chosen objective creates vulnerabilities and challenges as well as clear benefits.

---

[2]For a detailed exposition of this framework, see C. K. Prahalad and Yves Doz, *The Multinational Mission* (New York: Free Press, 1987).

Multinational Flexibility   A worldwide company faces an operating environment characterized by its diversity and volatility. Some of the opportunities and risks generated by this environment are endemic to all firms; others, however, are unique to companies operating across national borders. A key element of worldwide competitiveness, therefore, is multinational flexibility—the ability of a company to manage the risks and to exploit the opportunities that arise from the diversity and volatility of the global environment.[3]

Although there are many sources of diversity and volatility, it is worth highlighting four that we regard as particularly important. First, there are *macroeconomic risks* that are completely outside the control of the MNC, such as changes in prices, wages, or exchange rates caused by wars or natural calamities. Second, there are *political risks* that arise from policy actions of national governments, such as managed changes in exchange rates or interest rate adjustments. Third, there are *competitive risks* arising from the uncertainties of competitors' responses to the MNC's own strategies. And finally, there are *resource risks,* such as the availability of raw materials, capital, or managerial talent. In all four categories, the common characteristic of the various types of risks is that they all vary across countries and change over time. This makes flexibility the key strategic management requirement, because the diversity and volatility create attendant opportunities that must be considered jointly.

In general, multinational flexibility requires management to scan its broad environment to detect changes and discontinuities, and then respond to that new situation in the context of the worldwide business. MNCs following this approach exploit their exposure to diverse and dynamic environments to develop strategies in more-general and more-flexible terms so as to be robust to different international environmental cenarios.

Worldwide Learning   Most existing theories of the MNC view it as an instrument to extract additional revenues from internalized capabilities. The assumption is that the firm goes abroad to make more profits by exploiting its technology, brand name, or management capabilities in different countries around the world. And most traditional theory assumed that the key competencies resided at the MNC's center.

Although the search for additional profits or the desire to protect existing revenues may explain why MNCs come to exist, it does not provide a complete explanation of why some of them continue to grow and flourish. As we suggested in Chapter 1, an alternative view may well be that a key asset of the multinational is the diversity of environments in which it operates. This diversity exposes the MNC to multiple stimuli, allows it to develop diverse capabilities, and provides it with a broader learning opportunity than is available to a purely domestic firm. Furthermore, its initial stock of knowledge provides the MNC with the strength that allows it to create such organizational diversity in the first place. Chapter 5 provides a detailed discussion of the approaches that MNCs use to deliver on the objective of worldwide learning.

---

[3]This issue of multinational flexibility is discussed more fully in Bruce Kogut, "Designing Global Strategies: Profiting from Operating Flexibility," *Sloan Management Review,* Fall 1985, pp. 27–38.

The Means: National Differences, Scale, and Scope Economies

There are three fundamental tools for building worldwide competitive advantage: exploiting differences in sourcing and market potential across countries, exploiting economies of scope, and exploiting economies of scale. In this section we explore each of them in more depth.

National Differences   In the absence of efficient markets, the fact that different nations have different factor endowments (for example, abundance of labor, land, materials) leads to intercountry differences in factor costs. Because different activities of the firm, such as R&D, production, or marketing, use various factors to different degrees, a firm can gain cost advantages by configuring its value chain so that each activity is located in the country that has the least cost for its most intensively used factor. R&D facilities may be placed in the United Kingdom because of the available supply of high-quality, yet modestly paid scientists; manufacturing of labor-intensive components may be undertaken in Taiwan to capitalize on the low-cost, efficient labor force; and software development is concentrated in India where skilled software engineers are paid a fraction of Western salaries.

National differences may also exist in output markets. As we have discussed, customer tastes and preferences may be different in different countries, as may distribution systems, government regulations applicable to the concerned product markets, or the effectiveness of different promotion strategies. A firm can obtain higher prices for its output by tailoring its offerings to fit the unique requirements in each national market.

Scale Economies   Microeconomic theory provides a strong basis for evaluating the effect of scale on cost reduction, and the use of scale as a competitive tool is common in industries ranging from roller bearings to semiconductors. Whereas scale, by itself, is a static concept, there may be dynamic benefits of scale through what has been variously described as the experience or learning effect. The higher volume that helps a firm exploit scale benefits also allows it to accumulate learning, and this leads to progressive cost reduction as the firm moves down its learning curve. So while emerging Korean electronics firms were able to match the scale of experienced Japanese competitors, they were unable to compensate for the innumerable process-related efficiencies the Japanese had learned after decades of operating their global-scale plants.

Scope Economies   The concept of scope economies is based on the notion that certain economies arise from the fact that the cost of the joint production (or development, or distribution) of two or more products can be less than the cost of producing them separately.[4] Such cost reductions can take place because of many reasons—for example, resources such as information or technologies once acquired for use in producing one item may be available without cost for production of other items.

The strategic importance of scope economies arises from a diversified firm's ability to share investments and costs across the same or different value chains—a source of

---

[4]For a detailed exposition of scope economies, see W. J. Baumol, J. C. Panzer, and R. D. Willig, *Contestable Markets and the Theory of Industry Structure* (New York: Harcourt Brace Jovanovich, 1982).

economies competitors without such internal and external diversity cannot match. Such sharing can take place across segments, products, or markets, and may involve joint use of different kinds of assets (see Table 3-1).

Mapping Ends and Means: Building Blocks for Worldwide Advantage

Table 3-2 shows a mapping of the different goals and the different means for achieving worldwide competitiveness. Each goals–means intersection suggests some of the factors that can enhance a company's strategic position. Although the factors are only illustrative,

Table 3-1   Scope Economies in Product and Market Diversification

	Sources of Scope Economies	
	Product Diversification	**Market Diversification**
Shared physical assets	Factory automation with flexibility to produce multiple products (Ford)	Global brand name (Coca-Cola)
Shared external relations	Using common distribution channels for multiple products (Matsushita)	Servicing multinational customers worldwide (Citibank)
Shared learning	Shared R&D in computer and communications business (NEC)	Pooling knowledge developed in different markets (Procter & Gamble)

Table 3-2   Worldwide Advantage: Goals and Means

	Sources of Competitive Advantage		
Strategic Objectives	**National Differences**	**Scale Economies**	**Scope Economies**
Achieving efficiency in current operations	Benefiting from differences in factor costs—wages and cost of capital	Expanding and exploiting potential scale economies in each activity	Sharing of investments and costs across markets and businesses
Managing risks through multinational flexibility	Managing different kinds of risks arising from market- or policy-induced changes in comparative advantages of different countries	Balancing scale with strategic and operational flexibility	Portfolio diversification of risks and creation of options and side bets
Innovation, learning, and adaptation	Learning from societal differences in organizational and managerial processes and systems	Benefiting from experience—cost reduction and innovation	Shared learning across organizational components in different products, markets, or businesses

it may be useful to study them carefully and to compare them against the proposals of the different articles mentioned at the beginning of the chapter. It will become apparent that each author is focusing on a specific subset of factors—essentially, some of the different goals–means combinations—and the differences among their prescriptions can be understood in terms of the differences in the particular aspect of worldwide competitive advantage that they focus on.

Multinational, International, Global, and Transnational Strategies

In Chapter 2, we described some of the traditional approaches to managing worldwide operations that we designated multinational, international, global, and transnational strategies. The distinction among these different approaches as well as their respective strengths and vulnerabilities can be further elaborated in terms of the different goals–means combinations we have just described.

Multinational Strategy

The multinational strategic approach focuses primarily on one of the different means— national differences—to achieve most of its strategic objectives. Companies adopting this approach tend to focus on the revenue side, usually by differentiating their products and services in response to national differences in customer preferences, industry characteristics, and government regulations. This leads most of these companies to depend on local-for-local innovations, a process requiring the subsidiary not only to identify local needs but also to use its own local resources to respond to those needs. Carrying out most activities within each country on a local-for-local basis also allows those adopting a multinational strategy to match costs and revenues on a currency-by-currency basis.

Many European companies such as Unilever, ICI, Philips, and Nestlé have traditionally followed this strategic model. In these companies, assets and resources historically were widely dispersed, allowing overseas subsidiaries to carry out a wide range of activities from development and production to sales and services. Their self-sufficiency was typically accompanied by considerable local autonomy. But, although such independent national units were unusually flexible and responsive to their local environments, they inevitably suffered problems of inefficiencies and an inability to exploit the knowledge and competencies of other national units.

International Strategy

Companies adopting this broad approach focus on creating and exploiting innovations on a worldwide basis, using all the different means to achieve this end. As we describe in the next chapter, MNCs headquartered in large and technologically advanced countries often adopted this strategic approach but limited it primarily to exploiting home-country innovations to develop competitive positions abroad. The international product cycle theory we described in Chapter 1 describes both the strategic motivation and competitive posture of these companies: At least initially, their internationalization process relied heavily on transferring new products, processes, or strategies developed from the home country to less-advanced overseas markets.

This approach was common among U.S.-based MNCs such as Kraft, Pfizer, Procter & Gamble, and General Electric. Although these companies built considerable strengths out of their ability to create and leverage innovations, many suffered from deficiencies of both efficiency and flexibility because they did not develop either the centralized and high-scale operations of companies adopting global strategies or the very high degree of local responsiveness that multinational companies could muster through their autonomous, self-sufficient, and entrepreneurial local operations.

Global Strategy

Companies adopting the classic global strategic approach, as we have defined it, depend primarily on developing global efficiency. They use all the different means to achieve the best cost and quality positions for their products.

This has been the classic approach of many Japanese companies such as Toyota, Canon, Komatsu, and Matsushita. As these and other similar companies have found, however, such efficiency comes with some compromise of both flexibility and learning. For example, concentrating manufacturing to capture global scale may also result in a high level of intercountry product shipments that can raise risks of policy intervention, particularly by host governments in major importer countries. Similarly, companies that centralize R&D for efficiency reasons often find they are constrained in their ability to capture new developments in countries outside their home markets or to leverage innovations created by foreign subsidiaries in the rest of their worldwide operations. And finally, the concentration (most often through centralization) of activities like R&D and manufacturing to achieve global scale exposes such companies to high sourcing risks, particularly in exchange rate exposure.

Transnational Strategy

Beneath each of these traditional approaches lie some implicit assumptions on how best to build worldwide competitive advantage. The global company assumes that the best-cost position is the key source of competitiveness; the multinational company sees differentiation as the primary way to enhance performance; and the international company expects to use innovations to reduce costs, enhance revenues, or both. Companies adopting the transnational strategy recognize that each of these traditional approaches is partial: that each has its own merits but none represents the whole truth.

To achieve worldwide competitive advantage, costs and revenues have to be managed simultaneously, both efficiency and innovation are important, and innovations can arise in many different parts of the organization. Therefore, instead of focusing on any subpart of the set of issues shown in Table 3-2, the transnational company focuses on exploiting each and every goals–means combination so as to develop layers of competitive advantage by exploiting efficiency, flexibility, and learning simultaneously.

To achieve this ambitious strategic approach, however, the transnational company must develop a very different configuration of assets and capabilities than is typical of the traditional multinational, international, and global company structures. The global company tends to concentrate all its resources—either in its home country or in low-cost overseas locations—so as to exploit the scale economies available in each activity. The multinational company typically disperses its resources among its different national operations so as to be able to respond to local needs. And the international company tends to centralize those resources that are key to developing innovations, but decentralizes others to allow its innovations to be adapted worldwide.

The transnational, however, must develop a more sophisticated and differentiated configuration of assets and capabilities. It first decides which key resources and capabilities are best centralized within the home-country operation, not only to realize scale economies, but also to protect certain core competencies and to provide the necessary supervision of corporate management. Basic research, for example, is often viewed as such a capability, with core technologies kept at home for reasons of strategic security as well as competence concentration. For different reasons, the global account team or international management development responsibility may be located centrally to facilitate top-management control over these key corporate resources.

Certain other resources may be concentrated but not necessarily at home—a configuration that might be termed "excentralization" rather then decentralization. World-scale production plants for labor-intensive products may be built in a low-wage country such as Mexico or Malaysia. The advanced state of a particular technology may demand concentration of relevant R&D resources and activities in Japan, Germany, or the United States. Such flexible specialization—or "ex-centralization"—complements the benefits of scale economies with the flexibility of accessing low input costs or scarce resources, and the responsiveness of accommodating national political interests. This approach can also apply to specific functional activities. For example, Sony relocated its treasury operations to London to improve its access to the financial markets.

Some other resources may be best decentralized on a regional or local basis, either because potential economies of scale are small, or because of the need to create flexibility by avoiding exclusive dependence on a single facility. Local or regional facilities may not only afford protection against exchange rate shifts, strikes, natural disasters, and other disruptions, but also reduce logistical and coordination costs. An important side benefit provided by such facilities is the impact they can have in building the motivation and capability of national subsidiaries, an impact that can easily make small efficiency sacrifices worthwhile.

A classic example is provided by GE Medical Systems' (GEMS) reconfiguration of its worldwide resources beginning in 1997. Whereas basic research remained concentrated in the U.S., development and engineering capabilities were being actively expanded in Hungary, India, Korea, and China where technical expertise was both available and inexpensive. In an even more dramatic transformation, GEMS aimed to reduce its material costs by 20 percent and its manufacturing labor cost by 50 percent by developing its own "centers of excellence" (COEs) and outsourced suppliers in low-cost countries. Over several years, much of its final manufacturing was relocated from Milwaukee to Mexico, from Paris to Budapest, and from Tokyo to Shanghai.

As in any transnational organization, the result is a complex configuration of assets, resources, and capabilities that centralizes some resources at home, "ex-centralizes" some abroad, and distributes yet others among its many national operations. Furthermore, the company integrates these dispersed yet specialized resources through strong interdependencies. World-scale component plants in locations such as India, Israel, and

Table 3-3   Strategic Orientation and Configuration of Assets and Capabilities in Multinational, International, Global, and Transnational Companies

	Multinational	International	Global	Transnational
Strategic orientation	Building flexibility to respond to national differences through strong, resourceful, and entrepreneurial national operations	Exploiting parent-company knowledge and capabilities through worldwide diffusion and adaptation	Building cost advantages through centralized, global-scale operations	Developing global efficiency, flexibility, and worldwide learning capability simultaneously
Configuration of assets and capabilities	Decentralized and rationally self-sufficient	Sources of core competencies centralized, others decentralized	Centralized and globally scaled	Dispersed, interdependent, and specialized

Mexico supply specialized manufacturing plants in countries as diverse as Hungary, China, and the United States. Furthermore, subsidiary operations were set up in reciprocal supply relationships in which, for example, China became the global source for low-end CT scanners, but depended on the Korean COE for its x-ray machines, and on the United States for high-end equipment. Through such complex configurations, transnationals such as GEMS can leverage many more of the ways for building competitive advantage shown in Table 3-2 than its multinational, international, or global counterparts. Table 3-3 summarizes the differences in the asset configuration that support the different strategic approaches of the various MNC models.

◼ Worldwide Competitive Advantage: The Strategic Tasks

In the final part of this chapter, we look at how a company can respond to the strategic challenges we have described. The task will clearly be very different depending on the company's international posture and history. Companies that are among the major worldwide players in their businesses must focus on defending their dominance, while also building new sources of advantage. For companies that are smaller but aspire to worldwide competitiveness, the task is one of building the resources and capabilities needed to challenge the entrenched leaders. And, for companies that are focused on their national markets and lack either the resources or the motivation for international expansion, the challenge is to protect their domestic positions from others that have the advantage of being MNCs.

Defending Worldwide Dominance

The shifting external forces we have described resulted in severe difficulties—even for those MNCs that had enjoyed strong historical positions in their businesses worldwide. Typically, most of these companies pursued the traditional multinational, international, or global strategies, and their past successes were built on the fit between their specific strategic capability and the dominant environmental force in their industries. In multinational industries such as branded packaged products where forces for national responsiveness were dominant, companies such as Unilever developed strong worldwide positions by adopting multinational strategies. In contrast, in global industries like consumer electronics or semiconductor chips, companies such as Matsushita or Hitachi built leadership positions by adopting global strategies.

In the emerging competitive environment, however, these companies could no longer rely on their historic ability to exploit global efficiency, multinational flexibility, or worldwide learning. As an increasing number of industries developed what we have termed transnational characteristics, companies faced the need to master all three capabilities simultaneously. The challenge for the leading companies was to protect and enhance the particular strength they had, while simultaneously building the other capabilities.

For many MNCs, the initial response to this new strategic challenge was to try to restructure the configuration of their assets and activities to develop the capabilities they lacked. Global companies with highly centralized resources sought to develop flexibility by dispersing resources among their national subsidiaries; multinational companies, in contrast, tried to emulate their global competitors by centralizing R&D, manufacturing, and other scale-intensive activities. In essence, these companies tried to find a new "fit" configuration by drastic restructuring of their existing configuration.

Such a zero-based search for the ideal configuration not only led to external problems such as conflict with host governments over issues such as plant closures, but also resulted in a great deal of trauma inside the company's own organization. The greatest problem of such an approach, however, was that it tended to erode the particular competency the company already had without effectively adding the new strengths they sought.

The complex balancing act of protecting existing advantages while building new ones required companies to follow two fairly simple principles. First, they had to concentrate at least as much on defending and reinforcing their existing assets and capabilities as on developing new ones. Their approach tended to be one of building on—and eventually modifying—their existing infrastructure instead of radical restructuring. To the extent possible, they relied on modernizing existing facilities rather than dismantling the old and creating new ones.

Second, these companies looked for ways to compensate for their deficiency or approximate a competitor's source of advantage, rather than trying to imitate its asset structure or task configuration. In searching for efficiency, multinational companies with a decentralized and dispersed resource structure found it easier to develop efficiency by adopting new flexible manufacturing technologies in some of their existing plants and upgrading others to global sources rather than to close those plants and shift production to lower-cost countries to match the structure of competing global companies. Similarly, global companies found it more effective to develop responsiveness and flexibility by creating internal linkages between their national sales subsidiaries and their centralized development or manufacturing units rather than trying to mimic multinational companies by dispersing their resources to each country operation, and in the process undermining their core strength of efficiency.

Challenging the Global Leader

Over the last two decades, a number of companies have managed to evolve from relatively small national players to major worldwide competitors, challenging the dominance of traditional leaders in their businesses. Dell in the computer industry, Electrolux in the domestic appliances business, and Cemex in the cement industry are some examples of companies that have evolved from relative obscurity to global visibility within relatively short periods of time.

The actual processes adopted to manage such dramatic transformations vary widely from company to company. Electrolux, for example, grew almost exclusively through acquisitions while Dell built capabilities largely through internal development, and Cemex used a mix of greenfield investments and acquisitions. Similarly, whereas Dell built its growth on the basis of cost advantages and logistics capabilities, it expanded internationally because of its direct-selling business model and the ability to react quickly to changes in customer demand. Despite wide differences in their specific approaches, however, most of these new champions appear to have followed a similar step-by-step approach to building their competitive positions.

Each developed an initial toehold in the market by focusing on a narrow niche—often one specific product within one specific market—and by developing a strong competitive position within that niche. That competitive position was built on multiple sources of competitive advantage rather than on a single strategic capability.

Next, the toehold was expanded to a foothold by limited and carefully selected expansion along both product and geographic dimensions, and by extending the step-by-step improvement of both cost and quality to this expanded portfolio. Such expansion was typically focused on products and markets that were not of central importance to the established leaders in the business. By staying outside the range of the leaders' peripheral vision, the challenger could remain relatively invisible, thereby building up its strength and infrastructure without incurring direct retaliation from competitors with far greater resources. For example, emerging companies often focused initially on relatively low-margin products such as small-screen TV sets or subcompact cars.

While developing their own product portfolio, technological capabilities, geographic scope, and marketing expertise, challengers were often able to build up manufacturing volume and the resulting cost efficiencies by becoming original equipment manufacturer (OEM) suppliers to their larger competitors. Although this allowed the larger competitor to benefit from the challenger's cost advantages, it also developed the supplying company's understanding of customer needs and marketing strategies in the advanced markets served by the leading companies.

Once these building blocks for worldwide advantage were in place, the challenger typically moved rapidly to convert its low-profile foothold into a strong permanent position in the worldwide business. Dramatic scaling up of production facilities—increasing capacity 30-fold in five years as Matsushita did first in color TVs and later in VCRs—typically preceded a wave of new-product introduction and expansion into the key markets through multiple channels and their own brand names.

Protecting Domestic Niches

For reasons of resource or other constraints, some national companies may not be able to aspire to such worldwide expansion. Such companies are not insulated from the impact of global competition, however. Their major challenge is to protect their domestic niches from worldwide players with superior resources and multiple sources of competitive advantage.[5] This is particularly an issue in developing markets such as India and China where local companies face much larger, more aggressive, and deeper-pocketed competitors.

There are three broad alternative courses of action that can be pursued by such national competitors. The first approach is to defend against the competitor's global advantage. Just as MNC managers can act to facilitate the globalization of industry structure, so their counterparts in national companies can use their influence in the opposite direction. An astute manager of a national company might be able to foil the attempts of a global competitor by taking action to influence industry structure or market conditions to the national company's advantage. This might involve influencing consumer preference to demand a more locally adapted or service-intensive product; it could imply tying up key distribution channels; or it might mean preempting local sources of critical supplies. Many companies trying to enter the Japanese market claim to have faced this type of defensive strategy by local firms.

A second strategic option would be to offset the competitor's global advantage. The simplest way to do this is to lobby for government assistance in the form of tariff protection. A more ambitious approach is to gain government sponsorship to develop equivalent global capabilities through funding of R&D, subsidizing exports, and financing capital investments. As a "national champion," the company would theoretically be able to compete globally. However, in reality, it is very unusual for such a company to prosper. Airbus Industrie, which now shares the global market for large commercial airplanes with Boeing, is one of the few exceptions—rising from the ashes of other attempts by European governments to sponsor a viable computer company in the 1970s or to promote a European electronics industry a decade later.

The third alternative is to approximate the competitors' global advantages by linking up in some form of alliance or coalition with a viable global company. Numerous such linkages have been formed with the purpose of sharing the risks and costs of operating in a high-risk global environment. By pooling or exchanging market access, technology, and production capability, smaller competitors can gain some measure of defense against global giants. One example of such an approach is the way in which Siemens, ICL, and other small computer companies entered into agreements and joint projects with Fujitsu during the 1980s to enable them to maintain viability against the dominant transnational competitor, IBM.

Concluding Comments

Although these three strategic responses are not meant to cover every possible scenario, they highlight two important points from this chapter. First, the MNC faces a complex set of options in terms of the strategic levers it can pull to achieve competitive advantage, and the framework in Table 3-2 helps make sense of those options by separating out means and ends. Second, the competitive intensity in most industries today is such that a company cannot just afford to plough its own furrow. Rather, it is necessary to

[5]For a detailed discussion of such strategies, see N. Dhawar and T. Frost, "Competing with Giants: Survival Strategies for Local Companies Competing in Emerging Markets," *Harvard Business Review* 77, no. 2 (1999), pp. 119–130.

gain competitive parity on all relevant dimensions (efficiency, flexibility, learning) while also achieving differentiation on one. To be sure, the ability to achieve multiple competitive objectives at the same time is far from straightforward, and as a result we see many MNCs experimenting with new ways of organizing their worldwide activities. Which is the issue addressed in the next chapter.

Case 3-1 Caterpillar Tractor Co.

It was late afternoon on the twentieth of October 1981, and a positive mood pervaded the corporate headquarters of Caterpillar Tractor Co. (Cat) in Peoria, Illinois. Preliminary reports showed that Cat, the world's largest manufacturer of earth-moving equipment (EME), was headed for the best financial results in its history. Sales in 1981 were projected to reach $9.2 billion, exceeding the previous high of $8.6 billion achieved in 1980, and profits were expected to jump from the previous year's $565 million to about $580 million. A top management meeting had been called by Lee Morgan, chairman and chief executive officer, to review the preliminary results and appraise Caterpillar's competitive strategy for the next several years. Morgan wanted to know what measures were required to ensure that the company's impressive performance continued.

World Earth-Moving Equipment Industry in 1981

EME represented about 70% of the dollar sales of the construction equipment industry in 1981, encompassed a diverse range of machines such as excavators, bulldozers, graders, loaders, off-highway tractors and haulers. Some of these machines were available with wheels or crawler tracks, and most were available in a wide range of sizes and horsepower (hp) ratings.

This case was prepared by U. Srinivasa Rangan, Research Associate, under the supervision of Associate Professor Christopher A. Bartlett.

Copyright © 1985 by the President and Fellows of Harvard College. Harvard Business School case 385-276.

The Market Worldwide demand for EME had doubled between 1973 and 1980. Overall the United States exported roughly one-third of its production. (See Exhibit 1 for shipments by year including exports.) Estimates of worldwide market size varied between $14 and $15 billion for 1981, depending on the type of machines included.

Besides the original equipment, the world market for parts and attachments was substantial, accounting for as much as one-third of construction machinery sales volume. Most attachments were sold along with the prime mover at the time of sale and were included in the initial sales figures. Generally, profit margins were substantially higher for parts and attachments than for whole machines.

The Users The construction and mining industries were the key users of EME, the former representing over 60% of the market and the latter for almost 30%. Forestry accounted for the balance.

The term *construction industry* usually included work relating to buildings, dams, airports, roads, waste disposal, and so forth. The United States accounted for roughly 5% of world new-construction expenditures, or an estimated $230 billion in 1980. Repairs and maintenance expenditures were believed to be another $75 billion worldwide.

Since 1979, the construction industry in the United States had faced a major downturn. The Commerce Department considered the industry depressed, with a 12% drop in aggregate hours worked by construction workers and a seasonally adjusted unemployment rate of 16% in late 1981. (See Exhibit 2 for some data relating to the industry.)

Exhibit 1 U.S. Industry Shipments, Including Exports (number of units)

	Total Shipments					Export				
	1977	1978	1979	1980	1981*	1977	1978	1979	1980	1981*
Tractors										
Crawler	19,847	22,058	19,468	16,446	15,785	NA†	8,850	6,902	7,063	7,466
Wheel	2,798	6,013	4,962	6,895	4,254	1,591	2,285	2,289	1,381	1,733
Loaders										
Crawler	6,146	7,040	6,321	4,455	3,286	NA†	1,270	1,117	1,211	1,422
Wheel	14,331	18,214	21,628	17,103	13,168	3,626	3,352	3,213	5,710	4,645
Track Shovel	21,011	23,401	29,409	23,837	16,915	3,431	3,645	5,364	6,633	4,678
Hauler										
Rear Dump	2,816	2,330	2,486	1,877	1,930	1,007	816	1,051	1,163	1,190
Bottom Dump	60	2,775	NA†	3,187	2,855	NA†	388	NA†	NA†	NA†
Scrapers	4,898	5,012	4,075	2,571	2,403	1,211	1,187	1,253	1,156	1,317
Graders	6,117	7,372	7,257	7,165	5,947	2,606	2,537	2,183	3,074	3,062
Excavators										
Crawler	4,207	5,007	5,084	3,562	2,338	783	790	1,167	857	722
Wheel	855	995	645	410	460	145	150	NA†	66	69
Cable	214	127	165	82	60	46	46	31	62	30

*Estimated.
†Not available.
Source: Bureau of the Census; CIMA, *Outlook 1984.*

Exhibit 2 New Construction Output Indicators for the United States

Year	Total Value		As Percentage of GNP		Value per Capita Constant 1972$	Construction Index 1972 = 100
	Current $ ($ bil.)	Constant $ ($ bil.)	Current $ (%)	Constant $ (%)		
1970	94.9	107.0	9.7	9.9	522	88.6
1971	110.0	116.0	10.3	10.3	560	94.8
1972	124.1	123.9	10.6	10.4	593	100.0
1973	137.9	126.9	10.6	10.1	603	108.7
1974	138.5	109.1	9.8	8.7	515	126.9
1975	134.5	97.2	8.8	7.9	455	138.4
1976	151.1	105.0	8.9	8.1	488	143.9
1977	174.0	111.3	10.9	8.3	513	156.3
1978	205.5	116.9	9.7	8.1	535	175.7
1979	229.0	114.7	9.5	7.7	520	199.0
1980	228.7	103.5	8.7	6.9	465	221.7

Source: *Construction Review,* June 1981.

Table A   Worldwide Construction Expenditure (1981)

Region	Expenditure Percent	Projected Real Annual Growth Rates, 1982–1986
United States	50.0%	1%
Canada	3.5	2
Latin America	7.5	4
Europe	5.0	2
Middle East	7.5	5
Asia and Australia	26.5	6
Total	100.0%	

Source: Compiled data from various 1981 issues of *Engineering News Record* and *First Boston Research.*

The end of the interstate highways program in the late 1960s had shrunk the road construction market considerably.

The EME demand depended largely on the pace at which machines were substituting for labor. Thus, demand had traditionally been higher in developed countries than in developing ones. Recent trends, however, were changing the overall demand pattern. (See Table A.) Since the mid-1970s, the oil-rich Middle Eastern countries had witnessed a massive rise in construction activity. Among the less developed countries (LDCs) in general, considerable potential existed, since they required extensive infrastructure. Many, however, faced financing problems.

The construction industry was highly concentrated and U.S. dominated—although both these characteristics were changing. All of the industrialized nations had indigenous construction capabilities, and many had successfully expanded their operations overseas. Several of the "advanced developing countries" were also upgrading their construction services and entering the international market. Until recently, the U.S. contractors, who had a large domestic base and assured U.S. government-sponsored construction work abroad, had also won a large portion of the overseas construction contracts. A survey indicated that 29 companies accounted for 94% of non-U.S. construction and 54% of U.S.

construction in 1980. But these firms were facing increasing competition from Third World construction firms, which tended to use their low-cost labor as their main competitive weapon, shifting work crews to construction sites worldwide. Many observers felt that non-U.S. companies were better placed to bid for and perform contracts in developing countries since they did not face curbs similar to the U.S. Foreign Corrupt Practices Act (FCPA) of 1977 which forbade U.S. companies from indulging in unethical activities such as bribery and kickbacks in overseas dealings.

Third World contractors also benefited by being more flexible. A vice president of the leading Filipino construction firm was quoted as saying that his company looked for joint ventures with local firms in developing countries, since these arrangements enabled his company "to enjoy government treatment normally reserved for indigenous contractors." Many U.S. companies also noted that foreign companies received financial and diplomatic support from their home governments when bidding and favorable tax treatment on earnings outside their own countries. The South Korean government established an overseas construction fund of about $500 million "to help finance development of new markets and technology." Similarly, India coordinated the efforts of the Indian companies in pooling information on working conditions abroad and in pooling resources for joint ventures. (See Table B for Asian success in Middle Eastern contracts in recent years. For purposes of comparison, it should be noted that as late as 1975, U.S. companies claimed more than one-third of Middle Eastern construction contracts in dollar terms.)

Usually, in overseas projects, the machinery was brought in by the sole contractor or by one of the partners in a consortium, who also took responsibility for disposing of machines at the end of the contract. Frequently the heavy equipment was sold locally or shipped to nearby markets; sometimes it was moved to another site where the operating company or members of a consortium were working. This "overhang" of used equipment was large in the Middle East. The equipment's value was written off over varying periods, ranging from one to five years.

Table B   Middle Eastern Construction Contracts Awarded to Companies of Different Nationalities

Country or Region of Origin	1979	1980
1. Middle East	16.52%	27.38%
2. United States	16.86	6.88
3. Japan	17.32	9.89
4. France	14.84	19.67
5. West Germany	12.69	8.94
6. South Korea	9.45	12.82
7. United Kingdom	6.87	7.16
8. Eastern Europe	4.52	5.07
9. Philippines	0.93	2.19
	100.00%	100.00%
Amount (in $ millions)	$39,429	$33,967

Source: *Constructor,* January 1982.

Construction companies all over the world operated under severe cost and time constraints. Scheduling machine use efficiently and minimizing downtime were considered vital for success, and some companies used computerized systems to schedule parts changes. In the United States, high capital and energy costs had led some construction companies to use their equipment longer, and to rent, rather than buy, more equipment.

Equipment purchase decisions were generally made by committees of high-level management and technical personnel in large construction companies, and by a few top executives in smaller ones. A survey conducted in the late 1970s indicated that the manufacturer's reputation, machine performance and dealer capability were the most important criteria for decision making, followed closely by price and parts availability.

Governments were generally more price-sensitive than contractors and placed more reliance on the manufacturer's ability to deal directly with them to provide direct maintenance and repair facilities. In many developing countries, particularly in the Far East, the major buyers were a few large, state-owned enterprises. Their bids for machines specifically sought quotations which included prices for parts needed over the next two years.

The mining industry was another important user of EME. All types of open-pit mining made use of these machines, and new markets appeared as the search for energy alternatives to oil intensified with coal, oil from oil shale sands and nuclear power. But forecasting the demand for EME in the energy sector was extremely difficult. Four countries—the United States, USSR, China, and Australia—accounted for 60% of world reserves and current production of coal. Much of the coal production was by open-pit surface mining which was less costly, but also more capital-intensive and demanded more skilled labor. The U.S. coal industry, the world's largest and most export-oriented, was operating at 77% of installed capacity in 1981. Surface mining faced many environmental constraints, as did other fuel minerals such as oil-shale-sands development and uranium mining.

Six nonfuel minerals—iron, copper, aluminum, zinc, nickel and lead—accounted for roughly three-quarters of the total value of world mineral production in 1976. Since the late 1960s, mining of these minerals in almost all the developing countries had come under state control. The related expropriations of foreign mining companies' assets had led to the development of new mines in politically safe countries like Canada and Australia. The state-owned mining enterprises, lured by very high mineral prices in the early 1970s, had also undertaken large expansion and new capacity-creation projects.

One UN study on new mine-opening expenditures concluded that between 1978 and 1990 about $12 billion (1977 dollars) would be spent annually in the developed and developing countries, of which the latter's share would be $4 billion.

Distribution   Internationally, EME manufacturers sold through dealers, who provided direct and after-sales service. Even when the sale was made direct, it was often the dealer who provided the service. The rule of thumb was that a crawler tractor, over its six-year economic life, would require service and parts equal to its initial cost.

Normal competitive practice had been to franchise dealers by means of a separate sales agreement for each product line handled. Many manufacturers believed that a full-line franchise not only hindered dealer specialization, but also limited the manufacturer's ability to get maximum market coverage for all its products.

Because most dealerships carried their inventories on their own accounts, they were characterized by high capitalization and required relatively high dollar sales volume. Individual sales had high per unit value and generally demanded greater service than, say, agricultural equipment. Customers stressed dealer relationships and/or dealer reputation as an important factor in their purchasing decisions.

The Suppliers   The EME industry began in the late 1800s with the development of steam-powered equipment, developing as a derivative of the agricultural tractor. Except for Cat, most of the world's major EME manufacturers were also leaders in the agricultural equipment market.

Rather than high-technology breakthroughs, the industry had focused more on constant improvement of existing products to make them more energy efficient, comfortable, or suitable for specific kinds of jobs. In 1981, U.S. construction equipment manufacturers spent $432 million on sales of about $17 billion. In comparison, the automobile industry spent 4.9% of sales on R&D, and heavy machinery manufacturers 2.3%.

About two-thirds of the total product cost of construction equipment was in heavy components—engines, axles, transmissions, and hydraulics—whose manufacturing was capital intensive and highly sensitive to economies of scale. Because of the secrecy surrounding the operations of EME manufacturers, it was difficult to quantify scale effects. Some industry observers tended to compare the EME industry with the agricultural tractor industry, however, where it was estimated that the optimum scale of operation was about 90,000 units a year and the costs fell by 11% between 60,000 and 90,000 units. Although others questioned the validity of the comparison, there appeared to be general

Table C Cost Structure of a Large Bulldozer (Equivalent to Cat D-6)	
	Percent of Cost
Labor	35.0%
Components and subassemblies	12.4
Overhead	18.0
Assembly	4.6
Purchased materials and components	49.6
Overhead	15.4
	100.0%

Source: Boston Consulting Group.

agreement that economies of scale did exist up to a level of 90,000 units, but there was considerable disagreement over the extent of cost disadvantage resulting from lower output levels.

The cost structure of a typical large bulldozer appears in Table C. Except for some highly specialized products, the basis for profitable operation was believed to be volume production. Many manufacturers had also integrated backward into components such as engines and axles. Steel purchases were particularly important since they represented approximately 15% of the product cost. Steel prices varied widely, with Japanese steel costing on average about 30% less than U.S.-made steel.

Several large developing countries, such as Mexico, Brazil, Argentina and India, had demanded at least partial manufacture of EME sold in their markets. Other countries erected nontariff barriers, such as specification requirements, that pressured EME companies to build offshore plants.

Competition   In 1981 there were seven major contenders in the EME industry and a myriad of smaller, local specialists. The majors—Caterpillar (Cat), J.I. Case (a division of Tenneco), John Deere, Clark Equipment, Fiat-Allis, International Harvester and Komatsu (of Japan)—accounted for more than 90% of dollar sales worldwide. Their market shares through the 1970s are shown in Exhibit 3.

Exhibit 3 Market Share Positions of Major Earth-moving Equipment Producers

	1971	1972	1973	1974	1975	1976	1977	1978	1979	1980
Caterpillar*	56.0%	55.0%	53.0%	53.0%	54.4%	56.1%	53.6%	51.9%	50.0%	53.3%
Komatsu	10.3	10.9	11.6	9.0	9.2	11.3	11.8	14.3	14.8	15.2
J.I. Case	6.7	6.9	8.9	8.3	7.2	7.4	8.5	9.4	10.5	10.3
Fiat-Allis†	4.3	4.0	3.8	7.3	7.7	6.3	6.5	6.1	5.8	5.7
Deere	5.8	6.2	6.3	6.1	4.7	5.2	6.6	6.7	7.1	6.6
International Harvester	11.0	10.0	10.1	9.7	10.0	7.6	7.2	6.6	7.1	5.1
Clark	5.9	6.0	6.3	6.6	6.8	6.1	5.8	5.0	4.7	3.8
Total	100.0%	100.0%	100.0%	100.0%	100.0%	100.0%	100.0%	100.0%	100.0%	100.0%
IBH‡	—	—	—	—	0.5	0.5	0.6%	0.7	1.4	4.2
Total sales (millions)§	$4,063	$4,954	$6,190	$7,651	$8,840	$8,773	$10,130	$12,841	$14,027	$14,916
Year-to-year change	—	21.3%	24.9%	23.6%	15.5%	−0.8%	15.5%	26.8%	9.2%	6.3%
Price increase‖	4%	5%	12%	10%	18%	6%	8%	9%	11%	12%
Real growth‖	—	16	13	13	(3)	(7)	7	18	(2)	(6)

Note: The figures relating to Massey-Ferguson Limited have not been included in this table. MF held less than 2% of the market in 1980, and in the previous years, it seldom held more than 3.5%.

*Includes sales from Caterpillar-Mitsubishi joint venture net of sales to and from Caterpillar.

†Allis-Chalmers only prior to 1974.

‡IBH Holding AG—founded in 1975 with growth through acquisitions of ten European equipment manufacturers through 1980. In 1980 IBH acquired Hymac (U.K.) and Hanomag (Germany). In 1981 IBH acquired Terex from General Motors.

§Excludes IBH.

‖Wertheim & Co., Inc. estimates.

Source: Wertheim & Co., Inc.

All companies had to contend with Cat's dominance in almost all market segments. This had encouraged the smaller firms to approach these markets indirectly. As one industry participant put it, their strategy was to "nibble away, moving in as Cat moved up to bigger equipment, forcing Cat to protect its heels here and head there." Some manufacturers chose to offer a full line of only one type of product, such as loaders or scrapers, while others chose to offer one product of each type. Often competitors brought out either a larger or a smaller version of a Cat product. (The major competitors' positions in various product segments appear in Exhibit 4.)

International Harvester (IH) IH was a large U.S. firm with its basic products in three industries: heavy-duty trucks, agricultural equipment and con-struction equipment. In the heavy-duty truck sector (45% of sales in 1980), it faced tough competitors such as GM and Ford, who were low-cost produc-ers in an industry where competition was often on price. In the mature and cyclical agricultural equip-ment sector, competition centered on having a strong dealer network. IH was second to John Deere in market share in the U.S., with 30%, com-pared with Deere's 36%. In 1980, 40% of IH's sales came from the farm sector. In construction equip-ment, IH competed head-on with Cat. It had a strong distribution system, with 70 dealers and 200 outlets worldwide, but particularly strong in Asia and in Eastern Bloc countries. After Cat, IH had the second broadest product line. It produced some components, like engines, castings, fasteners and bearings, and purchased 50–70% of its parts re-quirements. In 1980, IH's sales in EME were

Exhibit 4   Position of Competitors in Product Segments

	Cat	Komatsu	J.I. Case*	Int'l. Harv.	Deere	IBH†	Fiat-Allis	Clark
Backhoes‡			XXX	X	XX	XX	X	
Excavators§	XXX	XX	XX		XX			
Tractors								
Crawler over 90 hp	XXX	XX	X	XX	X	X	XX	
Crawler under 90 hp	XX	XX	XX	XX	XXX	X	X	
Wheel‖	XXX	X	X	XX	X	X	X	XX
Graders	XXX	X			XX		X	X
Loaders								
Crawler	XXX	XX	X	X	XX	X	X	
Wheel	XXX	XX	X	XX	XX	X	X	XX
Off-highway trucks#	XX	X	X	XX	X	XX	X	XX
Scrapers	XXX	X		X	X	X	X	X
Other**	XXX	XX	X	XX	X	X	X	XX

Note: XXX denotes leading position; XX denotes major participation; X denotes minor participation.
*A subsidiary of Tenneco, Inc.
†IBH Holding, A.G.-founded in 1975 with growth through acquisitions of ten European equipment manufacturers through 1980.
‡Other participants include J.C. Bamford in the U.K., Ford Motor, and Volvo in Sweden.
§Other participants include Koehring Co., Poclain (40% owned by J.I. Case) in France, Hitachi and Mitsubishi in Japan, Orenstein & Koppel (O&K) and Liebherr in Germany, and J.C. Bamford and Priestman (Acrow) in the U.K.
‖Other participants include Ford Motor, Volvo, O&K, J.C. Bamford, and Leyland.
#Other participants include Unit Rig & Equipment Co. (private), Volvo, Euclid (Daimler-Benz), and Leyland.
**Includes skidders, compactors and attachments.
Source: Wertheim & Co., Inc.

$750 million (12% of sales). IH's results in recent years had been poor, and the company was reported to be in financial difficulty.

J. I. Case   Case was an independent farm equipment company before it was purchased by Tenneco in 1970. It had since diversified away from the very competitive, highly cyclical farm equipment industry. By 1981, construction equipment represented 67% of Case's sales. Many of the company's eleven plants in the U.S. produced components and finished products for both agricultural and construction equipment, and the same distribution channels were used to distribute both. Case's network of 1,200 independent dealers and 219 company-owned retail outlets were almost all in the United States and Canada. Its product strategy focused on a few products and offered a wide array of machines in each category. For instance, in the hydraulic excavator segment, Case offered 13 models, with horsepowers ranging from 120 to 445. This compared with Cat's offering of five models between 85 and 325 hp and John Deere's two models within the same range. Acquiring a 40% interest in Poclain of France in 1977, Case gained access to the technology of a leading hydraulic excavator producer. Poclain's European marketing subsidiaries and Brazilian excavator assembly operation came with the acquisition.

John Deere   Deere led the world in farm equipment manufacture, offering a full line with a concentration on large horsepower tractors. More than 85% of Deere's sales of $5,450 million in 1981 came from farm equipment, and the balance from construction equipment. In the latter the company offered a full line, but only one or two models for each product. Deere reportedly has over 25% of the U.S. crawler market. The company's loyal 2,300 dealer network was a major asset, and according to one report, Deere was rapidly expanding its small base of overseas distributors. The same report said that Deere aimed to be number two in the United States in construction equipment and number four worldwide. In the farm sector, the company was reputed to be a low-cost producer. Although Deere

depended heavily on outside sourcing for components, there was extensive integration of manufacturing, especially in engines, transmissions, and components linked to Deere designs and specifications. Deere had manufacturing and/or assembly operations in a number of countries, including France, Germany, Brazil, South Africa, Australia, and Spain, although only the French operation was related to construction equipment. Deere spent heavily on R&D, devoting 4.4% of sales to it in 1981. The company had industry production "firsts" such as the dual-path hydrostatic drive for tracked equipment and microcomputers to control some transmission functions. It was implementing CAD/CAM programs to lower its manufacturing costs further.

Komatsu   This company dominated the Japanese construction equipment industry and was the second largest EME company worldwide. It held 60% market share within Japan, but was a distant second to Caterpillar worldwide. Until the late 1960s, Komatsu had been a small Japanese EME producer with a limited line of inferior-quality products. In the mid-1960s, when Caterpillar announced a joint venture with Mitsubishi, Komatsu's management was motivated to revitalize the company. Through licensing agreements with Cummins for diesel engines, International Harvester for large wheel loaders and Bucyrus-Erie for excavator designs, the company developed its technology. With the benefit of a labor cost advantage relative to U.S. and European competitors, and the postwar Japanese construction boom, Komatsu not only survived but also prospered over the next decade. When domestic demand slowed in the mid-seventies, the company looked towards export markets. Komatsu exported mainly whole machines although, responding to government requests, it had set up assembly plants in Mexico and Brazil in the 1970s. It cultivated cordial relationships with governments in communist and Third World countries.

Outside Japan, Komatsu lacked an effective dealer network. In the large U.S. market, for instance, it had to rely on nonexclusive dealerships which generally catered to small contractors. Komatsu's machines were often cheaper than Cat's. Said Lee Morgan, Cat's CEO, "Generally speaking, Komatsu's products are priced at least 10% to 15% below Caterpillar's. That says clearly what they believe our value is versus theirs."

Other Competitors   Among other major manufacturers, Clark Equipment focused on one type of product, the loader. The company faced severe competition from low-cost producers, and the recession had not helped. Fiat-Allis competed with a full line, emphasizing heavier models. The company tended to compete on price but was not considered a serious competitive threat due to its poor reputation for quality and reliability.

Since 1975, a new German-based company, IBH Holding Company (IBH), burgeoned. It had been put together through the acquisition of a handful of money-losing French, German, and American operations by a 37-year-old entrepreneur and Harvard MBA, Dieter Esch. He planned to make the company a full-line competitor and felt that it would be "the No. 2 company in the industry after Caterpillar." In early 1981 IBH acquired Terex Corporation, a GM subsidiary that specialized in making a wide range of EME, giving IBH a much-needed U.S. manufacturing and marketing base. Only six months after the acquisition, IBH had already turned Terex around. IBH had integrated several sets of distributors (some 600 worldwide) and found it difficult to manage spare parts inventories and to keep service levels high. Moreover, IBH did not make most parts itself, and it had an equity base of only $70 million.

Besides these larger companies, smaller national competitors were particularly strong in some countries. J.C. Bamford, for instance, held a 40% share of the U.K. market. The company planned to increase its overseas sales, taking advantage of the falling pound sterling.

Cat's Background

Headquartered in Peoria, Illinois, Cat was a multinational company that designed, manufactured, and marketed products in two principal categories: (1) earth-moving, construction, and materials-handling machinery and equipment and related parts; and (2) engines for earth-moving and construction machines, on-highway trucks, and for marine, petroleum, agricultural, industrial, and other applications, and electric power generation systems. Cat was the world's largest manufacturer of EME. Of the company's expected $9.2 billion in sales in 1981, 57% would be overseas. (See Exhibits 5, 6, and 7.) Products and components manufactured in the United States accounted for 68% of these non-U.S. sales. Cat's large geographic base and its broad product line were intended to protect it from a dependence on the domestic business cycle. Estimated parts sales represented about 35% to 45% of total revenue, although their exact contribution was never revealed by the company.

Cat's rise to global dominance stemmed from a mixture of good luck, shrewd judgment and world history. The company was fortunate to be based in the United States, where the proliferation of highways that followed the development of the auto industry led to strong demand for EME. In the late 1920s Raymond Force, a far-sighted chief executive, pulled Cat out of the overcrowded farm equipment business to concentrate on this growing EME segment. World War II created tremendous demand for earth-moving machines, and the U.S. Army decided to standardize on Cat's bulldozers. From 1941 to 1944, Cat's sales tripled. When the U.S. Army withdrew from Europe and Asia after the war, it left behind the bulky machines for local use. Foreign users became familiar with Cat machines and foreign mechanics learned to service Cat equipment, thereby laying the foundation for the emergence of a formidable worldwide EME producer.

The company's management engaged in careful strategic analysis and tried to take a long-term view of its business. In more than half a century, Cat had suffered only one year of loss; and that was 1932, the height of the Depression. The strength of the company's classic strategic posture of high-quality products backed by effective service was well understood throughout the company, and management was

Exhibit 5 Income Statement ($ millions)

Fiscal Year	1976 $	%	1977 $	%	1978 $	%	1979 $	%	1980 $	%	1981* $	%
Net sales	$5,042.30	(100.0)	$5,848.90	(100.0)	$7,219.20	(100.0)	$7,613.20	(100.0)	$8,597.80	(100.0)	$9,154.50	(100.0)
Cost of goods sold	3,720.20	(73.8)	4,312.00	(73.7)	5,349.30	(74.1)	5,888.50	(77.3)	6,627.10	(77.1)	6,933.30	(75.7)
SG&A†	453.20	(9.0)	489.20	(8.4)	586.00	(8.1)	662.00	(9.7)	769.50	(8.9)	868.70	(9.5)
Depreciation and amortization	184.10	(3.7)	210.50	(3.6)	257.10	(3.6)	311.80	(4.1)	370.20	(4.3)	448.40	(4.9)
Net operating income	684.80	(13.6)	837.20	(14.3)	1,026.80	(14.2)	750.90	(9.9)	831.00	(9.7)	904.10	(9.9)
Nonoperating income (Expense)	0.00		0.00		48.00		80.00		112.60		107.30	
Interest expense	42.50	(0.8)	60.10	(1.0)	111.90	(1.6)	139.10	(1.8)	173.20	(2.0)	224.80	(2.5)
Pretax income	643.30	(12.8)	779.20	(13.3)	963.20	(13.3)	725.50	(9.5)	796.70	(9.3)	802.80	(8.8)
Income taxes	260.10	(5.2)	334.10	(5.7)	396.90	(5.5)	233.90	(3.1)	231.90	(2.7)	223.90	(2.4)
Current taxes	271.60		308.30		395.90		271.60		243.50		240.30	
Deferred income taxes	(11.50)		25.80		1.00		(37.70)		(11.60)		(16.40)	
Profit after tax	383.20	(7.6)	445.10	(7.6)	566.30	(7.8)	491.60	(6.5)	564.80	(6.6)	578.90	(6.3)
Common dividends per share	$1.46		$1.58		$1.88		$2.10		$1.33		NA‡	

*Estimated.
†Selling, general, and administrative expenses.
‡NA means not available.
Source: Annual reports.

(continued)

Exhibit 5 Caterpillar Balance Sheet ($ millions) *(concluded)*

As of December 31:	1976	1977	1978	1979	1980	1981*
Assets						
Current assets	$2,096.90	$2,252.30	$2,628.30	$2,606.90	$2,932.90	$3,544.40
Cash and equivalents	88.10	209.40	244.50	147.20	104.00	81.00
Receivables	604.60	648.10	767.80	692.70	912.40	994.30
Inventories	1,244.90	1,288.60	1,522.30	1,670.20	1,749.60	2,213.80
Other current assets	159.30	106.20	93.70	96.80	166.90	255.30
Fixed assets	1,797.00	2,093.30	2,402.80	2,796.40	3,165.30	3,740.50
Long-term investments	78.30	72.50	58.80	35.30	103.50	120.00
Net plant	1,698.60	1,999.10	2,281.40	2,687.80	3,008.50	3,396.20
Accumulated depreciation	1,082.60	1,222.10	1,418.50	1,638.00	1,822.90	2,154.60
Deferred charges	0.00	0.00	0.00	23.50	0.00	0.00
Intangibles	0.00	0.00	0.00	0.00	0.00	146.40
Other assets	20.10	21.70	62.60	49.80	53.30	77.90
Total assets	3,893.90	4,345.60	5,031.10	5,403.30	6,098.20	7,284.90
Liabilities and stockholders' equity						
Current liabilities	821.20	955.80	1,237.10	1,386.10	1,711.50	2,369.50
Short-term debt	59.90	99.90	146.90	463.20	446.60	847.60
Notes payable	30.90	87.30	112.60	404.20	430.30	747.00
Current long-term debt	29.00	12.60	34.30	59.00	16.30	100.60
Accounts payable	622.70	677.70	724.00	645.00	890.00	1,120.90
Income taxes payable	138.60	178.20	236.70	133.40	198.10	189.40
Other current liabilities	0.00	0.00	129.50	144.50	176.80	211.60
Deferred taxes	11.30	36.00	23.90	0.00	23.10	97.70
Long-term debt	1,034.10	1,011.00	1,018.00	951.90	931.60	960.90
Total liabilities	1,866.60	2,002.80	2,279.00	2,338.00	2,666.20	3,428.10
Stockholders' equity	2,027.30	2,342.80	2,752.10	3,065.30	3,432.00	3,856.80
Total liabilities and net worth	3,893.90	4,345.60	5,031.10	5,403.30	6,098.20	7,284.90

*Estimated.
Source: Annual reports.

Exhibit 6   Distribution of Caterpillar's Overseas Sales

	1973	1977	1978	1979	1980	1981
Africa and Middle East	14%	30%	25%	23%	26%	36%
Asia/Pacific	12	14	17	20	19	19
Europe	50	25	27	28	26	19
Latin America	13	20	19	17	18	17
Canada	11	11	12	12	11	9
Total	100%	100%	100%	100%	100%	100%
Overseas sales as percent of Cat's total sales	49.1%	50.7%	48.1%	53.8%	57.1%	56.6%

Source: Form 10-K reports.

Exhibit 7   Mix of Caterpillar Sales by Third World Region ($ millions)

	1977	1978	1979	1980	1981
Latin America					
Exports from U.S.	$438	$506	$476	$617	$654
Sales of foreign mfd. pdt.	162	168	240	262	249
Total sales	600	674	716	879	903
Exports percent of total sales	73%	75%	66%	70%	72%
Africa/Mideast					
Exports from U.S.	$509	$497	$580	$765	$1,236
Sales of foreign mfd. pdt.	376	370	380	517	650
Total sales	885	867	960	1,282	1,886
Exports percent of total sales	58%	57%	60%	60%	66%
Asia/Pacific*					
Exports from U.S.	$291	$398	$528	$641	$687
Sales of foreign mfd. pdt.	119	168	236	280	239
Total sales	410	566	764	921	929
Exports percent of total sales	71%	70%	69%	70%	74%
Third World Total					
Exports from U.S.	$1,238	$1,401	$1,584	$2,023	$2,577
Sales of foreign mfd. pdt.	557	706	856	1,059	1,138
Total sales	1,795	2,107	2,440	3,082	3,715
Exports percent of total sales	65%	66%	65%	66%	69%
Caterpillar worldwide sales	$5,848	$7,219	$7,613	$8,598	$9,154
Exports to Third World percent of Cat	21%	19%	21%	24%	28%
Third World sales percent of Cat	30%	29%	32%	36%	40%

*Includes Australia and New Zealand.
Source: Form 10-K reports.

committed to its maintenance and defense. A senior executive said in an interview: "Our management strengths are a hell of a hurdle for competitors to overcome. We not only have a strong defensible strategic position, we just know our business better than anyone else, and we work harder at it."

Marketing   Cat seized the postwar opportunity with both hands, establishing independent dealerships to service the machines left in Europe and Asia. These dealers quickly became self-sustaining, and along with the strong U.S. dealership network, they became the core of Cat's marketing strategy. In 1981, the company had 129 full-line independent dealers overseas operating 605 branches worldwide, each branch capable of providing service and spare parts backup. In the United States, the corresponding figures were 87 dealers and 284 branches. These dealers' combined net worth was nearly equal to that of Caterpillar itself (see Exhibit 8).

Cat tied the dealers close to it by enhancing their position as entrepreneurs. When one of the U.S. dealers had established a production line to rebuild Cat engines, and a shop that refurbished track shoes and other tractor parts, Cat management supported the efforts despite the fact that customers could buy rebuilt parts that lasted about 80% as long as new ones at half the cost.

Cat helped the dealers maintain appropriate inventory levels. The company established a national computer network that enabled its U.S. dealers to order any part from the central distribution depot in Illinois for delivery the next day. Cat offered to repurchase parts or equipment dealers could not sell. When introducing new products, the company first built up a two-month supply of spare parts. Cat guaranteed that if parts were not delivered within 48 hours anywhere in the world, the customer got them free.

The company conducted regular training programs for dealers and product demonstrations for their customers. It even conducted a course in Peoria for dealers' children to encourage them to remain in the family business. Caterpillar's chairman summed up his company's attitude: "We approach our dealers as partners in the enterprise, not as agents or middlemen. We worry as much about their performance as they do themselves."

An average Cat dealer had a net worth of $4 million and annual sales of $100 million in the United States. The field population of Cat machines approached 20 times that of the nearest competitor. Because of his financial strength, an average dealer could expand his selling and service capabilities at the same pace that Cat expanded its product line. In 1980, Cat dealers spent more than $200 million on

Exhibit 8   Data on Caterpillar Dealers in 1981

Cat Dealers	Inside U.S.	Outside U.S.	Worldwide
Full-line dealers	87	129	216
Lift-truck dealers exclusively	12	4	16
Branch stores	284	605	889
Employees	24,913	53,657	78,570
Service bays	4,708	5,117	9,825
Investment in new facilities and equipment in last five years ($ millions)	$375	$515	$890
Floor space added for sales, service, and parts in last five years (square feet in millions)	7.4	5.2	12.6
Total dealer floor space (square feet in millions)	16.4	16.9	33.3
Combined net worth ($ millions)	$1,400	$2,197	$3,597

Source: Annual report.

new buildings and equipment. No Cat dealer had failed in recent years. In fact some of the largest dealerships abroad were held by other multinationals, like General Electric (in Colombia and Venezuela) and Unilever (in Africa). Although no reliable figures were available, it was believed that dealers received a margin of 25% on list (retail) prices of Caterpillar machines, and considerably higher margins on parts.

Cat advertised its products heavily in specialist magazines like the *Engineering News Record.* Mostly its advertisements focused on a single product, often a new introduction.

Manufacturing   The second leg of Cat's strategy was its concentration on manufacturing excellence. All Cat products were substantially the same, wherever made. Cat invested heavily in a few large-scale, state-of-the-art component manufacturing facilities—many of them near Peoria—to meet worldwide demand. The company then used these centralized facilities to supply overseas assembly plants that also added local features. Local plants not only avoided the high transportation cost of end products but also helped the company respond to the demands of local governments for manufacturing investment.

The company manufactured in 22 plants in the United States, three in the United Kingdom, two each in Brazil, Canada, and France, and one each in Australia and Belgium. It also manufactured through 50%-owned ventures in Japan and India and a 49%-owned company in Mexico. Another 50/50 joint venture was being negotiated in Indonesia. Five of the U.S. plants made mainly engines, both for incorporation into Cat's machines, and for sale to other equipment manufacturers and dealers. Five U.S. plants made only turbine-engine and related system components for Solar Turbines Incorporated, a wholly owned subsidiary. All other U.S. plants produced various EME machines.

Throughout the 1970s, Cat continued to expand its plants, although it typically operated at less than 75% capacity. In 1981 Cat had an estimated $12 billion of sales capacity (both machines and engines). To achieve break-even the company had to sell about $6.8 billion each year. According to senior management, it was better to shave profit margins in times of soft demand than to risk losing customers because shipments were late or products were poorly made. The company was highly integrated backward, with nearly 90% of its components and parts made in-house.

Cat's commitment to manufacturing excellence showed in its capital spending program. (See Table D for recent trends in capital expenditure programs.) Much of the capital spending was motivated by an internal Caterpillar study in late 1970s that concluded there was enormous growth potential in the earth-moving industry. Another aspect of this ambitious capital spending program was Caterpillar's commitment to flexible manufacturing systems. Obsolete equipment was being replaced by more up-to-date, electronically controlled equipment.

Quality control also attracted management's attention. In 1980, Cat started experimenting with quality circles, an approach that encouraged assembly line workers to form problem-solving groups to identify and analyze problems and recommend solutions. The company had also used employee newsletters to emphasize the importance of increasing productivity in order to meet foreign competition, especially from Japan.

Cat's use of automation to achieve productivity gains was not well received by its workers. In 1979, the company and the United Auto Workers union (UAW) went through an unusually bitter strike which led to an 11-week walkout by 40,000 workers in Peoria, and a 7-week stoppage at other U.S. plants. In 1980, the company laid off 5,600 workers, further souring management-labor relations. Many observers felt that labor relations was Cat's Achilles' heel. In recent press releases, Cat contended that its workers were paid an average of $20 per hour, compared to the $11 Komatsu paid its workers. Since labor costs accounted for nearly two-thirds of the value added at Caterpillar, management felt it was imperative that costs be contained. (See Table E for a comparison of the value-added structures.)

Table D   Cat's Capital Expenditure Program ($ millions)

Year	Capital Expenditures	Gross Plant	Cap. Exp. as Percent Gross Plant (at previous year-end)
1981*	$713.2	$5,454.3	15.0%
1980	749.2	4,750.8	17.8
1979	675.9	4,209.7	18.6
1978	543.4	3,637.0	17.2
1977	516.5	3,165.6	18.9
1976	495.0	2,734.5	21.8
1975	446.0	2,266.9	24.0
1974	349.7	1,856.4	22.6
1973	263.7	1,543.2	20.2
1972	132.8	1,303.5	9.8
1971	123.6	1,361.1	9.9
1970	$113.2	$1,251.5	9.7%

*Estimated.
Source: First Boston.

Table E   Value-Added Structure at Caterpillar and Komatsu

	Cat	Komatsu*
Labor costs	66.4%	50.2%
Depreciation	10.2	10.4
Interest expenses	5.1	−4.8
Net income	13.2	17.1
Taxes	5.1	25.2
Other	—	1.9
Total	100.0%	100.0%

*About half of the total domestic sales of Komatsu were derived from direct sales to end-users who usually purchased machines under installment credit. This enabled Komatsu to earn interest at a rate higher than its borrowings. Further, Komatsu had substantial marketable securities as liquid assets.
Source: Nomura Securities.

Cat's manufacturing system was not without its critics. One industry observer remarked:

Cat's engineers are terrific in engineering but not in organizing. They know that if they let production go overseas, the U.S. operations will have to act as a buffer, causing production to yo-yo. They would prefer to use exports from the United States to keep production levels constant. Their approach is to keep volume concentrated so that they can automate and cut labor.

The observer also criticized Cat's production system, terming it as being "five years behind the production systems used in Japan" resulting in "high overheads and setup costs."

Overseas Expansion   Cat's top management had developed a world view of their business. Initially, overseas dealers depended on the parts business of U.S. construction companies, shuttling machines around the world from job to job. Through its long-term commitment to international markets, however, Cat cemented its relationship with its dealers and encouraged them to devote primary attention to Cat products. The typical overseas dealer did more than half of his business in Cat's products. In the United States and Canada, the proportion was 80%.

During the 1950s and 1960s Cat opened offices in the United Kingdom, Europe, Brazil, Canada, Mexico, and Australia. It built manufacturing facilities in the United Kingdom, France, and Canada in the mid-1950s, and in Brazil, Belgium, and Australia in the early 1960s. The late 1960s saw the establishment of the Mexican joint venture. Although some of the foreign expansion was motivated by the fear of being locked out of markets through protectionist measures, most moves were the result of a management belief that wherever a market existed in an industrially advanced country, a local competitor would eventually emerge to serve it and later move abroad. Thus, unless Cat itself were on the scene, it would not be able to compete effectively.

In the early 1960s the company tried to enter the Japanese market. First it attempted to link up with Komatsu, but Komatsu wanted only a licensing agreement. Cat then began talking to Mitsubishi. Immediately, Komatsu went to the Ministry of International Trade and Industry (MITI) and asked it to block the new venture until Komatsu upgraded its product line. MITI obliged. After Komatsu had concluded a deal with Cummins Engine for the manufacture of engines under license, MITI permitted the Cat-Mitsubishi joint venture.

Because it saw its domestic and international operations as being closely linked, Cat preferred to maintain complete managerial control over all subsidiaries through 100% ownership. It agreed to joint ventures only when required by host government policies, and until 1981, had not set up a minority-owned subsidiary abroad. Furthermore, Cat ensured strategic unity in the worldwide operations by sending some of its best senior managers abroad to manage the operations of its subsidiaries. When they returned to Peoria, these managers took more of a world view of the company's operations. The executive compensation system for expatriates put considerable stress on their contribution to Cat's worldwide performance.

Cat's international marketing operations viewed the world in three parts. North and South America were served by the U.S. operation as well as by the Brazilian, Mexican, and Canadian facilities. Europe, the Middle East, and Africa were served by the European facilities. The Far East received its products from Japan, Australia, and India, although the large Australian market was served mostly from the United States. Despite these regional options, many of the large machines and a number of key components, such as transmissions, were sourced only from the United States.

This division of the world led to friction between Mitsubishi and Cat. For instance, in the 1970s an independent dealer in British Columbia imported Mitsubishi-Cat machines and started selling them at a lower price and yet making profits. The regular Cat dealer for the region complained to Peoria, and Cat management directed the Japanese venture to refrain from selling direct in North America. In Australia, a similar situation prevailed.

The company's international sales efforts were coordinated by the sales managers based in Peoria, directing Cat's field representatives who in turn, communicated with the dealers. The sales managers tried to maintain consistent worldwide pricing and dealer policies, but industry observers felt that Cat's prices in the United States were consistently higher than in overseas markets. "They have never known an acceptable return on European production—even in the best years," said one analyst. In 1981, according to the same analyst, Caterpillar's operating margin abroad was about 7% vs. 20% in the United States.

Product Development Research and development expenditures at Cat were substantial—$363 million in 1981. Most research was targeted directly toward product development, product improvement, and applied research. Cat undertook basic research when it needed materials or components that its suppliers could not provide. For instance, it developed a beadless tire for its big loaders, then licensed the technology to Goodyear.

A senior executive summed up the company's approach to product development: "Unless a product is highly capital-intensive, will benefit from high technology, and is marketable through our current distribution system, it will not fit our product development strategy." Cat was rarely the first with a new offering, preferring to let other companies go through the trial-and-error stage, then following quickly with the most trouble-free product in the market. One of the company's vice presidents said: "Market share for us is not an objective. Building sophisticated, durable, reliable products and providing good support is." By constant adaptation, Cat engineers had created 120 different machines serving almost as many market segments.

Pricing   Cat's products were usually priced at a premium of 10% to 20% over the nearest competitive model, but management felt that its product quality and service excellence merited such a premium. It tried to avoid overpricing, and did not factor in some costs, such as new plant start-up costs, into its pricing calculations. This had meant lower profit margins in recent years of major capacity expansion. Because of Cat's uniform pricing policy, dealers all over the world were billed in dollars, irrespective of the origin of the machines. The prices were often based on U.S. manufacturing cost, but when the dollar was strong, Cat had to be flexible.

In the EME industry, a large part of the profit was in spare parts. A large crawler tractor cutting into rocks in an iron ore mine will use up parts worth as much as the original equipment within two years or so. Although Cat never revealed the data, one industry estimate was that Cat's profit margin on parts was at least twice that on original equipment.

Diversification   Cat's stated objective was to grow 6% to 7% a year in real terms throughout the 1980s. Because its domestic construction business was becoming increasingly mature, the company decided to achieve this through related diversification. In mid-1981, the company purchased the Solar Turbines Division from financially troubled IH for $505 million. Solar made turbine engines, natural gas compressors, generators and power drives; 80% of its sales went to the oil and natural gas industry with more than 50% outside the United States.

Cat's competitive strategy in engines built on a huge captive base; the company was the world's largest consumer of engines over 400 hp. In addition, since the late 1960s, it had developed and supplied engines for Ford trucks, and by 1981 supplied over a third of Ford's truck engine needs. It aimed to become the low-cost producer by using up-to-date technologies and factories. The capital expenditure record of the engines division detailed in Exhibit 9 shows the company's commitment.

Exhibit 9   Caterpillar Engine Division's Operating Record ($ millions)

Year Ends December 31	Net Sales	Operating Profit	Operating Margin (%)	Total Engine Sales*	Engine Division Capital Spending	Outside Sales as % Cat's Sales
1981[†]	2,049	364	17.8	2,983[‡]	410	22/24[‡]
1981[§]	1,805	389[‖]	21.6	2,492	NA	20
1980	1,400	218	15.6	2,156	214	16
1979	1,138	124	10.9	1,680	183	15
1978	1,057	234	22.1	1,644	146	15
1977	771	156	20.1	1,259	168	17
1975	482	NA	NA	NA	NA	10
1970	174	NA	NA	NA	NA	8

Note: NA means not available.
*Including internal usage at transfer price.
[†]Including Solar, estimated.
[‡]As if Solar, purchased in July 1981, had been present for a full year.
[§]Excluding; Solar, estimated.
[‖]Estimated; reflects absence of $25 million write-down at Solar after acquisition.
Source: First Boston.

Cat's purchase of Solar Turbines came 16 years after its previous acquisition (in 1965, it bought Towmotor to gain a foothold in the lift truck business). Lee Morgan explained why his company had not followed the acquisition route of competitors like Clark Equipment and Massey-Furguson:

> Most companies look at diversification as a proliferation of products in many different lines, but that misses the point. A tractor does not really care whether it works in agriculture, oil exploration, or road building, and that is the essence of diversification—being involved in many sectors of the economy.

Financial Policies   Cat was a financially conservative company with a low dependence on debt. It traditionally offered low dividend payout ratios, using retained earnings for financing. The company used the last-in, first-out (LIFO) method of inventory valuation, and treated its R&D costs as expenses in the years incurred.

Cat's balance sheet was not as tight as some competitor's due to the company's manufacturing policies. One supplier estimated that half of his and Cat's work-in-progress inventory maintained by Cat and its suppliers resulted from a safety stock to guard against quality problems. In early 1981, Lee Morgan singled out the Japanese inventory control systems as one of the keys to Japanese success in manufacturing. "What the factory needs today should be either made today or delivered today."

Personnel and External Relations Policies   Cat hired only individuals who expressed a willingness to work their way up from the factory and dedicate their entire careers to the company. It hired management recruits directly from college, often people with technical degrees. As a rule, the company did not hire MBAs. Over two-thirds of Caterpillar's top executives were born in Illinois or neighboring states. Morgan joined the company in 1946, after graduating from the University of Illinois, and spent most of his career in sales. The company president, Robert Gilmore, was a forty-four-year company veteran who rose through the ranks via an apprenticeship in manufacturing after graduating from high school. The company conducted its own in-house management development programs.

This approach to recruitment and training had led to a close-knit management group (inbred in the view of critics) who worked, lived, and socialized together. They were so dedicated to their work that they were sometimes described as having "yellow paint in their veins," a reference to the ubiquitous yellow of Cat's machines. This approach was carried abroad as well. Most employees in the company's sales subsidiary in Geneva lived in one suburb referred to locally as "Caterpillar Village." In Japan, all of the company's American employees were housed in one Tokyo apartment complex and traveled to work together in one bus. This clubbiness was reinforced by the company's close-mouthed conduct of its business. It routinely refused to provide information to the press unless it thought it absolutely necessary. The same treatment was meted out to security analysts and even the industry association, the Construction Industry Manufacturers Association (CIMA). The company also discouraged its dealers from joining the Association of Equipment Distributors.

An important feature of Cat's operations was the extent to which the company dominated the economy of Illinois in general and Peoria in particular. Cat's high wages had provided the region with Illinois' third highest per-capita income. Cat was proud of its contribution to the local community, and its senior managers often reiterated the company's commitment to Peoria. In 1981, the company was in the midst of constructing a training center in downtown Peoria as well as a huge addition to its Morton worldwide parts distribution center nearby. With considerable reluctance, Cat reduced its local work force from a peak of 36,000 in 1979 to its 1981 level of 33,500. This represented over 20% of the area's work force, and was more than 15 times the payroll of Peoria's second-largest employer.

Management Systems and Style   The key element in Cat's management systems was what the company called being "severally responsible." Under this value system, all staff and operating people in a department were responsible for obtaining results. The company believed this promoted a cooperative, team-building approach. "This is no place for individual star performers," said Morgan. "We encourage an uncommon amount of subordination of personal wishes to the good of the company." In keeping with that tradition of excising the cult of personality, the public relations department put out no personal profile of Lee Morgan or any other top manager.

Cat was one of the first companies to respond constructively to the Lee emerging criticisms of multinational corporations. Morgan said: "At Caterpillar, we seek friendly, cooperative relationships with governments. To that end, we are willing to make some substantial commitments—not only in terms of capital, but also in terms of operating principles." Those operating principles were spelled out in the *Caterpillar Code of Worldwide Business Conduct,* first published in 1974, two years before the OECD guidelines on multinational enterprises came into being. The code set a high standard of behavior for its business managers and set forth the company's expectations of fair treatment by host governments.

Another aspect of Cat's management style had been its consistent willingness to take a long-term view of the company's fortunes and spend today for tomorrow's growth. Lee Morgan again: "In our business, the lead times are long. It takes ten years or more to develop and introduce a new product. To us, short-term planning means the next five years." To further the long-term approach, the company strove toward a simple management structure that encouraged easy and informal communications. Said Morgan: "The root of our organizational process is the ability of anyone to walk into my office. . . . We try to see to it that the rate of bureaucracy does not get out of hand here."

Cat had long resisted the idea of a separate corporate planning office, believing that its line managers throughout the organization understood the company's well-established strategic principles and functional policies. At the core of its strategy was a defense of its dominant competitive position through continuous product development and long-term investment in its production facilities and marketing channels.

Typically, top management decisions were arrived at by consensus. For instance, product development was monitored through a product control department comprising representatives from manufacturing, marketing, and engineering that assessed potential competition and forecast sales volumes for five years. The final decision rested with a committee composed of the chairman, some executives from his office, and several key vice presidents. "People begin bouncing ideas off one another in a series of meetings," said Morgan. "I am presumably the guy who makes the decision, but I am greatly influenced by the consensus."

There was no question, however, that Peoria dominated the entire company. Besides maintaining strong central financial and production controls, headquarters kept constant tabs on the company's operation worldwide, and no problem was considered undeserving of its attention. In fact, no management promotion above the level of department head was authorized without the chairman's personal approval.

Situation in October 1981   In late 1981 Caterpillar faced an unsettled economic environment. Since 1979, the U.S. economy had been in a downturn. The Federal Reserve's anti-inflationary tight money policy, which had raised interest rates, had severely affected the construction industry. The 1982 consensus forecast among economists predicted deeper recession and gradually declining interest rates. Having benefited from the depreciation of the dollar in the late 1970s, Cat management was also concerned about forecasts of a continued strengthening of the U.S. currency.

The 1979 oil shock had stimulated construction in some of the oil-rich countries. By late 1981, however, the oil price rise had forced a recession on non-oil-developing countries. Meanwhile, demand for crude had softened, and some economists predicted an oil glut in the 1980s. This threatened to upset the massive development plans of countries like Nigeria and Mexico.

In late 1981 much talk also circulated in the world financial press about the global debt crisis. Many large developing countries, such as Mexico, Brazil, Argentina, Nigeria, and South Korea, were facing a severe liquidity crunch, and international banks were reportedly reluctant to increase their already large exposure to LDCs. Simultaneously, developed countries were proposing reductions in foreign aid, and commodity prices were also registering steep declines.

The Far East and Australia was the only region showing hopeful signs. The ASEAN countries—Singapore, Malaysia, Indonesia, the Philippines, and Thailand—had been growing impressively over the last five years, and this trend was expected to continue. South Korea, Taiwan, and Japan were also prospering. Australia's minerals-led boom, temporarily dampened by the world recession, was expected to reassert itself through the 1980s.

In 1981 the U.S. EME industry was operating at about 60% of capacity. Capacity utilization rates for the last few years had been around 65%. In 1980, the industry had employed about 190,000 people; it was estimated that by the end of 1981, the number would have fallen to about 152,000.

Future Strategy   Morgan opened his management meeting with the news that the UAW delegates had given advance notice that in light of Cat's outstanding financial results, the union would be asking for substantial increases at next year's triennial contract negotiation. It also expected to recoup the benefits lost after the bitter 1979 strike.

As well as beginning to think about the company's approach to these demands, Morgan also wanted to engage his managers in a discussion of how Cat might respond to the changing industry and emerging competitive environment.

Case 3-2   Komatsu Limited

In late January 1985 Chairman Ryoichi Kawai of Komatsu Limited, the world's second-largest earth-moving equipment (EME) company, saw the quarterly financial results of Caterpillar Tractor Co. (Cat), its archrival. With his understanding of the industry and of his competitor's problems, he was not surprised to see Cat's losses continuing but was not expecting the figure to be so high. The $251 million fourth-quarter loss brought the company's full-year loss to $428 million, closing out Cat's third straight unprofitable year. Although it meant that Komatsu appeared to be closing in on a competitor that had dominated the industry for so long, Kawai knew his competitor well enough to understand that Cat would fight hard to regain its preeminent position.

The realization that the industry structure was changing led Kawai to reflect on Komatsu's position. Since his company had become a major player in the industry, it might be necessary to reappraise its competitive strategy. "After all," mused Kawai, "one important lesson to be drawn from Cat's decline is that success today does not necessarily imply success tomorrow."

World EME Industry

The demand for EME depended mainly on the general level of construction and mining activities, and both industries had undergone considerable change during the 1970s.[1] In the construction industry, for example, it became increasingly clear that in most developed countries the major nonrecurring construction expenditures such as highway programs, water management programs, land clearing, and housing had been largely completed. In the last quarter of the century, developing countries would

▌ This case was prepared by Associate Professor Christopher A. Bartlett and Research Associate U. Srinivasa Rangan.
▌ Copyright © 1985 by the President and Fellows of Harvard College. Harvard Business School case 385-277.

▌ [1]A detailed industry review is contained in the companion case, "Caterpillar Tractor, Co." HBS Case No. 9-385-276, and only a brief summary of the key issues is presented here.

probably provide most of the large remaining infrastructure projects.

Among developing countries, financing considerations played a significant part in buying decisions for all capital equipment. Further, the state sector was often a significant buyer, and for EME, the buying behavior typically stressed up-front bidding procedures that regularly included not only machines but also spare parts for a period of two years or more.

The mining industry had also undergone considerable change during the 1970s. In many less developed countries (LDCs) mining belonged to the state sector. This contributed to the surplus production and widely gyrating prices of many minerals. The economic uncertainty and political instability in several of the traditional source countries caused mining companies to explore mineral development in developed countries such as Australia. In the energy sector, the oil crises of 1973 and 1979 triggered a construction boom in the Middle East, and major developments elsewhere as other sources of energy were tapped.

The worldwide EME industry had traditionally been dominated by a handful of firms, almost all of them North American. The industry giant was Cat, based in Peoria, Illinois. Throughout the 1960s and the 1970s the company held a market share of over 50%. (Exhibit 1 shows the market share trend from 1971 to 1984.) The company built an unmatched reputation for quality and service in construction equipment. Its dealer network in North America and abroad, particularly in Europe and Latin America, had been an important source of its strength. The company's carefully planned competitive strategy emphasized the building of advanced, enduring machines using components made in specialized plants (mostly in the United States), selling them at premium prices, and offering fast, high-quality field service. Cat's high point came in 1981, when the sales and profits hit record levels of $9.2 billion and $580 million, respectively.

Industry Developments since 1981   As the U.S. recession deepened in the early 1980s, the value of contracts signed by the top 400 U.S. construction companies fell by a third from $170 billion in 1981 to $115 billion in 1983. Much of Europe and Latin America was also in the throes of a recession, and the overseas portion of U.S. construction companies' contracts fell by 45% from 1981 to 1983.

During the same period many LDCs, particularly in Latin America and Africa, faced uncertain economic environments with low commodity prices, problems associated with debt servicing and new borrowing, and recession in their principal export markets such as the United States and Western Europe. Furthermore, the softening of oil prices meant that the Middle East no longer remained the center of activity for large construction contracts as it had been in the 1970s. The only economies with much economic resilience were in the Far East.

The competition in the EME industry had intensified during this period. The substantial capacity built during the more prosperous years of the late 1970s far exceeded industry demand. IBH, a German firm formed through the acquisition of many smaller European companies, registered extraordinary growth for several years. By 1983, however, this major European competitor faced bankruptcy proceedings. International Harvester (IH), an industry veteran, was forced to sell its EME business to Dresser in 1983. Almost all the companies had suffered losses since 1981, with U.S. exporters particularly hurt by a dollar that appreciated 40% between 1981 and 1984 in trade-weighted terms.

Cat's performance, however, held the attention of most industry observers. Although it had been known to pay generous hourly rates to its workers, Cat's labor relations had deteriorated. In the October 1982 wage negotiations, the company, citing the labor cost differential of more than 45% compared with its Japanese rival, sought to contain costs. Cat's treasurer was quoted as saying, "We can handle a 10% to 15% differential but not 45%."

The United Auto Workers union (UAW) would have none of it. Citing Cat's extraordinarily good performances in prior years, the UAW demanded a share in the prosperity. However, considering the company's worries about future prospects, the

Exhibit 1 Market Shares of Major EME Producers

	1971	1972	1973	1974	1975	1976	1977	1978	1979	1980	1981	1982	1983	1984‖
Cat*	56.0%	55.0%	53.0%	53.0%	54.4%	56.1%	53.6%	51.9%	50.0%	53.3%	50.8%	45.7%	43.9%	43.0%
Komatsu	10.3	10.9	11.6	9.0	9.2	11.3	11.8	14.3	14.8	15.2	16.1	19.6	23.6	25.0
J.I. Case	6.7	6.9	8.9	8.3	7.2	7.4	8.5	9.4	10.5	10.3	9.7	9.9	9.6	10.0
Fiat-Allis†	4.3	4.0	3.8	7.3	7.7	6.3	6.5	6.1	5.8	5.7	5.3	5.8	4.8	4.3
Deere	5.8	6.2	6.3	6.1	4.7	5.2	6.6	6.7	7.1	6.6	5.0	4.8	5.9	6.5
International Harvester	11.0	10.0	10.1	9.7	10.0	7.6	7.2	6.6	7.1	5.1	4.7	3.5	3.3	3.0
Clark	5.9	6.0	6.3	6.6	6.8	6.1	5.8	5.0	4.7	3.8	3.2	2.9	3.1	3.5
Total	100%	100%	100%	100%	100%	100%	100%	100%	100%	100%				
IBH‡	—	—	—	—	0.5	0.5	0.6	0.7	1.4	4.2	5.3	7.8	5.8	4.7
Total industry sales (mil.)§	$4,063	$4,954	$6,190	$7,651	$8,840	$8,773	$10,130	$12,841	$14,027	$14,916	$14,788	$12,098	$10,956	$13,956
Year-to-year change	—	21.3%	24.9%	23.6%	15.5%	−0.8%	15.5%	26.8%	9.2%	6.3%	−0.9%	−23.3%	−9.4%	27.3%
Price increase‖	4%	5%	12%	10%	18%	6%	8%	9%	11%	12%	9%	5%	3%	0%
Real growth‖	—	16	13	13	(3)	(7)	7	18	(2)	(6)	(10)	(28)	(12)	27

*Includes sales from Mitsubishi-Cat joint venture net of sales to and from Cat.
†Allis-Chalmers only before 1974.
‡IBH Holding AG—founded in 1975 with growth through acquisitions of 10 European equipment manufacturers through 1980. In 1980 IBH acquired Hymac (U.K.) and Hanomag (Germany). In 1981 IBH acquired Terex from General Motors.
§Excludes IBH up to 1980 but includes it thereafter.
‖Wertheim & Co., estimates.
Source: Wertheim & Co., Inc.

UAW made what in other days would have been a generous offer: to continue the old contract for three years with cost-of-living allowances (COLAs) continued as before plus 3% raises annually, but no new add-ons. The company turned down the union proposal and stuck to its offer: no basic pay increases for three years; COLA for two of the three years but at a trimmed-down rate. Further, Cat wanted reductions in paid time off and more management flexibility in work scheduling between areas without having to consider workers' seniority.

A bitter 204-day strike (one of the largest on record against a major U.S. company) was finally broken in May 1983. Facing inventory shortages and the prospect of its dealer network not being able to meet customer demand, Cat conceded to almost all the union's demands except the additional 3% annual increase in COLA. Said one industry analyst, "The settlement will do little to ameliorate what has become a hostile relationship between Cat and the UAW."

With the strike behind it, the company was optimistic that it would post a profit in 1984. Indeed, a robust U.S. economic recovery lifted Cat's domestic sales 30% above 1983 levels. Foreign sales also increased 11% in 1984, with strong gains in Canada, Australia, Japan, and Europe offsetting overall declines in developing countries. Although total physical volume increased 26% over 1983 levels, sales revenue rose by only 21% due to "intense price competition." Cat managers blamed excess industry capacity and the strength of the U.S. dollar for this situation.

In response to continuing losses, Cat initiated a cost-reduction program in 1982, and management claimed that its 1984 costs were 14% below 1981 levels adjusted for inflation and volume. Furthermore, the company consolidated the operations of five U.S. plants and halted the construction of a national parts warehouse, resulting in 1984 write-offs of $226 million. In late 1984 management decided to close five other facilities. The full benefits of the consolidations and closings were not reflected in 1984's results, but management indicated that its efforts "could permit the company to be moderately profitable in 1985," acknowledging

that this implied gaining sales at the expense of competitors. (Selected financial data for the period from 1979 to 1984 appear in Exhibit 2.)

Komatsu Limited

In 1983 Komatsu Limited, the Osaka-based Japanese company with its headquarters in Tokyo, had consolidated net sales of $3.2 billion, with 81% of the sales emanating from the EME sector and the balance from a diversified base of manufactures, such as diesel engines, presses, machine tools, industrial robots, solar batteries, and steel castings. Yet, only two decades earlier, Komatsu had been just one of many small local equipment manufacturers living in the shadow of Cat.

Background   Komatsu was established in 1921 as a specialized producer of mining equipment. The company's basic philosophy since its earliest days emphasized the need to export. The founder of the company, Mr. Takeuchi, had stressed in his management goals statement as early as 1921 the requirement for management to have two important perspectives—an "overseas orientation" and a "user orientation." A year later Komatsu acquired an electric furnace and started producing steel castings. In 1931 the company successfully produced a two-ton crawler type of agricultural tractor, the first in Japan. During the Second World War Komatsu became an important producer of bulldozers, tanks, howitzers, and so forth.

In the postwar years the company reoriented itself toward industrial EME. The company's bulldozer was much in demand in the late 1950s as Japan's postwar reconstruction started in earnest. There was little competitive pressure on Komatsu either to augment its product line or to improve the quality of products. The company president acknowledged, "The quality of our products in terms of durability during that period was only half that of the international standards." Unable to persuade dealers to sell its equipment, the company set up its own branch sales offices and authorized small local repair shops to be Komatsu service agents. Given the poor quality of the machines, it is not surprising that customers complained of the company's

Exhibit 2   Selected Financial Data on Caterpillar ($ in millions, except per share amounts)

	1984	1983	1982	1981	1980	1979
Sales	$6,576	$5,424	$6,469	$9,154	$8,598	$7,613
Profit (loss) for year—consolidated	$(428)	$(345)	$(180)	$579	$565	$492
Profit (loss) per share of common stock	$(4.47)	$(3.74)	$(2.04)	$6.64	$6.53	$4.92
Return on average common stock equity	(138.8)%	(10.0)%	(4.9)%	15.9%	17.4%	16.9%
Dividends paid per share of common stock	$1.25	$1.50	$2.40	$2.40	$2.325	$2.10
Current ratio at year-end	1.5:1	2.5:1	2.87:1	1.50:1	1.71:1	1.88:1
Total assets at year-end	$6,223	$6,968	$7,201	$7,285	$6,098	$5,403
Long-term debt due after one year at year-end	$1,384	$1,894	$2,389	$961	$932	$952
Capital expenditures for land, buildings, machinery, and equipment	$234	$324	$534	$836	$749	$676
Depreciation and amortization	$492	506	$505	$448	$370	$312
Research and engineering costs	$345	$340	$376	$363	$326	$283
Average number of employees	59,776	58,402	73,249	83,455	86,350	89,266
Average number of shares of common stock outstanding	95,919,938	92,378,405	87,999,086	87,178,522	86,458,748	86,406,162

Source: Annual reports.

poor service capability. Thus, despite the booming demand and the tariff-sheltered market, by 1963, Komatsu remained a puny, $168 million manufacturer of a limited line of EME, lacking technical know-how to produce sophisticated machines.

The turning point came in 1963, when the Japanese Ministry of International Trade and Investment (MITI) decided to open the EME industry to foreign capital investment. MITI felt it was necessary to continue to protect the emerging Japanese auto and electronics industries. As a quid pro quo, the EME industry was to be opened up since MITI officials believed that Japan did not possess a long-run competitive advantage in this industry. Cat decided to take advantage of the opportunity, and Komatsu was suddenly faced with a formidable competitor in its own backyard. Komatsu opposed the proposed Mitsubishi-Cat joint venture, but MITI was only willing to delay the project for two years. Yashinari Kawai, Komatsu's president, decided he must immediately take advantage of the Japanese government's policies, which demanded that foreign companies help the Japanese companies in return for access to Japan's markets. He planned to make his company a competitor of world standards.

The 1960s   In his single-minded drive for survival, Kawai set two goals: the acquisition of the necessary advanced technology from abroad and the improvement of product quality within the company. A manager who had been at Komatsu during this time recalled:

Our mission was made very clear by the president. There was no question that the rapid upgrading of quality standards was the priority task that had to be promoted. It was the only way Komatsu could survive the crisis.

The company entered licensing arrangements with two major EME manufacturers in the United States—International Harvester and Bucyrus-Erie. The former was well known for its wheel-loader technology, and the latter was a world leader in excavator technology. Komatsu also concluded a licensing and technology collaboration agreement with Cummins Engine in the United States, which led the world in diesel engine development. Komatsu paid a substantial price for this technological access, not only in financial payments but also in restrictions on exports that it had to agree to as part of the arrangements. Recognizing that its dependence on these licensees left it vulnerable, the company established its first R&D laboratory in 1966 to focus on the application of electrical engineering developments.

Komatsu also launched a quality upgrading program in its factories. The program, one of the first to reflect the Total Quality Control (TQC) concept, was an adaptation and extension of the well-known Japanese quality-control-circles system in manufacturing operations. The objective of TQC was to ensure the highest quality in every aspect of Komatsu's operations. A company spokesperson explained, "The TQC umbrella spreads over all our activities. Virtually everything necessary to develop, to produce, and to service our products—and to keep customers around the world satisfied with those products' high performance, reliability, and durability—is incorporated into our scheme of Total Quality Control." All personnel—from top management to every worker on the assembly line—was expected to strive for TQC. Komatsu management was proud of receiving the highly coveted 1964 Deming Prize for quality control within three years of launching TQC.

In 1964 the company also began Project A. The project aimed to upgrade the quality of the small and medium-sized bulldozers, Komatsu's primary domestic market product. A top manager recalled, "The president commanded the staff to ignore the costs and produce world-standard products. He told us to disregard the Japanese Industrial Standards [JIS]." The first batch of upgraded products reached the market in 1966. The project produced spectacular results. The durability of the new products was twice that of the old ones, and despite the fact that Komatsu doubled the length of its warranty period, the number of warranty claims actually decreased by 67% from the previous level.

At this stage the company launched the second phase of Project A as cost reductions took precedence. Every aspect of design, production facilities, parts assembly, assembly-line systems, and the operation processes was subjected to thorough scrutiny, and costs were pared down. Between 1965 and 1970 the company increased its domestic market share from 50% to 65% despite the advent of the Mitsubishi-Caterpillar joint venture in Japan.

The company also benefited in other ways as reflected by the company president's comments:

> The product quality improvement activities greatly improved the quality of work within the company. A crisis atmosphere prevailed in the company when the project was being implemented, resulting in a spirit of unity between the management and staff. This was perhaps the most valuable achievement of the project.

The Early 1970s   By the early 1970s Komatsu's management sensed the need for aggressive expansion abroad. The company had achieved dominance within Japan. With domestic construction activity leveling off, however, it appeared as if the EME market was reaching maturity with little prospect of substantial growth. Meanwhile, management was aware of the rise of natural resources activities throughout the world, and particularly the construction boom in the Middle East in the post-1974 period.

Up until the 1960s the company's exports were largely based on inquiries received from abroad. The first large export order came from Argentina in 1955. During the early 1960s the company began opening a market in Eastern bloc countries. Yashinari Kawai was committed to promoting Japan's trade relations with the USSR and China. He and his son Ryoichi, a promising young Komatsu manager, conducted extensive negotiations in both countries and developed excellent relations with many high-level officials.

In the mid-1960s the company turned its attention to Western Europe. Large-scale shipments to Italy were followed by exports to other countries. In 1967 Komatsu Europe was established as a European marketing subsidiary, to better coordinate the delivery of parts and the provision of field service. In the same year the first Komatsu machines were exported to the United States. In 1970 Komatsu America was established to develop business in the huge North American market. In most of these markets Komatsu concentrated on selling a limited product line, typically crawler-tractors and crawler-loaders, which were the most common equipment on construction sites. By pricing 30% to 40% below similar Cat equipment, the company soon established a foothold in most target markets.

Unlike Cat, whose servicing dealer network covered the globe, Komatsu had no such sales and service system. Even in Japan the company was trying to supplement its company-owned branches and small repair shops with an independent dealer structure. Overseas, Komatsu found it even more difficult to establish strong sales and service capabilities. Companies with the resources and skills to be strong dealers were already locked into one of the competitive EME distribution networks. To ensure good service by those dealers it had signed up, Komatsu maintained extensive parts inventories in each country—"a deliberate overkill," according to one dealer. When it could not get dealers, however, Komatsu handled the sales function directly, at least initially. Its links with Japanese trading companies helped to locate important projects, and the company's overseas subsidiaries would often follow these up to sell directly to government agencies or large companies.

In 1972 Komatsu launched a new project called Project B. This time the focus was on the exports. The large bulldozer, the company's main export item, was chosen for improvement. The aim was similar to Project A's: to upgrade the quality and reliability of its large bulldozer models and bring them up to world standards, then work on cost reductions. Once these aims were realized, the company planned to launch similar efforts for the other lines of export products such as power shovels. Although Project B's main objective was to develop the company's overseas markets, the new machines were also offered in Japan and further reinforced Komatsu's domestic position.

The mid-1970s also saw the beginnings of efforts to penetrate the markets of LDCs, and in particular the fast-growing industrializing countries in Asia and Latin America. In 1974 the company established a new presale service department that provided assistance from the earliest stage of planned development projects in LDCs. The services that the department made available to LDCs free of cost included advice on issues such as site investigation, feasibility studies, planning of projects, selections of machines, training of operators, and so on. Komatsu also started developing its own exclusive dealer network in some of the large LDCs. In Southeast Asia and Africa, where payment terms for imported machines often involved some form of countertrade, the company also used the services of Japanese trading companies. With all these efforts, Komatsu's ratio of exports to total sales grew from 20% in 1973 to 41% in 1974 and to 55% in 1975.

During the early 1970s the company's R&D efforts continued apace with some attention to basic research as well as product development. Much of the effort, however, focused on the needs of the domestic market since the licensing arrangements constrained export efforts in some important new product areas. New excavator models were brought onto the market in this period, as were completely new products such as pipe layers, large dump trucks, and hydroshift vehicles.

The Late 1970s   By 1976 the Japanese market was highly concentrated, with Komatsu taking a 60% share and the Mitsubishi-Cat joint venture left with slightly over 30%. However, there was no indication of much market growth in the near future, since worldwide demand for construction equipment was slowing. Komatsu management decided to focus on improving the competitiveness of its products.

A four-part cost-reduction plan was initiated, the first part being dubbed the "V-10 campaign." The V-10 goal was to reduce the cost by 10% while maintaining or improving product quality. The second part of the overall plan called for reducing the number of parts by over 20%. The third part aimed at value engineering, specifically focusing on redesigning the products to gain economies in materials or manufacturing. The fourth part was a rationalization of the manufacturing system. By the end of the decade the company was well on its way to achieving all these goals.

As Komatsu planned this ambitious cost-reduction plan, an unexpected development occurred that required immediate management attention. In the fall of 1977 the Japanese yen began appreciating rapidly against most major currencies. For example, the yen/dollar exchange rate went from 293 at the end of 1976 to 240 a year later. Management responded by adopting a policy of using a pessimistic internal yen/dollar exchange rate of 180 for planning purposes. Manufacturing was responsible for achieving a cost structure that could be profitable even at this "worst-scenario" rate. After trading at a high of ¥179 to the dollar in mid-1978, the yen weakened considerably against the dollar and most other currencies in 1979 (see Figure A).

During the late 1970s Komatsu also accelerated its product development program. Between 1976 and 1981 the number of models offered in the five basic categories of EME (bulldozers, excavators, dump trucks, loaders, and graders) increased from 46 to 77. When Komatsu introduced its off-highway dump trucks and hydraulic excavators earlier than Cat, management proudly hailed the company's new leadership in technical development and innovation. "We are not content to produce the same type of equipment year after year," said one technical manager, "but are always looking at the latest technical developments and are trying to see how we can adapt them to our products." An example of this approach was the application of electronic technology to all types of machinery. Komatsu had the distinction of introducing the world's first radio-controlled bulldozer, amphibious bulldozer, and remote-controlled underwater bulldozer. These unique products were aimed at special uses such as toxic dump sites and underwater mining.

The 1980s   Until 1980 Komatsu was impeded by the narrow product line it offered abroad. According to a senior manager, the market for EME could be divided into the bidding market (dominant in most developing countries) and the commercial market (dominant in most developed countries). Although Komatsu's bulldozers and loaders were generally adequate to meet the needs of the former, demand in such markets was highly erratic. Any company that aspired to become a global competitor needed to gain a strong foothold in the commercial market, and to do so, it was almost a competitive necessity to be a full-line manufacturer with an extensive sales and service network.

The decision to become a full-line supplier, however, meant that Komatsu had to reevaluate its licensing relationships with technology suppliers. In exchange for help in obtaining essential know-how from Bucyrus-Erie and International Harvester for the manufacture of excavators and loaders, Komatsu signed agreements giving American licensers a tight grip over Komatsu's exports of its products and a veto over the introduction of competing products in Japan. In 1980 Komatsu objected to Bucyrus-Erie's terms restricting the export of two new products using the latter's technology. When Bucyrus demurred, Komatsu appealed to Japan's fair trade commission. After appropriate deliberations, the government agency agreed with Komatsu that it was a restrictive business practice that impaired competition. This finding allowed Komatsu to buy its way out of the contract, paying Bucyrus $13.6 million to get the data it wanted and another $6 million for royalties on the balance of the contract in May 1981. In early 1982 Komatsu had an opportunity to buy out of its obligations to International Harvester. When financially strapped Harvester was looking for cash, Komatsu bought back IH's half interest in its loader business for $52 million.

Figure A   Currency Movements: Effective Exchange Rates (1975 average = 100)

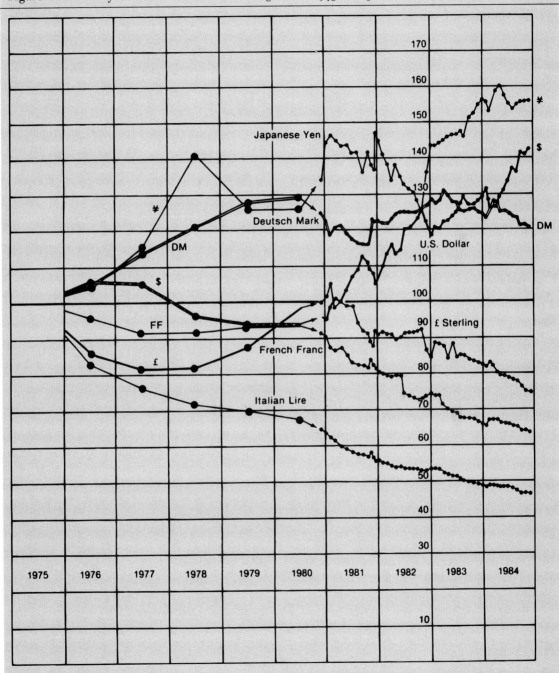

One senior manager of Komatsu summed up the approach very matter-of-factly, "Komatsu had digested its licensed technology and had established its own technology. Therefore, we just got out of the various licensing agreements." Freed of the constraints of the licensing agreements, Komatsu could sell hydraulic excavators and wheel loaders to world markets. The company emerged as a full-line competitor.

In the early 1970s Komatsu started to reorganize its distributor network worldwide, aiming to supplement the direct sales offices with more servicing dealers similar to Cat's. In 1983 the company had 8 marketing subsidiaries abroad, more than 20 overseas offices, and some 160 distributors in foreign countries. It maintained liaison offices in Havana, Warsaw, Moscow, and Peking (Beijing). In the United States, its established five regional centers for parts distribution and service. At each of these centers Japanese engineers were available to help dealers' repair departments with significant problems.

Komatsu management recognized that its 56 dealers in the United States were no match for the Cat distribution system. On average, only 30% of a Komatsu-America dealer's sales were of the company's products. Without exception, they all carried other lines as well, such as Clark and Fiat-Allis. Dealers were reluctant to become exclusive, often citing the small field population of Komatsu machines and its narrow product line. As the company broadened its product range, it began a heavy advertising campaign in specialist trade magazines, stressing its full-line capability and its product reliability.

Komatsu celebrated its sixtieth anniversary in 1981. That year it launched a new product called "EPOCHS," which stood for "Efficient Production-Oriented Choice Specifications." The project's theme was reconciliation of two contradictory demands. The aim was to "improve production efficiency without reducing the number of product specifications required by the market." The overseas expansion in the 1970s taught management that cus-

tomer requirements varied widely by market and by application. For example, in Australia prospects were excellent in coal and iron-ore mining, but the tough operating requirements surpassed the capabilities of machines designed for Japanese construction applications. Komatsu responded by designing bulldozers, power shovels, and dump trucks adapted to mining conditions in Australia. To better its competition, it sent field engineers to survey Australian miners and elicited their comments and complaints about the equipment. The company then incorporated the needed improvements into its products.

As its export market increased, the company faced demands to adapt its products to suit the user requirements in different countries and diverse applications. These requirements varied with each country's environmental conditions and legal requirements. Such adaptations, however, were costly in terms of production efficiency, parts inventory, and field service management. The purpose of the EPOCHS project was to allow the company to respond to the diverse market needs without compromising its cost position.

The project focused attention on the linkages between production and marketing requirements, thereby reinforcing the spirit of TQC, which emphasized the connection between user needs and product development. The EPOCHS project led to the development of a standardized core module for major products and the required number of parts to create the market-determined variety of finished models. This approach was expected to reconcile the contradictory needs of the production and marketing departments.

By the end of 1983 the company's manufacturing had become fully integrated, producing almost all of its components and parts in-house (it was the largest producer of steel castings in Japan, for example). Komatsu prided itself on what it called the "integrated" and "concentrated" production system. From the selection of raw materials to the production and assembly of finished products, it was all part of a single, coordinated system. Further, main components of Komatsu products, regardless of size, were manufactured exclusively in individual plants.

Komatsu products were manufactured in 14 separate plants, 13 of them in Japan. The fully owned Brazilian subsidiary produced medium-sized bulldozers for Brazil and other countries in the region. In 1975 the company established a 49%-owned Mexican joint venture for the production of large-scale bulldozers for Mexico and neighboring countries.

Komatsu continued to emphasize its commitment to R&D. By 1982 four separate research labs specialized in production engineering, design engineering, electrical applications, and electronic applications. Product development centers were located in four major plants. A new research laboratory integrating the engineering and electrical labs was in the offing in 1982. The R&D expenditures as a percentage of sales increased from 4.3% in 1981 to 5.3% in 1982 and to 5.8% in 1983. In comparison, the average for the Japanese mechanical equipment industry was 1.7% in 1982.

The R&D staff was elated when the company decided in 1981 that it was ready to participate in the International Construction Equipment Exposition (Conexpo) in Houston. Komatsu displayed some machines not previously seen—prototypes of products that would be marketed in 1982 or later. One of the main attractions at Conexpo was Komatsu's 1,000 hp bulldozer, bigger than Cat's top-of-the-line 700 hp machine. Officially, Cat's response was cool, saying that it had no plans to follow suit. But according to Komatsu managers, the most interested observers at their exhibit were Cat technicians. One Komatsu manager reportedly photographed four Cat managers examining and measuring the company's equipment at the exposition. "Ten years ago," he smiled, "we would have been the ones caught doing that."

Nonetheless, concern persisted about the depressed state of the construction industry worldwide, and Komatsu managers began talking increasingly about other business opportunities. In 1979 top management launched a companywide project called "F and F." The abbreviation stood for "Future and Frontiers," and its objective was to develop new products and new businesses. The project encouraged suggestions from all employees, asking them to consider both the needs of society and the technical know-how of the company. Management followed up on many of the 3,500 suggestions submitted, eventually leading to the development of such diverse new products as arc-welding robots, heat pumps, an excavating system for deep-sea sand, and amorphous silicon materials for efficient exploitation of solar energy.

Komatsu's R&D laboratories played an important role in this new diversification thrust, and the company planned to quadruple the number of research professionals within five years. Further, a joint research agreement with Cummins Engine provided for the sharing of information on diesel equipment improvements, including a heat pump Komatsu had developed that reportedly cut fuel costs by about 40%. The company also announced a breakthrough in developing a cast-iron alloy that was superior to the conventional aluminum alloy in heat resistance, noise generation, and fuel economy for use in high-speed diesel engines.

In the early 1980s Japanese-made industrial robots accounted for 80% of the world market, and Komatsu was already one of the top manufacturers focusing on arc-welding and material-handling robots, which it also put to use in its own factories.

Komatsu in 1984   By 1984 Komatsu managers had good reason to be proud of their company's record of the previous two decades. (See Exhibit 3 for a summary of the financial results of the company.) It still held a 60% market share in Japan, helped in part by sales to its fully owned construction and real estate subsidiaries. The company's domestic sales and service network was acknowledged to be the most extensive and efficient in Japan. Sales activities were conducted by 10 regional offices, 50 branch offices, and over 100 other sales offices. In addition, 100 independent dealers handled Komatsu products and were backed by the

Exhibit 3   Selected Consolidated Financial Data on Komatsu Limited (millions of yen)

	1984	1983	1982	1981	1980	1979	1978
Net sales	¥713,472	¥750,530	¥810,379	¥703,705	¥647,773	¥558,229	¥479,732
Net income	22,642	26,265	32,639	33,257	27,766	23,746	19,617
Earnings per common share	27.2	32.6	41.9	44.0	37.8	32.8	27.6
Cash dividends per common share	8.0	8.0	8.0	8.0	8.0	8.0	8.5
Working capital at year-end	154,466	120,829	119,695	63,705	58,469	43,496	26,927
Property, plant and equipment at year-end	157,617	143,182	134,223	120,225	110,579	107,767	110,459
Total assets at year-end	943,806	888,324	930,685	877,544	830,773	792,847	739,031
Long-term debt—less current maturities at year-end	80,722	57,442	67,731	48,443	62,755	76,925	70,871

Yen per U.S. Dollar

	1984	1983	1982	1981	1980	1979	1978
Exchange rates							
Rate at year-end	252	232	234	220	203	239	191
Average rate	239	238	248	222	225	220	204
Range of high and low rate	223–252	227–247	230–278	206–240	203–251	200–249	179–240

Note: Komatsu had a number of subsidiaries involved in construction, real estate development, overseas sales, and other activities in addition to the parent company, which was involved in earth-moving equipment manufacture.
Source: Annual reports and Form 20F reports.

company's computerized parts supply system, which guaranteed a replacement part within 48 hours anywhere in the world.

Exports expanded so that they represented well over half of Komatsu's total sales in 1983. The company continued to strengthen its relationships with the Eastern bloc and had a backlog of orders for equipment for the Siberian natural resource project. The Reagan administration's embargo in December 1981 on the sale of Cat pipe-laying equipment to Russia handed the total business to the Japanese company. Komatsu also signed a contract with the Soviets to develop a scraper based on a Russian design, using Japanese components, and was collaborating with the Russians on a big crawler-dozer and dump truck. Komatsu's sales to the Soviet Union were soon expected to overtake Cat's.

Worldwide, the company's marketing efforts gathered momentum. In Australia, its products were well received in mining circles. Referring to his company's decision to buy Komatsu's machines, the managing director of one of the largest mining companies in Australia said:

Having come to consider the market its monopoly, Caterpillar became very offhand with its customer relations. Our analysis suggested that the Komatsu machines offered significant dollar savings and outperformed the equivalent Caterpillar equipment. Komatsu's spares backup should be rated good. The operators also seemed to like the machines.

Despite competitors' suggestions to the contrary, Komatsu dealers generally denied that they were still competing mainly on price. A U.S. dealer commented:

> When you're selling against number one, you need some price advantage. But we tell contractors we can give them 10% more machine for 10% less money. That's not selling price in my book.

Although Komatsu had undoubtedly been highly successful over the previous two decades, the company's senior management felt that stagnant world demand would lead to fierce competition in the EME industry and could threaten Komatsu's growth. The internal consensus was that the existing distribution network represented a point of vulnerability. Almost inevitably, a senior Komatsu marketing executive compared his company with Cat:

> We have some gaps in our overseas sales network. Caterpillar's distribution network surpasses that of Komatsu in terms of capital, assets, number of employees, and experience. Caterpillar has greater strength in user financing and sales promotion. Indeed, some of our major dealers went bankrupt in the 1980 recession, and that taught us a major lesson about the need for financially strong dealers.

Managers hoped that Komatsu's continued efforts to produce new and differentiated products would help it to build a network of exclusive distributors overseas. Although the company could point to some progress on this objective in Europe, Asia, and Australia, it faced a much tougher task in the United States, where its market share was only 5% in 1983 (see Exhibit 4).

Responding to the demands of local governments, the company had commenced assembly operations in Brazil and Mexico. It was also working on a joint-venture proposal with its local dealer in Indonesia, where it held a 70% market share in the EME business. But Komatsu's preference had consistently been to design, manufacture, and export machines from Japan, despite the potential problems related to such a highly centralized production system. The rise of trade frictions between the European Community and the United States on the one hand and Japan on the other represented the most obvious risk in the early 1980s. A dumping complaint had been filed against Komatsu in Europe, and the EEC Commission was considering the imposition of countervailing duties. Another risk for a centrally sourced company was the possible loss of competitive position due to adverse exchange-rate movements. And finally, the logistical economics of shipping heavy equipment around the world could become a burden. According to the president of Komatsu-America Corporation, freight for bulldozers and loaders amounted to 6% to 7% of Komatsu's landed cost in the United States. For other machines it could be 10% or more.

Again, Komatsu managers compared their company with Cat:

> Caterpillar has production throughout the world. It is easier for them to shift production in response to protectionism, exchange-rate fluctuations, and changes

---

Exhibit 4   Komatsu's Sales by Geographic Region

	1977	1978	1979	1980	1981	1982	1983
Japan	57.7%	62.4%	62.6%	56.7%	50.7%	41.8%	46.1%
Asia and Oceania	11.2	11.6	15.8	18.3	22.5	30.6	30.5
America (North and South)	18.7	15.7	12.3	11.8	11.8	7.8	7.5
Europe, Middle East, and Africa	12.4	10.3	9.3	13.2	15.0	19.8	15.9
Total	100.0	100.0	100.0	100.0	100.0	100.0	100.0

Source: Form 20F reports.

in other competitive factors. Komatsu has production plants only in a few developing countries, where it had to establish them [due to local government pressures]. Consequently, Komatsu has less flexibility in the face of changes in competitive factors.

Komatsu's market approach continued to emphasize the twin orientations toward overseas markets and consumer satisfaction laid down 60 years earlier by the founder. During the 1970s two additional themes had emerged. A senior manager described them succinctly, "The first is vertical integration based on the philosophy that you must start with good raw materials if you want to manufacture good machines. The second is the Total Quality Control [TQC] practices that pervade all our actions."

At Komatsu TQC went beyond just management practice. It epitomized management philosophy, representing the value system of the workers and managers alike. According to one top manager:

It is the spirit of Komatsu. For every issue or problem, we are encouraged to go back to the root cause and make the necessary decisions. Not only does TQC help us resolve short-run management problems, but it also lays the foundation for future growth. Thus, it is a key to management innovation.

Komatsu extended its quality commitment to its dealers and suppliers. Working closely with suppliers, the company trained them in adopting its TQC system. The dealers were also encouraged to take advantage of its offer of free services to help implement such a system in their companies. In 1981 Komatsu achieved the distinction of being awarded the Japan Quality Control Prize, considered by many to be the world's supreme quality-control honor. Furthermore, its quality-control circle at the Osaka plant had twice won gold medals from the Union of Japanese Scientists and Engineers, topping the 178,000 quality-control circles of all companies in Japan.

The management practice of relying on the TQC system was supplemented by another system called the "PDCA" management cycle. The initials stood for Plan, Do, Check, and Act. The starting point for the PDCA cycle was the long-term plan announced by the top management team, and the company president's policy statement issued at the beginning of the year. Company president Ryoichi Kawai referred to this as "management by policy." He said:

Personally, I believe that a company must always be innovative. To this end, the basic policy and value of the target must be clarified so that all the staff members can fully understand what the company is aiming for in a specific time period. This is the purpose of the management by policy system.

The policy statements became the basis for management focus and follow-up action. As one of the managers described the PDCA system:

A plan is made, it is executed, its results are checked, and then new actions are planned. Every activity is based on this cycle, including companywide management control systems, production, marketing, and R&D. Because of this, the corporate ability to achieve the targets set improves. These steps also improve the workers' morale and management's leadership.

The management team at Komatsu believed that the intertwined system of TQC, PDCA, and management by policy contributed to company performance and employee development. In the words of one senior manager:

Tangible results from these systems have been twofold—increasing market share through quality improvement and productivity improvement leading to cost reduction. But equally important is the achievement of the intangibles such as improved communications among departments and setting up of clear common goals.

Ryoichi Kawai again:

A human being donates his energy to work in order to enjoy and lead an enriched and satisfying life. . . . We think that it is necessary to satisfy the workers' monetary as well as other needs simultaneously. First of all, there is the satisfaction of achievement in work. Second, there is the satisfaction of cooperating with a colleague and receiving the approval of others. Third, there is the satisfaction of witnessing an institution grow and achieve maturity. It is satisfaction, pride, and consciousness toward participation that make workers feel that they are contributing to a great objective and are doing important work in the company.

As a result, Komatsu had a long history of good labor relations, and the company believed this had been important in its ability to improve productivity and achieve cost competitiveness. Statistics compiled by Nomura Securities showed that between 1976 and 1981 labor productivity rose at an annual compound rate of 15.2% at Komatsu compared with the 10.6% annual rate at Cat. Both companies were investing heavily in plant capital expenditure during the period.

Despite the high productivity of its workers, the average Komatsu employee earned only 55% of the wages paid to Cat employees. Together with lower raw material costs (particularly steel), this low-cost, high-productivity labor force was clearly one of Komatsu's basic assets (see Tables A and B).

Pondering the Future   It was quite in character for Ryoichi Kawai, the chairman of Komatsu, to ponder the future direction for the company that he had headed since 1964, succeeding his father, Yashinari Kawai. Like his father, he had graduated from the elite Tokyo University and had served in the government bureaucracy. He became the

Table B   Steel Price Comparison: U.S./Japan ($/ton)

	U.S.	Japan*	Japan/U.S.
Hot-rolled mill coil	494	359	73%
Hot-rolled steel plate	635	445	70%

Note: Assumed yen-dollar rate is $1 = ¥220.
*Contracted price. Actual prices are often lower due to negotiations between suppliers and the users.
Source: Boston Consulting Group.

youngest department head in MITI's history before joining Komatsu in 1954. Like every other company executive, he had spent time with workers on the factory floor and was familiar with the company's products and production processes.

Kawai had been described in the press as a "workaholic," who often spent his lunch time at his desk partaking of the $3 box lunch from the company cafeteria. He traveled abroad frequently to pursue business deals. Although considered a mild and gentle person, he reportedly had a tight grip on the company. In an interview with *Fortune* magazine, he hinted at his philosophy of life. "In the government you are only requested to do your best. In a company, it is one's duty to earn money and pay your workers. You can't get there by just doing your best."

Kawai greatly admired Cat and often spoke of modeling his company after it. Despite his generous praise of his American competitor, however, he seemed to cherish the idea of beating Cat some day. He likened the competition to a tennis match. "As you know, in a tennis tournament, you can be losing in the middle of the game but win at the late stage." This spirit of competition with Cat pervaded the entire company. Komatsu's in-house slogan was "Maru-C," which roughly translated meant "Encircle Caterpillar." Reportedly, the company continuously monitored events in Peoria, and one of the main jobs of Komatsu's executives in the United States was to keep tabs on any and all

Table A   Cost Structure of a Large Bulldozer (equivalent to CAT D-6)

		Percent of Cost
Labor		35.0%
Components and subassemblies	12.4	
Overhead	18.0	
Assembly	4.6	
Purchased materials and components		49.6
Overhead		15.4
		100.0%

Source: Boston Consulting Group.

relevant press reports. Cat's monthly in-house letter to its employees, which featured new product introductions and other company-related news, was required reading for all Komatsu executives, and copies were sent by express mail to Tokyo for analysis at the corporate headquarters.

As Kawai continued to think about the possible changes in Komatsu's competitive strategy, he kept reminding himself that complacency is one vice his company had to guard against. "Eternal vigilance is not the price of liberty alone. It is also the price of prosperity."

Case 3-3   BSkyB

People watch bucketfuls of tv in this country. It's cold, it's rainy, the weather's miserable outside. There's nothing else to do really . . .

British Television Executive

Early in 1983 Rupert Murdoch's News Corporation bought a floundering British company called Satellite Television and renamed it Sky. Though scorned at the time by industry analysts and media barons, Sky quickly became an undeniable powerhouse in British television. It pioneered the development of the British satellite broadcasting industry, handily defeating the better connected, better capitalized consortium that was designed to destroy it. It wrested control of viewing rights to some of Britain's most coveted programming, including coverage of the country's Premier League soccer.[1] It won a series of regulatory challenges to its growing market presence and had even begun, in less than a decade, to threaten the position of the indomitable BBC (British Broadcasting Corporation). By 1997, Murdoch's Sky was the most profitable broadcaster in the United Kingdom and one of Britain's top 20 corporations.[2]

Yet, just as Sky was buttressing its place in the British market, the rules of the game began to shift again. In Britain as elsewhere the fundamental nature

of broadcasting was changing. Analogue transmission was giving way to digital formats and the Internet, satellite, video-on-demand and narrowcasting all promised to overwhelm the role of traditional broadcasters and television stations. To some observers, it was a situation ripe for Sky and the industry-defying brashness that defined Murdoch's career. Others felt it was the beginning of the end. Sky had prospered in large part by writing the rules of its own game. What would happen to its power as the rules began to change?

Rupert Murdoch and the Creation of Newscorp

Sky from the start was the brainchild of Rupert Murdoch. Already one of the most influential men in British media, Murdoch had built his improbable empire from an Australian newspaper started by his father. After consolidating his father's assets, Murdoch created *The Australian* in the mid-1960s, the nation's first serious national newspaper. He then diversified into television, acquiring stations in Australia, New Zealand, and Hong Kong. In 1968 Murdoch began to expand northwards as well, purchasing *News of the World,* a British tabloid. During the 1970s, Murdoch continued his push, acquiring both additional tabloid (or lower-market) papers such as the *National Star* and the *New York Post,* and higher-end papers such as the *Village Voice* and *New York*

---

[1]Called football in Britain.

[2]See Mathew Horsman, "Sky: The Inside Story," *The Guardian,* November 10, 1997, p. 4.

Professor Debora Spar and Paula Zakaria, MBA 1997, prepared this case as the basis for class discussion rather than to illustrate either effective or ineffective handling of an administrative situation.

Copyright © 1998 by the President and Fellows of Harvard College. Harvard Business School case 798-077.

magazine. By the end of the 1980s, Murdoch's News Corporation owned the *Times* and *Sunday Times* in Britain; the *Boston Herald* and *Chicago Sun Times* in the United States, and Hong Kong's *South China Morning Post.* And those were only the highest profile publications. News Corporation had also purchased the Twentieth Century Fox film studio and Metromedia television stations, combining their assets to create Fox Broadcasting, the fourth national television network in the United States.

Television in Britain

Before Sky, the British television industry had evolved in a slow and rather predictable fashion. For most of this time, the market was dominated by the venerable BBC, an institution respected in Britain and around the world for its high quality programming and technical leadership. As was the pattern across most of Europe, the BBC was government-run and financed. Funding for the broadcasts came from the proceeds of a £89.50 license fee paid annually by all British television owners regardless of their viewing preferences. In 1996, the license fee, and thus the BBC's "revenue," came to £1.8 billion. In return for these proceeds, the BBC was expected to serve a public mission, informing and elevating the British public in addition to entertaining them. The BBC was also required to comply with government standards for content and distribution. In general, both viewers and the government regarded the system as a success. With a staff of thousands of writers, directors, producers and reporters, the BBC was roundly seen as a national treasure, an integral part of Britain's cultural heritage and a high-profile mouthpiece to the world. Or as one industry insider described its role: "Television provided a public service for the good of the people. The broadcasters and the government were quite certain they knew what was best for the masses."[3]

Eventually, though, some of the masses began to protest against the BBC's monopoly over British television. In 1954 the government complied with requests for an expanded variety of programming and allowed for the creation of an independent, advertising-sponsored channel, named Independent Television (ITV). In 1981 a second channel, Channel 4, was added as well. Though free of the BBC's public service mandate, the new channels were still closely linked to the British government and its various regulatory agencies. ITV was essentially a conglomerate of private, regional stations, financed by commercial advertising but still under strict regulation by an Independent Broadcasting Authority (IBA).[4] The IBA, in turn, owned Channel 4, which was funded by taxes on the ITVs and devoted to minority audiences and niche programming.

The competition that emerged from this structure was limited and unthreatening. The ITVs and BBC competed for market share but not funding; the regionally-based ITVs rarely competed for the same advertising revenue; and the BBC, with its massive staff and license fee, retained its traditional preeminence in expensive, high quality programming.

The advent of cable television did little to affect this basic structure. In 1984 the Cable and Broadcasting Act allocated cable franchises to petitioning firms, but restricted the provision of cable television only to those regions where geography made terrestrial broadcasting (the traditional ground-based tower system) impossible. As a result, cable "passed by" less than one percent of Britain's television households in 1985. In the United States, by contrast, 36% of households subscribed to cable in that same year.[5]

For the next decade, cable expanded only slowly. Restricted by their geographical limits and without an obvious source for programming, cable companies had little competitive advantage against the far better entrenched BBC and ITVs. So they continued to lay cable and offer their services, but without seeing any significant growth in their market penetration. By 1994, a decade after the Cable and

---

[3]Personal interview, London, July 1997.

[4]Pankaj Ghemawat, "British Satellite Broadcasting versus Sky Television," Harvard Business School Case 9-794-031.

[5]From Willis Emmons and David Grossman, "Note on Cable Television Regulation," Harvard Business School Case 9-391-022.

Broadcast Act, only 650,000 British homes were connected to any form of cable.[6]

This was the world of British television—quiet, staid, high quality and comfortable. Until Rupert Murdoch came along.

Sky Takes Off

In the early 1980s, satellite television in Britain was even less developed than cable. Technologically, satellite broadcasts had been possible since the late 1960s, when scientists first succeeded in launching data transmission satellites into stationary orbit. Essentially, these are transmitters that hover exactly 22,300 miles above earth—the point at which their revolution precisely matches the earth's rotation. From this point, the satellite's transmission can consistently reach a specified region of the earth—the satellite's "footprint"—24 hours a day.

In an effort to extend and control the commercial use of satellites, a multilateral organization known as the World Administrative Radio Council had parsed out the world's known satellite space in 1977. Each of the participating countries received five channels on existing broadcast satellites at that time, plus a certain amount of space for future satellites. While most European governments wrestled with the allocation of these channels, Britain moved particularly slowly. By the mid-1980s, the British government had still not allocated its channels to any domestic broadcaster. The BBC had declined the government's initial approach, protesting that they did not have the funds to support the additional programming and sales effort that a satellite channel would require, much less the resources to build and launch a dedicated satellite.

And thus the field was wide open in 1981, when an independent producer named Brian Haynes launched Satellite Television plc (SATV). Rather than petitioning for a piece of Britain's allocated space, Haynes persuaded the European Space Agency to allow him to rent space on an underutilized telecommunications satellite whose footprint included most of Europe and England. Because this was a communications satellite rather than a broadcast satellite, it was not covered by any of Britain's broadcast regulations.

Haynes's vision was to emulate American satellite pioneers Ted Turner (of CNN) and Jerry Levin (of HBO). Like them, he intended to transmit programming via satellite to cable stations, which would then redistribute the shows to individual households. Eventually, Haynes hoped, the development of smaller and cheaper receiving dishes would enable him to bypass the cable operators and transmit directly to his customers' homes. But in the meantime Haynes quickly found himself in a treacherous position. With only a small budget behind him, he could not afford to make or buy the programming that might lure subscribers or cable operators to his new channel. And without a solid subscriber base, he could not earn sufficient revenues to fund his operations or his programming. Repeatedly, Haynes was forced to search for new investors. It was on one of those searches that he discovered Rupert Murdoch's News Corporation.

In 1983, News Corp. paid £10 million for a majority interest in SATV. Rapidly, News coined the new name Sky and replaced Haynes and his management team with television executives skilled in the programming side of the business.[7] For the next four years, Sky broadcast a news and entertainment channel to subscribers in 20 European countries. The channel broadcast 18 hours a day and reached over 10 million households via local cable systems.[8] Total investment over the four years was £40 million.

It wasn't until 1986, five years after Haynes's SATV and a decade after Britain had obtained satellite broadcasting capacity, that British broadcasters at last grew interested in satellite television. In April of that year, the IBA publicly invited applicants to lease three of the country's five government-owned satellite transmitters. Sky, the

[6]"Survey of Cable TV and Satellite Broadcasting," *Financial Times,* October 6, 1993, p. 4.

[7]William Shawcross, *Murdoch* (New York: Simon & Schuster, 1992), p. 207.

[8]Ghemawat, p. 3.

only applicant with experience in satellite television, lost out to a hastily-assembled consortium called British Satellite Broadcasting (BSB). BSB was a high-powered group with ambitious plans. It included two of the country's ITVs (Granada and Anglia Television) plus Pearson, a diversified information and entertainment company, Richard Branson's Virgin Records and Amstrad a marketer and distributor of consumer electronics. Together the consortium aimed to provide Britain's first direct-to-home satellite channel. To maintain the noncommercial image built by the BBC, BSB planned to earn its revenues from subscription rather than advertisement. Its transmission standard would be based on D-MAC, a technologically ambitious standard that the European Union had recently endorsed for all government-owned broadcast satellites. Unlike older transmission standards, D-MAC would be compatible with the long-awaited high definition television (HDTV). By employing a D-MAC-based system, BSB planned to leapfrog existing transmission standards and position itself to dominate the next generation of television broadcast in Britain. It also planned to sell cutting-edge "squarials," small square receiving dishes that would epitomize the company's technological prowess. Start-up costs for the venture were estimated at half a billion dollars for a three channel service. Amid great fanfare, BSB predicted a launch date of October 1989.

As BSB hired some of the country's top managers and television programmers, Sky scrambled unceremoniously to relaunch its own satellite service. On June 8, 1988, Murdoch announced that Sky, too, would soon offer a direct-to-home (DTH) satellite service, complete with its own small receiving dishes and popular new programming. To transmit the DTH channels, Sky would lease four transmitters on a new Astra communications satellite. Unlike BSB, Sky would employ an older transmission standard, dubbed PAL.

Compared with BSB's lofty ambitions, Sky's was nearly an old-fashioned plan. PAL was considered an inferior technical standard and would never be compatible with HDTV transmission. Sky's

dishes were also lower-tech than those proposed by BSB, and its satellite provider was barely a player in the European satellite industry. By the late 1980s, nearly all of Europe's satellites were high powered, national direct broadcast systems similar to that which the British government had allocated to BSB. Astra, by contrast, was launched by Societe Europeene des Satellites (SES), a small private company based in Luxembourg. It was only a medium-powered satellite by emerging standards—but it was private, foreign, and officially a communications, rather than a broadcast, satellite. Britain's regulators had no jurisdiction over anything transmitted from Luxembourg's satellite space.

Murdoch made his break from the British regulators transparent and loud. With Sky's DTH service, he proclaimed, "We are seeing the dawn of an age of freedom for viewing and freedom for advertising. Broadcasting in this country has for too long been the preserve of the old Establishment that has been elitist in its thinking and in its approach to programming."[9] He vowed to begin broadcasting in February 1989, only six months after the announcement of Sky's plans—and eight months prior to BSB's launch.

Once the dual announcements had been made, the rivals raced to acquire precious programming rights. Not surprisingly, both headed straight to Hollywood, hoping to lock in the British distribution of popular U.S. films. After an expensive bidding war, Sky paid a reported £270 million to acquire the rights to films from Orion, Touchstone, Warner Brothers, and News Corp's own Twentieth Century Fox. BSB negotiated a £550 million deal for the rights to movies from Paramount, Universal, MGM/United Artists and Columbia Pictures.[10] As part of his negotiations, Murdoch agreed to what would become a critical arrangement. Because Sky's footprint spread across the European continent, its broadcast could be received outside the United Kingdom. To preserve their viewing rights

[9]Shawcross, p. 343.

[10]Shawcross, p. 345; Ghemawat, p. 8; and "The Battle of Britain Is Taking Its Toll on the Media Barons," *Business Week,* February 5, 1990, pp. 38–9.

in Europe, the studios thus insisted that Murdoch encrypt their films, restricting Sky's viewership to paying subscribers. In response, Murdoch shifted from an advertising-based business plan (his original intent) to a subscription-based plan. He also rushed to acquire the requisite technologies: a means to encrypt and de-scramble Sky's broadcasts and to manage a complicated mix of subscriber preferences.

Sky launched its new service as promised, in February of 1989. It then began a blitzkreig sales effort with a direct marketing organization and over 1000 salespeople. After failing to sell its home receivers at retail outlets, the company literally went door to door, with an initial deal that included free subscription to Sky's movie channel, installation of the dish and receiver and free maintenance.[11] BSB, meanwhile, was slowing down, dragged by technical problems with the untested D-MAC format. When BSB finally launched in April 1990, Sky was already in 1.1 million households; approximately 600,000 via satellite dishes and the remainder through cable.[12]

By this point, BSB was already the second most expensive British start-up in history, topped only by the Channel Tunnel. Launched with $700 million, the consortium had raised an additional $1.5 billion at the start of 1990. Under the terms of the debt covenant, the group needed to sign half a million subscribers by December in order to receive the next infusion of capital. And Sky was already capturing the market.

BSB fought Sky on two simultaneous fronts: with subscribers and with the British regulatory authorities. In a highly public campaign, BSB charged that Sky had circumvented British regulation through "technological wizardry," using its perch above Luxembourg to exempt its programming from British regulation.[13] The consortium also urged that the existing Broadcasting Act of 1981 be expanded to include cable and satellite broadcasters;

if it were, then the Australian-born Murdoch, whose News Corp already owned two of Britain's largest national newspapers, would be in violation of British laws prohibiting foreign ownership of television and cross-ownership, by anyone, of newspapers and television.

By October, it had become clear that BSB had lost both the regulatory and the subscriber battles. With only 120,000 household subscribers, the consortium was roughly half a million short of its goal and losing £8 million a week.[14] The critical last tranche of financing would be withheld. Meanwhile, when Margaret Thatcher's government passed the Broadcasting Act of 1990, Sky emerged unscathed. The law extended ownership rules to terrestrial television broadcasters and to satellite broadcasters who employed high powered satellites like Astra's, however, were not covered under the new regulation. Late in October, BSB and Sky began formal negotiations. In November, the two companies merged to form BSkyB. With a 50% share of the new company, News Corp was clearly the controlling force. Sky had won.

In the aftermath of the deal, controversy swept through the British broadcasting industry. The chairman of the IBA, who only learned about the merger an hour before its signing, declared the deal "illegal and brutal." Canceling the BSB's formal contract to transmit, he proclaimed, "It is clear to the IBA that the completion of the merger, for which the IBA's consent was neither obtained nor sought, gave rise to a serious breach of BSB's program contract."[15] Echoing these sentiments, the Labour party's broadcasting spokesperson asserted that "This merger is a skyjack. We are totally opposed to a satellite monopoly, particularly when controlled by a non-EC national."[16] The Office of Fair Trade, Britain's anti-monopoly watchdog, declared its intention to investigate whether having a

---

[11]Richard Lander, "The Satellite War; Low Tech against High Tech," *The Independent,* March 25, 1990, p. 10.
[12]Ghemawat, p. 9.
[13]Shawcross, p. 382.

[14]Shawcross, p. 383; "How BSB Was Koed," *The Economist,* November 10, 1990, p. 79.
[15]"UK: The Marketing Story," *Marketing,* November 8, 1990. (Reprinted from Reuter Textline.)
[16]Ibid.

single satellite provider was anti-competitive.[17] Even the usually pro-business *Economist* joined the anti-Murdoch fray, calling the deal a "Wapping in the Air," and referring to Murdoch's previous success in breaking the once-powerful British printing union.[18]

Yet Murdoch and his new BSkyB remained largely unaffected by the uproar. Under the terms of the 1990 Broadcasting Act, the IBA was to be replaced by a new regulatory agency, the Independent Television Commission (ITC). During the transition, the IBA was effectively a lame duck. So threats from that direction carried little weight. More importantly, Thatcher's government remained strongly supportive of the Act and of Murdoch. Thatcher herself defended the need to introduce more competition into the staid world of British broadcasting. She acknowledged having a conversation with Murdoch two days before the announcement of BSkyB, but insisted that no "specifics" had been discussed.[19] A member of Thatcher's cabinet was perhaps more forthcoming in describing the government's response. "Once the merger happened," he explained, "the choice was between no satellite company and the merged company. We could have stopped Sky by amending the Broadcast Act to keep News Corp out of satellite or we could have made it illegal to advertise on satellite. If we had done that we would have finished up with no satellite television and we would have irritated Murdoch, the worst of all outcomes. He was our friend and he supported us. We owed him for Wapping and for his support. And, Murdoch was people we could not bully. Look at the *Sun.* Look at the *Times.* We needed his political support." [20]

In the end, no formal proceedings were brought against the merger and BSkyB set out to establish itself as Europe's leading provider of satellite television.

BSkyB Takes Off

The next several years were extremely busy for the newly formed company. It consolidated its operations, substantially expanded program offerings, grew its subscriber base, and pioneered cutting edge computer systems. With Murdoch turning his energies to other corners of his empire, the management of BSkyB fell increasingly to Sam Chisholm, a former managing director at Australia's Nine Network, who had been appointed chief executive late in 1990. Chisholm came to Sky with a reputation for legendary programming instincts and a ruthless managerial style. As one associate described him: "Chisholm came out of a truly competitive television environment. The whole of his strategy was that if any piece of programming looked like it might have value at any time in the future, you should buy it and grow it or buy it and kill it."[21] When Chisholm came on board, BSkyB was losing £5 million a week.[22] Murdoch hired his fellow Australian to turn the network around. While moving rapidly on all fronts, Chisholm concentrated on two key aspects of BSkyB's strategy: controlling content and controlling access.

Controlling Content   In April 1991 BSkyB was formally relaunched, complete now with five channels of programming: Sky One, Sky News, The Movie Channel, Sky Movies Plus, and Sky Sports. Before year end, four more channels were added: The Children's Channel, MTV, Screensport, and Lifestyle. Unlike the first five, Sky did not own the content of these latter channels. It merely bought the rights to them, and transmitted them from the Astra satellite, free of charge, to Sky subscribers.

[17]Andy Fry and Mat Toor, "Sky's the Limit for Satellite TV," *Marketing,* November 8, 1990.

[18]"Broadcasting: Wapping in the Air," *The Economist,* November 10, 1990, p. 72.

[19]Georgina Henry, "UK: Prime Minister Knew of Satellite TV Merger," *The Guardian,* November 12, 1990. (Reprinted from Reuter Textline.)

[20]Case writer interview, London, July, 1997.

[21]Quoted in Mathew Horsman, "Rupert's Sam Missile," *The Guardian,* November 10, 1997, p. 2.

[22]Estimates about these losses vary considerably. The £5 million figure is from "The Gambler's Last Throw," *The Economist,* March 9, 1996, p. 68. Horsman claims losses of £14 million in "Sky: The Inside Story: He Barks and Bites," *The Guardian,* November 10, 1997, p. 4.

Chisholm and his negotiators also returned to Hollywood where, as the sole satellite provider in Britain, they were now in a better bargaining position. After a year of discussion, Sony, Columbia Pictures, Warner Brothers and Disney's Touchstone all agreed to improved terms for Sky: by the end of the year, BSkyB controlled the British rights to more than 90% of Hollywood's first run movies. Reportedly, the five-year deals cost Sky well over a billion dollars. It was widely rumored in the industry that Sky had convinced the studios to link licensing fees to subscriber levels, thereby deferring payments while pre-empting their competitors from buying future film rights away from Sky.

With movies in its pocket, Sky turned next to sports. Early in 1992, the company bought the exclusive rights to Cricket's World Cup. Almost at once, sales of its satellite dishes doubled to 100,000 a month.[23] In May, Sky announced a £304 million deal for the exclusive rights to televise all games of Britain's Premier League soccer (a 22 member group of the country's best teams) for four years. Previously, these rights had been held by the ITVs, which generally paid roughly £55 million for the same contract. Now, if soccer fans wanted to see their games, they had to subscribe to Sky. Satellite dish sales skyrocketed and subscribers grew by 30% in 1992. "Soccer," as Murdoch later modestly described it, "was very important to BSkyB."[24]

In September of 1992, Sky Sports became a premium channel, meaning that subscribers had to pay an extra fee above the basic package. Meanwhile, News Corp continued to acquire sporting rights. By the end of 1996, BSkyB owned the rights to the Ruby League, the Football League (the three levels of Britsh soccer below the Premier League), Britain's overseas cricket tours, and Ryder Cup golf. Each year, because of Sky's aggressive bidding, the price of these rights soared higher. By 1996, when Sky rebid for the Premier League's four year contract the bill came to £670 million.

As BSkyB expanded its program content, its product offerings grew increasingly complicated. In 1990, it had provided all subscribers with the same basic channels for a flat fee. By 1996, subscribers could choose from a wide range of choices, picking (and paying) for what they wanted to see. From its original three channels, Sky now had thirty "basic" channels, six premium channels, and a smattering of pay-per-view events. To manage this increased complexity, the company relied on a increasingly sophisticated system of conditional access.

Controlling Access   Pioneered largely by Sky, a conditional access system is the brains of a home satellite system. So long as a satellite service derives its revenues primarily from advertising, conditional access is not really a concern. The company can simply broadcast its programs "free to air," and not worry about the precise number or identity of its viewers. When a system is based on subscriber revenues, however, the identity of these viewers becomes critical: those who watch must pay. When a system offers, like Sky, a wide and diverse menu of programming, each viewer must be able to choose precisely what he or she wants; each must receive precisely what they've ordered; and each must pay what they owe. Managing this system thus becomes a critical part of the channel's business strategy.

Sky first developed a conditional access system early in 1990, when its arrangements with the Hollywood studios forced the company to encrypt its programming and rely on a subscription-based business model. To develop the encryption software, Sky approached Adi Shamir, a mathematician at the Weizmann Institute of Science in Israel and also a founder of RSA Data Security, a leader in digital security software. Together with Yeda Research and Development, the company through which the Weizmann Institute commercialized its technologies, News formed News Data Security Products. Through a somewhat complex trading relationship, News then created a subsidiary, News Datacom, to receive exclusive license to NDSP's encryption technology and focus wholly on encryption and subscriber management. In July, 1992, News bought out all other shareholders. In December of that year Stephen Barden, formerly general manager at BSkyB, was brought in as CEO.[25]

Essentially, Sky's conditional access system consisted of two integrated parts—a set-top box and a subscriber management system. The subscriber management system functions somewhat like a credit card processing center. It receives orders from new customers; processes change requests or specific choices from existing customers; and keeps track of payment. Every day, customized computer programs process thousands of requests and changes. As these requests are processed, a customer service center codes the information and sends it to a broadcast receiver. The receiver then sends a scrambled signal to the "smart card" installed in each customer's set top box. Though the card looks like a simple credit card, it actually contains a powerful microprocessor which contains the code necessary to unscramble the particular channels ordered by a subscriber. The card thus "tells" the set top box which portions of the satellite transmission to receive and decipher.[26]

Technologically, the system created and installed by News Datacom is extremely sophisticated. It employs cutting edge encryption algorithms to manage what its engineers claim to be pirate-proof digital broadcasting systems. It enables BSkyB to match precisely its viewers' preferences and payments, and to control access to its valuable program rights. It also gives the company an inordinately powerful competitive edge. Once subscribers are hooked into the Sky system, switching is difficult and relatively unlikely. Since the receiving dish is installed to face only the Astra satellite, it can not pick up signals from other transmitters. If it is moved, it will no longer receive Sky. Similarly, Sky's payment and conditional access

system only processes Sky's subscriptions. To receive other encrypted signals, Sky viewers would need to install a second set top box, as well as a second satellite. A possible choice—but not a likely one.

Not surprisingly, then, most would-be competitors to Sky decided in the early- and mid-1990s to piggyback on Sky's existing infrastructure rather than compete against it. Along with MTV and the Children's Channel, VH1, Nickelodeon, the Family Channel and Bravo all eventually added their own content to Sky's programming. As of 1997, BSkyB was still the only satellite television company in Britain. Approximately 15% of Britain's households subscribed to some package of Sky's programming, and many more bought Sky channels through cable distributors. In June of 1996, BSkyB's revenues crossed the billion pound mark for the first time. Its profits that year were more than £300 million. As CEO Chisholm summarized the company's position "subscribers are switching on to Sky in record numbers . . . BSkyB is now extremely well positioned to capitalize on the introduction of digital television and the significant benefits that will flow from this new technology."[27] Other observers, however, were less sanguine. Reviewing the digital landscape, one member of the European Parliament worried that Sky's clear dominance threatened the very "democracy and culture" of Europe. "Whoever controls the decoder controls the gateway, and rules governing access by broadcasters to the decoder will determine what goes on the set. There is fear that Sky's stranglehold will continue into the digital age."[28]

Challenges

Murdoch and Sky seemed invincible. But then, late in the 1990s, rapid developments in the British broadcasting industry raised a number of new and unforeseen challenges. Three in particular

[25]Barry Fox, "Murdoch's Cryptic Vision for Global TV," *New Scientist,* September 11, 1993, p. 20; William Lewis, "TV Smart Cards," *Financial Times,* May 2, 1996, p. 12.

[26]See "Murdoch's News Datacom at Cutting Edge of Digital Broadcasting," *Jerusalem Post,* October 21, 1996, p. 3.

[27]"The Sky's the Limit for BSkyB," *New Media Age,* March 6, 1997, pp. 10–11.

[28]David Brown, "Watch with Big Brother," *The Scotsman,* December 4, 1996, pp. 39–40.

threatened to encroach upon Sky's well-embedded market position: the growing reach and ambition of Britain's cable companies; the advent of digital transmission formats; and the changing nature of regulation in Britain.

Cable Competition   As described earlier, the cable television industry in Britain had grown more slowly and conservatively than it had elsewhere. Hampered by geographical restrictions, outpowered by the BBC and then Sky, British cable companies had never developed an independent source of programming or a dedicated subscriber base. Instead, they leased proprietary content from BSkyB or elsewhere and simply delivered it across their direct-to-home cable network. This arrangement essentially robbed the companies of any competitive advantage or market flexibility. They were forced to buy content at whatever price—and Sky, more often than not, was setting the prices. Reportedly, Sky refused to permit any of the cable companies to purchase discrete blocks of desired programming. Instead, they had to purchase pre-bundled packages, where popular premium shows (sports, news) came together with less broadly attractive programming. Because Sky had the content, it generally did not suffer much negotiation about the price. It set prices, and the cable companies had little choice but to accept. Typically, Sky charged the cable providers 59% of the retail price paid by Sky's own subscribers. Commenting on this pricing structure, one cable executive complained, "My typical cost of sales is 65%. If I am paying 59% to Sky, where do I make my money? I still have to pay to transmit. They are a brutal monopolist."[29]

Throughout the 1990s, the cable companies endeavored to compete with this "brutal monopolist" not through programming or pricing, but on the basis of differentiated service. Technologically, Britain's is the Rolls Royce of cable systems. It employs a highly sophisticated broadband cable infrastructure, capable of carrying not just television signals but also phone communication and high speed Internet connections. The system can also be converted to a digital format easily and inexpensively. Thus, Britain's leading cable operators had positioned themselves as multiple providers. To their subscribers they offered not just television programming but *both* cable and telephone service for a low combined rate. As the Director General of one cable firm explained his long term strategy: "In the short term we are gaining market share by providing good prices. In the long term we can compete on services because our existing technology will allow us to provide all kinds of interactive services such as banking and shopping. Satellite technology simply cannot provide the kind of interactivity that we can."[30]

Going Digital   If cable's boasts had occurred against a backdrop of constant technology, their threat might well have been limited. But in 1995 and 1996, the advent of digital technologies was suddenly calling into question the very notion of broadcasting and the shape of Britain's existing regulatory environment.

Technically, digital television (like all digital applications) involves the transmission of data in a simple binary form. In analogue transmissions, data is sent from the source to the recipient as a wave, with a fair amount of information redundancy required to reproduce the transmitted image accurately. In digital transmission, by contrast, the data is encoded in a binary language using ones and zeroes, with no information redundancy whatsoever. These digits are then reconfigured (into an image or sound) at the receiving site. Commercially, the beauty of digital formats is that they allow for a greater clarity of reproduction: digital compact discs have a clearer sound than vinyl LPs; digital television provides a sharper and more accurate picture. More importantly, perhaps, techniques for digital compression dramatically increase the carrying capacity of nearly all transmission media (often referred to simply as "pipes"). With digital signals transmitted in a compressed

---

[29]Case writer interview with cable company executive, London, June, 1997.

[30]Case writer interview with cable company executive, London, June, 1997.

form, television frequencies, for example, can carry five to six, even ten times as many channels as they could in the analogue world. So can radio frequencies, short wave radio frequencies and even old-fashioned fiber optic cables. The much-lauded "500 channel universe" was entirely a creation of digital compression: by squeezing television (and other) signals into ever-narrower bands of data, digital compression vastly multiplied the potential distribution of movies, news, television programming. Of anything, indeed, that could be converted into a electronic stream of binary digits.

In the United States, the focus of the "Digital Revolution" in the 1990s was largely the Internet. In Britain, by contrast, the television and media markets received the lion's share of attention. And BSkyB was a central figure. Before the move to digital, Britain's television spectrum supported five traditional analogue channels: three BBC channels, Channel 4, and ITV. All were standard terrestrial broadcasters: they used television towers to send analogue signals "free to air" to any viewer equipped with a receiving aerial. Digital compression meant that these five analogue channels could carry instead 36 digital channels. To receive the new (and presumably improved) digital picture, customers would need either a new digital television set, or a set top box that could convert the digital signal for their older analogue set. Cable companies could also convert (quite easily) to digital formats, expanding their capacity to over 150 channels. And satellite had basically the same expansive potential.

The question, of course, was who would fill these expanded digital "pipes," and with what. In the summer of 1996, the British Parliament published the Broadcast Act of 1996, setting forth its plans for the allocation of digital terrestrial licenses. The core of the policy was the creation of six "multiplexes," frequency channels capable of transmitting between three and six digital channels. Two of the multiplexes would be reserved for existing analogue stations (one for the BBC; the other for services of Channels 3 and 4). The remainder would be awarded as 12-year licenses to interested applicants. Digital service from these channels was expected to commence in July 1998.[31]

In the eyes of many observers, the allocation of the multiplexes would at last create some competition for both BBC and BSkyB. By creating whole new avenues for distribution, the digital channels could break Sky's stranglehold on the pay TV market and bring new blood into what had become again a fairly staid and stable industry. The opportunity, as one observer asserted, "was to exploit the cultural richness of television as a mass medium and to give a much needed boost to media diversity in Britain."[32]

But Murdoch, not surprisingly, had other plans. When British regulatory agencies first trumpeted their plans for a new 36-channel digital universe, Murdoch countered with a far more ambitious agenda. In August 1995 he first announced his intention to launch 120 digital channels from a new digitally-equipped satellite. One year later he pushed the ante up, promising to deliver 200 digital channels from the end of 1997, with an eventual total of 500.[33]

Further complicating the picture (and Sky's position) was the related issue of set top boxes. All of the plans for digital television—be it cable, terrestrial, satellite or even wireless—involved set top boxes. It was the boxes that would control access to multiple offerings, descrambling the channels that viewers had chosen and paid to receive. It was the boxes that would be the brains for a multiple channel, pay-per-view world. And Sky, through its News Datacom subsidiary, was the only company in Britain that owned the rights to set top boxes. It was also the only company that already had an installed base of set top boxes: its existing 3.5 million direct-to-home subscribers.[34]

[31]For more on the details of the 1996 Act, see Helen Burton, "Digital Broadcasting in the United Kingdom," *Computer and Telecommunications Law Review,* vol. 1 (1997), pp. 33–42.

[32]"A Brave New World: A Brave New Decision," *The Guardian,* April 14, 1997, p. 4.

[33]See Stephen Barden, "Let's get digital," *The Independent,* December 8, 1996.

[34]"Sky's the Limit," *New Media Age,* March 6, 1997, p. 10.

On the surface, then, BSkyB appeared to be entering the digital age from an unassailably strong position. It had the programming; it had the channel potential; it had the boxes. It also, as of May, 1997, had a bid to become one of Britain's new digital multiplex providers.[35] Together with two of the country's most powerful ITVs, Carlton and Granada, Sky formed a new consortium, British Digital Broadcasting (BDB), to launch a proposed digital terrestrial service. With a planned investment of £300 million, BDB would target a mass television audience with a combined menu of sports, movies, and news programming—content that the three participating firms already controlled. In its bid, BDB asked to be considered either for all three available multiplexes or for one. Their only major competitor was Digital Television Network (DTN), an unlikely consortium of International Cable Tel, a U.S. cable operator, and United News and Media, a British broadcaster.[36] Unlike BDB, DTN had no existing access to broad market programming. Instead, it proposed to serve a highly segmented minority subscriber base and offer a variety of two-way communications services such as shopping and information retrieval. If BDB was the old guard, DTN was clearly the long shot. And few in 1996 had much confidence in its long term prospects. BDB was thus the front runner in the bid for Britain's digital multiplexes.

Obviously, then, the threat to Sky did not come from the digital technologies themselves. On the contrary, the move to digital left Sky, if anything, in an even stronger competitive position. The threat came from the regulatory changes that the technology had created.

The Regulators   Traditionally, television in Britain has fallen under the overlapping jurisdiction of three regulatory agencies. The primary agency is the Independent Television Commission (ITC),

which oversees and licenses all commercial television services, including terrestrial, cable and satellite.[37] Its central function is to ensure fair competition among broadcasters and hold them to agreed standards for program and advertising content. If a broadcaster violates the regulatory norms of the ITC, the agency has the ability to revoke or alter the broadcast license. The second regulator, the Office of Fair Trade (OFT), has a broader mandate. As Britain's overarching watchdog of competition, it has authority to discipline television broadcasters for unfair or anti-competitive. The third regulator, OFTEL (Office of Telecommunications), is not even officially related to the television industry. Yet because its bailiwick covers all of Britain's telecommunications industry, and because telephone and cable in Britain share a common wiring system, OFTEL's authority frequently laps into the field of television. Indeed, since the advent of cable television, many within the television industry have regarded OFTEL as a more powerful regulator than either the ITC or the OFT.

In the mid-1990s, each of these regulatory bodies was reviewing, at some level, complaints against BSkyB's entrenched market position. In December of 1995, a rash of complaints from cable operators compelled OFT to conduct a formal review of BSkyB's conduct in the pay television market. OFT reviewed Sky's exclusive rights to sports and movie programming, its conditional access system and its control over most of the available transponder space. In December 1996 it concluded that although Sky had a leadership position in all elements of its pay television business, its leadership did not constitute an abuse of power.[38] Six months later, following another round of complaints from the cable companies, ITC agreed to conduct a similar investigation of Sky. The European Commission, meanwhile, had responded to the advent of digital technologies with the publication of an Advanced Television Standards

[35]Keith Weir, "UK Media Heavyweights Team Up for TV Fight," *European Business Report* May 2, 1997. (Reprinted from Reuter Textline.)

[36]"Aerial Combat," *The Economist,* May 24, 1997, pp. 63–4.

[37]The ITC effectively replaced the IBA as of January 1990.

[38]See Office of Fair Trading, "The Director General's Review of BSkyB's Position in the Wholesale Pay TV Market," London, December, 1996.

Directive. A long and often highly technical document, the Directive sought to lay the framework for the development of digital television in Europe. It stressed the importance of inter-operability of standards, allowing consumers to "receive all their digital TV through one box."[39] It also was quite explicit on the topic of set top boxes. It required that, in the digital environment, conditional access services would have to be available to all broadcasters on a "fair and reasonable basis." As interpreted, this meant that all broadcasters would have to have equal access to a set top box, even if they did not own the box or its conditional access software.

Behind this rather complicated technological provision lay a key strategic demand—and months of political maneuvering. Much of BSkyB's power at this point lay in its network of set top boxes. So long as Sky controlled the boxes, it wielded leverage over both its customers and its competitors. Customers needed Sky boxes to receive Sky's popular content and competitors needed to piggyback on Sky's infrastructure if they wanted to reach its ever-expanding base of subscribers. For years, many in the British television industry (and particularly the BBC and cable operators) had bristled against the competitive position embedded in Sky's boxes. They hoped to use the advent of digital technologies (and the corresponding wave of new regulation) to break what they saw as Sky's unfair stranglehold over British television. Accordingly, many in Britain (and Europe as well) began to advocate the development of a "common interface," a plug-in conditional access system that would enable a variety of broadcasters to share a common set top box. Sky, of course, disagreed. Arguing that a common interface simply did not make sense either commercially or technologically, Sky joined a European-wide industry forum, the DVB (Digital Video Broadcasting Project) to reconsider the issues surrounding digital transmission and conditional access. After several years of discussion, the group, which was composed primarily of

engineers, proposed a set of digital television standards that rejected a common interface in favor of a "Simulcrypt" option. With Simulcrypt, broadcasters would incorporate encryption data into their transmissions and then allow a decoder (presumably an existing one) to receive and descramble their signal. DVB also agreed to work towards a common interface, but did not suggest making such an interface mandatory.[40] These standards, proposed to the European Commission, were eventually incorporated into the Advanced Television Standards Directive.

To Sky, the Commission's decision merely reinforced the reasonableness of its own position and the commercial impossibility of trying to squeeze various smart cards and payment systems into one already-complicated box. Others in the industry, however, saw the Directive as yet another political victory for Sky, evidence of its power even in Brussels and in the impending world of digital television.

Under the terms of the Directive, Sky (and other conditional access providers in Europe) would have to offer all digital broadcasters non-discriminatory access to their systems. They also were required to keep accounts for their access services separate from their other businesses, and to refrain from prohibiting equipment manufacturers from including common interface systems in their boxes. In Britain, responsibility for implementing the Directive fell to OFTEL, which rapidly declared its intent to defend the availability of access on a "fair and reasonable basis."[41] How this provision would translate to commercial reality, however, remained unclear.

The Summer of '97

In April of 1997, Britain's ITC began reviewing proposals for the digital multiplexes. With only DTN and BDB in the running, the industry concurred that BDB was the only possible choice. Sky would thus receive a platform for digital terrestrial broadcasts.

---

[39]"TV Standards Directive Signals Digital TV Lift-off Towards Information Society," Press Release, Commission of the European Communities, July 25, 1995.

[40]See Burton, p. 39.

[41]OFTEL Review of Conditional Access Systems, December 1996.

Exhibit 1   Satellite and Broadband Cable Development in the United Kingdom, 1989–1996

	1989	1990	1991	1992	1993	1994	1995	1996
Total TV homes (000s)	21,214	21,518	22,007	22,046	22,145	22,303	22,412	23,436
Direct to Home Satellite								
DTH	497	1,278	1,734	2,097	2,477	2,754	3,138	3,566
Penetration (%)	2.3	5.9	7.9	9.5	11.2	12.3	14.0	15.2
Broadband Cable								
Homes passed	557	828	1,016	1,567	2,327	3,336	4,968	7,157
Homes connected (TV)	87	149	192	331	473	708	1,044	1,523
Penetration (%)	15.6	18.0	18.9	21.1	20.3	21.2	21.0	21.3

Source: Office of Fair Trading, "The Director General's Review of BSkyB's Position in the Wholesale Pay TV Market," London, December 1996, p. 25; Andrew Bailes, "The UK Cable and Satellite Market," *Financial Times Telecoms and Media Publishing: An FT Marketing Brief,* London, 1997, p. 67.

Its rivals, particularly the cable companies, were lobbying vigorously for someone to clip Sky's wings. But OFT was moving slowly and OFTEL was largely preoccupied with parallel developments in the telecommunications sector. A formal regulatory check on Sky seemed highly unlikely. Then something unusual happened. Late in the spring, British authorities made a formal request to the Competition Directorate of the European Commission, asking for an inquiry into Sky's participation in the BDB consortium. Two aspects of the request were noteworthy. First, that the regulators were directly targeting Sky. And second that they asked the Commission for an inquiry *before* choosing a bid winner. Although this violated standard policy, the Commission agreed to review Sky's position.

Defining what competition meant in a rapidly developing industry was not easy. In general, policy-makers within the Directorate appreciated the advantages of scale in capital-intensive industries such as telephony, television, telecommunications and computing. After decades of watching the separate European nations protect their own small and often uncompetitive "national champions," the general view in the EU was to allow strong European firms to grow unfettered and to resist taking any regulatory actions that might stifle competition or innovation. At the same time, however, the Competition Directorate wanted to prevent any single dominant player from controlling its market—particularly if that market lay at the intersection of any of the new or converging industries.[42] On June 3 Karel Van Miert, the EU's Commissioner for Competition formally announced his discomfort with the BDB bid. "There is a problem so far as the pay TV business is concerned," he asserted, "because there could be an enhancement of an already-dominant position."[43] Two weeks later, the ITC announced that it would only consider the BDB bid if BSkyB relinquished its equity stake in the consortium. Sky was out.

Within the week, BDB structured a new deal. Sky withdrew from the consortium with £75 million and a five year contract for the supply of programming to the new venture. According to Morgan Stanley's estimates, the programming contract would provide Sky with roughly £300 million a year in incremental operating profits.

Meanwhile, Sky was also active on the technology front. It consolidated News Datacom and its subscriber management system into a new company,

[42]Case writer interview, Brussels, July 1997.

[43]"EU Raises Doubts on Digital TV License Bid," *Financial Times,* June 4, 1997.

Exhibit 2   Market Share of Total Viewer Hours in the British Television Market, 1992–1996

	Percentage of Total Viewer Hours				
	1992	1993	1994	1995	1996
Terrestrial					
BBC1	33.7	32.7	32.4	32.1	32.5
BBC2	10.5	10.3	10.6	11.2	11.6
ITV	40.8	39.9	39.5	37.2	35.1
Channel 4	10.1	11.0	10.7	11.0	10.8
Total Terrestrial	95.1	93.9	93.2	91.5	89.9
BSkyB					
Sky One	1.1	1.4	1.1	1.2	1.3
Sky News	.3	.3	.2	.4	.3
Sky Sports	.5	.6	.7	.9	1.0
Movie Channel	.5	.6	.7	.8	.8
Sky Movies	.9	.9	.8	.9	.9
Nickelodeon/Paramount			.2	.4	.5
Total BSkyB	3.3	3.8	3.7	4.6	4.8
Other					
Discovery/TLC	.2	.2	.3		
Eurosport	.3	.3			
MTV	.2	.3	.3.	.2	.2
Children's Channel	.2	.2	.1	.2	.2
TNT and Cartoon	.4	.6	.8		
UK Gold		.6	.6	.6	.6
Total Other	.4	1.1	1.6	2.1	2.4

Source: Toby Syfret, "UK Trends in Multi Channel Audiences and Advertising Revenue," *Financial Times Media and Telecoms: An FT Marketing Brief,* London, 1997, p. 38.

NDS, and purchased Digi-Media Vision, a firm with cutting edge technologies for video compression and multiplexing. Soon thereafter, the company demonstrated a prototype of a new digital set top box, one that could simultaneously employ several different scrambling systems.[44] Together with Matsushita, British Telecom (BT) and Midland Bank, Sky also formed British Interactive Broadcasting, a novel and ambitious interactive venture.

According to the company's plans, BIB would manufacture set top boxes capable of interactive services. Using either phone lines or television connections, BIB boxes would enable customers to shop on line, conduct bank transactions, and so forth. To attract these customers, the new venture planned to spend £600 million to subsidize the retail price of the new digital set top box.[45] BIB was expected to launch in the summer of 1998.

[44]Junko Yoshida, "Mogul Maneuvers for Digital TV Presence on a Grand Scale," *Electronic Engineering Times,* June 16, 1997.

[45]"Battle of the Boxes," *The Economist,* October 4, 1997, p. 73.

Exhibit 3   Pay Television Channels Available in Britain, 1996

Channel	Owner	Description	% Share of Pay TV Audience
Encrypted Basic Channels			
Sky One	BSkyB	Entertainment	14
Sky News	BSkyB	News	3
Sky Travel	BSkyB	Travel	<1
Sky Soap	BSkyB	Entertainment	<1
QVC	QVC/BSkyB	Home Shopping	na
MTV	Viacom	Music	2
VH-1	Viacom	Music	2
Nickelodeon	Viacom/BSkyB	Children's	4
Children's Channel	Flextech/Pearson	Children's	2
Bravo	Flextech	Entertainment	1
Family Channel	IFE/Flextech	Entertainment	1
Discovery/Learning	Discovery	Documentary	4
CMT Europe	Consortium	Country Music	<1
UK Gold	Consortium	Entertainment	6
UK Living	Consortium	Women's Lifestyle	3
History Channel	A & E/BSkyB	Entertainment	na
Paramount Channel	Viacom/BSkyB	Entertainment	<1
EBN	Tel. Inc/Dow Jones	Business News	<1
Sci-Fi Channel	Viacom	Entertainment	na
Encrypted Premium Channels			
Sky Movies	BSkyB	Films	9
The Movie Channel	BSkyB	Films	8
Sky Movies Gold	BSkyB	Films	2
Sky Sports	BSkyB	Sports	na
Sky Sports 2	BSkyB	Sports	13
Sky Sports Gold	BSkyB	Sports	<1
Disney Channel	Disney	Entertainment	3
The Racing Channel	SIS	Sports	na
The Adult Channel	Graff PPV	Adult	na
Playboy	Playboy/BSkyB	Adult	na
Fantasy Channel	Northern and Shell	Adult	na
JSTV	NA	Japanese	na
Chinese Channel	Pacific/Shaw	Chinese	na
ZeeTV	Zee TV	Asian	na
Free-to-Air Channels			
TNT	Turner	Entertainment	1
Cartoon Network	Turner	Children's	7
CNN	Turner	News	na
CNE	NA	Chinese	na
Eurosport	TFI/Canal+/ESON	Sports	2

Source: Office of Fair Trading, "The Director General's Review of BSkyB's Position in the Wholesale Pay TV Market," London, December 1996, pp. 141–42.

Exhibit 4   Cable Only Channels in Britain, 1996

Channel	Owner	Description
Basic Channels		
The Parliament	Consortium	Parliament
Performance	Daily Mail	Arts
Travel	Landmark	Travel
Identity	Black Ent.	West Indian
Asia Net	NA	Asian
Channel One	Daily Mail	Regional
Live TV	Mirror Group	Regional/Gossip
The Box	TCI	Music
Euronews	France TV/RAI	News
Channel Guide	Picture Apps	Programme Listings
MBC	Private	Middle East
Landscape Channel	Landscape	Music
Vision	NA	Christian
NBC Superchannel	NBC/Marcucci	Entertainment
Selec TV	Carlton	Education
Worldnet	NA	Entertainment
Mid Extension	Jones Cable	Education
Bloomberg TV	Private	Information
Premium Channels		
Namaste	NA	Asian
HVC	Graff PPV	Movies

Source: Office of Fair Trade, "The Director General's Review of BSkyB's Position in the Wholesale Pay TV Market," London, December 1996, p. 142.

Exhibit 5   BSkyB Financial Highlights, 1992–1996 (£ millions)

	1992	1993	1994	1995	1996
Revenue					
DTH Subscribers	154	263	407	582	728
Cable	19	33	48	75	122
Advertising	44	64	78	92	110
Other	16	20	17	29	49
Total Revenue	233	380	550	778	1,008
Operating Expenses	280	318	380	533	693
Operating Profit	(47)	62	170	245	315

Source: BSkyB Annual Reports.

Exhibit 6   BSkyB Direct to Home Prices, 1991–1996 (£)

	1991	1992	1993	1994	1995	1996
Multi Channel				6.99	9.99	10.99
Sky Sports			5.99	11.99	14.99	15.99
One Movie Channel	9.99	11.99	11.99	11.99	14.99	15.99
Two Movie Channels	14.99	16.99	16.99	16.99	19.99	21.99
One Movie Channel and Sky Sports			16.98	16.99	19.99	21.99
Two Movie Channels and Sky Sports			19.98	19.99	22.99	24.99

Source: Office of Fair Trading, "The Director General's Review of BSkyB's Position in the Wholesale Pay TV Market," London, December 1996, p. 32.

The market, however, had reacted sharply to news of Sky's forced withdrawal from the BDB consortium. By August of 1997, BSkyB's stock was at a one year low, having lost more than a billion dollars of market value since the ITC announcement. The Premier League, the jewel of Sky's sporting empire, had also indicated its interest in severing links with Sky and broadcasting its own events. And several Hollywood studios had recently mentioned that, in the impending 500-channel universe, they might begin to sell their pay-per-view rights to an overlapping set of television providers.

Sky, it appeared, was at a crossroads. In June its long-time head Sam Chisholm resigned, citing health concerns. Many in the industry murmured, however, that his departure had far more to do with the arrival of Elisabeth Murdoch, Rupert's 27-year-old daughter and heir apparent at Sky. Industry analysts clamored that the end of Sky was near, that the EU had at last broken its stranglehold on Britain's pay television market, and that changing technologies would soon eliminate any vestiges of its competitive advantage. But BSkyB had heard many of these predictions before.

Case 3-4   General Electric Medical Systems, 2002

In early 2002, Joe Hogan, president and CEO of Milwaukee-based General Electric Medical Systems Division (GEMS), the world's leading manufacturer of diagnostic imaging equipment, faced a difficult challenge. Hogan was tapped to lead GEMS in November, 2000, when his former boss, Jeff Immelt, was named to replace the legendary

Jack Welch in the top position at GEMS' celebrated corporate parent, General Electric (GE). By 2002, GE had the world's largest market capitalization ($400 billion), built on its much-admired six-sigma and globalization initiatives, and its competitive culture (Exhibits 1 and 2). GE was *Fortune*'s Global Most Admired Company in 1998, 1999, and 2000.

Meanwhile, GEMS, as the leader in global practices within GE, had built a formidable global presence, especially on the backs of the Global Product Company (GPC) concept, implemented during Immelt's time. GPC's philosophy was to concentrate manufacturing—and ultimately other

‖ ProfessorTarun Khanna and James Weber, Senior Researcher, Global Research Group, prepared this case. HBS cases are developed solely as the basis for class discussion. Cases are not intended to serve as endorsements, sources of primary data, or illustrates of effective or ineffective management.
‖ Copyright © 2002 President and Fellows of Harvard College. Harvard Business School case 702-428.

Exhibit 1   GE Corporate Financial Data

	For Years Ended December 31					
	1996	1997	1998	1999	2000	2001
Revenues						
Sales of goods	$36,106	$40,675	$ 43,749	$47,785	$54,828	$52,677
Sales of services	11,791	12,729	14,938	16,283	18,126	18,722
Other income (note 2)	638	2,300	649	798	436	234
Earnings of GECS	—	—	—	—	—	—
GECS revenues from service (note 3)	30,544	35,136	41,133	46,764	56,463	54,280
Total revenues	79,179	90,840	100,469	111,630	129,853	125,913
Costs and expenses (note 4)						
Cost of goods sold	26,298	30,889	31,772	34,554	39,312	35,678
Cost of services sold	8,293	9,199	10,508	11,404	12,511	12,419
Interest and other financial charges	7,904	8,384	9,753	10,013	11,720	11,062
Insurance losses and policyholder and annuity benefits	6,678	8,278	9,608	11,028	14,399	15,062
Provision for losses on financing receivables (note 14)	1,033	1,421	1,603	1,671	2,045	2,481
Other costs and expenses	17,898	21,250	23,483	27,018	30,993	28,162
Minority interest in net earnings of consolidated affiliates	269	240	265	365	427	348
Total costs and expenses	68,373	79,661	86,992	96,053	111,407	106,212
Earnings before income taxes	10,806	11,179	13,477	15,577	18,446	19,701
Provision for income taxes (note 7)	(3,526)	(2,976)	(4,181)	(4,860)	(5,711)	(5,573)
Net earnings	$7,280	$8,203	$9,296	$10,717	$12,735	$13,684
Total assets (millions)	$272,402	$304,012	$355,935	$405,200	$437,006	$495,023

General Electric Co. **Balance Sheet ($ millions)**	DEC 1996	DEC 1997	DEC 1998	DEC 1999	DEC 2000	DEC 2001
Total assets	$272,402	$304,012	$355,935	$405,200	$437,006	$495,023
Total debt	129,446	144,678	175,041	201,773	201,312	232,882
Total equity	31,125	34,438	38,880	42,557	50,492	54,824
Fiscal year-end stock price	16.479	24.458	34	51.583	47.938	40.08

Source: *General Electric 2001 Annual Report.*

activities—wherever in the world it could be carried out to GE's exacting standards most cost-effectively. Yet opportunities in China were stressing the GPC model. Hogan wondered whether he should modify GPC by adopting an "In China for China" policy so as to focus squarely on the Chinese market.

In parallel, technological changes—represented by advances in genomics and healthcare information technology—were making personalized medicine and personalized diagnostics possible. These could radically alter GEMS' business model, by demanding that the organization embrace a move

Exhibit 2   Summary of Operating Segments

				For Years Ended December 31 (in millions)				
	1994	1995	1996	1997	1998	1999	2000	2001
Revenues								
GE								
Aircraft engines	$5,830	$6,098	$6,302	$7,799	$10,294	$10,730	$10,779	$11,389
Appliances	5,204	5,137	5,586	5,801	5,619	5,671	5,887	5,810
Industrial Products and Systems	9,375	10,209	10,401	10,984	11,222	11,555	11,848	11,647
NBC	3,361	3,919	5,232	5,153	5,269	5,790	6,797	7,069
Plastics	5,681	6,647	6,509	6,695	6,633	6,941	7,776	5,769
Power Systems	5,357	6,962	7,704	7,986	8,500	10,089	14,861	20,211
Technical Products and Services[a]	4,285	4,430	4,700	4,861	5,323	6,863	7,915	9,011
All others	253	292	—	—	—	—	—	—
Eliminations	(1,068)	(1,082)	(1,093)	(1,247)	(1,401)	(1,767)	(2,075)	(2,900)
Total GE segment revenues	39,278	42,612	45,341	48,032	51,459	55,882	63,788	68,006
Corporate items	1,135	1,154	1,407	3,227	771	619	517	445
GECS[b] earnings	2,085	2,415	2,817	3,256	3,796	4,443	5,192	5,586
Total GE revenues	42,498	46,181	49,565	54,515	56,026	60,944	69,497	74,037
GECS segment revenues	19,875	26,492	32,713	39,931	48,694	55,749	66,177	58,353
Eliminations	(2,264)	(2,645)	(3,099)	(3,606)	(4,251)	(5,063)	(5,821)	(6,477)
Consolidated revenues	$60,109	$70,028	$79,179	$90,840	$100,469	$111,630	$129,853	$125,913
Segment profit								
GE								
Aircraft engines	$987	$1,135	$1,214	$1,366	$1,769	$2,104	$2,464	$2,609
Appliances	704	682	748	771	755	655	684	643
Industrial Products and Systems	1,305	1,488	1,587	1,789	1,880	2,095	2,187	1,843
NBC	540	797	1,020	1,216	1,349	1,576	1,797	1,596
Plastics	981	1,435	1,443	1,500	1,584	1,651	1,923	1,602
Power Systems	1,354	782	1,189	1,275	1,338	1,753	2,809	5,182
Technical Products and Services	805	810	855	988	1,109	1,359	1,718	1,970
All others	245	285	—	—	—	—	—	—
Total GE operating profit	5,922	7,414	8,056	8,905	9,784	11,193	13,582	15,445
GECS net earnings	2,085	2,415	2,817	3,256	3,796	4,443	5,192	5,586
Total segment profit	9,007	9,829	10,873	12,161	13,580	15,636	18,774	21,031
Corporate items and eliminations	(800)	(548)	(703)	(1,351)	(584)	(902)	(1,429)	(1,893)
GE interest and other financial charges	(410)	(649)	(595)	(797)	(883)	(810)	(811)	(817)
GE provision for income taxes	(1,882)	(2,059)	(2,295)	(1,810)	(2,817)	(3,207)	(3,799)	(4,193)
Consolidated net earnings	$5,915	$6,573	$7,280	$8,203	$9,296	$10,717	$12,735	$13,684

[a]Technical Products and Services is primarily GEMS, but also includes some other GE businesses.

[b]"GECS" means General Electric Capital Services, Inc. and all of its affiliates and associated companies. The segment profit measure for GE's industrial business is operating profit (earnings before interest and other financial charges, and income taxes). The segment profit measure for GECS is net earnings, reflecting the importance of financing and tax considerations to its operating activities.

Source: *General Electric 2001 Annual Report.*

Exhibit 3   Country Healthcare Statistics

Country	% GDP Spent on Healthcare (1997)[a]	Healthcare Expenditures per Capita (1997, $)[a]	Number of Hospitals[b]	Hospital Beds per 1000 Capita[b]	% of Population Over Age 65[a]	Medical Device Exp. per Capita ($)[b]
United States	13.9	4,095	6,100	3.5	12.7	174
Japan	7.2	1,760	8,400	10.1	14.6	109
Germany	10.7	2,364	2,300	7.3	15.6	86
France	9.6	2,047	3,300	8.8	15.4	68
United Kingdom	6.8	1,391	1,600	4.9	15.6	50
Canada	9.2	2,175	1,200	5.7	12.0	75
Mexico	4.7	363	3,700	1.2	4.1	6
China	4.0[b]	27[b]	68,000	2.3	7.1[c]	1
India	5.6	69	15,000	1.0	4.7[c]	1

Sources: a = Walter W. Wieners, editor, *Global Healthcare Markets: A Comprehensive Guide to Regions, Trends, and Opportunities Shaping the International Healthcare Arena* (San Francisco: Jossey-Bass, 2001), p. 26 and p. 36.

b = Company documents.

c = The World Factbook, Central Intelligence Agency, on-line edition, November 19, 2001: <www.odci.gov/cia/publications/factbook>.

away from its engineering heritage toward bio-chemistry, and learn to compete intensely with entrepreneurial software companies. Demographic changes complicated matters further. Populations were aging in advanced nations, and global information flows made healthcare disparities between developed and developing nations more stark, and unacceptable. Ultimately, GE demanded that GEMS grow annually at 20% and return on capital rise from its current 26% to 35%. The spotlight was on GEMS as Immelt moved toward a technology-focused 21st century GE.

Healthcare Systems around the World

There were wide variations in the world's health-care systems at the beginning of the 21st century, even as medical expertise, drugs, and technologies spread across national boundaries at varying rates (Exhibit 3). Healthcare spending as a percentage of GDP had increased worldwide over the previous three decades. The worldwide aging of populations implied fewer working-age people to pay for more intense care. The emerging middle-classes of Asia,

Eastern Europe and Latin America were increasingly aware of, and needed, better healthcare.

The United States   The United States spent more than any other country on healthcare, overall and on a per capita basis. Roughly 45% of total expenditures came from government programs primarily for the elderly, poor, and disabled, 33% came from private insurance, 17% were out-of-pocket expenses paid by patients, and the remainder came from other private sources.[1] Employers paid the majority of private insurance premiums with a significant minority portion paid by the covered employees. The United States was the only wealthy, industrialized country to fund the majority of its healthcare from private sources. Because there was no government-funded universal healthcare coverage and because coverage through employer plans was not mandated, over 15% of the population had no health insurance.[2] Nearly all individuals with

[1]Walter W. Wieners, ed., *Global Healthcare Markets: A Comprehensive Guide to Regions, Trends, and Opportunities Shaping the International Healthcare Arena* (San Francisco: Jossey-Bass, 2001), p. 386.

[2]Ibid., p. 382.

insurance were covered for diagnostic testing. Both the new equipment and replacement markets were growing slowly.

Through for-profit managed care organizations (MCO), government and employer payers had demanded cost cutting over the past decade. Increasingly, coverage was provided primarily through MCOs, with less use for indemnity plans—fee-for-service plans where doctors could order any medically necessary procedure and insurers were obligated to pay. MCOs were consolidating and demanding price reductions from providers and equipment manufacturers. But there was mounting dissatisfaction about MCOs occasionally using this power to inappropriate supersede physician authority in determining appropriate treatment.

Approximately 70% of hospitals were private, not-for-profit institutions, much of the remainder were private for-profit, and a small percentage were government-owned.[3] An increasing portion of care was provided by out-patient clinics, nearly all of which were privately owned and many were for-profit. Some clinics specialized in providing diagnostic imaging services and were often owned by the doctors who referred patients to them. Many hospitals faced difficult economic times. Increased outpatient and in-home care and shorter hospital stays had created excess capacity in the hospital sector. In 1999, the Balanced Budget Act reduced reimbursement rates for Medicare payments, further eroding hospital profits and tightening capital budgets.

Japan   Japan provided universal health coverage. However, the majority of individuals received coverage through workplace-based insurance societies. Workers had payroll deductions that paid for their own insurance and contributed to insurance pools that covered retirees and other segments of the population. Additionally, those seeking care made significant co-payments. Hospitals were owned by doctors and were mostly for-profit, though Japanese law prohibited distributing profits to outside shareholders. Hospitals also tended not to specialize in particular medical disciplines. Finally, they were reimbursed through a regulated fee-for-service system which stifled price competition, and encouraged competition through the acquisition of advanced medical technologies. The system's historical success had made it well-liked. But it was also increasingly unsuited to the ongoing demographic changes. By 2025, Japan was projected to have 27% of its population older than age 65 compared with 20% for the United States.[4]

France   The government-sponsored universal healthcare insurance system was funded largely through payroll contributions by employers, and paid for approximately 75% of the nation's total healthcare costs.[5] Additionally, many people purchased supplemental insurance. Roughly 20% of overall costs were paid out-of-pocket by patients. This helped check healthcare costs in a system that allowed patients to choose doctors and specialists on their own and where doctors were paid on a fee-for-service basis. Most hospitals were government-owned and funded with a global budget while most ambulatory care services were privately provided. In the mid- to late-1990s, a number of modest reforms were introduced in an effort to slow the growth of healthcare costs. Ultimately, these reforms, modeled on U.S. cost control efforts, were expected to introduce restrictions on patient choice, employ primary care providers to serve as gatekeepers, adopt capitation funding, and slow the introduction of expensive new technologies

India   Very few people had private health insurance coverage in India. There was considerable variation in the public health amenities across India's various states. Overall, the poor quality of such amenities as existed led those that could afford it to chose private healthcare providers and pay out-of-pocket. Individuals paid 75% as out-of-pocket expenses.[6] The vacuum of poor healthcare was (very) partly filled by a few academic hospitals,

---

[3]Ibid., p. 391.

[4]Ibid., p. 360.
[5]Ibid., p. 166.
[6]Ibid., p. 340.

some hospitals run by charities, and several for-profit hospital chains that had emerged in the 1990s to serve the economically well-off. In the late 1990s, India instituted a number of market reforms that would allow the development of a private healthcare insurance market and encourage foreign investment. The healthcare industry was expected to grow at 13% annually.[7] As in other major developing nations, this growth included a transformation in focus from the major communicable diseases, maternity and infant illnesses, to chronic conditions generally faced by an older population. The treatment of such medical conditions required enhanced use of sophisticated diagnostic equipment.

China   Prior to the early 1980s, the Chinese government both paid for and delivered the majority of healthcare services in China. In the years since, many health programs had been discontinued. By the end of the 1990s, individuals largely paid for their own healthcare as out-of-pocket expenses. Roughly half the urban population and 10% of the rural population had some level of health insurance.[8] The health services that were still provided by the government were largely done at the provincial and other local levels with very little funding by the central government. The government continued to run some 70,000 hospitals, a large fraction of the total number, where patients paid out-of-pocket.[9] A miniscule 1% of these were large and well-funded.[10] Private hospitals had been established recently, sometimes financed by Taiwanese investors. The central government set the prices that providers could charge patients at one-quarter to one-half of the actual costs of the service. To make up the shortfall, providers took cash under the table, or prescribed drugs and diagnostic testing since these were not subject to price controls. The same lack of price regulations on testing led investor groups, some of which were foreign, to form diagnostic testing centers that purchased or leased high-tech diagnostic testing equipment. Hospitals' reputations came to be based on the ownership of such equipment. Demand for diagnostic equipment was high in proportion to the overall amount spent on healthcare, even though the installed base was still low. In countries like China and India, some opined that it made more sense to focus on expanding basic coverage rather than on emphasizing high-technology medicine.

Key Technological Trends in Healthcare

Two emerging ideas in healthcare had the potential to revolutionize the practice of medicine in coming decades: personalized medicine and a move from a focus on cure to a focus on prevention. Personalized medicine involved developing drugs for a specific individual, or small group, based on the individual's genetic code, rather than drugs aimed at entire populations. In the future, it would be possible to look for genetic indicators of disease preemptively, and treat preventively. Both trends required advances in diagnostic imaging.

Genomics   Genomics and proteomics were broad terms used to describe the study of hereditary traits and potential abnormalities of cells and cell function. Genes, which were found in the cell's DNA, determined cell function by controlling various proteins. Gene therapy involved replacing faulty DNA in diseased cells with healthy DNA. The basic steps included identifying the defective portion of the DNA, growing the corrected genes, and inserting the new genes into the appropriate cells using "vectors," which were typically viruses made harmless. Each step in the process had high failure rates—the vector might not survive long enough, the new gene might not arrive at the correct cells, might not get inside the cell nucleus to access the DNA, and might not function if they did get inside. Because of this failure rate, and because the technology of genetic diagnosing had advanced further than genetic therapies, physicians were debating whether it was ethical to tell patients they would contract diseases for which there was no treatment.

[7]Ibid., p. 348.
[8]Ibid., p. 324.
[9]Ibid., p. 321.
[10]Ibid., p. 321.

For these embryonic techniques to progress, significant advances in diagnostic imaging capabilities were required. Traditional imaging techniques, such as X-ray and MRI, did not have an image resolution high enough to see whether the gene therapy was performing correctly or which step in the process might be breaking down (see the Appendix). Newer techniques, such as PET scanning, held promise. Researchers had created reporter genes that tracked the movement and activity of the corrective gene and were visible to the PET machines.

Developing these new imaging techniques would challenge medical equipment manufacturers. Manufacturers' expertise typically lay in the areas of engineering and physics, however, the newer techniques called for expertise in biomedical sciences. Further, companies would be required to collaborate with the pharmaceutical companies that developed the viruses and chemical reagents that the imaging equipment had to detect. Joint technological development could also complicate the regulatory approval process for equipment makers. Imaging companies working jointly with pharmaceutical companies would likely be subject to the latter's longer regulatory approval cycles.

Such factors were expected to force changes in the business model for imaging equipment companies. Traditional revenue streams consisted of a sizeable up-front payment, at the time of initial equipment sale, and an ongoing and very profitable servicing revenue stream. Overall operating margins, with three-to-five year development cycles, could be as high as 20%. In contrast, in some chemical-intensive businesses, equipment was sold "at cost" and most profits were made from ongoing sale of chemical reagents. In pharmaceutical companies, operating margins were closer to 30%, product development times were about 10 years, and the "hit rate" of successful products was very low compared with 90% for imaging equipment makers. One GEMS senior manager cautioned that, while regulatory factors were country-specific, ultimately "the great thing is that we are all, country and race notwithstanding, genetically much more similar than we are not. It is a global opportunity."

Healthcare IT   The generation of massive amounts of data, and the associated need for managing it appropriately, had created an information technology (IT) market that was approximately $3 billion in size in the United States and growing at 20% per year, with the worldwide market estimated to be twice as big.[11] The majors competitors—GEMS, Siemens, and Philips—had focused attention on this new market and, by 2002, controlled 80% of what in the mid-1990s had been a fragmented market.

Digital Imaging   Digital imaging—at the simplest level, viewing images on computer screens instead of X-ray films—was responsible for a flood of new data. Observing the actual functioning of an organ, often in three dimensions, required the generation of thousands of images. Digital imaging could also be combined with computer-aided detection software, so that clinicians could manipulate images, combine them with images from other detection equipment, and integrate them with other patient health data to achieve a far more detailed and meaningful picture of the disease state. Promising applications were already in various stages of development. For example, it was hoped that digital X-rays of particular organs could automatically be computer-searched for signs of other abnormalities. Newer imaging technologies were expected to be able to "light up" contrast agents, injected into the patient, that attached themselves to particular diseased cell receptors, thus facilitating more precise diagnoses than currently feasible. It might also be possible to verify whether or not specific drugs were reaching the targeted areas, as had begun to be the case in treatments of brain lesions that characterized Alzheimer's disease.

Electronic Patient Records   Electronic patient records (EPR) allowed patient data to be easily stored and accessed remotely. They held out the prospect of addressing the frustrating fact that

---

[11]This refers to the market for information technology for clinicians. It is distinct from administrative IT systems used in the healthcare sector, which are no different from systems used in other industries. The latter was a $20 bn market in the U.S.

patient records often were not in one central place, either physically or on-line. To illustrate this problem, an industry executive described a hypothetical situation often faced by diabetics:

> Diabetes requires constant monitoring. Often a patient who is not in a location near his or her regular physician or endocrinologist is in trouble because patient records are hard to locate. The physician has to make decisions based on inadequate data. When the patient goes on vacation, changes in dietary habits or exercise levels cause fluctuations in blood sugar levels. The patient decides to wait to see a doctor since it is unlikely that adequate treatment will be provided by someone unfamiliar with the case. Such a patient could go into potentially fatal insulin shock. EPRs partly address such problems by centralizing records and enabling remote access, though they create concerns about patient privacy and data ownership.

Because electronic records would enable clinicians to get maximum medical value from diagnostic images, creating unified, compatible database technologies had become a focus of imaging technology companies. By developing healthcare IT systems, imaging companies could ensure that the images from their own diagnostic equipment would be compatible with hospital IT systems.

Disease Management Systems Healthcare IT systems were also expected to play a key role in developing disease management systems which helped payers and providers assist patients with chronic conditions follow prescribed treatment plans. Industry experts noted that IT systems impacted disease management programs at several stages including patient selection, data acquisition and transmission, data evaluation and storage, and education and intervention.[12] Further, the creation of EPRs meant that patients could be tracked over several years and, with accumulation of sufficient data across potentially millions of individuals, clinical pathways leading to particular diseases could be identified.

Competitors

Each of GEMS' principal competitors—divisions of Siemens, Philips and Toshiba—had broad product lines and each accounted for under 10% of its parent company's revenues. These firms were just four of 10 prominent full-line diagnostics players in the early 1980s.[13] By 1995, GEMS' market share had reached 21%, and GEMS, Siemens and Philips collectively had a 52% share.[14] By 2002, GEMS' share was just shy of 50%, and the three leaders accounted for over 80% of worldwide sales.

Siemens Medical Solutions Siemens Medical Solutions, based in Germany, held the number two market share position worldwide and led in several product segments (Exhibit 4). It had revenues of $4 billion with parent company revenues at $78 billion. Siemens obtained roughly half of its medical sales in the U.S. market and located the headquarters of three of its ten divisions in the country. One-third of sales were from the European market with nearly 20% in Germany. Siemens had close relations with German regulators and was well positioned in the future growth markets of the developing world, with special access to Eastern Europe. In 1996, Siemens formed a health services division to provide consulting and other services. Siemens made two major acquisitions of U.S.-based companies in 2000—Shared Medical Systems (SMS) for $2 billion to help its healthcare IT effort, and Acuson for $700 million to bolster its ultrasound offering. GEMS executives estimated that Siemens' 10% margins in 2000 (up from a loss in 1997) were driven by a 5% margin in equipment sales, 15% in services, and 3% in information technology related services, and generated a return on total capital of 9%. Part of Siemens strategy was to "win business at any cost" by offering low prices.

Philips Medical Systems Philips Medical Systems, based in The Netherlands, held a strong

[12]Alin Adomeit, Axel Baur, and Rainer Salfeld, "A New Model for Disease Management," *The McKinsey Quarterly,* Number 4, 2001.

[13]"Diagnostic Imaging Industry-Update," Joseph Eichinger, The Investext Group Boston, MA, November 16, 1983, p. 5.
[14]Electrical Equipment report, Ann M. Schwetje and Heve Francois, Smith Barney, April 24, 1995, p. 20.

Exhibit 4   Global Market Share Leaders by Modality

Modality	Number 1 Market Share	Number 2 Market Share	Number 3 Market Share
X-ray	GEMS	Philips	Siemens
Computed tomography	GEMS	Philips	Siemens
Magnetic resonance	GEMS	Siemens	
Nuclear medicine	Siemens	GEMS	Philips
PET	GEMS	Siemens	
Ultrasound	GEMS	Philips	Siemens
Healthcare IT	Siemens	GEMS	
Patient monitoring	Philips	GEMS	
Cardiology	GEMS		

Source: Company documents.

overall third place market share, led in nuclear medicine and ultrasound, and was particularly strong in vascular and cardiologic X-ray. Philips' sales by region pattern nearly matched that of Siemens: roughly half U.S., one-third Europe, and 15% Asia. In recent years, Philips had aggressively expanded through acquisition, including the 2001 acquisitions of Marconi Medical Systems and Agilent. Once these acquisitions were completed later in 2001, Philips would have doubled in size in the past couple years, surpassing Siemens and taking the number two market share position with nearly $5 billion in sales. Over the coming year, Philips planned to focus on restructuring and integrating its recent acquisitions which had under-performed in the recent past. The company was also pushing into the healthcare IT segment, but was not a major competitor in this segment in 2001. Margins at Philips had fluctuated in recent years between 2% to 3% losses to gains of nearly 9%—driven by 3% margins in equipment sales and 10% margins in services—and return on total capital was 6%. Philips spent approximately 8% of sales on R&D.

Toshiba Medical Systems   Toshiba Medical Systems, headquartered in Japan, had the fourth largest market share position with sales estimated at $2.3 billion. Toshiba was particularly strong in the ultrasound and CT modalities, was known for

producing cost effective and reliable products, and had the second largest market share in Asia. It recently began developing its own imaging equipment service business whereas previously it had contracted with an outside vendor. Toshiba was also growing its healthcare IT business and had recently formed a joint venture with an applications service provider. Its margins were estimated to be in the range of 5%, and it was considered an acquisition target.

Separately, there was competition in providing after-sales services. In the United States, each of the four principal rivals serviced equipment from any OEM, and were labeled "multi-vendors." Other OEMs serviced their own equipment only. There were also independent service organizations (ISO) who were typically multi-vendors, and who often received contracts from insurance companies who specialized in insuring the diagnostic equipment of their hospital customers. In 2002 OEMs share in the U.S. had increased to 77%, while that of ISOs and in-house staff had fallen to 10% and 13% respectively, with insurers falling by the wayside.[15] The services sector was organized quite differently outside the United States. Since many nations'

[15]Some information in this paragraph comes from "Total Medical Imaging Equipment Services Market," a report by Frost and Sullivan, 2002.

authorities insisted that OEMs serviced their own products, there was little scope for multi-vendors to exist.

General Electric Medical Systems

GEMS' strong performance under Jeff Immelt from 1997 to 2000 had been a factor in his promotion to chairman of GE. GEMS' roots began in the 1940s with the purchase of an X-ray business in Chicago. Long an industry innovator, GEMS developed CT technology in the 1970s and MR in the 1980s, and competed in all medical imaging modalities in over 100 countries by 2002. It boasted the number one position in MR and CT imaging worldwide, and had the leading market share in all regions (Americas, Europe/Africa, and Asia).

Most revenues were earned in high-cost, industrialized countries while manufacturing was increasingly carried out in low cost, developing nations. Profits tended to be highest in developed nations where reimbursement rates were higher and where demand for higher-end products was greater. GEMS executives expected each of its main modalities to reach $1 billion in worldwide sales. By 2001, both the CT and MR businesses had exceeded this mark, and nuclear medicine and the PET business were growing rapidly. (See Exhibit 5 for GEMS financial data.)

Global Evolution of GEMS   The evolution of GEMS from a U.S. company to one whose non-U.S. revenues exceeded 50% in 2002 was a multi-stage process. GEMS' first major step outside the United

Exhibit 5   GEMS Financial Data ($ millions)

	1995	1996	1997	1998	1999	2000	2001
Sales	3,665	3,960	4,100	4,620	6,170	7,240	8,400
Operating margin	500	570	690	825	1,055	1,280	1,485
Net income	305	345	400	480	615	760	890
Funds flow	245	290	310	(845)	—	15	170
Cash from operating activities	340	545	470	565	820	915	965
P&E reinvestment ratio	2.1	2.0	1.7	1.6	1.0	1.0	1.0
Working capital—5 pt. average	601	577	489	485	780	830	930
Product line sales							
Ultrasound		190			550	750	900
CT		615			825	1,000	1,150
MR		735			1,010	1,140	1,200
X-Ray		620			650	1,005	1,240
Functional Imaging (NM/PET)		55			200	235	390
IT		—	50	130	850	1,000	1,300
Service		1,520			1,950	2,020	2,220
Other		225			135	90	—
Total Sales		3,960			6,170	7,240	8,400
Regional sales							
Americas		2,200		2,850	3,945	4,640	5,230
Europe		850		885	1,075	1,200	1,510
Asia		910		885	1,150	1,400	1,660
Total Sales		3,960		4,620	6,170	7,240	8,400

Source: Company documents.

States was a joint venture in the early 1980s with Yokogawa Medical Systems to build and sell MRI products in Japan. In 1988, GEMS gained a foothold in the European market, by exchanging GE's consumer electronic business (televisions) with the medical devices business unit of the French company Thomson.

In 1987, John Trani, newly-named GEMS head, set out more formally to create a global company. Trani emphasized the training and development of business leaders in global management and brought in a number of leading academics to develop a program. This consisted partly of forming small teams of American, Asian, and European managers and having them train together in each of the three regions. By 1992, nearly 300 of GEMS' top managers had been through the program. Initially, the majority of GEMS' international managers were American nationals working outside the United States. The development program, however, sought to identify and develop local managers, of whom some were brought to the United States to hold management positions. In the 1990s, Trani also invested in developing the Asian market organization outside of Japan. This consisted primarily of the India and China markets that, although small, had enormous growth potential. GEMS became a leader within GE in terms of developing a global business.[16] Trani responded to reductions in healthcare reimbursement in the late 1980s to mid 1990s by emphasizing cost reductions.

Immelt inherited a $4 billion company. His first major effort was to step up acquisitions. Size, Immelt believed, would be critical to obtaining sufficient capital to invest in emerging businesses. In 2000, one of the acquired companies formed the basis for GEMS-IT, a new subsidiary focused on healthcare IT. Second, he spearheaded an initiative called the Global Products Company (GPC) that was geared towards cutting costs by shifting manufacturing activities, and eventually design and

engineering activities, out of high cost countries and moving them into low cost countries (described below). Third, he invested in developing marketing and sales organizations within key markets. Activities such as hosting symposia deepened GEMS' relationships with local opinion leaders and make GEMS more than just an equipment company in the eyes of its customers. Greg Lucier (HBS MBA '90), CEO of GEMS-IT, referred to this as being "more German than the Germans."

Consistent with this emphasis on local sales and marketing was GEMS' new organization structure. GEMS was organized around three groups: the poles, the businesses, and the functions. The poles were three geographically based sales, marketing and service organizations: the Americas—North and South America; Europe—including Eastern Europe and Africa; and Asia—including Australia. Each pole was headed by a regional vice president reporting to Hogan. GEMS also had eight business heads, such as the MR and CT businesses, reporting to Hogan. The head of GEMS-IT also reported to Hogan. Finally, functional heads—running manufacturing, engineering, R&D, global supply chain, customer advocacy, legal, finance, and HR—reported to Hogan.

Current Strategy   Salient features of key activities are described below.

Manufacturing   Since the launch of GPC in 1997, manufacturing was shifted from high cost to low cost countries. Each product was to be built in one or two "Centers of Excellence (COE)" that could then be shipped anywhere in the world (Exhibit 6). Between 60% and 96% of product made in a COE ended up being sold elsewhere. GEMS, with its extensive sales and marketing organizations around the world, was ideally positioned among GE divisions to pioneer GPC. By 2001, manufacturing had moved from Paris to Budapest, from Milwaukee to Mexico City, and from Tokyo to Shanghai and Bangalore.

A high portion of GEMS production activities consisted of the assembly of parts and sub assemblies manufactured by outside suppliers. Marc

---

[16]In June 2001, Yoshiaki Fujimori, an early participant in GEMS global training and development program and a GEMS manager throughout the 1990s, become the first non-American to run a major GE business when he was named president and CEO of GE's plastics division.

Exhibit 6   Global Product Company

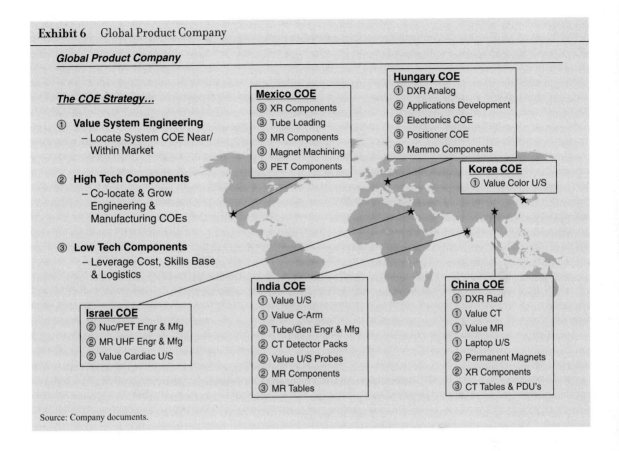

Global Product Company

The COE Strategy...

① **Value System Engineering**
   – Locate System COE Near/
     Within Market

② **High Tech Components**
   – Co-locate & Grow
     Engineering &
     Manufacturing COEs

③ **Low Tech Components**
   – Leverage Cost, Skills Base
     & Logistics

Mexico COE
③ XR Components
③ Tube Loading
③ MR Components
③ Magnet Machining
③ PET Components

Hungary COE
① DXR Analog
② Applications Development
② Electronics COE
③ Positioner COE
③ Mammo Components

Korea COE
① Value Color U/S

Israel COE
② Nuc/PET Engr & Mfg
② MR UHF Engr & Mfg
② Value Cardiac U/S

India COE
① Value U/S
① Value C-Arm
② Tube/Gen Engr & Mfg
② CT Detector Packs
② Value U/S Probes
② MR Components
③ MR Tables

China COE
① DXR Rad
① Value CT
① Value MR
① Laptop U/S
② Permanent Magnets
② XR Components
③ CT Tables & PDU's

Source: Company documents.

Onetto, the vice president of GEMS' global supply chain, stated, "Because we buy so many things, the game for us is very much a supply chain game and not a manufacturing game" (Exhibit 7). These assembly "inputs" were not simple parts like bolts, resistors, or metal frames, but rather complex, high-value added assemblies such as computer boards, precision machined assemblies, and complex molded plastics. Onetto explained that the only things that GEMS made were the "crown jewels," the proprietary heart of each of the company's products.

Inputs purchased from vendors accounted for roughly $2 billion of GEMS $2.3 billion in total variable costs for manufacturing and a significant majority (85%) of these inputs were manufactured in high cost countries. Significant savings were expected if GEMS could successfully switch to using suppliers based in low cost countries. Manufacturing costs were approximately 80% material and 20% labor. GEMS had set a goal of having 50% of its direct material purchases from low cost countries, and 60% of its manufacturing activities located there, up from roughly 15% and 40% in 2001. Lucier guessed that GEMS was about 60% of the way to getting to its ultimate goal to save 10–30% on materials and 50% on labor. Brian Worrel, head of finance, commented, "While GPC moves into a country entail some fixed costs, the payback has been within two years typically, partly because much of the plant and equipment can be sourced locally."

Onetto, however, explained that the biggest challenge to such a transition was the development of

Exhibit 7   Global Supply Chain

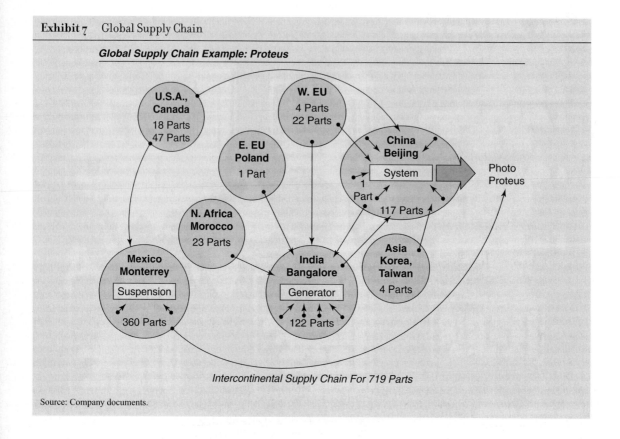

Global Supply Chain Example: Proteus

Intercontinental Supply Chain For 719 Parts

Source: Company documents.

suppliers in low cost countries. "You just can't go to the local chamber of commerce in India or China and find workable suppliers—it must be a long term strategy." GEMS' eight year relationship with Bharat Electronics Ltd. (BEL) of India was an example of the time and commitment needed to develop a supplier. A 20-person sourcing team of GEMS engineers spent 25% of their time working with BEL and a seven person GEMS quality team spent 50% of its time with BEL. Onetto gave a six-sigma class to BEL's CEO and senior management team. GEMS initially purchased simpler, less critical parts from BEL and over time bought more complex parts. By 2001, BEL was supplying parts to all of GEMS that used to only be made in the United States and Japan. Onetto further explained that because GEMS wanted truly independent suppliers and not quasi-GE plants, GEMS had not provided financing to its developing suppliers, but noted that the existence of a GEMS contract enabled suppliers to obtain their own financing. First-year cost savings of moving to a low cost country were about 30%, with expectations of further ongoing cost reductions of 10% annually.

Offsetting these gains were GPC-specific costs. These included inventory, logistic, documentation and import duty costs relating to moving materials and products around the world. It was costly to rely on a less experienced workforce in the new location. Each time an operation shifted to a low cost country, employees from both the old location and headquarters endured long trips from home. For example, when one printed circuit board plant was moved to Budapest, six to eight employees had to practically move there for six months. Those left behind often lost their jobs, creating a human toll on the workforce. Despite this, total GEMS employment in the United States was higher due to the company's growth and increased need for knowledge workers. Reinaldo Garcia, head of GEMS Europe, commented that managing reduced investment in countries like France, Spain and Italy, had involved extensive, and often difficult, communications with various public entities. Moving away from developed countries also meant losing the concessions these countries often provided to encourage export-generating investment. On the other hand, Lucier emphasized offsetting broad benefits, "GPC has been a great way to attract talent from new regions as it is our first major step in many countries. It tends to make us insiders in countries that have considerable nationalistic pride."

Aware of the difficulties inherent in moving production from one location to another, GEMS used a "pitcher-catcher" concept to facilitate the moves. For each move, a pitching team at the site of the existing plant worked with a catching team at the new site. Managers were measured on the effectiveness of the move and a move was not considered complete until the performance of the catching team met or exceeded that of the pitching team. The pitcher-catcher concept had been developed elsewhere within GE and had subsequently diffused throughout the company. Indeed, Lucier believed there were other opportunities to learn from GE. For example, the Industrial Products division had developed a measurement called "span" that looked at whether a shipment was sent before or after the targeted ship date as a means of controlling factory throughputs. "Design for reliability" techniques, advanced in the Aircraft Engines division, were also relevant.

John Chiminski observed that this infrastructure was supported by an efficient parts organization,

> We use 90 warehouses across five continents to ship two million parts annually. There are half a million different types of parts, of which 80,000 will ship in any given year, with half of these repeating the following year. In general, demand is spiky. No use for several years will be followed by demand surges of uncertain duration. We measure our performance by the 'span,' or the time it takes to fulfil a certain percentage of the demand for our services. Seventy-five percent of our demand is met in 4 hours, and 95% is met within 75 hours. Stated differently, it takes no more than 24 hours to ship intra-region, and no more than 48 hours to ship from outside the region.

Mark Ship, global logistics manager, observed that the supply chain worked sufficiently well that, in the wake of the 9/11 tragedy, despite air freight to major manufacturing sites stopped for five days, there were no plant shutdowns and no missed customer commitments. This required several GE business units working with U.S. customs, chartered planes and van lines, and local police and the FBI, with 24*7 communication within and outside GEMS, as the world cleared air and other freight backlogs over the next ten days.

R&D and Product Design   GEMS typically spent 7% to 9% of sales on R&D projects and held the philosophy that the best technology would always win in the marketplace. New products within existing platforms might take a year or two to develop and cost $5 million to $10 million. New platforms might take three years to develop while significant breakthroughs might take 10 years. Often longer-term projects focused on more basic research were done at the GE corporate R&D level. The corporate R&D group had invented CT technology in the 1970s, for example. More recently, it had invested over $100 million to develop digital detectors for X-ray machines that would replace the need for X-ray film. Corporate R&D had also been involved in the development of remote monitoring and diagnostic technologies that GEMS used in their equipment service activities. This technology linked the diagnostic imaging equipment installed at customer sites with GEMS servicing centers which made it possible to observe the operating performance of the equipment and diagnose problems before sending out a service technician. In some cases, equipment problems could be solved remotely. The technology had since diffused throughout GE to be used wherever GE had assets in the field, as in aircraft engines and power systems.

GPC philosophy had begun to seep through to the R&D function, causing product design responsibility to gravitate towards countries with talented but under-utilized human capital. Steve Patscot, the human resources manager for GEMS-IT, recalled, "I took a trip through Eastern Europe a couple years ago and found highly capable engineers with masters degrees making $1.50 per hour. There was nothing for them to do after the Cold War and the collapse of the aerospace and military industries. We had to learn to harness this talent pool." The ability to absorb new talent pools would be fundamental going forward as Patscot opined that "GEMS is not likely to be beaten by existing competitors, but more by some unforeseeable coalition."

Shifting knowledge bases of relevance certainly created the potential for being blindsided. Gene Saragnese, vice president of technology, described the changes:

> Five years ago we built boxes (MR, CT, X-ray) and R&D was comprised largely of electrical engineers, mechanical engineers, and physicists. Then we added integrated solutions and we brought in a lot of software engineers. Tomorrow we will move into the biochemical world and we will need different skills. Each evolution brings broader market development and in theory broader revenues.

Lucier envisioned a possible two-step transition to make GEMS relevant in this biochemical world of diagnostics. Step one involved collaborating with pharmaceutical companies to develop equipment capable of detecting the reagents developed by the pharmaceutical companies. Step two entailed, in some sense, a return to the business of selling and servicing equipment, albeit of a different kind. There were two ways to make this two-step transition. Organic growth over the five-to-ten year period would likely entail capital outlays of the order of $100 million per year. Alternatively, a multibillion dollar acquisition of an appropriate company could get GEMS started down this road.

Sales   GEMS treated sales as a local operation. Local expertise and relationships were needed to deal with governmental regulatory bodies, healthcare infrastructures, and customers in each country.

Given the high price of GEMS products, often in excess of $1 million, the sales process was long and typically involved managers at multiple levels within the hospital, clinic, or other healthcare organization. Depending on the cost of the equipment and the size of the hospital budget, approval decisions might be made anywhere from the department head level to the board of directors. Members of the sales team met with financial managers to discuss costs, reimbursements, and financing; with heads of radiology departments to discuss and demonstrate image quality and throughput (number of procedures per time period); and with technicians to discuss how the equipment was operated. Increasingly, sales team members also met with physicians, such as cardiologists, to discuss ways in which the images could be used. Often, the radiology department head wrote a business plan indicating the need for the equipment, the types and numbers of patients to be served, and the reimbursement values from insurance providers. The level of reimbursement, typically set by a government health agency, and the equipment throughput, were big factors in determining the price the purchaser could afford. The sales process typically took six to 12 months. The imaging equipment had a life cycle of approximately seven years in most western countries and a bit longer in poorer nations. While the equipment itself, with proper maintenance, could last much longer, it became technically obsolete.

Garcia explained that GEMS usually relied on a wholly-owned direct sales organization, especially if the market was large enough to support such an infrastructure. As an example, GEMS had arm's-length dealings with distributors in Egypt a decade ago, but, as demand rose and the installed base of GEMS products increased, GEMS bought out the major distributors and accelerated its investments in developing the Egyptian market. African countries, with the exception of South Africa and Egypt, continued to primarily be served through arm's-length dealings.

Overall, GEMS earned roughly 60% of its revenues through equipment sales with the remainder consisting of services such as equipment repair, healthcare IT systems, and productivity improvement consulting with customers. Service contracts earned significantly higher margins than did equipment sales. With the larger installed base of equipment, service contract sales were proportionally higher in the mature markets. Paul Mirabella, head of the worldwide healthcare solutions group, pointed out two recent changes in the way GEMS viewed services. First, they had tried to move away from a purely price-based discussion about a maintenance contract to one that focused on value-added services. Second, they had moved toward thinking of in-house service providers as a different kind of customer, rather than as competitors.

Marketing   There were at least three different marketing challenges—customizing products to suit country needs, marketing used products, and marketing newer generation products and services (Healthcare IT).

GEMS believed that customers and patients were basically the same around the world, but at the same time realized that some customization of products was required for each country. The desire to follow GPC to drive down costs had to be reconciled with the need to recognize differences between countries. Beyond the obvious differences in languages that might appear on a machine, richer countries tended to buy more sophisticated equipment. Some advanced-country buyers also chose lower priced and used equipment. There were differences in cultural feelings as well. France, for example, tended to do proportionally more MR exams than CT scans because of concerns about the amount of X-ray exposure. Other countries used less nuclear medicine due to health concerns. Complicating things further were nationalist beliefs that caused purchasers from some countries to avoid buying equipment made in certain other countries. Though GEMS designed products to be easily adaptable to the different markets, engineers in one country did not always understand the needs of others. Mike Jones, GEMS' global business and market development manager, stated, "People in the U.S. can't design a low end product for China. They will add needless bells and whistles and they just won't get it right. Similarly, China can't design a product for the Mayo Clinic."

Another form of customization was necessary to cater to the needs of developing nations, lacking the 'soft' infrastructure needed for diagnostic healthcare delivery. Garcia explained:

> GEMS held a round-table for Eastern European customers in Budapest last year. The Croatian contingent made clear that their radiologists needed to be trained to use advanced equipment. It became apparent to us that a real differentiation opportunity exists here. We plan to hold seminars for users, regardless of whether or not they are using our products currently. We also spend a lot of time marketing to the regulators, explaining to them that it is not cost effective to save on capital investment in, say, MR machines.

GEMS had put in place a "Gold Seal" program to market used equipment. Bob Cancalosi, Global General Manager for Gold Seal, described the pre-owned market as having two parts. The "as-is-where-is" business entailed GEMS acquiring used equipment from one location and relocating it. The refurbishing business acquired used equipment satisfying stringent criteria—using state-of-the-art digitized databases—brought it back to OEM specs, and re-sold it. Traditionally GEMS refurbished only its own products, though it was in the midst of acquiring a large refurbisher of non-GEMS products. Cancalosi commented,

> This is a $1 billion global market, growing at 15% per year. We have a 30% share of it already, and are moving in the direction of doing more refurbishing rather than as-is-where-is work. I can't get my hands on enough pre-owned assets to satisfy demand we know exists. We run facilities in Milwaukee, Paris and Tokyo, and are so far out of capacity that we are considering another facility in Bangalore. Ten percent of used sales that we complete crosses national borders, though my guess is that cross-border potential business as a fraction of the total used business is more in the range of 30%. The one thing that scares me most

about this business is the 800-odd broker/dealers with whom we compete, with no passion for six-sigma type quality and very low overheads.

Different challenges presented themselves in marketing healthcare IT products to clinicians. Vik Khetarpal described a spectrum of possible products. At one extreme were the "if we build it they will come" type of products, with a clear value proposition for the adopters. This included products that replaced illegible white-board handwriting with products to help with emergency room patient-tracking, and products that replaced manual monitoring with centralized, simultaneous, automated surveillance of dozens of patients in an obstetrics environment. Image-archiving products that helped fulfil the legal requirements of maintaining extremely data-intensive records for long time-periods were also eagerly adopted. Most of these products involved gathering and processing existing data more efficiently. At the other extreme were products that required physicians to change behavior. Physician order-entry provided the classic example. System-wide costs would be greatly reduced if computer entry occurred, but most doctors continued to prefer to hand-write their orders, often illegibly. GEMS estimated that it would take three to five years to get hospitals to move from the former to the latter kind of product. Even in 2002, only a handful of U.S. hospitals had automated order-entry, and these only because they had mandated the change for medical students. Khetarpal commented,

> Our ideal customer is one operating multiple facilities that are geographically dispersed, with a mobile patient population. It turns out that these are found globally. Germany, Malaysia and U.K. have all been hot markets for us. It was a pleasant surprise to find that interacting with doctors was quite similar worldwide, in the sense that they had similar needs. Vital signs, meds, and disease markers are the same; the ICU feels the same worldwide. But understanding doctors' incentives to embrace products is important. Hospitals act differently around the world. For example, ER medicine is more advanced in the U.S. than anywhere else. In Germany, you have ER hospitals, rather than ER rooms in each hospital.

Managing the Regulatory Interface Keith Morgan, senior legal counsel, explained:

> The key to healthcare is understanding that it is halfway between a utility and a free market enterprise. Government involvement is ubiquitous and spans the spectrum from provider to payor to regulator. Government tends to get more involved as society develops. Look at the U.S. The Food and Drug Administration regulates equipment for efficacy and safety, the manner in which we promote our products, and our business practices. Health and Human Services administers Medicare and has a huge impact on our economics.

Wilson described his role as combining "defense and offense." Defense involved ensuring across-the-board compliance, complicated by variations in rules across countries. It also included ensuring a level playing field against domestic competitors in other countries. Offence included trying to influence evolving rules and regulations, especially in the "wild west show" that tended to characterize newer regulatory systems in some countries.

Human Resources Under Welch, GE emphasized developing highly competent technical and managerial talent. The company was known for having a very deep bench. Executives in one division regularly selected its own managers from other parts of GE. Naren Gursahaney, GEMS' current Asia head, was a typical example. His six years in several GE businesses were followed by a two-year stint at GE corporate in Connecticut. Within GEMS, he first ran service operations in Asia, moved back to Milwaukee to a staff position for a short while, and returned to Tokyo to his current position. Hogan said, "For senior GEMS management positions, I always ask whether the individual can run a GE company—not just GEMS—and whether the GEMS position in question develops the person. Who runs GEMS is ultimately Jeff Immelt's call."

Within GEMS, extensive emphasis had been placed on developing managers capable to succeed in a global environment. This included both moving managers around from one country to another, and also developing local managers within each country. Steve Patscot, GEMS' HR director who had been at GEMS since the late 1980s, noted, "To be a truly global company you must surrender national identity." Indeed, GEMS headcount had increased tenfold in China since 1995, five-fold in India, and thrice-over in Mexico and Eastern Europe, while remaining roughly stable elsewhere. The average cost of a GE engineer had fallen steadily in the late 1990s because of international sourcing of talent, especially from India, by several GE business units, including GEMS.

Lucier acknowledged that reallocating human resources away from mature segments toward newer ones was a perennial human resources challenge. GEMS addressed this partly by creating new units, such as GEMS-IT, to separate the businesses. Lucier highlighted two challenges that GEMS-IT had faced in recent times. Both converting the talent that GEMS-IT acquired as part of its acquisitions, and converting them into "leaders" in the GE sense, required considerable ongoing effort. Yet, as Lucier put it, "Working with cutting-edge technology at a leading company to help save people's lives is a compelling value proposition for talent, and has allowed us to maintain lower than usual attrition rates."

Managing Acquisitions   Although several key acquisitions had been made in the 1980s to launch globalization at GEMS, there were very few major acquisitions prior to Immelt's arrival at GEMS in 1997. Under Immelt, GEMS then purchased nearly 100 businesses ranging in value from $1 million to nearly $1 billion. This was several times over similar activity at any of the major competitors. Many of these acquisitions were outside of the United States. Because of this acquisition strategy and successful post-acquisition integration, GEMS had been growing at over 25% in some markets that were growing at less than 10%. While GE Capital was the one GE division that had made more acquisitions than GEMS, its acquisitions did not have to be as fully integrated into the rest of the division as did acquisitions at GEMS.

Often, an acquisition, particularly of foreign distributors, occurred after some period of a growing relationship. Such a relationship might evolve from a joint venture to partial ownership before a full acquisition was completed. Aside from growth, GEMS acquired companies to obtain new product lines and associated technical expertise to fill gaps in its own product offerings, to gain access to new markets, and to achieve efficiency gains to keep up with the ever present pressures from equipment purchasers to reduce prices. Jones stated, "Many times, the companies we buy are not global, but a big part of the value that we bring is to be able to leverage our existing infrastructure, our distribution and service capabilities around the world, and take those products and services global." Thus, Lunar Corporation, which made equipment to measure bone density to detect osteoporosis, had little international presence. GEMS planned to grow it by 20% annually and expand its presence in the women's healthcare segment. GEMS acquired Marquette—a leader in diagnostic cardiology, patient monitoring devices, and clinical information systems—and made it a key piece in the newly formed GEMS-IT division. GEMS-IT planned to spend anywhere from $0.5–$1 billion annually on acquisitions for several years to continue to build its businesses.

Pulling the Activities Together   GEMS' introduction of Signa, its open MR system, served as an example of how all the functions came together to develop and launch a new product line. Traditional MR systems involved patients having to slide on a table into a cylindrical scanning tunnel. Claustrophobic or very large patients often found this uncomfortable. In the mid-1990s, a competitor developed a MR system with magnets above and below the exam table, but not surrounding it. The magnetic field strength of the competitor's product was low and the resulting image quality was far below traditional MR systems. GEMS then invested some $50 million over two and one-half years to develop what it believed was a far better system that put them a couple years ahead of the competition. Lucier noted that GEMS was only able to do this because it had already spent some $1 billion in the MR business.

GEMS launched the Signa simultaneously all over the world. Previous products were launched in the United States first, then in Europe and Japan, and eventually elsewhere. The product was sold by convincing radiologists that they would attract more patients because it was a more comfortable system, and it produced great images. GEMS assisted hospitals and clinics target specific markets with promotional advertisements aimed at medical consumers using words such as "no more fears." GEMS spent between $10 million and $15 million on the product rollout and marketing campaigns.

GEMS sold 300 units in 18 months at approximately $1.5 million each. Actual selling prices varied widely in different countries depending on reimbursement rates for the various procedures that the Signa could perform. Americans, Lucier explained, seemed willing to pay more to live longer and had the highest reimbursement rates. Japan and Europe paid less well. For markets such as China, and other sites with restricted funding opportunities, GEMS had designed a less powerful Signa machine that sold for half as much. Hospitals and clinics increased profits by increasing the numbers of patients they imaged. Service contracts were particularly profitable as GEMS could receive $100,000 per year for what usually amounted to minor adjustments to the machines. The service was provided largely by GEMS 7,000 worldwide field service engineers who were supplemented by a few contractors in some markets. GEMS expected then to acquire used units at about $300–$400K each, to spend $100K in refurbishing, and to resell these for $800K with a year's warranty included. They would also sell five-year contracts to customers at $125K/year, plus accessories sales as and when demanded.

GEMS in China
GEMS sold its first CT unit in China in 1979 in response to an order placed directly with its Milwaukee headquarters. Subsequent developments included a Hong Kong office, followed by a "rep office" in China in 1986, and a 1991 manufacturing joint venture to get around import quotas. In 1995, following the elimination of quotas, the China team competed aggressively with other GE teams for the rights to become the "Center of

Excellence" for low-end CT manufacturing within GE. Chih Chen, head of GEMS' China effort for the past five years, commented, "Korea and India, and a newly acquired unit in Japan, all wanted the same position. Within GE, there is extensive market competition. We won after a year and a half of inspections of competing GE factories worldwide."

Separate joint ventures were established for CT, X-Ray and Ultrasound involving partnerships with multiple regulatory authorities (Ministry of Health, and the State Drug Administration—SDA) and their subsidiary manufacturing units. Chen described the challenges of these ventures. "In one joint venture, the partner firm would receive orders for equipment, and then service the orders from its separately wholly-owned factory, thus cutting us out. We couldn't stop this practice. So we had to renegotiate." By 2002, GE had acquired 100% ownership of two of the ventures and 90% of the third.

There were three categories of products at GEMS China—locally made products for local use, locally made products for sale by GEMS around the world, and products imported from other GEMS plants worldwide. In 2002, 70% of GEMS China's production was for export, up from 60% three years ago. In contrast, the Siemens JV in China, which predated GEMS' arrival, was solely set up to manufacture for the local market. GEMS had a 40% market share, greater than the sum of Siemens' and Philips' shares. The remaining market was populated with hundreds of assemblers and trading companies, many of which had tried to set up manufacturing facilities but with limited success. Chen—a native of Taiwan, U.S.-educated Ph.D., and veteran of GE postings in Silicon Valley, Singapore, Taiwan and Beijing—attributed the leadership position to knowing how to "work in the jungle." Keith Morgan also pointed out that GEMS tried to constructively influence the evolution of business practices in China:

> Some years ago, brokers purchased used medical equipment from the west and dumped it in China. The Chinese government deemed this insulting and banned the sale of used equipment. We spent a lot of time suggesting that the problem was not with the

equipment but with the lack of rules governing its use. Without such equipment, rural hospitals would be denied functionality. Even the U.S. allows a regulated used equipment market.

Chen explained that the importance of the China market to GEMS was a function of its size and composition:

China is already the third largest market for medical diagnostics worldwide, behind the U.S. and Japan, and growing the fastest of these three. It also has the largest demand for low-end medical diagnostic products. For example, we sell a CT-Economy scanner for $300,000 in China, whereas the U.S. model costs $1 million. These low-end products can be used all over the world ultimately, even in some parts of rich countries. The low-end probably accounts for 20% of worldwide industry revenues, with the high end and middle-tier accounting for 45% and 35% respectively. To succeed in the high-end and middle-tier, you have to be in the U.S. and Japan respectively; to succeed in the low-end, you will have to own the Chinese market.

Chen's team advocated an "In China for China" policy, which would involve bending the tenets of the GPC policies that had propelled GEMS through its recent successes. It would entail moving plants already in low cost countries to China, partly duplicating existing infrastructure, under the logic that domestic production would have greater demand. As an example, Exhibit 8 shows the per unit and total economics of the part of a patient monitoring

Exhibit 8	Economics of Patient Monitoring Device Made in Mexico for the Chinese Market	
	$ Millions	**$/Unit**
Sales	$2.6	$3,300
Total variable cost	2.1	2,570
Variable margin	0.6	730
Incremental fixed cost	0.0	
Profit	0.6	
Number of units	800	

Source: Company documents.

product made in Mexico for the Chinese market. The product was sold in developing countries around the world and to individual clinics in advanced economies, and was a simpler version of a networked monitoring device sold worldwide. Demand in China was such that a drop in price of 10% could probably raise sales by 50%. Moving the production to China would not require incremental fixed costs of more than $1 million, since physical space was already available. Incrementally smaller variable costs could be expected—of the order of 2%—by avoiding duties and tariffs and by local sourcing, limited in the immediate term.

Looking Ahead   The challenges facing GEMS, under the new stewardship of Hogan, varied extensively around the world. For example, the strategic issues could not be more different from Japan to Hungary. The former, trapped in decade-long economic stasis, was unlikely to support high growth rates; the latter was on the cusp of becoming a major market for medical diagnostics, where GEMS, and other major diagnostic imaging firms had the opportunity to shape usage patterns. In Europe's lead market, Germany, GEMS had eaten away gradually at Siemens' lead, and seen its share rise from 5% to 25% over the past decade. Becoming an "insider" in Germany had been a slow process and involved creating relationships with universities, acquiring German companies, and understanding the needs of German doctors. But Siemens' continued dominance rankled. But perhaps the greatest challenge had to do with China. China demanded attention. Hogan realized that the "In China for China" policy represented a continued allocation of resources away from other parts of Asia—especially Japan—toward China. Further, he had to consider the excitement of continued technological ferment in the core markets and the prospect of scrutiny from the omniscient corporate parent, GE.

◼ Appendix: Major Modalities of Diagnostic Imaging Competitors

X-Ray   X-rays were the original imaging technology and represented over half of all diagnostic images taken. The equipment consisted of a radiation generator and a detector. Various body tissues absorbed or transmitted X-rays sent by the generator to various degrees. A two-dimensional contrasting image showing internal body structures thus formed on the detector. X-ray systems were useful for viewing structural abnormalities, such as broken bones or tumors, but less adept at viewing soft tissues. Images were still pictures and often contained structures above and below the area of interest. The introduction of digital X-rays in the 1990s enabled images to be stored and shared electronically, rather than on film, and constituted a major advance.

Computed Tomography (CT)   CT imaging systems, which included computer-axial tomography (CAT) systems, were an advanced form of X-ray imaging. In a CT system, an X-ray generator was located in one side of a donut shaped (toroidal) cabinet and an X-ray detector was located in the opposite side. The patient lay on a table that slid through the donut hole. As the patient moved through the hole, the X-ray generator and X-ray detector rotated inside the cabinet and around the patient to take multiple images from many different angles. The image data was computer processed into two-dimensional views of the body. As with X-ray systems, CT images were based on differences in tissue density. CT was used in facial reconstruction, tumor detection and the treatment of various traumas and blood vessel blockages.

Magnetic Resonance Imaging (MR)   MR imaging involved a patient lying on a table inside a cylindrical tunnel. The tunnel walls contained high powered magnets, radio wave generators, and radio wave detectors. The magnetic field and radio waves generated by the MR system caused the hydrogen atoms in the patient's water molecules to line up in a single direction. When the MR radio waves were turned off, the hydrogen atoms return to their original positions and in the process they emitted their own radio waves. These waves were detected by the MR system and used to create detailed two-dimensional and three-dimensional images. The 1990s development of open MR systems increased patient comfort by placing magnets above and below the patient table rather than surrounding the table. Higher strength MR systems formed higher quality images more quickly than lower strength systems. MR systems were used to view soft tissues, particularly heart and circulatory systems, and muscular/skeletal abnormalities. Increasingly, MR systems were viewing in functional imaging where organs could be viewed in action.

Nuclear Medicine Imaging (NM)   Radioactive isotopes were injected, ingested, or inhaled into the patient. Various tissues absorbed varying amounts of the isotopes that emitted gamma radiations. Gamma cameras detected the emissions which were then computer processed and displayed on a monitor. NM imagers were used in functional imaging of organs, body systems, and disease condition, and not snapshot structural imaging. The images provided exceptional detail to the cellular level and could be used to detect diseases much earlier than other modalities. The radio isotopes could be purchased or in some cases manufactured on site. Positron emission tomography (PET) systems, a recent advancement in the NM field, produced images with significantly higher resolutions. However, PET systems were more expensive (approaching $2 million compared with less than $1 million for NM) and additionally required short-lived isotopes that had to be produced on site using $2 million cyclotrons.

Ultrasound   Ultrasound systems used a transducer to transmit ultrasound waves into the body. Internal organs and structures reflected the sound back to the transducer, were computer processed, and then displayed on a video monitor. While ultrasound systems were continually being improved and could produce detailed structural images, system costs remained low compared with other modalities. Typical applications included viewing heart function, blood flow, various organs, and pregnancy conditions.

Non Imaging Diagnostic Segments

Patient Monitoring   Patient monitoring was a broad field of products used to monitor various patient conditions within a variety of hospital settings. Patient monitoring devices included neonatal monitoring, fetal monitoring, anesthesiology and other products.

Cardiology   Cardiology diagnostic equipment also covered a broad range and was often divided into invasive and non-invasive segments. Invasive cardiology products included equipment for catheter procedures that tested various aspects of a heart's electrical systems. Non-invasive cardiology covered electrocardiograph (ECG) equipment and ambulatory devices that recorded heart electrical function through wires attached to the body, and also stress test equipment and heart defibrillators.

Reading 3-1   The Globalization of Markets

Theodore Levitt

A powerful force drives the world toward a converging commonality, and that force is technology. It has proletarianized communication, transport, and travel. It has made isolated places and impoverished peoples eager for modernity's allurements. Almost everyone everywhere wants all the things they have heard about, seen, or experienced via the new technologies.

The result is a new commercial reality—the emergence of global markets for standardized consumer products on a previously unimagined scale of magnitude. Corporations geared to this new reality benefit from enormous economies of scale in production, distribution, marketing, and management. By translating these benefits into reduced world prices, they can decimate competitors that still live in the disabling grip of old assumptions about how the world works.

Gone are accustomed differences in national or regional preference. Gone are the days when a company could sell last year's models—or lesser versions of advanced products—in the less-developed world. And gone are the days when prices, margins, and profits abroad were generally higher than at home.

The globalization of markets is at hand. With that, the multinational commercial world nears its end, and so does the multinational corporation.

The multinational and the global corporation are not the same thing. The multinational corporation operates in a number of countries, and adjusts its products and practices in each—at high relative costs. The global corporation operates with resolute constancy—at low relative cost—as if the entire world (or major regions of it) were a single entity; it sells the same things in the same way everywhere.

Which strategy is better is not a matter of opinion but of necessity. Worldwide communications carry everywhere the constant drumbeat of modern possibilities to lighten and enhance work, raise living standards, divert, and entertain. The same countries that ask the world to recognize and respect the individuality of their cultures insist on the wholesale transfer to them of modern goods, services, and technologies. Modernity is not just a wish but also a widespread practice among those who cling, with unyielding passion or religious fervor, to ancient attitudes and heritages.

Who can forget the televised scenes during the 1979 Iranian uprisings of young men in fashionable French-cut trousers and silky body shirts thirsting

▌ Reprinted by permission of *Harvard Business Review*. "The Globalization of Markets" by Theodore Levitt, (May/June 1983).
▌ Copyright © 1983 by the President and Fellows of Harvard College; all rights reserved.

with raised modern weapons for blood in the name of Islamic fundamentalism?

In Brazil, thousands swarm daily from pre-industrial Bahian darkness into exploding coastal cities, there quickly to install television sets in crowded corrugated huts and, next to battered Volkswagens, make sacrificial offerings of fruit and fresh-killed chickens to Macumban spirits by candlelight.

During Biafra's fratricidal war against the Ibos, daily televised reports showed soldiers carrying blood stained swords and listening to transistor radios while drinking Coca-Cola.

In the isolated Siberian city of Krasnoyarsk, with no paved streets and censored news, occasional Western travelers are stealthily propositioned for cigarettes, digital watches, and even the clothes off their backs.

The organized smuggling of electronic equipment, used automobiles, Western clothing, cosmetics, and pirated movies into primitive places exceeds even the thriving underground trade in modern weapons and their military mercenaries.

A thousand suggestive ways attest to the ubiquity of the desire for the most advanced things that the world makes and sells—goods of the best quality and reliability at the lowest price. The world's needs and desires have been irrevocably homogenized. This makes the multinational corporation obsolete and the global corporation absolute.

Living in the Republic of Technology

Daniel J. Boorstin, author of the monumental trilogy, *The Americans,* characterized our age as driven by "the Republic of Technology [whose] supreme law . . . is convergence, the tendency for everything to become more like everything else."

In business, this trend has pushed markets toward global commonality. Corporations sell standardized products in the same way everywhere—autos, steel, chemicals, petroleum, cement, agricultural commodities and equipment, industrial and commercial construction, banking and insurance services, computers, semiconductors, transport, electronic instruments, pharmaceuticals, and telecommunications, to mention some of the obvious.

Nor is the sweeping gale of globalization confined to these raw material or high-tech products, where the universal language of customers and users facilitates standardization. The transforming winds whipped up by the proletarianization of communication and travel enter every crevice of life.

Commercially, nothing confirms this as much as the success of McDonald's from the Champs Elysées to the Ginza, of Coca-Cola in Bahrain and Pepsi-Cola in Moscow, and of rock music, Greek salad, Hollywood movies, Revlon cosmetics, Sony televisions, and Levi jeans everywhere. "High-touch" products are as ubiquitous as high-tech.

Starting from opposing sides, the high-tech and the high-touch ends of the commercial spectrum gradually consume the undistributed middle in their cosmopolitan orbit. No one is exempt and nothing can stop the process. Everywhere everything gets more and more like everything else as the world's preference structure is relentlessly homogenized.

Consider the cases of Coca-Cola and Pepsi-Cola, which are globally standardized products sold everywhere and welcomed by everyone. Both successfully cross multitudes of national, regional, and ethnic taste buds trained to a variety of deeply ingrained local preferences of taste, flavor, consistency, effervescence, and aftertaste. Everywhere both sell well. Cigarettes, too, especially American-made, make year-to-year global inroads on territories previously held in the firm grip of other, mostly local, blends.

These are not exceptional examples. (Indeed their global reach would be even greater were it not for artificial trade barriers.) They exemplify a general drift toward the homogenization of the world and how companies distribute, finance, and price products.[1] Nothing is exempt. The products and methods of the industrialized world play a single tune for all the world, and all the world eagerly dances to it.

---

[1] In a landmark article, Robert D. Buzzell pointed out the rapidity with which barriers to standardization were falling. In all cases they succumbed to more and cheaper advanced ways of doing things. See "Can You Standardize Multinational Marketing?" *HBR,* November–December 1968.

Ancient differences in national tastes or modes of doing business disappear. The commonality of preference leads inescapably to the standardization of products, manufacturing, and the institutions of trade and commerce. Small nation-based markets transmogrify and expand. Success in world competition turns on efficiency in production, distribution, marketing, and management, and inevitably becomes focused on price.

The most effective world competitors incorporate superior quality and reliability into their cost structures. They sell in all national markets the same kind of products sold at home or in their largest export market. They compete on the basis of appropriate value—the best combinations of price, quality, reliability, and delivery for products that are globally identical with respect to design, function, and even fashion.

That, and little else, explains the surging success of Japanese companies dealing worldwide in a vast variety of products—both tangible products like steel, cars, motorcycles, hi-fi equipment, farm machinery, robots, microprocessors, carbon fibers, and now even textiles, and intangibles like banking, shipping, general contracting, and soon computer software. Nor are high-quality and low-cost operations incompatible, as a host of consulting organizations and data engineers argue with vigorous vacuity. The reported data are incomplete, wrongly analyzed, and contradictory. The truth is that low-cost operations are the hallmark of corporate cultures that require and produce quality in all that they do. High quality and low costs are not opposing postures. They are compatible, twin identities of superior practice.[2]

To say that Japan's companies are not global because they export cars with left-side drives to the United States and the European continent, while those in Japan have right-side drives, or because they sell office machines through distributors in the United States but directly at home, or speak

Portuguese in Brazil, is to mistake a difference for a distinction. The same is true of Safeway and Southland retail chains operating effectively in the Middle East, and to not only native but also imported populations from Korea, the Philippines, Pakistan, India, Thailand, Britain, and the United States. National rules of the road differ, and so do distribution channels and languages. Japan's distinction is its unrelenting push for economy and value enhancement. That translates into a drive for standardization at high quality levels.

Vindication of the Model T   If a company forces costs and prices down and pushes quality and reliability up—while maintaining reasonable concern for suitability—customers will prefer its world-standardized products. The theory holds, at this stage in the evolution of globalization, no matter what conventional market research and even common sense may suggest about different national and regional tastes, preferences, needs, and institutions. The Japanese have repeatedly vindicated this theory, as did Henry Ford with the Model T. Most important, so have their imitators, including companies from South Korea (television sets and heavy construction), Malaysia (personal calculators and microcomputers), Brazil (auto parts and tools), Colombia (apparel), Singapore (optical equipment), and yes, even from the United States (office copiers, computers, bicycles, castings), Western Europe (automatic washing machines), Rumania (housewares), Hungary (apparel), Yugoslavia (furniture), and Israel (pagination equipment).

Of course, large companies operating in a single nation or even a single city don't standardize everything they make, sell, or do. They have product lines instead of a single product version, and multiple distribution channels. There are neighborhood, local, regional, ethnic, and institutional differences, even within metropolitan areas. But although companies customize products for particular market segments, they know that success in a world with homogenized demand requires a search for sales opportunities in similar segments across the globe in order to achieve the economies of scale necessary to compete.

---

[2]There is powerful new evidence for this, even though the opposite has been urged by analysts of PIMS data for nearly a decade. See "Product Quality: Cost Production and Business Performance—A Test of Some Key Hypotheses" by Lynn W. Phillips, Dae Chang, and Robert D. Buzzell, Harvard Business School Working Paper No. 83-13.

Such a search works because a market segment in one country is seldom unique; it has close cousins everywhere precisely because technology has homogenized the globe. Even small local segments have their global equivalents everywhere and become subject to global competition, especially on price.

The global competitor will seek constantly to standardize his offering everywhere. He will digress from this standardization only after exhausting all possibilities to retain it, and he will push for reinstatement of standardization whenever digression and divergence have occurred. He will never assume that the customer is a king who knows his own wishes.

Trouble increasingly stalks companies that lack clarified global focus and remain inattentive to the economics of simplicity and standardization. The most endangered companies in the rapidly evolving world tend to be those that dominate rather small domestic markets with high value-added products for which there are smaller markets elsewhere. With transportation costs proportionately low, distant competitors will enter the now-sheltered markets of those companies with goods produced more cheaply under scale-efficient conditions. Global competition spells the end of domestic territoriality, no matter how diminutive the territory may be.

When the global producer offers his lower costs internationally, his patronage expands exponentially. He not only reaches into distant markets, but also attracts customers who previously held to local preferences and now capitulate to the attractions of lesser prices. The strategy of standardization not only responds to worldwide homogenized markets but also expands those markets with aggressive low pricing. The new technological juggernaut taps an ancient motivation—to make one's money go as far as possible. This is universal—not simply a motivation but actually a need.

The Hedgehog Knows

The difference between the hedgehog and the fox, wrote Sir Isaiah Berlin in distinguishing between Dostoevski and Tolstoy, is that the fox knows a lot about a great many things, but the hedgehog knows everything about one great thing. The multinational corporation knows a lot about a great many countries and congenially adapts to supposed differences. It willingly accepts vestigial national differences, not questioning the possibility of their transformation, not recognizing how the world is ready and eager for the benefit of modernity, especially when the price is right. The multinational corporation's accommodating mode to visible national differences is medieval.

By contrast, the global corporation knows everything about one great thing. It knows about the absolute need to be competitive on a worldwide basis as well as nationally and seeks constantly to drive down prices by standardizing what it sells and how it operates. It treats the world as composed of few standardized markets rather than many customized markets. It actively seeks and vigorously works toward global convergence. Its mission is modernity and its mode, price competition, even when it sells top-of-the-line, high-end products. It knows about the one great thing all nations and people have in common: scarcity.

Nobody takes scarcity lying down; everyone wants more. This in part explains division of labor and specialization of production. They enable people and nations to optimize their conditions through trade. The median is usually money.

Experience teaches that money has three special qualities: scarcity, difficulty of acquisition, and transience. People understandably treat it with respect. Everyone in the increasingly homogenized world market wants products and features that everybody else wants. If the price is low enough, they will take highly standardized world products, even if these aren't exactly what mother said was suitable, what immemorial custom decreed was right, or what market-research fabulists asserted was preferred.

The implacable truth of all modern production—whether of tangible or intangible goods—is that large-scale production of standardized items is generally cheaper within a wide range of volume than small-scale production. Some argue that CAD/CAM will allow companies to manufacture customized products on a small scale—but cheaply. But the argument misses the point. If a company treats the world as one or two distinctive product markets, it can serve the world more economically than if it treats it as three, four, or five product markets.

Why Remaining Differences?   Different cultural preferences, national tastes and standards, and business institutions are vestiges of the past. Some inheritances die gradually; others prosper and expand into mainstream global preferences. So-called ethnic markets are a good example. Chinese food, pita bread, country and western music, pizza, and jazz are everywhere. They are market segments that exist in worldwide proportions. They don't deny or contradict global homogenization but confirm it.

Many of today's differences among nations as to products and their features actually reflect the respectful accommodation of multinational corporations to what they believe are fixed local preferences. They *believe* preferences are fixed, not because they are but because of rigid habits of thinking about what actually is. Most executives in multinational corporations are thoughtlessly accommodating. They falsely presume that marketing means giving the customer what he says he wants rather than trying to understand exactly what he'd like. So they persist with high-cost, customized multinational products and practices instead of pressing hard and pressing properly for global standardization.

I do not advocate the systemic disregard of local or national differences. But a company's sensitivity to such differences does not require that it ignore the possibilities of doing things differently or better.

There are, for example, enormous differences among Middle Eastern countries. Some are socialist, some monarchies, some republics. Some take their legal heritage from the Napoleonic Code, some from the Ottoman Empire, and some from the British common law; except for Israel, all are influenced by Islam. Doing business means personalizing the business relationship in an obsessively intimate fashion. During the month of Ramadan, business discussions can start only after 10 o'clock at night, when people are tired and full of food after a day of fasting. A company must almost certainly have a local partner; a local lawyer is required (as, say, in New York), and irrevocable letters of credit are essential. Yet, as Coca-Cola's Senior Vice President Sam Ayoub noted, "Arabs are much more capable of making distinctions between cultural and religious purposes on the one hand and economic realities on the other than is generally assumed. Islam is compatible with science and modern times."

Barriers to globalization are not confined to the Middle East. The free transfer of technology and data across the boundaries of the European Common Market countries are hampered by legal and financial impediments. And there is resistance to radio and television interference ("pollution") among neighboring European countries.

But the past is a good guide to the future. With persistence and appropriate means, barriers against superior technologies and economics have always fallen. There is no recorded exception where reasonable effort has been made to overcome them. It is very much a matter of time and effort.

A Failure in Global Imagination

Many companies have tried to standardize world practice by exporting domestic products and processes without accommodation or change—and have failed miserably. Their deficiencies have been seized on as evidence of bovine stupidity in the face of abject impossibility. Advocates of global standardization see them as examples of failures in execution.

In fact, poor execution is often an important cause. More important, however, is failure of nerve—failure of imagination.

Consider the case for the introduction of fully automatic home laundry equipment in Western Europe at a time when few homes had even semiautomatic machines. Hoover, Ltd., whose parent company was headquartered in North Canton, Ohio, had a prominent presence in Britain as a producer of vacuum cleaners and washing machines. Due to insufficient demand in the home market and low exports to the European continent, the large washing machine plant in England operated far below capacity. The company needed to sell more of its semiautomatic or automatic machines.

Exhibit 1   Consumer Preferences as to Automatic Washing Machine Features in the 1960s

Features	Great Britain	Italy	West Germany	France	Sweden
Shell dimensions*	34″ and narrow	Low and narrow	34″ and wide	34″ and narrow	34″ and wide
Drum material	Enamel	Enamel	Stainless steel	Enamel	Stainless steel
Loading	Top	Front	Front	Front	Front
Front porthole	Yes/no	Yes	Yes	Yes	Yes
Capacity	5 kilos	4 kilos	6 kilos	5 kilos	6 kilos
Spin speed	700 rpm	400 rpm	850 rpm	600 rpm	800 rpm
Water-heating system	No[†]	Yes	Yes[‡]	Yes	No[†]
Washing action	Agitator	Tumble	Tumble	Agitator	Tumble
Styling features	Inconspicuous appearance	Brightly colored	Indestructible appearance	Elegant appearance	Strong appearance

*34″ height was (in the process of being adopted as) a standard work-surface height in Europe.
[†]Most British and Swedish homes had centrally heated hot water.
[‡]West Germans preferred to launder at temperatures higher than generally provided centrally.

Because it had a "proper" marketing orientation, Hoover conducted consumer preference studies in Britain and each major continental country. The results showed feature preferences clearly enough among several countries (see Exhibit 1).

The incremental unit variable costs (in pounds sterling) of customizing to meet just a few of the national preferences were:

	£	s*	d[†]
Stainless steel versus enamel drum	1	0	0
Porthole window		10	0
Spin speed of 800 rpm versus 700 rpm		15	0
Water heater	2	15	0
6 versus 5 kilos capacity	1	10	0
	£6	10s	0d
	$18.20 at the exchange rate of that time.		

*s = shillings.
[†]d = pence.

Considerable plant investment was needed to meet other preferences.

The lowest retail prices (in pounds sterling) of leading locally produced brands in the various countries were approximately:

U.K.	£110
France	114
West Germany	113
Sweden	134
Italy	57

Product customization in each country would have put Hoover in a poor competitive position on the basis of price, mostly due to the higher manufacturing costs incurred by short production runs for separate features. Because Common Market tariff reduction programs were then incomplete, Hoover also paid tariff duties in each continental country.

How to Make a Creative Analysis   In the Hoover case, an imaginative analysis of automatic washing machine sales in each country would have revealed that:

1. Italian automatics, small in capacity and size, low-powered, without built-in heaters, with porcelain enamel tubs, were priced aggressively

low and were gaining large market shares in all countries, including West Germany.

2. The best-selling automatics in West Germany were heavily advertised (three times more than the next most promoted brand), were ideally suited to national tastes, and were also by far the highest priced machines available in that country.

3. Italy, with the lowest penetration of washing machines of any kind (manual, semiautomatic, or automatic) was rapidly going directly to automatics, skipping the pattern of first buying hand-wringer, manually assisted machines and then semiautomatics.

4. Detergent manufacturers were just beginning to promote the technique of cold-water and tepid-water laundering then used in the United States.

The growing success of small, low-powered, low-speed, low-capacity, low-priced Italian machines, even against the preferred but highly priced and highly promoted brand in West Germany, was significant. It contained a powerful message that was lost on managers confidently wedded to a distorted version of the marketing concept according to which you give the customer what he says he wants. In fact the customers *said* they wanted certain features, but their behavior demonstrated they'd take other features provided the price and the promotion were right.

In this case it was obvious that, under prevailing conditions, people preferred a low-priced automatic over any kind of manual or semiautomatic machine and certainly over higher priced automatics, even though the low-priced automatics failed to fulfill all their expressed preferences. The supposedly meticulous and demanding German consumers violated all expectations by buying the simple, low-priced Italian machines.

It was equally clear that people were profoundly influenced by promotions of automatic washers; in West Germany, the most heavily promoted ideal machine also had the largest market share despite its high price. Two things clearly influenced customers to buy: low price regardless of feature preferences and heavy promotion regardless of price.

Both factors helped homemakers get what they most wanted—the superior benefits bestowed by fully automatic machines.

Hoover should have aggressively sold a simple, standardized high-quality machine at a low price (afforded by the 17% variable cost reduction that the elimination of £6-10-0 worth of extra features made possible). The suggested retail prices could have been somewhat less than £100. The extra funds "saved" by avoiding unnecessary plant modifications would have supported an extended service network and aggressive media promotions.

Hoover's media message should have been: *this is the machine that you, the homemaker, deserve to have to reduce the repetitive heavy daily household burdens, so that you may have more constructive time to spend with your children and your husband.* The promotion should also have targeted the husband to give him, preferably in the presence of his wife, a sense of obligation to provide an automatic washer for her even before he bought an automobile for himself. An aggressively low price, combined with heavy promotion of this kind, would have overcome previously expressed preferences for particular features.

The Hoover case illustrates how the perverse practice of the marketing concept and the absence of any kind of marketing imagination let multinational attitudes survive when customers actually want the benefits of global standardization. The whole project got off on the wrong foot. It asked people what features they wanted in a washing machine rather than what they wanted out of life. Selling a line of products individually tailored to each nation is thoughtless. Managers who took pride in practicing the marketing concept to the fullest did not, in fact, practice it at all. Hoover asked the wrong questions, then applied neither thought nor imagination to the answers. Such companies are like the ethnocentricists in the Middle Ages who saw with everyday clarity the sun revolving around the earth and offered it as Truth. With no additional data but a more searching mind, Copernicus, like the hedgehog, interpreted a more compelling and accurate reality. Data do not yield information except with the intervention of the mind. Information does not yield meaning except with the intervention of imagination.

Accepting the Inevitable

The global corporation accepts for better or for worse that technology drives consumers relentlessly toward the same common goals—alleviation of life's burdens and the expansion of discretionary time and spending power. Its role is profoundly different from what it has been for the ordinary corporation during its brief, turbulent, and remarkably protean history. It orchestrates the twin vectors of technology and globalization for the world's benefit. Neither fate, nor nature, nor God but rather the necessity of commerce created this role.

In the United States two industries became global long before they were consciously aware of it. After over a generation of persistent and acrimonious labor shutdowns, the United Steelworkers of America have not called an industrywide strike since 1959; the United Auto Workers have not shut down General Motors since 1970. Both unions realize that they have become global—shutting down all or most of U.S. manufacturing would not shut out U.S. customers. Overseas suppliers are there to supply the market.

Cracking the Code of Western Markets   Since the theory of the marketing concept emerged a quarter of a century ago, the more managerially advanced corporations have been eager to offer what customers clearly wanted rather than what was merely convenient. They have created marketing departments supported by professional market researchers of awesome and often costly proportions. And they have proliferated extraordinary numbers of operations and product lines—highly tailored products and delivery systems for many different markets, market segments, and nations.

Significantly, Japanese companies operate almost entirely without marketing departments or market research of the kind so prevalent in the West. Yet, in the colorful words of General Electric's chairman John F. Welch, Jr., the Japanese,

coming from a small cluster of resource-poor islands, with an entirely alien culture and an almost impenetrably complex language, have cracked the code of Western markets. They have done it not by looking with mechanistic thoroughness at the way markets are different but rather by searching for meaning with a deeper wisdom. They have discovered the one great thing all markets have in common—an overwhelming desire for dependable, world-standard modernity in all things, at aggressively low prices. In response, they deliver irresistible value everywhere, attracting people with products that market-research technocrats described with superficial certainty as being unsuitable and uncompetitive.

The wider a company's global reach, the greater the number of regional and national preferences it will encounter for certain product features, distribution systems, or promotional media. There will always need to be some accommodation to differences. But the widely prevailing and often unthinking belief in the immutability of these differences is generally mistaken. Evidence of business failure because of lack of accommodation is often evidence of other shortcomings.

Take the case of Revlon in Japan. The company unnecessarily alienated retailers and confused customers by selling world-standardized cosmetics only in elite outlets; then it tried to recover with low-priced world-standardized products in broader distribution, followed by a change in the company president and cutbacks in distribution as costs rose faster than sales. The problem was not that Revlon didn't understand the Japanese market; it didn't do the job right, wavered in its programs, and was impatient to boot.

By contrast, the Outboard Marine Corporation, with imagination, push, and persistence, collapsed long-established three-tiered distribution channels in Europe into a more focused and controllable two-step system—and did so despite the vociferous warnings of local trade groups. It also reduced the number and types of retail outlets. The result was greater improvement in credit and product-installation service to customers, major cost reductions, and sales advances.

In its highly successful introduction of Contac 600 (the timed-release decongestant) into Japan, SmithKline Corporation used 35 wholesalers instead of the 1,000-plus that established practice required. Daily contacts with the wholesalers and key retailers, also in violation of established practice, supplemented the plan, and it worked.

Denied access to established distribution institutions in the United States, Komatsu, the Japanese manufacturer of lightweight farm machinery, entered the market through over-the-road construction equipment dealers in rural areas of the Sunbelt, where farms are smaller, the soil sandier and easier to work. Here inexperienced distributors were able to attract customers on the basis of Komatsu's product and price appropriateness.

In cases of successful challenge to prevailing institutions and practices, a combination of product reliability and quality, strong and sustained support systems, aggressively low prices, and sales-compensation packages, as well as audacity and implacability, circumvented, shattered, and transformed very different distribution systems. Instead of resentment, there was admiration.

Still, some differences between nations are unyielding, even in a world of microprocessors. In the United States almost all manufacturers of microprocessors check them for reliability through a so-called parallel system of testing. Japan prefers the totally different sequential testing system. So Teradyne Corporation, the world's largest producer of microprocessor test equipment, makes one line for the United States and one for Japan. That's easy.

What's not so easy for Teradyne is to know how best to organize and manage, in this instance, its marketing effort. Companies can organize by product, region, function, or by using some combination of these. A company can have separate marketing organizations for Japan and for the United States, or it can have separate product groups, one working largely in Japan and the other in the United States. A single manufacturing facility or marketing operation might service both markets, or a company might use separate marketing operations for each.

Questions arise if the company organizes by product. In the case of Teradyne, should the group handling the parallel system, whose major market is the United States, sell in Japan and compete with the group focused on the Japanese market? If the company organizes regionally, how do regional groups divide their efforts between promoting the parallel versus the sequential system? If the company organizes in terms of function, how does it get commitment in marketing, for example, for one line instead of the other?

There is no one reliably right answer—no one formula by which to get it. There isn't even a satisfactory contingent answer.[3] What works well for one company or one place may fail for another in precisely the same place, depending on the capabilities, histories, reputations, resources, and even the cultures of both.

The Earth Is Flat

The differences that persist throughout the world despite its globalization affirm an ancient dictum of economics—that things are driven by what happens at the margin, not at the core. Thus, in ordinary competitive analysis, what's important is not the average price but the marginal price; what happens not in the usual case but at the interface of newly erupting conditions. What counts in commercial affairs is what happens at the cutting edge. What is most striking today is the underlying similarities of what is happening now to national preferences at the margin. These similarities at the cutting edge cumulatively form an overwhelming, predominant commonality everywhere.

To refer to the persistence of economic nationalism (protective and subsidized trade practices, special tax aids, or restrictions for home market producers) as a barrier to the globalization of markets is to make a valid point. Economic nationalism does have a powerful persistence. But, as with the present almost totally smooth internationalization

---

[3]For a discussion of multinational reorganization, see Christopher A. Bartlett, "MNCs: Get Off the Reorganization Merry-Go-Round," *HBR,* March–April 1983, p. 138.

of investment capital, the past alone does not shape or predict the future.

Reality is not a fixed paradigm, dominated by immemorial customs and derived attitudes, heedless of powerful and abundant new forces. The world is becoming increasingly informed about the liberating and enhancing possibilities of modernity. The persistence of the inherited varieties of national preferences rests uneasily on increasing evidence of, and restlessness regarding, their inefficiency, costliness, and confinement. The historic past, and the national differences respecting commerce and industry it spawned and fostered everywhere, is now subject to relatively easy transformation.

Cosmopolitanism is no longer the monopoly of the intellectual and leisure classes; it is becoming the established property and defining characteristic of all sectors everywhere in the world. Gradually and irresistibly it breaks down the walls of economic insularity, nationalism, and chauvinism. What we see today as escalating commercial nationalism is simply the last violent death rattle of an obsolete institution.

Companies that adapt to and capitalize on economic convergence can still make distinctions and adjustments in different markets. Persistent differences in the world are consistent with fundamental underlying commonalities; they often complement rather than oppose each other—in business as they do in physics. There is, in physics, simultaneously matter and anti-matter working in symbiotic harmony.

The earth is round, but for most purposes it's sensible to treat it as flat. Space is curved, but not much for everyday life here on earth.

Divergence from established practice happens all the time. But the multinational mind, warped into circumspection and timidity by years of stumbles and transnational troubles, now rarely challenges existing overseas practices. More often it considers any departure from inherited domestic routines as mindless, disrespectful, or impossible. It is the mind of a bygone day.

The successful global corporation does not abjure customization or differentiation for the requirements of markets that differ in product preferences, spending patterns, shopping preferences, and institutional or legal arrangements. But the global corporation accepts and adjusts to these differences only reluctantly, only after relentlessly testing their immutability, after trying in various ways to circumvent and reshape them as we saw in the cases of Outboard Marine in Europe, Smith-Kline in Japan, and Komatsu in the United States.

There is only one significant respect in which a company's activities around the world are important, and this is in what it produces and how it sells. Everything else derives from, and is subsidiary to, these activities.

The purpose of business is to get and keep a customer. Or, to use Peter Drucker's more refined construction, to *create* and keep a customer. A company must be wedded to the ideal of innovation—offering better or more preferred products in such combinations of ways, means, places, and at such prices that prospects *prefer* doing business with the company rather than with others.

Preferences are constantly shaped and reshaped. Within our global commonality enormous variety constantly asserts itself and thrives, as can be seen within the world's single largest domestic market, the United States. But in the process of world homogenization, modern markets expand to reach cost-reducing global proportions. With better and cheaper communication and transport, even small local market segments hitherto protected from distant competitors now feel the pressure of their presence. Nobody is safe from global reach and the irresistible economies of scale.

Two vectors shape the world—technology and globalization. The first helps determine human preferences; the second, economic realities. Regardless of how much preferences evolve and diverge, they also gradually converge and form markets where economies of scale lead to reduction of costs and prices.

The modern global corporation contrasts powerfully with the aging multinational corporation. Instead of adapting to superficial and even entrenched differences within and between nations, it will seek sensibly to force suitably standardized products and practices on the entire globe. They are exactly what the world will take, if they come also with low prices, high quality, and blessed reliability. The global company will operate, in this regard, precisely as Henry Kissinger wrote in *Years of Upheaval* about the continuing Japanese economic success—"voracious in its collection of information, impervious to pressure, and implacable in execution."

Given what is everywhere the purpose of commerce, the global company will shape the vectors of technology and globalization into its great strategic fecundity. It will systematically push these vectors toward their own convergence, offering everyone simultaneously high-quality, more or less standardized products at optimally low prices, thereby achieving for itself vastly expanded markets and profits. Companies that do not adapt to the new global realities will become victims of those that do.

Reading 3-2   Global Strategy . . . in a World of Nations?

George S. Yip

Whether to globalize and how to globalize, have become two of the most burning strategy issues for managers around the world. Many forces are driving companies around the world to globalize by expanding their participation in foreign markets. Almost every product market in the major world economies—computers, fast food, nuts and bolts—has foreign competitors. Trade barriers are also falling; the recent United States/Canada trade agreement and the impending 1992 harmonization in the European Community are the two most dramatic examples. Japan is gradually opening up its long barricaded markets. Maturity in domestic markets is also driving companies to seek international expansion. This is particularly true of U.S. companies that, nourished by the huge domestic market, have typically lagged behind their European and Japanese rivals in internationalization.

Companies are also seeking to globalize by integrating their worldwide strategy. Such global integration contrasts with the multinational approach whereby companies set up country subsidiaries that design, produce, and market products or services tailored to local needs. This multinational model (also described as a "multidomestic strategy") is now in question.[1] Several changes seem to increase the likelihood that, in some industries, a global strategy will be more successful than a multidomestic one. One of these changes, as argued forcefully and controversially by Levitt, is the growing similarity of what citizens of different countries want to buy.[2] Other changes include the reduction of tariff and nontariff barriers, technology investments that are becoming too expensive to amortize

George S. Yip is visiting associate professor at the School of Business Administration, Georgetown University, and also director of the PIMS Global Strategy Program. Dr. Yip holds the B.A. and M.A. degrees from Cambridge University, the M.B.A. degree from Cranfield Institute of Technology, and the M.B.A. and D.B.A. degrees from the Graduate School of Business Administration, Harvard University. His business experience includes marketing and advertising responsibilities with Unilever and Lintas and management consulting with Price Waterhouse and the MAC Group. He is the author of *Barriers to Entry* and of numerous articles.

[1]See T. Hout, M. E. Porter, and E. Rudden, "How Global Companies Win Out," *Harvard Business Review,* September–October 1982, pp. 98–108. My framework, developed in this article, is based in part on M. E. Porter's pioneering work on global strategy. His ideas are further developed in M. E. Porter, "Competition in Global Industries: A Conceptual Framework," in *Competition in Global Industries,* ed. M. E. Porter (Boston: Harvard Business School Press, 1986). Bartlett and Ghoshal define a "transnational industry" that is somewhat similar to Porter's "global industry." See: C. A. Bartlett and S. Ghoshal, "Managing across Borders: New Strategic Requirements," *Sloan Management Review,* Summer 1987, pp. 7–17.

[2]T. Levitt, "The Globalization of Markets," *Harvard Business Review,* May–June 1983, pp. 92–102.

Figure 1   Total Global Strategy

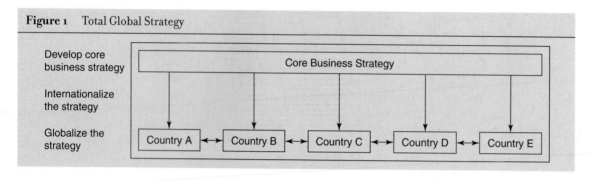

Figure 2   Framework of Global Strategy Forces

in one market only, and competitors that are globalizing the rules of the game.

Companies want to know how to globalize—in other words, expand market participation—and how to develop an integrated worldwide strategy. As depicted in Figure 1, three steps are essential in developing a total worldwide strategy:

- Developing the core strategy—the basis of sustainable competitive advantage. It is usually developed for the home country first.
- Internationalizing the core strategy through international expansion of activities and through adaptation.
- Globalizing the international strategy by integrating the strategy across countries.

Multinational companies know the first two well. They know the third step less well since globaliza-

tion runs counter to the accepted wisdom of tailoring for national markets.[3]

This article makes a case for how a global strategy might work and directs managers toward opportunities to exploit globalization. It also presents the drawbacks and costs of globalization. Figure 2 lays out a framework for thinking through globalization issues.[4]

Industry globalization drivers (underlying market, cost, and other industry conditions) are external determined, while global strategy levers are choices

---

[3]These obstacles are laid out in one of the rejoinders provoked by Levitt's article. See: S. P. Douglas and Y. Wind, "The Myth of Globalization," *Columbia Journal of World Business,* Winter 1987, pp. 19–29.

[4]For a more theoretical exposition of this framework see: G. S. Yip, "An Integrated Approach to Global Competitive Strategy," in *Frontiers of Management,* ed. R. Mansfield (London: Routledge, forthcoming).

Table 1   Globalization Dimensions/Global Strategy Levers

Dimension	Setting for Pure Multidomestic Strategy	Setting for Pure Global Strategy
Market participation	No particular pattern	Significant share in major markets
Product offering	Fully customized in each country	Fully standardized worldwide
Location of value-added activities	All activities in each country	Concentrated—one activity in each (different) country
Marketing approach	Local	Uniform worldwide
Competitive moves	Stand-alone by country	Integrated across countries

available to the worldwide business. Drivers create the potential for a multinational business to achieve the benefits of global strategy. To achieve these benefits, a multinational business needs to set its *global strategy levers* (e.g., use of product standardization) appropriately to industry drivers, and to the position and resources of the business and its parent company.[5] The organization's ability to implement the strategy affects how well the benefits can be achieved.

What Is Global Strategy?

Setting strategy for a worldwide business requires making choices along a number of strategic dimensions. Table 1 lists five such dimensions or "global strategy levers" and their respective positions under a pure multidomestic strategy and a pure global strategy. Intermediate positions are, of course, feasible. For each dimension, a multidomestic strategy seeks to maximize worldwide performance by maximizing local competitive advantage, revenues, or profits: a global strategy seeks to maximize worldwide performance through sharing and integration.

Market Participation   In a multidomestic strategy, countries are selected on the basis of their stand-alone potential for revenues and profits. In a

global strategy, countries need to be selected for their potential contribution to globalization benefits. This may mean entering a market that is unattractive in its own right, but has global strategic significance, such as the home market of a global competitor. Or it may mean building share in a limited number of key markets rather than undertaking more widespread coverage. A pattern of major share in major markets is advocated in Ohmae's USA-Europe-Japan "triad" concept.[6] In contrast, under a multidomestic strategy, no particular pattern of participation is required—rather, the pattern accrues from the pursuit of local advantage. The Electrolux Group, the Swedish appliance giant, is pursuing a strategy of building significant share in major world markets. The company aims to be the first global appliance maker. In 1986, Electrolux took over Zanussi Industries to become the top producer of appliances in Western Europe. Later that year, Electrolux acquired White Consolidated Industries, the third largest American appliance manufacturer.

Product Offering   In a multidomestic strategy, the products offered in each country are tailored to local needs. In a global strategy, the ideal is a standardized core product that requires minimal local adaptation. Cost reduction is usually the most important benefit of product standardization. Levitt has made the most extreme case for product

[5]The concept of the global strategy lever was first presented in: G. S. Yip, P. M. Loewe, and M. Y. Yoshino, "How to Take Your Company to the Global Market," *Columbia Journal of World Business,* Winter 1988, pp. 37–48.

[6]K. Ohmae, *Triad Power: The Coming Shape of Global Competition* (New York: Free Press, 1985).

standardization. Others stress the need for flexibility, or the need for a broad product portfolio, with many product varieties in order to share technologies and distribution channels.[7] In practice, some multinationals have pursued product standardization to a greater or lesser extent.[8] Differing worldwide needs can be met by adapting a standardized core product. In the early 1970s, sales of the Boeing 737 began to level off. Boeing turned to developing countries as an attractive new market, but found initially that its product did not fit the new environments. Because of the shortness of runways, their greater softness, and the lower technical expertise of their pilots, the planes tended to bounce a great deal. When the planes bounced on landing, the brakes failed. To fix this problem, Boeing modified the design by adding thrust to the engines, redesigning the wings and landing gear, and installing tires with lower pressure. These adaptations to a standardized core product enabled the 737 to become the best-selling plane in history.

Location of Value-Added Activities   In a multidomestic strategy, all or most of the value chain is reproduced in every country. In another type of international strategy—exporting—most of the value chain is kept in one country. In a global strategy, costs are reduced by breaking up the value chain so each activity may be conducted in a different country. One value chain strategy is partial concentration and partial duplication. The key feature of a global position on this dimension is the strategic placement of the value chain around the globe.

Many electronics companies now locate part or all of their manufacturing operations in Southeast Asia because of that region's low-cost, skilled labor. In addition, a key component (the semiconductor chip) is very cheap there. Under the United States-Japan Semiconductor Agreement, the Japanese agreed not to sell chips in the United States below cost. But in an industry plagued by overcapacity, the chips had to go somewhere. The agreement resulted in Japanese chips being sold below cost in Southeast Asia. The lower cost of chips combined with the lower labor cost has attracted many manufacturers of computers and other electronic equipment to Southeast Asia.

Marketing Approach   In a multidomestic strategy, marketing is fully tailored for each country, being developed locally. In a global strategy, a uniform marketing approach is applied around the world, although not all elements of the marketing mix need be uniform.[9] Unilever achieved great success with a fabric softener that used a globally common positioning, advertising theme, and symbol (a teddy bear), but a brand name that varied by country. Similarly, a product that serves a common need can be geographically expanded with a uniform marketing program, despite differences in marketing environments.

Competitive Moves   In a multidomestic strategy, the managers in each country make competitive moves without regard for what happens in other countries. In a global strategy, competitive moves are integrated across countries. The same type of move is made in different countries at the same time or in a systematic sequence: A competitor is attacked in one country in order to drain its resources for another country, or a competitive attack in one country is countered in a different country. Perhaps the best example is the counterattack in a competitor's home market as a parry to an attack on one's own home market. Integration of competitive strategy is rarely practiced, except perhaps by some Japanese companies.[10]

[7]G. Hamel and C. K. Prahalad, "Do You Really Have a Global Strategy?" *Harvard Business Review,* July–August, 1985, pp. 139–148; B. Kogut, "Designing Global Strategies: Profiting from Operational Flexibility," *Sloan Management Review,* Fall 1985, pp. 27–38.

[8]P. G. P. Walters, "International Marketing Policy: A Discussion of the Standardization Construct and Its Relevance for Corporate Policy," *Journal of International Business Studies,* Summer 1986, pp. 55–69.

[9]For a discussion of the possibilities and merits of uniform marketing see: R. D. Buzzell, "Can You Standardize Multinational Marketing?" *Harvard Business Review,* November–December 1968, pp. 102–13; and J. A. Quelch and E. J. Hoff, "Customizing Global Marketing," *Harvard Business Review,* May–June 1986, pp. 59–68.

[10]P. Kotler et al., *The New Competition* (Englewood Cliffs, N.J.: Prentice Hall, 1985), p. 174.

Bridgestone Corporation, the Japanese tire manufacturer, tried to integrate its competitive moves in response to global consolidation by its major competitors—Continental AG's acquisition of Gencorp's General Tire and Rubber Company, General Tire's joint venture with two Japanese tire makers, and Sumitomo's acquisition of an interest in Dunlop Tire. These competitive actions forced Bridgestone to establish a presence in the major U.S. market in order to maintain its position in the world tire market. To this end, Bridgestone formed a joint venture to own and manage Firestone Corporation's worldwide tire business. This joint venture also allowed Bridgestone to gain access to Firestone's European plants.

Benefits of a Global Strategy

Companies that use global strategy levers can achieve one or more of these benefits (see Figure 3):[11]

- Cost reductions;
- Improved quality of products and programs;
- Enhanced customer preference; and
- Increased competitive leverage.

Cost Reductions   An integrated global strategy can reduce worldwide costs in several ways. A company can increase the benefits from economies of scale by *pooling production or other activities* for two or more countries. Understanding the potential benefit of these economies of scale, Sony Corporation has concentrated its compact disc production in Terre Haute, Indiana, and Salzburg, Austria.

A second way to cut costs is by *exploiting lower factor costs* by moving manufacturing or other activities to low-cost countries. This approach has, of course, motivated the recent surge of offshore manufacturing, particularly by U.S. firms. For example, the Mexican side of the U.S.-Mexico border is now crowded with "maquiladoras"—manufacturing plants set up and run by U.S. companies using Mexican labor.

Global strategy can also cut costs by *exploiting flexibility*. A company with manufacturing locations in several countries can move production from location to location on short notice to take advantage of the lowest costs at a given time. Dow Chemical takes this approach to minimize the cost of producing chemicals. Dow uses a linear programming model that takes account of international differences in exchange rates, tax rates, and transportation and labor costs. The model comes up with the best mix of production volume by location for each planning period.

An integrated global strategy can also reduce costs by *enhancing bargaining power*. A company whose strategy allows for switching production among different countries greatly increases its bargaining power with suppliers, workers, and host governments. Labor unions in European countries are very concerned that the creation of the single European market after 1992 will allow companies to switch production from country to country at will. This integrated production strategy would greatly enhance companies' bargaining power at the expense of unions.

Improved Quality of Products and Programs Under a global strategy, companies focus on a smaller number of products and programs than under a multidomestic strategy. This concentration can improve both product and program quality. Global focus is one reason for Japanese success in automobiles. Toyota markets a far smaller number of models around the world than does General Motors, even allowing for its unit sales being half that of General Motors's. Toyota has concentrated on improving its few models while General Motors has fragmented its development funds. For example, the Toyota Camry is the U.S. version of a basic worldwide model and is the successor to a long line of development efforts. The Camry is consistently rated as the best in its class of medium-sized cars. In contrast, General Motors's Pontiac Fiero started out as one of the most successful small sports cars, but was recently withdrawn. Industry observers blamed this on a failure to invest development money to overcome minor problems.

---

[11]Figure 3 is also presented in Yip (forthcoming).

Figure 3 How Global Strategy Levers Achieve Globalization Benefits

Global Strategy Levers	Benefits				Major Drawbacks
	Cost Reduction	Improved Quality of Products and Programs	Enhanced Customer Preference	Increased Competitive Leverage	All Levers Incur Coordination Costs, Plus
Major market participation	Increases volume for economies of scale		Via global availability, global serviceability, and global recognition	Advantage of earlier entry Provides more sites for attack and counterattack, hostage for good behavior	Earlier or greater commitment to a market man warranted on own merits
Product standardization	Reduces duplication of development efforts Allows concentration of production to exploit economies of scale	Focuses development and management resources	Allows consumers to use familiar product while abroad Allows organizations to use same product across country units	Basis for low-cost invasion of markets	Less responsive to local needs
Activity concentration	Reduces duplication of activities Helps exploit economies of scale Exploits differences in country factor costs Partial concentration allows flexibility versus currency charges, and versus bargaining parties	Focuses effort Allows more consistent quality control		Allows maintenance of cost advantage independent of local conditions	Distances activities from the customer Increases currency risk
Uniform marketing	Reduces design and production costs of marketing programs	Focuses talent and resources Leverages scarce, good ideas	Reinforces marketing messages by exposing customer to same mix in different countries		Reduces adaptation to local customer behavior and marketing environment
Integrated competitive moves				Provides more options and leverage in attack and defense	Local competitiveness may be sacrificed

Enhanced Customer Preference   Global availability, serviceability, and recognition can enhance customer preference through reinforcement. Soft drink and fast food companies are, of course, leading exponents of this strategy. Many suppliers of financial services, such as credit cards, must have a global presence because their service is travel-related. Manufacturers of industrial products can also exploit this benefit. A supplier that can provide a multinational customer with a standard product around the world gains from worldwide familiarity. Computer manufacturers have long pursued this strategy.

Increased Competitive Leverage   A global strategy provides more points from which to attack and counterattack competitors. In an effort to prevent the Japanese from becoming a competitive nuisance in disposable syringes, Becton Dickinson, a major U.S. medical products company, decided to enter three markets in Japan's backyard. Becton entered the Hong Kong, Singapore, and Philippine markets to prevent further Japanese expansions.[12]

▌ Drawbacks of Global Strategy

Globalization can incur significant management costs through increased coordination, reporting requirements, and even added staff. It can also reduce the firm's effectiveness in individual countries if overcentralization hurts local motivation and morale. In addition, each global strategy lever has particular drawbacks.

A global strategy approach to *market participation* can incur an earlier or greater commitment to a market than is warranted on its own merits. Many American companies, such as Motorola, are struggling to penetrate Japanese markets, more in order to enhance their global competitive position than to make money in Japan for its own sake.

Product standardization can result in a product that does not entirely satisfy *any* customers. When

companies first internationalize, they often offer their standard domestic product without adapting it for other countries, and suffer the consequences. For example, Procter & Gamble stumbled recently when it introduced Cheer laundry detergent in Japan without changing the U.S. product or marketing message (that the detergent was effective in all temperatures). After experiencing serious losses, P&G discovered two instances of insufficient adaptation. First, the detergent did not suds up as it should because the Japanese use a great deal of fabric softener. Second, the Japanese usually wash clothes in either cold tap water or bath water, so the claim of working in all temperatures was irrelevant. Cheer became successful in Japan only after the product was reformulated and the marketing message was changed.

A globally standardized product is designed for the global market but can seldom satisfy all needs in all countries. For instance, Canon, a Japanese company, sacrificed the ability to copy certain Japanese paper sizes when it first designed a photocopier for the global market.

Activity concentration distances customers and can result in lower responsiveness and flexibility. It also increases currency risk by incurring costs and revenues in different countries. Recently volatile exchange rates have required companies that concentrate their production to hedge their currency exposure.

Uniform marketing can reduce adaptation to local customer behavior. For example, the head office of British Airways mandated that every country use the "Manhattan Landing" television commercial developed by advertising agency Saatchi and Saatchi. While the commercial did win many awards, it has been criticized for using a visual image (New York City) that was not widely recognized in many countries.

Integrated competitive moves can mean sacrificing revenues, profits, or competitive position in individual countries, particularly when the subsidiary in one country is asked to attack a global competitor in order to send a signal or to divert that competitor's resources from another country.

▌ [12]M. R. Cvar, "Case Studies in Global Competition," in Porter (1986).

Figure 4. Globalization Potential of Industry versus Globalization Strategy

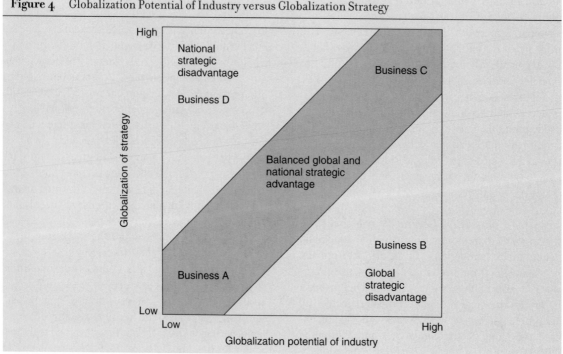

Finding the Balance

The most successful worldwide strategies find a balance between overglobalizing and underglobalizing. The ideal strategy matches the level of strategy globalization to the globalization potential of the industry. In Figure 4 both Business A and Business C achieve balanced global and national strategic advantage. Business A does so with a low level of strategy globalization to match the low globalization potential of its industry (e.g., frozen food products). Business C uses a high level of strategy globalization to match the high globalization potential of its industry (e.g., computer equipment). Business B is at a global disadvantage because it uses a strategy that is less globalized than the potential offered by its industry. The business is failing to exploit potential global benefits such as cost savings via product standardization. Business D is at a national disadvantage because it is too

globalized relative to the potential offered by its industry. The business is not tailoring its products and programs as much as it should. While there is no systematic evidence, executives' comments suggest that far more businesses suffer from insufficient globalization than from excessive globalization. Figure 4 is oversimplified in that it shows only one overall dimension for both strategy and industry potential. As argued earlier, a global strategy has five major dimensions and many subdimensions. Similarly, the potential of industry globalization is multidimensional.

Industry Globalization Drivers

To achieve the benefits of globalization, the managers of a worldwide business need to recognize when industry globalization drivers (industry conditions) provide the opportunity to use global strategy levers. These drivers can be grouped in four categories: market, cost, governmental, and competitive. Each industry globalization driver affects the potential use of global strategy levers (see Figure 5).

Market Drivers   Market globalization drivers depend on customer behavior and the structure of distribution channels. These drivers affect the use of all five global strategy levers.

- *Homogeneous Customer Needs*. When customers in different countries want essentially the same type of product or service (or can be so persuaded), opportunities arise to market a standardized product. Understanding which aspects of the product can be standardized and which should be customized is key. In addition, homogeneous needs make participation in a large number of markets easier because fewer different product offerings need to be developed and supported.

- *Global Customers*. Global customers buy on a centralized or coordinated basis for decentralized use. The existence of global customers both allows and requires a uniform marketing program. There are two types of global customers: national and multinational. A national global customer searches the world for suppliers but uses the purchased product or service in one country. National defense agencies are a good example. A multinational global customer also searches the world for suppliers, but uses the purchased product or service in many countries. The World Health Organization's purchase of medical products is an example. Multinational global customers are particularly challenging to serve and often require a global account management program. Companies that implement such programs have to beware of global customers using the unified account management to extract lower global prices. Having a single global account manager makes it easier for a global customer to negotiate a single global price. Typically, the global customer pushes for the lowest country price to become the global price. But a good global account manager should be able to justify differences in prices across countries.

- *Global Channels*. Analogous to global customers, channels of distribution may buy on a global or at least a regional basis. Global channels or middlemen are also important in exploiting differences in prices by buying at a lower price in one country and selling at a higher price in another country. Their presence makes it more necessary for a business to rationalize its worldwide pricing. Global channels are rare, but regionwide channels are increasing in number, particularly in European grocery distribution and retailing.

- *Transferable Marketing*. The buying decision may be such that marketing elements, such as brand names and advertising, require little local adaptation. Such transferability enables firms to use uniform marketing strategies and facilitates expanded participation in markets. A worldwide business can also adapt its brand names and advertising campaigns to make them more transferable, or, even better, design global ones to start with. Offsetting risks include the blandness of uniformly acceptable brand names or advertising, and the vulnerability of relying on a single brand franchise.

Cost Drivers   Cost drivers depend on the economics of the business; they particularly affect activity concentration.

- *Economies of Scale and Scope*. A single-country market may not be large enough for the local business to achieve all possible economies of scale or scope. Scale at a given location can be increased through participation in multiple markets combined with product standardization or concentration of selected value activities. Corresponding risks include rigidity and vulnerability to disruption.

In the past few years, the economics of the electronics industry have shifted. As the cost of circuits has decreased, the economic advantage has gone to companies that can produce the lowest-cost components. Size has become a major asset. Thomson, the French electronics firm, understands the need to have a worldwide presence in an industry characterized by economies of scale. In 1987, Thomson greatly increased both its operating scale and its global coverage by acquiring the RCA television business from General Electric.

Figure 5 Effects of Industry Globalization Drivers on the Potential Use of Global Strategy Levers

			Strategy Levers		
Industry Drivers	Major Market Participation	Product Standardization	Activity Concentration	Uniform Marketing	Integrated Competitive Moves
Market					
Homogeneous needs	Fewer varieties needed to serve many markets	Standardized product is more acceptable			Allows sequenced invasion of markets
Global customers			Marketing process has to be coordinated	Marketing content needs to be uniform	
Global channels			Marketing process has to be coordinated	Marketing content needs to be uniform	
Transferable marketing	Easier to expand internationally			Allows use of global brands advertising, etc.	
Cost					
Economies of scale and scope	Multiple markets needed to reach economic scale	Standardization needed to reach economic scale	Concentration helps reach economic scale	Uniform marketing cuts program development and production costs	Country interdependence affects overall scale economies
Learning and experience	Multiple markets accelerate learning	Standardization accelerates learning	Concentration accelerates learning		
Sourcing efficiencies			Centralized purchasing exploits efficiencies		
Favorable logistics	Easier to expand internationally		Allows concentrated production		Allows export competition

Cost					
Differences in country costs and skills			Exploited by activity concentration		Increase vulnerability of high-cost countries
Product development costs	Multiple markets needed to pay back investment	Standardization reduces development needs	Concentration cuts cost of development		
Government					
Favorable trade policies	Affects nature extent of participation	May require or prevent product features	Local content rules affect extent of concentration possible		Integration needed to deal with competitive effects of tariffs/subsidies
Compatible technical standards	Affects markets that can be entered	Affects standardization possible			
Common marketing regulations				Affects approaches possible	
Competitive					
Interdependence of countries	More participation leverages benefits	Accept tradeoffs to get best global product	Locate key activities in lead countries	Use lead country to develop programs	Integration needed to exploit benefits
Competitors globalized or might globalize	Expand to match or preempt	Match or preempt	Match or preempt	Match or preempt	Integration needed to exploit benefits

• *Learning and Experience.* Even if economies of scope and scale are exhausted, expanded market participation and activity concentration can accelerate the accumulation of learning and experience. The steeper the learning and experience curves, the greater the potential benefit will be. Managers should beware, though, of the usual danger in pursuing experience curve strategies—overaggressive pricing that destroys not just the competition but the market as well. Prices get so low that profit is insufficient to sustain any competitor.

• *Sourcing Efficiencies.* Centralized purchasing of new materials can significantly lower costs. Himont began as a joint venture between Hercules Inc. of the United States and Montedison Petrolchimica SpA of Italy, and is the leader in the global polypropylene market. Central to Himont's strategy is global coordination among manufacturing facilities in the purchase of raw materials, particularly monomer, the key ingredient in polypropylene production. Rationalization of raw material orders significantly strengthens the venture's low-cost production advantage.

• *Favorable Logistics.* A favorable ratio of sales value to transportation cost enhances the company's ability to concentrate production. Other logistical factors include nonperishability, the absence of time urgency, and little need for location close to customer facilities. Even the shape of the product can make a crucial difference. Cardboard tubes, such as those used as cores for textiles, cannot be shipped economically because they are mostly air. In contrast, cardboard cones are transportable because many units can be stacked in the same space.

• *Differences in Country Costs and Skills.* Factor costs generally vary across countries; this is particularly true in certain industries. The availability of particular skills also varies. Concentration of activities in low-cost or high-skill countries can increase productivity and reduce costs, but managers need to anticipate the danger of training future offshore competitors.[13]

Under attack from lower-priced cars, Volkswagen has needed to reduce its costs. It is doing so by concentrating its production to take advantage of the differences in various country costs. In Spain, hourly labor costs are below DM 20 per hour, while those in West Germany are over DM 40 per hour. To take advantage of this cost differential, the company moved production of Polos from Wolfsburg to Spain, freeing up the high-wage German labor to produce the higher-priced Golf cars. Another example of this concentration occurred when Volkswagen shut down its New Stanton, Pennsylvania, plant that manufactured Golfs and Jettas. The lower end of the U.S. market would be served by its low-wage Brazilian facility that produced the Fox. The higher end of the product line (Jetta and Golf) would be exported from Europe. This concentration and coordination of production has enabled the company to lower costs substantially.

• *Product Development Costs.* Product development costs can be reduced by developing a few global or regional products rather than many national products. The automobile industry is characterized by long product development periods and high product development costs. One reason for the high costs is duplication of effort across countries. The Ford Motor Company's "Centers of Excellence" program aims to reduce these duplicating efforts and to exploit the differing expertise of Ford specialists worldwide. As part of the concentrated effort, Ford of Europe is designing a common platform for all compacts, while Ford of North America is developing platforms for the replacement of the midsized Taurus and Sable. This concentration of design is estimated to save "hundreds of millions of dollars per model by eliminating duplicative efforts and saving on retooling factories."[14]

Governmental Drivers Government globalization drivers depend on the rules set by national governments and affect the use of all global strategy levers.

[13]See: C. C. Markides and N. Berg, "Manufacturing Offshore Is Bad Business," *Harvard Business Review,* September–October 1988, pp. 113–20.

[14]"Can Ford Stay on Top?" *Business Week,* September 28, 1987, pp. 78–86.

• *Favorable Trade Policies.* Host governments affect globalization potential through import tariffs and quotas, nontariff barriers, export subsidies, local content requirements, currency and capital flow restrictions, and requirements on technology transfer.[15] Host government policies can make it difficult to use the global levers of major market participation, product standardization, activity concentration, and uniform marketing; they also affect the integrated-competitive-moves lever.

National trade policies constrain companies' concentration of manufacturing activities. Aggressive U.S. government actions including threats on tariffs, quotas, and protectionist measures have helped convince Japanese automakers and other manufacturers to give up their concentration of manufacturing in Japan. Reluctantly, Japanese companies are opening plants in the United States. Honda has even made a public relations virtue out of necessity. It recently gave great publicity to the first shipment of a U.S.-made Honda car to Japan.

The easing of government restrictions can set off a rush for expanded market participation. European Community regulations for banking and financial services will be among those harmonized in 1992. The European Community decision to permit the free flow of capital along member countries has led European financial institutions to jockey for position. Until recently, the Deutsche Bank had only 15 offices outside of Germany, but it has recently established a major presence in the French market. In 1987, Deutsche Bank also moved into the Italian market by acquiring Bank of America's 100 branches there. Other financial organizations, such as J. P. Morgan of the United States, Swiss Bank Corporation, and the S. P. Warburg Group in Britain have increased their participation in major European markets through acquisitions.

• *Compatible Technical Standards.* Differences in technical standards, especially government-imposed standards, limit the extent to which products can be standardized. Often, standards are set with protectionism in mind. Motorola found that many of their electronics products were excluded from the Japanese market because these products operated at a higher frequency than was permitted in Japan.

• *Common Marketing Regulations.* The marketing environment of individual countries affects the extent to which uniform global marketing approaches can be used. Certain types of media may be prohibited or restricted. For example, the United States is far more liberal than Europe about the kinds of advertising claims that can be made on television. The British authorities even veto the depiction of socially undesirable behavior. For example, British television authorities do not allow scenes of children pestering their parents to buy a product. And, of course, the use of sex is different. As one extreme, France is far more liberal than the United States about sex in advertising. Various promotional devices, such as lotteries, may also be restricted.

Competitive Drivers Market, cost, and governmental globalization drivers are essentially fixed for an industry at any given time. Competitors can play only a limited role in affecting these factors (although a sustained effort can bring about change, particularly in the case of consumer preferences). In contrast, competitive drivers are entirely in the realm of competitor choice. Competitors can raise the globalization potential of their industry and spur the need for a response on the global strategy levers.

• *Interdependence of Countries.* A competitor may create competitive interdependence among countries by pursuing a global strategy. The basic mechanism is through sharing of activities. When activities such as production are shared among countries, a competitor's market share in one country affects its scale and overall cost position in the shared activities. Changes in that scale and cost will affect its competitive position in all countries dependent on the shared activities. Less directly, customers may

---

[15]Three public sector activities that can protect domestic competitors are blocking access to the domestic market, providing subsidies, and creating spillovers in research and development. See: M. A. Spence, "Industrial Organizational and Competitive Advantage in Multinational Industries," *American Economic Review* 74 (May 1984), pp. 356–60.

view market position in a lead country as an indicator of overall quality. Companies frequently promote a product as, for example, "the leading brand in the United States." Other competitors then need to respond via increased market participation, uniform marketing, or integrated competitive strategy to avoid a downward spiral of sequentially weakened positions in individual countries.

In the automobile industry, where economies of scale are significant and where sharing activities can lower costs, markets have significant competitive interdependence. As companies like Ford and Volkswagen concentrate production and become more cost competitive with the Japanese manufacturers, the Japanese are pressured to enter more markets so that increased production volume will lower costs. Whether conscious of this or not, Toyota has begun a concerted effort to penetrate the German market: Between 1984 and 1987, Toyota doubled the number of cars produced for the German market.

• *Globalized Competitors.* More specifically, attaching or preempting individual competitor moves may be necessary. These moves include expanding into or within major markets, being the first to introduce a standardized product, or being the first to use a uniform marketing program.

The need to preempt a global competitor can spur increased market participation. In 1986, Unilever, the European consumer products company, sought to increase its participation in the U.S. market by launching a hostile takeover bid for Richardson-Vicks Inc. Unilever's global archrival, Procter & Gamble, saw the threat to its home turf and outbid Unilever to capture Richardson-Vicks. With Richardson-Vicks's European system, P&G was able to greatly strengthen its European positioning. So Unilever's attempt to expand participation in a rival's home market backfired to allow the rival to expand participation in Unilever's home markets.

In summary, industry globalization drivers provide opportunities to use global strategy levers in many ways. Some industries, such as civil aircraft, can score high on most dimensions of globalization.[16] Others, such as the cement industry, seem to be inherently local. But more and more industries are developing globalization potential. Even the food industry in Europe, renowned for its diversity of taste, is now a globalization target for major food multinationals.

Changes over Time   Finally, industry evolution plays a role. As each of the industry globalization drivers changes over time, so too will the appropriate global strategy change. For example, in the European major appliance industry, globalization forces seem to have reversed. In the late 1960s and early 1970s, a regional standardization strategy was successful for some key competitors.[17] But in the 1980s the situation appears to have turned around, and the most successful strategies seem to be national.[18]

In some cases, the actions of individual competitors can affect the direction and pace of change; competitors positioned to take advantage of globalization forces will want to hasten them. For example, a competitor with strong central manufacturing capabilities may want to accelerate the worldwide acceptance of a standardized product.

More than One Strategy Is Viable

Although they are powerful, industry globalization drivers do not dictate one formula for success. More than one type of international strategy can be viable in a given industry.

Industries vary across drivers. No industry is high on every one of the many globalization drivers. A particular competitor may be in a strong position to exploit a driver that scores low on globalization. For example, the dominance of national government customers offsets the globalization potential from other industry drivers, because government customers typically prefer to do business with their own nationals. In such an industry a competitor with a

---

[16]M. Y. Yoshino, "Global Competition in a Salient Industry: The Case of Civil Aircraft," in Porter (1986).

[17]Levitt (May–June 1983).

[18]C. Baden Fuller et al., "National or Global?" *The Study of Company Strategies and the European Market for Major Appliances* (London: London Business School Centre for Business Strategy, working paper series, No. 28, June 1987).

global strategy can use its other advantages, such as low cost from centralization of global production, to offset this drawback. At the same time, another multinational competitor with good government contacts can pursue a multidomestic strategy and succeed without globalization advantages, and single-country local competitors can succeed on the basis of their very particular local assets. The hotel industry provides examples both of successful global and of successful local competitors.

Global effects are incremental. Globalization drivers are not deterministic for a second reason: The appropriate use of strategy levers adds competitive advantage to existing sources. These other sources may allow individual competitors to thrive with international strategies that are mismatched with industry globalization drivers. For example, superior technology is a major source of competitive advantage in most industries, but can be quite independent of globalization drivers. A competitor with sufficiently superior technology can use it to offset globalization disadvantages.

Business and parent company position and resources are crucial. The third reason that drivers are not deterministic is related to resources. A worldwide business may face industry drivers that strongly favor a global strategy. But global strategies are typically expensive to implement initially even though great cost savings and revenue gains should follow. High initial investments may be

needed to expand within or into major markets, to develop standardized products, to relocate value activities, to create global brands, to create new organization units or coordination processes, and to implement other aspects of a global strategy. The strategic position of the business is also relevant. Even though a global strategy may improve the business's long-term strategic position, its immediate position may be so weak that resources should be devoted to short-term, country-by-country improvements. Despite the automobile industry's very strong globalization driver, Chrysler Corporation had to deglobalize by selling off most of its international automotive businesses to avoid bankruptcy. Lastly, investing in nonglobal sources of competitive advantage, such as superior technology, may yield greater returns than global ones, such as centralized manufacturing.

Organizations have limitations. Finally, factors such as organization structure, management processes, people, and culture affect how well a desired global strategy can be implemented. Organizational differences among companies in the same industry can, or should, constrain the companies' pursuit of the same global strategy. Organization issues in globalization are a major topic, and cannot be covered in the space here.[19]

▌[19]See: Yip et al. (1988); and C. K. Prahalad and Y. L. Doz. *The Multinational Mission: Balancing Local Demands and Global Vision* (New York: Free Press, 1987).

Reading 3-3   Competition in Global Industries: A Conceptual Framework

Michael E. Porter

International competition ranks high on the list of issues confronting firms today. The growing im-

▌This reading has benefited from comments by Richard A. Rawlinson, M. Therese Flaherty, and Louis T. Wells, Jr.
▌Reprinted from *Competition in Global Industries,* M. E. Porter (ed.), with permission from Harvard Business School Publishing.

portance of international competition is well recognized both in the business and academic communities, for reasons that are clear when one examines just about any data set that exists on international trade or investment. Figure 1, for example, compares world trade and world GNP.

Figure 1   Growth of World Trade

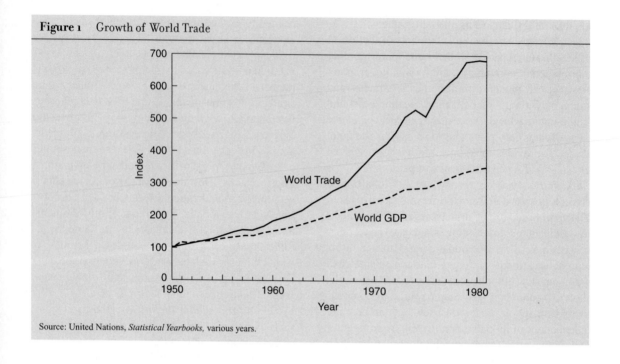

Source: United Nations, *Statistical Yearbooks*, various years.

Something interesting started happening around the mid-1950s, when the growth in world trade began to exceed significantly the growth in world GNP.[1] A few years later, by 1963, foreign direct investment by firms in developing countries began to grow rapidly.[2] The 1950s marked the beginning of a fundamental change in the international competitive environment. The change has been accelerated by the emergence across a wide range of industries of potent new international competitors, from countries such as Japan, Korea, and Taiwan, calling into question theories of international competition that placed advanced nations in the driver's seat. It is a trend that continues to cause sleepless nights for many business managers.

The subject of international competition is far from new. A large body of literature rooted in the principle of comparative advantage has investi-

gated the many implications of the various theoretical models of international trade.[3] Considerable research on the multinational firm exists, reflecting the growing importance of the multinational since the turn of the century. I think it is fair to characterize this work as resting heavily on the multinational's ability to exploit know-how and expertise gained in one country's market in other countries at low costs, thereby offsetting the unavoidable extra costs of doing business in a foreign country.[4] A related body of knowledge also exists in companies and in writing on the problems of entry into foreign markets and the life cycle of how a firm should

---

[1]Intra-industry trade, where a country both exports and imports goods in the same industry, has grown markedly as well. The reasons will be made clear by the framework below.

[2]United Nations Center on Transnational Corporations (1984).

[3]For a survey, see Caves and Jones (1985).

[4]See, particularly, the work of Hymer, Kindleberger, and Caves. There are many books on the theory and management of the multinational, which are too numerous to cite here. For an excellent survey of the literature, see Caves (1982). A more recent stream of literature emphasizes how the multinational firm internalizes transactions to circumvent imperfections in various intermediate markets, most importantly the market for knowledge. Prominent examples of this work are Buckley and Casson (1976) and Teece (1981). For a survey and extension, see Teece (1985).

compete abroad, beginning with export of licensing and ultimately moving to the establishment of foreign subsidiaries.[5] Finally, many of the functional fields in management have their branch of thinking about international issues, for example, international marketing, international finance. Most attention is concentrated, by and large, on the problems of doing business in a foreign country.

As rich as it is, however, our knowledge of international competition does not address some pressing questions facing today's international firms. Though research and practice have provided some guidance for considering incremental investment decisions to enter new countries, at best we have an incomplete view of how to conceive of a firm's overall international strategy and how such a strategy should be selected. Put another way, we know more about the problems of becoming a multinational than about strategies for managing an established multinational.[6]

This article seeks to explore the implications of international competition for competitive strategy. In particular, what are the distinctive questions for competitive strategy that are raised by international, as opposed to domestic, competition? Many of the strategy issues for a company competing internationally are very much the same as for one competing domestically: a firm must still analyze its industry structure and competitors, understand its buyer and the sources of buyer value, diagnose its relative cost position, and seek to establish a sustainable competitive advantage within some competitive scope, whether it be across the board or in an industry segment. These are subjects I have written about extensively.[7] But there are some questions for strategy that are peculiar to international competition, and that add to rather than replace those examined by other authors. These questions all revolve, in one way or another, around how what a firm does in one country affects or is affected by what is going on in other countries—the degree of connection among country competition.

Patterns of International Competition

The appropriate unit of analysis in setting international strategy is the industry, because the industry is the arena in which competitive advantage is won or lost. The pattern of international competition differs markedly from industry to industry. Industries vary along a spectrum from *multidomestic* to *global* in their competitive scope.

In multidomestic industries, competition in each country (or small group of countries) is essentially independent of competition in other countries. A multidomestic industry is one that is present in many countries (e.g., there is a consumer banking industry in Sri Lanka, one in France, and one in the United States), but one in which competition occurs on a country-by-country basis. In a multidomestic industry, a multinational firm may enjoy a competitive advantage from the one-time transfer of know-how from its home base to foreign countries. However, the firm modifies and adapts its intangible assets in order to employ them in each country, and the competitive outcome over time is then determined by conditions in each country. The competitive advantages of the firm, then, are largely specific to the country. The international industry becomes a collection of essentially domestic industries—hence the term multidomestic. Industries where competition has traditionally exhibited this pattern include retailing, consumer packaged goods, distribution, insurance, consumer finance, and caustic chemicals.

At the other end of the spectrum are what I term global industries. The term global—like the word "strategy"—has become overused and perhaps

---

[5]Knickerbocker's (1973) work on oligopolistic reaction adds an important dimension to the process of entering foreign markets through illuminating bunching in the timing of entry into a country by firms in an industry and relating this to defensive considerations. Vernon's product cycle of international trade combines a view of how products mature with the evolution in a firm's international activities to predict the patterns of trade and investment in developed and developing countries (Vernon 1966). Vernon himself, among others, has raised questions about how general the product cycle pattern is today.

[6]There are some notable exceptions to the general paucity of thinking on the strategy of established multinationals. See, for example, Stopford and Wells (1972), Franko (1976), Stobaugh et al. (1976).

[7]Porter (1980, 1985a).

misunderstood. The definition of a global industry employed here is an industry in which a firm's competitive position in one country is significantly affected by its position in other countries or vice versa.[8] Therefore, the international industry is not merely a collection of domestic industries but a series of linked domestic industries in which the rivals compete against each other on a truly worldwide basis. Industries exhibiting or evolving toward the global pattern today include commercial aircraft, TV sets, semiconductors, copiers, automobiles, and watches.

The implications for international strategy of this distinction between multidomestic and global are quite profound. In a multidomestic industry, a firm can and should manage its international activities like a portfolio. Its subsidiaries or other operations around the world should each control all the important activities necessary to do business in the industry and should enjoy a high degree of autonomy. The firm's strategy in a country should be determined largely by the competitive conditions in that country; the firm's international strategy should be what I term a country-centered strategy.

In a multidomestic industry, competing internationally is discretionary. A firm can choose to remain domestic or can expand internationally, if it has some advantage that allows it to overcome the extra costs of entering and competing in foreign markets. The important competitors in multidomestic industries will either be domestic companies or multinationals with stand-alone operations abroad. Such is the situation in each of the multidomestic industries listed earlier. In a multidomestic industry, then, international strategy collapses to a series of domestic strategies. The issues that are uniquely international revolve around how to do business abroad, how to select good countries in which to compete (or assess country risk), and how to achieve the one-time transfer of know-how or

expertise. These are questions that are relatively well developed in the literature.

In a global industry, managing international activities like a portfolio will undermine the possibility of achieving competitive advantage. In a global industry, a firm must in some way integrate its activities on a worldwide basis to capture the linkages among countries. This integration will require more than transferring intangible assets among countries, though it will include such transfer. A firm may choose to compete with a country-centered strategy, focusing on specific market segments or countries where it can carve out a niche by responding to whatever local country differences are present. However, it does so at some considerable peril from competitors with global strategies. All the important competitors in the global industries listed above compete worldwide with increasingly coordinated strategies.

In international competition, a firm has to perform some functions in each of the countries in which it competes. Even though a global competitor must view its international activities as an overall system, it still has to maintain some country perspective. It is the balancing of these two perspectives that becomes one of the essential questions in global strategy.[9]

---

[8]The distinction between multidomestic and global competition and some of its strategic implications were first described in Hout, Porter, and Rudden (1982).

[9]Perlmutter's (1969) concept of ethnocentric, polycentric, and geocentric multinationals is an interesting but different one. It takes the firm, not the industry, as the unit of analysis and is decoupled from industry structure. It focuses on management attitudes, the nationality of executives, and other aspects of organization. Perlmutter presents ethnocentric, polycentric, and geocentric as stages of an organization's development as a multinational, with geocentric as the goal. A later paper (Wind, Douglas, and Perlmutter 1973) tempers this conclusion based on the fact that some companies may not have the required sophistication in marketing to attempt a geocentric strategy. Products embedded in the lifestyle or culture of a country are also identified as less susceptible to geocentrism. The Perlmutter et al. view does not attempt to link management orientation to industry structure and strategy. International strategy should grow out of the net competitive advantage in a global industry of different types of worldwide coordination. In some industries, a country-centered strategy, roughly analogous to Perlmutter's polycentric idea, may be the best strategy irrespective of company size and international experience. Conversely, a global strategy may be imperative given the competitive advantage that accrues from it. Industry and strategy should define the organization approach, not vice versa.

Figure 2   The Value Chain

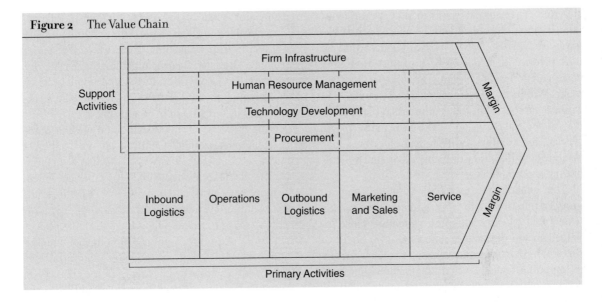

Causes of Globalization

If we accept the distinction between multidomestic and global industries as an important taxonomy of patterns of international competition, a number of questions arise. When does an industry globalize? What exactly do we mean by a global strategy, and is there more than one kind? What determines the type of international strategy best suited to a particular industry?

An industry can be defined as global if there is some competitive advantage to integrating activities on a worldwide basis. To make this statement operational, however, we must be very precise about what we mean by activities and also what we mean by integrating. To diagnose the sources of competitive advantage in any context, whether it be domestic or international, it is necessary to adopt a disaggregated view of the firm, which I call the value chain.[10] Every firm is a collection of discrete activities performed to do business in its industry—I call them value activities. The activities performed by a firm include such things as salespeople selling the product, service technicians performing repairs, scien-

tists in the laboratory designing products or processes, and accountants keeping the books. Such activities are technologically and, in most cases, physically distinct. It is only at the level of these discrete activities, rather than the firm as a whole, that competitive advantage can be truly understood.

A firm may possess two types of competitive advantage: (1) *low cost,* or (2) *differentiation.* These grow out of the firm's ability to perform the activities in the value chain either more cheaply or in a unique way relative to its competitors. The ultimate value a firm creates is what buyers are willing to pay for what the firm provides, which includes its physical product in addition to any ancillary services or benefits, such as design assistance, repair or more timely delivery than competitors. Profit results if the value created through performing the required activities exceeds the collective cost of performing them. Competitive advantage is a function of either providing comparable buyer value more efficiently than competitors (low cost), or performing activities at comparable cost but in unique ways that create more buyer value than competitors and, hence, command a premium price (differentiation).

The value chain, shown in Figure 2, provides a systematic means of displaying and categorizing

---

[10]Porter (1985*a*) describes value chain theory and its use in analyzing competitive advantage.

activities. The activities performed by a firm in any industry can be grouped into the nine generic categories shown. The labels may differ based on industry convention, but every firm performs these basic categories of activities in some way or another. Within each category, a firm typically performs a number of discrete activities that are particular to the industry and to the firm's strategy. In service, for example, firms typically perform such discrete activities as installation, repair, parts distribution, and upgrading.

The generic categories of activities can be grouped into two broad types. Along the bottom are what I call *primary* activities, which are those involved in the physical creation of the product or service, its delivery and marketing to the buyer, and its support after sale. Across the top are what I call *support* activities, which provide inputs or infrastructure that allow the primary activities to take place on an ongoing basis.

Procurement is the obtaining of purchased inputs, such as raw materials, purchased services, machinery, and so on. Procurement stretches across the entire value chain because it supports every activity, that is, every activity uses purchased inputs of some kind. There are typically many different discrete procurement activities within a firm, often performed by different people. Technology development encompasses the activities involved in designing the product as well as in creating and improving the way the various activities in the value chain are performed. We tend to think of technology in terms of the product or manufacturing process. In fact, every activity involves a technology or technologies, which may be simple or sophisticated, and a firm has a stock of know-how about how to perform each activity. Technology development typically involves a variety of different discrete activities, some performed outside the R&D department.

Human resource management is the recruiting, training, and development of personnel. Every activity involves human resources, and thus human resource management activities span the entire chain. Finally, firm infrastructure includes activities such as general management, accounting, legal, finance, strategic planning, and all the other activities outside of specific primary or support activities but essential to enable the entire chain's operation. Each category of activities is of differing relative importance to competitive advantage in different industries, although they are present in all industries.

Activities in a firm's value chain are not independent, but are connected through what I call linkages. The way one activity is performed frequently affects the cost or effectiveness of other activities. If more is spent on the purchase of a raw material, for example, a firm may lower its cost of fabrication or assembly. There are many linkages that connect activities, not only within the firm but also with the activities of its suppliers, channels, and ultimately its buyers. The firm's value chain resides in a larger stream of activities that I term the value system. Suppliers have value chains that provide the purchased inputs to the firm's chain; channels have value chains through which the firm's product or service passes; buyers have value chains in which the firm's product or service is employed. The connections among activities in this system also become essential to competitive advantage. For example, the way suppliers perform particular activities can affect the cost or effectiveness of activities within the firm.

A final important building block in value chain theory, necessary for our purposes here, is the notion of *competitive scope*. Competitive scope is the breadth of activities the firm performs in competing in an industry. There are four basic dimensions of competitive scope: segment scope, or the range of segments the firm serves (e.g., product varieties, customer types); industry scope, or the range of related industries the firm competes in with a coordinated strategy; vertical scope, or what activities are performed by the firm versus suppliers and channels; and geographic scope, or the geographic regions in which the firm operates with a coordinated strategy. Competitive scope is vital to competitive advantage because it shapes the configuration of the value chain, how activities are performed and whether activities are shared among units.

International strategy is an issue of geographic scope. Its analysis is quite similar to that of whether and how a firm should compete locally, regionally, or nationally within a country. In the international context, government tends to have a greater involvement in competition and there are more significant variations among geographic regions in buyer needs. Nevertheless, these differences are matters of degree and the framework here can be readily applied to the choice of strategy by firms who compete in large countries consisting of several regions or cities.

International Configuration and Coordination of Activities

A firm that competes internationally must decide how to spread the activities in the value chain among countries. A distinction immediately arises between the activities labeled downstream on Figure 3, and those labeled upstream activities and support activities. The location of downstream activities, those more related to the buyer, is usually tied to where the buyer is located. If a firm is going to sell in Japan, for example, it usually must provide service in Japan and it must have salespeople stationed in Japan. In some industries it is possible to have a single sales force that travels to the buyer's country and back again; some other specific downstream activities such as the production of advertising copy can sometimes also be performed centrally. More typically, however, the firm must locate the capability to perform downstream activities in each of the countries in which it operates. Upstream activities and support activities, conversely, could conceptually be decoupled from where the buyer is located in most industries.

This distinction carries some interesting implications. First, downstream activities create competitive advantages that are largely country specific: a firm's reputation, brand name, and service network in a country grow largely out of a firm's activities in that country and create entry/mobility barriers largely in that country alone. Competitive advantage in upstream and support activities often grows more out of the entire system of countries in which a firm competes than from its position in any one country.

Second, in industries where downstream activities or other buyer-tied activities are vital to competitive advantage, there tends to be a more multidomestic pattern of international competition. In many service industries, for example, not only

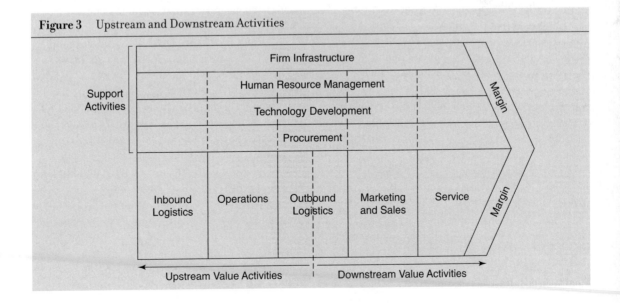

Figure 3 Upstream and Downstream Activities

Table 1   Illustrative Configuration of Activities Globally for a U.S. Company

Activities	U.S.	Canada	U.K.	France	Germany	Japan
Inbound logistics	X		X		X	X
Operations						
Components	X		X			
Assembly	X				X	X
Testing	X				X	X
Outbound logistics						
Order processing	X					
Physical distribution	X	X	X	X	X	X
Marketing and sales						
Advertising	X	X	X	X	X	X
Sales force	X	X	X	X	X	X
Promotional materials	X					
Service	X	X	X	X	X	X
Procurement	X					X
Technology development	X					X
Human resource management	X	X	X	X	X	X
Firm infrastructure	X					

downstream activities but frequently upstream activities are tied to buyer location, and global strategies are comparatively less common.[11] In industries where upstream and support activities such as technology development and operations are crucial to competitive advantage, global competition is more common. In global competition, the location and scale of these potentially footloose activities is optimized from a worldwide perspective.[12]

The distinctive issues in international, as contrasted to domestic, strategy can be summarized in two key dimensions of how a firm competes internationally. The first I call the *configuration* of a firm's activities worldwide or the location in the world where each activity in the value chain is performed, including in how many places. The second dimension I call *coordination*, which refers to how like or linked activities performed in different countries are coordinated with each other. If, for example, there are three plants—one in Germany, one in Japan, and one in the United States—how do the activities in those plants relate to each other?

A firm faces an array of options in both configuration and coordination for each activity in the value chain. Configuration options range from *concentrated*—performing an activity in one location and serving the world from it, for example, one R&D lab, one large plant—to *dispersed*, that is, performing the activity in every country. In the extreme case, each country would have a complete value chain. Table 1 illustrates an example of configuration of worldwide activities in an industry.[13] A firm need not concentrate all its activities in the same country. Today, in fact, it has become

[11]There is a growing globalization of service firm strategies, however, as service firms serve multinational buyers. Developments in information technology raise the importance of R&D, and automation pervades the primary activities of service firms. Service firms tend to draw advantages from a global strategy largely in the support activities in the value chain.

[12]Buzzell (1968), Pryor (1965), and Wind, Douglas, and Perlmutter (1973) point out that national differences are in most cases more critical with respect to marketing than with production and finance. This generalization reflects the fact that marketing activities are often inherently country based. However, this generalization is not reliable because in many countries, production and other activities are widely dispersed.

[13]In practice, a diagram such as Table 1 would involve each important discrete activity (not broad categories) and include all the countries in which a firm operates.

Table 2   Configuration and Coordination Issues by Category of Activity

Value Activity	Configuration Issues	Coordination Issues
Operations	Location of production facilities for components and end products	Allocation of production tasks among dispersed facilities Networking of international plants Transferring process technology and production know-how among plants
Marketing and sales	Product line selection Country (market) selection Location of preparation of advertising and promotional materials	Commonality of brand name worldwide Coordination of sales to multinational accounts Similarity of channels and product positioning worldwide Coordination of pricing in different countries
Service	Location of the service organization	Similarity of service standards and procedures worldwide
Technology development	Number and location of R&D centers	Allocation of research tasks among dispersed R&D centers Interchange among R&D centers Developing products responsive to market needs in many countries Sequence of product introductions around the world
Procurement	Location of the purchasing function	Locating and managing suppliers in different countries Transferring knowledge about input markets Coordinating purchases of common items

common to concentrate activities in many different countries.

Coordination options range from none to many. For example, a firm producing in three plants could at one extreme allow each plant to operate with full autonomy, including different production steps and different part numbers. At the other extreme, the plants could be tightly coordinated by employing the same information system, the same production process, the same parts, specifications, and so forth. Options for coordination in an activity are typically more numerous than the configuration options, because there are many possible types of coordination and many different facets of an activity on which to coordinate.

Table 2 lists some of the configuration issues and coordination issues for several categories of value activities. In technology development, for example, the configuration issue is where R&D is performed: at one location or two or more locations and in what countries? The coordination issues have to do with such things as the allocation of tasks among R & D centers, the extent of interchange among them, and the location and sequence of product introduction around the world. There are configuration issues and coordination issues for every activity.[14]

Figure 4 is a way of summarizing these basic choices in international strategy geographically on a single diagram, with coordination of activities on the vertical axis and configuration of activities on

[14]M. Therese Flaherty provided helpful comments that clarified the configuration/coordination distinction.

Figure 4 The Dimensions of International Strategy

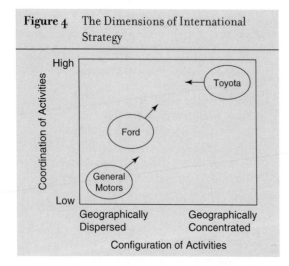

Configuration of Activities

the horizontal axis. The firm has to make a set of choices for each activity. If a firm employs a very dispersed configuration, placing an entire value chain in every country (or small group of contiguous countries) in which it operates and coordinating little or not at all among them, then the firm is competing with a country-centered strategy.[15] The domestic firm, operating in only one country, is the extreme case of a firm with a country-centered strategy. As we move from the lower left-hand corner of the diagram up or to the right, we have strategies that are increasingly global. Figure 4 can be employed to map strategic groups in an international industry because its axes capture the most important sources of competitive advantage from an international strategy.[16]

Figure 5 illustrates some of the possible variations in international strategy. The simplest global strategy is to concentrate as many activities as possible in one country, serve the world from this home base, and tightly coordinate through standardization those activities that must inherently be performed

near the buyer. This is the pattern adopted by many Japanese firms in the 1960s and 1970s, such as Toyota. The position of Toyota is plotted on Figure 4 along with key competitors. However, the options apparent in Figures 5 and 6 make it clear that there is no such thing as one global strategy.

There are many different kinds of global strategies, depending on a firm's choices about configuration and coordination throughout the value chain. In copiers, for example, Xerox has until recently concentrated R&D in the United States, but dispersed other activities, in some cases using joint-venture partners to perform them. On dispersed activities, however, coordination has been quite high. The Xerox brand, marketing approach, and servicing procedures have been quite standardized worldwide. Canon, on the other hand, has had a much more concentrated configuration of activities through somewhat less coordination of the dispersed activities. The vast majority of Canon's support activities plus most manufacturing have been performed in Japan. Aside from the requirement to use the Canon brand, however, local marketing subsidiaries have been given quite a bit of latitude in each region of the world.

Competitors with country-centered and global strategies can co-exist in an industry, but global strategies by some competitors frequently force other firms to follow suit. In automobiles, for example, Toyota has employed a relatively simple global strategy to achieve the position of low-cost producer. General Motors has historically competed with a country-centered international strategy, with separate manufacturing facilities and even separate brand names in different regions, while Ford has practiced only regional coordination. As the arrows indicate, all three companies are modifying their international strategies today—the U.S. firms toward more global strategies and Toyota toward becoming more dispersed as its international position grows.

A global strategy can now be defined more precisely as one in which a firm seeks to *gain competitive advantage from its international presence through either a concentrated configuration, coordinating among dispersed activities, or both.* The

---

[15]Here, the firm makes only a one-time transfer of knowledge in establishing each subsidiary, which gives it an advantage over local firms. Transaction costs dictate the multinational form rather than market transactions.

[16]Strategic groups are described in Porter (1980), chapter 7.

Figure 5   Types of International Strategy

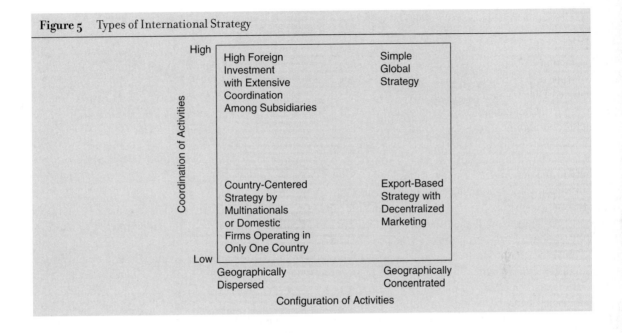

one-time transfer of intangible assets, emphasized in the literature, is just one of many ways. Measuring the presence of a global industry empirically must reflect both dimensions and not just one. Market presence of firms in many countries and some export and import of components and end products are characteristic of most global industries. Hence, intraindustry trade is a good sign of the presence of global competition, and its growth is one indication that the incidence of global industries has increased. High levels of foreign investment or the mere presence of multinational firms are not reliable measures, however, because firms may be managing foreign units like a portfolio.

Configuration/Coordination and Competitive Advantage   Understanding the competitive advantages of a global strategy and, in turn, the causes of industry globalization, requires that we specify the conditions under which concentrating activities globally and/or coordinating dispersed activities leads to either lower cost or differentiation. In each case, there are structural characteristics of an industry that work for and against globalization.

The factors that favor concentrating an activity in one or a few locations to serve the world are as follows:

- Economies of scale in the activity;
- A proprietary learning curve in the activity;
- Comparative advantage of one or a few locations for performing the activity;
- Coordination advantages of co-locating linked activities such as R&D and production.

The first two factors relate to *how many* sites an activity is performed at, while the last two relate to *where* these sites are. Comparative advantage can apply to any activity, not just production. There may be some locations in the world that are better places than others to perform other activities such as research or creation of advertising materials. India has become a center for software writing, for example. Government can promote the concentration of activities by providing subsidies or other incentives to employ a particular country as an export base—in effect altering comparative advantage—a role many governments are attempting to play today.

There are also structural characteristics that favor dispersion of an activity to many countries, because they create concentration costs. Local product needs may differ, nullifying the advantages of scale or learning from one-site operation of an activity. Dispersing a range of activities in a country may facilitate marketing in that country by signaling commitment to local buyers and/or providing greater local responsiveness. Dispersing an activity may facilitate learning or gaining know-how in the activity, as a number of sites increases information flow and managers get closer to more markets. Transport, communication, and storage costs can make it inefficient to concentrate the activity in one location.

Government is also frequently a powerful force for dispersing activities, through tariffs, nontariff barriers, and nationalistic purchasing (nationalistic purchasing can exist without a direct government role as well). Governments typically want firms to locate the entire value chain in their country, because this creates benefits and spillovers to the country that often go beyond local content.[17] Dispersing some activities may sometimes allow the concentration of others, through placating governments or through linkages among activities that will be described below. Dispersion is also encouraged by the risks of performing an activity at one place: exchange rate risk, political risk, risk of interruption, and so on. The balance between the advantages of concentrating and dispersing an activity normally differ for each activity (and industry). The best configuration for R&D is different from that for component fabrication, and this is different from that for assembly, installation, advertising, and procurement.[18]

The desirability of coordinating like or linked activities that are dispersed involves a similar balance of structural factors. Coordination potentially allows the sharing and accumulation of know-how and expertise among dispersed activities. If a firm learns how to operate the production process better in Germany, transferring that learning may make the process run better in U.S. and Japanese plants. Differing countries, with their inevitably differing conditions, provide a fertile basis for comparison as well as opportunities for arbitrating knowledge, obtained in different places about different aspects of the business. Knowledge may accumulate not only in product or process technology but also about buyer needs and marketing techniques. A firm coordinating internationally may also receive early warning of industry changes by spotting them in one or two leading countries before they become broadly apparent and transferring the knowledge to guide other activities elsewhere. The initial transfer of knowledge in establishing a foreign subsidiary is recognizable as one case of coordination among dispersed activities. However, it is clear that knowledge is continually created and can flow among all subsidiaries. The ability to accumulate and transfer this knowledge among units is a potent advantage of the global competitor over domestic or country-centered competitors.[19]

Coordination among dispersed activities also potentially improves the ability to reap economies of scale in activities if subtasks are allocated among locations to allow some specialization, for example, each R&D center has a different area of focus. This illustrates how the way a network of foreign locations is managed can have a great influence on the ability to reap the benefits of any given configuration of activities. Viewed another way, close coordination is frequently a partial offset to dispersing an activity.

Closely related to this is the relationship between international coordination in one activity and

[17]For example, governments may desire national autonomy in decision making and the spillovers from domestic R&D and training of skilled workers.

[18]A number of authors have framed the globalization of industries in terms of the balance between imperatives for global integration and imperatives for national responsiveness, a useful distinction. See Prahalad (1975), Doz (1976), and Bartlett (1979). I relate that distinction here to more basic issues of where and how a firm performs the activities in the value chain internationally.

[19]Transactional failures make coordination between independent firms or coalition partners even more difficult than the initial transfer of knowledge in establishing a foreign subsidiary, not to mention ongoing coordination among subsidiaries.

the configuration of another. For example, coordination in the marketing activity involving information exchange about buyer needs in many countries may allow a central R&D facility to design a standard or easy-to-modify product for sale worldwide, unlocking the scale economies of a concentrated configuration in R&D and production. Such a linkage among separate activities has been exploited by Canon in the design of its personal copier. Similarly, dispersing procurement may allow concentrating manufacturing, since sourcing from many countries can open up the opportunity to export to them.

Coordination may also allow a firm to respond to *shifting* comparative advantage, where movements in exchange rates and factor costs are significant and hard to forecast. For example, incrementally increasing production at the location currently enjoying favorable exchange rates can lower costs. Coordination can also reinforce a firm's brand reputation with buyers through ensuring a consistent image and approach to doing business on a worldwide basis. This is particularly valuable if buyers are mobile or information about the industry flows freely around the world. Coordination may also differentiate the firm with multinational buyers if it allows the firm to serve them anywhere and in a consistent way. Coordination (and a global approach to configuration) enhances leverage with local governments if the firm is able to grow or shrink activities in one country at the expense of others. Finally, coordination yields flexibility in responding to competitors, by allowing the firm to respond to them differently in different countries and to retaliate in one country to a challenge in another. A firm may choose, for example, to compete aggressively in the country from which a challenger draws its most important volume or cash flow in order to reduce the competitors' strength in other countries. IBM and Caterpillar have practiced this sort of defensive behavior in their Japanese operations.

Coordination of dispersed activities usually involves costs that differ by form of coordination and by industry. Local conditions in countries may vary in ways that may make a common approach across countries suboptimal. For example, if every plant in the world is required to use the same raw material, the firm pays a penalty in countries where that raw material is expensive relative to satisfactory substitutes. Business practices, marketing systems, raw material sources, local infrastructures, and a variety of other factors may differ across countries as well, in ways that may mitigate the advantages of a common approach or of the sharing of learning. Governments may restrain the flow of information required for coordination, or impose other barriers to it. Transaction costs of coordination among countries can also be high. International coordination involves long distances, language problems, and cultural barriers to communication. Such problems may mean in some industries that coordination is not optimal. They also suggest that forms of coordination that involve relatively infrequent decisions, such as adopting common service standards or employing the same raw materials, will enjoy advantages over forms of coordination involving ongoing interchange such as transshipping components and end products among facilities.

There are also substantial organizational challenges involved in achieving cooperation among subsidiaries, because of difficulties in aligning subsidiary managers' interests with those of the firm as a whole. The German branch does not necessarily want to tell the U.S. branch about their latest breakthroughs on the production line because it may make it harder for them to outdo the Americans in the annual comparison of operating efficiency among plants. These vexing organizational problems mean that country subsidiaries often view each other more as competitors than collaborators.[20] As with configuration, a firm must make an activity-by-activity choice about where there is net competitive advantage to coordinating in various ways.

Some factors favoring dispersion of activities also impede coordination, while others do not. Transport costs raise few barriers to coordination,

---

[20]The difficulties in coordinating across business units competing in different industries within the diversified firm is described in Porter (1985a), chapter 11.

for example, while product heterogeneity creates substantial ones. Product heterogeneity and the actions of government often have the special characteristics of impeding *both* concentration and coordination, giving them a particularly strategic role in affecting the pattern of international competition.

Coordination in some activities may be necessary to reap the advantages of configuration in others as noted earlier. The use of common raw materials in each plant, for example, allows worldwide purchasing. Moreover, tailoring some activities to countries (not coordinating) may allow concentration and standardization of others. For example, tailored marketing in each country may allow the same product to be positioned differently and hence sold successfully in many countries, unlocking possibilities for reaping economies of scale in production and R&D. Thus, coordination and configuration interact.

Diversification into related industries can also shape the best global configuration/coordination in a single industry. For example, a diversified firm may be able to produce a number of related products in dispersed plants, instead of concentrating production of one product in a single plant, and still achieve economies of scale. This reflects the fact that sharing activities among units competing in related industries may serve the same strategic purpose as sharing them in competing in many countries—namely, scale or learning economies.[21]

Diversification can also create new options for bargaining with governments. For example, exports in one business unit can be traded for the ability to import in another. IBM follows this approach, seeking a balance of trade in each country in which it operates. Diversification in a variety of industries may also facilitate bartering. Conversely, diversification may raise a firm's overall commitment to a country, increasing the host government's leverage. For all these reasons, the extent of a firm's diversification should be a consideration in its choice of international strategy.

Configuration/Coordination and the Pattern of International Competition   Industries globalize when the benefits of configuring and/or coordinating globally exceed the costs of doing so. The way in which an industry globalizes reflects the specific benefits and costs of global configuration and/or coordination of each value activity. The activities in which global competitors gain competitive advantage will differ correspondingly. Configuration/coordination determines the ongoing competitive advantages of a global strategy, growing out of a firm's overall international position. These are additive to competitive advantages a firm derives/possesses from its domestic market positions. An initial transfer of knowledge from the home base to subsidiaries, is thus one, but by no means the most important, advantage of a global competitor.[22]

In some industries, the competitive advantage from a global strategy comes in technology development, and firms gain little advantage from concentrating primary activities which means that they are dispersed around the world. A good example is the manufacture of glass and plastic containers, where transport cost leads to a dispersion of plants but opportunities to perform R&D centrally and to transfer production know-how among plants yield significant advantages to global firms. In other industries, such as cameras or videocassette recorders, firms gain advantages from concentrating production to achieve economies of scale and learning, but give subsidiaries much more autonomy in sales and marketing. Finally, in some industries there is no net advantage to a global strategy

---

[21]For a discussion, see Porter (1985a), chapter 9.

[22]Empirical research has found a strong correlation between R&D and advertising intensity and the extent of foreign direct investment (for a survey, see Caves 1982). Both these factors have a place in our model of the determinants of globalization, but for quite different reasons. R&D intensity suggests scale advantages for the global competitor in developing products or processes that are manufactured abroad either due to low production scale economies or government pressures, or that require investments in service infrastructure. Advertising intensity, however, is much closer to proxying the possibilities for the classic transfer of marketing knowledge to foreign subsidiaries. High advertising industries are also frequently those where local tastes differ and manufacturing scale economies are modest, both reasons to disperse many activities.

and country-centered strategies dominate; the industry is multidomestic.

An industry such as commercial aircraft represents an extreme case of a global industry (e.g., placement in the upper right-hand corner of Figure 4). Three competitors, Boeing, McDonnell Douglas, and Airbus, all have global strategies. In value activities important to cost and differentiation in the industry, there are compelling net advantages to concentrating most activities to serve worldwide markets and coordinating the dispersed activities extensively. Yet, host governments have a particular interest in the commercial aircraft industry because of its large trade potential, defense implications, and R&D spillovers. The competitive advantages of a global strategy are so great that all the successful aircraft producers have sought to achieve and preserve them. In addition, the power of government to intervene has been mitigated by the paucity of viable worldwide competitors and the enormous barriers to entry created, in part, by the advantages of a global strategy. The result has been that firms have been able to assuage government through procurement. Boeing, for example, is very careful about where it buys components. Boeing seeks to develop suppliers in countries that are large potential customers. This requires a great deal of extra effort by Boeing to transfer technology and to work with suppliers to ensure that they meet its standards. Boeing realizes that this is preferable to compromising the competitive advantage of its strongly integrated worldwide strategy. It is willing to employ one value activity (procurement), where the advantages of concentration are modest, to help preserve the benefits of concentration in other activities. Recently, commercial aircraft competitors have entered into joint ventures and other coalition arrangements with foreign suppliers to achieve the same affect, as well as to spread the risk of huge development costs.

Segments and vertical stages of an industry frequently vary in their pattern of globalization. In aluminum, the upstream (alumina and ingot) stages are global industries. The downstream stage, semi-fabrication, is a group of multidomestic businesses, because product needs vary by country, transport costs are high, and intensive local customer service is required. Scale economies in the value chain are modest. In lubricants, automotive motor oil tends to be a multidomestic industry, while marine engine lubricants is a global industry. In automotive oil, countries have varying driving standards, weather conditions, and local laws. Production involves blending various kinds of base oils and additives, and is subject to few economies of scale but high shipping costs. Distribution channels are important to competitive success and vary markedly from country to country. Country-centered competitors, such as Castrol and Quaker State, are leaders in most countries. In the marine segment, conversely, ships move freely around the world and require the same oil everywhere. Successful competitors are global. A third and different industry is lodging, where most segments are multidomestic because the majority of activities in the value chain are tied to buyer location and country differences lead to few benefits from coordination. In high-priced business-oriented hotels, however, competition is more global. Global competitors such as Hilton, Marriott, and Sheraton have dispersed value chains, but employ common brand names, common service standards, and worldwide reservation systems to gain advantages in serving highly mobile business travelers.[23]

Just as the pattern of globalization may differ by segment or industry stage, so may the pattern differ by groups of countries. There are often *subsystems* of countries within which the advantages of configuration/coordination are greater than with other countries. For example, configuration/coordination possibilities may be high in competing in countries with similar climatic conditions (such as the Nordic countries) because they have similar product needs. Subsystems can be based on geographic regions, climatic conditions, language, state of economic development, extent of government intervention in competition, and historical or

---

[23]This description draws on a study of the incidence of multinationals in the hotel industry by Dunning and McQueen (1981).

current political ties. In the record industry, for example, possibilities for coordination are great among the Spanish-speaking countries and countries with a large Spanish-speaking population such as the United States. Where there is extreme government intervention, geographic isolation, or very unusual product needs, countries can be effectively outside the global system or any subsystem.

International strategy has often been characterized as a choice between worldwide standardization and local tailoring, or as the tension between the economic imperative (large-scale efficient facilities) and the political imperative (local content, local production). It should be clear from the discussion so far that neither characterization captures the complexity of a firm's international strategy choices. A firm's choice of international strategy involves the search for competitive advantage from global configuration/coordination throughout the value chain. A firm may standardize (concentrate) some activities and tailor (disperse) others. It may also be able to standardize and tailor at the same time through the coordination of dispersed activities, or use local tailoring of some activities (e.g., different product positioning in each country) to allow standardization of others (e.g., production). Similarly, the economic imperative is not always for a global strategy—in some industries a country-centered strategy is the economic imperative. Conversely, the political imperative in some industries may be to concentrate activities where governments provide strong export incentives and locational subsidies.

The essence of international strategy is not to resolve tradeoffs between concentration and dispersion, but to eliminate or mitigate them. This implies concentrating and dispersing different value activities depending on industry structure, dispersing some activities to allow concentration of others, and minimizing the tradeoff between concentration and dispersion by coordinating dispersed activities.[24]

---

[24]There is an analogy here between the Lawrence and Lorsch (1967) idea that differentiation of functions within a firm along with providing effective integration improves performance, a point suggested by M. Therese Flaherty.

The Process of Industry Globalization   Industries globalize because the net competitive advantage of a global approach to configuration/coordination becomes significant. Sometimes this is due to exogenous environmental changes, such as shifts in technology, buyer needs, government policy, or country infrastructure. In automotive supply, for example, the industry is globalizing as buyers (the auto producers) become increasingly global competitors. In other industries, strategic innovations by a competitor can unlock the potential for globalization. For example, a firm may perceive a means of providing local content without dispersing scale-sensitive value activities, such as local installation and testing. Other tools to unlock globalization include: reducing the cost of modifying a centrally designed and produced product to meet local needs, such as modularizing the power supply in an otherwise standard product; increasing product homogeneity by designing a product that incorporates the features demanded by every significant country; or homogenizing worldwide demand through product repositioning. In electronic products such as communications switching equipment, for example, Northern Telecom, NEC Corporation, and Ericsson have benefited from product architectures which permit modularization of software and relatively low-cost modification to fit different country needs. Environmental changes and strategic insights frequently go hand in hand in changing the pattern of international competition.

There may be problems in the transition from multidomestic to global competition in industries where domestic or country-centered competitors have already established entry or mobility barriers that are market-specific. The possession by country-centered or domestic competitors of strong brand names, strong distribution channel relationships, or long-standing buyer relationships, will retard the penetration of global firms. Firms also face difficulties in shifting from country-centered to global strategies if they have a legacy of dispersed worldwide activities and organizational norms that place great authority at the country level. Domestic firms can sometimes be more successful than established multinationals in becoming global competitors, because they start with a cleaner slate than do firms who must rationalize and reorient their international activities.

The ultimate leaders in global industries are often first movers: the first firms to perceive the possibilities for a global strategy and move to implement one. For example, Boeing was the first global competitor in aircraft, as was Honda in motorcycles, IBM in computers, Kodak in film, and Becton Dickinson in disposable syringes. First movers gain scale and learning advantages that make competing with them difficult. First-mover effects are particularly important in global industries, because of the association between globalization and economies of scale, learning, and flexibility achieved through worldwide configuration/coordination. Global leadership can shift if industry structural change provides the opportunity for leapfrogging to new products or new technologies that nullify past leaders' scale and learning; again, the first mover to the new generation/technology often wins.

Global leaders often begin with some advantage at home, whether it be low labor cost or a product design or marketing advantage. They use this as a lever to enter foreign markets. Once there, however, the global competitor converts the initial home advantage into competitive advantages that grow out of its overall worldwide system, such as production scale economies or the ability to amortize R&D costs. While the initial advantage may have been hard to sustain, the global strategy creates *new* advantages that can be much more durable.

A good example is automobiles, where Toyota and Nissan initially competed in simple, small cars on the basis of low labor costs. As these companies achieved worldwide penetration, however, they gained economies of scale and accelerated down the learning curve. World scale allowed aggressive investments in new equipment and R&D. Today, the Korean competitor Hyundai competes in small, simple cars based on low labor costs. Toyota and Nissan have long since graduated to broad lines of increasingly differentiated cars, drawing on the advantages of their worldwide positions.

Global Strategy and Comparative Advantage   It is useful to pause and reflect on the relationship between the frame work I have presented and the notion of comparative advantage. Is there a difference? The traditional concept of comparative advantage is that factor-cost or factor-quality differences among countries lead to production in countries with advantages in a particular industry which export the product elsewhere in the world. Competitive advantage, in this view, grows out of *where* firms perform activities.

The location of activities is clearly one source of potential advantage in a global firm. The global competitor can locate activities wherever comparative advantage lies, decoupling comparative advantage from the firm's home base or country of ownership. Indeed, the framework presented here suggests that the comparative advantage story is richer than typically told, because it not only involves production activities (the usual focus of discussions) but also applies to other activities in the value chain, such as R&D, processing orders, or designing advertisements. Comparative advantage is specific to the *activity* and not the location of the value chain as a whole.[25] One of the potent advantages of the global firm is that it can spread activities to reflect different preferred locations, something a domestic or country-centered competitor does not do. Thus, components can be made in Taiwan, software written in India, and basic R&D performed in Silicon Valley, for example. This international specialization and arbitrage of activities within the firm is made possible by the growing ability to coordinate and configure globally, and can be difficult to accomplish through arm's-length or quasi-arm's-length transactions because of risks of contracting with independent parties as well as high transaction costs.

[25]It has been recognized that comparative advantage in different stages in a vertically integrated industry sector such as aluminum can reside in different countries. Bauxite mining will take place in resource-rich countries, for example, while smelting will take place in countries with low electrical power cost (see Caves and Jones 1985, p. 142). The argument here extends this thinking *within* the value chain of any stage, and suggests that the optimal location for performing individual activities may vary as well.

While my framework suggests a more complex view of comparative advantage, it also suggests, however, that many forms of competitive advantage for the global firm derive less from *where* it performs activities than from *how* it performs them on a worldwide basis; economies of scale, proprietary learning, and differentiation with multinational buyers are not tied to countries but to the configuration and coordination of the firm's worldwide system. While these advantages are frequently quite sustainable, traditional sources of comparative advantage can be very elusive sources of competitive advantage for an international competitor today, because comparative advantage frequently shifts. A country with the lowest labor cost is overtaken within a few years by some other country; as has happened repeatedly in shipbuilding as Japan has replaced Europe only to be replaced by Korea. Moreover, falling direct labor cost as a percentage of total costs, increasingly global markets for raw materials and other inputs, and freer flowing technology have diminished the role of traditional sources of comparative advantage.

My research on a broad cross-section of industries suggests that the achievement of sustainable world leadership follows a more complex pattern than the exploitation of comparative advantage per se. A competitor may start with a comparative-advantage-related edge that provides the basis for penetrating foreign markets, but this edge is rapidly translated into a broader array of advantages that arise from the global approach to configuration and coordination described earlier. Japanese firms, for example, have done a masterful job in many industries of converting fleeting labor-cost advantages into durable systemwide advantages because of scale and proprietary know-how. Over time, these systemwide advantages are further reinforced with country-specific advantages such as brand identity in many countries as well as distribution channel access.

Many Japanese firms were fortunate enough to make their transitions from country-based comparative advantage to global competitive advantage in a buoyant world economy while nobody paid much attention to them. European and U.S. competitors were willing to cede market share in "less desirable" segments such as the low end of the product line, or so they thought. The Japanese translated these beachheads into world leadership by broadening their lines and reaping advantages in scale and proprietary learning. The Koreans and Taiwanese, the latest entrants in consumer electronics and other industries with low-price strategies, may have a hard time replicating Japan's success. Products have standardized and growth is slow, while Japanese and U.S. competitors are alert to the threat. Japanese firms enjoyed first-mover advantages in pursuing their strategies that the Koreans and Taiwanese do not.

Global Platforms The interaction of the home country conditions and competitive advantages from a global strategy that transcend the country suggest a more complex role of the country in firm success than implied by the theory of comparative advantage. To understand this more complex role of the country, I define the concept of a "global platform." A country is a desirable global platform in an industry if it provides an environment yielding firms domiciled in that country an advantage in competing globally in that particular industry. The firm need not necessarily be owned by investors in the country, but the country is its home base for competing in a particular industry. An essential element of this definition is that it hinges on success *outside* the country, and not merely country conditions that allow firms to successfully master domestic competition. In global competition, a country must be viewed as a platform and not as the place where all a firm's activities are performed.

There are two broad determinants of a good global platform in an industry, which I have explored in more detail elsewhere.[26] The first is comparative advantage, or the factor endowment of the country as a site to perform particular important activities in the industry. Today, *simple factors* such as

---

[26]See Porter (1985*b*). The issues in this section are the subject of a major current research project involving nine countries.

low-cost unskilled labor and natural resources are increasingly less important to global competition than *complex factors* such as skilled scientific and technical personnel as well as advanced infrastructure. Direct labor is a minor proportion of cost in many manufactured goods and automation of nonproduction activities is shrinking it further, while markets for resources are increasingly global and technology has widened the number of sources of many resources. A country's factor endowment is partly exogenous but partly endogenous, the result of attention and investment in the country.

The second determinant of the attractiveness of a country as a global platform in an industry are the characteristics of a country's demand and local operating environment. A country's demand conditions include the size and timing of its demand in an industry, factors recognized as important by authors such as Linder and Vernon.[27] They also include, however, the sophistication and power of local buyers and channels, and the particular product features and attributes demanded. These latter factors are frequently more important today than size and timing of demand, because income differences among many developed countries are relatively small and industries develop simultaneously in many countries. Local operating conditions relevant to investment success include the customs and conditions for doing business in a particular industry as well as the intensity of local competition. Strong local competition frequently benefits a country's success in international competition rather than impedes it, a view sometimes used to advocate the creation of "national champions." Japanese machine tool and electronic firms, Italian ski boot manufacturers, German high performance automakers, and American minicomputer companies all illustrate the spur of local competition to success abroad.

Local demand and operating conditions provide a number of potentially powerful sources of competitive advantage to a global competitor based in

that country. The first is first-mover advantages in perceiving and implementing the appropriate global strategy. Pressing local needs, particularly peculiar ones, lead firms to embark early to solve local problems and gain proprietary know-how. This is then translated into scale and learning advantages as firms move early to compete globally. The second benefit is motivation. Sophisticated, powerful customers, tough operating problems, and a formidable local rival or two promote rapid progress down the learning curve and conceiving of new ways of competing. The final potential benefit of local demand conditions is a baseload of demand for product varieties that will be sought after in international markets. The role of the country in the success of a firm internationally, then, is in the interaction between conditions of local supply, the composition and timing of country demand, and the nature of the local operating environment with economies of scale and learning.

The two determinants of country competitiveness in an industry interact in important and sometimes counterintuitive ways. Local demand and needs frequently influence private and social investment in endogenous factors of production. A nation with oceans as borders and dependence on sea trade, for example, is more prone to have universities and scientific centers dedicated to oceanographic education and research. Similarly, factor endowment seems to influence local demand. The per capita consumption of wine is highest in winegrowing regions, for example.

"Comparative disadvantage" in some factors of production can be an advantage in global competition when combined with pressing local demand. Poor growing conditions have led Israeli farmers to innovate in irrigation and cultivation techniques, for example. The shrinking role of simple factors of production relative to complex factors such as technical personnel seem to be enhancing the frequency and importance of such circumstances. What is important today in international success is unleashing innovation in the proper direction, instead of passive exploitation of a country's static cost advantages, which shift rapidly and can be overcome.

[27] See Linder (1961), Vernon (1966), and Gruber, Mehta, and Vernon (1967).

International success today is a dynamic process resulting from continued development of products and processes. The forces that guide firms to undertake such activity are central to the success of a country's firms in international competition.

A good example of the interplay among these factors is the television set industry. In the United States, early demand was in large screen console sets because TV sets were initially luxury items kept in the living room. As buyers began to purchase second and third sets, sets became smaller and more portable. They were used increasingly in the bedroom, the kitchen, the car, and elsewhere. As the TV set industry matured, table model and portable sets became the universal product variety. Japanese firms, because of the small size of Japanese homes, gained early experience in small sets. They dedicated most of their R&D to developing small picture tubes and compact sets. The Japanese also faced a compelling need to reduce power consumption of sets because of the existing energy crisis, which led them to rapid introduction of solid-state technology. This, in turn, facilitated reducing the number of components and automating manufacturing. The whole process was accelerated by the more rapid saturation of the Japanese home market than the American market and a large number of Japanese competitors who were competing fiercely for the same pie.

In the process of naturally serving the needs of their home market and dealing with local problems, then, Japanese firms gained early experience and scale in segments of the industry that came to dominate world demand. U.S. firms, conversely, pioneered large-screen console sets with fine furniture cabinets. As the industry matured, the experience base of U.S. firms centered on a segment that was small and isolated to a few countries, notably the United States. Aided by intense competitive pressure, Japanese firms were able to penetrate world markets in a segment that was not only uninteresting to foreign firms but also one in which the Japanese had initial-scale learning- and labor-cost advantages. Ultimately the low-cost advantage disappeared as production was automated, but global

scale and learning economies rapidly took over as the Japanese advanced product and process technology at a rapid pace. This example illustrates how early demand for TV sets in the United States proved to be a disadvantage rather than the advantage that some views of international competition paint it to be. Moreover, Japan's comparative disadvantage in energy proved to be an advantage in TV sets (and a number of other industries).

The two broad determinants of a good global platform rest on the interaction between country characteristics and firms' strategies. The literature on comparative advantage, through focusing on country factor endowments, minimizing the demand side, and suppressing the individual firm, is most appropriate in industries where there are few economies of scale, little proprietary technology or technological change, or few possibilities for product differentiation.[28] While these industry characteristics are those of many traditionally traded goods, they describe few of today's important global industries.

The Historical Evolution of International Competition

Having established a framework for understanding the globalization of industries, I am now in a position to view the phenomenon in historical perspective. This discussion provides a way of validating the framework and isolating important issues for global competitors today. If one goes back far enough, relatively few industries were global. Around 1880, most industries were local or regional in scope. The reasons are rather self-evident in the context of my framework. There were few economies of scale in production until fuel-powered machines and assembly-line techniques emerged. There were heterogeneous product needs among regions within countries, much less among countries. There were few if any national media; the *Saturday Evening Post* was the first important national magazine in the United States and developed in the teens and

---

[28]Where it does recognize scale economies, trade theory views them narrowly as arising from production in one country.

twenties. Communication between regions was difficult before the telegraph, telephone, and railroad systems became well developed.

These structural conditions created little impetus for the widespread globalization of industry. Those industries that were global reflected classic comparative-advantage considerations. Goods were simply unavailable in some countries who imported them from others, or differences in the availability of land, resources, or skilled labor made some countries desirable suppliers to others. Export of goods produced locally was the predominant form of global strategy adapted. There was little need for widespread government barriers to international trade during this period, although trade barriers were quite high in some countries for some commodities.

Developments around the 1880s, however, marked the beginnings of what today has blossomed into the globalization of many industries. The first wave of modern global competitors grew up in the late 1800s and early 1900s. Many industries went from local (or regional) to national in scope, and some began globalizing. Firms such as Ford, Singer, Gillette, National Cash Register, Otis, and Western Electric had commanding world market shares by the teens, and operated with integrated worldwide strategies. Early global competitors were principally U.S. and European companies.

Driving this first wave of modern globalization were rising production scale economies, because of the advancements in technology that outpaced the growth of the world economy. Product needs also became more homogenized in different countries as knowledge and industrialization diffused. Transport improved, first through the rail-road and steamships and later in trucking. Communication became more efficient with the telegraph, telephone, and efficient mail service. At the same time, trade barriers were either modest or overwhelmed by the strong competitive advantages of the new large-scale firms.

The burst of globalization soon slowed, however. Most of the few industries that were global moved increasingly toward a multidomestic pattern. Multi-

nationals remained, but between the 1920s and 1950 many evolved toward becoming federations of autonomous subsidiaries. The principal reason was a strong wave of nationalism and resulting high-tariff barriers, partly caused by the world economic crisis and world wars. Another barrier to global strategies was a growing web of cartels and other interfirm contractual agreements. These limited the geographic spread of firms.

The early global competitors began rapidly dispersing their value chains. The situation of Ford Motor Company is no exception. While in 1925 Ford had almost no production outside the United States, by World War II its overseas production had risen sharply. Firms that first became multinationals during the interwar period tended to adopt country-centered strategies. European multinationals, operating in a setting where there were many sovereign countries within a relatively small geographical area, were very early to establish self-contained and quite autonomous subsidiaries in many countries. A more tolerant regulatory environment also encouraged European firms to form cartels and other cooperative agreements among themselves, which limited their foreign market entry.

Between the 1950s and the late 1970s there was a strong reversal of the interwar trends. As the outcome in Figure 1 implied, there have been very strong underlying forces driving the globalization of industries. The important reasons can be understood using the configuration/coordination framework. The competitive advantage of competing worldwide from concentrated activities rose sharply, while concentration costs fell. There was a renewed rise in scale economies in many activities because of advancing technology. The minimum efficient scale of an auto assembly plant more than tripled between 1960 and 1975, for example, while the average real cost of developing a new drug more than quadrupled. The pace of technological change has increased, creating more incentive to amortize R&D costs over worldwide sales.

Product needs have continued to homogenize among countries, as income differences have narrowed, information and communication has flowed more freely around the world, and travel has increased.[29] Growing similarities in business practices and marketing systems (e.g., chain stores) in different countries have also been a facilitating factor in homogenizing needs. Within countries there has been a parallel trend toward greater market segmentation, which some observers see as contradictory to the view that product needs in different countries are becoming more similar. However, segments today seem based less on country differences and more on buyer differences that transcend country boundaries, differences such as demographic, user-industry, or income groups. Many firms successfully employ global segmentation strategies in which they serve a narrow segment of an industry worldwide, as do Daimler-Benz and Rolex.

Another driver of post–World War II globalization has been a sharp reduction in the real costs of transportation. This has occurred through innovations in transportation technology including increasingly large bulk carriers, container ships, and larger more efficient aircraft. At the same time, government impediments to global configuration have been falling in the postwar period. Tariff barriers have gone down, international cartels and patent-sharing agreements have disappeared, while regional economic pacts such as the European Community have emerged to facilitate trade and investment, albeit imperfectly.

The ability to coordinate globally has also risen markedly in the postwar period. Perhaps the most striking reason is falling communication costs, in voice, data, and travel time for individuals. The ability to coordinate activities in different countries has also been facilitated by growing similarities among countries in marketing systems, business practices, and infrastructure; country after country has developed supermarkets and mass distributors, TV advertising, and so on. Greater international mobility of buyers and information has raised the payoff to coordinating how a firm does business around the world. Increasing numbers of firms who are themselves multinational have created growing possibilities for differentiation by suppliers who

were global. Growing volatility of exchange rates has raised the advantage of coordinating production in an international plant network.

The forces underlying globalization have been self-reinforcing. The globalization of firms' strategies has contributed to the homogenization of buyer needs and business practices. Early global competitors must frequently stimulate the demand for uniform global varieties, for example, as Becton Dickinson has done with disposable syringes and Honda did with motorcycles. Globalization of industries begets globalization of supplier industries. The increasing globalization of semiconductor manufacturers is a good example. Pioneering global competitors also stimulate the development and growth of international telecommunication infrastructure as well as the creation of global advertising media, for example, *The Economist* and *The Wall Street Journal*.

Japan has clearly been the winner in the postwar globalization of competition. Japan's firms not only had an initial labor cost advantage but the orientation and skills to translate this into more durable competitive advantages such as scale and proprietary technology. The Japanese context also offered an excellent platform for globalization in many industries, given postwar environmental and technological trends. With home market-demand conditions favoring compactness, a compelling need to cope with high energy costs, and a national conviction to raise quality, Japan has proved a fertile incubator of global leaders.

Japanese multinationals had the advantage of embarking on international strategies in the 1950s and 1960s when the imperatives for a global approach to strategy were beginning to accelerate, but without the legacy of past international investments and modes of behavior.[30] Japanese firms also had an orientation toward highly concentrated activities that fit the strategic imperative of the time. Most European and many U.S. multinationals, conversely, were well established internationally before

---

[29]Levitt's (1983) article provides a supporting view.

[30]Japan's limited prewar international sales were handled largely through trading companies. Trading companies still handled a good portion of Japanese exports in the 1970s but have become less important in newer and high-technology industries.

the war. They had legacies of local subsidiary autonomy that reflected the interwar environment. As Japanese firms spread internationally, they dispersed activities only grudgingly and engaged in extensive global coordination. European and country-centered U.S. companies struggled to rationalize overly dispersed configurations of activities and to boost the level of global coordination among foreign units. They found the decentralized organization structures so fashionable in the 1960s and 1970s to be a hindrance.

▉ Strategic Implications of Globalization

When the pattern of international competition shifts from multidomestic to global in an industry, there are many implications for the strategy of an international firm. At the broadest level, globalization casts new light on many issues that have long been of interest to students of international business. In areas such as international finance, marketing, and business-government relations, the emphasis in the literature has been on the unique problems of adapting to local conditions and ways of doing business in a foreign country.

In a global industry these concerns must be supplemented with an overriding focus on the ways and means of international configuration and coordination. In government relations, for example, the focus must shift from stand-alone negotiations with host countries (appropriate in multidomestic competition) to a recognition that negotiations in one country will both affect other countries and be shaped by possibilities for performing activities in other countries. In finance, measuring the performance of subsidiaries must be modified to reflect the contribution of one subsidiary to another's cost position or differentiation in a global strategy, instead of viewing each subsidiary as a stand-alone unit. In battling with global competitors, it may be appropriate in some countries to accept low profits indefinitely— in multidomestic competition this would be unjustified.[31] In global industries, the overall system matters as much or more than the country.

Overall International Strategy   The most basic question raised by the globalization of an industry is what overall international strategy a firm should adopt. In a global industry, a global strategy that captures the particular advantages of configuration/ coordination present in that industry is necessary to attain a leading position. The firm must examine each activity in the value chain to see if there is a competitive advantage to concentrating and/or to coordinating the activity globally in various ways. However, many firms may not have the resources or initial position to pursue a global strategy, particularly domestic competitors. It is important, as a result, to explore strategic options short of a full-blown global strategy that may be present in global industries.

Abstracting from the particular configuration/ coordination a firm adopts for competing internationally, there are four broad types of possible strategies in a global industry, illustrated schematically in Figure 6. Any strategy involves a choice of the type of competitive advantage sought (low cost or differentiation) and the competitive scope within which the advantage is to be achieved.[32] In global industries, competitive scope involves both the industry segments in which a firm competes and whether it seeks the benefits of configuration/coordination across countries or chooses instead a country-centered approach to competing. These dimensions lead to four broad strategies, illustrated in Figure 6:

Global Cost Leadership or Differentiation: seeking the cost or differentiation advantages of global configuration/coordination through selling a wide line of products to buyers in all or most significant country markets. Global cost leaders (e.g., Toyota, Komatsu) tend to sell standardized products and reap scale advantages in technology development, procurement, and production. Global differentiators (e.g., IBM, Caterpillar) often use their scale and learning advantages to lower the cost of differentiating (e.g., offering many models and frequent model changes) and exploit their worldwide position to reinforce their brand reputation and/or product differentiation with multinational buyers.

▉ [31]For a discussion, see Hout, Porter, and Rudden (1982). For a recent treatment, see Hamel and Prahalad (1985).

▉ [32]For a discussion, see Porter (1985*a*), chapters 1 and 2.

Figure 6   Strategic Alternatives in a Global Industry

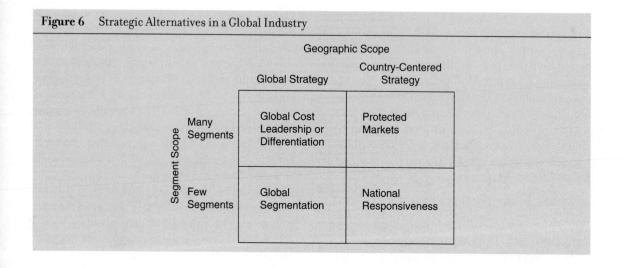

Global Segmentation: serving a particular industry segment worldwide, such as Toyota in lift trucks and Mercedes in automobiles. A variant of this strategy is competing in a subset of countries where the advantages of concentration/coordination are particularly great. In some industries, global segmentation is the only feasible global strategy because the advantages of a global configuration/coordination exist only in particular segments (e.g., high-priced business hotels). A global strategy can make entirely new segmentations of an industry possible, because serving a segment worldwide overcomes scale thresholds that make serving the segment in one country impractical.

Global segmentation, which captures the advantages of a global strategy but marshalls resources by focusing on a narrow segment, is frequently a viable option for a smaller multinational or domestic competitor. The strategy has been quite common among multinationals from smaller countries such as Finland and Switzerland. It is also frequently the first step in a sequenced strategy to move from a domestic to a global strategy. In industries such as motorcycles, farm tractors, and TV sets, for example, initial beachheads were established by Japanese firms following global segmentation strategies

focused on the smaller-sized end of the product line, later expanded into full-line positions.

Protected Markets: seeking out countries where market positions are protected by host governments. The protected markets strategy rests on government impediments to global competition such as high tariffs, stringent import quotas, and high local content requirements, which effectively isolate a country from the global industry. Protected markets strategies usually imply the need for *early* foreign direct investment in a country and can encompass only a subset of countries, because if government impediments were pervasive the industry would be multidomestic. They are generally most feasible in developing countries with protectionist industrial policies such as India, Mexico, and Argentina, though developed countries such as France and Canada offer havens for protected markets strategies in selected industries.

National Responsiveness: focus on those industry segments most affected by local country differences though the industry as a whole is global. The firm aims to meet unusual local needs in products, channels, and marketing practices in each country, foregoing the competitive advantages of a global strategy. The national responsiveness strategy may imply that a firm compete only in those countries where segments with unusual needs are significant in size. The national responsiveness strategy is based on *economic* impediments to global configuration/coordination, while the protected markets strategy rests on government impediments. National responsiveness and protected markets can be pursued simultaneously if government protection only covers certain segments.

Protected markets or national responsiveness strategies rest on the costs of global configuration/coordination that remain even in industries that globalize. They rely on careful focus on certain segments/countries to hold off global competitors, and represent natural options for domestic firms without the resources to become international as well as multinationals who lack the resources or skills to concentrate/coordinate their activities worldwide. The sustainability of a national responsiveness strategy depends on continued national differences in some segments as well as the price differential between locally tailored and global varieties. If the extra cost to buy a better performing global variety is small or the price premium to buy a tailored local variety is too great, global competitors may overtake country-centered ones. Moreover, there is a tendency for global competitors to widen their product lines over time as they overcome market-specific barriers to entry in a country, even into segments that appear subject to local differences. In motorcycles, for example, global Japanese competitors eventually entered the large bike segment even though it is insignificant in size in Japan and many other countries. They employed shared dealer networks, brand names, and production facilities built up through competing in the global small bike segment.[33]

The sustainability of the protected markets strategy rests on continued government impediments to global competitors as well as the sanctity of a firm's favored status. Governments often invite additional competitors into their markets as the markets grow, however, and also escalate their demands on a firm once it has sunk investments in a country. Because protected markets strategies lack a competitive advantage in economic terms, their choice depends on a sophisticated prediction about future government behavior.

In many industries, two or more of the strategies can co-exist.[34] Segments with strong national differences and/or countries with high levels of protection lead to situations where there are global competitors, country-centered multinationals, and domestic firms all competing in the industry. Timing plays an important role in the industry structures observed. Early entry by a global competitor often retards the development of country-centered multinationals and domestic firms. Conversely, first-mover advantages garnered by country-centered or domestic firms can erect country-specific entry/mobility barriers that offset the advantages of a global competitor. The importance of timing suggests that multiple outcomes may be possible.

The Future of International Competition

Since the late 1970s, there have been some gradual but significant changes in the pattern of international competition that carry important implications for international strategy. Foreign direct investment has been growing more rapidly and flowing in new directions, while growth in trade has slowed. This article's framework provides a template with which I can examine these changes and probe their significance. The factors shaping the global configuration of activities by firms are developing in ways that contrast with the trends of the previous thirty years.

Homogenization of product needs among countries appears to be continuing, though segmentation within countries is as well. As a result, consumer packaged goods are becoming increasingly prone toward globalization, though they have long been

---

[33]A key consideration in the sustainability of national responsiveness strategies is the ability of broad-line competitors to share activities among segments. See Porter (1985a), chapter 7, for a generic treatment.

[34]Mixed strategies are also observed in which a firm employs a global strategy in one group of countries and country-centered strategies in others. In the sewing machine industry, for example, otherwise global competitions product pedal-powered sewing machines that meet local needs in developing countries with high levels of protection.

characterized by multidomestic competition. There are also signs of globalization in some service industries as the introduction of information technology creates scale economies in support activities and facilitate coordination in primary activities. Global service firms are reaping advantages in hardware and software development as well as in procurement.

In many industries, however, limits have been reached in this scale economies that have been driving the concentration of activities. These limits grow out of classic diseconomies of scale that arise in very large facilities, as well as new, more flexible technology in manufacturing and other activities that is often not as scale sensitive as previous methods. At the same time, though, flexible manufacturing allows the production of multiple varieties (to serve different countries) in a single plant. This may encourage new movement toward globalization in industries in which product differences among countries have remained significant and have blocked globalization in the past. Another important change is the declining labor content in many industries due to automation of the value chain, which is reducing the incentive to locate activities in low-wage countries such as South Korea and Singapore.

There also appear to be some limits to further decline in transport costs, as innovations such as containerization, bulk ships, and larger aircraft have largely run their course. However, a parallel trend toward smaller, lighter products and components may keep some downward pressure on transport costs. The biggest change in the benefits and costs of concentrated configuration has been the sharp rise in protectionism in recent years and the resulting rise in nontariff barriers akin to the 1920s. As a group, these factors point to less need and less opportunity for highly concentrated configurations of activities and explain why growth in direct investment has been outpacing growth in trade. Falling labor content also suggests that more foreign investment will flow to developed countries (to secure market access) instead of low-wage countries.

When the coordination dimension is examined, the picture looks quite different. Communication and coordination costs are dropping sharply, driven by breathtaking advances in information systems and telecommunication technology. We have just seen the beginning of developments in this area, which are spreading throughout the value chain.[35] Boeing, for example, is employing computer-aided design technology to jointly design components on-line with foreign suppliers. Engineers in different countries are communicating via computer screens. Marketing systems and business practices continue to homogenize, facilitating the coordination of activities in different countries. The mobility of buyers and information is also growing rapidly, greasing the international spread of brand reputations and enhancing the importance of consistency in the way activities are performed worldwide. Increasing numbers of multinational and global firms are begetting globalization by their suppliers. There is also a sharp rise in the computerization of manufacturing as well as other activities throughout the value chain, which greatly facilitates coordination among dispersed sites.

The imperative of global strategy is shifting, then, in ways that will require a rebalancing of configuration and coordination. Concentrating activities is less necessary in economic terms, and less possible as governments force more dispersion. These forces are pushing firms to intermediate positions on the configuration axis as shown in Figure 7. At the same time, the ability to coordinate globally throughout the value chain is increasing dramatically through modern technology. The need to coordinate is also rising to offset greater dispersion and to respond to buyer needs. Moreover, intermediate configurations often require greater coordination, and coordination can neutralize some of the costs of dispersion forced on firms by governments. These considerations imply an upward movement in Figure 7. Thus, simpler first generation global strategies (e.g.,

[35]For a discussion, see Porter and Millar (1985).

Figure 7 Future Trends in International Competition

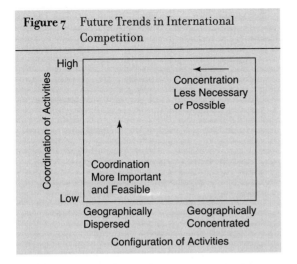

concentration and export) seem to be giving way to more complex global strategies involving multiple though coordinated R&D activities, sophisticated networking of overseas plants, worldwide procurement, and so on.

Thus, today's game of global strategy seems increasingly to be a game of coordination—getting dispersed production facilities, R&D laboratories, and marketing activities to truly work together. Widespread coordination remains the exception rather than the rule today in many multinationals. Successful international competitors in the future will be those who can seek out competitive advantages from global configuration/coordination anywhere in the value chain, and overcome the organizational barriers to exploiting them.

References

Bartlett, C. A. "Multinational Structural Evolution: The Changing Decision Environment in the International Division." D.B.A. diss., Harvard Graduate School of Business Administration, 1979.

Buckley, P. J., and M. C. Casson. *The Future of the Multinational Enterprise.* London: Holms and Meier, 1976.

Buzzell, R. D. "Can You Standardize Multinational Marketing?" *Harvard Business Review* (November/December 1968): 102–13.

Casson, M. C. "Transaction Costs and the Theory of the Multinational Enterprise," in A. Rugman, ed., *New Theories of the Multinational Enterprise.* London: Croom Helm, 1982.

Caves, R. E. *Multinational Enterprise and Economic Analysis.* Cambridge, England: Cambridge University Press, 1982.

Caves, R. E., and R. W. Jones. *World Trade and Payments,* fourth edition. Boston: Little, Brown, 1985.

Doz, Y. "National Policies and Multinational Management." D.B.A. diss., Harvard Graduate School of Business Administration, 1976.

Dunning, J., and M. McQueen. "The Eclectic Theory of International Production: A Case Study of the International Hotel Industry." *Managerial and Decision Economics* 2 (December 1981): 197–210.

Franko, L. G. *The European Multinationals: A Renewed Challenge to American and British Big Business.* Stanford, Conn.: Greylock, 1976.

Gruber, W., D. Mehta, and R. Vernon. "The R&D Factor in International Trade and Investment of United States Industries." *Journal of Political Economy* (February 1967): 20–37.

Hamel, G., and C. K. Prahalad. "Do You Really Have a Global Strategy?" *Harvard Business Review* (July/August 1985): 139–48.

Hirsch, S. "Technological Factors in the Composition and Direction of Israel's Industrial Exports," in Vernon, R., ed., *Technological Factors in International Trade.* New York: National Bureau of Economic Research, 1970, 365–408.

Hladik, K. "International Joint Ventures: An Empirical Investigation into the Characteristics of Recent U.S.-Foreign Joint Venture

Partnerships." Ph.D. diss., Business Economics Program, Harvard University, 1984.

Hout, T., M. E. Porter, and E. Rudden. "How Global Companies Win Out." *Harvard Business Review* (September/October 1982): 98–108.

Knickerbocker, F. *Oligopolistic Reaction and Multinational Enterprise.* Cambridge, Mass.: Harvard University Press, 1973.

Lawrence, P. R., and J. W. Lorsch. *Organization and Environment.* Boston: Division of Research, Harvard Graduate School of Business Administration, 1967.

Levitt, T. "The Globalization of Markets." *Harvard Business Review* (May/June 1983): 92–102.

Linder, S. *An Essay on Trade and Transformation.* New York: John Wiley, 1961.

Perlmutter, H. V. "The Tortuous Evolution of the Multinational Corporation." *Columbia Journal of World Business* (January/February 1969): 9–18.

Porter, M. E. *Competitive Strategy: Techniques for Analyzing Industries and Competitors.* New York: Free Press, 1980.

———. *Competitive Advantage: Creating and Sustaining Superior Performance.* New York: Free Press, 1985*a*.

———. "Beyond Comparative Advantage." Working Paper, Harvard Graduate School of Business Administration, August 1985*b*.

Porter, M. E., and V. Millar. "How Information Gives You Competitive Advantage." *Harvard Business Review* (July/August 1985): 149–60.

Prahalad, C. K. "The Strategic Process in a Multinational Corporation." D.B.A. diss., Harvard Graduate School of Business Administration, 1975.

Pryor, M. H. "Planning in a World-Wide Business." *Harvard Business Review* 43 (January/February 1965): 130–9.

Ronstadt, R. C. "International R&D: The Establishment and Evolution of Research and Development Abroad by Seven U.S. Multinationals. *Journal of International Business Studies* (Spring/Summer 1978): 7–23.

Stobaugh, R. B., et al. "Nine Investments Abroad and Their Impact at Home: Case Studies on Multinational Enterprise and the U.S. Economy." Boston: Division of Research, Harvard Business School, 1976.

Stopford, J. J., and L. T. Wells, Jr. *Managing the Multinational Enterprise: Organization of the Firm and Overlap of Subsidiaries.* New York: Basic Books, 1972.

Teece, D. J. "Multinational Enterprise: Market Failure and Market Power Considerations." *Sloan Management Review* 22, no. 3 (September 1981): 3–17.

———. "Transaction Cost Economics and the Multinational Enterprise: An Assessment." Working Paper IB-3, Business School, University of California at Berkeley, January 1985.

United Nations Center on Transnational Corporations, *Salient Features and Trends in Foreign Direct Investment.* United Nations, New York, 1984.

Vernon, R. "International Investment and International Trade in the Product Cycle." *Quarterly Journal of Economics* 80 (May 1966): 190–207.

Williamson, O. *Markets and Hierarchies.* New York: Free Press, 1975.

Wind, Y., S. P. Douglas, and H. B. Perlmutter. "Guidelines for Developing International Marketing Strategies." *Journal of Marketing* 37 (April 1973): 14–23.

CHAPTER 4

Developing Coordination and Control:
The Organizational Challenge

In the earlier chapters we described how changes in the international operating environment have forced MNCs to optimize global efficiency, national responsiveness, and worldwide learning simultaneously. For most companies, this new challenge implied not only a fundamental strategic reorientation, but also a major change in organizational capability.

Implementing such a complex three-pronged strategic objective would be difficult under any circumstances, but in a worldwide company the task is complicated even further. The very act of "going international" multiplies a company's organizational complexity. Most companies find it difficult enough balancing product divisions or business units with corporate staff functions. The thought of adding geographically oriented management and maintaining a three-way balance of organizational perspectives and capabilities among product, function, and region is intimidating. The difficulty is further increased because the resolution of tensions among the three different management groups must be accomplished in an organization whose operating units are divided by distance and time and whose key members are separated by barriers of culture and language.

Beyond Structural Fit

Because the choice of a basic organizational structure has such a powerful influence on the management process in an MNC, much of the earlier attention of managers and researchers alike was focused on trying to find which formal structure provided the right "fit" under various conditions. The most widely recognized study on this issue was John Stopford's research on the 187 largest U.S.-based MNCs in the late 1960s.[1] His work resulted in a "stages model" of international organization structure that defined two variables to capture strategic and administrative complexity that faced most companies as they expanded abroad: the number of products sold internationally ("foreign product diversity" in Figure 4-1) and the importance of international sales to the company ("foreign sales as a percentage of total sales"). Plotting the structural change in his sample of 187 companies, he found that worldwide corporations typically adopt different organizational structures at different stages of international expansion.

---

[1]Stopford's research is described in John M. Stopford and Louis T. Wells, *Managing the Multinational Enterprise* (New York: Basic Books, 1972).

Figure 4-1   Stopford and Wells's International Structural Stages Model

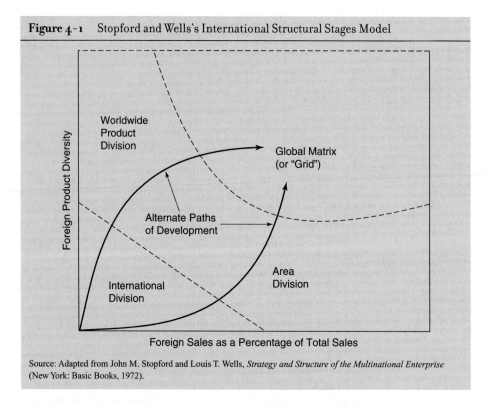

Source: Adapted from John M. Stopford and Louis T. Wells, *Strategy and Structure of the Multinational Enterprise* (New York: Basic Books, 1972).

According to this model, worldwide companies typically manage their international operations through an international division at the early stage of foreign expansion. Subsequently, those companies that expand their sales abroad without significantly increasing foreign product diversity typically adopt an area structure (for example, European region, Asia-Pacific region, etc.). Other companies that expand by increasing their foreign product diversity tend to adopt the worldwide product division structure (for example, chemicals division, plastics division, etc.). Finally, when both foreign sales and foreign product diversity are high, companies resort to a global matrix in which a French chemicals manager might report to both the European regional head and the global chemicals division president.

Although these ideas were presented as a descriptive model, consultants and managers soon began to apply them prescriptively. For many companies, it seemed that structure followed fashion more than strategy. And in the process, the debate was often reduced to generalized discussions of the comparative value of product- versus geography-based structures on one hand, and to simplistic choices between "centralization" and "decentralization" on the other.

Confronted with the increasing complexity, diversity, and change in the 1980s, managers in many worldwide companies looked for ways to restructure. Conventional wisdom provided a ready solution: the global matrix. But for most companies, the result was disappointing. The promised land of the global matrix turned out to be an organizational quagmire from which they were forced to retreat.

Failure of the Matrix

In theory, the solution should have worked. Having frontline managers report simultaneously to different organizational groups (such as the French chemicals manager in the example above) should have enabled the companies to maintain the balance among centralized efficiency, local responsiveness, and worldwide knowledge transfer. The multiple channels of communication and control promised the ability to nurture diverse management perspectives, and the ability to shift the balance of power within the matrix theoretically gave it great flexibility. The reality turned out to be otherwise, however, and the history of companies that built formal global matrix structures was an unhappy one.

Dow Chemical, a pioneer of global matrix organization, eventually returned to a more conventional structure with clear lines of responsibility being given to geographic managers. Citibank, once a textbook example of the global matrix, also discarded this mode of dual reporting relationships after a few years of highly publicized experimentation. And so too did scores of other companies that tried to manage their worldwide activities through this complex and rather bureaucratic structure.

Most encountered the same problems. The matrix amplified the differences in perspectives and interests by forcing all issues through the dual chains of command so that even a minor difference could become the subject of heated disagreement and debate. Dual reporting led to conflict and confusion; the proliferation of channels created informational logjams; and overlapping responsibilities resulted in turf battles and a loss of accountability. Separated by barriers of distance, time, language, and culture, managers found it virtually impossible to clarify the confusion and resolve the conflicts. As a result, in company after company, the initial appeal of the global matrix structure quickly faded into a recognition that a different solution was required.

Building Organizational Capability

The basic problem underlying a company's search for a structural fit was that it focused on only one organizational variable—formal structure—and this single tool proved to be unequal to the task of capturing the complexity of the strategic task facing most MNCs. First, as indicated earlier, this focus often forced managers to ignore the multidimensionality of the environmental forces as they made choices between product- versus geographically based structures. Second, structure defined a static set of roles, responsibilities, and relationships in a dynamic and rapidly evolving task environment. And finally, restructuring efforts often proved harmful, as organizations were bludgeoned into a major realignment of roles, responsibilities, and relationships by overnight changes in the structure.

In an increasing number of companies, managers now recognize that formal structure is a powerful but blunt instrument of strategic change. Structural fit is becoming both less relevant and harder to achieve. To develop the vital multidimensional and flexible capabilities, a company must reorient managers' thinking and reshape the core decision-making systems. In doing so, the company's entire management process—the administrative system, communication channels, and interpersonal relationships—becomes the tools for managing such change.

In this chapter, we will explore some of the more subtle and sophisticated ways of thinking about and dealing with the organizational challenges facing managers in worldwide companies. As a first step, we will examine how administrative heritage—a company's history and its embedded management culture—influences its organization and its ability and willingness to change. Next, we will describe the characteristics of the transnational organization that can operate effectively in the complex international environment. Finally, we will describe the tools and processes that can be used to develop the required organizational capability and suggest how these tools might be used to manage the process of strategic and organizational change.

Administrative Heritage

Whereas industry analysis can reveal a company's strategic challenges and market opportunities, its ability to fulfill that promise will be greatly influenced—and often constrained—by its existing asset configuration and resource distribution, its historical definition of management responsibilities, and its ingrained organizational norms. A company's organization is shaped not only by current external task demands, but also by past internal management biases. In particular, each company is influenced by the path by which it developed—its organizational history—and the values, norms, and practices of its management—its management culture. Collectively, these factors constitute a company's administrative heritage.

Administrative heritage can be, at the same time, one of the company's greatest assets—the underlying source of its key competencies—and also a significant liability, because it resists change and thereby prevents realignment. As managers in many companies have learned, often at considerable cost, although strategic plans can be scrapped and redrawn overnight, there is no such thing as a zero-based organization. Companies are, to a significant extent, captives of their past, and any organizational transformation has to focus at least as much on where the company is coming from—its administrative heritage—as on where it wants to get to.

The importance of a company's administrative heritage can be illustrated by contrasting the development of a typical European MNC whose major international expansion occurred in the decades of the 1920s and 1930s, a typical American MNC that expanded abroad in the 1940s and 1950s, and a typical Japanese company that made its main overseas thrust in the 1960s and 1970s. Even if these companies were in the same industry, their different heritages led to their adopting some very different strategic and organizational models.

Decentralized Federation

Expanding abroad in a period of rising tariffs and discriminatory legislation, the typical European company was forced to build local production facilities to compete effectively with local competitors. With their own plants, national subsidiaries were able to modify products and marketing approaches to meet widely differing local market needs. The increasing independence of these self-sufficient national units was reinforced by the transportation and communications barriers that existed in that era, limiting the head-quarters' ability to intervene in the management of the company's spreading worldwide operations.

The emerging configuration of distributed assets and delegated responsibility fit well with the ingrained management norms and practices in many European companies. European companies, particularly those from the United Kingdom, the Netherlands, and France, developed an internal culture that emphasized personal relationships (an "old boys network") rather than formal structures, and financial controls more than coordination of technical or operational detail. This management style tended to reinforce companies' willingness to delegate more operating independence and strategic freedom to their foreign subsidiaries. Highly autonomous national companies were often managed more as a portfolio of offshore investments rather than as a single international business.

The resulting organization pattern was a loose federation of independent national subsidiaries, each focused primarily on its local market. As a result, many of these companies adopted what we have described in the earlier chapters as the multinational strategy and managed it through a decentralized federation organization model that is represented in Figure 4-2(a).

Figure 4-2   Organizational Configuration Models

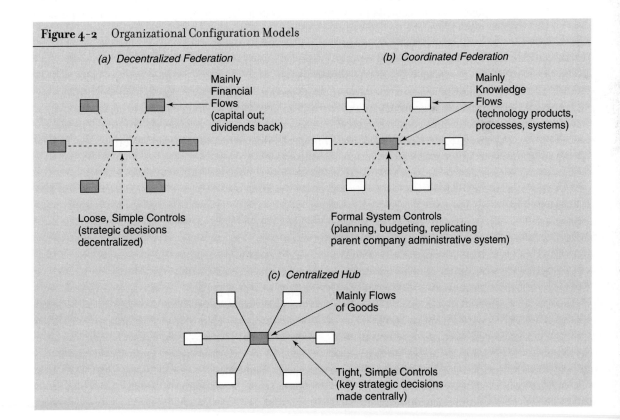

(a) Decentralized Federation

Mainly Financial Flows (capital out; dividends back)

Loose, Simple Controls (strategic decisions decentralized)

(b) Coordinated Federation

Mainly Knowledge Flows (technology products, processes, systems)

Formal System Controls (planning, budgeting, replicating parent company administrative system)

(c) Centralized Hub

Mainly Flows of Goods

Tight, Simple Controls (key strategic decisions made centrally)

Coordinated Federation

United States companies, many of which enjoyed their fastest international expansion in the 1940s and 1950s, developed under very different circumstances. Their main strength lay in the new technologies and management processes they had developed as a consequence of being located in the world's largest, richest, and most technologically advanced market. After the war, their foreign expansion focused primarily on leveraging this strength, giving rise to the international product cycle theory referred to in Chapter 1.

Reinforcing this strategy was a professional managerial culture in most U.S.-based companies that contrasted with the "old boys network" that typified the European companies' processes. The management approach in most U.S.-based companies was built on a willingness to delegate responsibility, while retaining overall control through sophisticated management systems and specialist corporate staffs. The systems provided channels for a regular flow of information to be interpreted by the central staff and used by top management for coordination and control.

The main handicap such companies faced was that parent-company management often adopted a parochial and even superior attitude toward international operations, perhaps because of the assumption that new ideas and developments all came from the parent. Despite corporate management's increased understanding of its overseas markets, it often seemed to view foreign operations as appendages whose principal purpose was to leverage the capabilities and resources developed in the home market.

Nonetheless, the approach was highly successful in the postwar decades, and many U.S.-based companies adopted what we have described as the international strategy and a coordinated federation organizational model shown in Figure 4-2(b). Their foreign subsidiaries were often free to adapt products or strategies to reflect market differences, but their dependence on the parent company for new products, processes, and ideas dictated a great deal more coordination and control by headquarters than in the decentralized federation organization. This was facilitated by the existence of formal systems and controls in the headquarters–subsidiary link.

Centralized Hub

In contrast, the typical Japanese company, making its main international thrust since the 1960s, faced a greatly altered external environment and operated with very different internal norms and values. With limited prior overseas exposure, it chose not to match the well-established local marketing capabilities and facilities of its European and U.S. competitors. (Indeed, well-established Japanese trading companies often provided it with an easier means of entering foreign markets.) However, it had new, efficient, scale-intensive plants, and it was expanding into a global environment of declining trade barriers. Together, these factors gave it the incentive to develop a competitive advantage at the upstream end of the value-added chain. Its competitive strategy emphasized cost advantages and quality assurance, demanding tight control over product development, procurement, and manufacturing. A centrally controlled, export-based internationalization strategy represented a perfect fit with the external environment and the company's competitive capabilities.

Such an approach also fit the cultural background and organizational values in the emerging Japanese MNC. At the foundation of the internal processes were the strong national cultural norms that emphasized group behavior and valued interpersonal harmony reflected in management practices such as *nemawashi* (consensus building) and *ringi* (shared decision making). By keeping primary decision making and control at the center, the Japanese company could retain this culturally dependent management system that was so communications-intensive and people-dependent. In addition, international growth through exporting made it possible for Japanese MNCs to retain their system of lifetime employment. As a result, these companies adopted what we have described as a global strategy, and developed a centralized hub organizational model, shown in Figure 4-2(c), to support this strategic orientation.

The Transnational Challenge

In Chapters 2 and 3, we advanced the hypothesis that many worldwide industries were transformed in the 1980s from traditional multinational, international, and global forms toward a transnational form. Instead of demanding efficiency, or responsiveness, or learning as the key capability for success, these businesses now require participating firms to achieve the three capabilities simultaneously to remain competitive.

Table 4-1 summarizes the key characteristics of the decentralized federation, coordinated federation, and centralized hub organizations we have described in this chapter as the supporting forms for companies pursuing the multinational, international, and global strategies. A review of these characteristics immediately reveals the problems each of the three archetypal company models might face in responding to the transnational challenge.

With its resources and capabilities consolidated at the center, the global company achieves efficiency primarily by exploiting potential scale economies in all its activities.

Table 4-1 Organizational Characteristics of Decentralized Federation, Coordinated Federation, and Centralized Hub Organizations

	Decentralized Federation	**Coordinated Federation**	**Centralized Hub**
Strategic approach	Multinational	International	Global
Key strategic capability	National responsiveness	Worldwide transfer of home country innovations	Global-scale efficiency
Configuration of assets and capabilities	Decentralized and nationally self-sufficient	Sources of core competencies centralized, others decentralized	Centralized and globally scaled
Role of overseas operations	Sensing and exploiting local opportunities	Adapting and leveraging parent-company competencies	Implementing parent-company strategies
Development and diffusion of knowledge	Knowledge developed and retained within each unit	Knowledge developed at the center and transferred to overseas units	Knowledge developed and retained at the center

In such an organization, however, the national subsidiaries' lack of resources and responsibilities may undermine their motivation and their ability to respond to local market needs, whereas the central groups often lack adequate understanding of the market needs and production realities outside their home market. These are problems that a global organization cannot overcome without jeopardizing its trump card of global efficiency.

The classic multinational company suffers from other limitations. Although its dispersed resources and decentralized decision making allows national subsidiaries to respond to local needs, the fragmentation of activities also leads to inefficiency. Learning also suffers, because knowledge is not consolidated and does not flow among the various parts of the company. As a result, local innovations often represent little more than the efforts of subsidiary management to protect its turf and autonomy, or reinventions of the wheel caused by blocked communication or the not-invented-here (NIH) syndrome.

In contrast, the international company is better able to leverage the knowledge and capabilities of the parent company (but is still not very good at learning from its foreign operations). However, its resource configuration and operating systems make it less efficient than the global company, and less responsive than the multinational company.

The Transnational Organization

There are three important organizational characteristics that distinguish the transnational organization from its multinational, international, or global counterparts: It builds and legitimizes multiple diverse internal perspectives; its physical assets and management capabilities are distributed internationally, but are interdependent; and it has a robust and flexible internal integrative process. In the following paragraphs, we will describe and illustrate each of these characteristics.

Multidimensional Perspectives

Managing in an environment in which strategic forces are both diverse and changeable, the transnational company must create the ability to sense and analyze the numerous and often conflicting opportunities, pressures, and demands it faces worldwide. Strong national subsidiary management is needed to sense and represent the changing needs of local consumers and the increasing pressures from host governments; capable global business management is required to track the strategy of global competitors and to provide the coordination necessary to respond appropriately; and influential functional management is needed to concentrate corporate knowledge, information, and expertise, and facilitate its transfer among organizational units.

Unfortunately, in many companies, power is concentrated with the particular management group that has historically represented the company's most critical strategic tasks—often at the cost of allowing other groups representing other needs to atrophy. For example, in multinational companies, key decisions were usually dominated by the country management group because they made the most critical contribution to achieving national responsiveness. In global companies, by contrast, managers in worldwide product divisions were typically the most influential, because strong business management played the key role in the company's efforts to seek global efficiency. And in international companies, functional management groups often came to assume this position of dominance because of their roles in building, accumulating, and transferring the company's skills, knowledge, and capabilities.

In transnational companies, however, biases in the decision-making process are consciously reduced by building up the capability, credibility, and influence of the less-powerful management groups while protecting the morale and capabilities of the dominant group. The objective is to build a multidimensional organization in which the influence of each of the three management groups is balanced. Some of the cases in this book focus explicitly on this issue of developing and maintaining such a balanced and multidimensional organization.

Distributed, Interdependent Capabilities

Having sensed the diverse opportunities and demands it faces, the transnational organization must then be able to make choices among them and respond in a timely and effective manner to those that are deemed strategically important. When a company's decision-making process and organizational capabilities are concentrated at the center—as they are in the global organization's centralized hub configuration—it is often difficult to respond appropriately to diverse worldwide demands. Being distant from the frontline opportunities and threats, the central group's ability to act in an effective and timely manner is constrained by its reliance on complex and intensive international communications. On the other hand, multinational organizations with their response capabilities spread throughout the decentralized federation of independent operations suffer from duplication of effort, inefficiency of operations, and barriers to international learning.

In transnational organizations, management breaks away from the restricted view that assumes the need to centralize activities for which global scale or specialized knowledge is important. They ensure that viable national units achieve global scale by specializing their activities and giving them the responsibility of becoming the company's world source for a given product or expertise. And by securing the cooperation and involvement of the individuals in the relevant national units, they tap into important technological advances and market developments wherever they are occurring around the globe.

One major consequence of the distribution of assets and responsibilities is that the interdependence of worldwide units automatically increases. Simple structural configurations like the decentralized federation, the coordinated federation, and the centralized hub are inadequate for the task facing the transnational corporation. What is needed is a structure we term the integrated network (see Figure 4-3).

In the integrated network configuration, management regards each of the worldwide units as a source of ideas, skills, capabilities, and knowledge that can be harnessed for the benefit of the total organization. Efficient local plants may be converted into international production centers; innovative national or regional development labs may be designated the company's "center of excellence" for a particular product or process development; and creative subsidiary marketing groups may be given a lead role in developing worldwide marketing strategies for certain products or businesses.

Figure 4-3   Integrated Network Model

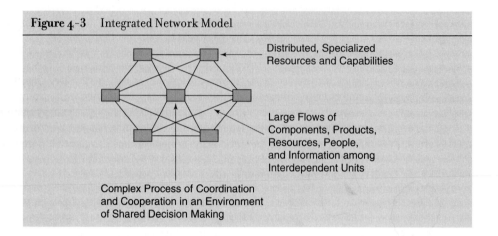

Distributed, Specialized Resources and Capabilities

Large Flows of Components, Products, Resources, People, and Information among Interdependent Units

Complex Process of Coordination and Cooperation in an Environment of Shared Decision Making

Flexible Integrative Process

Finally, the transnational organization requires a management process that can resolve the diversity of interests and perspectives and integrate the dispersed responsibilities. However, it cannot be bound by the symmetry of organizational process that follows when the task is seen in simplistic or static terms (for example, "Should responsibilities be centralized or decentralized?"). It is clear that the benefits to be gained from central control of worldwide research or manufacturing activities may be much more important than those related to the global coordination of the sales and service functions. We have also seen how the pattern of functional coordination varies by business and by geographic area (aircraft engine companies need central control of more decisions than multinational food packagers; operations in developing countries may need more central support than those in advanced countries). Furthermore, all coordination needs to be able to change over time.

Thus, management must be able to differentiate its operating relationships and change its decision-making roles by function, across businesses, among geographic units, and over time. The management process must be able to change from product to product, from country to country, and even from decision to decision. This requires the development of rather sophisticated and subtle decision-making machinery based on three different but interdependent management processes. The first is a focused and constrained escalation process that allows top management to intervene directly in the content of key decisions (for example, major resource allocation commitments)—a subtle and carefully managed form of *centralization*. The second is a process in which management structures individual roles and administrative systems to influence specific decisions (typically repetitive or routine activities like setting transfer prices) through *formalization*. The third is a self-regulatory capability in which top management's role is to establish a broad culture and set of relationships that provide a supportive organizational context for delegated decisions—a sophisticated management process driven by *socialization*.

Anatomy, Physiology, and Psychology of the Transnational

The kind of organization we have described as a transnational clearly represents something quite different from its predecessors—the multinational, international, and global organizations. Building such an organization requires much more than choosing between a product or a geographic organization structure; and managing it implies much more than centralizing or delegating decisions By viewing the organizational challenge as one of creating and managing a decision process that responds to the company's critical task demands, the MNC manager is forced to adopt a very different approach from someone who defines the problem as one of discovering and installing the ideal structure.

If the structural stages model no longer provides a helpful description of international organization development, we need a different way to conceptualize the more complex array of tools and processes discussed in our earlier descriptions of transnational organizations. The simple but useful framework adopted here is to describe the organization in terms of a physiological model. To be effective, change in an organization's anatomy (the formal structure of its assets, resources, and responsibilities) must be complemented by adaptations to its physiology (the organization's systems and decision processes) and to its psychology (the organization's culture and management mentality). The different tools and processes used to build and manage the transnational will be described using this physiological model.

Structuring the Organizational Anatomy

The traditional approach to MNC organization problems tended to be defined in macrostructural terms that focused on simple but rather superficial choices, such as the classic product versus area structure debate. As we have seen, however, the development of a transnational organization requires management to pay equal attention to designing and developing a supporting structure that both supplements and counterbalances the innate power of the line structure.

Having carefully defined the structure and responsibilities of all management groups, the next challenge is to ensure that particularly those without line authority have appropriate access to and influence in the mainstream of the management process. Microstructural tools such as task forces or committees become important in creating supplemental decision-making forums that often allow nonline managers to assume responsibility and be given authority in a way that is not possible within the formal line organization.

Where once task forces and special committees were considered ad hoc, or quick-fix devices, companies building transnational organizations use them as legitimate and important structural tools through which top management can modify or fine-tune their basic structure. To stretch our anatomical analogy, if the formal line structure is the organization's backbone, then the nonline structure is its rib cage, and these microstructural tools are the muscle and the cartilage that give the organizational skeleton its flexibility.

Building the Organizational Physiology

One of the key roles of management is to influence the structure of the communication channels through which the organization's decision-making process operates. By adapting the various administrative systems, hierarchical channels, and informal relationships, they can exert a powerful influence—and even control—over the volume, content, and direction of information flows. This flow of information that is the lifeblood of all management processes defines the organizational physiology.

Many researchers have shown the link between the need for information and the complexity and uncertainty of the tasks to be performed. In the integrated network configuration, task complexity and uncertainty are very high. Operating an interdependent system in such a setting requires large volumes of complex information to be gathered, exchanged, and processed. In the complex integrated network that frames a transnational organization, formal systems alone cannot support their huge information processing needs. Such companies are forced to look beyond the traditional tools and the conventional.

For years, managers have recognized that a great deal of information exchange and even decision making—perhaps the majority—occurs through the organization's innumerable informal channels and relationships. Yet this part of the management process has often been dismissed as either unimportant ("office gossip" or "rumor mill") or unmanageable ("disruptive cliques" or "unholy alliances"). In the management of transnational organizations, such biases need to be reexamined. Not only is it more important for managers of international operations to exert some control and influence over informal systems, because organizational units are widely separated and because information is scarce it is also more feasible to do so.

Getting started is often remarkably easy, requiring managers to do little more than use their daily involvement in the ongoing management processes to shape the nature and quality of communications patterns and relationships. The nature and intensity of informal relationships respond remarkably quickly to changes in the frequency and agenda of management trips and corporate meetings, the pattern of one's committee assignments, and the track of one's career development. In addition, management can also recognize, legitimize, and reinforce existing informal relationships that are contributing to the corporate objective.

Developing the Organizational Psychology

In addition to an anatomy and a physiology, each organization also has a psychology (that is, a set of explicit or implicit corporate values and shared beliefs) that greatly influences the way it operates. For companies operating in an international environment, this is a particularly important organizational attribute. When employees come from a variety of different national backgrounds, management cannot assume that all will share common values and relate to common norms. Furthermore, in an operating environment in which managers are separated by distance and time barriers, shared management understanding is often a much more powerful tool than formal structure and systems in coordinating diverse activities.

Of the numerous tools and techniques that can affect an organization's psychology, our review of transnational organizations has highlighted three that are particularly important. The first is the need for a clear, shared understanding of the company's mission and objectives. Matsushita's 250-year vision of its role in a world society, Nokia's commitment to "Connecting People," and Bill Gates's aspiration to create a world with "a computer on every desk and in every home running on Microsoft software" represent variants of this approach applied at different strategic and operational levels.

The second important tool is the visible behavior and public actions of senior management. Particularly in a transnational organization where other signals may be diluted or distorted, top management's actions speak louder than words and tend to have a powerful influence on the company's culture. They represent the clearest role model of behavior and a signal of the company's strategic and organizational priorities. When Sony Corporation founder and CEO, Akio Morita, relocated to New York to build the company's U.S. operations personally, he sent a message about Sony's commitment to its overseas businesses that could not have been conveyed as strongly by any other means.

The third and most commonly used set of tools for modifying organizational psychology in the transnational organization is nested in the company's personnel policies, practices, and systems. A company can develop a multidimensional and flexible organization process only if its personnel systems develop and reinforce the appropriate kinds of people. In Eli Lilly, we saw a good example of such an approach. Its recruiting and promotion policies emphasized the importance of good interpersonal skills and flexible, nonparochial personalities; its career path management was used not only to develop skills and knowledge, but also to broaden individual perspectives and interpersonal relationships; and its measurement and reward systems were designed to reinforce the thrust of other organization-building efforts.

Although the process of adapting an organization's culture, values, or beliefs is slow and the techniques are subtle, this tool plays a particularly important role in the development of a transnational organization, because change in the organizational anatomy and physiology without complementary modifications to its psychology can lead to severe organizational problems.

Managing the Process of Change

Particularly in the United States, many managers have assumed that organizational change was driven and dominated by changes in the formal structure. One of the most dramatic examples was Westinghouse's reorganization of its operations. Dissatisfied with the worldwide product organization, top management assigned a team of executives to study the company's international organization problems for 90 days. Its proposal that Westinghouse adopt a global matrix was accepted, and the team was then given three months to "install the new structure."

The example is far from unusual—literally hundreds of other companies have done the same thing. The managers involved seemed to assume that changes in formal roles and reporting relationships would force changes in the organizational relationships and decision processes, which in turn would reshape the way individual managers think and act. This model of the process of organizational change is illustrated in Figure 4-4.

But such an approach loses sight of the real organization behind the boxes and lines on the chart. The boxes that are casually shifted around represent people with abilities,

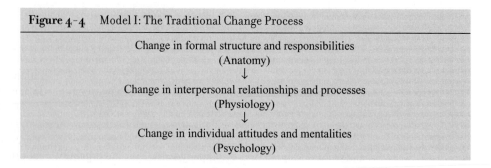

Figure 4-4   Model I: The Traditional Change Process

Change in formal structure and responsibilities
(Anatomy)
↓
Change in interpersonal relationships and processes
(Physiology)
↓
Change in individual attitudes and mentalities
(Psychology)

motivations, and interests, not just formal positions with specified roles. The lines that are redrawn are not just formal reporting channels, but interpersonal relationships that may have taken years to develop. As a result, forcing changes in organizational process and management mentality by altering the formal structure can have a high cost. The new relationships defined in the reorganized structure will often take months to establish at the most basic level, and a year or more to become truly effective. Developing new individual attitudes and behaviors will take even longer, because many employees will be frustrated, alienated, or simply unequal to the new job requirements.

Most European and Japanese companies tend to adopt a very different approach in managing organizational change. Top management in these companies consciously uses personnel assignments as an important mechanism of organizational change. Building on the informal relationships that dominated their earlier management processes, European companies often use assignments and transfers to forge interpersonal links, build organizational cohesion, and develop policy consistency. And Japanese companies typically place enormous emphasis on socializing the individual into the organization and shaping his or her attitudes to conform with overall corporate values. Organizational change in these companies is often driven more by intensive education programs than by reconfigurations of structure or systems.

Although the specific change process and sequence must vary from one company to the next, the overall process adopted in these companies for managing change is very different from the process driven by structural realignment. Indeed, the sequence is often the reverse. The first objective for many European and Japanese companies seeking major change is often to influence the understanding and the perceptions of key individuals. Then follows a series of changes aimed at modifying the communication flows and decision-making processes. Only in a final stage are the changes consolidated and confirmed by structural realignment. This process is represented by the model in Figure 4-5.

Of course, these two models of organizational change in worldwide companies are both oversimplifications of the process and overgeneralizations of national difference. All change processes inevitably involve substantial overlap and interaction in the alterations in organizational autonomy, physiology, and psychology; the two sequences merely reflect differences in the relative emphasis on each set of tools during the process. Furthermore, although the two models reflect historical national biases, those differences seem to be eroding. United States, European, and Japanese companies appear to be learning from one another.

Figure 4-5   Model II: The Emerging Change Process

Change in individual attitudes and mentalities
↓
Change in interpersonal relationships and processes
↓
Change in formal structure and responsibilities

Although the more gradual change process is much less organizationally traumatic, in times of crisis—chronic poor performance, a badly misaligned structure, or major structural change in the environment, for example—radical restructuring may be necessary to achieve rapid and sweeping change. For most organizations, however, dramatic structural change is also highly traumatic and can distract managers from their external tasks as they focus on the internal realignment. Fortunately, most change processes can be managed in a more evolutionary manner, focusing first on modification of individual perspectives and interpersonal relationships before tackling the formal redistribution of responsibilities and power.

The Transnational Organization in Transition

Over the past decade or so, political, competitive, and social pressures have reinforced the need for MNCs to create organizations that can sense and respond to complex yet often conflicting demands. Yet, as more and more companies confront the need to build worldwide organizations that are both multidimensional and flexible, the form of the transnational organization they are creating continues to adapt. Among the most widespread transnational organizational trends we have observed in recent years are the disenchantment with formal matrix structures, the redefinition of their primary organizational dimensions, and the changing role of functional management in transnationals.

Disenchantment with Formal Matrix Structures

As an increasing number of managers recognized the need to develop the multidimensional organizational capabilities that characterize a transnational organization, the initial reaction of many was to impose the new model through a global matrix structure. Widespread press coverage of ABB's decade-long global expansion through such an organization encouraged some to believe that this structure was the key to exploiting global scale efficiencies while simultaneously responding to local market needs. But as many soon discovered, the strategic benefits provided by such a complex organization came at an organizational cost.

Although some companies were able to create the culture and process that were vital to the success of the matrix structure—in ABB's case, they supported the company's ambitious global expansion for more than a decade—others were much less successful. One such failure was P&G's much publicized Organization 2005, which boldly imposed a global product structure over the company's historically successful geographic organization. The global matrix so installed created problems that eventually cost CEO Durk Jager his job.

But despite continuing nervousness about the global matrix structure, most MNCs still recognize the need to create multidimensional and flexible organizations. The big lesson of the 1990s was that such organizations are best built by developing overlaid processes and supportive cultures and not just by formalizing multiple reporting relationships. A. G. Lafley, P&G's new CEO, put it well when he said, "We built this new house, then moved in before the plumbing and wiring were connected. You cannot change organization with structure alone."

Redefinition of Key Organization Dimensions

Historically the dominant organization dimensions around which most MNCs built their worldwide operations were business or product management on one side, and country or regional management on the other. But over the past decade or so, the primary organizational characteristics that defined the transnational corporation began to change, with the global customer dimension becoming increasingly important in many worldwide organizations.

The pressure to create such customer-driven organizations grew gradually during the 1990s. First, as global customers began demanding uniform prices and service levels from their suppliers, MNCs were forced to respond by creating dedicated global account managers who would take responsibility for all sales to their customers around the world. Then, as customers expected increasing levels of value-added services, companies began to shift from "selling products" to "providing solutions." These and similar forces led to the creation of transnational organizations in which front-end customer-facing units would bundle together products from back-end product-driven units. A good example of this was IBM's Global Services Organization, one of the most successful customer-facing organizations that grew rapidly because of its ability to supply customers with a combination of IBM's products, consulting services, and often an additional package of related outsourced products and services.

Changing the Functional Management Role

In transnational organizations built around business, geography, and more recently customer, the functional managers responsible for finance, human resources, logistics, and other cross-business and cross-organizational specialties were typically relegated to secondary staff roles. However, with the expansion of the information-based, knowledge-intensive service economy, the resources and expertise that resided in these specialized functions became increasingly important sources of competitive advantage. As a result, in recent years they have seen their roles become increasingly important in many transnational organizations.

Managers of finance, HR, and IT functions gained importance because of their control of the scarce strategic resources that were so critical to capture and leverage on a worldwide basis. With the globalization of financial markets, for example, the finance function was often able to play a critically important role in lowering the cost of capital for the MNC. Even more dramatic has been the role of the human resource experts as MNCs tapped into scarce knowledge and expertise outside the home country and leveraged it for global competitive advantage. Similarly, the recent rise of chief knowledge officers reflects the importance that many companies are placing in the organization's ability to capture and leverage valuable information, best practice, or scarce knowledge wherever it exists in the company.

Once again, this is creating a need for transnational companies to create organizational overlays supplemented by new channels of communication and forums of decision making that allow the MNC to develop and leverage its competitive advantage through its sophisticated organizational capabilities. The form and function of the transnational organization continues to adapt as MNC managers seek new ways to develop and deliver layers of competitive advantage.

Concluding Comments

In this chapter we have looked at the organizational capabilities that the MNC has to build to operate effectively in the fast-changing business environment of the 1990s and 2000s. The strategic challenge, as we have described it, requires the MNC to optimize global efficiency, national responsiveness, and worldwide learning simultaneously. To deliver on this complex and conflicting set of demands, a new form of organization is required, that we call the transnational. The transnational is characterized by its legitimization of multidimensional perspectives, its distributed and interdependent capabilities, and its flexible integrative processes.

Case 4-1   Philips and Matsushita 1998: Growth of Two Global Companies

Throughout their long histories, N.V. Philips (Netherlands) and Matsushita Electric Industrial (Japan) had followed very different strategies and emerged with different organizational capabilities. Philips had built its success on a worldwide portfolio of responsive national organizations while Matsushita had built its global competitiveness on its centralized, highly efficient operations in Japan.

During the 1980s, both companies experienced major challenges to their historic approaches that forced major strategic and organizational changes, and throughout the 1990s, both companies were struggling to reestablish their competitiveness. With the twenty-first century around the corner,

observers were divided on the effectiveness of the massive strategic and organizational changes both companies had taken, and how it would affect their long-running competitive battle.

Philips: Background

In 1892, Gerard Philips and his father opened a small light bulb factory in Holland. When their Eindhoven-based venture almost failed, they recruited Gerard's brother, Anton, an excellent salesman and manager, to join the company. By 1900, Philips was the third largest light bulb producer in Europe.

From its founding, Philips developed a tradition of caring for workers. In Eindhoven, it built company houses, bolstered education, and provided local services; and it paid its employees so well that

This case was prepared by Professor Christopher A. Bartlett.
Copyright © 1999 by the President and Fellows of Harvard College.
Harvard Business School case 399-102.

other local employers complained. When Philips incorporated in 1912, it set aside 10% of profits for employees.

Technological Competence and Geographic Expansion

While larger electrical products companies were racing to diversify, Philips & Co. made only light bulbs. This one-product focus and Gerard's technological prowess enabled the company to create significant innovations. Company policy was to scrap old plant and use new machines or factories whenever advances were made in new production technology. Anton wrote down assets rapidly and set aside substantial reserves for replacing outdated equipment. Philips also became a leader in industrial research, established physics and chemistry labs to address production problems as well as more abstract scientific ones. The labs developed a tungsten metal filament bulb that was a great commercial success and gave Philips the financial strength to compete against its giant rivals.

Holland's small size soon forced Philips to look beyond Dutch borders for enough volume to mass produce, and in 1899, Anton hired the company's first export managers. The managers spent 8 to 10 months a year traveling in such diverse places as Japan, Australia, Canada, Brazil, and Russia to establish new markets. In 1912, as the electric lamp industry started to show signs of overcapacity, Philips started building sales organizations in the United States, Canada, and France, and other cartel-free countries. All other functions remained highly centralized in Eindhoven. In many foreign countries, Philips created joint ventures with domestic companies to gain acceptance in local markets.

In 1919, Philips entered into the "Principal Agreement" with General Electric, giving each company the use of the other's patents. The agreement also divided the world into "three spheres of influence": General Electric would control North America; Philips would control Holland; both companies agreed to compete freely in the rest of the world. (General Electric also took a 20% stake in Philips.) After this time, Philips began evolving from a highly centralized company whose sales were conducted through third parties to a decentralized sales organization with autonomous marketing companies in 14 European countries, China, Brazil, and Australia.

During this period, the company also broadened its product line significantly. In 1918, it began producing electronic vacuum tubes; eight years later its first radios appeared, capturing a 20% world market share within a decade; and during the 1930s, Philips began producing X-ray tubes. The Great Depression brought with it trade barriers and high tariffs, and Philips was forced to build local production facilities to protect its foreign sales of these products.

▌ Philips: Organizational Development

One of the earliest traditions at Philips was a shared but competitive leadership by the commercial and technical functions. Gerard, an engineer, and Anton, a businessman, began a subtle competition where Gerard would try to produce more than Anton could sell and vice versa. Nevertheless, the two agreed that strong research was vital to Philips' survival.

During the late 1930s, in anticipation of the impending war, Philips transferred its overseas assets to two trusts, British Philips and the North American Philips Corporation; it also moved most of its vital research laboratories to Redhill in Surrey, England, and its top management to the United States. Supported by the assets and resources transferred abroad, and isolated from their parent, the individual country organizations became more independent during the war.

Because waves of Allied and German bombing had pummeled most of Philips' industrial plant in the Netherlands, the management board decided to build the postwar organization on the strengths of the national organizations (NOs). Their greatly increased self-sufficiency during the war had allowed most to become adept at responding to country-specific market conditions—a capability that became a valuable asset in the postwar era. For example, when international wrangling precluded any agreement on television transmission standards, each nation decided at different times whether to adopt PAL, SECAM, or NTSC standards. Furthermore, consumer preferences and economic conditions varied: in some countries, rich, furniture-encased TV sets were the norm; in others sleek, contemporary models dominated the market. In the United Kingdom, the only way to penetrate the market was to establish a rental business; in richer countries, a major marketing challenge was overcoming elitist prejudice against television. In this environment, the independent NOs had a great advantage in being able to sense and respond to the differences.

Eventually, responsiveness extended beyond adaptive marketing. As NOs built their own technical capabilities, product development often became a function of local market conditions. For example, Philips of Canada created the company's first color TV; Philips of Australia created the first stereo TV; and Philips of the United Kingdom created the first TVs with teletext.

While NOs took major responsibility for financial, legal, and administrative matters, fourteen product divisions (PDs), located in Eindhoven, were formally responsible for development, production, and global distribution. (In reality, the NOs' control of assets and the PDs' distance from the operations often undercut this formal role.) The research function remained independent and expanded internationally with eight separate laboratories in Europe and the United States.

While formal corporate-level structure was represented as a type of geographic/product matrix, it was clear that NOs had the real power. NOs reported directly to the management board, which Philips enlarged from 4 members to 10 to ensure that top management remained in control of the vital NO operations. To lead the expanded management board, a four-man "presidium" was created. The board encouraged interaction with the highly autonomous NOs. Each NO sent envoys to Eindhoven to represent its interests, and top management, most of whom had been with the company for their entire careers, typically including multiple foreign tours of duty, made frequent country visits. In 1954, the International Concern Council was established to formalize regular meetings among the principal managers from all the NOs and the board of management.

Within the NOs, the management structure mimicked the legendary joint technical and commercial leadership of the two Philips brothers. NOs were led by a technical manager and a commercial manager. In some locations, a finance manager filled out the top management triad that typically reached key decisions collectively. This cross-functional co-ordination capability was reflected throughout the organization. On the front lines, product teams, comprising junior managers from the commercial and technical functions, set product policies and carried out administrative functions. Cross-functional coordination also occurred at the product group level through group management teams, whose technical and commercial members met monthly to review progress and resolve inter-functional differences. Finally, the senior management committee of each subsidiary (with top commercial, technical and financial managers) reviewed progress to ensure that product group directions fit with national strategies and priorities.

The overwhelming importance of foreign operations to Philips, the commensurate status of the NOs within the corporate hierarchy, and even the cosmopolitan appeal of many of the subsidiaries' locations encouraged many Philips managers to take extended foreign tours duty, working in a series of two or three year posts. This elite group of expatriate managers identified strongly with each other and with the NOs as a group, and had no difficulty representing their strong, country-oriented views to corporate management.

Philips: Attempts at Reorganization

In the 1960s, the creation of the Common Market eroded trade barriers within Europe and diluted the rationale for maintaining independent, country-level subsidiaries. New transistor- and printed circuit-based technologies demanded larger production runs than most national plants could justify, and many of Philips' competitors were moving production of electronics to new facilities in low-wage areas in East Asia and Central and South America. Despite its many technological innovations, Philips' ability to bring products to market began to falter. In the 1960s, the company invented the audiocassette but let its Japanese competitors capture the mass market. Almost 20 years later, Philips developed the V2000 videocassette format—superior technically to Sony's Beta or Matsushita's VHS—but could not successfully market the product. Indeed, North American Philips rejected the V2000, choosing instead to outsource, brand, and sell a VHS product under license from Matsushita. Within three years, Philips was forced to abandon V2000 and produce a VHS product.

Over three decades, five chairman experimented with reorganizing the company to deal with its growing problems. Yet in the late 1990s, Philips' financial performance remained poor and its global competitiveness was still in question. (See Exhibits 1 and 2.)

Van Reimsdijk and Rodenburg Reorganizations, 1970s

Concerned about what *Management Today* described as "continued profitless progress," newly appointed CEO Hendrick van Reimsdijk created an organization committee to prepare a policy paper on the division of responsibilities between the PDs and the NOs. Their report, dubbed the "Yellow Booklet," outlined the disadvantages of Philips' matrix organization in 1971:

> Without an agreement [defining the relationship between national organizations and product divisions], it is impossible to determine in any given situation which of the two parties is responsible. . . . As operations become increasingly complex, an organizational form of this type will only lower the speed of reaction of an enterprise.

On the basis of this report, van Reimsdijk proposed rebalancing the managerial relationships between PDs and NOs—"tilting the matrix" in his words—to allow Philips to increase the scale of production, decrease the number of products marketed, concentrate production, and increase the flow of goods among national organizations. He proposed closing the least efficient local plants and converting the best into International Production Centers (IPCs), each supplying many NOs. In so doing, van Reimsdijk hoped that PD managers would gain control over manufacturing operations. Due to the political and organizational difficulty of closing local plants, however, implementation was slow. By the end of the decade, several IPCs had

been established, but the NOs seemed as powerful and independent as ever.

In the late 1970s, his successor CEO, Dr. Rodenburg, continued this thrust. He reinforced matrix simplification by replacing the dual commercial and technical leadership with single management at both the corporate and national organizational levels. Yet the power struggles continued.

Wisse Dekker Reorganization, 1982

Unsatisfied with the company's slow response and concerned by its slumping financial performance, upon becoming CEO in 1982, Wisse Dekker outlined a new global strategy. Aware of the cost advantage of Philips' Japanese counterparts, he created more IPCs and closed inefficient operations—particularly in Europe where 40 of the company's more than 200 plants were shut. He focused on core operations by selling some businesses (e.g., welding, energy cables, and furniture) while acquiring an interest in Grundig and Westinghouse's North American lamp activities. Dekker also supported technology-sharing agreements and pushed alliances in offshore manufacturing.

To deal with the slow-moving bureaucracy, he continued his predecessor's initiative to replace dual leadership with single general managers. He also continued to "tilt the matrix" by giving PDs formal product management responsibility, but leaving NOs responsible for local profits. And, he energized the management board by reducing its size, bringing on directors with strong operating experience, and creating subcommittees to deal with difficult issues. Finally, Dekker redefined the product planning process to incorporate input from the NOs, but gave global PDs the final decision on long-range direction. Still sales declined and profits stagnated.

Van der Klugt Reorganization, 1987

When Cor van der Klugt succeeded Dekker as chairman, Philips had lost its long-held industry leadership position to Matsushita, and was one of only two non-Japanese consumer electronics companies in the world's top ten. Its profit margins of 1% to 2% not only lagged behind General Electric's 9%, but even its highly aggressive Japanese competitors' slim 4%.

Exhibit 1 Philips Group Summary Financial Data, 1970–1997 (millions of guilders unless otherwise stated)

	1997	1996	1995	1990	1985	1980	1975	1970
Net sales	F76,453	F69,195	F64,462	F55,764	F60,045	F36,536	F27,115	F15,070
Income from operations (excluding restructuring)	5,065	2,537	4,090	2,260	3,075	1,577	1,201	1,280
Income from operations (including restructuring)	4,960	1,812	4,044	−2,389	NA	NA	NA	NA
As a percentage of net sales	6.5%	2.6%	6.3%	−4.3%	5.1%	4.3%	4.5%	8.5%
Income after taxes	3,278	685	2,889	F−4,447	F1,025	F532	F341	F446
Net income from normal business operations	3,291	723	2,684	−4,526	NA	328	347	435
Stockholders' equity (common)	19,457	13,956	14,055	11,165	16,151	12,996	10,047	6,324
Return on stockholders' equity	16.6%	5.0%	20.2%	−30.2%	5.6%	2.7%	3.6%	7.3%
Distribution per common share, par value F 10 (in guilders)	F2.00	F1.60	F1.60	F0.0	F2.00	F1.80	F1.40	F1.70
Total assets	59,441	55,072	54,683	51,595	52,883	39,647	30,040	19,088
Inventories as a percentage of net sales	18.6%	17.9%	18.2%	20.7%	23.2%	32.8%	32.9%	35.2%
Outstanding trade receivables in month's sales	1.7	1.7	1.6	1.6	2.0	3.0	3.0	2.8
Current ratio	1.7			1.4	1.6	1.7	1.8	1.7
Employees at year-end (in thousands)	270	263	265	273	346	373	397	359
Wages, salaries and other related costs				F17,582	F21,491	F15,339	F11,212	F5,890
Exchange rate (period end; guilder/$)	2.02	1.74	1.60	1.69	2.75	2.15	2.69	3.62

Selected Data in Millions of Dollars:

	1997	1996	1995	1990	1985	1980	1975	1970
Sales	$39,207	$40,944	$40,039	$33,018	$21,802	$16,993	$10,098	$4,163
Operating profit	2,543	1,072	2,512	1,247	988	734	464	NA
Pretax income	2,174	541	2,083	−2,380	658	364	256	NA
Net income	2,940	(349)	1,667	−2,510	334	153	95	120
Total assets	29,426	31,651	32,651	30,549	19,202	18,440	11,186	5,273
Shareholders' equity (common)	9,632	8,021	8,784	6,611	5,864	6,044	3,741	1,747

Source: Annual reports; Standard & Poors' *Compustat*; Moody's Industrial and International Manuals.

Exhibit 2 Philips Group, Sales by Product and Geographic Segment, 1985–1997 (million guilders)

	1997		1996		1995		1990		1985	
Net Sales by Product Segment:										
Lighting	F10,024	13%	F8,860	13%	F8,353	13%	F7,026	13%	F7,976	12%
Consumer electronics	23,825	31	24,039	35	22,027	34	25,400	46	16,906	26
Domestic appliances	—		—						6,644	10
Professional products/systems	12,869	17	11,323	16	11,562	18	13,059	23	17,850	28
Components/semiconductors	15,003	20	11,925	17	10,714	17	8,161	15	11,620	18
Software/services	13,009	17	11,256	16	9,425	15				
Miscellaneous	1,723	2	1,783	3	2,381	4	2,118	4	3,272	5
Total	76,453	100%	69,195	100%	64,462	100%	F55,764	100%	F64,266	100%
Operating Income by Sector:										
Lighting	1,151	23%	702	39%	983	24%	419	18%	F 910	30%
Consumer electronics	772	16	10	1	167	4	1,499	66	34	1
Domestic appliances	—		—				—		397	13
Professional products/systems	502	10	0	0	157	4	189	8	1,484	48
Components/semiconductors	2,262	46	1,496	83	2,233	55	−43	−2	44	1
Software/services	1,173	24	490	27	886	22				
Miscellaneous	188	4	199	11	423	10	218	10	200	7
Increase not attributable to a sector	(1,090)	(22)	(1,085)	(60)	(805)	(20)	−22	−1	6	0
Total	4,960	100%	1,812	1,006	4,044	100%	2,260	100%	F3,075	100%

Notes: Totals may not add due to rounding.
Product sector sales after 1988 are external sales only, therefore no eliminations are made; sector sales before 1988 include sales to other sectors, therefore eliminations are made.
Data are not comparable to consolidated financial summary due to restating.
Source: Annual reports.

Van der Klugt set a profit objective of 3%–4% and made beating the Japanese companies a top priority.

As van der Klugt reviewed Philips' strategy, he designated various businesses as core (those that shared related technologies, had strategic importance, or were technical leaders) and non-core (stand-alone businesses that were not targets for world leadership and could eventually be sold if required). Of the four businesses defined as core, three were strategically linked: Components, Consumer Electronics, and Telecommunications and Data Systems. The fourth, Lighting, was regarded as strategically vital because cash flow funded development. The non-core businesses included domestic appliances and medical systems which van der Klugt spun off into joint ventures with Whirlpool and GE, respectively.

In continuing efforts to strengthen the PDs relative to the NOs, van der Klugt restructured Philips around the four core global divisions rather than the former 14 PDs. This allowed him to trim the management board, appointing the displaced board members to a new policy-making Group Management Committee. Finally, he sharply reduced the 3,000 strong headquarters staff, reallocating many of them to the PDs.

To link PDs more directly to markets, van der Klugt dispatched many product line managers to Philips' most competitive markets. For example, management of the digital audio tape and electric shaver product lines were relocated to Japan, while the medical technology and domestic appliances lines were moved to the United States.

Such moves, along with continued efforts at globalizing product development and production efforts required that the parent company gain firmer control over NOs, especially the giant North American Philips Corp. (NAPC). Although Philips had obtained a majority equity interest after World War II, the U.S. company did not always respond to directives from the center. Referring to its much publicized choice of Matsushita's VHS video cassette format over its parent's V2000 format, NAPC's chairman said, "We made the best decisions for the parochial interests of our stockholders. They were not always parallel with those of Philips worldwide." To prevent replays of such experiences, in 1987 van der Klugt repurchased publicly owned NAPC shares for $700 million.

Reflecting the growing sentiment among some managers that R&D was not market-oriented enough, van der Klugt halved spending on basic research to about 10% of total R&D. To manage R&D's tendency "to ponder the fundamental laws of nature," he made R&D the direct responsibility of the businesses being supported by the research. This required that each research lab become focused on specific business areas (see Exhibit 3).

Finally, van der Klugt continued the effort to build efficient, specialized, multi-market production facilities by closing 75 of the company's 420

Exhibit 3   Philips Research Labs by Location and Specialty, 1987

Location	Size (staff)	Specialty
Eindhoven, The Netherlands	2,000	Basic research, electronics, manufacturing technology
Redhill, Surrey, England	450	Microelectronics, television, defense
Hamburg, Germany	350	Communications, office equipment, medical imaging
Aachen, West Germany	250	Fiber optics, X-ray systems
Paris, France	350	Microprocessors, chip materials and design
Brussels, Belgium	50	Artificial intelligence
Briarcliff Manor, New York	35	Optical systems, television, superconductivity, defense
Sunnyvale, California	150	Integrated circuits

Source: Philips, in *Business Week*, March 21, 1988, p. 156.

remaining plants worldwide. He also eliminated 38,000 of its 344,000 employees—21,000 through divesting businesses, shaking up the myth of lifetime employment at the company. He anticipated that all these restructurings would lead to a financial recovery by 1990. Unanticipated losses for that year, however—more than 4.5 billion Dutch guilder ($2.5 billion)—provoked a class action law suit by angry American investors, who alleged that positive projections by the company had been misleading. In a surprise move, on May 14, 1990, van der Klugt and half of the management board were replaced.

Timmer Reorganization, 1990   The new president, Jan Timmer, had spent most of his 35-year Philips career turning around unprofitable businesses. In an early meeting with his top 100 managers he distributed a hypothetical—but fact-based—press release announcing that Philips was bankrupt. (There had already been rumors of a takeover or a government bailout.) "So what action can you take this weekend?" he challenged.

Under "Operation Centurion," headcount was reduced by 68,000 or 22% over the next 18 months, earning Timmer the nickname "The Butcher of Eindhoven." Because European laws required substantial compensation for layoffs—Eindhoven workers received 15 months' pay, for example—the first round of 10,000 layoffs alone cost Philips $700 million. To spread the burden around the globe, and to speed the process, Timmer asked his PD managers to negotiate cuts with NO managers. According to one report, however, country managers were "digging in their heels to save local jobs." But the cuts came—many from overseas operations. In addition to the job cuts, Timmer vowed to "change the way we work." He established new performance rules and asked hundreds of top managers to sign contracts that committed them to specific financial goals. Those who broke those contracts were replaced—often with outsiders.

To focus resources further, Timmer sold off various businesses including integrated circuits to Matsushita, minicomputers to Digital, defense electronics to Thomson and the remaining 53% of appliances to Whirlpool. Yet profitability was still well below the modest 4% on sales he promised. In particular, consumer electronics lagged with slow growth in a price-competitive market. The core problem was identified by a 1994 McKinsey study that estimated that value added per hour in Japanese consumer electronic factories was still 68% above that of European plants.

After three years of cost-cutting, in early 1994 Timmer presented a new growth strategy to the board. His plan was to expand software, services and multimedia to become 40% of revenues by 2000. Earlier, he had recruited Frank Carrubba, Hewlett-Packard's director of research, and encouraged him to focus on developing 15 core technologies. The list, which included interactive compact disc (CD-i), digital compact cassettes (DCC), high-definition television (HDTV) and multimedia software, was soon dubbed "the president's projects." But his earlier divestment of some of Philips's truly high-tech businesses and a 37% cut in R&D personnel left the company with few who understood the technology of the new priority businesses.

Boonstra Reorganization, 1996   By 1996, it was clear that Philips's HDTV technology would not become industry standard, that its DCC gamble had lost out to Sony's Minidisc, and that CI-i was a marketing failure. While costs were lower, so too was morale, particularly among middle management. Critics claimed that the company's drive for cost-cutting and standardization had led it to ignore new worldwide market demands for more segmented products and higher consumer service. When Timmer stepped down in October 1996, the board decided to replace him with a radical choice for Philips—an outsider whose expertise was in marketing and Asia rather than technology and Europe.

Cor Boonstra was a 58-year-old Dutchman whose years as CEO of Sara Lee, the U.S. consumer products firm, had earned him a reputation as a hard driver and a marketing genius. Joining

Philips in 1994, he had headed the Asia Pacific region and the lighting division before being tapped as CEO. Unencumbered by tradition, he immediately announced sweeping changes. "There are no taboos, no sacred cows," he said. "The bleeders must be turned around, sold or closed. And we must change an organization that has been a closed system."

Within six months Boonstra had sold off 18 businesses he described as "bleeders" and had reduced commitments to 13 more perpetual loss makers, including a withdrawal from troubled German giant, Grundig. To reach his target of increasing return on invested capital from 17% to 24% by 1999, he also initiated a major restructuring of Philips' worldwide operations, promising to transform a structure he described as "a plate of spaghetti" into "a neat row of asparagus." He said:

> How can we compete with the Koreans? They don't have 350 companies all over the world. Their factory in Ireland covers Europe and their manufacturing facility in Mexico serves North America. We need a more structured and simpler manufacturing and marketing organization to achieve a cost pattern in line with those who do not have our heritage. This is still one of the biggest issues facing Philips.

Within a year, he had begun to rationalize the global structure and redeploy its resources. Over and above the restructuring, 3,100 jobs were eliminated in North America and 3,000 employees were added in Asia Pacific during 1997, emphasizing Boonstra's determination to shift production to low-wage countries and his broader commitment to Asia. ("With Europe's slow growth, Asia is key to our rebuilding task," he said.) And he restructured the company around 100 business units, each responsible for its profits, worldwide, effectively eliminating the old PD/NO matrix. Finally, to the shock of most employees, he announced that the 100-year-old Eindhoven headquarters would be relocated to Amsterdam.

By early 1998, he was ready to announce his strategy. Despite early speculation that he might abandon consumer electronics, he proclaimed it as the center of Philips's future. Betting on the "digital revolution," he planned to focus on established technologies such as cellular phones (through joint ventures with Marantz and Lucent), digital TV, digital videodisc and web TV. More radically, he committed major resources to marketing, including a 40% increase in advertising to raise awareness and image of the Philips brand.

Record profits in 1997 boosted spirits in Philips, but, as *The Financial Times* pointed out, from such a low profit base, "the first few percentage points are comparatively easy to achieve."

Matsushita: Background

In 1918, Konosuke Matsushita (or "KM" as he was affectionately known), a 23-year-old inspector with the Osaka Electric Light Company, invested ¥100 to start production of double-ended sockets in his modest home. The company grew rapidly, expanding into battery-powered lamps, electric irons, and radios. On May 5, 1932, Matsushita's 14th anniversary, KM announced to his 162 employees a 250-year corporate plan broken into 25-year sections, each to be carried out by successive generations. His plan was codified in a company creed and in the "Seven Spirits of Matsushita" (see Exhibit 4), which, along with the company song, continued to be woven into morning assemblies worldwide and provided the basis of the "cultural and spiritual training" all new employees received during their first seven months with the company.

In the post-war boom, Matsushita introduced a flood of new products: TV sets in 1952; transistor radios in 1958; color TVs, dishwashers and electric ovens in 1960. Capitalizing on its broad line of 5,000 products (Sony produced 80), the company opened 25,000 domestic retail distribution outlets. With more than six times the outlets of rival Sony, the ubiquitous "National Shops" represented about 40% of all appliance stores in Japan in the late 1960s. These not only provided assured sales volume, but also gave the company direct access to market trends and consumer product reaction.

Exhibit 4   Matsushita Creed and Philosophy
(excerpts)

Creed

Through our industrial activities, we strive to foster progress, to promote the general welfare of society, and to devote ourselves to furthering the development of world culture.

Seven Spirits of Matsushita

Service through Industry
Fairness
Harmony and Cooperation
Struggle for Progress
Courtesy and Humility
Adjustment and Assimilation
Gratitude

KM's Business Philosophy (Selected Quotations)

"The purpose of an enterprise is to contribute to society by supplying goods of high quality at low prices in ample quantity."

"Profit comes in compensation for contribution to society. . . . [It] is a result rather than a goal."

"The responsibility of the manufacturer cannot be relieved until its product is disposed of by the end user."

"Unsuccessful business employs a wrong management. You should not find its causes in bad fortune, unfavorable surroundings or wrong timing."

"Business appetite has no self-restraining mechanism. . . . When you notice you have gone too far, you must have the courage to come back."

Source: "Matsushita Electric Industrial (MEI) in 1987," Harvard Business School case 388-144.

When post-war growth slowed, however, Matsushita had to look beyond its expanding product line and excellent distribution system for growth. After trying many tactics to boost sales—even sending assembly line workers out as door-to-door salesmen—the company eventually focused on export markets.

The Organization's Foundation: Divisional Structure   Plagued by RI health, KM wished to delegate more authority than was typical in Japanese companies. In 1933, Matsushita became the first Japanese company to adopt the divisional structure, giving each division clearly defined profit responsibilities while creating a "small business" environment to maintain growth and flexibility. Under its "one-product-one division" system, each product line was managed by a separate autonomous division to be operated almost like an independent corporation. Corporate management provided it with initial funds, deliberately underestimating working capital requirements to motivate divisions to work hard for their retained earnings. Divisional profitability was determined after deductions for central services such as R&D, and interest on internal borrowings. KM expected uniform performance across the company's 36 divisions, and division managers whose operating profits fell below 4% of sales for two successive years were replaced.

Matsushita ran its corporate treasury like a commercial bank, reviewing divisions' loan requests for which it charged slightly higher-than-market interest, and accepting deposits on their excess funds. Each division paid 60% of earnings to headquarters and financed all additional working capital and fixed asset requirements from the retained 40%. Transfer prices were based on the market and settled through the treasury on normal commercial terms.

While basic technology was developed in a central research laboratory (CRL), product development and engineering occurred in each of the product divisions. Matsushita intentionally underfunded the CRL, forcing it to compete for additional funding from the divisions. Annually, the CRL publicized its major research projects to the product divisions, which then provided funding in exchange for technology for marketable applications.

This divisional structure generated competition among divisions, spurring them to drive growth by leveraging their technology assets into new products. After the innovating division had earned substantial profits on its new product, however, company policy was to spin it off as a new division to maintain the "hungry spirit."

Matsushita: Internationalization

Although the establishment of overseas markets was a major thrust of the second 25 years in the 250-year plan, in an overseas trip in 1951 KM had been unable to find any American company willing to collaborate with Matsushita. The best he could do was a technology exchange and licensing agreement with Philips. Nonetheless, the push to internationalize continued.

Expanding through Color TV   In the 1950s and 1960s, trade liberalization and lower shipping rates made possible a healthy export business built on black and white TV sets. In 1953, the company opened its first overseas branch office— the Matsushita Electric Corporation of America (MECA). With neither a distribution network nor a strong brand, the company could not access traditional retailers, and had to resort to selling its products under their private brands through mass merchandisers and discounters.

During the 1960s, pressure from national governments in developing countries led Matsushita to open manufacturing facilities in several countries in Southeast Asia and Central and South America. As manufacturing costs in Japan rose, Matsushita shifted more basic production to these low-wage countries, but almost all high-value components and subassemblies were still made in Japan. By the 1970s, projectionist sentiments in the West forced the company to establish plants in the Americas and Europe. In 1972, it opened a plant in Canada; in 1974, it bought Motorola's TV business and started manufacturing its Quasar brand in the United States; and in 1976, it built a plant in Cardiff, Wales to supply the Common Market.

Building Global Leadership: Dominating through VCRs   The birth of the videocassette recorder (VCR) propelled Matsushita into first place in the consumer electronics industry during the 1980s. Recognizing the potential mass-market appeal of the VCR—developed by Californian broadcasting company, Ampex, in 1956—engineers at Matsushita began developing VCR technology. After six years of development work, Matsushita launched its commercial broadcast video recorder in 1964, and introduced a consumer version two years later.

In 1975, Sony introduced the technically superior "Betamax" format, and the next year JVC launched a competing "VHS" format. Under pressure from MITI, Mitsushita agreed to give up its own format and adopt the more popular VHS. During Matsushita's 20 years of VCR product development, various members of the VCR research team had moved from central labs to the product divisions' development labs and eventually to the plant. In 1976, as sales at home and abroad began to take off, Matsushita celebrated the unit's first profitable year.

The company quickly built production to meet its own needs as well as OEM customers like GE, RCA and Zenith who decided to forgo self-manufacture. Between 1977 and 1985, capacity was increased 33-fold to 6.8 million units. (In parallel, the company aggressively licensed the VHS format to other manufacturers, including Hitachi, Sharp, Mitsubishi and, eventually, Philips.) Increased volume enabled Matsushita to slash prices 50% within five years of product launch, while simultaneously improving quality on several carefully monitored dimensions. By the mid-1980s, VCRs accounted for 30% of sales—over 40% of overseas revenues—and provided 45% of profits.

Matsushita: Managing International Operations

In the mid-1980s, the growing number of overseas companies reported to Japan in one of two ways: wholly owned, single-product global plants reported directly to Matsushita's product divisions, while overseas sales and marketing subsidiaries and overseas companies producing a broad product line for local markets, reported to Matsushita Electric

Exhibit 5   Organization of METC, 1985

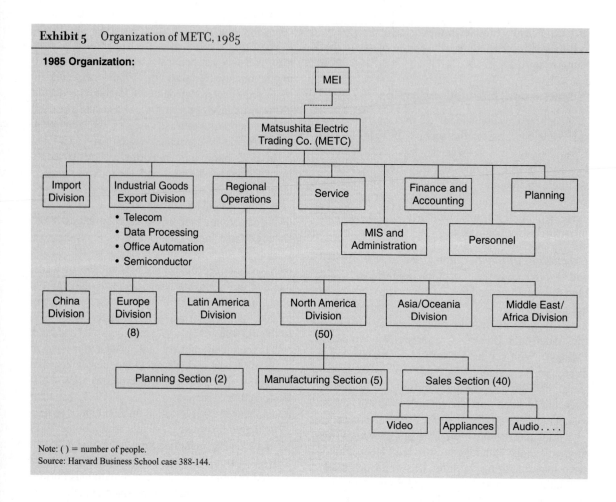

Note: ( ) = number of people.
Source: Harvard Business School case 388-144.

Trading Company (METC), a separate legal entity. (See Exhibit 5 or METC's organization.)

Changing Systems and Controls   Throughout the 1970s, the central product divisions maintained strong operating control over their offshore production units. Overseas operations used plant and equipment designed by the parent company, followed manufacturing procedures dictated by the center, and used materials from Matsushita's domestic plants. Growing trends toward local sourcing, however, gradually weakened the divisions' direct control. By the 1980s, instead of controlling inputs, they began to monitor measures of output (e.g., quality, productivity, inventory levels).

About the same time, product divisions began receiving the globally consolidated return on sales reports that had previously been consolidated in METC statements. By the mid-1980s, as worldwide planning was introduced for the first time, corporate management required all its product divisions to prepare global product strategies.

Headquarters-Subsidiary   Relations   Although METC and the product divisions set detailed sales and profits targets for their overseas subsidiaries, local managers were told they had complete autonomy on how to achieve the targets. "Mike" Matsuoko, president of the company's largest European production subsidiary in Cardiff, Wales, however, emphasized that failure to meet targets forfeited freedom: "Losses show bad health and invite many doctors from Japan who provide advice and support."

In the mid-1980s, Matsushita had over 700 expatriate managers and technicians on foreign assignment for four to eight years, but defended that high number by describing their pivotal role. "This vital communication role," said one manager, "almost always requires a manager from the parent company. Even if a local manager speaks Japanese, he would not have the long experience that is needed to build relationships and understand our management processes."

Expatriate managers were located throughout foreign subsidiaries, but there were a few positions that were almost always reserved for them. The most visible were subsidiary general managers whose main role was to translate Matsushita philosophy abroad. Expatriate accounting managers were expected to "mercilessly expose the truth" to corporate headquarters; and Japanese technical managers were sent to transfer product and process technologies and provide headquarters with local market information. These expatriates maintained relationships with senior colleagues at headquarters who acted as career mentors, evaluated performance (with some input from local managers), and provided expatriates with information about parent company developments.

General managers of foreign subsidiaries visited headquarters at least two or three times each year— some as often as every month. Corporate managers reciprocated these visits, and on average, major operations hosted at least one headquarters manager each day of the year. Face-to-face meetings were considered vital: "Figures are important," said one manager, "but the meetings are necessary to develop judgment." Faxes and after-hour phone calls between headquarters and expatriate colleagues were a vital management link.

In the mid-1980s, offshore production subsidiaries gained some flexibility. They were free to buy minor parts from local vendors as long as quality could be assured, but still had to buy key components from internal sources. Subsidiaries now carried out routine production tasks independently, calling on corporate technical personnel when plans called for major expansion or change. Similarly, sales subsidiaries had some choice over the products they sold. Each year the company held a two-week internal merchandising show and product planning meeting, where sales subsidiary managers negotiated over features, quantities, and even prices of the products they wanted to buy from the parent's product divisions. Corporate managers, however, could overrule the subsidiary if they thought introduction of a particular product was strategic.

Yamashita's Operation Localization   Although international sales kept rising, as early as the early 1980s growing host country pressures caused concern about the company's highly centralized operations. In 1982, newly appointed company President Toshihiko Yamashita launched "Operation Localization" to boost offshore production from less than 10% of value added to 25%, or half of overseas sales, by 1990. To support the target, he set out a program of four localizations—personnel, technology, material, and capital.

Over the next few years, Matsushita increased the number of local nationals in key positions. In the United States, for example, U.S. nationals became the presidents of three of the six local companies while in Taiwan, the majority of production divisions were replaced by Chinese managers. In each case, however, local national managers were still supported by senior Japanese advisors who maintained a direct link with the parent company. To localize technology and material, the company developed its national subsidiaries' expertise to source equipment locally, modify designs to meet local requirements, and incorporate local components, and adapt corporate processes and technologies to accommodate these changes while maintaining the company's quality standards.

The overall localization thrust sparked opposition from managers in Japan. In a low-growth environment, increased foreign production would come at the expense of export sales. "What will that mean for employment in Japan?" said one senior manager. "Protecting the interests of employees is one of our greatest moral commitments. We cannot sacrifice that for any reason." Even some foreign subsidiary managers feared it would reduce their access to central resources and expertise. If localized operations caused export income to contribute less, they reasoned, the central product division managers could give priority to domestic needs over foreign operations.

Nonetheless, between 1980 and 1988, Matsushita added 21 manufacturing companies and 12 sales companies abroad to bring those respective totals to 60 and 41. In 1990, Matsushita employed 50,000 workers overseas, twice the number of a decade earlier. Despite these efforts, in 1990 overseas production stood at only ¥600 billion—still less than half Matsushita's 25% target. (See Exhibits 6 and 7.)

President Yamashita had also hoped that Operation Localization would help Matsushita's overseas companies develop the innovative capability and entrepreneurial initiatives that he had long admired in the national organizations of rival Philips. (Past efforts to develop such capabilities abroad had failed. For example, when Matsushita acquired Motorola's TV business in the United States, its highly innovative technology group atrophied as American engineers resigned in response to what they felt to be excessive control from Japan's highly centralized R&D operations.) In an unusual act for a Japanese CEO, Yamashita publicly expressed his unhappiness with the lack of initiative at the TV plant in Cardiff. Despite the transfer of substantial resources and the delegation of many responsibilities, he felt that the plant remained too dependent on the center.

Tanii's Integration and Expansion   Yamashita's successor, Akio Tanii, expanded on his predecessor's initiatives. In part because Matsushita's product divisions received only 3% royalties for foreign production against at least 10% return on sales for exports from Japan, he felt that product divisions were not giving their full attention to

developing operations outside Japan. To correct the situation, he brought all foreign subsidiaries of Matsushita under the control of METC in 1986, thus consolidating the company's international operations in one administrative entity. To further integrate domestic and overseas operations, in April 1988, Tanii merged METC into the parent company. Then, to shift operational control nearer to local markets, he relocated major regional headquarters functions from Japan to North America, Europe, and Southeast Asia. Yet still he was frustrated that the overseas subsidiary companies acted as the implementing agents of the Osaka-based product divisions.

Through all these changes, however, Matsushita's worldwide growth continued generating huge reserves. With $17.5 billion in financial assets at the end of 1989, the company was referred to as the "Matsushita Bank." Several top executives felt that if they could not develop innovative overseas companies, they should buy them. Flush with cash and international success, in early 1991 the company acquired MCA, the U.S. entertainment giant for $6.1 billion, with the objective of obtaining a media software source for its hardware. Within a year, however, Japan's bubble economy had burst, wiping out $2.6 trillion in stock market value and plunging the economy into recession. Almost overnight, Tanii had to shift the company's focus from expansion to cost containment.

Morishita's Restructuring   Despite Tanii's best efforts to cut costs, the problems ran too deep. The company's huge capacity, its full line of products, and its network of 27,000 retailers turned from assets to liabilities. With 1992 profits less than half their 1991 level, Tanii was forced to resign in February 1993.

His replacement, Yoichi Morishita—at 56 the most junior of the firm's executive vice presidents—immediately implemented a major restructuring designed "to eliminate laxness and extravagance." Central to his effort was a commitment to cut headquarters staff and decentralize responsibility to operating units, including overseas companies.

Exhibit 6 Matsushita, Summary Financial Data, 1990–1997*

	1997	1996	1995	1990	1985	1980	1975	1970
In Billions of Yen and Percent:								
Sales	¥7,676	¥6,795	¥6,948	¥6,003	¥5,291	¥2,916	¥1,385	¥932
Income before tax	332	77	232	572	723	324	83	147
As percentage of sales	4.3%	1.1%	3.3%	9.5%	13.7%	11.1%	6.0%	15.8%
Net income	¥138	¥(58)†	¥90	¥236	¥216	¥125	¥32	¥70
As percentage of sales	1.8%	(0.8%)	1.3%	3.9%	4.1%	4.3%	2.3%	7.6%
Cash dividends (per share)	12.50	12.50	13.50	¥10.00	¥9.52	¥7.51	¥6.82	¥6.21
Total assets	8,696	8,011	8,202	7,851	5,076	2,479	1,274	735
Stockholders' equity	3,696	3,398	3,255	3,201	2,084	1,092	573	324
Capital investment	415	381	316	355	288	NA	NA	NA
Depreciation	345	292	296	238	227	65	28	23
R&D	435	399	378	346	248	102	51	NA
Employees (units)	270,651	265,538	265,397	198,299	175,828	107,057	82,869	78,924
Overseas employees	116,279	107,530	112,314	59,216	38,380	NA	NA	NA
As percentage of total employees	43%	40%	42%	30%	22%	NA	NA	NA
Exchange rate (fiscal period end; ¥/$)	124	106	89	159	213	213	303	360
In Millions of Dollars:								
Sales	$61,902	$64,102	$78,069	$37,753	$24,890	$13,690	$4,572	$2,588
Operating income before depreciation	3,015	2,495	2,924	4,343	3,682	1,606	317	NA
Operating income after depreciation	2,678	723	2,609	2,847	2,764	1,301	224	NA
Pretax income	1,112	(536)	1,017	3,667	3,396	1,520	273	408
Net income	70,128	75,583	92,159	1,482	1,214	584	105	195
Total assets	29,804	32,053	36,575	49,379	21,499	11,636	4,206	2,042
Total equity				20,131	10,153	5,129	1,890	900

*Data prior to 1987 are for the fiscal year ending November 20; data 1988 and after are for the fiscal year ending March 31.
†1996 results include a write-off of ¥164 billion in losses stemming from the sale of MCA in June 1995.
Source: Annual reports; Standard & Poors' *Compustat*; Moody's Industrial and International Manuals.

Exhibit 7 Matsushita, Sales by Product and Geographic Segment, 1985–1990 (billion yen)

	1997		1996		1995		FY 1990		FY 1985	
By Product Segment:										
Video equipment	¥1,342	17%	¥1,225	18%	¥1,272	18%	¥1,598	27%	¥1,947	37%
Audio equipment	576	8	518	8	555	8	561	9	570	11
Home appliances	1,026	13	914	13	916	13	802	13	763	14
Communication and industrial equipment	2,492	32	2,013	<30	1,797	26	1,375	23	849	16
Electronic components	1,055	14	1,020	15	893	13	781	13	573	11
Batteries and kitchen-related equipment	472	6	405	6	374	4	312	5	217	4
Others	710	9	700	10	530	8	573	10	372	7
Total	7,676	100%	6,795	100%	6,948	100%	¥6,003	100%	¥5,291	100%
By Geographic Segment:										
Domestic	4,046	53%	3,727	55%	3,455	50%	¥3,382	56%	¥2,659	50%
Overseas	3,630	47	3,068	45	3,493	50	2,621	44	2,632	50

Notes: Total may not add due to rounding.
Source: Annual reports.

Under the slogan "simple, small, speedy and strategic," over the next 18 months he eliminated a layer of management and transferred 6,000 corporate staff to operating jobs. To the shock of many, he even began questioning the sanctity of lifetime employment. By contrast, he consolidated 20 research centers into nine, centralizing decisions to speed up new product introductions. Unwilling to respond to MCI's management pressure for more funding and greater independence, Matsushita sold off 80% of the company to Seagram at a $1.2 billion loss in early 1995.

Meanwhile, stimulated by a rising yen that raised the export prices, product divisions were aggressively moving value added offshore, particularly to Southeast Asia. Attracted by booming markets, lower costs and strong local partners, the company began investing in major production facilities, not just the knockdown assembly plants of the 1970s and 1980s. For example, production of all 1.5 million of Matsushita's export air conditioners was transferred to Malaysia. In that country alone,

Matsushita had established 16 companies producing a wide range of products and employing 20,000 people. Subsequently, the air conditioning and television companies expanded their commitment by establishing substantial Malaysian design and development centers. Similar levels of commitment were also being made to facilities in China, India and Vietnam.

By fiscal year 1997, profit margins had risen from 2.8% when Morishita took over to 4.3%. Besides restructuring the company, he had successfully repositioned its product portfolio, reducing low margin consumer electronics from 50% to 35% of sales and moving into digital technologies such as cellular phones, digital cameras and digital video discs. Yet Morishita was still discouraged that still less than 50% of overseas sales were manufactured abroad. Equally troubling was the company's slow transition to local senior-level management in its overseas companies, and the even less successful attempts to integrate foreign managers at senior levels in the parent company.

Case 4-2   Becton Dickinson: Worldwide Blood Collection Team

In the spring of 1993, Bill Kozy, president of Becton Dickinson VACUTAINER Systems (BDVS) division, discussed the challenges he foresaw for the Worldwide Blood Collection Team (WBCT) he led. Over his four and a half years chairing this team of managers drawn from BDVS operations around the globe, Kozy had seen great growth in the business. (See Exhibit 1.) He was particularly proud of the role the WBCT played in BDVS's two major new product introductions—the HEMO-

GARD safety closure and the plastic PLUS TUBE line—because they represented the first products developed and launched through the transnational management approach he was trying to develop.

But Kozy knew that he still faced difficult organizational issues as worldwide blood collection evolved from an international business treating overseas operations as appendages, to a genuinely transnational business managing its worldwide portfolio of resources and capabilities as strategic assets. Three major issues concerned him. First, there was the structure of the worldwide blood collection business. As Becton Dickinson's business grew outside the United States and the U.S. market matured, Kozy wondered if the configuration of roles and

▌ Research Associate Kathleen Scharf prepared this case, under the supervision of Professor Christopher A. Bartlett, as the basis for class discussion rather than to illustrate either effective or ineffective handling of an administrative situation.
▌ Copyright © 1993 by the President and Fellows of Harvard College. Harvard Business School case 394-072.

Exhibit 1 Becton Dickinson & Company—Income Statement ($000s)

Division and Strategy Center	1985 Actual $	1986 Actual $	1987 Actual $	1988 Actual $	1989 Actual $	1990 Actual $	1991 Actual $	1992 Actual $
Worldwide Blood Collection (including specimen collection)								
Net trade sales	$144,371	$172,770	$198,790	$236,736	$264,533	$293,940	$329,837	$363,376
Gross profit	62,815	77,902	90,443	109,201	118,353	133,234	147,000	163,714
Total expenses	37,188	40,156	46,897	55,114	59,518	65,436	75,970	82,614
OIBT[a]	23,046	34,950	41,441	48,680	52,562	60,110	60,344	72,732
RONA (pretax—average)	23.94%	30.60%	32.20%	31.00%	25.90%	23.00%	18.00%	23.00%
U.S. Blood Collection								
Net trade sales	$92,921	$102,823	$110,269	$123,018	$140,886	$149,910	$162,217	$170,670
Gross profit	44,400	48,327	50,723	56,711	62,595	66,860	71,375	74,753
Total expenses	22,780	22,218	22,975	25,013	27,269	38,693	32,759	34,712
OIBT[a]	19,421	23,978	25,955	29,730	32,990	35,539	33,559	36,529
RONA (pretax—average)	41.70%	41.10%	42.10%	41.70%	35.90%	29.60%	21.20%	25.30%
Europe Blood Collection								
Net trade sales	$30,204	$44,862	$56,669	$71,879	$75,275	$93,106	$111,751	$130,174
Gross profit	8,683	17,865	25,501	32,921	33,874	42,829	51,182	60,140
Total expenses	9,661	12,518	15,283	18,869	19,800	23,177	27,448	30,504
OIBT[a]	(1,055)	5,309	10,218	11,400	11,226	16,144	19,435	25,769
RONA (pretax—average)	(2.8%)	12.20%	20.00%	18.40%	13.00%	14.70%	14.30%	20.30%
Japan Blood Collection								
Net trade sales	$2,213	$3,421	$5,719	$7,438	$8,654	$9,074	$11,452	$14,735
Gross profit	1,237	2,382	3,380	4,626	5,338	4,339	4,972	7,100
Total expenses	1,084	1,532	3,883	5,130	4,978	4,877	6,149	6,692
OIBT[a]	154	850	(501)	(732)	95	(817)	(1,555)	(92.4)
RONA (pretax—average)	8.50%	45.00%	(16.7%)	(13.7%)	1.50%	(10.7%)	(17.3%)	(0.8%)

Note: Although data have been disguised, key relationships have been retained.
[a] Operating Income Before Taxes for 1985–1987 includes little or no GCE for international units.

resources was appropriate. WBCT members were increasingly involved in discussions and negotiations over complex issues of where R&D resources and capabilities should be developed.

Kozy's second issue concerned the need to align human resource systems with the new worldwide strategies, the changing structures such as the WBCT, and the evolving processes for key decisions such as development of worldwide products. He had experienced the difficulties inherent in chairing a team of unevenly matched and skilled managers. And as larger numbers of managers became involved in decisions and actions beyond their traditional areas of responsibility, he wondered how they should be measured and evaluated in terms of their contributions to BD's worldwide businesses.

Finally, Kozy was aware that some of his colleagues still wondered whether the WBCT was the right mechanism for managing BDVS's worldwide business in accordance with transnational concepts. While he believed this body had played a vital role particularly as it clarified its responsibilities in recent years, perhaps it was time to reevaluate its future role.

History and Context of BD's International Business

Founded in 1897 as a manufacturer of clinical thermometers, Becton Dickinson and Company (BD) was a supplier of medical products and diagnostic systems to hospitals, physicians' offices, clinical and research laboratories, and pharmacies. BD had 10 core businesses organized into two product sectors: medical and diagnostic. Major medical sector products included hypodermic needles and syringes, medical gloves, diabetic products, and intravenous catheters. Diagnostic products included blood collection devices, prepared plated media, automated systems to detect and identify bacteria, rapid manual tests for doctors' offices, blood cell analysis systems, and immunocytometry products for cellular analysis.

Although about half of BD's 1992 sales of $2 billion were generated outside the United States, the company's international business had been

developed relatively recently. In 1960, BD began to build a European organization whose central role was to expand the market for the very successful line of products the company had developed for the U.S. market. The European operation was built as a portfolio of country subsidiaries whose general managers reported to an area president who, in turn, was part of the corporate-level international group. Country managers were responsible for sales, marketing, distribution, administration, and compliance with local regulations, whereas U.S. division presidents managed R&D, manufacturing, and other operational issues. (See Exhibit 2.)

During the 1970s, BD transferred the locus of power from the functionally dominated regional office to the national subsidiaries, giving the country managers clear mandate to maximize sales in their countries. Evaluation and compensation still gave country managers little incentive to risk short-term local results in the service of longer-term corporate goals for international market development. Their main complaint was that their performance was often limited because U.S. division managers often filled international orders only when the U.S. demands were covered, and routinely refused to consider new product requests from abroad.

European SBUs   In 1980, BD's senior executives saw the need to respond to several important developments. As the U.S. market matured, growing opportunities in Europe became increasingly attractive. At the same time, several international medical technology companies were focusing their attention on Europe, posing a threat to BD's position not only in those markets but in the United States as well. As a result, pressure was increasing to reorganize sales and marketing activities in support of international growth, to rationalize international product flows, and to achieve more uniform cost and quality standards worldwide.

Expanding on the Strategic Business Unit (SBU) concept that had been overlaid on the U.S. product divisions to provide them with more strategic focus and discipline, top management decided to create corresponding European SBUs. The head of each

Exhibit 2   Organization Chart, 1979 ·

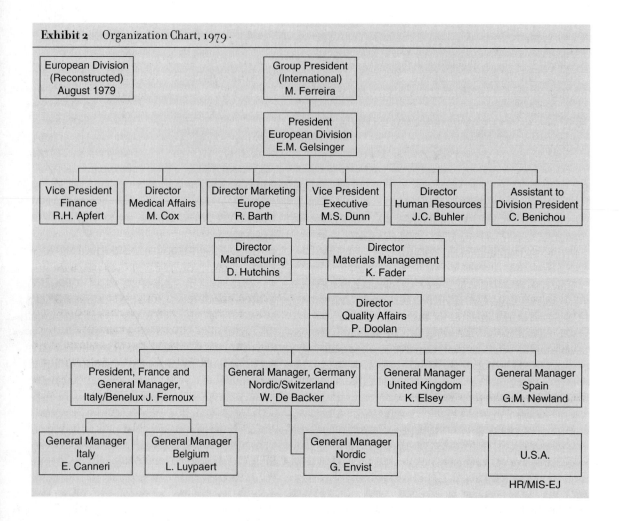

European SBU was given the title of president, and treated similarly to a division president in the United States. This status level was higher than that accorded to country managers in Europe. Country level sales and marketing personnel for these products now reported directly to the European SBU presidents rather than to their country manager. The country organizations retained responsibility for accounting, finance, human resource, and other administrative functions; BD's European headquarters coordinated these functions on a Europe-wide basis. The country presidents were still compensated based on their country P&L results, whereas SBU

managers were rewarded for their SBU's results Europe-wide.

Although senior managers worked to prepare European managers for the new structure, a manager involved recalled making complex presentations to "a largely unresponsive audience." European managers had just adjusted to a shift from a regionally dominated functional organization to a stronger country system. Now they were being asked to buy into a regionally driven structure once again. The changes were traumatic. Under the new hybrid structure, many country presidents felt their roles had greatly diminished. Although they were still

BD's legal representatives and managed relationships with local regulatory agencies, unions, medical advisory panels, and the like, their role in broader strategy development, planning, and decision-making processes was unclear. In this environment, border disputes among SBU managers, country managers, and regional and corporate staff departments erupted frequently.

Differences over many issues such as marketing plans, sourcing, or managing manufacturing assets, arose periodically between U.S. and non-U.S. managers. But it was the conflict over new product development issues that often became the most emotional flashpoint for issues of autonomy, competence, and cultural bias. Because the U.S. divisions still controlled R&D, Europeans accused the U.S. divisions of a strong bias for products with U.S. markets. The U.S. division presidents, on the other hand, found most European product requests poorly documented and reflective of incomplete understandings of the real resource costs of the product development cycle.

Toward Transnational Management   Despite the continued spectacular growth of its European sales and market share, BD Europe posted operating losses for FY 1983–1984. The company was in an investment mode with respect to its European businesses, and the Plymouth plant, which had been built in 1981 as a regional plant for Europe, was not expected to turn a profit until the late 1980s. But senior managers feared that cost and quality goals would be difficult to achieve with the conflict that existed among pivotal players and organizational units, and it seemed unlikely that BD's European situation would permit it to contend successfully with a growing field of competitors.

By 1985, some senior managers were ready to reassess how the company managed its worldwide operations. As a result, BD engaged a consulting company to study the problem. The consultant produced two alternative models ("The Worldwide Product Division" and "Europe as Equal Partner"), each described in great detail as to the structural change required. Senior management decided it was not ready for another restructuring, with all the implied turf battles and inwardly focused energy. Instead they sought a solution that would respond to the external forces for more cross-border coordination, but that would not compromise the country organizations' entrepreneurship and motivation, undermine their excellent relationships with their local markets, or interfere with their need to negotiate with national regulatory, medical and labor groups.

It was in this context that some senior managers met with Harvard Professor Christopher Bartlett, then undertaking a research project with his colleague Sumantra Ghoshal on worldwide organization.[1] In several sessions with the top team, Bartlett emphasized three core findings from the study:

- The strategic need for companies to build global efficiency, national responsiveness, and a worldwide innovation and learning capacity;
- The need of this multilayered strategic capability for a multidimensional organization, not one structured around traditional dichotomous choices between product and geography, centralization and decentralization; and
- The building of such organizations by changing management culture and values and developing organizational processes and relationships, and not just by changing formal structural design.

International Sector President Clateo Castellini, an Italian national, and Group President Ralph Biggadike, a British national, strongly advocated Bartlett's transnational approach because they saw it as providing a balance between the country structure and the SBU structure debated within BD. After many months of discussion, BD senior managers agreed to make the transnational approach the subject of the 1986 senior management conference. Then in a series of three-day management conferences in 1986 and 1987, Bartlett exposed over 150 of BD's managers to transnational concepts.

---

[1]Reported in Christopher A. Bartlett and Sumantra Ghoshal, *Managing Across Borders: The Transnational Solution* (Boston: HBS Press, 1989).

Exhibit 3   Task Responsibility Framework: Vacutainer Systems*

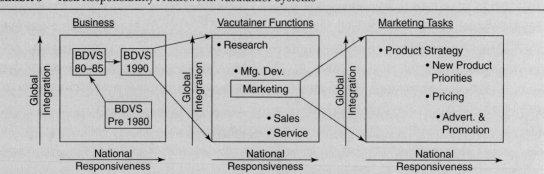

*This reflects the preliminary discussions and analysis done at the early transitional management seminars, where managers began to negotiate, business by business, function by function, and task by task, which responsibilities needed to be managed primarily by SBUs in a global manner (the northwest quadrant), which needed to be managed primarily by subsidiaries in a local manner (the southeast quadrant), and which <u>few key issues</u> needed to be handled in off-line forums where global and local managers could engage in the more intensive discussions and negotiations that transnational management required (the northeast quadrant). This analysis illustrates the outcomes on discussions about allocation of responsibility for marketing tasks in the Vacutainer Systems business. Similar discussions and analysis were undertaken to determine responsibility for key tasks in all major functions on a business by business basis.

After analyzing the changes occurring in their businesses, the managers quickly realized the need to build multiple sources of competitive advantage and that doing so would require strong management capability in both the local and global dimensions.

Using frameworks similar to those illustrated in Exhibit 3, the managers spent most of the conference discussing and negotiating what needed to be managed in a more globally integrated manner, what needed to be handled in a more nationally responsive way, and what few issues needed to be handled jointly. As the exhibit suggests, they quickly discovered that there was no single formula and that they had to decide business by business, function by function, and even decision by decision.

Although most issues could be clearly allocated to country or business management, a few vital issues need to be managed in a shared fashion. To provide a forum for these decisions, as well as a means to develop relationships between key managers, in late 1986 Worldwide Teams were established for each of the key worldwide businesses. Because each of the businesses had defined its organizational tasks ·differently, no attempt was made to impose a uniform set of responsibilities on the teams. Instead, senior management challenged each team to define its own role in helping manage the worldwide business. Some quickly became active in initiating worldwide projects and coordinating joint decision-making processes; others met less frequently and slipped into the role of communication forums.

▉ The Changes at VACUTAINER Systems

One of the businesses affected by all the changes was the BD VACUTAINER Systems (BDVS) Division. BDVS included the U.S. business, which housed all R&D, and the European operations. Manufacturing plants in the United States and Europe reported to the BDVS president through the divisional director of Manufacturing. In Asia and Latin America, however, the VACUTAINER business still reported to the country presidents. (See Exhibit 4.)

BDVS as a Worldwide Business   The first formal "worldwide" meeting of BDVS managers occurred in Annecy, France in 1982. The meeting was quite

Exhibit 4 Organization Chart, 1986

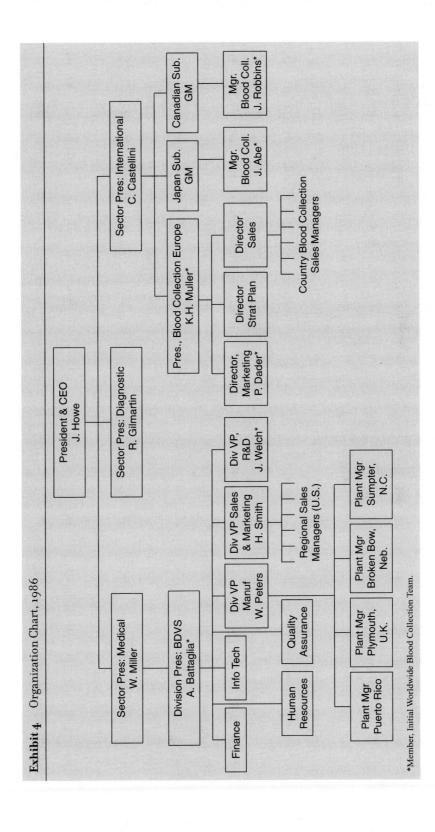

*Member, Initial Worldwide Blood Collection Team.

formal, with the U.S. group explaining to the Europeans procedures for new product development, product support, and other divisional functions. In response, the Europeans explained the nature of their market with its diverse pattern of medical practice.

Encouraged by their influence as a united group, the Europeans continued to meet on a somewhat informal and *ad hoc* basis throughout the early 1980s. Then European BDVS President Karlheinz Müller, described the spirit of the group:

> After that [Annecy meeting] we had fairly regular meetings and product training for our sales force. It was a relationship we benefited mutually from, initiated really by the people, and tolerated by management.

Through this process of opening communication channels, the non-U.S. managers became conscious that they might be able to have an input into BD's worldwide strategy. This encouraged managers in Europe and Japan to propose new product ideas to the worldwide SBU group in the mid-1980s. The initial response, however, was greatly disappointing for both non-U.S. groups, and by 1985 there was growing cynicism that the worldwide meetings were little more than a means of imposing U.S. strategy on overseas operations.

The stories of the development of two products—HEMOGARD and the PLUS TUBE—will illustrate the challenges BD faced in developing an integrated worldwide management approach.

HEMOGARD^TM*: The European Proposal*   In 1980, BD's European sales force began a push to convert European customers from conventional syringes to the VACUTAINER^TM blood collection system that had been a major success in the U.S. market. In Europe, however, there was some resistance because of perceived blood exposure safety problems for laboratory personnel removing the VACUTAINER^TM rubber stopper, which had to be popped off in order to remove blood for testing. Because this action broke the vacuum in the tube, there was some danger blood would "aerosol"—spray out of the tube onto the worker's skin—or that the tube would actually break, posing a danger of

cuts and infection with blood-transmitted diseases such as hepatitis.

The issue became a major topic of discussion in early 1983 at a VACUTAINER^TM Europe sales meeting in St. Paul de Vence, France. Several sales and marketing managers reported that some of BD's competitors were developing closures that reduced the danger of worker contamination. Furthermore, they confirmed that BD's ability to convert was being slowed down most in the high-potential markets of the United Kingdom, Germany, and Italy, where safety concerns were the greatest. Following their diagnosis, the group developed drawings and preliminary specifications for the screw-on plastic closure device they envisioned and sent them off to Joseph Welch, head of BDVS's R&D department.

The proposal met with little response due to a number of factors. There were no formal organizational means to translate regional interests into potential R&D priorities. Even new product and product extension ideas generated in the United States were not placed on a clearly prioritized list for R&D attention. Since the proposed screw-on cap represented an expensive product development commitment, U.S. marketing people saw little reason to develop it, believing it would be a niche product with limited demand, even in Europe. Furthermore, BDVS had several large-scale projects on the board, and the Americans saw little need to take a major risk without strong support within R&D and with thinly documented paybacks.

As Müller later acknowledged:

> Since we had 100 million [annual unit sales of tubes] versus 500 million for the United States, it was hard to interest R&D. And our marketing group was not very effective then in submitting the Project Initiation Review properly. Without formal processes, it all had to be done through an informal relationship with Joe Welch.

Nonetheless, within Europe there was a growing sense of frustration as time passed and the screw-on closure was not forthcoming from U.S. R&D. The promise of truly worldwide management seemed hollow.

In June of 1984, after considerable pressure from Müller and his team, Welch agreed to a compromise. He directed his R&D department to develop a mold for an interim product, a press-on plastic cap called the Safety Cap that could be added to existing VACUTAINER products for use in hematology labs. The design was a good deal simpler than the European proposal, and the mold itself was produced in a weekend in BD's machine shop.

In October of 1984, four months after the first Safety Cap molds were produced, Alfred Battaglia became BDVS president and committed himself to "lighting a fire" under the division's product development process. He saw his new division's R&D function as one with many projects but no clear sense of their relative importance and business potential. Instead of relying on personal contacts and the "squeaky wheel" approach that had been the division's *de facto* research priority system, Battaglia encouraged his staff to pursue a clearer and more informed approach to allocating BDVS's resources. To help in this regard, he developed and began to use an R&D priority matrix on which proposed projects were ranked based on a combination of development cost and potential return.

Early in 1985, BDVS began to ship small quantities of Safety Caps for field trials in Europe. The company's accounts were protected more against the incursions of competing safety products, and field data could be fed back to the U.S. R&D engineers still working on the project. Unfortunately, the trials were not very successful, as an engineer involved with the project recalled:

> The Safety Caps didn't exactly take off. They didn't fit in everybody's holders. They didn't fit with competitive needles. We didn't have a very good needle at the time, so a lot of places were using our tube with someone else's needle. . . . It was a son of a gun to push on; it took about 30 pounds of force to put it on . . . [and] it was very smooth and straight-sided, so it was hard to grip with a wet glove.

As BDVS engineers went back to work on the project, Battaglia urged the R&D group to look at the project as one with worldwide significance. Not only did it respond to a growing concern for health care workers' safety, but it also offered a differentiating benefit that could allow BDVS to standardize on a smaller global blood collection tube size, thereby reducing costs.

From the European perspective, however, all they saw was a further delay. Therefore, when key U.S. and European figures met in 1985 at BD's plant in Plymouth, England, Müller expressed his frustration to Battaglia. By this stage, the European team had buttressed its initial proposal with market studies and physicians' endorsements and lined up significant support for the product through direct contacts at the U.S. corporate level. (Müller later characterized his own approach as "table banging.") Battaglia was sympathetic and agreed to commit to the project.

Following this meeting, Welch assigned more R&D resources to the project and moved more aggressively to secure agreement to specifications. New European trials provided input into design decisions, and by March 1986, marketing groups in the United States, Canada, Europe, and Japan had signed off on the specifications for the Safety Cap. Now the challenge was to implement the launch of a product called HEMOGARD™.

PLUS TUBE: The Japanese Proposal   When members of the Blood Collection SBU met in Tokyo in 1985, Japanese managers talked with leading team members about what they saw as a key to VACUTAINER market share in Japan: unbreakable specimen collection tubes. Breakability was much more than an issue of safety to Japanese users. Because of a strong cultural aversion to blood loss, recollecting specimens because of tube breakage was a major problem, and resistance to breakability was seen as a core measure of overall product quality. Although European management viewed the plastic tube as a less urgent, longer-term need, the Japanese group saw it as an urgent priority to defend BD's fragile market share against competitive Japanese products already selling well.

Many BDVS observers realized that demand for relatively light, unbreakable collection tubes would grow as environmental and safety concerns increased worldwide. In both Austria and Japan, local firms had already introduced plastic tubes, and although their market share was small and localized, they looked to be potential threats to BD's penetration of these markets.

Again, the sense of local Japanese managers was that their requests had fallen on deaf ears. Japanese managers felt they had struggled against uncertain supplies and inattention to quality concerns for several years; between 1982 and 1984 BD actually lost part of its small market share in Japan. From their perspective, the HEMOGARD™ project had finally captured attention, and by 1985, was "winning" development resources while their project (dubbed the PLUS TUBE) "lost" because of the originating market's small size. U.S. R&D managers rejected this view and pointed out that the costs and technical challenges entailed in the two projects differed greatly. Whereas HEMOGARD could be developed with existing technologies, the projected plastic tube would require substantial re-tooling and the location or development of high-performing polymer materials that would not only meet medical standards but also guarantee shelf life, transparency, and other performance characteristics glass tube users had come to expect.

The Worldwide Blood Collection Team

The frustration and confusion managers were experiencing on the HEMOGARD and PLUS TUBE projects were symptomatic of the interpersonal tension that existed as BD struggled with how best to manage international expansion. The transnational organizational structure designated to help BD deal with these issues was the Worldwide Blood Collection Team (WBCT) in 1986. (See Exhibit 5.) It was hoped that the new organizational structure, and the changed management approach it required, would help resolve some of the problems.

Early Years: Defining the WBCT's Role   Although the WBCT decided to focus on strategic issues, its ability to fulfill that objective was limited by two factors. First, worldwide plans were part of the U.S. division's strategic/operational/financial planning process (SOF), developed by the U.S. staff

---

Exhibit 5   Worldwide Blood Collection Team, 1986

- Alfred Battaglia, President, BDVS US
- Hank Smith, Vice President, Sales/Marketing BDVS
- Joe Welch, Vice President/R&D BDVS
- Bill Peters, Vice President/Manufacturing BDVS
- Karlheinz Muller, President, Blood Collection Products Europe
- Pierre Dader, Director of Marketing, Blood Collection Products Europe
- Jun Abe, Manager, Blood Collection and Diabetic Products Japan
- Canadian representative (rotating)

Periodic attender:

- Representative, Latin America

---

with limited worldwide consultation. And second, few non-U.S. managers had been trained in BD's strategic planning system, which senior BD managers viewed as central to the firm's management system.

As a consequence, during the first two years of the WBCT's official existence, the team was seen largely as an information-sharing group. Basically, the organization continued to operate as it had under the old SBU model: the U.S. division determined strategy, directed R&D, and controlled manufacturing resources, while overseas operations focused on sales and marketing. Non-U.S. WBCT members, designated by their country or regional managers, tended to be junior to the U.S. team members and less able to commit their own organizations to the WBCT agenda. Some regions' delegates appeared irregularly at team meetings, changed frequently, and did not always command English well enough to participate fully in discussions. As a result, for both HEMOGARD and the PLUS TUBE, continued progress was determined by the originating region's ability to convince the BDVS president and R&D director of the projects' potential.

The creation of the WBCT, however, soon had an impact on the development of the HEMOGARD project. In 1986, it was becoming clear to U.S.

Exhibit 6   Worldwide Blood Collection Team Role, 1992

- Develop the worldwide strategy and the strategic goals for the Blood Collection Strategy Center.
- Support development of the regional strategies congruent with the worldwide strategy.
- Recommend the worldwide resource allocation to achieve the maximized effectiveness and efficiency in implementation of the worldwide strategy.
- Review the worldwide business performance to monitor the progress to worldwide strategic goals and to recommend the corrective strategies, if necessary.
- Develop and update the worldwide competitive strategies by integrating the competitive information from the worldwide regions.
- Support developing the regional competitive strategies by releasing the collected competitive information to the worldwide regions.
- Evaluate and prioritize the new product concepts in the worldwide R&D agenda to maintain the optimum resource allocation in PACE.
- Support non-PACE regional product development requirements based upon specifically local customer needs by the worldwide technical support function in the BDVS organization.
- Coordinate worldwide product strategies and rollouts.
- Make recommendations on "global" vs. "local" business activities.
- Coordinate transfer of key skills/capabilities from "Centers of Excellence" to regions.
- Maintain good communications with regional senior managements to help them to develop and implement the well-integrated regional operations strategy with the Blood Collection Strategy Center strategy.
- Identify and locate medical/QA/RA support to the worldwide regions.
- Identify and allocate technical/selling skill training support to the worldwide regions.

Source: *Worldwide Blood Collection Operating Manual.*

---

epidemiologists and to the general public that the AIDS virus outbreaks were early warnings of a pandemic, and the worldwide humanitarian and business potentials of a safety tube closure became more obvious. A BDVS R&D engineer explained:

> The driver was Europe originally, and even in 1984 and 1985 . . . Europeans tended to have a longer view of some trends. They knew about AIDS, and that it was important, and would get worse. In the United States, we were a year or two behind on that curve; awareness peaked around 1986. . . . It was only after the scare hit the United States that we really started cranking [HEMOGARD] up.

With this more widespread support for HE-MOGARD, the WBCT provided a useful forum in which to discuss and drive the project. At the team's urging, BDVS R&D director Joe Welch pursued the project aggressively. The WBCT also decided to use the Plymouth, England, plant as the major source for the product.

The PLUS TUBE found a more difficult time claiming the WBCT's attention. First, the team's role was unclear in its early days, and nobody seemed sure of what function to play. Second, the project overlapped with the HEMOGARD launch, and the BDVS R&D and manufacturing staffs were heavily involved with both.

Japanese managers were convinced that the HE-MOGARD closure on a glass tube had no future in Japan. They were also greatly alarmed by news that Terumo, BD's major competitor in Japan, was working steadily toward a plastic tube. While the persistent Japanese concerns convinced the U.S. managers to raise the priority of getting a viable product into Japan, even without the breakthrough in plastic technology they had been seeking, there was continuing debate within the WBCT about the worldwide application of plastic tube strategy. In contrast to HEMOGARD, which everyone believed eventually would be a crucial product worldwide, PLUS TUBE was seen by many as a uniquely Japanese product. Most of the Europeans, for instance, were unconvinced that rapid plastic tube development was necessary to their short-term regional strategy, although some, like Eckhard Lachenauer, believed it would be a key competitive product by 1995. A U.S. participant recalled the flavor of the discussion in 1987 and 1988:

> There seemed to be two camps about whether plastic was necessary. There was a lot of discussion of profits and ROA. We also had to decide how fast we would push the plastic tube, if we did decide to develop it. That was very important because in some instances the coexistence of glass and plastic was an important business strategy for us.

The division and the corporation agreed in 1987 to a staged development scheme, which aimed at supplying the Japanese market as quickly as possible, and moved on toward ultimate goals of shelf life, appearance, cost, and other factors with the help of BD's Research Center in North Carolina.

The debate of PLUS TUBE in the WBCT meetings did serve to increase overall awareness of the project and, as a result, led to some progress in locating suppliers. BD managers in Europe and in Japan ferreted out promising suppliers, licensers, and business partners able to supply technology and materials. For example, Müller introduced Welch to representatives of Greiner, the Austrian company manufacturing plastic blood collection tubes, and Jun Abe of BD's Japanese company put him in touch with Sekisui, a Japanese company interested in a marketing partnership for its plastic technology. In 1987, BD agreed to purchase Greiner's molds and Sekisui's plastic technology.

The Maturing WBCT: Launching World Products

In October of 1988, when Battaglia was promoted to group president, Bill Kozy became BDVS president. By this time the WBCT composition and role had evolved considerably, and Kozy saw the team as a major means to achieve the ambitious growth in international business he and BD expected.

However, from his first meeting with the WBCT, Kozy was aware that it was still struggling with the notion of "transnational management." It was difficult for managers to grasp and embody a change process that was focused not on a structural prescription but on changing processes and relationships and on broadening management mentalities ("creating a matrix in managers' minds," as the transnational model proposed). Kozy described the division's early operating committee discussions:

> In terms of worldwide roles and responsibilities, no one had a clue. A bunch of basically command and control people suddenly became "team members" or "team leaders." Everyone wanted to know what his role was, what he was responsible for. People were still in the political mode of "If you're not going to develop my products, I'm going to tell."

To spark discussion on the team's role, Kozy asked his entire senior staff to read Bartlett and Ghoshal's book *Managing Across Borders,* so that the group could discuss it chapter by chapter during its regular meetings. The new division president saw the reading and discussions as a valuable exercise, although some of his staff greeted references to it with wry laughter.

Kozy himself recounted an epiphany of sorts that occurred on a plane during a conversation with his Japanese seatmate. The two men discussed the challenges of international business management, and the Japanese manager said Kozy was lucky to work for a company with the patience to adopt an approach like transnational management, which would clearly require at least 10 years to implement. The extent to which transnational management really was built on changing managers' mentalities and relationships rather than just restructuring reporting relationships suddenly struck Kozy with full force, and the amount of time required to achieve genuine transnational management became clear. He realized that it probably *was* a 10-year process, and that his own division had been struggling with it for only three or four years.

Kozy's commitment to clarify the WBCT's responsibilities and increase its role as a key forum for transnational management exchange was greatly facilitated by the ongoing operations relating to the two new products under development.

HEMOGARD Launch   As the HEMOGARD launch neared, the WBCT was increasingly involved in marketing decisions, some of which did not meet with field sales approval. For technical reasons and to reduce manufacturing costs, BDVS wanted to minimize the number of individual HEMOGARD catalogue numbers. But every time they reduced the size of the product line, the European marketing group would have to lower its forecasts, triggering long debate within the group. Eckhard Lachenauer described the WBCT discussions of the number of VACUTAINER products to be offered with HEMOGARD closures and debates over sales projections as "a constant battle."

Finally, the HEMOGARD line was launched in July 1989. European Director of Operations John Hanson described the launch as the most successful in which he had ever participated, representing to him a truly cross-functional and trans-Atlantic team effort. He recalled the plan's execution:

> By the end of 1988 the real final stage was to involve the plants to bring the product to market. That was the part that was highly successful. It was the first real transnational effort that brought the product to a very aggressive launch date of June 1989. And we slipped by only one month, to July 1989. That I always quote as being truly successful in a worldwide team sense— the plants, R&D, the Supply Chain group, sales and marketing. We had very detailed plans, and they actually happened—that's the amazing part.

Hanson attributed the success of the HEMO-GARD launch effort to two central characteristics. First, team roles were made an integral part of members' regular jobs rather than side assignments:

> All of the team assignments and the additional responsibilities these jobs implied were formalized within the framework of their job description. People did the job as they were meant to, this meant that rather than being asked to take on a team assignment on the side.

Second, Hanson believed the launch process was effective because project participants agreed to

bypass any existing management information systems that were slow and bureaucratic. For example, new materials management models were developed on local personal computers because existing systems seemed unlikely to support the manufacturing schedules BD contemplated. Furthermore, minutes of the meetings of far-flung teams and committees were faxed to Kozy and Welch within hours. In turn, these managers and their staff responded rapidly to queries, requests, and issues. Hanson recalled:

> The whole key was focus and communication and holding people responsible for what they're actually supposed to do. There's no project now with that weekly communication and weekly meetings. The coordination is not as clear and crisp.

PLUS TUBE Launch   The launch of the PLUS TUBE went less smoothly, but the WBCT's role was also critical in bringing this product to market. The main problem stemmed from BDVS R&D's agreeing to a launch date schedule before completely understanding how challenging a shift from glass to plastic would be. The molds purchased from Greiner produced tubes that did not fit the HEMOGARD closure and had to be modified. In making adjustments, the group quickly learned that plastic was a very different material from glass. But having the WBCT forum at least allowed the problems to be identified quickly and for corrective action to be agreed on and assigned.

Although BDVS originally planned to release the first PLUS TUBEs in late 1988 or 1989, by that date they had not even begun the first Japanese field trials. Eventually trials were conducted and the first products were shipped in 1991. The division and the WBCT were learning that agreement to a marketing strategy did not produce manufacturing capability, as one manager pointed out:

> It took us a year to figure out how to make it work; the schedules were very aggressive. We have learned from this. For the PLUS TUBE we put schedules on products before we figured out how to do it. We're now using a planning method that won't let you commit to a date until you've proved a technology.

Exhibit 7   Transnational Organizational Concept, September 1992

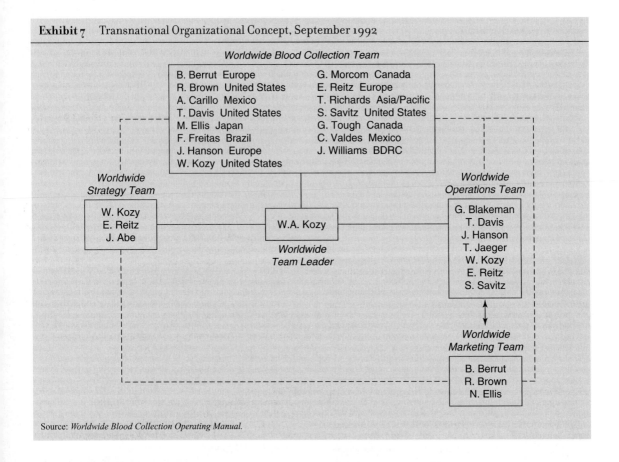

Worldwide Blood Collection Team

B. Berrut Europe	G. Morcom Canada
R. Brown United States	E. Reitz Europe
A. Carillo Mexico	T. Richards Asia/Pacific
T. Davis United States	S. Savitz United States
M. Ellis Japan	G. Tough Canada
F. Freitas Brazil	C. Valdes Mexico
J. Hanson Europe	J. Williams BDRC
W. Kozy United States	

Worldwide
Strategy Team

W. Kozy
E. Reitz
J. Abe

W.A. Kozy
*Worldwide
Team Leader*

Worldwide
Operations Team

G. Blakeman
T. Davis
J. Hanson
T. Jaeger
W. Kozy
E. Reitz
S. Savitz

Worldwide
Marketing Team

B. Berrut
R. Brown
N. Ellis

Source: *Worldwide Blood Collection Operating Manual.*

Structural Change in the WBCT   At the same time the WBCT was handling the implementation of the two new product launches, it was also engaged in a variety of other issues that required the input and involvement of managers worldwide. Meanwhile, the size and diversity of team membership had grown substantially. By 1990, a few of the most active and influential team members felt that the WBCT was too large and too diversely skilled to make all of the decisions the team's projects required. As Lachenauer explained, "Bill (Kozy) and I realized one day that we could not make all the decisions in the big team. It was taking too much time on tactics and not enough on strategy." The decision was made to form three smaller subteams that could move more efficiently to deal with the strategic,

operating, and marketing issues that were becoming increasingly important. (See Exhibits 7 and 8.)

In 1991 the three members of the Worldwide Strategy Team—Kozy, Lachenauer, and Abe—embarked on a worldwide profiling tour, using BD's long-established strategic profiling process to examine regional strategic potentials and advise regional managers on their role in the worldwide business unit's international strategy. The trio met in Tokyo with managers in BD's Japanese and Asia Pacific blood collection businesses, in Mexico City with their Brazilian and Mexican counterparts, with Canadian managers, and with managers in Europe and the United States. They visited customers in Brazil and Japan. The visits exposed the Strategy Team to the realities of the business outside its major

Exhibit 8   Worldwide Blood Collection
Team, 1992

- President, BDVS US
- President, Blood Collection Europe
- Vice President/R&D BDVS
- Director of Marketing, BDVS
- Director, Worldwide Manufacturing and Logistics
- Vice President, Worldwide Business Development
- Corporate Medical Director
- Marketing Director, Blood Collection Europe
- Vice President/General Manager, Diagnostic Canada
- Marketing Manager, Blood Collection Canada
- Sales and Marketing Director, Blood Collection Japan
- Business Director, Blood Collection Asia Pacific
- Sales and Marketing Director, Diagnostic Mexico
- Sales and Marketing Director, Blood Collection Brazil
- Director, Manufacturing Europe (Director, Plymouth plant)

Worldwide Strategy Team

- President, BDVS
- President, Blood Collection Europe
- Vice President, Worldwide Business Development

Leads Worldwide Strategy Development in the Worldwide Blood Collection Team.

Worldwide Operations Team

- Director, Worldwide Manufacturing and Logistics (Chair)
- President, BDVS US
- President, Blood Collection Europe
- Plant Manager, Sumter, North Carolina
- Director, Manufacturing Europe
- Vice President/R&D, BDVS

Acts as Worldwide Operations Management Team for Manufacturing, R&D, and Supply Chain Management.

Worldwide Marketing Team

- Director of Marketing, BDVS
- Director of Marketing, Blood Collection Europe
- Director of Marketing, BDVS Japan

Speaks for "Worldwide Marketing" on key product strategies or new product decisions.

Source: *Worldwide Blood Collection Operating Manual.*

markets, and Kozy returned newly impressed by the potential of markets such as Latin America.

The trip also sensitized the team to the different needs of local markets (e.g., Japanese needs for smaller tubes and some labeling changes). In fact, the Strategy Team members were engaged enough in the problems presented by the Brazilian business that they arranged to visit Brazil. As these visits and exchanges continued, managers recognized that a new level of understanding and cooperation was emerging in subsequent WBCT meetings. Abe commented:

> Before when we talked about "worldwide strategy" we really didn't know—we talked only about surface things. That really changed; there were much better suggestions, and much better advice. Now we could see how to use U.S. and even European resources to help.

The other major structural changes related to the management of R&D and technology support. As the HEMOGARD and PLUS TUBE experiences had shown, overseas managers had often experienced difficulty in getting support from the U.S.-based R&D group. The situation was even more difficult for those trying to get technology assistance for older products no longer marketed in the United States, because most R&D staff were tied up in current projects.

The situation gradually began to improve in the late 1980s, particularly after the arrival of Steven Sous, a BDVS quality assurance (QA) specialist. As a sideline to his domestic responsibilities, Sous took on the role of QA liaison to Japan and from that base gradually expanded his international role. Because of the personal contacts he made during those meetings and in trips to BD locations outside the United States, Sous was increasingly identified as the best person to contact for technical support—especially in the problematic area of support for products deemphasized or discontinued in the United States. As issues in which he was involved came up, he began to attend the WBCT meetings in an unofficial capacity, eventually attending regularly.

When Joseph Welch left BDVS in January of 1990 to become president of BD Labware, and

Steven Savitz took his place as VP of R&D, Savitz defined his role as "doing worldwide R&D for the division." His non-U.S. colleagues viewed him as "genuinely transnational." Savitz strengthened the international role Steven Sous had taken, in 1991 giving him the new title of manager, Research and Development Worldwide Technical Support. Sous and his group were responsible for working with the non-U.S. businesses to support and extend products, including responsibility for relatively small projects such as label changes, producing VACUTAINER tubes for high-altitude applications, and packaging variations necessitated by government regulations or differences in device-dispensing practices. Most of these "do it now" projects did not require large financial investment and did not need to wend their way through the division's major project approval and resource allocation process. To deal with demand, Sous hoped to expand his staff by four permanent positions in FY 1992.

During the same period, Kozy and Savitz responded to Lachenauer's long-term lobbying for a Europe-based R&D manager by appointing Chris Dufresne, Manager R&D VACUTAINER Systems Europe in BD's European headquarters. He reported to Lachenauer with a dotted line to Savitz, and was responsible for helping to manage the interface between European management and the U.S. R&D organization, particularly for expediting European new product and product extension ideas. Dufresne's position was a compromise between the European desire to be fully integrated vertically and the U.S. division's desire to maintain control over worldwide R&D efforts.

Dufresne lost no time in becoming a champion for European products. During the May 1992 meetings, he presented an ordered list of potential products for European applications. Many present agreed that his reputation and U.S. experience increased the likelihood that European ideas would be accorded serious consideration by the WBCT and by Kozy and Savitz.

During the May 1992 Toronto meeting, members of the WBCT discussed two important new developments in their technology management.

First, BDVS was working with a consultant to refine the project approval and project management processes. Second, they discussed the need for greater non-U.S. participation in the R&D function. Although budget constraints prevented him from further expansion of the R&D organizations in regions outside the United States and Europe, Kozy was sympathetic to the requests. After much discussion, he and WBCT members from Mexico and Japan developed the idea of creating a position within the U.S. R&D organization to be funded jointly by Mexico and Japan.

All WBCT members saw clear evolution toward genuine transnational management in the team's operation. Roles and structures were clarified in practice and in the "Worldwide Blood Collection Manual" (on which Exhibits 6, 7, and 8 are based). But historic difficulties in achieving a real balance between the power of the U.S. division staff and the rest of the company's interests persisted. During the 1992 Toronto meetings, Lachenauer and Kozy and his staff clearly dominated many discussions from which their non-U.S. colleagues sometimes seemed disengaged. A rapid assessment of the development costs and sales potential of a list of proposed new products and product extensions yielded a priority list intended to guide the U.S. R&D function in its work over the company year, but some team members wondered privately whether they had either the time or the expertise to assess every project fairly. They cited examples of products such as the European-sponsored SEDITAINER tube, whose further development still languished in the face of the American medical directors' disapproval and American marketers' indifference.

The WBCT in 1993: Achievements and Challenges

After the WBCT met in Geneva in May of 1993, many participants sensed that the group was continuing to evolve toward a genuinely transnational position. Where they once struggled to achieve consensus around uniform global strategies and goals, they were now comfortable with regional variations consistent with overall worldwide strategies and business goals. For example, because European members preferred a marketing strategy that emphasized choice between glass and plastic, the group discussed selling the PLUS TUBE under another name in Europe to avoid implying invidious comparisons to the glass tubes they planned to sell alongside plastic for a few years. U.S. participant Tom Jaeger saw this and other local market-specific discussions as good indications of the WBCT's evolution toward a genuine transnational mentality:

> Even in the most recent meeting before this, we felt there had to be a worldwide consensus on business strategy; now a consensus has arisen that we can have different strategies . . . we need to have everyone understand, and decide on a regional basis exactly what to do. I believe in that—that everyone is the keeper of their own markets.

Furthermore, the WBCT's ability to respond rapidly to worldwide needs had developed considerably. When members representing Japan pushed for rapid expansion of catalogue numbers to include smaller tubes and a wider range of coatings and additives, many were elated by a six-month concept-to-release process for a new additive tube for Japan undertaken in 1992, remarking that without the R&D proposal review and priority-setting capacities of the evolving WBCT, such speed would have been inconceivable.

The group also broadened international participation in R&D decision-making. The European director of Operations and a senior European marketing manager joined the worldwide Project Approval Committee, thereby bringing the group to U.S./ European parity. Furthermore, WBCT members had already agreed to place sponsored engineers from Europe, Japan, and Latin America on the U.S. R&D staff.

Members saw considerable change in WBCT team members' ability to communicate and negotiate shared and divergent strategies and operational parameters. A frequent WBCT participant with both R&D and manufacturing experience at BD observed that each member's understanding of the whole range of the business had deepened, and that members had learned how to argue for the projects they supported:

> Because of the Worldwide Team meetings, each of the different regions now looks at their marketplace a little bit differently because at meetings they have to explain to people from other parts of the world what's really going on. They have to get outside their tunnel vision, put a perspective on the whole thing. Someone can't just say, "This is the way it is," so he prepares his data to explain why his perspective might be different from theirs.

However, as he reviewed the WBCT's achievements, Kozy could not help wondering what additional changes would be required to keep the group operating effectively. Questions that particularly concerned him were:

- Does the business have the right configuration of assets and resources? In particular, what are the implications of our recent changes in the R&D function for the future of that key task? Should we try to keep our resources concentrated in the United States and expand the "sponsored liaison" positions, or should we yield to the European lobby for a more fully integrated European development capability? How can we balance the large-scale businesses in the United States and Europe, against the smaller businesses in the rest of the world?

- What changes do we need to make in our human resource policies and practices to move us further towards transnational management? What changes can we make to our human resource management system so we can send people on overseas assignment with some assurance that their careers won't be compromised? The new compensation system has been favorably received [see Exhibit 9], and should help us get over the conflict between the WBCT and the regions caused by regional managers' being rewarded for maximizing the local budget, but what else can be done to increase WBCT effectiveness?

- Finally, how should the WBCT's role evolve as we move into the future? Is there need for more

Exhibit 9   Senior Management Bonus Plan Changes, 1993

Corporate Officers	Sector Presidents	Division Heads
Old Formula		
50% Company (65% EPS vs. budget, 35% strategic)	25% Company (65% EPS vs. budget, 35% strategic)	25% Company (65% EPS vs. budget, 35% strategic)
25% Strategic (function/company)	50% Sector (65% OIBT vs. budget, 35% strategic)	50% Unit (65% OIBT vs. budget, 35% strategic)
25% Individual performance	25% Individual performance	25% Individual performance
New Formula		
75% Company EPS[a] budget	25% Company EPS[a] vs. Budget	25% Sector (65% OIBT vs. budget, 35% strategic)
	50% Sector OIBT	50% Unit OIBT
25% Strategic (function/company)	25% Strategic (worldwide sector)	25% Strategic (worldwide teams)

[a]As reported for executive officers; FX neutral for other corporate officers.

structure and more clearly defined roles as some advocated, or should it continue to be managed on a more flexible process-driven manner? What impact will changing membership have on its operation, and can such personal dependencies be managed? Do a few strong managers dominate team meetings, and do we need to find ways to foster broader participation?

Case 4-3   Schneider Electric Global Account Management

Fritz Keller, international account manager (IAM) in Schneider Electric (Switzerland) S.A., was preparing for his first account manager workshop with one of his new global accounts, Calchem,

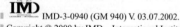

IMD-3-0940 (GM 940) V. 03.07.2002.

Copyright © 2000 by IMD—International Institute for Management Development, Lausanne, Switzerland. Not to be used or reproduced without written permission directly from IMD.

Research Associate Anne-Valerie Ohlsson prepared this case under the supervision of Professor Joe DiStefano as a basis for class discussion rather than to illustrate either effective or ineffective handling of a business situation.

Please note that some numbers and percentages have been altered and that the names of individuals and client accounts have been disguised.

worldwide manufacturer of specialty chemicals. One of the standard challenges in introducing a new account to the advantages of the global relationship was reflected by the fact that, until a week before the meeting, Keller had been unable to persuade representatives from Calchem's head office in Basel to attend the two-day meeting in Nice. Keller believed that Calchem had never had as close a supplier relationship as he was proposing and felt uncomfortable with the idea. On the other hand, with 30% of Calchem billings originating from the US operations, one of Calchem's senior US executives had been quick to accept Keller's invitation. Then, a week before the meeting, the head of automation had accepted the invitation, and two days before the meeting, the VP of group purchasing had called to say that he would attend the second day of the two-day meeting.

After two years on the job, Fritz Keller was a strong supporter of Schneider's global account management (GAM), which he was convinced brought mutual advantages to customers and to Schneider. But the challenge with Calchem wasn't the only issue he had identified as an important concern for him and his 60 IAM counterparts around the globe. Among other things that kept him busy were:

- Gaining the necessary cooperation from Schneider's local companies, which served Calchem accounts in their country's marketing structure.
- Getting timely information from Schneider's information systems, which had been established in the French headquarters to serve the large and growing number of global accounts that had been so successful in increasing Schneider's worldwide revenues.
- Finding the time to network with his IAM counterparts and getting to know important Schneider managers in key countries around the world who could make or break his promises to Calchem when special assistance was needed.
- Getting the support of his own boss to add the necessary people in Switzerland to take full advantage of the GAM opportunities of other multinationals based in Switzerland.

Schneider Electric Background

Schneider Electric was founded in 1782 as an industrial equipment company. During its first years, the company grew rapidly, surviving both the French Revolution and the Napoleonic Wars. Under the leadership of brothers Adolphe and Eugene Schneider, the company built the first French locomotive in 1836.

By 1914 the company had become one of France's most important heavy industry companies and, as such, played an important role in France's war effort during World War I. Schneider entered the electrical contracting business in 1929. During World War II many Schneider factories were either destroyed or commandeered. Following the war, and supported by the French government, the organization was restructured as a holding company. The new holding's operating units were grouped into three subsidiaries: civil and electrical engineering, industrial manufacturing and construction.

In 1969, three years after going public (the last family member passed away in 1950), Schneider merged with Empain to form the Empain-Schneider group. The merger was followed by a period of extensive acquisition and diversification, including ski equipment, fashion, publishing and travel.

The diversification strategy was not as successful as expected and, between 1980 and 1993, Schneider went through a complete reorganization. In 1993 the company merged with its former parent company, Société Parisienne d'Entreprises et de Participation. New stocks were issued to existing shareholders; operations were streamlined. Merlin Gerin (acquired in 1975) and Telemecanique (acquired in 1988) became Schneider Electric in Europe. Square D (acquired in 1991) represented Schneider's North American operations. The brands continued to be identified globally,[1] while operational synergies were obtained by shared facilities on a country or regional basis.

In a continued effort to refocus and expand, in 1996 Schneider set up the first totally French-owned company in China. In 1997 it sold Spie Batignolles, its electrical contracting subsidiary, and in 1999 it paid US$1.1 billion to acquire Lexel[2] in a move to broaden its household equipment offering. That year, the group also changed its name globally to Schneider Electric. By 2000 Schneider Electric was one of the largest electrical manufacturers in the world, operating 150 manufacturing and marketing facilities in 130 countries. It served

---

[1]The brand names were retained, as in most markets there was greater customer recognition for the individual brands than there was for the Schneider brand.

[2]A joint venture owned by Finland's Ahlstrom and Denmark's NKT Holding.

the electrical power, industrial, infrastructure and construction markets. Selected applications included electrical power in residential, industrial and commercial buildings, infrastructures for airports, road and rail networks, merchant marine and naval facilities and monitoring systems for power generation substations and distribution grids.

Shifting from Local to Global Account Management

Communication, reliability, speed and service to local customers are what make us successful as a team. We do not win customers with the technology—it is common to all the companies in the field. We win with the relationship-building and by delivering on the relationship.

Fritz Keller, *International Account Manager (Switzerland)*

In 1992 Schneider Global Business Development (SGBD) was created as a worldwide sales organization, parallel to the country-based sales force. One objective was to significantly expand business with the company's global, strategic clients.

Schneider first ventured into global account management with Copiato, an American company with which it had a long-standing relationship. By developing a deeper understanding of Copiato's needs, Schneider could tailor products that better suited Copiato's market. The two companies identified mutually beneficial initiatives in product development, reduction of project cycle time, improvement of productivity, minimization of down-times, savings in maintenance costs and reduction of inventory and purchasing costs. Working together around the globe helped ensure global consistency in product offering and service quality. As an indicator of the success and quality of the relationship, Copiato and Schneider were jointly awarded the 1995 Arthur Anderson Best of the Best Award for Channel Management. Subsequently, Schneider became Copiato's first and only globally certified electrical supplier.

The global account structure developed gradually. The shift from local to global account management came with a number of challenges: global account management was expensive, pricing and contracting became far more complicated and overcoming regional differences and "parochialism" represented a significant challenge.

Other challenges were the large degree of customization the company wanted to provide the client and the shift from standardized manufacturing to client-led manufacturing. In responding to a favored customer's needs, for example, Schneider had to invest in special equipment to design the product to the client's requirements. In turn, the client made Schneider its sole supplier for that group of products. As trust developed, increasingly rich relationships followed.

The high level of communication and customer interaction necessary to make the partnership successful involved a new way of working. In the most mature relationships, Schneider and its clients designed products together, forming product-development teams with members from both organizations. This required high involvement from senior management in both organizations and high trust. (Refer to Exhibit 1 for an example of the realignment of relationships.)

Definition of a Global Strategic Account

Schneider had set a requirement for companies that wanted to be considered as a strategic global account: the client had to offer the potential of sourcing at least 50% of its global business from Schneider. This allowed Schneider to recover the startup costs of the relationship over time. As François LeBlanc, head SGBD for the past five years, noted,

> Part of the problem is that your clients are also at different levels of globalization. You have to be patient, but you must also be able to amortize your costs. That's why there is a 50% entry barrier. Within the first two years of an alliance you get really fast growth, say from 5% to 20%. But the real challenge is to obtain more than 20% of your client's total business. The only way to achieve this is to provide consistent productivity improvements to your client. Winning the next 30% or more of your client's business will take you another three years. So, if after five years you do not have 50% of that client's business, you should seriously reconsider the relationship.

Exhibit 1   Evolution of Customer-Supplier Relationship

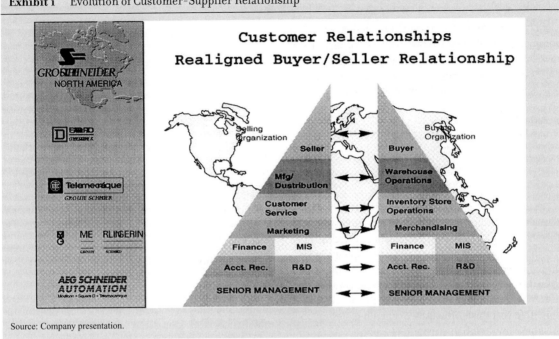

Source: Company presentation.

In addition, the client had to meet a number of pre-established conditions set by Schneider. The client had to help Schneider understand its challenges, needs and services. It had to agree to share early project information and make purchasing commitments. Other factors Schneider considered were compatibility of goals, values, styles and time horizons. A preferred relationship also included the cost-saving benefit of neither party having to go through a bidding process for a new project.

Building a Structure for Global Account Management

The structure of Schneider's global account management could be likened to a web (refer to Figure 1). In the center was Schneider Electric's Paris headquarters. International account managers reported through a matrix structure: they were responsible for the global accounts through SGBD's regional structure, but they also reported to the line organization through the country heads. Headquar-

ters coordinated global R&D, marketing, solutions and services, and provided SGBD with preferential support. The plants, located around the world, had responsibility for service contracts, time-to-market, training and maintenance. Wholesalers were in charge of pricing agreements, stocking, delivery times and technical training. The OEM/Systems Integration department managed service programs, conversion and provided technical training.

The headquarters of each global strategic account (GSA) was involved in the process. The IAM in charge of the account was based in the country of the GSA's headquarters. Together, Schneider and the client developed coordinated strategies and discussed potential reductions of overall costs.

The international account manager could obtain support from marketing resources dedicated to SGBD and from the industry expert teams in various geographical locations (e.g., Silicon Valley for the microelectronic specialists). The IAM provided Schneider's local country correspondents

Figure 1 International SGBD Network

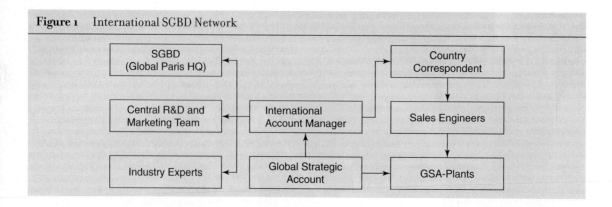

(international account correspondents, or IACs) with account information. The IACs shared this information with their local engineers and fed information back to the IAM. The engineers spent a large amount of time at the local plants of the GSAs. The GSA headquarters dealt directly with the IAM.

Performance Measures and Reward Systems

The IAMs were reviewed every year at the annual planning and review meeting. The meeting included the IAM's corporate sponsor[3] and the cluster[4] director. The review covered three areas: key objectives (including soft, general issues such as the number of projects developed with a key account), sales forecasts and critical issues or support needed. IAM performance was measured through a globally oriented management-by-objectives system. Profits were evaluated at net-price levels to ensure that products were not given away to win the account. As LeBlanc noted:

> In countries where sensitivity to quotas and incentives is very high (such as in the US), IAMs can receive an additional 20% to 50% of their salary as bonus. In general, I consider that the amount tied to local turnover is still too high relative to global turnover. The main challenge with the reward systems

is that we need to encourage both global account managers and local sales forces to look for a win-win situation.

In addition to the annual planning and review meetings, each cluster held its own annual meeting with all cluster IAMs and a number of local IACs. These meetings served the purpose of sharing information and ideas and providing industry updates. The meetings were held in a different country every year so that five to six local IACs could attend. A global SGBD meeting, including all IAMs and the SGBD central supporting team, was also held yearly.

The cost of measuring the benefits of a GSA was very high. Consequently, three to four accounts were chosen for closer scrutiny on an ad hoc, yearly basis. Corporate auditors and the corporate controller carried out an in-depth P&L analysis of these selected accounts. This independent, corporate performance measure allowed Schneider to check the validity of the approach and the margins on each GSA over years. Lou Primo, who divided his time between Paris and the US as director of international business development for SGBD, explained some of the difficulties Schneider experienced at the time:

> The issue of measurement of IAM and IAC effectiveness continues to be a difficult one for us. The same is true for measuring the worth of a GSA to Schneider Electric. While we would very much like to be able to measure these things, our current business systems are not well suited to providing data for this purpose.

---

[3] Each IAM had a senior executive from the parent corporation who was a top-level contact with the global strategic accounts associated with that IAM and who served as a mentor for the IAM. Fritz Keller's corporate sponsor was François LeBlanc, the head of the SGBD organization.

[4] A cluster was a business area. For Schneider these included food & beverages, automotive, pharmaceuticals, and microelectronics.

As a result of this lack of good business systems, we tend to take an intuitive approach to the evaluation of our IAMs, IACs and our GSAs. We rely heavily on the opinion of the country management in this regard. While we have continued to grow the number of accounts that we consider as GSAs, we have also de-listed three or four accounts which we felt did not measure up to our expectations.

A major problem in the senior and country management of Schneider Electric was the perception that large accounts often meant high volume with low margins. After several years of activity, SGBD was able to prove with actual revenue and margin figures that this was untrue. However, this perception was hard to change, and SGBD management always had to be ready to prove that global strategic accounts could yield higher-than-average margins to the overall benefit of both the account and Schneider Electric.

Training

Specific skills necessary to be a successful IAM included the ability to influence without authority and the ability to work across cultures.

Schneider's global account managers were expected to exhibit the following behaviors and skills[5]:

- Clear vision and mission statements.
- Empowerment:
  - Executive global nomination
  - Reporting structure
  - Internal awareness, and
  - Cooperation for local implementation.
- Effective communication network with identified regional managers at several levels and a formalized matrix structure.
- "Solution-selling" competence.
- Cultural adaptability.

Development activities were conducted in a variety of ways. Some centralized training was conducted at SGBD headquarters in Paris; other development occurred at client workshops. In addition to the formal training programs, the corporate spon-

sors and senior regional executives from SGBD worked with IAMs as on-the-job mentors. One of the gurus of GAM in Schneider, Harry Smith, who had started the Copiato account, was also renowned for his colorful coaching of IAMs, both at the client workshops he often attended and when he met with the IAMs in the field at US customer offices. Smith had taken a particular interest in Fritz Keller—he had taken Keller fishing during a visit to Smith's home in upstate New York. Smith explained why he believed in mentoring:

> The ability to network within the Schneider organization is not intuitive and there is no roadmap. Networking skills and contacts are extremely important as the IAM is a matrix manager and as such must gain support through consensus rather than edict. When an IAM networks with senior client management, senior VPs of manufacturing, engineering, purchasing, quality, finance, etc., the dialog changes as does the need set of the client. Our IAMs each have one senior Schneider manager assigned as an executive sponsor/mentor to help the IAM determine what Schneider management resource is most appropriate for each of the customer contact types identified above. Most of the time the most appropriate action for the IAM is to enable the conversation between peer members rather that conduct the meeting himself.

Schneider's Competitors and Their Relative Strengths in GAM

Schneider's main competitors included global players such as ABB, Alstom, Cuttler Hammer, General Electric, Rockwell and Siemens. Many of the company's main competitors embraced a project approach, rather than a solutions-oriented one. Others pursued a "stepping-stone" approach. They developed planned sequences of advertising and promotional events tightly linked to their sales, marketing and field service plans. These events were linked to calls for action that led customers to the next milestone in a desired relationship, while explicitly seeking awareness and credibility for solving specific customer business goals. (Refer to Exhibit 2 for an example of a competitor strategy.)

Schneider reacted to this range of strategies by developing entry and exit barriers for its clients.

[5]Lane, H. W., J. J. DiStefano, and M. L. Maznevski, *International Management Behavior,* 3rd ed. (Cambridge, Mass.: Blackwell Publishers, 1997), p. 192.

Exhibit 2   Example of Competitor Strategy

Competitor X

Earn Trust	Set Entry Barriers	Establish Exit Barriers	Solve Problems Together
New Smart Technology Advertisements Control View Compatible Software Advertisements	Application White Papers Conversion Programs "Channel Authorization" Programs Automation Fair Exhibit & Conference Program Automation Solutions Partners ISA tradeshow Exhibit	Application Assistance Teams MIS Network Support for "Enabled Products" SPC/MIS Application Support for Software	**Integrated Manufacturing**
Broad Product Offer Ads	Nationwide Distributor Directories Free Guide and Conversion Selectors Integrated Supply White Paper	Integrated Supply Guidelines/Programs Consortiums and Affiliations	**Integrated Logistics**
Global Advertisement	Worldwide Application Service and Support Directories	Global Systems Integration Support	**Globalization**

Source: Company presentation.

Entry barriers included product superiority, service superiority, networking relationships, joint long-term planning, joint product-design assistance, consignment inventory, common software systems and pricing agreements. Exit barriers included volume-based rebates, technical support, customer clubs, specialized training, formal long-term contracts, financial support and shared facilities. High switching costs made it difficult for competitors to convert their customers and for customers to convert their suppliers. (Refer to Exhibit 3 for Schneider's competitor defense strategy.)

The Situation in 2000

Reporting Structure and Funding Processes
The head of the SGBD reported to the senior management of Schneider Electric. If there were irresolvable differences between SGBD and geographic or business unit managers, the issues were resolved at this level.

Funding for SGBD was a function of annual requests accumulated from SGBD, which were reviewed and revised within that part of the organization. Geographic division vice presidents then reviewed the total request and contributed their share to the central SGBD budget. Amounts from the geographic heads were in rough proportion to overall sales volume of the geographic division, but were not automatically transferred to the SGBD organization within that geography. Instead, the "internal" SGBD budget allocations were made on the basis of global account sales and potential. This allowed smaller countries to participate in global account management without the local operating organizations having to contribute disproportionately to their resources. In effect, larger divisions subsidized SGBD activities in smaller countries.

By 2000 Schneider had a group of 60 international account managers, in addition to SGBD international account correspondents, in over

Exhibit 3   Schneider's Competitor Defense Strategy

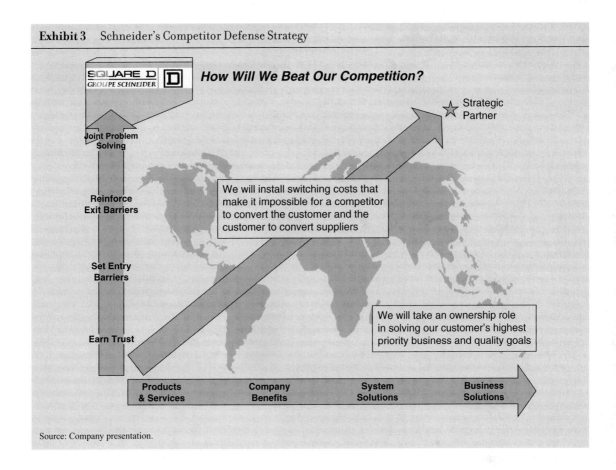

Source: Company presentation.

90 countries. (Refer to Exhibit 4 for the organization of the overall company and the SGBD structure in February 2001.) The accounts were organized in four main clusters including food and beverage, automotive, pharmaceuticals and microelectronics. The center for food and beverage expertise was in France, for automotive, Germany, and pharma and microelectronics in the US. A fifth cluster included those clients who did not belong to one of the above-mentioned industries. The individual industry experts for these clusters performed two functions: As experts, their knowledge could be called upon from any country in the world, but they also managed large accounts in their clusters.

Within each country with a GSA headquarters were IAMs. In countries where the GSA had oper-

ations, Schneider designated IACs. In Austria the IAC managed six accounts belonging to four clusters. The correspondent managed sales for all six clients, but was accountable to different senior executives responsible for the different clusters who resided in different countries.

The Calchem-Schneider Relationship

Calchem developed and manufactured specialty chemicals for the paper, paint and plastics industry. The company had operations in 130 countries. Its cost structure was both power intensive and power sensitive. In the mid-1990s the company had moved away from a price-based "black boxes" approach to purchasing in order to reduce plant downtime and decrease energy costs. This focused

Exhibit 4   Schneider Organizational Design

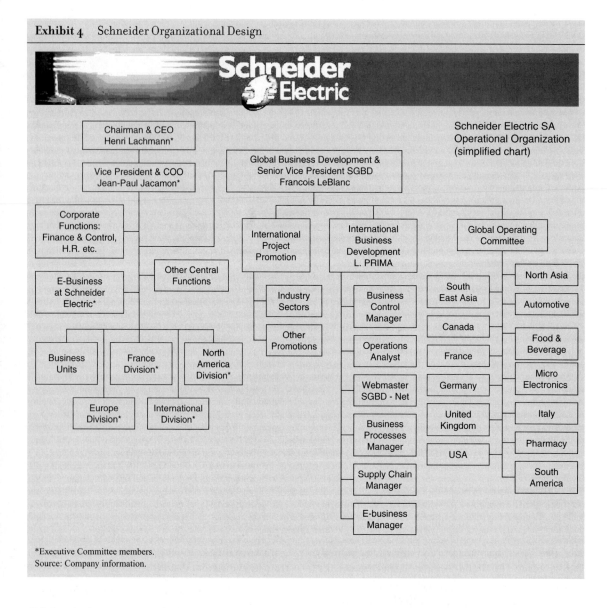

*Executive Committee members.
Source: Company information.

Calchem's interest on solutions providers rather than on equipment and software providers.

The two companies shared a long-standing relationship, especially in the automation field. Calchem met the requirements defined by Schneider for its strategic accounts—global presence and a potential for over $15 million in revenue. In addition, Calchem's purchasing policy was based on technology, relationship and service before price, which mirrored the SGBD philosophy.

Prior to becoming a GSA, Calchem had purchased SFr 3 to 4 million in Schneider products (exclusively from its automation product-line). The projects and purchases were neither coordinated internationally nor across business areas. A year later, with the development of common strategies and a high degree of information sharing (coordinated by the IAM), purchasing orders amounted to SFr 10 million, with a realistic possibility for another SFr 20 to 25 million in the near future.

Convincing Calchem of the added-value of becoming a GSA was not easy. Keller recalled some of his early meetings with Calchem:

> Companies may be interested in the GAM advantages in terms of pricing deals, but they are sometimes less ready to invest the time and initial costs required to launch a global process. Yet we are actually helping the customer understand his business better by giving him a global picture of it. For example, Calchem did not know the total value of its orders with us, nor were they fully aware of the breadth of our services, product lines and solutions. The interesting thing is that some customer subsidiaries understand this better than their own headquarters. In the case of Calchem, headquarters was initially reluctant to send participants to the joint meeting in Nice, while their US subsidiary, representing 30% of the business with Schneider, jumped at the opportunity to participate.

Calchem requested status as a global strategic account at the end of 1999. Schneider and the client met several times to define needs and prepare the first single-source order. A Schneider team made up of IAMs, IACs and technical experts from the Paris headquarters visited the client's engineering centers and participated in several engineering meetings. LeBlanc, as corporate sponsor, met with senior executives from Calchem to discuss the strategic aspects of the relationship. This pairing of very senior people ensured that common goals were achieved and that the relationship was reinforced at all levels of the client organization.

The Calchem-Schneider Electric Workshop

Normally, company-supplier workshops were held once or twice yearly with Schneider's strategic accounts. The meetings were arranged and sponsored by Schneider. All the IAMs and IACs involved with the account were invited to attend. (Refer to Exhibit 5 for some of the Do's and Don'ts suggested by Harry Smith to IAMs and IACs attending

---

Exhibit 5   Do's and Don'ts for IAMs and IACs

Do's and Don'ts

Do:
- Network—get to know as many Client people as you can, especially ones outside of the normal sales cycle, get their business card.
- Think of yourself as a Client Account Manager.
- Be very open and share information in the joint session.
- Think of your Client as a business ally not just a client to whom we sell product.
- Get Names.
- Copy Harry Smith on all correspondence.
- Follow-up, if you tell a Client contact that you will telephone or write or send a sample, make sure you do.
- Make sure that you spend time talking one on one with the various Client Managers, learn that they are easy to work with and welcome your advice.
- Have Fun.

Do's and Don'ts

Don't:
- Bring up orders you did not get from the Client.
- Schedule meetings with the Client—get their card and call them after the meeting.
- Make excuses about our not being able to fill an order or deliver a particular product. If something like that comes up and it probably will in the joint session, find out what the Client wants and then start to find ways to fill their order.
- Try to impress the Client with the business you are doing.
- Refer to your clients as customers, customers buy goods from an attendant, clients seek the advice of a professional.

Source: Company presentation.

---

the workshops.) On the customer side, country managers and heads of purchasing were also invited. As different issues emerged in the relationship, different customer executives participated in these meetings to plan ahead, solve problems and review past performance.

In the case of the upcoming Calchem meeting to be held in June 2000, the objectives for the workshop included reinforcing the relationship among Calchem's six engineering centers, the plants and Schneider on a global basis, analyzing and understanding Calchem's future needs, providing the best offering, developing new solutions and enhancing local service. (Refer to Exhibit 6 for a list of countries and roles presented at the meeting.) Above all, the objective was to close the perception gap that prevailed in some Calchem divisions that believed, "We have a strategic alliance with Schneider, but we are the ones who make all the decisions!" Keller hoped that the two executives from Calchem would provide new information about their strategy. Since the VP for group purchasing was new to Calchem, he hoped to learn about how compatible his approach to purchasing was with Schneider's SGA philosophy.

Within Schneider's own organization the meeting also served to increase the effectiveness of cross-national teamwork among the Calchem IACs

and the effectiveness of interactions with the client. In this regard, since Calchem's senior US executive was coming to the meeting, Keller had also invited a senior manager from Graybar, Schneider's main US distributor, and the country manager from Switzerland.

The meeting was expected to reinforce the message to Calchem that Schneider as a whole was strongly committed to global account management and to their needs in particular. To demonstrate this even more clearly, Smith, who worked closely with their US operations, and Primo, who oversaw all the SGBD service functions in Paris, were also making presentations at the Nice meeting. Their presence, together with attendance and participation by senior Calchem executives, would also reinforce internal commitment and understanding among the Schneider IACs in attendance. The workshop was designed to address existing issues and to highlight future challenges. For example, in this workshop, Keller knew that Smith would openly accept the blame for a design problem

Exhibit 6   Participants in the Schneider/Calchem/Lactal Workshop

Country	Schneider SGBD	IAC for Calchem	IAC for Lactal	Calchem	Lactal	Distributor
Canada		1	1			
Switzerland		1	3	2	2	
Czechoslovakia		1	1			
Spain		1	1			
Finland		1				
France	2	1	1			
Germany		1	1			
Italy		1	2			
Mexico		1				
The Netherlands			1			
Poland		1	1			
Turkey		1				
Republic of South Africa			1			
United Kingdom		1	2			
USA	4	4	3	1	1	1
Total	**6**	**16**	**18**	**3**	**3**	**1**

Source: Company information.

encountered by Calchem in the US in order to defuse the client's anger about what had been a sensitive issue in the relationship. He would also use the occasion to underscore, for both Calchem and the Schneider IACs, how the problem had been satisfactorily resolved. Keller anticipated that some of the IACs would likely disagree with his counterpart's mea culpa approach. That was one of the reasons he had built into the program a half-day training session on cross-cultural understanding, using a professor who had worked at other GSA-Schneider workshops.

Keller's Challenges

This expected negative reaction from one or two of the IACs from Latin cultures reflected one of the issues facing Keller as he attempted to sell the global approach to local sale forces. As Keller put it:

> The local service and sales engineers are essential to our local presence. With the GAM approach, they are afraid of losing power and independence, and tend to resist its implementation in their area. My job is to help them understand that I bring with me the resources of the whole company to support their needs.

He added:

> In many projects, one or two delivering countries will benefit from the business, while other countries will provide support without benefiting from the business generated. These countries may feel that they have had costs at no advantage. However, they receive sales credits for their involvement. The country of delivery (country who gets the order), country of influence (the one who provides the equipment), country of engineering and country of destination all receive sales credits.

Primo supported this view:

> Consistency of account coverage is always important with any account, but this is even more important for global strategic accounts (GSA). Global strategic accounts become very dependent upon the IAM and IAC once a strong relationship and a sense of trust are built up. This relationship-building and the gaining of the trust of the global strategic account may take several years in both the home country and in other countries. For this reason it is important to have the same

people calling on the GSA over a span of years. In the major large country organizations this is usually not much of an issue. However, in smaller country organizations with higher turnover of personnel, it is sometimes hard to keep the same IAC calling on the GSA for more then a year or two.

For example, during the same week as the Calchem workshop, Keller organized a two-day workshop with Lactal, the second Swiss-based multinational qualified as a GSA. This saved travel costs since most of the IAC and SGBD attendees would be participating in both meetings. Schneider Mexico did not plan to send any participants to the Lactal workshop despite Keller's attempt to convince the Mexicans of the value of their attendance. He had tried to demonstrate the value by insisting on the importance of the Lactal account in Mexico. Although both Switzerland (as the country of the client HQ) and the US (as the provider of the equipment) would be rewarded for participating in the process, Schneider's Mexican subsidiary would receive a sales credit of 20% for further growth of the business in the country.

The biggest tensions arose with countries that did not run highly profitable organizations and therefore could not support the costs of an IAM or an IAC. LeBlanc gave the example of a European subsidiary that hosted the headquarters of two global accounts, but could not or would not support an IAM.

> In this specific case, I sent the country manager an ultimatum: should he continue to resist investing in an IAM, the two accounts would be disqualified. Disqualification of an account could have serious repercussions. In most cases a country covers both a global account and that account's key suppliers. So losing an account often means losing more than one client.

He added:

> The high degree of commitment by Schneider senior management to GAM sends a clear message throughout the organization that management at all levels needs to support the concept. To assist the less profitable countries, a regional head may decide to support an IAM for a local subsidiary and carry him for a year. The four executive vice presidents for Schneider's

world regions sit on SGBD's executive committee. We meet three to four times a year and address unresolved resource allocation issues such as this one. This helps IAMs like Keller to do their jobs more effectively.

Networking within Schneider was an equally important challenge for Keller, who noted:

The main task of an international account manager is the development of a network that will enable him to bring the value of the whole company, 64,000 people, to the service of the customer. When I travel to France or the US I spend a lot of time in the engineering centers meeting engineers and software developers—the very people who are crucial in delivering a customized solution to the client. I get to know them and their capacities and they get to understand how I can connect them to customers. For example, while I was in Canada working to expand our opportunities with a Swiss-based company I am trying to add to our GSA list, I added several days to my trip to introduce myself to key Schneider manufacturing managers in the US Midwest.

Keeping up with the heavy information requirements of the GAM system was also an issue. Finding an effective process for updating and accessing information that was fast and simple required designing a new information system. In the words of Primo:

Information systems to support the international account managers are a critical element in our success with global strategic accounts. In a networked virtual organization such as ours, the sharing and communication of information between all parties involved in support of the account is key. Development of these systems is not easy. It is vital to identify the most important pieces of information needed. This avoids overloading the account managers and others with requests for too much information. It also keeps the databases from getting too large.

The initial system, based on Lotus Notes, was far too heavy and complicated and many account managers avoided using it as much as possible. As Keller described it:

The account plan "main menu" includes an executive summary with general customer information about headquarters, products, organization, strategy and a consolidation of the local country files, e.g., sales to the account, contacts, locations, etc. Each IAC can read all the information, but is only able to enter information into his own country file. An important part is the discussion forum, which allows sharing of information on projects, new solutions, presentations, etc. In the

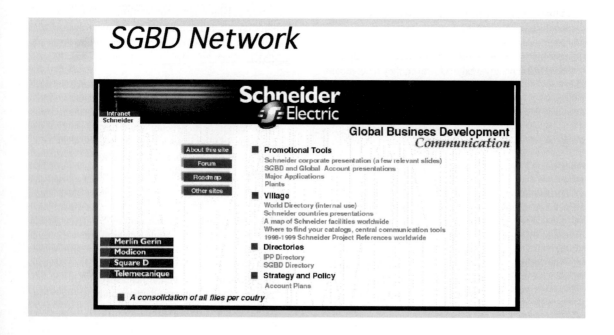

SGBD headquarters, it is possible to consolidate all GSA information and analyze geographic, cluster or business unit sales development. It is a very useful internal tool, but also has some disadvantages. First, since it is primarily for internal use, it doesn't give direct added-value to the customer. Second, since many IACs are responsible for four to eight accounts in one country, the requirement to update local actions is a heavy task. It requires the IAM to provide very strong motivation to the IAC to keep the data current.

Therefore Keller developed a number of simplified paper-based solutions using various worksheets. These tools provided information that also added direct value to the customer. They included an Excel contact list that showed each of the customer's engineering centers and their locations, together with their sub-suppliers and the corresponding Schneider contacts. A project list and several presentations for IACs and local sales engineers were also available in PowerPoint format. In the early project phases, these types of information helped convince engineers and sub-suppliers of Schneider's close relationship with and knowledge about Calchem.

In addition, the SGBD network provided corporate and country presentations, information about references and applications and various directories.

Receiving support from his local boss to develop the IAM activity in Switzerland represented a further challenge to Keller. The Swiss president focused on P&L; naturally, he concentrated mainly on the Swiss business, the full range of Schneider products and services, and was therefore less prone to absorb the costs of additional IAMs, the benefits of which would be deferred. Additionally none of Calchem's 160 plants was located in Switzerland, which meant no direct revenue was credited to the Swiss P&L.

While Keller was already carrying more than his share by supporting two GSAs (as opposed to the usual "one account one IAM" approach in Schneider), he had already identified further business opportunities in Switzerland. Local sales forces were in contact with a large construction company, headquartered in Switzerland, for which Keller had identified a potential $40 million contract at three sites in Canada and the US. Keller had met the local IACs but felt that his concentrating on this additional account diluted his efforts with his two existing GSAs. To reap the benefits of this additional GSA he would need support from an additional IAM based in Switzerland. This revealed the generic problem between measurement and rewards from the country heads as profit centers based on local P&L versus the investment needed initially to generate new revenues and profit from the global account.

As he looked ahead to the excitement of the workshop in Nice, Keller also knew that he should be thinking about these challenges during the meetings, too. Some ways of dealing with the issues might well emerge from the discussions with the various people he was looking forward to seeing.

Case 4-4   ABB's Relays Business: Building and Managing a Global Matrix

It was a casual conversation between the chairmen of Asea and Brown Boveri in 1987 about the dismal state of the utilities equipment market that eventually led to merger talks between these two giant

▍ This case was prepared by Professor Christopher A. Bartlett.
▍ Copyright © 1993 by the President and Fellows of Harvard College. Harvard Business School case 394-016.

power equipment companies. Within weeks of the announcement in August 1987, Percy Barnevik, the CEO of Asea who was asked to lead the combined operations, had articulated a strategic vision for Asea Brown Boveri (ABB). Convinced that the decade-long decline in new power generation capacity would soon reverse itself, he believed that the new technologies and scale economies required to meet the new demand could only be developed by companies operating on a global scale. At the same time, however, he felt that because of the high level of government ownership or control of power companies, the vast majority of new orders would continue to go to companies with a strong national presence. His strategy was to build a company that could exploit these two major industry trends.

Having articulated his broad vision, Barnevik formed a 10-person top management work group to analyze how the operations of Asea and Brown Boveri could best be linked to achieve it. Because ABB would start operating as a merged company on January 1, 1988, Barnevik wanted quick action. Within two months, the top management team had decided on a matrix structure that would balance the global business focus of an organization built on approximately 60 global business areas (BAs) with the national market focus provided by 1,300 local companies grouped under the umbrella of several country-based holding companies (see Exhibit 1).

Barnevik then set about selecting the management team that would staff the new organization. To select the 300 key managers who would lead the change process, Barnevik personally interviewed hundreds of Asea and Brown Boveri executives. He was seeking those with good technical and commercial backgrounds who were "tough skinned, fast on their feet, and able to lead" yet also "open, generous, and capable of thinking in group terms."

In January 1988, he assembled this handpicked group of 300 for a three-day meeting in Cannes. In presentations supported with 198 overhead transparencies (an approach that was to become a signature of his communications-intensive management style), Barnevik detailed industry trends, analyzed market opportunities, and profiled ABB's economics and cost structures. But mostly he focused on how the new organization would allow ABB to manage three contradictions—to be global and local, big and small, radically decentralized with central control. (Exhibit 2 presents excerpts from

---

Exhibit 1   ABB Matrix Concept

The ABB organization is built on a federation of 1,300 operating companies charged with managing the front-line operations. In each major country or region, these companies are administered through a national holding company, which is responsible for ensuring effective performance of ABB's total market presence. At the same time, each operating company reports to one of 58 Business Areas (BAs) responsible for developing global strategies.
    Conceptually, the matrix operates as follows:

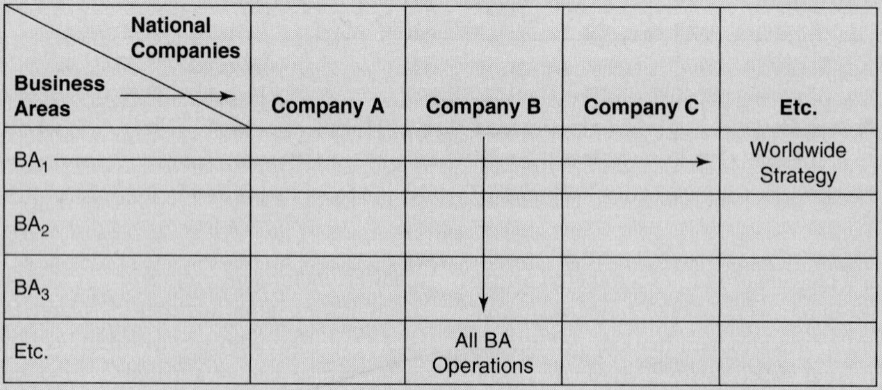

Business Areas \ National Companies	Company A	Company B	Company C	Etc.
BA$_1$				Worldwide Strategy
BA$_2$				
BA$_3$				
Etc.		All BA Operations		

Source: Company documents.

Exhibit 2   Cannes Top Management Meeting—Excerpts from Barnevik's Slides

BA Management Responsibilities
- Worldwide result and profitability
- Establishing a management team—preferably consisting of members from different countries
- Developing a worldwide strategy
- Basic development (typically CAD)
- Coordinating delegated development
- Market allocation scheme and/or tender coordination

Country Management Responsibilities
- Size and complexity of local structure in line with ABB's business presence
- In smaller countries: single company with departments
- In larger countries: holding structure with many subsidiaries and operating units
- Local entities serve their respective markets in line with BA objectives, strategies, and guidelines—they have responsibility for operational results

General Principles of Management Behavior
1. To take action (and stick out one's neck) and do the right things obviously the best behavior
2. To take action and do the wrong things is next best (within reason and a limited number of times)
3. Not to take action (and lost opportunities) is the only unacceptable behavior

Policies for Change
- Identify necessary changes implemented as fast as possible. Small risk that negative changes not considered enough
  - Concentrate on the ones with biggest profit improvements (80-20 rule)
  - 10 times more common to delay than the opposite
- Get over with "negative" changes in a lump sum and avoid prolonging the process and cut it up in pieces. Packages with "positive" and "negative" changes desirable. Important to quickly focus on new opportunities. Means earlier focus on positive changes
- No "fair" reduction in terms of equality between locations—improvements of group profitability counts as main criteria in a broad sense
- Most major changes must be started first year
  - "Honeymoon" of small changes would be detrimental
  - What is not started in the first year will be a lot more difficult later
- The merger creates unique possibilities ("excuses") to undertake long overdue actions which should have been undertaken anyway
- Upcoming merger problems must be resolved fast and on lowest possible level
- Example
  - First cutting capacity, merging and streamlining costs
  - Then with increased competitiveness—growth and new opportunities
- Volume increase is solution to cost problems

some of his overhead slides.) At the end of the meeting, each manager received a 21-page "policy bible" outlining the major policies and values to be communicated to the next level of the organization.

Barnevik's management model focused on the twin principles of decentralized responsibility and individual accountability. To emphasize the former, he ensured that most of ABB's key resources were controlled directly by the federation of 1,300 front-line companies, whenever possible set up as separate legal entities. To ensure that managers inherited their results from year to year, he gave them

Exhibit 3   ABB Key Performance Data: 1988–1991

	1988	1989	1990	1991
Revenues	17,832	20,560	26,688	28,883
Operating earnings after depreciation	854	1,257	1,790	609
Net income	386	589	590	609
Acquisition expenditures	544	3,090	677	612
Property, plant, and equipment expenditure	736	783	961	1,035
R&D expenditure	1,255	1,361	1,931	2,342
Operating earnings/revenues	4.8%	6.1%	6.7%	6.6%
Return on equity	12.5	16.8	4.5	13.9
Return on capital employed	13.6	17.0	19.7	17.1
Number of employees	169,459	189,493	215,154	214,399

control over their balance sheets, including the right to borrow and the ability to retain up to 30% of earnings. Furthermore, he implemented his "30/30/30 rule" in which he decreed that all headquarters organizations—from corporate to business area to regional—should be dramatically downsized by relocating 30% of the headquarters personnel to the front-line companies, by having another 30% provide their value added as outsourced services, and by laying off an additional 30%. To set the example, the staffing level at ABB's combined corporate headquarters was reduced from over 2,000 to only 150.

To ensure accountability, Barnevik assigned a team to develop a new transparent reporting system which aimed at "democratizing information." Dubbed ABACUS, the system was designed to collect uniform dollar-dominated performance data at the level of ABB's 4,500 profit centers. By allowing comparisons against budget and forecast to be aggregated and disaggregated, ABACUS facilitated analysis within and across businesses, countries, and companies or profit centers.

Given control over key resources and provided with current relevant information, managers on the front-lines were expected to act. Barnevik's "7-3 formula" reinforced the notion that it was better to decide quickly and be right seven times out of ten than to delay or to search for the perfect solution. "Better roughly and quickly than carefully and

slowly," he said. "The only thing we cannot accept is people who do nothing."

He took these and other aspects of his strongly held beliefs and values out to the field, traveling some 200 days a year, always with his large bag of overhead transparencies. Through continued acquisition and rejuvenated internal growth, within four years ABB grew to become a $29 billion company with over 200,000 employees worldwide—the giant of its industry, dominating previous first-tier players like Siemens, Hitachi, and General Electric (see Exhibit 3). To understand how this rapid growth and geographic expansion was managed, this case focuses on the birth and development of one of ABB's almost 60 business areas (BAs) (Exhibit 4).

Building the Relays Organization

In August 1987, Göran Lindahl, Asea's executive vice president responsible for power transmission, found himself on Barnevik's 10-person top management transition team. After presenting a proposal for merging the two power transmission businesses, Lindahl was tapped to head this important segment for ABB as of January 1, 1988.

Creating the Management Team   In the relays business, as in each of the other eight BAs reporting to him, Lindahl's first task was to identify the managers who would drive the integration and capture the synergies that were fundamental to

Exhibit 4 ABB Organization Structure (1991)

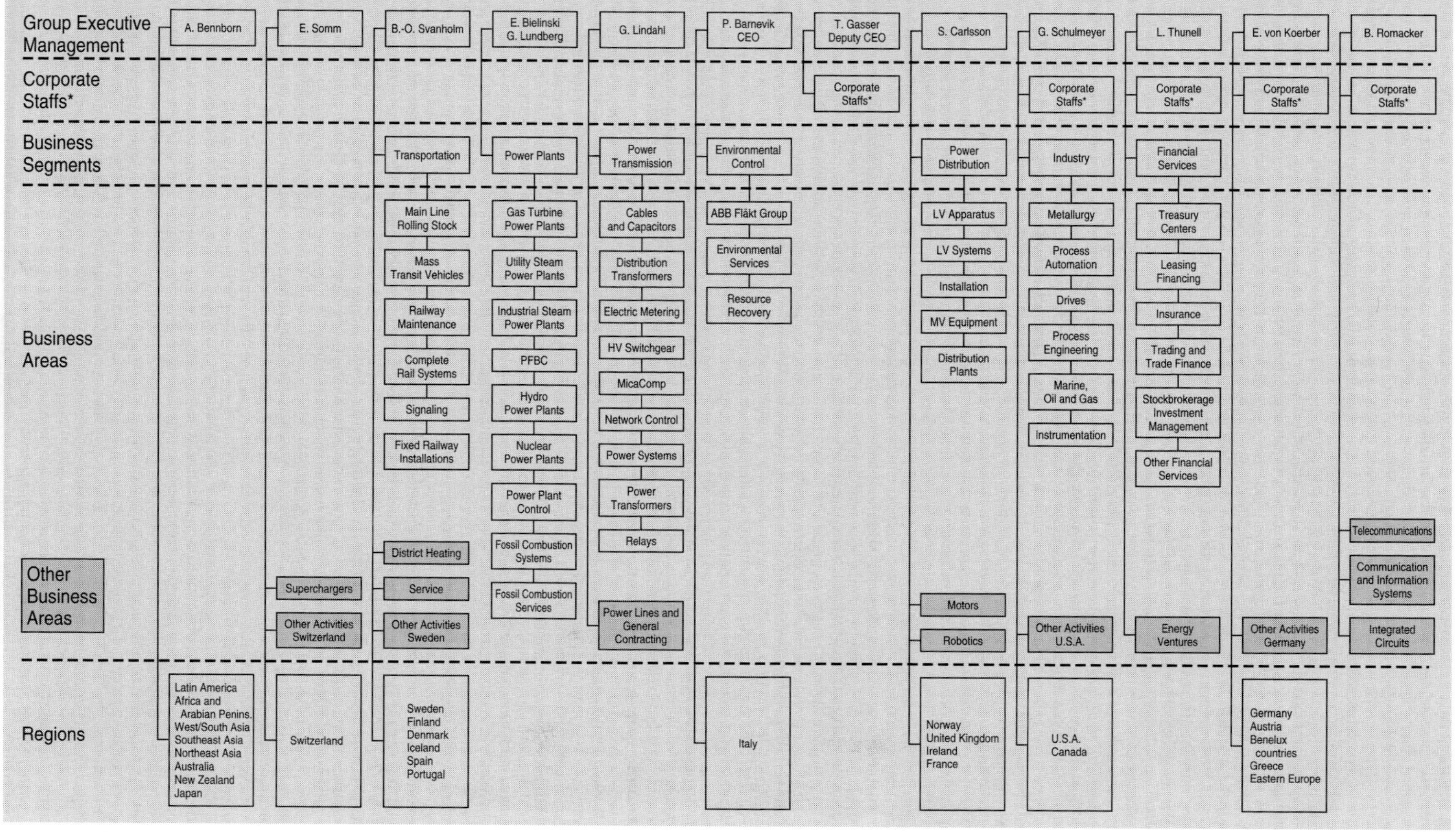

Group Executive Management: A. Bernborn · E. Somm · B.-O. Svanholm · E. Bielinski / G. Lundberg · G. Lindahl · P. Barnevik CEO · T. Gasser Deputy CEO · S. Carlsson · G. Schulmeyer · L. Thunell · E. von Koerber · B. Romacker

Corporate Staffs*: Corporate Staffs* (under P. Barnevik / T. Gasser, S. Carlsson, G. Schulmeyer, L. Thunell, E. von Koerber, B. Romacker)

Business Segments:
- Transportation (B.-O. Svanholm)
- Power Plants (E. Bielinski / G. Lundberg)
- Power Transmission (G. Lindahl)
- Environmental Control (P. Barnevik)
- Power Distribution (S. Carlsson)
- Industry (G. Schulmeyer)
- Financial Services (L. Thunell)

Business Areas:

Transportation:
- Main Line Rolling Stock
- Mass Transit Vehicles
- Railway Maintenance
- Complete Rail Systems
- Signaling
- Fixed Railway Installations

Power Plants:
- Gas Turbine Power Plants
- Utility Steam Power Plants
- Industrial Steam Power Plants
- PFBC
- Hydro Power Plants
- Nuclear Power Plants
- Power Plant Control
- Fossil Combustion Systems
- Fossil Combustion Services

Power Transmission:
- Cables and Capacitors
- Distribution Transformers
- Electric Metering
- HV Switchgear
- MicaComp
- Network Control
- Power Systems
- Power Transformers
- Relays
- Power Lines and General Contracting

Environmental Control:
- ABB Fläkt Group
- Environmental Services
- Resource Recovery

Power Distribution:
- LV Apparatus
- LV Systems
- Installation
- MV Equipment
- Distribution Plants

Industry:
- Metallurgy
- Process Automation
- Drives
- Process Engineering
- Marine, Oil and Gas
- Instrumentation

Financial Services:
- Treasury Centers
- Leasing Financing
- Insurance
- Trading and Trade Finance
- Stockbrokerage Investment Management
- Other Financial Services

Other Business Areas:
- Superchargers
- Other Activities Switzerland
- District Heating
- Service
- Other Activities Sweden
- Motors
- Robotics
- Other Activities U.S.A.
- Other Activities Germany
- Energy Ventures
- Telecommunications
- Communication and Information Systems
- Integrated Circuits

Regions:
- Latin America and Africa and Arabian Penins. West/South Asia Southeast Asia Northeast Asia Australia New Zealand Japan
- Switzerland
- Sweden Finland Denmark Iceland Spain Portugal
- Italy
- Norway United Kingdom Ireland France
- U.S.A. Canada
- Germany Austria Benelux countries Greece Eastern Europe

ABB's strategy. He described the process:

> For me, the key qualifications were proven performance in their business, and broad experience in more than one discipline. But, as important as their career background was their personality—their flexibility, integrity, and statesmanship.

He named Anders Fraggstedt, general manager of Asea's relays business based in Västerås, Sweden, to assume the additional role of BA head for ABB's relays business worldwide. To support Fraggstedt in his new role (and also to help minimize the number of decisions escalated to the corporate level for resolution), Lindahl created a BA board with Fraggstedt as chairman and the relays business managers from Baden, Switzerland, and Vasa, Finland, as the two other members. (The Vasa business had come as part of the acquisition of Stromberg, the Finnish electrical giant.)

At the same time, Lindahl felt that he needed to keep a close personal involvement in the process. But this did not imply that he had an army of staff to monitor operations and control performance against targets. Like others at the group executive level, Lindahl maintained a small staff to help manage his $5 billion global business. Besides himself, it numbered four persons—two controllers, a business development manager, and a secretary.

He saw his key role as providing an environment in which those below him could be most effective. As a first step, he believed he had to create the uncertainty necessary to encourage "unlearning" of old assumptions and behaviors. Through what he referred to as "the framework," Lindahl set challenging goals and objectives for his newly appointed managers—tightly defined at first, but gradually expanding and loosening:

> People are as good as you make them. We have about 8,000 engineers in our 35,000-person segment. They are bright, capable people who make excellent managers. My first task is to provide the frameworks to help them develop as managers; the next challenge is to loosen and expand the framework to let them become leaders.

In his definition, leaders were the individuals who had displayed the requisite personal characteristics (which he identified as flexibility, statesmanship and generosity), and who were ready to take responsibility for setting their own objectives and standards. "When I have developed all the managers into leaders," he said, "we will have a self-driven, self-renewing organization."

Communicating the New Philosophy and Values
As he met with his new team, one of the most important items on Lindahl's agenda was to communicate the company's guiding principle of decentralization. He explained:

> The newspapers may describe ABB's power transmission power segment as a $5 billion operation with 35,000 employees, but I think of it as almost two hundred operating companies further divided into 700 profit centers each with about 50 employees and $7 million in revenues. Although the BAs play a vital role in setting strategy, only the local companies can implement the plans and achieve the objectives.

The message was well received by most front-line managers. Don Jans, who had come with Westinghouse's power transmission and distribution business when ABB acquired it in early 1989, reflected the attitude among his colleagues at the time:

> The prevailing view when ABB acquired our business was that we'd lost the war. We were resigned to the fact that the occupying troops would move in and we'd move out. But to our surprise, they not only asked us to stay on, they gave us the opportunity to run the whole relays business—even the Allentown operation that was ABB's own facility in the United States.

To do so, however, required Jans and his colleagues to make major changes in their business assumptions, organizational practices, and management styles. In Westinghouse, Jans had five layers of management between himself and the CEO; in ABB there were only two. In Westinghouse, he had been constantly frustrated by the bureaucracy imposed by a 3,000-person headquarters; in ABB he had to adjust to the need for self-sufficiency in an organization with only 150 people at corporate. In Westinghouse, decisions had been top-down and shaped by political negotiations; in ABB Jans found many more were delegated and were driven by data and results. He described the first few meetings when he and his colleagues were exposed to the ABB philosophy and values as "an exhilarating experience":

> It was amazing. We were constantly seeing the top guys in meetings and seminars—Barnevik, Lindahl, Schulmeyer (the North American regional VP). They came with stacks of transparencies and could talk for hours about how the industry was developing, where ABB wanted to be, how it was going to get there, and so on. It was spellbinding; a real education.
>
> Just as important was their willingness to listen to our proposals and invest in the relays business. In Westinghouse, capital allocations had always been tightly managed, but after the mid-1970s, it seemed as if they were even less willing to invest in old core businesses like relays. Not so after 1989. ABB is really committed to this business, and if we can justify an investment, we can usually get the resources.

One of Lindahl's main objectives in his nonstop communications was to instill a clear and strong value system to guide management action. "In the end," he said, "managers are loyal not to a particular boss or even to a company, but to a set of values they believe in and find satisfying." He identified the core values as being an emphasis on quality, not only in products but also in organizational processes and relationships; a commitment to excellence in technology to ensure the business remained at the forefront of the industry; a dedication to productivity

and performance not just in the plants but at all levels of the organization; and a belief in people—both customers and employees—as the means to achieving the first three.

Lindahl also used his company visits to emphasize the importance of individual accountability. The company's broad philosophies were translated into specific task requirements for managers at all levels, and Lindahl devoted a substantial amount of time to communicating the appropriate roles, responsibilities, and relationships summarized in a chart that he had discussed with every profit center manager in his segment (see Exhibit 5). While BA management was responsible for setting worldwide strategy and overall operating objectives, local company managers controlled operations and were responsible for profits. The integration of the different interests took place through a rigorous planning and budgeting process; the assurance of appropriate implementation through a sophisticated set of formal and informal controls. Because he believed firmly in the need to control performance against "the framework," one of Lindahl's earliest and most important appointments was "a controller who was sensitive to operations rather than just a number cruncher."

Defining the Agenda   In the early days, Lindahl's "framework" was fairly tight. He wanted his businesses to focus on restructuring themselves

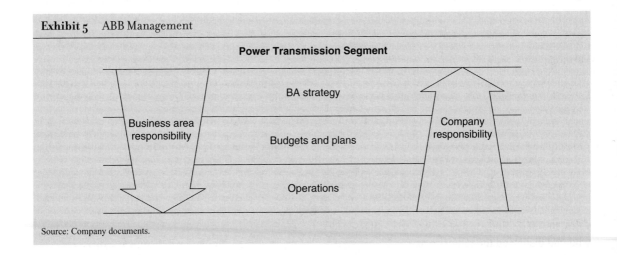

Exhibit 5   ABB Management

Power Transmission Segment

Business area responsibility

BA strategy

Budgets and plans

Operations

Company responsibility

Source: Company documents.

rapidly:

> If you want to bring about change, you need to force it, and that means giving the organization a clear vision of your expectations and pushing for results. Eventually, the change process becomes natural and develops its own momentum. I told each BA board that our objective was to conquer the globe in power transmission. At the same time, I kept reminding them of the need to focus on the customers, watch competitors, and deliver current results. To do that, they would have to deal with the overcapacity we clearly had, and capitalize on the best technology in the combined operations. Which plants were the most efficient? Which technology should become standard? It was a huge undertaking to do all the analysis and negotiate sensitive agreements.

In the early stages of the restructuring process, Lindahl reported getting lots of issues coming up for his review and resolution, but typically he pushed them back down for further discussion. Many such issues involved the painful process of closing plants, reallocating historical market relationships, or cutting traditional product lines. He saw his major job as trying to convert the "winner/loser" mentality into a recognition that the new organization could become "winner/winner."

After a full year of difficult analysis, discussion and negotiation, Anders Fraggstedt and his relays BA board decided on the BA's basic restructuring concept. Vasa, Finland, would assume the leadership role in developing and manufacturing relays for distribution protection of the lower-voltage products that had been Stromberg's specialty and for which it was clearly the technological leader. In high-voltage protection, where both Asea and BBC had strong capabilities, the major overlap in development, manufacturing, and marketing was resolved by giving Västerås, Sweden, primary responsibility for high-voltage products, and Baden, Switzerland, the lead role for project and systems deliveries that engineered multiple products into integrated forms or turnkey installations. Furthermore, to eliminate marketing overlap, Sweden would assume overall responsibility for sales into Europe, North America, and Australia, where bids were mostly for individual relays products, while Switzerland would focus its marketing efforts on Latin America, Africa, and Asia, where project business was more important.

A senior manager of the Swiss relays company reflected on the outcome for his unit:

> Sure, there was concern in Baden. People talked about the Swedes dominating the management, they were concerned that most of our production was being transferred out, and they complained that we lost well-established markets like Germany and France while retaining only the "poor man's countries" in the developing world. But the company was committed to keeping the existing know-how, and Mr. Fraggstedt reassured us that our relays R&D group would be retained. After a long talk with Mr. Lindahl, I was convinced, and I took on the job of persuading the organization to look at the changes more positively.

Restructuring the Business   In December 1988, Göran Lindahl approached Ulf Gundemark, the manager of ABB's Swedish low-voltage switch gear operations, and offered him the opportunity to replace Anders Fraggstedt as the business area head for ABB's $250 million worldwide relays business. It was an attractive opportunity for a 37-year-old engineer who had spent 10 years of his 12-year career with Asea in its relays business.

Like other BA heads, Gundemark would continue to be responsible for his national company's operations, but would also wear a second hat as a worldwide BA manager. To assist him in this new role, he would have a staff of two—a controller and a coordination/business development manager. His first challenge was to integrate the disparate relays operations of Asea, Brown Boveri, Stromberg, and now Westinghouse.[1] It would be a difficult task to integrate companies that not only had vastly different management cultures, but also had been bitter competitors.

Gundemark saw his first priority being to communicate the broad rationalization principles that

---

[1] In January 1989, ABB acquired a 45% share of Westinghouse's transmission and distribution business with an option to buy the remaining 55%. The joint venture was fully integrated into the ABB. In relays, for example, Don Jans, the ex-Westinghouse relays head, joined the relays BA board now chaired by Gundemark.

Exhibit 6   Relays BA Organization

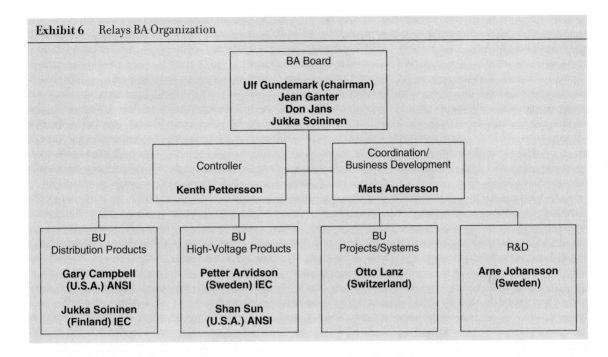

had been hammered out in a year-long negotiation process and to implement the major changes. Recognizing that ABB planned to take a one-time restructuring charge against its 1989 results, he initiated the Revaba Project (Restructure Västerås and Baden) to implement the most difficult part of the rationalization plans as quickly as possible. Overall coordination of the project was assigned to a team headed by the R&D manager at Baden and the production manager at Västerås. After allowing the team to set its own goals within the framework defined by the board, Gundemark held all members accountable for achieving their results, reviewing progress every two weeks.

Due to the complexity of Revaba and the acquisition of the Westinghouse operations, the restructuring project took longer than expected. By the end of 1990, however, the new structure of ABB's worldwide relays business was emerging. Production was specialized in four global production centers, development activities in each company were coordinated by a worldwide R&D head, and local manufacturing and engineering activities were defined and legit-

imized in the 12 non-core relays companies around the world (see Exhibits 6 and 7).

The process linking the worldwide structure was developed and defined by scores of day-to-day decisions that continually confronted Gundemark and his BA board. Soon after the production rationalization had been implemented, for example, Gundemark found himself confronting questions about the recently negotiated allocations of export markets. The issue was raised around the Swiss company's responsibility for coordinating sales into Mexico, which earned it a markup on products sourced from other ABB relays operations. Several senior managers felt the company had to shorten the company's lines to its customers and minimize the non-value-added work in the system. Gundemark delegated the issue to a team composed of the marketing managers from the four key supply companies and asked them to develop a proposal. After considerable negotiations, the team reported to the BA board that they could not find a solution. Gundemark pushed the task back to them for further discussion and analysis. Some days later, the team

Exhibit 7   Relays BA Worldwide Operations

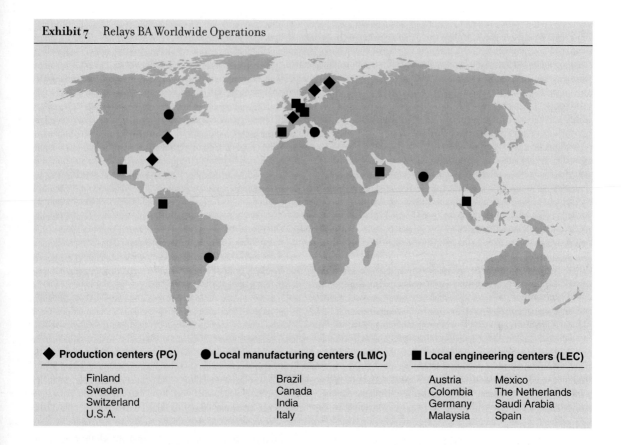

◆ Production centers (PC)	● Local manufacturing centers (LMC)	■ Local engineering centers (LEC)	
Finland	Brazil	Austria	Mexico
Sweden	Canada	Colombia	The Netherlands
Switzerland	India	Germany	Saudi Arabia
U.S.A.	Italy	Malaysia	Spain

indicated they had reached a majority recommendation supported by three of the four members. Again Gundemark rejected the proposal, demanding a unanimous recommendation. Finally, after three full and exhausting days of negotiation, the marketing managers decided that local companies with strong engineering capabilities should be able to order directly on any production center. Another piece of policy and structure was in place.[2]

New Organizational Structures and Processes
While he was overseeing the restructuring, Gundemark knew there would be significant coordination of operations built on a foundation of spe-

cialized yet interdependent operations. In 1989, the only effective integrating mechanism was the BA board Lindahl had established, and Gundemark was concerned that it had become a monthly forum swamped with current operating issues. He wanted to create an organization that would not only relieve this pressure, but also be truer to ABB's decentralization philosophy.

Building on an Asea practice in place for many years, Gundemark established a steering committee for each of the national relays companies. These were, in effect, small local boards with membership drawn from the local relays company, other closely related ABB units, the national holding company, and the corporate relays BA management. Two to four times a year, each steering committee met to discuss its local relays company's operating performance and long-term strategy. At the operating level,

---

[2]This process reflected a widespread company philosophy of resolving problems at the lowest levels. As Barnevik often told his managers, "You can escalate a problem to me once, you can escalate it to me twice, but if you escalate it three times, I will probably know it's time to replace you."

Exhibit 8   Partial Matrix Relationships in Relays BA

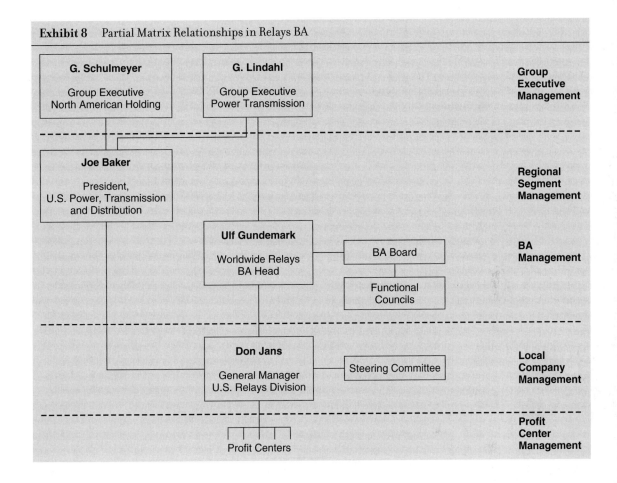

such meetings became vital forums for senior-level business and regional managers to review the operations of the local units, and to ensure that the objectives and priorities they were given to those front-line operations were consistent. To the company general managers, they offered an important opportunity to communicate key issues and problems, elicit input and support, and reconcile conflicts.

Although he was relatively new to ABB, U.S. relays general manager Don Jans was quickly becoming accustomed to ABB's collaborative team management style.[3] He found the steering committee to

be a "powerful concept." In addition to himself, his relays steering committee, which met quarterly, consisted of Ulf Gundemark as the BA representative, the strategic planning manager, marketing manager, and controller from the U.S. power transmission and distribution (T&D) regional headquarters, and the general manager of the closely related network control company. It was chaired by Joe Baker, the regional ABB Power T&D head, who reported both to Göran Lindahl, his business boss, and to Gerhard Schulmeyer, the president of the U.S. holding company, ABB Inc. (See Exhibit 8 for a representation of the matrix relationships.)

Relays steering committee chairman Baker, a 39-year veteran of Westinghouse, had entered ABB via the acquisition as a self-admitted skeptic of the

---

▌ [3]As well as serving on Gundemark's relays BA Board, he was also a member of the steering committee for his own relays company, ABB's network control company in the United Sates, and for the relays subsidiaries in Canada and Puerto Rico.

matrix organization. In 1979, Westinghouse had imposed a matrix structure on its international division and the results had been "a complete failure," according to Baker. Eventually, however, he began to acknowledge that the ABB system seemed to be working, and he reflected on the differences:

> In Westinghouse, we recruited first-class people, did an outstanding job of management development, then wasted all that investment by constraining them with a highly authoritarian structure. In ABB, we spent much of our first year thrashing out how we would work together. . . . In the end, it was this culture of delegated responsibility and intensive communication that made this organization work. . . . It was an amazing change; I felt like I'd rediscovered management after 39 years.[4]

In addition to providing local companies with more guidance, Gundemark also wanted to exploit synergies, particularly across the four core companies. To achieve this, he formed functional councils for R&D, total quality, and purchasing and charged each with the task of developing policy guidelines that captured "best practice." Each council was composed of specialists from several operating units, including the four major centers. They met quarterly, usually at a different site not only to expose managers to the various local practices, but also to send a clear signal to the organization. Chairpersons of the councils also rotated on an annual basis, allowing different national units to share the leadership.

All three councils were extremely successful in creating contacts among specialists in diverse geographic locations and providing them with a forum at which to share knowledge. For example, Bill Wallace, manager of total quality in the U.S. relays business, reported enthusiastically on the value created by the council on which he served:

It's had an enormous impact. There is a lot of cross-fertilization going on. For example, we had been working on time-based management for several years and had delivered impressive reductions in cycle time and inventory levels. In 1990, a team from Finland visited Coral Springs to see what we were doing. Nine months later on a plant tour during a council meeting in Vasa, I was amazed to see how they adapted and successfully implemented our JIT and Kan Ban system.

Larry Vanduzer, Coral Springs purchasing manager, was equally proud of progress on the council on which he served:

> Because material costs can represent 35%–40% of sales value, there is huge potential for economies. Even in our first year when we were focusing mainly on developing the appropriate metrics to evaluate purchasing, we still squeezed out $1 million in cost savings. Now we work mainly on setting goals, certifying and consolidating suppliers, and sharing our learning. Each year we report back to the BA board on progress, and I'd have to say the measurement has created some healthy internal competition. Vasa reduced its lead time to an average 10-day delivery, and we want to challenge them!

New Strategic Process   Having delegated most operating responsibilities to the steering committees, Gundemark wanted to change the role of the BA board to a quarterly forum for discussing strategy, policies, and overall objective-setting. In introducing this longer-term focus, he was determined not to make strategic planning the hollow exercise he had both seen and experienced:

> I wanted to sweep aside a lot of the old assumptions about strategy we inherited from the 1970s and 1980s—that it was defined primarily by top management, that it was communicated through confidential copies kept in locked files, and that it was updated annually, but usually without challenging the underlying assumptions or objectives. I wanted it to become a process that involved all levels of management, was widely communicated, and constantly open to challenge.

In March 1990, he formed a nine-person task force with members drawn from the high-potential middle managers of companies in Brazil, Germany,

---

[4]After seeing how quickly ABB turned around a business they had struggled for years, senior management at Westinghouse invited Baker to explain how they did it. After he described the change in organization culture and management philosophy that had revitalized the business, a Westinghouse EVP said, "We can't manage with so little direction and so much conflict." Replied Baker, "That's the problem."

Exhibit 9   Relays BA Strategy 2000: Excerpts and Overview

Vision

Our vision is to contribute to a better living standard for the world by producing technically advanced products which are essential to ensure the safe and reliable supply of electric power.

Key Concepts (Excerpts)

- We must communicate our organization, vision, strategy, and results to all employees and tie their activities to the BA goals.
- Employees must feel they have jobs with personal development opportunities and team spirit.
- We will expand . . . through aggressive marketing, refined segmentation . . . and innovative sales concepts.
- Management will communicate a commitment to total quality . . . and we will improve total performance through systematic measurement and analysis of key elements of total quality.
- We will make customer focus plans and follow performance to bring the customer focus culture to all employees.
- We will create a team spirit and make teamwork the method for working together.
- We will push responsibility and authority to the operational level.
- We will have volume growth of 6% per annum and a return on capital employed of 40%.
- We will reduce product development cycle times to one year by 1994.
- Will develop COMSYS as a evolutionary process for creating modular, locally acceptable products using common tools, methods, and design.

Source: Company documents.

Finland, the United States, Sweden, and Switzerland, and charged them with the task of creating a clear vision for the relays BA. He set the tone by raising sensitive but important questions that he knew the team would have to confront if they were to develop a worthwhile proposal: How well are each of the companies implementing their new organizational responsibilities? Are we becoming too short-term focused? Is there too much of a Swedish bias in our management? He urged them to be bold, direct, and creative in taking a completely fresh look at the business, and to report back to the BA board in six months.

In September, propelled by a request from Göran Lindahl for a clear global relays strategy by year's end, the BA board heard the group's presentation, which proposed a broad vision focused on seven core elements of the relays business future development (total quality, customer focus, technology, human assets, organization, image, and growth). With further input and refinement by the BA management team, the task force's broad conclusions were developed into a 24-page document titled "Strategy 2000." Once approved, Strategy 2000 was formally unveiled at a worldwide relays management meeting and, within weeks, communicated to the entire organization via specially prepared materials and presentations (see Exhibit 9 for an overview).

Lindahl saw his role in the strategic process as much more than the approver of formal business plans such as the one developed by Gundemark's team. He saw strategy as an ongoing part of management and used his bi-monthly transmission segment management meetings to shape the strategic thinking of his key executives. Here he not only reviewed current performance, but also challenged his nine BA heads (like Gundemark) and 10 major regional managers (like Baker) to stretch their thinking. He would present them with issues such as environmental legislation, trade barriers, or north-south political conflicts and ask them to develop scenarios for how such issues might affect their businesses and how they might deal with the changes. "I try to make such exercises fun," he said, "but you always have to be thinking a little bit ahead."

New Systems and Controls   Throughout this period of orienting and restructuring, Gundemark and other BA managers in the power transmission segment were constantly being reminded by Lindahl not to let the internal changes distract the organization from the marketplace. The historic performance of ABB's various relays units was mixed, with the portfolio of profits and losses about equalizing each other at the time of the merger. After 1989, his big challenge would be to get consistent profitability across all operations, while building an organization that could leverage the restructured business.

With ABACUS in place, budgeting had become a serious and demanding process. In May, Lindahl and his staff prepared a tentative broad gauge budget by BA and by region for the following year. The BA and regional managers in turn allocated their proposed breakdowns to the local company level. By August, a bottom-up response was returned to the corporate office, where it was consolidated and tested. Lindahl would identify gaps or concerns and contact the local manager and the BA head to challenge and negotiate, typically asking what additional support they needed to reach the proposed target. It was a communications-intensive process.

Throughout the year, Lindahl tracked the monthly results, and with the help of his controller, tried to identify trends or uncover problems. He had no problem in reaching across levels in the formal organization to check up on emerging problems. Typically, he asked managers "What went wrong? What are you doing about it? What can we do to help?" This ongoing awareness of current business developments and involvement in key decisions throughout the organization was what Lindahl described as "fingers in the pie" management:

> Many companies, particularly in the United States, have evolved towards a kind of abstract management approach with senior executives controlling operations through sophisticated systems. I try to deal directly with the critical issues and the people managing them, and that means I need to put my hands on major changes. Even if I'm wrong, I need to initiate the change, to shake things up, to create an environment of learning. Once that process is initiated, it gains its own momentum.

At the BA level, Gundemark also exploited the new system by supplementing the broad budgeting process with more tailored reporting formats which he selected from the 30 measures tracked by ABACUS. For example, he created a Relays Performance League, which rank-ordered the companies on the basis of their quarterly gross margin, expenses, inventory, and net income percentages. In an effort to motivate managers to seek out best practice, the comparative data was circulated to all relays profit centers, and an award was given for the best overall performance of the year (see Exhibit 10). Those on the bottom of the league table desperately sought out ways to improve their standing, seeking input and support from their higher-ranked colleagues.

But Gundemark emphasized that Göran Lindahl was constantly asking him questions and proposing targets that were not measured by the formal systems. He commented:

> ABACUS is fine, but it can only provide historical financial information. To manage the business properly—and to respond to questions from Göran—I need to be able to anticipate problems and understand alternative courses of corrective action. And that requires a strong personal management network. We work intensely at that!

Management Challenges

At the end of 1991, Göran Lindahl seemed satisfied with the record that the relays BA had racked up in its first four years. The restructuring of assets and resources had largely been accomplished, and with help of the new operating systems and controls, current performance had been greatly improved. From 1988, when half the relays companies were losing money, within four years all 16 major companies worldwide were contributing to the significantly improved profits. Return on capital employed had almost doubled.

Exhibit 10   Relays BA Performance League: Letter to Local BA Managers

February 22, 1991

Dear Friends:

BA Performance League: Actual, 1990

First of all, congratulations on a very successful year. As you know, we exceeded the budget for orders received, revenues, and earnings after financial items (EAFI). This year we reached an important milestone—having all Relays operations contributing with positive earnings.

Congratulations to Attila Magyar and his team in Austria. They have won the 1990 Performance League, outperforming the budget on three of the four measures. . . . The prize, a Minolta camera, will be presented at the next Steering Committee meeting.

- Digging into the year's results, we recognize:
- 67% of the units achieved over-budget gross margins. Good!
- 80% of the units beat their budgets in EAFI. Excellent!
- Only 40% of the units, however, have been able to keep S&A costs below budget.
- And only two countries reached their budgeted inventory and receivable goals.

We are concerned about these developments on the cost and capital side. . . . We suggest that these items be brought up at your next Steering Committee meetings, and that targets and action plans be agreed on so we can together break these negative trends.

Finally, thank you once again for a very positive year. We look forward to a 1991 as successful as 1990.

Yours sincerely,
Ulf Gundemark

Position	Gross Margin (%) (Rank)		S&A/ Revenues (%) (Rank)		Inv. & Rec./ Revenues (%) (Rank)		EAFI/ Revenues (%) (Rank)		Total Points (Ranking)	
1. Austria	35,3	(02)	15,2	(05)	38,5	(06)	20,0	(02)	15	(1)
2. Finland	32,0	(04)	18,9	(06)	41,8	(08)	17,3	(03)	21	(2)
3. Canada	30,9	(05)	19,4	(08)	28,6	(02)	14,4	(07)	22	(3)
4. Allentown	43,3	(01)	29,4	(15)	38,0	(05)	20,1	(01)	22	(4)
5. Spain	29,5	(06)	13,7	(04)	48,6	(09)	17,2	(04)	23	(5)
6. Coral Springs	35,1	(03)	23,3	(14)	31,7	(04)	15,2	(06)	27	(6)
7. Mexico	21,5	(14)	13,0	(03)	12,1	(01)	12,2	(11)	29	(7)
8. Brazil	28,4	(08)	19,4	(08)	56,3	(10)	15,8	(05)	31	(8)
9. Germany	25,1	(11)	19,3	(07)	28,6	(02)	6,9	(13)	33	(9)
10. Saudi Arabia	23,7	(13)	11,2	(02)	87,9	(14)	14,1	(08)	37	(10)
11. Sweden	25,4	(10)	19,9	(11)	41,1	(07)	13,3	(10)	28	(11)
12. Italy	28,7	(07)	20,0	(12)	78,9	(13)	13,6	(09)	41	(12)
13. India	12,1	(15)	8,0	(01)	124,9	(15)	6,9	(13)	44	(13)
14. Netherlands	26,6	(09)	21,1	(13)	68,2	(12)	8,1	(12)	46	(14)
15. Switzerland	25,0	(12)	19,7	(10)	62,2	(11)	5,7	(15)	48	(15)

Note: All figures from ABACUS.

As in most other businesses, ABB's relays management was still trying to fine-tune both its strategy and its organization. In Coral Springs, for example, Don Jans was proud of his unit's achievement since becoming part of ABB: revenues were up 45%, on-time shipments had jumped from 70% to 99%, cycle time had been cut by 70% and inventories had been slashed by 40%. But he was still adjusting to life in a matrix and the conflicts that it created. In particular, he was wrestling with Comsys, a BA-sponsored project to create a common product platform.

Adjusting the New Organization   Although Jans was enthusiastic about the opportunities created by ABB's unique organization structure and management philosophy, he was also becoming increasingly aware of the difficulties of making it work effectively. While acknowledging that ABB's matrix organization brought his relays business much more attention and support than it had received in the old Westinghouse hierarchy, he was becoming aware that the process of obtaining such commitments could often be difficult and frustrating:

> This kind of structure becomes frustrating when your two bosses' priorities don't coincide. For example, we recently got strong support from Gundemark to invest in people to push forward our long-term technical development priorities, but Joe Baker says he needs current operating profit and has crunched down on our proposed development funds. I'm not sure where we will end up, but right now it's confusing and frustrating.

Joe Baker agreed that the situation was frustrating, but felt that such negotiations were inevitable:

> At Ulf Gundemark's urging, Don asked for approval for $1.5 million for new hires in product development, and at the time I indicated it looked OK. But I live in the matrix too, and when our regional transmission performance started slipping behind budget, I started hearing from Lindahl and Schulmeyer. Don understands that if one business is down, another one has to step up to the plate. I didn't tell him he had to cut R&D, but I did ask him to help with our shortfall.

> Well, Don got really mad and wrote me a strong letter. In Westinghouse he probably would have been removed, but here we encourage people to kick back. I didn't like it, but I'm glad he did it. In the end, I talked to Ulf and suggested that if he really wanted the R&D done, maybe he could support it out of Sweden.

The issue arose again at the next Steering Committee Meeting for Jans's U.S. relays company. After further debate, Gundemark agreed to transfer two Swedish technical managers to Coral Springs to initiate Jans's program. In turn, Baker agreed to include the increased development expenditure in the next year's budget.

The Comsys Challenge   Although Jans was very supportive of ABB's philosophy of coordinating key strategy decisions across national boundaries, he had serious concerns about a major BA development project known as the common systems (or Comsys) project. Soon after announcing its formation in 1990, Gundemark challenged the relays R&D council to develop a common platform for future product development across units. As he described the problem:

> Despite our coordination and specialization, we are still too compartmentalized. We are captives of our history, and each company tries to position and protect itself by creating products for its assigned markets. Rather than emphasizing differences in the needs across the European, American, and developing countries markets, we need to develop a common base of hardware and software that can be adapted to local needs and individual customers.

To implement the Comsys project, a cross-country team was formed consisting of two technical experts from each of the four major centers. By early 1992, the nine sub-project teams were still hammering out the details of product design, operating standards, and overall project implementation, and the feeling was that they were years away from having tangible results. Because most local development had been curtailed to focus resources on Comsys, the grumblings of many front-line profit center managers were becoming more audible. Said Gundemark:

> It was essential to get middle managers from the various countries involved rather than doing this centrally, even if it does slow things down. But these missionaries are confronting the old views back in their home organizations and are having a hard time selling the new ideas. It may mean we lose some time initially, but we will gain that back multiplied when we get everyone pulling in the same direction.

Don Jans felt that the Comsys problem was not only polluting his team's growing feeling of independent initiative, it was also compromising his unit's current performance by holding up local development projects. Yet he felt conflicted about his response. Should he wear his BA board member's hat and tell his managers to buckle down and make the project work? Or should he put on his company general manager's hat and defend the interests of his Coral Springs profit centers and ask Gundemark for relief from Comsys to focus more local resources back on projects to meet the immediate market needs?

The Future   As Jans prepared for the quarterly BA board meeting in early 1992, he drafted a "balance sheet" of achievements and challenges that would become the basis of a presentation he would make to his colleagues on the relays integration process to date (Exhibit 11). He was pleasantly surprised with the length of the asset side of his balance sheet but realized that most management attention needed to be focused on the "liabilities" side. Jans wondered what the company could do to deal with the kinds of problems he faced. It was a concern that was shared by Ulf Gundemark and Göran Lindahl.

Exhibit 11   Evaluation of Relays BA Integration: Excerpts from Don Jan's Presentation to BA Board, February 1992

Success Elements	Areas for Strengthening
• Clear vision and expectations from the top • Responsibility push down—consensus teams not "top down" • Good collaborative managers without strong egos—mutual respect • Strong ethic of "what/how/deadline" • Synergy through integrating devices (Boards, Councils, Centers of Excellence) • Linking world capability (market access, technology, etc.) to become world class • Best practices-internal benchmarking—internal competition • Key program as share knowledge, provide focus (TQM, TMB, Supplier Partnering, Customer Focus, etc.) • Constant communication	• Tension between BA and country management (long-term vs. short-term) • Internal competition (marketing and technology) • Profit center concept creates unmet resource needs—psychological impact • Tension between meeting operating objectives and participating in time-consuming integration processes • Barriers to technology sharing • Still resistance to lead centers taking leadership in market/business planning • Reduce inventories through better support of engineering centers, reduce lead time, and on-time shipments • Need more people exchanges through benchmarking

Reading 4-1   Tap Your Subsidiaries for Global Reach

Christopher A. Bartlett and Sumantra Ghoshal

In 1972, EMI developed the CAT scanner. This technological breakthrough seemed to be the innovation that the U.K.–based company had long sought in order to relieve its heavy dependence on the cyclical music and entertainment business and to strengthen itself in international markets. The medical community hailed the product, and within four years EMI had established a medical electronics business that was generating 20% of the company's worldwide earnings. The scanner enjoyed a dominant market position, a fine reputation, and a strong technological leadership situation.

Nevertheless, by mid-1979 EMI had started losing money in this business, and the company's deteriorating performance eventually forced it to accept a takeover bid from Thorn Electric. Thorn immediately divested the ailing medical electronics business. Ironically, the takeover was announced the same month that Godfrey Hounsfield, the EMI scientist who developed the CAT scanner, was awarded a Nobel Prize for the invention.

How could such a fairy-tale success story turn so quickly into a nightmare? There were many contributing causes, but at the center were a structure and management process that impeded the company's ability to capitalize on its technological assets and its worldwide market position.

The concentration of EMI's technical, financial, and managerial resources in the United Kingdom made it unresponsive to the varied and changing needs of international markets. As worldwide demand built up, delivery lead times for the scanner stretched out more than 12 months. Despite the protests of EMI's U.S. managers that these delays were opening opportunities for competitive entry,

‖ Reprinted by permission of *Harvard Business Review.* "Tap Your Subsidiaries for Global Reach" by Christopher A. Bartlett and Sumantra Ghoshal, (November/December 1986).
‖ Copyright © 1986 by the President and Fellows of Harvard; all rights reserved.

headquarters continued to fill orders on the basis of when they were received rather than on how strategically important they were. Corporate management would not allow local sourcing or duplicate manufacturing of the components that were the bottlenecks causing delays.

The centralization of decision making in London also impaired the company's ability to guide strategy to meet the needs of the market. For example, medical practitioners in the United States, the key market for CAT scanners, considered reduction of scan time to be an important objective, while EMI's central research laboratory, influenced by feedback from the domestic market, concentrated on improving image resolution. When General Electric eventually brought out a competitive product with a shorter scan time, customers deserted EMI.

In the final analysis, it was EMI's limited organizational capability that prevented it from capitalizing on its large resource base and its strong global competitive position. The company lacked:

The ability to sense changes in market needs and industry structure occurring away from home.

The resources to analyze data and develop strategic responses to competitive challenges that were emerging worldwide.

The managerial initiative, motivation, and capability in its overseas operations to respond imaginatively to diverse and fast-changing operating environments.

While the demise of its scanner business represents an extreme example, the problems EMI faced are common. With all the current attention being given to global strategy, companies risk underestimating the organizational challenge of managing their global operations. Indeed, the top management in almost every one of the MNCs we have studied has had an excellent idea of what it needed to do to become more globally competitive; it was less clear on how to organize to achieve its global strategic objectives.

United Nations Model and HQ Syndrome

Our study covered nine core companies in three industries and a dozen secondary companies from a more diverse industrial spectrum. They were selected from three areas of origin—the United States, Europe, and Japan. Despite this diversity, most of these companies had developed their international operations around two common assumptions on how to organize. We dubbed these well-ingrained beliefs the "U.N. model assumption" and the "headquarters hierarchy syndrome."

Although there are wide differences in importance of operations in major markets like Germany, Japan, or the United States, compared with subsidiaries in Argentina, Malaysia, or Nigeria, for example, most multinationals treat their foreign subsidiaries in a remarkably uniform manner. One executive we talked to termed this approach "the U.N. model of multinational management." Thus, it is common to see managers express subsidiary roles and responsibilities in the same general terms, apply their planning control systems uniformly system-wide, involve country managers to a like degree in planning, and evaluate them against standardized criteria. The uniform systems and procedures tend to paper over any differences in the informal treatment of subsidiaries.

When national units are operationally self-sufficient and strategically independent, uniform treatment may allow each to develop a plan for dealing with its local environment. As a company reaches for the benefits of global integration, however, there is little need for uniformity and symmetry among units. Yet the growing complexity of the corporate management task heightens the appeal of a simple system.

The second common assumption we observed, the headquarters hierarchy syndrome, grows out of and is reinforced by the U.N. model assumption. The symmetrical organization approach encourages management to envision two roles for the organiza-

tion, one for headquarters and another for the national subsidiaries. As companies moved to build a consistent global strategy, we saw a strong tendency for headquarters managers to try to coordinate key decisions and control global resources and have the subsidiaries act as implementers and adapters of the global strategy in their localities.

As strategy implementation proceeded, we observed country managers struggling to retain their freedom, flexibility, and effectiveness, while their counterparts at the center worked to maintain their control and legitimacy as administrators of the global strategy. It's not surprising that relationships between the center and the periphery often became strained and even adversarial.

The combined effect of these two assumptions is to severely limit the organizational capability of a company's international operations in three important ways. First, the doctrine of symmetrical treatment results in an overcompensation for the needs of smaller or less crucial markets and a simultaneous underresponsiveness to the needs of strategically important countries. Moreover, by relegating the national subsidiaries to the role of local implementers and adapters of global directives, the head office risks grossly underutilizing the company's worldwide assets and organizational capabilities. And finally, ever-expanding control by headquarters deprives the country managers of outlets for their skills and creative energy. Naturally, they come to feel demotivated and even disenfranchised.

Dispersed Responsibility

The limitations of the symmetrical, hierarchical mode of operation have become increasingly clear to MNC executives, and in many of the companies we surveyed we found managers experimenting with alternative ways of managing their worldwide operations. And as we reviewed these various approaches, we saw a new pattern emerging that suggested a significantly different model of global organization based on some important new assumptions and beliefs. We saw companies experimenting with ways of selectively varying the roles and responsibilities of their national organizations to reflect explicitly the differences in external environments and internal capabilities. We also saw them modifying central administrative systems to legitimize the differences they encountered.

Such is the case with Procter & Gamble's European operations. More than a decade ago, P&G's European subsidiaries were free to adapt the parent company's technology, products, and marketing approaches to their local situation as they saw fit— while being held responsible, of course, for sales and earnings in their respective countries. Many of these subsidiaries had become large and powerful. By the mid-1970s, economic and competitive pressures were squeezing P&G's European profitability. The head office in Cincinnati decided that the loose organizational arrangement inhibited product development, curtailed the company's ability to capture Europewide scale economies, and afforded poor protection against competitors' attempts to pick off product lines country by country.

So the company launched what became known as the Pampers experiment—an approach firmly grounded in the classic U.N. and HQ assumptions. It created a position at European headquarters in Brussels to develop a Pampers strategy for the whole continent. By giving this manager responsibility for the Europewide product and marketing strategy, management hoped to be able to eliminate the diversity in brand strategy by coordinating activities across subsidiary boundaries. Within 12 months, the Pampers experiment had failed. It not only ignored local knowledge and underutilized subsidiary strengths but also demotivated the country managers to the point that they felt no responsibility for sales performance of the brand in their areas.

Obviously, a different approach was called for. Instead of assuming that the best solutions were to be found in headquarters, top management decided to find a way to exploit the expertise of the national units. For most products, P&G had one or two European subsidiaries that had been more creative, committed, and successful than the others. By extending the responsibilities and influence of these organizations, top management reasoned, the company could make the success infectious. All that

was needed was a means for promoting intersubsidiary cooperation that could offset the problems caused by the company's dispersed and independent operations. For P&G the key was the creation of "Eurobrand" teams.

For each important brand the company formed a management team that carried the responsibility for development and coordination of marketing strategy for Europe. Each Eurobrand team was headed not by a manager from headquarters but by the general manager and the appropriate brand group from the "lead" subsidiary—a unit selected for its success and creativity with the brand. Supporting them were brand managers from other subsidiaries, functional managers from headquarters, and anyone else involved in strategy for the particular product. Team meetings became forums for the lead-country group to pass on ideas, propose action, and hammer out agreements.

The first Eurobrand team had charge of a new liquid detergent called Vizir. The brand group in the lead country, West Germany, had undertaken product and market testing, settled on the package design and advertising theme, and developed the marketing strategy. The Eurobrand team ratified all these elements, then launched Vizir in six new markets within a year. This was the first time the company had ever introduced a new product in that many markets in so brief a span. It was also the first time the company had gotten agreement in several subsidiaries on a single product formulation, a uniform advertising theme, a standard packaging line, and a sole manufacturing source. Thereafter, Eurobrand teams proliferated; P&G's way of organizing and directing subsidiary operations had changed fundamentally.

On reflection, company managers feel that there were two main reasons why Eurobrand teams succeeded where the Pampers experiment had failed. First, they captured the knowledge, the expertise, and most important, the commitment of managers closest to the market. Equally significant was the fact that relationships among managers on Eurobrand teams were built on interdependence rather than on independence, as in the old organization, or on dependence, as with the Pampers experiment. Different subsidiaries had the lead role for different brands, and the need for reciprocal cooperation was obvious to everyone.

Other companies have made similar discoveries about new ways to manage their international operations—at NEC and Philips, at L. M. Ericsson and Matsushita, at ITT and Unilever, we observed executives challenging the assumptions behind the traditional head office–subsidiary relationship. The various terms they used—lead-country concept, key-market subsidiary, global-market mandate, center of excellence—all suggested a new model based on a recognition that their organizational task was focused on a single problem: the need to resolve imbalances between market demands and constraints on the one hand and uneven subsidiary capabilities on the other. Top officers understand that the option of a zero-based organization is not open to an established multinational organization. But they seem to have hit on an approach that works.

Black Holes, etc. The actions these companies have taken suggest an organizational model of differentiated rather than homogeneous subsidiary roles and of dispersed rather than concentrated responsibilities. As we analyzed the nature of the emerging subsidiary roles and responsibilities, we were able to see a pattern in their distribution and identify the criteria used to assign them. Exhibit 1 represents a somewhat oversimplified conceptualization of the criteria and roles, but it is true enough for discussion purposes.

The strategic importance of a specific country unit is strongly influenced by the significance of its national environment to the company's global strategy. A large market is obviously important, and so is a competitor's home market or a market that is particularly sophisticated or technologically advanced. The organizational competence of a particular subsidiary can, of course, be in technology, production, marketing, or any other area.

Strategic Leader This role can be played by a highly competent national subsidiary located in a strategically important market. In this role, the

Exhibit 1 Roles for National Subsidiaries

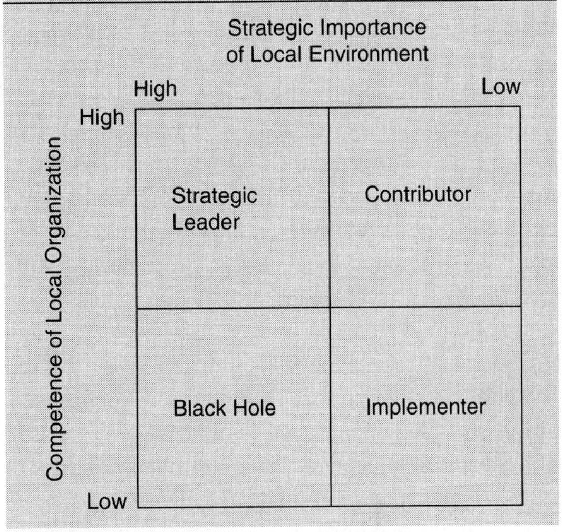

subsidiary serves as a partner of headquarters in developing and implementing strategy. It must not only be a sensor for detecting signals of change but also a help in analyzing the threats and opportunities and developing appropriate responses.

The part played by the U.K. subsidiary of Philips in building the company's strong leadership position in the teletext-TV business provides an illustration. In the early 1970s, the BBC and ITV (an independent British TV company) simultaneously launched projects to adapt existing transmission capacity to permit broadcast of text and simple diagrams. But teletext, as it was called, required a TV receiver that would accept and decode the modified transmissions. For TV set manufacturers, the market opportunity required a big investment in R&D and production facilities, but commercial possibilities of teletext were highly uncertain, and most producers decided against making the investment. They spurned teletext as a typical British toy—fancy and not very useful. Who would pay a heavy premium just to read text on a TV screen?

Philips' U.K. subsidiary, however, was convinced that the product had a future and decided to pursue its own plans. Its top officers persuaded Philips' component manufacturing unit to design and produce the integrated-circuit chip for receiving teletext and commissioned their Croydon plant to build the teletext decoder.

In the face of poor market acceptance (the company sold only 1,000 teletext sets in its first year), the U.K. subsidiary did not give up. It lent support to the British government's efforts to promote teletext and make it widely available. Meanwhile, management kept up pressure on the Croydon factory to find ways of reducing costs and improving reception quality—which it did.

In late 1979, teletext took off, and by 1982 half a million sets were being sold annually in the United Kingdom. Today almost three million teletext sets are in use in Britain, and the concept is spreading abroad. Philips has built up a dominant position in markets that have accepted the service. Corporate management has given the U.K. subsidiary formal responsibility to continue to exercise leadership in the development, manufacture, and marketing of teletext on a companywide basis. The Croydon plant is recognized as Philips' center of competence and international sourcing plant for teletext-TV sets.

Contributor   Filling this role is a subsidiary operating in a small or strategically unimportant market but having a distinctive capability. A fine example is the Australian subsidiary of L. M. Ericsson, which played a crucial part in developing its successful AXE digital telecommunications switch. The down-under group gave impetus to the conversion of the system from its initial analog design to the digital form. Later its engineers helped construct several key components of the system.

This subsidiary had built up its superior technological capability when the Australian telephone authority became one of the first in the world to call for bids on electronic telephone switching equipment. The government in Canberra, however, had insisted on a strong local technical capability as a condition for access to the market. Moreover, heading this unit of the Swedish company was a willful, independent, and entrepreneurial country manager who strengthened the R&D team, even without full support from headquarters.

These various factors resulted in the local subsidiary having a technological capability and an R&D resource base that was much larger than subsidiaries in other markets of similar size or importance. Left to their own devices, management worried that such internal competencies would focus on local tasks and priorities that were unnecessary or even detrimental to the overall global strategy. But if the company inhibited the development activities of the local units, it risked losing these special skills. Under the circumstances, management saw the need to co-opt this valuable subsidiary expertise and channel it toward projects of corporate importance.

Implementer   In the third situation, a national organization in a less strategically important market has just enough competence to maintain its local operation. The market potential is limited, and the corporate resource commitment reflects it. Most national units of most companies are given this role. They might include subsidiaries in the developing countries, in Canada, and in the smaller European countries. Without access to critical information, and having to control scarce resources, these national organizations lack the potential to become contributors to the company's strategic planning. They are deliverers of the company's value added; they have the important task of generating the funds that keep the company going and underwrite its expansion.

The implementers' efficiency is as important as the creativity of the strategic leaders or contributors—and perhaps more so, for it is this group that provides the largest leverage that affords MNCs their competitive advantage. The implementers produce the opportunity to capture economies of scale and scope that are crucial to most companies' global strategies.

In Procter & Gamble's European introduction of Vizir, the French company played an important contributing role by undertaking a second market test and later modifying the advertising approach. In the other launches during the first year, Austria, Spain, Holland, and Belgium were implementers; they took the defined strategy and made it work in their markets. Resisting any temptation to push for change in the formula, alteration of the package, or adjustment of the advertising theme, these national subsidiaries enabled P&G to extract profitable efficiencies.

The Black Hole   Philips in Japan, Ericsson in the United States, and Matsushita in Germany are black holes. In each of these important markets, strong local presence is essential for maintaining the company's global position. And in each case, the local company hardly makes a dent.

The black hole is not an acceptable strategic position. Unlike the other roles we have described, the objective is not to manage it but to manage one's way out of it. But building a significant local presence in a national environment that is large, sophisticated, and competitive is extremely difficult, expensive, and time consuming.

One common tack has been to create a sensory outpost in the black hole environment so as to exploit the learning potential, even if the local business potential is beyond reach. Many American and European companies have set up small establishments in Japan to monitor technologies, market trends, and competitors. Feedback to headquarters, so the thinking goes, will allow further analysis of the global implications of local developments and will at least help prevent erosion of the company's position in other markets. But this strategy has often been less fruitful than the company had hoped. Look at the case of Philips in Japan.

Although Philips had two manufacturing joint ventures with Matsushita, not until 1956 did it enter Japan by establishing a marketing organization. When Japan was emerging as a significant force in the consumer electronics market in the late 1960s, the company decided it had to get further into that market. After years of unsuccessfully trying to penetrate the captive distribution channels of the principal Japanese manufacturers, headquarters settled for a Japan "window" that would keep it informed of technical developments there. But results were disappointing. The reason, according to a senior manager of Philips in Japan, is that to sense effectively, eyes and ears are not enough. One must get "inside the bloodstream of the business," he said, with constant and direct access to distribution channels, component suppliers, and equipment manufacturers.

Detecting a new development after it has occurred is useless, for there is no time to play catchup. One needs to know of developments as they emerge, and for that one must be a player, not a spectator. Moreover, being confined to window status, the local company is prevented from playing a strategic role. It is condemned to a permanent existence as a black hole.

So Philips is trying to get into the bloodstream of the Japanese market, moving away from the window concept and into the struggle for market share. The local organization now sees its task as winning market share rather than just monitoring local developments. But it is being very selective and focusing on areas where it has advantages over strong local competition. The Japanese unit started with coffee makers and electric shavers. Philips' acquisition of Marantz, a hi-fi equipment producer, gives it a bid to expand on its strategic base and build the internal capabilities that will enable the Japanese subsidiary to climb out of the black hole.

Another way to manage one's way out of the black hole is to develop a strategic alliance. Such coalitions can involve different levels of cooperation. Ericsson's joint venture with Honeywell in the United States and AT&T's with Philips in Europe are examples of attempts to fill up a black hole by obtaining resources and competence from a strong local organization in exchange for capabilities available elsewhere.

Shaping, Building, Directing   Corporate management faces three big challenges in guiding the dispersion of responsibilities and differentiating subsidiaries' tasks. The first is in setting the strategic direction for the company by identifying its mission and its business objectives. The second is in building the differentiated organization, not only by designing the diverse roles and distributing the assignments but also by giving the managers responsible for filling them the legitimacy and power to do so. The final challenge is in directing the process to ensure that the several roles are coordinated and that the distributed responsibilities are controlled.

Setting the Course   Any company (or any organization, for that matter) needs a strong, unifying sense of direction. But that need is particularly strong in an organization in which tasks are differentiated and responsibilities dispersed. Without it, the decentralized management process will quickly degenerate into strategic anarchy. A visitor to any NEC establishment in the world will see everywhere the company motto "C&C," which stands for computers and communications. This simple pairing of words is much more than a definition of NEC's product markets; top managers have made it the touchstone of a common global strategy. They emphasize it to focus the attention of employees on the key strategy of linking two technologies. And they employ it to help managers think how NEC can compete with larger companies like IBM and AT&T, which are perceived as vulnerable insofar as they lack a balance in the two technologies and markets.

Top management at NEC headquarters in Tokyo strives to inculcate its worldwide organization with an understanding of the C&C strategy and philosophy. It is this strong, shared understanding that permits greater differentiation of managerial processes and the decentralization of tasks.

But in addition to their role of developing and communicating a vision of the corporate mission, the top officers at headquarters also retain overall responsibility for the company's specific business strategies. While not abandoning this role at the heart of the company's strategic process, executives of many multinational companies are co-opting other parts of the organization (and particularly its diverse national organizations) into important business strategy roles, as we have already described. When it gives up its lead role, however, headquarters management always tracks that delegated responsibility.

Building Differentiation   In determining which units should be given the lead, contributor, or follower roles, management must consider the motivational as well as the strategic impact of its decisions. If unfulfilled, the promise offered by the new organization model can be as demotivating as the symmetrical hierarchy, in which all foreign subsidiaries are assigned permanent secondary roles.

For most national units, an organization in which lead and contributor roles are concentrated in a few favorite children represents little advance from old situations in which the parent dominated the decision making. In any units continually obliged to implement strategies developed elsewhere, skills atrophy, entrepreneurship dies, and any innovative spark that existed when it enjoyed more independence now sputters.

By dealing out lead or contributing roles to the smaller or less developed units, even if only for one or two strategically less important products, the headquarters group will give them a huge incentive. Although Philips N.V. had many other subsidiaries closer to large markets or with better access to corporate know-how and expertise, headquarters awarded the Taiwan unit the lead role in the small-screen monitor business. This vote of confidence gave the Taiwanese terrific motivation to do well and made them feel like a full contributing partner in the company's worldwide strategy.

But allocating roles isn't enough; the head office has to empower the units to exercise their voices in the organization by ensuring that those with lead positions particularly have access to and influence in the corporate decision-making process. This is not a trivial task, especially if strategic initiative and decision-making powers have long been concentrated at headquarters.

NEC discovered this truth about a decade ago when it was trying to transform itself into a global enterprise. Because NTT, the Japanese telephone authority, was dragging its feet in converting its exchanges to the new digital switching technology, NEC was forced to diverge from its custom of designing equipment mainly for its big domestic customer. The NEAC 61 digital switch was the first outgrowth of the policy shift; it was aimed primarily at the huge, newly deregulated U.S. telephone market.

Managers and engineers in Japan developed the product; the American subsidiary had little input. Although the hardware drew praise from customers, the switch had severe software deficiencies that hampered its penetration of the U.S. market.

Recognizing the need to change its administrative setup, top management committed publicly to becoming "a genuine world enterprise" rather than a Japanese company operating abroad. To permit the U.S. subsidiary a greater voice, headquarters helped it build a local software development capability. This plus the unit's growing knowledge about the Bell operating companies—NEC's target customers—gave the American managers legitimacy and power in Japan.

NEC's next-generation digital switch, the NEAC 61-E, evolved quite differently. Exercising their new influence at headquarters, U.S. subsidiary managers took the lead in establishing its features and specifications and played a big part in the design.

Another path to empowerment takes the form of dislodging the decision-making process from the home office. Ericsson combats the headquarters hierarchy syndrome by appointing product and functional managers from headquarters to subsidiary boards. The give-and-take in board meetings is helpful for both subsidiary and parent. Matsushita holds an annual review of each major worldwide function (like manufacturing and human resource management) in the offices of a national subsidiary it considers to be a leading exponent of the particular function. In addition to the symbolic value for employees of the units, the siting obliges officials from Tokyo headquarters to consider issues that the front lines are experiencing and gives local managers the home-court advantage in seeking a voice in decision making.

Often the most effective means of giving strategy access and influence to national units is to create entirely new channels and forums. This approach permits roles, responsibilities, and relationships to be defined and developed with far less constraint than through modification of existing communication patterns or through shifting of responsibility boundaries. Procter & Gamble's Eurobrand teams are a case in point.

Directing the Process   When the roles of operating units are differentiated and responsibility is more dispersed, corporate management must be prepared to deemphasize its direct control over the strategic content but develop an ability to manage the dispersed strategic process. Furthermore, headquarters must adopt a flexible administrative stance that allows it to differentiate the way it manages one subsidiary to the next and from business to business within a single unit, depending on the particular role it plays in each business.

In units with lead roles, headquarters plays an important role in ensuring that the business strategies developed fit the company's overall goals and priorities. But control in the classic sense is often quite loose. Corporate management's chief function is to support those with strategy leadership responsibility by giving them the resources and the freedom needed for the innovative and entrepreneurial role they have been asked to play.

With a unit placed in a contributor role, the head-office task is to redirect local resources to programs outside the unit's control. In so doing, it has to counter the natural hierarchy of loyalties that in most national organizations puts local interests above global ones. In such a situation, headquarters must be careful not to discourage the local managers and technicians so much that they stop contributing or leave in frustration. This has happened to many U.S. companies that have tried to manage their Canadian subsidiaries in a contributor role. Ericsson has solved the problem in its Australian subsidiary by attaching half the R&D team to headquarters, which farms out to these engineers projects that are part of the company's global development program.

The head office maintains tighter control over a subsidiary in an implementor role. Because such a group represents the company's opportunity to capture the benefits of scale and learning from which it gets and sustains its competitive advantage, headquarters stresses economy and efficiency in selling the products. Communication of strategies developed elsewhere and control of routine tasks can be carried out through systems, allowing headquarters to manage these units more efficiently than most others.

As for the black hole unit, the task for top executives is to develop its resources and capabilities to make it more responsive to its environment. Managers of these units depend heavily on headquarters for help and support, creating an urgent need for intensive training and transfer of skills and resources.

Firing the Spark Plugs

Multinational companies often build cumbersome and expensive infrastructures designed to control their widespread operations and to coordinate the diverse and often conflicting demands they make. As the coordination and control task expands, the typical headquarters organization becomes larger and more powerful, while the national subsidiaries are increasingly regarded as pipelines for centrally developed products and strategy.

But an international company enjoys a big advantage over a national one: it is exposed to a wider and more diverse range of environmental stimuli. The broader range of customer preferences, the wider spectrum of competitive behavior, the more serious array of government demands, and the more diverse sources of technological information represent potential triggers of innovation and thus a rich source of learning for the company. To capitalize on this advantage requires an organization that is sensitive to the environment and responsive in absorbing the information it gathers.

So national companies must not be regarded as just pipelines but recognized as sources of information and expertise that can build competitive advantage. The best way to exploit this resource is not through centralized direction and control but through a cooperative effort and co-option of dispersed capabilities. In such a relationship, the entrepreneurial spark plugs in the national units can flourish.

Reading 4-2   Making Global Strategies Work

W. Chan Kim
Renée A. Mauborgne

It is hardly a novel insight that global competitive forces compel multinationals to fully leverage the distinctive resources, knowledge, and expertise residing in their subsidiary operations. Questions of what are "winning" global strategic moves for the modern multinational have increasingly intoxicated international executives.[1] Yet for all the fanfare about global strategies and their increasingly undeniable link to multinational success, little has been said or written about how to make global strategies work. The key question we address here is just that: What does it take for multinationals to successfully execute global strategies?

Our research results paint a striking picture of the importance of the strategy-making process itself for effective global strategy execution. Over the

❚ W. Chan Kim is associate professor of strategy and international management, INSEAD. Renée A. Mauborgne is research associate of management and international business, INSEAD.
❚ Special thanks are due to Sumantra Ghoshal, Philippe Haspeslagh, and Michael Scott Morton. Their comments greatly improved this paper. Special thanks are also due to INSEAD, especially Associate Dean Yves Doz, for generous financial support of this research.
❚ Copyright ©1993 by the SLOAN MANAGEMENT REVIEW Association. All rights reserved.

❚ [1]For an excellent review of the literature on global strategy, see:
S. Ghoshal, "Global Strategy: An Organizing Framework," *Strategic Management Journal* 8 (1987): 425–440.

last four years, we have done extensive research to understand how multinationals can successfully implement global strategies. Because subsidiary top managers are the key catalysts for, or obstacles preventing, global strategy execution, we asked them directly just what it was that motivated them to execute or to defy their companies' global strategic decisions.

Subsidiary top managers were quick to rattle off a series of well-established implementation mechanisms: incentive compensation, monitoring systems, and rewards and punishments. They were equally quick to add that they did not believe these control mechanisms alone to be either sufficient or that effective. The general consensus was that these mechanisms were not particularly motivating and were easy to dodge and cheat. Even more recurrent in our discussions, however, were the dynamics of the global strategic decision-making process itself. When deciding whether or to what extent to carry out global strategies, subsidiary top managers accorded great importance to the way in which those strategies were generated. Their overriding concern involved a deceptively simple though evidently profound principle: due process should be exercised in the global strategic decision-making process.

In practical terms, due process means: (1) that the head office is familiar with subsidiaries' local situations; (2) that two-way communication exists in the global strategy-making process; (3) that the head office is relatively consistent in making decisions across subsidiary units; (4) that subsidiary units can legitimately challenge the head office's strategic views and decisions; and (5) that subsidiary units receive an explanation for final strategic decisions.

In short, we observed that, in the absence of these factors, subsidiary top managers were often upset and negatively disposed toward resulting strategic decisions. However, in the presence of these factors, the reaction was just the reverse. Subsidiary top managers were favorably disposed toward resulting decisions, thought them wise, and were motivated to implement them even if, and here is the biggest benefit of all, these decisions were not in line with their individual subsidiary units' interests.

We begin this paper by probing in depth just what subsidiary top managers mean by due process and why they judge its exercise important in the global strategy-making process. Next we examine what leads subsidiary top managers to view traditional implementation mechanisms as increasingly insufficient for global strategies. Finally, we trace the real effects of due process in global strategy making on global strategy execution and explore why they are so profound.

The Meaning of Due Process

To get to the heart of how multinationals can make global strategies work, we held extensive interviews with sixty-three subsidiary presidents.[2] Our initial objective was to get subsidiary presidents' honest evaluation of the factors that drove them to carry out or resist their organizations' global strategic decisions. As the interviews progressed, the one tendency that stood out was the subsidiary presidents' natural inclination to discuss how global strategies were generated. Time and again, the dynamics of the global strategy-making process itself were the centerpiece of their discussions. Their principal concern was whether due process was exercised. That is, was the strategy-making process fair from the subsidiary unit perspective?

Through these interviews, we identified the five characteristics above that, taken together, defined due process in global strategic decision making (see Figure 1).[3] What is interesting is that these five characteristics were important regardless of the industry or the subsidiary's strategic importance. Appendix A profiles our sixty-three subsidiary presidents and discusses how they were selected. Here we discuss each of the characteristics and

[2] For an extensive discussion on our field study, see: W.C. Kim and R.A. Mauborgne, "Implementing Global Strategies: The Role of Procedural Justice," *Strategic Management Journal* 12 (1991): 125–143; and W.C. Kim and R.A. Mauborgne, "Procedural Justice Theory and the Multinational Organization," in *Organization Theory and the Multinational Corporation,* eds. S. Ghoshal and E. Westney (London: MacMillan, 1993a).

[3] The Q-sort technique was used to define the meaning of due process in global strategic decision making. For a detailed explanation of this process, see: Kim and Mauborgne (1991 and 1993a).

Figure 1   What Is Due Process in Global Strategic Decision Making?

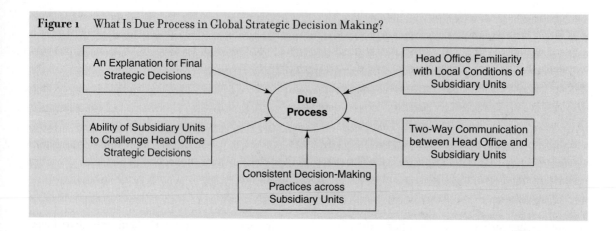

examine through the eyes of subsidiary top managers what makes each of them vital.

Head Office's Familiarity with Local Conditions

> The head office does not know a damn thing about what's going on down here. They tell me to further push their global "core" products even at the expense of our existing product lines. And you know what I tell them? I tell them they're crazy. They don't realize that not only don't these "core" products sell in our local market but that we are already losing sales on our existing product lines from tough local competitors due to our lack of push on them.

This statement indicates subsidiary top managers' attitudes when the head office lacks knowledge of the local market. One manager explains why local familiarity is important:

> The head office needs to invest in understanding the local market. How can I respect their decisions and follow them if I don't believe that they are made with an understanding of the local market?

When subsidiary managers believe the head office has a reasonable grasp of the local situation, they are apt to make statements like this one:

> I have tremendous faith and trust in the head office's strategic decisions. They know the local market. When they make a decision, they understand the ramifications of that decision, be those ramifications good or bad. Whether I like their decisions or not, there's at least a method to their madness.

What it comes down to is that in the absence of local familiarity, subsidiary top managers do not judge the head office to be competent and sincere. They tend to think of the head office instead as incapable and apathetic toward their foreign operation. As a consequence, these managers have little respect for the decisions coming down. They quickly become skeptical of the soundness and quality of the resulting global strategies. This provides an excellent excuse for not only why they do not implement global strategies but why they should not. As one executive put it, "To not follow the global strategic decisions handed down to a subsidiary unit is not a curse but a blessing in disguise. Those decisions aren't based on reality; they are based on air." At the most, local familiarity gives confidence that global strategies are based on thoughtful analyses; at the least, it prevents subsidiary managers from using this seemingly reasonable justification for not executing global strategic decisions.

Two-Way Communication   When global strategic decisions are being made that affect a subsidiary unit, subsidiary top managers value the ability to voice their opinion and work back and forth with the head office in decision formulation. This communication symbolizes the respect the head office has for subsidiary units as well as the confidence it places in subsidiary managers' opinions and insights.

Our observation is that this respect and confidence is quickly reciprocated by subsidiary top managers as well. Although two-way communication often results in heated debates, it also builds a profound spirit of comradeship, unity, and mutual trust among the head office and subsidiary top management teams. Moreover, when subsidiary managers participate in global strategic decision making, they come to view the decisions as their own. As a result, they often defend and uphold these decisions. As one executive commented:

> The open exchange of information and ideas is critical in global strategy making. It opens the ears of managers in both the head office and subsidiary units and typically results in better value judgments. When we [subsidiary managers] feel that our views are given sufficient attention, we are less likely to be dissatisfied with global strategic decisions or to feel antagonistic toward the head office and are better motivated to act rigorously to carry out the agreed-upon plan of action.

Consistent Decision-Making Practices Consider two opposing comments made by different executives. One says:

> Our global strategic decision making is a very political process. If you are on the "inside track," the head office treats you as a relatively important element of global strategic decision making. But if not, you and your unit are likely to be completely overlooked and just slapped with a set of strategic decisions that are supposed to be implemented. At times, I think the whole process is just a scam, a politicians' arena where strategic decisions reflect not competitive and economic dynamics but the dynamics of political interplay.

The other says:

> Admittedly subsidiary units don't walk away with symmetric decision outcomes—one subsidiary unit may get what seems to be a windfall allocation of resources while another may take a cut. But all subsidiary units are treated relatively consistently when it comes to how these decisions are reached. It's a fair process. There doesn't seem to be much favoritism or political jockeying in this decision-making process.

These two comments shed light on why consistent decision-making practices across subsidiary units are a prized aspect of due process. Basically, they are thought to minimize the degree of politics and favoritism in the strategy generation process. Subsidiary managers are confident that there is a level playing field across subsidiary units. And this is important. Subsidiary managers do not expect the strategic decisions made across subsidiary units to be identical, as they understand that units are not equally important for the organization. But they do view the consistent application of decision-making rules as an essential element of due process.

In the absence of consistency, subsidiary managers are quick to judge the decision-making process as arbitrary, politically rigged, and hence not to be trusted. They find the confusion and uncertainty extremely frustrating, and they are inclined to attribute unfavorable strategic decisions to unfair decision rules as opposed to competitive and economic dynamics. Consequently, they become bitter and resentful and more apt to want to undermine resulting decisions.

Ability to Refute Decisions Having the ability to refute the head office's strategic views and decisions also makes subsidiary managers feel that due process is being exercised. Admittedly this can be traced in part to managers' perceived increase in influence over strategic decisions, but our discussions suggest another reason why the ability to refute is important. It makes managers feel that the process is fair simply because they can clearly point out possible misperceptions or wrong assumptions made by head office managers concerning local conditions or subsidiary operations. But more than this, the ability to challenge head office decisions inspires subsidiary managers to more willingly follow these decisions because they know that if the decisions should prove unreasonable or wrong-headed, the possibility always exists to correct them. As one executive explained:

> When I know I have the right to openly challenge the head office's decisions, that automatically tells me that the head office is confident in their decisions, that they have faith that their underlying logic and

analyses can stand the test of open scrutiny. But it also tells me that, despite the head office's confidence, they also recognize that being removed from the local market opens up the possibility that they will judge the local situation incorrectly. Not only do I respect the head office for this, but it in turn gives me confidence that the intentions and global strategic decisions of the head office are truly made in the interests of the overall organization and not based on politics.

An Explanation for Final Decisions   Subsidiary top managers think it only fair that the head office give them an explanation for final global strategic decisions. And they consider it an important aspect of due process. In short, subsidiary managers need an intellectual understanding of the rationale driving ultimate decisions. They want to know why they should carry out the decisions. This is especially true if those decisions override their expressed views or seem unfavorable to their own unit. To quote one executive:

> When the head office provides an explanation for why decisions are made as they are, they provide evidence that they acted in a fair and impartial manner. This signals to me that the head office has at least considered the subsidiary point of view before they may have rejected it. When I understand why final strategic decisions are made as they are, I'm more inclined to implement those decisions even if I don't particularly view them as favorable.

What Makes Due Process Important for Global Strategy Execution

As our interviews with subsidiary presidents progressed and the meaning of due process became clear, a second equally important trend became visible: those managers who believed that due process was exercised in the firms' global strategy-making process were the same executives who trusted their head offices significantly, who were highly committed to their organizations, who felt a sense of comradeship or unity with the corporate center, and who were motivated to execute not only the letter but also the spirit of the decisions. That is, not only did subsidiary presidents articulate the importance of due process in global strategy making, but their attitudes and behavior were significantly affected

by its perceived presence or absence. And not just any attitudes or behavior, but attitudes and behavior that determine the success or failure of global strategy execution.

A review of some of the most popular global strategic prescriptions makes this point clear. They are as follows: locate each value-added activity in the country that has the least cost for the factor that activity uses most intensely;[4] dexterously shift capital and resources across national markets, cross-subsidizing global units, to knock out global competitors;[5] institutionalize fully standardized product offerings, marketing approaches, and commonly used distribution systems worldwide to allow for maximum global efficiencies;[6] and, as argued recently, consciously consolidate worldwide knowledge, technology, marketing, and production skills to build reservoirs of distinctive core competencies that can act as engines for continuous new business development, innovation, and enhanced customer value.[7]

Each of these global strategic prescriptions is different. There is no one formula for success. Different global competitive and economic dynamics will always dictate different and multiple routes to success. Yet a fundamental thread runs through and unites each of these prescriptions, and that is the underlying condition necessary for the effective execution of each strategy.

Ask about any of these purported global strategies: What does it take to successfully execute it? Time and again the answer involves three underlying requirements: (1) the increasing sacrifice of subsystem for system priorities and considerations;

[4]B. Kogut, "Designing Global Strategies: Comparative and Competitive Value-Added Chains," *Sloan Management Review,* Summer 1985, pp. 15–28; and M.E. Porter, "Competition in Global Industries: A Conceptual Framework," in *Competition in Global Industries,* ed. M.E. Porter (Boston: Harvard Business School Press, 1986).

[5]G. Hamel and C.K. Prahalad, "Do You Really Have a Global Strategy?" *Harvard Business Review,* July–August 1985, pp. 139–148; and W.C. Kim and R.A. Mauborgne, "Becoming an Effective Global Competitor," *The Journal of Business Strategy,* January–February 1988, pp. 33–37.

[6]T. Levitt, "The Globalization of Markets," *Harvard Business Review,* May–June 1983, pp. 92–102; and G.S. Yip, "Global Strategy . . . In a World of Nations?" *Sloan Management Review,* Fall 1989, pp. 29–41.

[7]C.K. Prahalad and G. Hamel, "The Core Competence of the Corporation," *Harvard Business Review,* May–June 1990, pp. 79–91.

(2) swift actions in a globally coordinated manner; and (3) effective and efficient exchange relations among the nodes of the multinational's global network. Which is to say that to implement global strategies, multinationals need subsidiary managers with a sense of commitment, trust, and social harmony. Organizational commitment inspires these managers to identify with the multinational's global objectives and to exert effort, accept responsibility, and exercise initiative on behalf of the overall organization—despite potential "costs" at the subsidiary unit level. Trust is essential to work out mutual wills in the multinational. It inspires subsidiary managers to more readily accept in good faith the intentions, actions, and decisions of the head office instead of second guessing, procrastinating, and opportunistically haggling over each directive. Which is to say that trust is necessary for quick and coordinated global actions. Lastly, social harmony is essential to strengthen the social fabric among members of global units. It encourages efficient and effective exchange relations, which have fast become indispensable to effective global strategy execution.

These salutary attitudes, however, are not in and of themselves sufficient to make global strategies work. Beyond this, multinationals need to ensure that subsidiary managers actually engage in not only compulsory but also voluntary execution of strategic decisions. By compulsory execution, we mean carrying out the directives of global strategic decisions in accordance with the multinational's formally required standards—satisfying, to the letter, the stipulated responsibilities. In contrast, by voluntary execution, we mean exerting effort beyond that which is formally required to execute decisions to the best of one's abilities. Put differently, it is the effort subsidiary top managers exert beyond the call of duty to implement global strategic decisions.[8]

---

[8]For an extensive discussion of these two forms of compliance, both the conceptual distinction between them and their theoretical root, see: C. O'Reilly and J. Chatman, "Organizational Commitment and Psychological Attachment: The Effects of Compliance, Identification, and Internalization on Prosocial Behavior," *Journal of Applied Psychology* 71 (1986): 492–499; and P.M. Blau and W.R. Scott, *Formal Organizations* (San Francisco, California: Chandler Publishing Company, 1962), pp. 140–141.

What all this suggests is that the exercise of due process in global strategic decision making represents a potentially powerful though unexplored route to the implementation of global strategies. Not only do subsidiary top managers emphasize the importance of fairness and impartiality in global strategic decision making, they are so obsessed by the existence or nonexistence of due process that it profoundly affects their attitudes and behavior—attitudes and behavior that are virtually indispensable to making global strategies work. We are talking about commitment, trust, social harmony, and the motivation to execute not only the letter but also the spirit of decisions—that is, to engage in compulsory and voluntary execution of strategic decisions.

But what about other implementation mechanisms? Are traditional implementation mechanisms alone not sufficient for the effective execution of global strategies? If not, how does due process support these traditional mechanisms to make global strategies work?

Traditional Implementation Mechanisms

As mentioned earlier, when we asked subsidiary presidents what motivated them to implement or to defy global strategic decisions, they typically began with a list of well-established administrative mechanisms. Most of them mentioned incentive compensation, monitoring systems, the fist of the head office, and the magnitude and precision of rewards and punishments. But as our discussions progressed, we found subsidiary presidents eager to add that they did not believe these implementation tools alone to be either sufficient or effective. For one thing, they were not particularly motivating. For another, the tools were increasingly easy to dodge and cheat.

Not Motivating?

I am not saying that rewards and punishments and auditing systems are useless in the implementation process. They certainly are useful. If the head office could assess exactly to what extent I followed global strategic decisions and rewarded me based precisely on that behavior, it would be a lie to say that this would not act as an incentive to execute global strategies. It would. It's just that this would not motivate me to do more than is absolutely necessary to satisfy the minimum requirements of global strategic decisions. It wouldn't inspire me to exert energy, exercise initiative, or to take on tasks that I am not directly compensated for in the execution of global strategies.

This comment, made by one executive, is representative of the general opinion of most of the subsidiary presidents we interviewed. Save for a few specific cases, we discovered that a reliance on instrumental approaches produced a utilitarian, contractual attitude toward compliance.[9] Stated succinctly: to the extent that subsidiary top managers judge that the head office can carefully monitor their behavior and will accurately allocate rewards and punishments, managers have an incentive to satisfy the minimum requirements of global strategic decisions. No more, no less. Instrumental approaches have the power to encourage only compulsory execution—execution to the letter, not to the spirit, of the decisions. The trouble, as we have already argued, is that to make global strategies work, subsidiary managers cannot simply "execute this" or "undertake that" in some highly prescribed manner. Their actions must be secured less by rational calculations of individual gain than by kinship obligations. What we are talking about is voluntary execution. An example will bring this to life.

The Case of Global Learning

Global learning—the ability of a multinational to transfer the knowledge and expertise developed in each part of its global network to all other parts worldwide—has fast become an essential strategic asset.[10] For global learning to be actualized, we argue that nothing less than an affirmative attitude toward cooperation will suffice—that is, voluntary execution. One reason for this is that knowledge and expertise are often viewed as power and as such are not easily shared. Another reason is that the major benefits of internal diffusion of know-how accrue to recipients, not transmitters. Of course, were it possible for subsidiary units to "sell" their knowledge and expertise to other subsidiary units, these problems might be overcome. However, this is often and perhaps usually infeasible. As know-how is largely an intangible asset, its value to a "purchasing" unit cannot be known until the purchaser has it, but once the knowledge is disclosed, the purchaser has acquired it without cost.[11] In the absence of economic incentives and with the presence of perceived power disincentives to diffuse knowledge and expertise, it follows that full-blown global learning will not transpire as long as quid pro quo attitudes toward strategy execution prevail. Rather, the hoarding and withholding of knowledge and expertise are far more likely.

Easy to Dodge and Cheat?

Beyond the fact that subsidiary managers do not consider these instrumental approaches to be that motivating is the reality that managers increasingly find these tools easy to dodge and cheat. And if they are easy to dodge and cheat, they are truly ineffective. Basically, the decline in their effectiveness can be explained by the collapse of the three distinctive features of hierarchy in the modern multinational. These three features are: (1) appraisal and control capability; (2) the power of the head office; and (3) common values and expectations.[12] Traditional implementation tools are increasingly easy to dodge as these hierarchical features collapse.[13] Let us take a quick look at the forces leading to the demise of these features.

Collapse of Appraisal and Control Capability

International executives are witnessing a collapse in the multinationals' appraisal and control capability.

---

[9]That a reliance on instrumental approaches to compliance leads to utilitarian contractual attitude toward involvement relations finds strong support in the award-winning article: J. Kerr and J.W. Slocum, "Managing Corporate Culture through Reward Systems," *Academy of Management Executive* 1 (1987): 99–108.

[10]C.A. Bartlett and S. Ghoshal, "Managing across Borders: New Strategic Requirements," *Sloan Management Review,* Summer 1987, pp. 7–16; and S. Ghoshal and C.A. Bartlett, "Creation, Adoption, and Diffusion of Innovations by Subsidiaries of Multinational Corporations," *Journal of International Business Studies,* Fall 1988, pp. 365–388.

[11]K.J. Arrow, "The Organization of Economic Activity," *The Analysis and Evaluation of Public Expenditure: The PPB System* (Joint Economic Committee, Ninety-first Congress, First Session, 1969), pp. 59–73.

[12]For a brilliant discussion on the distinctive powers of hierarchy and internal organization, see: O.E. Williamson, *Markets and Hierarchies: Analysis and Antitrust Implications* (New York: Free Press, 1975).

[13]See the perspicacious article by Hedlund for further support for this argument: G. Hedlund, "The Hypermodern MNC-A Heterarchy?" *Human Resource Management* 25 (1986): pp. 9–25.

Although, in theory, information systems can be designed to meet the complexity of any organization or situation, in reality, they are having a tough time meeting the modern multinational's demands. The predominant reason for this is the rapid increase in horizontal linkages and interdependencies across subsidiary units. As subsidiary units increasingly share resources and work together on single projects to realize global economies of scale and scope, the unique performance and contribution of each subsidiary unit is increasingly difficult to decipher.[14] Distinctions between faulty and meritorious performance are becoming tenuous. Confusion opens the door for shirking, opportunistic behavior and conflict. Moreover, this problem is made even more severe by the escalating size of most multinationals. The corporate center is limited in its ability to make accurate evaluations of each subsidiary unit.

Eroding Power of the Head Office No longer do centrally directed orders elicit easy obedience from subsidiary units. One reason for the erosion in the head office's hierarchical power is subsidiary units' increasing size and resource parity. Subsidiaries are less reliant on the head office, and the head office is more dependent on subsidiary units. To the extent that dependence decreases power, the corporate center and overseas units are converging in power.[15] This situation is aggravated further by the mounting intensity of direct subsidiary-to-subsidiary linkages, which lessens the head office's centrality.[16]

Decline in Common Values and Expectations As subsidiary units have increasingly accumulated distinct resources and capabilities in response to their different task environments, they have developed values and behavioral norms distinct from those in the home office.[17] On top of this, the nontrivial physical and psychic distances increasingly separating overseas units from corporate centers fuel even further the emergence of subcultures and countercultures within the modern multinational. The result is more antagonistic relations between head office and subsidiary top management teams and a natural inclination on the part of subsidiary managers to pursue subsidiary-level objectives.[18]

The upshot of all this is that the distinctive features of hierarchy in the multinational used to support traditional implementation mechanisms are increasingly collapsing. As shown in Figure 2, the emergence of a monitoring problem, the intensification of sub- and countercultures, and mounting control loss increasingly plague the multinational, making its traditional implementation tools less and less effective.

How Does Due Process Support Traditional Implementation Mechanisms? Although traditional implementation tools have become on the whole less effective, the extent to which this is true appears to be contingent in part on whether due process is exercised. Recall for a moment the due process characteristics. Two-way communication, the ability to refute the head office's viewpoints, and an accounting for final strategic decisions all foster open interaction and intensive information exchange between head office and subsidiary top managers. This open interaction almost forces the head office to keep rewards, punishments, and appraisal and control systems aligned with strategic decisions. An example will make this point clear.

One subsidiary president we interviewed had been requested to institute an aggressive price-reductions policy in his local market. The strategic aim was to counter an assertive price attack launched by global competitor in his company's home market. The subsidiary president understood that the

---

[14]For an extensive discussion on the ways in which interdependencies and joint efforts confound accountability and create monitoring difficulties, see: G.R. Jones and C.W.L. Hill, "Transaction Cost Analysis of Strategy-Structure Choice," *Strategic Management Journal* 9 (1988): 159–172.

[15]For an excellent discussion on the inverse relationship between power and dependence, see, for example: R.M. Emerson, "Power-Dependence Relations," *American Sociological Review* 27 (1962): 31–41.

[16]For a discussion on the ways in which centrality affects power relations, see: L.C. Freeman, "Centrality in Social Networks: Conceptual Clarification," *Social Networks* 2 (1979): 215–239.

[17]That business units or divisions accumulation of distinct capabilities and tasks reinforces distinct values and behavioral norms was empirically validated. See: P.R. Lawrence and J.W. Lorsch. *Organization and Environment* (Boston: Harvard University Press, 1967).

[18]See Hedlund (1986) for further elaboration of this point.

Figure 2   The Collapse of Hierarchy in the Modern Multinational Corporation

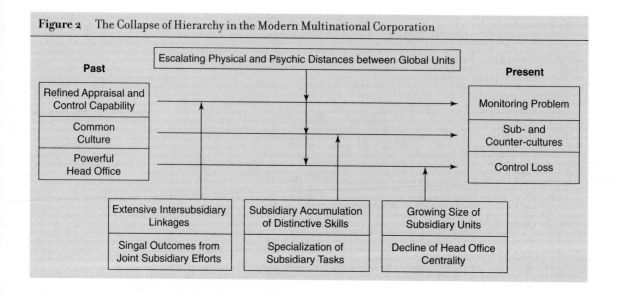

execution of such a policy would benefit the overall organization—it would drain the resources of the global competitor's profit sanctuary, its home market. He also knew, however, that the policy would likely result in negative financial performance by his local operation.

The open interaction between him and the head office allowed him to address his concern directly. He stated that he understood why it was necessary for his unit to institute such a policy and that he would accept such a global strategic mission. But he argued that the execution of this mission would invalidate a sole reliance on "stand-alone" financial criteria for assessing his subsidiary unit's performance. He proposed having his unit's performance evaluated also by the strategic contribution it made to the overall organization. The head office managers and subsidiary president were able to develop a mutually acceptable set of performance evaluation criteria for his unit. In this way, the exercise of due process spurs the head office to keep traditional implementation tools aligned with strategic decisions.

Lessons from Our Field Observations

We can draw two overriding lessons from our field observations. The first is that the multinational increasingly faces a dilemma in executing its global strategies. On the one hand, the effective implementation of global strategies requires a sense of community and cooperation among all the nodes of the multinational's global network. On the other hand, multinationals are experiencing a loss in hierarchical control and an increasing independence of subsidiary units, which creates an environment of calculative, utilitarian, and frictional interunit relations. This is not particularly conducive to efficient and effective exchange. In the face of this *multinational dilemma,* we need more than traditional implementation mechanisms to make global strategies work.

The second lesson is that the exercise of due process in global strategy making seems to be a powerful, yet unexplored, way to overcome the multinational dilemma and make global strategies work. This is traceable to two sources. The first is that due process helps to overcome the exchange difficulties in the multinational by inspiring a sense of commitment, trust, and social harmony among subsidiary top managers. The second is that, beyond these salutary attitudes, the exercise of due process inspires subsidiary top managers to more readily execute strategic decisions to not only the letter but also the spirit with which they were set forth.

▩ The Tangible Effect of Due Process

At the end of our interviews, we presented our findings to the subsidiary presidents' head office managers. These head office managers found our results fascinating and provocative. They were intrigued by our proposition that instrumental calculations of gains and losses were not the dominant driver behind subsidiary managers' actions and found it particularly interesting that subsidiary managers had placed so much emphasis on the importance of due process in global strategy making. According to these executives, it was a challenging proposition that the presence or absence of due process had the power to influence not only the important attitudes of commitment, trust, and social harmony but also subsidiary managers' actual execution of resulting decisions.

Nonetheless, despite the executives' overall excitement with our findings, underneath this ran a current of hesitation. To quote one executive:

> Your findings are provocative. But to institute due process in global strategy making is a time-consuming, difficult task. Before I start to embark on such an attempt, I would like to have more evidence of the tangible benefits of due process than just the observations made and insights gained from your field research.

This hesitation was valid. It challenged us to go beyond our field work and empirically test our propositions. This meant conducting an extensive mail survey to develop a bigger database that could test the validity of our field observations. In short, we set out to examine whether due process exercised a positive overall effect not only on the commitment, trust, and social harmony of subsidiary top managers but also on compulsory and voluntary execution. We also set out to test whether these effects were significantly stronger or particularly potent in those subsidiary managers who received unfavorable strategic decision outcomes vis-à-vis those who received favorable outcomes. Appendix B presents a profile of our sample population, the measurements used to estimate each variable, and the type of analyses we employed.

The Results   The results of our regression analyses confirmed our observation that due process in global strategy making is indeed positively related to subsidiary managers' sense of organizational commitment, trust in head office management, and social harmony between them and the head office. All slope coefficients proved to be statistically significantly ($p < .01$),[19] which is to say that the more subsidiary managers believe that due process is exercised in the global strategy-making process, the more positive attitudes they have toward head office management and the organization as a whole.

Beyond this, we also found a positive relationship between due process and compulsory and voluntary execution. All slope coefficients again proved to be statistically significant ($p < .01$). This provides evidence that the exercise of due process does more than inspire positive attitudes. It also triggers subsidiary managers to "go the extra mile" and carry out the spirit of global strategic decisions.

More interesting from an implementation perspective, however, are the results of another analysis. We wanted to see the effect of due process when subsidiary managers judged strategic decisions to be favorable or unfavorable for their unit. By strategic decisions we mean the strategic roles, resources, and responsibilities received by subsidiary units as a result of the last annual global strategy-making process.

During the course of our interviews, one of the most fascinating things we observed was that the effect of due process on subsidiary managers' attitudes and behavior was particularly strong precisely in those individuals who received decision outcomes viewed as unfavorable. Put differently, due process provided an especially strong "cushion of support" that mitigated the negative ramifications of

---

▌ [19] That the exercise of due process or, as it is often referred to, procedural justice, has the power to effectuate the higher-order attitudes of commitment, trust, and social harmony finds theoretical and empirical support in other settings. See, for example: S. Alexander and M. Ruderman, "The Role of Procedural and Distributive Justice in Organizational Behavior," *Social Psychology Research* 1 (1987): 177–198; and R. Folger and M. Konovsky, "Effects of Procedural and Distributive Justice on Reactions to Pay Raise Decision," *Academy of Management Journal* 32 (1989): 115–130; and E.A. Lind and T.R. Tyler, *The Psychology of Procedural Justice* (New York: Plenum, 1988).

Figure 3a   Due Process and Organizational Commitment

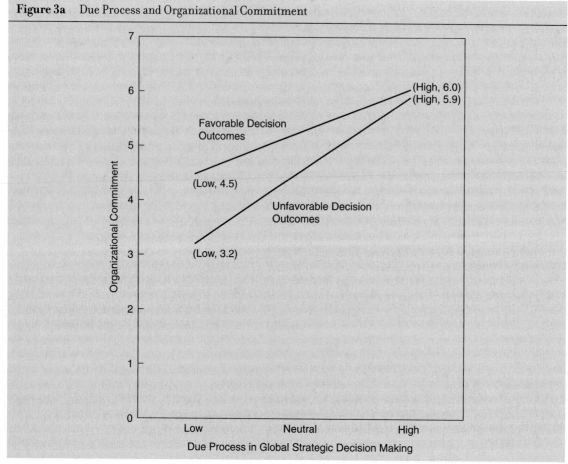

unfavorable decisions by significantly inflating positive attitudes and behavior within recipients of unfavorable outcomes.[20] Figures 3a through 3c show the average commitment, trust, and social harmony scores for subsidiary top managers receiving favorable versus unfavorable strategic decision outcomes. As the figures consistently reveal, when decision outcomes were viewed as unfavorable, the exercise of due process did much to check discontent and to

give "loser" subsidiary managers powerful reasons to stay committed to their organization (in Figure 3a, the mean commitment score increases from 3.2 to 5.9; $p < .01$), to have trust in head office management (in Figure 3b, the mean trust score increases from 2.0 to 5.3; $p < .01$), and to cultivate an atmosphere of social harmony between them and the head office (in Figure 3c, the mean social harmony score increases from 2.3 to 4.7; $p < .01$). On the other hand, when outcomes were viewed as favorable, the due process effect, although undeniably present, was not as potent as with unfavorable outcomes. In particular, as due process heightened, the mean score for commitment increased from 4.5 to 6.0 ($p < .01$), that for trust from 4.4 to 5.6 ($p < .05$), and that for

---

[20]This "cushion of support" effect not only finds support in the existing procedural justice literature but is recognized to be one of the most important effects of procedural justice or due process. See, for example: Lind and Tyler (1988); and T.R. Tyler, *Why People Obey the Law: Procedural Justice, Legitimacy, and Compliance* (New Haven, Connecticut: Yale University Press, 1990).

Figure 3b   Due Process and Trust in Head Office Management

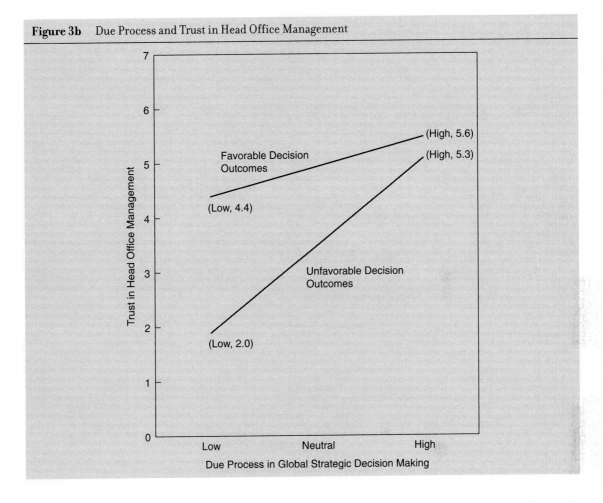

social harmony from 3.5 to 4.8 (p < .05). For all three salutary attitudes, the slope coefficient differential between the favorable outcome and the unfavorable outcome group also proved to be statistically significant (p < .01).[21]

[21]We examined and confirmed the statistical difference in the due process effect between the favorable outcome and the unfavorable outcome group for organizational commitment, trust in head office management, and social harmony. This was done using what econometricians call the Chow test, which is able to examine the statistical significance in slope differentials between the groups. In our case, test statistics of F values for all three salutary attitudes were significant at the 1 percent level and hence indicated to reject the null hypotheses that no slope coefficient difference exists between the favorable outcome and the unfavorable outcome group. For a detailed discussion on the Chow test, see: G.C. Chow, "Tests of Equality between Subsets of Coefficients in Two Linear Regression," *Econometrica* (1960): 591–605.

Figures 4a and 4b present the average compulsory and voluntary execution scores for subsidiary top managers receiving favorable versus unfavorable strategic decision outcomes. As Figure 4a reveals, the use of due process in global strategic decision making indeed appears to boost compulsory execution in managers who receive unfavorable decision outcomes to a greater extent than in those who received favorable outcomes. Specifically, when decision outcomes were judged unfavorable, the exercise of due process did much to motivate subsidiary managers to perform the strategic roles and responsibilities assigned to their unit in accordance with the organization's formal requirements (mean compulsory execution score increased from

Figure 3c   Due Process and Social Harmony

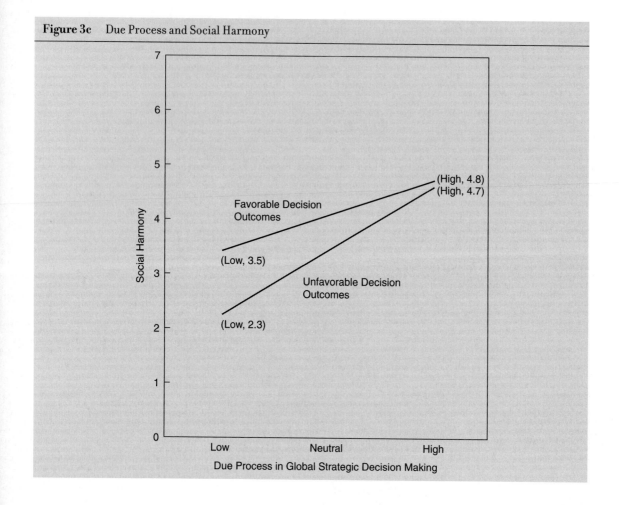

3.8 to 5.7; p < .01). On the other hand, when outcomes were viewed as favorable, the due process effect on compulsory execution, although undeniably present, was not as potent (mean score increased from 5.2 to 6.2; p < .05). The slope coefficient differential between the favorable outcome and the unfavorable outcome group proved to be statistically significant (p < .05).[22]

The same cannot be said, however, for voluntary execution. On the one hand, the voluntary execution of all subsidiary top managers significantly escalates as due process increases (in Figure 4b, mean voluntary execution score increases from 2.4 to 5.2 for recipients of unfavorable outcomes and from 2.9 to 5.5 for recipients of favorable outcomes; both significant at p < .01). On the other hand, the effect of due process on voluntary execution does not vary whether the decision outcomes are favorable or not. For voluntary execution, the slope coefficient differential between the favorable outcome and the unfavorable outcome group proved to be statistically not significant

---

[22] The F value for compulsory execution was significant at the 5 percent level and hence indicated to reject the null hypothesis that no slope coefficient difference exists between the favorable outcome and the unfavorable outcome group. Ibid.

Figure 4.a   Due Process and Compulsory Execution

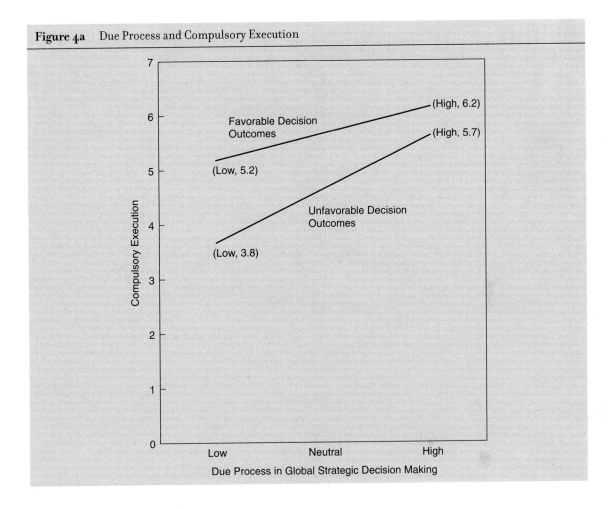

(p > .10).[23] These findings indicate that although decision outcomes do not seem to affect subsidiary managers' voluntary execution, the exercise of due process does inspire these managers to go beyond the call of duty to implement strategic decisions. This is further supported by our regression result that decision outcomes had no relationship with voluntary execution; the regression coefficient for this relationship was not statistically significant (p > .10).

In summary, except in the case of voluntary execution, with a low level of due process, there is a big gap between the attitudes and behavior of subsidiary top managers with favorable and unfavorable decision outcomes.[24] As expected, with a low level of due process, subsidiary managers with unfavorable decision outcomes were generally dissatisfied with the head office and the overall organization and consequently felt a low level of commitment, trust, and social harmony. Not surprisingly, these same managers were not highly

[23] The F value for voluntary execution was not significant (p > .10) and hence indicated not to reject the null hypothesis that no slope coefficient difference exists between the favorable outcome and the unfavorable outcome group. Ibid.

[24] Variance analysis was employed to assess the statistical significance in the mean difference between the groups.

Figure 4.b   Due Process and Voluntary Execution

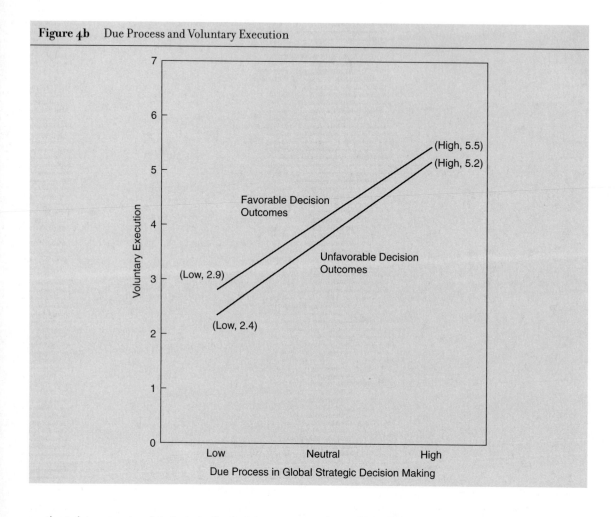

motivated to execute global strategic decisions to the letter or spirit with which they were set forth.

However, with a high level of due process, the picture was different. There was little gap between those managers who had received favorable and unfavorable decision outcomes in their reported scores of commitment, trust, and social harmony and compulsory and voluntary execution; all these gaps proved to be statistically not significant (p > .10). Hence, the gap was significantly reduced as due process heightened. Which is to say that the power of due process is strong enough to overcome the negative ramifications of unfavorable outcomes and even inspires in those subsidiary top managers

the positive disposition necessary for global strategy execution. Moreover, whether managers received favorable or unfavorable outcomes, their degree of commitment, trust, and social harmony and compulsory and voluntary execution was much higher when due process was exercised in global strategy making than when it was not. Hence, our empirical tests strongly support our field observations.

Conclusion

How can multinationals make global strategies work? The results of this research suggest that the answer resides in the quality of the global strategy-making process itself. When deciding whether or not or to what extent to carry out global strategic decisions, subsidiary top managers accord great importance to the way in which global strategies are generated. Their overriding concern: Is due process exercised in the global strategy-making process?

In the presence of due process, subsidiary managers are motivated to implement global strategies. They feel a strong sense of organizational commitment, trust in head office management, and social harmony with their head office counterparts. These attitudes are not only important, they are the fundamental requirements for making global strategies work. Further, the exercise of due process translates directly into a high level of compulsory and voluntary execution, which is to say that due process motivates managers not only to fulfill corporate standards but also to exert voluntary effort to implement strategic decisions to the best of their ability. The power of due process in this regard is more remarkable when we consider our finding that voluntary execution was induced only by due process and not by the instrumental value of decision outcomes. In the absence of due process, the effect is just the reverse. Subsidiary top managers are frustrated with the head office, the overall organization, and the resulting global strategic decisions. This diminishes fast their willingness to execute global strategies.

But beyond this, what makes due process particularly significant for global strategy execution is that its effect on salutary attitudes and implementation behavior is especially strong in managers who receive unfavorable decision outcomes. This is one of the most critical tasks for global strategy execution. After all, it is precisely those managers who are inclined to subvert, undermine, and even sabotage global strategic decisions. This is a significant issue because the intensity of global competition and the requirements of winning global strategies require an increasing number of decisions that are perceived as unfavorable.

Examples Abound There are many examples of unfavorable decisions. In one multinational we studied, subsidiary units were recently asked to forgo their national products in favor of global core products that many units considered to be either overstandardized or overpriced for their national markets. In another multinational, the U.S. subsidiary was required to transfer a large portion of its export sales to its sister European subsidiaries. Although this substitution substantially increased capacity utilization rates in Europe and decreased the losses suffered from overcapacity there, as one U.S. executive put it, "The transfer was nothing but a loss for us." And so the list goes, endlessly on. To cite one executive:

> Our modern enterprises live in a world of global competition. The key to win here is to think globally and fully leverage our globally dispersed resources, skills, and knowledge. It is important to maximize our efficiency at the global level. To achieve this, it is unavoidable that an increasing number of subsidiaries will end up receiving unfavorable decision outcomes from their individual standpoints. No doubt, these subsidiary units will be more inclined to foot-drag and exert counterefforts than to execute global strategies. The question is then, how can we turn around these negative attitudes and inspire subsidiary units to follow and implement a global approach?

To make global strategies work, head office executives need to pay greater attention to the way they generate global strategic decisions. Although the exercise of due process by itself does not make difficult head office–subsidiary issues vanish, it does motivate subsidiary managers to accept and implement global strategies. The image of the subsidiary manager that emerges here stands in marked contrast with that of the organization man who is driven overridingly by concerns of instrumental and economic maximization. It seems that subsidiary managers are both sensitive and responsive to issues of fairness in decision-making processes. Given that both our field observations and our empirical study consistently support the importance of due process, maybe it is time that companies seriously reflect on just what they have been doing to motivate their subsidiary top managers to implement global strategies. They need to pay more heed to the importance of due process in global strategy making.

Appendix A

How did we conduct our field research? We solicited the participation of twenty-five multinationals by means of direct and indirect personal contacts with head office senior executives. Nineteen of these multinationals agreed to support this research, and they gave us the names of the subsidiary presidents heading their ten largest subsidiary operations in terms of annual sales. The dominant industries of these nineteen multinationals were: computers (five firms), packaged foods (four), electrical products (four), pharmaceuticals (three), automobiles (one), paper and wood products (one), and textiles (one).

We were able to successfully contact, via telephone, 141 of the subsidiary presidents. We guaranteed that all comments would be held strictly confidential and used solely for scientific research and that their head office managers would not be informed as to which subsidiary presidents ultimately participated in our study. Sixty-three of these subsidiary presidents were willing to participate. The remaining subsidiary presidents declined, most frequently because of a lack of time. We then held extensive interviews.

Appendix B

Sample Population We distributed the mail questionnaire to 195 subsidiary top managers. This pool comprised the 63 subsidiary presidents who participated in our field research and 132 other subsidiary top managers who directly participated in the last annual global strategic decision-making process between the head office and their national unit. The latter were also members of our nineteen original participation multinationals; their names were supplied by the 63 subsidiary presidents.[25] The titles of the subsidiary top managers ranged from president to executive vice president to director. These executives were considered to represent the key catalysts for global strategy execution in their national units.

We distributed the questionnaire within six weeks of the completion of the last annual global strategic decision-making process of our nineteen participating multinationals. Of the 195 questionnaires distributed, 142 were returned to the researchers. The questionnaire assessed the extent of due process in the last strategy-making process, subsidiary top managers' attitudes of organizational commitment, trust, and social harmony, and the perceived favorability of strategic decision outcomes.

Ten months later, just before the start of another annual global strategic decision-making process, we distributed a second questionnaire to the 142 managers who responded to our first-round questionnaire. In this one, we assessed subsidiary top managers' compulsory and voluntary execution of the global strategic decisions resulting from the preceding annual strategy-making process. Of these, 119 questionnaires were returned to the researchers and used in our analysis of the relationship between due process and compulsory and voluntary execution.[26]

Measurements

Due Process   To assess whether or to what extent due process was exercised in global strategic decision making, we used a five-item measure in our survey questionnaire.[27] This involved having subsidiary top managers evaluate on a seven-point Likert-type scale each of the five identified aspects of due process, in short: (1) the extent to which the head office is knowledgeable of the subsidiary unit's local situation; (2) the extent to which two-way communication exists in the process; (3) the extent to which the head office is fairly consistent in making global strategic decisions across subsidiary units; (4) the extent to which subsidiary top managers can legitimately challenge the strategic views

---

[25]For an extensive discussion on the design and administration of our mail questionnaire, see: Kim and Mauborgne (1991 and 1993a).

[26]For an extensive discussion on the design and administration of the second-wave questionnaire of our longitudinal study on subsidiary top managers' strategy execution, see: W.C. Kim and R.A. Mauborgne, "Procedural Justice, Attitudes, and Subsidiary Top Management Compliance with Multinationals' Corporate Strategic Decisions," *Academy of Management Journal,* forthcoming, June 1993b.

[27]Kim and Mauborgne (1991 and 1993a).

and decisions of the head office; and (5) the extent to which subsidiary top managers receive a full explanation for global strategic decisions.[28] The Cronbach's coefficient alpha for this five-item scale was .86.[29]

Organizational Commitment Nine items were used to assess the top managers' organizational commitment.[30] Sample items include, "I am willing to put in a great deal of effort beyond that normally expected in order to help this organization be successful," and "This organization really inspires the very best in me in the way of job performance." All items were assessed on a seven-point scale with anchors labeled (1) strongly disagree and (7) strongly agree. The Cronbach's coefficient alpha for this nine-item scale was .91.

Trust in Head Office Management To measure the trust subsidiary top managers have in the head office, we used four questions.[31] These are:

1. How much confidence and trust do you have in head office management?
2. Head office management at times must make decisions that seem to be against the interests of your unit. When this happens, how much trust do you have that your unit's current sacrifice will

be justified by the head office's future support for your unit?
3. How willing are you to accept and follow those strategic decisions made by head office management?
4. How free do you feel to discuss with head office management the problems and difficulties faced by your unit without fear of jeopardizing your position or having your comment "held against" you later on?

Again, all four items were measured on seven-point scales. The Cronbach's coefficient alpha for this four-item scale was 94.

Social Harmony A four-item measure assessed the perceived social harmony between head office and subsidiary top managers.[32] The managers were asked to think of their relations with head office management when answering the following items: (1) how well they help each other out; (2) how well they get along with one another; (3) how well they stick together; and (4) the extent to which conflict characterizes their relations. These items were measured on seven-point scales with the fourth item reversely scored. The Cronbach's coefficient alpha for this four-item scale was .87.

Strategic Decision Outcome Favorability Four items assessed the perceived favorability of global strategic decisions received by subsidiary units as a result of the last annual global strategic decision-making process.[33] Subsidiary top managers were asked to assess the extent to which the global strategic roles, responsibilities, and resources allocated to their unit: (1) reflected their unit's individual performance achieved; (2) mirrored their unit's relative contribution to the overall organization;

---

[28] We averaged the scores for these multiple items to estimate our due process measure. The same procedure was used for all of our other multi-item measures: organizational commitment, trust, social harmony, and strategic decision outcome favorability. For a detailed discussion on why this simple averaging approach yields an unbiased estimate, see: H.M. Blalock, "Multiple Indicators and the Causal Approach to Measurement Error," *American Journal of Sociology* 75 (1969): 264–272.

[29] The Cronbach's coefficient alpha indicates the internal consistency reliability of a scale. Generally, a multi-item scale can be judged to be reliable when the value of its Cronbach alpha exceeds 0.70. Notice here that besides our due process measure, all of our other multi-item scales can be said to be reliable. For a detailed discussion on a measure's reliability, see: J. Nunnally, *Psychometric Methods* (New York: McGraw-Hill, 1978).

[30] The nine-item measure used to assess organizational commitment was developed by: R.T. Mowday, R.M. Steers, and L.W. Porter, "The Measurement of Organizational Commitment," *Journal of Vocational Behavior* 14 (1979): 224–247.

[31] The items used to measure trust were drawn from the interpersonal trust measures of: W.H. Read, "Upward Communication in Industrial Hierarchies," *Human Relations* 15 (1962): 3–15; and R. Likert, *The Human Organization* (New York: McGraw-Hill, 1967).

[32] The indicators used to measure social harmony were drawn from the cohesiveness index developed by: S.E. Seashore, *Group Cohesiveness in the Industrial Work Group* (Ann Arbor: University of Michigan Press, 1954); and C. Cammann, M. Fichman, G. Douglas, and J.R. Klesh, "Assessing Attitudes and Perceptions of Organizational Members," in *Assessing Organizational Change,* eds. S.E. Seashore, E.E. Lawler, P.H. Mirvis, and C. Cammann (New York: John Wiley & Sons, 1983).

[33] The four-item measure used to assess strategic decision outcome favorability was originally developed by: Kim and Mauborgne (1991).

(3) exceeded their unit's expectations; and (4) were absolutely favorable. All four items were measured on seven-point scales. The Cronbach's coefficient alpha for this four-item scale was .83.

Compulsory Execution   To assess the extent to which each subsidiary top manager carried out global strategic decisions in accordance with their formally required corporate standards, two questions were posed. First, for each of eight major activities (marketing and sales, research and development, manufacturing, purchasing, cost-reduction programs, general cash-flow utilization, human resource management, and other administrative activities), subsidiary top managers were asked to respond on a seven-point (1 = not at all, 7 = completely) scale to the following question: "Please try to recall as accurately as possible your overall behavior and actions taken since the preceding annual global strategic-decision process between the head office and your national unit. Then for each of the eight outlined activities indicate the extent to which you executed these decisions in accordance with your organization's required standards. Note that you should not include in this assessment any efforts that may have been extended beyond your organization's required standards in order to achieve optimum performance in these activities." Organization was defined here as the multinational.

For each of these eight activities, we then had subsidiary top management rate on a five-point scale, ranging from "1 = not important" to "5 = extremely important," the degree of importance of each of these activities to the successful fulfillment of their overall job requirements. This assessment is important because although each of our respondents was a top manager with overarching responsibilities for and involvement in overall subsidiary unit operations across these activities, many reported having full responsibility for some activities but having only limited responsibility in the sense of giving final approval in other activities. Accordingly, to assess the extent of each manager's compulsory execution, these importance ratings were used as weights to reflect each activity's relative

contribution or importance to the fulfillment of each manager's overall job requirements. Using these weights, we then obtained each manager's weighted-average compulsory execution score. Specifically, for each manager, we first multiplied the manager's compulsory execution score on each of the eight activities by his or her corresponding importance ratings and then added these weighted execution scores. Finally, we divided this added figure back by the sum of these importance ratings to arrive at each manager's weighted-average compulsory execution score.[34]

Voluntary Execution   To assess the extent to which subsidiary top managers exerted voluntary effort to carry out global strategic decisions to the best of their abilities, we used a similar approach to that used in our assessment of compulsory execution. First, for each of the eight major activities, the managers were asked to respond on a seven-point scale (1 = not at all, 7 = greatly) to the following question: "Please try to recall as accurately as possible your overall behavior and actions taken since the preceding annual global strategic decision process between the head office and your national unit. Then for each of the eight outlined activities indicate the extent to which you voluntarily exerted effort beyond the formally required standards of your organization to execute global strategic decisions to the best of your abilities. Rephrased, to what extent did you willingly exert energy, exercise initiative, and devote your effort beyond that which is formally required to achieve optimum performance in your execution of global strategic decisions in each of these activities?"

Using the same question on dimensional importance described above for compulsory execution to

---

[34]The use of a multidimensional approach with criterion weights to measure both compulsory and voluntary execution is in line with Steer's advice and seemed particularly appropriate for taking into account subsidiary top managers' different levels of involvement in carrying out these activities and hence their different levels of contribution to the execution of these activities in accordance with their formal job requirements. See: R.M. Steers, "Problems in the Measurement of Organizational Effectiveness," *Administrative Science Quarterly* 20 (1975): 546–558.

obtain weights, we derived a weighted-average measure of each manager's voluntary execution of global strategic decisions. The process used to derive this weighted-average measure of voluntary execution mirrors that used to arrive at our weighted-average measure of compulsory execution.[35]

Analyses   We used two tests to establish the effect of due process on the managers' attitudes and behavior. First, we performed regression analyses to see whether due process positively correlated with the managers' attitudes of organizational commitment, trust in head office management, and social harmony between them and head office management and whether due process was also related to the managers' compulsory and voluntary execution of the resulting decisions.

Second, we tested whether due process produces a "cushion of support" that enhances salutary attitudes and execution to a greater extent in those managers who received unfavorable decision outcomes than those who received favorable outcomes. To perform this test, we first divided respondents into two groups based on the perceived favorability or unfavorability of strategic decision outcomes

received in the last annual strategy-making process. Those managers with outcome favorability scores above the sample mean were classified as recipients of favorable strategic-decision outcomes; those below the sample mean were classified as recipients of unfavorable outcomes. We then further split our respondents based on the perceived degree of due process exercised. Respondents with due process scores above the sample mean were treated as experiencing a high level of due process, whereas those having due process scores below the sample mean were treated as experiencing a low level of due process. Finally, we calculated and compared the mean levels of reported organizational commitment, trust in head office management, social harmony, and compulsory and voluntary execution for each of our four groups: the high outcome favorability–high due process group; the high outcome favorability–low due process group; the low outcome favorability–high due process group; and the low outcome favorability–low due process group. As is described in the article, we used variance analysis and the slope coefficient differential test to test differences between these four groups. We observed no evidence for systematic differences in contextual variables such as industry type and subsidiary size across these four groups.

[35]Ibid.

Reading 4-3   Can Selling Be Globalized? The Pitfalls of Global Account Management

David Arnold, Julian Birkinshaw, Omar Toulan

To international companies, there is something both inevitable and desirable about the trend towards global account management, the establishment of structures and processes to service major

By David Arnold, Harvard Business School; Julian Birkinshaw, London Business School; Omar Toulan, McGill University. *California Management Review* 44, no. 1 (2001).

customers on a global basis. Inevitable because major business customers are generally well down the road to globalization, especially in their procurement and operations functions, and so increasingly demand from their major suppliers worldwide contracts with standardized terms in areas such as product specification, price and service standards. Desirable because the institution of global customer management is in line with trends like customer relationship management and building customer-centric organizations, ideas which currently hold much sway with top executives and may well be he subject of ongoing initiatives within the company.

But vendor companies should think carefully before jumping on the global customer bandwagon. These relationships can turn out very differently from expectations, and in many cases vendors are finding that unanticipated costs outweigh the benefits. Over the last two years we have conducted field research into global account management in Europe and North America, from the vendor's perspective, and in over half the corporations we found management struggling to figure out how to make this sys-

tem work. In many cases, the major change resulting from categorizing a customer as a global account was increasing downward pressure on prices, because consolidated sales triggered requests for greater volume discounts, and because the reliance of the vendor on the account became more salient. In addition, we found that many vendor companies were paying increased sales commission, since now both global account teams and local sales teams were involved in sales. And top sales executives were having to accept lower standards of account management than they knew from national account times—not one of the companies we researched, for example, had developed a system for measuring account profitability on a global scale. The box, "Implementing Global Account Management: Two

Implementing Global Account Management: Two Cautionary Tales

Whitegoods Corporation is a European manufacturing company which designated a number of global account managers in response to the centralized purchasing demands of major retail customers. These individuals negotiated the whole package with their customers—product specifications, prices, even local installation and service agreements. Unfortunately, Whitegoods sales organization was still managed on a country-by-country basis. Local sales people prioritized the higher-margin business they got through local customers. Some disregarded the frame agreement altogether, with the result that global account managers found themselves "policing" the deal. And in a few countries, local sales managers were not even informed about the global accounts and only found out about them via their customers. The result: delays and disagreements on local installation and a soured relationship between national sales managers and global account managers. Prices were squeezed down as a result of the global agreement, but the projected sales volume increases did not materialize.

Computer Corporation, a US-based manufacturer, had negotiated a similar agreement with a major global account in the financial services sector. The German subsidiary of that customer approached Computer Corp.'s German subsidiary for quotes on a major order for 500 workstations, required as the firm switched its European headquarters from London to Frankfurt. It wanted a price below the minimum specified in the global agreement, arguing that extra volume discounts were appropriate since the order was large, non-recurring, and all intended for local German offices. Computer Corp.'s German subsidiary, a profit center, with much to gain from accepting the order in what was proving a difficult recessionary year in Germany, eventually succumbed to the temptation and accepted the order. It proved to be less substantive than promised, with only 100 units being purchased, a good number of which it suspected were re-exported to Eastern Europe. The global agreement, meanwhile, had fallen apart as other subsidiaries of the customer got word of the lower price obtained in Germany.

Cautionary Tales" provides detailed examples from two of the companies involved in the research.

This paper reports on a two-year research project in which we looked at the approaches taken by sixteen large companies in developing global account management structures.[1] In the following section we describe the research approach, and provide an overview of the statistical findings from the study. In the latter sections we describe the key insights that emerged around two issues—strategy and implementation. These, we argue, are the key areas where international companies need to make some tough decisions <u>before</u> entering global account relationships. Companies need to be aware of the pitfalls, and set themselves clear criteria against which relationships are examined before commitments are made. If these steps are taken, then the rewards of global relationships with customers can be substantial. If not, the relationship can become imbalanced, and in these cases it is almost always the buyer who benefits at the expense of the vendor.

Overview of the Research

Our research was conducted in two stages. Stage one involved face-to-face interviews with 35 managers in 10 companies—typically a mixture of global account managers, national sales managers, and executives responsible for overseeing global account organisations. In stage two we administered questionnaires to the same three groups of people in 16 companies, resulting in 107 completed questionnaires from global account managers, 55 from na-

tional sales managers, and 10 from executives responsible for overseeing the global account organization in their company. Taken together, these multiple sources of data provided us with a fairly complete picture of the strategic and operational issues associated with global account management. And in particular, by getting the perspectives of national sales managers we were able to compare global accounts with non-global accounts.[2]

It is worth providing a quick overview of the statistical findings from the questionnaires. Focusing first on the global account managers, the basic story that emerged was that sales to their global account had grown strongly (average 10–15% per year), but that the average price of goods sold to that account had gone down slightly. Table 1 provides a complete breakdown of these numbers. In terms of how the accounts were organized, the typical model was that certain key decisions, including pricing, became the primary responsibility of the global account manager, but most local sales and service activity continued to be done at the local level (again, see Table 1). Obviously this split created some tension, as we shall see later.

We also surveyed 55 national sales managers, who are the individuals ultimately responsible for all sales in their national market, including those that go through global accounts. They were divided into three groups, according to the importance of global accounts in their national market. The first group had less than 20% of their sales made through global accounts, so we designated them as "Non-Global." The second group had between 20% and 50% of their sales made through global

[1] For further reading on global account management and the antecedent literature on key account management see McDonald, M., T. Millman & B. Rogers (1997), Key Account Management: Theory, Practice and Challenges, *Journal of Marketing Management,* 13, 737–757; Napolitano, L. (1998), Global Account Management: The New Frontier. *NAMA Journal* 34, 3 (Summer); Weilbaker, D.C., & W.A. Weeks (1997) The Evolution of National Account Management: A Literature Perspective, *Journal of Personal Selling & Sales Management* XVII, 4 (Fall); Yip, G. & T. Madsen (1996), Global Account Management: The New Frontier in Relationship Marketing, *International Marketing Review* 13(3), 24–42; Birkinshaw, J.M., O. Toulan and D. Arnold (2001), Global Account Management in Multinational Corporations, theory and evidence, *Journal of International Business Studies* (forthcoming) and the special issue of *Thexis,* 1999 (4).

[2] There is a methodological issue here, which is worth clarifying. Ideally one would seek to understand the impact of global account management structures on the vendor by comparing a sample of "global accounts" with a matched sample of "non-global accounts." In practice, however, this is almost impossible to do. By definition global accounts are created because they meet certain criteria in terms of importance or size that makes their comparison with non-global accounts highly suspect. And our attempts to study companies that had not introduced global account structures proved to be fruitless because there was no-one responsible for the international customers in question, and they did not perceive the issue as important. Instead, we decided to undertake the comparison of global and non-global accounts by asking national sales managers, because they typically had to deal with some combination of the two.

Table 1   Characteristics of Global Accounts, Opinions of Global Account Managers

Question	Possible Responses	Number
How fast have sales to this global customer grown during the past 3 years?	0% per year or less	6
	5% per year	26
	10% per year	24
	15% per year	18
	20% per year	11
	>20% per year	18
What is the average price of goods sold to your global customer, relative to 3 years ago?	Much lower	27
	Slightly lower	21
	No change	25
	Slightly higher	27
	Much higher	4
Who is responsible for pricing decisions relating to the global account?	Primarily country sales manager	10
	Country sales manager and GAM jointly	66
	Primarily GAM	30
To what extent are sales and support in your company . . .	Coordinated globally	4
	Partially globally coordinated	21
	Done locally, some central coordination	51
	Done exclusively on a local basis	28

accounts so we called them "Mixed." The final group we called "Global" because over 50% of their sales were made through global accounts. There were similar numbers of respondents in each group.

Comparing these three groups on the same dimensions as above, some interesting patterns emerged (see Table 2). Sales growth was similar in all three, typically around 15% per year. But in terms of the price of goods sold, the Global group experienced "much lower" or "slightly lower" prices, whereas the Non-Global group indicated "no change" in prices. In other words, the price erosion appeared to be significantly worse in the global accounts than in the non-global accounts. In terms of where responsibilities lay for various activities, pricing decisions were made on a more central basis in the Global group, and sales and service activities were undertaken on a more local basis in the Non-Global group. These findings are much as one would expect, but they are important nonetheless. Essentially they suggest that Global accounts represent a centralization of certain activities, often as a result of the demands of the customer, resulting in a similar overall level of sales growth but a downward pressure on prices.

The following two sections play out this basic insight in much greater detail. While the text is expressed in qualitative terms, it is worth observing that the findings emerged from a detailed statistical analysis of the data that was collected. References are made where applicable to the underlying analysis.

Strategy—Selecting and Designing Global Account Relationships

The key strategic questions facing the vendor company are whether to create global accounts at all, and if the decision is made to do so, which customer relationships should be selected. Of course, this decision is to some shaped dictated by the preferences of your customers, but to the extent it is possible to choose, our argument is that vendor companies should take a highly selective approach to the introduction of global account structures. It is better to start from the skeptical viewpoint that, for

Table 2   Characteristics of Global Accounts Compared with Other Accounts, Opinions of National Sales Managers (n = 55)

Focus of Customer Base	Non-Global (less than 20% of national sales come from formally designated "global accounts")	Mixed (between 20% and 49% of national sales come from formally designated "global accounts")	Global (50% of national sales or more come from formally designated "global accounts")
How fast have total sales in this country grown during the past 3 years? (1 = 0% per year or less, 2 = 5% per year, 3 = 10% per year, 4 = 15% per year, 5 = 20% per year, 6 = >20% per year)	4.09	4.18	4.00
How do the average price of goods sold by your subsidiary compare to 3 years ago? (1 = Much lower, 2 = Slightly lower, 3 = No change, 4 = Slightly higher, 5 = Much higher)	2.91	2.41	1.73*
Who is responsible for pricing decisions relating to global accounts in your country? (1 = Primarily country sales manager, 2 = Jointly by country sales manager and global account manager, 3 = Primarily by global account manager)	1.92	1.76	2.24*
To what extent are sales and support in your company done on a local basis? (1 = Coordinated globally, 2 = Partially globally coordinated, 3 = Done locally, some central coordination, 4 = Done exclusively on a local basis)	3.67	3.82	3.00*

*Note that on the latter three questions, the Global group number is significantly different to the Mixed and Non-Global group.

vendors, such relationships are inherently dangerous. In selecting the right customers to designate as global accounts, the two most important criteria are the balance of power in the relationship, and the potential for strategic synergies.

Assess the Balance of Power   The shark lurking in the waters of global account management is the bargaining power logic of centralized purchasing. A professional buyer looking for standard worldwide pricing is, of course, looking for the lowest price to be applied everywhere. Beyond this, a customer consolidating purchases from several countries will, reasonably, expect volume discounts against previously prevailing prices. And the fact is that, in most companies, the purchasing function is considerably more globally coordinated than the sales function, since it shows greater return to scale than the more execution-sensitive function of managing customer relationships. It's not surprising, then, that so many global account relationships favor the customer at the expense of the vendor.

The key determinant of the balance of power in global account negotiations is the degree of internationalization of the two partners. In many cases, for example, companies admitted to us that they simply did not have the systems to calculate worldwide sales to a given customer: in some countries, sales went through distributors, and could not be tracked by end customer; and in others, sales to an affiliate or partner or subsidiary of a customer were not tracked as part of the same account.

If the customer is more globally coordinated than the vendor, then pressure for price cuts will soon surface, something we identify as a "price squeeze" (see Figure 1). For example, one company's advertising agency had managed to identify all advertising expenditures worldwide with the titles and channels belonging to one of the largest global media groups. The fragmentation typical of these media groups meant that they were surprised by the information, and unable to resist the demand for lower prices on the basis of global volume.

Figure 1   Vendor-Customer Fit (prospects for an effective global account relationship?)

	Vendor's International Coordination	
	Low	**High**
Low	**Country-by-Country Relationship** Non-existent Potential	**Hollow Agreement** Low Potential
High	**Price Squeeze** Low Potential	**Global Fit** High Potential

(Customer's International Coordination — vertical axis, Low at top to High at bottom)

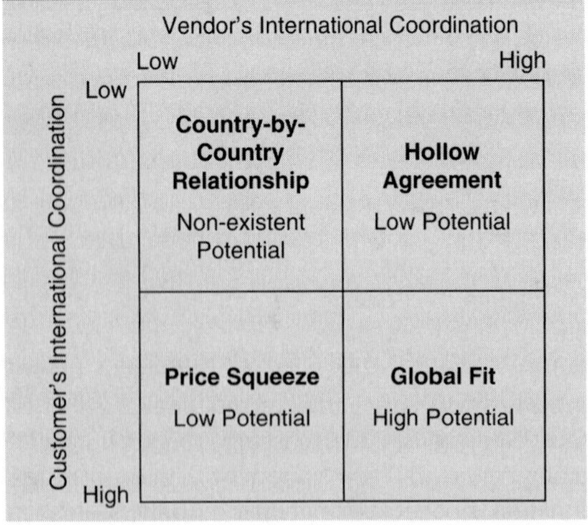

The other problem that surfaces when you are working with a more global customer is that you can end up servicing agreements in countries where you have no presence. Imagine the surprise of one vendor we interviewed when he received a call demanding service from a global account at their plant in Indonesia. The vendor had no sales or service organization in that country, nor did he realize that the customer was using products there, because they were sold to the Singapore buying office and then shipped on to the factory in Indonesia. Rather than antagonize the customer, this vendor flew someone out from a neighboring country, but it was an expensive solution to a problem that probably should have been foreseen.

To be clear, this scenario does not guarantee that the vendor will face a price squeeze. Many far-sighted customers will choose to build a win-win relationship with their vendors rather than squeeze them on price in the short-term. And some vendors are skilful at increasing their power over their customers in other ways. But our research makes it very clear that if the vendor is "under-globalised" in relation to the customer, it will be in a rather vulnerable position. In such a situation, the best approach is to improve the international coordination of your sales and support organization, rather than rely on enlightened and far-sighted customers.

If the vendor is more coordinated than the customer the prospect of a global account relationship might look more attractive, but experience indicates that this imbalance will imperil the partnership in different ways, something we describe as a "hollow agreement." The customer's corporate procurement executives will negotiate a global agreement even though the company is not globalized enough to make local procurement executives comply with the agreement. The result? An agreement that exists only in name. The standardized products and service agreements are unlikely to take hold in the customer organization. Local buyers, without any incentive to switch suppliers, will continue to use their own local sources; some will see this as a turf issue, resenting the imposition of terms agreed by corporate executives. The customer, in other words, cannot deliver. Meanwhile, of course, the cost of serving the account has increased because of the addition of the global account organization.

In contrast, when the two sides are well-matched in their internationalization, a global account relationship can work very well. Consider the case of Ericsson's relationship with Cable and Wireless. Both companies have long established global operations. Cable and Wireless views Ericsson as its most important supplier of telecoms equipment. In return, Ericsson rates Cable and Wireless as one of its top ten customers worldwide. Ericsson has put in place a large global account team dedicated to working with Cable and Wireless around the world as they bid for new licenses and install leading-edge equipment. While the global account relationship exists primarily at the headquarters level in London, there are also local relationships between Ericsson and Cable and Wireless operations in a further 20 countries around the world.

Assess the Customer as a Strategic Partner, Not Just a Sales Account   In our field research, the more successful global account relationships were almost all ones that had been initiated by the vendor for strategic reasons. Their motivation for doing so, of course, was to increase their share of the customer's business, either through guaranteed minimum levels of business, or account penetration in country-markets where the share of the customer's business had been low because of local factors. But this objective only proved achievable if there was a strategic logic behind the partnership, such as the development of innovative and/or customized offerings that benefited both parties. 3M, for example, actively targets key customers in the electronics sector as partners in its product development initiatives—the targeted customers not only pass the business volume criterion, but are judged to have resources or competencies from which 3M will benefit in the product development process. In return, the customer benefits from involvement in a relevant R&D project which will deliver customized (and in some cases exclusive) new products. Another example is Electrolux's commercial

refrigeration business, which has strategic partnering relationships with Shell and other big oil companies on a global basis. For Shell, an important part of their global strategy is a common *Retail Visual Identity* (RVI)—which means that the gas station forecourt and shop look the same wherever you go. Electrolux is working on a range of large commercial refrigerators that fit Shell's RVI—and which pushes their product development further at the same time.

The reason to push for a strategic relationship are clear—if the relationship has no rationale other than sales, then the negotiations will center on price and the globalization of the relationship will result in pressure for volume discounts. The broadening of the relationship to include strategic development projects, such as new product development or customized service agreements is the only way to make global accounts pay for the vendor.

How then should vendors assess the strategic potential of customers as global partners? Our research suggests that such relationships need to operate well on three different levels, and if any of these is missing problems are likely to emerge.[3]

Strategic Importance   Does this relationship really matter to you? And does it matter to your customer? There are two important measures of importance. The first, familiar to all experienced sales executives, is the share of business accounted for by the relationship: do we have over half of the customer's purchases in this category? If a customer buys less than half their supplies from us and still asks to be a global account, it is likely to be a price squeeze they have in mind. Second, is the customer a lead user of our products? This is the rationale behind 3M's approach. Any supplier should be in a closer learning relationship with its lead users, even

---

[3]This set of findings come from a research paper, "The Role of Interorganisational Fit in Global Account Management" by O. Toulan, J. Birkinshaw and D. Arnold (2001). This paper shows that significant predictors of account performance are the "fit" between vendor and customer on (1) the strategic importance of the account, (2) the level of executive support, (3) the international marketing strategy adopted, and (4) the international coordination of activities.

if the sales volumes do not make this customer the largest.

Marketing and Sales Strategy   Global account relationships cannot work unless both partners are committed to global marketing. While this may seem a statement of the obvious, our experience indicates that in many cases there is a serious mismatch between vendor and customer on the extent to which global consistency is part of the marketing strategy. For example, British Telecom has built a series of alliances and joint ventures around Europe in order to offer "one-stop shopping" to its international business customers. However, the reality of managing a portfolio of alliances, each with its own local partners, is that their approach varies from country to country. As a result, BT cannot yet offer the standardized solutions its business customers would like.

To be clear, global account management does not require that everything is centralized, but it is important that there is a compelling demand for a consistent worldwide platform for the agreement. The extent to which the customer's local marketing units are free to adapt marketing mix elements, especially products, is a good predictor of their attachment to localized purchasing.

Top Executive Support   At what level in your organization, and in your customer's organization, does the account relationship exist? As with any sort of key account, the relationship shifts from price negotiations to strategic issues as you move through the customer's hierarchy. So catching the eye of the VP of supply chain management, or similar, is important. But equally critical is executive support on the vendor side, as a means of increasing the legitimacy of the program in both the vendor and customer organizations. For example, a manager we spoke to in Hewlett Packard's test and measurement organization (now Agilent) was frustrated that one of their largest accounts was being managed in what he termed a "transactional" way. He was pushing to make it a strategic account, but he acknowledged that the existing account manager—a great sales manager but not a strategic

thinker—was the wrong person to take it to that level. What this account needed, and what the most successful cases in our study already had in place, was ownership at a senior level. Global account *executives* are assigned, as mentors to the global account *managers,* and these individuals can get together with their counterparts in the customer organization to explore opportunities for long-term collaboration.

Implementation—Putting the Right Systems and People in Place

The second big challenge with global accounts revolves around effective implementation. Sales has traditionally been a local responsibility, even in the largest multinationals, because it was regarded as execution-sensitive, and not susceptible to the economies of scale and control which have motivated globalization in other functions of the business. Global account management, in effect, turns this rationale upside down. We saw in most corporations we interviewed signs of tension of who "owns" the customer. In fact, the major problem we encountered in all our research was the conflict between the newly instituted international customer management organization, usually a corporate unit with global responsibility, and the management of a national subsidiary. Country managers are generally measured on sales revenues, and the removal of responsibility for a major customer is therefore a tangible loss. In some cases, country management were compensated for sales to the global account originating in their country even if they played no part in the sale. But the global account team also needed compensating, of course, and so in many cases the vendor organization resigned itself to double-counting orders for the purposes of compensation.

The situation is made more complex by the fact that country management involvement is still necessary in managing such a customer. Delivery and after-sales service has to be managed locally. In addition, managers assigned to the global account team are often located in the field, not in corporate units, because their location is determined by the customer organization rather than by their own. For the purposes of much day-to-day management, such as expense management, office services, and human resource issues, they are regarded as part of the national subsidiary organization.

So how do you avoid these sorts of implementation problems? There is no silver bullet here, because as one executive noted, "there is a constant tug between global management and country management that cannot be solved—you just have to manage it." And managing the tension means a lot of hard work building up the necessary capabilities in the global sales organization, and the supporting systems and structures. Here are five lessons that came out of our research.[4]

Clarify the Role of the Global Account Management Team   In many companies, global account management starts out as an exercise in internal coordination—as a way of making salespeople in different parts of the company aware of what each other is doing. This is OK as a first step, but as an end state it is not enough. If the global account management program is worth establishing, it needs teeth, and that means having a global line of reporting as well as a local one. For example, in Hewlett Packard's global account program, the Nortel Networks account manager reports to his sales manager in Canada *and* to the vice president of global accounts in Palo Alto. The value of this matrix-like arrangement is that when conflicts arise (should he spend time developing the Nortel business in Europe?), the global account manager has someone back in HQ to help make his case. To be clear, there should be no hard rules about when the global wins out over the local. But what should be avoided at all costs is the situation where the global

account managers (in name) are simply slotted in to the country-based sales organization.

Make Incentive Structure Realistic   Global account management organizations sit alongside pre-existing national sales organizations, rather than replacing them, and both units have a vital role in managing the account. Sales orders will still be booked through the local sales force, for example, and delivery and service are still a local job. So who should get the sales commission when a global account places an order? We found this to be one of the thorniest problems facing vendors. In almost all cases we encountered, the organization was resigned to simply paying the commission twice: once to the global account managers based on global sales, and a local payment for each order taken. This expensive solution is tolerable only if the global account program results in increased business with the customer (i.e., if the strategy is right). While several companies had learned the dangers of splitting the incentives, none of those we researched had found a solution other than multiple rewards. The lesson is clear—even if the decisions are split between global and local units, the incentive structure must be replicated at both levels as if it were a purely local responsibility.

Pick the Right Global Account Managers: Not Just Super-Salesmen   Most global account managers are recruited from the sales organization—from positions like regional sales manager, or national sales manager in small countries. But this approach is misguided, because a global account is very different from a portfolio of regional or national accounts. True, many regional account managers *do* make good global account managers, but they have to learn some new skills to make the transition—internal coordination, taking a long term perspective, nurturing the account not milking it, and so on. One company we studied took the opposite approach, by appointing executives with senior line-management experience as global account managers. These individuals had all the necessary skills, and were able to give the global account program its much-needed visibility.

[4]This set of findings come from the following paper: Birkinshaw, J.M., O. Toulan and D. Arnold (2001), Global Account Management in Multinational Corporations, Theory and Evidence, *Journal of International Business Studies,* volume 32, pp. 321–348. To be specific, we find that the performance of the global account is significantly associated with (1) the functional scope of the account, (2) the level of communication between the global account manager and counterparts in the two organisations, and (3) the support systems provided by the vendor.

Create a Strong Support Network   Global account management can be a lonely job, because as a matter of definition you don't really belong in any one country. So to make the role viable, global account managers need a strong support network. They need mentors back at head office, they need information systems and communication materials to broadcast their activities, and they need regular meetings with each other at which they can compare notes and swap war stories. Indeed, our research suggested that the strength of the internal support system was the single best predictor of a successful global account. Consider the case of Ericsson's enterprise networks business, which sells PBXs and office services to multinational customers. The global account managers are based in the home-countries of their customers, but located in Stockholm there is an extensive set of support activities—an order desk, marketing and customer relations, corporate network management, special project support, and internal network building. These are services that would be too expensive to spread all over the world. But perhaps more importantly, they provide the visibility and political legitimacy that the global account managers need to get their work done.

Make Sure the Customer Relationship Operates at More than One Level   We have already talked about the need for support at a senior executive level, and this usually gets established quite quickly. But what usually gets neglected is the establishment of relationships *underneath* the global account manager. And this is a serious problem, because the best-laid plans in the world are useless if your organization cannot deliver on them. Consider the comments of one local sales manager, on the efforts of his global account manager: "He negotiated a frame agreement with the customer, but then he did not follow through. I only found out about the agreement when I got a call from the customer. I was made to look like an idiot, because I didn't know what he was talking about."

How do you avoid blunders like this? Ideally, you want to "mirror" your customer's organization from the global account executive right down to the local field and support team, but the reality is that except for the largest accounts (with their own dedicated people) you have to make do with your existing country-based sales organization. A popular way of solving the problem is to create two organizations within any country: a global customer unit which reports to the corporate locus of responsibility for that client, and the territoritally-defined national sales organization. This is not unlike the split between national accounts and sales districts, or between direct and 'distribution' business. But is creates enormous problems of transition, and cuts across the profit-and-loss responsibility and accountability given to most national subsidiaries.

Conclusion

Global account management represents an interesting new challenge to multinational corporations. Until now, globalization has occurred mainly in "upstream" activities such as production, R&D, and financing, where benefits of scale and control are most evident. Customer management, and the wider field of marketing, has until now generally been the responsibility of local subsidiaries, in order to maximize responsiveness to the heterogeneous demands of different markets. And the structure of multinationals has reflected this configuration of activities: subsidiary responsibility for marketing and sales within their territory maximizes local responsiveness, and, by placing responsibility for revenue generation at the national level, provides a basis for the company's measurement and control systems.

The trend towards global customer management undermines much of this traditional logic, and indeed cuts against the traditional lines of organization in most large firms. Our recommendation is that companies think hard about whether global account management is right for them, because while there can be great benefits there are also considerable downside risks in going down that route.

To oversimplify the case, companies tend to fall into three different camps in their approach to global account management. Some like 3M are ahead of their customers, typically because they are seeking to build strategic relationships through which new technologies and products can be developed. This group essentially has nothing to fear, because they are creating global accounts on their own terms. The second group is moving at the same speed as its customers. These companies are typically reacting to the initiatives of their customers, but quickly getting to grips with the challenge and putting programs in place to deliver on their customers' demands. For this group, the advice is to be selective. Global account management may be inevitable in your industry, but by figuring out your bargaining power and the degree of fit between your company and your leading customers, you can influence the way such accounts are established, and which ones you want to focus your efforts on.

Finally, there is a group of companies that are lagging behind their customers, typically through reluctance to acknowledge the changes underway in their industry. Global account management is a real threat to these companies, because they either find themselves scrambling to deliver a global account program for which they are ill-equipped, or they can find themselves losing business to better-organized competitors. For this group, the need to get to grips with the issues raised in the article is of paramount importance. While global account relationships may well result in lower margins in key product areas, at least you will be able to go into them with a better understanding of the risks, and what needs to be done to implement such relationships effectively.

CHAPTER 5

Creating and Leveraging Knowledge:
The Worldwide Learning Challenge

In Chapter 3, we described how companies competing in today's global competitive environment are being required to build layers of competitive advantage—in particular, the ability to capture global scale efficiencies, local market responsiveness, and worldwide learning capability. But in the closing years of the 20th century, as MNCs found ways to match each other in the more familiar attributes of global scale efficiency and local responsiveness, the leading-edge competitive battles shifted to companies' ability to link and leverage their resources to capture advantage through worldwide learning.

In a competitive environment in which the ability to develop and rapidly diffuse innovation around the world is vital, MNCs can no longer regard their overseas operations simply as the means to access low-cost labor or capture incremental markets. Today, offshore subsidiaries must act as the sensors of new market trends or technological developments; they must be able to attract scarce talent and expertise; and they must be able to act collectively with other subsidiaries to exploit the resulting new products and initiatives worldwide, regardless of where they originated.

Yet developing this capability to create, leverage, and apply knowledge worldwide is not a simple task for most large MNCs. Despite the fact that people are innately curious and naturally motivated to learn from each other, most modern corporations are constructed in a way that constrains and sometimes kills this natural human instinct. In this chapter, we focus on one of the most important current challenges facing MNC management—how to develop and diffuse knowledge in a way that supports effective worldwide innovation and learning.

Central, Local, and Transnational Innovation

Traditionally, MNCs' innovative capabilities were dominated by one of two classic processes. In the *center-for-global* innovation model, the new opportunity was usually sensed in the home country; the centralized resources and capabilities of the parent company were brought to bear to create the new product or process; and implementation involved driving the innovation through subsidiaries whose role it was to introduce the innovation to their local market. Pfizer's development of Viagra or Intel's creation of Pentium processors are two classic examples of this model.

In contrast, *local-for-local* innovation relies on subsidiary-based knowledge development. Responding to perceived local opportunities, subsidiaries use their own resources and capabilities to create innovative responses that are then implemented in the local market. Unilever's development of a detergent bar for the Indian market's need for a product suitable for stream washing is a good illustration of the process, as is Philippines-based Jollibee's strategy of adapting its fast-food products to local market preferences of each country it entered.

Most MNCs have tried to develop elements of both models of innovation but the tension that exists between the knowledge management processes supporting each usually means that one dominates. Not surprisingly, the center-for-global innovation tends to dominate in companies we describe as global or international, whereas local-for-local processes fit more easily into the multinational strategic model. However, in recent years the traditional strategic mentalities have been evolving into two new transnational innovation processes we describe as *locally leveraged* and *globally linked*. Locally leveraged innovation involves ensuring that the special resources and capabilities of each national subsidiary are available not only to that local entity, but also to other MNC units worldwide. For example, two of Sara Lee Corporation's biggest new brands in the household and body care division in the 1990s—Sanex and Ambi pur—were first developed in Spain, and subsequently rolled out on a worldwide basis. Globally linked innovation pools the resources and capabilities of many different units—at both the parent company and subsidiary level—to jointly create and manage an activity. For example, the idea for Volkswagen's New Beetle came originally out of the U.S. head office in Detroit, the design was done in the company's design studios in California, and the development and engineering work was conducted at corporate headquarters in Wolfsburg, Germany.

Both these transnational innovation models rest on a sophisticated ability to take market intelligence developed in one part of the organization, perhaps link it to specialized expertise located in a second entity and a scarce resource in a third, before eventually diffusing the new product or proposal worldwide. This was the kind of innovative process Procter and Gamble first developed through the creation of "Eurobrand" development teams, that resulted in the creation of the heavy-duty liquid detergent, Vizir. Recognizing the power of this cross-unit innovation and learning capability, the company gradually built it into a core competence that it now regards as the centerpiece of its global competitive strategy.

Although these processes are becoming more widespread, they have supplemented rather than replaced the traditional central and local innovation processes. In a competitive environment, most companies recognize the need to engage their resources and capabilities in as many ways as they can. The challenge is to build an organization that can simultaneously facilitate all four processes of innovation and learning. This requires that they understand not only the power of each, but also their limitations:

- The greatest risk of center-for-global innovation is market insensitivity and the accompanying resistance of local subsidiary management to what they view as inappropriate new products and processes.
- Local-for-local innovations often suffer from needless differentiation and "reinvention of the wheel" caused by resource-rich subsidiaries trying to protect their independence and autonomy.

- Locally leveraged innovations can be threatened by the "not-invented-here" syndrome that often blocks the successful transfer of products and processes from the innovative subsidiary to others in the company.
- And the major impediment to globally linked innovation tends to be the high coordination cost required to link widely dispersed assets, resources, and capabilities into an effective integrated network of free-flowing ideas and innovations. Building a portfolio of innovative processes to drive worldwide learning requires that the companies overcome two related but different problems. Not only must companies avoid the various pitfalls associated with each process, they must also find ways to overcome the organizational contradictions among them as they try to manage all the sources of innovation simultaneously.

▪ Making Central Innovations Effective

The key strength on which many Japanese companies built their global leadership positions in a diverse range of businesses, from zippers to automobiles, lay in the effectiveness of their center-for-global innovations. This is not to say that many did not use some of the other operative modes but, in general, the Japanese became the champion managers of centralized innovation in the 1980s and have remained so.

Three factors stand out as the most important explanations of their success in managing the center-for-global process: (1) gaining the input of subsidiaries into centralized activities, (2) ensuring that all functional tasks are linked to market needs, and (3) integrating value chain functions such as development, production, and marketing by managing the transfer of responsibilities among them.

Gaining Subsidiary Input: Multiple Linkages

The two most important problems facing a company with highly centralized operations are that those at the center may not understand market needs, and that those in the subsidiaries required to implement the central innovation are not committed to it. These problems are best addressed by building multiple linkages between headquarters and overseas subsidiaries not only to give headquarters managers a better understanding of country-level needs and opportunities, but also to give subsidiary managers greater access to and involvement in centralized decisions and tasks.

Matsushita, for example, does not try to limit the number of linkages between headquarters and subsidiaries or focus them through a single point as many companies do for the sake of efficiency. Rather, it tries to preserve the different perspectives, priorities, and even prejudices of its diverse groups worldwide, and ensure that they have linkages to those in the headquarters who can represent and defend their views.

Responding to National Needs: Market Mechanisms

Like many other companies, Matsushita has created an integrative process to ensure that headquarters managers responsible for R&D, manufacturing, marketing, and so on, are not sheltered from the constraints and demands felt by managers in the front line of the operations. One of the key elements in achieving this difficult organizational task is the company's willingness to use internal "market mechanisms" for directing and regulating the central activities.

For example, approximately half of Matsushita's total research budget is allocated not to the research laboratories but to the product divisions. The purpose of the split budget is to create a context in which technologically driven and market-led ideas can compete for attention. Each year, the product divisions suggest a set of research projects that they would like to sponsor. At the same time, the various research laboratories hold annual exhibitions and write specific proposals to highlight research projects that they would like to undertake. The engineering and development groups of the product divisions mediate the subsequent contracting and negotiation process. Specific projects are sponsored by the divisions and are allocated to the laboratories or research groups of their choice, along with requisite funds and other resources.

Managing Responsibility Transfer: Personnel Flow

In local-for-local innovation processes, cross-functional integration across research, manufacturing, and marketing is facilitated by the smaller size and closer proximity of the units responsible for each stage of activity. Because this is not true where parent company units take the lead role in the development and manufacture of new products and processes, more centralized organizations must build alternative means for integrating the different tasks.

At Matsushita, for example, the integrative systems rely heavily on the transfer of people. The career paths of research engineers are structured to ensure that a majority of them spend about five to eight years in the central research laboratories engaged in pure research, then another five years in the product divisions in applied research and development, and finally in a direct operational function, such as production or marketing, wherein they take line-management positions for the rest of their working lives. More important—and in stark contrast to the approach in most Western companies—each engineer usually makes the transition from one department to the next along with the transfer of the major project on which he or she has been working. This ensures that specific knowledge about the project moves with the individual.

Another mechanism for cross-functional integration in Matsushita works in the opposite direction. Wherever possible, the company tries to identify the manager who will head the production task for a new product under development and makes him or her a full-time member of the research team from the initial stage of the development process. This system not only injects direct production expertise into the development team, but also facilitates transfer of the project after the design is completed. Matsushita also uses this mechanism as a way of transferring product expertise from headquarters to its worldwide sales subsidiaries.

Making Local Innovations Efficient

If the classic global companies in Japan are the champion managers of central innovation, the archetypal multinational companies from Europe are often masters at managing local innovations. Of the many factors that facilitate local-for-local innovations in

European companies, there are three that are the most significant—their ability to empower local management in national subsidiaries, to establish effective mechanisms for linking these local managers to corporate decision-making processes, and to force tight cross-functional integration within each subsidiary.

Empowering Local Management

Perhaps the most important factor supporting local innovations is the dispersal of the organizational assets and resources and the delegation of authority that occur so easily in decentralized federation companies. Since it was founded in 1891, for example, Philips has recognized the need to expand its operations beyond its small domestic market, but the successive barriers—poor transport and communication linkages in the early decades of the century, protectionist pressures in the 1930s, and the disruption of World War II—encouraged the company to build national organizations with a substantial degree of autonomy and self-sufficiency. Such dispersed managerial and technological resources coupled with local autonomy and decentralized control over the resources enable subsidiary managers to be more effective in managing local development, manufacturing, and other functional tasks.

Linking Local Managers to Corporate Decision-Making Processes

Whereas local resources and autonomy make it feasible for subsidiary managers to be creative and entrepreneurial, linkages to corporate decision-making processes are necessary to make these local-for-local tasks effective for the company as a whole. In many European companies, a cadre of entrepreneurial expatriates play a key role in developing and maintaining such linkages.

In Philips, many of the best managers spend most of their careers in national operations, working for three to four years in a series of subsidiaries—jobs that are often much larger and have higher status than the small home country market of the Netherlands.

Not surprisingly, such a career assignment pattern has an important influence on managerial attitudes and organizational relationships. The expatriate managers tend to identify strongly with the national organization's point of view, and this shared identity creates a strong bond and distinct subculture within the company. In contrast to Philips, Matsushita has been able to generate very little interaction among its expatriate managers who tend to regard themselves as parent-company executives temporarily on assignment in a foreign company.

Integrating Subsidiary Functions

Finally, local innovativeness of decentralized federation organizations is enhanced because of the strong cross-functional integration that typically exists within each national operation. Most Philips subsidiaries use integration mechanisms at three organizational levels. First, for each project, there is what Philips calls an article team consisting of relatively junior managers from the commercial and technical functions. It is the responsibility of this team to evolve product policies and to prepare annual sales plans and budgets.

At the product level, cross-functional coordination is accomplished through a product group management team of technical and commercial representatives which meets once a month to review results, suggest corrective actions, and resolve any interfunctional differences. Keeping control and conflict resolution at this level facilitates sensitive and rapid response to initiatives and ideas generated at the local level.

The highest subsidiary-level coordination forum is the senior management committee (SMC), consisting of the top commercial, technical, and financial managers in the subsidiary. Acting essentially as a local board, the SMC coordinates effort among the functional groups and ensures that the national operation retains primary responsibility for its own strategies and priorities. Each of these three forums facilitate local initiave by encouraging issues to be resolved without escalation for approval or arbitration.

Making Transnational Processes Feasible

The complexity of the innovation and learning processes in a multinational corporation is significantly exacerbated by the fact that new opportunities can emerge from anywhere, and often a long way from either the complementary capability or the key decision makers. For example, in 2001, when General Motors' global product head saw the new sports coupe that GM's Australian subsidiary had launched as the Holden Monaro, he decided it was the ideal car to introduce in the United States as a resurrection of the Pontiac GTO. With a domestic demand of only 5,000 Monaros, General Motors Holden had to significantly expand its capacity to the expected export volume of 18,000 Pontiacs after the 2003 U.S. launch of the GTO.

In a case such as this, the transnational company needs to embrace a mind-set in which subsidiary managers are encouraged to take initiative, and headquarters managers are more accepting of the capabilities and potential of their overseas operations. And it needs to build linkages among different units of the company (for example, between the Australian design and production operations and GM's Detroit-based global marketing and sales operation) to leverage existing resources and capabilities, regardless of their locations, and to exploit opportunities that arise in any part of the company's dispersed operations.

In many MNCs, three simplifying assumptions have traditionally blocked organizational capabilities necessary for managing such transnational operations. The need to reduce organizational and strategic complexity made these assumptions extremely widespread among large MNCs:

- An often implicit assumption that roles of different organizational units are uniform and symmetrical. This leads companies to manage very different businesses, functions, and national operations in essentially the same way.
- An assumption, conscious or unconscious, is that headquarter-subsidiary relationships should be based on clear and unambiguous patterns of dependence or independence.
- The assumption that corporate management has a responsibility to exercise decision making and control uniformly.

Companies that are most successful in developing transnational innovations challenge these assumptions. Instead of treating all businesses, functions, and subsidiaries the same, they systematically differentiate tasks and responsibilities. Instead of seeking organizational clarity by basing relationships on dependence or independence, they build and manage interdependence among the different units of the companies. And, instead of considering control their key task, corporate managers search for complex mechanisms to coordinate and co-opt the differentiated and interdependent organizational units into sharing a vision of the company's strategic tasks.

From Symmetry to Differentiation

Like many other companies, Unilever built its international operations with an implicit assumption of organizational symmetry. Managers of diverse local businesses, with products ranging from packaged foods to chemicals and detergents, all reported to strongly independent national subsidiary managers, who in turn reported through regional directors to the board. In the post–World War II era, as management began to recognize the need to capture potential economies across national boundaries and to transfer learning worldwide, product-coordination groups were formed at the corporate center. Under the assumption of organizational symmetry, the number of coordination groups grew from 3 in 1962, to 6 in 1969, and 10 by 1977.

By the early 1980s, however, there was a growing recognition that different businesses faced different demands for integration and responsiveness. Whereas standardization, coordination, and integration paid high dividends in the chemical and detergent businesses, for example, important differences in local tastes and national cultures impeded the same degree of coordination in foods.

As Unilever tackled the challenge of managing some businesses in a more globally coordinated manner, it was also confronted with the question of what to coordinate. Historically, most national subsidiaries chose to develop, manufacture, and market products they thought appropriate. Over time, however, decentralization of all functional responsibilities became increasingly difficult to support. For the sake of cost control and competitive effectiveness, Unilever needed to break with tradition and begin centralizing European product development and purchasing, but was less compelled to pull local sales and promotional responsibilities to the center.

In addition to differentiating the way they managed their various businesses and functions, most companies eventually recognized the importance of differentiating the management of diverse geographic operations. Despite the fact that various national subsidiaries operated with very different external environments and internal constraints, the operations in Sydney, Singapore, and Shanghai often reported through the same channels, were managed through standardized planning and control systems, and worked under a set of common and generalized subsidiary mandates.

Recognizing that such symmetrical treatment could constrain strategic capabilities, many companies made changes. At Unilever, for example, Europe's highly competitive markets and closely linked economies led management to gradually increase the role of European product coordinators until they eventually had direct line responsibility for all operating companies in their businesses. In Latin America, however, national management maintained its historic line-management role, and product coordinators acted only as advisers. Unilever has thus moved in sequence from a symmetrical organization managed through a uniformly decentralized federation to a much more differentiated one: differentiating first by product, then by function, and finally by geography.

From Dependence or Independence to Interdependence

As we described in Chapter 4, national subsidiaries in decentralized federation organizations enjoyed considerable independence from the headquarters, whereas those in centralized hub organizations remained strongly dependent on the parent company for resources and capabilities. But the emerging strategic demands make organizational models based on such simple interunit dependence or independence inappropriate.

Independent units risk being picked off one by one by competitors whose coordinated global approach gives them two important strategic advantages—the ability to integrate scale-efficient operations, and the opportunity to cross-subsidize the losses from battles in one market with funds generated by profitable operations in others. On the other hand, foreign operations that depend totally on a central unit risk being unable to respond effectively to strong national competitors or to sense potentially important local-market or technical intelligence.

But it is not easy to change relationships of dependence or independence that were built over a long history. Most companies found that attempts to improve interunit collaboration by adding layer upon layer of administrative mechanisms to foster greater cooperation were disappointing. Independent units feigned compliance while fiercely protecting their independence, and dependent units found that the new cooperative spirit bestowed little more than the right to agree with those on whom they depended.

To create an effective interdependent organization, two requirements must be met. First, the company must develop a configuration of resources that is neither centralized nor decentralized, but is both dispersed and specialized. Such a configuration lies at the heart of the transnational company's integrated network mode of operations, as we have already discussed in Chapter 4.

The second requirement is to build interunit integration mechanisms to ensure that task interdependencies lead to the benefits of synergy rather than the paralysis of conflict. Above all else, interunit cooperation requires good interpersonal relations among managers in different units. The experiences of Ericsson, the Swedish telecommunications company, suggest that the movement of people is one of the strongest mechanisms for breaking down local dogmas. Ericsson achieved this with a long-standing policy of transferring large numbers of people back and forth between headquarters and subsidiaries. Whereas its Japanese competitor NEC may transfer a new technology through a few key managers sent on temporary assignment, Ericsson will send a team of 50 or 100 engineers and managers for a year or two; NEC's flow is primarily from headquarters to subsidiary, Ericsson's is a balanced two-way flow with people coming to the parent company not only to learn but also to bring their expertise; and NEC's transfers are predominantly Japanese, Ericsson's multidirectional process involves all nationalities.

However, any organization in which there are shared tasks and joint responsibilities requires additional decision-making and conflict-resolution forums. In Ericsson, often-divergent objectives and interests of the parent company and the local subsidiary are exchanged in the national company's board meetings. Unlike many companies whose local boards are designed solely to satisfy national legal requirements, Ericsson uses its local boards as legitimate forums for communicating objectives, resolving differences, and making decisions.

From Unidimensional Control to Differentiated Coordination

The simplifying assumptions of organizational symmetry and dependence (or independence) allowed the management processes in many companies to be dominated by simple controls—tight operational controls in subsidiaries that depend on the center, and a looser system of administrative or financial controls in decentralized units. When companies began to challenge the assumptions underlying organizational relationships, however, they found they also needed to adapt their management processes. The growing interdependence of organizational units strained the simple control-dominated systems and underlined the need to supplement existing processes with more-sophisticated ones.

As organizations became, at the same time, more diverse and more interdependent, there was an explosion in the number of issues that had to be linked, reconciled, or integrated. But the costs of coordination are high, both in financial and human terms, and coordinating capabilities are always limited. Most companies, though, tended to concentrate on a primary means of coordination and control—"the company's way of doing things."

In analyzing how managers might develop a coordination system that would best fit the needs for various functions and tasks, it is helpful to think about the various flows between organization units that are involved in the execution of each task. Three flows are the lifeblood of any organization, but are of particular importance in a transnational company. The first is the flow of goods: the complex interconnections through which companies source their raw materials and other supplies, link flows of components and subassemblies, and distribute finished goods. The second is the flow of resources, which encompasses not only the allocation of capital and repatriation of dividends, but also the transfer of technology and the movement of personnel throughout the system. The third is the flow of valuable information and knowledge—from raw data and analyzed information to accumulated knowledge and embedded expertise—which companies must diffuse throughout the worldwide network of national units.

It can be very difficult to coordinate the flows of *goods* in a complex integrated network of interdependent operations. But in most companies, this coordination process can be managed effectively at lower levels of the organization when clear procedures and strong systems are set up, or in other words through a *formalized* management process. For example, within its network of manufacturing plants in different countries, Ericsson learned to coordinate product and materials flows by standardizing as many procedures as possible and formalizing the logistics control.

It is more difficult to coordinate flows of financial, human, and technological *resources*. Allocation of these scarce resources represents the major strategic choices the company makes and must therefore be controlled at the corporate level. We have described the transnational company as an organization of diverse needs and perspectives, many of which are conflicting and all of which are changing. In such an organization, only managers with an overview of the total situation can make the critical decisions on the funding of projects, the sharing of scarce technological resources, and the allocation of organizational skills and capabilities. Managing the flows of resources is a classic example of the need for coordination by *centralization*.

Perhaps the most difficult task is to coordinate the huge flow of strategic information and proprietary *knowledge* required to operate a transnational organization. The diversity and changeability of the flow make it impossible to coordinate through formal systems; and the sheer volume and complexity of information would overload headquarters if coordination were centralized. The most effective way to ensure that worldwide organizational units are analyzing their diverse environments appropriately is to sensitize local managers to the broader corporate objectives and priorities. That goal is best reached by transferring personnel with the relevant knowledge or creating organizational forums that allow for the free exchange of information and foster interunit learning. In short, the *socialization* process is the classic solution for the coordination of information flows.

Naturally, none of these broad characterizations of the fit between flows and processes is absolute, and companies use a variety of coordinative mechanisms in managing all three flows. Goods flows may be centrally coordinated, for example, for products under allocation, when several plants are operating at less than capacity or if cost structures or host government demands change. And as information flows become routine, they can be coordinated through formalization if appropriate management information systems are installed.

■ Concluding Comments

The approaches to innovation in MNCs have changed considerably over the last 20 years. Where once MNCs relied on simple models of centralized or localized innovation, the vast majority now find it necessary to build their innovation processes around multiple operating units and geographically disparate sources of knowledge. In this chapter we have identified three generic approaches to innovation, and for each we have identified its typical limitations, and the approaches MNCs can use to overcome those limitations. To be clear, there is no one right way of managing the innovation process in the MNC, because each company has its own unique administrative heritage that it cannot and should not disavow. Nonetheless, it is possible to identify certain principles—around differentiation of roles, interdependence of units, and modes of control—that underpin the development of an effective transnational organization.

Case 5-1   P&G Japan: The SK-II Globalization Project

In November 1999, Paolo de Cesare was preparing for a meeting with the Global Leadership Team (GLT) of P&G's Beauty Care Global Business Unit (GBU) to present his analysis of whether a prestige Japanese skincare line called SK-II could become a truly global brand by expanding into new markets in China and/or Europe. As president of Max Factor Japan, the hub of P&G's fast-growing cosmetics business in Asia, and previously in charge of the company's European skincare business, de Cesare had considerable credibility in the GLT. Yet, as he readily acknowledged, there were significant risks in P&G's first-ever proposal to expand a Japanese brand into new markets worldwide.

Chairing the GLT meeting was Alan ("A. G.") Lafley, head of P&G's Beauty Care GBU to which de Cesare reported. In the end, it was his organization—and his budget—that would support such a global expansion. Although he had been an early champion of SK-II in Japan, Lafley would need strong evidence of the transferability of a brand that had succeeded in a culture where the consumers, distribution channels, and competitors were vastly different from those in most other countries. Another constraint facing de Cesare was the fact that P&G's global organization was in the midst of the bold but disruptive Organization 2005 restructuring program. As GBUs took over profit responsibility historically held by P&G's country-based organizations, management was still trying to negotiate their new working relationships. In this context, de Cesare, Lafley, and other GLT members struggled to answer some key questions: Did SK-II have the potential to develop into a major global brand? If so, which markets were the most important to enter

now? And how should this be implemented in P&G's newly reorganized global operations?

P&G's Internationalization: Engine of Growth

De Cesare's reflections about globalizing a Japanese product was just the latest step in an internationalization process that P&G had begun three quarters of a century earlier. But it was the creation of the Overseas Division in 1948 that drove three decades of rapid expansion. Growing first in Europe, then Latin America and Asia, by 1980, P&G's operations in 27 overseas countries accounted for over 25% of its $11 billion worldwide sales. (Exhibit 1 summarizes P&G's international expansion.)

Local Adaptiveness Meets Cross-Market Integration   Throughout its early expansion, the company adhered to a set of principles set down by Walter Lingle, the first VP of overseas operations. "We must tailor our products to meet consumer demands in each nation," he said. "But we must create local country subsidiaries whose structure, policies and practices are as exact a replica of the U.S. Procter & Gamble organization as it is possible to create." Under the Lingle principles, the company soon built a portfolio of self-sufficient subsidiaries run by country general managers (GMs) who grew their companies by adapting P&G technology and marketing expertise to their knowledge of their local markets.

Yet, by the 1980s, two problems emerged. First, the cost of running all the local product development labs and manufacturing plants was limiting profits. And second, the ferocious autonomy of national subsidiaries was preventing the global rollout of new products and technology improvements. Local GMs often resisted such initiatives due to the negative impact they had on local profits for which the country subsidiaries were held accountable. As a result, new products could take a decade or more to be introduced worldwide.

▌ Professor Christopher A. Bartlett prepared this case. HBS cases are developed solely as the basis for class discussion. Cases are not intended to serve as endorsements, sources of primary data, or illustrations of effective or ineffective management. Certain data have been disguised but key relationships have been retained.
▌ Copyright © 2002 President and Fellows of Harvard College. Harvard Business School case 303–003.

Exhibit 1 P&G's Internationalization Timetable	
Year	**Markets Entered**
1837–1930	United States and Canada
1930–1940	United Kingdom, Philippines
1940–1950	Puerto Rico, Venezuela, Mexico
1950–1960	Switzerland, France, Belgium, Italy, Peru, Saudi Arabia, Morocco
1960–1970	Germany, Greece, Spain, Netherlands, Sweden, Austria, Indonesia, Malaysia, Hong Kong, Singapore, Japan
1970–1980	Ireland
1980–1990	Columbia, Chile, Caribbean, Guatemala, Kenya, Egypt, Thailand, Australia, New Zealand, India, Taiwan, Korea, Pakistan, Turkey, Brazil, El Salvador
1990–2000	Russia, China, Czech Republic, Hungary, Poland, Slovak Republic, Bulgaria, Belarus, Latvia, Estonia, Romania, Lithuania, Kazakhstan, Yugoslavia, Croatia, Uzbekistan, Ukraine, Slovenia, Nigeria, South Africa, Denmark, Portugal, Norway, Argentina, Yemen, Sri Lanka, Vietnam, Bangladesh, Costa Rica, Turkmenistan

Source: Company records.

Consequently, during the 1980s, P&G's historically "hands off" regional headquarters became more active. In Europe, for example, Euro Technical Teams were formed to eliminate needless country-by-country product differences, reduce duplicated development efforts, and gain consensus on new technology diffusion. Subsequently, region-wide coordination spread to purchasing, finance, and even marketing. In particular, the formation of Euro Brand Teams became an effective forum for marketing managers to coordinate region-wide product strategy and new product rollouts.

By the mid-1980s, these overlaid regional coordinating processes were formalized when the VPs responsible for each of the three European regions were also given coordinative responsibility for a product category. While these individuals clearly had organizational influence, profit responsibility remained with the country subsidiary GMs. (See Exhibit 2 for the 1986 European organization.)

Birth of Global Management   In 1986, the seven divisions in P&G's domestic U.S. organization were broken into 26 categories, each with its own product development, product supply, and sales and marketing capabilities. Given the parallel development of a European category management structure, it was not a big leap to appoint the first global category executives in 1989. These new roles were given significant responsibility for developing global strategy, managing the technology program, and qualifying expansion markets—but not profit responsibility which still rested with the country subsidiary GMs.

Then, building on the success of the strong regional organization in Europe, the company replaced its International Division with four regional entities—North America, Europe, Latin America, and Asia—each assuming primary responsibility for profitability. (See Exhibit 3 for P&G's structure in 1990.) A significant boost in the company's overseas growth followed, particularly in opening the untapped markets of Eastern Europe and China.

By the mid-1990s, with operations in over 75 countries, major new expansion opportunities were shrinking and growth was slowing. Furthermore, while global category management had improved cross-market coordination, innovative new products such as two-in-one shampoo or compact detergent were still coming through the pipeline very slowly. And even when they did, they were taking many years to roll out worldwide. To many in the organization, the matrix structure seemed an impediment to entrepreneurship and flexibility.

Exhibit 2 P&G European Organization, 1986

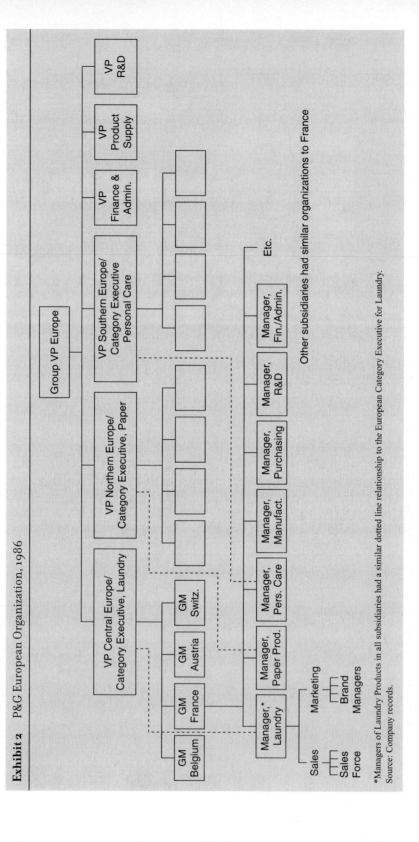

*Managers of Laundry Products in all subsidiaries had a similar dotted line relationship to the European Category Executive for Laundry.

Source: Company records.

Exhibit 3 P&G's Worldwide Organization Structure, 1990

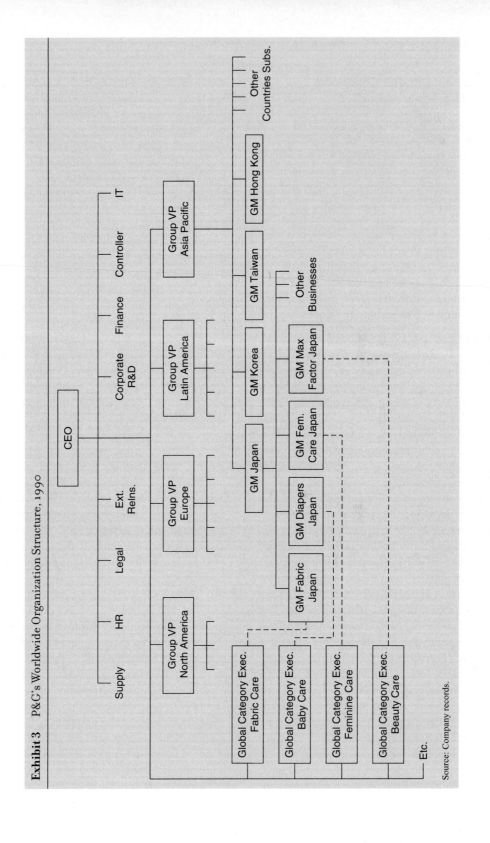

Source: Company records.

P&G Japan: Difficult Childhood, Struggling Adolescence

Up to the mid-1980s, P&G Japan had been a minor contributor to P&G's international growth. Indeed, the startup had been so difficult that, in 1984, twelve years after entering the Japan market, P&G's board reviewed the accumulated losses of $200 million, the ongoing negative operating margins of (75%), and the eroding sales base—decreasing from ¥44 billion in 1979 to ¥26 billion in 1984—and wondered if it was time to exit this market. But CEO Ed Artzt convinced the board that Japan was strategically important, that the organization had learned from its mistakes—and that Durk Jager, the energetic new country GM, could turn things around.

The Turnaround   In 1985, as the first step in a program called "Ichidai Hiyaku" ("The Great Flying leap"), Jager analyzed the causes of P&G's spectacular failure in Japan. Among his key findings was that the company had not recognized the distinctive needs and habits of the very demanding Japanese consumer. (For instance, P&G Japan had built its laundry detergent business around All Temperature Cheer, a product that ignored the Japanese practice of doing the laundry in tap water, not a range of water temperatures.) Furthermore, he found that they had not respected the innovative capability of Japanese companies like Kao and Lion who turned out to be among the world's toughest competitors. (After creating the market for disposable diapers in Japan, for example, they watched Pampers market share drop from 100% in 1979 to 8% in 1985 as local competitors introduced similar products with major improvements.) And he concluded that they had not adapted to the complex Japanese distribution system. (For instance, after realizing that its 3,000 wholesalers were providing little promotional support for P&G products, the company resorted to aggressive discounting which, in turn, triggered distributor disengagement and competitive price wars for several years.)

Jager argued that without a major in-country product development capability, P&G could never respond to the demanding Japanese consumer and the tough technology-driven local competitors. Envisioning a technology center that would support product development throughout Asia and even take worldwide leadership roles, he persuaded his superiors to grow P&G's 60 person R&D team into an organization that could compete with competitor Kao's 2,000 strong R&D operation.

Over the next four years, radical change in market research, advertising, and distribution resulted in a 270% increase in sales which, in turn, reduced unit production costs by 62%. In 1988, with laundry detergents again profitable, and Pampers and Whisper (the Japanese version of P&G's Always feminine napkin) achieving market leadership, Jager began to emphasize expansion through more new product introductions, and a bold expansion into the beauty products category. When P&G implemented its new region-based reorganization in 1990, Jager became the logical candidate to assume the newly created position of group VP for Asia, a position he held until 1991 when he went to run the huge U.S. business.

The Relapse   In the early 1990s, however, P&G Japan's strong performance began eroding. The problems began when Japan's "Bubble Economy" burst in 1991. More troubling, however, was the fact that, even within this stagnating market, P&G was losing share. Between 1992 and 1996 its Yen sales fell 3% to 4% annually for a cumulative 20% total decline, while in the same period competitor Unicharm's annual growth was 13% and Kao's was 3%.

Even P&G's entry into the new category of beauty care served to worsen rather than improve the situation. The parent company's 1991 acquisition of Max Factor gave P&G Japan a foothold in the $10 billion Japanese cosmetics market. But in Japan, sales of only $300 million made it a distant number five competitor, its 3% market share dwarfed by Shiseido's 20% plus. Then, in 1992 P&G's global beauty care category executive announced the global launch of the Max Factor Blue, a top end self-select color cosmetic line to be sold through general merchandise and drug stores. But

in Japan, over 80% of the market was sold by trained beauty counselors in specialty stores or department store cosmetics counters. The new self-select strategy, coupled with a decision to cut costs in the expensive beauty-counselor distribution channel led to the Japanese cosmetics business recording a 15% decline in sales. The previous breakeven performance became a negative operating margin of (10%) in 1993. Things became even worse the following year, with losses running at $1 million a week.

In 1994, the Japanese beauty business lost $50 million on sales of less than $300 million. Among the scores of businesses in the 15 countries reporting to him, A. G. Lafley, the newly arrived VP of the Asia region, quickly zeroed in on Max Factor Japan as a priority problem area. "We first had to clean up the Max Factor Blue mass market mess, then review our basic strategy," he said. Over the next three years, the local organization worked hard to make Max Factor Japan profitable. Its product line was rationalized from 1400 SKUs to 500; distribution support was focused on 4,000 of the previous 10,000 sales outlets; and sales and marketing staff was cut from 600 to 150. It was a trying time for Max Factor Japan.

▌ Organization 2005: Blueprint for Global Growth

In 1996, Durk Jager, now promoted to chief operating officer under CEO John Pepper, signaled that he saw the development of new products as the key to P&G's future growth. While supporting Pepper's emphasis on expanding into emerging markets, he voiced concern that the company would "start running out of white space towards the end of the decade." To emphasize the importance of creating new businesses, he became the champion of a Leadership Innovation Team to identify and support major company-wide innovations.

When he became CEO in January 1999, Jager continued his mission. Citing P&G breakthroughs such as the first synthetic detergent in the 1930s, its introduction of fluoride toothpaste in the 1950s, and

its development of the first disposable diaper in the 1960s, he said, "Almost without exception, we've won biggest on the strength of superior product technology. . . . But frankly, we've come nowhere near exploiting its full potential." Backing this belief, in 1999 he increased the budget for R&D by 12% while cutting marketing expenditures by 9%.

If P&G's growth would now depend on its ability to develop new products and roll them out rapidly worldwide, Jager believed his new strategic thrust had to be implemented through a radically different organization. Since early 1998 he and Pepper had been planning Organization 2005, an initiative he felt represented "the most dramatic change to P&G's structure, processes, and culture in the company's history." Implementing O2005, as it came to be called, he promised it would bring 13% to 15% annual earnings growth and would result in $900 million in annual savings starting in 2004. Implementation would be painful, he warned: in the first five years it called for closing of 10 plants and the loss of 15,000 jobs—13% of the worldwide workforce. The cost of the restructuring was estimated at $1.9 billion, with $1 billion of that total forecast for 1999 and 2000.

Changing the Culture   During the three months prior to assuming the CEO role, Jager toured P&G's sites worldwide. He concluded that P&G's sluggish 2% annual volume growth and its loss of global market share was due to a culture he saw as slow, conformist, and risk-averse. (See Exhibit 4 for P&G's financial performance.) In his view, employees were wasting half their time on "non value-added work" such as memo writing, form filling, or chart preparation, slowing down decisions and making the company vulnerable to more nimble competition. (One observer described P&G's product development model as "ready, aim, aim, aim, aim, fire.") He concluded that any organizational change would have to be built on a cultural revolution.

With "Stretch, Innovation, and Speed" as his watchwords, Jager signaled his intent to shake up norms and practices that had shaped generations of highly disciplined, intensely loyal managers often

Exhibit 4 P&G Select Financial Performance Data 1980–1999

	June 1999	June 1998	June 1997	June 1996	June 1995	June 1990	June 1985	June 1980
Annual Income Statement ($ millions)								
Sales	38,125	37,154	35,764	35,284	33,434	24,081	13,552	10,772
Cost of Goods Sold	18,615	19,466	18,829	19,404	18,370	14,658	9,099	7,471
Gross Profit	19,510	17,688	16,935	15,880	15,064	9,423	4,453	3,301
Selling, General, and Administrative Expense *of which:*	10,628	10,035	9,960	9,707	9,632	6,262	3,099	1,977
Research and Development Expense	1,726	1,546	1,469	1,399	1,148	693	400	228
Advertising Expense	3,538	3,704	3,466	3,254	3,284	2,059	1,105	621
Depreciation, Depletion, and Amortization	2,148	1,598	1,487	1,358	1,253	859	378	196
Operating Profit	6,734	6,055	5,488	4,815	4,179	2,302	976	1,128
Interest Expense	650	548	457	493	511	395	165	97
Non-Operating Income/ Expense	235	201	218	272	409	561	193	51
Special Items	−481	0	0	75	−77	0	0	0
Total Income Taxes	2,075	1,928	1,834	1,623	1,355	914	369	440
Net Income	3,763	3,780	3,415	3,046	2,645	1,554	635	642
Geographic Breakdown: Net Sales								
Americas	58.4%	54.7%	53.8%	52.9%	55.1%			
United States						62.5%	75.4%	80.9%
Europe, Middle East and Africa	31.9%	35.1%	35.3%	35.2%	32.9%			
International						39.9%	22.3%	22.4%
Asia	9.7%	10.2%	10.9%	11.9%	10.8%			
Corporate					1.2%	−2.1%	2.3%	−3.3%
Number of Employees	110,000	110,000	106,000	103,000	99,200	94,000	62,000	59,000
Abbreviated Balance Sheet ($ millions)								
ASSETS								
Total Current Assets	11,358	10,577	10,786	10,807	10,842	7,644	3,816	3,007
Plant, Property & Equipment, net	12,626	12,180	11,376	11,118	11,026	7,436	5,292	3,237
Other Assets	8,129	8,209	5,382	5,805	6,257	3,407	575	309
TOTAL ASSETS	32,113	30,966	27,544	27,730	28,125	18,487	9,683	6,553
LIABILITIES								
Total Current Liabilities	10,761	9,250	7,798	7,825	8,648	5,417	2,589	1,670
Long-Term Debt	6,231	5,765	4,143	4,670	5,161	3,588	877	835
Deferred Taxes	362	428	559	638	531	1,258	945	445
Other Liabilities	2,701	3,287	2,998	2,875	3,196	706	0	0
TOTAL LIABILITIES	20,055	18,730	15,498	16,008	17,536	10,969	4,411	2,950
TOTAL EQUITY	12,058	12,236	12,046	11,722	10,589	7,518	5,272	3,603
TOTAL LIABILITIES & EQUITY	32,113	30,966	27,544	27,730	28,125	18,487	9,683	6,553

Source: SEC Filings, Standard & Poor's Research Insight.

referred to within the industry as "Proctoids." "Great ideas come from conflict and dissatisfaction with the status quo," he said. "I'd like an organization where there are rebels." To signal the importance of risk taking and speed, Jager gave a green light to the Leadership Innovation Team to implement a global rollout of two radically new products: Dryel, a home dry cleaning kit, and Swiffer, an electrostatically-charged dust mop. Just 18 months after entering their first test market, they were on sale in the United States, Europe, Latin America, and Asia. Jager promised twenty more new products over the next eighteen months. "And if you are worried about oversight," he said, "I am the portfolio manager."

Changing the Processes   Reinforcing the new culture were some major changes to P&G's traditional systems and processes. To emphasize the need for greater risk taking, Jager leveraged the performance-based component of compensation so that, for example, the variability of a vice president's annual pay package increased from a traditional range of 20% (10% up or down) to 80% (40% up or down). And to motivate people and align them with the overall success of the company, he extended the reach of the stock option plan from senior management to virtually all employees. Even outsiders were involved, and P&G's advertising agencies soon found their compensation linked to sales increases per dollar spent.

Another major systems shift occurred in the area of budgets. Jager felt that the annual ritual of preparing, negotiating, and revising line item sales and expenses by product, by country was enormously time-wasting and energy-sapping. And the episodic nature of separate marketing, payroll, and initiative budgets had become even more inefficient. Going forward, Jager argued for an integrated business planning process where all budget elements of the operating plan could be reviewed and approved together.

Changing the Structure   In perhaps the most drastic change introduced in O2005, primary profit responsibility shifted from P&G's four regional organizations to seven global business units (GBUs) that would now manage product development, manufacturing and marketing of their respective categories worldwide. The old regional organizations were reconstituted into seven market development organizations (MDOs) that assumed responsibility for local implementation of the GBU's global strategies.[1] And transactional activities such as accounting, HR payroll, and much of IT were coordinated through a global business service unit (GBS). (See Exhibit 5 for a representation of the new structure.)

Beyond their clear responsibility for developing and rolling out new products, the GBUs were also charged with the task of increasing efficiency by standardizing manufacturing processes, simplifying brand portfolios, and coordinating marketing activities. For example, by reducing the company's twelve different diaper manufacturing processes to one standard production model, Jager believed that P&G could not only reap economies but might remove a major barrier to rapid new product rollouts. And by axing some of its 300 brands and evaluating the core group with global potential, he felt the company could leverage its resources more efficiently.

The restructuring also aimed to eliminate bureaucracy and increase accountability. Overall, six management layers were stripped out, reducing the levels between chairman and the front line from 13 to 7. Furthermore, numerous committee responsibilities were transferred to individuals. For example, the final sign-off on new advertising copy was given to individual executives not approval boards, cutting the time it took to get out ads from months to days.

New Corporate Priorities Meet Old Japanese Problems

The seeds of the major strategic and organizational changes began sprouting long before Durk Jager assumed the CEO role in January 1999. For years, Jager had been pushing his belief in growth through innovation, urging businesses to invest in new products and technologies. Even the organizational review that resulted in the O2005 blueprint had

---

[1]In an exception to the shift of profit responsibility to the GBUs, the MDOs responsible for developing countries were treated as profit centers.

Exhibit 5   P&G Organization, 1999 (Post "O2005" Implementation)

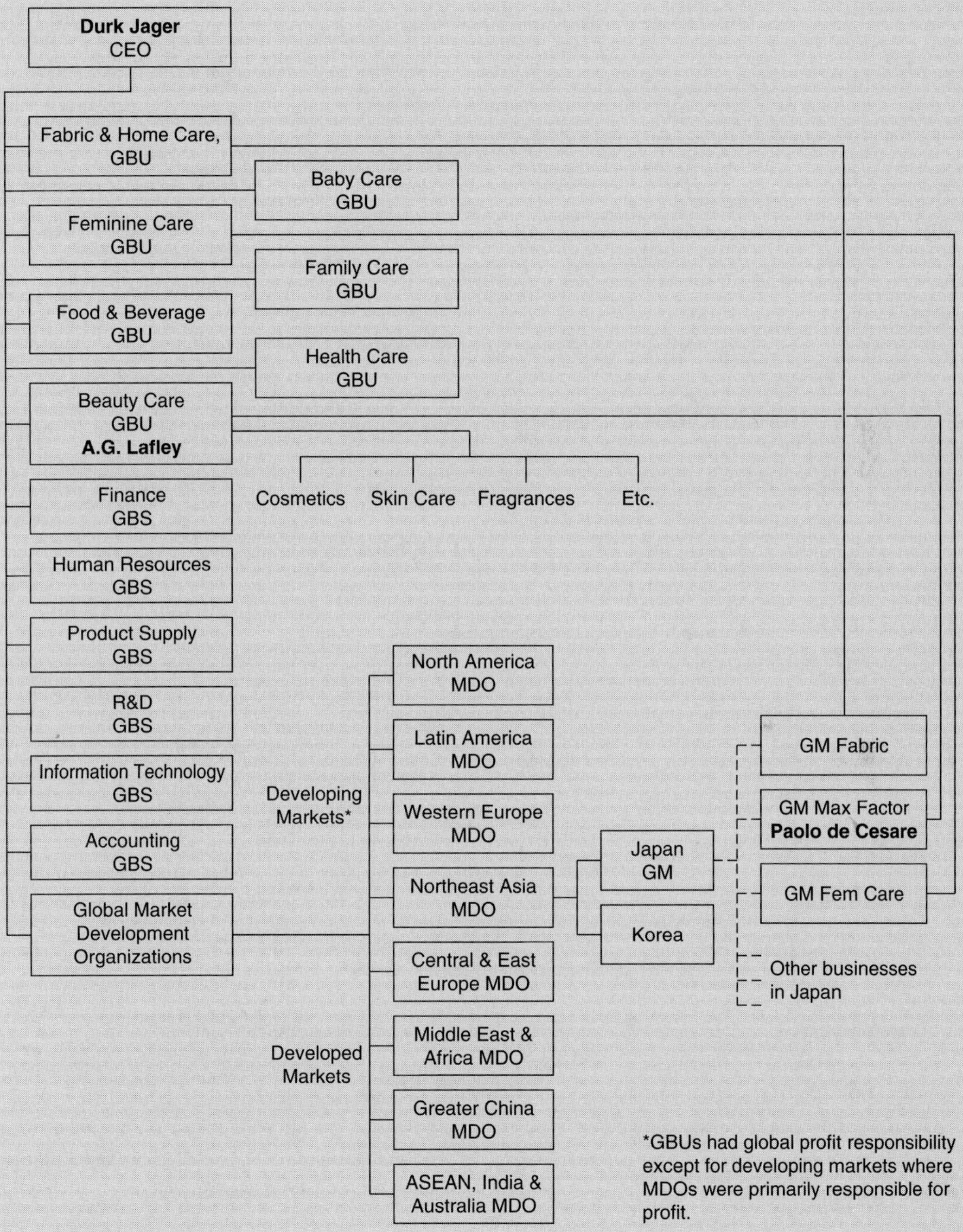

| Durk Jager |
| CEO |

Fabric & Home Care, GBU

Baby Care GBU

Feminine Care GBU

Family Care GBU

Food & Beverage GBU

Health Care GBU

Beauty Care GBU **A.G. Lafley**

Cosmetics   Skin Care   Fragrances   Etc.

Finance GBS

Human Resources GBS

Product Supply GBS

R&D GBS

Information Technology GBS

Accounting GBS

Global Market Development Organizations

Developing Markets*

North America MDO

Latin America MDO

Western Europe MDO

Northeast Asia MDO

Central & East Europe MDO

Developed Markets

Middle East & Africa MDO

Greater China MDO

ASEAN, India & Australia MDO

Japan GM

Korea

GM Fabric

GM Max Factor **Paolo de Cesare**

GM Fem Care

Other businesses in Japan

*GBUs had global profit responsibility except for developing markets where MDOs were primarily responsible for profit.

Source: Company records.

Exhibit 6   Beauty Counselor Work Flow

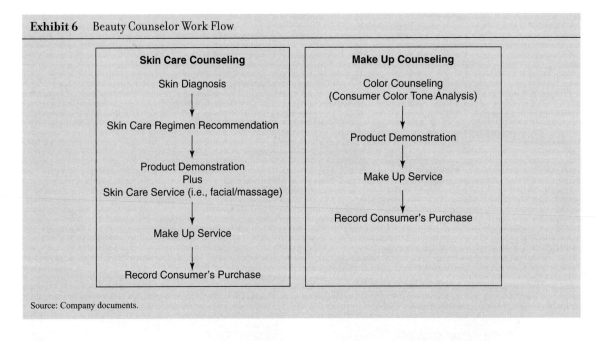

Source: Company documents.

begun a year before he took over. The winds of change blew through all parts of the company, including the long-suffering Japanese company's beauty care business which was finally emerging from years of problems.

Building the Base: From Mass to Class   By 1997 the Japanese cosmetics business had achieved breakeven. With guidance and support from A. G. Lafley, the VP for the Asia region, the Japanese team had focused its advertising investment on just two brands—Max Factor Color and a prestige skin care brand called SK-II. "Poring through the Japanese business, we found this little jewel called SK-II," recalled Lafley. "It became the cornerstone of our new focus on the prestige beauty-counselor segment."[2] Max Factor Japan began rebuilding its beauty counselor channels, which involved signifi-

cant investments in training as well as counter design and installation (see Exhibits 6 and 7). Supporting these investments was a bold experiment in TV advertising featuring a well respected Japanese actress in her late 30s. In three years SK-II's awareness ratings rose from around 20% to over 70%, while sales in the same period more than doubled.

Building on this success, management adapted the ad campaign for Hong Kong and Taiwan, where SK-II had quietly built a loyal following among the many women who took their fashion cues from Tokyo. In both markets, sales rocketed, and by 1996/97, export sales of $68 million represented about 30% of the brand's total sales. More important, SK-II was now generating significant operating profits. Yet within P&G, this high-end product had little visibility outside Japan. Paolo de Cesare, general manager of P&G's European skincare business in the mid 1990s, felt that, because the company's skin care experience came from the highly successful mass market Olay brand, few outside Japan understood SK-II. "I remember some people saying that SK-II was like Olay for Japan," he recalled. "People outside Japan just didn't know what to make of it."

[2] SK-II was an obscure skin care product that had not even been recognized, much less evaluated, in the Max Factor acquisition. Containing Pitera, a secret yeast-based ingredient supposedly developed by a Japanese monk who noticed how the hands of workers in sake breweries kept young looking, SK-II had a small but extremely loyal following of users. Priced at ¥15,000 ($120) or more per bottle, it clearly was at the top of the skin care range.

Exhibit 7   In-Store SK-II Counter Space

Source: Company documents.

Responding to the Innovation Push   Meanwhile, Durk Jager had begun his push for more innovation. Given his firmly held belief that Japan's demanding consumers and tough competitors made it an important source of leading-edge ideas, it was not surprising that more innovative ideas and initiatives from Japan began finding their way through the company. For example, an electrostatically charged cleaning cloth developed by a Japanese competitor became the genesis of P&G's global rollout of Swiffer dry mops; rising Japanese sensitivity to hygiene and sanitation spawned worldwide application in products such as Ariel Pure Clean ("beyond whiteness, it washes away germs"); and dozens of other ideas from Japan—from a waterless car washing cloth to a disposable stain-removing pad to a washing-machine-based dry cleaning product—were all put into P&G's product development pipeline.

Because Japanese women had by far the highest use of beauty care products in the world, it was natural that the global beauty care category management started to regard Max Factor Japan as a potential source of innovation. One of the first worldwide development projects on which Japan played a key role was Lipfinity, a long-lasting lipstick that was felt to have global potential.

In the mid-1990s, the impressive but short-lived success of long-lasting lipsticks introduced in Japan by Shiseido and Kenebo reinforced P&G's own consumer research which had long indicated the potential for such a product. Working with R&D labs in Cincinnati and the United Kingdom, several Japanese technologists participated on a global team that developed a new product involving a durable color base and a renewable moisturizing second coat. Recognizing that this two-stage application would result

in a more expensive product that involved basic habit changes, the global cosmetics category executive asked Max Factor Japan to be the new brand's global lead market.

Viewing the task as "translating the breakthrough technology invention into a market-sensitive product innovation," the Japanese product management team developed the marketing approach—concept, packaging, positioning, communications strategy, etc.—that led to the new brand, Lipfinity becoming Japan's best selling lipstick. The Japanese innovations were then transferred worldwide, as Lipfinity rolled out in Europe and the United States within six months of the Japanese launch.

O2005 Rolls Out   Soon after O2005 was first announced in September 1998, massive management changes began. By the time of its formal implementation in July 1999, half the top 30 and a third of the top 300 were new to their jobs. For example, A. G. Lafley, who had just returned from Asia to head the North American region, was asked to prepare to hand off that role and take over as head of the Beauty Care GBU (Global Business Unit). "It was a crazy year," recalled Lafley. "There was so much to build, but beyond the grand design, we were not clear about it should operate."

In another of the hundreds of O2005's senior management changes, Paolo de Cesare, head of P&G's European skincare business, was promoted to the VP level and asked to move to Osaka and head up Max Factor Japan. Under the new structure he would report directly to Lafley's Beauty Care GBU, and on a dotted-line basis to the head of the MDO (Market Development Organization) for Northeast Asia.

In addition to adjusting to this new complexity where responsibilities and relationships were still being defined, de Cesare found himself in a new global role. As President of Max Factor Japan he became a member of the beauty care global leadership team (GLT), a group comprised of the business general managers from three key MDOs, representatives from key functions such as R&D, consumer research, product supply, HR, and finance, and chaired by Lafley as GBU head. These meetings

became vital forums for implementing Lafley's charge to focus investment on the top brands with the potential to become global assets. The question took on new importance for de Cesare when he was named global franchise leader for SK-II and asked to explore its potential as a global brand.

A New Global Product Development Process
Soon after arriving in Japan, de Cesare discovered that the Japanese Max Factor organization was increasingly involved in new global product development activities following its successful Lipfinity role. This process began under the leadership of the beauty care GLT when consumer research identified an unmet consumer need worldwide. A lead research center then developed a technical model of how P&G could respond to the need. Next, the GLT process brought in marketing expertise from lead markets to expand that technology "chassis" into a holistic new product concept. Finally, contributing technologists and marketers were designated to work on the variations in ingredients or aesthetics necessary to adapt the core technology or product concept to local markets.

This global product development process was set in motion when consumer researchers found that, despite regional differences, there was a worldwide opportunity in facial cleansing. The research showed that, although U.S. women were satisfied with the clean feeling they got using bar soaps, it left their skin tight and dry; in Europe, women applied a cleansing milk with a cotton pad which left their skin moisturized and conditioned, but not as clean as they wanted; and in Japan, the leading habit of using foaming facial cleansers left women satisfied with skin conditioning but not with moisturizing. Globally, however, the unmet need was to achieve soft, moisturized, clean-feeling skin, and herein the GBU saw the product opportunity—and the technological challenge.

A technology team was assembled at an R&D facility in Cincinnati, drawing on the most qualified technologists from its labs worldwide. For example, because the average Japanese woman spent 4.5 minutes on her face-cleansing regime, compared to 1.7 minutes for the typical American woman,

Japanese technologists were sought for their refined expertise of cleansing processes, and their particular understanding of how to develop product with the rich, creamy lather.

Working with a woven substrate technology developed by P&G's paper business, the core technology team found that a 10 micron fiber, when woven into a mesh, was effective in trapping and absorbing dirt and impurities. By impregnating this substrate with a dry-sprayed formula of cleansers and moisturizers activated at different times in the cleansing process, they felt they could develop a disposable cleansing cloth that would respond to the identified consumer need. After this technology "chassis" had been developed, a technology team in Japan adapted it to allow the cloth to be impregnated with a different cleanser formulation that included the SK-II ingredient, Pitera.

A U.S.-based marketing team took on the task of developing an Olay product concept using the basic impregnated cloth technology. Identifying their consumers' view of a multi-step salon facial as the ultimate cleansing experience, this team came up with the concept of a one-step routine that offered the benefits of cleansing, conditioning, and toning—"just like a daily facial." Meanwhile, another team had the same assignment in Japan, which became the lead market for the SK-II version. Because women already had a five or six step cleansing routine, the SK-II version was positioned as a "foaming massage cloth" that built on the ritual experience of increasing skin circulation through a massage while boosting skin clarity due to the micro fibers' ability to clean pores and trap dirt. (See Exhibit 8 for illustration with other core SK-II products.)

Because of its premium pricing strategy, the SK-II Foaming Massage Cloth was packaged in a much more elegant dispensing box that sold for ¥6,000 ($50) compared to $7 for the Olay Facial Cloth in the United States. And Japan assigned several technologists to the task of developing detailed product performance data that was communicated to Japanese beauty magazines which took a much more scientific approach to their product reviews than their Western counterparts. In the end, each market ended up with a distinct product built on a common technology platform. Marketing expertise was also shared—the Japanese performance analysis and data was widely used in Europe, for example—allowing the organization to leverage its local learning.

▌ The SK-II Decision: A Global Brand?

After barely six months in Japan, de Cesare recognized that he now had three different roles in the new organization. As president of Max Factor Japan, he was impressed by the turnaround this local company had pulled off, and was optimistic about its ability to grow significantly in the large Japanese beauty market. As GLT member on the beauty care GBU, he was proud of his organization's contribution to the GBU-sponsored global new product innovation process, and was convinced that Japan could continue to contribute to and learn from P&G's impressive technology base. And now as global franchise leader for SK-II, he was excited by the opportunity to explore whether the brand could be expanded into the $10 billion worldwide prestige skin care market. (See Exhibit 9.)

When he arrived in Japan, de Cesare found that SK-II's success in Taiwan and Hong Kong (by 1998/99 they accounted for 45% of total SK-II sales) had already encouraged management to begin expansion into three other regional markets—Singapore, Malaysia, and Korea. But these were relatively small markets, and as he reviewed data on the global skin care and prestige beauty markets, he wondered if the time was right to make a bold entry into one or more major markets. (See Exhibits 10 and 11 for global market and consumer data.)

As he reviewed the opportunities, three alternatives presented themselves. First, the beauty care management team for Greater China was interested in expanding on SK-II's success in Taiwan and Hong Kong by introducing the brand into mainland China. Then, at GLT meetings, de Cesare had discussed with the head of beauty care in Europe the possibilities of bringing this brand into a large Western market. His third option—really his first, he realized—was to focus first on building on the

Exhibit 8   SK-II Product Line Illustration

pitera soak

FACIAL TREATMENT ESSENCE
Skin Balancing Essence

The heart of the SK-II range, the revolutionary **Facial Treatment Essence** is the second point in your Ritual. This unique Pitera-rich product helps boost moisture levels to improve texture and clarity for a more beautiful, glowing complexion.

Women are so passionate about **Facial Treatment Essence** that they describe it as their 'holy' water. It contains the most concentrated amount of Pitera of all our skincare products—around 90% pure SK-II Pitera. It absorbs easily and leaves your skin looking radiant, with a supple, smooth feel.

FOAMING MASSAGE CLOTH
Purifying Cleansing Cloth

These innovative **Foaming Massage Cloths** leave your skin feeling smooth and velvety. A single sheet offers the outstanding effects of a cleanser, facial wash and massage. It gently washes away impurities, excess oil and non-waterproof eye make-up, leaving your skin clean, pure and refreshed.

FACIAL TREATMENT CLEAR LOTION
Clear Purifying Lotion

For a perfectly conditioned and ultra-fresh skin, use the **Facial Treatment Clear Lotion** morning and evening after cleansing your face and neck. The final part of your cleansing process, this Lotion helps remove residual impurities and dead skin cells.

Source: Company brochure.

successful business in SK-II's home market by exploiting some of the significant potential in his rich and proven Japanese market.

The Japanese Opportunity Japanese women were among the most sophisticated users of beauty products in the world and on a per capita basis, they were the world's leading consumers of these products. Despite its improved performance in recent years, Max Factor Japan could claim less than a 3% share of this $10 billion market. "It's huge," boasted

Exhibit 9   Global Prestige Market: Size and Geographic Split

Global Prestige Market
(Fragrances, Cosmetics, Skin) = $15 billion at
retail level (of which approximately 60% is skin care)

United States	26%
Canada	2
Asia/Pacific[a]	25
United Kingdom	5
France	5
Germany	5
Rest of Europe	16
Rest of World	16%

[a]Japan represented over 80% of the Asia/Pacific total.
Source: Company data.

Exhibit 10   Global Cosmetics and Skin Care Market Size—CY1999

Skin Care (Main market and prestige)

Region/Country	Retail Sales ($ million)	Two-Year Growth Rate
Western Europe	$8,736	7%
France	2,019	7
Germany	1,839	14
United Kingdom	1,052	17
North America	6,059	18
U.S.A.	5,603	18
Asia/Pacific	11,220	2
China	1,022	28
Japan	6,869	6
South Korea	1,895	9
Taiwan	532	18
Hong Kong	266	6%

Source: Company data.

one local manager. "Larger than the U.S. laundry market."

Although SK-II had sales of more than $150 million in Japan in 1999, de Cesare was also aware that in recent years its home market growth had slowed. This was something the new manager felt he could change by tapping into P&G's extensive technological resources. The successful experience of the foaming massage cloth convinced him that there was a significant opportunity to expand sales by extending the SK-II line beyond its traditional product offerings. For example, he could see an immediate opportunity to move into new segments by adding anti-aging and skin-whitening products to the SK-II range. Although this would take a considerable amount of time and effort, it would leverage existing capabilities internally and existing brand image externally. Compared to the new market entry options, investment would be quite low.

An exciting development that would support this home market thrust emerged when he discovered was that his SK-II technology and marketing teams had come together to develop an innovative Beauty Imaging System (BIS). Using the Japanese technicians' skills in miniaturization and software development, they were working to create a simplified version of scientific equipment used by P&G lab technicians to qualify new skin-care products by measuring improvements in skin condition. The plan was to install the modified BIS at SK-II counters and have beauty consultants use it to boost the accuracy and credibility of the vital skin diagnosis step of their counseling process. The project fit perfectly with de Cesare's vision for SK-II to become the brand that provided individual solutions to skin care problems. He felt it could have significant impact in building loyalty in the analytically inclined Japanese consumer, and immediately boosted support for the project.

With such a small share of such a rich market, de Cesare felt that a strategy of product innovation and superior in-store service had the potential to accelerate a growth rate that had slowed to 5% per annum over the past three years. Although Shiseido could be expected to put up a good fight, he felt SK-II should double sales in Japan over the next six or seven years. In short, de Cesare was extremely excited about SK-II's potential for growth in its home market. He said: "It's a fabulous opportunity. One loyal SK-II customer in Japan already spends about

Exhibit 11   Skin Care and Cosmetics Habits and Practices: Selected Countries

Product Usage (% Past 7 Days)	United States[a]	Japan[a]	China[b]	United Kingdom[a]
Facial Moisturizer—Lotion	45%	95%	26%	37%
Facial Moisturizer—Cream	25	28	52	45
Facial Cleansers (excluding Family Bar Soap)	51	90	57	41
Foundation	70	85	35	57
Lipstick	84	97	75	85
Mascara	76%	27%	13%	75%

[a]Based on broad, representative sample of consumers.
[b]Based on upper income consumers in Beijing City.
Source: Company data.

$1,000 a year on the brand. Even if you were a regular consumer of all P&G's other products—from toothpaste and deodorant to shampoo and detergent—all together you would spend nowhere near that amount annually."

The Chinese Puzzle A very different opportunity existed in China, where P&G had been operating only since 1988. Because of the extraordinarily low prices of Chinese laundry products, the company had uncharacteristically led with beauty products when it entered this huge market. Olay was launched in 1989 and, after early problems, eventually became highly successful by adopting a nontraditional marketing strategy. To justify its price premium—it was 20 to 30 times the price of local skin-care products—Shivesh Ram, the entrepreneurial beauty-care manager in China, decided to add a service component to Olay's superior product formulation. Borrowing from the Japanese Max Factor model, he began selling through counters in the state-owned department stores staffed by beauty counselors. By 1999, Olay had almost 1,000 such counters in China and was an outstanding success.

As the Chinese market opened to international retailers, department stores from Taiwan, Hong Kong, and Singapore began opening in Beijing and Shanghai. Familiar with Olay as a mass-market brand, they questioned allocating it scarce beauty counter space alongside Estee Lauder, Lancôme, Shiseido, and other premium brands that had al-

ready claimed the prime locations that were critical to success in this business. It was at this point that Ram began exploring the possibility of introducing SK-II, allowing Olay to move deeper into second-tier department stores, to stores in smaller cities, and to "second floor" cosmetics locations in large stores. "China is widely predicted to become the second largest market in the world," said Ram. "The prestige beauty segment is growing at 30 to 40% a year, and virtually every major competitor in that space is already here."

Counterbalancing Ram's enthusiastic proposals, de Cesare also heard voices of concern. Beyond the potential impact on a successful Olay market position, some were worried that SK-II would be a distraction to P&G's strategy of becoming a mainstream Chinese company, and its competitive goal of entering 600 Chinese cities ahead of Unilever, Kao, and other global players. They argued that targeting an elite consumer group with a niche product was not in keeping with the objective of reaching the 1.2 billion population with laundry, hair care, oral care, diapers, and other basics. After all, the four step regimen of SK-II—a three month supply—could cost more than one month's salary for the average woman working in a major Chinese city.

Furthermore, the skeptics wondered if the Chinese consumer was ready for SK-II. Olay had succeeded only by educating its customers to move from a one-step skin-care process—washing with bar soap and water—to a three-step cleansing and

moisturizing process. SK-II relied on having women develop a four- to six-step regimen, something the doubters felt was unrealistic. But as Ram and others argued, within the target market, skin care practices were quite developed and penetration of skin care products was higher than in many developed markets.

Finally, the Chinese market presented numerous other risks from the widespread existence of counterfeit prestige products to the bureaucracy attached to a one-year import registration process. But the biggest concern was the likelihood that SK-II would attract import duties of 35% to 40%. This meant that even if P&G squeezed its margin in China, SK-II would have to be priced significantly above the retail level in other markets. Still, the China team calculated that because of the lower cost of beauty consultants, they could still be profitable. (See Exhibit 12 for cost estimates.)

Despite the critics, Ram was eager to try, and he responded to their concerns:

> There are three Chinas—rural China, low income urban China, and sophisticated, wealthy China concentrated in Shanghai, Beijing, and Guangzhou. It's as big a target consumer group as in many developed markets. If we don't move soon, the battle for that elite will be lost to the global beauty-care powerhouses that have been here for three years or more.

Ram was strongly supported by his regional beauty care manager, and by the Greater China MDO president. Together, they were willing to experiment with a few counters in Shanghai, and if successful, to expand to more counters in other major cities. Over the first three years, they expected to generate $10 to $15 million in sales, by which time they expected the brand to achieve breakeven. They estimated the initial investment to build counters, train beauty consultants, and support the introduction would probably mean losses of about 10% of sales over that three-year period.

The European Question   As he explored global opportunities for SK-II, de Cesare's mind kept returning to the European market he knew so well. Unlike China, Europe had a relatively large and sophisticated group of beauty-conscious consumers who already practiced a multi-step regimen using various specialized skin-care products. What he was unsure of was whether there was a significant group willing to adopt the disciplined six- to eight-step ritual that the devoted Japanese SK-II users followed.

The bigger challenge, in his view, would be introducing a totally new brand into an already crowded field of high-profile, well respected competitors including Estee Lauder, Clinique, Lancôme, Chanel, and Dior. While TV advertising had proven highly effective in raising SK-II's awareness and sales in Japan, Taiwan, and Hong Kong, the cost of television—or even print—made such an approach prohibitive in Europe. And without any real brand awareness or heritage, he wondered if SK-II's mystique would transfer to a Western market.

Exhibit 12   Global SK-II Cost Structure (% of net sales)[a]

FY1999/2000	Japan	Taiwan/ Hong Kong	PR China Expected	United Kingdom Expected
Net sales	100%	100%	100%	100%
Cost of products sold	22	26	45	29
Marketing, research and selling/ administrative expense	67	58	44	63
Operating income	11%	16%	11%	8%

[a]Data disguised.
Source: Company estimates.

As he thought through these issues, de Cesare spoke with his old boss, Mike Thompson, the head of P&G's beauty business in Europe. Because they sold primarily to mass distribution outlets, Thompson did not think the Max Factor salesforce provided SK-II the appropriate access to the European market. However, he explained that the fine fragrances business was beginning to do quite well. In the United Kingdom, for example, its own 25-person salesforce was on track in 1999 to book $1 million in after-tax profit on sales of $12 million. Selling brands like Hugo Boss, Giorgio, and Beverly Hills to department stores and Boots, the major pharmacy chain, its sales approach and trade relationship was different from the SK-II model in Japan. Nevertheless, Thompson felt it was a major asset that could be leveraged.

Furthermore, Thompson told de Cesare that his wife was a loyal SK-II user, and reasoned that since she was a critical judge of products there would be other women who would discover the same benefits she did. He believed that SK-II provided the fine fragrance business a way to extend its line in the few department stores that dominated U.K. distribution in the prestige business. He thought they would be willing to give SK-II a try. (He was less optimistic about countries like France and Germany, however, where prestige products were sold through thousands of perfumeries, making it impossible to justify the SK-II consultants who would be vital to the sales model.)

Initial consumer research in the United Kingdom had provided mixed results. But de Cesare felt that while this kind of blind testing could provide useful data on detergents, it was less helpful in this case. The consumers tested the product blind for one week, then were interviewed about their impressions. But lacking the beauty counselors' analysis and advice, and without the full skin care regimen, he felt the results were not a good predictor of SK-II's potential.

In discussions with Thompson, de Cesare concluded that he could hope to achieve sales of $10 million by the fourth year in the U.K. market. Given the intense competition, he recognized that he would

have to absorb losses of $1 million to $2 million annually over that period as the startup investment.

The Organizational Constraint   While the strategic opportunities were clear, de Cesare also recognized that his decision needed to recognize the organizational reality in which it would be implemented. While GBU head Lafley was an early champion and continuing supporter of SK-II, his boss, Durk Jager, was less committed. Jager was among those in P&G who openly questioned how well some of the products in the beauty-care business—particularly some of the acquired brands—fit in the P&G portfolio. While he was comfortable with high volume products like shampoo, he was more skeptical of the upper end of the line, particularly fine fragrances. In his view, the fashion-linked and promotion-driven sales models did not play well to P&G's "stack it high, sell it cheap" marketing skills nor leverage its superior technologies.

The other organizational reality was that the implementation of O2005 was causing a good deal of organizational disruption and management distraction. This was particularly true in Europe as Mike Thompson explained:

> We swung the pendulum 180 degrees from a local to a global focus. Marketing plans and budgets had previously been developed locally, strongly debated with European managers, then rolled up. Now they were developed globally—or at least regionally—by new people who often did not understand the competitive and trade differences across markets. We began to standardize and centralize our policies and practices out of Geneva. Not surprisingly, a lot of our best local managers left the company.

One result of the O2005 change was that country subsidiary general managers were now focused more on maximizing sales volume than profits, and this had put the beauty care business under significant budget pressure. Thompson explained the situation in Europe in 1999:

> One thing became clear very quickly: it was a lot easier to sell cases of Ariel [detergent] or Pampers [diapers] than cases of cosmetics, so guess where the

salesforce effort went? At the same time, the new product pipeline was resulting in almost a "launch of the month" and with the introduction of new products like Swiffer and Febreze, it was hard for the MDOs to manage all of these corporate priorities. . . . Finally, because cosmetics sales required more time and effort from local salesforces, more local costs were assigned to that business, and that has added to profit pressures.

Framing the Proposal   It was in this context that de Cesare was framing his proposal on the global

potential of SK-II as a brand, and his plans to exploit the opportunities he saw. But he knew Lafley's long ties and positive feelings towards SK-II would not be sufficient to convince him. The GBU head was committed to focusing beauty care on the core brands that could be developed as a global franchise, and his questions would likely zero in on whether de Cesare could build SK-II into such a brand.

Case 5-2   McKinsey & Company: Managing Knowledge and Learning

In April 1996, halfway through his first three-year term as managing director of McKinsey & Company, Rajat Gupta was feeling quite proud as he flew out of Bermuda, site of the firm's second annual Practice Olympics. He had just listened to twenty teams outlining innovative new ideas they had developed out of recent project work, and, like his fellow senior partner judges, Gupta had come away impressed by the intelligence and creativity of the firm's next generation of consultants.

But there was another thought that kept coming back to the 47-year-old leader of this highly successful $1.8 billion consulting firm (see Exhibit 1 for a twenty-year growth history). If this represented the tip of McKinsey's knowledge and expertise iceberg, how well was the firm doing in developing, capturing, and leveraging this asset in service of its clients worldwide? In his mind, the task of knowledge development had become much more complex over the past decade or so due to three intersecting forces. First, in an increasingly information and knowledge-driven age, the sheer volume and rate of change of new knowledge made the task much more complex; second, clients' ex-

pectations of and need for leading-edge expertise were constantly increasing; and third, the firm's own success had made it much more difficult to link and leverage the knowledge and expertise represented by 3,800 consultants in 69 offices worldwide. Although the Practice Olympics was only one of several initiatives he had championed, Gupta wondered if it was enough, particularly in light of his often stated belief that "knowledge is the lifeblood of McKinsey."

■ The Founders' Legacy[1]

Founded in 1926 by University of Chicago professor, James ("Mac") McKinsey, the firm of "accounting and engineering advisors" that bore his name grew rapidly. Soon Mac began recruiting experienced executives and training them in the integrated approach he called his General Survey outline. In Saturday morning sessions he would lead consultants through an "undeviating sequence" of analysis—goals, strategy, policies, organization, facilities, procedures, and personnel—while still encouraging them to synthesize data and think for themselves.

▌ This case was prepared by Prof. Christopher A. Bartlett.
▌ Copyright © 1996 by the President and Fellows of Harvard College. Harvard Business School case 396-357.

▌[1]The Founders' Legacy section draws on Amar V. Bhide, "Building the Professional Firm: McKinsey & Co., 1939–1968," HBS Working Paper 95-010.

Exhibit 1   McKinsey & Company: 20-Year Growth Indicators

Year	Number Office Locations	Number Active Engagements	Number of CSS*	Number of MGMs†
1975	24	661	529	NA
1980	31	771	744	NA
1985	36	1823	1248	NA
1990	47	2789	2465	348
1991	51	2875	2653	395
1992	55	2917	2875	399
1993	60	3142	3122	422
1994	64	3398	3334	440
1995	69	3559	3817	472

*CSS = Client Service Staff (all professional consulting staff)
†MGM = Management Group Members (partners and directors)
Source: Internal McKinsey & Company documents.

In 1932, Mac recruited Marvin Bower, a bright young lawyer with a Harvard MBA, and within two years asked him to become manager of the recently opened New York office. Convinced that he had to upgrade the firm's image in an industry typically regarded as "efficiency experts" or "business doctors," Bower undertook to imbue in his associates the sense of professionalism he had experienced in his time in a law partnership. In a 1937 memo, he outlined his vision for the firm as one focused on issues of importance to top-level management, adhering to the highest standards of integrity, professional ethics, and technical excellence, able to attract and develop young men of outstanding qualifications, and committed to continually raising its stature and influence. Above all, it was to be a firm dedicated to the mission of serving its clients superbly well.

Over the next decade, Bower worked tirelessly to influence his partners and associates to share his vision. As new offices opened, he became a strong advocate of the One Firm policy that required all consultants to be recruited and advanced on a firmwide basis, clients to be treated as McKinsey & Company responsibilities, and profits to be shared from a firm pool, not an office pool. And through dinner seminars, he began upgrading the size and

quality of McKinsey's clients. In the 1945 New Engagement Guide, he articulated a policy that every assignment should bring the firm something more than revenue—experience or prestige, for example.

Elected Managing Partner in 1950, Bower led his ten partners and 74 associates to initiate a series of major changes that turned McKinsey into an elite consulting firm unable to meet the demand for its services. Each client's problems were seen as unique, but Bower and his colleagues firmly believed that well-trained, highly intelligent generalists could quickly grasp the issue, and through disciplined analysis find its solution. The firm's extraordinary domestic growth through the 1950s provided a basis for international expansion that accelerated the rate of growth in the 1960s. Following the opening of the London Office in 1959, offices in Geneva, Amsterdam, Düsseldorf, and Paris followed quickly. By the time Bower stepped down as Managing Director in 1967, McKinsey was a well-established and highly respected presence in Europe and North America.

A Decade of Doubt

Although leadership succession was well planned and executed, within a few years, the McKinsey growth engine seemed to stall. The economic

turmoil of the oil crisis, the slowing of the division-alization process that had fueled the European expansion, the growing sophistication of client management, and the appearance of new focused competitors like Boston Consulting Group (BCG) all contributed to the problem. Almost overnight, McKinsey's enormous reservoir of internal self-confidence and even self-satisfaction began to turn to self-doubt and self-criticism.

Commission on Firm Aims and Goals   Concerned that the slowing growth in Europe and the U.S. was more than just a cyclical market down-turn, the firm's partners assigned a committee of their most respected peers to study the problem and make recommendations. In April 1971, the Commission on Firm Aims and Goals concluded that the firm has been growing too fast. The authors bluntly reported, "Our preoccupation with the geographic expansion and new practice possibilities has caused us to neglect the development of our technical and professional skills." The report concluded that McKinsey had been too willing to accept routine assignments from marginal clients, that the quality of work done was uneven, and that while its consultants were excellent generalist problem solvers, they often lacked the deep industry knowledge or the substantive specialized expertise that clients were demanding.

One of the Commission's central proposals was that the firm had to recommit itself to the con-tinuous development of its members. This meant that growth would have to be slowed and that the MGM-to-associate ratio be reduced from 7 to 1 back to 5 or 6 to 1. It further proposed that empha-sis be placed on the development of what it termed "T-shaped" consultants—those who supplemented a broad generalist perspective with an in-depth in-dustry or functional specialty.

Practice Development Initiative   When Ron Daniel was elected Managing Director in 1976—the fourth to hold the position since Bower had stepped down nine years earlier—McKinsey was still strug-gling to meet the challenges laid out in the Commis-sion's report. As the head of the New York office

since 1970, Daniel had experienced firsthand the rising expectations of increasingly sophisticated clients and the aggressive challenges of new com-petitors like BCG. In contrast to McKinsey's local office-based model of "client relationship" consult-ing, BCG began competing on the basis of "thought leadership" from a highly concentrated resource base in Boston. Using some simple but powerful tools, such as the experience curve and the growth-share matrix, BCG began to make strong inroads into the strategy-consulting market. As McKinsey began losing both clients and recruits to BCG, Daniel became convinced that his firm could no longer succeed pursuing its generalist model.

One of his first moves was to appoint one of the firm's most respected and productive senior part-ners as McKinsey's first full-time director of train-ing. As an expanded commitment to developing consultants' skills and expertise became the norm, the executive committee began debating the need to formally updating the firm's long-standing mission to reflect the firm's core commitment not only to serving its clients but also to developing its consul-tants. (Exhibit 2.)

But Daniel also believed some structural changes were necessary. Building on an initiative he and his colleagues had already implemented in the New York office, he created industry-based Clientele Sectors in consumer products, banking, industrial goods, insurance, and so on, cutting across the geo-graphic offices that remained the primary organi-zational entity. He also encouraged more formal development of the firm's functional expertise in areas like strategy, organization and operations where knowledge and experience were widely dif-fused and minimally codified. However, many—including Marvin Bower—expressed concern that any move towards a product-driven approach could damage McKinsey's distinctive advantage of local presence which gave partners strong connections with the business community, allowed teams to work on site with clients and facilitated implemen-tation. It was an approach that they felt contrasted sharply with the "fly in, fly out" model of expert-based consulting.

Exhibit 2   McKinsey's Mission and Guiding Principles (1996)

McKinsey Mission

To help our clients make positive, lasting, and substantial improvements in their performance and to build a great Firm that is able to attract, develop, excite, and retain exceptional people.

Guiding Principles

Serving Clients

Adhere to professional standards.
Follow the top management approach.
Assist the client in implementation and capability building.
Perform consulting in a cost-effective manner.

Building the Firm

Operate as one Firm.
Maintain a meritocracy.
Show a genuine concern for our people.
Foster an open and nonhierarchical working atmosphere.
Manage the Firm's resources responsibly.

Being a Member of the Professional Staff

Demonstrate commitment to client service.
Strive continuously for superior quality.
Advance the state-of-the-art management.
Contribute a spirit of partnership through teamwork and collaboration.
Profit from the freedom and assume the responsibility associated with self-governance.
Uphold the obligation to dissent.

Nonetheless, Daniel pressed ahead, and the industry sectors quickly found a natural client base. Feeling that functional expertise needed more attention, he assembled working groups to develop knowledge in two areas that were at the heart of McKinsey's practice—strategy and organization. To head up the first group, he named Fred Gluck, a director in the New York office who had been outspoken in urging the firm to modify its traditional generalist approach. In June 1977, Gluck invited a

"Super Group" of younger partners with strategy expertise to a three-day meeting to share ideas and develop an agenda for the strategy practice. One described the meeting:

> We had three days of unmitigated chaos. Someone from New York would stand up and present a four-box matrix. A partner from London would present a nine-box matrix. A German would present a 47-box matrix. It was chaos. . . . but at the end of the third day some strands of thought were coming together.

At the same time, Daniel asked Bob Waterman who had been working on a Siemens-sponsored study of "excellent companies" and Jim Bennett, a respected senior partner, to assemble a group that could articulate the firm's existing knowledge in the organization arena. One of their first recruits was an innovative young Ph.D. in organizational theory named Tom Peters.

Revival and Renewal

By the early 1980s, with growth resuming, a cautious optimism returned to McKinsey for the first time in almost a decade.

Centers of Competence   Recognizing that the activities of the two practice development projects could not just be a one-time effort, in 1980 Daniel asked Gluck to join the central small group that comprised the Firm Office and focus on the knowledge-building agenda that had become his passion. Ever since his arrival at the firm from Bell Labs in 1967, Gluck had wanted to bring an equally stimulating intellectual environment to McKinsey. Against some strong internal resistance, he set out to convert his partners to his strongly held beliefs— that knowledge development had to be a central, not a peripheral firm activity; that it needed to be ongoing and institutionalized, not temporary and project based; and that it had to be the responsibility of everyone, not just a few.

As one key means of bringing this about, he created 15 Centers of Competence (virtual centers, not locations) built around existing areas of functional expertise like marketing, change management, and

systems. In a 1982 memo to all partners, he described the role of these centers as twofold: to help develop consultants and to ensure the continued renewal of the firm's intellectual resources. For each Center, Gluck identified one or two highly motivated, recognized experts in the particular field and named them practice leaders. The expectation was that these leaders would assemble from around the firm, a core group of partners who were active in the practice area and interested in contributing to its development. (See Exhibit 3 for the 15 Centers and 11 Sectors in 1983.)

To help build a shared body of knowledge, the leadership of each of the 15 centers began to initiate a series of activities primarily involving the core group and less frequently, the members of the practice network. A colleague commented on his commitment to establishing the centers:

> Unlike industry sectors, the centers of competence did not have a natural, stable client base, and Fred had to work hard to get them going. . . . He basically told the practice leaders, "Spend whatever you can—the cost is almost irrelevant compared to the payoff."

Exhibit 3   McKinsey's Emerging Practice Areas: Centers of Competence and Industry Sectors, 1983

Centers of Competence	Clientele Sectors
Building institutional skills	Automotive
Business management unit	Banking
Change management	Chemicals
Corporate leadership	Communications and
Corporate finance	information
Diagnostic scan	Consumer products
International management	Electronics
Integrated logistics	Energy
Manufacturing	Health care
Marketing	Industrial goods
Microeconomics	Insurance
Sourcing	Steel
Strategic management	
Systems	
Technology	

There was no attempt to filter or manage the process, and the effect was "to let a thousand flowers bloom."

Gluck also spent a huge amount of time trying to change an internal status hierarchy based largely on the size and importance of one's client base. Arguing that practice development ("snowball making" as it became known internally) was not less "macho" than client development ("snowball throwing"), he tried to convince his colleagues that everyone had to become snowball makers *and* snowball throwers. In endless discussions, he would provoke his colleagues with barbed pronouncements and personal challenges: "Knowing what you're talking about is not necessarily a client service handicap" or "Would you want your brain surgery done by a general practitioner?"

Building a Knowledge Infrastructure   As the firm's new emphasis on individual consultant training took hold and the Clientele Sectors and Centers of Competence began to generate new insights, many began to feel the need to capture and leverage the learning. Although big ideas had occasionally been written up as articles for publication in newspapers, magazines, or journals like *Harvard Business Review,* there was still a deep-seated suspicion of anything that smacked of packaging ideas or creating proprietary concepts.

This reluctance to document concepts had long constrained the internal transfer of ideas and the vast majority of internally developed knowledge was never captured.

This began to change with the launching of the McKinsey Staff Paper series in 1978, and by the early 1980s the firm was actively encouraging its consultants to publish their key findings. The initiative got a major boost with the publication in 1982 of two major best-sellers, Peters and Waterman's *In Search of Excellence* and Kenichi Ohmae's *The Mind of the Strategist.* But books, articles, and staff papers required major time investments, and only a small minority of consultants made the effort to write them. Believing that the firm had to lower the barrier to internal knowledge communication,

Gluck introduced the idea of Practice Bulletins, two-page summaries of important new ideas that identified the experts who could provide more detail. A partner elaborated:

> The Bulletins were essentially internal advertisements for ideas and the people who had developed them. We tried to convince people that they would help build their personal networks and internal reputations. . . . Fred was not at all concerned that the quality was mixed, and had a strong philosophy of letting the internal market sort out what were the really big ideas.

Believing that the firm's organizational infrastructure needed major overhaul, in 1987 Gluck launched a Knowledge Management Project. After five months of study, the team made three recommendations. First, the firm had to make a major commitment to build a common database of knowledge accumulated from client work and developed in the practice areas. Second, to ensure that the databases were maintained and used, they proposed that each practice area (Clientele Sector and Competence Center) hire a full-time practice coordinator who could act as an "intelligent switch" responsible for monitoring the quality of the data and for helping consultants access the relevant information. And finally, they suggested that the firm expand its hiring practices and promotion policies to create a career path for deep functional specialists whose narrow expertise would not fit the normal profile of a T-shaped consultant.

The task of implementing these recommendations fell to a team led by Bill Matassoni, the firm's director of communications and Brook Manville, a newly recruited Yale Ph.D. with experience with electronic publishing. Focusing first on the Firm Practice Information System (FPIS), a computerized database of client engagements, they installed new systems and procedures to make the data more complete, accurate, and timely so that it could be accessed as a reliable information resource, not just an archival record. More difficult was the task of capturing the knowledge that had accumulated in the practice areas since much of it had not been

formalized and none of it had been prioritized or integrated. To create a computer-based Practice Development Network (PDNet), Matassoni and Manville put huge energy into begging, cajoling, and challenging each practice to develop and submit documents that represented their core knowledge. After months of work, they had collected the 2,000 documents that they believed provided the critical mass to launch PDNet.

Matassoni and his team also developed another information resource that had not been part of the study team's recommendations. They assembled a listing of all firm experts and key document titles by practice area and published it in a small book, compact enough to fit in any consultant's briefcase. The Knowledge Resource Directory (KRD) became the McKinsey Yellow Pages and found immediate and widespread use firm-wide. Although the computerized databases were slow to be widely adopted, the KRD found almost immediate enthusiastic acceptance.

Making the new practice coordinator's position effective proved more challenging. Initially, these roles were seen as little more than glorified librarians. It took several years before the new roles were filled by individuals (often ex-consultants) who were sufficiently respected that they could not only act as consultants to those seeking information about their area of expertise, but also were able to impose the discipline necessary to maintain and build the practice's databases.

Perhaps the most difficult task was to legitimize the role of a new class of consultants—the specialist. The basic concept was that a professional could make a career in McKinsey by emphasizing specialized knowledge development rather than the broad-based problem-solving skills and client development orientation that were deeply embedded in the firm's value system. While several consultants with deep technical expertise in specialties like market research, finance, or steel making were recruited, most found it hard to assimilate into the mainstream. The firm seemed uncomfortable about how to evaluate, compensate, or promote these individuals, and many either became isolated or disaffected. Nonetheless, the partnership continued to support the notion of a specialist promotion track and continued to struggle with how to make it work.

Matassoni reflected on the changes:

> The objective of the infrastructure changes was not so much to create a new McKinsey as to keep the old "one firm" concept functioning as we grew. . . . Despite all the talk of computerized databases, the knowledge management process still relied heavily on personal networks, old practices like cross-office transfers, and strong "One Firm" norms like helping other consultants when they called. And at promotion time, nobody reviewed your PD documents. They looked at how you used your internal networks to have your ideas make an impact on clients.

Managing Success

By the late 1980s, the firm was expanding rapidly again. In 1988, the same year Fred Gluck was elected managing director, new offices were opened in Rome, Helsinki, São Paulo, and Minneapolis bringing the total to 41. From the partners' perspective, however, enhancing McKinsey's reputation as a thought leader was at least as important as attracting new business.

Refining Knowledge Management   After being elected MD, Gluck delegated the practice development role he had played since 1980 to a newly constituted Clientele and Professional Development Committee (CPDC). When Ted Hall took over leadership of this committee in late 1991, he felt there was a need to adjust the firm's knowledge development focus. He commented:

> By the early 1990s, too many people were seeing practice development as the creation of experts and the generation of documents in order to build our reputation. But knowledge is only valuable when it is between the ears of consultants and applied to clients' problems. Because it is less effectively developed through the disciplined work of a few than through the spontaneous interaction of many, we had to change the more structured "discover-codify-disseminate" model to a looser and more inclusive "engage-explore-apply-share" approach. In other

words, we shifted our focus from developing knowledge to building individual and team capability.

Over the years, Gluck's philosophy "to let 1,000 flowers bloom" had resulted in the original group of 11 sectors and 15 centers expanding to become what Hall called "72 islands of activity," (Sectors, Centers, Working Groups, and Special Projects) many of which were perceived as fiefdoms dominated by one or two established experts. In Hall's view, the garden of 1,000 flowers needed weeding, a task requiring a larger group of mostly different gardeners. The CPDC began integrating the diverse groups into seven sectors and seven functional capability groups (see Exhibit 4). These sectors and groups were led by teams of five to seven partners (typically younger directors and principals) with the objective of replacing the leader-driven knowledge creation and dissemination process with a "stewardship model" of self-governing practices focused on competence building.

Client Impact   With responsibility for knowledge management delegated to the CPDC, Gluck began to focus on a new theme—client impact. On being elected managing director, he made this a central theme in his early speeches, memos, and his first All Partners Conference. He also created a Client Impact Committee, and asked it to explore the ways in which the firm could ensure that the expertise it was developing created positive measurable results in each client engagement.

One of the most important initiatives of the new committee was to persuade the partners to redefine the firm's key consulting unit from the engagement team (ET) to the client service team (CST). The traditional ET, assembled to deliver a three- or four-month assignment for a client was a highly efficient and flexible unit, but it tended to focus on the immediate task rather than on the client's long-term need. The CST concept was that the firm could add long-term value and increase the effectiveness of individual engagements if it could unite a core of individuals (particularly at the partner level) who were linked across multiple ETs, and commit them to working with the client over an extended period. The impact was to broaden the classic model of a single

Exhibit 4   Group Framework for Sectors and Centers

Functional Capability Groups	Clientele Industry Sectors
Corporate Governance and Leadership	*Financial Institutions*
Corporate organization	Banking
Corporate management processes	Insurance
Corporate strategy development	Health care payor/provider
Corporate relationship design and management	
Corporate finance	*Consumer*
Post-merger management	Retailing
	Consumer industries
Organization (OPP/MOVE)	Media
Corporate transformation design and leadership	Pharmaceuticals
Energizing approaches	
Organization design and development	*Energy*
Leadership and teams	Electrical utilities
Engaging teams	Petroleum
	Natural gas
Information Technology/Systems	Other energy
To be determined	
	Basic Materials
Marketing	Steel
Market research	Pulp and paper
Sales force management	Chemicals
Channel management	Other basic materials
Global marketing	
Pricing	*Aerospace, Electronics, and Telecom*
Process and sector support	Telecom
	Electronics
Operations Effectiveness	Aerospace
Integrated logistics	
Manufacturing	*Transportation*
Purchasing and supply management	
	Automotive, Assembly, and Machinery
Strategy	Automotive
Strategy	Assembly
Microeconomics	
Business dynamics	
Business planning processes	
Cross-Functional Management	
Innovation	
Customer satisfaction	
Product/technology development and	
commercialization	
Core process redesign	

Source: Internal McKinsey & Company document.

partner "owning" a client to a group of partners with shared commitment to each client.

Although client impact studies indicated the new structure led to a longer-term focus and deeper understanding of issues, it also raised some concerns. Some felt that the new approach biased resource allocation to the largest clients with the biggest CSTs. Others felt that CSTs tended to be more insular, guarding proprietary concepts and reaching out less often for firm-wide knowledge.

The latter concern in part reflected changes in the locus of knowledge development being advocated by CPDC. In response to concerns within the partnership about a gradual decline in associates' involvement in intellectual capital development, the CPDC began to emphasize the need for CSTs to play a central role in the intellectual life of McKinsey. (See Exhibit 5 for a CPDC conceptualization.) Believing that the CSTs (by 1993 about 200 firm-wide) represented the real learning laboratories, the CPDC sent memos to the new industry sector and capabil-

ity group leaders advising them that their practices would be evaluated by their coverage of the firm's CSTs. They also wrote to all consultants emphasizing the importance of the firm's intellectual development and their own professional development, for which they had primary responsibility. Finally, they assembled data on the amount of time consultants were spending on practice and professional development by office, distributing the widely divergent results to partners in offices worldwide.

Developing Multiple Career Paths   Despite (or perhaps because of) all these changes, the specialist consultant model continued to struggle. Over the years, the evaluation criteria for the specialist career path had gradually converged with the mainstream generalist promotion criteria. For example, the specialist's old promotion standard of "world-class expertise" in a particular field had given way to a more pragmatic emphasis on client impact; the notion of a legitimate role as a consultant to teams had evolved

Exhibit 5   CPDC Proposed Organizational Relationships

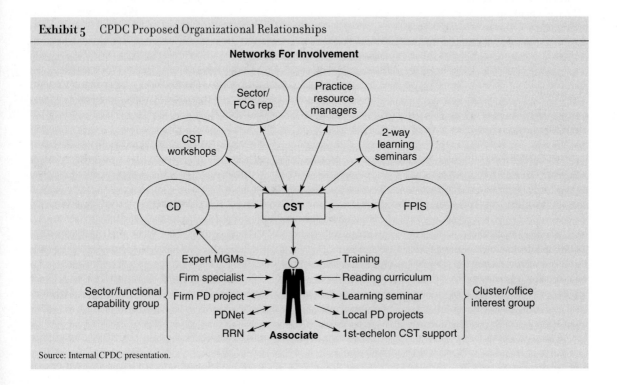

Source: Internal CPDC presentation.

Exhibit 6   Alternative Career Path Focus and Criteria

Career Paths/Roles			
CSS Paths		*CSSA Paths*	
General Consulting	**Specialized Consulting**	**Practice Expertise**	**Practice Management Administration**
Focus			
Perform general problem solving and lead implementation Develop client relationships	Apply in-depth practice knowledge to studies Develop client relationships Build external reputation	Leverage practice knowledge across studies Create new knowledge	Codify and transfer knowledge Help administer practice

Source: Internal McKinsey & Company presentation.

to a need for specialists to be "engagement director capable"; and the less pressured evaluation standard of "grow or go" was replaced by the normal associate's more demanding "up or out" requirement, albeit within a slightly more flexible timeframe.

Although these changes had reduced the earlier role dissonance—specialists become more T shaped—it also diluted the original objective, and in late 1992 the Professional Personnel Committee decided to create two new career paths for client service support and administrative (CSSA) staff:

- The first reaffirmed a path to partnership for practice-dedicated specialists who built credibility with clients and CSTs through their specialized knowledge and its expert application. Their skills would have them in high demand as consultants to teams (CDs) rather than as engagement directors (EDs).
- The second new option was the practice management track designed to provide a career progression for practice coordinators, who had a key role in transferring knowledge and in helping practice leaders manage increasingly complex networks. Valuable administrators could also be promoted on this track.

Despite the announcement of the new criteria and promotion processes, amongst associates and specialists alike there was still a good deal of skepticism and confusion about the viability of the specialist track to partnership. (See Exhibit 6 for an overview comparison.)

Throughout the period of change, Gluck kept returning to his long-term theme that, "it's all about people." He said:

> There are two ways to look at McKinsey. The most common way is that we are a client service firm whose primary purpose is to serve the companies seeking our help. That is legitimate. But I believe there is an even more powerful way for us to see ourselves. We should begin to view our primary purpose as building a great institution that becomes an engine for producing highly motivated world-class people who in turn will serve our clients extraordinarily well.

Knowledge Management on the Front

To see how McKinsey's evolving knowledge management processes were being felt by those on the firm's front lines, we will follow the activities of three consultants working in three diverse locations and focused on three different agendas.

Jeff Peters and the Sydney Office Assignment
John Stuckey, a director in McKinsey's Sydney office, felt great satisfaction at being invited to bid for a financial services growth strategy study for one of

Australia's most respected companies. Yet the opportunity also created some challenges. As in most small or medium-sized offices, most consultants in Sydney were generalists. Almost all with financial industry expertise had been "conflicted out" of the project due to work they had done for competing financial institutions in Australia.

Stuckey immediately began using his personal network to find how he might tap into McKinsey's worldwide resources for someone who could lead this first engagement for an important new client. After numerous phone calls and some lobbying at a directors' conference he identified Jeff Peters, a Boston-based senior engagement manager and veteran of more than 20 studies for financial institutions. The only problem was that Peters had two ongoing commitments that would make him unavailable for at least the first six weeks of the Australian assignment.

Meanwhile, Stuckey and Ken Gibson, his engagement director on the project, were working with the Sydney office staffing coordinator to identify qualified, available, and nonconflicted associates to complete the team. Balancing assignments of over 80 consultants to 25 ongoing teams was a complex process that involved matching the needs of the engagement and the individual consultants' development requirements. A constant flow of consultants across offices helped buffer constraints, and also contributed to the transfer of knowledge. At any one time 15 to 25 Australian consultants were on short- or long-term assignments abroad, while another 10 to 15 consultants from other offices were working in Australia. (Firm-wide, nearly 20% of work was performed by consultants on inter-office loans.)

They identified a three-person team to work with Peters. John Peacocke was a New Zealand army engineer with an MBA in finance from Wharton and two years of experience in McKinsey. Although he had served on a four-month study for a retail bank client in Cleveland, since returning to Australia he had worked mostly for oil and gas clients. Patty Akopianz was a one-year associate who had worked in investment banking before earning an MBA at Harvard. Her primary interest and her developing expertise was in consumer marketing. The business analyst was Jonathan Liew, previously an actuary who was embarking on his first McKinsey assignment.

With Peters' help, Stuckey and Gibson also began assembling a group of internal specialists and experts who could act as consulting directors (CDs) to the team. James Gorman, a personal financial services expert in New York, agreed to visit Sydney for a week and to be available for weekly conference calls; Majid Arab, an insurance industry specialist committed to a two-week visit and a similar "on-call" availability; Andrew Doman, a London-based financial industry expert, also signed on as a CD. Within the Sydney office, Charles Conn, a leader in the firm's growth strategies practice, agreed to lend his expertise, as did Clem Doherty, a firm leader in the impact of technology.

With Gibson acting more as an engagement manager than an engagement director, the team began scanning the Knowledge Resource Directory, the FPIS and the PDNet for leads. (Firm-wide, the use of PDNet documents had boomed in the eight years since its introduction. By early 1996, there were almost 12,000 documents on PDNet, with over 2,000 being requested each month.) In all, they tracked down 179 relevant PD documents and tapped into the advice and experience of over 60 firm members worldwide. A team member explained:

> Ken was acting as EM, but he was not really an expert in financial services, so we were even more reliant than usual on the internal network. Some of the ideas we got off PDNet were helpful, but the trail of contacts was much more valuable. . . . Being on a completely different time zone had great advantages. If you hit a wall at the end of the day, you could drop messages in a dozen voicemail boxes in Europe and the United States. Because the firm norm is that you respond to requests by colleagues, by morning you would have seven or eight new suggestions, data sources, or leads.

At the end of the first phase, the team convened an internal workshop designed to keep client management informed, involved, and committed to the emerging conclusions. Out of this meeting, the team was focused on seven core beliefs and four viable options that provided its agenda for the next phase of the project. It was at this point that Peters was able to join the team:

> By the time I arrived, most of the hard analysis had been done and they had been able to narrow the focus from the universe to four core options in just over a month. It was very impressive how they had been able to do that with limited team-based expertise and a demanding client.... With things going so well, my main priority was to focus the team on the end product. Once we got a clear logical outline, I assigned tasks and got out of the way. Most of my time I spent working on the client relationship.... It was great learning for John and Patty, and both of them were ready to take on a management role in their next engagements.

In November, the team presented its conclusions to the board, and after some tough questioning and challenging, they accepted the recommendations and began an implementation process. The client's managing director reflected on the outcome:

> We're a tough client, but I would rate their work as very good. Their value added was in their access to knowledge, the intellectual rigor they bring, and their ability to build understanding and consensus among a diverse management group. . . . If things don't go ahead now, it's our own fault.

John Stuckey had a little different post-engagement view of the result:

> Overall, I think we did pretty good work, but I was a bit disappointed we didn't come up with a radical breakthrough.... We leveraged the firm's knowledge base effectively, but I worry that we rely so much on our internal expertise. We have to beware of the trap that many large successful companies have fallen into by becoming too introverted, too satisfied with their own view of the world.

Warwick Bray and European Telecoms After earning his MBA at Melbourne University, Warwick Bray joined McKinsey's Melbourne office in 1989. A computer science major, he had worked as a systems engineer at Hewlett Packard and wanted to leverage his technological experience. For two of his first three years, he worked on engagements related to the impact of deregulation on the Asia-Pacific telecommunications industry. In early 1992, Bray advised his group development leader (his assigned mentor and adviser) that he would be interested in spending a year in London. After several phone discussions the transfer was arranged, and in March the young Australian found himself on his first European team.

From his experience on the Australian telecom projects, Bray had written a PD document, "Negotiating Interconnect," which he presented at the firm's annual worldwide telecom conference. Recognizing this developing "knowledge spike," Michael Patsalos-Fox, telecom practice leader in London, invited Bray to work with him on a study. Soon he was being called in as a deregulation expert to make presentations to various client executives. "In McKinsey you have to earn that right," said Bray. "For me it was immensely satisfying to be recognized as an expert."

Under the leadership of Patsalos-Fox, the telecom practice had grown rapidly in the United Kingdom. With deregulation spreading across the continent in the 1990s, however, he was becoming overwhelmed by the demands for his help. Beginning in the late 1980s, Patsalos-Fox decided to stop acting as the sole repository for and exporter of European telecom information and expertise, and start developing a more interdependent network. To help in this task, he appointed Sulu Soderstrom, a Stanford MBA with a strong technology background, as full-time practice coordinator. Over the next few years she played a key role in creating the administrative glue that bonded together telecom practice groups in offices throughout Europe. Said Patsalos-Fox:

> She wrote proposals, became the expert on information sources, organized European conferences, helped with cross-office staffing, located expertise and supported and participated in our practice development work. Gradually she helped us move from an "export"-based hub and spokes model of information sharing to a true federalist-based network.

In this growth environment and supported by the stronger infrastructure, the practice exploded during the 1990s. To move the knowledge creation beyond what he described as "incremental synthesis of past experience," Patsalos-Fox launched a series of practice-sponsored studies. Staffed by some of the practice's best consultants, they focused on big topics like "The Industry Structure in 2005," or "The Telephone Company of the Future." But most of the practice's knowledge base was built by the informal initiatives of individual associates who would step back after several engagements and write a paper on their new insights. For example, Bray wrote several well-received PD documents and was enhancing his internal reputation as an expert in deregulation and multimedia. Increasingly he was invited to consult to or even join teams in other parts of Europe. Said Patsalos-Fox:

> He was flying around making presentations and helping teams. Although the internal audience is the toughest, he was getting invited back. When it came time for him to come up for election, the London office nominated him but the strength of his support came from his colleagues in the European telecom network.

In 1996, Patsalos-Fox felt it was time for a new generation of practice leadership. He asked his young Australian protégé and two other partners— one in Brussels, one in Paris—if they would take on a co-leadership role. Bray reflected on two challenges he and his co-leaders faced. The first was to make telecom a really exciting and interesting practice so it could attract the best associates. That meant taking on the most interesting work, and running our engagements so that people felt they were developing and having fun.

The second key challenge was how to develop the largely informal links among the fast-growing European telecom practices. Despite the excellent job that Soderstrom had done as the practice's repository of knowledge and channel of communication, it was clear that there were limits to her ability to act as the sole "intelligent switch." As a result, the group had initiated a practice-specific intranet link designed to allow members direct access to the practice's knowledge base (PD documents, conference proceedings, CVs, etc.), its members' capabilities (via home pages for each practice member), client base (CST home pages, links to client web sites), and external knowledge resources (MIT's Multimedia Lab, Theseus Institute, etc.). More open yet more focused than existing firm-wide systems like PDNet, the Telecom Intranet was expected to accelerate the "engage-explore-apply-share" knowledge cycle.

There were some, however, who worried that this would be another step away from "one firm" towards compartmentalization, and from focus on building idea-driven personal networks towards creating data-based electronic transactions. In particular, the concern was that functional capability groups would be less able to transfer their knowledge into increasingly strong and self-contained industry-based practices. Warwick Bray recognized the problem, acknowledging that linkages between European telecom and most functional practices "could be better":

> The problem is we rarely feel the need to draw on those groups. For example, I know the firm's pricing practice has world-class expertise in industrial pricing, but we haven't yet learned how to apply it to telecom. We mostly call on the pricing experts within our practice. We probably should reach out more.

Stephen Dull and the Business Marketing Competence Center   After completing his MBA at the University of Michigan in 1983, Stephen Dull spent the next five years in various consumer marketing jobs at Pillsbury. In 1988, he was contacted by an executive search firm that had been retained by McKinsey to recruit potential consultants in consumer marketing. Joining the Atlanta office, Dull soon discovered that there was no structured development program. Like the eight experienced consumer marketing recruits in other offices, he was expected to create his own agenda.

Working on various studies, Dull found his interests shifting from consumer to industrial marketing issues. As he focused on building his own expertise, however, Dull acknowledged that he did not pay enough attention to developing strong client relations. "And around here, serving clients is what really counts," he said. So, in late 1994—a time when he might be discussing his election to principal—he had a long counseling session with his group development leader about his career. The GDL confirmed that he was not well positioned for election, but proposed another option. He suggested that Dull talk to Rob Rosiello, a principal in the New York office who had just launched a business-to-business marketing initiative within the marketing practice. Said Dull:

> Like most new initiatives, "B to B" was struggling to get established without full-time resources, so Rob was pleased to see me. I was enjoying my business marketing work, so the initiative sounded like a great opportunity. . . . Together, we wrote a proposal to make me the firm's first business marketing specialist.

The decision to pursue this strategy was not an easy one for Dull. Like most of his colleagues, he felt that specialists were regarded as second-class citizens—"overhead being supported by real consultants who serve clients," Dull suggested. But his GDL told him that recent directors meetings had reaffirmed the importance of building functional expertise, and some had even suggested that 150%–20% of the firm's partners should be functional experts within the next five to seven years. (As of 1995, over 300 associates were specialists, but only 15 of the 500 partners.) In April 1995, Dull and Rosiello took their proposal to Andrew Parsons and David Court, two leaders of the Marketing practice. The directors suggested a mutual trial of the concept until the end of the year and offered to provide Dull the support to commit full time to developing the B to B initiative.

Dull's first priority was to collect the various concepts, frameworks, and case studies that existed within the firm, consolidating and synthesizing them in several PD documents. In the process, he and Rosiello began assembling a core team of interested contributors. Together, they developed an agenda of half a dozen cutting-edge issues in business marketing—segmentation, multi-buyer decision

making and marketing partnerships, for example—and launched a number of study initiatives around them. Beyond an expanded series of PD documents, the outcome was an emerging set of core beliefs, and a new framework for business marketing.

The activity also attracted the interest of Mark Leiter, a specialist in the Marketing Science Center of Competence. This center, which had developed largely around a group of a dozen or so specialists, was in many ways a model of what Dull hoped the B to B initiative could become, and having a second committed specialist certainly helped.

In November, another major step to that goal occurred when the B to B initiative was declared a Center of Competence. At that time, the core group decided they would test their colleagues' interest and their own credibility by arranging an internal conference at which they would present their ideas. When over 50 people showed up including partners and directors from four continents, Dull felt that prospects for the center looked good.

Through the cumulative impact of the PD documents, the conference and word of mouth recommendations, by early 1996 Dull and his colleagues were getting more calls than the small center could handle. They were proud when the March listing of PDNet "Best-Sellers" listed B to B documents at numbers 2, 4, and 9 (see Exhibit 7). For Dull, the resulting process was enlightening:

> We decided that when we got calls we would swarm all over them and show our colleagues we could really add value for their clients. . . . This may sound strange—even corny—but I now really understand why this is a profession and not a business. If I help a partner serve his client better, he will call me back. It's all about relationships, forming personal bonds, helping each other.

While Dull was pleased with the way the new center was gaining credibility and having impact, he was still very uncertain about his promotion prospects. As he considered his future, he began to give serious thought to writing a book on business to business marketing to enhance his internal credibility and external visibility.

Exhibit 7   PDNet "Best-Sellers": March and Year-to-Date, 1996

Number Requested	Title, Author(s), Date, PDNet #	Functional Capability Group/Sector
March 1996		
21	**Developing a Distinctive Consumer Marketing Organization** *Nora Aufreiter, Theresa Austerberry, Steve Carlotti, Mike George, Liz Lempres (1/96, #13240)*	Consumer Industries/ Packaged Goods; Marketing
19	**VIP: Value Improvement Program to Enhance Customer Value in Business to Business Marketing** *Dirk Berensmann, Marc Fischer, Heiner Frankemölle, Lutz-Peter Pape, Wolf-Dieter Voss (10/95, #13340)*	Marketing; Steel
16	**Handbook For Sales Force Effectiveness—1991 Edition** *(5/91, #6670)*	Marketing
15	**Understanding and Influencing Customer Purchase Decisions in Business to Business Markets** *Mark Leiter (3/95, #12525)*	Marketing
15	**Channel Management Handbook** *Christine Bucklin, Stephen DeFalco, John DeVincentis, John Levis (1/95, #11876)*	Marketing
15	**Platforms for Growth in Personal Financial Services (PFS201)** *Christopher Leech, Ronald O'Hanley, Eric Lambrecht, Kristin Morse (11/95, #12995)*	Personal Financial Services
14	**Developing Successful Acquisition Programs to Support Long-Term Growth Strategies** *Steve Coley, Dan Goodwin (11/92, #9150)*	Corporate Finance
14	**Understanding Value-Based Segmentation** *John Forsyth, Linda Middleton (11/95, #11730)*	Consumer Industries/ Packaged Goods; Marketing
14	**The Dual Perspective Customer Map for Business to Business Marketing** *(3/95, #12526)*	Marketing
13	**Growth Strategy—Platforms, Staircases and Franchises** *Charles Conn, Rob McLean, David White (8/94, #11400)*	Strategy
Cumulative Index (January–March)		
54	**Introduction to CRM (Continuous Relationship Marketing)—Leveraging CRM to Build PFS Franchise Value (PFS221)** *Margo Geogiadis, Milt Gillespie, Tim Gokey, Mike Sherman, Marc Singer (11/95, #12999)*	Personal Financial Services
45	**Platforms for Growth in Personal Financial Services (PFS201)** *Christopher Leech, Ronald O'Hanley, Eric Lambrecht, Kristin Morse (11/95, #12995)*	Personal Financial Services
40	**Launching a CRM Effort (PFS222)** *Nick Brown, Margo Georgiadis (10/95, #12940)*	Marketing
38	**Building Value Through Continuous Relationship Marketing (CRM)** *Nich Brown, Mike Wright (10/95, #13126)*	Banking and Securities
36	**Combining Art and Science to Optimize Brand Portfolios** *Richard Benson-Armer, David Court, John Forsyth (10/95, #12916)*	Marketing; Consumer Industries/Packaged Goods
35	**Consumer Payments and the Future of Retail Banks (PA202)** *John Stephenson, Peter Sands (11/95, #13008)*	Payments and Operating Products
34	**CRM (Continuous Relationship Marketing) Case Examples Overview** *Howie Hayes, David Putts (9/95, #12931)*	Marketing
32	**Straightforward Approaches to Building Management Talent** *Parke Boneysteele, Bill Meehan, Kristin Morse, Pete Sidebottom (9/95, #12843)*	Organization
32	**Reconfiguring and Reenergizing Personal Selling Channels (PFS213)** *Patrick Wetzel, Amy Zinsser (11/95, #12997)*	Personal Financial Services
31	**From Traditional Home Banking to On-Line PFS (PFS211)** *Gaurang Desai, Brian Johnson, Kai Lahmann, Gottfried Leibbrandt, Paal Weberg (11/95, #12998)*	Personal Financial Services

Source: *Month By Month* (McKinsey's internal staff magazine).

▌ A New MD, A New Focus

In 1994, after six years of leadership in which firm revenue had doubled to an estimated $1.5 billion annually, Fred Gluck stepped down as MD. His successor was 45-year-old Rajat Gupta, a 20-year McKinsey veteran committed to continuing the emphasis on knowledge development. After listening to the continuing debates about which knowledge development approach was most effective, Gupta came to the conclusion that the discussions were consuming energy that should have been directed towards the activity itself. "The firm did not have to make a choice," he said. "We had to pursue *all* the options." With that conclusion, Gupta launched a four-pronged attack.

He wanted to capitalize on the firm's long-term investment practice development driven by Clientele Industry Sectors and Functional Capability Groups and Supported by the knowledge infrastructure of PDNet and FPIS. But he also wanted to create some new channels, forums, and mechanisms for knowledge development and organizational learning.

Building on an experiment begun by the German office, Gupta embraced a grass-roots knowledge-development approach called Practice Olympics. Two- to six-person teams from offices around the world were encouraged to develop ideas that grew out of recent client engagements and formalize them for presentation at a regional competition with senior partners and clients as judges. The 20 best regional teams then competed at a firm-wide event. Gupta was proud that in its second year, the event had attracted over 150 teams and involved 15% of the associate body.

At a different level, in late 1995 the new MD initiated six special initiatives—multi-year internal assignments led by senior partners that focused on emerging issues that were of importance to CEOs. The initiatives tapped both internal and external expertise to develop "state-of-the-art" formulations of each key issue. For example, one focused on the shape and function of the corporation of the future, another on creating and managing strategic growth, and a third on capturing global opportunities.

Gupta saw these initiatives as reasserting the importance of the firm's functional knowledge yet providing a means to do longer term, bigger commitment, cross-functional development.

Finally, he planned to expand on the model of the McKinsey Global Institute, a firm-sponsored research center established in 1991 to study implications of changes in the global economy on business. The proposal was to create other pools of dedicated resources protected from daily pressures and client demands, and focused on long-term research agendas. A Change Center was established in 1995 and an Operations Center was being planned. Gupta saw these institutes as a way in which McKinsey could recruit more research-oriented people and link more effectively into the academic arena.

Most of these initiatives were new and their impact had not yet been felt within the firm. Yet Gupta was convinced the direction was right:

> We have easily doubled our investment in knowledge over these past couple of years. There are lots more people involved in many more initiatives. If that means we do 5–10% less client work today, we are willing to pay that price to invest in the future. Since Marvin Bower, every leadership group has had a commitment to leave the firm stronger than it found it. It's a fundamental value of McKinsey to invest for the future of the firm.

▌ Future Directions

Against this background, the McKinsey partnership was engaged in spirited debate about the firm's future directions and priorities. The following is a sampling of their opinions:

> I am concerned that our growth may stretch the fabric of the place. We can't keep on disaggregating our units to create niches for everyone because we have exhausted the capability of our integrating mechanisms. I believe our future is in developing around CSTs and integrating across them around common knowledge agendas.

> Historically, I was a supporter of slower growth, but now I'm convinced we must grow faster. That is the

key to creating opportunity and excitement for people, and that generates innovation and drives knowledge development. . . . Technology is vital not only in supporting knowledge transfer, but also in allowing partners to mentor more young associates. We have to be much more aggressive in using it.

There is a dark side to technology—what I call technopoly. It can drive out communication and people start believing that e-mailing someone is the same thing as talking to them. If teams stop meeting as often or if practice conferences evolve into discussion forums on Lotus Notes, the technology that has supported our growth may begin to erode our culture based on personal networks.

I worry that we are losing our sense of village as we compartmentalize our activities and divide into specialties. And the power of IT has sometimes led to information overload. The risk is that the more we spend searching out the right PD document, the ideal framework, or the best expert, the less time we spend thinking creatively about the problem. I worry that as we increase the science, we might lose the craft of what we do.

These were among the scores of opinions that Rajat Gupta heard since becoming MD. His job was to sort through them and set a direction that would "leave the firm stronger than he found it."

Case 5-3   Skandia AFS: Developing Intellectual Capital Globally

Jan R. Carendi, deputy chief executive officer (CEO) of Skandia Insurance Company Ltd. (Skandia) and chief operating officer (COO) of Skandia's Assurance and Financial Services (AFS) division, smiled as he reviewed a report on his unit's growth during his 10 years at the helm. Over this time, AFS's sales of private long-term savings and insurance products had grown 45% per year. Once a small unit in the international division of the 140-year-old Stockholm-based insurance and financial services company, AFS currently accounted for almost 50% of Skandia's gross premium revenues. (See Exhibit 1 for Skandia and AFS results 1986–1995.)

Yet to many, Carendi was a maverick who had continually defied conventional wisdom. By redefining the nature of the business, and restructuring it around alliances, some thought he had hollowed out the business and made it less robust than

conventional and fully integrated companies. Others in this traditional industry questioned his radical approach of refocusing his managers on intellectual capital—looking at the organization's knowledge rather than finances as its key resources. While the payoffs of his approach were evident, the critics insisted there were also risks.

Carendi recognized that his bold actions were likely to raise eyebrows, but to date AFS's strong performance had been sufficient to quiet his critics. However, he was aware that in the turbulent segment of the market his company had carved out, past performance was no guarantee of future success. While financial analysts were focused on the 30% fall in premium income of AFS's flagship U.K. operation in 1995, to Carendi, premium growth was a relative measure, and only one indicator of long-term success. His immediate concern was AFS's ability to maintain service quality when resources were constrained by rapid expansion. And long term, he was uncertain how the ability of the Internet to provide increasingly sophisticated consumers with direct access to insurance products would affect the

▌ This case was prepared by Professor Christopher A. Bartlett and Research Associate Takia Mahmood.
▌ Copyright © 1996 by the President and Fellows of Harvard College. Harvard Business School case 396-412.

Exhibit 1   Financial Results for Skandia and AFS: 1986–1995

Million Swedish Kronor (MSEK)	1986	1987	1988	1989	1990	1991	1992	1993	1994	1995
Kronor per U.S.$	7.1	6.3	6.1	6.4	5.9	6.0	5.8	7.8	7.7	7.1
*Gross Premium Income (MSEK)**										
Skandia Group	4,381	4,731	5,282	18,519	24,853	29,031	36,525	43,503	52,248	52,241
AFS:	—	1,919	1,524	1,979	2,868	5,483	7,891	17,240	25,888	23,961
Unit-link assurance	—	1,841	1,464	1,807	2,683	4,306	6,089	16,939	23,898	20,706
Life assurance	—	78	60	172	185	1,083	1,664	119	1,754	3,016
Management Operating Result (MSEK)†										
Skandia Group	4,773	(1,013)	4,410	4,044	(3,205)	(1,098)	(3,721)	4,069	(1,715)	815
AFS:	—	33	28	3	(33)	110	100	389	625	707
Unit-link assurance	—	25	15	(13)	(47)	88	80	386	530	595
Life assurance	—	8	13	16	14	22	20	3	91	99
Return on Net Asset Value (percent)										
Skandia Group	60	(10)	38	24	(19)	(10)	(30)	31	(8)	7
AFS	—	NA	NA	NA	NA	NA	6.5	17.6	19.2	17.6

*Beginning in 1989, Skandia Group results include Skandia International. Results in years 1989–1992 include American Skandia Reinsurance (Life Insurance sold in 1993), and in 1994–1995 include Intercaser (Spanish Life Insurance Company).
†Management operating results include changes in surplus values for investments.
Source: Skandia.

broker-based distribution network his organization had spent a decade building.

Skandia Company Background

Skandia was founded in 1855 and almost immediately began expanding internationally, opening offices in Norway, Denmark, Russia, Germany, and the Netherlands within a year. It entered the U.S. market in 1900, becoming the first non-British insurance company to do so. However, following the losses incurred in the 1906 San Francisco earthquake and World War I, Skandia's interest in international markets waned, remaining fairly dormant until the 1960s when it entered another period of growth, at home and abroad. Despite some acquisitions of a few small foreign life assurance companies, most of Skandia's international business was

in reinsurance.[1] The few foreign operations were managed as a portfolio of companies through International Life Operations, a small division of Skandia International.

In keeping with common industry practice, Skandia had developed as a fully integrated organization, focused primarily on its domestic market. The company was comprised of four core value-adding activities, undertaken by a corporate staff located in Stockholm:

- An actuarial function whose key role was to make the risk assessments required to design insurance products to meet targeted consumer needs

[1]Reinsurance was business accepted from another company to allow it to distribute its risk.

- A sales and marketing group that identified market opportunities and sold products to consumers primarily through company representatives and exclusive agents
- An investment management function that invested premium income, and applied earnings to fund benefit payment, cover operating expenses, and generate profits
- An administrative group that managed the substantial customer, accounting, and regulatory paperwork generated by the system

Like most other insurance companies, Skandia had been a pioneer in the use of computer technology to facilitate the complex actuarial calculations, track huge investment portfolios, and support the heavy customer service and other administrative requirements. From the 1960s through the 1980s, it had followed the industry trend of building massive mainframe capacity at the central office, a location through which all data flowed. Many in the industry saw these huge infrastructure investments and the complex systems required to manage them as a barrier to entry in this highly regulated environment. Even for existing companies, it was estimated that the support structure and systems required for new market entry could cost millions of dollars and involve hundreds of man years of effort to establish.

In the late 1980s, however, many of Skandia's existing practices and management assumptions were being challenged by a newcomer to the corporate headquarters. In less than a decade, Jan Carendi had built an organization that had created a whole new business for Skandia. His international rollout of the unit-linked assurance annuity business grew to represent almost half the company's premium income by 1994, and become its dominant engine of future growth.[2]

---

[2]Unit-linked (or mutual fund-linked) assurance is a variable life assurance product that allows the policyholder to invest the savings portion of the premium in a variety of investment vehicles offered by the company (various combinations of stock, bond, and money market investments with different risk-return profiles). While broadening the appeal of insurance products, these instruments created more complex demands on product development, sales, investment, and administration than the standard life assurance policies.

Jan Carendi and the Rebirth of AFS

Born in Argentina of Swedish parents, Jan Carendi spoke fluent Spanish and felt more comfortable in the free-wheeling Latin environment than in the more restrictive Swedish culture. With a degree from the School of Economics in Gothenberg, Sweden, Carendi had joined Skandia as an executive trainee in 1970, taking an entry-level job in Skandia's Mexican regional headquarters in 1971. Based on his open and flexible style, he developed a great deal of trust within the Mexican entity and worked his way up to become controller and, ultimately, deputy chief executive in 1981.

In 1974, Carendi met Lars Lekander, a manager at Skandia and well-respected internal expert in organizational design, who had been sent to Mexico to help straighten out the subsidiary's managerial and organizational problems. Lekander immediately recognized Carendi as a highly effective manager and a "natural problem solver" who had taken responsibilities far beyond his controller's job. Carendi appeared to delegate responsibility easily, perhaps too easily at times—a trait that often made him impatient with traditional organizational forms and management practices. When the unexpected death of the head of Skandia's International Life Operations (ILO) in 1986 led to the search for a replacement, Lekander recommended Carendi, who by that time had become the president and CEO of Skandia's subsidiary in Colombia.

Lessons from the United Kingdom   ILO was a small division of Skandia International which had over 90% of its business in the high-risk reinsurance sector and was losing money. Carendi's plan was to clean up this core business, using the proceeds to fund growth in the primary life assurance business. However, when corporate management decided to spin off the reinsurance operation, ILO was viewed as an organization orphan. Its business portfolio consisted of a 50% share of a primary insurance company in Spain, with 37 shareholders fighting over its future direction, and a 60% share of an entrepreneurial life assurance venture in the United Kingdom.

The U.K. organization had been established in 1979 by a group of young entrepreneurs who had left an established insurance company to start a new business. Their objective was to take advantage of the opportunity created by regulatory changes that allowed savings to be linked to investment-backed variable life assurance policies. The entrepreneurs approached Skandia for financial backing for a venture to sell variable unit-linked annuities directly to the public. As the new company grew increasingly successful, the founders became ferociously independent and strongly resisted any intervention from the parent company. But Carendi wanted to learn more about the innovative unit-linked product that he saw as having potential in other markets.

He decided to gain control of the U.K. company by buying back 100% of the equity, and to support the U.K. team as it continued to develop its innovative product. One problem that the young company experienced was that its best in-house funds managers often left for higher pay elsewhere. It also experienced similar turnover problems with a sales force of dedicated agents. To stem the outflow of talent, the U.K. managers decided to externalize both the fund management and sales functions. They selected local retailers (independent brokers and banks), who were well known to the market, and entered into cooperative alliances with them for customer networking and distribution. They did the same with a wide range of highly visible local unit-trust (mutual fund) investment managers who had superior track records.

Eventually, Carendi began to see in this alliance-based structure, the foundation of a new business model upon which he could build a new worldwide Assurance and Financial Service (AFS) business. In this new configuration, he saw that AFS would need to redefine its role as the linkage between the distribution and investment functions. It would add value by packaging long-term savings products for brokers and their clients, and by bringing wholesale distribution to brand name money managers. In describing his new business concept, he said, "We must begin to think of ourselves less as insurance specialists, and more as 'specialists in collaboration'." (See Exhibit 2.)

Transferring the Model: The U.S. Start-Up   By the late 1980s, the insurance industry was undergoing major change worldwide. In many countries, deregulation was opening the industry to banks and other financial and nonfinancial institutions. At the same time, cuts in government-sponsored pension and social security schemes were leading many people to question their ability to depend on such programs for their retirement security. In some countries, governments were actively encouraging greater long-term self-reliance by creating tax incentives for insurance-backed long-term savings. Behind all of these changes was a worldwide demographic trend towards an aging population that was not only contributing to the crisis in social security programs, but simultaneously creating new insurance market opportunities. It was against this background that Carendi wanted to expand his business abroad as quickly and aggressively as he could, initially aiming at one new market entry a year.

Based on a feasibility study done by the U.K. company, in 1988 Carendi decided to leverage the U.K.'s success to enter the very competitive American life assurance market. To build the new business, he hired an experienced U.S. industry manager and gave him the support of three relocated executives with specialized expertise—the two U.K. executives who had headed the U.S. market study, and Leif Reinius, AFS's international systems controller.

Reinius had been working on a PC-based, modular, software system, designed to support the U.K. investment-linked product and its "partnership model" of management. The software was designed to capture the company's essential administrative processes and coordinative mechanisms, such as policyholder applications, fund selection, daily pricing, commission management, and statements of accounts. Unfortunately, when he tested it in the U.S. environment, Reinius found that the system was inflexible and inappropriate in a market with a different set of consumer needs and regulatory requirements.

Exhibit 2 The "Specialists in Collaboration" Organization Concept

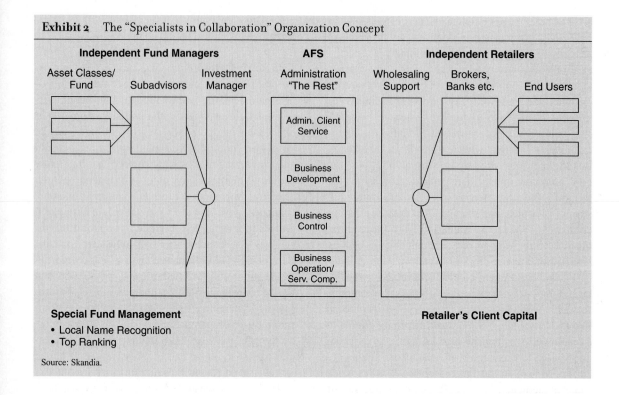

Source: Skandia.

At the same time, American Skandia was having difficulty establishing the external visibility it needed to attract new customers and the internal credibility it needed to obtain continued corporate support. The newly established U.S. company had spent $5 million per year in 1988 and 1989, but had booked no business and had few prospects. Some in the parent company were beginning to question whether AFS should continue to invest in the struggling operation. Carendi decided it was time for a shakeup. In 1989, he removed the U.S. head and some other managers and took on the role of subsidiary president himself.

Formalizing the Prototype Although the initial transfer of the U.K.-based systems had not been successful, Carendi became increasingly convinced of the power of the concept of a transportable software package that Reinius was developing. By capturing cumulative experience, the huge start-up costs of

new market entry—to define new products, support distribution efforts, and provide an administrative infrastructure—could be greatly reduced. As he explained: "Applying prototype concepts to business development should enable us to design products and develop administrative processes for a specific market in half the time, and at a quarter of the cost."

At the end of 1989, Reinius returned to Stockholm to continue working on the "core prototype system." His objective was to make it parameter-driven—so that those in new operations could input variables on risk factors, savings percentage, charges, and other factors—and to make it more flexible—so that it could be adapted to local restrictions, reporting requirements, and language. The first chance to use the new prototype came in 1990 when AFS expanded into the Swiss market. Breaking away from the model of traditional insurance companies, the AFS prototype was designed to operate on smaller IBM/AS400 computers rather than large mainframes. Its core chassis of various financially and administratively oriented modules—for applications such as policy administration, product definition, distribution, asset management, accounting, billing, and collection—now comprised a comprehensive yet flexible operating framework. (See Exhibit 3.)

Despite the excitement that the growth was generating within AFS, Carendi's unconventional approach found its detractors within Skandia. Senior level IT executives were concerned about his investments in nonmainframe-based systems development; others saw his reliance on loose, unfocused teams as a risk in a structured, financially

Exhibit 3   Systems Prototype: Components and Integration

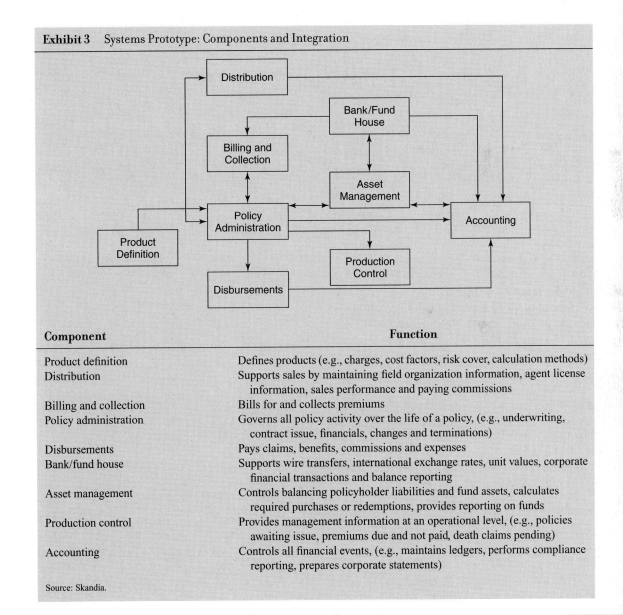

Component	Function
Product definition	Defines products (e.g., charges, cost factors, risk cover, calculation methods)
Distribution	Supports sales by maintaining field organization information, agent license information, sales performance and paying commissions
Billing and collection	Bills for and collects premiums
Policy administration	Governs all policy activity over the life of a policy, (e.g., underwriting, contract issue, financials, changes and terminations)
Disbursements	Pays claims, benefits, commissions and expenses
Bank/fund house	Supports wire transfers, international exchange rates, unit values, corporate financial transactions and balance reporting
Asset management	Controls balancing policyholder liabilities and fund assets, calculates required purchases or redemptions, provides reporting on funds
Production control	Provides management information at an operational level, (e.g., policies awaiting issue, premiums due and not paid, death claims pending)
Accounting	Controls all financial events, (e.g., maintains ledgers, performs compliance reporting, prepares corporate statements)

Source: Skandia.

conservative company. These doubts gained additional credibility because AFS was still reporting negative results. Because sales of these products typically generated more expenses than premiums income in early years (due to the heavy front loading of commissions, administrative set-up expenses, etc.), Carendi faced the dilemma that the faster he grew, the more losses he created. Despite American Skandia's sales growth from $6.3 million in 1989 to $141 million in 1991, Hans Dalborg, the head of Skandia International, of which AFS was still a part, continued to express concern about the ongoing negative results in the United States. It was only in 1991, when Dalborg left the company and AFS was made a separate unit reporting directly to Björn Wolrath, the president and CEO of Skandia Group and a strong supporter of AFS strategy, that Carendi won full support for his radically different approach to international expansion.

Leveraging the Model: The European Thrust   In 1991, with the fall of the Berlin wall, Carendi and his team decided to open a company in Germany. To develop some expertise in analyzing new market entry and starting up new subsidiaries, Carendi tapped Ann-Christin Pehrsson, a young woman he had met at a conference. Impressed by the quality of her thinking, he pursued her until he could convince her to leave her job and join AFS. Looking for a role that would challenge her and use her talents, he named Pehrsson AFS's Director of Business Development, a one-person function based in Stockholm. With the help of local contacts, she developed a three-phase analysis of the new market opportunity: a market study, a legal requirements analysis, and a report on local distribution and money management networks. Pehrsson described why the analysis was so important for the German startup:

> Germans hesitate to speculate and take financial risks. This is a problem which is conditioned by culture, so it's important to interest people in the advantages of a variable annuity—still a relatively unknown form of long-term savings. . . . We faced similar challenges in changing the distribution channels. The German market is traditionally a captive

agent market, and the agents cooperate loyally with domestic companies and sell traditional life insurance products. Broker distribution is a new activity we had to help grow.

With the lessons taken from the Swiss entry and with the understanding generated by Pehrsson's business development analysis, Reinius and his team improved the systems prototype, allowing even greater flexibility to adapt to Germany's tax regulations and reporting requirements. Eventually, each local company hired its own IT people to make such adjustments and to maintain its systems, although the staff was kept quite small—three in Germany, three in Switzerland.

Managing the New Business Model

As he pursued his international expansion strategy built on the three-legged stool of unit-linked annuity products, the partnership-based business model, and the prototype-based learning processes, Carendi started to articulate a management philosophy that was radically different from the traditional Skandia approach. He became convinced that AFS would have to compete on its ability to maintain what he called a "permanent state of advanced readiness." He told his organization:

> Today, creating bullet-proof products isn't as important as building the ability to constantly develop and deploy new products that responded to changing customer needs. You have to be able to get in and out of products and services with the competitive energy of a kid playing a video game rather than with the analytical consistency of a grand master trying to hang on in a three-day chess match.

To create such a flexible and dynamic capability, he believed he had to create different internal organization framework, new performance metrics, and radically different ways of managing people.

The Federative Organization   For years Carendi had been working to transform AFS into Lekander's ideal of a "federative organization." The concept fit well with Carendi's evolving management philosophy based on delegated responsibility and individual initiative. As a result, when a local company began to develop particular capabilities in a vital function or activity from which other units might learn, Carendi recognized its achievements by designating it a strategic competence center. For instance, Spain became a competence center for bank product design, the United States for information technology, and Colombia for administrative support and back-office functions. But no designation was permanent and lasted only until another local company sped by it on the learning curve.

Since there was no formal structural linkage to connect the federation of national units in which AFS's expertise resided, Carendi worked hard to create informal connections that encouraged information and knowledge sharing across units. One common way was to draw people together to work on project teams not only in the start-up of new subsidiaries, but also in the ongoing management of the business. The project team Carendi assembled to define the specifications of a system to deliver payouts for annuities was typical. Representatives from several subsidiaries not only captured diverse expertise from multiple country units, but also ensured that the system was designed so that the amount of adaptation required when it was deployed would be minimal.

Insisting that vital information available in any part of the organization should be accessible by all AFS companies, Carendi commissioned the IT units at AFS in Stockholm and Shelton, Connecticut to create an integrative global area network (GAN) infrastructure. Initially providing the capability for electronic mail and document and file sharing, even to those traveling within AFS offices, the GAN later expanded to serve as a conduit for core business applications and to provide an electronic venue for the exchange of ideas and experiences. For instance, the Austrian subsidiary ran part of its operations on the server in Switzerland, while Mexico used the GAN to access programs housed in the United States.

As he developed this linked federation, Carendi was careful to keep the AFS Stockholm staff at a minimum. Consisting of approximately 40 of the company's 1,700 employees, this group worked on the construction of the IT infrastructure, cross-border sales and marketing projects, business development, and accounting and financial control, leveraging resources decentralized to the country units. For example, there were five major centers in the IT federation, located in Germany, Colombia, Spain, England, and the United States, each of which not only supported its local operation but also contributed to the broader AFS development priorities. The Stockholm staff also organized knowledge-sharing activities and functioned as the center of AFS communications, particularly of its values. "We don't refer to Stockholm as the *head* office," said one senior manager. "The brain power is out in the field. If anything, the center acts as the *heart* office, maintaining the values of the group and helping pump information—our lifeblood—around the organization. It certainly avoids prescribing how businesses should be conducted around the world."

Measuring Intellectual Capital   The more Carendi became convinced of the competitive value of AFS's knowledge assets, the more he became frustrated with the inability of traditional financial reports to focus management on the critical task of building and leveraging intellectual capital. Because traditional accounting measures did not even recognize, let alone try to measure such assets, he gave top priority to finding a way of describing and measuring the effectiveness of investments in non-capital assets and resources.

To help him with this challenge, in 1991, Carendi hired Leif Edvinsson, Senior Vice President of Training and Development at a Swedish bank, with an MBA from the University of California at Berkeley, and named him the world's first director of Intellectual Capital. Edvinsson observed that many companies on the Stockholm Stock Exchange were valued at three to eight times their book value, and in the United States at even higher multiples. He argued that these huge hidden values were largely accounted for by a company's intellectual capital:

Hidden value is the root system of the corporate tree. Healthy, strong roots provide the nutrients and nourishment necessary for its growth and production of fruit. The quality of the fruit—the results you can see—is dependent on the roots, which you cannot see. . . . From this perspective, the bottom-line financial results are really the top-line results. The real bottom-line is renewal and development, which is the foundation for the future.

To help him translate the broad concept of "intellectual capital" into management specifics, Edvinsson classified it into human capital (the knowledge, skill, and capability of employees in meeting the needs of customers) and structural capital (codified brainpower embedded over time in databases, customer files, software, manuals, trademarks, and organizational structures). (See Exhibit 4.) Edvinsson believed that the key management task was developing intellectual capital, which involved leveraging its human capital, and transforming it into structural capital, thereby creating value for cus-

tomers, investors, and other stakeholders. Said Edvinsson, "The real aim is to convert IQ into ECU [the European Currency Unit]. Focusing on managing financial resources using only information from their accounting systems is a bit like driving into the future while looking in the rearview mirror."

Edvinsson realized, however, that his task extended far beyond defining terms and developing concepts. To implement his ideas and influence into the ongoing decision-making processes, he obtained Carendi's approval to employ the world's first controller for Intellectual Capital whose full-time job was to define measures, gather data, and publish reports that would calibrate AFS's effectiveness in developing and exploiting its human and structural capital. Beginning with modest quarterly reports, Edvinsson and his controller gradually expanded the number of categories of intellectual capital and the means of measuring

Exhibit 4 The Building Blocks of Intellectual Capital

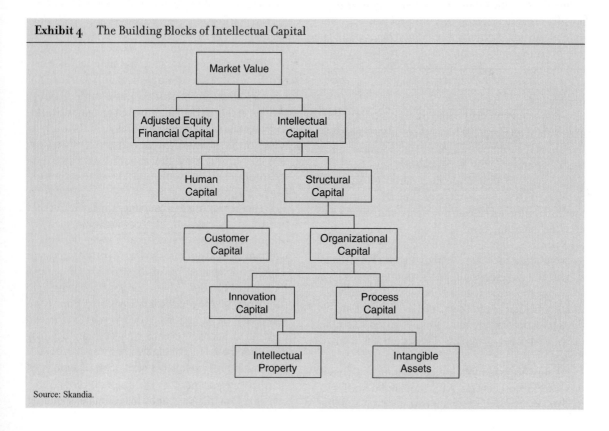

Source: Skandia.

them, culminating in the publication of AFS's first annual report on intellectual assets for 1993. The report provided baseline measurements of many nontraditional inputs and performance measures including information technology as a percentage of total expenses, the number of IT-literate employees as a percentage of all employees, gross insurance premiums per employee, and changes in savings per account.

Edvinsson's work touched off a debate within AFS about the utility of using scarce resources, first to identify and define the new indicators, (which were less universal and less readily apparent than traditional financial measures), and then to develop the infrastructure to capture the new data and analyze it. Some suggested that although they understood the effort conceptually, they were unclear about how the additional data would be used—in setting priorities, allocating resources, or determining compensation, for example. Even those who saw the value of highlighting the "hidden assets" in their operations, wondered if that would not be better managed by focusing on the knowledge-building process itself, rather than on creating a standardized "intellectual" balance sheet. "The concept of intellectual capital helps you see what else to do to stay competitive," said one senior manager. "But accounting for intellectual assets in the same way year after year—that would just be boring."

Despite the skepticism, Edvinsson continued his mission, eventually developing a new measurement model called the Business Navigator. This tool tracked changes in performance ratios on five key dimensions:

- The financial focus which represented yesterday's performance;
- The customer focus, the human focus, and the process focus, which represented today's performance;
- The renewal and development focus, which represented tomorrow's performance.

Edvinsson pointed out, "What's interesting is to measure not just the numbers, but the changes—because direction is more important than precision.

It is better to be roughly right than precisely wrong. That is why we call it navigation."

In 1993, Carendi announced that each AFS unit would begin to report quarterly performance according to intellectual capital measures along with the standard financial ones, and that both sets of data would be used in resource allocation and priority setting decisions. (See Exhibit 5 for its application in American Skandia.) Use of the measures soon started to spread outside AFS, and Skandia's top management team decided to make this a corporate-wide initiative. In 1994, Skandia became the first company in the world to publish a formal report on intellectual capital (IC), as a supplement to its annual report.

Managing Employees as Volunteers   Carendi's commitment to developing intellectual capital was reflected in his attitude to AFS employees: "All my assets are in their heads, yet they can walk away. If I want them to give me their best ideas and share their biggest dreams, I have to treat them as volunteers."

Carendi described his own role as having two key functions—coach of the team and agent of change. Far from seeing his job as sitting at the apex of the organization, he took on multiple jobs, infiltrating the organization at all levels. In addition to his job as head of AFS, he served as a member of the parent company's five-person executive committee (the Direktionen), as CEO of American Skandia, and as Board Chairman of AFS's holding companies: a continental company that controlled the Swiss, German, and Austrian group; a Mediterranean company that managed the Spanish and Italian groups; a South American company responsible for the group in Colombia; and an American company that controlled the U.S. and Mexican groups. (See Exhibit 6.) Describing himself as "a civil servant in his own organization," Carendi spent 90% of his time internally, and only 10% of his time on outside-focused activities. (However, he expected all of his company managers to be highly attuned to their external environments.) He traveled constantly, more than 200 days a year by his estimate, spending

Exhibit 5   The AFS Business Navigator

Indicators of American Skandia Life

In this report we have decided to excerpt and illustrate a sampling of indicators for one of AFS's units, the U.S. operating unit American Skandia Life Assurance Corporation.

Since its start in 1989, American Skandia has seen gross premium volume rise to more than MSEK 10,240. The company is thus the 14th largest in the U.S. variable annuity market. The rate of development is high and has resulted in the launching of two to four significant new products or services a year.

Financial Focus

	1994	1993	1992
Return on net asset value	12.2%	24.3%	16.5%
Result of operations (MSEK)	115	96	19
Value added/empl. (SEK 000)	1,666	1,982	976

Comments: American Skandia's growth remains strong, despite slowing growth in the overall market.

Customer Focus

	1994	1993	1992
Number of contract	59,089	31,997	12,123
Savings/contract (SEK 000)	333	371	281
Surrender ratio	4.2%	3.6%	8.0%
Points of sale	11,573	4,805	2,768
Number of fund managers	19	11	8
Number of funds	52	35	24

Comments: American Skandia has a growing network of brokers, banks and fund managers. All of these have shown growth of about 100 percent since last year. This growth adds to American Skandia's structural capital.

Human Focus

	1994	1993	1992
Number of employees (full-time)	220	133	94
Number of managers	62	n.a.	n.a.
of whom, women	13	n.a.	n.a.
Training exp./employee (SEK 000)	9.8	10.6	4.0

Comments: American Skandia's work force has grown rapidly. Many new employees are young. 72 percent of the employees are under 40 years of age.

Process Focus

	1994	1993	1992
Contracts/employee	269	241	129
Adm. expense/gross premium	2.9%	2.6%	4.8%
PC/employee	1.3	1.4	1.1
IT expense/adm. expense	8.8%	4.7%	13.3%

Comments: An aggressive IT focus during the year has resulted in low administrative expenses despite a concurrent growth in volume.

(continued)

Exhibit 5 *(concluded)*

Renewal & Development Focus

	1994	1993	1992
Premium from new launches	11.1%	5.2%	49.7%
Increase in net premium	17.8%	204.8%	159.1%
Business development exp./ administrative expense	11.6%	9.8%	3.0%
Share of empl. below age 40	72%	74%	n.a.

Comments: American Skandia has sustained its rapid pace of growth and presence in a highly competitive total market. The rate of business development is very high, which has become a hallmark of American Skandia. The rate of renewal can be credited among other things to IT investments and the build-up of the federative structure

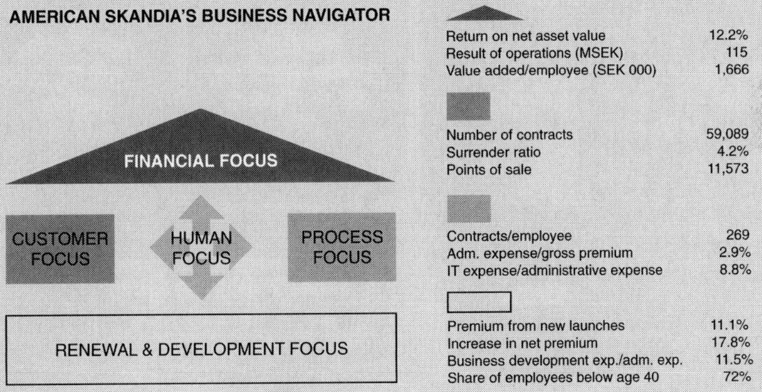
AMERICAN SKANDIA'S BUSINESS NAVIGATOR
FINANCIAL FOCUS
CUSTOMER FOCUS
HUMAN FOCUS
PROCESS FOCUS
RENEWAL & DEVELOPMENT FOCUS
Return on net asset value 12.2%
Result of operations (MSEK) 115
Value added/employee (SEK 000) 1,666
Number of contracts 59,089
Surrender ratio 4.2%
Points of sale 11,573
Contracts/employee 269
Adm. expense/gross premium 2.9%
IT expense/administrative expense 8.8%
Premium from new launches 11.1%
Increase in net premium 17.8%
Business development exp./adm. exp. 11.5%
Share of employees below age 40 72%

*n.a. = not available
Source: Skandia.

approximately 40% of his time in the United States, 30% in Sweden, and 30% in the rest of the world.

By taking on so many roles and traveling, Carendi believed he had to manage his various formal positions with a light hand, leaving lots of room for others. In a management style he described as "thrust and trust," he outlined the board priorities or thrust, then empowered people to take action. If someone raised an issue, he was likely to recall an old Swedish adage that if you asked a question you owned the question. When things went wrong, Carendi encouraged open discussion of the problems amongst peers, giving rise to a culture in which people owned up to their errors and the lessons to be drawn from them. "As long as it's based on good faith and careful thinking, it's OK to make a mistake," he explained.

Carendi believed that this strong philosophy of delegation and learning by mistakes put a high premium on recruiting excellent people. "You hire the best people and leave them alone," he said. "If you're not going to leave them alone, you don't need to hire the best people." He often signed on people ahead of any defined need, as he did with Pehrsson, and let them poke around the organization until they found a role. Viewing people selection as his greatest strength, Carendi retained the right to veto hiring decisions two levels below him. Beyond openness, honesty, willingness to question, and an ability to

Exhibit 6   Skandia and AFS: Organizational Structure

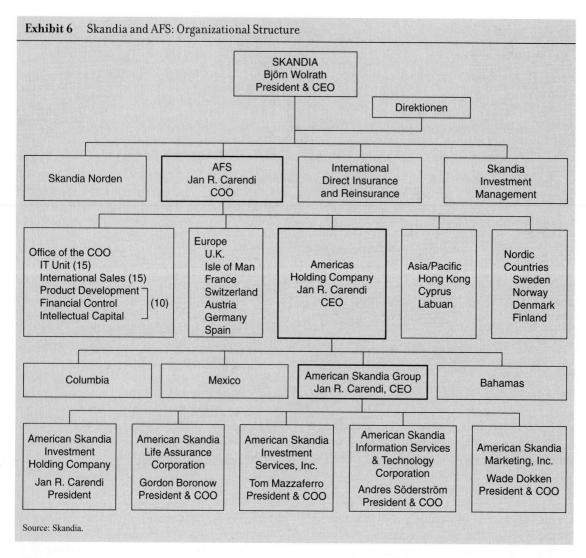

Source: Skandia.

release the potential in others, he looked for personal "chemistry," asking himself "Would I like to have dinner with this person?"

Carendi also established a well-understood norm that "individuals had the responsibility to develop their own capabilities, and the company had the responsibility not to waste them." In keeping with that belief, people could volunteer to be on one of the numerous teams that were constantly being assembled in AFS, even if they were in areas outside their own expertise. When forming teams, managers typically

sent out e-mail messages to relevant departments, and people nominated themselves. Before defining the final team, managers held an informal election among the nominees to get their input on who could best serve the team.

To fully utilize the potential of those he recruited, developed, and empowered, Carendi believed he had to maintain AFS's informal and entrepreneurial culture—one that was distinctly different from that of the parent company. "We are a tent in a palace pitched right on top of the Iranian carpet," he said.

"When circumstances change, we just take our tent down and put it up somewhere else." Starting in 1992, Carendi began to formalize and communicate his ideas about how the organization should work in a series of "white papers" published in the internal newspaper. Among the key aspirations of the management model he wrote about were:

- A "high trust" culture characterized by shared values, transparent communications, and the encouragement for people to accept responsibility and take risk.
- A challenging work environment in which learning was driven by people pushing each other in open, honest disagreement.
- An organization built on identifying and improving processes that were unique to AFS, and could become a source of competitive differentiation.

Current Operations, New Challenges

As the functional units in some AFS companies began to adapt and apply IC measures into their front-line operations, the new structure, processes, and culture were affecting the way front-line managers made decisions.

Changes in American Skandia   After modifying the Business Navigator for his unit, Anders Söderström, the head of American Skandia's IT unit, discovered that he was not investing enough in training his employees in new rapidly changing technologies. (See Exhibit 7 for his unit's Business Navigator.) "We noticed that our ratio of IT training expenses to IT expense was certainly lower than what we had planned, and lower relative to where we thought our competitors were," said Söderström. "The IC measures pointed me in exactly the opposite direction than the financial measures. While I was minimizing my expenses, I was putting at risk the knowledge and competence of my people at using current and future technologies to their fullest. The Business Navigator let me see that sometimes what looks good is bad, short-term thinking."

Other American Skandia units were doing likewise. The customer service area began to work on the customer focus dimension of the Navigator,

Exhibit 7   The American Skandia IT Business Navigator

American Skandia's It Business Navigator

IT expense/administrative expense	19%
Value added*/IT employees	117
Investments in IT	2,927

Number of internal IT customers	552
Number of external IT customers	14
Number of contracts/IT employees	1,906
Corporate IT literacy	+7%

IT capacity (CPU & DASD)		
AS/400	168,300 trans./hour	47 GB
PC/LAN	14,055 MIPS	199 GB
Change in IT inventory		3,639

IT development expense/IT expense	60%
IT expenses on training/IT expense	1%
R&D resources/total resources	5%

All amount in USD 000s.

*Change in IT inventory.
Source: Skandia.

developing measures and monitoring trends relating to the promptness and accuracy of responses to telephone requests from the wholesalers and brokers. It was piloting a project where, based on the results, representatives could win instant cash awards, based upon the performance of their customer service team. And in the marketing and sales department, management was trying to measure and monitor the development of customer capital. For instance, they started tracking number of brokers who wrote new business, or became inactive, each quarter, displaying the results on a bulletin board. Just by highlighting the data, they believed they made it manageable.

Reflecting his belief that "strategic ability begins and ends with serving the needs of the customer," Carendi urged the American Skandia marketing organization to redirect the bulk of systems development efforts towards meeting the needs of the company's key brokers and banks. At first, the focus was simply on providing them with excellent service and support. One initiative was the creation of a "concierge desk" to help brokers with whatever they needed: hotel reservations, lost credit cards, theater tickets. "Now the broker thinks of American Skandia when he has a problem to solve," said Carendi. "And the likelihood is that he will also think of us when he has business to write." At the same time, the customer-service function was reorganized into teams with the objective of providing personal service and building lifetime relationships with their assigned brokers and wholesalers. Carendi also invested in the professional development of his sales partners, establishing a Leaders College offering bi-monthly sessions in an array of financial and professional development topics.

Envisioning a day when a broker would provide much greater perceived value to the client by filtering and interpreting the confusing amount of information in the marketplace, American Skandia developed a PC-based software product called ASSESS. Launched in 1994, ASSESS helped brokers become experts on 35 different investment options by providing access to a variety of data sources, including analyst reports, stock listings, and standard indices. It also included an in-depth online questionnaire that helped the broker understand the client's needs, and educate them about the relationship of risk and return and the benefits of long-term investing. The software, which was mailed free to 20,000 brokers in the United States, freed them of tedious administrative tasks and allowed them to spend more time advising the client—addressing questions, completing paperwork, and closing the deal right away, rather than weeks later when interest might have cooled off.

To reduce the rate of turnover in its sales networks, American Skandia's sales and marketing division also made a sizable investment in creating a database on 250,000 brokers. The largest such repository in the industry, the database tracked by broker, the types of annuities sold, the commission structure, annual sales, and even the type of software each preferred. The area was also developing systems ranging from one that that signaled a slow-down in a broker's underwriting activity, predicted the need for support, and even sent out automatic thank-yous. "I want to create a process where we're communicating and building an emotional tie with the broker," said the subsidiary's marketing chief Dokken. "I want to make him think twice about leaving us."

Staying Ahead   Despite AFS's successful growth, Carendi was continually trying to identify and test strategic opportunities—what he described as a "dress rehearsal for the future." Recognizing that the world was becoming too complex and dynamic for him to develop clear foresight alone, he began more aggressively tapping into the ideas of his employees who were not only closer to the market, but also knew more about AFS and its capabilities. The more he thought about it, the more Carendi wanted to structure a formal process around future scanning. To help him implement, he enlisted the help of his Director of Intellectual Capital, Edvinsson.

Edvinsson hand-picked a pilot team of nine people from the United States, the United Kingdom, Colombia, Germany, and Sweden, deliberately focusing on AFS's "Generation X," the twenty-somethings who were the seed corn of the future leadership. He gave them a full-time three-month assignment to develop scenarios of the future for the company and the industry and to be prepared to present their conclusions to the company's Strategic Advisory Board (SAB). After an initial brainstorming session, the team settled on four areas of investigation: the customer, the "Egonomy" (economy at both the personal and macro levels), corporate reality (AFS's resources and constraints), and "valutics," (political systems and national values).

After weeks of intensive reading and discussion to flesh out their ideas, the team made their presentation to the SAB in Stockholm. The Generation Xers foresaw a future in which the customer would be more knowledgeable, have access to information at any time and any place, and demand product flexibility to fit their fast-paced and changing lifestyles. "We will have to offer a totally customized product," said one member of the team. "In other words, there will be no product. There will be as many products as there are clients. The client will be the creator." They then challenged senior managers to accept their scenarios at face value, and to come up with the best response for AFS. The Generation X team and the SAB then compared notes and were surprised at how convergent their ideas were—with one major exception. While the generation Xers could foresee a fragmented market undermining AFS's carefully designed network, top management believed that there was still value to be added by brokers because they made clients aware of the need for financial planning.

With the success of the pilot attempt in 1995, Carendi supported and enlarged the concept of future scanning through the creation of the Skandia Future Centers (SFC) division, appointing Edvinsson in charge. The Centers would act as a meeting place and "greenhouse" for dialog and collaboration. The first iteration created five "future teams," each composed of five full-time members drawn from three populations—the "in power" generation, the "potential" generation, and "Generation X." The groups would meet over several months, convening frequently for a day or two to discuss their assigned issues—the future of information technology, organization and leadership, changing demographics, changes in the insurance market, and the future of the world economy. In addition, the groups would invite "rolodex groups" of outside experts to present their perspectives on broad conceptual issues in a variety of fields related or not to insurance and financial services. The knowledge gained would be shared throughout the organization via the GAN. The first future center was to be inaugurated near Stockholm in May 1996, and other locations were planned.

Current Issues   In 1996, AFS was a worldwide organization, with an impressive array performance statistics. Despite a downturn in 1995, premium income had grown 45% annually during the past five years. Between 1992 and 1995, its customer base had grown from 100,000 to 785,000, its alliance network of brokers, fund managers, and other partners had expanded from 15,000 to 46,000, and its employee base had expanded from 1,130 to 1,700. With only one out of twenty-seven people working for it on its payroll, some began to describe AFS as a "virtual corporation." By its own estimate, the company's network-based organization and its use of cutting-edge information technology had reduced its administrative costs to one-third those of its competitors.

Yet, despite these accomplishments, Carendi was focused on how to defend and improve AFS's position as a leader in its chosen business. Many of AFS's practices were now being imitated widely as other companies built cooperative alliances for money management and distribution. Still others had released their own versions of the ASSESS software, and cloned AFS's products. Furthermore, deregulation had lowered barriers to entry into the market, and most major mutual fund families now offered annuity insurance products. All of this meant that customer loyalty was eroding. As Carendi explained:

> Competition could come from anywhere. Today, we compete with mutual funds. Tomorrow, we are going to compete with software houses. . . .
>
> Consumers couldn't care less about established relationships today if they can get it cheaper elsewhere, and at the time of day that suits their schedule rather than when the banker or broker's office is open.

Carendi was particularly intrigued by the ideas generated by the "Generation X" pilot team's future scenario in which potential policyholders would buy insurance very differently than they did in the past. Was the AFS model he had so carefully constructed still viable? if not, how should it be changed? And how should such profound decisions be made?

Case 5-4a   Meridian Magnesium: International Technology Transfer

Len Miller was in the midst of planning a trip to Meridian Magnesium's U.S. and Italian production facilities. He was visiting the plants to learn how to improve Meridian's internal transfers of technology. While Meridian was the leading supplier worldwide of magnesium die-cast components to the automotive parts industry, differences in performance among Meridian plants were stark. Miller, a vice-president (VP) at Meridian, wondered what he might do to bring the performance of the U.S. and Italian facilities up to the same level as the Canadian facility. Part of the problem seemed to be that the U.S. and Italian facilities resisted the technological innovations that were benefiting the Canadian plant. Miller not only needed to understand the reasons for these differences, but also needed to develop a game plan that resolved the issues before Meridian's annual board meeting in two weeks' time.

The Automotive Parts Industry

The global automotive parts industry, servicing the world's original equipment manufacturers (OEMs), was projected to have sales of over US$519[1] billion

[1]*Unless otherwise stated, all amounts are in Canadian dollars.*

Ken Cole prepared this case under the supervision of Professor Tima Bansal solely to provide material for class discussion. The authors do not intend to illustrate either effective or ineffective handling of a managerial situation. The authors may have disguised certain names and other identifying information to protect confidentiality.

Ivey Management Services prohibits any form of reproduction, storage or transmittal without its written permission. This material is not covered under authorization from CanCopy or any reproduction rights organization. To order copies or request permission to reproduce materials, contact Ivey Publishing, Ivey Management Services, c/o Richard Ivey School of Business, The University of Western Ontario, London, Ontario, Canada, N6A 3K7; phone (519) 661-3208; fax (519) 661-3882; e-mail cases@ivey.uwo.ca.

One-time permission to reproduce granted by Ivey Management Services on February 6, 2003.

IVEY

Copyright © 2001, Ivey Management Services
Version: (A) 2001-11-12.

Richard Ivey School of Business
The University of Western Ontario

in 2000. Canadian manufacturers were expected to account for approximately US$39 billion of that amount.

In the 1990s, the automotive industry witnessed three major trends: consolidation, outsourcing and globalization. It had been predicted that by 2010, consolidation would result in as few as six global OEMs and approximately 50 major global parts suppliers. Consolidation and outsourcing provided automotive parts purchasers with incredible purchasing leverage that resulted in strong discount pressures on suppliers. In response, suppliers focused on developing value-added pre- and post-production services, including design, engineering, machining, finishing and assembly. For large international suppliers, the challenge was to ensure that all production facilities, regardless of geographic location, were using the most efficient, lowest cost technologies and processes.

The automotive parts industry was comprised primarily of three materials: steel, plastics and aluminum. These suppliers represented billions of dollars in annual sales, strong research and development (R&D) capabilities, and full customer design and engineering support. Magnesium autoparts suppliers, on the other hand, while growing quickly, were relatively small with just over one billion dollars cumulative global sales in 1999. Steel and aluminum autoparts generally competed on price, while magnesium and plastics autoparts generally competed on design, integration with other materials and quality. Magnesium was much lighter than steel and one-third lighter than aluminum. It was also stronger than either plastics or aluminum. However, recent alliances between plastics and steel companies, to produce a hybrid lighter-weight material, had left aluminum and magnesium die-casters uneasy and increased their sense of urgency to lower costs to remain competitive.

Meridian Magnesium Incorporated— Corporate History

Meridian Magnesium, originally Webster Manufacturing, began in the 1930s as a zinc die-casting operation based in London, Ontario, and focused primarily on small-machine parts. In the 1960s, with the signing of the automotive trade pact, the owner, John Webster, saw the opportunity to die-cast automotive parts. Webster's automotive business grew, and by the early 1970s, sales surpassed $20 million. At that time, Webster was approached by Ford to consider die-casting in magnesium, the lightest structural metal. Ford was interested in reducing the weight of vehicles due to the OPEC crisis and the emergence of corporate average fuel economy (CAFE) standards during that decade. In 1980, the company sold its first magnesium product: a "remote control mirror bezel" for the Ford Mustang.

The success of this first product convinced Webster to convert much of its zinc business to magnesium. In 1981, Webster built its first magnesium die-casting plant, moving four magnesium die-casting machines from London to Strathroy, Ontario. After John Webster's retirement in the early 1980s, the company changed hands several times, eventually becoming Meridian Magnesium Inc. and going public in 1989. Meridian attracted significant attention in the markets, particularly from two companies that, by 1998, had secured almost equal ownership. The first, with 49 per cent of Meridian shares, was Norsk Hydro, the Norwegian public utility company and one of the world's largest producers of magnesium ingots and alloys. The second, with 51 per cent ownership, was Teksid, an Italian-based world leader in the foundry (melting of metals) industry. In 1998, Norsk and Teksid took Meridian private once again and signed a shareholders' agreement providing for equal decision-making power on Meridian's board of directors. Both owners planned to provide Meridian with significant technological support; Norsk in areas related to magnesium metal and alloys, and Teksid in areas related to foundry processes.

Meridian in 2000

By the late 1990s, Meridian was the largest automotive supplier of magnesium die-cast components to both original equipment manufacturers (OEMs) and Tier 1 suppliers (major global suppliers), with approximately 55 per cent of the global market for magnesium automotive parts. Meridian had sales in excess of $300 million and was a "big fish" in the "small pond" of magnesium automotive parts. Meridian's mission statement declared that, ". . . Meridian is committed to being the leading full service supplier of magnesium die-casting components and assemblies in the global automotive market."

The company had three plants, Magnesium Products Division (MPD) in Strathroy, Ontario, Magnesium Products of America (MPA) in Eaton Rapids, Michigan, and a smaller plant, Magnesium Products of Italy (MPI) in Valle d'Aosta in northeast Italy. Meridian was the industry's lowest-cost producer and the process technology leader. Meridian had a very strong market position in North America, with leading levels of magnesium know-how, strong shareholder support, good labor relations and few capital restraints due to a strong debt/equity position. The plants produced numerous products, including fully integrated instrument panels, cross-car beams, transfer cases and steering components. Meridian also had business development offices throughout North America and Western Europe. These offices developed and maintained contacts with customer engineering and design groups.

Meridian's Goals

As part of its 10-year plan, Meridian had set some aggressive growth targets for 2010 including:

- Annual growth rate of 15 per cent
- Return on capital employed exceeding 15 per cent
- Maintaining a 40 per cent share of global market
- Sales exceeding $1 billion
- Earnings of greater than $100 million
- Continuing to be the lowest-cost producer

Other more general goals included expanding operations to make sub-assemblies and modules;

expanding product offerings into body, structural and powertrain applications; and the development of new technologies to provide Meridian with more sources of sustainable competitive advantage. In the short term, technological goals included the improvement of foundry systems and the development of "in-cell" recycling capabilities.

Recognized weaknesses in the Meridian organization included a lack of employee retention due to a very tight labor market. People with strong process and production knowledge were in very short supply. Furthermore, the Italian and U.S. facilities did not perform as well as the Canadian facility, which was partly attributable to the difficulty in retaining knowledgeable people.

Len Miller and GTO

Upon assuming office in 1998, Meridian's chief executive officer (CEO), Paolo Maccario, had redesigned Meridian's management structure and appointed three VPs and a president (see Exhibit 1 for

details). Based in Strathroy, Len Miller was responsible for Meridian's Global Technologies Organization (GTO). Miller had joined Meridian as the assistant general manager of MPD at the Strathroy plant in 1996, and had worked hard to improve operating efficiencies. In December of 1996, Miller was promoted to general manager and in early 1999, became VP of Meridian's recently created (January 1998) GTO division.

As Meridian had expanded to a multiplant, international organization in the 1990s, it became apparent that the company could benefit from the centralization of some of the "knowledge" components within the business. At that time, each plant had its own R&D budget and developed its own technologies and solutions, and there was no formal system of communication between plants. GTO's mandate was to "facilitate the identification and communication of best practices between the plants" and to help the plants realize their business objectives as defined by the corporate strategy and growth

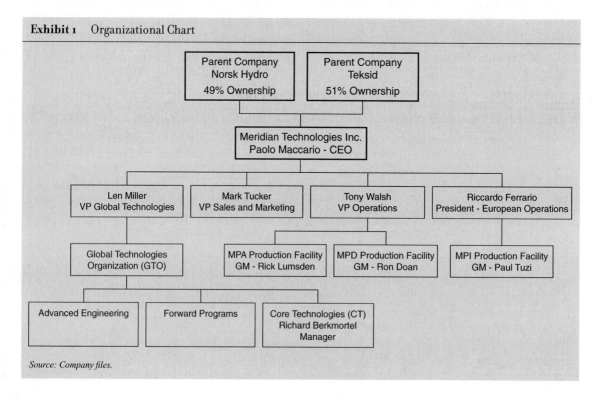

Exhibit 1   Organizational Chart

Source: Company files.

targets. GTO was not a profit centre, and therefore it relied on the plants to finance its activities. GTO grew rapidly in its first three years of operations, from 11 to more than 55 employees. In 1998, GTO's budget was between $2 million to $3 million, but was increased to $7.5 million in 2000.

In the summer of 2000, GTO staff moved into a separate facility across the street from the MPD plant in Strathroy. The two-story, "Global Technology Centre (GTC)" was equipped with leading-edge technology solutions, sophisticated design program software, complete Intranet and Internet connectivity and powerful servers, accessible worldwide. Separated from the plants in this new facility, the organization quickly developed a reputation for being a "great place to get promoted to," and many in the Meridian organization began to refer to GTC as the "Good Times Club."

When GTO was created, Miller had great hopes that the centralized development of best practices would generate significant benefits. He believed that the plants would readily participate in projects to improve operating efficiencies and lower costs. Instead, after more than two years of GTO operations, the plants continued to resist implementing some proven best practices. The NIH Syndrome (Not Invented Here), as Miller liked to call it, was pervasive at Meridian. But to Miller, the problem was even more complex than a mere question of where or how the technology was developed. Numerous organizational and cultural issues had developed as a result of Meridian's rapid international expansion, leaving Meridian struggling to develop and implement companywide standards.

There were other issues as well. According to Mark Tucker, Meridian's VP of sales and marketing, "One of the biggest things is that people don't understand the roles and responsibilities of GTO at the operations level, the business level . . . because today, I would bet, you go to any one of the plants and half the people there wouldn't even know what goes on here at GTO."

Miller also recognized that GTO had some other weaknesses that continually interfered with efforts to improve production efficiencies across all plants. According to Miller, ". . . The largest failure to date has been the failure to improve relationships between GTO and the U.S. facility. This is a failure at the vice-presidential level, but it is also a failure at the organizational level, at the level of the plant employees and the GTO staff."

Despite these problems, Miller felt that over all, GTO had enjoyed success. The core technologies group within GTO had done an excellent job developing in-house recycling. All the plants had implemented the process and were realizing significant savings. According to Miller, "The true measure of success for GTO is in the value delivered."

Core Technologies (CT)

Within GTO, Core Technologies was directly responsible for the centralized development and communication of best practices between the plants (see Exhibit 2 for CT objectives). CT also had a

---

Exhibit 2   Core Technology Objectives

- Serve as a Meridian "Centre of Expertise" and technical training resource for Business Units
- Ensure a consistent application of Meridian's best process practices by coordinating and evaluating plant innovation and strong plant relations
- Assist implementation of latest technology at Meridian plants
- Research, benchmark and evaluate alternative technologies, products and materials
- Gather and disseminate competitive intelligence
- Set and achieve aggressive targets for speed to market—50 per cent reductions for specific core technologies that can capture the heart of the industry
- Relentless pursuit of low cost producer status within the process context to achieve a sustainable competitive advantage

supporting role in other GTO functions, including assisting other GTO departments with business development, product engineering and product launch co-ordination. CT's primary focus, however, was on assisting with cost reductions, safety-related projects and new technologies.

Miller had spent his first three months as VP trying to figure out how the Meridian organization really worked. He saw the need to build a strong CT team and find strong leadership. He envisioned a team that would be able to do anything technology-related within the fields of magnesium, die-casting and auto parts. Leadership was critical, and Miller chose Richard Berkmortel, a mechanical engineer with manufacturing and product engineering experience, and promoted him to manager of CT. Berkmortel had been at MPD for six years, his last two years as a business unit manager in Strathroy's operations.

The CT unit was comprised of Berkmortel, two PhD metallurgists, two process engineers with extensive "shop-floor" experience and three other engineers with specific areas of expertise. Four of the existing CT staff were promoted from the Strathroy production facility; three were external hires and one was hired from the U.S. facility. Three of the eight who were promoted internally had 15 or more years experience in the industry. Berkmortel himself had eight years of die-casting experience and the remainder of his team had, on average, five years of experience.

Communication between CT and the plants was largely informal, as it had been before GTO was formed. This informal style seemed to fit the practical "get the job done" mindset that was so prevalent at the plant level. Formal communication occurred at the monthly operations meetings where Miller often reviewed ongoing CT projects with the other VPs and the plant managers. On an irregular basis, GTO distributed an internal newsletter that highlighted developments and successes.

CT was respected for its development and implementation of in-house recycling of magnesium metal. This project, undertaken in 1998 and completed at all plants in late 2000, yielded significant savings to the plants and had been implemented companywide as quickly as possible.

Another project, gas displacement pumps, had not fared so well. While CT expended considerable resources to develop the pumps which were adopted by the Canadian facility, the U.S. facility independently developed siphon tubes. Despite some evidence that the gas displacement pumps were more efficient and led to cost savings, the U.S. facility continued to use siphon tubes. Other projects included "in-cell" recycling and the development of better systems for the delivery of SF6 (Sulpher Hexaflouride) that Meridian used as a cover gas to protect melted magnesium. The eventual replacement of SF6, a "greenhouse" gas, with a substitute cover gas was another ongoing CT project.

Meridian Products Division (MPD)— Strathroy, Ontario, Canada

MPD began magnesium die-casting in 1981 and, by 1999, was the flagship of the Meridian organization. While employee retention at MPD was an issue, it was less so than at the other plants. Management believed that keeping good people from the predominantly rural farming communities surrounding the Strathroy facility was easier than in Michigan's extended suburbs and bedroom communities. Retention was a significant advantage since it took several years to develop significant levels of process expertise. MPD was non-union and had been since its inception. Relations between management and employees were strong and marked by frequent, frank and open communication. The plant had a strong relationship with GTO, and according to Ron Doan, the plant manager, collaboration on projects in the past had been fruitful.

Meridian Products of America (MPA)— Eaton Rapids, Michigan

Approximately a three-hour drive from MPD, MPA was located in the heart of Michigan's famous automotive region. MPA began magnesium die-casting production in 1995 as an expansion project from MPD. From 1999 through 2005, MPA was slated to launch a number of new magnesium products. "Launch mode," with its numerous uncertainties, tough deadlines and growing pains, was predicted to significantly stretch plant resources.

Meridian Products of Italy (MPI)— Verres, Valle d'Aosta, Italy

MPI began in 1995 as a joint venture between Teksid and Meridian to build the Fiat/Lancia "Epsilon" seat for SEPI, the seat division of Fiat Auto. Originally the business required four die-cast machines, but eventually production estimates resulted in expansion to nine machines. Unfortunately, the

developing industrial region, and the unions were pleased to have the jobs there. Salaries were similar across all industries in the region so the union had little effect on salary costs. But working conditions in the plant were always an issue, especially since the region's largest employer was the nearby casino, offering cleaner and "more glamorous" work. Of MPI's 130 employees, 20 were in business development or were GTO transferees assigned to MPI to help develop processes and technologies. In the future, MPI planned to expand production to 7,400 tonnes by 2003.

Plant Comparisons Comparative figures for each of Meridian's three production facilities are as follows:

Comparative Figures, 1999	MPD (Canada)	MPA (United States)	MPI (Italy)
Tonnes Mg produced	14,000 gross metric tonnes	11,000 gross metric tones	3,000 gross metric tones
Die cast machines	20 from 800 to 2,500 tonnes	17 from 800 to 3,000 tonnes	9 from 420 to 2,500 tonnes
Employees	370	350	130
1999 revenues (US$)	180 million	140 million	60 million
1999 EBIT* (US$)	40 million	12 million	(Loss)
Secondary operations	Machining, finishing and assembly	Machining, drilling and assembly	None—Value added work currently outsourced

*EBIT—Earnings before Interest and Taxes.

seat project was subsequently cancelled, but Fiat chose Meridian to produce the cross-car beam for the Bravo Brava. The financial terms were highly unfavorable for Meridian, which had very little leverage, given MPI's significant excess capacity as a result of the cancellation of the seat project. After this inauspicious beginning, MPI struggled to turn a profit.

MPI was unionized, as were most Italian companies. Only 10 per cent of the employees, however, were card-carrying union members, and the relationship between the union and management was "very smooth." The Aosta Valley was a newly

Notes from an Interview with Richard Berkmortel

Miller had spoken to Berkmortel, the manager of Core Technologies, to understand his perspective on why the technologies developed by the CT division were not being adopted universally by Meridian plants. Several comments from his conversation with Berkmortel had stuck in Miller's mind.

Plant Attitudes

According to Berkmortel, while CT was meant to be a centre of knowledge and best practices and to share information and innovations with the plants "... very little of this actually occurs in a formal, organized way and some of the plants are slightly proprietary about good ideas and innovations." Berkmortel believed that CT had failed to break down the "negative—NIH—attitudes at the plants" and to get the plants to adopt common values toward technological developments.

Choosing Technology Projects

With respect to choosing the projects on which CT worked, Berkmortel reflected,

A lot of innovations have to come from the plants. I think it is more efficient for them to do it. They have a specific need to resolve immediately, and that need, along with the time expediency, will drive innovation. A lot of the time, they are the best equipped to understand what their needs are and to resolve them.

The plants may have an issue, and they have a lot of their own resources that they can put toward that issue. For MPA and MPI, it is more difficult since they are somewhat removed from us (CT) in terms of distance. Typically, I see that the plant managers find it difficult to ask for assistance from Miller since they are often unsure of GTO's role or are unwilling to accept support. Also at times, there is outside support that is better equipped to deal with a technical issue, such as the original equipment manufacturer could assist with their own piece of equipment.

A Successful Project— In-House Recycling

In-house recycling was a major success because everybody wanted it. The plants wanted it for financial reasons . . . the goals fit closely with plant philosophies, strength in foundries, and every part of the company wanted the project to go ahead . . . so there was full support and there was no disagreement as to what direction we should be taking. So that went a long ways to facilitating the initial steps of development. A pilot operation was set up at MPD. That facility was chosen due to location, location, location.

Today at MPD, all scrap is recycled . . . and that technology represents a significant savings on raw material costs. We had no problems in getting the other plants to adopt it. MPA wanted the project to go ahead immediately since it was seen as a corporate project, a Meridian project. MPI was also a relatively smooth transition. MPI came third since they had other priorities they needed to implement beforehand. Part of the delay at MPI was also related to resources, since the implementation team was working at MPA and had to finish there before they could begin working at MPI.

A More Typical Project—SF6 Pulse System

Berkmortel discussed a typical project related to improving foundry design.

The particular project was the SF6 pulse system. The plants, MPD in particular, had been complaining about corrosion on the pots and SF6 prices were rising. A study was done by CT on MPD's pots with the help of an outside gas analysing company. Plant participation from MPD and MPA was relatively minor. In the end, a new system was developed that reduced pot corrosion and SF6 consumption. The improvements were communicated directly from plant to plant at the operations meetings. MPA saw the positive effect on MPD's financials and requested the information directly from MPD. MPA is now probably at about 50 to 60 per cent implementation. MPI has been very slow to react and does not have the process implemented yet . . . information and drawings have been sent several times, along with the equipment and they have yet to install the equipment, approximately one year later.

According to Berkmortel,

MPI is not adopting SF6 pulse systems because their foundry knowledge is somewhat lacking. They do not yet understand their process enough for the pulse system to be useful since they have a number of other foundry issues to improve before the technology would help them to save money. I don't understand why their foundry technology is different from that of MPD and MPA since numerous people have been sent to assist and improve their systems.

A "Failed" Project—Gas Displacement Pumps

In speaking about CT's biggest disappointment to date, Berkmortel identified gas displacement pumps.

> Gas displacement pumps were a CT project and a plant project at MPD. Our work resulted in up to 25 per cent improvement in some areas. At MPD these improvements were measurable and cost savings were evident. But the other plants refused to implement the technology. MPA did not accept it since they felt that they could get the same benefit from siphon tubes and that there would be less disruption in the plant since they would not have to reengineer their foundry processes. The financial benefits of gas displacement pumps were not as evident as they were with recycling. The process was a three-year process, and both the siphon tubes and the gas displacement pumps were being improved simultaneously . . . even if the data indicate that the fourth generation of gas displacement pumps are vastly superior for some products or some machines, it is unlikely that there will be enough evidence coming out of MPD to convince the other plants to make the investment.

Communications

With respect to communications, Berkmortel indicated that cultural and language differences imposed barriers between North America and Italy, but that other problems existed between MPA and CT despite similarities in culture and language.

> In the beginning, communication with MPI was difficult, but it has improved significantly over the last six months. The message that CT wants to give to the plants is that there is some benefit to seeking assistance from CT. CT definitely has the most success when the plant comes to CT with a problem to resolve. When they feel that they have a need and they come to us, it works. On projects, plant people are automatically respected . . . we have started to pull people from the "customers" to start to add credibility to the process.

Improving CT

Berkmortel also believed that some of the issues were resource related.

> Development of new processes, like in-house recycling, has consumed the majority of CT's resources, especially our human resources, or more so than expected, so our role in supporting the plants has been lower than 25 per cent. I would say only 10 per cent of our time has been spent on this and only when the plants have requested that we do so.

In terms of the future, Berkmortel believed that,

> The focus needs to be on "big"—Meridian projects with direct financial impact. Smaller projects are harder to focus on because the resources have been allocated to priority items where we can have the most impact. We maybe need a slightly larger group of people where we can dedicate people to non-core projects. In terms of allocating people, there are millions of projects that the plant would like done, and often I don't have people with the right knowledge or enough people to respond to all of those needs.
>
> Typically, CT works for a particular customer. We have looked at working in cross-plant teams. That goes back to communication—how we communicate with the plants. It has typically been done at operations meetings. The plant managers raise an issue that they believe CT should deal with, and CT reports back on how they could deal with the issue, and the teams are set up afterwards.

Understanding the Plants' Perspectives

Miller needed to find out why some technologies that had been adopted by MPD were not being adopted by the U.S. and Italian facilities. He had scheduled meetings with the managers of MPD, MPA and MPI over the next two weeks. Miller needed to get to the root of the problem and identify ways in which these issues could be resolved.

This case was the first place winner of the 2001 Indiana University Center for International Business Education and Research (IUCIBER) International Case Competition. IUCIBER is funded by a grant from the U.S. Department of Education.

Case 5-4b Meridian Magnesium: The American Perspective

Notes from Interview with Rick Lumsden, Plant Manager—Magnesium Products of America (MPA)

Len Miller spoke with Rick Lumsden, plant manager for MPA. In his conversations, Lumsden was characteristically succinct.

MPA Goals

The goals of MPA were all specified in the business plan and are related to safety targets, quality targets and performance targets. My particular challenges include improving productivity in terms of reduced cycle times, lower scrap levels and less production downtime. I am also working to improve labor efficiencies and tooling and equipment levels.

See Exhibit 1 for MPA year 2000 Objectives. Environmental issues were also on his list of projects.

Choosing Technology Projects

According to Lumsden,

The best way to meet these challenges is through careful planning and the use of best possible planning prac-

▌ Ken Cole prepared this case under the supervision of Professor Tima Bansal solely to provide material for class discussion. The authors do not intend to illustrate either effective or ineffective handling of a managerial situation. The authors may have disguised certain names and other identifying information to protect confidentiality.

▌ Ivey Management Services prohibits any form of reproduction, storage or transmittal without its written permission. This material is not covered under authorization from CanCopy or any reproduction rights organization. To order copies or request permission to reproduce materials, contact Ivey Publishing, Ivey Management Services, c/o Richard Ivey School of Business, The University of Western Ontario, London, Ontario, Canada, N6A 3K7; phone (519) 661-3208; fax (519) 661-3882; e-mail cases@ivey.uwo.ca.

▌ One-time permission to reproduce granted by Ivey Management Services on February 6, 2003.

IVEY Copyright © 2001, Ivey Management Services
Version: (A) 2001-11-12.

Richard Ivey School of Business
The University of Western Ontario

Exhibit 1 Objectives for MPA

1. Meet business plan EBIT and EVA targets
2. Achieve GPU target of 63%
3. Meet plant scrap rate target of 6.6%
4. Launch the following new programs
   - UN 152 Case and Cover
   - RS Upper
   - Explorer IP
5. Complete in-house recycling project
6. Achieve safety goals (Frequency + 2.47 & severity = 20)
7. Strengthen customer relationships through improved PPM9<50 and delivery performance (100% on time)
8. Meet productivity improvement targets
9. Remain union free
10. Continue to develop team-based organization

tices. This would include identifying and prioritizing issues in conjunction with the plants, and then doing the necessary research to justify potential improvements before developing implementation methods.

Core Technologies (CT) could best assist in this process by co-ordinating activities between all plants and CT, and by helping the plants problem solve when required. Teams at CT need to be proactive in their efforts to work with the plants. Much of this should be driven by the plants and their needs. The goal of CT should be to service the plants and to develop and implement the best technology, from ingot to finished products. They could study the plants and determine what processes are currently being used and then determine of those, which are the best. Decisions should not be based on price.

Communications

According to Lumsden,

There is no structure in the communication between GTO and the plants, or between one plant and the others. I really have no idea what CT are doing today; they do not communicate what they do. But CT and the development of technologies is a good way to bring people together. Right now, plant-to-plant communication on these issues is pretty good. Tony Walsh, as vice-president of operations, makes sure that the plants are well connected. There is no official structure for communicating with CT, it's a very unofficial, non-structured transfer of best practices.

Improving CT

Lumsden believed that CT could best improve its operations by defining its roles and responsibilities, being accountable to the plants in areas of plant support, holding regular meetings with plant technology people and participating at the floor-level in the plants to gain knowledge.

The best process for communication, in Lumsden's opinion, would be the semi-annual, off-site meeting. These meetings would allow plant people to define priorities with the engineers and the team leaders from the plants.

Lumsden also felt that there was a real need for quantitative analysis: "CT needs to crunch the numbers for example, gas displacement pumps versus siphon tubes, to determine which is more efficient."

Case 5-4c   Meridian Magnesium: The Canadian Perspective

Notes from Interview with Ron Doan, Plant Manager—Magnesium Products Division (MPD)

Ron Doan spoke to Len Miller about his plant's priorities, his experiences with Core Technologies (CT) and how he believed the organization might be improved.

MPD Goals

The goals for MPD have been set by Paolo Maccario and the board. We are to have impeccable safety records and be a world-class supplier of quality parts. We need a squeaky clean record with the customers . . . zero customer concerns. Employee focus first, followed by customer focus. Maccario not only wants to eliminate long-term accidents, but he doesn't want anyone to have even the minor scrapes, burns and cuts . . . total elimination, zero.

To do these things, you need to evolve the technology . . . whether that be equipment, metal you are using, the training levels of your people, etc. . . . so that when you turn a machine on, it runs and makes good parts. The ultimate goal is to be like some of the plastic manufacturers, where one person runs five or six machines from a control room, walks in in the morning, turns the machines on, and then turns them off and goes home at night and knows that they have made nothing but perfect parts all day long and never stopped . . . ideal world . . . how do we get there?

▌ Ken Cole prepared this case under the supervision of Professor Tima Bansal solely to provide material for class discussion. The authors do not intend to illustrate either effective or ineffective handling of a managerial situation. The authors may have disguised certain names and other identifying information to protect confidentiality.
▌ Ivey Management Services prohibits any form of reproduction, storage or transmittal without its written permission. This material is not covered under authorization from CanCopy or any reproduction rights organization. To order copies or request permission to reproduce materials, contact Ivey Publishing, Ivey Management Services, c/o Richard Ivey School of Business, The University of Western Ontario, London, Ontario, Canada, N6A 3K7; phone (519) 661-3208; fax (519) 661-3882; e-mail cases@ivey.uwo.ca.
▌ One-time permission to reproduce granted by Ivey Management Services on February 6, 2003.

IVEY   Copyright © 2001, Ivey Management Services
Version: (A) 2001-11-12.

Richard Ivey School of Business
The University of Western Ontario

Plant Attitudes

Proximity (for MPD to the Global Technologies Organization [GTO]) is a major advantage . . . I see CT people several times per week and if I have a problem, I can call them up and they come over . . . I can utilize them the same way as I use my own people in the plant . . . but for Magnesium Products of America [MPA] or Magnesium Products of Italy [MPI], they don't get that response . . . they may have to send a picture of a problem rather than just having the guys come over and look at it.

I think the other plants are very receptive to initiatives coming from CT, but it is very hard to transfer the technology if you don't have the infrastructure to support it, not just in the plant, but also in the region, so they struggle more with the technology . . . and they have the learning curve, especially at MPI.

Choosing Technology Projects

Rick [Lumsden, plant manager of MPA] and I have sat down two or three times and come up with a list of things that needed to be done and the list got lost in "Never-Never Land" . . . probably because priorities change . . . plant priorities and CT priorities. I am not sure if they changed the list or we changed the list, it is a moving target.

I really do not think we need help on the day-to-day making of a magnesium die-castings. We have more expertise in-house than CT has. CT needs to work on projects related to what will help me four, five or 10 years from now, not next year . . . for example, is there a better way to pre-heat ingots, are there additives that we can put in the magnesium to better dross the pots, what's the alternate gas for SF6 . . . those types of projects.

The Gas Displacement Pump Project

We have, for instance, gas displacement pumps . . . we struggled with siphon tubes for a long time and made lots of improvements, but it still boiled down to raising and lowering the tube all the time for safety reasons. Norsk had developed a gas displacement pump that we brought in-house here, before there was a CT . . . so are they driving it? No, they are just helping us out. They have provided another brain . . . a smart person . . . and also their metallur-

gist has helped us with metal issues. They have supported and continue to support us on the project . . . we suffered for months in development but where we are today, there is no reason why MPA can't use the pumps. MPI can't use them yet because they use round, rather than bathtub-shaped pots . . . it would be more difficult to use gas displacement pumps there. But you can tell in the organization that there is a big question mark because we haven't purchased gas displacement pumps for the new plant. They are using siphon tubes in the new facility that is being built since they see that as "easy" technology and they see the success of MPA with the siphon tubes.

In-House Recycling Project

Recycling . . . they [CT] did a marvelous job. They were successful because they were very focused, knew exactly what they had to do, were very logical in their process and their approach to eliminating roadblocks at all levels, even the customer levels. They also have set up a very good process; simple, but it works. They have made a process window that is so huge that even with the human factor, you still make good recycled metal all the time.

Communications

I don't think that they have had any failures, to my knowledge . . . but they don't market themselves. For instance, in our operations meetings, the Forward Programs group is represented, CT is not. Now does Len Miller handle the CT projects? Sure. Do we ever get to them? No! Or only in a very rapid manner . . . I don't know, and maybe I don't need to know, what Richard [Berkmortel] and his guys are working on . . . but I don't really know where their priorities are, I have no idea, like I said, they don't market themselves. They are an unknown, and if they are an unknown to us guys over here, then MPA and MPI don't have a clue.

Improving CT

They have nine projects listed in their report on projects, and it would be better if they worked on only two or three if they are going to keep their human resources where they are.

Once we have all the same goals, at the plant levels, and Rick, myself and Paul [Tuzi] are working on it . . . it will mean a whole lot for CT because when you only have a very small number of people, they have to be very focused, they can't be working on 14 projects because then none of them get done well. We are going to say, these are where we are really lacking today. Please take us to the future.

Case 5-4d   Meridian Magnesium: The Italian Perspective

Notes from Interviews with Riccardo Ferrario, President, and Paul Tuzi, General Manager (GM)—Magnesium Products of Italy (MPI)

Len Miller reflected upon his conversations with Riccardo Ferrario and Paul Tuzi.

Plant Attitudes

According to Ferrario, there were significant differences between the North America plant and the Italian one.

The plants started in two completely different places, and the problem is the market. In effect, there are many more original equipment managers (OEMs) in Europe, the volume for each single model is much smaller, the scale is much lower, costs are higher and there is less profit. As well, many languages in Europe complicate things and add costs, as do external factors. For instance, corporate average fuel economy (CAFÉ) standards are not an issue in Europe but recycling legislation applies different pressures.

The weakest resource at MPI is experience, especially in production and in management where the managers are good quality, but young and inexperienced. The teamwork concept was started in 1998 . . . 80 per cent of my managerial team is new since 1999. Business development has been a stable function, but the plant has at least 12 to 15 per cent annual turnover in employees.

Choosing Technology Projects

Ferrario continued,

There should be centralized research and development (R&D) for such functions as melt, metal transfer, shot and other core processes. Best practices should be spread from the centre of R&D to the individual plants. As for other "non-core" processes, each plant should develop the system that works best for that plant, and CT can act as a facilitator for the transfer of those technologies. There are two levels of technology, the main river, key processes and the secondary contributory technologies. The main river (see Exhibit 1) is that in which the new technologies must be shared, but then there are numerous feeder streams that contribute to the process, that can be done differently from plant to plant. It is GTO's responsibility to develop R&D processes that contribute to enhancing the productivity of the main river of technologies and controlling these technologies by defining and communicating best practices throughout the organization.

Ken Cole prepared this case under the supervision of Professor Tima Bansal solely to provide material for class discussion. The authors do not intend to illustrate either effective or ineffective handling of a managerial situation. The authors may have disguised certain names and other identifying information to protect confidentiality.

Ivey Management Services prohibits any form of reproduction, storage or transmittal without its written permission. This material is not covered under authorization from CanCopy or any reproduction rights organization. To order copies or request permission to reproduce materials, contact Ivey Publishing, Ivey Management Services, c/o Richard Ivey School of Business, The University of Western Ontario, London, Ontario, Canada, N6A 3K7; phone (519) 661-3208; fax (519) 661-3882; e-mail cases@ivey.uwo.ca.

One-time permission to reproduce granted by Ivey Management Services on February 6, 2003.

IVEY *Copyright © 2001, Ivey Management Services Version: (A) 2001-11-12.*

Richard Ivey School of Business
The University of Western Ontario

Exhibit 1   Ferrario's "Main River" of Technology

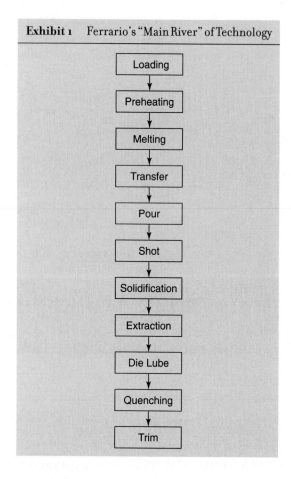

Improving CT

In terms of the how to improve CT Ferrario believed that "first you have to get agreement between the plants as to what is a core technology, and then how best to develop the technology, and then decide how that should be spread throughout the organization."

Paul Tuzi

Miller also spoke with Tuzi, MPI's newly appointed GM, to determine his perspective on MPI, and on how CT could help the organization realize its goals. Tuzi had several goals for MPI. Short-term, he wished to stabilize the new management team and work towards increasing production efficiencies, including GPU (good piece uptime) and decreasing scrap levels. In the medium term, he wanted to make the departments at MPI self-sufficient and prepare the facility for upcoming product launches.

MPI's Technological Goals

In Tuzi's opinion, to achieve its goals, MPI needed to improve in three technological areas:

- Improve MPI's internal capacity for continuous improvement of existing capabilities;
- Improve MPI's ability to troubleshoot existing operations; and
- Develop and improve MPI's abilities in secondary operations.

Communications

In Tuzi's opinion, technology transfer required not only having the knowledge, but also having the right people to inform and train his employees.

> Technology transfer is the transfer of both information and know-how—if information is transferred to groups that are not capable or insufficiently trained, then the information will not be used. CT can most help us by being able to transfer over best practices and by assisting in implementation.

Improving CT

Tuzi was very pleased with the results of the in-house recycling project, but was unsure of the progress being made on in-cell recycling.

> No one has followed up on the in-cell recycling project—how are the results at other plants? CT needs to improve its presence at other facilities. And let us know, when things don't get completed, why they did not get completed. They have to tell us if language is an issue. They also need to tell us what are the clear objectives for the upcoming year.

Reading 5-1   Unleash Innovation in Foreign Subsidiaries

Julian Birkinshaw and Neil Hood

The challenge of going global is not simply to sell products wherever customers are but to take advantage of bright ideas wherever they spring up. Indeed, growth-triggering innovation often emerges in foreign subsidiaries—from employees closest to customers and least attached to the procedures and politesse of the home office. NCR's automatic teller business, for instance, took off only when the development team shifted activities from corporate headquarters in Dayton, Ohio, to Dundee, Scotland. Under the guidance of a charismatic leader with scrappy persistence, NCR's Scottish operation became the largest manufacturer of ATMs in the world and brought the moribund Dundee manufacturing center back from the brink of extinction.

But as every multinational manager knows, making the most of foreign subsidiaries is tricky. Too often, heavy-handed responses from headquarters squelch local enthusiasm and drive out good ideas—and good people. Even when headquarters tries to do the right thing by democratizing the innovation process and ceding more power to subsidiaries, the results are not always stellar. (See the box "A Worst-Case Scenario.")

For the last eight years, we have studied more than 50 multinational corporations to understand what companies can do differently to encourage

❚ *Julian Birkinshaw is an associate professor of strategy and international management at London Business School. Neil Hood is a professor of business policy and codirector of the Strathclyde International Business Unit at the University of Strathclyde in Glasgow, Scotland.*

❚ Reprinted by permission of *Harvard Business Review.* "Unleash Innovation in Foreign Subsidiaries" by Julian Birkinshaw and Neil Hood (March 2001).

❚ Copyright © 2001 by Harvard Business School Publishing Corporation. All rights reserved.

innovation in foreign subsidiaries—what we call "innovation at the edges." Our observations suggest that when companies start to think of foreign subsidiaries as peninsulas rather than as islands—as extensions of the company's strategic domain rather than as isolated outposts—innovative ideas flow more freely from the periphery to the corporate center. (We first heard the peninsula concept articulated by managers at Monsanto Canada as they grappled with the challenge of redefining their role after the 1989 Free Trade Agreement with the United States.) But even more than a change in mind-set, corporate executives require a new set of practices, with two aims: to improve the formal and informal channels of communication between headquarters and subsidiaries and to give foreign subsidiaries more authority to see their ideas through. Only then can companies ensure that bright ideas—and the smart people who dream them up—don't end up marooned on desert islands.

Peninsulas, Not Islands

Fostering innovation in foreign subsidiaries is a familiar goal, but it is extremely difficult to achieve in real life. In the past, multinationals recognized the need to tap into a few select subsidiaries, but today successful corporate executives recognize that good ideas can come from any foreign subsidiary. (See the box "Three Eras of the Multinational.") The challenge is to find ways to liberalize, not tighten, internal systems and to delegate more authority to local subsidiaries. It isn't enough to ask subsidiary managers to be innovative; corporate managers need to give them incentives and support systems to facilitate their efforts. That's more easily

A Worst-Case Scenario

To illustrate the challenges that entrepreneurs in subsidiaries typically face, consider the story of Scott McTaggart, a 29-year-old business development manager in the Canadian subsidiary of a diversified industrial company.

He couldn't have seen it coming, but when McTaggart joined the subsidiary in the mid-1990s, he was in for a rocky ride. With a reputation for decentralization and programs that encouraged individual initiative, the U.S.-based business was one of the most reliably profitable companies in the world. Not only were employees encouraged to practice an informal style of management, but the company had also established several initiatives that encouraged frontline employees to play active roles in improving business processes. These programs resulted in large cost savings, and, perhaps even more important, they spawned a new creativity and enthusiasm among employees—an atmosphere, you would think, in which entrepreneurs could thrive.

At the Canadian subsidiary where McTaggart worked, however, the glory days were largely a thing of the past. As the oldest of 30 international subsidiaries, the Canadian group had once operated as a miniature replica of its parent company with a CEO who was fully responsible for the profits of the Canadian operating divisions. But in the 1980s, the parent company had moved to a more integrated model for North American operations. It created a dozen strategic business units, all headquartered in the United States. Thus the role of the Canadian CEO was reduced to that of mere figurehead, and the Canadian subsidiary was left to deal with mundane issues such as new legislation and tax accounting. It was only through a small business-development group that entrepreneurial activities were formally encouraged.

Soon after his arrival, McTaggart identified an opportunity to bid for a massive, government-sponsored energy management project that entailed the installation and financing of energy-efficient lightbulbs, motors, and other electrical equipment in 150 federal buildings throughout Canada. With potential revenues in the billions, energy management was a great opportunity, in McTaggart's view, not just for the Canadian subsidiary but for the entire company. Lacking a budget of his own, McTaggart convinced one division president to provide $1 million in seed money to test the market. Elated, McTaggart quickly put together a small project team and started to go after business.

That's when the problems began. A few months after McTaggart's initiative got under way, the business unit went through a dramatic reorganization. Following the abrupt resignation of the unit's president, the new president withdrew support for the energy management project. Suddenly orphaned, McTaggart found a new sponsor in another business unit after a series of emphatic presentations and 11th-hour phone calls.

Even as McTaggart scrambled for funds, the fledgling business was becoming a player in the energy management business—several pilot projects were completed and four new contracts were secured. But again problems emerged. McTaggart and his new sponsor came to realize at virtually the same painful moment that even though energy management fit well with the existing business's product lines, the energy management business's life cycle was wildly out of sync with the rest of the division's product portfolio.

Clearly, McTaggart needed to make a number of up-front investments and take several calculated risks to grow his business. But his new sponsor, obsessed with controlling costs and intent on being involved in day-to-day decisions (or so it seemed to McTaggart), kept urging McTaggart to curb his growth expectations. Finally, matters came to a head: faced with yet another demand to scale back his projections, McTaggart decided to resign. The energy management business limped along for another 18 months but never regained its previous pace. A disillusioned McTaggart started his own company, this time better equipped, he hoped, to control its destiny.

McTaggart's experience is all too common. His idea was consonant with the company's entrepreneurial spirit and was aligned with corporate growth targets, but McTaggart faced obstacle after obstacle: lack of fit with existing businesses, changing agendas at the top, risk-averse managers, culture clashes, and time lost fighting internal resistance. He lost a great opportunity to take his ideas to the limit, and the company wasted time, money, and that precious commodity, initiative.

---

said than done, of course, but our observations suggest four approaches:

- Give seed money to subsidiaries.
- Use formal requests for proposals.
- Encourage subsidiaries to be incubators.
- Build international networks.

When these practices are set in motion, we can expect far more creative and genuinely innovative ideas to emerge from the edges of the corporation. Let's take a look at each approach.

Give Seed Money to Subsidiaries   It's easy to argue that subsidiary companies need access to seed money, but corporate executives must strike a balance between demanding that subsidiaries meet short-term results and granting them sufficient freedom to pursue new ideas. Put too much focus on the former, and you know that subsidiaries will hide profits—not to pursue their new ideas but to protect themselves in case of a rainy day. Put too much emphasis on the latter, and there will be a proliferation of so-called strategic projects whose returns will fall below target levels. One way to achieve the necessary balance is to give subsidiaries discretionary budgets to test ideas within limits imposed by corporate headquarters. But it's also a matter of who holds the purse strings for which types of investments. Major investments can and should be made at a corporate level. But seed money can be handled on a more decentralized basis by giving local subsidiaries discretionary budgets to test ideas.

For example, in the late 1980s, Hilary Smith, a market development manager at 3M Canada, identified a market for systems that would allow library visitors to check out books without assistance. Her proposal fell on deaf ears at corporate headquarters, partly because the market for traditional library security machines in the United States was still growing rapidly. She pursued it anyway, using seed funding from the Canadian R&D budget to put together a prototype. At the American Library Association meeting where the prototype debuted, she discovered that 3M Australia had been working on a similar product. Hearing enthusiastic comments from potential customers, she and her Australian counterpart agreed to work together to bring out a single 3M product. Additional funding was supplied by the U.S.-based library systems business unit, and Smith was given worldwide responsibility for the product's launch. Manufacturing was transferred to St. Paul, Minnesota, where the U.S. business unit was based. The Australian subsidiary retained product and business development rights in Australia and New Zealand. SelfCheck is now one of the main products in 3M Library Systems' portfolio—thanks in no small part to the initial funding from the Canadian and Australian divisions.

It often happens, of course, that an idea seeded by a business unit, having developed into a viable business, is eventually abandoned because it doesn't fit well with the rest of the unit. Corporate-sponsored development projects therefore are an important alternative to business-unit-level investments. ABB, the global engineering and technology firm with headquarters in Zurich, provides both seed money at the subsidiary level and corporate funding for new ideas that cross the boundaries of existing business units. In ABB's 12 corporate research centers, located around the world, employees are encouraged to propose "high impact" projects—those with

Three Eras of the Multinational

Multinationals have evolved through three phases over the past 50 years, both in terms of their geographic scope and the roles played by their foreign subsidiaries:

Paternalism   In the first half of the twentieth century, the dominant model for multinationals was to innovate in the home country and then roll out new products across the corporate empire. U.S. companies like Caterpillar, IBM, and Procter & Gamble became masters of this model. But as foreign markets for the established multinationals became more sophisticated and as the foreign subsidiaries in those countries grew stronger, it gradually became apparent that the home country did not have a monopoly on innovation and leading-edge thinking.

Expansionism   In the 1970s and 1980s, many multinational corporations set up "scanning units" to tap into the ideas coming out of key foreign markets, and they built R&D sites abroad to gain access to scientific communities. But welcome as they were, corporate investments of this type represented but a halfhearted attempt to tap into the ideas and opportunities in foreign markets. There were two major problems. First, scanning units and foreign R&D labs were attractive in principle but difficult to manage effectively. For example, many European multinationals,

including Volkswagen, Volvo, and Ericsson, established development centers in California, but in most cases the units struggled to successfully transfer and integrate their ideas with those of their parent companies. Second, by defining certain units as responsible for picking up new ideas, corporate managers were implicitly signaling to all other foreign units that they did not have to bother. Such an approach limited growth opportunities to a few select markets or technologies and dampened the initiative of subsidiary managers in other foreign units.

Liberalism   A third model, now emerging, takes a more democratic approach to the pursuit of new opportunities. It builds on two basic arguments: first, useful new business ideas can emerge from anywhere in the world, particularly those parts of the organization that are in direct contact with customers, suppliers, and other external parties. Second, the greater the distance from the center, the less constrained individuals are by the traditions, norms, and belief structures of the corporation. This is the argument that subsidiaries should be viewed as peninsulas rather than islands. As multinationals take such an approach, we can expect far more creative and genuinely innovative ideas to emerge from the edge of the corporation than from the center. The challenge becomes one of tapping into the ideas and leveraging them effectively.

broad, cross-business-unit applications—which are then funded from a corporate budget. One such project led to the creation of a state-of-the-art electrical transformer factory in Athens, Georgia. Dubbed the "factory of the future," the test factory is fully automated, from ordering through production to the delivery of the finished product. The results have been truly spectacular: labor costs have been cut by half, cycle times have been cut by 90%, and time from order entry to shipping has been reduced from 30 days to one day.

Use Formal Requests for Proposals   Providing seed money to subsidiaries is a start, but funds alone won't generate valuable innovations from a passive subsidiary manager. Executives must also find ways to increase the demand for seed money. To that end, it helps to think of subsidiaries as freelance contractors that are granted licenses to manufacture or develop certain products. When you want to make a new investment, you send out a request for proposal (RFP), which may yield three or four competing bids. Volkswagen's decision to

manufacture the New Beetle in Puebla, Mexico, for example, was the result of a lengthy review in which the Puebla site was compared with sites in Germany and Eastern Europe. It also required heavy-duty championing from executives in Mexico and the United States, who saw a local production base as essential to their plans for reviving the VW brand in North America.

An RFP approach can also stimulate subsidiaries to develop creative solutions to corporate challenges. Monsanto's Canadian management team picked up on a tentative corporate plan to build a dry-formulation plant for its Roundup herbicide and pushed hard for that investment to be made in Canada. In preparing their proposal, they were able to shape the product's specifications—as any contracting company knows, that's the only way to win competitive tenders. But the members of the Canadian group knew they wouldn't get the nod based on cost alone, so they developed their proposal around such innovative practices as self-directed work teams, empowerment, and outsourcing. Their proposal focused on the competencies of the Canadian operation and demonstrated how the investment could help forestall a threat from another company rumored to be developing a competing product in central Canada. Consequently, the Canadian proposal won the contract, beating out a Monsanto site in Louisiana and an independent manufacturer in Iowa.

We have seen this approach to new investments work well in a variety of multinational companies. But we have also seen companies shy away from it because the costs of reviewing and evaluating multiple bids can be prohibitive. The best approach is to limit the list of competing proposals to three or four—as long as the narrowing process is designed to increase, rather than suppress, variance. It is best to avoid formal reviews in which two mediocre options are set up alongside the preferred candidate for the sake of appearances. This happens all too often, and it is a splendid way of killing the initiative of subsidiary managers.

Encourage Subsidiaries to Be Incubators   Subsidiary managers often comment that their distance from headquarters makes it hard for them to attract attention. But distance can become an advantage. It allows foreign subsidiaries to experiment with unconventional or unpopular projects that would be closed down if they were more visible to headquarters. It allows them to become incubators that can provide shelter and resources for businesses that are not yet strong enough to stand on their own.

Consider the actions of Ulf Borgström, manager of the Swedish subsidiary of a U.S. minicomputer manufacturer. The company was struggling in the early 1990s because of a weak product line, and the Swedish subsidiary was on the verge of bankruptcy. Borgström was able to turn around the operation by disregarding orders from headquarters and pursuing whatever business he could find in the Swedish market. Unable to sell his own company's products, he decided to offer service contracts on competitors' products. Needless to say, his superiors in the home office immediately discredited his strategy, but Borgström persevered, and the service contracts proved to be a significant factor in the subsidiary's revival. By 1997, headquarters had come around to his way of thinking, and the Swedish subsidiary was hailed as a success story.

Or take Ericsson as another example. Outsiders know that Ericsson has successfully caught two of the biggest waves in the telecommunications business in recent years: the emergence of second-generation digital radio technology and the subsequent boom in the handsets business. Insiders admit, however, that both businesses struggled to gain acceptance while they were being developed and would have been killed if their sponsors had not been persistent. In fact, in the latter case, Åke Lundqvist, the president of the nascent handsets unit, moved himself and his team to southern Sweden, which gave him the time and space to get the business going without interference from corporate executives. More recently, Ericsson has created a new unit called Ericsson Business Innovation, whose mandate, in the words of its director, Jöran Hoff, "is to create the next core business" for the corporation. It acts as a venture fund by providing seed money and management expertise to promising new

projects—not just Stockholm-based projects, but those in places as diverse as southern California, North Carolina, and Finland.

The subsidiary-as-incubator model is promising, but as with all corporate venturing, there is a risk that a new business idea won't find a home within the corporate portfolio. The critical success factor is typically how well the project champion is connected with other parts of the corporation. Hence the importance of international networks.

Build International Networks   As every corporate executive—and entrepreneur, for that matter—knows, it's essential to give would-be innovators access to professional and informal networks. But such networks are not easily manufactured. Some companies have tried to build international networks by creating employee rotation programs, but too often these personnel moves have been ineffective because they've been artificial—they haven't been linked to practical business initiatives. If employees don't do real work during their overseas assignments, they never become part of local teams or become integrated into networks. A number of corporations, however, now deploy talented employees on short-term overseas assignments that are tied to tangible business goals. In the short term, these assignments furnish useful resources for current projects; in the long term, they increase the number and variety of professional networks from which the next ideas are likely to emerge.

For example, when ABB acquired Taylor Instruments, a Rochester, New York-based automation and controls company, the entire management team of ABB's automation and controls business was temporarily moved from Sweden to ABB's U.S. headquarters in Stamford, Connecticut, to oversee the integration process and help develop a new identity for the business. After three years, the management team, which by then included a couple of Americans, was moved back to Sweden.

Similarly, Hewlett-Packard often brings in an experienced management team from corporate headquarters to get new subsidiary operations started.

The team's job is to get performance on track, bring a local management team up to speed, and move on to another project. At both companies, the creation of strong international networks is the by-product of real work rather than an end in itself.

Multinationals also need to create roles for what we have come to think of as idea brokers. In a crowded marketplace, brokers add value through their ability to bring buyers and sellers together. For innovation at the edges to thrive, entrepreneurs in foreign subsidiaries need to be linked with sources of funding, complementary assets, and sponsors in other parts of the company. That's where idea brokers come into the picture. With their wealth of contacts and experiences, they play three important roles.

First, they link seed money with new ideas. Consider the story of Mats Leijon, an electrical engineer in one of ABB's corporate research labs who came up with a disruptive technology called the Powerformer—a high-voltage generator that allows power to go directly from the generator to overhead cables without a step-up transformer. Without the assistance of Harry Frank, the head of one of ABB's corporate research labs, Leijon's invention might never have seen the light of day, especially given that the Powerformer promised to wipe out more than one of ABB's core businesses. Frank brokered the idea by translating it into business terms, and Leijon's project received funding from the Swedish country manager, Bert-Olof Svanholm. It was launched in 1998. Today, several leading ABB customers are adopting the Powerformer, and the story of Mats Leijon's innovation has become a touchstone for other entrepreneurs at ABB.

Second, idea brokers help find the right organizational home for new ideas. In one product development group in Hewlett-Packard's Canadian subsidiary, initial funding for a new software product came from HP Canada, which was enough to get the product to market. But for the business to grow, the development group's general manager realized he needed to find a home for his product in one of HP's major divisions. He began to sound out his contacts, including several group vice presidents

who were able to use their broad knowledge of the HP businesses to put him in touch with various parent divisions. After one false start, he found the right home in a small, Seattle-based division that was selling to the same customer sectors as his group. In HP, the group vice presidents are the idea brokers, and a significant part of their time is spent balancing the portfolio of businesses—splitting up large divisions, merging small divisions, shifting emerging businesses between divisions to create better opportunities for growth, and so on.

The third role idea brokers play is in cross-selling products and services among businesses. Skandia AFS, the financial services group, provides a good example. It is organized as a federation of national businesses, each of which is free to develop its own product lines for the local marketplace (they share a common business model and information system). Recognizing that a country-centered approach could restrict the transfer of new ideas across borders, Skandia created an internal brokering unit called the International Support Unit (ISU). Its role is to take new products developed in one country and cross-sell them into other countries; managed as a profit center, Skandia ISU earns its revenues through commissions on cross-border product sales.

In an era in which new business ideas are as likely to come from Stockholm as from Silicon Valley, multinational companies cannot afford to limit their creative gene pools to corporate R&D labs or a few select outposts. They must find ways to tap into the diverse and multifaceted opportunities that exist in foreign operations. Taken together, the four practices we've outlined can help corporate executives unleash innovation at the edges and fulfill, at last, the promise of going global.

Reading 5-2   Integrating the Enterprise

Sumantra Ghoshal and Lynda Gratton

One of the most fundamental and enduring tensions in all but very small companies arise from the conflicting needs of subunit-level autonomy and empowerment, on the one hand, and for overall organizational integration and cohesion, on the other.[1] These tensions increase with increasing complexity of the organization, and assume their most intense form in the context of large, diversified global companies.[2]

Creating relatively autonomous subunits with their own empowered management brings the benefits of both an entrepreneurial flair that can flourish within those entities, and also the establishment of a relatively simple and clear system for monitoring and evaluating their individual performance.

▌ *Sloan Management Review*. "Integrating the Enterprise" by Sumantra Ghoshal and Lynda Gratton (2002). London Business School, Sussex Place, Regent' Park, London NW1 4SA, U.K. Phone: 44-0207-262-5050, Fax: 44-0207-724-7875. Email: sghoshal@london.edu, Lgratton@london.edu.
▌ Please do not quote or cite without prior approval of authors. Comments are welcome and can be directed to either author.
▌ [1]For a theory-grounded analysis of this tension, see R. P. Rumelt, "Inertia and Transformation," in C. M. Montgomery (ed.), *Resource-Based and Evolutionary Theories of the Firm,* Boston: Kluwer Academic Publishers, 1995.

▌ [2]For a rich description and analysis of this tension in the specific context of large, diversified global companies, see C. K. Prahalad and Y. Doz, *The Multinational Mission: Balancing Local Demands and Global Vision,* New York: Free Press, 1987.

Table 1   Integration Drivers and Illustrative Examples

Integration Drivers	Illustrative Examples
1. Customer satisfaction and relationship management	ABB (engineering and automation), OgilvyOne (direct marketing), Oracle (software)
2. Technological convergence and innovation management	Sony (home entertainment), Oracle, OgilvyOne
3. Growth and globalization	BP (petroleum and chemicals), Goldman Sachs (financial services), LVMH (luxury and fashion)
4. Corporate restructuring and M & A	BP, OgilvyOne, Nicholas Piramal (pharmaceuticals)

Indeed, it is precisely because of these benefits that many large companies around the world have, over the last decade, broken up their organizational behemoths into small units, allowing their managers considerable freedom to manage their own operations and holding them accountable for achieving their performance goals.[3] Some, though not all, of these companies have achieved significant benefits from such restructuring. Freed from bureaucratic central controls, these empowered units have improved both the speed and the quality of their responsiveness to market demands, and the spirit of entrepreneurship has led to new initiatives and innovations. At the same time, corporate-level overhead costs have been reduced and internal governance processes have become more transparent because of the reduced complexity.

These benefits have come at a cost, however. Autonomy and empowerment of subunits have led to fragmentation, and to deficiencies in internal integration and cohesion. The autonomous and empowered managers of the different subunits find few incentives for sharing knowledge or other resources, particularly when the performance management processes focus only or even primarily on the performance of their own pieces of the company, rather than on the performance of the whole.

Now, in company after company, we are finding that the focus of management attention has moved to the integration and cohesion side of the tension. Having cleaned up the businesses, and having achieved the benefits that could be extracted from focusing on the competitiveness of each unit, the next round of performance improvement must come from better integration across those units.[4] Different companies we have studied[5] are experiencing this pressure for integration in different ways (see Table 1).

For some companies, the main impetus for integration is coming from the demands of customers whose needs cut across the company's internal boundaries. In ABB, the 1300 small companies created by Percy Barnevik in the late 1980s have been consolidated by the current CEO Jurgen Centerman into 400, primarily to be able to serve global customers more effectively. We saw the same pressure in OgilvyOne, the largest direct marketing agency in the world. The launch of American Express' new blue card required global rollout, across multiple

[4]This sequential process of performance improvement—first building the strength of the units and then building integration mechanisms across them—was described in S. Ghoshal and C. A. Bartlett, "Rebuilding Behavioral Context: A Blueprint for Corporate Renewal," *Sloan Management Review,* Vol. 37, No. 2, Winter 1996.

[5]This article is based on our case research over the last five years in 15 large, global companies including the 8 listed in the table. We have interviewed large numbers of managers in each of these companies, and all quotations in this article are derived from these interviews. We have also had access to documents from both public sources and from the companies themselves. For each company, we have written up our observations in a case study, and copies of these cases can be obtained from either author.

[3]For description of companies who followed this strategy of creating small units to rekindle frontline entrepreneurship, see S. Ghoshal and C. A. Bartlett, *The Individualized Corporation,* New York: Harper Collins, 1997.

media, in six months. This would have been completely impossible in the fragmented and internally competitive OgilvyOne of the past.

For some other companies, technological changes and their effects on management of innovation are the primary drivers of the need for integration. As home entertainment is shifting away from stand-alone, analog-technology based consumer electronics products to web-based, digitised content delivery, Japan's Sony Corporation is facing the need to integrate its historically autonomous product divisions to ensure that all its audio and video products can work with each other, and can be accessed directly through a personal computer, a game machine, a PDA, or a mobile phone, together with the software available through its music and movie businesses. To respond to this fundamental technological change, Sony has had to enter the personal computer business—the established gateway to the internet—and develop a more integrated innovation process to ensure that its VAIO PCs can work seamlessly with all its other products and services.

For companies like Oracle, Goldman Sachs and LVMH, rapid growth and globalization over the last decade are now demanding consolidation and integration. Oracle, for example, has internationalised at a phenomenal pace, with little time to develop its organizational systems and processes. As a result, each of its overseas units developed its own unique system to cater to the needs of its local customers. Over the last two years, the company has been working hard to standardize and integrate all these diverse systems, so as to achieve the benefits of both efficiency and better global coordination.

In BP, the need for integration is driven by another very different demand. Its merger with Amoco, Arco and Castrol had created a highly fragmented organization with an amalgam of many different management styles and philosophies. Integration has been vital to make the 100,000 employees of the merged entity focus away from the differences of their separate pasts to the possibilities of their common and shared future. Nicholas Piramal, one of the largest pharmaceutical companies in India that has grown rapidly through a spate of acquisitions, is confronting the same need, as is OgilvyOne, in its efforts to integrate a number of recently acquired small internet marketing companies within its traditional direct marketing businesses.

Old Chestnut, but in a New Context

At one level, there is nothing new here. The need for integration to counterbalance internal differentiation is about as old an organizational chestnut as there is.[6] But, while the problem is old and familiar, the circumstances companies face today are different from those of the past. The new circumstances both create some new possibilities and eliminate some historical options.

The most important change is the web, and the IT capabilities that surround it. The crux of integration has always been the sharing of information, and the new technologies enable organizational responses to the integration needs in ways that were simply not available even five years ago.[7]

While technology has created some new possibilities, some historical tools of integration have also been dulled by the changed circumstances. For example, movement of people and the structuring of career paths were the most vital means of organizational integration in companies as diverse as Unilever, Matsushita and Hewlett Packard.[8] Each of these companies had built up a pool of managers

---

[6]For a classic analysis of this need, see P. R. Lawrence and J. W. Lorsch, *Organization and Environment,* Boston: Division of Research, Harvard Business School, 1967.

[7]This impact of the web on integration opportunities can be easily inferred from the analysis of R. L. Daft and R. H. Lengel, "Organizational Information Requirements, Media Richness, and Structural Design," *Management Science* 32:554–571, 1986. For a more focused discussion on the role of IT in facilitating communication, see A. D. Shulman, "Putting Group Information Technology in Its Place: Communication and Good Work Group Performance," in S. R. Clegg, C. Hardy and W. R. Nord (eds.), *Handbook of Organization Studies,* London: Sage, 1996, pp. 357–374.

[8]See R. G. Edstrom and J. R. Galbraith, "Transfer of Managers as a Coordination and Control Strategy in Multinational Organizations," *Administrative Science Quarterly,* Vol. 222, June 1977.

who had worked across different functions, businesses and geographies of the company, and their collective personal networks created the glue that held the company together. While to an extent this is still a powerful tool for socializing people and building organizational cohesion, it is increasingly not available to many companies either because, like Oracle, they are too young, or because, as in HP, lifetime careers and on-demand mobility of people can no longer be assumed or planned for.

The drastic pruning of middle management that many companies have undertaken over the last decade has deprived them of another important, if often unrecognized source of organizational integration.[9] Historically, mid-level managers within the businesses and in support functions played boundary-spanning and coordinating roles. With the elimination of these roles, companies have lost the slack resources that acted as the linking mechanisms within their organizations.

But perhaps the most important difference lies in a changed management philosophy with regard to organizational integration. In the past, integration was managed primarily through vertical processes. The way to make different business, functional or geographical units to share resources and coordinate their activities was to bring them under a common boss and a common planning and control system.[10] While there has always been a recognition of the relevance of horizontal integration mechanisms,[11] in practice they have typically been seen as secondary; as reinforcement to the primary vertical processes.

The most fundamental change we have observed in the ways in which companies are now responding to the integration needs is a move away from the traditional vertical mechanisms of hierarchy and formal systems to a primary reliance on horizontal processes, so as to build integration on top of subunit level autonomy and empowerment rather than as a replacement. The secondary has now become primary.

What then, are some of the ways in which companies are responding to this need for putting it all together again, without destroying the vitality of the parts? In our research, we have found four areas of action: operational integration through standardization of the technological infrastructure, intellectual integration through the development of a shared knowledge base, social integration through building collective bonds of performance and emotional integration through the creation of a common identity and purpose (see Figure 1). While all four areas are distinct, they are also inter-related and the challenge of integrating the enterprise is the challenge of managing these inter-relationships in a synergistic manner.[12]

Operational Integration through Standardized Technological Infrastructure

Influenced in part by the reengineering wave, many companies have, over the 1990s, made significant progress in rationalizing their production and distribution infrastructures. The primary focus of operational integration has now shifted to support functions such as finance, HR, planning and service. The most critical bottleneck in rationalizing and

---

[9]This important but often ignored role of middle managers in organizational integration has been described in R. M. Kauter, *The Change Masters,* New York: Simon and Schuster, 1983.

[10]Such vertical processes of organizational integration lay at the heart of the divisionalized organizational model: for perhaps one of the richest and best-known expositions, see A. D. Chandler, *Strategy and Structure: Chapters in the History of American Industrial Enterprise,* Cambridge: MIT Press, 1962.

[11]See J. Galbraith, *Designing Complex Organizations,* Reading, MA: Addison-Wesley, 1973. In the context of large, global companies—of the kind that are used to illustrate the arguments in this paper—the use of such horizontal mechanisms has been described in C. A. Bartlett and S. Ghoshal, *Managing Across Borders: The Transnational Solution,* Boston: The Harvard Business School Press, 1988.

[12]Our focus in this paper is on the challenges of internal integration across existing and established units within large, complex organizations. Clearly, there are other important integration contexts—that of integrating strategic alliances, joint ventures, upstream and downstream partners on the value chain, and so on. While we do not deal with these contexts in this paper, interested readers can find comprehensive treatments of these topics elsewhere—in Y. Doz and G. Hamel, *Alliance Advantage,* Boston: Harvard Business School Press, 1998, on integration across strategic alliances and partnerships, for example. Even within the organization, integration of new ventures poses an unique set of challenges, which we do not deal with. Readers interested in this specific topic, can find an outstanding analysis in C. Christensen, *The Innovators Dilemma,* Boston: Harvard Business School Press, 1997.

Figure 1   A Framework for Organizational Integration

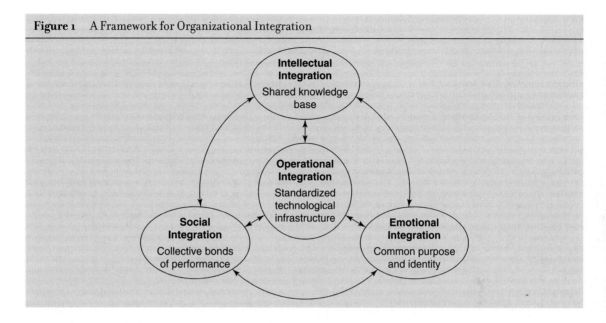

integrating these activities lies in the IT systems of companies.

While many companies have recognized this constraint, and have made some progress in harmonizing their historically fragmented IT infrastructure, they are still far away from the kind of standardization that is necessary for fully exploiting the integration potential available in these support functions.

As an example of what is possible, consider the case of Oracle. As we indicated earlier, the breakneck speed of Oracle's international expansion had led to the creation of highly autonomous national subsidiaries that had developed completely different systems to manage their own operations. Even as late as 1997, the company had 97 e-mail servers running 7 different and mutually incompatible versions. Each country had its own unique ERP system and its own website in the local language. They had even changed the colour of the Oracle logo, based on the taste of the local managers.

Despite having the same products worldwide, the Oracle organization had packaged, bundled and priced them differently in each market, creating an explosion of offerings. It was not possible to know exactly how many people Oracle employed world-

wide on any day. To find that out, someone had to scout through 60 databases, with no consistent format, and consolidate the number. By the time this could be done, the answer would have changed in the fast growing company.

It was at this time that CEO Larry Ellison articulated the direction of the company in the next phase of evolution of the IT industry. He envisioned the computer industry to turn into an utility, rather like electricity or water: the hardware, data and applications residing in a central location with customers being able to use these at will over the internet with only a PC and a browser. In this world, Oracle would become a provider of integrated services, covering a full range of applications including Enterprise Resource Planning (ERP), Customer Relationship Management (CRM), Supply Chain Management (SCM) and Human Resource Management (HRM). Beyond its database products, customers could buy all their application requirements, all mutually compatible, from one source—Oracle. As Ellison described, "if you want to buy a car, would you get an engine from BMW, a chassis from Jaguar, windshield wipers from Ford? No, of course not. Right now with the software out there, you need a glue gun—or hire all these consultants to put it together. They call it best-of-breed. I call it a mess."

To create credibility among customers about his vision of a whole set of standardized and integrated applications being used over the Internet, Ellison decided to make Oracle its own beta test site. "Eat your own dogfood" was his metaphor, and he publicly announced a target of saving $1 billion in costs—10% of revenues—by adopting this new approach to building a company's operating infrastructure.

This is precisely what Oracle has done between 2000 and 2001. All the different e-mail systems have been consolidated into one standardized, global e-mail system, using only two servers located in Oracle headquarters in California, instead of 97 servers spread all over the world. Historically, pricing was completely a local preserve; now all prices and discounts are standardized globally and can be viewed over the Internet. The different ERP customisations in every country in Europe have been standardized, and is operated from a single central source. All the different websites have been replaced by a single global site, Oracle.com, run out of the U.S. in multiple languages.

Observers may quibble over how much exactly Oracle has saved, but most estimates are close to the original $1 billion target. Over the two years of implementation of these standardized, global operating platforms, Oracle's operating margin has improved from 14 to 35 percent. Ellison has now upped the ante from $1 billion in savings to $2 billion, and the company is going through the next round of rationalization of its operating infrastructure in order to achieve the new goal.

What has such drastic standardization and centralization done to frontline entrepreneurship? According to Jeff Henley, Oracle's CFO, it has actually enhanced their ability to act entrepreneurially. "The question is what kind of entrepreneurship? It would be goofy to let people do as they please in building and managing a local IT operation to support internal processes. By standardizing those, we have channelled that entrepreneurship where it adds value—in serving customers. We think it is a good idea if a sales person spends time selling product benefits rather than negotiating prices and discounts."

Why has Oracle been so successful in such a radical effort to standardize its technological infrastructure while most companies are only able to make incremental progress? The single most important factor has been the total commitment of a powerful CEO. Ellison made this initiative his absolute and only priority. To overcome objections from country managers, he allowed them to participate in the designing of the standardized systems—so that their special needs as well as unique contributions could be accommodated—and then gave them a simple choice: they could either adopt the standardized and centrally operated systems completely free of cost, or they could continue with the local systems, bearing full costs, but with no adjustment in return expectations.

Standardizing operating processes has always been seen as a powerful integrating device. Historically, it was simply not possible to create centrally managed standard systems; now it is. The real benefits flow only at the extreme, not with half-measures. While Oracle's business perhaps allows it to go further than, say, Unilever, we believe that the need for integration will require that most companies go much further than they have in standardizing their operating platforms.

Intellectual Integration through Shared Knowledge Base

Under the garb of "knowledge management" many companies have developed IT-based systems that are essentially databases, enabling sharing and usage of information on an organization-wide basis. This however is only the first step in establishing a shared knowledge base that truly integrates a company's intellectual capital. To create an user-pull to supplement the technology-push, effective integration of knowledge requires the edge of a clear link with strategy and the support of extensive conversation and dialogue.[13]

---

[13]Several authors have highlighted this need of a social structure to support IT-based systems for effective knowledge management in distributed organizations: see, for example, the discussion on "Social Ecology" in V. Govindarajan and A. Gupta, *The Quest for Global Dominance,* San Francisco: Jossey-Bass, 2001.

In OgilvyOne, the direct marketing business of Ogilvy and Mather, the need for integration had sprung to the fore in the early 1990s when American Express, an old client that had earlier abandoned the agency, returned to its fold and IBM, in an unprecedented move, offered OgilvyOne its entire account. Both clients demanded integrated services, as well as business solutions that combined interactive media with traditional direct marketing. Unlike the 1980s, when advertising agencies used costly mass media campaigns on television to attract customers, in the 1990s the challenge was to grab the attention of "the anarchic customer" who had a choice among an almost infinite range of channels. OgilvyOne's historically fragmented organization, with highly autonomous divisions such as Data Consult, Direct Mail and Ogilvy Interactive simply could not effectively respond to these needs for integrated service delivery.

To respond to this challenge, OgilvyOne developed a new strategy focused on customer ownership and 360° brand stewardship. Both strategies were built on proprietary tools designed to build and support trust and relational capital with clients and their final consumers.

Customer ownership tools, such as QuickScan, enabled Ogilvy's creative professionals to develop better understanding of the clients' customers. It questioned the client's assumptions and allowed focused targeting of desired segments. For example, the use of this technique revealed that only 16% of customers of Nestle Pet Foods accounted for 90% of the customer value for Friskies, a major cat food brand. 360° brand stewardship similarly incorporated a set of tools and techniques that could be used to understand, develop and enhance the relationship between a customer and a brand.

The usage of these tools and techniques, however, were conditional upon the development of mechanisms for the creation, sharing and exchange of knowledge across different parts of the company. The company had to harness the brainpower of the marketing gurus, the mathematics PhD's, the expert statisticians, the strategy consultants and the individualistic creatives that comprised the organization. To do so, OgilvyOne developed "Truffles."

The name came from a famous statement of David Ogilvy, the founder: "I prefer the discipline of knowledge to the anarchy of ignorance, and we pursue knowledge the way a pig pursues truffles." Supported by 60 knowledge officers across the entire company, Truffles was the product of years of documentation that represented the accumulated intellectual capital of the company. But it was also much more. It was a living forum for creating and sharing new ideas. The rise of OgilvyOne as the world's largest direct marketing company owes a tremendous amount to Truffles, according to Reimer Thedens, the firm's CEO.

What made Truffles work was not just the world-class IT infrastructure, nor the tremendous effort and investment to constantly keep it current in terms of information and ideas, but the direct link between the system and the firm's strategy focused on customer ownership and 360° brand stewardship. It was this link that made both senior managers and the creatives use the system. With both the tools and techniques and the relevant data being available on Truffles, the system served as the link between research and ideas, on the one hand, and "actionable stuff," on the other. It was this direct link that overcame initial resistance to its use.

The other aspect behind Truffle's success were the "soft bonds" that were established to support the spirit of sharing and using knowledge. The company invested heavily in creating conversation forums—from Friday morning breakfast meetings to top-level Board Away Days—to build interpersonal relationships. With the motto that "the most important role of managers is to create friendships," the senior leaders of the company invested enormous amounts of their personal time to develop the internal trust that underlies intellectual integration. In an extreme example of this investment, Nigel Howlett, the Chairman of OgilvyOne's London office, spent half a day a week for many months simply building a relationship with Tim Carrigan, the CEO of NoHo Digital, an interactive marketing company Howlett wanted to buy. The discussions were as much personal as they were strategic. The result of the friendship they built was manifest immediately after the acquisition was finalized. Within two weeks, NoHo's employees were not only using Truffles, but were also contributing new information and techniques to the database for use by all Ogilvy employees.

Social Integration through Collective Bonds of Performance

In most companies, learning and sharing are seen as best done horizontally, in peer-to-peer forums, while performance management and resource allocation are still the preserve of boss-subordinate relationships. What we found in our research were the enormous advantages that could be achieved when the role of peer-to-peer interactions were extended to these preserves of vertical processes. In the words of Lord John Browne, the CEO of BP, "One theme we observed was the very different interaction between people of equal standing, if you will, when they reviewed each other's work, than there was when a superior reviewed the work of a subordinate. We concluded that the way to get the best answers would be to get peers to challenge and support each other, than to have a hierarchical challenge process."

BP's use of peer groups—essentially groups of managers who manage similar businesses—to drive learning and knowledge sharing through the "Peer Assist" process has received widespread attention.[14] This process allows the manager of an under-performing unit to have the benefit of the expertise of his or her peers to improve performance. However, over the last two years, BP has refined and extended "Peer Assist" to "Peer Challenge" wherein the power of the peer groups are used to drive the performance management and resource allocation processes.

BP's performance management system is essentially simple. The managers of each of its autonomous business units enter into an annual performance contract with the top management, and they are then free to achieve the results in whatever way they wish. What peer challenge requires is that they get their plans, including investment plans, approved by their peers, before finalizing the performance contract with top management. "The peers must be satisfied that you are carrying your fair share of the heavy water buckets," said Rodney Chase, BP's Deputy Chief Executive. "The old issue of sandbagging management is gone. The challenge now comes from peers, not from management."[15]

"The peer challenge," as described by Polly Flinn, one of BP's Business Unit Heads, "is about convincing people in similar positions to support your investment proposal knowing that they could invest the same capital elsewhere, and going eyeball to eyeball with them—and then having to reaffirm whether you have made it or not over the coming months or quarters." The process gets its teeth from the fact that 50% of the unit manager's bonus depends on the performance of his or her unit, and the remaining 50% on the performance of the peer group.

In an added twist, BP has now extended the peer process even further—the three top performing business units in a peer group have now been made responsible for improving the performance of the bottom three. "We had not-invented-here raised to an art form," said Rodney Chase. With peer assist and peer challenge, "what we have raised to an art form is that if I have a good idea, my first responsibility is to share it with my peers, and if I am performing poorly, I will get the peer group to help me."

What BP has achieved is a powerful force of integration and knowledge sharing by bringing the peers together in a collective bond of performance. According to John Browne, "people do not learn, at least in a corporate environment, without a target. You can implore people to learn, and they will to some extent. But if you say, "look the learning is necessary in order to cut the cost of drilling a well by 10%," then they will learn with purpose." What is special about BP's peer groups is the effectiveness of transferring, sharing and leveraging cumulative learning by this direct link with performance.

[14]See, for example, T. Hansen, and Bolko von Oetinger, "Introducing T-Shaped Managers: Knowledge Management's Next Generation," *Harvard Business Review,* March 2001.

[15]This is essentially a sophisticated use of social control—see W. G. Ouchi, "A Conceptual Framework for the Design of Organizational Control Mechanisms," *Management Science* 25: 833–848, 1979.

Emotional Integration through Shared Identity and Meaning

Ultimately, the acid test of organizational integration lies in the domain of collective action. Unless a shared knowledge base translates into coordinated and aligned action across the different parts of an organization, it serves as nothing more than an expensive library. Unless peer relationships based on trust and friendship allow excellence of collective execution, they create no value other than the comforts of an exclusive country club.[16]

It is in this coordination and alignment of actions that the hierarchy had historically proven to be such a good thing. A common boss could align the activities of different parts both through direct orders and through formal planning and control.[17] Yet, for most companies, this tried and tested method is no longer as effective not only because it destroys frontline initiative and the spirit of entrepreneurship but also because of its inability to cope with uncertainty and rapid change.[18] In OgilvyOne, this distinction is highlighted through a metaphor: "While classical orchestras follow a conductor and a musical score, in a rigid and formal manner, jazz bands—like webmarketeers—must be fluid, flexible, improvised and should always trust the requests and applause of their audience."[19]

Beyond standardized infrastructure, shared knowledge and mutual trust, fluid and flexible collective action requires emotional integration through the creation of a common purpose and identity. And it is precisely this strength of emotional integration that has historically been the primary driver of success for companies such as Goldman Sachs.

Teamwork has always been a core value in the world's premier investment bank because, in the words of Hank Paulson, Goldman Sach's CEO, "Quite simply, none of us is as smart as all of us." It is this entrenched tradition of teamwork that undergirds the firm's reputation for excellence in execution. "Everywhere and in every country around the world, when a Goldman Sachs banker walks into the room, all of Goldman Sachs comes with him or her," said Robin Neustein, Head of the firm's Private Equity Group. "That, in turn, is the outcome of constant work on maintaining the one-firm identity and the internal challenge to be the best and help each other be the best, and all sharing in the one reputational capital of the firm name."

This emotional alignment among individuals and between them and the firm is the product of three very distinct characteristics of the firm. First, the culture of success is built on a relentless focus on client relationships. Anyone who ever steps inside the firm can palpably feel this obsession with building and maintaining close and trusting relationships with clients. In the words of Neustein again, "At Goldman Sachs, honour comes in the form of client service. . . . That is why if you try to make a lot of money without putting your client first, it is not a mark of success, it is a mark of shame."

Stories of how the firm's legendary leaders—Sidney Weinberg, Gus Levy, John Whitehead and others—went to extreme lengths, such as having six dinners in one night, are told and retold within the firm to protect this pride in being seen as a "trusted advisor" by the most influential politicians, industrialists and wealthy individuals all over the world. Client focus acts as an instrument of integration rather than of protective individual ownership, however, because of the explicit focus on long-term retention. "Clients are simply in your custody,"

[16] For an elaborate analysis of these pathologies that are all too common in companies, see J. Pfeffer and R. I. Sutton, *The Knowing-Doing Gap: How Smart Companies Turn Knowledge into Action,* Cambridge; MA: Harvard Business School Press, 2000.

[17] These benefits of hierarchy provide the theoretical basis for influential economic analysis of why firms exist: one of the most well-known of such analyses being O. E. Williamson's *Markets and Hierarchies: Analysis and Antitrust Implications,* New York: Free Press, 1975.

[18] For a discussion on the limitations of a hierarchical system in coping with uncertainty and rapid change, see S. L. Brown and K. M. Eisenhardt, *Competing on the Edge,* Boston: Harvard Business Press, 1998.

[19] This metaphor of an organization as a jazz band, emphasizing flexibility, fluidity and improvisation, is very consistent with current research on the important role of communication, both verbal and nonverbal, in achieving integrated, cooperative "performance." For the foundational statement on this perspective of organizational innovation, see K. E. Weick, *The Social Psychology of Organizing,* Reading, MA: Addison-Wesley, 1969, and also his article "Theorizing about Organizational Communication," in F. M. Jublin, L. L. Putman, K. H. Roberts and L. W. Porter (eds.), *Handbook of Organizational Communication,* CA: Sage, 1987, pp. 97–122.

John Weinberg consistently reminded all employees. "Someone before you established the relationship and someone after you will carry it on."

While client focus provides a force for emotional integration from the outside, enormous pride in the quality of colleagues is an equally powerful force of emotional integration from the inside. As a *Fortune* magazine survey revealed, 99% of Goldman Sachs employees were proud to work for the firm. Extraordinary levels of investment in recruiting only the most talented people around the globe, and then in continuous training and development for excellence has, over decades, created the mystique about the firm as a magnet for talent that, in turn, undergirds this pride of belonging.

It is not just the salary that has allowed the firm to become this magnet for talent. Inherently linked to the identity—shaping pride of belonging lies a belief about a broader sense of purpose that emotionally connects each individual to the ethos of the firm. As described by John Thornton, Goldman Sach's President and Co-Chief Coordinating Officer, "Anyone with any depth and talent has to ask the question 'what am I doing with my life?' The purpose of my life is to use my talent for some larger and better purpose." In Goldman Sachs, a broader purpose has historically been at the heart of this positive cycle of building emotional integration through the linkage between purpose, talent and the pride of belonging. As one young Vietnamese recruit told us "If shareholder capitalism works better than any other kind, then we are not just mercenaries but the potential benefactors of the regions we serve. There is a huge amount of work that has to be done in making shareholder capitalism the basis of innovation and entrepreneurialism in countries around the world. I believe we genuinely have this superior vision of capitalism, and I am excited by the possibility of contributing to rebuilding these economies from the ground up."

Finally, the third contributor to emotional integration in Goldman Sachs is the one-firm mentality that is supported both by ensuring that some things, such as the evaluation and selection of partners, are done on a firm-wide rather than divisional or product basis, and a compensation system that, till very recently, relied on the overall P&L of the firm to determine each partner's fortunes. At the beginning of the year, each partner was allotted a fixed proportion of whatever the income for the year would be, with no discretionary payment at all based on any aspect of the partner's or his or her unit's performance. "We all had a piece of the action," said Phil Murphy, co-Head of Investment Management. "We didn't care where the action came from. There was no disincentive to take that call from Hong Kong to help me out . . . you and I didn't care who got the credit for it, we knew we would both share the benefits." Even after becoming a public company, this link between overall firm performance and each partner's compensation is still maintained though 60% rather than 100% of the rewards are now based on the common pool.

The Co-evolution of Autonomy and Horizontal Integration

In the companies we have described in this article, what we found was that individual and subunit level autonomy and horizontal integration co-evolved in a dynamic process, over time. It is in this dynamic evolution that horizontal integration plays a very different role than vertical integration. Instead of smothering bottom-up initiatives, it creates a reinforcing process through which, over time, both autonomy and integration can flourish (see Figure 2). We will describe this process as it unfolded in one company—BP—but the actual evolution was very similar in all the others.

As the CEO of Sohio, BP's North American subsidiary, John Browne had conducted a careful experiment to test his growing belief in creating a spirit of entrepreneurship in a big company by breaking it up into relatively small, empowered units. He had restructured a chronically loss-making operation into a separate unit, allocated to it managers who represented the "normal" talent levels available to the company—so as to avoid the possibility that the outcome would be purely a result of outstanding local leadership—and given complete autonomy to those managers to run the operation, freed from the company's traditional central controls. The dramatic improvement in the performance

Figure 2   The Co-evolution of Autonomy and Horizontal Integration

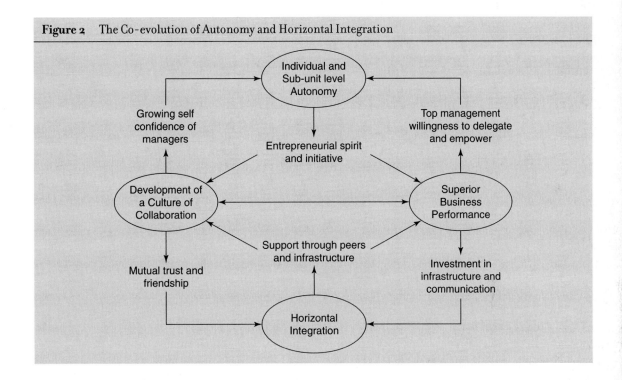

of this unit had become a key lesson for him, by the time he took over as the CEO of BP in 1996.

As the corporate CEO, Browne acted on this lesson by restructuring the company into 150 business units, and yielding to the managers of these units a great deal of freedom to run their operations, subject to the conditions that they respect a set of "boundaries"—essentially the core values of the company—and deliver on their performance contracts. Simultaneously, he either drastically downsized or completely eliminated much of the staff-supported vertical command and control infrastructure in BP, abolishing the offices of country presidents and several of the company's functional departments in London.

Instead, as a support to the empowered and fully accountable business unit leaders, he created the peer groups we have described earlier in this paper. Grouping together managers who ran similar businesses, the peers were made responsible to help one another in order to improve both individual and collective performance.

The "peer assist" process took about two years to become effective. Much of BP's quite dramatic improvement in business performance came from the combination of the entrepreneurial spirit and sense of ownership within the business units, and the collective sharing of learning and mutual support that were engendered by the peer groups. For example, the managing director of the company's retail business in Poland, Polly Flinn—then a young manager from Amoco with no experience of working outside the United States—drew on the active help of several members of the marketing peer group to turn around the business from a loss of £20 million per year to a profit of £6 million.

As the business performance improved through this combination of empowerment and support, it led to two outcomes. First, top level managers including Browne, Rodney Chase and others developed growing confidence in their strategy of delegating authority to the business unit leaders. Second, the company found greater resources to invest in developing the integration infrastructure, including IT systems, and in building the conversation and communication mechanisms. These investments, in truth, further strengthened the mechanisms and processes of horizontal integration.

As this symbiotic effects of autonomy and horizontal integration evolved, a culture of collaboration gradually emerged. Rodney Chase, BP's Deputy CEO, described this process of culture change as follows; "In our personal lives—as fathers, mothers, brothers or sisters—we know how much we like to help someone close to us to succeed. Why didn't we believe that the same can happen in our business lives? That is the breakthrough, and you get there, when people take enormous pride in helping their colleagues to succeed."

As this culture evolved, it led to two inter-related but separate outcomes. First, the self-confidence of the managers grew. As they set themselves tough but achievable targets and achieved them through their own initiatives and the support of their peers, they developed the confidence to set slightly tougher targets, and so on.[20] In that process, they

strengthened their sense of autonomy and their spirit of entrepreneurship. Second, the culture also led to the reinforcement of mutual trust and friendship, which strengthened the peer group processes of horizontal integration.

One crucial feature of this symbiotic co-evolution of autonomy and horizontal integration is that the process takes time to mature. Vertical integration—bringing different units under a common boss and a common planning and control system, for example—can be implemented relatively quickly. Developing self-confidence in people and building trust and friendship, on the other hand, can only be achieved through persistent action and reinforcement over long periods of time. For top-level leaders of companies, this is the greatest challenge in building horizontal integration: while they have to be relentless in driving the process, they also have to be patient in their expectations of results. For those who can respond to this challenge, the ultimate benefits can be very significant: durable enhancement of organizational capability and sustainable improvement of business performance.

---

[20]This is very similar to the development of self-efficacy: see A. Bandura, *Self-Efficacy: The Expertise of Control,* New York: Freeman, 1997.

Reading 5-3   The Knowledge-Creating Company

Ikujiro Nonaka

In an economy where the only certainty is uncertainty, the one sure source of lasting competitive advantage is knowledge. When markets shift, technologies proliferate, competitors multiply, and

Ikujiro Nonaka is professor of management at the Institute for Business Research of Hitotsubashi University in Tokyo, Japan. His last HBR article, written with Hirotaka Takeuchi, was "The New New Product Development Game" (January–February 1986).
Reprinted by permission of *Harvard Business Review.* "The Knowledge-Creating Company" by Ikujiro Nonaka (November–December 1991).
Copyright © 1991 by the President and Fellows of Harvard College. All rights reserved.

products become obsolete almost overnight, successful companies are those that consistently create new knowledge, disseminate it widely throughout the organization, and quickly embody it in new technologies and products. These activities define the "knowledge-creating" company, whose sole business is continuous innovation.

And yet, despite all the talk about "brainpower" and "intellectual capital," few managers grasp the true nature of the knowledge-creating company—let alone know how to manage it. The reason: they misunderstand what knowledge is and what companies must do to exploit it.

Deeply ingrained in the traditions of Western management, from Frederick Taylor to Herbert Simon, is a view of the organization as a machine for "information processing." According to this view, the only useful knowledge is formal and systematic—hard (read: quantifiable) data, codified procedures, universal principles. And the key metrics for measuring the value of new knowledge are similarly hard and quantifiable—increased efficiency, lower costs, improved return on investment.

But there is another way to think about knowledge and its role in business organizations. It is found most commonly at highly successful Japanese competitors like Honda, Canon, Matsushita, NEC, Sharp, and Kao. These companies have become famous for their ability to respond quickly to customers, create new markets, rapidly develop new products, and dominate emergent technologies. The secret of their success is their unique approach to managing the creation of new knowledge.

To Western managers, the Japanese approach often seems odd or even incomprehensible. Consider the following examples.

- How is the slogan "Theory of Automobile Evolution" a meaningful design concept for a new car? And yet, this phrase led to the creation of the Honda City, Honda's innovative urban car.
- Why is a beer can a useful analogy for a personal copier? Just such an analogy caused a fundamental breakthrough in the design of Canon's revolutionary mini-copier, a product that created the personal copier market and has led Canon's successful migration from its stagnating camera business to the more lucrative field of office automation.
- What possible concrete sense of direction can a made-up word such as "optoelectronics" provide a company's product-development engineers? Under this rubric, however, Sharp has developed a reputation for creating "first products" that define new technologies and markets, making Sharp a major player in businesses ranging from color televisions to liquid crystal displays to customized integrated circuits.

In each of these cases, cryptic slogans that to a Western manager sound just plain silly—appropriate for an advertising campaign perhaps but certainly not for running a company—are in fact highly effective tools for creating new knowledge. Managers everywhere recognize the serendipitous quality of innovation. Executives at these Japanese companies are *managing* that serendipity to the benefit of the company, its employees, and its customers.

The centerpiece of the Japanese approach is the recognition that creating new knowledge is not simply a matter of "processing" objective information. Rather, it depends on tapping the tacit and often highly subjective insights, intuitions, and hunches of individual employees and making those insights available for testing and use by the company as a whole. The key to this process is personal commitment, the employees' sense of identity with the enterprise and its mission. Mobilizing that commitment and embodying tacit knowledge in actual technologies and products require managers who are as comfortable with images and symbols—slogans such as Theory of Automobile Evolution, analogies like that between a personal copier and a beer can, metaphors such as "optoelectronics"—as they are with hard numbers measuring market share, productivity, or ROI.

The more holistic approach to knowledge at many Japanese companies is also founded on another fundamental insight. A company is not a machine but a living organism. Much like an individual, it can have a collective sense of identity and fundamental purpose. This is the organizational equivalent of self-knowledge—a shared understanding of what the company stands for, where it is going, what kind of world it wants to live in, and, most important, how to make that world a reality.

In this respect, the knowledge-creating company is as much about ideals as it is about ideas. And that fact fuels innovation. The essence of innovation is to re-create the world according to a particular vision or ideal. To create new knowledge means quite literally to re-create the company and everyone in it in a nonstop process of personal and organizational self-renewal. In the knowledge-creating company, inventing new knowledge is not a specialized activity—the province of the R&D department or marketing or strategic planning. It is a way of behaving, indeed a way of being, in which everyone is a knowledge worker—that is to say, an entrepreneur.

The reasons why Japanese companies seem especially good at this kind of continuous innovation and self-renewal are complicated. But the key lesson for managers is quite simple: much as manufacturers around the world have learned from Japanese manufacturing techniques, any company that wants to compete on knowledge must also learn from Japanese techniques of knowledge creation. The experiences of the Japanese companies discussed below suggest a fresh way to think about managerial roles and responsibilities, organizational design, and business practices in the knowledge-creating company. It is an approach that puts knowledge creation exactly where it belongs: at the very center of a company's human resources strategy.

The Spiral of Knowledge

New knowledge always begins with the individual. A brilliant researcher has an insight that leads to a new patent. A middle manager's intuitive sense of market trends becomes the catalyst for an important new product concept. A shop-floor worker draws on years of experience to come up with a new process innovation. In each case, an individual's personal knowledge is transformed into organizational knowledge valuable to the company as a whole.

Making personal knowledge available to others is the central activity of the knowledge-creating company. It takes place continuously and at all levels of the organization. And as the following example suggests, sometimes it can take unexpected forms.

In 1985, product developers at the Osaka-based Matsushita Electric Company were hard at work on a new home bread-making machine. But they were having trouble getting the machine to knead dough correctly. Despite their efforts, the crust of the bread was overcooked while the inside was hardly

done at all. Employees exhaustively analyzed the problem. They even compared X rays of dough kneaded by the machine and dough kneaded by professional bakers. But they were unable to obtain any meaningful data.

Finally, software developer Ikuko Tanaka proposed a creative solution. The Osaka International Hotel had a reputation for making the best bread in Osaka. Why not use it as a model? Tanaka trained with the hotel's head baker to study his kneading technique. She observed that the baker had a distinctive way of stretching the dough. After a year of trial and error, working closely with the project's engineers, Tanaka came up with product specifications—including the addition of special ribs inside the machine—that successfully reproduced the baker's stretching technique and the quality of the bread she had learned to make at the hotel. The result: Matsushita's unique "twist dough" method and a product that in its first year set a record for sales of a new kitchen appliance.

Ikuko Tanaka's innovation illustrates a movement between two very different types of knowledge. The end point of that movement is "explicit" knowledge: the product specifications for the bread-making machine. Explicit knowledge is formal and systematic. For this reason, it can be easily communicated and shared, in product specifications or a scientific formula or a computer program.

But the starting point of Tanaka's innovation is another kind of knowledge that is not so easily expressible: "tacit" knowledge like that possessed by the chief baker at the Osaka International Hotel. Tacit knowledge is highly personal. It is hard to formalize and, therefore, difficult to communicate to others. Or in the words of the philosopher Michael Polanyi, "We can know more than we can tell." Tacit knowledge is also deeply rooted in action and in an individual's commitment to a specific context—a craft or profession, a particular technology or product market, or the activities of a work group or team.

Tacit knowledge consists partly of technical skills—the kind of informal, hard-to-pin-down skills captured in the term "know-how." A master craftsman after years of experience develops a wealth of expertise "at his fingertips." But he is often unable to articulate the scientific or technical principles behind what he knows.

At the same time, tacit knowledge has an important cognitive dimension. It consists of mental models, beliefs, and perspectives so ingrained that we take them for granted, and therefore cannot easily articulate them. For this very reason, these implicit models profoundly shape how we perceive the world around us.

The distinction between tacit and explicit knowledge suggests four basic patterns for creating knowledge in any organization.

1. *From Tacit to Tacit.* Sometimes, one individual shares tacit knowledge directly with another. For example, when Ikuko Tanaka apprentices herself to the head baker at the Osaka International Hotel, she learns his tacit skills through observation, imitation, and practice. They become part of her own tacit knowledge base. Put another way, she is "socialized" into the craft.

But on its own, socialization is a rather limited form of knowledge creation. True, the apprentice learns the master's skills. But neither the apprentice nor the master gain any systematic insight into their craft knowledge. Because their knowledge never becomes explicit, it cannot easily be leveraged by the organization as a whole.

2. *From Explicit to Explicit.* An individual can also combine discrete pieces of explicit knowledge into a new whole. For example, when a comptroller of a company collects information from throughout the organization and puts it together in a financial report, that report is new knowledge in the sense that it synthesizes information from many different sources. But this combination does not really extend the company's existing knowledge base either.

But when tacit and explicit knowledge interact, as in the Matsushita example, something powerful happens. It is precisely this exchange *between* tacit and explicit knowledge that Japanese companies are especially good at developing.

3. *From Tacit to Explicit.* When Ikuko Tanaka is able to articulate the foundations of her tacit knowledge of bread making, she converts it into explicit knowledge, thus allowing it to be shared with her project-development team. Another example might be the comptroller who, instead of merely compiling a conventional financial plan for his company, develops an innovative new approach to budgetary control based on his own tacit knowledge developed over years in the job.

4. *From Explicit to Tacit.* What's more, as new explicit knowledge is shared throughout an organization, other employees begin to internalize it—that is, they use it to broaden, extend, and reframe their own tacit knowledge. The comptroller's proposal causes a revision of the company's financial control system. Other employees use the innovation and eventually come to take it for granted as part of the background of tools and resources necessary to do their jobs.

In the knowledge-creating company, all four of these patterns exist in dynamic interaction, a kind of spiral of knowledge. Think back to Matsushita's Ikuko Tanaka:

1. First, she learns the tacit secrets of the Osaka International Hotel baker (socialization).
2. Next, she translates these secrets into explicit knowledge that she can communicate to her team members and others at Matsushita (articulation).
3. The team then standardizes this knowledge, putting it together into a manual or workbook and embodying it in a product (combination).
4. Finally, through the experience of creating a new product, Tanaka and her team members enrich their own tacit knowledge base (internalization). In particular, they come to understand in an extremely intuitive way that products like the home bread-making machine can provide genuine quality. That is, the machine must make bread that is as good as that of a professional baker.

This starts the spiral of knowledge all over again, but this time at a higher level. The new tacit insight about genuine quality developed in designing the home bread-making machine is informally conveyed to other Matsushita employees. They use it to formulate equivalent quality standards for other new Matsushita products—whether kitchen appliances, audiovisual equipment, or white goods. In this way, the organization's knowledge base grows ever broader.

Articulation (converting tacit knowledge into explicit knowledge) and internalization (using that explicit knowledge to extend one's own tacit knowledge base) are the critical steps in this spiral of knowledge. The reason is that both require the active involvement of the self—that is, personal commitment. Ikuko Tanaka's decision to apprentice herself to a master baker is one example of this commitment. Similarly, when the comptroller articulates his tacit knowledge and embodies it in a new innovation, his personal identity is directly involved in a way it is not when he merely "crunches" the numbers of a conventional financial plan.

Indeed, because tacit knowledge includes mental models and beliefs in addition to know-how, moving from the tacit to the explicit is really a process of articulating one's vision of the world—what it is and what it ought to be. When employees invent new knowledge, they are also reinventing themselves, the company, and even the world.

When managers grasp this, they realize that the appropriate tools for managing the knowledge-creating company look very different from those found at most Western companies.

▌From Metaphor to Model

To convert tacit knowledge into explicit knowledge means finding a way to express the inexpressible. Unfortunately, one of the most powerful management tools for doing so is also among the most frequently overlooked: the store of figurative language and symbolism that managers can draw from to articulate their intuitions and insights. At Japanese companies, this evocative and sometimes extremely poetic language figures especially prominently in product development.

In 1978, top management at Honda inaugurated the development of a new-concept car with the slogan, "Let's gamble." The phrase expressed senior executives' conviction that Honda's Civic and the Accord models were becoming too familiar. Managers also realized that along with a new postwar generation entering the car market, a new generation of young product designers was coming of age with unconventional ideas about what made a good car.

The business decision that followed from the "Let's gamble" slogan was to form a new-product development team of young engineers and designers (the average age was 27). Top management charged the team with two—and only two—instructions: first, to come up with a product concept fundamentally different from anything the company had ever done before; and second, to make a car that was inexpensive but not cheap.

This mission might sound vague, but in fact it provided the team an extremely clear sense of direction. For instance, in the early days of the project, some team members proposed designing a smaller and cheaper version of the Honda Civic—a safe and technologically feasible option. But the team quickly decided this approach contradicted the entire rationale of its mission. The only alternative was to invent something totally new.

Project team leader Hiroo Watanabe coined another slogan to express his sense of the team's ambitious challenge: Theory of Automobile Evolution. The phrase described an ideal. In effect, it posed the question: If the automobile were an organism, how should it evolve? As team members argued and discussed what Watanabe's slogan might possibly mean, they came up with an answer in the form of yet another slogan: "man-maximum, machine-minimum." This captured the team's belief that the ideal car should somehow transcend the traditional human-machine relationship. But that required challenging what Watanabe called "the reasoning of Detroit," which had sacrificed comfort for appearance.

The "evolutionary" trend the team articulated eventually came to be embodied in the image of a sphere—a car simultaneously "short" (in length) and "tall" (in height). Such a car, they reasoned, would be lighter and cheaper, but also more comfortable and more solid than traditional cars. A sphere provided the most room for the passenger while taking up the least amount of space on the road. What's more, the shape minimized the space taken up by the engine and other mechanical systems. This gave birth to a product concept the team called "Tall Boy," which eventually led to the Honda City, the company's distinctive urban car.

The Tall Boy concept totally contradicted the conventional wisdom about automobile design at the time, which emphasized long, low sedans. But the City's revolutionary styling and engineering were prophetic. The car inaugurated a whole new approach to design in the Japanese auto industry based on the man-maximum, machine-minimum concept, which has led to the new generation of "tall and short" cars now quite prevalent in Japan.

The story of the Honda City suggests how Japanese companies use figurative language at all levels of the company and in all phases of the product development process. It also begins to suggest the different kinds of figurative language and the distinctive role each plays.

One kind of figurative language that is especially important is metaphor. By "metaphor," I don't just mean a grammatical structure or allegorical expression. Rather, metaphor is a distinctive method of perception. It is a way for individuals grounded in different contexts and with different experiences to understand something intuitively through the use of imagination and symbols without the need for analysis or generalization. Through metaphors, people put together what they know in new ways and begin to express what they know but cannot yet say. As such, metaphor is highly effective in fostering direct commitment to the creative process in the early stages of knowledge creation.

Metaphor accomplishes this by merging two different and distant areas of experience into a single, inclusive image or symbol—what linguistic philosopher Max Black has aptly described as "two ideas in one phrase." By establishing a connection between two things that seem only distantly related, metaphors set up a discrepancy or conflict. Often, metaphoric images have multiple meanings, appear logically contradictory or even irrational. But far from being a weakness, this is in fact an enormous

strength. For it is the very conflict that metaphors embody that jump-starts the creative process. As employees try to define more clearly the insight that the metaphor expresses, they work to reconcile the conflicting meanings. That is the first step in making the tacit explicit.

Consider the example of Hiroo Watanabe's slogan, Theory of Automobile Evolution. Like any good metaphor, it combines two ideas one wouldn't normally think of together—the automobile, which is a machine, and the theory of evolution, which refers to living organisms. And yet, this discrepancy is a fruitful platform for speculation about the characteristics of the ideal car.

But while metaphor triggers the knowledge-creation process, it alone is not enough to complete it. The next step is analogy. Whereas metaphor is mostly driven by intuition and links images that at first glance seem remote from each other, analogy is a more structured process of reconciling contradictions and making distinctions. Put another way, by clarifying how the two ideas in one phrase actually are alike and not alike, the contradictions incorporated into metaphors are harmonized by analogy. In this respect, analogy is an intermediate step between pure imagination and logical thinking.

Probably the best example of analogy comes from the development of Canon's revolutionary mini-copier. Canon designers knew that for the first personal copier to be successful, it had to be reliable. To ensure reliability, they proposed to make the product's photosensitive copier drum—which is the source of 90% of all maintenance problems— disposable. To be disposable, however, the drum would have to be easy and cheap to make. How to manufacture a throwaway drum?

The breakthrough came one day when task-force leader Hiroshi Tanaka ordered out for some beer. As the team discussed design problems over their drinks, Tanaka held one of the beer cans and wondered aloud, "How much does it cost to manufacture this can?" The question led the team to speculate whether the same process for making an aluminum beer can could be applied to the manufacture of an aluminum copier drum. By exploring how the drum actually is and is not like a beer can, the mini-copier development team was able to come up with the process technology that could manufacture an aluminum copier drum at the appropriate low cost.

Finally, the last step in the knowledge-creation process is to create an actual model. A model is far more immediately conceivable than a metaphor or an analogy. In the model, contradictions get resolved and concepts become transferable through consistent and systematic logic. The quality standards for the bread at the Osaka International Hotel lead Matsushita to develop the right product specifications for its home bread-making machine. The image of a sphere leads Honda to its Tall Boy product concept.

Of course, terms like "metaphor," "analogy," and "model" are ideal types. In reality, they are often hard to distinguish from each other; the same phrase or image can embody more than one of the three functions. Still, the three terms capture the process by which organizations convert tacit knowledge into explicit knowledge: first, by linking contradictory things and ideas through metaphor; then, by resolving these contradictions through analogy; and, finally, by crystallizing the created concepts and embodying them in a model, which makes the knowledge available to the rest of the company.

From Chaos to Concept: Managing the Knowledge-Creating Company

Understanding knowledge creation as a process of making tacit knowledge explicit—a matter of metaphors, analogies, and models—has direct implications for how a company designs its organization and defines managerial roles and responsibilities within it. This is the "how" of the knowledge-creating company, the structures and practices that translate a company's vision into innovative technologies and products.

The fundamental principle of organizational design at the Japanese companies I have studied is redundancy—the conscious overlapping of company information, business activities, and managerial responsibilities. To Western managers, the term "redundancy," with its connotations of unnecessary duplication and waste, may sound unappealing.

And yet, building a redundant organization is the first step in managing the knowledge-creating company.

Redundancy is important because it encourages frequent dialogue and communication. This helps create a "common cognitive ground" among employees and thus facilitates the transfer of tacit knowledge. Since members of the organization share overlapping information, they can sense what others are struggling to articulate. Redundancy also spreads new explicit knowledge through the organization so it can be internalized by employees.

The organizational logic of redundancy helps explain why Japanese companies manage product development as an overlapping process where different functional divisions work together in a shared division of labor. At Canon, redundant product development goes one step further. The company organizes product-development teams according to "the principle of internal competition." A team is divided into competing groups that develop different approaches to the same project and then argue over the advantages and disadvantages of their proposals. This encourages the team to look at a project from a variety of perspectives. Under the guidance of a team leader, the team eventually develops a common understanding of the "best" approach.

In one sense, such internal competition is wasteful. Why have two or more groups of employees pursuing the same product-development project? But when responsibilities are shared, information proliferates, and the organization's ability to create and implement concepts is accelerated.

At Canon, for example, inventing the mini-copier's low-cost disposable drum resulted in new technologies that facilitated miniaturization, weight reduction, and automated assembly. These technologies were then quickly applied to other office automation products such as microfilm readers, laser printers, word processors, and typewriters. This was an important factor in diversifying Canon from cameras to office automation and in securing a competitive edge in the laser printer industry. By 1987—only five years after the mini-copier was introduced—a full 74% of Canon's revenues came from its business machines division.

Another way to build redundancy is through strategic rotation, especially between different areas of technology and between functions such as R&D and marketing. Rotation helps employees understand the business from a multiplicity of perspectives. This makes organizational knowledge more "fluid" and easier to put into practice. At Kao Corporation, a leading Japanese consumer-products manufacturer, researchers often "retire" from the R&D department by the age of 40 in order to transfer to other departments such as marketing, sales, or production. And all employees are expected to hold at least three different jobs in any given ten-year period.

Free access to company information also helps build redundancy. When information differentials exist, members of an organization can no longer interact on equal terms, which hinders the search for different interpretations of new knowledge. Thus Kao's top management does not allow any discrimination in access to information among employees. All company information (with the exception of personnel data) is stored in a single integrated database, open to any employee regardless of position.

As these examples suggest, no one department or group of experts has the exclusive responsibility for creating new knowledge in the knowledge-creating company. Senior managers, middle managers, and frontline employees all play a part. Indeed, the value of any one person's contribution is determined less by his or her location in the organizational hierarchy than by the importance of the information he or she provides to the entire knowledge-creating system.

But this is not to say that there is no differentiation among roles and responsibilities in the knowledge-creating company. In fact, creating new knowledge is the product of a dynamic interaction among three roles.

Frontline employees are immersed in the day-today details of particular technologies, products, or markets. No one is more expert in the realities of a company's business than they are. But while these employees are deluged with highly specific information, they often find it extremely difficult to turn that information into useful knowledge. For one thing, signals from the marketplace can be vague and ambiguous. For another, employees can be-

come so caught up in their own narrow perspective, that they lose sight of the broader context.

What's more, even when employees *do* develop meaningful ideas and insights, it can still be difficult to communicate the import of that information to others. People don't just passively receive new knowledge, they actively interpret it to fit their own situation and perspective. Thus what makes sense in one context can change or even lose its meaning when communicated to people in a different context. As a result, there is a continual shift in meaning as new knowledge is diffused in an organization.

The confusion created by the inevitable discrepancies in meaning that occur in any organization might seem like a problem. In fact, it can be a rich source of new knowledge—*if* a company knows how to manage it. The key to doing so is continuously challenging employees to reexamine what they take for granted. Such reflection is always necessary in the knowledge-creating company, but it is especially essential during times of crisis or breakdown, when a company's traditional categories of knowledge no longer work. At such moments, ambiguity can prove extremely useful as a source of alternative meanings, a fresh way to think about things, a new sense of direction. In this respect, new knowledge is born in chaos.

The main job of managers in the knowledge-creating company is to orient this chaos toward purposeful knowledge creation. Managers do this by providing employees with a conceptual framework that helps them make sense of their own experience. This takes place at the senior management level at the top of the company and at the middle management level on company teams.

Senior managers give voice to a company's future by articulating metaphors, symbols, and concepts that orient the knowledge-creating activities of employees. They do this by asking the questions: What are we trying to learn? What do we need to know? Where should we be going? Who are we? If the job of frontline employees is to know "what is," then the job of senior executives is to know "what ought to be." Or in the words of Hiroshi Honma, senior researcher at Honda: "Senior managers are romantics who go in quest of the ideal."

At some of the Japanese companies I have studied, CEOs talk about this role in terms of their responsibility for articulating the company's "conceptual umbrella": the grand concepts that in highly universal and abstract terms identify the common features linking seemingly disparate activities or businesses into a coherent whole. Sharp's dedication to optoelectronics is a good example.

In 1973, Sharp invented the first low-power electronic calculator by combining two key technologies—liquid crystal displays (LCDs) and complementary metal oxide semiconductors (CMOSs). Company technologists coined the term "optoelectronics" to describe this merging of microelectronics with optical technologies. The company's senior managers then took up the word and magnified its impact far beyond the R&D and engineering departments in the company.

Optoelectronics represents an image of the world that Sharp wants to live in. It is one of the key concepts articulating what the company ought to be. As such, it has become an overarching guide for the company's strategic development. Under this rubric, Sharp has moved beyond its original success in calculators to become a market leader in a broad range of products based on LCD and semiconductor technologies, including: the Electronic Organizer pocket notebook, LCD projection systems, as well as customized integrated circuits such as masked ROMs, ASICs, and CCDs (charge-coupled devices, which convert light into electronic signals).

Other Japanese companies have similar umbrella concepts. At NEC, top management has categorized the company's knowledge base in terms of a few key technologies and then developed the metaphor "C&C" (for "computers and communications"). At Kao, the umbrella concept is "surface active science," referring to techniques for coating the surface area of materials. This phrase has guided the company's diversification into products ranging from soap detergents to cosmetics to floppy disks—all natural derivatives of Kao's core knowledge base.

Another way top management provides employees with a sense of direction is by setting the standards for justifying the value of the knowledge that is constantly being developed by the organization's members. Deciding which efforts to support and develop is a highly strategic task.

In most companies, the ultimate test for measuring the value of new knowledge is economic—increased efficiency, lower costs, improved ROI. But in the knowledge-creating company, other more qualitative factors are equally important. Does the idea embody the company's vision? Is it an expression of top management's aspirations and strategic goals? Does it have the potential to build the company's organizational knowledge network?

The decision by Mazda to pursue the development of the rotary engine is a classic example of this more qualitative kind of justification. In 1974, the product-development team working on the engine was facing heavy pressure within the company to abandon the project. The rotary engine was a "gas guzzler," critics complained. It would never succeed in the marketplace.

Kenichi Yamamoto, head of the development team (and currently Mazda's chairman), argued that to stop the project would mean giving up on the company's dream of revolutionizing the combustion engine. "Let's think this way," Yamamoto proposed. "We are making history, and it is our fate to deal with this challenge." The decision to continue led to Mazda's successful rotary-engine sports car, the Savanna RX-7.

Seen from the perspective of traditional management, Yamamoto's argument about the company's "fate" sounds crazy. But in the context of the knowledge-creating company, it makes perfect sense. Yamamoto appealed to the fundamental aspirations of the company—what he termed "dedication to uncompromised value"—and to the strategy of technological leadership that senior executives had articulated. He showed how the rotary-engine project enacted the organization's commitment to its vision. Similarly, continuing the project reinforced the individual commitment of team members to that vision and to the organization.

Umbrella concepts and qualitative criteria for justification are crucial to giving a company's knowledge-creating activities a sense of direction. And yet, it is important to emphasize that a company's vision needs also to be open-ended, susceptible to a variety of different and even conflicting interpretations. At first glance, this may seem contradictory. After all, shouldn't a company's vision be unambiguous, coherent, and clear? If a vision is *too* unambiguous, however, it becomes more akin to an order or an instruction. And orders do not foster the high degree of personal commitment on which effective knowledge creation depends.

A more equivocal vision gives employees and work groups the freedom and autonomy to set their own goals. This is important because while the ideals of senior management are important, on their own they are not enough. The best that top management can do is to clear away any obstacles and prepare the ground for self-organizing groups or teams. Then, it is up to the teams to figure out what the ideals of the top mean in reality. Thus at Honda, a slogan as vague as "Let's gamble" and an extremely broad mission gave the Honda City product-development team a strong sense of its own identity, which led to a revolutionary new product.

Teams play a central role in the knowledge-creating company because they provide a shared context where individuals can interact with each other and engage in the constant dialogue on which effective reflection depends. Team members create new points of view through dialogue and discussion. They pool their information and examine it from various angles. Eventually, they integrate their diverse individual perspectives into a new collective perspective.

This dialogue can—indeed, should—involve considerable conflict and disagreement. It is precisely such conflict that pushes employees to question existing premises and make sense of their experience in a new way. "When people's rhythms are out of sync, quarrels occur and it's hard to bring people together," acknowledges a deputy manager for advanced technology development at Canon. "Yet if a group's rhythms are completely in unison from the beginning, it's also difficult to achieve good results."

As team leaders, middle managers are at the intersection of the vertical and horizontal flows of information in the company. They serve as a bridge between the visionary ideals of the top and the often chaotic market reality of those on the front line of the business. By creating middle-level business and product concepts, middle managers mediate between "what is" and "what should be." They remake reality according to the company's vision.

Thus at Honda, top management's decision to try something completely new took concrete form at the level of Hiroo Watanabe's product-development team in the Tall Boy product concept. At Canon, the company aspiration, "Making an excellent company through transcending the camera business," became a reality when Hiroshi Tanaka's task force developed the "Easy Maintenance" product concept, which eventually gave birth to the personal copier. And at Matsushita, the company's grand concept, "Human Electronics," came to life through the efforts of Ikuko Tanaka and others who developed the middle-range concept, "Easy Rich," and embodied it in the automatic bread-making machine.

In each of these cases, middle managers synthesized the tacit knowledge of both frontline employees and senior executives, made it explicit, and incorporated it into new technologies and products. In this respect, they are the true "knowledge engineers" of the knowledge-creating company.

CHAPTER 6

Managing across Boundaries:
The Collaborative Challenge

In the early 1980s, the strategic challenge for a company was viewed primarily as one of protecting its potential profits from erosion through either competition or bargaining. Such erosion of profits could be caused not only by the actions of competitors, but also by the bargaining powers of customers, suppliers, and governments. The key challenge facing a company was assumed to be its ability to maintain its independence by maintaining firm control over its activities. Furthermore, this strategic approach emphasized the defensive value of making other entities depend on it by capturing critical resources, building switching costs, and exploiting other vulnerabilities.[1]

A decade later, this view of strategy underwent a sea change. The need to pursue multiple sources of competitive advantage simultaneously (see Chapter 3) led not only to the need for building an interdependent and integrated network organization within the company (Chapter 5), but also to the need for building collaborative relationships externally with governments, competitors, customers, suppliers, and a variety of other institutions.

This important shift in strategic perspective was triggered by a variety of factors including rising R&D costs, shortening product life cycles, growing barriers to market entry, increasing need for global-scale economies, and the expanding importance of global standards. Such dramatic changes led managers to recognize that many of the human, financial, and technological resources they needed to compete effectively lay beyond their boundaries, and were often—for political or regulatory reasons—not for sale. This led many to shift their strategic focus away from an all-encompassing obsession with preempting competition to a broader view of building competitive advantage through selective and often simultaneous reliance on both collaboration and competition.

The previously dominant focus on value appropriation that characterized all dealings across a company's organizational boundary changed to simultaneous consideration of both value creation and value appropriation. Instead of trying to enhance their bargaining power over customers, companies began to build partnerships with them, thereby bolstering the customer's competitive position and, at the same time, leveraging their own competitiveness and innovative capabilities. Instead of challenging or, at best, accommodating the interests of host governments, many MNCs began actively pursuing cooperative relationships with government agencies and administrators.

---

[1] For the most influential exposition of this view, see Michael E. Porter, *Competitive Strategy* (New York: Free Press, 1980).

However, perhaps the most visible manifestation of this growing role of collaborative strategies lies in the phenomenon often described as strategic alliances: the increasing propensity of MNCs to form cooperative relationships with their global competitors. As described by Carlo de Benedetti, the ex-chairman of Olivetti and the key instigator of the variety of partnerships that Olivetti had developed with companies such as AT&T and Toshiba, "We have entered the age of alliances. . . . In the high-tech markets of the 1990s, we will see a shaking out of the isolated and a shaking in of the allied." It was a prediction that was proved quite accurate, and by the turn of the century strategic alliances had become central components of most MNC strategies.

Although our analysis of the causes and consequences of such collaborative strategies in this chapter focuses on the phenomenon of strategic alliances among global competitors, some of our arguments can be applied to a broader range of cooperative relations including those with customers, suppliers, and governments. We begin with a discussion of the key motivations for forming strategic alliances, then analyze the considerable risks such alliance arrangements carry, before proposing ideas about how managers might think about the key challenges and tasks involved in building and managing such alliances. The final section provides some brief conclusions.

■ Why Strategic Alliances?

The term strategic alliance has become widely used to describe a variety of different interfirm cooperation agreements ranging from shared research to formal joint ventures and minority equity participation. But regardless of the definitional vagueness, many recent studies have shown that large numbers of firms worldwide, including many industry leaders, are becoming increasingly involved in strategic alliances. Furthermore, several of these surveys have suggested that such partnerships are distinguishable from the traditional foreign investment joint ventures in several important ways.

Classically, the traditional joint ventures were formed between a senior multinational headquartered in an industrialized country and a junior local partner in a less-developed or less-industrialized country. The primary goal that dominated their formation was to gain new market access for existing products. In this classic contractual agreement, the senior partner provided existing products while the junior partner provided the local marketing expertise, the means to overcome any protectionist barriers, and the governmental contacts to deal with national regulations. Both partners benefited: The multinational achieved increased sales volume, and the local firm gained access to new products and often learned important new skills from its partner.

In contrast, the scope and motivations for the modern form of strategic alliances are clearly broadening. There are three trends that are particularly noteworthy. First, present-day strategic alliances are increasingly between firms in industrialized countries. Second, the focus is frequently on the creation of new products and technologies rather than the distribution of existing ones. And third, the present-day strategic alliances are often forged during industry transitions when competitive positions are shifting and the very basis for building and sustaining competitive advantage is being defined.

All of these characteristics make the new form of strategic alliances considerably more strategically important than the classic joint ventures they succeeded, and today the opportunity for competitive gain and loss through partnering is substantial. In the following paragraphs, we discuss in more detail why this rapidly developing form of business relationship is becoming so important by focusing on five key motivations that are driving the formation of strategic alliances: technology exchange, global competition, industry convergence, economies of scale, and alliances as an alternative to merger.

Technology Exchange

Various studies have confirmed that technology transfer or R&D collaboration is the major objective of over half the strategic alliances formed in recent years. The reason that technological exchange has become such a strong driver of alliances is simple: as more and more breakthroughs and major innovations increasingly are based on interdisciplinary and interindustry advances, the formerly clear boundaries between different industrial sectors and technologies become blurred. As a result, the necessary capabilities and resources are often beyond the scope of a single firm, making it increasingly difficult to compete effectively on the strength of one's own internal R&D efforts. The need to collaborate is further intensified by shorter product life cycles that increase both the time pressure and risk exposure while reducing the potential payback of massive R&D investments.

Not surprisingly, technology-intensive sectors such as telecommunications, information technology, electronics, pharmaceuticals, and specialty chemicals have become the central arenas for major and extensive cooperative agreements. Companies in these industries face an environment of accelerating change, short product life cycles, small market windows, and multiple vertical and lateral dependencies in their value chains. Because interfirm cooperation has often provided a solution to many of these strategic challenges, much of the technological development in each of these industries is now being driven by some form of R&D partnership.

Even mainstream industrial MNCs have employed strategic alliances to meet the challenge of coordinating and deploying discrete pools of technological resources without sacrificing R&D and commercialization scale advantages. For example, several advanced material suppliers have teamed up with global automotive companies to transfer their specialized technology across geographic borders. One typical example was the key role GEC played in transferring the Ford Xenoy bumper technology from Europe and adapting it to the U.S. market.

Global Competition

Over the past decade or so, fast-growing and widespread perception has emerged that global competitive battles will increasingly be fought out between teams of players aligned in strategic partnerships. Robert P. Collin, head of the U.S. subsidiary of a joint venture between General Electric and Fanuc, the Japanese robot maker, was blunt in his evaluation of the importance of using alliances as a key tool in competitive positioning. "To level out the global playing field," he said, "American companies will have to find partners." In the new game of global networks, successful MNCs from any country of origin may well be those that have chosen the best set of corporate allies.

Particularly in industries where there is a dominant worldwide market leader, strategic alliances and networks allow coalitions of smaller partners to compete more effectively against a global "common enemy" rather than each other. For example, the Symbian alliance among Psion, Ericsson, Nokia, and Motorola was created as a response to Microsoft's entry into the personal digital assistant (PDA) market. The partners recognized that their only hope of challenging Microsoft's new PDA operating system, Windows CE, was by developing a common standard in mobile phone and PDA operating systems.

Industry Convergence

Many high-technology industries are converging and overlapping in a way that seems destined to create a huge competitive traffic jam. Producers of computers, telecommunications, and components are merging; bio and chip technologies are intersecting; and advanced materials applications are creating greater overlaps in diverse applications from the aerospace to the automotive industry. Again, the preferred solution has been to create cross-industry alliances.

Furthermore, strategic alliances are sometimes the only way to develop the complex and interdisciplinary skills necessary in the competitive time frame required. Through such collaboration, alliances also become a way of shaping competition by reducing competitive intensity, by excluding potential entrants and isolating particular players, and by building complex integrated value chains that can act as a barrier to those who chose to go it alone.

Nowhere are the implications of this cross-industry convergence and broad-based collaboration clearer than in the case of high-definition television (HDTV). As with many other strategically critical technologies of the future—biotechnology, superconductivity, advanced ceramics, artificial intelligence—HDTV not only dwarfs previous investment requirements, but also extends beyond the technological capabilities of even the largest and most diversified MNCs. As a result, the development of this important new industry segment has been undertaken almost exclusively by country-based, cross-industry alliances of large powerful companies. In Japan, companies allied together to develop the range of products necessary for a system offering. At the same time, a European HDTV consortium was banded together to develop a competitive system. But in the United States, the legal and cultural barriers that prevented companies from working together in such partnerships threatened to compromise U.S. competitiveness in this major new industry.

Economies of Scale and Reduction of Risk

There are several ways in which strategic alliances and networks allow participating firms to reap the benefits of scale economies or learning—advantages that are particularly interesting to smaller companies trying to match the economic benefits that accrue to the largest MNCs. First, partners can pool their resources and concentrate their activities to raise the scale of activity or the rate of learning within the alliance significantly over that of each firm operating separately. Second, alliances allow partners to share and leverage the specific strengths and capabilities of each of the other participating firms.

Third, trading different or complementary resources between companies can also result in mutual gains and save each partner the high cost of duplication.

Beyond the scale benefits, companies are also motivated by the risk-sharing opportunities of such partnerships. This is particularly true in R&D where product life cycles are shortening and technological complexity is increasing. At the same time, R&D expenses are being driven sharply higher by personnel and capital costs. Because none of the participating firms bear the full risk and cost of the joint activity, alliances are often seen as an attractive risk-hedging mechanism.

One alliance driven by these motivations is the Renault-Nissan partnership. These two companies came together in 1999, with Renault taking a 36% in Nissan and installing Carlos Ghosn as its chief operating officer. Although Nissan's perilous financial position was evidently a key factor in their decision to bring in a foreign partner, the underlying driver of the alliance was the need—on both sides—for greater economies of scale and scope to achieve competitive parity with GM, Ford, and Toyota. The alliance led to a surprisingly fast turnaround of Nissan's fortunes, largely through Ghosn's decisive leadership, and subsequently to a broad set of projects to deliver synergies in product development, manufacturing, and distribution. Although still much smaller than GM or Ford, Renault-Nissan is now thought likely to be one of the long-term surviving players in the global automobile industry.

Alliance as an Alternative to Merger

Finally, there are still many industry sectors where political, regulatory, and legal constraints limit the extent of cross-border mergers and acquisitions. In such cases, companies often create alliances, not because they are inherently the most attractive organizational form but because they represent the best available alternative to merger.

The classic example of this phenomenon is the airline industry. Most countries still preclude foreign ownership of their domestic airlines. But a simple analysis of the economics of the industry—in terms of potential economies of scale, concentration of suppliers, opportunities for standardization of services, and competitive dynamics—would point to the availability of substantial benefits from global integration. So as a means of generating at least some of the benefits of global integration, while not breaking the rules against foreign ownership, airlines have formed themselves into marketing and code-sharing partnerships including Star Alliance and OneWorld.

Alliances of this type often lead to full-scale global integration if restrictions on foreign ownership are lifted. For example, as the telecommunications industry was gradually deregulated during the 1990s, alliances such as Concert and Unisource gave way to the emergence of true multinational players such as Worldcom, France Telecom, and Deutsche Telekom.

◼ The Risks and Costs of Collaboration

Because of these different motivations, there was an initial period of euphoria in which partnerships were seen as the panacea for most of the MNCs' global strategic problems and opportunities. Particularly in the 1980s, a large number of companies rushed to form polygamous relationships with a variety of partners around the world. The euphoria was fueled by two fashionable management concepts of the period: triad power[2] and stick to your knitting.[3]

The triad power concept emphasized the need to develop significant positions in the three key markets of the United States, western Europe, and Japan as a prerequisite for competing in global industries. Given the enormous costs and difficulties of independently accessing any one of these developed and highly competitive markets, many companies with unequal legs to their geographic stool saw alliances as the only feasible way to develop this triadic position.

The stick-to-your-knitting prescription in essence urged managers to disaggregate the value chain and focus their investments, efforts, and attention on only those tasks in which the company had a significant competitive advantage. Other operations were to be externalized through outsourcing or alliances. The seductive logic of both arguments, coupled with the rapidly evolving environmental demands, led to an explosion in the formation of such alliances during the 1980s. According to one study, the number of cooperative agreements between companies in different regions (U.S.–Japan, EU–Japan, U.S.–EU) rose from close to zero in 1979 to more than 360 in 1985.[4]

Since then, the experience companies gathered through such collaborative ventures highlighted some of the costs and risks of such partnerships. Some risks arise from the simultaneous presence of both collaborative and competitive aspects in such relationships. Others arise from the higher levels of strategic and organizational complexity of managing cooperative relationships outside the company's own boundaries.

The Risks of Competitive Collaboration

Many strategic alliances—including some of the most visible—involve partners who are fierce competitors outside the specific scope of the cooperative venture. Such relationships create the possibility that the collaborative venture might be used by one or both partners to develop a competitive edge over the other, or at least that the benefits from the partnership would be asymmetrical to the two parties, thereby changing their relative competitive positions. There are several factors that might cause such asymmetry.

A partnership is often motivated by the desire to join and leverage complementary skills and resources. For example, the two partners may have access to different technologies that can be combined to create new businesses or products. For example, SonyEricsson was created to bring together Sony's world-leading capabilities in consumer electronics and design with Ericsson's advanced technological know-how in mobile phones and strong relationships with mobile operators. Such an arrangement for competency pooling inevitably entails the possibility that, in the course of the partnership, one of the partners will learn and internalize the other's skills while carefully protecting its own, thereby creating the option of ultimately discarding the partner and appropriating all the benefits created by the partnership. This possibility becomes particularly salient

[2]See Kenichi Ohmae, *Triad Power* (New York: Free Press, 1985)

[3]One of the lessons developed in the highly influential book by Thomas Peters and Robert Waterman, *In Search of Excellence* (New York: Harper & Row, 1982).

[4]See M. Hergert and D. Morris, "Trends in International Collaborative Agreements," in *Cooperative Strategies in International Business,* eds. F. Contractor and P. Lorange (Lexington, Mass.: Lexington Books, 1988), p. 101.

when the skills and competencies of one of the partners are tacit and deeply embedded in complex organizational processes (and thereby difficult to learn or emulate), whereas those of the other partner are explicit and embodied in specific individual machines or drawings (and thereby liable to relatively easy observation and emulation).

When General Foods entered into a partnership with Ajinimoto, the Japanese food giant, it agreed to make available its advanced processing technology for products such as freeze-dried coffee. In return, its Japanese partner would contribute its marketing expertise to launch the new products on the Japanese market. After several years, however, the collaboration deteriorated and was eventually dissolved when Ajinomoto had absorbed the technology transfer and management felt it was no longer learning from its American partner. Unfortunately, General Foods had not done such a good job learning about the Japanese market and left the alliance with some bitterness.

The other predatory tactic might involve capturing investment initiative in order to use the partnership to erode the other's competitive position. In this scenario, the company ensures that it, rather than the partner, makes and keeps control over the critical investments. Such investments can be in the domain of product development, manufacturing, marketing, or wherever the most strategically vital part of the business value chain is located. Through these tactics, the aggressive company can strip its partner of the necessary infrastructure for competing independently and create one-way dependence on the collaboration that can be exploited at will.

Although they provide lively copy for magazine articles, such Machiavellian intentions and actions remain the exception, and the vast majority of cross-company collaborations are founded on a basis of mutual trust and shared commitment. Yet experience has shown that even the most carefully constructed strategic alliances can become highly risky and problematic ventures. Although many provide short-term solutions to some strategic problems, they can also serve to hide the deeper and more fundamental deficiencies that cause those problems. The short-term solution takes the pressure off the problem without solving it and makes the company highly vulnerable when the problem finally resurfaces, now in a more extreme and immediate form.

Furthermore, because such alliances typically involve sharing of tasks, each company almost inevitably loses some of the benefits from "learning by doing" for the tasks that it externalizes to its partner. Finally, even in the best-case scenario of a partnership that fully meets all expectations, the very success of partnership leads to some benefits for each partner and, therefore, to some strengthening of one's competitor. Behind the success of the alliance, therefore, lies the ever-present possibility that a competitor's newly acquired strength will be used against its alliance partner in some future competitive battle.[5]

The Cost of Strategic and Organizational Complexity

Cooperation is difficult to attain even in the best of circumstances. One of the strongest forces facilitating such behavior within a single company's internal operations is the understanding that the risks and rewards ultimately accrue to the company's own accounts, and therefore, either directly or indirectly, to the participants. This basic motivation is greatly diluted in strategic alliances. Furthermore, the scope of most alliances and the

---

[5]These potential risks of competitive collaboration are the focus of Reading 6-2—Gary Hamel, Yves L. Doz, and C. K. Prahalad, "Collaborate with Your Competitor—and Win," *Harvard Business Review.*

environmental uncertainties they inevitably face often prevent clear understanding of the risks that might be incurred or rewards that might accrue in the course of the partnership's evolution. As a result, cooperation in the context of allocated risks and rewards and divided loyalties inevitably creates additional strategic and organizational complexity that, in turn, involves additional costs for managing those complexities.

International partnerships bring together companies that are often products of vastly different economic, political, social, and cultural systems. Such differences in the administrative heritages of the partner companies, each of which brings its own strategic mentality and managerial practices to the venture, further exacerbate the organizational challenge. For example, tensions between Xerox and Fuji Xerox—a successful but often troubled relationship documented in Case 6-1—were as much an outgrowth of the differences in the business systems in which each was located as differences in the corporate culture between the U.S. company and its Japanese joint venture.

Biases and set perspectives even affect whole economies. Protected against takeover possibilities by a variety of legal and institutional factors, many Dutch, Swiss, or Japanese companies are continually bewildered by what they have perceived as the "accounting mentality" of their British or U.S. partners. Subject to the expectations of "The City" or "The Street" and forever under the threat of a hostile bid, the British and U.S. partners have been equally puzzled by their Swiss or Japanese partners' insensitivity to stock price effects of announcements and actions. Many alliances have been undone by what one side perceives as its partners' naïveté in financial and planning matters, and the other party views as short-term accounting games.

Organizational complexity that is due to the very broad scope of operations typical of many strategic alliances also contributes to the added difficulties. As we described in the introduction to this chapter, one of the distinguishing characteristics of present-day alliances is that compared to the narrower and more focused goals of earlier joint ventures, they often cover a broad range of activities. This expansion of scope requires partners not only to manage the many areas of contact within the alliance, but also to coordinate the different alliance-related tasks within its own organization. And the goals, tasks, and management processes for the alliance must be constantly monitored and adapted to changing conditions.

▪ Building and Managing Collaborative Ventures

As we have described in the preceding sections, alliances are neither conventional organizations with fully internalized activities, nor are they well-specified transaction relationships through which externalized activities are linked by market-based contracts. Instead, they combine elements of both. The participating companies retain their own competitive strategies and performance expectations as well as their national ideological and administrative identities. Yet, to obtain the required benefits out of the partnership, diverse organizational units in different companies and in different countries must effectively and flexibly coordinate their activities.

There are numerous reasons why such collaborative ventures inevitably present some very significant management challenges: strategic and environmental disparities among the partners, lack of a common experience and perception base, difficulties in interfirm communication, conflicts of interest and priorities, and inevitable personal differences among individuals who manage the interface. As a result, although it is manifest to most managers that strategic alliances can provide great benefits, they have also begun to realize that there is a big difference between making alliances and making them work.

The challenge can be considered in two parts, reflecting the prealliance tasks of analysis, negotiation, and decision making and the postalliance tasks of coordination, integration, and adaptation.

Building Cooperative Ventures

Alliances are like marriages. Just as the foundations of the relationship established during the dating process influences the quality and durability of the marriage, so the quality of the prealliance processes of partner selection and negotiation influence the clarity and reciprocity of mutual expectations from the alliance. There are three aspects of the prealliance process to which managers must pay close attention if the alliance is to have the best possible chance of success: partner selection, escalating commitment, and alliance scope.[6]

Partner Selection: Strategic and Organizational Analysis   The process of analyzing a potential partner's strategic and organizational capabilities is perhaps the most important yet also the most difficult of the prealliance tasks. Several factors impede the quality of the choice-making process.

The most important constraint lies in the availability of information required for an effective evaluation of the potential partner. Effective prealliance analysis needs data on the partner's relevant physical assets (such as the condition and productivity of plant and equipment), as well as on less-tangible assets (including the strength of brands, the quality of customer relationships, and the level of technological expertise) and organizational capabilities (such as managerial competence, employee loyalty, and shared values). The difficulty of obtaining such information in the short time limits in which most alliances are finalized is further complicated by the barriers of cultural and physical distance that MNCs must also overcome.

One key lesson emerging from the experience of most strategic alliances is that changes in each partner's competitive positions and strategic priorities have crucial impacts on the viability of the alliance over time. Even if the strategic trajectories of two companies cross at a particular point of time creating complementarities and the potential for a partnership, their paths may be so divergent as to make such complementarities too transient for the alliance to have any lasting value.

Although it is difficult enough to make a static assessment of a potential partner's strategic and organizational capabilities, it is almost impossible to make an effective prealliance analysis of how those capabilities are likely to evolve over time. Fuji Xerox again provides an interesting example. When the joint venture was formed, Xerox was clearly the senior partner from a technological point of view, so processes were created to facilitate knowledge transfer to Fuji Xerox, such as allowing Fuji Xerox scientists ("residents") to visit Xerox's Rochester and Palo Alto laboratories for extended periods.

---

[6]The prealliance process is in many ways similar to the preacquisition process and shares the same needs. See the article by David B. Jemison and Sim B. Sitkin, "Acquisitions: The Process Can Be a Problem," *Harvard Business Review*, no. 2 (1986): 107–14.

Xerox, on the other hand, did not see any value in being able to send its scientists over to Japan during the first two decades of partnership, so no such transfers were negotiated. Today, the fortunes of the two companies have changed, and it is arguably Fuji Xerox that has the technological edge. But the "resident" program for Fuji Xerox scientists to visit Xerox (and not vice versa) still exists.

Although there is probably no solution to this problem, companies that recognize alliances as a permanent and important part of their future organization have made monitoring for partners an ongoing rather than ad hoc process. Some have linked such activities into their integrated business intelligence system set up to monitor competitors. By having this group not only to analyze their competitors' potential strategies, but also to assess their value as acquisition or alliance candidates, these companies find themselves much better prepared when a specific alliance opportunity arises.

Escalating Commitment: Thrill of the Chase   The very process of alliance planning and negotiations can cause unrealistic expectations and wrong choices. In particular, some of the managers involved in the process can build up a great deal of personal enthusiasm and expectations in trying to sell the idea of the alliance within their own organization. This escalation process is similar to a process observed in many acquisition decisions where, in one manager's words, "The thrill of the chase blinds pursuers to the consequences of the catch." Because the champions of the idea—those most often caught in a spiral of escalating commitment—may be different from the operational managers who are later given responsibility for making the alliance work, major problems arise when the latter are confronted with inevitable pitfalls and less-visible problems.

The most effective way to control this escalation process is to ensure that at least the key operating managers likely to be involved in the implementation stage of the alliance are involved in the predecision negotiation process. Their involvement not only ensures greater commitment, but also creates a continuity between the pre- and postalliance actions. But the greatest benefit accrues to the long-term understanding that must develop between the partners. By ensuring that the broader strategic goals that motivate the alliance are related to specific operational details in the negotiation stage, the companies can enhance the clarity and the consistency of both the definition and the understanding of the alliance's goals and tasks.

Alliance Scope: Striving for Simplicity and Flexibility   All too often, in an effort to show commitment at the time of the agreement, partners press for broad and all-encompassing corporate partnerships and equity participation or exchange. Available experience, on the other hand, suggests that the key to successful alliance building lies in defining as simple and focused a scope for the partnership as is adequate to get the job done, and to retain at the same time the possibility to redefine and broaden the scope if needed. This is because alliances that are more complex also require more management attention to succeed and tend to be more difficult to manage.

Three factors add to the management complexity of a partnership: complicated cross-holdings of ownership or equity, the need for cross-functional coordination or integration, and breadth in the number and scope of joint activities. Before involving any alliance in such potentially complicated arrangements, management should ask the question: "Are these conditions absolutely necessary, given our objectives?" If a simple

OEM (original equipment manufacturer) arrangement can suffice, it is not only unnecessary to enter into a more committed alliance relationship but it is also undesirable because the added complexity will increase the likelihood of problems and difficulties in achieving the objectives of the partnership.

At the same time, it might be useful to provide some flexibility in the terms of the alliance for renegotiating and changing the scope, if and when found necessary. Even when a broad-based and multifaceted alliance is seen as the ultimate goal, many companies have found that it is preferable to start with a relatively simple and limited partnership whose scope is expanded gradually as both partners develop both better understanding of and greater trust in each other's motives, capabilities, and expectations.

Managing Cooperative Ventures

In personal relationships, whereas the mutual understanding and shared expectations developed during the courtship period affect the quality of the relationship after marriage, it is the ongoing commitment and flexibility of each partner that has the greater influence on determining the durability and success of such a union. Similarly, in corporate relationships, although the prealliance analysis and negotiation processes are important, it is a company's ability to manage the ongoing relationship that tends to be the key determining factor for the success or failure of an alliance. Among the numerous issues that influence a company's ability to manage a cooperative venture, there are three that appear to present the greatest challenges: managing the boundary, managing knowledge flows, and providing strategic direction.

Managing the Boundary: Structuring the Interface   There are many different ways in which the partners can structure the boundary of the alliance and manage the interface between this boundary and their own organizations. At one extreme, an independent legal organization can be created and given complete freedom to manage the alliance tasks. Alternatively, the alliance's operations can be managed by one or both parents with more substantial strategic, operational, or administrative controls. In many cases, however, the creation of such a distinct entity is not necessary, and simpler, less bureaucratic governance mechanisms such as joint committees may often be enough to guide and supervise shared tasks.

The choice among alternative boundary structures depends largely on the scope of the alliance. When the alliance's tasks are characterized by extensive functional interdependencies, there is a need for a high level of integration in the decision-making process relating to those shared tasks. In such circumstances, the creation of a separate entity is often the only effective way to manage such dense interlinkages. On the other hand, an alliance between two companies with the objective of marketing each other's existing products in noncompetitive markets may only need a few simple rules determining marketing parameters and financial arrangements, and a single joint committee to periodically review the outcomes.

Managing Knowledge Flows: Integrating the Interface   Irrespective of the specific objectives of any alliance, the very process of collaboration creates flows of information across the boundaries of the participating companies and creates the potential for learning from one another. Managing these knowledge flows involves two kinds of tasks for the participating companies. First, they must ensure full exploitation of the learning potential so created. Second, they must also prevent outflow of any information or knowledge they do not wish to share with their alliance partners.

In terms of the first point, the key problem is that the individuals managing the interface may often not be the best users for such knowledge. To maximize its learning from the partnership, a company must effectively integrate its interface managers into the rest of its organization. The gatekeepers must have knowledge of and access to the different individuals and management groups within the company who are likely to benefit most from the diverse kinds of information that flow through an alliance boundary. Managers familiar with the difficulties in managing information flows within the company's boundaries will readily realize that such cross-boundary learning is unlikely to occur unless specific mechanisms are created to make it happen.

The well-known NUMMI partnership between GM and Toyota illustrates this challenge. Located in Fremont, California, NUMMI quickly became one of the highest-productivity auto plants in North America. Yet despite the active involvement of hundreds of GM managers in running the plant, and GM's stated intention of learning from Toyota, the American partner never created an effective mechanism for transferring the knowledge gained in NUMMI to other GM plants.

Selection of appropriate interface managers is perhaps the single most important factor for facilitating such learning. Interface managers should have at least three key attributes: They must be well versed in the company's internal organizational process; they must have the personal credibility and status necessary to access key managers in different parts of the organization; and they must have a sufficiently broad understanding of the company's business and strategies to be able to recognize useful information and knowledge that might cross their path.

Merely placing the right managers at the interface is not sufficient to ensure effective learning, however. Supportive administrative processes must also be developed to facilitate systematic transfer of information and to monitor the effectiveness of such transfers. Such support is often achieved most effectively through simple systems and mechanisms such as task forces or periodic review meetings.

While exploiting the alliance's learning potential, however, each company must also manage the interface to prevent unintended flows of information to its partner. It is a delicate balancing task for those playing the gatekeeper role to ensure the free flow of information across the organizational boundaries while effectively regulating the flow of people and data to ensure that sensitive or proprietary knowledge is appropriately protected.

Providing Strategic Direction: The Governance Structure   The key to providing leadership and direction, ensuring strategic control, and resolving interorganizational conflicts is an effective governance structure. Unlike acquisitions, alliances are often premised on the equality of both partners, but an obsession to protect such equality often prevents companies from creating an effective governance structure for the partnership. Committees consisting of an equal number of participants from both companies and operating under strict norms of equality are often incapable of providing clear directions or forcing conflict resolution at lower levels. Indeed, many otherwise well-conceived alliances have floundered because of their dependence on such committees for their leadership and control.

To find their way around such problems, partners need to negotiate on the basis of what is termed "integrative" rather than "distributive" equality. Under such an agreement, each committee would be structured with clear single-handed leadership, but with each company taking the lead responsibility for different tasks. However, such delicately balanced arrangements can work only if the partners can agree on specific individuals, delegate the overall responsibility for the alliance to these individuals, and protect their ability to work to the best interests of the alliance itself rather than those of the parents.

Concluding Comments

Perspectives on strategic alliances have oscillated between the extremes of euphoria and disillusionment. Finally, however, there seems to be recognition that although such partnerships may not represent perfect solutions, they are often the best solution available to a particular company, at a particular point in time.

Easy—but Often Not the Best Solution

Perhaps the biggest danger for many companies is to pretend that the "quick and easy" option of a strategic alliance is also the best or the only option that is available. Cooperative arrangements are perhaps too tempting in catch-up situations where the partnership might provide a façade of recovery that masks serious problems.

Yet, while going it alone may well be the best option for any specific objective or task in the long term, almost no company can afford to meet all of its objectives in this way. When complete independence and self-sufficiency are not possible because of resource scarcity, lack of expertise, or time, or any other such reason, strategic alliances often become the second-best option.

Alliances Need Not Be Permanent

Another important factor that is commonly misunderstood is that dissolution of a partnership is not synonymous with failure. Many companies appear to have suffered because of their unwillingness or inability to terminate partnership arrangements when changing circumstances made those arrangements inappropriate. All organizations create internal pressures for their own perpetuation, and an alliance is no exception to this enduring reality. One important task for senior managers of the participating companies is to periodically ask the question why the alliance should not be terminated and to continue with the arrangement only if they can find compelling reasons to continue.

Flexibility Is Key

The original agreement for a partnership is typically based on limited information and unrealistic expectations. Experience from the actual process of working together provides the opportunity for fine-tuning and often for finding better ways of achieving higher levels of joint value creation. In such circumstances, the flexibility to adapt the goals, scope, and management of the alliance to changing conditions is essential. Besides, changing environmental conditions often make obsolete the original intentions and plans. Effective partnering requires the ability to monitor these changes and allow the partnership to evolve in response.

An Internal Knowledge Network: Basis for Learning

Finally, learning is one of the main benefits that a company can derive from a partnership, irrespective of whether it is one of the formal goals. For such learning to occur, however, a company must be receptive to the knowledge and skills available from the partner and must have an organization able to diffuse and leverage such learning. In the absence of an internal knowledge network, information obtained from the partner cannot be transferred and applied irrespective of potential value. Thus, building and managing an integrated network organization described in Chapter 4 is an essential prerequisite not only for effective internal processes, but also for effective management across organizational boundaries.

Case 6-1 Xerox and Fuji Xerox

We are committed to strengthening the strategic and functional coordination of Xerox and Fuji Xerox so that we will compete effectively against strong and unified global competitors.

Paul Allaire, *President and CEO of Xerox Corporation*
Yotaro Kobayashi, *President and CEO of Fuji Xerox*

Fuji Xerox, the joint venture between Xerox and Fuji Photo Film, was at a pivotal point in its 28-year history in 1990. Many considered it the most successful joint venture in history between an American and a Japanese company. Originally a sales organization for Xerox products in Japan, Fuji Xerox had evolved into a fully integrated operation with strong research, development, and manufacturing capabilities. As its sales and capabilities evolved, so did its importance within the Xerox Group: Its 1989 revenues of $3.6 billion represented 22% of the Xerox Group's worldwide revenue.[1] Furthermore, Fuji Xerox supplied the rest of the Xerox Group with low- to mid-range copiers. In Japan, the home country of Xerox's major competitors, Fuji Xerox held 22% of the installed base of copiers and 30% of revenues in the industry.

Yotaro "Tony" Kobayashi, Fuji Xerox's president and CEO, ascribed a good deal of the company's success to the autonomy that the joint venture had enjoyed from the beginning. Fuji Xerox was not "the norm" for joint ventures, he contended, adding that "the degree to which Xerox let us run was very unusual." Yet, paradoxically, as the company grew to represent a larger portion of Xerox's worldwide business (Exhibit 1), this situation seemed to be changing. "We have to begin to pay more attention to what our actions mean to Xerox," explained Kobayashi.

Paul Allaire, Xerox's president and CEO, added that Fuji Xerox's autonomy had been an important factor not only in its own success, but also in its growing contribution to the Xerox Group:

> The fact that we had this strong company in Japan was of extraordinary importance when other Japanese companies started coming after us. Fuji Xerox was able to see them coming earlier, and understood their development and manufacturing techniques.

---

[1]The Xerox Corporation (XC) is referred to in this case simply as Xerox. The combination of Rank Xerox (RX), Fuji Xerox (FX), and the Xerox Corporation is referred to as the Xerox Group. The revenues of Rank Xerox were consolidated into those of Xerox Corporation, but Fuji Xerox revenues were not. As described below, Xerox Corporation received 66% of RX earnings, which in turn included half of FX earnings.

This case was prepared by Benjamin Gomes-Casseres and Krista McQuade.

Copyright © 1991 by the President and Fellows of Harvard College. Harvard Business School case 391-156.

Exhibit 1   Growth of Xerox Corporation and Fuji Xerox, 1968–1989

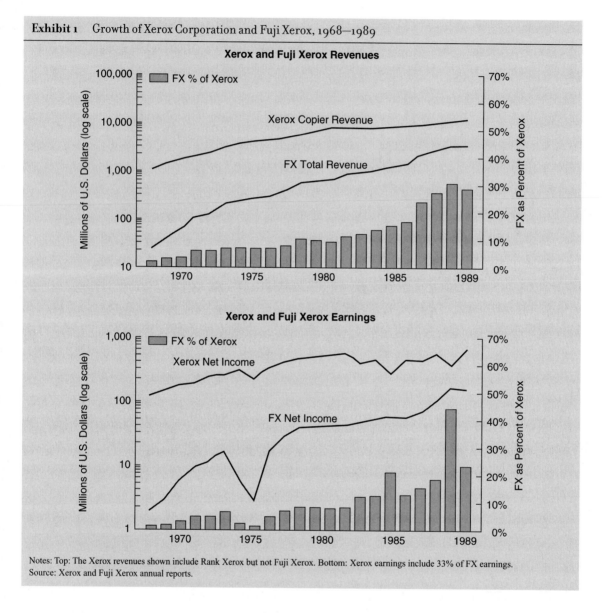

Notes: Top: The Xerox revenues shown include Rank Xerox but not Fuji Xerox. Bottom: Xerox earnings include 33% of FX earnings. Source: Xerox and Fuji Xerox annual reports.

We have excellent relationships with Fuji Xerox at the research, development, manufacturing, and managerial levels. Yet, because of this close relationship, there is a greater potential for conflict. If Fuji Xerox were within our organization, it would be easier, but then we would lose certain benefits. They have always had a reasonable amount of autonomy. I can't take that away from them, and I wouldn't want to.

Over the years, Fuji Xerox saw its local competitors grow rapidly through exports. The terms of its technology licensing agreements with Xerox, however, limited Fuji Xerox's sales to Japan and certain Far Eastern territories. As Canon, in particular, grew to challenge Xerox worldwide in low-end copiers, laser printers, and color copiers, Fuji

Xerox began to feel constrained by the relationship. "Fuji Xerox has aspirations to be a global company in marketing, manufacturing, and research," explained Jeff Kennard, who had managed the relationship between Xerox and Fuji Xerox since 1977. Kobayashi elaborated:

> The goals of Xerox and Fuji Xerox can be described as mostly compatible and partly conflicting. There *are* serious issues facing us. We often compare our situation with that of Canon or Ricoh, companies that have a single management organization in Japan. Are we as efficient and effective in the worldwide management of our business as we could be?
>
> Some of Fuji Xerox's products, such as facsimile machines, are managed like Canon's—with single-point design and manufacturing. But now there are external conditions in the United States and Europe that call for local manufacturing and development. Rank Xerox and Xerox are able to reach efficient volumes in their marketplaces. If Fuji Xerox manufactures only for Japan and adjacent markets, our volume will be too small, but Xerox is insisting on this. It is a tough challenge that we have to face together.

How should Fuji Xerox's aspirations be managed within the context of the Xerox Group? This was one of the questions facing the Codestiny Task Force commissioned in 1989 to review the capabilities and goals of Xerox and Fuji Xerox. Composed of senior managers from both companies, the task force would seek ways to enhance the strategic relationship between Xerox and Fuji Xerox for the 1990s. This was the third such review; Codestiny I (1982) and Codestiny II (1984) had both resulted in changes in contracts and agreements between the firms. With the basic technology licensing contract between Xerox and Fuji Xerox due to be renegotiated in 1993, participants in Codestiny III knew that their analysis could well lead to a substantial restructuring of the strategic relationship between the companies.

Xerox's International Expansion

When Chester Carlson tried to sell the rights to the revolutionary xerographic technology that he invented in 1938, GE, IBM, RCA, and Kodak all turned him down. Instead, the Haloid Corporation—a small photographic paper firm in Rochester, NY—agreed in 1946 to fund further research, and 10 years later acquired the full rights to the technology. By the time the company introduced its legendary 914 copier in 1959, xerographic products had come to dominate its business; in 1961 Haloid's name was changed to Xerox Corporation. The 914 was the world's first automatic plain paper copier (PPC), and produced high-quality copies four times faster than any other copier on the market. These advantages, coupled with an innovative machine rental scheme, led Xerox to dominate the industry for nearly 20 years. Company revenues rose from $40 million in 1960 to nearly $549 million in 1965, and to $1.2 billion in 1968, breaking the American record for the fastest company to reach $1 billion in sales. Net income grew from $2.6 million in 1960 to $129 million in 1968. In a mere decade, the name Xerox had become synonymous with copying.

Xerox moved quickly to establish an international network. Lacking the funds to expand alone, it formed a 50/50 joint venture in 1956 with the Rank Organization of Britain. Xerox would be entitled to about 66% of the profits of Rank Xerox. Rank operated a lucrative motion picture business and was seeking opportunities for diversification. Rank Xerox (RX), the new joint venture, was to manufacture xerographic products developed by Xerox and market them exclusively worldwide, except in the United States and Canada. By the early 1960s, Rank Xerox had established subsidiaries in Mexico, Italy, Germany, France, and Australia. In 1964, Xerox bought back the right to market xerographic products in the Western hemisphere.

Japanese firms immediately inquired about obtaining xerography licenses from Rank Xerox, but they were refused on the grounds that the technology was not commercially mature. By 1958, however, RX executives had turned their sights to the Japanese market. Aware of Japanese government regulations that required foreign firms to sell through local licensees or joint ventures, they sought a strong partner. Twenty-seven Japanese firms jockeyed for the position; Fuji Photo Film

(FPF) was the only nonelectronics firm in this group. Still, the company was chosen, partly because of the personal relationship and trust that had developed between RX President Thomas Law and FPF Chairman Setsutaro Kobayashi.

Fuji Photo Film was a manufacturer of photographic film since the early 1930s and second only to Kodak in that field. The company was trying to diversify its business away from silver-based photography, and was convinced that its technical expertise was well suited to the requirements of xerography. Under the direction of Nobuo Shono, the company had already begun experimenting with xerography; by 1958, it had invested 6 million yen in research and manufacturing facilities for the copiers that it hoped to license from Rank Xerox. As negotiations between the two companies intensified, Rank Xerox insisted on a joint venture instead of simply a license to Fuji Photo Film.

The Establishment of Fuji Xerox   Fuji Xerox, the 50/50 joint venture established by Fuji Photo Film and Rank Xerox in 1962, was originally intended to be a marketing organization to sell xerographic products manufactured by Fuji Photo Film. When the Japanese government refused to approve a joint venture intended solely as a sales company, however, the agreement was revised to give Fuji Xerox manufacturing rights. Fuji Xerox—not Fuji Photo Film—then became the contracting party with Rank Xerox, and received exclusive rights to xerographic patents in Japan. Fuji Xerox, in turn, subcontracted Fuji Photo Film to manufacture the products. As part of its technology licensing agreements with Rank Xerox, Fuji Xerox had exclusive rights to sell the machines in Japan, Indonesia, South Korea, the Philippines, Taiwan, Thailand, and Indochina. In return, Fuji Xerox would pay Rank Xerox a royalty of 5% on revenues from the sale of xerographic products. Rank Xerox would also be entitled to 50% of Fuji Xerox's profits.

Nobuo Shono became Fuji Xerox's first senior managing director, and Setsutaro Kobayashi, its president. Shono and Kobayashi drew their core executive staff, later known as the "Seven Samurai," from the ranks of Fuji Photo Film. A board of directors consisting of representatives from Rank Xerox and Fuji Photo Film was established to decide policy matters, while day-to-day operations were left to the Japanese management. The Xerox Corporation itself was to have no direct relationship with Fuji Xerox, and would participate in the profits of the joint venture only through its share in Rank Xerox.

Although Fuji Xerox adopted a number of business practices from Xerox, including organizational structure and the rental system, it remained distinctly Japanese throughout its history. Hideki Kaihatsu, managing director and chief staff officer at Fuji Xerox, explained:

> Employees are typically rotated through many functions before rising to the level of general management, and compensation and lifetime employment practices are similar to those of other Japanese firms. We emphasize long-term planning, teamwork, and we follow bottom-up decision making, including the "ringi" system. Furthermore, in procuring parts we follow the Japanese practice of qualifying a small group of vendors and working closely with them.

The Development of Fuji Xerox's Capabilities

Well before negotiations for the joint venture were finalized, engineers at Fuji Photo Film geared up for the production of Xerox copiers. Xerox machines were disassembled and studied to determine the equipment and supplies necessary for production. Three FPF engineers spent two months touring Xerox and Rank Xerox production facilities. At the establishment of the joint venture, a specific schedule was agreed upon, calling first for the sale of imported machines, then the assembly of imported knocked-down kits, and finally the domestic production of copiers. Import restrictions in Japan and government pressure to source locally accelerated this schedule, and the first Japanese-produced Xerox 914 was completed in September 1962; by 1965, 90% of the parts for the 914 came from local suppliers.

Fuji Xerox's first sales plan targeted financial institutions, large manufacturing corporations, and central government agencies. At the time of the introduction of the 914, 85% of the market was held by the inexpensive diazo type of copier. Although these copiers were difficult to operate and produced poor quality copies, they had been enormously successful in Japan, as the large number of characters in the Japanese language made typewriters difficult to use, and made copiers essential even for small offices. Ricoh, Copyer, and Mita had sold diazo copiers since the 1940s. By the early 1960s, Ricoh held an estimated 75% share of the market. A diazo copy was often referred to as a "Ricopy" in Japan.

Though Fuji Xerox had intended to sell the 914 copier outright, at Rank Xerox's insistence it implemented Xerox's trademark rental system. Within a year, the back-order list for the copier was five months' long. Output rose fivefold in five years, and Fuji Photo Film soon built a second production facility. In 1967, Fuji Xerox's sales passed those of Rank Xerox's French and German subsidiaries. Fuji Xerox's product line expanded to include other models, including a faster version of the 914, and a smaller desktop model. The 2400, capable of making 40 copies per minute (cpm),[2] was introduced in 1967. Sales subsidiaries were established throughout Fuji Xerox's licensed territory.

By the late 1960s, Fuji Xerox dominated the high-volume segment of the Japanese copier market. Ricoh, however, had made great inroads into the middle segment with an electrostatic copier based on an RCA technology, and was squeezing Fuji Xerox's market from below. In addition to the threat of substitute technologies, Fuji Xerox faced the end of its monopoly in plain paper copying; some of Xerox's core patents were scheduled to expire between 1968 and 1973. FX managers were already aware of efforts by several Japanese firms to develop plain paper copiers. In response to these pressures, Peter McColough, Xerox's president and CEO at the time, proposed to transfer the manufacture of copiers from Fuji Photo Film to Fuji Xerox, and in this way combine manufacturing and marketing activities under one roof. McColough described

the rationale for this decision:

> Fuji Xerox had to develop its own manufacturing capability. It had built up a good marketing organization, but had no assured source of supply. That left the company vulnerable. Fuji Photo Film initially resisted this idea because it would lose manufacturing volume and product revenues. They realized in the end that the issue went to the heart of the joint venture. Looking back, that was the most difficult period in our relationship.

In 1971, Fuji Photo Film transferred its copier plants to Fuji Xerox. That same year, Fuji Xerox completed the construction of a 160,000-square-foot manufacturing and engineering facility. From then on, Fuji Photo Film had little direct role in Fuji Xerox's operations. Yoichi Ogawa, senior managing director at Fuji Xerox in 1989 and one of the Seven Samurai, explained why Fuji Photo Film remained a passive partner after 1971:

> According to Fuji Photo Film's agreement with Xerox, the company, as a shareholder, could collect information from Fuji Xerox, but it could not use it in its own operations. In addition, a technology agreement between Fuji Xerox and Xerox provided that any technology acquired by Fuji Xerox from outside sources (including from Fuji Photo Film) could be freely passed on to Xerox.

In a separate development, Rank Xerox also lost much of its direct role in Fuji Xerox's operations. In December 1969, Xerox bought an additional 1% share of Rank Xerox from the Rank Organization, giving it 51% control of that joint venture. From then on, Rank Xerox would be managed as a Xerox subsidiary. Moto Sakamoto, an FX resident at Rank Xerox at the time, noticed an immediate change: "Things changed instantly as the Americans started coming in . . . gone was the old British style of management." Sakamoto was transferred to Xerox's main facility in Rochester, NY, as Fuji Xerox began to deal directly with Xerox. Rank Xerox's ownership share in Fuji Xerox remained at 50%, and the Xerox Corporation continued to receive 66% of Rank Xerox's profits, and therefore 33% of Fuji Xerox's.

Product Development at Fuji Xerox   The transfer of production facilities to Fuji Xerox and the

---

[2]The copier market was typically divided into low-, mid-, and high-volume segments. In the 1960s, the 2400 was considered a high-volume model; the original 914 copier made seven copies per minute. In the 1980s, copiers making less than 25 cpm were generally considered low-volume, while those making over 90 cpm were considered high-volume.

direct relationship established between Fuji Xerox and Xerox contributed to a continued strengthening of FX technical capabilities. Fuji Photo Film engineers had already been making modifications to Xerox designs in order to adapt the copiers to the local market; Japanese offices, for example, used different sized paper than American offices. Nobuo Shono, however, advocated the development of long-term R&D capabilities that would enable the company to develop its own products. In particular, he envisioned a high-performance, inexpensive, compact machine that could copy books. At the time, Xerox's priorities were different. Tony Kobayashi explained:

> We had been insisting that the Xerox Group needed to develop small copiers as an integral part of its worldwide strategy. However, Xerox's attitude was that the low end of the market was not a priority. . . . On the other hand, we were seeing rising demand for small copiers in Japan.[3]

Shono's development group produced four experimental copiers, each with projected manufacturing costs approximately half those of Xerox's smallest machine. When they first heard of the effort, engineers at Rank Xerox and Xerox doubted that these models could become commercially viable. Shono persisted, and in 1970 took a working prototype to London, where its performance amazed Rank Xerox executives. The machine was slow (5 cpm), but substantially smaller and lighter than comparable Xerox models. This demonstration immediately boosted Fuji Xerox's technical reputation within the Xerox Group, and for the first time Xerox allowed Fuji Xerox a small budget for R&D. In 1973, the FX2200—the world's smallest copier—was introduced in Japan with the slogan: "It's small, but it's a Xerox." The speed of the FX2200 was doubled in 1977 by the FX2202, and the basic model was improved further by the FX2300 and the FX2305.

Mushrooming Competition   The FX2200 appeared just in time to face an avalanche of new and serious competition. Canon was the first Japanese company to enter the plain paper copier market, introducing its low end "New Process" copiers in 1970; these machines were developed in-house and did not infringe on any Xerox patent. Ricoh and Konica, Fuji Photo Film's chief Japanese rivals in film, followed with their own technologies. In 1972, Canon made another major move by introducing copiers using liquid instead of dry toner. This technology was later licensed to Saxon, Ricoh, and Copyer. Liquid-toner copiers had the advantage of being smaller and less expensive to manufacture than dry-toner copiers like Xerox's, but they were cumbersome to use. They were introduced as a cheap alternative to Xerox dry copiers. Minolta, Copia, Mita, Sharp, and Toshiba also entered the plain paper copier industry; by 1975, 11 companies competed in the Japanese market.

In addition to developing small machines for its local market, Fuji Xerox tried to stem the competitive onslaught with more aggressive sales strategies. The company began to offer two- and three-year rental contracts as well as its standard one-year contract, and provided price incentives that were tied to contract length. It also began to offer three of its new low-priced copiers for outright sale, as the competition had been doing. Matazo Terada, one of the Seven Samurai, recalled that when the company tried to sell copiers before, Xerox management resisted:

> Xerox insisted on uniform policies—every country had to be managed like the U.S. firm. That was successful only while we were protected from competitors because of our monopoly. If Xerox had been more flexible from the beginning, we might have captured a larger market. That was a lost opportunity.

By 1977, Ricoh accounted for 34% of the number of copiers installed in Japan. Fuji Xerox followed with 25%, Canon with 15%, and Konica with 10%. In terms of copy volume, however, Fuji Xerox led the competition with more than 50% of the market, followed by Ricoh with 20%, and Canon and Konica with 10% each. In the low end of the market, Ricoh accounted for 50% of copy volume, compared to 10% for Fuji Xerox.

---

[3]Quoted in "Fuji Xerox Company, Ltd." Translation of a case study prepared by the Nomura School of Advanced Management in Tokyo.

Fuji Xerox's TQC Movement   Partly as a response to the new competition of the 1970s, as well as the oil shock and recession of 1973–1975, Fuji Xerox launched a Total Quality Control (TQC) program. Fuji Photo Film had operated a successful statistical quality control program, and in 1956 won the prestigious Deming Prize, awarded to companies that had shown outstanding quality management throughout their organization. Fuji Xerox's New Xerox Movement had three primary aims: to speed up the development of products that matched customer needs; to reduce costs and eliminate waste; and to adopt aggressively the latest technologies.

The focal point of the campaign was the development of "dantotsu," roughly translated as the "Absolute No. 1 Product." Company executives challenged the marketing and engineering departments to develop a product fitting this description in less time and at a lower cost than the competition. For six months, project proposals were turned down until the basic concept for the new product emerged in 1976: a compact, 40-cpm machine manufactured for half the price of any comparable machine, with half the number of parts of previous models, and developed in two years, compared to Xerox's typical four. Setsutaro's son, Tony Kobayashi, who became FX president in 1978 after his father died, explained:

> This was the first time Fuji Xerox had developed a copier based on our own design concept. The FX2200 copier we previously developed was an improved adaptation of a model developed in the United States. The American system of development was well established in our company. However, the U.S. way of developing new products on a step-by-step basis was too time consuming for our dynamic environment. The competition in the Japanese market required us to study the development systems of our rivals. . . . We found that we had been spending too much time in development. That is why we formulated the design concept for the new model and committed the entire company's resources to its development within a very limited timetable.[4]

The FX3500 was indeed introduced two years later, and by 1979, it had broken the Japanese record for the number of copiers sold in one year.

Ricoh and Canon rushed to develop copiers that could compete in the FX3500's market segment. Largely because of Fuji Xerox's effort to develop the FX3500, the company won the Deming Prize in 1980. In addition, the FX3500 firmly established Fuji Xerox as a technologically competent member of the Xerox Group. David Kearns, who would become Xerox's president in 1977, was amazed when he first saw a demonstration of the FX3500 prototype, and spontaneously broke out in applause.

Later, some observers labeled the FX3500 Fuji Xerox's "declaration of independence." The FX3500 project came after Xerox canceled a series of low- to mid-volume copiers on which Fuji Xerox was depending. Code-named SAM, Moses, Mohawk, Elf, Peter, Paul, and Mary, they were each canceled in mid-development, even though Fuji Xerox had gaps in its product range in the Japanese market. Jeff Kennard remembered that when Tony Kobayashi was told about the cancellation of Moses, he was also asked to stop work on the FX3500 project. "Tony refused," Kennard recalled, adding that Kobayashi said, in effect, "As long as I am responsible for the survival of this company, I can no longer be totally dependent on you for developing products. We are going to have to develop our own."

Xerox's Lost Decade

During the 1970s, competition in the U.S. and European copier markets changed radically. Prior to that period, Xerox had had a virtual monopoly because of its xerography patents. But beginning in 1970, one competitor after another entered the industry, often with new and improved PPC technologies. The Xerox Group share of worldwide PPC revenues fell from 93% in 1971 to 60% in 1975, and 40% in 1985 (Exhibit 2). This was Xerox's "lost decade"—an era of increasing competition, stagnating product development, and costly litigation.

New Competition High and Low   The proliferation of PPC vendors that started in Japan in the early 1970s soon appeared in the United States and Europe. By 1975, approximately 20 PPC manufacturers operated worldwide, including re-prographic companies (Xerox, Ricoh, Mita, Copyer, A.B. Dick,

---

[4]Quoted in "Fuji Xerox Company, Ltd."

Exhibit 2	Copier Sales of Leading Vendors Worldwide, 1975–1985 (millions of U.S. dollars except share data)		
	1975	1980	1985
Xerox Group	$3,967	$7,409	$8,903
U.S. and Americas	2,340	3,866	4,770
Rank Xerox	1,350	2,856	2,400
Fuji Xerox	277	687	1,733
Canon	87	732	2,178
Ricoh	290	1,092	1,926
Kodak	1	300	900
IBM	310	680	700
Minolta	25	387	743
3M	380	575	400
Oce	178	680	600
Savin	52	430	448
Konishiroku	85	302	470
Nashua	155	401	278
Agfa	115	268	200
Pitney Bowes	52	129	204
A.B. Dick	35	55	60
Saxon	56	127	20
AM International	59	23	10
Other Japanese	155	1,220	2,846
Other	596	792	1,115
Total	$6,598	$15,602	$22,001

Shares of Leading Firms in World Total

Xerox Group	60%	47%	40%
Americas	35	25	22
Rank Xerox	20	18	11
Fuji Xerox	4	4	8
Canon	1	5	10
Ricoh	4	7	9
Kodak	0	2	4
IBM	5	4	3
Minolta	0	2	3

Source: Donaldson, Lufkin & Jenrette, Inc.

AM, and 3M), paper companies (Dennison, Nashua, and Saxon), office equipment companies (IBM, SCM, Litton, and Pitney Bowes), photographic equipment companies (Canon, Konica, Kodak, and Minolta), and consumer electronics companies (Sharp and Toshiba).

Canon's New Process copiers were the first to hit the U.S. market, followed by a wave of liquid-toner copiers. The new Japanese machines were priced aggressively, and sold outright through independent dealers. On average, these machines broke down half as often as Xerox copiers. Canon sold under its own brand name, taking advantage of its reputation for quality photographic products, and supported its dealers through extensive financing, and sales and service training. Ricoh sold its machines through Savin Business Machines and the Nashua Corporation. Savin, primarily a marketing company, had funded the Stanford Research Institute's development of a liquid-toner copier, and subsequently had licensed Ricoh to manufacture the machines. The first Ricoh machines using this new technology were introduced in 1975 and were an instant success. Konica, Toshiba, Sharp, and Minolta entered the U.S. market through OEM relationships, as well as with their own brands.

Despite the entrance of so many Japanese competitors into the U.S. market, Xerox initially did little to respond to them. These competitors targeted the low end of the market, leaving Xerox's most important segments seemingly unaffected. Furthermore, Xerox continued to dominate the world copier market, with revenues that rose each year by more than Savin's total copiers sales. Xerox executives were more concerned by the entrance of IBM and Eastman Kodak into the copier industry, as these companies targeted the mid- and high-volume segments. (See Exhibit 3.)

IBM's introduction of its Copier I in 1970 signaled the end of Xerox's monopoly in its home market. Although IBM's first model was not successful because of a combination of high price and performance problems, the Copier II, introduced in 1972, began to take market share away from Xerox. These machines were marketed by IBM's office products sales force on a rental basis, supported by heavy advertising. IBM introduced the Copier II in Europe and Japan in 1975, and by 1976 had installed 80,000 copiers worldwide, against Xerox's estimated 926,000. IBM's high-volume Copier III

Exhibit 3   Copier Unit Placements of Xerox and Major Competitors

	Thousands of Units Placed by Market Segment (net)*					Share of Net Placements in Each Market Segment*				
	PCs	Low	Mid	High	Total	PCs	Low	Mid	High	Total
In the United States:										
Xerox										
1975	—	9	−8†	1	2	—	29%	—	100%	6%
1980	—	34	6	6	46	—	11	22	52	13
1985	—	66	27	15	108	0%	10	21	53	10
1989	12	101	53	13	179	5	14	27	45	15
Kodak and IBM										
1975	—	—	10	—	10	—	0	213	0	27
1980	—	—	5	5	11	—	0	20	48	3
1985	—	—	2	13	14	0	0	2	46	1
1989	—	—	5	9	13	0	0	2	31	1
Canon										
1975	—	3	—	—	3	—	10	0	0	8
1980	—	46	4	—	50	—	15	14	0	14
1985	176	107	17	—	300	86	16	13	0	29
1989	141	106	19	4	270	62	15	10	13	23
Others										
1975	—	19	3	—	22	—	61	55	0	59
1980	—	237	12	—	249	—	75	44	0	70
1985	30	514	81	—	625	14	75	64	0	60
1989	75	513	123	3	714	33	71	61	11	61
Total for all vendors										
1975	—	31	5	1	37					
1980	—	317	27	11	355					
1985	206	687	126	28	1,047					
1989	227	710	200	29	1,176					
In Western Europe:										
Rank Xerox										
1980	—	40	4	4	48	—	11	22	100	13
1984	—	54	19	9	82	0	9	25	74	10
1989	18	73	49	4	144	7	10	29	34	12
Kodak										
1980	—	—	4	—	4	—	0	22	0	1
1984	—	—	—	3	3	0	0	0	26	0
1989	—	—	2	2	3	0	0	1	13	0
Canon										
1980	—	36	4	—	40	—	10	21	0	11
1984	115	81	8	—	204	90	15	10	0	26
1989	130	110	25	3	268	49	15	15	26	22

(continued)

Exhibit 3   (*concluded*)

	Thousands of Units Placed by Market Segment (net)*					Share of Net Placements in Each Market Segment*				
	PCs	**Low**	**Mid**	**High**	**Total**	**PCs**	**Low**	**Mid**	**High**	**Total**
In Western Europe:										
Total for all vendors										
1980	—	351	19	4	374					
1984	128	578	76	12	794					
1989	268	752	168	11	1,199					
In Japan:										
Fuji Xerox										
1986					112					20
1989					142					21
Canon										
1986					138					25
1989					195					28
Others‡										
1986					311					55
1989					354					51
Total for all vendors										

*"Net Placements" are sales and new rentals minus old rentals returned to the vendor. Volume segments are defined as follows:

    PC = Less than 12 cpm (average price about $1,000)
    Low = 12 to 30 cpm (average price about $3,000)
    Mid = 31 to 69 cpm (average price about $8,500)
    High = Over 70 cpm (average price about $55,000)

†Indicates that, on balance, 8,000 rental units were returned.
‡Ricoh was particularly strong in Japan, with a 32% share in 1989.
Source: Dataquest Incorporated.

came out in 1976, but was withdrawn because of reliability problems. It was reintroduced as a mid-volume machine early in 1978, but IBM's copier business suffered permanently from the setback.

Eastman Kodak's main facilities were located across town from Xerox's in Rochester, NY. Kodak's success as a high-technology, chemistry-based, American firm had been a model for Xerox's founders and early leaders. When Kodak introduced the high-end Ektaprint 100 copier in 1975, however, admiration quickly turned to intense rivalry. Unlike the IBM Copier I, Kodak's first machine was extremely innovative. In particular, it featured a microcomputer that monitored the performance of the copier and alerted operators to problems through a digital display. A central computer at Kodak monitored the trouble signals and dispatched service people to a machine before breakdown. The machines were also capable of excellent reproduction. The Ektaprint series was well accepted in the marketplace, and quickly gained a reputation for the highest-quality image reproduction in the field.

Xerox's Stagnation   In its first competitive actions against IBM, Kodak, and the Japanese entrants, Xerox could not come up with a winning strategy. It focused R&D on developing a super-high-speed copier and field-tested its first color copier in 1971; neither became a commercial success. Xerox's mid-volume 4000 and 3100 series, introduced in the early 1970s, suffered from reliability problems and were also commercial failures. Even when the price of the 3100 was slashed from $12,000 to $4,400, it did not sell well. Ricoh/Savin became the top seller in the U.S. market in 1976, and Xerox's market share in the United States continued to fall. However, the seriousness of Xerox's situation was slow to sink in, according to David Kearns:

> We dominated the industry we had created. We were convinced that we were providing the world with high-quality machines, and our convictions were reinforced by the broad acceptance of Xerox products by our customers. We had always been successful, and we assumed that we would continue to be successful. Our success was so overwhelming that we became complacent.[5]

About 1978, Fuji Xerox offered to sell its FX2202 copier to Xerox and Rank Xerox to help them counter Japanese competition in the United States and Europe. Rank Xerox purchased 25,000 of the machines, but Xerox Corporation refused to buy any.[6] Bill Glavin, the managing director at Rank Xerox at that time, noted:

> We had never placed such a large order before and expected to sell them in 12 months. Two thousand machines per month was an incredible rate of sales, but we did it. For Tony Kobayashi, that order must have represented a substantial part of his production that year. We worked closely with them, and they gave us top-notch support.

This first successful cooperation led Rank Xerox to import more of the FX machines. In addition, Kodak had delayed its entry into Europe by two years, giving Rank Xerox time to formulate a defensive marketing strategy for the high end. As for IBM, its excellent distribution network and reputation in Europe could not make up for a generally inferior product. As Wayland Hicks, the general manager of Rank Xerox's U.K. operating company in the late 1970s, noted, "If IBM had Kodak's product, Xerox would have been dead." Rank Xerox was able to defend its market share while Xerox's U.S. share continued to decline.

In 1979, largely because of Rank Xerox's success with the FX product, Xerox began to import the FX2202, and later the FX2300 and the FX2350. Typically, in the year that the products were introduced in the U.S. market, the machines were assembled by Fuji Xerox before export. Then, acceding to union demands in the United States, Fuji Xerox exported them as knock-down units to be assembled at Xerox. "Some of our people had been reluctant to import FX machines," recalled Peter McColough. "Our engineers felt that they had developed xerography, and that the first FX machines weren't good enough."

Courtroom Battles   Xerox became involved in the 1970s in a series of courtroom battles. Immediately after IBM came out with its Copier I in 1970, Xerox sued for patent infringement, and IBM countersued. The companies argued 12 separate counts in the United States and Canada. Xerox won some of these suits and the rest were settled in 1978, when the firms agreed to an exchange of patents covering all information-handling products and to a $25 million payment to Xerox. Two other American firms, the SCM Corporation and Van Dyk Research, sued Xerox for alleged antitrust violations in 1973 and 1975, respectively, each claiming $1.5 billion in damages. Both lost their suits in 1978–1979.

More damaging still, the Federal Trade Commission (FTC) initiated action against Xerox in 1973, charging that the firm controlled 95% of the plain paper copier industry, and that its pricing, leasing, and patent-licensing practices violated the Sherman Antitrust Act. The FTC demanded that Xerox offer unrestricted, royalty-free licenses on all its copier patents, that it divest itself of Rank Xerox and Fuji Xerox, and that it allow third parties to service, maintain, and repair copiers leased from Xerox. In 1975, Xerox settled out of court by signing a consent decree with the FTC, in which it agreed to

---

[5]David T. Kearns, "Leadership Through Quality," *Academy of Management Executive,* vol. 4 (1990): 86–89.

[6]Although Xerox had acquired equity control of Rank Xerox in 1969, the line operations of the two firms were not integrated until 1978. Rank Xerox could thus make this decision in relative autonomy.

license more than 1,700 past and future patents for a period of 10 years. Competitors were permitted to license up to three patents free of royalties, to pay 0.5% of revenues on the next three, and to license additional patents royalty free. Xerox also agreed to forgive past patent infringements, to cease offering package-pricing plans on machines and supplies, and to begin outright sales of machines.

Kodak, IBM, Canon, Ricoh, and other Japanese firms were among the firms to secure Xerox licenses under this arrangement. At this point, the Japanese firms that had entered the market with liquid-toner copiers switched to Xerox's dry-toner process.

Adjusting the Relationship between Xerox and Fuji Xerox

As Fuji Xerox's business grew and Xerox's came under increasing pressure at home, the relationship between the two companies changed. The original joint venture and technology assistance agreements of the early 1960s were updated in 1976 and in 1983, and numerous interim agreements were signed to adjust policies on such issues as procurement and relations to third parties (Exhibit 4). Bob Meredith, a lawyer by training and Xerox's resident director in Tokyo, described the role of these contracts:

> The legal contracts are flexible. We don't follow an adversarial, arm's-length approach, where you might try to gain short-term advantage or act opportunistically. The equity commitment focuses our relationship on one main objective: What is the profit-maximizing thing to do?

Technology agreements and other contracts between Xerox and Fuji Xerox provided guidelines for the relationship. In addition, the contracts specified royalties and transfer pricing procedures. In 1976, a Technology Assistance Contract (TAC) had been signed by Xerox and Fuji Xerox, which maintained the 5% royalty that Xerox received from Fuji Xerox's xerographic sales, and that was to last 10 years. During the Codestiny I discussions, however, the royalty structure of the contract was revised. The 1983 TAA established a basic royalty on

Fuji Xerox's total sales, representing Fuji Xerox's right to use the Xerox tradename and technology in its licensed territory. The royalty on xerographic sales, however, was set to decline annually between 1983 and 1993. In addition, for the first time Fuji Xerox would begin receiving a manufacturing license fee (MLF), designed to compensate it for its development and manufacturing investments. In particular, an MLF of up to 20% could be added to the unit costs of FX machines exported in knocked-down form and assembled and sold by Xerox.

These and other subtle changes in the relationship between the two firms tended to reinforce Fuji Xerox's autonomy. David Kearns recalled how he worked to "unfetter" Fuji Xerox in the late 1970s:

> Xerox was attempting to control so many aspects of Fuji Xerox's operations. We were reviewing their marketing strategies, what products they were going to develop, and so on. But it didn't make sense to me to try to run the business from thousands of miles away. So, I encouraged them to pursue their own strategies and develop their own products. Of course, they were moving in that direction anyway.

Turning Around Xerox

In 1979, Xerox began to formalize a strategy based on the reality of its declining position in the copier industry. Kearns recalled the initial shock of the necessity to do so:

> The Japanese were selling products in the United States for what it cost us to *make* them. We were losing market share rapidly, but didn't have the cost structure to do anything about it. I was not sure if Xerox would make it out of the 1980s.

One of Xerox's strategies was to diversify out of copiers by acquiring a number of financial services companies between 1983 and 1988. Financial services, Kearns believed, would provide "an anchor in a nonmanufacturing business, and one in which Japanese companies were not active overseas." Before the financial services industry went sour at the end of the decade, this line of business was a steady source of earnings for Xerox, providing more than

---

Exhibit 4   Major Agreements between Xerox and Fuji Xerox

1960 Joint Enterprise Contract and Articles of Incorporation (1962)

- Established equal ownership of FX by Rank Xerox and Fuji Photo Film
  - Defined FX's exclusive license to Xerography in its territory: Japan, Taiwan, Philippines, the Koreas, Indonesia, Indochina
  - FX nonexclusive license to nonxerographic products in territory
  - Specifies terms of technology assistance: royalty due Rank Xerox—5% of net sales of xerographic products

1976 Joint Enterprise Contract (JEC)

- Agreement between Rank Xerox and Fuji Photo Film, updating 1960 JEC
- Specified Board of Directors composition
- FX management to be appointed by Fuji Photo Film
- Agreements on technology transfer, royalties, and transfer pricing
- Identified matters requiring Xerox concurrence, including:
    Financial policy, including major capital expenditures
    Business and operating plans
    Relations with third parties
    Sales outside of FX licensed territory

1976 Technological Assistance Contract (TAC)

- 10-year agreement between Xerox and Fuji Xerox
- Revised technology assistance agreements of 1960, 1968, and 1971
- Maintained 5% royalty on xerographic products

1978 R&D Reimbursement Agreement

- Defines reimbursement to FX for R&D on FX products marketed by Xerox: 100% to 120% of design cost

1983 Technology Assistance Agreement (TAA)

- 10-year agreement between Xerox and Fuji Xerox
- Replaced 1976 technology transfer agreements
- Revised royalty rates:
    Basic Royalty on total FX revenue, plus
    Royalty on xerographic revenues to decline annually from 1983 to 1993

1983 Product Acquisition Policy

- Provided guidelines for intercompany transfer pricing
- Established concept of reciprocal Manufacturing License Fee (MLF), designed to reimburse FX for development and manufacturing costs:
    Up to 25% markup on assembled machines supplied by FX
    Up to 20% markup on unit cost for FX machines assembled by XC
    Specific designs and services required by Xerox reimbursed 100%

1985 Procurement Policy

- Provided guidelines for Xerox procurement in FX licensed territory:
    FX right to bid first
    Procurement from third party to be coordinated with FX

1986 Arrangements Strategy Agreement

- Defined parameters for negotiating alliances with third parties

Source: Compiled from Xerox Corporation documents.

$2 billion in profits in five years. In 1989, however, financial services' earnings declined significantly and substantial assets were written off.

Kearns also began to take a closer look at the strategies of Fuji Xerox and other Japanese companies. Upon importing the first FX products, Xerox engineers had been amazed by a reject rate for parts that was a mere fraction of the American rate, and by substantially lower manufacturing costs. Visits to FX facilities introduced Xerox executives to the practice of "benchmarking," or systematically tracking costs and performance in all areas of operations against those of the best in the field. The findings from Xerox's own benchmarking efforts helped fuel Kearns's efforts to infuse his organization with new vision and determination.

In 1981, Kearns announced a companywide initiative for "business effectiveness," and two years later formally launched Xerox's Leadership Through Quality program. Xerox's program was based on the experience of Fuji Xerox, and throughout the effort, Kearns called upon Kobayashi and others at Fuji Xerox for help. Xerox hired Japanese consultants recommended by Fuji Xerox, and some 200 high-level Xerox and Rank Xerox managers visited Fuji Xerox in later years to learn first-hand about its TQC management and philosophy. The Leadership Through Quality program emphasized high employee involvement in attaining five major goals: (1) increased market research and competitive benchmarking; (2) just in-time manufacturing to decrease costs; (3) faster product development; (4) development of state-of-the-art technology; and (5) a devotion to quality in all areas.

The rallying point for Xerox's quality movement was the development of the 10 Series, a new family of copiers. Wayland Hicks, in charge of this development effort, stated: "The Xerox turnaround started on September 22, 1982, at the announcement of the 1075 in New York." Led by this mid-volume machine, the 10 Series became the most successful line of copiers in Xerox history, and served to restore the company's finances and morale. The series—dubbed the "Marathon" family of copiers—represented a new generation of machines aimed primarily at the mid-volume segment of the market. Altogether, 14 models were introduced between 1982 and 1986, 6 of which were still sold in 1990. Fuji Xerox designed and produced the low end models in the 10 Series—the 1020, 1035, and the 1055, the latter drawing on basic technologies developed for the FX3500. The 1075 became the first American-made product to win Japan's Grand Prize for Good Design. Because at that time Xerox's Japanese competitors were not strong in mid-volume copiers, the 10 Series forestalled their move into that segment of the market and helped Xerox win back market share. The company regained 2–3 percentage points in 1983, and 12 points in 1984. By the end of 1985, more than 750,000 10 Series machines had been rented or sold, accounting for nearly 38% of Xerox's worldwide installed base.

Throughout the 1980s, Xerox continued to change the way it did business. For example, over 100,000 employees went through three days of off-site training to unite the entire organization behind the quality effort. The program achieved significant improvements in Xerox operations. After reducing its supplier base, the company reduced its purchased parts' costs by 45% and their quality was improved dramatically. Xerox's average manufacturing costs were reduced by 20% and the time-to-market for new products was cut by 60%. Xerox's progress was recognized by the U.S. Commerce Department in 1989, when the company's Business Products and Systems division received the Malcolm Baldrige National Quality Award for its "preeminent quality leadership." (Xerox's 1971–1989 financial results are in Exhibit 5.)

Xerox and Fuji Xerox in the 1990s

The Canon Challenge   A number of factors were expected to continue to draw Fuji Xerox and Xerox closer to each other in the 1990s. One was the continuously rising capabilities of the Xerox Group's competitors, particularly Canon. While Xerox's precipitous decline in the 1970s had been stemmed and many of the competitors from that decade had faded away, Canon's copier business continued to expand. From 1980 to 1989, Canon's total sales

Exhibit 5   Key Financial Data for Xerox and Fuji Photo Film (millions of U.S. dollars except financial ratios and where noted)

	1971	1976	1981	1982	1983	1984	1985	1986	1987	1988	1989
Xerox Corporation											
Total revenues	1,954	4,515	8,180	8,073	10,463	11,400	11,994	13,287	15,108	16,441	17,635
Document processing			8,013	7,895	8,223	8,714	9,068	9,744	10,834	11,688	12,431
Financial services			167	178	2,240	2,686	2,926	3,543	4,274	4,753	5,204
Operating income	785	1,486	2,071	1,654	1,444	1,557	1,502	1,327	1,376	2,154	2,031
Net income	213	365	598	424	466	291	475	465	578	388	704
Total assets	2,250	4,959	7,674	7,668	14,064	15,154	16,838	19,050	22,450	26,441	30,088
Long-term debt	425	1,000	870	850	1,461	1,614	1,583	1,730	1,539	5,379	7,511
Stockholders' equity	1,052	2,179	3,728	3,724	4,664	4,543	4,828	5,129	5,547	5,667	6,116
R&D expenses	96	226	511	541	529	555	597	650	722	794	809
Employees (millions)	66	100	112	103	108	111	113	112	112	113	111
Earnings/Share (U.S. dollars)	2.85	4.35	6.25	4.06	4.5	3.26	3.42	4.48	5.3	3.49	6.56
Dividend/Share (U.S. dollars)	0.80	1.10	3.00	3.00	3.00	3.00	3.00	3.00	3.00	3.00	3.00
Document processing revenues as share of total	*	*	98%	98%	79%	76%	76%	73%	72%	71%	70%
Operating income/Revenue	40%	33%	25%	20%	14%	14%	13%	10%	9%	13%	12%
Operating income/Assets	35	30	27	22	10	10	9	7	6	8	7
Operating income/Equity	75	68	56	44	31	34	31	26	25	38	33
Net income/Revenue	10.9	8.1	7.3	5.3	4.5	2.6	4.0	3.5	3.8	2.4	4.0
Net income/Assets	9.5	7.4	7.8	5.5	3.3	1.9	2.8	2.4	2.6	1.5	2.3
Net income/Equity	20.2	16.8	16.0	11.4	10.0	6.4	9.8	9.1	10.4	6.8	11.5
R&D expense/Revenue	4.9	5.0	6.2	6.7	5.1	4.9	5.0	4.9	4.8	4.8	4.6
Long-term debt/Assets	19	20	11	11	10	11	9	9	7	20	25
Equity/Assets	47	44	49	49	33	30	29	27	25	21	20
Dividends/Earnings	28	25	48	74	67	92	88	67	57	86	46
Fuji Photo Film											
Total revenue							3,136	4,504	5,636	6,833	6,732
Net income							600	801	1,030	1,217	1,210
Dividends							21	30	35	41	36
Net income/Revenue							19%	18%	18%	18%	18%
Dividends/Earnings							3.5%	3.7%	3.4%	3.4%	3.0%

*Practically 100%.
Source: Company annual reports.

grew from $2.9 billion to $9.4 billion, a growth rate of 14% per year. Canon's R&D spending grew even more rapidly at 24% per year, from $77 million to $525 million. By 1989, Canon was no longer primarily a camera company—40% of its revenues came from copiers, and 20% from laser printers.

In the second half of the 1980s, Canon developed a dominating presence in the low end laser printers that were becoming ubiquitous companions to microcomputers. Laser printing technology was closely related to plain paper copying technology, and as digital copying systems were introduced, the importance of laser printing in the PPC market was bound to increase. Canon's laser printing engines were the core of the highly successful Hewlett-Packard Laserprinter series, which accounted for about 50% of laser printer sales in the United States. This OEM business was thought to yield Canon some $1 billion in revenues. In the rest of the world, Canon sold printers under its own brand name.

In copiers, Canon was strong in the low end of the market, and had recently developed a growing business in color copiers, where it held 50% of the market by 1989. Analysts pointed out that Canon was introducing twice as many products as the Xerox Group, although it spent less than $600 million on R&D annually, compared to Xerox's $800 million and Fuji Xerox's $300 million. Canon's goal was to become a $70 billion company by the year 2000, implying a 22% annual growth rate in the 1990s. A significant portion of this growth was projected to come from Xerox's heartland—high- and mid-volume copiers and printers.

Xerox, however, was determined to be aggressive in its response. Hicks, who in 1989 had become the executive vice president for worldwide marketing at Xerox, hung a framed blow-up of a 1984 *Fortune* article on Canon in his office. It was entitled "And Then We Will Attack"; below it Hicks hung a sign that read: "And Then They Will Lose."

Xerox Group strategists saw the relationship between Xerox and Fuji Xerox as a critical element in competing worldwide against Canon. Canon had a strong presence in all major world markets, as did the Xerox companies (Exhibit 6). But Xerox CEO

Paul Allaire highlighted a major difference in the two firms' global networks: "When we negotiate with Fuji Xerox, we can't just represent ourselves. We need to find what is fair and equitable to essentially three partners. Canon is 100% owned by one company."

The Fuji Xerox Challenge   Another trend drawing Fuji Xerox and Xerox closer was the growth of Fuji Xerox itself (Exhibit 7). Fuji Xerox's dollar revenues grew faster than Xerox's in the 1980s, and represented a more significant portion of the Xerox Group's worldwide revenues than it had previously. Fuji Xerox's financial contribution to Xerox's net earnings in the form of royalties and profits had also grown sharply—from 5% in 1981 to 22% in 1988. And throughout the decade, Fuji Xerox had been an important source of low end copiers for Xerox. Between 1980 and 1988, Fuji Xerox's sales to Xerox and Rank Xerox grew from $32 million to $620 million (Exhibit 8). "Fuji Xerox is a critical asset of Xerox," concluded Allaire.

Fuji Xerox developed its technological capabilities further in the 1980s, investing heavily in R&D (Exhibit 9). While it continued to rely on Xerox for basic research on new technologies, by the late 1980s very few of the models sold by Fuji Xerox in Japan had been designed by Xerox (Exhibit 10). For the most part, they were high-end models, working at speeds of above 120 cpm. Heavy investment by Fuji Xerox during the late 1980s had produced many low end models, and even a few in the 60–90 cpm range. Many of these were exported to or manufactured by Xerox and Rank Xerox. In 1980, 70% of the low-volume units sold by Xerox and Rank Xerox were of their own design, and 30% were of Fuji Xerox design; by 1987, 94% were of Fuji Xerox design. Even in 1989, however, all of Xerox and Rank Xerox's mid- and high-volume copiers were of their own design.

All these factors led Fuji Xerox and Xerox to intensify their cooperation on research, product development, manufacturing, and planning in the 1980s. Bill Glavin and Jeff Kennard worked together to launch "strategy summits." Glavin

Exhibit 6   Global Configuration of Xerox Group and Canon in 1989

	United States	Japan	Western Europe	Other
Share of world GNP	26%	14%	21% (4 largest countries)	39%
Share of world PPC market (units)	33%	20%	34%	14%

Xerox Group

	United States	Japan	Europe	Americas
Revenues	$6.6 billion	$3.5 billion	$4.0 billion	$1.7 billion
Employees	54,000	19,600	29,000	16,000
Production:				
PPC	149,000	180,000	176,400	39,100
Printers	15,000	60,000	15,700	—
Systems	8,000	18,000	1,900	—
Faxes	—	95,000	—	—
Percent of market (units):				
PPCs	15%	22%	12%	
R&D centers	2	1	1	1
Alliances	—	Fuji Photo Film	Rank Organization	

Canon

	North America	Japan	Europe	Other
Revenues	$2.9 billion	$2.9 billion	$2.9 billion	
Employees	4,500	27,500	6,500	
Production:				
PPC	60,000	700,000	370,000	
Other	Laser printers and engines	Cameras, printers		Cameras in China
Percent of market (units):				
PPCs	23%	26%	23%	
Laserprinting	70			
Color PPCs	50			
R&D centers	0	1	0	
Alliances	HP ($1B OEM) Kodak, NeXT	—	Olivetti	

Source: Xerox and industry sources.

described why:

> We needed the senior management of research, engineering, manufacturing, and planning from both companies to come together, and begin discussing the issues that affected them jointly. The talks included people from all product lines—copiers, printers, and systems. We tried to agree on common strategies and allocate who should do what.

These top management summits were held about twice a year during the 1980s, and led to further meetings between the functional organizations on each side. Fuji Xerox's organization mirrored Xerox's: A corporate research group did basic and applied research; machines were designed and built by the development and manufacturing organization; and products were sold and serviced by

Exhibit 7 Key Financial Data for Fuji Xerox (millions of U.S. dollars at yearly average exchange rates, except financial ratios and where noted)

	1971	1976	1981	1982	1983	1984	1985	1986	1987	1988	1989
Revenues	107	307	872	962	1,111	1,282	1,456	2,303	2,955	3,570	3,554
Operating expenses	79	259	754	813	970	1,125	1,304	2,093	2,673	3,197	3,180
R&D	—	13	49	47	84	109	117	151	194	242	292
S, G, and A	38	119	308	333	399	443	507	801	1,041	1,296	1,324
Operating income	27	47	117	150	141	157	152	210	282	373	374
Net income	10	17	46	50	56	61	59	71	106	173	162
Total assets	176	405	897	931	1,046	1,199	1,276	1,883	2,457	3,186	3,093
Total equity	49	121	324	325	388	440	487	744	959	1,237	1,285
Retained earnings	33	84	270	277	338	390	439	680	885	1,154	1,131
Depreciation and amortization	16	63	131	113	130	155	153	218	266	271	278
Capital expenditure	65	64	196	178	230	217	244	296	284	297	512
Employees (thousands)	4.9	7.7	9.8	11.3	12.6	13.9	15.1	16.5	17.2	18.0	19.6
Dividends paid out	1	7	9	8	8	8	8	12	14	18	30
Financial Ratios											
Operating income/Revenues	25%	15%	13%	16%	13%	12%	10%	9%	10%	10%	11%
Operating income/Assets	15	12	13	16	13	13	12	11	11	12	12
Net income/Revenues	9.1	5.6	5.3	5.2	9.1	4.8	4.1	3.1	3.6	4.9	4.5
Net income/Assets	5.5	4.3	5.1	5.3	5.4	5.1	4.6	3.7	4.3	5.4	5.2
Net income/Equity	19.9	14.3	14.2	15.3	14.6	13.8	12.2	9.5	11.1	14.0	12.6
R&D expense/Revenues	—	4.4	5.6	4.9	7.6	8.5	8.0	6.5	6.6	6.8	8.2
Capital expenditure/Revenues	61.2	20.9	22.5	18.5	20.7	16.9	16.8	12.9	9.6	8.3	14.4
Total equity/Assets	28	30	36	35	37	37	38	40	39	39	42
Dividends paid/Total equity	1.6	6	3	2	2	2	2	2	1	1	2
Dividends/Earnings	8.2	41	20	16	14	13	14	17	13	10	19
Average exchange rate (yen per U.S. dollar)	348	297	221	249	238	238	239	169	145	128	138

Note: Fiscal year ending October 20.
Source: Fuji Xerox annual reports; exchange rate from the IMF.

Exhibit 8 Intra-Firm and Bilateral Trade in Copiers

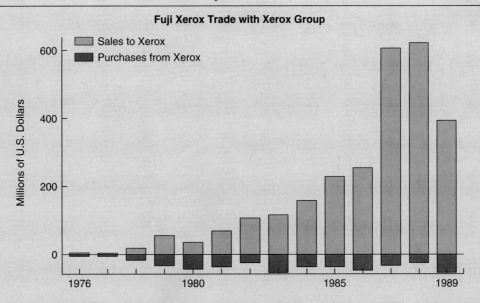

Fuji Xerox Trade with Xerox Group

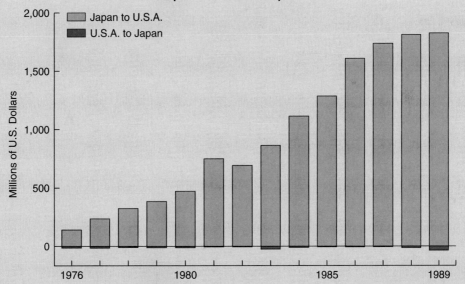

Japan–U.S. Trade in Copiers

Notes: Top: Includes finished machines, parts, and knock-down kits. Bottom: Includes copiers (SITC 75182) and copier parts and accessories (SITC 75919).

Source: Fuji Xerox annual report; and United Nations, *SITC Trade Data Base.*

Exhibit 9   Fuji Xerox Technology Spending and Receipts, 1968–1989

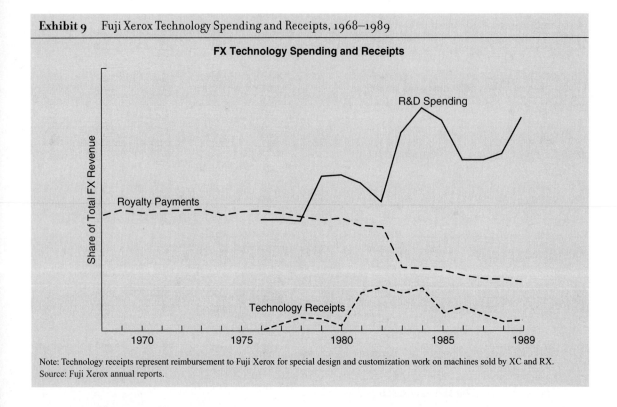

Note: Technology receipts represent reimbursement to Fuji Xerox for special design and customization work on machines sold by XC and RX.
Source: Fuji Xerox annual reports.

the marketing organization. Collaboration between Xerox and Fuji Xerox seemed to be most successful in research, and harder to implement in development and manufacturing; there was no coordination at all between marketing groups, as each had a different licensed territory. Of course, there was some tendency to protect traditional turfs. "On both sides you cannot totally dismiss the NIH syndrome," commented Tony Kobayashi. "It is another form of parochialism." Still, where the incentives for collaboration were high, the companies launched joint projects, agreeing on who would take "lead" and "support" roles and eliminating overlapping activities. Bill Spencer, Xerox vice president of technology at the time, described the rationale behind one of these joint research projects:

It is an attempt to combine American ingenuity with the manufacturing skills of the Japanese. Xerox has excellent basic research and software capabilities, and

Fuji Xerox is good at development and hardware design. Together, we should be able to develop better products quicker than alone.

The functional collaboration between the companies was reinforced by exchanges of personnel and by an evolving communication process. Since the 1970s, personnel from Fuji Xerox had spent time as residents at Xerox and engineers from both companies had frequently crossed the Pacific to provide on-the-spot assistance. These personnel ex-changes had, in fact, been an important channel for the transfer of technology from Xerox to Fuji Xerox. By 1989, an estimated 1,000 young, high-potential FX employees had spent three years each as residents at Xerox, and some 150 Xerox people had done this at Fuji Xerox. These residents were directly involved in the work of their host companies. Every year there were also some 1,000 shorter visits by engineers and managers. These exchanges

Exhibit 10   Growth of Fuji Xerox's Technical Capabilities, 1970–1989

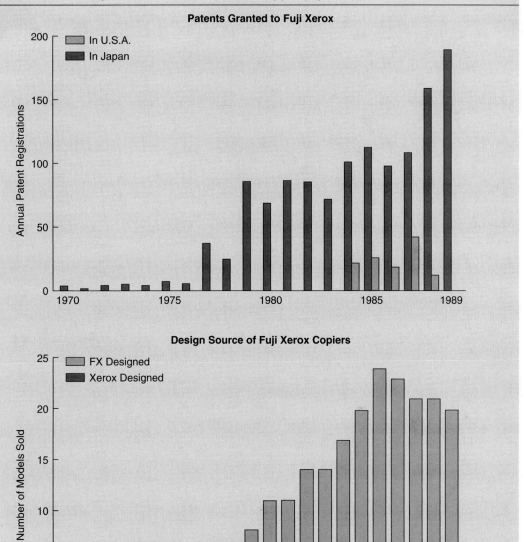

Notes: Top: Utility models included in Japan. Bottom: Based on product introductions, assuming that every product has a commercial life of four years.
Source: Fuji Xerox.

and the summit meetings contributed to a constructive relationship. "Whenever a problem came up, we established a process to manage it," explained Jeff Kennard. "The trust built up between the companies has been a key factor in the success of this relationship. It enables one to take on short-term costs in the interest of long-term gains for the group."

By the mid-1980s, most Xerox managers also had mixed feelings of challenge and admiration toward Fuji Xerox, which were echoed by Kennard:

> It seems that every time Xerox blinks and retracts, Fuji Xerox forges ahead. Fuji Xerox continues to be the agent for change. They have great corporate vision and they target what is strategically important. Then they take tough decisions and make the needed investment.

The Management Challenge   In this context, Allaire and Kobayashi commissioned the Codestiny III Task Force, charging it with developing a framework for cooperation between the two companies in the 1990s. The task force consisted of top planners in each company and was to report to the two CEOs within a year of its formation. Roger Levien, Xerox's vice president for strategy and head of the Codestiny III talks, described the motivation for the project:

> Fuji Xerox had certain issues they wanted to discuss, and we agreed to do so in the Codestiny process. One of their desires was to get the worldwide market for the low end. They also wanted to develop a more symmetric relationship with us. We wanted to spell everything out, identify all of the alternatives, and leave the final decision to top management.

One of the issues to be addressed by the Codestiny team was Fuji Xerox's aspirations to expand its markets in Asia. Under the existing technology licensing contracts, Fuji Xerox had the right to sell in Indonesia, South Korea, the Philippines, Taiwan, and Thailand (total GDP in 1989: $570 billion), and it had indeed established sales subsidiaries in each of these markets. But Rank Xerox in London was responsible for managing sales in what it called the South Pacific Operations— Australia (1989 GDP: $280 billion), New Zealand ($45 billion), Singapore ($28 billion), Malaysia ($37 billion), China ($420 billion), and Hong Kong ($63 billion). Since the early 1980s, Fuji Xerox had

argued that this arrangement led to inefficiencies in serving the South Pacific markets. At that time, knock-down kits were sometimes shipped from Fuji Xerox to Britain for assembly, and then shipped back to Asia for sale. Furthermore, Rank Xerox followed a very different marketing strategy in these markets than Fuji Xerox did in its neighboring Asian markets. Rank Xerox emphasized high profit margins and sales of high-end machines, whereas Fuji Xerox put greater emphasis on market share and low-end products. As a result, when Fuji Xerox urged Rank Xerox in the late 1970s to adopt a more aggressive sales strategy in Australia before Canon entered that market, Rank Xerox refused. Although Rank Xerox managed the South Pacific countries out of a regional office in Hong Kong, Fuji Xerox's sales subsidiaries were usually joint ventures with local partners, and so drew more on local management talent.

Another key issue for the Codestiny team was how the Xerox Group should manage the low-end laser printer business in the United States. This market segment was receiving renewed attention in 1989, following the appointment of Bill Lowe as Xerox's executive vice president for development and manufacturing. Lowe came to Xerox from IBM, where he had been in charge of the personal computer business. Soon after arriving at Xerox, he began to focus on the problems in the low end copier and printer businesses, where Fuji Xerox typically developed and manufactured products sold by Xerox.

> Both companies were trying to get full profit out of it, even though the margins were slim. Fuji Xerox's policy was to mark up costs; Xerox's was to get an acceptable gross profit. Furthermore, each product had a different mark-up scheme, and many sideline deals confounded the issues. This fostered sharp dealings between the partners. So, most of our energy was focussed on each other, not on Canon. We were pointing fingers and frustrating ourselves.

The Codestiny team analyzed these specific issues within a broad framework, and began by outlining the various options available for cooperation in marketing, research, and development and manufacturing (Exhibit 11). The team considered the

Exhibit 11   Relationship Options Identified by Codestiny Task Force

Marketing

A. Independent and overlapping

Act as two separate companies serving the world market, with some coordination on business direction and strategy. No geographic constraints.

B. Independent and separate

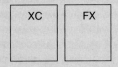

Concentrate efforts on licensed territories for core products, with multinational business as required.

C. Separate with exceptions

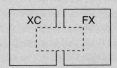

Same as B, but with joint or overlapping activities across territorial boundaries on case-by-case basis.

D. Coordinated global product mandates

Worldwide and exclusive responsibility for products or product ranges manufactured under special licenses.

Research

A. Independent

Each pursues own interest and becomes self-sufficient.

B. Coordinated

Coordinated group research programs of XC and FX, with both self-sufficiency and overlap.

C. Joint

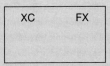

Single research organization without overlap.

D. Complementary

Separate organizations operating on exclusive products.

(continued)

Exhibit 11   *(concluded)*

Development and Manufacturing

A. Independent

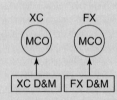

Each development and manufacturing (D&M) organization supplies its own marketing organization (MCO).

B. Complementary without overlap

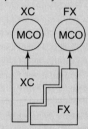

Assign development roles to each organization, with no overlap allowed in development projects.

C. Complementary with overlap

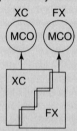

Same as B, but with overlap in development projects.

D. Joint

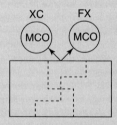

Single development and manufacturing organization with individual projects targeted to needs of separate marketing organizations.

Source: Compiled from Xerox documents.

advantages and disadvantages of each of these options and began to develop possible strategies for the South Pacific Operations and for the low end printer business in the United States.

But there was much more at stake than decisions in these two areas. The central question facing Xerox and Fuji Xerox was: How should the relationship between the two companies be structured and managed in the new global environment of the 1990s?

Case 6-2   Renault/Nissan: The Making of a Global Alliance

▌Renault's Point of View

Geneva, March 3, 1999. International Motor Show   As a traditional get-together for the leading automobile manufacturers, the Geneva International Motor Show provides an opportunity to unveil new prototypes and gauge market trends. This year, however, conversations in the main hall of the exhibition focused as much on the strategic movements of international companies as on products. For since the start of the year, major manœuvres had been under way to form an alliance with Nissan, Japan's second-biggest manufacturer, and they had to be finalised before March 30, which marks the end of the tax year in Japan.

Two candidates were in the ring. In one corner, the French group Renault, the world's ninth-largest manufacturer with 4.3% of the market, which had been negotiating with Nissan for more than 10 months; in the other, German-American giant DaimlerChrysler, the fifth-largest manufacturer with 8.4% of the world market, which began taking an interest in December 1998.

▌ The cases were written by:

▌ **Renault's point of view:** Olivier Masclef, Doctoral Students; EM Lyon.

▌ **Nissan's point of view:** LBS MBA students Naoko Hida and Ashok Krishnan (FT-2000), under the joint supervision of Professor Asakawa of Keio Business School, Professor Gomez of Lyon Business School and Professor Korine of London Business School. The financial support of the Strategic Leadership Research Programme at LBS, the *"Rodolphe Mérieux"* Foundation for Research in Venturing at EM Lyon, and overseas case development fund at Keio Business School are gratefully acknowledged.

▌ The cases are based on interviews conducted in Paris and Tokyo during the Spring of 2000 with the following executives:

▌ **Renault's point of view:** MM. Dassas *VP, finance* De Andria *VP, corporate planning,* Douin *EVP, Alliance coordinator* Husson *VP, legal* Levy *EVP, finance* Schweitzer *Chairman and CEO.*

▌ **Nissan's point of view:** MM. Anraku, *managing director in charge of finance and accounting* Shiga, Sugino, Suzuki, *Nissan Corporate Planning,* Hanawa *Chairman and CEO.*

For Renault, it was a difficult bout. For a start, DaimlerChrysler's financial clout made it the favourite. Second, Renault's previous attempt to form such an alliance, with Swedish manufacturer Volvo six years earlier, had ended in a resounding defeat after years of negotiations. Daimler and Chrysler, on the other hand, had just rocked the automobile sector by pulling off a spectacular merger less than a year earlier. And an alliance with an Asian partner seemed a vital part of Daimler-Chrysler's international strategy to complete the consolidation of a company with a strong presence in all three of the world's major economic centres.

Tension mounted with the arrival in Geneva of Jürgen Schremp, Co-Chairman of DaimlerChrysler, and Louis Schweitzer, Chairman and C.E.O. of the Renault Group. Everyone was certain that the future of Nissan would be decided in the days to come. Most economic observers were expecting to see a new giant formed: DaimlerChrysler-Nissan.

But Renault's bosses were convinced that the struggle was not yet over. Looking beyond superficial reasoning, they felt that the potential synergies between Renault and Nissan were greater than those between DaimlerChrysler and Nissan because they did not simply concern commercial and technological issues. Despite the size difference between the two rivals, Renault did have some noteworthy advantages. Was it a question of personal conviction or objective reasons? While only a few days were left to convince the Nissan executives, the force of Renault's arguments and the ability to communicate them had already been established by the relationship built up by the company's teams of negotiators over several months.

Renault's Strategic Alternative   In the spring of 1997, Georges Douin, Executive Vice President in charge of corporate strategy, had submitted an international development plan to Renault's

Management Committee, at the request of Louis Schweitzer. Major changes were taking place on the world automobile stage. A round of large-scale mergers had begun, with Volkswagen AG taking the initiative in Europe, but now the Asian slow-down called the Japanese car companies' potential into question, particularly regarding finance. New opportunities for international cooperation began to take shape. The shift towards the globalisation of the industry looked irreversible.

Against this background, the plan referred to the strengths and weaknesses of the Renault group, as well as its prospects for expansion. The company could choose between remaining a significant but restricted player in the European market, with a share of around 5% of the world market, or become a major player helping to define the rules of the game, which would mean winning 10% of market share worldwide and extending its product range. The second choice would mean a strategy of alliances with partners in the other main economic regions.

The collapse of a recently attempted merger with the Swedish group Volvo in 1993 had left its mark on the company. The operation, which had been the subject of extremely careful negotiations between February 1990 and December 1993, had been based on shared synergies between the two companies. It formed part of European industrial policy, and was encouraged by the authorities because Renault was owned by the French state. The industry minister had played a part in the negotiations and brought the country's political influence into the balance. Both partners were Europeans, with relatively close national cultures. After a long period of rapprochement, it was expected that Renault and Volvo would merge. The matter appeared to have been finalised when, in December 1993, Volvo shareholders voted against the agreement.

> "Our partner did not appreciate the strong involvement of the French state. For our part, there was also a lack of diplomacy and an over-eagerness to take control." (Mr Dassas, VP, Financial Operations)

So the merger never took place. Renault found itself thrown back five years in the race to gain international stature. As time went by, the need to come up with an alliance policy became more pressing. The plan put forward by Georges Douin stressed the need for the firm to position itself chiefly in the Asian market. One scenario introduced some potential partners, including Subaru, Mitsubishi, Suzuki and Nissan. Apart from Nissan, they were all smaller than Renault and therefore appeared to be within its reach, especially as the company had been privatised in 1996 and the French state now had only a 46% stake. Attitudes in France had changed significantly and the separation of political and economic influences was the order of the day. Renault could therefore count on its shareholders to give the management a totally free hand to implement its chosen strategy.

Louis Schweitzer weighed up the dangers and difficulties of the strategic choice that had to be made. Staying European meant condemning the company to obey the market rules imposed by the biggest firms, with perhaps a loss of independence in the long term due to inadequate resources. But failing once more to form an international alliance would be disastrous for Renault's credibility, not to mention the wasted effort and strategic and financial losses involved. Time was running out because opportunities for alliances were bound to become increasingly infrequent and hard to negotiate. The chairman made a decision: Renault's expansion would be international and would include an alliance in Asia. The plan was approved. But how should Renault set about finding the right partner?

Patient Prospecting   Renault had been keeping a close watch on the Asian market since the mid-1980s. Although it had not yet worked out an alliance policy, the group was monitoring opportunities and familiarising itself both with the Asian motor industry and with Asian negotiating methods. One man embodies that policy: Georges Douin, first as technical director, then as the person in charge of orchestrating Renault Group projects from 1992 to 1997. He is currently EVP, Product & Strategic Planning and International Operations.

"We must be constantly on the alert (. . .). It's true that the Renault-Nissan negotiations were brought to a conclusion in nine months—they took place between June 1998 and April 1999—but in fact they were based on a great deal of work behind the scenes by Renault, which was a pioneer in the field, as well as on a solid foundation of relations with the Japanese." (Georges Douin, EVP)

Between 1985 and 1995, therefore, contacts were occasional but continual. In 1987 Renault planned a research programme on diesel engines with Honda which never came to fruition. New relations were established in 1995 on other joint research projects. Around the same time talks were held with the Korean companies Daewoo and Samsung. Like the Japanese, the Korean companies were looking for ways to penetrate the European market, which was protected by quotas restricting imports of Asian vehicles, by forming alliances with local manufacturers. One particularly clear opportunity presented itself in 1993. One of the issues on the table during the ongoing talks between Volvo and Renault was what would happen to Volvo's partner Mitsubishi. The Renault teams, led by Georges Douin, went to Japan to evaluate potential synergies with the Japanese company, in what was a fresh opportunity to understand how the country's businesses worked and to make contacts with their executives.

"In the proposed alliance with Volvo, part of the Volvo "package," was Mitsubishi (. . .) I went to see them several times. They quickly took the decision to buy some Renault engines—that made our relations easier too—we sold diesel engines to Mitsubishi, we sold them gearboxes (. . .). So I was 'very Mitsubishi'" (Georges Douin, EVP)

However, relations with Mitsubishi were interrupted by the failure of the Renault-Volvo merger. Further contacts were made in 1996, with the Korean company Daewoo. All the possible synergies were discussed as well, but the talks ended abruptly after four months.

So Asia and Japan were not totally unknown territory to Renault when its international development plan was introduced. It was already familiar with the industry, and personal ties had been forged with its leaders. But restricted projects and continual failures showed that Asia was still a difficult market for European manufacturers to enter. Had Renault's strategic monitoring allowed it to build up sufficient experience for it to grasp the opportunity of an alliance when the time was right?

An Unexpected Hunt   After the international strategic plan was approved, a Renault delegation began to canvass Japanese companies in April 1998.

"I had been on an assignment to meet Japanese banks, and even Japanese motor industry analysts, to see how things were going for the country's manufacturers. I had seen four or five big international banks and met with automobile specialists (. . .). It was an exploratory mission, to see how many problems the Japanese motor industry had . . . and which Japanese manufacturers were most likely to be interested in alliances." (Mr Dassas, VP, Financial Operations)

Some Japanese manufacturers could be eliminated as potential partners very quickly. General Motors has a large stake in Suzuki, and Subaru offered few opportunities for synergies because of its technological originality. After the assignment, two companies stood out as the most likely candidates for an alliance: Mitsubishi and Nissan. Georges Douin went to Japan to look further into the opportunities for working with the two manufacturers. Mitsubishi looked like the favourite because of its size and its previous cooperation with Renault during the Volvo episode. Nissan seemed too big to be a potential partner. Nonetheless, the Renault delegation members were struck by the attentiveness of the Japanese representatives and the interest they showed for cooperating with the French.

"It was Renault that took the initiative of contacting them, which produced the very positive reaction that in a way surprised us at first (. . .). The surprise was to see that Nissan was perfectly willing to start talks with us." (Mr De Andria, VP, Strategic Planning)

So the names of the two potential partners were put to Mr Schweitzer. At around the same time, a major piece of news broke in the automobile industry: the merger between Daimler-Benz and Chrysler.

"Obviously, we were surprised by the Daimler-Chrysler merger in April-May 1998. Mr Schweitzer learned it from the press" (Georges Douin, EVP). "Daimler-Chrysler was a major shake-up. And it was against that background that the alliance was formed" (Mr De Andria, VP, Strategic Planning). "Daimler-Chrysler was a shock in the automobile world, especially in France. We were aware that things were moving very quickly and that there were no taboos any more." (Mr Husson, VP, General Counsel)

The deal meant that globalisation suddenly speeded up, and therefore the need to make or grasp the best opportunities very quickly. In June 1998 DaimlerChrysler started negotiating with Nissan with a view to taking over the group's truck division, Nissan Diesel. Meanwhile, Louis Schweitzer wrote to the chairmen of Mitsubishi and Nissan outlining the terms of a possible partnership between Renault and each company.

"In June I wrote a letter saying *'I believe we should be thinking strategically. Can we do that together?'* Obviously, before writing that I had decided to take action should the opportunity present itself. I was ready to reach agreement on a system along the lines of the one we ended up with, in other words acquisition of a stake in the other company, and possibly a reciprocal one, which would not lead to a complete merger." (Louis Schweitzer, Chairman)

While Mitsubishi took a long time to get back to Renault, Nissan reacted quickly.

"Bankers came to see us saying: 'We know someone who can talk to someone who can talk to someone who can talk to Nissan, so we might be able to establish a relationship between you and Nissan in a few months. But of course if you write to them, that's the best way to make sure of failure because it's unthinkable, it simply isn't done.' Well, I wrote to Hanawa in June and he answered in July." (Louis Schweitzer, Chairman)

Straight away, a French delegation was sent to Japan to draw up a shopping list. At the end of July, Louis Schweitzer met Nissan's chairman, Yoshikazu Hanawa, in Tokyo. A relationship of trust was quickly established between the two men.

"Mr Schweitzer and Mr Hanawa learned to trust each other very quickly. I think that this trust between the chairmen has lasted all the way through, with no stumbling blocks, deviations or betrayals" (Georges Douin, EVP). "There was a sort of mutual respect and complementarity between Hanawa and Schweitzer. Those are very important factors. The first handshake decides everything." (Mr Husson, VP, General Counsel). "I think they [the Japanese] greatly appreciated Mr Schweitzer's style. An article published in the Japanese press commented: *'But it's incredible! We've found a boss in the automobile sector who isn't a brute!'*" (Mr Dassas, Finance Director)

In July and August the two companies pinpointed about 20 potential opportunities for joint synergies: geographical distribution of their markets, complementarity of their product ranges and the possibility of sharing common platforms. Matters moved quickly enough for the chairmen to sign a memorandum on September 10 concerning the financial evaluation and joint costing of those synergies with a view to a possible strategic alliance. At the same time, Louis Schweitzer decided to make no further approaches to the Mitsubishi group.

"I described that once in an interview by saying that we went hunting for rabbits and we found a deer." (Mr De Andria, VP, Strategic Planning)

The planned alliance concerned only Nissan Motors, Nissan's automobile division, and an exclusive negotiation clause until the end of December 1998 was included in the memorandum. Amid the greatest secrecy, the two companies started a campaign to pinpoint and cost cooperation opportunities. At Renault, the campaign was given the code name *Operation Pacific*.

But could the French company ensure rapid success with its new partner after failing with a better known and culturally closer potential partner like Volvo?

Operation Pacific   Twenty Franco-Japanese teams were given the task of evaluating the main issues that would shape an alliance between Renault and Nissan. The process, which lasted until November

1998, took the form of a series of joint studies. The team leaders were chosen from the company that had the most experience of the subject being studied. In all, about 100 people from each company were involved. The joint studies played a fundamental role in creating a climate of confidence at the grass roots between the two manufacturers. Two main types of issue emerged rapidly.

The first was the question of synergies. In this respect, Renault gradually discovered that the situation was exceptionally promising, surpassing its expectations. First of all the companies' product ranges were extremely complementary. Renault was ahead of the field in mid-range cars and light commercial vehicles, while Nissan Motors specialised in mid-range vehicles and the four-wheel-drive vehicles and pickups typical of the American light commercial vehicles market, in which Renault was not represented. The outlook was equally good on a geographical level. Renault was firmly established in Western Europe and South America, while Nissan had the strongest foothold in North and Central America, Asia, Japan and Africa. In terms of expertise, Renault had achieved excellent cost control, formalised a global strategy for platforms and purchasing, and was known for designing vehicles of innovative style and appearance. Nissan stood out more through its quality control, R&D programmes and technology.

Between September and December the two companies evaluated synergies, assessed their financial value and the technical feasibility of working together more closely. The French and Japanese teams exchanged information about their know-how, expertise and projects. Their work showed that the potential synergies should yield, on paper, savings of 51.5 million euros in 2000, 1 billion euros in 2001 and 1.5 billion euros in 2002 through the rationalisation of platforms and a joint purchasing and distribution policy.

"It was extraordinary in terms of synergies. We really believed in it, or at least those taking part in the negotiations did. . . . Quite frankly, we were so complementary in terms of geography, products, personality (. . .). So we had great confidence. The maps of where we were established were completely different (. . .) Their products are of extraordinarily high quality. Two of the best factories in the world belong to Nissan, one in England and one in the United States (. . .). Our engineers were full of admiration for Nissan's manufacturing processes." (Mr Dassas, VP, Financial Operations)

Nonetheless, although the industrial outlook was promising, the same could not be said of organisational matters. In 1998 Nissan Motors was a company with major financial problems. A succession of years showing losses had left the company with total debts of 23 billion euros and a list of annual repayments that was becoming increasingly difficult to respect. The reason was a complex combination of internal management problems: Nissan headed a Keiretsu which had been built up gradually over the years. The company had never established a rational purchasing policy or system of relations with suppliers. Manufacturing costs were high and its product range was too diverse. Quality came at a high price. Moreover, Nissan's global market share had slumped from 6.4% in 1990 to 4.9% in 1998.

Engineering culture took precedence over managerial culture, while the quest for performance and quality won out over costing. Promotion was based entirely on length of service. Apparently, Mr Hanawa was acutely aware that the company was heading towards bankruptcy. He set a symbolic date, March 30, 1999, as a deadline. It was the end of the Japanese financial year, when short-term credit lines were to be renegotiated.

"That seemed to me both highly artificial and extremely useful. Artificial because it was tied in with the end of the fiscal year, and the end of the fiscal year only exists on the day accounts are published. So it seemed to me a completely artificial deadline (. . .). But it was useful because, in any negotiations, failure to set a deadline has many disadvantages because the talks may drag on and on (. . .). Nissan's rating was a subject that Mr Hanawa brought up frequently." (Louis Schweitzer, Chairman) "They were afraid that their Japanese rating would fall too. Now that would have been a disaster because they could not have coped with the resulting increase in their expenses." (M. Dassas, VP, Financial Operations)

Such a decline would have meant official recognition of the company's ailing finances. So Nissan found itself in the paradoxical situation of being justly proud of its products and technological capacity while sustaining financial losses that could lead to its collapse or to it falling into the hands of a competitor. The need to "save face," a basic requirement in the balance of Japanese company relations, was one of the keys to understanding the negotiations.

Nissan had to join forces with a partner which would bail it out financially in the short term, on condition that this went along with sufficient restructuring to reorganise the production system, purchasing policy and its Keiretsu generally so that the company would remain competitive on a world scale.

> "The Japanese executives had understood that, looking more closely, Renault's expertise included a number of complementary factors that would be easier to implement than those with Daimler. In other words, the restructuring processes that we introduced, Renault's expertise in cost reduction, purchasing, production sites, engineering, services . . . And probably Renault's expertise in marketing and product innovation too. . . . Those factors counterbalanced the fact that the DaimlerChrysler group may have looked stronger financially on the surface but . . . Renault could really help Nissan to find the way out of its difficulties. . . . When the Japanese said that it was better to learn to catch fish than to be given them, I think that was what they meant. Without a doubt, Daimler was in a position to be able to give them fish, but there was no guarantee that they would teach them to catch their own. Renault was more likely to teach them the art of fishing." (Mr Lévy, EVP)

Japanese-style corporate governance tends to water down the responsibility of individual managers into a system of collective responsibility. It is difficult in such circumstances to define strategies through which the managers would have to call themselves into question.

> "There were no decision-makers outside Nissan. Identifying the person who made a decision was extremely difficult. Because we've all read the literature that says a Japanese company is managed collectively, that the Board of Directors has 37 members (. . .). But, when you come down to it, why would an independent company bigger than Renault enter an agreement under which it became equal to Renault, at most? In a way, it meant acknowledging a need that is not natural for any kind of management." (Louis Schweitzer, Chairman)

Did Renault have sufficient credibility to face not just the industrial challenge but also the financial and managerial challenge at Nissan?

The Big Picture: Pass or Fail   While the French negotiators were surprised by the quality of the relationship that was being built with their opposite numbers at Nissan and by the speed with which talks on manufacturing issues were progressing, the French were also perfectly aware of their handicaps. They pinpointed three main ones: Renault's lack of a strong image in Japan, its low capital compared to Nissan and its history as a public-sector company with large financial deficits.

As a mainly European company, Renault was little known on the Japanese market. This meant that the acquisition of Japan's second-biggest company by an unknown French firm would not give Nissan's partners the impression of a prestigious alliance, which might have made up for the humiliation of being bought by a foreigner. Moreover, Renault's financial position would not enable it to wipe out the Japanese manufacturer's debts. Its participation could only be partial and would have to be accompanied by firm guarantees about Nissan's ability to rebalance its books. The danger was that Nissan's deficit might also drag Renault into the red after the spectacular economic recovery of the previous ten years. Breaking with its past as a public company, Renault had modernised production, rationalised its purchasing network and become one of the world's most efficient manufacturers. Its ultra-modern research centre just outside Paris was a potent symbol of its capacity for innovation. Going further, one man was a symbol of that economic rationalisation policy: Carlos Ghosn, who was EVP at the time of the negotiations. His reputation as a 'cost killer' highlighted both the radical financial modernisation of Renault and the attention the company paid to staying on a sound footing. In those circumstances, an alliance with a partner whose Keiretsu-style organisation and cost management was the opposite of Renault's did not look promising.

Very early on, in October 1998, Mr Schweitzer had a clear view of the feasibility of the alliance between Renault and Nissan. He felt it had to be based on two principles over which there could be no compromise: equal status and participation in management.

> "We had to move closer strategically, but it could not be a simple acquisition or a merger, because a Franco-Japanese merger is no easy matter." (. . .) "I suggested to him [Mr Hanawa] that three people from Renault should become members of the Nissan Board of Directors: the COO, the VP Product Planning and the Deputy Chief Financial Officer. (. . .) I told Ghosn: *"I won't do this deal if you don't go to Japan!"* Before proposing the COO position, I had to have someone (. . .). In my opinion, I didn't have anyone else who could do the job." (Louis Schweitzer, Chairman)

Mr Schweitzer waited for the right moment to talk about his idea to Mr Hanawa. At the end of October, the two men discussed a draft for what might become Renault's letter of intent at the end of the negotiating period.

> "Well, they don't really understand what a COO is because there's no such thing in Japan. There's no word in Japanese to describe a COO. But there were no talks about that. I only asked for those three, I didn't ask for any other jobs except those three and he [Mr Hanawa] didn't try to argue about any of them." (Louis Schweitzer, Chairman)

However, the entire Nissan management still had to be convinced that only an alliance offering a global solution to its problems was feasible and that this could only be concluded on the basis of the principles put forward by Renault. So far the joint studies had done a considerable amount of work in the field to establish trust between the teams. But the strategic negotiations had only involved a few people at Nissan: Mr Hanawa and the three corporate planning executives, Mr Shiga, Mr Suzuki and Mr Sugino.

> "Mr Hanawa talked to me, but I don't know how he managed to achieve a consensus at Nissan (. . .). Throughout my negotiations with Nissan, I never knew who was 'for' and who was 'against,' and I never knew who made the decisions." (Louis Schweitzer, Chairman)

It was agreed that the French would submit the outlines of a proposed capital alliance to the Nissan Management Committee. This was Operation Big Picture. In Tokyo, on November 11, 1998, Louis Schweitzer, Georges Douin and Carlos Ghosn spent three hours explaining their strategic outlook, Nissan's need for an alliance and the conditions for it to succeed, and describing at length the stages of Renault's recovery in earlier years. They felt that it was a decisive moment because they were revealing the situation quite openly, and it was not favourable to the Japanese.

> "It shook them up quite a bit, obviously, because we were showing them that they had rather too many factories, rather too many employees and rather too many business activities in rather too many difficult areas (. . .). They were shocked that anyone outside the company should be speaking to them so frankly. At the time we were afraid that our approach might cause a breakdown in the talks because they seemed so affected" (Mr De Andria, VP, Strategic Planning). "By that point, I was perspiring heavily! I really felt that we had plunged headlong into an attitude of arrogance" (Louis Schweitzer, Chairman). "We knew we were playing with fire. We had the growing impression of being on slippery ground, not to say enemy territory (. . .). We weren't at all sure we could pull it off—that was certain." (Mr Douin, Vice-Chairman)

As agreed earlier, no discussion followed the case put forward by the French, and the two sides took their leave in silence. The Japanese had until the end of December before the exclusive negotiating period ran out to reach a conclusion about the strategic viewpoint defended by Renault.

Tokyo, December 23, 1998. Renault's official letter of intent defining the general conditions of the alliance was due to be discussed when a sudden new development occurred. Behind the scenes, Mr Hanawa warned his French counterpart that Renault's proposal had to cover all Nissan's business activities—not just Nissan Motors but also Nissan Diesel. Until then only the automobile division had been mentioned and Renault knew nothing about the trucks division. And for the final round of negotiations aimed at reaching agreement on an alliance in March 1999, Renault's exclusivity clause was not renewed.

A new player had come on the scene: Daimler-Chrysler. Had the Japanese understood only too well the lesson they had been given by the French?

Competition for an Alliance   DaimlerChrysler had been negotiating the acquisition of Nissan Diesel since June. The loss-making Japanese trucks subsidiary was in a critical condition which is why, after months of evaluation, the German-American group suggested taking over the entire Nissan group, acquiring a majority stake in the company. The financial soundness and prestige of Daimler-Chrysler could solve Nissan's problems and ensure that its absorption by an international company controlled by the German Daimler-Benz was accepted by the Japanese.

The French did not change their stand in any respect. They maintained their proposal for an equal alliance that would guarantee Nissan's independence and give Renault a 36% stake in the group. They stressed their proposed involvement in restructuring Nissan's management, and their experience in that area, and agreed without hesitation that Nissan Diesel would be included in the deal.

"Keeping 40% of Nissan Diesel raised a number of problems for us so what we did was this: we told them Nissan Motors): *'We're going to buy from you part of your share of Nissan Diesel so that we own 22.5% each.'* This had the advantage of being a simple financial holding for Renault (. . .), and secondly it also prevented us from having to consolidate a larger stake in our accounts. It was a shrewd piece of accounting." (Mr Lévy, EVP)

The due diligence period began in January 1999. It was difficult because the French did not know what was being negotiated with DaimlerChrysler, so their hopes fluctuated. The Renault teams continued to apply the negotiating rules laid down by top management since the start of negotiations: treating the people at Nissan as equals, avoiding all forms of arrogance, remaining attentive while maintaining the two principles put forward by Mr Schweitzer as conditions for a win-win situation for both sides of the alliance.

"And that was where our retrospective assessment of all our previous experiences was very useful to us (. . .). Above all we tried—even if we didn't manage it 100%—to avoid putting ourselves forward as the company making an acquisition, the side that comes out on top. We always wanted to have due regard for form, to have due consideration for the Japanese (. . .). We kept in view the lessons that could be learned from our previous experiences." (Mr De Andria, VP, Strategic Planning).

Urged on by the rivalry with DaimlerChrysler, Renault found itself in the role of outsider which encouraged the French to underline their strengths and show their willingness to adapt further to Japanese sensitivities. They felt that they were putting forward the more appropriate answer to Nissan's situation compared to the German-American steamroller twice their size. Even so, while the technical teams continued to make progress in evaluating future cooperation, the strategic teams had the impression that they were working mainly for form's sake. Nissan had to choose between a merger and a partnership, and its choice would depend on what clauses to preserve its identity were being negotiated at DaimlerChrysler headquarters in Stuttgart.

No details leaked out of the discussions between the Japanese and the Germans, but international motor industry experts gave DaimlerChrysler a decisive advantage. Only the Germans had the financial capacity to absorb Nissan's deficits and take charge of an industrial restructuring that seemed bound to be long, difficult and expensive against the notoriously opaque background of Japanese finances and labour relations.

In Geneva, everyone was waiting for the statement that would start a new chapter in the story of the globalisation of the motor industry. It was early March, and the French had absolutely no idea what the outcome would be.

> "The situation was very tense. . . . We felt that they were tempted by the German proposal (. . .). The impression we had had during the negotiations, when apparently they were no longer interested by what we were saying, when we thought their minds were elsewhere . . . now we said: 'That was it. It was the Germans.' It was mainly with regard to the Germans that our hopes waxed and waned" (Mr Dassas, VP, Financial Operations). "There was a week when we just lost all faith (. . .). It was at the start of March, I believe (. . .). We gave up hope. It was all over. The negotiations were awful. Nothing happened, nothing at all . . . it was distressing." (Mr Husson, VP, General Counsel)

The Outcome   Geneva, March 10, 1999. Jürgen Shremp, CEO of DaimlerChrysler called a press conference.

> "This is the result of a three-month period where both parties assess the strengths and financial options of a global cooperation. We had to accept that the opportunities a close relationship with Nissan offer are not achievable as quickly and smoothly as initially expected." (Jürgen Schremp, Co-Chairman of Daimler-Chrysler)

The news came as a surprise to most observers. DaimlerChrysler had proved unable to grasp the opportunity to form an alliance with Nissan and had left the door open for Renault. Now there was nothing to stand in the way of Renault signing the alliance on the terms put forward by Louis Schweitzer, who insisted that none of the company's original proposals be changed.

> "The decision we made during the final negotiations was not to change our position. It was an important choice on our part to say: *'It's not because Daimler is no longer around that we are changing our proposal.'* In other words, it wasn't because there was no-one else to up the stakes that we were planning to change the conditions of the deal, because we knew that they would have to make a deal with someone and there was nobody against me. I decided not to do that because I felt it would destroy the relationship of trust which was indispensable for us to work together (. . .). It seemed

more important to show that we were loyal, stable and reliable partners." (Louis Schweitzer, Chairman)

News of the breakdown of the Daimler talks surprised the team of French negotiators as they got off the plane in Tokyo, where they were due to continue talks on the legal aspects of the alliance. In the big meeting hall, the atmosphere was solemn.

> "We went to Ginza and met our Japanese friends. We said to them: 'We have learned of the event that has changed the circumstances of our negotiations. We note the withdrawal of Daimler-Chrysler. From now on, we want you to know that it isn't Renault's style and culture to take advantage of its partner's problems.' Mr Shiga got up, he did this [mime of the Japanese salute] and sat down again." (Mr Husson, VP, General Counsel)

The alliance between Renault and Nissan was concluded on March 27, 1999. Both companies retained their independence. Three French representatives left Renault to become members of the Nissan Board: Carlos Ghosn, COO, Patrick Pélata, who is responsible for strategy, and Thierry Moulonguet, who is in charge of finance. A Global Alliance Committee was set up to meet monthly to manage the alliance. Eleven global teams were formed to start work in the field on the various aspects. The world's fourth-biggest automobile manufacturer was born, with 9.4% of the international market and strong prospects for growth. In the autumn of 1999, Carlos Ghosn submitted the Nissan Revival Plan.

Nissan's Point of View

Ginza, June 1998   On a hot June morning in 1998, Nissan President Yoshikazu Hanawa arrived for work at the company headquarters in the Ginza district of downtown Tokyo. He was greeted by the uniformed employees at the reception desk and walked past a 1957 Datsun convertible to the elevator that exclusively served the executive offices on the 15th floor.

Entering his office, he was informed by an executive vice president of Renault's interest in a potential partnership with Nissan.

Problems Facing Nissan (1996–1998)   Hanawa had come to power in the middle of the recession in Japan. As of 1996, Nissan had accumulated a debt to sales ratio of 62%. Nissan had sustained continued losses since 1992. This also was having profound effects on the approximately 1400 holding suppliers, dealerships and other subsidiaries of Nissan, throwing them into financial disarray.

Over the first two years of Hanawa's tenure, the situation continued to deteriorate. For the fiscal year ending in March 1998, Nissan reported losses of 14 billion yen, with the debt to sales ratio rising to 66%.

Nissan's problems need to be understood in the context of the changes taking place in the automotive industry. One major factor was the world-wide over-capacity in the car market. It was estimated that automakers had a capacity to produce 70 million vehicles, while demand amounted to only 52 million units.[1] The second factor affecting the automotive industry was the stricter environmental and safety regulations that increased R&D costs per car.

Global over-capacity within the automotive industry and rising costs per vehicle made it increasingly important for industry players to seek size through strategic partnerships or mergers. Ford's acquisition of Volvo in 1998 and the merger of Daimler and Chrysler in the same year sent signals to the industry that served to accelerate the trend.

History   Nissan Motor Co. Ltd. was established in 1933 by Yoshisuke Aikawa to manufacture and sell small Datsun passenger cars and auto parts.

(i) Prewar   The first small-size Datsun passenger car rolled off the assembly line at the Yokohama Plant in April 1935, and vehicle exports to Australia were also launched that same year. The slogan "The Rising Sun as the flag and Datsun as the car of choice"[2] was originated at that time, symbolising Japan's rapid industrialisation.

In 1936, as the signs of the war grew stronger, production emphasis shifted from small-size Datsun passenger cars to military trucks.

(ii) Postwar   Nissan suffered from a major loss of sales force in the early postwar period. This was due to the fact that many leading auto dealerships, previously affiliated with the old Nissan network, switched to Toyota after the dissolution of Japan Motor Vehicle Distribution Co. Ltd., which had monopolised vehicle distribution during the war.

Nissan resumed production of Nissan trucks in 1945 and Datsun passenger cars in 1947. Post-war progress was swift. By 1958, the Datsun 210 could be entered in the grueling Australian Rally, and, by 1960, the company received the Deming Prize for engineering excellence.

(iii) 1960s   The 1959 Bluebird and the 1960 Cedric captivated the imagination of Japanese car buyers and quickened the pace of motorization in Japan. The Sunny was introduced in 1966 during the "my car" era in Japan. Nissan's model lines during the 1960s were indicative of the company's competition with Toyota: the Bluebird lined up against Toyota's Corona, and the Cedric against Toyota's Crown.[3]

This was a period of growth for Nissan. In 1961, the company established Nissan Mexicana, S.A. de C.V., its first overseas manufacturing operation. Nissan also set up two state-of-the-art manufacturing facilities in Japan, the Oppama Plant in 1962 and the Zama Plant in 1965. In the mid-60s, the Japanese government suggested a merger of Nissan and Prince Motor Co. Ltd. to create a larger company that would be better equipped to handle any hostile takeover attempts by foreign companies, leading to the 1966 merger between Nissan Motor and Prince Motor. Nissan maintains a strong link with the Japanese government and to this day provides a large percentage of government limousines.

(iv) 1970s   The two energy crises of the 1970s increased the demand for small Japanese cars worldwide and led to a surge in exports. In 1973, the Sunny ranked first in the fuel and economy tests conducted by the U.S. Environmental Protection Agency and thus gained instant popularity in the U.S. market under the advertising slogan of

---

[1]Nissan estimates.
[2]Nissan corporate web-site.

[3]Nissan Fact File 1999.

"Datsun saves." The sporty Z car also built a large following in the U.S. during the 1970s.

In 1975, Nissan opened the Kyushu Plant, a leading edge facility that today can still boast of the most advanced automation technology in the world.

(v) 1980s   During the 1980s, Nissan was the second Japanese car company, following Honda, to establish a manufacturing base in the U.S. (1980; Nissan Motor Manufacturing Corp., U.S.A) and Datsun Truck and Sentra production began in the U.S. Nissan then moved to establish a manufacturing base in Europe, the first among the Japanese car companies to do so (1984; Nissan Motor Manufacturing Corp. UK).

Rapid overseas expansion was initiated by the 11th Nissan President, Takashi Ishihara (1977–1985). During the 1980s, Nissan's domestic sales began to fall. In order to stem declining sales, Ishihara sought out opportunities in overseas markets and started establishing new plant facilities in the U.S. and the UK. But declining sales in the domestic market remained unsolved, leading Nissan into a vicious cycle of over-capacity, falling sales, and domestic price cuts. This caused conflicts between the Japanese unions and the management. Nissan employees protested against the idea of increasing production capacity overseas when their domestic plants itself were under utilised. However, Ishihara did not stop to hear these voices and continued with his plan for global expansion. This was an example of Ishihara's so called "impulsive management strategy" and unilateral approach.

The continuous conflict with the union badly affected the image of Nissan. The 12th Nissan President, Yutaka Kume (1985–1992) realised the need to stimulate the Nissan brand image and focused on new model introductions. The up-market Cima for the executive class and the sporty Silvia for the younger generation, were introduced in the late 1980s as part of a brand enhancement scheme. With the help of a booming economy, the cars became extremely popular.

In addition, Kume realised that the internal health of the company was also a reflection of the Nissan brand. By the time of his designation as President, employees had become tired of the continuous conflict between the management and the unions during the previous Ishihara era. Kume emphasized improving the environment of the workers, up to the point of creating an organisation in which people would not feel hesitant to call him by his name, Kume-san, rather than by his title.

(vi) 1990s   Kume, who focused on creating a better image for Nissan, had once said, "I want to make the cars more attractive for the younger generation. Therefore, I believe when a concept for a new model is being developed, the voices have to come from the bottom up." However, the bottom-up approach seemed to lead to a loss of direction in the overall policy for model developments. Moreover, since 50% of Nissan dealerships were owned by Nissan (Toyota owned only 10% of its dealerships), dealers had no autonomy in selecting car models, market feedback was poor. This prompted Kume to worry that "Nissan cars are becoming further and further away from the true voice of our customers."[4]

With the burst of Japan's bubble economy, Nissan's profits plummeted from 101.3 billion in March 1992 to a loss of 166 billion yen by March 1995. The 13th Nissan President, Yoshifumi Tsuji (1992–1996), who had spent most of his career on the production side, focused on improving domestic sales. He made frequent visits to all of the domestic dealerships, meeting with dealer representatives, sales board members and sales regional managers. The meetings with the dealer representatives had little effect. Domestic sales appeared to be declining not because Nissan lacked in sales capability, but because there was a fundamental flaw in the concept and the style of the product per se. Without combating the fundamental problem of product improvement, Tsuji presented a drastic down-sizing plan in February 1993 with a target to reduce costs by 200 billion yen by year 1995 in order to obtain profitability even at a low 2 million unit production level.

The Hanawa Era   In 1996, Yoshikazu Hanawa became the 14th President of Nissan. After obtaining

---

[4]"Toyota's Ambition and Nissan's Commitment" by Yoshio Tsukuda.

an economics degree at the University of Tokyo in 1957, he joined Nissan to start his first assignment in the Human Resource Department. He later became involved in Nissan's overseas operations and was designated as head of the committee responsible to establish Nissan's Tennessee plant in the US. By 1985, he was promoted as the first and youngest director in the Corporate Planning Department. He was also involved in numerous restructuring plans such as the closure of the Zama plant in 1995. Many of the Nissan top managers were Tokyo University graduates, and Hanawa had the ideal profile to become the President of Nissan.

(i) Hanawa's Mission

In one of his first interviews upon becoming President, Hanawa said,

> Nissan must cooperate and integrate all efforts towards one vector in order to show better results. We must change the "Nissan Bureaucracy" which has long been our image. . . .[5]

When Hanawa took over as President, Nissan's domestic market share had dropped to 15.9%,[6] only half of that of Toyota. Hanawa's initial plans focused on new car development, with the aim of recovering domestic market share and an objective of 25%[7] by the year 2000. When announcing this target, he said, "It is not a healthy situation both for the companies as well as for the customers for one car company to dominate sales. I would like to establish an era for two mutual companies so that both Toyota and Nissan can stimulate one another and grow together."[8]

(ii) Internal Organisation

From the early stages of Hanawa's time as President, his main concern was to change the culture of the organisation. Hanawa was deeply concerned that Nissan had become complacent and lacked a sense of "urgency," despite the economic distress experienced in Japan after the burst of the bubble economy and the poor market and financial performance of the company.

When Hanawa joined Nissan in 1957, Nissan was still a small operating company, fresh with new ideas and innovation. Recalling his early days at Nissan, Hanawa said, "As Nissan grew larger in scale, a new culture took over. Most employees became more concerned with their own line of business or function and did not know where value was being added for Nissan as a whole. The company lacked both in cross-functional and cross-regional communication. The passive internal culture was reflected in our cars, making them unattractive and far away from customers' taste. Nissan had always thought that as long as there is quality, our cars will sell at a high price. But that logic is no longer true in today's market. It is more about designing, and it is more about customer orientation. But there is a bureaucratic culture rooted into our organisation, which makes it very difficult to implement change. . . . but we needed a change, and one solution was to bring in a new wind."

(iii) Global Business Reform Plan

Shortly after the end of the 1998 Japanese fiscal year, Nissan's Corporate Planning Department presented a "Global Business Reform Plan" to Hanawa and the board. 1998 had resulted in net losses of 14 billion yen on a consolidated basis, tracable to a fall in domestic vehicle demand, the write-down in the carrying value of vehicles in the U.S. lease portfolio, and evaluation losses on marketable securities.[9]

It was evident to the employees that Nissan's future was not very bright. Nissan had been showing consecutive losses since 1992. Everyone knew that something had to be done about it, but nobody seemed to know what or who should take the initiative to unwind the bad cycle the company had become trapped in.

The "Global Business Reform Plan" presentation proposed to achieve a consolidated operating profit to sales ratio of 5% in the fiscal year ending March 2001 and 6% in the fiscal year ending March 2003. There were two options presented in this plan in order to realise these targets. One approach was

‖ [5]"Will Nissan Revive?" by Nikkei Shinbunsha.
‖ [6]The figure includes mini-cars.
‖ [7]The figure excludes mini-cars.
‖ [8]"Will Nissan Revive?" by Nikkei Shinbunsha.

‖ [9]Nissan Press Release (27 May 1998).

to implement an independent survival plan by drastic down-sizing; through reduced development costs, integration of platforms, streamlining sales channels, divesting non-core business assets and other cost cutting strategies. The second approach was to form a global alliance and to survive through increased scale.

It was in this context that a global strategic alliance was proposed.

Another Joint Cooperation with Renault? Hanawa contacted Yutaka Suzuki, Director & General Manager at Corporate Planning Department, to respond to the proposal from Renault. Suzuki and Toshiyuki Shiga, Senior Manager at the Corporate Planning Department, were specifically told by Hanawa to proceed with an immediate investigation on Renault. Shiga was responsible for dealing with all external proposals such as technology alliances and joint cooperation. In fact, when Shiga was contacted by Hanawa regarding the proposal from Renault, he first thought of previous talks for a possible joint development with Renault. Shiga had met André Douin, head of Renault's Planning Department, in Paris in September 1997 concerning a possibility for Renault to produce pickup trucks under a Nissan license in the Mercosur area. Therefore, not only did Shiga already know something of Renault, but also thought that this was merely an extension of the possible joint cooperation Renault was seeking with Nissan since the previous year.

However, Renault was not merely asking for another joint cooperation this time. Renault wanted to know if Nissan might be interested in pursuing a global alliance at the corporate level. Nevertheless, when Shiga received orders to study this proposal from Hanawa, he was not surprised. Nissan had received cooperation proposals in the past from various car companies and it was his task to investigate the potential of each proposal.

The Alliance Process

(i) Phase I: Preliminary Study (July–September 1998) Nissan's Corporate Planning Department was the right place to start off the investigation for a global alliance possibility. It was the only department that included representatives from each of the main functional departments within Nissan: production, purchasing, development, overseas sales, domestic sales, financial affairs, legal and HR. The Corporate Planning Department rolled out the investigation plan in the following manner.

The Research Group within the Corporate Planning Department conducted a thorough internal study of Renault. It was the first time they had conducted such an in-depth analysis on a European car company.

Taiji Sugino, manager at the Corporate Planning Department with a background in international law and corporate governance, had been involved in the research and commented:

> My task was to get to know more about Renault as a company. Renault was not very well known in Japan and we knew very little to start with. Before considering an alliance, we needed to gain an understanding of how it might be possible to integrate with Renault from a business cooporation perspective. We also needed to see the economic benefits of forming an alliance. I conducted a competitor intelligence gathering exercise, a SWOT analysis and further strategic studies to understand the potential synergy effects on a daily basis.

On the strength of this research, Nissan saw considerable potential in the alliance. There were three main reasons for optimism: first, the two companies showed strength in different regions of the world (Nissan in Asia and the US, Renault in Europe), and collaboration between the two companies would give increased geographical coverage. Second, Renault was better at making smaller cars, while Nissan was better at making larger cars. However, despite the fact that the two companies' cars were not in direct competition with one another, there was strong potential for platform integration, indicating a possibility of reduced costs and increased efficiency for both companies. Third, the size of the two companies in terms of market capitalization and number of units produced was very similar as of 1998, lessening threats of future dominance or possible take over from either side.

Sugino said,

> "We marvelled at the success of Renault, because light and small vehicles generate much smaller margins compared to Nissan's large size vehicles. Nevertheless, Renault had managed to turn around its performance in a very short span of time [on the basis of small cars]." Sugino, manager at the Corporate Planning.

At the time the alliance formation process was begun (1998), Renault had an earnings before tax margin (EBT) of 4.6%. Since the loss-making year of 1996 (EBT: 3.6%), Renault had managed to become profitable and grow total sales from 184,078 million FF to 243,934 million FF (1998).

However, Renault faced limitations for future growth. With over 80% of their sales coming from Europe, Renault wanted to broaden coverage, gain scale, and solidify its market position.

When the potential for a global alliance became clearer, the investigation was forwarded to the Strategic Group within the Corporate Planning Department at Nissan. There, the people got together to develop a shopping list of potential joint projects which could possibly take place between Nissan and Renault.

The Planning Department at Renault had developed a similar shopping list. In July 1998, Suzuki, Shiga and Keiichi Maekawa, an engineering manager from the Corporate Planning Department, left for Paris to exchange the two shopping lists. Initially, the combined shopping lists had approximately 100 possible joint projects, of which ultimately 21 projects were prioritised after numerous negotiations between the two Planning Departments during the months of July and August. With this list in hand, the three Nissan representatives went back to Japan and reported to Hanawa on the progress of their investigation.

(ii) Phase II: Joint Study Teams (September–December 1998)   In September 1998, Suzuki was asked by Hanawa to proceed with the 21 joint projects by forming "Joint Study Teams" between Nissan and Renault.

Now, for the first time, the operational level became involved in joint studies. However, the

Corporate Planning Department was given strict orders of confidentiality by Hanawa. They were told not to reveal the purpose of the studies to the engineers involved and that the teams should not know of each other or of the bigger picture that their work fit into. They were to think that this was just like other joint study projects previously undertaken. There had been joint study projects in the past, for example the Volkswagen Santana project. Under this proposal, Nissan would have assembled VW cars at the Zama Plant. The cooperation with VW fell through because engineers at VW and Nissan did not work well together. It was therefore very important to assess the soft elements, such as operational fit at the engineering level, in the joint study teams.

The Corporate Planning Department was also not informed of the purpose nor the direction with which Hanawa was planning to proceed with the joint studies. They only received repeated emphasis by Hanawa that from this stage onwards, the engineers should take complete control in order to allow room for in-depth studies.

Faced with many uncertainties and a very short deadline for results (December 1998), the Corporate Planning Department of Nissan in cooperation with Renault quickly formed the following teams:

Group A:	Regional Operation Group
	A-1) European Team
	A-2) Asian Team
	A-3) Mexico Team
	A-4) South African Team
	A-5) Mercosur Team
Group B:	Product Group
Group C:	Platform Integration Group
Group D:	Powertrain Group
Total:	21 Joint Study Teams

The 21 joint study teams worked under team leaders, and 10 operational people from each company participated in the typical team.

Within teams, questions did arise about the level of cooperation. For example, the Nissan A-3 team members asked why Nissan should allow

Renault into their Mexico Plant. Suzuki responded to them:

> "If we allow Renault into our Mexico Plant, then perhaps we can gain access to Renault's Brazil/Argentina Plant. We need to take a give and take perspective." Suzuki, Shiga and Sugino were responsible for answering all questions raised by the teams from the Nissan side.

Synergy meant two things for Nissan; complementarity and mutual efficiency. It made no sense for Nissan if two companies having the same capability got together. It only made sense if the companies complemented one another bringing overall efficiency and benefits for both companies.

There was a great amount of secrecy between the two companies initially. However, in order to see the synergy effect and the actual benefits for both companies, the facts had to be revealed as Renault and Nissan progressed with their joint studies. Shiga recalled, "The kind of information that we were sharing with each other prior to the alliance agreement was a very rare case."

For example, one joint study was made on the development of a 1 liter gasoline engine. Based on the joint study conducted by the joint study teams, Nissan calculated the NPV of this investment. In addition to this, Nissan had projected a reference case on this development if it had been conducted separately with the different research capabilities that Nissan and Renault individually had. If the combined NPV of Renault and Nissan had exceeded the NPV resulted by the joint study teams, it made no sense to proceed with the joint project. The difference of the two resulting NPVs, was what Nissan called the "synergy effect."

There were a few "win-lose" projects but most of the projects resulted in a "win-win" projection. The aim was to achieve benefits for both sides.

(iii) Phase III: Reporting   The 21 Joint Study Teams produced a progress report each month between October and December. Shiga reported the results to Hanawa and Suzuki.

As Renault and Nissan progressed with their joint studies, the two Planning Departments had come down to a common strategy,

> "The two Planning Departments of Renault and Nissan agreed that after identifying a strategic link through the joint studies, we must form a common strategy in order to achieve profitable growth for both companies. The basic policy for the alliance strategy would be to distinguish the brand identity from any kind of synergy. We saw the possibility of manufacturing integration but not brand integration, just as we saw possibilities of back office integration but not front office integration. In other words, Renault and Nissan felt that we should integrate only the processes that were far away from customers." (Shiga, manager at the Corporate Planning)

On 15 December 1998, a final report produced by the 21 Joint Study Teams was submitted to Hanawa.

(iv) Alliance Formation Process (January–March)   In the beginning of 1999, the negotiation became more aggressive and rapid, focusing on the re-structuring of the organisation as well as financial and legal affairs. Due diligence commenced on 15 January 1999 for the purpose of validating mutual claims. Shiga commented on the alliance formation process,

> Since both sides had strong individual needs to make themselves stronger, the joint study took place "sincerely." It was not just a handshake between the top managers.

Sugino added his perspective on the alliance formation process,

> For Nissan, the negotiations and the execution of the alliance contract were a process and not an objective. The objective was not to finalise the contract wording but to examine how to share best practices. For example, it was evident that Renault had strengths in two things: cost management and customer satisfaction. Nissan had strengths in technology, productivity, quality control, and global-level operations. Nissan wanted to know how Renault managed to maintain such a low cost structure, but Renault would not reveal this information unless an alliance was formed. Therefore, forming an alliance was a means of obtaining this know-how, and not an objective per se. Agreement finalisation was only the starting point of the alliance.

(v) Employee Involvement   Sugino explained the relationship between Renault and Nissan at the operational level to be the following,

> Nissan employees thought of Renault as a company that placed emphasis on communication improvement rather than negotiation.

Because of Renault's emphasis on communication, it was easy for Nissan to understand Renault. However, Sugino thought that the situation was quite the opposite for Renault.

> "The only point of contact on the Nissan side, who really knew the entire picture, was Mr. Hanawa, and hence I think that it must have been difficult for Renault to understand Nissan. (. . .) 'All of us were not really well aware of what was happening apart from what could be found in the papers. I knew in January 1999 because I had to prepare for due diligence. But I think most directors did not know about it until the day of announcement in March 1999. Only board members, Mr. Shiga and Mr. Sugino were informed by Mr. Hanawa." (Anraku, managing director in charge of finance and accounting)

Hanawa, always at the center of control, was very quick to respond to his lieutenants: Suzuki, Shiga and Sugino.

> "He would normally respond within the day. His decision making was very quick. That's when I sensed that Mr. Hanawa and Mr. Schweitzer were talking to each other very frequently, otherwise Mr. Hanawa could not have responded to me so quickly." (Sugino, manager at the Corporate Planning)

Although the word "global alliance" was never spelled out to his lieutenants by Hanawa, they gradually grew convinced that Nissan would really form an alliance with Renault in the near future. Unusual actions such as Hanawa's frequent calls to the Corporate Planning Department for feedback on the joint projects, or getting the managers there actively involved instead of confiding to his board members, or even the rapid response from Hanawa concerning queries during the process, made Suzuki, Shiga and Sugino gain confidence that soon a big decision would be made by Hanawa.

There was also a sense of confidence building at the planning level. Although the decision would ultimately be made by Hanawa, the actions leading up to the alliance were taken by the Corporate Planning Department. As Suzuki said, "We made the alliance happen. We did it."

However, some people at Nissan wished that there were more key persons within the company involved during the discussions with Renault. This would have helped avoid the shock that followed and allowed Human Resources to have considered issues relating to post-alliance integration.

Hanawa and Schweitzer

(i) Letter (June 1998)   Hanawa explained that initially, he did not think that a global alliance was really necessary. But rather, he felt the need to strengthen Nissan's overseas operation through their central office in Japan. Hanawa commented, "At first I did not think of forming an alliance with Renault, but I did consider possible joint cooperation. After all, everybody was doing that."

> "I think Mr. Hanawa initially wanted to take the independent survival approach when the options were opened to him after the Global Business Reform Plan presentation in May 1998. During the months between July and December I think he tried to do both, but ultimately, came down to the global alliance approach." (Shiga, manager at the Corporate Planning)

(ii) Negotiation with Schweitzer (July–December 1998)   In July 1998, Hanawa decided to meet Louis Schweitzer, the Chairman of Renault. This was the first of many meetings to follow.

Between July and December, 1998, the two men met more than ten times in addition to numerous private telephone calls, to discuss the alliance. All of the meetings were one-on-one affairs, with Hanawa's long-time translator the only outsider present.

> "The relationship I had with Mr. Schweitzer was one of honesty. In fact, the first thing I said to Mr. Schweitzer when I met him in July was, 'I am going to be frank with you, whatever the negotiation

results may be. So let's be frank with each other.' But with many people around, it is difficult to tell each other the truth, that is why I decided to negotiate alone. This also avoids insider risk. I think Mr. Schweitzer, on the other hand, was more careful about opening up to me because of the previous experience with Volvo. I believe the process leading up to an alliance is all about telling the truth; dishonesty only makes the process longer." (Hanawa, President)

(iii) Proposal of Potential Synergies   During the course of their discussions, Hanawa and Schweitzer both agreed on the need to conduct joint studies prior to the alliance, in order to assess the organisational fit at the operational level. Both CEOs indicated to their Planning Departments to form a shopping list of possible joint projects and to perform these projects specifically in the form of "joint study teams." The CEOs wanted the potential synergies to be proposed by the operational level of both sides and set a year-end deadline for the results.

> "In a car company, when there's a problem, the problem normally rises from the engineering department. So engineers were selected from both sides to work on research topics for 3 months. Similar projects were performed for other departments as well. As a result, there seemed to be a good chemistry between Renault and Nissan." (Hanawa, President)

As the joint study progressed between Renault and Nissan, Schweitzer and Hanawa started to see an organisational fit between the two companies.

> "I was impressed with two things about Renault. Firstly, I was impressed with Mr. Schweitzer's courageous decision to embrace a new business opportunity, and secondly, the fact that we had agreed on the terms of equal position. This was important for me, as dominance destroys motivation. Once Nissan picks up, we will buy a share in Renault's equity. These are the terms that we both agreed on." (Hanawa, President)

Hanawa emphasised that the assessment from the joint study teams was the determining factor for the alliance.

> "Take for example, platform integration between Renault and Nissan. Nissan currently has 26 ranges of platforms and Renault has 8. If after the alliance, we can produce a common range of 10 platforms, it would reduce cost and increase efficiency. We all know that the concept is good, but we will never know if it is the right decision to make unless we do it. So I decided on the alliance to let actions take over. . . . Mr. Schweitzer told me about Carlos Ghosn's key role in the turn around of Renault three years back . . . I let him know that I wanted that man [to help Nissan]." (Hanawa, President)

(iv) Renault's "Big Picture" Presentation (10 November 1998)   In October 1998, Schweitzer met Hanawa and articulated his perspective on the potential alliance between the two companies. Hanawa commented, "I did not agree with it from the start of course. But I was not surprised. Through our discussions, I felt that Mr. Schweitzer always had a more comprehensive view of the partnership than I did. I took it as one opinion."

At this time, Schweitzer expressed an interest in sharing his views with a larger set of people at Nissan. Hanawa agreed to let Schweitzer and his team fly over to Japan and make a presentation about Renault's cost reduction experience, as well as the potential synergies to be gained from an alliance between the two companies. The presentation to Hanawa and some of Nissan's top executives was held on 10 November at Nissan headquarters. Schweitzer, Douin and Ghosn explained Renault's cost reduction capabilities and presented a comprehensive turn-around plan.

> "At the presentation, the participants were informed for the first time of the overall direction which the joint studies might be leading towards. But to be frank, I myself was amazed at the details of their study concerning the potential synergies. I was surprised at the level of research as well as the level of involvement with which Renault had progressed with the alliance plans. Because at Nissan, the negotiation was strictly kept between Mr. Schweitzer and I. This was the difference between Renault and Nissan. Renault knew exactly what they wanted from the beginning. I think our board only understood it as one possibility." (Hanawa, President)

(v) Final Meeting (21–23 December 1998)   On 15 December, the final reports from the joint study teams were submitted, and the "synergy effect" figures were presented. Based on these figures, Schweitzer and Hanawa met on 21–23 December to hold a final meeting on the alliance plans. On 23 December, Hanawa let Schweitzer know that the alliance talks would not be exclusive, and that Renault would be asked to bid for both Nissan Motor and Nissan Diesel.

In effect, DaimlerChrysler had been in negotiations with Nissan Diesel, Nissan's affiliate truck company, since May 1998. Juergen Hubbert, DaimlerChrysler board member for passenger cars remarked that, "Nissan Motor would help Daimler-Chrysler to achieve its aim of 20–25% of group sales being in Asia within 10 years. In the short-term we can do without a foothold in passenger cars in Asia, but we cannot do without one in trucks. Entering the Asian truck business is most urgent for DaimlerChrysler, but Nissan Diesel and Nissan Motor are interwoven in such a way that we are forced to talk about both."[10]

Hanawa later commented upon the interest of DaimlerChrysler,

> When Daimler and Chrysler merged in May 1998, Mr. Schremp talked about his interest in Nissan Diesel. This caused problems as it was supposed to be internal information, but by then, the Japanese press took it up as a great scoop.

Just a rumor?

> "Determining an alliance partner actually involves a lot of work, joint study teams, bottom-up reporting, etc. . . . In view of all the work that was put into the study process with Renault, I imagine that evaluating another alliance deal at the same time would really be a major undertaking." (Shiga, Corporate Planning)

(vi) Final Run   After December 23 and until March 13, when Renault and Nissan finalized the

basic alliance agreement, Hanawa and Schweitzer met only twice more. The core of the negotiations ended in December 1998.

> "Alliances are not a money-game, especially for car companies. We have responsibility for people at all levels. We all believed and trusted in Mr. Hanawa's decision. We believe he did the right thing." (Shiga, Corporate Planning).

On 15 January, due diligence commenced and the legal and finance departments took over. Hanawa had set a deadline of March because he felt that prolonging the process only created conflict and turmoil.

DaimlerChrysler ended all talks with Nissan on March 11, 1999. The Renault/Nissan alliance agreement was officially signed on 27 March 1999. This agreement aimed at strengthening Nissan's financial position and achieving profitable growth for both companies. On 28 May 1999, Renault invested 643 billion yen and acquired 36.8% of the equity of Nissan Motor and 22.5% of Nissan Diesel.

Appendices

Appendix 1	Global Ranking of Major Automakers (1998)	
	Volume Mil. Units	**Market Share**
Global Ranking		
General Motors	8.90	15%
Ford Motors	8.50	15%
Toyota Motors	6.40	10%
Renault/Nissan	4.80	9%
Volkswagen	4.30	9%
Daimler/Chrysler	4.00	8%

Source: Warburg Dillion Reed Global Auto Analyser (September 1999).

---

[10]*Financial Times,* March 8, 1999.

Appendix 2   Comparison: DaimlerChrysler, Nissan and Renault

	DaimlerChrysler	**Nissan**	**Renault**
Annual Revenue ($ mio)	147.745.000	50.212.000	41.349.000
Net income ($ mio)	5.404.000	−213.000	1.500.000
Work force	441.500	135.800	140.900
World market share (value)	8.4%	4.9%	4.3%
Vehicle production	3.9	2.6	2.1
(in millions—1998)	Daimler: 1.1		
	Chrysler: 2.8		

Appendix 3   Renault and Nissan around the World

	Renault		*Nissan*	
Vehicles Sold (1998)	**Volume**	**Market Share (value)**	**Volume**	**Market Share (value)**
Western Europe	1.798.160	11%	505.768	3.1%
North America	—	—	656.704	4%
South America	110.656	5.1%	—	—
Japan	—	—	902.968	15.3%
ASEAN	—	—	129.172	10.8%
Turkey, Middle East, North Africa	117.040	7.9%	116.512	9.1%
Rest of world	102.144		336.296	
Number of Plants (1998)	**Full-fledged Plants**	**Local Assembly Sites**	**Full-fledged Plants**	**Local Assembly Sites**
Europe	18	—	3	—
Japan	—	—	12	—
Asia	1 (China)	2	2	3
North America	1 (Mexico)	—	4	—
South America	3	2		
Africa	—	1 (Morocco)	1 (South Africa)	—

Appendix 4   Model Categories of Renault and Nissan

	Renault		*Nissan*	
Names	**Volume Sold (approx, 1998)**	**Model Categories**	**Volume Sold (approx, 1998)**	**Names**
Twingo	250.000	Entry level	—	—
Clio	600.000	Sub-compact	350.000	March, Micra, Cube
Mégane, Scénic, R19	800.000	Compact	550.000	Almera, Sunny
Laguna	250.000	Mid-size	350.000	Bluebird, Primera
Safrane, Spider	50.000	Luxury	500.000	Altima, Maxima, Infiniti, Q45, Cedric
Espace	100.000	Minivan	150.000	Quest, Elgrand, Prairie
—	—	4*4	250.000	Safari, Patrol, Terrano
—	—	Pick-up	250.000	Pick-up
Express, Kangoo, Trafic, Master	350.000	Utility	150.000	Atlas Civilian

Appendix 5   Competences of Renault and Nissan (recognized at alliance signing)

Renault	Nissan
Cost management	Engineering competence
Global platform and purchase strategies	Technology
Innovative products	Plant productivity
Marketing and design	Product and process quality management

Appendix 6   Platform Integration

Example: Common platform (Clio/Micra)

	Common Range of Platforms		
	Renault	**Nissan**	**Alliance**
Number of platforms	8	26	10
Volume per platform (000 units)	280	105	500

Example: Components (joint development of a small diesel engine)

	Common Range of Engines and Transmission Families		
	Renault	**Nissan**	**Alliance**
Number of engine platforms	7	20	8
Volume per platform (000 units)	320	140	630

Source: Schroders; Renault-Nissan Strategic Alliance Report (April 1999).

Appendix 7   History of Renault

1898:   Renault Frères founded in Boulogne, at Billancourt (production: 1 vehicle).

1903:   Death of Marcel Renault. Louis Renault takes over (production: 778 vehicles).

1941:   Occupation and collaboration with Axis.

1944:   Arrest of Louis Renault by Allies (he dies september 24); factories are requisitioned.

1945:   Nationalization decreed because of collaboration. Creation of Régie Nationale des Usines Renault. President: Pierre Lefaucheux (production: 12.031 vehicles).

1969:   Creation of Renault-Finance to support international evolution (production: 1.047.986 vehicles).

1979:   22,8% participation taken in AMC (US). 10% participation in Volvo (Su) with an option for 20% (production: 1.872.526 vehicles).

1980:   Increased participation in AMC to 46,4% (production: 2.053.677 vehicles).

1981:   RVI (Renault Véhicules Industriels) buys Dodge Trucks (US) (production: 1.764.701 vehicles).

(continued)

Appendix 7   *(concluded)*

1983:	Agreement with Matra. Renault takes control of Mack (US) (production: 2.035.133 vehicles).
1984:	With debts of 57 billion francs (half annual revenue) and annual losses of 12,5 billion, Renault is virtually bankrupt (production: 1.740.737 vehicles).
1985:	Resignation of Bernard Hanon. Georges Besse becomes president puts in place a restructuring policy: recapitalisation of 8 billion by the French state, financial restructuring with RVI by 500 million francs, policy of disengagement and refocusing, 2.550 redundancies at RVI, plan to reduce headcount by 21.000 people in 2 years (production: 1.637.634 vehicles).
1986:	Georges Besse is assassinated by Action Directe on the 17 novembre. RVI announces 2.624 lay-offs, the Mexican factory of Sahagun is closed, 13.5 ha of factory space at Billancourt are put up for sale (production: 1.754.332 vehicles).
1987:	Raymond Lévy president of Renault. Further lightening: AMC is sold to Chrysler. Renault becomes a for-profit firm again and prepares to follow a logic of profit after a second phase of recapitalization (10 billion francs) by the French state and shareholder (production: 1.831.390 vehicles).
1990:	Renault becomes an SA (Société Anonyme) and Volvo now owns 20% of the capital (production: 1.848.078 vehicles).
1992:	Raymond Lévy reaches age limit and cedes his place to Louis Schweitzer on 27 may (production: 2.094.774 vehicles).
1993:	6 septembre: the merger Renault-Volvo is announced. December: Volvo abandons merger (production: 1.761.496 vehicles).
1994:	Renault goes public: the French state holds only 52,97% of the capital (production: 1.914.662 vehicles).
1996:	Privatization. First losses since the 1980s 80 (production: 1.804.910 vehicles).
1997:	Vilvorde factory (B) is closed (2.700 jobs). Return to profitability. French state: 46% of capital.

Appendix 8   Recovery of Renault (in FF mio)

	1983	1984	1985	1986
Revenue	104.145.000	110.274.000	117.584.000	122.138.000
Net income	−1.420.000	−1.576.000	−12.555.000	−10.897.000
CAF (MBA)	1.446.000	1.938.000	−6.481.000	−6.003.000
Equity	10.119.000	11.164.000	1.851.000	−7.365.000
Work force	215.000	219.805	213.725	196.414
	1988	**1989**	**1990**	**1995**
Revenue	147.510.000	161.438.000	174.477.000	178.537.000
Net income	3.256.000	8.834.000	9.289.000	3.636.000
CAF (MBA)	10.010.000	15.260.000	15.050.000	12.145.000
Equity	−5.726.000	14.012.000	22.466.000	42.784.000
Work force	188.900	181.715	174.573	138.279

Appendix 9 Renault S.A. (France)—Financial Snapshot

	Renault S.A. (France) (mil. FF)						
	12/31/1992	12/31/1993	12/31/1994	12/31/1995	12/31/1996	12/31/1997	12/31/1998
Sales	184,252	169,789	178,537	184,065	184,078	207,912	243,934
R & D expenses	6,190	6,902	7,707	7,904	9,125	9,038	10,189
Income before taxes	6,481	1,094	3,485	1,976	−5,645	4,095	11,145
EBT margin	3.52%	0.64%	1.95%	1.07%	−3.07%	1.97%	4.57%
No of shares (mil)	224	227	238	239	240	240	240
Earnings per share	28.93	4.09	15.65	9.02	−22.07	22.78	36.97
Total shareholders'	33,965	33,877	42,784	43,796	37,770	43,917	51,562
Total debt	8,727	7,851	−1,458	3,368	9,385	2,097	−12,650
Debt/equity ratio	26%	23%	−3%	8%	25%	5%	−25%
Debt/sales ratio	5%	5%	−1%	2%	5%	1%	−5%
R&D costs/sales	3.36%	4.07%	4.32%	4.29%	4.96%	4.35%	4.18%

Source: Renault Annual Report

Appendix 10 Japanese Automakers Profitability (1998)

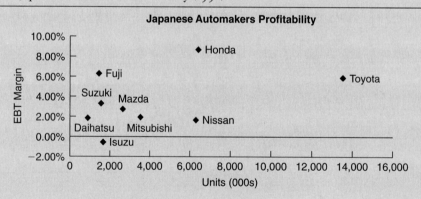

Source: Schroders; Renault-Nissan Strategic Alliance Report (April 1999).

Appendix 11 Structural Excess Capacity at Nissan (1998)

Region	No of Plants	Capacity	Production	Excess Capacity	%
Japan	4	2000000	1600000	400000	20%
Rest of Asia	3	260000	106000	154000	59%
N. America	3	720000	500000	220000	31%
Europe	2	430000	280000	150000	35%
Total		3410000	2486000	924000	27%

Source: *Automobile News.*

615

Appendix 12 Nissan Motor Co.—Financial Snapshot

Nissan Motor Co. (Mil. Yen)

	03/31/1992	03/31/1993	03/31/1994	03/31/1995	03/31/1996	03/31/1997	03/31/1998
Sales	6,417,931	6,197,599	5,800,857	5,834,123	6,039,107	6,658,875	6,564,637
Operating income (loss)	154,279	−5,417	−142,319	−102,717	43,235	199,880	84,346
Income (loss) before tax	166,371	−56,545	−101,331	−179,745	−81,454	101,073	−24,458
EBT margin	2.59%	−0.91%	−1.75%	−3.08%	−1.35%	1.52%	−0.37%
Total income taxes	67,859	7,842	−1,357	2,901	12,504	31,619	−6,842
Net income (loss)	101,295	−55,998	−86,915	−166,054	−88,418	77,743	−14,007
Number of shares (mil)	2,512	2,512	2,512	2,513	2,513	2,513	2,437
Net income (loss) per share	40.32	−22.28	−34.59	−66.09	−35.18	30.94	−5.57
Sales ('000 units)		2,813	2,691	2,700	2,671	2,710	2,568
Total long-term debt	2,045,135	2,331,172	2,680,736	2,209,000	3,728,000	3,839,000	4,342,000
Total shareholders' equity		1,580,000	1,429,000	1,429,000	1,356,000	1,356,000	1,282,000
Debt/Equity ratio		148%	188%	155%	275%	283%	339%
Debt/Sales ratio	32%	38%	46%	38%	62%	58%	66%

Source: *Nissan Annual Report.*

Appendix 13   Global Demand by Country

	1995	1996	1997	1998	1999(exp)	2000(exp)	2001(exp)
			Global Automobile Demand (000 units)				
United States	14800	15097	15115	15697	16900	16300	16300
% change		2.01%	0.12%	3.85%	7.66%	−3.55%	0.00%
Europe							
– Germany	3314	3508	3528	3740	3880	3980	3950
% change		5.85%	0.57%	6.01%	3.74%	2.58%	−0.75%
– France	1930	2132	1713	1944	2130	2160	2080
% change		10.47%	−19.65%	13.49%	9.57%	1.41%	−3.70%
– Italy	1720	1719	2412	2364	2350	2400	2420
% change		−0.06%	40.31%	−1.99%	−0.59%	2.13%	0.83%
– U.K.	1945	2026	2171	2247	2180	1950	1880
% change		4.16%	7.16%	3.50%	−2.98%	−10.55%	−3.59%
– Spain	833	909	1012	1191	1450	1450	1400
% change		9.12%	11.33%	17.69%	21.75%	0.00%	−3.45%
Total Europe	9742	10294	10836	11486	11990	11940	11730
% change		5.67%	5.27%	6.00%	4.39%	−0.42%	−1.76%
Asia							
– Japan	6865	6896	6726	5880	5886	6000	6200
% change		0.45%	−2.47%	−12.58%	0.10%	1.94%	3.33%
– China	912	976	1085	1027	1120	1305	1493
% change		7.02%	11.17%	−5.35%	9.06%	16.52%	14.41%
– Korea	1556	1644	1513	780	1092	1190	1273
% change		5.66%	−7.97%	−48.45%	40.00%	8.97%	6.97%
Total Asia	9333	9516	9324	7687	8098	8495	8966
% change		1.96%	−2.02%	−17.56%	5.35%	4.90%	5.54%
Latin America							
– Brazil	1579	1632	1827	1415	1100	1250	1450
% change		3.36%	11.95%	−22.55%	−22.26%	13.64%	16.00%
– Argentina	319	362	396	437	445	493	510
% change		13.48%	9.39%	10.35%	1.83%	10.79%	3.45%
Total Latin America	1898	1994	2223	1852	1545	1743	1960
% change		5.06%	11.48%	−16.69%	-16.58%	12.82%	12.45%
Rest of the World	5910	5446	6019	6000	6314	6765	6957
% change		−7.85%	10.52%	−0.32%	5.23%	7.14%	2.84%
World Total	41683	42347	43517	42722	44847	45243	45913
% change		1.59%	2.76%	−1.83%	4.97%	0.88%	1.48%

Source: Warburg Dillion Reed Global Auto Analyser (September 1999).

Appendix 14   Market Shares by Region

	1995	1996	1997	1998	1999(exp)
European Market Shares					
VW	18.30%	17.20%	17.20%	18.10%	18.90%
PSA	12.70%	12.00%	11.30%	11.40%	11.50%
Japanese	11.40%	11.10%	11.50%	11.70%	11.50%
GM	13.30%	12.50%	12.10%	1.50%	11.60%
Ford	12.40%	11.60%	11.30%	10.20%	11.50%
Renault	10.70%	10.10%	9.90%	10.70%	10.60%
Fiat	12.00%	11.10%	11.90%	10.90%	10.40%
BMW	6.40%	6.30%	6.10%	5.70%	5.20%
DaimlerChrysler	3.80%	3.60%	4.40%	5.00%	5.40%
US Market Shares					
GM	33.10%	31.70%	31.50%	29.40%	29.60%
Ford	36.20%	25.90%	25.70%	25.00%	24.70%
DaimlerChrysler	15.60%	17.30%	16.50%	17.70%	16.90%
Toyota	7.30%	7.70%	8.10%	8.70%	8.60%
Honda	5.40%	5.60%	6.20%	6.40%	6.30%
Nissan	5.20%	5.00%	4.80%	4.00%	3.90%
VW	0.90%	1.10%	1.10%	1.70%	2.20%
Mazda	1.90%	1.60%	1.50%	1.50%	1.50%
Koreans	90.00%	1.00%	1.10%	1.10%	1.90%
Japanese Market Shares					
Toyota	29.60%	30.50%	29.60%	28.90%	28.20%
Nissan	16.00%	15.90%	15.40%	15.30%	13.60%
Mitsubishi	11.90%	10.90%	10.10%	10.10%	10.20%
Honda	8.30%	10.20%	11.50%	11.60%	11.10%
Suzuki	9.00%	9.00%	8.90%	9.40%	10.50%
Daihatsu	6.00%	6.80%	6.70%	7.40%	9.10%
Mazda	5.30%	4.80%	5.00%	5.40%	5.40%
Fuji Heavy	5.00%	5.10%	4.50%	4.70%	5.10%
Imports	5.70%	6.20%	5.40%	4.70%	4.70%

Source: Warburg Dillion Reed Global Auto Analyser (September 1999).

Appendix 15   Global Automakers Profitability (EBIT Margin)

	1996	1997	1998	1999(exp)
GM	2.50%	−0.30%	3.50%	6.80%
Ford	3.40%	6.60%	6.70%	7.70%
DaimlerChrysler	5.20%	4.70%	5.60%	8.70%
VW	3.00%	3.00%	4.90%	5.00%
Renault	−3.30%	1.00%	4.40%	4.10%
Fiat	2.30%	3.90%	1.60%	1.40%
BMW	4.50%	5.50%	4.70%	5.20%
Toyota	4.90%	6.60%	6.30%	5.90%
Nissan	2.40%	1.70%	1.60%	1.60%
Honda	6.70%	9.80%	9.30%	8.70%
Suzuki	4.10%	3.50%	3.30%	3.30%

Source: Warburg Dillion Reed Global Auto Analyser (September 1999).

Case 6-3   Star Alliance (A): A Global Network

Miami, 3 December 2001—The heads of the Star Alliance member airlines assembled in Miami for their semi-annual Chief Executive Board meeting. As Star Alliance CEO Jaan Albrecht reflected on the events of 2001—the creeping economic recession and the terrorist attacks of September 11 that caused a sharp downturn of the airline industry— the focus of the meeting turned to how Star Alliance could enable member carriers to support each other through that current unprecedented turbulence.

"Our partnership is more important now than ever before as the global airline industry is facing the worst crisis in its history," he said. *"As much as Star Alliance has proven its value in good times, it is now demonstrating its value in current times of difficulty. By working together and leveraging the combined strengths of the alliance, the Star Alliance member airlines stand to gain collectively."*

▌ The Global Airline Industry

Since the start of commercial aviation, airlines came to symbolise national pride for countries all over the world. Having a "flag carrier" that travelled the globe to transport its citizens to new places and bring others to the home country was seen as a sign of economic prosperity and power. In many cases,

London Business School   This case was prepared by Angela Andal-Ancion, Research Assistant, with initial work by Claire Stravato, Research Assistant, under the direction of Professor George S. Yip, London Business School. This case was funded by the Centre for the Network Economy. © London Business School, 2002. To obtain permission to reproduce this case contact Anne Wilson, awilson@london.edu, Tel. +44 20 7262 5050, Fax. +44 20 7724 7875. LBS reference CS-02-039.

The opinions of the authors do not reflect the opinions of Star Alliance nor of the member carriers.

government-owned or controlled corporations ran these national carriers. With the huge capital investment needed to set up and run a fleet of aeroplanes, many airlines relied on their national governments to cough up the cash. Subsidies and state aid became the norm rather than the exception. A false sense of operational profitability thus resulted.

The trouble was that many of the flag carriers were seen as hidebound, inefficient operators, which had been propped up for years by governments.[1] Most had been partly privatised, dipping at least their toes into the icy waters of commercial reality. Only a handful remained fully state-owned, but most were seen as overweight and incapable of surviving the harsh realities of competition.

After many years of state aid, governments had enough and finally relented to seeing their flag carriers face the consequences of non-profitability. Swissair saw its aeroplanes grounded in October 2001 after the Swiss Government and financial institutions refused to inject more cash in the business. At the same period, Belgium's Sabena also filed for bankruptcy after it exhausted its government's rescue package and still failed to find new investors.

Deregulation of the Industry   The first signs of competition in the airline industry began in the late 1970s with deregulation, which ushered in a new era of opportunity and change. The U.S. Airline Deregulation Act was signed into law on 24 October 1978 and instituted the gradual reduction in the powers of the Civil Aeronautics Board, which until

---

▌ [1]See "Survival of the Fittest for Euro Airlines," BBC News Online, 3 October 2001.

then had regulated pricing, market entry and other airline functions. The call to aviation reform reflected the shared view among legislators that regulation had: (1) effectively prevented new entrants from operating in domestic, long-haul sectors; (2) protected the inefficiencies of the system which allowed labour and other operating costs to rise above reasonable levels; and (3) prevented significant price competition.

Deregulation in Europe followed a similar trend, albeit several decades behind the U.S. In April 1997, the last phase of the "Third Package," which was put into effect by the European Commission in 1993, ended constraints on European carriers from operating purely domestic routes beyond their national borders. This meant that for example, a French carrier could be permitted to operate services between two cities in Italy. Previously a French carrier could only offer domestic service within another EC state only as part of service originating or ending outside of that state.[2]

As deregulation unravelled, many international carriers entered into cooperative agreements with foreign partners to expand their route networks. These arrangements included joint purchasing and maintenance agreements, "blocked space" agreements under which a carrier bought a dedicated block of seats on a competitor's flight and designated them as its own; and marketing agreements that enabled two airlines to credit each other's frequent flyer programs.

In the international marketplace, air routes, frequency and fares were all governed by bilateral agreements,[3] which grew out of the 1944 Chicago Convention. The Convention brought together 52 member states with the objective of crafting a framework that would govern international air transport. A protectionist framework prevailed, which led to the industry's continued restriction from free market operation in many countries. For example, U.S. carriers were not able to organise additional services to Argentina, Japan and the United Kingdom because of the very restrictive nature of the bilaterals governing those services. The U.S. bilateral with Japan, while it was recently modified, was still quite restrictive. Officials from All Nippon Airways confirmed: *"The level of freedom we have is different. Carriers have antitrust immunity in the U.S. but we don't. Dealing with government can be quite hard—the Japanese government, for example, does not accept Open Skies."* Since only designated carriers could serve certain routes, non-designated carriers were only able to access these markets through a code-sharing alliance.

In the mid-1980s several airlines began a new cooperative practice on a limited number of routes called "code-sharing." This practice, which had to be periodically approved by the U.S. Department of Transportation (DOT), allowed airlines to offer their passenger routes under coordinated times in certain markets. Under code-sharing agreements, an airline used its two-character designator code to advertise the flight of another airline as its own. Because both airlines could list the same flight, it appeared two or more times, and thereby increased the flight's chances of being selected by travel agents.

Prior to deregulation in the U.S. and in Europe, there had been a long history of airline cooperation, including pooling of revenues and equity ownership. Two European carriers, KLM and British Airways, were among the pioneers. While BA initially set its sights on United and saw the deal subsequently fall apart, KLM targeted Northwest. KLM, then the world's 12th largest airline, bought a stake in Northwest in 1989. According to KLM's FY 1990 annual report: *"The Northwest investment provides KLM with an economic interest in fast-growing U.S. domestic and transpacific air transport markets. Through commercial cooperation in passenger and freight transport, both airlines aim to strengthen their international market positions. Cooperation has already started in a number of fields."*

In 1992 the governments of The Netherlands and the United States agreed to an "Open Skies"

---

[2] See American Express press release "Full European Airline Deregulation Nears, Posing Travel Management Challenges to U.S. Firms," 26 March 1997.

[3] In 2000, there were more than 4000 aviation bilaterals in force.

bilateral air treaty, which granted KLM and Northwest full antitrust immunity. The U.S. policy of Open Skies was at that time the latest weapon the DOT used to eliminate very restrictive bilateral agreements, with the ultimate goal of liberalising global air routes. Antitrust immunity allowed KLM and Northwest to act as one company with regard to designing, pricing and selling their product. At the time, the rest of the industry did not go so far as to deride KLM/Northwest, but many airline managements remarked that they did not think antitrust immunity meant very much. Exhibit 1 shows the U.S. Open Skies agreements.

Open Skies saw the free flow of people around the globe. Businesses thrived and the worldwide economy improved. As more and more people travelled, an interesting relationship emerged: what happened in the worldwide economy had a direct impact on the business of airlines. Global events/crises like wars and acts of terrorism pushed first the global airline industry into a tailspin, then led to

closure for some airlines. The Gulf War in 1991–92, which shot up the price of fuel, and brought business travel and tourism to a standstill, brought losses to the U.S. airline industry of $12.8 billion. Before it was over, two of the United States' largest airlines, Pan Am and Eastern disappeared from the skies.

But as global air traffic slumped 25% following the start of the Gulf War, it swiftly picked up again. Between the prosperous years of 1995 and 1998, the worldwide airline industry experienced a dramatic turnaround, with reported total net profits in excess of $25 billion.

The aviation industry was hit hard once more by the 11 September 2001 terrorist attacks in New York and Washington. Although many airlines were already under severe pressure from falling passenger traffic and ill-judged investments, the industry also had to face higher security costs following the terrorist attacks. The International Air Transport Agency (IATA) had initially forecast losses of

---

Exhibit 1   U.S. Open Skies Agreements

Americas	Asia/Pacific	Europe	Africa	Middle East
Argentina***	Australia**	Austria	Burkina Faso	Bahrain
Aruba	Brunei	Belgium	The Gambia	Jordan
Canada*	Malaysia	Czech Republic	Ghana	Qatar
Chile	New Zealand	Denmark	Namibia	United Arab Emirates
Costa Rica	Pakistan	Finland	Tanzania	
Dominican Republic	Singapore	Germany		
El Salvador	South Korea	Iceland		
Guatemala	Taiwan	Italy		
Honduras	Uzbekistan	Luxembourg		
Netherlands Antilles		Netherlands		
Nicaragua		Norway		
Panama		Portugal		
Peru		Romania		
		Slovak Republic		
		Sweden		
		Turkey		
		Switzerland		

*Open Transborder agreement; **Agreement only covers cargo services; ***Although accord reached in December 1999, the implementation has been delayed until 2001 at the earliest.
Source: U.S. State Department and Merrill Lynch Research.

Exhibit 2   International Air Traffic, 1976–2001 [AEA international scheduled traffic (RPK*)]

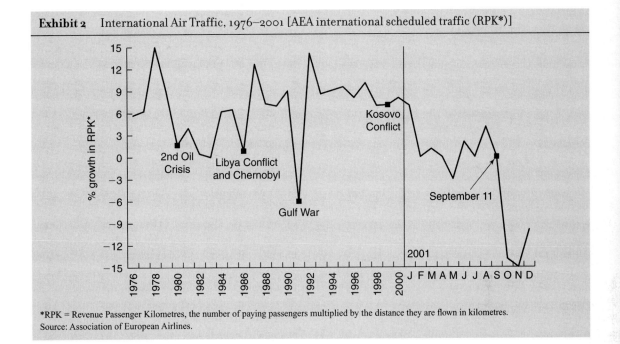

*RPK = Revenue Passenger Kilometres, the number of paying passengers multiplied by the distance they are flown in kilometres.
Source: Association of European Airlines.

$2.5 billion for 2001, but later increased its estimate to $7 billion. This assumed a 15% fall in traffic and capacity, which led to more than 200,000 job losses.[4]

Typical of European airlines, SAS greatly suffered from the 2001 decline of its home economy. Sweden was the largest market and accounted for 40% of SAS's total ticket sales. GDP growth in Sweden was 1% in 2001, compared with 2.5% in 2000. Exhibit 2 plots the international air traffic from 1976–2001.

"The truth is the industry was already bumping through turbulence, long before the tragedies in New York," revealed Lord Marshall, Chairman of British Airways.[5] *"Two things matter to airlines—the amount of empty seats on their planes, and the cost of getting those planes into the air. Reducing these two factors leads to profits, and in recent years, the industry has been struggling."*

Because the demand for air travel was inextricably linked to the overall strength of the economy, the airline industry had to manage a delicate balancing act between supply and demand to make sure that its industry capacity kept pace with traffic growth.

During the late 1990s, airlines ordered new aircraft at a rapid rate, well in excess of historical levels. With a strong economy pushing traffic demand up and up, there did not seem to be too much risk. It was commonly understood that if push came to shove, older aircraft could be parked to ease the excess capacity situation that developed. This aircraft-buying binge saw new deliveries average 1000 per year in four consecutive years, from 1998 to 2001.

The industry was profitable, although astute observers had noted that earnings actually had peaked a few years earlier and airlines were on the reverse slope of the profit cycle. It appeared that

[4]See "Airlines Losses Seen Trebling," BBC News Online, 9 October 2001.
[5]See Symonds, T., "Airlines to Embrace Consolidation," BBC News Online, 21 November 2001.

overcapacity[6] was the perennial root cause of the industry's problem. *"It almost always comes to the issue of capacity,"* observed former American Airlines and US Airways senior executive Randy Malin. *"You can go back and look at every business cycle. Airlines say, 'I'm never going to make that mistake again and pour on the capacity just because we have a couple of good years,' but inevitably they do."*

John Walsh, an analyst based in Annapolis, Maryland, agreed: *"The real endemic problem is too many aircraft. In the 1990s cycle you had recession and the Gulf War as catalysts . . . and I think you've got a similar situation in 2001: excess capacity and a situation where the September 11 incident and the recession that followed are catalysts."*

To some observers, the problem was that the industry started from the wrong premise—that traffic growth always represented unfulfilled demand—rather than recognising that growth was being achieved at the expense of profits. *"There is a theory in this industry that there is innate business demand that keeps growing with the population,"* said one analyst working for a large European airline. In his opinion, *"True business demand growth is close to zero. In a dot-com boom, that's really a positive 2%–3%. You could add 3% more planes and keep your margins. But in average years if you're looking over the business cycle, this is a mature industry for the hub carriers and the optimal income over the cycle is zero growth. That is, growth higher than that is worse than zero. Now the problem is, someone says, 'Oh look I made a lot of money. If I buy 10 more aeroplanes I can make even more.'"*

Rise of Budget Carriers   As the big network airlines bled from overcapacity and a false sense of operational profitability, low-cost point-to-point competitors expanded and tried to make permanent market share inroads.[7] Their low costs enabled them to make profits even in the worst of conditions that they managed to avoid losses in the fourth quarter of 2001, when the whole industry experienced a massive downturn. While the network airlines lay off employees and reduced capacity by 10%–20%, the point-to-point carriers cut back little or none at all. The network airlines deferred delivery of new aircraft in order to conserve cash in the following years. The point-to-point carriers continued to take deliveries.

In the United States, Southwest, the archetype of the low-cost point-to-point airlines continued to acquire aircraft—11 737–700s in 2002, 21 in 2003 and 94 more through 2007.

In Europe, cut-price operators led by Ryanair, easyJet and Go also continued experiencing good business. Ryanair, the second largest with around 10 million passengers in 2001, ordered up to 150 new Boeing 737s, which would more than triple its fleet. easyJet not only had plans to buy up to 75 aircraft from Boeing or Airbus, but also acquired rival airline Go, which was founded by British Airways, to become Europe's largest low-cost carrier.

These low-cost carriers depended for their success on much more than a simple, point-to-point service with no catering or other frills. They operated on a different business model to the traditional hub carriers—raising fares as advance bookings filled a flight boosted their yields, dispensing with travel agents, and selling direct over the Internet. They changed the rules of the game and showed signs of winning. Ryanair and easyJet revealed that 90% of their seats were sold on the Net, which was ten times the share of mainstream carriers.

"At present, low-cost carriers occupy a specific niche in the market," said Albrecht. *"Their business model is the exact opposite to that of worldwide, full-service airlines which make up the Star Alliance."*

Two factors have led to the success of these low-cost carriers: the Internet, and the changing behaviour and priorities of customers.

The Internet had a huge impact on the way airline tickets were purchased, distributed and marketed. Selling tickets via an airline's website lowered distribution costs and eliminated many

---

[6]See Flint, P., "Those Who Can't Remember the Past . . .," *Air Transport World* Feb 2002.

[7]See Bond, D., "Network Airlines Survive as Niche Carriers Profit," *Aviation Week & Space Technology,* 18 March 2002.

intermediaries that received a "cut" off the price of the traditional paper ticket (e.g., reservation fee and travel agents' commissions) and costs associated with processing the ticket (e.g., printing, mailing and revenue accounting).

The advent of the Internet also gave customers more access to information, which enabled them to expand their travelling horizons to new, more exciting and exotic destinations, and be savvier in seeing their demands for price and affordability met. Whereas air travel was originally a luxury item and a service that only the wealthy could afford, suddenly it was a form of mass transportation.

"In Lufthansa, we have debates about this," said Thomas Sattelberger,[8] executive vice president for Lufthansa products and services. *"Should we offer no frills or more frills? The issue for us is the competitiveness of our production platforms, i.e., the productivity of our aircraft, airport, alliance structures and human resource."*

Network Airlines' Response   As the post-deregulation era in the mid-90s saw many international carriers move into new phases of economic agreements in order to gain competitive advantages in their various markets, code-sharing practices expanded and were supplemented by alliances. Both economic agreements permitted airlines to add routes to their systems virtually overnight, and instantly enlarged their market share while still enjoying antitrust immunity.

A wave of mega-alliances around the world started. Besides code-sharing agreements, some of the strongest alliances included marketing arrangements, procurement policies, system commonality and even interchange of flight crew personnel and aircraft. Exhibit 3 summarises the different types of airline alliances.

More than 500 alliances were shaped in the late 1990s. Most were eventually consolidated into five multi-carrier alliances—the KLM/Northwest alliance, oneworld, the Qualiflyer Alliance, SkyTeam,

and the Star Alliance. Exhibit 4 shows the membership of these global airline alliances.

Star Alliance launched in May 1997. Lufthansa and United, along with Air Canada, SAS and Thai Airways expanded their already existing bilateral cooperation agreements into multiple partnerships. The airlines, all with different geographical areas of strength moved from the formal and reciprocal code-sharing, to coordination of flight schedules, joint advertising, integration of frequent-flyer programs, and common purchasing programmes.

In September 1998, American Airlines, British Airways, Cathay Pacific Airways and Qantas Airways announced a new, customer-driven global alliance with the unveiling of the oneworld brand and the launch of a multi-million programme designed to raise the standard of global air travel.

In the late 1990s, Swissair consolidated its frequent-flyer program, Qualiflyer, into an alliance of mainly European airlines, which it led with Sabena. However, both airlines went bankrupt in October 2001. They were later resurrected and renamed as SWISS and SN Brussels Airlines respectively, but kept their Qualiflyer alliance intact.

In August 2000, the SkyTeam global alliance was formed by Aeromexico, Air France, Delta Air Lines, Korean Air, Alitalia and CSA Czech Airlines. Their union generated shared access to major hubs positioned around the world, including Mexico City, Paris, Atlanta, and Seoul.

KLM and Northwest had launched their alliance in 1993. During 2001, KLM announced a planned partnership with Continental Airlines, which already cooperated with Northwest in the United States.

Between them, these alliances accounted for more than two-thirds of air travel. Competition in the airline industry thus turned increasingly among the alliance networks rather than among airlines. By 2001, 70% of the alliances had code sharing, 50% had integrated frequent-flyer programmes, but only 15% tried to save costs by sharing such activities as catering, training, maintenance and aircraft-buying.

In the aftermath of 11th September 2001, the quasi-mergers of the alliance world were seen as a safe and economical way to consolidate the global

---

[8]Thomas Sattelberger spoke at a London Business School MBA forum, London, 25 May 2002.

Exhibit 3   Types of Airline Alliances

The left column lists the different levels of alliance agreements in the airline industry, ranging from the most basic to the most integrated. The arrows on the right column illustrate the extent of alliance agreements entered by the leading airline alliances.

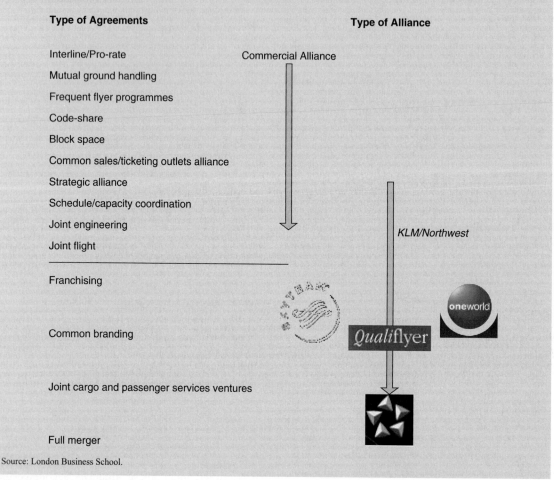

Source: London Business School.

airline industry and put the business back into shape. Even more than in the past, alliance meant survival in the industry as illustrated by Lufthansa's Chairman Jürgen Weber who said *"consolidation is what the business needs."*

Star Alliance

Where in the world do you want to go? With 729 airports in 124 countries worldwide, the Star Alliance is the largest airline network in the world. Whether you dream of lazy sunny days in Phuket, amazing adventures in the Amazon, visiting the family in Vancouver or stealing away to romantic Paris, there is always a Star Alliance airline waiting to take you there.

Star Alliance website (www.staralliance.com)

History   The Star Alliance network formally launched with 5 member airlines—Air Canada, Lufthansa, Thai, United and SAS—on 14 May 1997.

Exhibit 4   Global Airline Alliances

Alliance Brand	Core Members	World Market Share
Star Alliance	Air Canada (Canada) Air New Zealand (New Zealand) All Nippon Airways (Japan) Austrian Airlines Group* (Austria) bmi British Midland (United Kingdom) Lufthansa (Germany) Mexicana (Mexico) SAS (Scandinavia) Singapore Airlines (Singapore) Thai Airways (Thailand) United (United States) Varig (Brazil) Asiana (pending—2003) LOT Polish Airlines (pending—2003) SpanAir (pending—2003)	21%
oneworld	Aer Lingus (Ireland) American (United States) British Airways (United Kingdom) Cathay Pacific (Hong Kong) Finnair (Finland) Iberia (Spain) LanChile (Chile) Qantas (Australia)	16%
SkyTeam	AeroMexico (Mexico) Air France (France) Alitalia (Italy) CSA Czech Airlines (Czech Republic) Delta (United States) Korean Airlines (South Korea)	10%
KLM/NW	KLM (The Netherlands) Northwest Airlines (United States) Continental (United States)	7%
Qualiflyer**	SWISS—formerly Swissair & Crossair (Switzerland) SN Brussels Airlines—formerly Sabena & DAT (Belgium) Air Lib (France) Air Littoral (France) LTU—until 31.12.02 (Germany) TAP Air Portugal (Portugal)	4%

*Includes Austrian, Lauda Air and Tyrolean Airways.
**The Qualiflyer Alliance will be split up and cease to exist effective 1 January 2003. The members will revert to their individual frequent flyer programmes, namely Swiss International Airlines, SN Brussels Airlines and TAP Air Portugal.
   Some airlines (Others 38%), such as Virgin Atlantic, are not part of any global alliance, or are only partially aligned.

However, the inspiration to form a cohesive network seemed inherent among the member airlines even years before, as bilateral and trilateral agreements existed in different combinations among the 14 members (Exhibit 5).

Who's Who   They came together as one but the members of the Star Alliance network did not lose their individual identities. Exhibit 6 provides a brief description of each carrier as provided on one of their websites.

Strategic Objectives   The Star Alliance members had different objectives for entering into the alliance, but they all had a common theme: to expand their geographic network in the most cost-effective way. The airlines faced various challenges and scenarios in their business—how to enter new markets, how to extend market presence, and how to maintain presence in key markets, and together, they pondered on the best way forward. Exhibit 7 illustrates the geographic network of Star Alliance.

Star Alliance members agreed that the most important rationale for establishing an alliance was that it allowed an airline to increase the geographic scope of its network without sizable capital investment. *"In essence the alliance creates a network of virtual destinations,"* said a representative from bmi British Midland.

Since it joined the Alliance in July 2000, bmi was able to launch its first transatlantic service to Washington Dulles International and Chicago O'Hare by operating in conjunction with its Star Alliance partner, United. One of the many benefits of the cooperation agreement enabled customers to book with bmi to 29 onward destinations, connecting to United flights at Washington or Chicago.

Similarly on the other side of the world, ANA was able to market an integrated European offering to customers in Japan through its Star Alliance partner bmi, while gaining important market share from main competitor Japan Air Lines. The British carrier also saw major growth in traffic routing through Heathrow from Japan to a wide range of European destinations.

"Why is it so important to serve every corner of the world? So that a customer can fly to any major city worldwide without ever flying any other airline outside of the 'brand.' A single ticket, one major frequent flyer plan, clubrooms at every major airport, coordinated schedules and a product of consistent quality—these are the aims of the alliance network," bmi stressed.

For bigger carriers like United and Lufthansa, alliance networks were attractive to multinational corporations interested in a single travel vendor, as well as to the international business passenger, interested in the "ultimate" frequent flyer plan. *"The most comprehensive and developed network of airline alliances should be able to command a revenue premium for its airline members,"* shared a representative from United.

ANA saw this phenomenon in action in the area of conferences and conventions. *"We have organised bilateral agreements with convention organisers to appoint Star Alliance as the official carrier."* This arrangement not only allowed organisers to attract audiences from all over the world, but also built global awareness for the Star Alliance brand. Exhibit 8 shows an example of advertising material promoting Star Alliance Conventions Plus, the first ever global conventions service, which gave organisers and delegates a central point of access to a global network of airlines.

The Alliance's code-share agreements also led to an increase in route rationalisation among the member carriers. Lufthansa stopped its services to Australia in 2000, and instead relied on its partner Singapore Airlines to cover the routes. Being a member of Star Alliance, individual airlines could coordinate flight schedules and routes more freely with their fellow members.

Alliances were also an effective way to extend market presence in competitor and key destinations. The Star Alliance members leveraged their carriers' local strengths to build up the whole network's market presence. The alliance structure was also flexible in that it allowed members to strike agreements with other non-alliance members (e.g., Singapore Airlines and Virgin Atlantic code-share flights between

Exhibit 5 Evolution of Star Alliance

October 1992	Air Canada and United Airlines unveiled an alliance agreement.
September 1993	Varig and Lufthansa announced a marketing agreement including code-sharing.
October 1993	Lufthansa and United announced a comprehensive marketing agreement including code-sharing: the first Varig and Lufthansa code-share flights began.
June 1994	The first United and Lufthansa code-share flights began.
January 1995	Thai Airways International and Ansett Australia signed a Memorandum of Understanding to collaborate on code-sharing, schedule coordination and joint marketing.
May 1995	SAS and Lufthansa announced a far-reaching strategic alliance, which included code-sharing. United and Air Canada expanded code-sharing.
June 1995	SAS and Thai announced a code-sharing agreement from June 1996.
September 1995	United and SAS announced a cooperation agreement from June 1996.
October 1995	Thai and Lufthansa began code-sharing.
February 1996	Lufthansa and SAS began code-share flights between Germany and Scandinavia.
March 1996	Lufthansa and Air Canada announced a comprehensive alliance.
May 1996	The United-Lufthansa alliance received anti-trust immunity from the U.S. Department of Transportation.
June 1996	Air Canada and Lufthansa began code-share flights between Germany and Canada.
October 1996	Thai received U.S. approval for code-share services with United; SAS and Air Canada announced an alliance to start in 1997.
November 1996	United, Lufthansa and SAS were awarded trilateral anti-trust immunity by the U.S. Department of Transportation.
March 1997	Varig and United signed a comprehensive marketing agreement including code-sharing.
14 May 1997	Air Canada, Lufthansa, SAS, Thai Airways International and United Airlines launched the Star Alliance network.
September 1997	Air Canada and SAS began code-share flights.
October 1997	Varig joined the Star Alliance network.
October 1997	The first Varig and United code-share flights began.
October 1998	All Nippon Airways gained Observer status with the Star Alliance network, with plans to become a full member in October 1999.
March 1999	Thai and ANA signed a Memorandum of Understanding towards future co-operation.
March 1999	Ansett Australia and Air New Zealand joined the Star Alliance network.
July 1999	Mexicana gained Observer status, with plans to join in 2000.
October 1999	Star Alliance City Office in Paris opened; with an official launch event in Tokyo, ANA joined the Star Alliance network as Singapore Airlines gained Observer status to join in 2000.
November 1999	bmi gained Observer status to join Star Alliance in 2000.
March 2000	The Austrian Airlines Group, comprising Austrian Airlines, Lauda Air and Tyrolean Airways became the 10th member of Star Alliance.
April 2000	Singapore Airlines joined Star Alliance.
May 2000	The Star Alliance Business Centre opened in Los Angeles.
July 2000	bmi and Mexicana became the latest Star Alliance members.
August 2000	The Star Alliance Business Centre in Frankfurt opened.
September 2000	Star Alliance launched StarNet—a sophisticated IT solution that linked the various computer systems of the member airlines.
November 2000	Star Alliance announced the completion of its full-time Alliance Management Team (AMT)—the executive body for the partnership.
December 2000	Star Alliance Business Centre in Bangkok opened.
May 2001	Star Alliance announced the appointment of its CEO—Jaan Albrecht.
August 2001	The first Star Alliance lounge (in Zurich) opened.
14 September 2001	Ansett Australia ceased operation and membership from Star Alliance.
January 2002	Star Alliance was registered under German law as a limited liability company with 65 full-time management staff at its world headquarters in Frankfurt.

Source: Star Alliance website.

Exhibit 6   Star Alliance Member Profiles

AIR CANADA	Voted Best Passenger Airline in 1999 by Air Transport World magazine, Canada's flagship carrier maintains one of the youngest fleets in the world and is renowned for value-added customer service, technical excellence and passenger safety.
AIR NEW ZEALAND	Like its people, the national airline is known for the flair and warmth of its truly Pacific hospitality. Air New Zealand boasts an individual network covering 48 cities in 15 countries. Amongst many other accolades, it holds the 2000 *Travel Weekly* Annual Globe Award for Best Pacific Airline.
ANA	Operating more than 500 flights a day and serving over 30 international destinations, All Nippon Airways (ANA) is widely recognized for its outstanding service. It was the first airline to offer its First Class passengers 180° reclining seats.
AUSTRIAN AIRLINES	With a very special intermediary role linking Eastern and Western Europe, Austrian Airlines has grown significantly in recent years. The award-winning Grand Class service ensures passengers receive the very best Austria can offer.
bmi	Since 1990, bmi British Midland has received over 30 awards in recognition of the quality of its service. Flying to over 30 European destinations, it is the U.K.'s second largest airline. bmi holds 14% of all take-off and landing slots at London Heathrow, its main operational base.
Lauda	The Austrian carrier Lauda Air is renowned for its outstanding service, offering both Amadeus and Economy Class passengers the very best in comfort, cuisine and entertainment. Equipped with state-of-the-art technology, it has one of the youngest fleets in the world.
Lufthansa	With characteristic technical excellence and the highest standards of passenger comfort, Lufthansa boasts one of the world's most modern and environmentally friendly fleets.
MEXICANA	North America's pioneer airline is the fourth oldest in the world. Today Mexicana operates a fleet of over 57 aircraft and its staff look after 8 million passengers every year.
Scandinavian Airlines	An embodiment of innovation itself, SAS has one of the most environmentally advanced fleets in the world. It has also won the Best International Frequent Flyer Programme Award for the past four years.
SINGAPORE AIRLINES	Recognized throughout the industry as a leader and innovator, Singapore Airlines operates one of the youngest fleets, with an average age of just 5 years. Its fleet currently serves over 90 destinations in 40 countries.
Thai	Serving over 35 countries, Thai Airways is proud to take their culture wherever they go. The Royal Orchid Service extends a warm and traditional welcome to over 15 million passengers a year, including a fresh orchid flower to all its female passengers.
tyrolean	Tyrolean operates a 31-strong fleet with an average age of 3.5 years, one of the youngest and most modern fleets in Europe today. It was recently voted Regional Airline of the Year by *Air Transport World* magazine.
UNITED	With over 2,300 flights a day, United is one of the world's largest airlines. One of the most innovative too. It was the first with flight attendants, flight kitchens and the first to fly non-stop across the United States.
VARIG	Varig is dedicated to pioneering the highest standards of service, a quality that's been recognized with many awards. As Latin America's largest carrier, it serves 79 destinations within Brazil as well as 20 countries throughout the Americas.

Source: All Nippon Airways website.

Exhibit 7   Star Alliance's Geographic Network (nearly 80% of airline traffic flows are in the Northern Hemisphere).

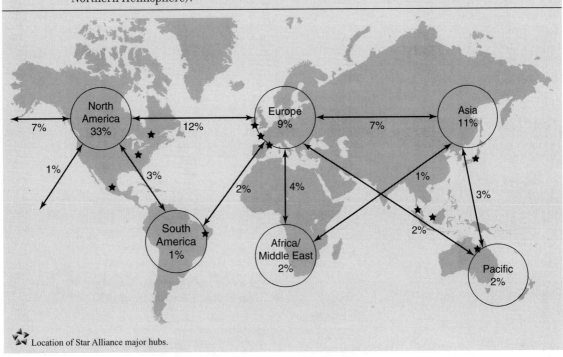

Location of Star Alliance major hubs.

Singapore and London,[9] with mileage points creditable to both frequent flyer programs).

London, the home market of British Airways (the UK's biggest airline) and the oneworld alliance, was a case in point. With bmi at the helm, Star Alliance initiated discussions with the British Airports Authority, owners and operators of London Heathrow Airport, on how Star Alliance could have an effective hub at Heathrow. bmi's Chairman Sir Michael Bishop[10] explained: *"(London) Heathrow is an important global hub for Star Alliance. It is also where we face some of our toughest competition. Oneworld has developed a strong alliance network, with members that we all respect as strong carriers. Our members are committed to ensuring*

[9]Source: Singapore Airlines Annual Report 2001–02.
[10]See bmi press release "Star Alliance Plans Major Customer Investments at London Heathrow Airport," 30 March 2001.

that Star Alliance becomes the premier alliance offering from Heathrow." He added that significant investment was required to consolidate activities of the Star Alliance airlines into one terminal, which was currently being conducted from Terminals 1 and 3.

The Star Alliance partners saw bmi's clout at Heathrow and allowed it take a leadership role in planning the future infrastructure of the airport so that Heathrow could be an effective hub that supported two competing global alliances. As the UK's second largest airline, bmi was able to deliver and coordinate a better service in the UK. *"bmi delivered the UK to Star,"* said Andrew Jansen, Star Alliance manager for bmi.

Hong Kong was another case in point. Herman Tiemens, United's marketing manager for Star Alliance, revealed that United's high brand awareness in Hong Kong offered a comparative alternative to

Exhibit 8   Advertising Collateral for Star Alliance Conventions Plus

Cathay Pacific (the home airline) at oneworld's home market. *"Hence, other Star Alliance carriers could effectively strengthen their presence in Hong Kong through us."*

In some cases a carrier possessed the route authority to serve a particular market, but was uncertain about how long it would take to reach an acceptable return. This was critical to the decision process since aircraft represented significant capital expenditure, especially aircraft flown on international routes. In these cases, joint venture agreements provided within the Alliance framework was the solution. For a joint venture between Air Canada and Lufthansa flight from Toronto to Frankfurt, the aircraft would effectively be split in two so that each airline had responsibility to sell seats in their half of the aircraft. Revenues were shared so that Lufthansa received 100% of revenues from sales of its part of the aircraft.

"Joint venture agreements are easier to handle from an operations perspective and more profitable. You've got two airlines marketing the same flight to customers, increasing chances of reaching full capacity. The only problem was that it's not consumer friendly. It could be quite confusing for the customer who has booked on a specific flight and carrier but was actually flown by a different carrier," said Louise McKenven, vice president for loyalty and marketing at Star Alliance.

Star Alliance's Mission and Vision   Star Alliance saw its mission as contributing to the long-term profitability of its members beyond their individual capabilities. *"We wanted to assist carriers improve*

their bottomline through collaboration—go beyond the results they could achieve on their own," said Albrecht. Its vision was to be the leading global airline alliance for the frequent international traveller.

Taking stock of its strategic objectives, United conducted research on what customers would want from a global airline network.

"We found 3 guiding principles," said John Schoff, Star Alliance Manager for United, *"customers want global access. United does not fly to South America and India but can provide these service through its affiliates. They also want their status to travel with them, so that frequent travellers with recognised status in United would receive the same level of premium service if they travelled with other airlines. More importantly, they want a seamless travel experience. If a passenger were travelling to multiple destinations, his or her checked baggage would be forwarded automatically to the right destination. We believe that following customer benefits would generate us revenue benefits."*

The addition of four new airline members in 2000 (Austrian Airlines Group, Singapore Airlines, bmi and Mexicana), and three more in 2002 (Asiana, LOT Polish Airlines and SpanAir) allowed Star Alliance to successfully further develop its global traffic system. In order to further increase value for the alliance's customers and members, and raise competitiveness, the intention was to take advantage of the alliance's size and global presence through further integration between members' networks, products and services, IT systems and other resources.

Governance   Star Alliance started as a virtual organisation with two headquarters—in Los Angeles (owned by United) and Frankfurt (owned by Lufthansa). A committee structure was put in place to manage the different aspects of running an airline, but in an integrated way.

The five pioneering members operated on the informal "gentleman's agreement" basis, but more formal processes were put in place as the alliance membership grew. *"There were certain things you could do with five carriers that you couldn't' do with fourteen,"* commented United.

Its quest to find the best way of working together led to the formation in January 2002 of a separate management company, Star Alliance Services GmbH, based in Frankfurt. The new unit, registered under German law as a limited liability company, had 65 full-time management staff that took on the strategic responsibilities for Star Alliance, as well as facilitated decision-making and implementation for Alliance-wide projects and issues. With nearly seventeen members by 2002, there was a need to have full-time staff to manage the process.

The new management company also changed its reporting structure. Each member airline became an equal shareholder in the new company.

Star Alliance CEO Jaan Albrecht, once a pilot for Mexicana Airlines, summarised: *"Star Alliance has gone through a fascinating evolution. Originally, our alliance was based on the concept of collaborating in committees and working groups. Then with the growing complexity of some of our projects, the first full-time resources, mainly in the IT sector, were installed. With a growing portfolio of joint projects, this developed into a complete organisation based in three business centres— Bangkok, Frankfurt and Los Angeles. In refining (the organisation) further and also reviewing our portfolio after September 11 (2001), we decided to concentrate the team in one location. We will maintain regional staff presence in Asia and America. I'm convinced Star Alliance Services GmbH, now in place in Frankfurt, has the right people, the right resources to assist member carriers in delivering alliance products on our work list agenda."*

"We are a small United Nations with our different nationalities and cultures. As CEO, I am also responsible for the strategy setting for Star Alliance, in coordination with the CEOs of the member carriers," he added.

Whereas there was equal representation among members when Star Alliance was a virtual organisation run by committees, the establishment of the management company changed the old set-up so that it was not always bound to consult the airlines on their every move.

Star Alliance still relied on the input and experience of its member airlines. It created a Supervisory Board, composed of senior managers from each of the member carriers. Their roles were typically senior vice president for Commercial, Alliances or International. The Board had a legal requirement to meet once a year, but operational meetings normally took place every two to three months. Most of these meetings took place in Frankfurt at the Star Alliance headquarters there. Frankfurt proved to be easily accessible for the Board members, as well as being more cost- and time-efficient as Star's HQ was situated in the Frankfurt Airport Centre.

"We were facing increasing complexity sticking to the committee system because of the number of members and the depth of projects. Too much time was spent getting unanimous buy-in from all the members, which was getting complicated and not cost-efficient," he said.

The old committee members thus assumed advisory roles rather than their previous role of hands-on decision-making. Eighteen advisory groups were set up to cover all the functional areas (e.g., marketing, procurement, operations, technology, etc.) of running an alliance.

"It was a difficult move for the airlines to hand over to a third party. The start-up was quite slow, but now we are, we are able to sign legal documents, things are moving much faster. The carriers are now recognising the benefits of having fulltime people responsible for project management and implementation," he said.

From day 1, Albrecht made it a point to listen to carriers—what they liked from the Alliance, and their frustrations. He established joint work plans with the carriers by spending 50% of his and his VPs' time travelling/visiting the member carriers. The remaining 50% of the time is spent at the Frankfurt HQ for coordination duties. There is also a normal rotation of Star senior managers visiting the carriers to ensure continuous process-management and exchange of information.

"My role as Star Alliance CEO mainly involves coordination. With 17 members to manage, I am busy making plans for the next year, and getting human and financial commitment from the airlines for our projects," he said.

"My first reaction upon joining as CEO was to understand how the Alliance was set-up, and then redefine the role of the organisation through new strategies. I understood the rationale behind an alliance, and what it could achieve beforehand."

As CEO, Albrecht also found he had to right size the organisation and lower the expectations of the carriers. *"It emerged that internally carriers did not have a clear understanding of the role of Star Alliance. They heard talks about creating a mega-carrier, which meant that their individual identities would be dropped in time. They had crazy ideas and expectations of what Star would do and not do,"* he shared.

There were clear limits on what Albrecht's organisation could decide on the carriers' behalf. Most of the decisions (e.g., picking projects) required the buy-in of all the carriers. Once the decisions were made, the day-to-day work/implementation was done by Star Alliance.

"We didn't want a top-down approach. We conceptualised projects with the carriers," he summed.

Competing and Collaborating Managing the group dynamic was a challenge. *"It was quite awkward for Thai when we first started because our four other partners were all transatlantic airlines. They all started talking transatlantic—Chicago to London, Chicago to Paris, and so on. Star Alliance to them was THE transatlantic alliance. We had to remind them that Asia mattered too. Let's not forget transpacific,"* said Serm Phenjati, Advertising and Promotions Manager for Thai Airways.

Phenjati saw the interaction and evolution of relationships within the alliance—transatlantic vs. Asian groupings, North America vs. South America, big vs. small. He noticed that the members constantly faced the challenge of finding the right balance between competition and collaboration.

An example cited was United's frequent flyer program, Mileage Plus. Having the biggest database of frequent flyers, United knew best how to run the program, and considered the expertise as a source of competitive advantage that must be carefully guarded. *"We were all individuals, we were still competitors, yet we were members of one alliance,"* commented Schoff.

The level of collaboration and competition within the Alliance varied according to the issue, but all member airlines were prohibited from executing hostile takeovers on fellow members while part of the Alliance. This rule ensured fair play and a constructive culture among the members.

For Air Canada, cooperation within Star Alliance helped them win some battles—for example winning route rights to Asia, and getting better opportunities to go after more routes. Pierre Charbonneau, director for Star Alliance from Air Canada narrated an incident when competition between Brazilian and Canadian regional jet manufacturers, Embraer and Bombardier, in Brazil had denied Air Canada route rights to Rio de Janeiro because they were a Canadian company. Through the lobbying support of alliance partner Varig, the Brazilian Government saw that the two battles were separate, and eventually allowed Air Canada's access to those route rights.

Charbonneau also shared how his airline decided on the most optimal and strategic solution to locate day-to-day activities. *"It's quite common for airlines to locate individual 'sacred cow' activities such as Marketing, Product Design, Scheduling (i.e., all the functions which define the 'uniqueness' of an airline) at home,"* he said. *"However, in term of Operations and Technical Services, airlines normally preferred to co-locate with other alliance members to extract synergies. Air Canada reached significant benefits in closing a specific Line Maintenance Facility specialized for one aircraft type only and contracting it out to a partner who has greater facility and cheaper costs in exchange for themselves contracting to Air Canada the maintenance of an aircraft type for which it offered a better deal. In terms of Airports and Reservations, Air Canada was actively working on moving operations with under one roof to ensure maximum utilisation of counters, baggage areas, connection times etc."*

The Canadian carrier felt that there would also be great value in centralizing sales units of the various Alliance members in the same cities, *"but there was still very much a sense of 'selling one's own metal' in the sales force. The main reason for this culture was the way performance targets were still designed for meeting goals for individual airlines as opposed to selling the 'Alliance,'"* he said.

Finally, most of the corporate/admin functions were still largely located at the respective airline headquarters, except in some cities an airline would have large buildings that could accommodate local partners.

Singapore Airlines made London and Frankfurt its main European hubs where it could rely on partners to serve onward destinations around Europe. *"We found that Star had greater complementarity and better global coverage than oneworld (to South America for example). Ideally, a new carrier should bring value-added, cover areas not already covered by existing partners. If there's too much overlap, then there will be too much repetition,"* said Clarence Pong, alliance manager for Singapore Airlines.

bmi was more bullish than some of the bigger partners about pursuing integration opportunities within Star Alliance. bmi believed that the strategy of joining an alliance must be to derive real benefits on the cost side, though it recognised this would take some time. *"There's no point being in an alliance just to be a cosy club. We've got to deliver real benefits,"* said Andrew Jansen, alliance manager at bmi. *"Big carriers were slower to integrate because of their size and probably because there's less financial pressure, whereas we're (bmi) so cost-conscious, we get finicky when we see waste."*

As a smaller airline, bmi also had limited resources compared to its bigger partners. *"We looked at costs and concentrated on getting involved where we could. This meant chilling out a bit on the strategy side, as this meant huge resource cost for us, but perhaps being more passionate and vocal on the purchasing side."*

bmi believed that although Star Alliance had global presence and recognition, the partners still needed to come together at the ground level. *"There is still a strong competitive mentality at the ground level, for example among airport managers and sales forces. They need to be convinced to think differently, to get the message to cooperate. They need to agree not to be so precious,"* explained Mark Reakes, international marketing manager at bmi. He thought that while some airlines made a big song and dance about "network," their people didn't really participate in the idea of alliance cooperation.

According to ANA, carriers encountered some conflicts on the subject of lounge consolidation to make the Star Alliance brand more tangible. It was easy to implement in markets not home to a Star partner. However, carriers still wanted to keep their lounges in their strategic or home markets.

For Air Canada, the decision to integrate depended on the strength of airlines' market presence in different markets. *"Where there's no dominant presence of a member airline (e.g., Zurich or Miami), it makes sense to promote the Star Alliance brand more strongly by having one lounge. This also generated cost savings and efficiency. But in cities where dominant carriers are present (e.g., Frankfurt—Lufthansa, Chicago—United, Montreal—Air Canada), the individual lounges stayed as is. It's difficult to give away 'sacred cows' which have received high brand investment from the individual airlines."*

"Customers tell us they want to experience the individual personalities of the airlines. They don't want to fly vanilla airlines. Like, they choose to fly Thai because of what Thai is," Schoff explained. Thai had the same ideas about lounge consolidation. *"If it's a thin market, then it would make sense to have common presence. For our key markets, it is worthwhile to keep the Thai experience intact."*

According to SAS, *"Scandinavian lounges are very much appreciated by Star travellers. It conveys our identity, so we would like to keep it that way. But of course, there's also a need for Star Alliance lounges, especially in third markets (i.e., not a home market of any Star Alliance member). SAS is sharing lounges with other members in third markets currently in the U.S. and Asia."*

Lufthansa found the level of collaboration frustrating when it came to sharing lounge access. *"Lufthansa is the 2nd largest lounge provider, and we have one of the best lounges in the industry. We opened all our lounges to all gold cardholders in the hope that all members would follow suit. We wanted all alliance customers to have the same access but only our European partners did the same. It was a big disappointment but we are working on it,"* shared Sattelberger.

CEO Albrecht offered an explanation: *"Carriers are still struggling to recognise the strength of the Star Alliance brand vs. their own carrier's brand in the industry. In lounges, both cost (of running individual lounges) and branding elements are significant. The question then is—how far are carriers willing to let their own image be replaced or overtaken by the Star Alliance image? It's a matter of maturity and time to get the airlines more comfortable with this integration scheme."*

Beyond lounge consolidation however, ANA felt that there were still huge opportunities where the Star Alliance carriers could cooperate—maintenance, fleet operation, industrial training of employees, and purchasing, to name a few.

Singapore Airlines echoed the same view: *"Being the biggest alliance, we have opportunities to work and negotiate as a group (e.g., insurance companies, currently offered by individual governments). In the UK for example, the UK Government underwrites the first £1 billion. This is important in the wake of September 11."*

"We've had some low hanging fruit successes," shared Albrecht. *"Our joint purchasing project in maintenance procurement and onboard products (e.g., catering, cutlery, china, pillows) is a case in point. This project is by voluntary participation. Carriers implement a master agreement for each area of procurement, mainly to standardise prices. In general, carriers still draw up their own contracts with suppliers, but they always use the master agreement as reference."*

There was no single catering company that serviced all the Star Alliance carriers. Rather, it was common to have four or five carriers using the same caterer based on the master agreement and their locations. However, there was still plenty of scope for differentiation. For example, carriers still choose their own menu.

Culture   Although Star Alliance had established a consensus-driven culture from the start, some thought there was still some lip service done to be politically correct in dealing with the members, especially making sure that all players had an equal part in the discussions and decision-making. Many saw the process as slow and cumbersome. Rolling out projects was a multi-faceted approach.

"It wasn't clean at all. It didn't work well," recalled United representatives. They discovered that being politically correct wasn't expedient in terms of rolling things out.

"It felt like (the movie) Groundhog Day,"[11] recalled Doreen Riley, one of the marketing coordinators from Air Canada. *"For the launch, we wanted an ad that would be simple, easy, short but with strong impact. We'd get everyone's approval one day, but it would all change the next. And then we'd start from scratch."*

"It was very micro," continued Riley. *"Lufthansa had reservations about the black colour that was to be used for the launch collateral. According to them it was reminiscent of war. But the choice of colour also could not favour one particular airline (e.g., red = Canada, purple = Thai)."*

Star Alliance's tagline "The airline network for Earth" encountered some debate as well. Should the "e" in earth be capitalised or not? It entailed a conference call to resolve the matter.

"We needed to get buy-in from the members. There were no shortcuts," Riley concluded.

Despite the tedious process of getting everyone's approval on everything, the members still persevered with the unanimous system. United favoured this consensus-driven approach to the alternative majority model. *"We would feel nervous if we could not have a say in the marketing of Star Alliance,*

even if we were fully in charge of purchasing. There is no trade-off," said Schoff.

SAS admitted that although the unanimous process took longer to arrive at a conclusion compared to making decisions individually, *"it was important that we got things right from the beginning. And many times there is a better result when there is a group decision rather than a single party making the decisions,"* said Stefan Bjurholm, SAS alliance marketing and communications manager.

Because cultures interacted on a daily basis, and on every facet of the alliance, the member carriers underwent a process of discovery and understanding before they found the optimum way of working with each other.

United saw its North American culture as a frustration as well as an advantage. *"It was a frustration because while we wanted to move things as quickly as possible, this wasn't always possible. Other cultures had a different sense of time. On the other hand, our culture was an advantage too. When it was our turn to lead, we did so in an efficient manner."*

bmi experienced similar challenges dealing with cultural differences—British vs. German, British vs. American, and British vs. Asian. "(But) *being a smaller airline, we are less political and can say things without offending other people. Also, we found that we are often allowed to say things on other partners' behalf."*

SAS saw the diversity of cultures as strength for the Alliance. *"We offered different perspectives on issues. It was interesting to see what was important to other airlines, as sometimes we tend to focus on different issues that we believe is important."*

For ANA, *"Fourteen different companies with different cultures made it very difficult to reach conclusions."* They described their European counterparts to have *"very theoretical decisions"* which they found difficult to grasp and apply on a realistic level.

But Air Canada summarised Star Alliance to be a *"very close-knit and fun group."* According to the Canadians, Lufthansa was like a cheerleader within Star Alliance but they didn't impose their ways, *"as*

---

[11]In the movie "Groundhog Day," the "hero" is forced to relive the same day over and over.

much as one would expect because of their culture and size." Referring to the normal battle for power among the heavyweights, Charbonneau recalled that *"United and Lufthansa were the biggest airlines in the Alliance, but there was no clash between them, unlike BA and AA in oneworld."*

"My biggest joy was how smooth and how little cross-cultural issues we encountered in Star," said Lufthansa's Sattelberger. *"Relations were not stereotyped, which was a good thing."*

Air Canada described the culture that existed within Star Alliance to have *"mutual respect and great bonding, which went beyond work."* When Air Canada faced a hostile take over by Onex Corporation in 1999, it received immediate and unsolicited support from Lufthansa to launch a counter attack. *"Lufthansa asked us, so what do WE do next?"* recalled Charbonneau.

Culture and corporate size were not the only things that differed within Star. Different airlines had different business philosophies too. *"Projects that cost a few hundred thousand could be signed off easily by bigger carriers without doing cost-benefit analysis, but we had to do our analysis. This difference in philosophies caused some frustration at times,"* recalled Jansen.

In matters of brand-building, United saw that *"everyone agreed that Star Alliance was important to promote, but there was a spectrum of how people saw their brands promoted, from being loosely connected where the individual brands got more prominence, to being virtually merged, where the individual brands came second to the Star Alliance brand."*

United used the analogy of the European Union in explaining the cultural dynamic that was going on. *"Some airlines felt the same way as Great Britain, which wants to remain 'British' because it values its identity. On the other hand, other airlines are behaving more like Belgium, which is happy to be called 'European' first and foremost."*

United further explained that the strength of the individual brands within the Alliance was different. *"United has higher brand recognition compared to Mexicana. It is thus very important for us to retain*

our brand in different parts of the world. We don't want to forfeit our identity for the sake of Star Alliance. Our airlines have recognition; Star Alliance has too. Mexicana derives a halo effect from Star Alliance. United in Hong Kong also leverages the Star Alliance brand, so a reciprocal benefit exists."

Thai described Star's culture aptly. *"It's all about being sensitive to one another. You had to take off your own hat and put on the Star Alliance hat,"* shared Phenjati. He summarised: *"The key thing for each partner is to have the willingness to adapt and absorb the differences in culture and thinking to the whole system."*

Coping with Crises   The biggest test in Star Alliance's cultural cohesion came after 11 September 2001, when the whole airline industry experienced the effects of the hijackings in the United States. Albrecht called all his CEOs to Frankfurt soon after the attacks. *"You are all facing unprecedented challenges. How can we help each other out? What can we do as a group to leverage our power?"*

"A taskforce was set up composed of cost specialists who identified areas where we could cut costs, which involved anything except labour," he explained. *"Examples of initiatives included consolidation of projects, joint purchasing, and avoiding the duplication of processes at airports and call centres. The goal was to identify quick hits and then lay the groundwork for longer-term cost savings."*

United, which was directly affected by the attacks, saw the Alliance network in action. *"We really pulled together,"* recalled Schoff. *"After September 11, there were hundreds of passengers stranded all over the world that we had to look after. We had to get our passengers home."*

"Air Canada handled the crisis very well," said Charbonneau. *"Over 270 aircraft were stranded in Canada's airports. They landed everywhere in Canada because they were diverted from their flights. We were the sole ground handler and contact for the thousands of stranded passengers. It was Canada helping the rest of the world."*

Charbonneau recalled how many United crewmembers were stranded in Vancouver and were given access to the Air Canada Lounge. *"We took care of ANA passengers who couldn't continue their flights to Asia."* And when the situation improved, Air Canada tried to prioritise Star Alliance passengers and partners as much as possible by flying them out first. *"We received letters from CEOs of our Star Alliance partners commending Air Canada for how it handled the crisis."*

But there was more work to be done after the initial challenge of safely delivering passengers to their destinations was achieved. United, as did most of its partner airlines, had to decrease its operations immediately after the attacks. The U.S. carrier kept its Star Alliance partners constantly informed of its operational plans, and also communicated any contingencies as it faced potential strikes from airline mechanics.

bmi agreed that Star Alliance coped well with September 11. *"We stayed in regular dialogue with each other. The financial situation was serious for all airlines. Marketing could have taken an important role then, but it was difficult as nobody knew what was going to happen next, plus there was huge pressure to cut costs."*

Reakes recalled that some airlines went out with individual messages to reassure their passengers to allay their fears on air travel safety. *"Perhaps it would've been better if we could have delivered a common message as Star Alliance. It would've been more powerful and cost-effective."*

According to Lufthansa, synergies were utilised well during those dark months. *"A key issue with Star Alliance was, it's a sunshine network but would it work in a crisis too? The answer is YES. Star Alliance enabled us to abandon low-density routes but keep our global network healthy and intact,"* said Sattelberger.

Benefits   Indeed, for members, one of the basic benefits of being part of an alliance was to see cost savings in their business. Inevitably though, the members had different motivations for participating, as well as different ways of viewing the benefits they derived. Many factors came into play—strategic/political, economic, cultural.

For the founding partners, there was high expectation from forming Star Alliance, though no one knew exactly how things would turn out. *"It was vague in the beginning. You have to remember, this was a new category. We (Star Alliance) really created and popularised the word ALLIANCE,"* shared Thai.

"All carriers have their own profitability to worry about. There's nothing stopping members to cluster, invest or buy into each other's business. You're allowed to do what needs to be done to be profitable," said SAS. Exhibit 9 shows profitability figures for member airlines.

SAS was strongly pushing for efficiencies and economies of scale across Star Alliance. One area that has been a success story was in sharing ground service resources. *"In all of Germany, we use Lufthansa check-in, baggage handling services for our flights. Our partners use SAS ground services too when they fly to Scandinavia,"* said Bjurholm.

For United, there were strong quantitative and qualitative benefits of being part of Star Alliance. Before 11 September 2001, United achieved about $200 million per year in net revenues from the Star Alliance network, and said that Lufthansa also attributed 25% of its annual revenues to the Alliance. On the qualitative side, Star Alliance consistently received top marks in Merrill Lynch's annual league table of airline industry alliances,[12] which was based on 5 categories: geographic network, market size, network density, financial strength, and regulatory freedom. See Exhibit 10 for Merrill Lynch's definitions and rankings.

Smaller members achieved some halo effect from the Alliance. *"Star Alliance has helped raise the Thai brand. It has given the airlines and Thailand as a country greater worldwide exposure. Most importantly, Star Alliance is an endorsement of a high quality product that is Thai,"* noted Phenjati.

---

[12]See Merrill Lynch Airline Industry Report, 29 September 2000.

Exhibit 9   Annual Average Figures of Star Alliance Members (all annual averages are based on February 2001 figures)

Airlines (ranked by revenue)	Financial Data		Profitability Data			Employee Data	
	Revenue (US$ billion)	% Total Revenue	RPK* in Billion	ASK* in Billion	Load*	Employees	% Total Employees
United	18.0	28.7	201.0	265.0	72.3%	100,414	32.1
Lufthansa	8.9	14.2	85.5	117.9	75.2%	31,305	10.0
ANA	8.6	13.7	60.9	93.8	64.9%	14,639	4.7
SAS	4.9	7.8	22.6	34.1	65.8%	27,200	8.7
Singapore Airlines	4.6	7.3	71.1	92.6	76.8%	28,000	9.0
Air Canada	4.4	7.0	35.6	49.2	72.4%	25,800	8.3
Air New Zealand-AnsettAustralia	3.7	5.8	20.9	30.1	71.9%	22,966	7.4
Thai	3.0	4.8	41.3	55.5	70.6%	24,148	7.7
Varig	3.0	4.8	26.5	36.6	73.0%	17,740	5.7
Austrian Airlines Group	2.0	2.8	14.5	21.3	68.2%	7,673	2.5
Mexicana	1.0	1.6	12.6			6,345	2.0
BMI	0.9	1.4	3.1		63.2%	6,309	2.0
Total	**62.7**	**100.0**	**595.6**	**796.1**		**312,539**	**100.0**

*See Glossary for definitions.

N.B. Need some kind of measure of performance over time, e.g. change in each airline's global market share since joining Star Alliance. Too sensitive?

Source: annual reports.

"We joined Star Alliance because Singapore is a small country and needs more global reach. So, getting access to a large network is necessary. We have achieved this through Star," shared Joey Seow, Singapore Airlines' alliance manager.

According to bmi's Reakes, the British carrier has benefited "quite a lot from the association with Star. Because we're small, we can leverage our position and strong association with carriers like Lufthansa, United and Singapore Airlines."

The global and quality network that became synonymous with Star Alliance filtered through to its main target audience: the frequent flyers. But from their perspective,[13] awareness of Star Alliance and

its benefits centred on (1) mileage accruals on frequent flyer programmes; (2) expanded international network; and (3) lounge access. Exhibit 11 highlights the benefits of Star Alliance to frequent flyers.

One bmi passenger remarked: "So what does the Star Alliance membership mean to me? If you travel frequently on the airlines mentioned above, you will now earn miles in your frequent flyer programme on all British Midland flights. If you are an elite level member (Star Alliance Gold Member), you will get access to the British Midland lounge, even if you fly economy. You will also get priority on waitlists and additional checked-in luggage allowances."

An Air Canada passenger said: "The Star Alliance membership is like GOLD. I've got enough frequent flyer miles to take myself anywhere in the world now, and with Star Alliance membership, you

[13]Customers' feedback/quotes taken from www.epinions.com and personal interviews.

	Flights Data					Interline Revenue from Star Alliance	
No. of Destinations	Passengers Yearly (million)	Flights Daily	% Total Flights	Fleet Size	% Total Fleet	Interline Revenue (US$ million)	As % of Company Revenue
138	87.0	2,475	26.0	600	28.3	235	1.3%
344	43.8	1,349	14.1	287	13.6		
62	27.0	571	6.0	142	6.7	100	1.2%
92	23.2	1050	11.0	190	9.0	96	2.0%
99	15.0	222	2.3	91	4.3	NA	NA
120	19.2	1,200	12.6	246	11.6	285	6.5%
10	21.8	1,000	10.5	191	9.0	100	2.7%
75	16.3	286	3.0	78	3.7		
120	11.4	453	4.8	87	4.1		
111	8.4	410	4.3	92	4.3	19.6	1.1%
52	8.3	207	2.2	54	2.6		
32	6.0	306	3.2	60	2.8		

can redeem at much lower values than with other airlines. A short-haul ticket costs 15,000 miles, not much at all, and gets you a ticket within eight days."

While collecting miles from the Star Alliance airlines was the most popular benefit that passengers perceived, the different frequent flyer programs within the Alliance also allowed them to compare and contrast on the service they were getting. United was generally recognised as having the best and biggest frequent flyer program—generous with frequent flyer bonus miles, having a low mileage requirement, which made it easier to redeem free tickets. As such, many Star Alliance frequent flyers preferred to consolidate the miles they earned from other member airlines to their Mileage Plus account, United's frequent flyer program.

On the other hand, many passengers were aware that Singapore Airlines' Kris Flyer Program had higher hurdles for award milestones than other Star Alliance partners. *"SIA has been very strict on how someone obtains miles on their flights. I get the feeling that they only truly value their full fare First and Business Class passengers, as they are the only ones that ever get miles,"* said one passenger, while another commented: *"Fortunately, SIA belongs to the Star Alliance now, so you can use your UA or Thai mileage to redeem SIA flights."*

The benefits of Star Alliance's global network were strong in the minds of its customers, especially for frequent flyers of the Alliance's smaller members. *"British Midland is one of the smaller airlines that operate in the UK. Having said that, they are now part of the Star Alliance with other carriers*

Exhibit 10   The Merrill Lynch Alliance Index

The investment bank Merrill Lynch has tried to measure the power of each alliance family through the Merrill Lynch Alliance Index. Measuring the strength of the network, the regulatory environment and certain financial metrics, the Index was based on five major categories utilising data from numerous sources including IATA operating statistics, OAG database, DOT statistics and company reports. The Index ranked and scored each alliance relative to all the others. As a consequence, one alliance could significantly outscore another in a particular category despite a very small difference in what was being measured.

The maximum score an alliance could achieve was 100 points. The lowest an alliance could score was 25 points (the starting point for the scoring), which acknowledged the fact that being part of an alliance was a competitive advantage vis-à-vis flying solo.

The Index was based on 5 categories:

a. Geographic network (25 points)

Geographic network measured the global reach of the alliance's network. Data used were the number of destinations, the number of unduplicated miles in the route network, the number of departures, total capacity and distance flown.

b. Market size (25 points)

In addition to focusing on the size of the market both in terms of revenues as well as passengers, the market size section of the Index had a feature called major market presence. Major market presence was based on each alliance's capacity share in the world's top 30 markets. Not only did each alliance reflect its major carriers' shares, but also included the capacity provided by all code-share partners. The largest markets were determined based on airport passenger traffic.

c. Network density (25 points)

Network density measured how intensely the network was being utilised by looking at such statistics as traffic per unduplicated route mile and number of departures per destination.

d. Financial strength (10 points)

Merrill Lynch assigned the smallest weighting to this category, as financial strength really is not a strong determinant of an alliance's success; clearly though, it is still an important category because an alliance's ability to exploit opportunities is adversely impacted if one or more of its partners are financially hobbled.

e. Regulatory freedom (15 points)

This category commented on whether the alliance enjoyed Open Skies and antitrust immunity.

Merrill Lynch Alliance Rankings (31 July 2001) (point ranking: 1 = greatest; 4 = least)

	Star	Wings	Oneworld	Skyteam
Geographic Network 25 Points				
Number of destinations	1,193	519	703	610
	1	4	2	3
Number of unduplicated route km	5,545,960	1,763,594	3,367,165	2,574,357
	1	4	2	3
Number of departures	3,061,927	1,241,757	1,808,616	1,880,159
	1	4	2	2

(continued)

Exhibit 10   *(concluded)*

	Star	Wings	Oneworld	Skyteam
ASKs (000s)	871,908,272	369,752,803	646,390,148	465,475,869
	1	4	2	3
Kilometers flown (000s)	4,407,948	2,069,937	3,143,408	2,512,640
	1	4	2	3
Points	**25.0**	**6.3**	**18.8**	**12.5**
Market Size 25 Points				
Major market presence	23.4%	14.1%	17.8%	12.0%
	1	3	2	4
US$ passenger revenues (mm)	54,365	21,816	40,319	27,311
	1	4	2	3
Number of passengers	294,292,015	118,805,637	183,406,244	195,811,678
	1	4	3	2
RPKs (000s)	615,398,493	272,820,827	454,622,133	332,617,552
	1	4	2	3
Points	**25.0**	**7.8**	**18.8**	**12.5**
Network Density 25 Points				
Pas. rev. per unduplicated route km	9,803	12,370	11,974	10,609
	4	1	2	3
RPKs per unduplicated route km	110,963	154,696	135,016	131,144
	4	1	2	3
ASKs per unduplicated route km	157,215	209,659	191,969	180,812
	4	1	2	3
No. of departures per destination	2,567	2,393	2,573	3,082
	3	4	2	1
Passenger revenue per ASK (cents)	6.24	5.90	6.24	5.87
	2	3	1	4
Points	**10.0**	**18.8**	**20.0**	**13.8**
Financial Strength 10 Points				
Pre-tax margin	5.0%	4.4%	4.8%	5.2%
	2	4	3	1
Debt as a % of capital	68.9%	85.5%	65.2%	70.5%
	2	4	1	3
Points	**7.5**	**2.5**	**7.5**	**7.5**
Regulatory Freedom 15 Points				
Open skies	2	1	3	2
Points	**9.4**	**15.0**	**3.8**	**9.4**
Total points	**76.9**	**50.3**	**68.8**	**56.9**

Note: The point totals above do not reflect each alliance's brand development. If we were to score accordingly, then Star and oneworld would clearly extend their lead over the other alliances.
Star Alliance Members: LH UA RG BD AN NZ AC CP SK NH OS SQ TG MX.
Wings Alliance Members: KL NW CO.
Oneworld Alliance Members: AA BA CX QF IB AY LA EI.
Sky Team Alliance Members: DL AF AM KE AZ.
Source: Merrill Lynch.

Exhibit 11   Benefits of Star Alliance to Frequent Flyers

Products and Services within Star Alliance™

- 15 partner airlines which serve nearly 900 destinations in 130 countries.
- Co-ordinated timetables with extensive code-sharing.
- Earn and redeem bonus points in Star Alliance members' respective loyalty programs.
- Program with alliance-wide identification of and service to priority passengers (check-in, baggage, etc.).
- Access to some 500 lounges worldwide for eligible passengers.
- All the alliance's flights and timetables available in all major electronic reservations systems.
- Round-the-world tickets and Europe flight passport.
- Star Alliance website with reservations service (www.staralliance.com).

- Star Alliance Convention Plus, a product program designed for conference organizers and participants worldwide.
- Joint ticket offices in selected major cities.
- Joint service functions at selected airports (ticket office, check-in, lounges, etc.).
- Star Connection Teams at selected airports.
- Improved through check-in to final destination.
- Development of IT infrastructure to support new products and service within the alliance.
- Functional and cultural training for alliance members' employees who work with customer service.
- Close cooperation on environmental and safety issues.

Star Alliance's launch press release highlighted the benefits of the new network to travellers: *"global network; hassle-free travel; frequent flyer benefits and recognition that we value them as a customer; integrated services designed to provide optimum connections and make use of common facilities and locations; a single, definable overall brand to signify a commitment to customer service. There are more benefits to come. If a customer is important as a regular traveller to one airline, he or she is important—and will be recognised as such—by all our airlines."*

such as Air Canada, Air New Zealand, Lufthansa, Singapore Airlines and United Airlines. This means that when you fly British Midland you can get almost anywhere either with them or one of their partners. But what does that really mean? Well, to tell you the truth, apart from a bit of code sharing, I'm not actually sure," said one bmi passenger.

"Since the advent of Star Alliance, Thai has been connecting more people in the network to and from Asia than any other airline ever could," observed a Thai passenger.

"Air Canada is safe, uneventful, clean and efficient, and with Star Alliance membership, is a virtual worldwide airline. Go for it!" said one Air Canada frequent flyer.

One United passenger recalled his experience flying with Star Alliance. "Since my itinerary involved a total of five airports and two airlines (United and SAS), it was important that I be properly connected for the entire journey. Star Alliance these days seems the most stable of the international alliances, and it offers service between Singapore and Toronto. I checked in once at each end, and everything was arranged properly. All my boarding passes were issued, my luggage was properly tagged, and everything connected seamlessly. Impressive."

"Through both United and its Star Alliance, there are simply more flights that you'd get on less popular airlines," said another United frequent flyer.

Lounge access, a benefit offered to Star Alliance's most valued passengers, received mixed reviews. Because airlines still operated individual lounges in key markets, there were occasions when the lounges' exclusivity excluded even the most exclusive customers of Star Alliance.

A Thai frequent flyer with Gold member status recalled his experience: "I recently flew to Kuala Lumpur on Singapore Airlines, but was denied entry to their Kris Flyer business class lounge because I was flying economy. This is in contradiction to Star Alliance policy of allowing their Gold members access to lounges even when flying economy class. Thai Airways' Orchid Lounge was next door—and they let me in after I showed them my card even if *though I was not flying Thai airways that day. I was impressed. Their lounge has hot Pad Thai, fresh fruits and a wide selection of beverages—even better than SIA's Kris Flyer lounge."*

Effectiveness   The other side of the story was also worth noting. Feedback from Star Alliance members and customers shed light on the effectiveness of Star Alliance as a global network.

Charbonneau summarised, *"The first five years were about achieving awareness, stressing on our positioning, global coverage growth, frequent flyer benefits and building good relationships with our customers."*

The Alliance felt that the real challenge ahead was to achieve their promise to customers. *"We have not fully delivered on our promise to provide customers with seamless travel experience as we still encounter large baggage issues,"* Charbonneau said. He recalled an experience where non-coordination of members' actions led to major hassles for its travellers. When Ansett Australia went bankrupt in September 2001, some alliance carriers failed to provide the same level of protection to Ansett customers as they should have, resulting in negative publicity for the whole alliance.

Member airlines also saw the need to integrate further as a key driver of its effectiveness as a network, to get the synergies within the alliance (e.g., facilities in airports, services in regions, IT systems).

SAS believed that Star Alliance's effectiveness could be shown by cost and revenue benefits from being in the Alliance. *"We need to pursue more actively initiatives that would result in economies of scale, for example joint purchasing. Also, continue to develop tools to measure how many passengers are brought into the system as a result of the Alliance, and equity from the Star Alliance brand."*

Air Canada concurred: *"Everyone knows that the Star Alliance has brought some value . . . I think the passenger feed has been easy to measure for every partner, but the difficulty has been to agree on some sort of consistent model to value Star between us. We can pinpoint the network value quite pre-*

cisely, but the halo effect from the brand for instance, is more difficult to measure."

Air Canada believed that moving forward, the Alliance should give less focus on attracting new partners and more focus on further integrating existing members, and faster. *"From baby-step approach, we need to draw a line in the sand, don't move that line and work backwards from there to achieve our goals,"* Charbonneau said.

According to the Canadians, achieving synergies from purchasing has been the most disappointing. *"We achieved great savings in purchasing fuel, but great failure in purchasing cups and napkins. The marketing folks couldn't agree!"* Charbonneau explained that branding all disposables like cups and napkins under "Star Alliance" saw a conflict emerge between the desire of individual airlines' marketing departments to create a unique product and identity, and the operational goals of achieving cost savings from joint purchasing.

For bmi, the real test of Star Alliance's effectiveness lay in being confident that this mixture of organisations and partners could deliver real tangible customer benefits, and on time, in order to ensure its competitive advantage over other alliances. bmi believed Star Alliance was an effective global network because partners allowed each other to take leadership in their home markets. Adopting the "landlord concept," bmi was the landlord in the UK and Ireland and facilitated opportunities for all members to work together. *"In Dublin, we very happily pooled things together—from the lounges, to check-in, through to using the same baggage handling company, and even sales, where the Star Alliance group is now looking at agency contracts."*

But SAS had a more realistic viewpoint. Bjurholm believed that airlines in the Alliance needed to also regularly reflect on the question "why should I be a member of Star Alliance?" *"Because of the fast changing environment, airlines like SAS should always monitor their strategic position, for example, if being a member is still in line with their objectives,"* he said.

On the customers' side, some pondered on what real value Star Alliance had given them beyond the frenzy of collecting and redeeming frequent flyer miles. Was Star Alliance just a marketing-led initiative that takes away the noise and hassle of customers having to deal with many individual airlines? Should not Star Alliance be more innovation-led to deliver real value adding service to its customers?

They wondered if Star Alliance focused more on benefits for their members—capturing logistical and operational synergies, rather than providing real benefits for customers. With the strong focus on marketing the brand and image of Star Alliance, these frequent travellers couldn't help thinking, "what's in it for me?"

And while low-cost carriers like Ryanair, Go and easyJet were busy rethinking the whole flying experience, attacking the core structure of the industry to deliver real innovation to passengers, were the network airlines simply doing more of the same? This sceptical sentiment seemed to have some basis because while all alliances promised a seamless travel experience, the truth was that it was easier said than done. *"None of the airlines have seamless service,"* said McKenven. *"It's a goal, but it's exceedingly hard to operate because of the difference and incompatibility of systems. You have to be able to read the other airlines' data to achieve seamless service."* Also according to McKenven, Star Alliance had begun to make progress towards its goal of achieving seamless travel. *"We started in Loyalty. Today, if you call United's Mileage Plus programme, you can redeem a Singapore Airlines ticket straightaway from United's end. This development has to be replicated in every part of the Alliance,"* she shared.

The Star Alliance website was also equipped with a centralised reservations system of the member airlines.

Strategic Positioning   Star Alliance had two dilemmas on its strategic position relative to competitors.

The first dilemma focused on integration. On the one hand, Star considered itself to be well integrated, with an advanced form of governance—a market leader that had no model to follow. But oneworld was better integrated in its IT system, which was run by Sabre. The AA/BA leadership also delivered faster decisions, but its dominance was detrimental to the culture of the alliance. SkyTeam was closer to Star Alliance in the sense that it too had a consensus-driven culture. Because of this and the strength of Air France, Star Alliance considered SkyTeam more of a threat than oneworld.

Star believed that the KLM/Northwest alliance was probably the most integrated of them all, and thus captured the benefits of synergy integration from its commercial functions. But its 2-member alliance created a trade-off in global coverage.

Star Alliance knew that its ideal position for the future was to obtain maximum global coverage with maximum global integration, but how was it going to get there?

The rise in popularity of low-cost travel was also a big concern. Scandinavia had been one of the most competitive markets for air travel since 1999. Low fare airlines like Ryanair and easyJet had been active competitors. According to SAS, the growing trend of budget travel has seen more passengers travelling, paying fares from their own pockets. *"This is a price sensitive market, and this trend will definitely stay."*

Other members also recognised the rising demand for price value but remained unfazed. *"Our primary concern is to keep our business passengers, our core customers, which brings high income for (in the form of high margins) for airlines. We do this by focusing on delivering a quality product/ brand, because these passengers don't just want to get from A to B, they want the whole experience of service and quality as well,"* SAS said.

However, some members like Air Canada and bmi were more adventurous in addressing the growing strength of these budget carriers. Air Canada saw that the shift of middle class travellers to budget travel as a threat to all the airlines in the Alliance. They saw that budget carriers had the ability to eat up the incumbent airlines' domestic networks. This meant that the traditional business model they were operating on was not relevant anymore. In November 2001, Air Canada established

Tango, a no-frills air travel alternative complementing Air Canada's full service operations.

On the other side of the Atlantic, bmi also reconsidered its marketing position—whether to continue offering full service or change to being a low-cost carrier. CEO Austin Reid came up with the answer: *"we have to be a full service carrier but with a low cost base. It is unrealistic for short-haul carriers like bmi to run on a high cost base. bmi needs to offer a European set of fares to remain competitive."*

On top of cutting costs, bmi also launched a low-cost venture in March 2002—bmibaby—flying out from East Midlands airport in England. bmibaby saw encouraging figures from its first month of operations.

The Challenges Ahead

As Star Alliance celebrated its fifth anniversary, its members contemplated the changing landscape of the airline industry, and the innovations it had to make to ensure not just survival, but also continuing success.

Albrecht pondered: *"After achieving the status of being the biggest and most global airline alliance in the world, what's next for Star Alliance? How can we continue leading in the industry, leveraging the benefits of the Alliance to cope with the changing industry?"*

Glossary of Technical Terms

Airline Profitability is influenced by 6 factors:

- Yield
- Load factor
- Capacity
- Fuel prices
- Foreign exchanges
- Labour costs

Yield is the average revenue per revenue passenger miles/kilometres or revenue tones miles/kilometres

Revenue Passenger Kilometres (RPK): Total number of revenue passengers carried multiplied by the number of kms they are carried.

Revenue Tons Kilometres (RTK): Total number of cargo tons carried multiplied by the kms they are carried

Passenger Load Factor: A measure of passenger capacity utilisation (derived by expressing revenue passengers miles as a percentage of available seat miles)

Available Seat Kilometres (ASK): A measure of passenger capacity calculated by multiplying the total number of seat available for revenue traffic by miles flown

---

Reading 6-1   The Global Logic of Strategic Alliances

Kenichi Ohmae

Companies are just beginning to learn what nations have always known: in a complex, uncertain world filled with dangerous opponents, it is best not to go it alone. Great powers operating across broad theaters

▌ Reprinted by permission of *Harvard Business Review.* "The Global Logic of Strategic Alliances" by Kenichi Ohmae (March/April 1989).
▌ Copyright © 1989 by the President and Fellows of Harvard College; all rights reserved.

of engagement have traditionally made common cause with others whose interests ran parallel with their own. No shame in that. Entente—the striking of an alliance—is a responsible part of every good strategist's repertoire. In today's competitive environment, this is also true for corporate managers.

But managers have been slow to experiment with genuinely strategic alliances. A joint venture here and there, yes, of course. A long-term contractual relationship, certainly. But the forging of entente, rarely. A real alliance compromises the fundamental independence of economic actors, and managers don't like that. After all, for them, management has come to mean total control. Alliances mean sharing control. The one precludes the other.

In stable competitive environments, this allergy to loss of control exacts little penalty. Not so, however, in a changeable world of rapidly globalizing markets and industries—a world of converging consumer tastes, rapidly spreading technology, escalating fixed costs, and growing protectionism. I'd go further. Globalization mandates alliances, makes them absolutely essential to strategy. Uncomfortable, perhaps—but that's the way it is. Like it or not, the simultaneous developments that go under the name of globalization make alliances—entente—necessary.

Why, then, the reluctance of so many companies either to experiment with alliances or to stick with them long enough to learn how to make them work? To some extent, both foot dragging and early exit are born of fear—fear that the alliance will turn out to be a Trojan horse that affords potential competitors easy access to home markets. But there is also an impression that alliances represent, at best, a convenience, a quick-and-dirty means of entry into foreign markets. These attitudes make managers skittish and impatient.

Unless you understand the long-run strategic value of entente, you will grow frustrated when it proves—as it must—not to be a cheap and easy way of responding to the uncertainties of globalization. If you expect more of your partners than is reasonable, you will blame them too quickly when things do not go as planned. Chances are your impatience will make you much less tolerant of them than you would be of your own subsidiary overseas.

When you expect convenience, you rarely have much patience for the messy and demanding work of building a strong competitive position. Nor do you remember all the up-front overseas investments that you did *not* have to make. And without memory or patience, you risk precipitating exactly what you fear most: an unhappy or unsatisfied partner

that decides to bow out of the alliance and try to tackle your markets on its own.

Alliances are not tools of convenience. They are important, even critical, instruments of serving customers in a global environment. Glaxo, the British pharmaceutical company, for example, did not want to establish a full business system in each country where it did business. Especially given its costly commitment to topflight R&D, it did not see how it could—or why it should—build an extensive sales and service network to cover all the hospitals in Japan and the United States. So it decided to link up with first-class partners in Japan, swap its best drugs with them, and focus its own resources on generating greater sales from its established network in Europe. *That* kind of value creation and delivery is what alliances make possible.

Few companies operating in the Triad of Japan, the United States, and Europe can offer such topflight levels of value to all their customers all the time all by themselves. They need partners. They need entente. They might wish things were otherwise. But deep down they know better. Or they should.

▎ The Californiaization of Need

To understand why alliances are a necessity and not just a fad or a fashion, you first have to understand *why* globalization makes them essential as vehicles for customer-oriented value.

The explanation begins with a central, demonstrable fact: the convergence of consumer needs and preferences. Whatever their nationality, consumers in the Triad increasingly receive the same information, seek the same kinds of life-styles, and desire the same kinds of products. They all want the best products available, at the lowest prices possible. Everyone, in a sense, wants to live—and shop—in California.

Economic nationalism flourishes during election campaigns and infects what legislatures do and what particular interest groups ask for. But when individuals vote with their pocketbooks—when they walk into a store or showroom anywhere in the Triad—they leave behind the rhetoric and the mudslinging and the trappings of nationalism.

Do you write with a Waterman or a Mont Blanc pen or travel with a Vuitton suitcase because of national sentiments? Of course not. It does not matter if you live in Europe or Japan or the United States. You buy these pens or pieces of luggage because they represent the kind of value that you're looking for.

At the cash register, you don't care about country of origin or country of residence. You don't think about employment figures or trade deficits. You don't worry about where the product was made. It does not matter to you that a "British" sneaker by Reebok (now an American-owned company) was made in Korea, a German sneaker by Adidas in Taiwan, or a French ski by Rossignol in Spain. All you care about is the product's quality, price, design, value, and appeal to you as a customer.

This is just as true for industrial customers. The market for IBM computers or Toshiba laptops is not defined by geographic borders but by the inherent appeal of the product to users, regardless of where they live. And with the proliferation of trade journals, trade shows, and electronic databases, users have regular access to the same sources of product information.

Chip makers buy Nikon steppers because they are the best, not because they are made by a Japanese company. Manufacturers buy Tralfa industrial robots for the same reason and not because they happen to be Norwegian. The same goes for robots made by De Vilbiss in the United States. Companies around the world use IBM's MRP and CIM systems to shorten production times and cut work-in-process. Because of the demands of contemporary production modes, they use Fujitsu Fanuc's machine tools made in Japan. In fact, this one company dominates the numerically controlled (NC) machine-tool market worldwide: its market share in Japan is 70%; around the globe, 50%. This is neither accident nor fashion. These NC machines deliver value, and everyone knows it. But the national identity of these products has effectively disappeared.

The Dispersion of Technology

Today's products rely on so many different critical technologies that most companies can no longer maintain cutting-edge sophistication in all of them. The business software that made IBM PCs such an instant hit—1–2–3—was not, of course, an IBM product. It was a creation of Lotus Development Corporation. Most of the components in the popular-priced IBM PC itself were outsourced as well. IBM simply could not have developed the machine in anywhere near the time it did if it had tried to keep it 100% proprietary. In fact, the heart of IBM's accomplishment with the PC lay precisely in its decision—and its ability—to approach the development effort as a process of managing multiple external vendors.

Lotus provided applications software, and Microsoft wrote the operating system on an Intel microprocessor. Of course, Lotus, Microsoft, and Intel don't want to sell only to IBM. Naturally, they want to sell their products to as wide a range of customers as possible. Just as IBM needs to rely on an army of external vendors, so each vendor needs to sell to a broad array of customers. The inevitable result is the rapid dispersion of technology. No one company can do it all, simultaneously. No one company can keep all relevant technologies in-house, as General Motors did during the 1930s and 1940s. And that means no one can truly keep all critical technologies out of the hands of competitors around the globe.

Even original equipment manufacturers with captive technology are not immune to this dispersion. NEC may develop a state-of-the-art memory chip for its own mainframes, but it can sell five times the volume to other computer makers. This generates cash, lowers unit costs, and builds up the experience needed to push the technology still further. It also gets them better information about its products: external customers provide tougher feedback than do internal divisions. To be a world-class producer, NEC must provide the best new technology to global customers.

In short order, the technology becomes generally available, making time even more of a critical element in global strategy. Nothing stays proprietary for long. And no one player can master everything. Thus, operating globally means operating with partners—and that in turn means a further spread of technology.

The Importance of Fixed Costs

The convergence of customer need, together with this relentless dispersion of technology, has changed the logic by which managers have to steer. In the past, for example, you tried to build sustainable competitive advantage by establishing dominance in all of your business system's critical areas. You created barriers to entry where you could, locked away market share whenever possible, and used every bit of proprietary expertise, every collection of non-replicable assets to shore up the wall separating you from competitors. The name of the game in most industries was simply beating the competition. If you discovered an ounce of advantage, you strengthened it with a pound of proprietary skill or knowledge. Then you used it to support the defensive wall you were building against competitors.

The forces of globalization turn this logic on its head. You can't meet the value-based needs of customers in the Triad entirely on your own. You can't do without the technology and skills of others. You can't even keep your own technology to yourself for very long. Having a superior technology is important, of course, but it is not sufficient to guarantee success in the market. Meeting customer needs is the key—no matter what the source of the technology. No wall you erect stands tall. No door you slam stays shut. And no road you follow is inexpensive.

To compete in the global arena, you have to incur—and somehow find a way to defray—immense fixed costs. You can't play a variable-cost game anymore. You need partners who can help you amortize your fixed costs, and with them you need to define strategies that allow you to maximize the contribution to your fixed costs.

The evidence for this lesson is overwhelming. As automation has driven the labor content out of production, manufacturing has increasingly become a fixed-cost activity. And because the cost of developing breakthrough ideas and turning them into marketable products has skyrocketed, R&D has become a fixed cost too. In pharmaceuticals, for instance, when it takes $50 million or more to come up with an effective new drug, R&D is no longer a variable-cost game. And you can't count on being able to license a new drug—a variable cost—from companies not operating in your primary markets. Not unless you have your own proprietary drug to offer in return. With globalization, all major players in your industry are—or may become—direct competitors. You can't be sure in advance that they (or you) will want to share a particular piece of technology. You need partners, but you need your own people and your own labs too. That's fixed cost.

In much the same way, building and maintaining a brand name is a fixed cost. For many products, a brand name has no value at all if brand recognition falls below certain levels. When a company decides to buy a paper copier, for example, it usually calls up two or three producers in the order of their brand familiarity. If your copier is not among them, you don't even get a chance to try to sell your product. You simply *have* to be there to enjoy a high level of awareness among customers. And that means you have to pay for the privilege.

Trying to save money on brand promotion makes no sense if what you're selling is a consumer "pull" product: you spend a little money but not enough to realize any "pull" benefits. And a half-baked, half-supported brand is worse than no brand at all. With some products, you can better use the same money to enhance commissions so that the sales force will push them. In branded competition, if you want to play, you have to ante up the fixed costs of doing so.

The past decade has seen a comparable movement toward fixed costs in sales and distribution networks. Sure, you can try to play the variable-cost game by going through dealers. You can, at least, to an extent. But your sales force still has to provide the support, the training, and the manuals. And all these are fixed costs.

You can also try to make some of these costs variable on your own. You can chase low-cost labor, for example, by moving production to developing countries, but that won't get you very far these days.

In the past, you could make costs variable with your computers and management information systems by time-sharing. But experience has shown that you can't use time-sharing if you want a system that's dedicated to your own needs, a system capable of providing competitive advantage. So today, information technology is pretty much a fixed cost. Over the long term, of course, all these fixed costs become variable through adjustments in investment (capital expenditure) levels. But for the short term, they remain fixed. And the need to bolster contribution to them points in a single, clear direction: toward the forging of alliances to share fixed costs.

This is a fundamental change from the competitive world of 15 or even 10 years ago. And it demands a new logic for management action. In a variable-cost environment, the primary focus for managers is on boosting profits by reducing the cost of materials, wages, labor hours. In a fixed-cost environment, the focus switches to maximizing marginal contribution to fixed cost—that is, to boosting sales.

This new logic forces managers to amortize their fixed costs over a much larger market base—and this adds yet more fuel to the drive toward globalization. It also forces managers to rethink their strategies as they search for ways to maximize contribution to these fixed costs. Finally, this logic mandates entente—alliances that both enable and facilitate global, contribution-based strategies.

In practice, this means that if you don't have to invest in your own overseas sales force, you don't do it. If you run a pharmaceutical company with a good drug to distribute in Japan but no sales force to do it, find someone in Japan who also has a good product but no sales force in your country. You get double the profit by putting two strong drugs through your fixed-cost sales network, and so does your new ally. Why duplicate such huge expenses all down the line? Why go head-to-head? Why not join forces to maximize contribution to each other's fixed costs?

Maximizing the contribution to fixed costs does not come naturally. Tradition and pride make companies want to be the best at everything, to do everything themselves. But companies can no longer afford this solitary stance. Take the machine-tool market. If a German manufacturer clearly excels in custom-made segments, why should highly automated Japanese producers like Mori Seiki and Yamazaki tackle those segments too? Why not tie up with the Germans and let them dominate those segments worldwide? Why not try to supply them with certain common components that you can make better—or more cheaply—than they do? Why not disaggregate the product and the business system and put together an alliance that delivers the most value to customers while making the greatest contribution to both partners' fixed costs?

Why not do this? Companyism gets in the way. So does a competitor-focused approach to strategy. So does not knowing what it takes to operate globally and how alliances help with fixed costs. Managers must overcome these obstacles. And that will not happen by chance.

Dangers of Equity

Global alliances are not the only valid mechanisms for boosting contribution to fixed costs. A strong brand umbrella can always cover additional products. You can always give heightened attention to, say, an expensive distribution system that you've already built in Japan or Europe. And there is always the possibility of buying a foreign company. Experience shows, however, that you should look hard—and early—at forging alliances. In a world of imperfect options, they are often the fastest, least risky, and most profitable way to go global.

You can expand brands and build up distribution yourself—you can do everything yourself—with enough time, money, and luck. But all three are in short supply. In particular, you simply do not have the time to establish new markets one-by-one throughout the Triad. The "cascade" model of expansion no longer works. Today you have to be in all important markets simultaneously if you are going to keep competitors from establishing their positions. Globalization will not wait. You need alliances and you need them now. But not the traditional kind.

In the past, companies commonly approached international expansion by doing it on their own, acquiring orders, or establishing joint ventures. Now, the latter two approaches carry important equity-related concerns. Let equity—the classic instrument of capitalism—into the picture, and you start to worry about control and return on investment. There is pressure to get money back fast for the money you put in and dividends from the paper you hold.

It's a reflex. The analysts expect it of you. So do the business press, colleagues, and stockholders. They'll nod politely when you talk about improved sales or long-term strategic benefits. But what everybody really wants in short order is chart-topping ROI.

No one's going to argue that dividends aren't nice to tuck in your pocket. Of course they are. But the pressure to put them there can wreak havoc with your initial goals, especially if they include competing successfully in global markets by maximizing the contribution to fixed costs.

Managers must also overcome the popular misconception that total control increases chances of success. Companies that have enjoyed successful joint ventures for years can have things quickly go sour when they move to a literal, equity- and contract-based mode of ownership. Naturally, details vary with the particular case, but the slide into disarray and disappointment usually starts with the typical arguments that broke up one transnational chemical joint venture.

(Soon-to-Be) New Owner:

You guys never make decisions on time.

(Soon-to-Be) Former Partner:

Speedy decisions are not everything. Consensus is more important.

NO:

Well, just tell the dealers that our products are the best in the world. Tell them that they sell everywhere except here.

FP:

But the dealers complain that your products are just okay, not great. Even worse, they are not really tailored to the needs or aesthetic preferences of local customers.

NO:

Nonsense. What customers buy, everywhere in the world, is the physical performance of the product. No one matches us in performance.

FP:

Perhaps. Still, the dealers report that your products are not neatly packaged and often have scratches on the surface.

NO:

But that has no effect on performance.

FP:

Tell that to the dealers. They say they cannot readily see—or sell—the performance difference you're talking about, so they have to fall back on aesthetics, where your products are weak. We'll have to reduce price.

NO:

Don't you dare. We succeeded in the United States and in Europe by keeping our prices at least 5% above those of our competitors. If we're having trouble in Japan it's because of you. Your obvious lack of effort, knowledge, even confidence in our products—that's what keeps them from selling. Besides, your parent keeps on sending our joint venture group a bunch of bumbling old incompetents for managers. We rarely get the good people. Maybe the idea is to kill off our relationships entirely so they can start up a unit of their own making imitation products.

FP:

Well, if you feel that way, there is not much point in our continuing on together.

NO:

Glad you said that. We'll buy up the other 50% of the equity and go it on our own.

FP:

Good luck. By the way, how many Japanese-speaking managers do you have in your company—that is, after we pull out all the "bumbling old incompetents" from our joint venture?

NO:

None. But don't worry. We'll just hire a bunch of headhunters and get started up in record time.

This is a disaster waiting—no, rushing—to happen. Back when this arrangement was a functioning joint venture, however, both partners, and especially the middle managers, really made an effort to have things work. Under a cloud of 100% control, things are different. You can buy a company's equity, but you cannot buy the mind or the spirit or the initiative or the devotion of its people. Nor can you just go hire replacements. In different environments, the availability of key professional services—managerial, legal, and so on—varies considerably.

The lesson is painful but inescapable: having control does not necessarily mean a better managed company. You cannot manage a global company through control. In fact, control is the last resort. It's what you fall back on when everything else fails and you're willing to risk the demoralization of workers and managers.

This need for control is deeply rooted. The tradition of Western capitalism lies behind it, a tradition that has long taught managers the dangerously incorrect arithmetic that equates 51% with 100% and 49% with 0%. Yes, of course, 51% buys you full legal control. But it is control of activities in a foreign market, about which you may know little as you sit far removed from the needs of customers in your red-carpeted office in Manhattan, Tokyo, or Frankfurt.

When Americans and Europeans come to Japan, they all want 51%. That's the magic number because it ensures majority position and control over personnel, brand decisions, and investment choices. But good partnerships, like good marriages, don't work on the basis of ownership or control. It takes effort and commitment and enthusiasm from both sides if either is to realize the hoped-for benefits. You cannot own a successful partner any more than you can own a husband or a wife.

In time, as the relationship between partners deepens and as mutual trust and confidence build, there may come a point when it no longer makes sense to remain two separate entities. Strategy, values, and culture might all match up so well that both sides want to finish the work of combination. Hewlett-Packard's presence in Japan started out in 1963, for example, as a 51–49 joint venture with Yokogawa Electric. Over two decades, enough confidence had built up that in 1983, Yokogawa Electric gave Hewlett-Packard another 24%.

The point is, it took two decades for Hewlett-Packard to reach a significant ownership position. Control was never the objective. All along, the objective was simply to do things right and serve customers well by learning how to operate as a genuine insider in Japan. As a result, Hewlett-Packard now owns 75% of a $750 million company in Japan that earns 6.6% net profit after tax.

An emphasis on control through equity, however, immediately poisons the relationship. Instead of focusing on contribution to fixed costs, one company imperialistically tells the other, "Look, I've got a big equity stake in you. You don't give me all the dividends I want, so get busy and distribute my product. I'm not going to distribute yours, though. Remember, you work for me."

This kind of attitude problem prevents the development of intercompany management skills, which are critical for success in today's global environment. But these skills must be learned. Peter L. Bonfield, chairman and managing director of International Computers Ltd., has a plastic name-card holder that he distributes to all his people who are in touch with Fujitsu, ICL's mainframe computer partner in Japan. On one side there is a place for the cards; on the other, a proven list of "*Do*s" for making such collaborative arrangements work. (See "ICL's *Do*s for Successful Collaboration.") Nothing here about 51% or establishing control.

Equity by itself is not the problem in building successful alliances. In Japan, we have a lot of "group companies," known as *keiretsu,* where an equity stake of, say, 3% to 5% keeps both partners interested in each other's welfare without threatening either's autonomy. Stopping that far short of a controlling position keeps the equity holder from treating the other company as if it were a subsidiary. Small equity investments like these may be the way to go.

Joint ventures may also work, but there are two obstacles that can trip them up. First, there is a contract, and contracts—even at their best—can only

ICL's *Dos* for Successful Collaboration

1. Treat the collaboration as a personal commitment. It's people that make partnerships work.
2. Anticipate that it will take up management time. If you can't spare the time, don't start it.
3. Mutual respect and trust are essential. If you don't trust the people you are negotiating with, forget it.
4. Remember that both partners must get something out of it (money, eventually). Mutual benefit is vital. This will probably mean you've got to give something up. Recognize this from the outset.
5. Make sure you tie up a tight legal contract. Don't put off resolving unpleasant or contentious issues until "later." Once signed, however, the contract should be put away. If you refer to it, something is wrong with the relationship.
6. Recognize that during the course of a collaboration, circumstances and markets change. Recognize your partner's problems and be flexible.
7. Make sure you and your partner have mutual expectations of the collaboration and its time scale. One happy and one unhappy partner is a formula for failure.
8. Get to know your opposite numbers at all levels socially. Friends take longer to fall out.
9. Appreciate that cultures—both geographic and corporate—are different. Don't expect a partner to act or respond identically to you. Find out the true reason for a particular response.
10. Recognize your partner's interests and independence.
11. Even if the arrangement is tactical in your eyes, make sure you have corporate approval. Your tactical activity may be a key piece in an overall strategic jigsaw puzzle. With corporate commitment to the partnership, you can act with the positive authority needed in these relationships.
12. Celebrate achievement together. It's a shared elation, and you'll have earned it!

Postscript

Two further things to bear in mind:

1. If you're negotiating a product OEM deal, look for a quid pro quo. Remember that another product may offer more in return.
2. Joint development agreements must include joint marketing arrangements. You need the largest market possible to recover development costs and to get volume/margin benefits.

reflect an understanding of costs and markets and technologies at the moment companies sign them. When things change, as they always do, the partners don't really try to compromise and adjust. They look to the contract and start pointing fingers. After all, managers are human. They are sweet on their own companies and tolerant of their own mistakes. Tolerance goes way down when partners cause mistakes.

The second problem with joint ventures is that parent companies behave as parents everywhere often do. They don't give their children the breathing space—or the time—they need to grow. Nor do they react too kindly when their children want to expand, especially if it's into areas the parents want to keep for themselves. "Keep your hands off" is the message they send, and that's not a good way to motivate anyone, let alone their own children.

This is not to say that joint ventures cannot work. Many work quite well. Fuji Xerox, for example, a very successful 50–50 arrangement between Rank Xerox and Fuji Film, earns high profits on its $3 billion annual sales and attracts some of the best people in Japan to work for it. Equally important, it has enough autonomy to get actively involved in new areas like digital-imaging technology, even though both parents have strong interests there themselves. The head of Fuji Xerox, Yotaro Kobayashi, who is the son of the founder of Fuji

Film, now sits on the board of Xerox, which has benefited greatly from Fuji Xerox's experience in battling the Japanese companies that have attacked Xerox's position in the medium- to low-end copier segments in the United States.

On balance, however, most parents are not so tolerant of their joint ventures' own ambitions. There have to be better ways to go global than a regular sacrifice of the firstborn. There are.

Going global is what parents should do together—through alliances that address the issue of fixed costs. They work. Nissan distributes Volkswagens in Japan; Volkswagen sells Nissan's four-wheel drive cars in Europe. Mazda and Ford swap cars in the Triad; GM and Toyota both collaborate and compete in the United States and Australia. Continental Tire, General Tire (now owned by Continental), Yokohama Rubber, and Toyo Tire share R&D and swap production. In the United States, for example, General Tire supplies several Japanese transplants on behalf of Yokohama and Toyo, both of which supply tires on behalf of General and Continental to car companies in Japan. No equity changes hands.

In the pharmaceutical industry, where both ends of the business system (R&D and distribution) represent unusually high fixed costs, companies regularly allow their strong products to be distributed by (potential) competitors with excellent distribution systems in key foreign markets. In the United States, Marion Laboratories distributes Tanabe's Herbesser and Chugai's Ulcerim; Merck, Yamanouchi's Gaster; Eli Lilly, Fujisawa's Cefamezin. In Japan, Shionogi distributes Lilly's Ceclor as Kefral (1988 sales: $700 million). Sankyo distributes Squibb's Capoten; Takeda, Bayer's Adalat; Fujisawa, SmithKline's Tagamet. Sales in Japan of each of these medicines last year were in the order of $300 million.

The distribution of drugs is a labor- and relationship-intensive process. It takes a force of more than 1,000 detail people to have any real effect on Japanese medicine. Thus, unless you are committed to building and sustaining such a fixed cost in Japan, it makes sense to collaborate with someone who has such a force already in place—and who can reciprocate elsewhere in the Triad.

Despite the typical "United States versus Japan" political rhetoric, the semiconductor industry has given rise to many forms of alliances. Most companies feel shorthanded in their R&D, so they swap licenses aggressively. Different forces prompted cooperative arrangements in the nuclear industry. General Electric, Toshiba, Hitachi, ASEA, AMU, and KWU (Siemens) banded together during the late 1970s to develop an improved nuclear boiling-water reactor. They shared their upstream R&D on a global basis but kept downstream construction and local customer relationships to themselves. During the 1980s, the first three (core) members of the alliance continued their R&D collaboration and, in fact, developed an advanced boiling-water reactor concept. This time around, they split the orders from Tokyo Electric Power, among others, one-third each. As confidence builds, the activities open to joint participation can begin to encompass the entire business system.

Hitachi Kenki, a maker of construction equipment, has a loose alliance in hydraulic excavators with Deere & Company in North America and with Fiat Allis in Europe. Because Hitachi's product line was too narrow for it to set up its own distribution networks throughout the Triad, it tied up with partners who have strong networks already in place, as well as good additional products of their own, like bulldozers and wheel loaders, to fill in the gaps in Hitachi's product line. So effective have these arrangements been that the partners are now even committed to the joint development of a new wheel loader.

In the oligopolistic sheet glass industry, there is a noteworthy alliance between PPG and Asahi Glass, which began in 1966 with a joint venture in Japan to produce polyvinyl chloride. In 1985, the same pair formed a joint automotive-glass venture in the United States in hopes of capturing the business of Japanese automakers with U.S. production facilities. They built a second such plant in 1988. That same year they set up a chloride and caustic soda joint venture in Indonesia, along with some local participants and Mitsubishi Trading Company. During all this time, however, they remained fierce global competitors in the sheet-glass business.

Another long-term relationship is the one between Brown Shoe and Nippon Shoe, which introduced a new technology back in 1962 to produce Brown's "Regal" shoes. Today the relationship encompasses several other brands of Brown's shoes. For Brown, this has proven a most effective way to participate in a Japanese market for leather goods that would be otherwise closed to them for both social reasons (historically, Japanese tanners have been granted special privileges) and reasons of appropriate skill (Brown's expertise in, for example, managing its own retail chains is not so relevant in an environment where sky-high real estate prices make direct company ownership of retail shops prohibitively expensive).

There are more examples, but the pattern is obvious: a prudent, non–equity-dependent set of arrangements through which globally active companies can maximize the contribution to their fixed costs. No surprise here. These alliances are an important part of the way companies get back to strategy.

■ The Logic of Entente

One clear change of mind necessary to make alliances work is a shift from a focus on ROI to a focus on ROS (return of sales). An ROS orientation means that managers will concern themselves with the ongoing business benefits of the alliance, not just sit around and wait for a healthy return on their initial investment. Indeed, equity investments almost always have an overtone of one company trying to control another with money. But few businesses succeed because of control. Most make it because of motivation, entrepreneurship, customer relationships, creativity, persistence, and attention to the "softer" aspects of an organization, such as values and skills.

An alliance is a lot like a marriage. There may be no formal contract. There is no buying and selling of equity. There are few, if any, rigidly binding pro-

visions. It is a loose, evolving kind of relationship. Sure, there are guidelines and expectations. But no one expects a precise, measured return on the initial commitment. Both partners bring to an alliance a faith that they will be stronger together than either would be separately. Both believe that each has unique skills and functional abilities the other lacks. And both have to work diligently over time to make the union successful.

When one partner is weak or lazy or won't make an effort to explore what the two can do together, things can come apart. One-sidedness and asymmetry of effort and attention doom a relationship. If a wife goes out and becomes the family's breadwinner *and* does all the housework *and* raises the children *and* runs the errands *and* cooks the meals, sooner or later she will rebel. Quite right. If the husband were in the same position, he'd rebel too. As soon as either partner starts to feel that the situation is unfair or uneven, it will begin to come apart. Alliances are like that. They work only when the partners do.

It's hard work. It's all too easy for doubts to start to grow. A British whiskey company used a Japanese distributor until it felt it had gained enough experience to start its own sales operation in Japan. Japanese copier makers and automobile producers have done this to their U.S. partners. It happens. There's always the danger that a partner is not really in it for the long haul.

But the odds run the other way. There is a tremendous cost—and risk—in establishing your own distribution, logistics, manufacturing, sales, and R&D in every key market around the globe. It takes time to build skills in your own people and develop good relations with vendors and customers. Nine times out of 10, you will want to stay in the alliance.

Inchcape, a British trading house with a strong regional base in Asia, distributes Toyota cars in China, Hong Kong, Singapore, elsewhere in the Pacific region, and in several European countries. It also distributes Ricoh copiers in Hong Kong and Thailand. This arrangement benefits the Japanese producers, which get access to important parts of the world without having to set up their own distribution networks. It also benefits Inchcape, which can leverage its traditional British connections in Asia while adding new, globally competitive products to its distribution pipeline to replace the less attractive offerings of declining U.K.–based industries.

In practice, though, companies do start to have doubts. Say you've started up a Japanese alliance, not invested all that much, and been able to boost your production at home because of sales in Japan. Then you look at the actual cash flow from those sales, and it doesn't seem all that great. So you compare it with a competitor's results—a competitor that has gone into Japan entirely on its own. It's likely that you've forgotten how little effort you've put in when compared with the blood, sweat, and tears of your competitor. All you look at are the results.

All of a sudden you start to feel cheated; you remember every little inconvenience and frustration. You yield to the great temptation to compare apples with oranges, to moan about revenues while forgetting fixed costs. You start to question just how much the alliance is really doing for you.

It's a bit like going to a marriage counselor and complaining about the inconveniences of marriage because, had you not married, you could be dating anyone you like. You focus on what you think you're missing, on the inconveniences, and forget entirely about the benefits of being married. It's a psychological process. Alliance partners can easily fall into this kind of destructive pattern of thought, complaining about the annoyances of coordination, of working together, of not having free rein. They forget the benefits.

Actually, they forget to *look* for the benefits. And most accounting and control systems only make this worse. For instance, if you are running your own international sales operation in Japan, you know where to look for accurate measures of performance. You know how to read an income statement, figure out the return on invested capital, consolidate the performance of subsidiaries.

But when you're operating through a partner in Japan and you're asking yourself how that Japanese operation is doing, you forget to look for the benefits at home in the contribution to the fixed costs of R&D, manufacturing, and brand image. The financials don't highlight them; they usually don't even capture them. Most of the time, these contributions—like the extra production volume for OEM export—are simply invisible, below the line of sight.

Companies in the United States, in particular, often have large, dominant home country operations. As a result, they report the revenues generated by imports from their overseas partners as their own domestic sales. In fact, they think of what they're doing not as importing but as managing procurement. Exports get recorded as overseas sales of the domestic divisions. In either case, the contribution of the foreign partner gets lost in the categories used by the U.S.–based accounting system.

It takes real dedication to track down the domestic benefits of a global alliance. And you're not even going to look for them if you spend all your time complaining. The relationship is never going to last. That's too bad, of course, if the alliance really does contribute something of value. But even when alliances are good, you can outgrow them. Needs change, and today's partner might not be the best or the most suitable tomorrow.

Financial institutions shift about like this all the time. If you're placing a major issue, you may need to tie up with a Swiss bank with deep pockets. If you need help with retail distribution, you may turn to Merrill Lynch or Shearson Lehman Hutton. In Japan, Nomura Securities may be the best partner because of its size and retail strength. You don't need to be good at everything yourself as long as you can find a partner who compensates for your weak points.

Managing multiple partners is more difficult in manufacturing industries but still quite doable. IBM in the United States has a few important allies; in Japan it has teamed up with just about everyone possible. (There has even been a book published in Japanese, entitled *IBM's Alliance Strategy in*

Japan.) It has links with Ricoh in distribution and sales of low-end computers, with Nippon Steel in systems integration, with Fiji Bank in financial systems marketing, with OMRON in CIM, and with NTT in value-added networks. IBM is not a jack-of-all-trades. It has not made huge fixed-cost investments. In the eyes of Japanese customers, however, it has become an all-around player. No wonder IBM has achieved a major "insider" position in the fiercely competitive Japanese market, along with handsome sales ($7 billion in 1988) and profits ($1.2 billion).

Sure, individual partners may not last. Every business arrangement has its useful life. But maintaining a presence in Japan by means of alliances *is* a permanent endeavor, an enduring part of IBM's strategy. And acting as if current arrangements are permanent helps them last longer. Just like marriage. If you start cheating on day two, the whole thing gets shaky fast.

Why does the cheating start? You're already pretty far down the slippery slope when you say to yourself, "I've just signed this deal with so-and-so to distribute my products. I don't need to worry about that anymore as long as they send me my check on time." You're not holding up your half of the relationship. You're not working at it. More important, you're not trying to learn from it—or through it. You're not trying to grow, to get better as a partner. You start to imagine all sorts of grievances. And your eye starts to wander.

One of Japan's most remarkable success stories is 7-Eleven. Its success, however, is not due to the efforts of its U.S. owner, Southland Corporation, but rather to the earnest acquisition of "know-how" by Ito-Yokado, the Japanese licensee. Faced with a take-over threat, Southland management collected something on the order of $5 billion through asset stripping and junk bond issues. The high-interest cost of the LBO caused the company to report a $6 million loss in 1987. Meanwhile, since the Japanese had completely absorbed the know-how for running 7-Eleven, the only thing Southland had left in Japan was its 7-Eleven brand.

When Southland's management asked Ito-Yokado to buy the 7-Eleven brand name for half a billion dollars, Ito-Yokado's counterproposal was to arrange an interest-free loan of ¥41 billion to Southland in exchange for the annual royalty payment of $25 million, with the brand name as collateral. Should something happen to Southland so that it cannot pay back the debt, it will lose the brand and its Japanese affiliation completely. Yes, Southland got as much as a half a billion dollars out of Japan in exchange for mundane know-how, so they should be happy as a Yukon River gold miner. On the other hand, the loss of business connections in Japan means that Southland is permanently out of one of the most lucrative retail markets in the world. That's not a marriage. It's just a one-night stand.

Another company, a U.S. media company, took 10% of the equity of a good ad agency in Japan. When the agency went public, the U.S. investor sold off 3% and made a lot of money over and above its original investment. It still had 7%. Then the stockholders started to complain. At Tokyo's crazy stock market prices, that 7% represented about $40 million that was just sitting in Japan without earning dividends. (The dividend payout ratio of Japanese companies is usually very low.) So the stockholders pushed management to sell off the rest and bring the money back to the United States, where they could get at least a money-market level of return. No growth, of course. No lasting position in the booming Japanese market. Just a one-time killing.

Much the same logic seems to lie behind the sale by several U.S.–based companies of their equity positions in Japanese joint ventures. McGraw-Hill (Nikkei–McGraw-Hill), General Electric (Toshiba), B.F. Goodrich (Yokohama Rubber), CBS (CBS–Sony), and Nabisco (Yamazaki–Nabisco), among others, have all realized handsome capital gains in this fashion. If they had not given up their participation in so lucrative a market as Japan, however, the value of their holdings would now be many times greater still. GE, for example, probably realized more than $400 million from its sale of Toshiba shares during the early 1980s. But those same shares would be worth roughly $1.6 billion today. Similarly, B.F. Goodrich's investment in Yokohama Rubber would now be worth nearly $300 million, compared with an estimated $36 million that it realized from selling its shares during the late 1970s and early 1980s. Of course, such funds have since found other opportunities for profitable investment, but they would have to do very well indeed to offset the loss of so valuable an asset base in Japan.

This kind of equity-based mind-set makes the eye wander. It sends the message that alliances are not a desirable—or effective—means of coping with the urgent and inescapable pressures of globalization or of becoming a genuine insider throughout the Triad market. It reinforces the short-term orientation of managers already hard-pressed by the uncertainties of a new global environment.

When a dispute occurs in a transnational joint venture, it often has overtones of nationalism, sometimes even racism. Stereotypes persist. "Americans just can't understand our market," complain some frustrated partners. "The Germans are too rigid," complain others. "Those mechanical Japanese may be smart at home, but they sure as hell are dumb around here." We've all heard the comments.

It does not take companies with radically different nationalities to have a "clash of cultures" in a joint venture. Most of the cross-border mergers that took place in Europe during the 1970s have resulted in divorce or in a takeover by one of the two partners. In Japan, mergers between Japanese companies—Dai-Ichi Kangyo Bank and Taiyo Kobe Bank, for example—have journalists gossiping about personal conflicts at the top between, say, ex-Kangyo and ex-Dai-Ichi factions lingering on for 10 years or more.

Good combinations—Ciba-Geigy and Nippon Steel (a combination of Yawata and Fuji), for example—are the exception, not the rule. Two corporate cultures rarely mesh well or smoothly. In the academic world, there is a discipline devoted to the study of interpersonal relationships. To my knowledge, however, there is not even one scholar who specializes in the study of *intercompany* relationships. This is a serious omission, given the importance of joint ventures and alliances in today's competitive global environment. We need to know much more than we do about what makes effective corporate relationships work.

Having been involved with many multicomplex situations, I do not underestimate this task. Still, we must recognize and accept the inescapable subtleties and difficulties of intercompany relationships. That is the essential starting point. Then we must focus not on contractual or equity-related issues but on the quality of the people at the interface between organizations. Finally, we must understand that success requires frequent, rapport-building meetings at least at three organizational levels: top management, staff, and line management at the working level.

This is hard, motivation-testing work. No matter what they say, however, many companies don't really care about extending their global reach. All they want is a harvesting of the global market. They are not interested in the hard work of serving customers around the world. They are interested in next quarter's ROI. They are not concerned with getting back to strategy or delivering long-term value or forging entente. They want a quickie. They want to feel good today and not have to work too hard tomorrow. They are not serious about going global or about the painstaking work of building and maintaining the alliances a global market demands.

Yet the relentless challenges of globalization will not go away. And properly managed alliances are among the best mechanisms that companies have found to bring strategy to bear on these challenges. In today's uncertain world, it is best not to go it alone.

Reading 6-2   Collaborate with Your Competitors—and Win

Gary Hamel, Yves L. Doz, and C. K. Prahalad

Collaboration between competitors is in fashion. General Motors and Toyota assemble automobiles, Siemens and Philips develop semiconductors, Canon supplies photocopiers to Kodak, France's Thomson and Japan's JVC manufacture videocassette recorders. But the spread of what we call "competitive collaboration"—joint ventures, outsourcing agreements, product licensings, cooperative research—has triggered unease about the long-term consequences. A strategic alliance can strengthen both companies against outsiders even as it weakens one partner vis-à-vis the other. In particular, alliances between Asian companies and Western rivals seem to work against the Western partner. Cooperation becomes a low-cost route for new competitors to gain technology and market access.[1]

Yet the case for collaboration is stronger than ever. It takes so much money to develop new products and to penetrate new markets that few companies can go it alone in every situation. ICL, the British computer company, could not have developed its current generation of mainframes without Fujitsu. Motorola needs Toshiba's distribution capacity to break into the Japanese semiconductor market. Time is another critical factor. Alliances can provide shortcuts for Western companies racing to improve their production efficiency and quality control.

We have spent more than five years studying the inner workings of 15 strategic alliances and monitoring scores of others. Our research (see the box

"About Our Research") involves cooperative ventures between competitors from the United States and Japan, Europe and Japan, and the United States and Europe. We did not judge the success or failure of each partnership by its longevity—a common mistake when evaluating strategic alliances—but

---

About Our Research
We spent more than five years studying the internal workings of 15 strategic alliances around the world. We sought answers to a series of interrelated questions. What role have strategic alliances and outsourcing agreements played in the global success of Japanese and Korean companies? How do alliances change the competitive balance between partners? Does winning at collaboration mean different things to different companies? What factors determine who gains most from collaboration? To understand who won and who lost and why, we observed the interactions of the partners firsthand and at multiple levels in each organization. Our sample included four European–U.S. alliances, two intra-European alliances, two European–Japanese alliances, and seven U.S.–Japanese alliances. We gained access to both sides of the partnerships in about half the cases and studied each alliance for an average of three years. Confidentiality was a paramount concern. Where we did have access to both sides, we often wound up knowing more about who was doing what to whom than either of the partners. To preserve confidentiality, our article disguises many of the alliances that were part of the study.

---

[1] For a vigorous warning about the perils of collaboration, see Robert B. Reich and Eric D. Mankin, "Joint Ventures with Japan Give Away Our Future," *HBR*, March–April 1986, p. 78.

Reprinted by permission of *Harvard Business Review*. "Collaborate With Your Competitors and Win" by Gary Hamel, C. K. Prahalad, and Yves Doz, January/February 1989.

Copyright © 1988 by the President and Fellows of Harvard College; all rights reserved.

by the shifts in competitive strength on each side. We focused on how companies use competitive collaboration to enhance their internal skills and technologies while they guard against transferring competitive advantages to ambitious partners.

There is no immutable law that strategic alliances *must* be a windfall for Japanese or Korean partners. Many Western companies do give away more than they gain—but that's because they enter partnerships without knowing what it takes to win. Companies that benefit most from competitive collaboration adhere to a set of simple but powerful principles.

Collaboration is competition in a different form. Successful companies never forget that their new partners may be out to disarm them. They enter alliances with clear strategic objectives, and they also understand how their partners' objectives will affect their success.

Harmony is not the most important measure of success. Indeed, occasional conflict may be the best evidence of mutually beneficial collaboration. Few alliances remain win-win undertakings forever. A partner may be content even as it unknowingly surrenders core skills.

Cooperation has limits. Companies must defend against competitive compromise. A strategic alliance is a constantly evolving bargain whose real terms go beyond the legal agreement or the aims of top management. What information gets traded is determined day to day, often by engineers and operating managers. Successful companies inform employees at all levels about what skills and technologies are off-limits to the partner and monitor what the partner requests and receives.

Learning from partners is paramount. Successful companies view each alliance as a window on their partners' broad capabilities. They use the alliance to build skills in areas outside the formal agreement and systematically diffuse new knowledge throughout their organizations.

Why Collaborate?

Using an alliance with a competitor to acquire new technologies or skills is not devious. It reflects the commitment and capacity of each partner to absorb the skills of the other. We found that in every case in which a Japanese company emerged from an alliance stronger than its Western partner, the Japanese company had made a greater effort to learn.

Strategic intent is an essential ingredient in the commitment to learning. The willingness of Asian companies to enter alliances represents a change in competitive tactics, not competitive goals. NEC, for example, has used a series of collaborative ventures to enhance its technology and product competences. NEC is the only company in the world with a leading position in telecommunications, computers, and semiconductors—despite its investing less in R&D (as a percentage of revenues) than competitors like Texas Instruments, Northern Telecom, and L.M. Ericsson. Its string of partnerships, most notably with Honeywell, allowed NEC to leverage its in-house R&D over the last two decades.

Western companies, on the other hand, often enter alliances to avoid investments. They are more interested in reducing the costs and risks of entering new businesses or markets than to acquiring new skills. A senior U.S. manager offered this analysis of his company's venture with a Japanese rival: "We complement each other well—our distribution capability and their manufacturing skill. I see no reason to invest upstream if we can find a secure source of product. This is a comfortable relationship for us."

An executive from this company's Japanese partner offered a different perspective: "When it is necessary to collaborate, I go to my employees and say, 'This is bad, I wish we had these skills ourselves. Collaboration is second best. But I will feel worse if after four years we do not know how to do what our partner knows how to do.' We must digest their skills."

The problem here is not that the U.S. company wants to share investment risk (its Japanese partner does too) but that the U.S. company has no ambition *beyond* avoidance. When the commitment to learning is so one-sided, collaboration invariably leads to competitive compromise.

Many so-called alliances between Western companies and their Asian rivals are little more than

Competition for Competence

In the article "Do You Really Have a Global Strategy?" (*HBR*, July–August 1985), Gary Hamel and C. K. Prahalad examined one dimension of the global competitive battle: the race for brand dominance. This is the battle for control of distribution channels and global "share of mind." Another global battle has been much less visible and has received much less management attention. This is the battle for control over key technology-based competences that fuel new business development.

Honda has built a number of businesses, including marine engines, lawn mowers, generators, motorcycles, and cars, around its engine and power train competence. Casio draws on its expertise in semiconductors and digital display in producing calculators, small-screen televisions, musical instruments, and watches. Canon relies on its imaging and microprocessor competences in its camera, copier, and laser printer businesses.

In the short run, the quality and performance of a company's products determine its competitiveness. Over the longer term, however, what counts is the ability to build and enhance core competences—distinctive skills that spawn new generations of products. This is where many managers and commentators fear Western companies are losing. Our research helps explain why some companies may be more likely than others to surrender core skills.

Alliance or Outsourcing?   Enticing Western companies into outsourcing agreements provides several benefits to ambitious OEM partners. Serving as a manufacturing base for a Western partner is a quick route to increased manufacturing share without the risk or expense of building brand share. The Western partners' distribution capability allows Asian suppliers to focus all their resources on building absolute product advantage. Then OEMs can enter markets on their own and convert manufacturing share into brand share.

Serving as a sourcing platform yields more than just volume and process improvements. It also generates low-cost, low-risk market learning. The downstream (usually Western) partner typically provides information on how to tailor products to local markets. So every product design transferred to an OEM partner is also a research report on customer preferences and market needs. The OEM partner can use these insights to read the market accurately when it enters on its own.

A Ratchet Effect   Our research suggests that once a significant sourcing relationship has been established, the buyer becomes less willing and able to reemerge as a manufacturing competitor. Japanese and Korean companies are, with few exceptions, exemplary suppliers. If anything, the "soft option" of outsourcing becomes even softer as OEM suppliers routinely exceed delivery and quality expectations.

Outsourcing often begins a ratchetlike process. Relinquishing manufacturing control and paring back plant investment leads to sacrifices in product design, process technology, and, eventually, R&D budgets. Consequently, the OEM partner captures product-development as well as manufacturing initiative. Ambitious OEM partners are not content with the old formula of "You design it and we'll make it." The new reality is, "You design it, we'll learn from your designs, make them more manufacturable, and launch our products alongside yours."

Reversing the Verdict   This outcome is not inevitable. Western companies can retain control over their core competences by keeping a few simple principles in mind.

A competitive product is not the same thing as a competitive organization. While an Asian OEM partner may provide the former, it seldom provides the latter. In essence, outsourcing is a way of renting someone else's competitiveness rather than developing a long-term solution to competitive decline.

Rethink the make-or-buy decision. Companies often treat component manufacturing operations as cost centers and transfer their output to assembly units at an arbitrarily set price. This transfer price is an accounting fiction, and it is unlikely to yield as high a return as marketing or distribution investments, which require less research money and capital. But companies seldom consider the competitive consequences of surrendering control over a key value-creating activity.

Watch out for deepening dependence. Surrender results from a series of outsourcing decisions that individually make economic sense but collectively amount to a phased exit from the business. Different managers make outsourcing decisions at different times, unaware of the cumulative impact.

Replenish core competencies. Western companies must outsource some activities; the economics are just too compelling. The real issue is whether a company is adding to its stock of technologies and competences as rapidly as it is surrendering them. The question of whether to outsource should always provoke a second question: Where can we outpace our partner and other rivals in building new sources of competitive advantage?

---

sophisticated outsourcing arrangements (see the box "Competition for Competence"). General Motors buys cars and components from Korea's Daewoo. Siemens buys computers from Fujitsu. Apple buys laser printer engines from Canon. The traffic is almost entirely one way. These OEM deals offer Asian partners a way to capture investment initiative from Western competitors and displace customer competitors from value-creating activities. In many cases this goal meshes with that of the Western partner: to regain competitiveness quickly and with minimum effort.

Consider the joint venture between Rover, the British automaker, and Honda. Some 25 years ago, Rover's forerunners were world leaders in small car design. Honda had not even entered the automobile business. But in the mid-1970s, after failing to penetrate foreign markets, Rover turned to Honda for technology and product-development support. Rover has used the alliance to avoid investments to design and build new cars. Honda has cultivated skills in European styling and marketing as well as multinational manufacturing. There is little doubt which company will emerge stronger over the long term.

Troubled laggards like Rover often strike alliances with surging latecomers like Honda. Having fallen behind in a key skills area (in this case, manufacturing small cars), the laggard attempts to compensate for past failures. The late-comer uses the alliance to close a specific skills gap (in this case, learning to build cars for a regional market). But a laggard that forges a partnership for short-term gain may find itself in a dependency spiral: as it contributes fewer and fewer distinctive skills, it must reveal more and more of its internal operations to keep the partner interested. For the weaker company, the issue shifts from "Should we collaborate?" to "With whom should we collaborate?" to "How do we keep our partner interested as we lose the advantages that made us attractive to them in the first place?"

There's a certain paradox here. When both partners are equally intent on internalizing the other's skills, distrust and conflict may spoil the alliance and threaten its very survival. That's one reason joint ventures between Korean and Japanese companies have been few and tempestuous. Neither side wants to "open the kimono." Alliances seem to run most smoothly when one partner is intent on learning and the other is intent on avoidance—in essence, when one partner is willing to grow dependent on the other. But running smoothly is not the point; the point is for a company to emerge from an alliance more competitive than when it entered it.

One partner does not always have to give up more than it gains to ensure the survival of an alliance. There are certain conditions under which mutual gain is possible, at least for a time.

The partners' strategic goals converge while their competitive goals diverge. That is, each partner allows for the other's continued prosperity in the shared business. Philips and Du Pont collaborate to develop and manufacture compact discs, but neither side invades the other's market. There is a clear upstream/downstream division of effort.

The size and market power of both partners is modest compared with industry leaders. This forces each side to accept that mutual dependence may have to continue for many years. Long-term collaboration may be so critical to both partners that neither will risk antagonizing the other by an overtly competitive bid to appropriate skills or competence. Fujitsu's 1 to 5 disadvantage with IBM means it will be a long time, if ever, before Fujitsu can break away from its foreign partners and go it alone.

Each partner believes it can learn from the other and at the same time limit access to proprietary skills. JVC and Thomson, both of whom make VCRs, know that they are trading skills. But the two companies are looking for very different things. Thomson needs product technology and manufacturing prowess; JVC needs to learn how to succeed in the fragmented European market. Both sides believe there is an equitable chance for gain.

How to Build Secure Defenses

For collaboration to succeed, each partner must contribute something distinctive: basic research, product development skills, manufacturing capacity, access to distribution. The challenge is to share enough skills to create advantage vis-à-vis companies outside the alliance while preventing a wholesale transfer of core skills to the partner. This is a very thin line to walk. Companies must carefully select what skills and technologies they pass to their partners. They must develop safeguards against unintended, informal transfers of information. The goal is to limit the transparency of their operations.

The type of skill a company contributes is an important factor in how easily its partner can internalize the skills. The potential for transfer is greater when a partner's contribution is easily transported (in engineering drawings, on computer tapes, or in

the heads of a few technical experts); easily interpreted (it can be reduced to commonly understood equations or symbols); and easily absorbed (the skill or competence is independent of any particular cultural context).

Western companies face an inherent disadvantage because their skills are generally more vulnerable to transfer. The magnet that attracts so many companies to alliances with Asian competitors is their manufacturing excellence—a competence that is less transferable than most. Just-in-time inventory systems and quality circles can be imitated, but this is like pulling a few threads out of an oriental carpet. Manufacturing excellence is a complex web of employee training, integration with suppliers, statistical process controls, employee involvement, value engineering, and design for manufacture. It is difficult to extract such a subtle competence in any way but a piecemeal fashion.

There is an important distinction between technology and competence. A discrete, stand-alone technology (for example, the design of a semiconductor chip) is more easily transferred than a process competence, which is entwined in the social fabric of a company. Asian companies often learn more from their Western partners than vice versa because they contribute difficult-to-unravel strengths, while Western partners contribute easy-to-imitate technology.

So companies must take steps to limit transparency. One approach is to limit the scope of the formal agreement. It might cover a single technology rather than an entire range of technologies; part of a product line rather than the entire line; distribution in a limited number of markets or for a limited period of time. The objective is to circumscribe a partner's opportunities to learn.

Moreover, agreements should establish specific performance requirements. Motorola, for example, takes an incremental, incentive-based approach to technology transfer in its venture with Toshiba. The agreement calls for Motorola to release its microprocessor technology incrementally as Toshiba delivers on its promise to increase Motorola's penetration in the Japanese semiconductor market. The greater Motorola's market share, the greater Toshiba's access to Motorola's technology.

Many of the skills that migrate between companies are not covered in the formal terms of collaboration. Top management puts together strategic alliances and sets the legal parameters for exchange. But what actually gets traded is determined by day-to-day interactions of engineers, marketers, and product developers: who says what to whom, who gets access to what facilities, who sits on what joint committees. The most important deals ("I'll share this with you if you share that with me") may be struck four or five organizational levels below where the deal was signed. Here lurks the greatest risk of unintended transfers of important skills.

Consider one technology-sharing alliance between European and Japanese competitors. The European company valued the partnership as a way to acquire a specific technology. The Japanese company considered it a window on its partner's entire range of competences and interacted with a broad spectrum of its partner's marketing and product-development staff. The company mined each contact for as much information as possible.

For example, every time the European company requested a new feature on a product being sourced from its partner, the Japanese company asked for detailed customer and competitor analyses to justify the request. Over time, it developed a sophisticated picture of the European market that would assist its own entry strategy. The technology acquired by the European partner through the formal agreement had a useful life of three to five years. The competitive insights acquired informally by the Japanese company will probably endure longer.

Limiting unintended transfers at the operating level requires careful attention to the role of gatekeepers, the people who control what information flows to a partner. A gatekeeper can be effective only if there are a limited number of gateways through which a partner can access people and facilities. Fujitsu's many partners all go through a single office, the "collaboration section," to request information and assistance from different divisions.

This way the company can monitor and control access to critical skills and technologies.

We studied one partnership between European and U.S competitors that involved several divisions of each company. While the U.S. company could only access its partner through a single gateway, its partner had unfettered access to all participating divisions. The European company took advantage of its free rein. If one division refused to provide certain information, the European partner made the same request of another division. No single manager in the U.S. company could tell how much information had been transferred or was in a position to piece together patterns in the requests.

Collegiality is a prerequisite for collaborative success. But *too much* collegiality should set off warning bells to senior managers. CEOs or division presidents should expect occasional complaints from their counterparts about the reluctance of lower level employees to share information. That's a sign that the gatekeepers are doing their jobs. And senior management should regularly debrief operating personnel to find out what information the partner is requesting and what requests are being granted.

Limiting unintended transfers ultimately depends on employee loyalty and self-discipline. This was a real issue for many of the Western companies we studied. In their excitement and pride over technical achievements, engineering staffs sometimes shared information that top management considered sensitive. Japanese engineers were less likely to share proprietary information.

There are a host of cultural and professional reasons for the relative openness of Western technicians. Japanese engineers and scientists are more loyal to their company than to their profession. They are less steeped in the open give-and-take of university research since they receive much of their training from employers. They consider themselves team members more than individual scientific contributors. As one Japanese manager noted, "We don't feel any need to reveal what we know. It is not an issue of pride for us. We're glad to sit and listen. If we're patient we usually learn what we want to know."

Controlling unintended transfers may require restricting access to facilities as well as to people. Companies should declare sensitive laboratories and factories off-limits to their partners. Better yet, they might house the collaborative venture in an entirely new facility. IBM is building a special site in Japan where Fujitsu can review its forthcoming mainframe software before deciding whether to license it. IBM will be able to control exactly what Fujitsu sees and what information leaves the facility.

Finally, which country serves as "home" to the alliance affects transparency. If the collaborative team is located near one partner's major facilities, the other partner will have more opportunities to learn—but less control over what information gets traded. When the partner houses, feeds, and looks after engineers and operating managers, there is a danger they will "go native." Expatriate personnel need frequent visits from headquarters as well as regular furloughs home.

Enhance the Capacity to Learn

Whether collaboration leads to competitive surrender or revitalization depends foremost on what employees believe the purpose of the alliance to be. It is self-evident: to learn, one must *want* to learn. Western companies won't realize the full benefits of competitive collaboration until they overcome an arrogance borne of decades of leadership. In short, Western companies must be more receptive.

We asked a senior executive in a Japanese electronics company about the perception that Japanese companies learn more from their foreign partners than vice versa. "Our Western partners approach us with the attitude of teachers," he told us. "We are quite happy with this, because we have the attitude of students."

Learning begins at the top. Senior management must be committed to enhancing their companies' skills as well as to avoiding financial risk. But most learning takes place at the lower levels of an alliance. Operating employees not only represent the front lines in an effective defense but also play a vital role in acquiring knowledge. They must be well briefed on the partner's strengths and weaknesses and understand how acquiring particular skills will bolster their company's competitive position.

This is already standard practice among Asian companies. We accompanied a Japanese development engineer on a tour through a partner's factory. This engineer dutifully took notes on plant layout, the number of production stages, the rate at which the line was running, and the number of employees. He recorded all this despite the fact that he had no manufacturing responsibility in his own company, and that the alliance didn't encompass joint manufacturing. Such dedication greatly enhances learning.

Collaboration doesn't always provide an opportunity to fully internalize a partner's skills. Yet just acquiring new and more precise benchmarks of a partner's performance can be of great value. A new benchmark can provoke a thorough review of internal performance levels and may spur a round of competitive innovation. Asking questions like, "Why do their semiconductor logic designs have fewer errors than ours?" and "Why are they investing in this technology and we're not?" may provide the incentive for a vigorous catch-up program.

Competitive benchmarking is a tradition in most of the Japanese companies we studied. It requires many of the same skills associated with competitor analysis: systematically calibrating performance against external targets; learning to use rough estimates to determine where a competitor (or partner) is better, faster, or cheaper; translating those estimates into new internal targets; and recalibrating to establish the rate of improvement in a competitor's performance. The great advantage of competitive collaboration is that proximity makes benchmarking easier.

Indeed, some analysts argue that one of Toyota's motivations in collaborating with GM in the much-publicized NUMMI venture is to gauge the quality of GM's manufacturing technology. GM's top manufacturing people get a close look at Toyota, but the reverse is true as well. Toyota may be learning whether its giant U.S. competitor is capable of closing the productivity gap with Japan.

Competitive collaboration also provides a way of getting close enough to rivals to predict how they will behave when the alliance unravels or runs its course. How does the partner respond to price changes? How does it measure and reward executives? How does it prepare to launch a new product? By revealing a competitor's management orthodoxies, collaboration can increase the chances of success in future head-to-head battles.

Knowledge acquired from a competitor-partner is only valuable after it is diffused through the organization. Several companies we studied had established internal clearinghouses to collect and disseminate information. The collaborations manager at one Japanese company regularly made the rounds of all employees involved in alliances. He identified what information had been collected by whom and then passed it on to appropriate departments. Another company held regular meetings where employees shared new knowledge and determined who was best positioned to acquire additional information.

▌ Proceed with Care—But Proceed

After World War II, Japanese and Korean companies entered alliances with Western rivals from weak positions. But they worked steadfastly toward independence. In the early 1960s, NEC's computer business was one-quarter the size of Honeywell's, its primary foreign partner. It took only two decades for NEC to grow larger than Honeywell, which eventually sold its computer operations to an alliance between NEC and Group Bull of France. The NEC experience demonstrates that dependence on a foreign partner doesn't automatically condemn a company to also-ran status. Collaboration may sometimes be unavoidable; surrender is not.

Managers are too often obsessed with the ownership structure of an alliance. Whether a company controls 51% or 49% of a joint venture may be much less important than the rate at which each partner learns from the other. Companies that are confident of their ability to learn may even prefer some ambiguity in the alliance's legal structure. Ambiguity creates more potential to acquire skills and technologies. The challenge for Western companies is not to write tighter legal agreements but to become better learners.

Running away from collaboration is no answer. Even the largest Western companies can no longer outspend their global rivals. With leadership in many industries shifting toward the East, companies in the United States and Europe must become good borrowers—much like Asian companies did in the 1960s and 1970s. Competitive renewal depends on building new process capabilities and winning new product and technology battles. Collaboration can be a low-cost strategy for doing both.

CHAPTER 7

Building Multidimensional Capabilities:
The Management Challenge

From the discussions in previous chapters and descriptions in earlier cases, it should be clear that the MNC in the early 21st century is markedly different from its ancestor of the pre–World War II era, and even from its immediate predecessor of the 1960s and 1970s. It has been transformed by an environment in which multiple, often conflicting, forces were accelerating simultaneously. The globalization of markets, the acceleration of product and technology life cycles, the renewed assertion of national governments' demands, and, above all, the intensification of global competition made the 1980s and 1990s decades of complexity, diversity, and change for most MNCs.

As we have seen, the ability to compete on the basis of a single dominant competitive advantage gave way to a need to develop multiple strategic assets: global-scale efficiency and competitiveness, national responsiveness and flexibility, and a worldwide innovation and learning capability. In turn, these new strategic-task demands put pressure on existing organization structures and management processes. Traditional hierarchical structures with their emphasis on either/or choices have evolved toward organizational forms we have described as transnational, characterized by integrated networks of assets and resources, multidimensional management perspectives and capabilities, and flexible coordinative processes.

The management implications of all this change are enormous. To succeed in the international operating environment of the present, managers must be able to sense and interpret the complex and dynamic environmental changes; they must be able to develop and integrate the multiple strategic capabilities; and they must be able to build and manage the complicated yet subtle new organizations required to deliver coordinated action on a worldwide basis. Unless those in key management positions are highly skilled and knowledgeable, companies simply cannot respond to the major new challenges they face.

Yet surprisingly little attention is devoted to the study of the implications of all these changes on the roles and responsibilities of those who manage today's MNCs. Academics, consultants, and even managers themselves focus an enormous amount of time and energy on analyzing the various international environmental forces, on refining the concepts of global strategy, and on understanding the characteristics of effective transnational organizations. But without effective managers in place, sophisticated strategies and subtle organizations will fail, and the great risk for most MNCs today is that they are trying to implement third-generation strategies through second-generation organizations with first-generation managers.

In this chapter, we examine the management roles and responsibilities implied by the new challenges facing MNCs—those that take the manager beyond the first-generation assumptions. The tasks differ considerably for those in different parts and in different levels of the organization, so rather than generalizing, we will focus on the core responsibilities of different key management groups. In this chapter, we examine the roles and tasks of three specific groups in the transnational company: the global business manager, the worldwide functional manager, and the country subsidiary manager. (Recall that in Chapter 4 we suggested that variations often occur in the nature of transnational structures. As a result, other key executives—global account managers, for example—may also have a seat at the table.) To close the chapter, we review the role of top management in integrating these often-competing perspectives and capabilities.

▣ Global Business Management

The challenge of developing global efficiency and competitiveness requires management to capture the various scale and scope economies available to the MNC as well as capitalizing on the potential competitive advantages inherent in its worldwide market positioning. This demands a perspective that can see opportunities and risks across national boundaries and functional specialties, and a skill to coordinate and integrate activities across these barriers to capture the potential benefits. This is the fundamental task of the global business manager.

In implementing this important responsibility, the global business manager will be involved in a variety of diverse activities, whose balance will vary considerably depending on the nature of the business and the company's administrative heritage. Nonetheless, there are three core roles and responsibilities that almost always fall to this key manager: he or she will be the global product or business strategist, the architect of worldwide asset and resource configuration, and the coordinator and controller of cross-border transfers.

Global Business Strategist

Because competitive interaction increasingly takes place on a global chessboard, only a manager with worldwide perspective and responsibility can assess the strategic position and capability in a given business. This requires that companies configure their information, planning, and control systems so that they can be consolidated into consistent, integrated global business reports. This is not to imply that the global business manager alone has the perspective and capability to formulate strategic priorities, or that he or she should undertake that vital task unilaterally. Depending on the nature of the business, there will almost certainly be some need to incorporate the perspectives of geographic and functional managers who will represent strategic interests that may run counter to the business manager's drive to maximize global efficiency. Equally important, the business strategy must fit within the broader corporate strategy that should provide a clear vision of what the company wants to be and explicit values of how it will accomplish its mission.

In the final analysis, however, the responsibility to reconcile the different views falls to the global business manager who needs to prepare an integrated strategy of how the company will compete in his or her particular business. In many companies, the manager's ability to do so was compromised by the fact that the position was created by anointing domestic product division managers with the title of global business manager. Overseas subsidiary managers often felt that these managers were not only insensitive to nondomestic perspectives and interests, but also that they were biased toward the domestic organization in making key strategic decisions like product development and capacity plans. In many cases, their concerns were justified.

In the true transnational company, the global business manager need not be located in the home country, and in many cases, great benefits can accrue to relocating several such management groups abroad. Asea Brown Boveri (ABB), the Swiss-based electrical engineering company, has deliberately tried to leverage the capabilities of its strong operating companies worldwide and to exploit their location in key strategic markets by locating its worldwide business area management wherever such organizational and strategic dimensions coincide. In its global power transmission business, for example, the business area manager for switchgear was located in Sweden, for power transformers in Germany, for distribution transformers in Norway, and for electric metering in the United States.

Even well-established MNCs with a tradition of close control of worldwide business strategy are changing. The head of IBM's $6 billion telecommunications business moved her division headquarters to London. She explained that the rationale was not only to move the command center closer to the booming European market for computer networking, but also "[to] give us a different perspective on all our markets."

Architect of Asset and Resource Configuration

Closely tied to the challenge of shaping an integrated business strategy is the global business manager's responsibility for overseeing the worldwide distribution of key assets and resources. Again, this does not mean that he or she can make such decisions unilaterally. The input of interested geographic and functional managers must also be weighed. It is the global business manager, however, who is normally best placed to initiate and lead the debate on asset configuration, perhaps through a global strategy committee or a world board with membership drawn from key geographic and functional management groups.

In deciding where to locate key plants or develop vital resources, the business manager can never assume a zero base. Indeed, such decisions must be rooted in the company's administrative heritage. In multinational companies like Philips, Unilever, ICI, or Nestlé, many of the key assets and resources that permitted these companies to expand internationally have long been located in national companies operating as part of a decentralized federation. Any business manager trying to shape such companies' future configurations must build on rather than ignore or destroy the important benefits that such assets and resources represent. And particularly in cases of plant closures, he or she has to demonstrate enormous political dexterity to overcome the inevitable resistance from local stakeholders.

The challenge to the business manager is to shape the future configuration by leveraging existing resources and capabilities and linking them into a configuration that resembles the integrated network form. GE Medical Systems' reconfiguration of its development centers and sourcing plants as described in Chapter 3 represents a classic model of the construction of such a distributed yet integrated transnational structure.

Cross-Border Coordinator

This leads directly to the third key role played by most global business managers, that of cross-border coordinator. Although less overtly strategic than the other two responsibilities, it is nonetheless a vital operating function, because it involves deciding on sourcing patterns and managing cross-border transfer policies and mechanisms.

The task of coordinating flows of materials, components, and finished products becomes extremely complex as companies build transnational structures and capabilities. Rather than producing and shipping all products from a fully integrated central plant (the centralized hub model) or allowing local subsidiaries to develop self-sufficient capabilities (the decentralized federation model), transnational companies specialize their operations worldwide, building on the most capable national operations and capitalizing on locations of strategic importance. The resulting integrated network of specialized operations is highly interdependent, perhaps linking high labor content component plants in Poland and Korea with highly skilled subassembly operations in Germany and Singapore, which in turn supply specialized finished-product plants in the United States, England, France, and Japan.

The coordination mechanisms available to the global business manager vary from direct central control over quantities shipped and prices charged to the establishment of rules that essentially create an internal market mechanism to coordinate cross-border activities. The former means of control is more likely for products of high strategic importance (for example, Pfizer's control over quantities and pricing of shipments of the active ingredients of Viagra, or Coca-Cola's coordination of the supply of Coke syrup worldwide).

As products become more commodity-like, however, global product managers recognize that internal transfers should reflect the competitive conditions set by the external environment. This has led many to develop internal quasi markets as the principal means of coordination.

For example, in the consumer electronics giant, Matsushita, once the parent company develops prototypes of the following year's models of video cameras, CD players, and so on, global product managers offer them internally to buyers at merchandise meetings that are, in effect, huge internal trade fairs. At these meetings, national sales and marketing directors from Matsushita sales subsidiaries worldwide enter into direct discussions with the global product managers, negotiating modifications in product design, price, and delivery schedule to meet their local market needs.

▨ Worldwide Functional Management

Worldwide functional management refers to individuals with responsibility for primary activities like R&D, manufacturing, and marketing, as well as those responsible for support activities, such as the chief financial officer and the chief information officer. Their job, broadly speaking, is to diffuse innovations and transfer knowledge on a worldwide basis. This vital task is built on knowledge that is highly specialized by function—technological capability, marketing expertise, manufacturing know-how, and so on, and to do it effectively requires that functional managers evolve from the secondary staff roles they often played and take an active role in transnational management.

The tasks facing functional managers vary widely by specific function (technology transfer may be more intensive than the transfer of marketing expertise, for example), and by business (companies in transnational industries such as telecommunications demand more functional linkages and transfers than do those in multinational industries such as retailing). Nonetheless, we will highlight three basic roles and responsibilities that most worldwide functional managers should play: worldwide scanner of specialized information and intelligence, cross-pollinator of "best practices," and champion of transnational innovation.

Worldwide Intelligence Scanner

Most innovations start with some stimulus driving the company to respond to a perceived opportunity or threat. It may be a revolutionary technological breakthrough, an emerging consumer trend, a new competitive challenge, or a pending government regulation. And it may occur anywhere in the world. A typical example occurred when the radical Green political party first began achieving important victories in gaining popular support for environmental protection in Germany in the late 1980s. Companies with good sensory mechanisms in Germany recognized the significance of this development and began adjusting their products, processes, and company policies. As these political forces and market demands spread worldwide during the 1990s, those companies without the benefit of advance warning systems found themselves trying to respond not only to the growing political and consumer pressures, but also to the more-responsive competitors touting that they had several years' start in developing more environment-friendly products and strategies.

Although strategically important information was often sensed in the foreign subsidiaries of classic multinational or global companies, it was rarely transmitted to those who could act on it, or was ignored when it did get through. The communication problem was due primarily to the fact that the intelligence was usually of a specialist nature that was not always well understood by the generalists who controlled the line organization. To capture and transmit such information across national boundaries required the establishment of specialist information channels that linked local national technologists, marketers, and production specialists with others who understood their needs and shared their perspective.

In transnational companies, functional managers are linked through informal networks that are nurtured and maintained through frequent meetings, visits, and transfers. Through such linkages, these managers develop the contacts and relationships that allow them to transmit information rapidly around the globe. The functional managers at the corporate level become the linchpins in this effort and play a vital role as facilitators of communication and repositories of specialist information.

Cross-Pollinator of "Best Practices"

Overseas subsidiaries can be more than sources of strategic intelligence, however. In a truly transnational company, they can be the source of capabilities, expertise, and innovation that can be transferred to other parts of the organization. Caterpillar's leading-edge flexible manufacturing first emerged in its French and Belgian plants, for example, and much of P&G's liquid detergent technology was developed in its European Technology Center. In both cases, this expertise was transferred to other countries with important global strategic impact. Such an administrative ability to transfer new ideas and developments requires a considerable amount of management time and attention to break down the not-invented-here (NIH) syndrome that often thrives in international business. In this process, those with worldwide functional responsibilities are ideally placed to play the central cross-pollination role. Not only do they have the specialist knowledge required to identify and evaluate leading-edge practices, they also tend to have a well-developed informal communications network developed with others in their functional area.

The corporate functional managers in particular can play a vital role in this important task. Through informal contacts, formal evaluations, and frequent travel, they can identify where the best practices are being developed and implemented. They are also in a position to arrange cross-unit visits and transfers, host conferences, form task forces, or take other initiatives that will expose others to the new ideas.

Champion of Transnational Innovation

The two previously identified roles ideally position the functional manager to play a key role in developing what we call transnational innovations. As described in Chapter 5, these are different from the predominantly local activity that dominated the innovation process in multinational companies, or the centrally driven innovation in international and global companies. The first (and simplest) form of transnational innovation is what we term locally leveraged. By scanning their companies' worldwide operations, corporate functional managers can identify local innovations that have applications elsewhere. In Unilever, for example, product and marketing innovation for many of its global brands occurred in national subsidiaries. Snuggle fabric softener was born in Unilever's German company, Timotei herbal shampoo originated in its Scandinavian operations, and Impulse body spray was first introduced by its South African unit. Recognizing the potential that these local innovations had for the wider company, the parent company's marketing and technical groups created the impetus to spread them to other subsidiaries.

The second type of transnational innovation, which we term globally linked, requires functional managers to play a more sophisticated role. This type of innovation fully exploits the company's access to worldwide information and expertise by linking and leveraging intelligence sources with internal centers of excellence wherever they may be located. For example, P&G's global liquid detergent was developed by managing a complex network of relationships among technical and marketing managers worldwide. The product's desired performance responded to the Europeans' need for water-softening capability, the Americans' desire for improved cleaning capability, and the Japanese sensing of an opportunity for a liquid detergent with cold-water effectiveness. The product was developed incorporating technological breakthroughs that had occurred in creating a bleach substitute and enzyme stabilizer from the European Technical Center, an improved surfactant developed in the corporate labs, and new low-temperature performance capabilities contributed by the International Technical Center. By linking and leveraging the company's intelligence and resources worldwide, P&G developed a product that was vastly superior to those being worked on locally and centrally. The new product was successfully introduced as Liquid Tide in the United States, Liquid Ariel in Europe, and Liquid Cheer in Japan.

Geographic Subsidiary Management

In many MNCs, a successful tour as a country subsidiary manager is often thought of as the acid test of general management potential. Indeed, it is often a necessary qualification on the résumé of any candidate for a top-management position. Not only does it provide frontline exposure to the realities of today's international business environment, but it also puts the individual in a position where he or she must deal with enormous strategic complexity from an organizational position that is severely constrained. Moreover, the role of "country manager" is, if anything, becoming more difficult as more MNCs move toward structures dominated by global business units and global customers. In such situations, the manager of the country is often held accountable for results, yet has only limited formal authority over the people and assets within his or her jurisdiction.

We have described the strategic challenge facing the MNC as one of resolving the conflicting demands for global efficiency, multinational responsiveness, and worldwide learning. The country manager is at the center of this strategic tension—defending the company's market positions against global competitors, satisfying the demands of the host government, responding to the unique needs of local customers, and leveraging its local resources and capabilities to strengthen the company's competitive position worldwide.

There are many vital tasks the country manager must play, but we have identified three that capture the complexity of the task and highlight its important linkage role: acting as a bicultural interpreter, becoming the chief advocate and defender of national needs; and the vital frontline responsibility as implementer of the company's strategy.

Bicultural Interpreter

The need for the country manager to become the local expert who understands the needs of the local market, the strategy of competitors, and the demands of the host government is clear. But his or her responsibilities are much broader than this. Because managers at headquarters do not understand the environmental and cultural differences in the MNC's diverse foreign markets, the country manager must be able to analyze the information gathered, interpret its implications, and even predict the range of feasible outcomes. This role suggests an ability not only to act as an efficient sensor of the national environment, but also to become a cultural interpreter able to communicate the importance of that information to those whose perceptions may be obscured by ethnocentric biases.

There is another aspect to the country manager's role as information broker that is sometimes ignored. Not only must the individual have a sensitivity to and understanding of the national culture, he or she must also be comfortable in the corporate culture at the MNC. Again, this bicultural role implies much more than being an information conduit communicating the corporation's goals, strategies, and values to a group of employees located thousands of miles from the parent company. The country subsidiary manager must also interpret those broad goals and strategies so they become meaningful objectives and priorities at the local level of operation, and must apply those corporate values and organizational processes in a way that respects local cultural norms.

National Defender and Advocate

As important as the communication role is, it is not sufficient for the country manager to act solely as an intelligent mailbox. Information and analysis conveyed to corporate headquarters not only must be well understood, but also must be acted upon. This is particularly important in MNCs where strong business managers are arguing for a more integrated global approach and corporate functional managers are focusing on cross-border linkages. The country manager's role is to counterbalance these centralizing tendencies and ensure that the needs and opportunities that exist in the local environment are well understood and incorporated into the decision-making process.

As the national organization evolves from its early independence to a more mature role as part of an integrated worldwide network, the country manager's normal drive for national self-sufficiency and personal autonomy must be replaced by a less parochial perspective and a more corporate-oriented identity. This does not imply, however, that he or she should stop presenting the local perspective to headquarters management or stop defending the national interests. Indeed, the company's ability to become a true transnational depends on having strong advocates for the need to differentiate its operations locally and to be responsive to national demands and pressures.

Two distinct but related tasks are implied by this important role. The first requires the country manager to ensure that the overall corporate strategies, policies, and organization processes are appropriate from the national organization's perspective. Where the interests of local constituencies are violated or where the subsidiary's position might be compromised by the global strategy, it is the country manager's responsibility to become the defender of the national needs and perspectives.

In addition to defending the need for national differentiation and responsiveness, the country manager must also become an advocate for his or her national organization's role in the corporation's worldwide integrated system of which it is a part. As MNCs develop more of a transnational strategy, national organizations compete not only for corporate resources, but also for roles in the global operations. To ensure that each unit's full potential is realized, country managers must be able to identify and represent their particular national organization's key assets and capabilities, and the ways in which they can contribute to the MNC as a whole.

It is the country manager's job to mentor local employees and support those individuals in their fight for corporate resources and recognition. In doing so they build local capability that can be a major corporate asset. As the former head of Digital Equipment

Corporation in Scotland observed, "It is my *obligation* to seek out new investment. No-one else is going to stand up for these workers at head office. They are doing a great job, and I owe it to them to build up this operation. I get very angry with some of my counterparts in other parts of the country, who just toe the party line. They have followed their orders to the letter, but when I visit their plants I see unfulfilled potential everywhere."

Frontline Implementer of Corporate Strategy

Although the implementation of corporate strategy may seem the most obvious of tasks for the manager of a frontline operating unit, it is by no means the easiest. The first challenge is provided by the multiplicity and diversity of constituents whose demands and pressures compete for the country manager's attention. Being a subsidiary company of some distant MNC seems to bestow a special status on many national organizations and subject them to a different and a more intense type of pressure than other local companies. Governments may be suspicious of their motives, unions may distrust their national commitment, and customers may misunderstand their way of operating. Compounding the problem is the fact that corporate management often underestimates the significance of these demands and pressures.

Second, the country manager's implementation task is complicated by the corporate expectation that he or she take the broad corporate goals and strategies and translate them into specific actions that are responsive to the needs of the national environment. As we have seen, these global strategies are usually complex and finely balanced, reflecting multiple conflicting demands. Having been developed through subtle internal negotiation, they often leave the country manager very little room for maneuvering.

Pressured from without and constrained from within, the country manager needs a keen administrative sense to plot the negotiating range in which he or she can operate. The action decided upon must be sensitive enough to respect the limits of the diverse local constituencies, pragmatic enough to achieve the expected corporate outcome, and creative enough to balance the diverse internal and external demands and constraints.

As if this were not enough, the task is made even more difficult by the fact that the country manager does not act solely as the implementer of corporate strategy. As we discussed earlier, it is important that he or she also plays a key role in its formulation. Thus, the strategy the country manager is required to implement will often reflect some decisions against which he or she lobbied hard. Once the final decision is taken, however, the country manager must be able to convince his or her national organization to implement it with commitment and enthusiasm.

▦ Top-Level Corporate Management

Nowhere are the challenges facing management more extreme than at the top of an organization that is evolving toward becoming a transnational corporation. Not only do these senior executives have to integrate and provide direction for the diverse management groups we have described, but in doing so, they first have to break with many of the norms and traditions that historically defined their role.

Particularly in the 1970s and 1980s, as increasingly complex hierarchical structures forced them further and further from the front lines of their businesses, top-management's role became bureaucratized in a rising sea of systems and staff reports. As layers of management slowed decision making and the corporate headquarters role of coordination and support evolved to one of control and interference, top-management's attention was distracted from the external demands of customers and competitive pressures and began to focus internally on an increasingly bureaucratic process.

The transnational organization of today cannot afford to operate this way. Like executives at all levels of the organization, top management must add value, and this means liberating rather than constraining the organization below them. For those at the top of the transnational, this means more than just creating a diverse set of business, functional, and geographic management groups and assigning them specific roles and responsibilities. It also means maintaining the organizational legitimacy of each group, balancing and integrating their often-divergent influences in the ongoing management process, and maintaining a unifying sense of purpose and direction in the face of often-conflicting needs and priorities.

This constant balancing and integrating role is perhaps the most vital aspect of top management's job. It is reflected in the constant tension they feel between ensuring long-term viability and achieving short-term results, or between providing a clear overall corporate direction and leaving sufficient room for experimentation. This tension is reflected in the three core top-management tasks we choose to highlight here. The first, which focuses on the key role of providing long-term direction and purpose, is in some ways counterbalanced by the second, which highlights the need to achieve current results by leveraging performance. The third key task of ensuring continual renewal again focuses on long-term needs, but at the same time may require the organization to challenge its current directions and priorities.

Providing Direction and Purpose

In an organization built around the need for multidimensional strategic capabilities and the legitimacy of different management perspectives, the diversity and internal tension can create an exciting free market of competing ideas and can generate an enormous amount of individual and group motivation. But there is always a risk that these same powerful centrifugal forces could pull the company apart. By creating a common vision of the future and a shared set of values that overarch and subsume managers' more parochial objectives, top management can, in effect, create a corporate lightning rod that captures this otherwise diffuse energy and channels it toward powering a single company engine.

We have identified three characteristics that distinguish an energizing and effective strategic vision from a catchy but ineffective public relations slogan. First, the vision must be clear, and simplicity, relevance, and continuous reinforcement are the key to such clarity. NEC's integration of computers and communications—C&C—is a good example of how clarity can make a vision more powerful and effective. Top management in NEC has applied the C&C concept so effectively that it describes the company's business focus, defines its distinctive source of competitive advantage over large companies like IBM and AT&T, and summarizes its strategic and organizational initiatives. Throughout the company, the rich interpretations of C&C are understood and believed in.

Continuity is the second key characteristic of a vision that can provide direction and purpose. Despite shifts in leadership and continual adjustments in short-term business priorities, top management must remain committed to the company's core set of strategic objectives and organizational values. Without such continuity, the unifying vision takes on the transitory characteristics of the annual budget or quarterly targets—and engenders about as much organizational enthusiasm.

Finally, in communicating the vision and strategic direction, it is critical to establish consistency across organizational units—in other words, to ensure that the vision is shared by all. The cost of inconsistency can be horrendous. At a minimum, it can result in confusion and inefficiency; in the extreme, it can lead individuals and organizational units to pursue agendas that are mutually debilitating.

Leveraging Corporate Performance

Although aligning the company's resources, capabilities, and commitments to achieve common long-term objectives is vital, top management must also achieve results in the short term to remain viable among its competitors and credible with its stakeholders. Top management's role is to provide the controls, support, and coordination to leverage resources and capabilities to their highest level of performance.

In doing so, top managers in transnational companies must abandon old notions of control that are based primarily on responding to below-budget financial results. Effective top managers rely much more on control mechanisms that are personal and proactive. In discussions with their key management groups, they ensure that their particular responsibilities are understood in relation to the overall goal, and that strategic and operational priorities are clearly identified and agreed upon. They set demanding standards and use frequent informal visits to discuss operations and identify new problems or opportunities quickly.

When such issues are identified, the old model of top-down interference must be replaced by one driven by corporate-level support. Having created an organization staffed by experts and specialists, top management must resist the temptation to send in the headquarters storm troopers to take charge at the first sign of difficulty. Far more effective is an approach of delegating clear responsibilities, backing them with rewards that align those responsibilities with the corporate goals, then supporting each of the management groups with resources, specialized expertise, and other forms of support available from the top levels of the company.

Perhaps the most challenging task for top management as it tries to leverage the overall performance of the corporation is the need to coordinate the activities of an organization deliberately designed around diverse perspectives and responsibilities. As described in Chapter 4, there are three basic cross-organizational flows that must be carefully managed—goods, resources, and information—and each demands a different means of coordination. Goods flows can normally be routinized and managed through formal systems and procedures. Decisions involving the allocation of scarce resources (for example, capital allocation or key personnel assignments) are usually centralized because top management wants to be involved directly and personally. And flows of information and knowledge are generated and diffused most effectively through personal contact.

These three flows are the lifeblood of any company, and any organization's ability to make them more efficient and effective depends on top management's ability to develop a rich portfolio of coordinative processes. By balancing the formalization, centralization, and socialization processes, they can exploit the company's synergistic potential and greatly leverage performance.

Ensuring Continual Renewal

Despite their enormous value, either of these first two roles, if pursued to the extreme, can result in a company's long-term demise. A fixation on an outmoded mission can be just as dangerous as a preoccupation with short-term performance. Even together they can lead a company to be doomed by its continuing success. This is especially likely where successful strategies become elevated to the status of unquestioned wisdom and where effective organizational processes become institutionalized as routines. As strategies and processes ossify, management loses its flexibility, and eventually the organization sees its role as protecting its past heritage.

It is top management's role to prevent this from occurring, and there are several important ways in which it can ensure that the organization continues to renew itself rather than just reinventing its past. First, by reducing the internal bureaucracy and constantly orienting the organization to its customers and benchmarking it against its best competitors, top management can ensure an external orientation.

Equally important is its role in constantly questioning, challenging, stirring up, and changing things in a way that forces adaptation and learning. By creating a "dynamic imbalance" among those with different objectives, top management can prevent a myopic strategic posture from developing. (Clearly, this is a delicate process that requires a great deal of top-management time if it is not to degenerate into anarchy or corporate politics.)

Finally, top management can ensure renewal by defining the corporate mission and values statements so that they provide some stretch and maneuverability for management, and also so that they legitimize new initiatives. More than this, those at the top levels must monitor closely the process of dynamic imbalance they create and strongly support some of the more entrepreneurial experimentation or imaginative challenges to the status quo that emerge in such a situation.

■ Concluding Comments

In this chapter we shifted the level of analysis down to the individual manager. Rather than think in terms of the changing nature of the business environment, or the conflicting strategic imperatives facing the MNC, we examined the new roles of three groups of managers—those responsible for a global business unit, a worldwide function (such as finance or marketing), and a geographic territory (typically a country). We also looked at the new role of top-level corporate management in integrating and providing direction for these three groups. Each role involves many familiar tasks but also several new ones. Worldwide functional managers, for example, need to become thought leaders in their discipline and active cross-pollinators of best practices across countries. And country managers need to develop the capacity to translate political and social trends in their local market into business imperatives for the MNC.

These new roles and responsibilities are hard to put in place because they require managers to rethink many of their traditional assumptions about the nature of their work. And this is ultimately the biggest challenge facing the transnational organization—to create a generation of managers that have the requisite skills and the sense of perspective needed to operate in a multibusiness, multifunctional, multinational system.

Case 7-1   BRL Hardy: Globalizing an Australian Wine Company

In January 1998, Christopher Carson smiled as he reviewed the Nielsen market survey results that showed Hardy was the top-selling Australian wine brand in Great Britain and held the overall number two position (to Gallo) among all wine brands sold in Britain's off-trade (retailers, excluding hotels and restaurants). As managing director of BRL Hardy Europe, Carson felt proud of this achievement that reflected a 10-fold increase in volume since his first year with Hardy in 1991.

But his mental celebration was short-lived. In front of him were two files, each involving major decisions that would not only shape the future success of the company in Europe but also have major implications for BRL Hardy's overall international strategy:

- The first file contained details of the proposed launch of *D'istinto,* a new line of Italian wines developed in collaboration with a Sicilian winery. Carson and his U.K. team were deeply committed to this project, but several questions had been raised by Australian management. Not least was their concern about *Mapocho,* another joint-venture sourcing agreement Carson had initiated that was now struggling to correct a dis-

appointing market launch and deteriorating relations with the Chilean sourcing partner.
- The second issue he had to decide concerned two competing proposals for a new entry-level Australian wine. His U.K.-based management had developed considerable commitment to *Kelly's Revenge,* a brand they had created specifically in response to a U.K. market opportunity. But the parent company was promoting *Banrock Station,* a product it had launched successfully in Australia which it now wanted to roll out as a global brand at the same price point.

Watching over these developments was Steve Millar, managing director of the South Australia-based parent company that had experienced a period of extraordinary growth, due in large part to BRL Hardy's successful overseas expansion (Exhibit 1). A great believer in decentralized responsibility, he wanted Carson to be deeply involved in the decisions. But he also wanted to ensure that the European unit's actions fit with the company's bold new strategy to become one of the world's first truly global wine companies. Neither did he want to jeopardize BRL Hardy's position in the critically important U.K. market that accounted for two-thirds of its export sales. For both Millar and Carson, these were crucial decisions.

Industry Background

Vines were first introduced into Australia in 1788 by Captain Arthur Phillip, leader of the group of

Professor Christopher A. Bartlett prepared this case. Some names and data have been disguised. HBS cases are developed solely as the basis for class discussion. Cases are not intended to serve as endorsements, sources of primary data, or illustrations of effective or ineffective management.
Copyright © 1999 President and Fellows of Harvard College. Harvard Business School case 300-018.

Exhibit 1   BRL Hardy Limited: Summary Group Financial Results—1992–1997 (Aus$millions)

	1992	1993	1994	1995	1996	1997
Sales revenue	151.5	238.3	256.4	287.0	309.0	375.6
Operating profit (before interest, tax)	16.7	26.6	30.2	34.0	39.3	49.2
Net after tax profit	8.8	13.3	15.8	17.4	21.2	28.4
Earnings per share	13.2¢	14.1¢	15.7¢	15.7¢	18.1¢	23.3¢
Total assets	216.8	234.6	280.7	329.0	380.6	455.5
Total liabilities	117.4	127.4	146.6	160.4	194.4	205.8
Shareholders' equity	99.4	107.2	134.1	168.6	186.2	249.7
Debt/equity ratio	70%	57%	57%	53%	58%	41%

Source: Company documents.

convicts and settlers who comprised the first fleet of migrants to inhabit the new British colony. A wave of European settlers attracted by the gold rush of the mid-nineteenth century provided a boost to the young industry, both in upgrading the availability of vintner skills and in increasing primary demand for its output. Still, the industry grew slowly, and as late as 1969 annual per capita wine consumption in this beer-drinking country was only 8.2 liters—mostly ports and fortified wines—compared with over 100 liters per person per annum in France and Italy.

In the following 25 years, however, the Australian wine industry underwent a huge transformation. First, demand for fortified wines declined and vineyards were replanted with table wine varieties. Then, as consumers became more sophisticated, generic bulk wine sales—often sold in the two-liter "bag in a box" developed in Australia—were replaced by bottled varietals such as cabernet sauvignon, chardonnay, and shiraz, the classic grape type increasingly associated with Australia. By the mid-1990s, domestic consumption stood at 18½ liters per capita, eighteenth in the world.

Over this two-century history, more than 1,000 wineries were established in Australia. By 1996, however, the 10 largest accounted for 84% of the grape crush and 4 controlled over 75% of domestic branded sales. Most of these were public corporations, the largest of which was Southcorp whose

brands included Penfolds, Lindeman, and Seppelt. The number two company was BRL Hardy Ltd. (BRLH), selling under the Hardy, Houghton, Leasingham, and other labels.

During the 1980s and 1990s changes in the global wine industry had a major impact on these emerging Australian companies. A rationalization and consolidation among wine wholesalers and retailers was increasing the power of historically fragmented distribution channels. At the same time, however, large-scale wine suppliers from New World countries such as United States, South America, South Africa, and Australia were exploiting modern viticulture and more scientific wine-making practices to produce more consistent high-quality wine. These developments were occurring in an environment of rapidly growing demand from new consumers in nontraditional markets.

During this period of change, Australian wines began to find large markets abroad, and by 1995 exports accounted for more than 27% of production. But despite its rapid growth, the Australian industry accounted for less than 2% of the world wine production by volume and 2.5% by value. However, because only A$13 billion of the total A$65 billion global wine sales was traded product (80% of wine was consumed in the country of production), the Australian companies' A$450 million in 1995 exports represented 3.5% of the world export market. But in an industry that was becoming increasingly

Exhibit 2   Australian Wine Export Forecasts—Selected Markets 1996–2025

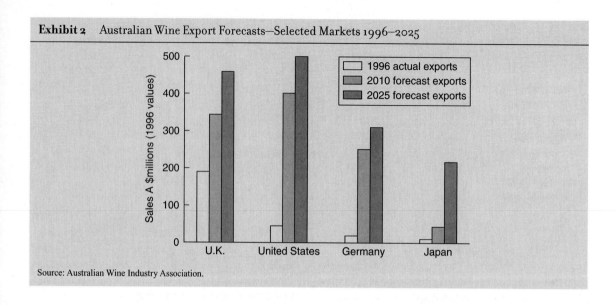

Source: Australian Wine Industry Association.

fashion-driven, Australian wine was becoming a "hot trend," and an ambitious industry association saw export potential growing to A\$2.5 billion by 2025—a 16% share of the projected traded value.[1] Together with an increase in domestic consumption, this translated to A\$4.5 billion in Australian wine sales and a doubling of production to 1.7 million tonnes by 2025.

The Australian industry association saw four export markets as key—the United Kingdom, the United States, Germany, and Japan. While the U.K. market would decrease in relative importance (in 1996 it was the world's largest wine importer and accounted for over 40% of Australian wine exports), over the next 25 years these four markets were expected to continue accounting for 60% of export sales. (See Exhibit 2.)

Company Background and History

BRLH's roots could be traced back to 1853 when Thomas Hardy, a 23-year-old English vineyard laborer, acquired land near Adelaide, South Australia, and planted it with vines. In 1857 he produced his

first vintage, exporting two hogsheads to England, and by 1882 he had won his first international gold medal at Bordeaux. When Hardy died in 1912, his company was Australia's largest winemaker.

Shortly after Hardy's death, in the Riverland region northeast of Adelaide, 130 Italian grape growers formed Australia's first cooperative winery in 1916, naming it the Renmano Wine Cooperative. In 1982 Renmano merged with the Riverland's largest winery and distillery, the Berri Cooperative to form Berri Renmano Limited (BRL). By the early 1990s, almost 500 member growers were delivering over 50,000 tonnes of grapes to BRL, giving it the second-largest crush in Australia. This huge-volume grape crush and its bulk-packaging operations led some to refer to BRL disparagingly as "the oil refinery of the wine industry."

Throughout their respective histories, Thomas Hardy & Sons and BRL followed quite different strategies and developed very different organizations. Hardy became known for award-winning quality wines, while the combined cooperatives specialized in fortified, bulk, and value wines. And in contrast to Hardy's "polite and traditional" values, BRL's culture was more "aggressive and commercial," according to one observer of both companies.

---

[1] All forecast values are in 1996 Australian dollars at wholesale prices. At 1996 year end, the exchange rate was A\$1 = US\$0.8.

International Roots   Although BRL experienced considerable success when it began selling abroad in the late 1980s (particularly in Scandinavia where it sold 6 million liters of bulk wines per annum), its efforts seemed quite modest when compared with Hardy's long history of exporting much higher-value-added bottled products and the huge additional commitments it was making in that same period. To expand on its U.K. sales base of 12,000 cases per annum, Hardy believed it needed to stop relying on importers, distributors, and agents who carried scores of brands from dozens of vineyards. After a long search, in 1989 it acquired Whiclar and Gordon, a respected U.K.-based wine importer-distributor, including its agency rights for a range of French, Chilean, and South African wines.

This move led management to begin talking about the possibility of buying European wineries that could provide their newly acquired distributors with the critical mass and credibility to give Hardy's wines greater access to Europe. Motivated by the looming 1992 target date for a unified European Community (EC) market, and stimulated by the notion that such alternative sources of supply could cushion the ever-present risk of a poor vintage in one region, Hardy's board felt this was an ideal time to invest. In contrast to the painstaking process of identifying acquisition targets for U.K. distribution, however, the vineyard purchasing decision seemed more opportunistic. In 1990, two Hardy directors visited the wine-growing regions in France and Italy, looking at properties on the market. Passing through southern France, they acquired the century-old Domaine de la Baume, a winery with extensive sources in the Languedoc region and several established domestic and export brands. Six months later, they took over Brolio de Ricasoli, a beautiful castle on a Tuscan hillside that made a well-known Chianti and was reputed to be Italy's oldest winery.

Almost immediately, however, problems surfaced in all three of the European acquisitions and soon they were bleeding the parent company of millions of dollars. Combined with a recession-driven market slowdown at home, these problems plunged Hardy into losses. Meanwhile, BRL was also struggling and was looking for ways to expand and upgrade its business. When one of Hardy's banks called in a loan and the company was forced to look for a financial partner, BRL was there. Despite its own marginal financial performance, BRL management decided to propose a merger. Said one ex-BRL manager, "We had access to fruit, funds, and disciplined management; they brought marketing expertise, brands, and winemaking know-how. It was a great fit if we could learn to work together." Others, however, were less sanguine. Despite the fact that together the companies accounted for 22% of the Australian wine market and 17% of national wine exports, the dismissive industry view was, "When you put two dogs together, all you get is louder barking." Nonetheless, the companies merged in June 1992 and three months later became a publicly listed company.[2]

New Management, New Strategies

Following the merger, ex-BRL executives assumed the majority of top jobs in BRLH: the newly merged company's deputy-chairman, CEO, operations and technical director, and the international trading director all came from BRL. From the other side, only Hardy's managing director (who became BRLH's business development director) and the Australian sales and marketing manager survived as members of the new top executive team. Steve Millar, formerly BRL's managing director and now CEO of the merged company, explained his early priorities:

> Our first task was to deal with the financial situation. Both companies had performed poorly the previous year, and although we thought our forecasts were conservative, the market was concerned we would not meet the promises made in our IPO [initial public offering]. . . . Then we had to integrate the two organizations. This meant selecting a management team that could both implement the necessary retrenchments and position us for growth. Since the Australian market accounted for the vast bulk of our profit, we

[2]The Italian Ricasoli operations were explicitly excluded from the merger due to their continued substantial losses and the likelihood they would continue.

initially concentrated our attention at home. . . . Only after getting these two priorities straight could we focus on our new strategy.

The Domestic Turnaround   The strategy that emerged was simple: the company would protect its share of the bulk cask business but concentrate on branded bottle sales for growth. This would require a commitment to quality that would support its brands. The initial management focus would be on the domestic market, first getting merger efficiencies, then implementing the new strategy.

As important as developing a clear strategy, in Millar's mind, was the need to change the company's culture and management style. His sense was that, although there was great potential in the company's middle management, much of it—particularly in the ex-Hardy team—had been held back by being resource constrained and excluded from major decisions. Millar's objective was to create a more decentralized approach, but to hold management accountable. He explained:

> It took time to get the message understood because Hardy management had tended to take a few big swings on high-risk decisions while keeping tight control over the small decisions. I wanted to delegate the small risks—to create a "have a go" mentality. The objective was to have us trying 20 things and getting 80% right rather than doing one or two big things that had to be 100% right.

The prerequisite to delegation, however, was that managers had to be willing to challenge the status quo, accept responsibility for the outcome of decisions that were delegated, and admit when they had made a mistake. David Woods, previously Hardy's national sales manager and now appointed to the same position in the merged company, recalled that the new management style was not easy for everyone to adopt: "Many of us from Hardy felt like outsiders, unsure if we would be allowed into meetings. It became easier after the first year or so when you had shown you could perform. But you definitely had to earn your stripes."

Woods "earned his stripes" by integrating the two sales forces, capturing the economies from the combination, and repositioning the product portfolio in line with the new strategy emphasizing quality branded bottle sales. The results were impressive with both domestic bottle market share and profitability increasing significantly in the first two years of BRLH's operation.

Relaunching International   Meanwhile, Millar had appointed Stephen Davies, an ex-BRL colleague who he regarded as a first-class strategic marketer, as group marketing and export manager for BRLH. A 12-year veteran of BRL, Davies had been responsible for establishing that company's export division in 1985 and had been credited with its successful expansion abroad. While the rest of top management's attention was focused on a major restructuring of the domestic operations, Davies began evaluating the company's international operations. What he found was a dispersed portfolio of marginal-to-weak market positions: a U.K. business selling a small volume of Hardy wines and just breaking even, a rapidly eroding BRL bulk business in Sweden, a weak Hardy-U.S. presence supported by a single representative, and a virtually nonexistent presence in Asia or the rest of Europe.

In Davies's mind, a few clear priorities began to emerge, many of which shadowed the domestic approach. The first priority had to be to clean up the operating problems that were the source of the financial problems. Only then would they focus on building on their strengths, starting with their position in the U.K. market. Making "Quality Wines for the World" the company's marketing slogan, Davies began to build the export strategy on the basis of a strong quality brand image. From the existing broad portfolio of exported products (see Exhibit 3), he initiated a program to rationalize the line and reposition a few key brands in a stepstair hierarchy from simple entry level products to fine wines for connoisseurs. At the mass market price points, for example, he focused the line on *Nottage Hill* and *Stamps* as the Hardy's "fighting brands," while at the top end he targeted the *Eileen Hardy* brand.

BRL Hardy in Europe

In the large, developed U.K. market, Davies found a turnaround had already begun under the leadership of Christopher Carson, managing director of

Exhibit 3   BRL Hardy Domestic versus Export Product Portfolio, 1993

Soft Pack (Cask) Wine

- 2 litre   Benmano and Stanley range
- 3 litre   Berri fortified range
- 4 and 5 litre   Stanley, Berri and Buronga Ridge range
- 10, 15, and 20 litre   Stanley and Berri Range

Bottled Table Wine

Less than $6.00

Brentwood range
Brown Bin 60
Hardy Traditional range
- Hardy Stamp Series
Spring Gully range
- Nottage Hill
Leasingham Hutt Creek
McLaren Vale hermitage

- $6.00 to $10.00

- Houghton White Burgandy
Hardy Siegersdorf range
- Leasingham Domaine range
- Houghton Wildflower Ridge range
Hardy Bird Series range
Hardy Tintara range
Moondah Brook Estate range
Renmano Chairman's Selection range
Redman Claret and Cabernet Sanvignon
Barossa Valley Estate range
Chais Baumiere range

- $10.00 to $15.00

- Hardy Collection range
- Houghton Gold Reserve range
- Chateau Reynella Stony Hill range

- Over $15.00

- Eileen Hardy range
Lauriston range
E&E Black Pepper Shiraz

Sparkling Wine

- Less than $6.00

Courier Brut
Hardy Grand Reserve
Chateau Reynella Brut

- $6.00 to $10.00   - Hardy's Sir James Cuvee Brut
- Over $10.00   Hardy's Classique Cuvee
Lauriston Methode Champenoise

Fortified Wine

- Less than $6.00

Brown Bin 60
Cromwell
- Tall Ships
Stanley 2 litre port soft pack (cask)

- $6.00 to $10.00   Rumpole
- Old Cave

- Over $10.00   Lauriston Port & Muscat
Hardy Show Port
Vintage Port
Chateau Reynella Vintage Port

Brandy

- Hardy Black Bottle
Berri
Renmano

All prices are based on the recommended retail price.
- Rationalized export line
Source: Company documents.

Exhibit 4   BRL Hardy Europe Ltd.: Key Historical Data (£'000)

		1990	1991	1992	1993	1994
Net sales turnover:	In GB £	£10,788	£12,112	£12,434	£15,521	£18,813
	In Australian $	A$22,243	A$24,973	A$29,965	A$33,830	A$37,946
Gross profit (after distribution expense)		£1,173	£1,429	£1,438	£1,595	£1,924
GP %/sales		10.9%	11.8%	11.6%	10.3%	10.2%
Administrative cost		£1,104	£1,261	£1,164	£1,172	£1,308
Admin %/sales		10.2%	10.4%	9.4%	7.6%	7.0%
Profit after tax		−£26	£6	£157	£266	£395
PAT %/sales		−0.2%	0.0%	1.3%	1.7%	2.1%
Average no. of employees		31	27	19	20	22
£ sales per employee		£348	£449	£654	£776	£855
Stock @ year end		£1,226	£1,043	£605	£897	£1,392
Stock turnover		7.8	10.2	18.2	15.5	12.1
Return on investment		−2.1%	0.5%	11.2%	17.9%	24.5%

Source: Company documents.

Hardy's U.K. company. Carson was an experienced marketing manager with over 20 years in the wine business and particular expertise in Italian wines. He had been hired by Hardy in October 1990 to head the U.K. company's sales and marketing function, including the two recently acquired distributors. Within a week of his joining, however, Carson realized that the financial situation in these companies was disastrous. He flew to Australia to tell Hardy's management that they would own a bankrupt U.K. organization unless drastic action was taken. He then proposed a series of cost-cutting steps.

In February 1991, Carson was appointed U.K. managing director and immediately began to implement his cost-cutting plan. Over the next 18 months, he pruned the product line from 870 items to 230 and reduced the headcount from 31 to 18 (including a separation with three of the six executive directors). He also installed strong systems, controls, and policies that put him firmly in charge of key decisions. As these actions were implemented, the 1990 losses became a breakeven operation in 1991, and by the time of the mid-1992 merger, it looked as if the European operations would be profitable again. (For BRLH Europe financials, see Exhibit 4.)

Developing the Headquarters Relationship   In his discussions with Davies in late 1992, Carson highlighted the key problems and priorities as he saw them. First was the need to build quickly on the 178,000 cases of Hardy-brand products that had represented less than a quarter of his total volume in 1991 (500,000 of his 700,000 case sales in 1991 were accounted for by a variety of low-margin French wines handled under agency agreements that had come with the purchase of Whiclar and Gordon). At the same time, if the company was going to restore the financial health of its French winemaker, Domaine de la Baume, he felt he would have to build substantially on the 10,000 cases of its product which he had sold in 1991. (He reported 1992 sales were on track to double their previous year's volume.) And finally, he wanted to protect an

			Forecast per BRLH Europe Strategic Plan			
1995	1996	1997	Plan 1998	Plan 1999	Plan 2000	Plan 2001
£27,661	£32,271	£40,100	£53,848	£66,012	£78,814	£91,606
A$57,734	A$69,532	A$82,680	A$111,027	A$136,107	A$162,503	A$188,878
£2,592	£3,202	£4,212	£5,453	£6,488	£7,630	£8,787
9.4%	9.9%	10.5%	10.1%	9.8%	9.7%	9.67%
£1,896	£2,118	£2,717	£3,649	£4,473	£5,340	£6,207
6.9%	6.8%	6.8%	6.8%	6.8%	6.8%	6.8%
£426	£723	£948	£1,087	£1,286	£1,460	£1,644
1.5%	2.2%	2.4%	2.0%	1.9%	1.9%	1.8%
24	28	34	48	62	76	91
£1,153	£1,153	£1,179	£1,122	£1,065	£1,037	£1,007
£1,265	£1,504	£1,500	£2,100	£2,600	£3,300	£3,900
19.8	19.3	23.9	23.0	22.9	21.6	21.2
23.5%	35.7%	39.7%	38.0%	37.8%	36.1%	37.2%

unstable imported Chilean product that had come as a Whiclar and Gordon agency. Carson told Davies of his plans to grow the high potential brand from 20,000 cases in 1991 to a forecast 60,000 cases for 1992.

Davies agreed with Carson's plans, particularly endorsing the focus on Australian brands. Yet the relationship was an uneasy one in the post-merger management uncertainties. The BRL-dominated headquarters management supported delegation, but only to those who had "earned their stripes." Within the Hardy-built European company, on the other hand, there were questions about whether their bulk-wine-oriented BRL colleagues understood international marketing. "There was a real tension," said one observer. "A real feeling of us versus them. I think Christopher and Stephen had some difficult conversations." The relationship was delicate enough that Steve Millar decided to have Carson report directly to him on the U.K. company's profit performance but through Davies for

marketing and brand strategy. (For BRLH international organization, see Exhibit 5.) But Millar did not want the shared reporting relationship to pull him into a role of resolving disputes on operating issues. Instead, he hoped for negotiation:

> Christopher had a good reputation and knew the market well. I assumed he would be a key player and was willing to let him prove it. He and Stephen just clashed, but confrontation can be healthy as long as it is constructive. I just kept urging them to work together—they could learn a lot from one another.

The biggest disputes seemed to emerge around marketing strategies, particularly branding and labeling issues. Although Hardy exported a dozen brands covering the full price range, its entry-level brands in the United Kingdom were Hardy's *Stamps,* blended red and white wines that then retailed for £2.99 and Hardy's *Nottage Hill,* a single varietal red and white at the £3.69 price point. Together, these two brands accounted for over 80% of Hardy brand sales by value and even more by

Exhibit 5   BRL Hardy's International Organization, 1993

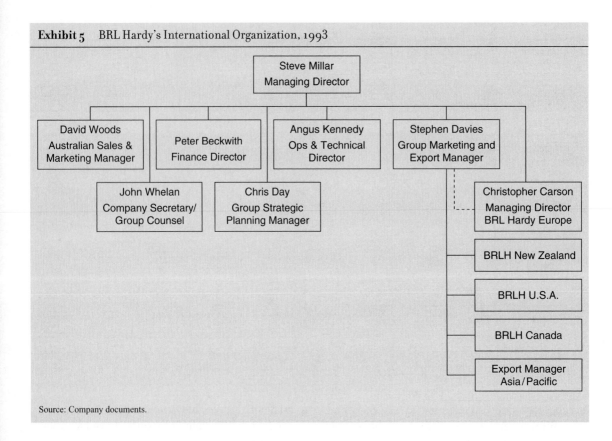

Source: Company documents.

volume. Carson was concerned that the image of these brands had eroded in the United Kingdom, and that he wanted to relabel, reposition, and re-launch them. But it was difficult to convince the home office, and he expressed his frustration:

> Australia controlled all aspects of the brand and they kept me on a pretty tight leash. When I took my message to Reynella [BRLH's corporate office near Adelaide], they didn't want to hear. They expect you to get runs on the board before they give you much freedom. . . . But we were in the U.K. market and they weren't. Finally they agreed, and in 1993 we relabeled and relaunched *Nottage Hill* and repositioned *Stamps*. By 1994 our volume of Hardy's brands quadrupled from 1992 and represented more than half our total sales. (See Exhibit 6.)

Davies acknowledged that he yielded on the *Stamps* and *Nottage Hill* decisions, believing "it

was better to let people follow a course they believe in—then the implementation will be better." But he became increasingly concerned about the demand for local control over branding, labeling, and pricing decisions, especially as the company's long-term strategy began to evolve.

The Evolving Strategy   In Reynella, by the mid-1990s, Millar and Davies began to conceive of BRL Hardy not as just a "quality exporter" but as an "international wine company" with worldwide product access backed by the marketing capability and distribution muscle to create global brands. As Millar explained:

> It was an important strategic shift. Most packaged goods businesses are dominated by multinational companies with global brands—like Coke or Kraft. We realized that there were no really established global wine

Exhibit 6   BRL Hardy Europe Ltd.: Case Summary History

In Std. 9 Liter Cases	1991	1992	1993	1994	1995	1996	1997
Hardy	178,500	194,303	411,084	856,876	1,031,071	1,383,772	1,763,698
Domaine de la Baume	10,000	19,564	49,698	63,540	89,256	155,608	158,587
Chile	20,000	58,848	24,855	76,775	112,954	120,540	50,537
French Agencies (AGW)	497,500	618,878	528,606	545,198	446,445	51,257	} 186,180
French Projects					2,162	58,744	
Grand total	706,000	891,593	1,014,243	1,542,389	1,681,888	1,769,921	2,159,002

Source: Company documents.

companies and, despite our newness at the game, we had a real chance to be one. . . . I began describing BRL Hardy to our shareholders as a company based on three core strengths: our world-class production facilities, our global brands, and our international distribution. Controlling those assets allows us to control our destiny in any major market in the world.

Within the industry, the notion of building global wine brands ran counter to the established wisdom. For example, Jean-Louis Duneu, the head of the Paris office of Lander, a branding consulting firm, recognized the potential of global branding, but was skeptical about its applicability to wine. "The promise of a brand is that it will be the same quality every time," he said. "That means that branded wine probably has to be blended to ensure consistency. The result is never as satisfying." Jonathan Knowles, another corporate identity consultant warned of another potential problem. "Wine lovers look for something they haven't heard of," he claimed. "There's almost an anti-branding mentality. When people who are not in the know get to know the brand name, people in the know no longer want the product."

That view also seemed widespread among traditional wine producers. In the highly fragmented European industry—there were 12,000 producers in Bordeaux alone—only a few top-of-the-market names like Lafite, d'Yquem, and Veuve Clicquot had achieved global recognition, but these held minuscule market shares. Of those that had attempted to build mass market global brands over the years, only a handful—Mateus Rosé, Blue Nun, Mouton

Cadet, and Hirondelle, for example—had succeeded. And of these, most had managed to capture only relatively small volumes and for brief periods of time. After years of trying, Gallo, the world's biggest wine brand, accounted for considerably less than 1% of global wine sales.

Nonetheless, Millar and Davies believed that changes in wine-making, the opening of global markets, and the changing consumer profile would all support their objective to become a truly international wine company built on a global branding capability. To implement this strategic shift, Davies felt the Reynella headquarters had to be the "global brand owners." He explained:

> Although we believe in decentralization and want to listen to and support overseas ideas and proposals, we also have to be clear about Reynella's role. Everyone has opinions on label design, but we'll lose control of the brand if we decentralize too much. Our role should be as brand owners deciding issues relating to labeling, pricing, and branding, and overseas should be responsible for sales, distribution, and promotion strategy.

Carson and his U.K. management team had some difficulty with this concept, and disagreements between the two executives continued through the mid-1990s. Carson tried to convince Davies that, unlike the Australian market where branded products accounted for 90% of sales mostly through hotels and bottle shops, the United Kingdom was not yet a branded wine market. Retailers' own labels dominated, particularly in the supermarkets that accounted for more than 50% of retail wine sales. Proximity to Continental sources meant that another big segment was claimed by a proliferation of tiny vineyard or village labels with little or no brand recognition, leaving only 12% of sales to recognized proprietary branded wines in 1995. In such a market, Carson argued, it would be hard to support a brand-driven strategy. He elaborated:

> We have to manage a progression from commodity to commodity brand to soft brand to hard brand. And at the early stage of that progression, distribution is key. It's more push than pull, and you need retailers' support to get your product on their shelves. That's why labeling is so important. Women represent 60% of the supermarket wine buyers and the label has to appeal to them.

As the decade rolled on, the debate between Carson and Davies continued. But, as Steve Millar put it, "With 70% growth, we could support the tension."

The 1997 Watershed Decisions

On the basis of the U.K. company's excellent performance, Carson was appointed chief executive of BRL Hardy Europe in 1995. He immediately began putting together some bold plans for the company's continued growth and, over the next couple of years, set in motion some initiatives that were to create a mixture of excitement and apprehension within the organization.

The Outsourcing Ventures   For the first five years following the merger, Carson had focused most of his attention on building sales of the Hardy brand wines. However, he remained acutely aware of the importance of the other non-Australian product lines he had inherited through the Whiclar and Gordon acquisition. Not only did the added volume bring scale economies to his sales and distribution operation, they also provided BRLH Europe with some other important strategic benefits.

As an agricultural product, every region's grape harvest was vulnerable to weather, disease, and other factors affecting the quality and quantity of a vintage. Carson recognized that sourcing from

Exhibit 7   Key Currency Fluctuations Affecting BRLH Europe

	$Aus/£	It Lira/£	Chilean Peso/£	$US/£
12/92	2.197	2239	NA	1.514
12/93	2.213	2516	NA	1.492
12/94	2.013	2546	NA	1.559
12/95	2.080	2455	630.8	1.541
12/96	2.088	2544	703.0	1.664
12/97	2.505	2892	727.1	1.659

Source: Company documents.

multiple regions was one way to minimize that risk. Furthermore, he became increasingly aware that major retailers—particularly grocery chains like Sainsburys—were trying to rationalize their suppliers. To simplify wine buying, they wanted to deal with only a few key suppliers who could provide them with a broad line of quality products. And finally, currency fluctuations exposed traded products like wine exports to currency-driven price variations that could substantially affect marketability, particularly for lower-priced products. (See Exhibit 7.)

For all these reasons, in 1997 Carson began to devote more of his time and attention to two non-Australian wine sources—a move that seemed to fit with Reynella's new emphasis on becoming "an international wine company." This shift was triggered by the unpleasant revelation in late 1996 that *Caliterra*, a brand he and his sales organization had built into the leading Chilean import in the United Kingdom, would not be renewing its distribution agreement. The supplier, Caliterra Limitade, had signed a joint venture agreement with U.S. winemaker Robert Mondavi.

Determined never again to invest in a brand he did not control, Carson initiated action on two fronts. In early 1997, he negotiated a 50/50 joint venture agreement with Jose Canopa y CIA Limitada under which the Chileans would provide the fruit and the winemaking facility while BRL Hardy would send in one of its winemakers to make several wines that it would sell in Europe under the *Mapocho* brand, using its marketing and distribution capabilities. Despite several mishaps, difficulties, and delays during the negotiations (including a near derailing when Carson's main contact left Canepa), by late 1997 the supply arrangements were in place.

At the same time he was finalizing the Chilean deal, Carson was also exploring alternative European sources, particularly for red wine. In March 1997, he made initial contact with Casa Vinicola Calatrasi, a family-owned winery in Sicily with links to a major grape grower's cooperative. After explaining his interest in developing a line of branded products to be sold through BRLH's distribution channels, he began analyzing product availability, volume forecasts, and prices.

Over the following months, he returned to Sicily a couple more times, meeting with the co-op farmers to explain how branding could give them security of demand and eventually better prices for their fruit. He told them of BRL Hardy's expertise in viticulture, and offered the help of the company's highly regarded technical experts to further enhance the value of their harvest through more productive vineyard techniques and new winemaking methods. Having experienced difficult negotiations with the Chilean joint venture, Carson wanted to avoid similar problems and emphasized that this would work only if it was a true partnership. He wanted the farmers' best fruit and their commitment to make the project work. At his first presentation, 60 farmers showed up. When the word spread, Carson found he had an audience of 135 receptive co-op members at his second presentation. "We all had a very good feeling about the relationship," said Carson. "It felt much more like a partnership than the Chilean JV where they were acting more like suppliers than part owners."

Returning to London, Carson engaged his organization in developing a strategy for the product code-named *Mata Hardy*. While detailed marketing plans were being developed internally, an external consultant began generating over 2,000 possible brand names. As Carson and his sales and marketing staff began narrowing the choices, they engaged a designer to develop labels and packaging that would capture the Mediterranean lifestyle they wanted the brand to reflect.

By July 1997, the marketing plans were developed to the point that Carson was ready to review his proposal with management in Reynella. He described how he wanted to offset projected Australian red wine shortages with alternative sources. Presenting his vision of sourcing from both the northern and southern hemispheres, he outlined his need for a full line to maximize his leverage as a distributor. He then described the broad objective of developing a brand that would respond to the average wine consumer who was interested in wine but not necessarily very knowledgeable about it. The new product was designed to give them the information they needed on appealing, easy-to-read labels with a pronounceable brand name. The objective was to give them a wine they would enjoy and a brand they would trust.

Carson then presented the portfolio of eight new Italian-sourced wines spread across the low and low-middle price points. At the baseline £3.49 price point would be wines made from less well known indigenous Sicilian grapes. At the next level would be blends of indigenous and premium varietals (a Catarrato-Chardonnay white and Nero d'Avola-Sangiovese red, for example) priced at £3.99. At £4.99 he planned to offer pure premium varietals such as Syrah and Sangiovese, while to top out the line he wanted to offer blends of super-varietals such as Cabernet-Merlot at £5.99.

The highlight of the presentation was when Carson unveiled his idea about creating a strong branded product, revealing both the final name choice—*D'istinto,* which translated as "instinctively"—and the boldly distinctive labels and other packaging designs. (See Exhibit 8.) (He swore all who saw the branding materials to secrecy since his intention was to reveal the new name and label with great fanfare just before its planned launch in early 1998.) The plan was to give *D'istinto* a unique image built around the Mediterranean lifestyle—passionate, warm, romantic, and relaxed—and to link it strongly to food. Each bottle would have a small booklet hung on its neck, describing the wine and inviting the buyer to write

Exhibit 8 *D'istinto* Proposed Packaging and Positioning

Capsule Product Position/Brand Image

- Value
- Quality
- Mass appeal

- Mediterranean lifestyle
- Food-friendly

- Relaxed
- Warm
- Romantic

Source: Company documents.

for free recipes. The intention was to create a database of wine-and-food-loving consumers to whom future promotions could be mailed. "This line can help us build BRLH Europe in size, impact, and reputation," said Carson. "We need to become known as a first-class branding company—a company able to leverage great distribution and strong marketing into recognized consumer brands."

In the meanwhile, however, early signs were that the *Mapocho* project was not going well. For months, Canepa managers had been raising doubts and concerns about the JV. For example, they claimed their costs went up, and wanted to renegotiate the supply price. By the time things got back on track, the Chilean company had made other commitments and the new venture lost its opportunity to get early access to the pick of the 1997 grape harvest. As a result, first samples of *Mapocho* sent to London by BRL Hardy's winemaker were disappointing. The Chileans thought the problem was

due to the winemaker sent from BRL Hardy being unfamiliar with Chilean wine, while he insisted they had not provided him with quality fruit. Early sales were disappointing and forecasts were that the first vintage would sell only 15,000 cases against the 80,000 originally planned. Unless there was a rapid turnaround, the company stood to lose up to £400,000. Despite this poor showing, however, the U.K. sales and marketing group was forecasting 1998 sales of 150,000 cases and the company was about to make a commitment to Canepa for this volume of their new vintage due in February. It was a forecast that made many in the Reynella headquarters very nervous.

As a consequence, while the Australians were impressed by Carson's ambitious ideas for *D'istinto,* many questions and doubts were raised and approval was slow in coming. Some senior management still had bad feelings about the Italian wine business left over from Hardy's earlier ill-fated Italian venture. Even those who had not lived through the Ricasoli losses had concerns about the troublesome ongoing experiment with the Chilean sourcing joint venture. And still others, including Stephen Davies, were concerned that the new Sicilian line could cannibalize Hardy's two fighting brands. *D'istinto* was initially proposed as a product to fill the price points that had been vacated as *Stamps* and *Nottage Hill* had become more expensive. But, as the Australian management pointed out, the extended Sicilian line now clearly overlapped with Hardy's core offerings—not only *Stamps* at £4.49 but even with *Nottage Hill* now selling for £5.49 (see Exhibit 9).

Finally, Steve Millar raised a more organizational concern. He was worried about the possibility of Carson losing his focus and about the strength of the European sales organization to carry another brand when it was already struggling with *Mapocho*. In the context of the U.K.'s overcommitment to the *Mapocho* launch, he was even more concerned when he saw *D'istinto's* projected sales of 160,000 cases in the first year rising to 500,000 by year four. "You will never do those numbers," said Millar. Carson's response was that

Exhibit 9 U.K. Product Price Point Matrix

Recommended Retail Price Point (£)	Hardy	Leasingham Chateau Reynella	Houghton	Mapocho	D'istinto
27.99	Eileen Hardy Shiraz Thomas Hardy Cab Sauv		Jack Mann Red		
24.99		E&E Black Pepper			
19.99		Classic Clare Shiraz			
12.99	Eileen Hardy Chardonnay	Ebenezer Shiraz Ebenezer Cab Merlot	Crofters Cab Merlot		
11.99		Ch Reynella Shiraz Ch Rey Cab Merlot			
9.99	Coonawarra Cab Sauv	Leasingham Shiraz Leas Cab Malbec			
8.99		Ebenezer Chardonnay Ch Rey Chard Leas Chard	Crofters Chardonnay		
7.99	Pathway Chardonnay	Domain Grenache	Wildflower Shiraz		
6.99	Bankside Shiraz	Leas Chardonnay Leas Semillon			
6.49	Bankside Chardonnay				
5.99	Nottage Hill Shiraz Stamps Sparkling		Wildflower Chardonnay Wildflower Chenin Blanc	Merlot	Cabernet Merlot
5.49	Nottage Hill Cab Shiraz				
4.99	Nottage Hill Chardonnay Nottage Hill Reisling Stamp Shiraz Cabernet Stamp Grenche Shiraz			Cab. Sauv. Chardonnay	Syrah Sangiovese
4.49	Stamp Chardonnay Sem Stamp ReislingG/Traminer			Sauv. Blanc	
3.99					Cataratto/Chardonnay Sangiovese/Merlot
3.49					Trebiano/Insolia Nero d'Aviola

Source: Company documents.

he thought *D'istinto* had global potential and could eventually reach a million cases. "By the next century, we'll even be exporting Italian wine to Australia!" he said.

Yet despite the lighthearted exchange with his boss, the widely expressed doubts he confronted in the Australian review meeting caused Carson to reflect. The financial investment in the branding, packaging, and launch expenses was relatively small—probably less than £100,000. But in a situation of continued difficulty with *Mapocho* sales, Carson understood that the real financial risk could come later in the form of contract commitments and excess inventory. Furthermore, he knew that the questions Steve Millar had raised about organizational capacity and his own risk of distraction were real. Would *D'istinto* overload human resources already stretched thin by the rapid expansion of the previous five years? And would it prove to be too big a competitor for management time, corporate funding, and eventually consumer sales? The questions were complicated by another decision Carson faced—one relating to the development of a new Australian product to extend the company's existing range of fighting brands.

The Australian Opportunity   As the *Stamps* and *Nottage Hill* brands gradually migrated upward to straddle the £4.49/£4.99/£5.49 price points, Carson believed there was an opening for a new low-end Australian brand to fill in the first rungs on the Hardy's price ladder below £4.49, the price points representing more than 80% of sales volume. Being fully occupied with the Chilean and Italian projects, however, he found himself unable to devote the time he wanted to developing a new Australian brand. To Steve Millar, this presented the ideal opportunity to push an agenda he had been urging on Carson for some time—the need to develop the senior levels of the U.K. organization, particularly on the marketing side. Said Millar:

> Christopher had done an amazing job of building the U.K. But he had driven much of it himself. . . . For a couple of years I'd been telling him, "Get people even

better than you *below* you." We'd even sent a few Australians to support him in marketing and help the communication back home. But most of them got chewed up pretty quickly.

Finding himself stretched thin, and recognizing he had to stand back from controlling operations, Carson agreed to take on a new expat Australian marketing manager. The person he chose was Paul Browne, an eight-year company veteran whose career had taken him from public relations to brand management in Australia. Most recently, he had been responsible for export marketing for the United States and Oceania, reporting to the president of BRL Hardy USA. Carson explained his choice:

> I wanted a driver. Someone who could take charge and get things done. As an Australian with an understanding of group level activities, Paul fit our need to fill the weakness in marketing. He roared into the business with great enthusiasm and linked up with our sales director and national accounts manager to understand the local market's needs.

Browne concluded that there was an opportunity for a Hardy's brand positioned at the £3.99 price point, but able to be promoted at £3.49. He felt the market was ready for a fun brand—even slightly quirky—which would appeal to a younger consumer, perhaps a first-time wine drinker who would later trade up to *Stamps* and *Nottage Hill*. The brand he came up with was *Kelly's Revenge,* named for an important character in the history of the Australian wine industry, but also suggestive of Ned Kelly, the infamous Australian bushranger (outlaw) of the early nineteenth century. With backing and support of the U.K. sales management, they pursued the concept, designing a colorful label and preparing a detailed marketing plan. (See Exhibit 10.) As excitement and enthusiasm increased, Carson stood back and gave his new product team its head.

Meanwhile, in Reynella, BRLH in Australia was developing a major new product targeted at a similar price point. In 1995, the company had acquired Banrock Station, a 1,800-hectare cattle grazing property in South Australia's Riverland district,

Exhibit 10   *Kelly's Revenge:* Label and Product Concept

Proposed Promotion Material/Back Label

It has taken 130 years for Dr. Alexander Kelly to have his revenge. Kelly was the first to recognize the wine growing potential to Australia's McLaren Vale region. His vision, however, was ahead of its time, and his eventual bankruptcy enabled the acquisition of the original Tintara Winery by Thomas Hardy. Hardy's wines eventually established the reputation of the McLaren Vale, winning tremendous praise at the Colonial and Indian Wine Exhibition in 1885. Kelly's descendents have continued to forge Hardy's wine-making tradition, and to this day Tintara Cellars are the home of Hardy's Wines, one of Australia's finest and most highly awarded winemakers. This wine is dedicated to the spirit of our pioneers.

Source: Company documents.

with the intention of converting a portion of it to viticulture. During the planting and development phase, visitors' universally positive reaction to BRLH's ongoing conservation efforts—planting only 400 hectares while returning the remaining land to its native state including the restoration of natural wetlands—convinced management that the property had brand potential. (See Exhibit 11.)

Positioned as an environmentally responsible product with part of its profits allocated to conservation groups, the *Banrock Station* brand was launched in Australia in 1996. The brand's image was reflected in its earth-tone labels and its positioning as an unpretentious, down-to-earth wine was captured by the motto "Good Earth, Fine Wine." Blended *Banrock Station* wines started at A$4.95, but the line extended up to premium varietals at A$7.95. In the United Kingdom, it would be positioned at the same price points as the proposed

Kelly's Revenge. The product was an immediate success in Australia, and soon thereafter became the largest-selling imported brand in New Zealand.

Convinced of *Banrock Station's* potential as a global brand, Davies and Millar urged BRLH companies in Europe and North America to put their best efforts behind it. Canadian management agreed to launch immediately, while in the United States, the decision was made to withdraw the *Stamps* product, which local management felt was devaluing the Hardy's image, and replace it with *Banrock Station.* But in Europe, where the *Kelly's Revenge* project was in its final development stages, the management team expressed grave doubts about *Banrock Station.* They argued that the label design was too dull and colorless to stand out on supermarket shelves, and that the product's environmental positioning would have limited appeal to U.K. consumers half a world away.

Exhibit 11   *Banrock Station:* Environmentally Responsible Product Positioning

Proposed Product Promotion Material

Banrock Station's precious soil is treated with respect and in return it nurtures the premium grape varieties that create our value-for-money, easy drinking wines of great character. Situated in the heart of South Australia's Riverland region, directly opposite the historic Cobb & Co. stage coach station, Banrock Station is a 4,500 acre property featuring some of the world's most picturesque scenery. In its midst lie 400 acres of premium sun-soaked vineyard.

Because we understand that good earth is the starting point for most of nature's bounty, we are working with like minded organizations to ensure this natural haven which surrounds the vineyards of Banrock Station is preserved for future generations to appreciate and enjoy. Every sip of Banrock Station fine wine gives a little back to the good earth from whence it came.

Banrock Station: Good Earth, Fine Wine.

Source: Company documents.

Steve Millar described the conflict that emerged around the competing concepts:

> I accept it as my mistake. I'd been pushing Christopher to delegate more and trying to get more Australians on his staff to help build links back to Australia. But Paul Browne became our biggest problem. He just didn't

have the skills for the job but he wanted to control everything. Then on top of that he started playing politics to block *Banrock Station*. When we asked him to give the new concept a try, he kept insisting it would never work. We got the feeling he had even organized customers to tell us how bad the label was. Instead of helping communications between Australia and Europe he became a major barrier.

Meanwhile, Browne presented his new *Kelly's Revenge* concept to the Australian management to a very skeptical reception. Davies's reaction was immediate, strong, and negative, seeing it as "kitsch, downmarket, and gimmicky." While ready to let the Europeans take the lead on Chilean or Italian products, he and his Reynella-based staff felt they knew more about marketing Australian wines. In Davies's words, "By decentralizing too much responsibility, we realized we risked losing control of brand issues. We wanted to take back more control as the brand owners."

Steve Millar recalled his reaction to the *Kelly's Revenge* proposal:

> I told them I thought it was terrible, but that it really didn't matter what I thought. I suggested we get the customers' reaction. When we took it to ASDA, the UK grocery chain, they were not enthralled. So I took that as an opportunity to suggest we give *Banrock Station* a try.

Although Christopher Carson had been backing his new marketing manager to this point, with *Banrock Station* succeeding elsewhere and senior management behind it as a global brand, the issue was becoming very complex. He knew the organization could not support both brands and felt the time had come when he would have to commit to one project or the other. For Steve Millar, the situation was equally complex. Given the U.K.'s strong performance, he wanted to give Carson as much freedom as possible, but also felt responsible for the implementation of the company's global strategy. Running through his mind was how he would respond if Carson and his U.K. organization remained firm in its commitment to *Kelly's Revenge* over *Banrock Station*.

Case 7-2   Silvio Napoli at Schindler India

"Monsieur Napoli, si vous vous plantez ici vous êtes fini! Mais si vous réussissez, vous aurez une très bonne carrière." (Translation: "Mr. Napoli, if you fall on your face here you are finished! But if you succeed, you will have a very nice career.") The words echoed off the walls of Silvio Napoli's empty living room and disappeared down the darkened hallway like startled ghosts. The parquet was still wet from the five inches of water that had flooded the first floor of the Napoli home in suburban New Delhi several days before, during one of the sewer system's periodic backups. Standing in the empty room were Napoli and Luc Bonnard, vice chairman, board of directors of Schindler Holdings Ltd., the respected Swiss-based manufacturer of elevators and escalators. It was November 1998, and Bonnard was visiting New Delhi for the first time to review progress on the start-up of the company's Indian subsidiary, which Napoli had been dispatched to run eight months earlier. Things were not going according to plan.

Napoli, a 33-year-old Italian former semiprofessional rugby player, had arrived in March with his pregnant wife and two young children and had quickly set about creating an entirely new organization from scratch. Since March, he had established offices in New Delhi and Mumbai, hired five Indian top managers, and begun to implement the aggressive business plan he had written the previous year while head of corporate planning in Switzerland. The plan called for a $10 million investment and hinged on selling "core, standardized products," with no allowance for customization. To keep costs

down and avoid India's high import tariffs, the plan also proposed that all manufacturing and logistics activities be outsourced to local suppliers.

Shortly before Bonnard's visit, however, Napoli was confronted with three challenges to his plan. First, he learned that for the second time in two months, his Indian managers had approved an order for a nonstandard product—calling for a glass rear wall in one of the supposedly standard elevators. At the same time, his business plan had come under intense cost pressures, first from a large increase in customs duties on imported elevator components, then from an unanticipated rise in transfer prices for the "low-cost" product lines imported from Schindler's European factories. Finally, as Napoli began accelerating his strategy of developing local sources for elevator components, he found that his requests for parts lists, design specifications, and engineering support were not forthcoming from Schindler's European plants.

As the implementation of his business plan stalled, Napoli wondered what he should do. Eight months in India and he still had not installed a single elevator, while his plan showed first-year sales of 50 units. And now Bonnard was visiting. Should he seek his help, propose a revised plan, or try to sort out the challenges himself? These were the thoughts running through Napoli's head as the vice chairman asked him, "So, how are things going so far, Mr. Napoli?"

▌Schindler's India Explorations

Schindler had a long and rather disjointed history with the Indian market. Although its first elevator in India was installed in 1925, the company did not have a local market presence until it appointed a local distributor in the late 1950s. Almost 40 years later, Schindler decided it was time to take an even bolder step and enter the market through its own wholly owned subsidiary.

▌Senior Research Associate Perry L. Fagan and Professor Michael Y. Yoshino prepared the original version of this case, "Silvio Napoli at Schindler India (A)," HBS No. 302-053 (Boston: Harvard Business School Publishing, 2002). This version was prepared by Professor Christopher A. Bartlett. HBS cases are developed solely as the basis for class discussion. Cases are not intended to serve as endorsements, sources of primary data, or illustrations of effective or ineffective management.
▌Copyright © 2003 President and Fellows of Harvard College. Harvard Business School case 303-086.

The Growing Commitment   Established in 1874 in Switzerland by Robert Schindler, the company began manufacturing elevators in 1889. Almost a century later, the 37-year-old Alfred N. Schindler became the fourth generation of the family to lead the company, in 1987. Over the next decade, he sought to transform the company's culture from that of an engineering-based manufacturing company to one of a customer-oriented service company.

By 1998, Schindler had worldwide revenues of 6.6 billion Swiss francs (US$4 billion) and was widely perceived as the technology leader in elevators. It was also the number one producer of escalators in the world. The company employed over 38,000 people in 97 subsidiaries but did not yet have its own operations in India, a market Alfred Schindler felt had great potential.

Although the first Schindler elevator in India was installed in 1925, it was not until 1958 that the company entered into a long-term distribution agreement with ECE, an Indian company. In 1985, Schindler terminated that agreement and entered into a technical collaboration with Mumbai-based Bharat Bijlee Ltd. (BBL) to manufacture, market, and sell its elevators. After acquiring a 12% equity stake in BBL, Schindler supported the local company as it became the number two player in the Indian elevator market, with a 10%–15% share a decade later.

On assuming the role of chairman in 1995, Alfred Schindler decided to take a six-month "sabbatical" during which he wanted to step back and review the long-term strategy of Schindler. As part of that process, he undertook to travel through several markets—China, Japan, and several other Far Eastern markets—that he felt were important to the company's growth. He spent several weeks in India, traveling over 3,000 kilometers in a small Ford rental car. "After his trip Mr. Schindler saw India as a second China," said a manager in Switzerland. "He saw huge growth potential. And once he targets something, he's like a hawk."

With the objective of raising its involvement, Schindler proposed to BBL that a separate joint venture be created for the elevator business, with Schindler taking management control. But negotiations proved difficult and eventually collapsed. In late 1996, collaboration with BBL ended, and the company began considering options to establish its own operation in India.

Silvio Napoli's Role   Meanwhile, after graduating from the MBA program at Harvard Business School, Silvio Napoli had joined Schindler in September 1994. He accepted a position at the company's headquarters in Ebikon, Switzerland, reporting directly to the CEO as head of corporate planning.

With its 120 years of history, Schindler was a formal Swiss company where the hierarchy was clear, politeness important, and first names rarely used. Napoli's office was on the top floor of the seven-story headquarters building, a floor reserved for the three members of the company's executive committee and the legal counsel. (For profiles of top management, see Exhibit 1.) "As soon as I arrived, I was aware that people were very responsive to my requests," said Napoli. "Just by my physical location, I generated fearful respect, and I realized I would have to manage my situation very carefully." A 20-year Schindler veteran recalled his reaction to Napoli's arrival: "He was the assistant to Mr. Schindler, so I knew I'd better be nice to him."

As head of corporate planning, Napoli was responsible for coordinating the annual strategic review process and undertaking external benchmarking and competitor analysis. But his most visible role was as staff to the corporate executive committee, the Verwaltungsrat Ausschuss (VRA)—which was composed of Alfred Schindler, Luc Bonnard, and Alfred Spöerri, the chief financial officer. As the only nonmember to attend VRA meetings, Napoli was responsible for taking meeting minutes and for following up on action items and special projects defined by the VRA.

The Swatch Project   In 1995, Napoli took on the Swatch Project, a major assignment that grew out of a concern by VRA members that margins on new-product sales were eroding as each competitor

Exhibit 1 Schindler Top Management Profiles

Name:	Alfred N. Schindler	Luc Bonnard	Alfred Spöerri
Position:	Chairman and Chief Executive Officer	Vice Chairman of the Board and Member of the Executive Committee	Member of the Board of Directors Member of the Executive Committee
Date of Birth:	March 21, 1949	October 8, 1946	August 22, 1938
Education:	*1976–1978:* MBA, Wharton, USA *1974–1976:* Certified Public Accountant School, Bern *1969–1974:* University of Basel—Law School (lic. jur.), Abschluss:lic.iur.	*1971:* Diploma in Electrical Engineering at ETH (Technical University), Zurich	
Experience:	*Since 1995:* Chairman of the Board and Chief Executive Officer *1985–1995:* Chairman of the Corporate Executive (CEO) *1984–1985:* Member of Corporate Management *1982–1984:* Head of Corporate Planning *1978–1979:* Deputy Head of Corporate Planning	*1996:* Vice Chairman *1991–1996:* Member of the Executive Committee *1986–1990:* COO Elevators and Escalators, Member Corporate Executive Committee *1985–1986:* Member, Executive Committee *1983–1985:* Group Management Member, North Europe *1973:* Management, Schindler, in France	*1991–1998:* Member, Executive Committee *1997–1998:* Chief Financial Officer *1979–1988:* Corporate Controller—Treasurer *1975–1979:* COO of Mexico *1971–1974:* Area Controller, Latin America *1968–1974:* Financial Officer of Mexico *1968:* Joined Schindler Group

Source: Schindler India.

strove to expand its installed base of elevators. Since such sales were a vital source of profitable long-term maintenance and service contracts, the project's imperative goal was to develop a standardized elevator at a dramatically lower cost than the existing broad line of more customized products.

It was a project that involved the young newcomer in sensitive discussions with Schindler's plants in Switzerland, France, and Spain to discuss design, determine costs, and explore sourcing alternatives. Napoli described the process and outcome of the Swatch Project:

> As you might imagine, I was viewed with some suspicion and concern. Here was this young MBA talking about getting costs down or outsourcing core tasks that the plants felt they owned. . . . In the end, we developed the S001, an elevator that could not be customized, used many parts obtained from outside suppliers, and incorporated processes never before seen in the group. All of this was unthinkable in the past. We redesigned the entire supply chain and halved the industry's standard 20- to 30-week cycle time.

The Indian Entry Project   Meanwhile, as negotiations with BBL broke down in India, the VRA decided to engage Boston Consulting Group (BCG) to identify and evaluate alternative local partners with whom Schindler might build a more significant business in India. As the company's point man on the project, Napoli worked with the consultants to narrow the list of 34 potential partners to eight candidates for review by the VRA.

As the team pursued the final choices, however, they found that there was no ideal partner. When it was determined that it was now legally and practically feasible to start up a 100% wholly owned company in India, the VRA asked Napoli and the head of Schindler's mergers and acquisitions department to explore that option.

Napoli contacted experts in India who helped him expand his understanding of the situation. Through discussions with market experts and studies by local consultants, Napoli spent nine months developing a detailed analysis of the market size,

legal environment, and competitive situation in the Indian elevator market. He integrated this into a business plan for Schindler's market entry and submitted it to the VRA. The plan was approved in October. Soon after, Napoli was offered the job of creating the Indian subsidiary. Napoli recalled his reaction:

> I realized that the future manager of the new company would be key to the success of the business plan I had been working on. Deep down, I knew I could do it and was conscious that my early involvement made me an ideal candidate. So when the offer came, I was not surprised. More surprising was the reaction of my headquarters' colleagues, who thought I was crazy to take such a high-risk career move that involved dragging my family to a developing country.

Bonnard explained the choice of Napoli:

> There are two possible profiles in a country like India. The first is a young guy [who] knows the company, people, and products; the second is someone who is 55 years old with grown kids looking for a new challenge. . . .
>
> Silvio knew lots of people. He was open to go new ways. We needed someone who could handle different cultures, who was young and flexible. We needed to trust the person we sent, and we trusted Mr. Napoli 100%. And we needed a generalist, not a pure specialist. We needed someone who had courage. Of course, we also needed to have someone who was willing to go. I spoke with other candidates with a similar profile to that of Mr. Napoli, but they didn't want to go. Finally, I believe that the people who make the business plan should have to realize it.

In November Napoli and his wife Fabienne, a French-German dual national, made their first trip to India. "We went on a 'look and see' visit, starting in Mumbai," Napoli recounted. "When we arrived in Delhi my wife looked around and said she would be more comfortable living here. After reaching an agreement on the relocation package back in Switzerland, I accepted the job."

Over the next several months, Napoli made three more trips to India to lay the groundwork for the move. In one key move, he engaged the executive search firm Egon Zehnder to identify candidates for his top management team. Although he had to await government approval to start the new company, when he moved to India, he wanted to have key managers in place.

Forming Schindler India

As vice president for South Asia, Napoli reported to the newly created India-Middle East region of Schindler's elevators and escalators division (see Exhibit 2). In March, Napoli officially relocated to India and began the task of building the company that would implement his business plan.

New Culture, New Challenges   On his first day in the Delhi office, Napoli got stuck in one of BBL's elevators. It proved to be an omen of things to come. He recalled:

> On our first morning in Delhi, six hours after the family had landed, my two-year-old daughter opened her forehead falling in the hotel room. The deep wound required hospitalization and stitching under total anesthesia. Two weeks later, Fabienne got infectious food poisoning, which required one-week hospitalization, threatening a miscarriage. The day she came back from hospital, my three-year-old son fell in the hotel bathroom and broke his front tooth. Rushing to an emergency dentist in a hotel car, I really wondered, for the only time in my life, whether I could stand this much longer.

Although Napoli and his family were in New Delhi, where he had opened a marketing and service office, he spent most of a typical week at the company's headquarters in Mumbai. "The first two months were really a hard-fought battle between family relocation and company start-up," he recalled. "Weeks were consumed shuttling between Delhi and Mumbai, hunting for office space, filing government registrations, and completing legal paperwork. On the family front, I had to get them started in a totally different system: housing, schools, doctors, grocery shopping . . . all things which are totally different in India."

In the process, Napoli found he had to adapt his management approach. "For example," he recalled,

"all types of characters started to approach me offering their services. They had heard that I was representing a Swiss firm about to invest in India. I soon learned to be careful in trusting anybody."

Recruiting the Team   Meanwhile, Egon Zehnder had identified several promising candidates for top positions in the new company. Mehar Karan ("M.K.") Singh, 42, was tapped for the role of managing director, a position that reported to Napoli but was viewed as a stepping stone to heading the subsidiary (for profiles of key Indian managers, see Exhibit 3). "At some point in your career you will report to someone younger than yourself," said Singh. "I decided that Schindler was an exciting opportunity to test this scenario."

Napoli explained the choice of Singh: "Having led construction projects for some of India's largest hotels, M.K. had firsthand experience in building an organization from scratch. But most of all, he had been on our customers' side. He would know how to make a difference in service." In addition, being 10 years older and having grown up in India, Singh brought valuable experience and a different perspective. He was also more sensitive to organizational power and relationships, as Napoli soon recognized:

> The first question M.K. asked me after joining the company was, "Who are your friends inside the company? Who doesn't like you?" I never thought about it this way. And I said to him: "Listen, you have to come out with a sense of that yourself. As far as I know, probably people are a little bit cautious of me because they know I used to work for the big bosses at headquarters."

To head field operations (sales, installation, and maintenance) Napoli hired T.A.K. Matthews, 35, who had worked for nine years at Otis India. Matthews recalled: "I had been approached before by elevator people, but after hearing a bit about Schindler's plans, I realized that you don't have a chance to get involved with a start-up every day." For Napoli, Matthews brought the business expertise he needed: "With M.K. and I as generalists,

Exhibit 2   Schindler Organization Chart, Elevator and Escalator Division

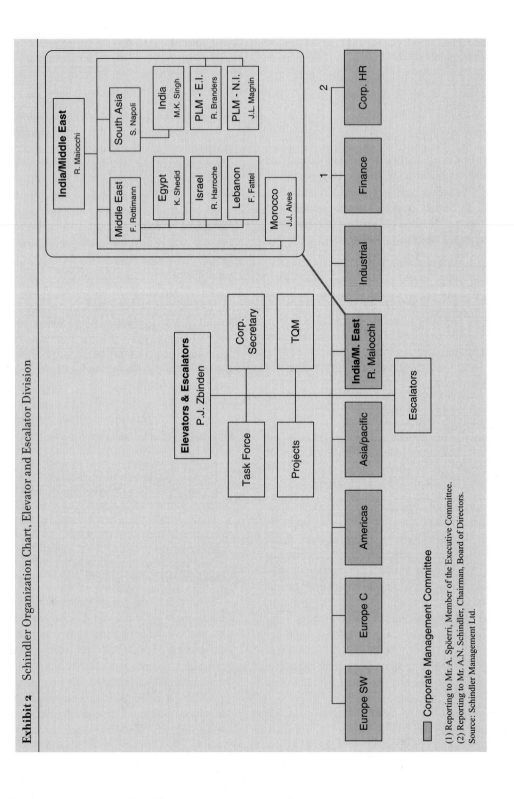

(1) Reporting to Mr. A. Spöerri, Member of the Executive Committee.
(2) Reporting to Mr. A.N. Schindler, Chairman, Board of Directors.
Source: Schindler Management Ltd.

Exhibit 3 Schindler India: Key Managers' Profiles

Name:	Silvio Napoli	Mehar Karan Singh	T.A.K. Matthews	Ronnie Dante	Jujudhan Jena
Position:	Vice President, Schindler South Asia	Managing Director	Vice President—Field Operations	General Manager—Engineering	Chief Financial Officer
Date of Birth:	August 23, 1965	April 12, 1955	March 12, 1964	November 3, 1959	March 3, 1967
Education:	*1992–1994:* MBA, Harvard University Graduate School of Business Administration, Boston, Massachusetts *1984–1989:* Graduate degree in Materials Science Engineering, Swiss Federal Institute of Technology (EPFL), Lausanne, Switzerland; Lausanne University rugby captain (1987) *1983–1984:* Ranked among top 20% foreign students admitted to EPFL, one-year compulsory selection program, Swiss Federal Institute of Technology (EPFL), Cours de Mathematiques Special, Lausanne, Switzerland	*1977:* B.E.—Mechanical Engineering; ranked top of his class in Indian Institute of Technology, Delhi, India *1979:* MBA, Indian Institute of Management, Ahmedabad, India (Awarded President of India's Gold Medal)	*1986:* B.Sc.—Civil Engineering, University of Dar-E-Salaam, Tanzania *1989:* MBA, Birla Institute of Technology, Ranchi, India	*1977:* HSC, D.G. Ruparel College, Mumbai, India	*1990:* Chartered Accountant, Institute of Chartered Accountancy, India

(*continued*)

Exhibit 3 *(concluded)*

Name:	Silvio Napoli	Mehar Karan Singh	T.A.K. Matthews	Ronnie Dante	Jujudhan Jena
Experience:	*Since 1998:* Vice President, South Asia, Schindler Management Ltd.	*Since 1998:* Managing Director, Schindler India Pvt. Ltd., Mumbai, India	*Since 1998:* Vice President—Field Operations, Schindler India Pvt. Ltd., Mumbai	*Since 1998:* General Manager—Engineering, Schindler India Pvt. Ltd., Mumbai	*Since 1998:* Chief Financial Officer, Schindler India Pvt. Ltd., Mumbai
	1994–1997: Vice President, Head of Corporate Planning, Schindler, Switzerland	*1979–1998:* Head of Projects and Development Group, Taj Group of Hotels, India (setting up hotels in India and abroad; joint ventures with state governments, local authorities, and international investors, including the Singapore Airlines, Gulf Cooperation Council Institutional investors. Responsible for financial restructuring of the international operations after the Gulf War, culminating with the successful 1995 GDR offering).	*1998:* Modernization Manager, Otis Elevator Company, Mumbai	*1995–1998:* National Field Engineering Manager, Otis Elevator, Mumbai	*1997–1998:* Financial Controller, Kellogg India Ltd., Mumbai
	1991–1992: Technical Market Development Specialist, Dow Europe, Rheinmuenster, Germany		*1989–1998:* Otis Elevator Company, New Delhi • Service & Service Sales Manager • Construction Manager • Assistant Construction Manager • Management Trainee	*1991–1995:* National Field Auditor, Otis Elevator, Mumbai	*1996–1997:* Group Manager, Procter & Gamble India Ltd., Mumbai
	1989–1991: Technical Service & Development Engineer, Dow Deutscheland, Rheinmuenster, Germany		*1986–1987:* Civil Engineer, Construction Companies, Tanzania	*1989–1991:* Supervisor, Otis Elevator	*1995–1996:* Treasury Manager, Procter & Gamble India Ltd.
	1989–1992: French Semi-Pro Rugby League (Strasbourg)			*1984–1989:* Commissioning of New Products, Otis Elevator, Singapore, Malaysia, and Mumbai	*1990–1995:* Financial Analyst, Procter & Gamble India Ltd.
				1982–1984: Commissioning Engineer, Otis Elevator Company, Gujarat	
				1977–1982: Apprentice, Otis Elevator Company, Maharashtra	

Source: Schindler India.

I absolutely needed someone with direct elevator experience to complement our management team. T.A.K. came across as a dynamic and ambitious hands-on manager waiting for the chance to exploit his potential."

Next, Napoli hired Ronnie Dante, 39, as his general manager for engineering. Dante had 24 years of experience at Otis. "Even with T.A.K., we missed a real hard-core elevator engineer capable of standing his ground in front of his European counterparts," said Napoli. "Such people are the authentic depositories of an unpublished science, and they are really very hard to find. Honestly, nobody in the group expected us to find and recruit someone like Ronnie. He is truly one of the best."

Hired to head the company's human resources department, Pankaj Sinha, 32, recalled his interview: "Mr. Napoli and Mr. Singh interviewed me together. There was a clarity in terms of what they were thinking that was very impressive." Napoli offered his assessment of Sinha: "Mr. Schindler had convinced me that the company really needed a front-line HR manager who was capable of developing a first-class organization. But I certainly did not want a traditional Indian ivory tower personnel director. Pankaj convinced us to hire him through his sheer determination to care about our employees."

Finally, he recruited Jujudhan Jena, 33, as his chief financial officer. (See Exhibit 4 for an organization chart.) Napoli explained his approach to hiring: "You try to see whether the character of the person is compatible with yours, whether you have a common set of values, which in our case range from high ethical standards, integrity, assiduousness to work, and drive. Mostly we were looking for people with the right attitude and energy, not just for elevator people."

Developing the Relationships As soon as the senior managers were on board, Napoli began working to develop them into an effective team. He recalled the early meetings with his new hires:

Because some of them were still finishing up their previous jobs, the first Schindler India staff meetings were held at night, in the Delhi Hotel lounge. I'll never forget working together on our first elevator project offer, late after holding a series of interviews for the first employees who would report to the top team. But most of those "undercover" sessions were dedicated to educating the new team about their new company and building consensus around our business plan. . . . The team was really forged through days of late work, fueled by the common motivation to see our project succeed.

In the team-forming process, the different management styles and personal characteristics of Schindler India's new leaders became clear. Even before he was assigned to India, Napoli was recognized as a "strong-headed and single-minded manager," as one manager at Swiss headquarters described him. "There couldn't have been a better environment to send Silvio than India," said another Swiss colleague. "He wants everything done yesterday. And in India, things don't get done yesterday."

Napoli acknowledged the personal challenge. "To survive in India you have to be half monk and half warrior," he said. "I was certainly more inclined to the warrior side, and when I left Switzerland, Mr. Bonnard told me, 'You will have to work on your monk part.'"

Napoli's Indian staff and colleagues described him as "driving very hard," "impulsive," "impatient," and at times "overcommunicative." "Mr. Napoli gets angry when deadlines are not met," added a member of his New Delhi staff. "He's a pretty hard taskmaster." The HR director, Sinha, was more circumspect: "Silvio has a lot of energy. When he focuses on an issue he manages to get everybody else's focus in that direction."

Descriptions of Napoli contrasted sharply with those of Singh, whom one manager saw as "friendly and easygoing." Another described him as "much more patient, but he can also be tough." Jena, the finance director, reflected on his first encounter with the two company leaders: "During the interview Silvio came across banging on the table, but I don't think that concerned me. Still, I remember wondering during the interview how two guys

Exhibit 4   Schindler India Organization Chart

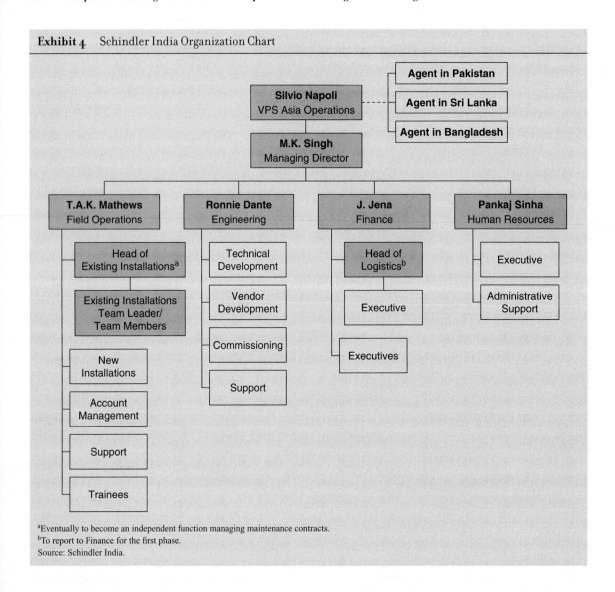

[a]Eventually to become an independent function managing maintenance contracts.
[b]To report to Finance for the first phase.
Source: Schindler India.

as different as M.K. and Silvio would fit together in a start-up." Matthews, the field operations manager, added another perspective:

> It's true that if you look at Silvio, M.K., and myself we are very different. At first we had sessions where the discussion would get pulled in every direction, but I think at the end of the day, it did bring about a balance. I would put it this way. Silvio came to India from Switzerland. But things here are very different:

You can't set your watch by the Indian trains. M.K. came from the hotel industry where even if you say "no," it's always made to sound like "yes."

"Silvio was the driver and clearly was the boss," said an Indian executive. "M.K. was great in helping Silvio understand the Indian environment. Having worked in the hotel industry he had a very good network. He had been on the customer side. But he had to learn the elevator business."

Exhibit 5   Indian Elevator Market, Structure, and Product Segmentation

Indian Market Structure	Segment	Stops	Speeds MPS	Schindler Products
	Manual	2–8	0.5–0.7	NIL
	Low rise	2–15	0.6–1.5	S001
	Mid rise	16–25	1.5	S300P
	High rise	>25	>1.5	S300P

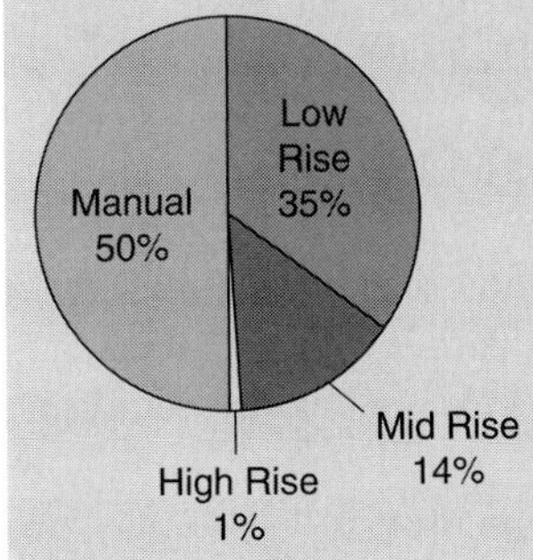

Low Rise 35%
Manual 50%
Mid Rise 14%
High Rise 1%

Source: Schindler India.

Out of this interaction emerged a company culture that employees described as "informal," "open," "responsive," and "proactive." It was also a lean, efficient organization. For example, furniture and office space were rented, and there were only two secretaries in the company—one for the Delhi office and one for Mumbai. "Everyone must do their own administrative work or they won't survive," said Singh.

The India Business Plan

As soon as his team was in place, Napoli worked to gain their commitment to his business plan. At its core were two basic elements: the need to sell a focused line of standard products, and the ability to outsource key manufacturing and logistics functions. This plan had been built on an analysis of the Indian market and competitive environment that Napoli also communicated to his team (see Exhibits 5 and 6 for data from the plan).

The Indian Elevator Market in 1998   Economic liberalization in India in the early 1990s had revived the construction industry, and along with it, the fortunes of the elevator industry. Roughly 50% of demand was for low-tech manual elevators, typically fitted with unsafe manual doors (see

Exhibit 5). A ban on collapsible gate elevators had been approved by the Indian Standards Institute, and, at the urging of the Indian government, individual states were making the ban legally enforceable. The low end of the market was characterized by intense competition among local companies. The ban, when fully implemented, was expected to make this market segment more interesting to major international players.

The middle segment of the market was promising due to India's rapid urbanization. The resulting shortage of space in Mumbai and fast-growing cities such as Bangalore, Pune, and Madras was leading to the development of low- and mid-rise buildings. Concurrently, traditional builders were becoming more sophisticated and professionalized, leading to an emphasis on better services and facilities and on higher quality, safer, and more technologically advanced elevators.

At the top end of the market, demand was growing for top-quality, high-rise office premises and housing facilities, particularly from multinational companies. Tourism was also expanding, greatly aiding the domestic hotel industry, a major buyer of top-line elevators. Although the top-end segment was small, the average value per elevator was five to six times that in the low end.

At the end of 1997, the installed base of elevators in India was 40,000, with an estimated 5,600 units sold during the year. Although this installed base was small compared with those of China (140,000 units) and Japan (400,000 units), India's growth potential was significant. The rapidly expanding residential segment accounted for 70% of the Indian market, followed by the commercial segment (office buildings and shopping centers) with a 20% share. The balance was accounted for by hotels (4%) and others (6%). Total revenues for the industry were US$125 million, including service income. For the first half of the decade, the market grew at a compound annual rate of 17% in units and 27% by value, but in 1996, a slump in the real estate market slowed unit growth to 10%. The unit growth forecast for 1998 was 5% but was expected to rise to 8%–12% in subsequent years. Together, Mumbai and New Delhi represented 60% of the total Indian elevator market.

In India, most sales were of single-speed elevators (65%), followed by two-speed (20%), variable frequency (13%), and hydraulic (2%). Sales of single-speed elevators dominated the residential market, while variable frequency was most commonly used in higher-end commercial applications. Although the Indian market was biased toward the simplest products, it was expected to shift gradually toward two-speed or higher technology in the future.

Competition   Napoli's business plan also documented that four major players accounted for more than three-quarters of the Indian market value: Otis (50%), BBL (8.6%), Finland's Kone (8.8%), and ECE (8.4%). Mitsubishi had recently begun importing premium elevators for hotels and commercial developments, and Hyundai Elevators had entered into a joint venture to manufacture high-end elevators in India. At this stage, however, they accounted for only 1% of sales. With the exception of Mitsubishi, all multinational players relied on local manufacturing for the majority of their components. The remaining 23% of the market—mostly the price-sensitive low end—was controlled by 25 regional players characterized by a lack of technical expertise and limited access to funds.

Otis India had an installed base of 26,000 elevators, 16,000 of which were under maintenance contracts. It manufactured its own components, spare parts, and fixtures at an aging plant in Mumbai and a new state-of-the art manufacturing plant near Bangalore. The company staffed 70 service centers, including a national service center in Mumbai, and held an estimated 85% of the high-end hotels and commercial segment. ("You couldn't name any building over 15 floors that did not have an Otis elevator," said ex-Otis employee Matthews. "Otis, Otis, Otis. Any special equipment, it goes Otis. Any fast elevator goes Otis.") Otis was reportedly one of the most profitable industrial companies in India, and its 3,500 employees had an average tenure of 20 years.

The Indian market was highly price sensitive, and there was agreement among industry analysts that elevators were becoming commodity products and that price pressures would increase. However, surveys indicated that service was also key to the builder's buying decision, as were the supplier's financial terms (Exhibit 6).

The elevator life cycle had seven distinct phases: engineering, production, installation, service, repair, modernization, and replacement. Over the 30-year life cycle of an elevator, the first three stages accounted for about one-third of the labor content but only 20% of the profits. In contrast, the latter four accounted for two-thirds of labor content but 80% of profits. As a result, annual maintenance contracts covering routine maintenance and breakdown service were vital. (High-margin spare parts were billed separately.) Service response time varied across segments. Most five-star hotels with multiple installations had a technician on call or on-site; for important commercial buildings and hospitals, the response time was usually within two hours, but many residential and some commercial customers reported an average response time of between six and eight hours.

The Standard Product Strategy　Napoli's analysis of the Indian environment coupled with his work on the Swatch Project led him to conclude that the most effective way for Schindler to enter this market would be to focus on a narrow product line of simple, standardized elevators. Although this was a radically different approach from that of his key competitors, he felt that Schindler could not compete just by matching what others did. It had to find its own unique source of advantage.

Exhibit 6　Market Research on Indian is Elevator Market, 1996

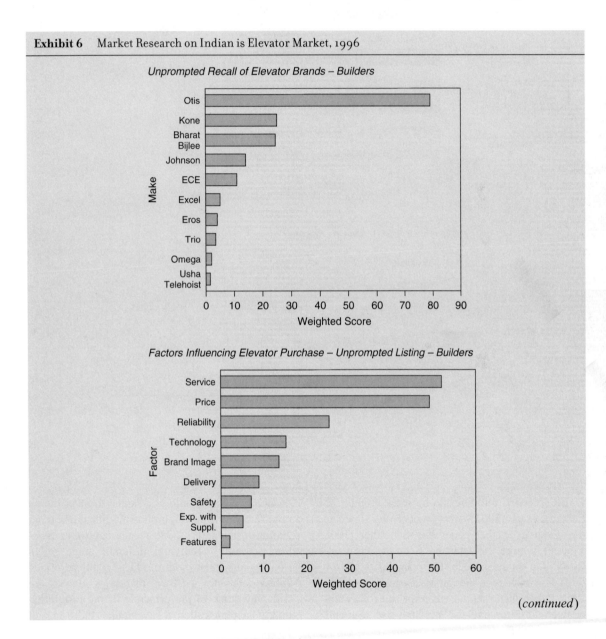

(*continued*)

Exhibit 6   *(concluded)*

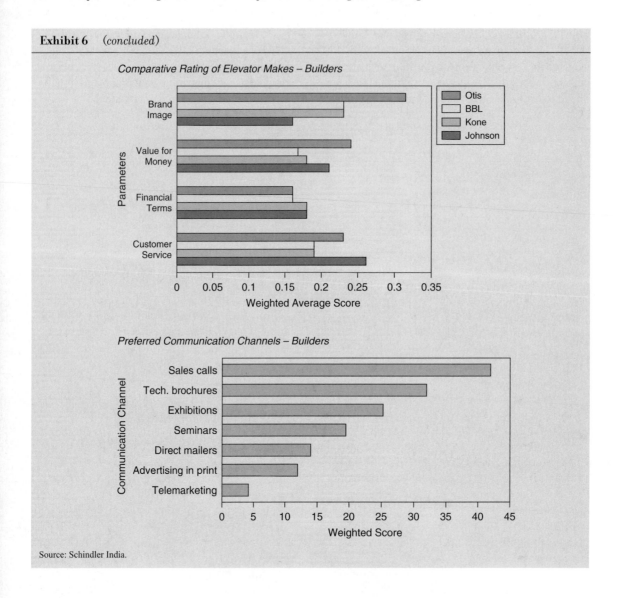

Comparative Rating of Elevator Makes – Builders

Preferred Communication Channels – Builders

Source: Schindler India.

He proposed building the business around the Schindler 001 (S001)—the product developed in the Swatch Project—and the Schindler 300P (S300P), a more sophisticated model being manufactured in southeast Asia. The plan was to use the S001 to win share in the low-rise segment as a primary target, then pick up whatever sales the company could in the mid-rise and high-rise segments with the S300P.

Both products could be adapted to meet Indian requirements with only minor modifications (e.g., adding a ventilator, a fire rescue controller function, a stop button, and different guide rails). Equally important, both products could be priced appropriately for the local market as long as the company stuck to the principle of no customization. The plan called for Schindler India to sell 50 units in the first year and to win a 20% share of the target segments in five years. It aimed to break even after four years and eventually to generate double-digit margins.

After communicating this strategy to his management team, Napoli was pleased when they came back with an innovative approach to selling the standard line. If the product was standardized, they argued, the sales and service should be differentiated. Singh's experience with hotel construction led him to conclude that projects were more effectively managed when one individual was responsible for designing, planning, contracting, and implementing. Yet, as Matthews knew, the traditional sales structure in the elevator industry had different specialists dedicated to sales, technical, and installation, each of whom handed the project off to the next person. Together, these managers proposed to Napoli that Schindler organize around an account-management concept designed to give the customer a single "hassle-free" point of contact.

The Outsourcing Strategy   India's high import duties had forced most foreign elevator companies to manufacture locally. But again, Napoli chose a different approach. To keep overheads low, his business plan proposed a radical sourcing concept: Schindler India would have no in-house manufacturing, no centralized assembly, no logistics infrastructure. Instead, the production of most components for the dominant S001 model would be outsourced to approved local suppliers. (The S300P would be wholly imported from southeast Asia.) Schindler would manufacture only safety-related components (the safety gear and speed governor, together representing 10% of the value), which would be imported from Europe. In addition, the entire logistics function would be outsourced to an internationally reputed logistics service provider. Some basic installation work—part of the on-site assembly of the drive, controller, car, doors, rails, and counterweight—would also be outsourced. However, maintenance contracts resulting from new sales would stay with Schindler.

Inspired by the local automotive industry—Mercedes outsourced most components of its

Indian vehicles—Napoli believed he could set up a local manufacturing network that would preserve Schindler's quality reputation. To ensure this, localization of each component would follow the same "product-creation process" criteria used by Schindler worldwide. Furthermore, before the first pre-series batch could be released, it would face an additional hurdle of testing and approval by experts from Schindler's European factories and competence centers.

From Analysis to Action: Implementing the Plan

By June, Napoli's management team members had settled into their roles, and the newly hired sales force was in the field. Almost immediately, however, the young expatriate leader began to experience questions, challenges, and impediments to his carefully prepared business plan.

Business Challenges   From the outset, several of Napoli's managers had questioned him on the feasibility of his plan. In particular, those from the elevator industry wondered how the company would survive selling only standard elevators. They also worried about the outsourcing strategy, since no other company in the industry worked this way. "Some of the doubts were expressed as questions," said Napoli. "Many more were unspoken, and my guess is they thought, 'We'll soon convince this crazy guy from Europe that we have to do something a bit less unusual.'"

In August, Napoli traveled to Italy to be with his wife when she gave birth to their third child. On one of his daily telephone calls to key managers in India, he discovered that the company had accepted an order for an expensive glass pod elevator that was to be imported from Europe. "I was at first just surprised, then pretty angry, since it clearly was a violation of the strategy we had all agreed on," said Napoli. "The project was committed, and it was too late to stop it. But I had a long talk with M.K. and followed it up with an e-mail reminding him and the others of our strategy."

After his return to India, Napoli was delighted when he heard that the company had won another order for four S001 elevators for a government building in Mumbai. It was only in later conversations with a field salesperson that he discovered that there was a possibility of a significant modification to the standard specification—once again involving a glass wall. Although the managers insisted that this was really a minor modification to an otherwise standard product, Napoli believed that installing it would be much more difficult than they expected.

The next challenge to his plan came when the first order for elevators was placed to Schindler's plants in Europe. Napoli was shocked when he saw the order confirmation listing transfer prices on the basic S001 30% above the costs he had used to prepare his plans. "When I called to complain, they told me that my calculations had been correct six months ago, but costs had increased, a new transfer costing system had been introduced subsequently," recalled Napoli.

The impact of the transfer price increase was made worse by the new budget the Indian government had passed during the summer. It included increased import duties on specific "noncore goods" including elevators, whose rates increased from 22% to 56%. Napoli recalled the impact:

> This was devastating to our planned break-even objectives. The first thing I did was to accelerate our plans to outsource the S001 as soon as possible. We immediately started working with the European plants to get design details, production specifications, and so on. Unfortunately, the plants were not quick to respond, and we were becoming frustrated at our inability to get their assistance in setting up alternative local sources.

Reflections of a Middle Manager   As darkness enveloped the neighborhood surrounding his townhouse, Napoli sat in his living room reflecting on his job. Outside, the night was filled with the sounds of barking dogs and the piercing whistles of the estate's security patrol. "Each family here has its own security guard," he explained. "But because guards fall asleep at their posts, our neighborhood association hired a man who patrols the neighborhood blowing his whistle at each guard post and waiting for a whistle in response. But now the whistling has gotten so bad that some families have begun paying this man not to whistle in front of their houses. Incredible, isn't it?"

Thinking back on his nine months in his new job, Napoli described the multiple demands. On one hand, he had to resolve the challenges he faced in India. On the other, he had to maintain contact with the European organization to ensure he received the support he needed. And on top of both these demands was an additional expectation that the company's top management had of this venture. Napoli explained:

> When we were discussing the business plan with Mr. Schindler, he said, "India will be our Formula One racing track." In the auto industry, 90% of all innovations are developed for and tested on Formula One cars and then reproduced on a much larger scale and adapted for the mass market. We are testing things in India—in isolation and on a fast track—that probably could not be done anywhere else in the company. The expectation is that what we prove can be adapted to the rest of the group.

While the viability of the Formula One concept was still unclear, Alfred Schindler commented on Napoli's experience:

> This job requires high energy and courage. It's a battlefield experience. This is the old economy, where you have to get involved in the nitty-gritty. We don't pay the big bucks or give stock options. We offer the pain, surprises, and challenges of implementation. The emotions start when you have to build what you have written. Mr. Napoli is feeling what it means to be in a hostile environment where nothing works as it should.

Napoli reflected, "You know the expression, 'It's lonely at the top?' Well, I'm not at the top, but I feel lonely in the middle. . . . I have to somehow swim my way through this ocean. Meanwhile, we have yet to install a single elevator and have no maintenance portfolio." At this point, Napoli's reflections were interrupted by the question of visiting vice chairman Luc Bonnard, "So, how are things going so far, Mr. Napoli?"

Case 7-3   The GE Energy Management Initiative (A)

In August 1992, Raj Bhatt, Business Development Manager for GE Canada, met with executives from GE Supply, a US-based distribution arm of GE. The purpose of the meeting was to discuss new business opportunities in Energy Efficiency, an industry that focused on the reduction of energy usage through the installation of energy-efficient technologies. Bhatt had recently gained pre-qualification for GE Canada to bid in a $1 billion program to install energy-efficient technologies in all Federal Government buildings. He was confident that GE's expertise in lighting, motors, appliances and financing was sufficient to win at least some of the contracts. Furthermore, he saw the program as a stepping stone to building a new GE business to service the Energy Efficiency needs of a range of clients.

The GE Supply executives informed Bhatt that they had already established a position in the US Energy Efficiency industry, through a joint venture with a new Energy Service Company (ESCo), and had retained the services of a full-time consultant to develop the business. They were interested in the Federal Buildings program that Bhatt had been working on, but felt that it would be more effi-

ciently run through a division of GE Supply, rather than as a locally managed Canadian venture. The meeting posed a dilemma for Bhatt. He was encouraged by the level of interest that already existed for Energy Efficiency within GE, but at the same time held certain misgivings about folding the Federal Buildings program into GE Supply's nascent business. Specifically, he was concerned that a lot of interesting Energy Efficiency opportunities existed in Canada which a US-focused business would not be in a position to exploit. Bhatt left the meeting uncertain how to proceed.

General Electric (GE)

GE, with $60 billion in revenues in 1991, was among the top ten industrial corporations in the world. From the early days of Thomas Edison, it had grown to be a diversified 54-business corporation by the early eighties. With 400,000 employees and a very strong corporate planning division, it exemplified the traditional strategic planning-oriented corporation of the 1970s.

In 1980, Jack Welch, the incoming CEO, made a series of sweeping changes. The corporate planning department was eliminated, layers of management were eliminated and the concepts of empowerment and customer focus became the new drivers behind GE's activities. Of the 54 businesses that Welch inherited, some were sold and others were amalgamated, leaving just 13. Welch's stated position was that the major criterion for holding on to a business was that it was number one or number two worldwide in its chosen industry.

The corporate structure under Welch was simplified and decentralised. Each division was autonomous, and was further subdivided into a number of operating companies. The head office for each division was in the US, but on average, 25% of GE's revenues came from its non-US operations. International operations, including Canada, were structured under the Vice Chairman, International

▌ Joseph N. Fry and Julian Birkinshaw prepared this case solely to provide material for class discussion. The authors do not intend to illustrate either effective or ineffective handling of a managerial situation. The authors may have disguised certain names and other identifying information to protect confidentiality.

▌ *Ivey Management Services prohibits any form of reproduction, storage or transmittal without its written permission. This material is not covered under authorization from CanCopy or any reproduction rights organization. To order copies or request permission to reproduce materials, contact Ivey Publishing, Ivey Management Services, c/o Richard Ivey School of Business, The University of Western Ontario, London, Ontario, Canada, N6A 3K7; phone (519) 661-3208; fax (519) 661-3882; e-mail cases@ivey.uwo.ca.*

▌ One-time permission to reproduce granted by Ivey Management Services on February 6, 2003.

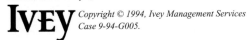

IVEY   *Copyright © 1994, Ivey Management Services Case 9-94-G005.*

Richard Ivey School of Business
The University of Western Ontario

Operations, but operating authority was held by the relevant division of GE. Thus, the lighting plant in Oakville, Ontario, reported to GE Lighting in Cleveland, Ohio, with only a secondary line of reporting through GE Canada.

Welch was committed to creating a more open and candid management style at GE. A central thrust of this commitment was the 'Work-Out' program, which he described as follows:

> The ultimate objective of Work-Out is clear. We want 300,000 people with different family aspirations, different financial goals, to share directly in this company's vision, the decision-making process and the rewards. We want to build a more stimulating environment, a more creative environment, a freer work atmosphere, with incentives tied directly to what people do. (*Harvard Business Review,* Sept 1989: 112–120)

Through a series of workshops and facilitated sessions, Work-Out's objective was to challenge the accepted practice at every level in every business. Work-Out sessions had already realized large cost savings by identifying non-essential practices that had gone undetected for years, but equally important, they had created a new level of creativity and enthusiasm among employees.

GE Canada   GE Canada was the longest-established international subsidiary of GE, with operations in 12 of the company's 13 businesses. In the 1970s, GE Canada operated as a "miniature replica" of its parent company: all functions were represented in Canada, and typically a full line of products was made, primarily for the Canadian market but with some exporting possibilities. The Canadian CEO was fully responsible for the profits of the Canadian operating divisions, and separate financial statements were prepared (GE held a 92% stake in GE Canada).

In the eighties, Jack Welch embarked on a major structural change to GE's North American business. Consistent with the increasingly global business environment that was taking shape, Welch recognized that maintaining separate country organizations could not be justified. Instead, an integrated organizational model emerged that became known as "direct-connect."[1] Essentially, this meant creating 13 strategic business units, and organizing them according to the global demands of the business rather than national interests. Typically, the general manager's role was eliminated in Canada, so that business leaders or functional managers reported directly to their business headquarters in the U.S., rather than through the Canadian organization. For example, the marketing manager for GE Lighting's Canadian operations reported directly to the GE Lighting marketing manager in Cleveland, Ohio. Profit responsibility was held by the global business unit. This arrangement ensured that business activities were effectively co-ordinated on a global basis. It also furthered Welch's objective of removing layers of management and empowering employees.

Matthew Meyer, CEO of GE Canada, had a vastly different role from his predecessors. With all operations reporting straight to their US divisional bosses, Meyer was directly responsible only for the activities of a very small number of employees. He had vice presidents in finance, environmental affairs, legal, human resources and government affairs. These managers were responsible for all the uniquely Canadian issues that cropped up, such as new legislation, tax accounting, government grants and so on. In addition, there was a small business development group, consisting of three managers. Traditionally, this group had been involved in feasibility studies and new market development for the business units in Canada. Following the shift to a 'direct-connect' structure, the role had become primarily one of looking for opportunities to leverage the strengths of Canadian activities on a global basis. They were also concerned with identifying new business opportunities in Canada. Bhatt, one of the business development managers, explained:

> Canada is a relatively small marketplace. Consequently, most U.S.-based business leaders have a limited awareness of the opportunities here because they have either a U.S. or a global focus. The role of business development is to attempt to identify investment

---

[1]The integration process was smoothed by the buyout of minority shareholders in GE Canada in 1989. The 1989 Free Trade agreement further streamlined the change.

or market opportunities here that they might find valuable.

There was some discussion among business development managers over the extent to which they should actively "sell" business opportunities to the GE businesses. Some felt that a proactive strategy of promoting Canadian opportunities was appropriate; others preferred to investigate only those cases where business development's involvement had been solicited. The recent decision to promote the VP, Business Development, but not replace him, added further to the uncertainty over the group's role.

Raj Bhatt   Bhatt was only 29. He had worked at GE for just one year, following a successful period at Northern Telecom and an MBA at the University of Western Ontario.

> Business development is quite a challenging experience. There are lots of good opportunities in Canada, but it is sometimes difficult to achieve the level of interest and buy-in necessary to attract the appropriate attention. The Oakville lighting plant, a global manufacturing mandate, is a planned $144 million investment and is certainly our biggest success so far, but there have been a lot of ideas that failed to materialize.

The business development manager typically held that post for only two years, after which he or she was expected to take a line position in one of the businesses. Bhatt had been given a number of attractive options, but had turned them down because he was afraid that his involvement was critical to a number of projects. Specifically, he was concerned that the Energy Efficiency business opportunity he had championed up to now would die because no one else had the knowledge of, or the enthusiasm for, that particular opportunity.

Energy Efficiency

Energy Efficiency covered the multitude of ways that energy usage could be optimised, including conservation, use of efficient appliances and off-peak usage. Energy Efficiency was originally conceived in the early 1970s as a response to rising oil prices. It recently saw a resurgence due to the environmental movement and the increasing need for cost competitiveness in the late eighties. Although strongly motivated by public opinion and government pressure, Energy Efficiency initiatives were usually sponsored by the energy supply utilities. They recognized that they could more effectively keep their investment down by reducing demand than by building expensive new power stations. There were also obvious benefits to consumers (in reduced costs) and to the environment.

The growth in utility-sponsored programs for Energy Efficiency was responsible for the formation of many Energy Service Companies (ESCos). These companies aimed to meet the demands and needs of their customers by utilizing these programs. Under the most common arrangement (called a performance contract), the ESCo would install energy-efficient technologies at no upfront cost to the client. The costs would be recouped from the savings realized. Such an arrangement could be very lucrative, but the ESCo bore all the risk in the event that the promised savings never materialized.

The ESCo Industry in Canada   The Canadian ESCo industry was among the most advanced in the world. Both Federal and Provincial governments had active energy-management programs to promote 'green' issues, and had targeted Energy Efficiency as a critical industry. Ontario Hydro and Quebec Hydro had budgets for Energy Efficiency of $800 million and $300 million, respectively, in comparison to the CDN$1.5 billion budget for all U.S. utilities combined.

As a result of the utilities' involvement, the Canadian ESCo industry was growing very rapidly; 1989 revenues of $20 million had grown to $100 million by 1992, and one estimate put the total market potential in the billions of dollars. Three major segments could be identified, each accounting for approximately one third of the total volume. They were *Commercial,* which consisted primarily of office buildings, hospitals and other public buildings; *Industrial,* which consisted of factories and production plants; and *Residential,* which consisted of single-family dwellings. So far the commercial sector had been the most rewarding to ESCos, largely due to the similarities between (for example) one hospital and another. Industrial also had potential, but required knowledge of the specific process technology used in each case.

Over the past decade, the ESCo industry in Canada had experienced mixed fortunes, as companies struggled to understand the dynamics of the market. Lack of technical and risk management experience, flawed contracts, lack of financial strength and energy price collapses had all led to very low levels of profitability among major players. The recent upsurge of interest in Energy Efficiency, however, had pushed the industry onto a more steady footing. Furthermore, a shake-out had occurred, leaving between 5 and 10 serious competitors in Canada.

ESCo Strategies   ESCos saw themselves as undertaking three useful functions with commercial and industrial customers. First, they could undertake energy audits of client sites and advise what forms of energy management were most appropriate. Second, they could engineer and provide access to a wide range of energy-efficient technologies that would normally be hard to get hold of. Third, they could install new energy-efficient equipment, under a performance contract or similar. In the Canadian industry, there were several hundred consulting engineers that participated in energy audits, but only seven "full-service" ESCos that undertook all three functions.

Of the three functions, programs such as performance contracting offered the greatest potential return to ESCos, but also the highest degree of risk. Following an installation, it took between five and ten years before the financial benefits were realized. ESCos were paid at the time of installation by their financing partners, who recovered their costs over the lifetime of the project, but in the event that the project was badly estimated, the shortfall in revenue would have to be made up by the ESCo. Access to capital at a reasonable cost was thus critical. Some ESCos had parent companies with deep pockets. The audit and supply functions, while less lucrative, were important elements of the ESCo's business because they established legitimacy in the

eyes of the customer. Many commercial clients were extremely sceptical of the estimated energy savings provided by ESCos, but if they agreed to an energy audit, there was a greater likelihood they could be sold on the merits of an installation. The credibility of the guarantee provided by the ESCo was thus of great importance.

The GE Energy Management Initiative

The Initial Opportunity   As GE Business Development Manager, Raj Bhatt received a communication from the Federal Government inviting ESCos to seek to be prequalified for the implementation of performance contracts in 50,000 federal buildings in Canada. The program had a potential total value of $1 billion, which was to be split into a number of smaller contracts. Bhatt was struck by the potential fit between GE's areas of expertise and the requirements of the program. ESCos had to be able to provide energy-efficient lighting, motors and controls and provide financing for the project; GE was a leading supplier of many of the required products and had a large financing division. Unlike rival firms that would have to form consortia between electrical and financing companies, GE could do many things in-house.

Bhatt submitted a proposal for the Federal Buildings program and, along with a number of other consortia, achieved "prequalification," meaning the right to bid on subsequent contracts that fell under the Federal Buildings umbrella. This success underlined the magnitude of the opportunity that GE was facing in the ESCo industry. Rather than limiting GE's involvement to the one-off Federal Buildings program, Bhatt thought there was potential for an ongoing GE business to meet the expected surge in demand for energy management services. He began to think through the best way of proceeding.

The GE Canada Executive Meeting   Bhatt's first move was to meet with the GE Canada executive group and get their reaction to his idea for an Energy Management Business. Attending were Matthew Meyer, Chairman & CEO, Mike Kozinsky, VP Finance, and Scott Larwood, VP Government

Relations. Larwood had already been heavily in-volved in the Federal Buildings program and was in favour of Bhatt's proposal.

Bhatt. GE Canada is very well-positioned to start an Energy Management business. We have a broader range of relevant products and services than any other ESCo, and the Ontario and Quebec Hydro pro-grams are among the most advanced in the world.

Kozinsky (Finance). But this is a systems busi-ness. We have never been very good at systems implementation.

Bhatt. I realize that we may have to find partners. We are working with a small ESCo on the Federal Buildings project which will do all the installation work. We can identify suitable future partners as things progress.

Kozinsky (Finance). But what is our experience in being a prime contractor? This seems to be very different from any business we have been involved with before.

Larwood (Government Relations). That's not quite true. The Apparatus Technical Service (ATS) business in Power Systems manages service con-tracts, and there is a lot of project experience in the States.

Meyer (CEO). But there seems to be a consider-able risk here. What happens if we pull down a load of asbestos when we're changing a lighting system? GE is an obvious target for legal action.

Kozinsky (Finance). And you stated earlier that there is some downside financial risk if the perfor-mance contract does not yield the expected savings.

Bhatt. True, but the estimates are conservative. The overall financial projections are very promising, and involve very little up-front cost. Apart from the salaries of three or four employees, most costs are on a contract-by-contract basis.

Meyer (CEO). Have you given any thought as to how this business would fit into the GE structure?

Bhatt. One of the strengths of GE Canada is that it already taps into all the different businesses. I would like to see the Energy Management business based in Canada, and drawing from the other GE businesses as required.

Bhatt received a lot of questioning and cautioning on various aspects of the proposal, but there was con-sensus at the end that the project was worth pursuing. Meyer recommended that Bhatt investigate the level of interest in the US businesses and at the corporate level before any formal proposal was put together.

The GE Supply Opportunity   In discussion with US colleagues, Bhatt discovered that three US divi-sions were attempting to establish their own ESCo-like initiatives. Two of them were at about the same stage of development as Bhatt. The third, GE Supply, was more advanced. They had been working with an ESCo for a number of months, and had retained a well-connected consultant to advise them. Up to now, the ESCo had assumed all the risk, with GE pro-viding their name, their products and some servicing expertise, but the division was planning to create a joint venture with the ESCo in the near future.

On hearing about the GE Supply initiative, Bhatt went to Connecticut to visit the GE Supply execu-tives to discuss their respective plans. Present at the meeting were Bhatt, Doug Taylor, CEO of GE Sup-ply, and Fred Allen, manager of the Energy Man-agement business.

Taylor (CEO). Last week we signed a formal al-liance agreement with Wetherwell Inc. to run for 18 months. We are now actively looking for contracts.

Allen (Energy Management). But the US market requires some education. How is the market in Canada?

Bhatt. There is a very promising opportunity that we are working on right now. Basically, the Federal

Government is looking for bidders on a $1 billion program, and we have already gained pre-qualification.

Allen (Energy Management). That beats anything we've got down here. I think there could be some real opportunities for us to work together. We have gained quite a lot of experience over the past 12 months, and combined with your market, we could have a winning combination.

Bhatt. I am certainly interested in exploring opportunities. How do you see a Canadian Energy Management business fitting with your business?

Taylor (CEO). We could manage the Canadian business out of our office here.

Bhatt. That causes me some concern. The business relies on close coordination with utilities and gov-

ernment bodies, and a strong local presence would definitely be necessary. I must admit, we considered that management of at least part of the business should be in Canada. The opportunities in Canada are unmatched.

Taylor (CEO). Well, there is some strength to your argument, but I don't see why this business should not fit the normal model.

Bhatt had some misgivings when the meeting came to a close. The business depended on close ties with government bodies, provincial utilities and local contractors to be really successful, and he felt that these would be lost if there was not a strong Canadian presence. Under the "direct-connect" system, he felt that would be more difficult to achieve.

Case 7-4   Genzyme's Gaucher Initiative: Global Risk and Responsibility

In June 1998, Tomye Tierney initiated an effort that led to the creation of Genzyme Corporation's Gaucher Initiative to provide the company's life-saving drug Cerezyme® enzyme[1] to sufferers of Gaucher disease worldwide, regardless of their ability to pay. Barely three years later, she faced a major decision that would determine the future of the bold experiment. Established as a partnership with the respected humanitarian organization Project HOPE, the Gaucher Initiative had been very

effective in locating and treating Gaucher patients in many less developed countries and had built a particularly strong program in Egypt. However, Genzyme's sales organization was becoming increasingly concerned that the fast-growing free distribution program in Egypt represented a barrier to their commercial objectives.

Although the company had grown rapidly in recent years, the high-risk biotech business required that it manage its resources carefully. (Exhibits 1 and 2 summarize Genzyme's financial history.) From the outset, therefore, Genzyme CEO Henri Termeer had told Tierney that the company's commitment to universal provision could not undermine its commercial viability. Specifically, he emphasized that the Gaucher Initiative was not to be viewed as a permanent solution to providing care in any country. Recognizing this, Tierney wondered if

[1]Genzyme®, Cerezyme®, and Ceredase® are registered trademarks of Genzyme Corporation. All rights reserved.

Professor Christopher A. Bartlett and Research Associate Andrew N. McLean prepared this case. HBS cases are developed solely as the basis for class discussion. Cases are not intended to serve as endorsements, sources of primary data, or illustrations of effective or ineffective management. Certain names and data have been disguised.

Copyright © 2002 President and Fellows of Harvard College. Harvard Business School case 303-048.

Exhibit 1 Genzyme Corp. Selected Consolidated Balance Sheets ($000s)

Year Ending December 31	2000	1999	1998	1997	1996	1991	1986	1981[a]
Assets								
Current assets								
Cash and equivalents	$ 236,213	$ 130,156	$ 118,612	$ 102,406	$ 93,132	$ 29,031	$ 2,309	$ 828
Short-term investments	104,586	255,846	175,453	51,259	56,608	78,147	19,496	—
Accounts receivable	205,094	166,803	163,042	118,277	116,833	31,838	2,728	—
Inventories	170,341	117,269	109,833	139,681	125,265	16,329	4,243	—
Prepaid expenses & other	37,681	18,918	31,467	17,361	100,287	3,688	299	—
Deferred tax assets—current	46,836	41,195	41,195	27,601	17,493	—	—	—
Non-current assets								
Net property, plant & equipment	504,412	383,181	382,619	385,348	393,839	32,057	4,020	—
Long-term investments	298,841	266,988	281,664	92,676	38,215	172,529	—	—
Notes receivable—related party	10,350	—	—	2,019	—	4,000	—	—
Net intangibles	1,539,782	253,153	279,516	271,275	247,745	13,362	—	—
Deferred tax assets—non-current		18,631	24,277	29,479	42,221	4,186	—	—
Investments in equity securities	121,251	97,859	51,977	30,047	—	—	—	—
Other non-current assets	42,713	37,283	30,669	28,024	38,870	5,371	—	2,098
Total assets	**$3,318,100**	**$1,787,282**	**$1,690,324**	**$1,295,453**	**$1,270,508**	**$390,538**	**$33,095**	**$2,926**
Liabilities and Stockholders' Equity								
Current liabilities								
Accounts payable	$ 26,165	$ 27,853	$ 27,604	$ 19,787	$ 22,271	$ 4,584	$ 1,004	—
Accrued expenses	139,683	73,359	72,370	72,103	70,124	10,964	548	—
Payable to joint venture	—	—	1,181	—	—	—	—	—
Income taxes payable	46,745	27,946	16,543	11,168	17,926	4,305	—	—
Deferred revenue	8,609	3,700	2,731	1,800	2,693	1,987	—	—
Current LT debt and lease obligations	19,897	5,080	100,568	905	999	1,484	225	—
Non-current liabilities								
Long-term debt and lease obligations	391,560	18,000	3,087	140,978	241,998	101,044	162	$ 382
Convertible notes and debentures	273,680	272,622	284,138	29,298	—	—	—	476
Deferred tax liability	230,384	—	8,078	—	—	—	—	—
Other non-current liabilities	6,236	2,330	—	7,364	12,188	6,298	176	1,924
Total liabilities	**$1,142,959**	**$ 430,890**	**$ 516,300**	**$ 283,403**	**$ 368,199**	**$130,666**	**$ 2,115**	**$2,782**
Stockholders' equity	2,175,141	1,356,392	1,172,554	1,012,050	902,309	259,872	30,979	180
	$3,318,100	**$1,787,282**	**$1,688,854**	**$1,295,453**	**$1,270,508**	**$390,538**	**$33,094**	**$2,962**

[a]1981 results cover the period from company inception on June 8, 1981. (Source: Genzyme 1986 IPO Prospectus.)
Source: Adapted by casewriters from Genzyme Corp. annual reports.

Exhibit 2 Genzyme Corp. Selected Consolidated Income Statement ($000s)

Year Ending December 31	2000	1999	1998	1997	1996	1991	1986	1981[a]
Revenues								
Product sales	$811,897	$683,482	$613,685	$529,927	$424,483	$ 72,019	$ 9,770	$2,167
Service sales	84,482	79,448	74,791	67,158	68,950	21,503	2,366	—
Revenue from R&D contracts	6,941	9,358	20,859	11,756	25,321	28,394	—	—
Total revenues	**$903,320**	**$772,288**	**$709,335**	**$608,841**	**$518,754**	**$121,916**	**$12,136**	**$2,167**
Expenses								
Cost of products sold	$232,383	$182,337	$211,076	$206,028	$155,930	$ 33,164	$ 5,421	$ 936
Cost of services sold	50,177	49,444	48,586	47,289	54,082	14,169	—	—
Selling, admin. & general	264,551	242,797	215,203	200,476	162,264	39,118	5,084	838
Research and development	169,478	150,516	119,005	89,558	80,849	27,232	2,285	57
Purchase of in-process R&D	200,191	5,436	—	7,000	130,639	—	—	—
Charge for impaired asset	4,321	—	—	—	—	—	—	—
Amortization of intangibles	22,974	24,674	24,334	17,245	8,849	—	—	—
Total expenses	**$944,075**	**$655,204**	**$618,204**	**$567,596**	**$592,613**	**$113,683**	**$12,790**	**$1,831**
Income (loss) before unusual items	**($40,755)**	**$117,084**	**$ 91,131**	**$41,245**	**($73,859)**	**$ 8,233**	**($654)**	**$336**
Investment income	$45,593	$36,158	$ 25,055	$11,409	$ 15,341	$12,371	$ 889	—
Interest expense	(15,710)	(21,771)	(22,593)	(12,667)	(6,990)	(2,088)	(194)	(92)
Equity in net loss of unconsolidated affiliates	(44,965)	(42,696)	(29,006)	(12,258)	(5,373)	—	—	—
Affiliate sale of stock	22,689	6,683	2,369	—	1,013	—	—	—
Sale of equity securities	15,873	(3,749)	(6)	—	1,711	—	—	—
Minority interest	4,625	3,674	4,285	—	—	—	—	—
Sale of product line	—	8,018	31,202	—	—	—	—	—
Sale of Gene-Trak	—	—	—	—	—	4,065	—	—
Credit from operating loss carryforward	—	—	—	—	—	8,387	—	—
Other revenue (expense)	5,188	14,527	—	(2,000)	(1,465)	2,726	—	—
Income (loss) before income taxes	**($7,462)**	**$117,928**	**$102,437**	**$25,729**	**($69,622)**	**$33,694**	**$ 41**	**$244**
Provision for income taxes	(55,478)	(46,947)	(39,870)	(12,100)	(3,195)	(12,848)	0	(165)
Net income (loss)	**($62,940)**	**$ 70,981**	**$ 62,567**	**$13,629**	**($72,817)**	**$20,846**	**$ 41**	**$ 79**

[a] 1981 results cover the period from company inception on June 8, 1981. (Source: Genzyme 1986 IPO Prospectus.)
Source: Adapted by casewriters from Genzyme Corp. annual reports.

the time had come to transfer the care of these patients to the government of Egypt. What if it refused to accept the responsibility? What if Project HOPE was unwilling to scale back its activities? In short, how exactly could the company balance the strong humanitarian and commercial principles it had built into its culture and values?

Birth of a Company

In contrast to other biotechnology firms that burst on the scene with impressive science-based, discovery-driven business models, Genzyme began by focusing on supplying raw materials—enzymes, fine chemicals, and reagents—to large research labs and pharmaceutical companies. Company co-founder Henry Blair had worked at the New England Enzyme Center of Tufts University School of Medicine and had many contacts in the research community. He founded the company in 1981 on the conservative belief that it should use revenues generated by selling reagents to generate cash flow and to create a track record that would allow it to fund further growth.

With a small pilot plant and office in a loft in Boston's Chinatown, Blair began searching for larger facilities to manufacture enzyme factors and reagents on a large scale. Within a year, he had located a company in the United Kingdom that was producing enzymes, substrates, and intermediates. Dissatisfied with the plant's efficiency and quality, Blair personally relocated to England to improve processes and increase yields. Within a few months the plant was profitable, and Genzyme was generating a positive cash flow. Sales in the first year were $2.2 million.

Laying the Foundation   Among all of Genzyme's early supply agreements, one had particular importance. Building on a long-term relationship he had with the National Institutes of Health (NIH), Blair obtained a contract to manufacture and supply the enzyme glucocerebrosidase (GCR) being used by Dr. Roscoe Brady in research on Gaucher (pronounced GO-shay) disease. Gaucher disease is an extremely rare and deadly condition caused by the body's inability to manufacture the GCR enzyme. Cells of the spleen, liver, lymph nodes, and bone marrow need GCR to break down and dispose of fatty residues from red blood cells' normal deterioration processes. Without this enzyme, fats collect and cause pain, fatigue, bone deterioration, fractures, and swelling of the affected organs.

Current estimates are that one in 400 of the general population carries the genetic mutations that cause Gaucher disease, but because both parents must pass on the mutation for a person to develop the disease, fewer than six of every one million people worldwide are predicted to have Gaucher disease. Of those 20,000 to 30,000 people, only about a quarter were thought to be ill enough to require treatment. (Populations with more intermarriage report a higher incidence of the disease. For example, among Jewish people of Eastern European ancestry, one in every 450 children is affected.) At the time of Brady's research, the treatment of choice was bone marrow transplantation, an extremely costly procedure with a 10% mortality rate.[2]

Throughout most of the 1970s, Brady's efforts to develop an enzyme replacement therapy had been unsuccessful, but in 1978, some members of his research team began suggesting that the large GCR molecule could better enter affected cells if the carbohydrate portion was modified, or "pruned." However, to put this idea into human trials involved expensive and risky protocols, and other team members expressed serious doubt that the modified molecule would work. After years of divisive internal debate, the NIH team put the "pruned molecule" hypothesis to the test in 1983. In its support role, Genzyme developed a production process for the enzyme required for the trials.

New Management, New Priorities   Meanwhile, Genzyme's top management was in transition. While Blair had been cleaning up the U.K. production processes, company co-founder Sheridan (Sherry)

[2]Estimates of prevalence were gathered from National Gaucher Foundation Web site, <http://www.gaucherdisease.org/prev.htm>, accessed July 18, 2002; and from "Genzyme Corp. Strategic Challenges with Ceredase," HBS Case No. 793-120 (Boston: Harvard Business School Publishing, 1994), pp. 7–8.

Snyder had been managing the financial and administrative side of the start-up. Although he had a background in the packaging business, Snyder was an entrepreneur and investor more than a professional manager, and the board decided the young company needed to engage a president to support him.

A search firm recommended Henri Termeer, a 36-year-old executive running a business making therapeutic products to treat hemophiliacs at medical products giant Baxter International. Termeer had joined Baxter in 1974 after completing his MBA and had built his reputation as an effective country manager of the company's German subsidiary. The search firm believed that his impressive management record, his broad industry knowledge, and his particular knowledge of blood-derived therapeutic treatment of genetic diseases made him an ideally qualified candidate.

Immediately upon joining Genzyme in October 1983, Termeer initiated a series of weekend discussions involving top management, members of the company's scientific advisory board of MIT and Harvard faculty, key investors, and a few outside advisors. Over several months they developed a few broad strategic principles that would guide Genzyme's future activities. First, Genzyme would be committed to building a diversified portfolio of targeted products and well-defined markets, with a particular focus on niches where needs were largely unmet. Equally important was its determination to remain independent by generating revenues from the start, by integrating vertically across the whole value chain, and by funding new development with internally generated funds or nonequity financial mechanisms.

While these meetings continued, Termeer was wrestling with some of the operating problems the company faced. Although he was aware that internal controls were all but nonexistent, the new president was still surprised to discover that one of the U.K. plants listed as an asset a particularly unsuccessful racehorse named Genzyme Gene. At that point he realized he had quite a job ahead in building a professional team and a sound management structure.

Betting the Ranch   As Termeer began his weekend sessions, Brady's new NIH trials were progressing. The results were disappointing yet tantalizing: only one patient out of the seven in the trial showed any response to the therapy, but his symptoms were dramatically reversed. The blind trial protocols masked the identity of the study participants, and critics of the modified enzyme in Brady's lab blocked the supporters' proposal to investigate the reason for the widely differing outcomes.

When the results of the trial became known, most within Genzyme were pessimistic about the prospects for this therapy. But Termeer was not ready to give up. After learning that the identity of the one patient who was in dramatic recovery was Ben Bryant, a 4-year-old boy from the Washington, D.C., area, he called the family.[a] Over the following months, he visited Ben and his family regularly and was very impressed that treatment resulted in a total reversal of symptoms, but when the injections stopped, Ben relapsed. Yet while Termeer became convinced the therapy could work, Genzyme's scientific advisory board was much less optimistic. For one whole day the scientists debated the issue with management, trying to answer three questions: Does it work? Is it safe? And could it be made profitable?

On the first question, the scientific advisors were doubtful, arguing that there was no strong indicator that this one case could have general implications. While agreeing with Termeer that Ben's recovery was extremely impressive, they did not share his belief that this was no aberration. The debate about safety was equally troubling. The enzyme used in the trial was extracted from the rare proteins found in human placentas collected from maternity wards in four large Boston hospitals. Growing publicity about risks of HIV and hepatitis C had led to widespread public concern about products derived from human tissue, leading the advisory board to suggest it would be more prudent to wait until biotechnology could create a recombinant version. Finally, there were major questions about whether a business

[a]Patient's name disguised.

could be created. Some raised concerns about accessing enough placentas, while others focused on the huge investment required to develop this product. Blair, conservative by nature, was worried it could bankrupt the company. Snyder also argued against the proposal.

Despite these many concerns, Termeer decided that it was unacceptable that product development should not proceed with a therapy potentially able to reverse this terrible disease. At this time, the company's best guess was that 2,000 patients worldwide could eventually use the product, with the potential of generating profits on a projected $100 million in annual sales—*if* further trials proved successful and *if* the product could qualify for "orphan drug" status, which would raise high entry barriers to any competing therapy for seven years. (Genzyme faced no patent barriers or licensing costs, since the government had decided not to patent the discovery of the modified GCR molecule to encourage further research.)

Throughout this process, Termeer and Blair had been talking to Scott Furbish, one member of the NIH team advocating the pruned molecule treatment. Frustrated by the infighting, Furbish was ready to quit NIH. They convinced him to join Genzyme and head up the research that would take his NIH work to fruition. But Termeer also took his scientific advisers' recommendation seriously and initiated parallel research on a recombinant form of the GCR enzyme.

Furbish and his team soon hypothesized that it was Ben Bryant's small size that allowed the therapy to succeed. By increasing the dosage to adult patients, they believed further clinical trials would show it was equally effective on them. Recalling all the uncertainties of 1985 as Genzyme made a new-drug application for Ceredase® enzyme under the Orphan Drug Act, Furbish said, "I would like to ask Henri how he had the guts to make that decision."

Going Public   By 1985, Termeer had tightened Genzyme's operations, set its broad strategic direction, strengthened its ongoing businesses, and committed to several important new research initiatives,

of which the Gaucher therapies were the boldest. With sales of 32 research reagents, diagnostic intermediaries, and fine chemicals generating almost $10 million in revenues, the company was approaching the financial break-even point. Termeer felt it was now time to take Genzyme public.

With the board's full support, he became CEO in late 1985 (Snyder had left the company) and soon after began planning an IPO for 1986. (See Exhibit 3 for excerpts from the prospectus.) Recognizing that most of the $27.4 million IPO cash infusion would be needed to finance the growth of existing operations, Termeer began exploring other means of funding product development. Unlike most other biotech companies, which financed research and development (R&D) by raising equity or entering into partnerships with large pharmaceutical companies, Genzyme elected to do so by creating a limited research partnership. Sales of the partnership units in 1987 raised a crucial $10 million to continue Ceredase development, splitting the risk and rewards of R&D but leaving Genzyme the option to buy back successful developments at a preset price.

Genzyme in Liftoff

By 1989 Ceredase approval seemed only a few years away, but public concern about the transmission of HIV from human-derived factors was growing. Recognizing that Genzyme could not develop a genetically engineered version of GCR quickly enough in-house, Termeer jumped at the opportunity to merge with Integrated Genetics (IG), a Massachusetts-based biotech firm with expertise in recombinant genetic engineering but an empty development pipeline following a patent-suit loss to Amgen.

Pursuing its strategy of diversification, Genzyme continued product development on multiple fronts—researching enzyme replacement for Fabry disease, developing genetic-screening tests, and working on therapies for cystic fibrosis, for example. With a continuing need for funding, a second limited research partnership in 1989 raised $36.7 million, followed by a second public stock offering for $39.1 million. In 1990 a special-purpose publicly traded research company was created, raising an

Exhibit 3   Excerpts from Genzyme's 1986 IPO Prospectus

The Company

- Genzyme develops, manufactures, and markets a variety of biological products used in human health care applications.
- Genzyme has additional human health care products under development. . . . [It] believes its practical experience in the production and sale of biological products will enhance its ability to manufacture and commercialize new products.
- As of March 1980, the company had 169 employees, of whom 39 are engaged in R&D.

Risk Factors

- Short operating history and losses . . . during each of its last few years.
- Regulation by government agencies . . . no assurance that . . . approvals will be granted.
- Uncertainty of product development.
- Patents with proprietary technology.
- Engaged in a segment of health care which is extremely competitive.
- Product liability.

Genzyme's Principal Products and Process Development Programs, 1986

Products and Processes	Applications	Status
Therapeutics		
Hyaluronic acid	Ophthalmic surgery	Development stage
	Soft-tissue implants	Development stage
	Surgical trauma	Research stage
	Joint disorders	Research stage
	Drug delivery	Research stage
Glycoprotein remodeling	Therapeutic glycoproteins	Research stage
Glucocerebrosidase	Treatment of Gaucher disease	NIH clinical trials
Ceramide trihexosidse	Treatment of Fabry disease	NIH development stage
Bulk pharmaceuticals	Active ingredients in branded and generic pharmaceuticals	Product sales
Diagnostics and reagents		
Diagnostic enzymes and substrates	Manufacture of diagnostic kits	Product sales
Research reagents	Lymphokine and glycoprotein research	Product sales
Fine chemicals		
Chiral compounds	Production of single isomer drugs	Development stage
Organic chemicals	Bioprocess compounds	Product sales

Source: Adapted by casewriters from Genzyme Corp. 1986 IPO Prospectus.

additional $47.3 million for targeted genetic research, including promising work on cystic fibrosis. But the real excitement at Genzyme focused on bringing Ceredase to market.

Building a Product Pipeline   As the Ceredase trials continued, the company worked to ensure prod-

uct supply. First-stage processing was contracted to the French Institute Merieux in Lyon, where rare proteins—among them GCR—were extracted from placentas shipped from the United States and all over Europe. (A year's supply of Ceredase for the average patient contained enzyme extracted and purified from 20,000 human placentas, or 27 tons of material.) Back in Boston, Genzyme modified the GCR enzyme then processed it to ensure its safety, purity, and concentration.

The U.S. Food and Drug Administration (FDA) finally approved Ceredase for marketing in the United States in 1991, giving Genzyme the momentum for another $143 million stock offering. Meanwhile, a team of biochemists from Genzyme and IG spliced the human gene responsible for producing GCR into cells cultured from Chinese hamster ovaries, producing recombinant GCR. Others worked on scaling up production from the two-and-a-half grams of product made in a one-liter container for the trials to a new proposed production facility with four bioreactors of 2,000 liters each.

In 1992, well before the production process was fully developed and more than a year before Genzyme would be ready to file the new-drug application for the product to be called Cerezyme, construction began on the new plant. To help finance the $180 million investment, a dramatic structure on the Charles River that stamped Genzyme's presence on Boston's skyline, Genzyme raised $100 million in debt. When commissioned, the plant's round-the-clock, 365-day-a-year production capacity would be six kilos of medicine annually—an output that would fit in a six-pack cooler but still sufficient for the 2,000 patients Genzyme hoped to treat worldwide.

Responding to Regulatory Pressures When Ceredase was approved, it had the distinction of being the most expensive therapy on the market. The complex extraction process, the limited availability of raw material, and the small number of patients combined to make production extremely costly. (Even when it was collecting 35% of all the placentas in the United States and over 70% of those in Europe, Genzyme could effectively supply Ceredase to only 1,000 to 1,500 patients.) Over one-third of this cost was attributable to acquiring and processing raw material, compared with raw material costs of 5% to 10% in typical drug manufacturing processes. (See Exhibit 4 for cost estimate.) Protocols called for patients with the severe form of the disease to initially receive 50 units of

Exhibit 4   Ceredase Cost and Profit Estimate, 1994

	$	$	%
Per patient annual price		$150,000	100%
Less cost of goods material	$47,900		
Mfg. Labor, overhead	5,300	$53,200	35
Gross Profit		$96,800	65
Less operating expenses			
Selling/reimbursement expense	$12,200		
Distribution	10,500		
R&D amortization	4,500		
Mfg. development amortization	2,000		
Corporate/admin. expenses	12,600		
Bad-debt provision	4,900		
Medicaid allowance	2,800		
Free goods	1,500	$51,000	34
Pretax operating profit		$45,800	31
Less state/federal taxes		14,600	10
Net income		$31,300	21

Note: Estimated average per patient revenue includes pediatric and adult patients on initial and maintenance treatments.
Source: Adapted by casewriters from Elyse Tanouye, "What Ails Us—What's Fair?" *The Wall Street Journal*, May 20, 1994, p. R11. (Source of data in the article given as Genzyme figures.)

Exhibit 5   Dosage Annual Cost Calculations for Ceredase and Cerezyme

Regimen and Patient Weight	Annual Cost
Initial treatment of	
50 units /kg.	
165 lbs. (75 kg.)	$360,750
110 lbs. (50 kg.)	240,500
33 lbs. (15 kg.)	72,150
Maintenance treatment of	
35 units /kg.	
165 lbs. (75 kg.)	$252,525
110 lbs. (50 kg.)	168,350
33 lbs. (15 kg.)	50,505

Note: Assumes biweekly infusions at $3.70 per unit medicine cost. Annual cost = price × dosage × weight × annual number of infusions.

Source: Prepared by casewriters with information supplied by Genzyme Corp.

Ceredase per kilo of body weight every two weeks. At $3.70 per unit, the first year's treatment could cost over $300,000, and although maintenance therapy could drop to roughly two-thirds of the initial dosage, the cost was high enough to attract the attention of regulators and politicians. (See Exhibit 5 for dosage calculations and costs.)

The political environment in which Ceredase was launched was a difficult one for pharmaceutical and biotech companies. The emphasis on healthcare reform in President Clinton's first term turned the spotlight on high-priced therapies, and along with a few other products such as Burroughs Welcome's AZT treatment for AIDS, Ceredase was singled out as an example of a drug that was seeking protection by exploiting the Orphan Drug Act.[3] Termeer's response was immediate and strong. (See Exhibit 6 for an editorial expressing his views.) He went to Washington and asked members of Congress and the regulatory authorities what they

wanted to know. He recalled: "I invited them to visit our operations and offered to open our books so they could see what it cost to develop and produce the product. I asked them for their suggestions—to tell me if we had done anything wrong. We would listen. Our approach was to be completely open and transparent. We were proud of what we had done and had nothing to hide."

In addition to showing his visitors the facilities and giving the Congressional Office of Technology Assessment (OTA) access to the books, Termeer also explained the company's philosophy: "Since the beginning, I have told this organization that our first responsibility is to treat patients with the disease, not to maximize financial returns. Regardless of where those people are or the financial circumstances they find themselves in, we take it as our responsibility to see they are treated."

To implement this "universal provision" philosophy, Genzyme created the Ceredase Assistance Program (CAP) even before Ceredase was approved to market. A CAP committee reviewed cases of extreme need—patients who had lost insurance coverage, for example—and where there was no alternative provided Ceredase free. But they always continued working with the patients to try to secure an ongoing supportive, paying party. In addition to Termeer, the CAP review committee consisted of medical, legal, and caseworker professionals.

After a detailed examination, the October 1992 OTA report concluded that, while NIH research had been used and while the Orphan Drug Act did reduce its risk, Genzyme had invested significantly in R&D and production facilities. Genzyme's pretax profit margin on the drug was determined to be in line with industry norms. (OTA's calculation excluded any R&D unrelated to Ceredase, bad debt, and free goods expenses.) Furthermore, OTA found that insurers were reimbursing the cost of the therapy because it was less expensive than surgery or extensive hospitalization.[4]

---

[3]Larry Thompson, "The High Cost of Rare Diseases: When Patients Can't Afford to Buy Lifesaving Drugs," *The Washington Post,* June 25, 1991, p. Z10; David Stipp, "Genzyme Counters Criticism over High Cost of Drug," *The Wall Street Journal,* June 23, 1992, p. B4; John Carey, "How Many Times Must a Patient Pay?" *Business Week,* February 1, 1993, p. 30.

[4]"Federal and Private Roles in the Development and Provision of Alglucerase Therapy for Gaucher Disease," Office of Technology Assessment, Washington, D.C.: Government Printing Office (1992).

Exhibit 6	*The Wall Street Journal* Op Ed Page, November 16, 1993, p. A28

The Cost of Miracles

Congress and the administration must ask the following question: If we impose price controls on breakthrough drugs, will we continue to get breakthrough drugs?

By Henri A. Termeer

As part of his continuing attack on the pharmaceutical industry, President Clinton has proposed establishing a federal committee to review the prices of "breakthrough" drugs, including those developed by the biotechnology industry. The Senate's Special Committee on Aging is scheduled to hold hearings today on the subject. Its chairman, Sen. David Pryor (D., Ark.), says the purpose of the hearings is to determine whether market forces are adequate to restrain prices.

The real danger, however, is not that the prices of new drugs will be too high, but that government controls, whether direct or indirect, will discourage investors from taking risks on biotechnology companies that develop new drugs.

The truth is that breakthrough drugs already face an onerous review: It's called the marketplace. Today, companies such as mine that develop breakthrough drugs can expect to have meaningful market exclusivity for only a few years. While a company's patent, or the special protection it can claim for its so-called orphan drugs, may preclude competitors from selling an identical product, it does not preclude others from designing and selling substantially similar products.

My own company's product, Ceredase, is an example of how market forces work. In the early 1980s, Genzyme was the only company working on a treatment for Gaucher's disease, a rare, inherited enzyme deficiency that causes crippling, and sometimes fatal, bone and organ deterioration. The CEO of another major biotechnology company had considered and rejected the idea of developing a treatment for such a rare disease because he could not imagine how his company could get an adequate return on a product intended for a few thousand patients.

Success Breeds Competition

Since Genzyme developed Ceredase, however, other companies have jumped into Gaucher's disease research. We are now competing with a company working on a variation of our drug, and two others are competing with us to develop gene-therapy approaches. There could be as many as four or five treatments for Gaucher's disease on the market within the next four years. If we hadn't taken the first step, there would be no market and no additional research on the disease.

My point is this: When an innovator company proves that its product works, and that a sufficient market exists to earn a return, it encourages other companies to develop similar products that enable them to compete for a share of that market. Given the breathtaking pace of biotechnology progress, it takes a relatively short time for other companies to develop substantially similar drugs. These will succeed, of course, only if they offer either price or therapeutic advantages over the innovator product.

Market forces are thus already creating price competition among pharmaceutical companies. A number of companies are implementing such programs as customer rebates and money-back guarantees. No government regulatory mechanism was necessary to induce this result.

In this respect, it is ironic that the same commentators who complain about pharmaceutical companies developing "me too" drugs (new versions of existing drugs) often fail to recognize that, at the very least, the introduction of such drugs helps constrain the prices of similar products, especially under a managed competition system in which insurance companies provide physicians with a greater incentive to consider the cost-effectiveness of the products they prescribe.

Congress should be less concerned about the possibility that a company might someday charge a high price for its AIDS vaccine for the two or three years before a competing product is available than about that company's ability to obtain the research-and-development funds needed to develop the vaccine in the first place. It is imperative that

(continued)

Exhibit 6   *(concluded)*

Congress and the administration consider the following question: If we alter market mechanisms by imposing price controls on breakthrough drugs, will we continue to get breakthrough drugs?

A breakthrough drug committee is not needed to ensure that drugs are priced reasonably. If a drug's benefit is not commensurate with its cost, physicians won't prescribe it, particularly under a managed competition system. From the patient's perspective, a committee's refusing to provide Medicare coverage for "excessively priced" drugs would substitute a bureaucrat's judgment for a physician's. It would also result in second-class medical care for aging Americans: Medicare patients would be denied access to drugs that are covered for the privately insured.

A breakthrough drug committee as proposed by Mr. Clinton is not only unnecessary, it is counterproductive. It will discourage investors from seeing the development of breakthrough drugs as an investment capable of reaping returns that are commensurate with the risks. Another Clinton proposal would allow the secretary of health and human services to negotiate prices for new drugs, under threat of excluding them from Medicare. Taken together, these proposals would constitute a price-control system that discriminates against biotechnology and other innovating pharmaceutical companies by threatening to blacklist their products unless government bureaucrats concur with company pricing decisions.

These Clinton proposals do little more than constrain our ability to develop breakthrough medicines. In the first eight months of this year, biotechnology stocks declined by 30%; and through initial public offerings and other investor appeals companies were able to raise only about 25% of the amount they spent during this period. Obviously, this is not sustainable for an industry that lost $3.6 billion last year.

My own company raised $100 million two years ago to fund its research and development of a treatment for cystic fibrosis, a common fatal genetic disease that kills the average patient at the age of 29. Even though we recently performed the first successful clinical trial of a gene-therapy treatment for cystic fibrosis, Genzyme would be hard-pressed to raise half that amount in today's investment environment. Yet we will need to make a total investment of more than $400 million to bring this product to market. If we succeed, we will be able to treat successfully 30,000 Americans who, in the severe phase of the disease, now receive annual medical care costing up to $50,000.

Proposals that discourage breakthrough drug development may be smart politics. But they are bad medicine and an ineffective means of cost control.

Japan, which has a single-payer system in which the government sets reimbursement rates for all health care products and services, uses government regulation of drug prices as a form of industrial policy to reward breakthrough drug development with a pricing premium. It is typical for the Japanese government to set prices for biotechnology drugs and other breakthrough pharmaceutical products at two to three times U.S. market prices, reflecting such a premium. On the other hand, the Japanese government cuts the prices of older pharmaceuticals annually according to a formula. The message to Japanese industry is clear: Innovate or die.

No Price Abuse
Sen. Pryor and the White House propose precisely the opposite—that breakthrough drugs be subject to government policies aimed at preventing "excessive" prices while old drugs continue to escalate in price at the general inflation rate.

In citing Japanese policy, I do not intend to suggest that the U.S. should adopt that system. To the contrary, I think that the relatively higher prices that the Japanese government willingly pays for breakthrough drugs are compelling evidence that American companies are not abusing the pricing freedom they enjoy in a system like ours.

Finally, let me note that the Japanese government has targeted biotechnology as an industry Japan wants to dominate by the year 2000. The U.S. will only forfeit its leadership position to Japan if its government encourages the development of breakthrough drugs and our own does not. The Japanese threat to our industry is not nearly as great as the threat from our own government.

Mr. Termeer is CEO of Genzyme Corp. in Cambridge, Mass.

Going to Market   Meanwhile, the company had been tackling the formidable task of bringing to market an extremely expensive therapy for a rare, poorly understood, and seldom-diagnosed disease. Termeer knew that once again he would have to attract different kinds of people to take on the challenge: "Recruiting the right people has been a key part of Genzyme's success. . . . I look for people with a passion to tackle things that seem impossible to solve. Practical dreamers who have a sense of compassion but believe they can change things. . . . And we attract people who see what we are doing as a worthwhile fight. There has to be a real personal involvement."

Drawing on the pool of biotech sales veterans in the Boston area, the company recruited an eight-person pioneering sales force with good industry knowledge whose members fit Termeer's "passionate practical dreamer" profile. In contrast to the traditional pharmaceutical model of making sales calls to doctors, pharmacies, and hospital purchasing agents, the Ceredase team focused on patients. After working to identify who they were, they educated them about the disease, organized them in support groups, and found treatment for them. They also educated physicians and reassured them about reimbursement.

Very quickly, the field sales force found the need for a support staff of caseworkers—typically, trained nurses and social workers—who advocated for patients with insurance companies. The caseworkers explained the therapy to the insurance representatives, provided supporting research materials, and handled the huge administrative demands for each submission. Said one of the early sales force members: "Because of insurance, it was a patient-oriented approach. Then, as the patient got better, the physician became motivated. We worked patient by patient, physician by physician. . . . This company is really about caring for our patients and doing the right thing for them. When a patient calls, you respond—it's the culture here."

The patient-oriented culture permeated the organization. Termeer explained that it was important for him personally to be in direct contact with patients, to feel emotionally involved in their suffering, and to use that to motivate himself and the organization to do something to help. Patient profiles were prominent in Genzyme's annual reports, photos of patients were pinned on cubicle walls in the offices, and company employees spoke passionately about how an individual or group of patients motivated them. Alison Lawton from regulatory affairs was typical: "Two months after I joined Genzyme, I went to a Gaucher patient meeting in Israel. . . . I cried my eyes out just seeing the patients and hearing them basically begging the Ministry to get them the therapy. . . . I remember thinking, 'I'm really going to make a difference if I can get this product registered here.'"

Yet some in the R&D labs claimed to be unmoved by Termeer's regular attempts to link their work to real patients' stories, believing their scientific training forced a more disciplined attitude. "If you are immersed in the science, you become intrigued by trying to figure out the problems," said one. "You're not inspired by stories of human tragedies or a picture of a kid on the wall." But others were. Furbish felt that most Genzyme scientists were different from others in the industry:

> There are clear philosophical divides in the biotech world. Technology looks down on sales and marketing, and Ph.D.s are trained to sneer at profit. But that doesn't hold at Genzyme. The patient focus builds from Henri down. His commitment is real and it affects everyone—even the Ph.D.s. Yet he also sets very aggressive business goals, and we come to appreciate that this is paying the bills as well as helping patients.

The same attitude had spread to the engineers and technicians in the plant. Blair Okita, vice president of Therapeutics Manufacturing and Development, found his experience at Genzyme much different from earlier stints at SmithKline Beecham and Merck: "Here we are motivated by a patient focus—right down to the technician level. For example, before doing their first run of the new Pompe product, our staff in the fill and finish area had a family with a child with Pompe's disease talk to them. . . . Each one of us is providing a life-saving therapy to a patient. That is a powerful motivating force."

As the network of educated patients and aware physicians expanded, sales of Ceredase grew rapidly. In 1993, after three years on the market, 1,000 patients were being treated, and cumulative sales were almost $250 million. Regulatory applications for Ceredase were pending in many international markets, and Cerezyme, the recombinant version of the therapy, was due for FDA approval in the United States in 1994. Genzyme's future looked promising indeed.

Opening Foreign Markets

Even before Ceredase was launched, Genzyme had been approached by companies wanting to cross-license or distribute the product abroad. True to his principle of controlling his business both upstream and downstream, Termeer refused. "International markets were an exciting opportunity," he said. "Besides, we were committed to seeking out and responding to Gaucher patients."

Pioneering Initiatives   In late 1990, Termeer called Tomye Tierney, an ex-colleague at Baxter, and convinced her to lead Genzyme's thrust into Europe. With her experience marketing Baxter's hemophilia products in many markets around the globe, Tierney had strong skills in building relationships with patients, physicians, and government officials. Said Termeer, "Tomye is one of those unusual people you can send into an impossible country where there are all kinds of roadblocks, and she can find a way."

Joining at the same time Genzyme was recruiting its U.S. sales force, Tierney had no sales model to build on. "Henri told me I would have to develop the international strategy," she recalled. "And when I asked him how long I had, he told me, 'Two weeks.'" She headed straight to Europe and within two months she had contacted her old physician friends, been referred to the few specialists working on Gaucher disease, located known patients in the United Kingdom, France, and the Netherlands, and begun connecting the network. Winning "investiga-

tional new drug" use approval, she made the first sales by December 1990.

Having set up the basic network, in September 1991 Tierney called another old Baxter colleague, Jan van Heek, and told him about Genzyme's European plans. Van Heek had just been offered a promotion at Baxter so was not very interested. "But I went to a patient and physician meeting and was astonished how much Genzyme meant to those people," he recalled. "There was an enormous sense of optimism and hope in the company, and I decided on the spot to join." By year's end, he had established Genzyme's temporary European headquarters—a rented house with a phone and a fax—and had hired the five entrepreneurial individuals who would develop the European market.

As the company pursued the long, complicated process of registration and approval in each of Europe's national health care systems, the high cost of Ceredase inevitably led to equally long and complex negotiations over price. But Genzyme's response was always simple, straightforward, and unwavering. The company had a universal global pricing policy. Termeer explained:

> We have only two prices—the commercial price or free. By taking an absolutely transparent global position, the discussion finishes quickly. We have not exploited our position by increasing prices—we have remained basically the same over that whole period. Our margin has gone up, but as it has we have taken on more responsibility to support patients around the world.

A Mobile Missionary   With van Heek running Europe, Termeer asked Tierney to become vice president and general manager of emerging markets with responsibility for developing opportunities in the rest of the world. Although she began initiatives in many markets, including Canada, Latin America, and Australia, it was the Middle East that captured much of her time and attention. Due to its high concentration of Gaucher patients, Israel was a priority market and in 1993 became the first country outside the United States to approve Ceredase. Another market that seemed to offer potential was

Egypt, and since 1990 Tierney had been in contact with Dr. Khalifa, a physician with an interest in Gaucher disease.

After four years, Tierney had built her widespread portfolio of markets into a $16 million business. In 1996, Termeer asked her to relocate to Asia, a market previously thought to have limited potential. Setting up her base in Singapore, she continued her missionary work. By that time, she had established a clear step-by-step approach to entering new markets. She explained:

> The key is to hire a smart local person to manage the process. For example, in Korea I found a pharmacist who had worked for the German drug company Boehringher. I connected him to a physician who we felt could be a local thought leader. She was treating a Gaucher patient willing to pay for his own treatment. This gave us the base to create a forum for patients and help them channel their frustration at not having access to therapy toward the government. Our local manager then worked with the patients, physicians, and government to enact orphan drug legislation and approve Cerezyme for reimbursement. It's a lot of work, but the Genzyme credo is "you've got to find a way."

As she opened markets in Japan, South Korea, Taiwan, Hong Kong, and other developed Asian countries, Tierney was increasingly aware that there were other, less developed economies—China, India, and Vietnam, for example—that simply could not afford this therapy. It was an issue that had become a growing concern for Termeer as well. For several years, patients from countries without access to Cerezyme had been coming to Boston to request free product from the CAP committee. (See Exhibit 7 for one well-publicized example.) This presented Termeer with a real dilemma: "The problem was we were having families moving to the United States asking to get free drug and treatment here forever. The real solution had to be to get treatment in their home country. It's less disruptive for the family and also educates the country about the therapy so more patients can be treated."

To the critics, however, the requirement to return home seemed to be a hard-hearted and even manipulative tactic designed to use patient needs to develop new market opportunities. It was a charge Termeer strongly refuted:

> What I will never tolerate is to create a blackmail situation where the patient is in the middle. There can be no circumstance where a patient on therapy is taken off therapy to create leverage. Or where a patient that needs therapy is denied it to create leverage. We have to make sure there is a critical need, then we must respond to the need. But we cannot take on the responsibility forever and we need to make people aware of the role they must play to help. . . . In the Peruvian family's case, we asked them to move back, then worked very hard with the government to get reimbursement in Peru. In the end we were able to help other Peruvian patients get the treatment also.

The Gaucher Initiative

As Termeer thought about how to address the question of providing treatment to Gaucher sufferers in less developed countries, he decided this would be an ideal next project for Tierney. But Tierney was not so sure. After nine months of persuasion and negotiation, she returned to Boston in June 1998 with a mandate to develop a humanitarian program for emerging markets—but without jeopardizing the company's existing or future commercial opportunities.

Setting Up the Program   As soon as Tierney returned, she scheduled a meeting with Termeer to review the parameters of her new assignment. She found he was deeply involved in the issues, and the meeting turned into the first of many brainstorming sessions she had with Termeer and Sandy Smith, the vice president of International, to whom she reported. The first issue Termeer addressed with Tierney was the charter of what they began calling the Gaucher Initiative. He recalled the guidelines clearly: "It was really just a continuation of the philosophy we had implemented through CAP. Where there is a critical need, we will respond. But we cannot take on the responsibility forever. Our goal must be to create a situation in which the country itself will eventually take responsibility for the treatment. That's where we need to get to."

Exhibit 7   *The Boston Sunday Globe* Article, April 11, 1993, p. 1

A Father, a Drug and an Ailing Son

By Philip Bennett
GLOBE STAFF

Justo Ascarza knows the logic of big business, of borders, of probable endings. But he lives by the logic of a parent whose child is dying, which is something else entirely.

"To struggle for the life of a child, for the life of a son, is to put yourself above rules, and even above laws," he said in a waiting room at Massachusetts General Hospital, impatient for his son to get better.

It was thinking like this that led Ascarza, without money, influence, or an understanding of English, across the globe to Boston to persuade doctors, hospitals, and Genzyme Corp. to save his son for free with one of the world's most costly drugs.

For a few months, Ascarza, a grade-school principal from Peru, made the system work for him. But, perhaps not surprisingly, it hasn't lasted. He says now that he is being made to work for the system, with the health of his son, Amaru, as leverage.

Ascarza and Genzyme are at odds over how long Amaru, 13, will receive free doses of Ceredase, the Cambridge biotechnology firm's premier drug, which the company says costs patients an average of $140,000 annually. Genzyme says the boy's next free dose, on Thursday, will be his last unless the Ascarzas return to Peru, where they would receive three more free months for introducing Ceredase to the country. The company then expects the government of Peru to pay for Amaru's treatment.

While the scheme might open a new South American market for Genzyme, Ascarza fears it may also result in suffering and death for his son. Peru is a country with shortages of medical resources and a surplus of tragedies. Ascarza, whose school salary is about $90 a month, asserts the government there will not pay for the drug, a claim supported even by the Lima physician Genzyme obtained for the family.

While the case is unusual, its issues are at the core of the health care debate, involving responsibility for care and its enormous expense and conflict over treatment that is costly to institutions but priceless for individuals and their families.

Because the Ascarzas are Peruvian, their case raises another, increasingly common question: should foreigners or unnaturalized immigrants living in the United States have the same rights to emergency care—some of it unavailable anywhere else—as U.S. citizens?

What nobody disputes is that Amaru Ascarza is very sick. He has Gaucher's disease, a rare genetic illness. Its symptoms include severe enlargement of the liver and spleen, excessive bleeding, and erosion of bones until they may start breaking. The disease can be fatal if untreated.

At 13, Amaru is 4 feet tall and weights 68 pounds. His abdomen is swollen grotesquely. His gums bleed. Struck with headaches, he presses his palms against his skull as if to hold the bone in place. His hands are delicate and tiny. He plays the flute and is a talented cartoonist.

He is a thoughtful and self-conscious teenager, usually quiet. His father says that prior to receiving Ceredase Amaru would often be prostrated by pain, wailing helplessly.

An effective treatment

Ceredase replaces an enzyme missing in Gaucher's victims, in many cases reversing the disease. Such has been the case with Amaru, who during three months of treatment has improved "miraculously," his father says, "inside and out."

"The medicine makes me feel better," Amaru said. "I go outside, do more things. When it wears off I feel sick again."

Since Ceredase was approved in the United States two years ago, it has been a bonanza for Genzyme. The company says that fewer than 6,000 of an estimated 20,000 Gaucher's patients worldwide can benefit from treatment with the drug, but its extraordinary cost has made it Genzyme's sales leader, generating $100 million last year.

The company currently has a monopoly on Ceredase under the Orphan Drug Law, which gives economic incentives to companies to develop drugs for rare diseases. And the drug attracts faithful customers: like insulin for diabetics, it is usually taken regularly for life.

Genzyme has been criticized for the cost of Ceredase, which can exceed $200,000 a year for patients. Executives say the drug is fairly priced. In addition, they say, no Gaucher's patient has been deprived of Ceredase for inability to pay, and they point by way of example to the day Justo Ascarza came to the door.

Exhibit 7   (*concluded*)

Ascarza, originally from a provincial town in the Andes, is an elementary school principal in a poor urban neighborhood in Lima. He speaks no English. He and his wife, Gladys, who joined him here recently, worry about their two other children, who remain in Peru. Yet with a relentlessness that can be breathtaking, he has made his case to any physician, attorney, government official, executive, or journalist who will listen.

His efforts have probably saved his son. In Peru, where no cases of Gaucher's had been previously noted, Amaru's condition went undiagnosed for five years. The Ascarzas were told their son might have leukemia until physicians correctly identified the illness and put the Ascarzas in touch with the National Institutes of Health, near Washington.

Company could benefit

Physicians studying Gaucher's disease invited the family to NIH last November. The Ascarzas persuaded American Airlines to donate airfare. A doctor there who examined Amaru found him seriously ill. But because he was not affected neurologically, he did not qualify for an NIH study that would have resulted in free treatment and was discharged.

It was then, with airfare donated by an NIH physician, that the Ascarzas with the help of a distant relative living in Cambridge, turned to Genzyme. They were accepted into a program of free treatment, "conditioned on the full cooperation of the parents and the patient," said Henri Termeer, Genzyme's chairman and chief executive.

In the Ascarzas' case, those conditions require them to return to Peru by the end of April in order to receive three more months of the drug for free. After that, the family must find financing, presumably from the government of Peru, to pay Genzyme an estimated $82,000 a year.

If the Ascarzas were to succeed in Peru, the benefits for Genzyme would be clear. Ceredase would presumably receive expedited approval for use. Publicity about the case would bring forward patients with Gaucher's disease who are currently undiagnosed. And, as in countries such as Brazil and Argentina, where Ceredase is now subsidized, the company would have a government guarantee of payment.

But Ascarza said he appealed to the wife of Peru's president, Alberto Fujimori, for aid and was turned down. Ceredase would be a great expense in a country where nurses at public hospitals earn less than $100 a month and tens of thousands of children die each year of dehydration caused by diarrhea because the government cannot afford to provide even the most basic care.

Question of responsibility

Genzyme executives, for their part, point out that they cannot solve the problems of health care in Peru and that the company is not a charity.

"We never give up on attempts to make the patient part of a safety net," said Termeer. But, he said, "We cannot do this in a way that we lose total leverage on the system. We cannot allow ourselves to be used in a way that takes everybody off the hook."

Genzyme has assured the Ascarzas that the company has arranged care from a respected Lima hematologist, Dr. Jose Galvez, and is ready to ship the Ceredase. Yet, in a telephone interview last week, Galvez was hardly reassuring.

"I don't know anything really," Galvez said. "His physician called me last week and told me about the patient and that they'd send me something in the mail. I'm just waiting. I just don't know anything else."

Asked whether he believed the Peruvian government would pay for the treatment, Galvez said: "I don't think so. I have to be honest with you. We have a lot of problems here and this is not a priority. Things are not good here."

Meanwhile, Ascarza said that he has been rebuffed only once for seeking free care for his son in the United States. Ironically, he said it came from a Peruvian doctor practicing here.

But the issue is more widespread.

"It's a horrible problem," said Dr. Norman Barton, who examined Amaru at the NIH. "To what extent do we as a society have the responsibility to provide advanced technologies to countries that have no means to pay for them?"

"I don't know, Ascarza said. "Maybe what I am doing is wrong. But it is my responsibility to guarantee that Amaru doesn't die because he didn't have the luck to be born in a developed country."

BOSTON GLOBE by PHILIP BENNETT. Copyright 1993 by GLOBE NEWSPAPER CO (MA). Reproduced with permission of GLOBE NEWSPAPER CO (MA) in the format Textbook via Copyright Clearance Center.

Implementation of this philosophy was complicated by the conjunction of the company's humanitarian commitment to universal provision and its commercial objective of a universal price. Recognizing that the humanitarian provision needed to be insulated from the commercial operations, Tierney and Termeer concluded they would need to work with an independent agency that had the infrastructure to distribute Cerezyme around the world. To ensure Genzyme's efforts would be both direct and discrete yet would not involve the company in decisions about who would receive treatment, they would also need an independent, medically qualified committee of experts to make case-by-case diagnoses and decisions about the relative needs of candidates for treatment.

As she developed the program design, Tierney worked with a corporate philanthropy consultant and shared development ideas with the program director for the Mectizan Donation Program, Merck's initiative to combat river blindness.[5] In October, after carefully screening several partner candidates suggested by the outside consultant, Tierney selected Project HOPE for its worldwide distribution network, long track record, emphasis on health education, and sterling reputation. Additionally, the organization had a strong presence in China and Egypt, markets which Tierney knew had a recognized need for this therapy. Project HOPE's emphasis on health-care development within a country, rather than ongoing charitable health-care provision, was also consistent with Genzyme's long-term commercial goals.

For its part, however, Project HOPE took some convincing. It wanted assurances that it would not be mixing a commercial agenda with its humanitarian mission and that the program would be run independently of Genzyme. Finally, an agreement was reached, and Tierney worked feverishly to get the program up and running by January 1, 1999. (See Exhibit 8 for memorandum of understanding highlights.)

▌[5]Peter Wehrwein, "Pharmaco-Philanthropy," *Harvard Public Health Review,* Summer 1999, pp. 32–39.

Implementing the Program   Tierney's first task was to work to establish a secretariat with a full-time program manager and an independent case review board. She then won Termeer's agreement to supplement the in-kind donation of Cerezyme with a yearly budget to support the program manager and secretariat and provide training, travel, and office peripherals for local treatment centers. Eager to begin shipment of the drug to Egypt and China, Tierney appealed to the quality control personnel at Genzyme to inspect and approve Project HOPE's delivery system immediately. With excitement about the new program running high at Genzyme (Termeer and Tierney had widely communicated the company's commitment to the Gaucher Initiative), plant personnel helped to bypass a two-month backlog, and the first product was shipped ahead of Tierney's year-end target date.

Working with Project HOPE, Tierney convened the independent six-member medical review board that would meet three times a year to establish patient-intake procedures, qualify new cases, and decide to terminate treatment for patients who did not respond to the therapy. The board consisted of three leading experts in Gaucher disease, Genzyme's chief medical officer, a Project HOPE staff member, and a medical ethicist, who quickly tested the board's independence.

As Project HOPE spread the word in Egypt and China, local doctors made case-by-case requests to the local Project HOPE office. Applications were forwarded to Genzyme, which coordinated a case docket for the medical advisory board. After medical advisory board approval, Genzyme prepared patient and dosage lists for distribution to Project HOPE, which then shipped the drug overseas in coolers. At its destination it was carried by truck— or sometimes by hand—to local hospitals, where it was reconstituted and prepared for infusion. Project HOPE qualified local doctors to administer the therapy and participate in the program. In its first year, the Gaucher Initiative treated 60 patients worldwide (37 in Egypt and 23 in China); by 2001 the number was 140.

Exhibit 8   Highlights of Gaucher Initiative Agreement

Program Objectives

- "To establish Expert Committee to provide technical, ethical and programmatic guidance."
- "To coordinate and facilitate training of eight physicians on the treatments of Gaucher disease."
- "To organize and carry out the timely shipment and delivery of Ceredase/Cerezyme to identified locations in the People's Republic of China and Egypt."
- "To provide treatment to approximately 60 patients" annually.

Project HOPE Responsibilities

- "Establish a Secretariat . . . to direct and manage the day-to-day activities and administration."
- Identify Project HOPE field staff to assist with implementation from the local level.
- "Establish an Expert Committee, which will meet bi-annually . . . to provide technical, ethical and programmatic guidance to the Gaucher Initiative. Provide a voting member to the Expert Committee."
- Coordinate and facilitate the training of four physicians from China, two from Egypt, and two from Project HOPE.
- "Arrange for the timely shipment and delivery of appropriate quantities of Ceredase/Cerezyme."
- "Provide liaison with participating hospitals and medical institutions, physicians and medical personnel, and the patients selected for participation in the Gaucher Initiative."
- "Collaborate with appointed Genzyme representatives to . . . publicize the Gaucher Initiative."
- "Submit to Genzyme quarterly financial and narrative reports on progress."

Genzyme Responsibilities

- "Identify patients . . . for selection by the Expert Committee for inclusion in the program."
- "Assist in the creation of the Expert Committee. Provide a voting member."
- "Donate to Project HOPE appropriate quantities of Ceredase/Cerezyme."
- "Facilitate the training of eight physicians . . . at the Gaucher workshop held at Genzyme."
- "Provide Project HOPE with technical assistance in the training aspects and treatment of Gaucher disease."
- "Collaborate with Project HOPE . . . to publicize the Gaucher Initiative."
- "Genzyme shall be responsible for funding the Gaucher Initiative."

Resolution of Disputes

- In the event of a dispute, "the parties shall first attempt to resolve the dispute through friendly discussions." After 14 days "the parties may mutually select a third party" for "non-binding mediation." After another 14 days "either party may refer the dispute to arbitration and withdraw from the Program" with 30 days' written notice.

Liability

- "Project HOPE will be responsible for obtaining liability insurance to protect the Expert Committee from any suits resulting from decisions concerning patient selection and program guidance."
- "Any liability associated with the products Ceredase/Cerezyme will be the responsibility of Genzyme."
- "Local liability concerning the treatment of patients will be the responsibility of the local physician."

Duration, Extension, and Termination

- Duration: five years.
- Extended by "mutual agreement and the signing of a letter defining the length of the extension."
- The agreement may be terminated "without cause upon giving 90 days' written notice."

Source: Adapted by casewriters from memorandum of understanding between Project HOPE and Genzyme Corp., effective January 1, 1999.

The Humanitarian/Commercial Tension   To the employees at Genzyme, the commitment to the Gaucher Initiative was another confirmation of the values they had heard Termeer espouse since the company's earliest days. Yet within the commercial organization, some voices of concern were emerging, particularly from those responsible for less developed markets. "We have a person who covers most of our Eastern European markets who was really concerned that if people began to understand we would give product away, it would be impossible to sell," Tierney recalled.

Christi van Heek, president of Genzyme's therapeutics division, reinforced the view that reimbursement could easily be lost if health-care providers felt they could obtain free product. She described how she had visited a physician in the Czech Republic who explained that his hospital lacked the money to buy Tylenol. Yet he eventually had six children on Cerezyme therapy. "He got reimbursement through the system," she said. "He had to fight for it, but this drug really works."

However, as the product penetration in developed nations approached saturation—sales growth increased only 6% between 2000 and 2001—the opportunities in markets outside the most developed economies began to attract more attention. (See Exhibit 9 for sales and patient growth.) Furthermore, Ceredase had come off orphan drug protection in 1998, and Cerezyme's would expire in 2001. Already competitors had applied for marketing approval for different therapies. Although Genzyme analysis cast doubts on their safety and effectiveness, it was a clear signal that this

Exhibit 9   Ceredase and Cerezyme Revenues and Patient Growth, 1991–2001

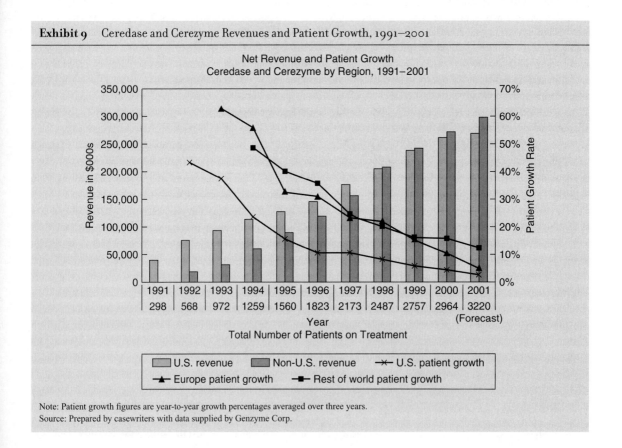

Note: Patient growth figures are year-to-year growth percentages averaged over three years.
Source: Prepared by casewriters with data supplied by Genzyme Corp.

larger-than-expected market was attractive to competitors. "The interesting question will be what the entry of competitors will do to this responsibility we have taken on," said Termeer. "Will it be a burden for us alone, or will it be a joint responsibility? We have not begun to sort that one out."

The Egyptian Dilemma

Even after she moved to Singapore, Tierney had kept her eye on the nascent opportunity in Egypt. It was a responsibility that would absorb much time and energy in coming years.

Building a Presence, Having an Impact In late 1996, Khalifa had informed her that he had obtained funding to treat a child with Gaucher disease. On a "named-patient basis," he also had obtained permission to import Cerezyme on humanitarian grounds even though it was not registered for sale in Egypt. However, several months later, when Tierney was visiting Egypt, she found that the funding was insufficient to cover the required treatment, and the patient was not responding to the low dosage provided. She immediately offered to request Genzyme's CAP program to sponsor a matching dose. Under this partial reimbursement arrangement, over the next two years Khalifa and Dr. Khaled, another physician now involved, had expanded treatment to a dozen patients, mostly children who were reimbursed under the government's Student Fund.

But now, with Tierney leading the Gaucher Initiative, responsibility for the Egyptian market was transferred to the general manager of Genzyme's Israel subsidiary, Zev Zelig. As a way of handing off her commercial responsibilities, Tierney introduced the Jordanian sales associate hired to cover Arab markets to her key physician and health insurance contacts. She also introduced him to the Project HOPE staff in Egypt. "The HOPE people were a little uncomfortable that we were actually making money on some of these patients," she explained. "They wanted a clear separation."

New Demands, New Expectations In Project HOPE's first year in Egypt, the number of patients grew from 12 to 37, many of them infants, since children under five were not covered by the government-financed Student Fund. Sales through the partial reimbursement program were also up, increasing from $82,200 in 1998 to $146,500 in 1999. But the growing number of "named patients" attracted the attention of regulatory authorities, and in early 2000 Zelig was told that Genzyme would have to register Cerezyme. Zelig asked one of the company's regulatory staff to help him assess the task, but after talking to the Egyptian authorities, they concluded that registration would be too expensive to be justified.

After the first quarter of 2000, sales stopped. Almost immediately, Tierney began to feel pressure from Zelig to scale back her program in Egypt. She recalled: "At our strategic planning meeting, Zev kept saying, 'I can't do it because she's giving away free drug.' And I'd come back, 'You need to hire an Egyptian sales associate and register in Egypt.' We went back and forth for almost a year."

Meanwhile, Project HOPE had just appointed Dr. John Howe as its new CEO. A well-respected cardiologist from Texas, Howe joined the organization with much energy and an ambition to expand its operations. "He told me he wanted to grow Project HOPE at least 50%," said Tierney. "And he was particularly interested in expanding the relationship with Genzyme."

Facing the Problem In early 2001, the tension between the commercial and humanitarian agendas in Egypt was still unresolved. While sales had stopped for a year, by May 2001 the Gaucher Initiative had expanded to 41 patients, with 5 more approvals about to start treatment. When Mike Heslop, Genzyme's vice president for global marketing, hired Tarek Ebrahim, an Egyptian physician, he made "sorting out the Egyptian issue" one of the newcomer's first assignments.

On May 25, Smith, Genzyme's vice president of International, convened a meeting to which he invited Heslop, Ebrahim, Zelig, and Tierney. Tierney recalled the discussion:

> The others were all from the commercial side and had been talking to Zev. So they were sitting there telling me to put a lid on the free drug program. Zev took the lead and said we had to get the word out that Project HOPE was not taking any more patients. I told them that the solution was to register the drug and get a local presence in Egypt. Then we could manage the transition. I told them I could not stop the program.

The meeting broke up with the proposal that Ebrahim go to Egypt, evaluate the situation, and return with his analysis and recommendation. Tierney liked and respected her new Egyptian marketing colleague but wondered how the situation could be resolved. How could she think through the problem? If Termeer were to be involved, what kind of recommendation could she make to him? And how could she and her colleagues implement the necessary changes?

Appendix A   Timeline of Selected Corporate Events, Genzyme Corp.

Year	Significant Events
1981	Genzyme founded by Henry Blair and Sherry Snyder, begins to supply NIH with GCR under contract.
1983	Genzyme hires Henri Termeer as president; becomes CEO, 1985. NIH launches first GCR enzyme-replacement trial.
1985	FDA designates Ceredase an orphan drug. Scientific advisory board (BIA) recommends against development of Ceredase.
1986	Genzyme IPO, June, raises $27.4 million cash for a company valuation of over $83 million.
1987	Forms R&D limited partnership, raising $10 million to develop Ceredase.
1989	Ceredase approved for seriously ill patients prior to marketing approval. Raises $39.1 million through public stock offering and $36.7 million through Genzyme Development Partners. Acquires Integrated Genetics (founded in 1981).
1990	Ceredase available outside United States on a named-patient basis. Forms Neozyme I, raises $47.3 million to fund R&D.
1991	Ceredase approved and receives orphan drug status. Raises $100 million in 10-year 6% debt, and raises $143 million in public stock offering.
1992	Begins work on gene therapy to treat cystic fibrosis. Congressional OTA report issued on the development of Ceredase. Forms Neozyme II, raises $85 million; purchases four research programs from Neozyme I for $49 million.
1993	New-drug application to FDA for Cerezyme.
1994	Cerezyme approved in United States, Germany, France, Holland, Australia, United Kingdom. Break-even on Ceredase.
1995	Ceredase sales approved in Portugal, Italy, New Zealand, Sweden, Spain. Genzyme General public offering raises $141 million.
1996	Japan approves Cerezyme.
1998	Genzyme General places $250 million 5.25% seven-year debt.
1999	Launches Gaucher Initiative.

Source: Adapted by casewriters from Genzyme Corp. sources.

Reading 7-1   Local Memoirs of a Global Manager

Gurcharan Das

There was a time when I used to believe with Diogenes the Cynic that "I am a citizen of the world," and I used to strut about feeling that a "blade of grass is always a blade of grass, whether in one country or another." Now I feel that each blade of grass has its spot on earth from where it draws its life, its strength; and so is man rooted to the land from where he draws his faith, together with his life.

In India, I was privileged to help build one of the largest businesses in the world for Vicks Vaporub, a hundred-year-old brand sold in 147 countries and now owned by Procter & Gamble. In the process, I learned a number of difficult and valuable lessons about business and about myself. The most important lesson was this: to learn to tap into the roots of diversity in a world where global standardization plays an increasingly useful role.

"Think global and act local," goes the saying, but that's only half a truth. International managers must also think local and then apply their local insights on a global scale.

The fact is that truths in this world are unique, individual, and highly parochial. They say all politics is local. So is all business. But this doesn't keep either from being global. In committing to our work we commit to a here and now, to a particular place and time; but what we learn from acting locally is often universal in nature.

This is how globalization takes place. Globalization does not mean imposing homogeneous solutions in a pluralistic world. It means having a global vision and strategy, but it also means cultivating roots and individual identities. It means nourishing local insights, but it also means reemploying communicable ideas in new geographies around the world.

The more human beings belong to their own time and place, the more they belong to *all* times and places. Today's best global managers know this truth. They nourish each "blade of grass."

Managerial basics are the same everywhere, in the West and in the Third World. There is a popular misconception among managers that you need merely to push a powerful brand name with a standard product, package, and advertising in order to conquer global markets, but actually the key to success is a tremendous amount of local passion for the brand and a feeling of local pride and ownership.

I learned these lessons as a manager of international brands in the Third World and as a native of India struggling against the temptation to stay behind in the West.

On Going Home

I was four years old when India became free. Before they left, the British divided us into two countries, India and Pakistan, and on a monsoon day in August 1947 I suddenly became a refugee. I had to flee east for my life because I was a Hindu in predominantly Muslim West Punjab. I survived, but a million others did not, and another 12 million were rendered homeless in one of the great tragedies of our times.

I grew up in a middle-class home in East Punjab as the eldest son of a civil engineer who built canals and dams for the government. Our family budget was always tight: after paying for milk and school fees, there was little left to run the house. My mother told us heroic stories from the *Mahabharata* and encouraged in us the virtues of honesty, thrift, and responsibility to country.

I grew up in the innocence of the Nehru age when we still had strong ideals. We believed in secularism, democracy, socialism, and the U.N.; and we were filled with the excitement of building a nation.

I came to the United States at the age of 12, when the Indian government sent my father to

❚ Reprinted by permission of *Harvard Business Review.* "Local Memoirs of a Global Manager" by Gurcharan Das, (March/April 1993).
❚ Copyright © 1993 by the President and Fellows of Harvard College; all rights reserved.

Washington, D.C., on temporary assignment. When my family returned to India a few years later, I won a scholarship to Harvard College and spent four happy years on the banks of the Charles River. My tutor taught me that the sons of Harvard had an obligation to serve, and I knew that I must one day use my education to serve India.

In 1964, in the towering confidence of my 21 years, I returned home. Some of my friends thought I had made a mistake. They said I should have gone on to graduate school and worked for a few years in the West. In fact, I missed the West in the beginning and told myself that I would go back before long; but I soon became absorbed in my new job with Richardson-Vicks in Bombay, and like the man who came to dinner, I stayed on.

From a trainee, I rose to become CEO of the company's Indian subsidiary, with interim assignments at Vicks headquarters in New York and in the Mexican subsidiary. When I became CEO, the Indian company was almost bankrupt, but with the help of a marvelous all-Indian organization, I turned it around in the early 1980s and made it one of the most profitable companies on the Bombay Stock Exchange. In 1985 we were acquired by Procter & Gamble, and so began another exciting chapter in my life. We successfully incorporated the company into P&G without losing a single employee, and we put ourselves on an aggressive growth path, with an entry first into sanitary napkins and then into one of the largest detergent markets in the world.

At three stages in my life, I was tempted to settle in the West. Each time I could have chosen to lead the cosmopolitan life of an expatriate. Each time I chose to return home. The first after college; the second when I was based in the New York office of Vicks, where I met my Nepali wife with her coveted Green Card (which we allowed to lapse); the third when I was in Mexico running our nutritional foods business, when once again I came home to earn a fraction of what I would have earned abroad.

Apart from a lurking wish to appear considerable in the eyes of those I grew up with, I ask myself why I keep returning to India. I have thrice opted for what appeared to be the less rational course in terms of career and money. The only remotely satisfying answer I have found comes from an enigmatic uncle of mine who once said, "You've come back, dear boy, because as a child you listened to the music of your mother's voice. They all say, 'I'll be back in a few years,' but the few years become many, until it is too late and you are lost in a lonely and homeless crowd."

Yet I think of myself as a global manager within the P&G world. I believe my curious life script has helped to create a mind-set that combines the particular with the universal, a mind-set rooted in the local and yet open and nonparochial, a mind-set I find useful in the global management of P&G brands.

On One-Pointed Success

I first arrived on the island of Bombay on a monsoon day after eight years of high school and college in America. That night, 15-foot waves shattered thunderously against the rocks below my window as the rain advanced from the Arabian sea like the disciplined forward phalanx of an army.

The next morning I reported for duty at Richardson-Vicks' Indian headquarters, which turned out to be a rented hole-in-the-wall with a dozen employees. This was a change after the company's swank New York offices in midtown Manhattan, where I had been interviewed. That evening my cousin invited me for dinner. He worked in a big British company with many factories, thousands of employees, and plush multistoried marble offices. I felt ashamed to talk about my job.

"How many factories do you have?" he wanted to know.

"None," I said.

"How many salesmen do you have?" he asked.

"None," I said.

"How many employees?"

"Twelve."

"How big are your offices?"

"A little smaller than your house."

Years later I realized that what embarrassed me that night turned out to be our strength. All 12 of our employees were focused on building our brands without the distraction of factories, sales forces, industrial relations, finance, and other staff departments. Our products were made under contract by Boots, an English drug company; they were distributed under contract by an outside distribution house with 100 salesmen spread around the country; our external auditors had arranged for someone to do our accounting; and our lawyers took care of our government work. We were lean, nimble, focused, and very profitable.

All my cousin's talk that night revolved around office politics, and all his advice was about how to get around the office bureaucracy. It was not clear to me how his company made decisions. But he was a smart man, and I sensed that with all his pride in working for a giant organization, he had little respect for its bureaucratic style.

If marketing a consumer product is what gives a company its competitive advantage, then it seems to me it should spend all its time building marketing and product muscle and employ outside suppliers to do everything else. It should spin off as many services as someone else is willing to take on and leave everyone inside the company focused on one thing—creating, retaining, and satisfying consumers.

There is a concept in Yoga called one-pointedness (from the Sanskrit *Ekagrata*). All 12 of us were one-pointedly focused on making Vicks a household name in India, as if we were 12 brand managers. I now teach our younger managers the value of a one-pointed focus on consumer satisfaction, which P&G measures every six months for all of its major brands.

Concentrating on one's core competence thus was one of the first lessons I learned. I learned it because I was face-to-face with the consumer, focused on the particular. Somehow I feel it would have taken me longer to learn this lesson in a glass tower in Manhattan.

As so often in life, however, by the time I could apply the lesson I had learned, we had a thousand people, with factories, sales forces, and many departments that were having a lot of fun fighting over turf. I believe that tomorrow's big companies may

well consist of hundreds of small decentralized units, each with a sharp focus on its particular customers and markets.

On the Kettle That Wrote My Paycheck

For months I believed that my salary came from the payroll clerk, so I was especially nice to her. (She was also the boss's secretary.) Then one day I discovered the most important truth of my career—I realized who really paid my salary.

Soon after I joined the company, my boss handed me a bag and a train ticket and sent me "up-country." A man of the old school, he believed that you learned marketing only in the bazaar, so I spent 10 of my first 15 months on the road and saw lots of up-country bazaars.

On the road, I typically would meet our trade customers in the mornings and consumers in the evenings. In the afternoons everyone slept. One evening I knocked on the door of a middle-class home in Surat, a busy trading town 200 miles north of Bombay. The lady of the house reluctantly let me in. I asked her, "What do you use for your family's coughs and colds?" Her eyes lit up, her face became animated. She told me that she had discovered the most wonderful solution. She went into the kitchen and brought back a jar of Vicks Vaporub and a kettle. She then showed me how she poured a spoon of Vaporub into the boiling kettle and inhaled the medicated vapors from the spout.

"If you don't believe me, try it for yourself," she said. "Here, let me boil some water for you."

Before I could reply she had disappeared into the kitchen. Instead of drinking tea that evening we inhaled Vicks Vaporub. As I walked back to my hotel, I felt intoxicated: I had discovered it was she who paid my salary. My job also became clear to me: I must reciprocate her compliment by striving relentlessly to satisfy her needs.

The irony is that all the money a company makes is made *outside* the company (at the point of sale), yet the employees spend their time *inside* the company, usually arguing over turf. Unfortunately, we don't see customers around us when we show up for work in the mornings.

When I became the CEO of the company I made a rule that every employee in every department had to go out every year and meet 20 consumers and 20 retailers or wholesalers in order to qualify for their annual raise. This not only helps to remind us who pays our salaries, we also get a payoff in good ideas to improve our products and services.

The ideal of being close to the customer may be obvious in the commercial societies of the West, but it was not so obvious 20 years ago in the protected, bureaucratic Indian environment. As to the lady in Surat, we quickly put her ideas into our advertising. She was the first consumer to show me a global insight in my own backyard.

Of Chairs, Armchairs, and Monsoons

Two years after I joined, I was promoted. I was given Vicks Vaporub to manage, which made me the first brand manager in the company. I noticed we were building volume strongly in the South but having trouble in the North. I asked myself whether I should try to fix the North or capitalize on the momentum in the South. I chose the latter, and it was the right choice. We later discovered that North Indians don't like to rub things on their bodies, yet the more important lesson was that it is usually better to build on your strength than to try and correct a weakness. Listen to and respect the market. Resist the temptation to impose your will on it.

We were doing well in the South partially because South Indians were accustomed to rubbing on balms for headaches, colds, bodyaches, insect bites, and a host of other minor maladies. We had a big and successful balm competitor, Amrutanjan, who offered relief for all these symptoms. My first impulse was to try to expand the use of Vaporub to other symptoms in order to compete in this larger balm market.

My boss quickly and wisely put a stop to that. In an uncharacteristically loud voice, he explained that Vaporub's unique function was to relieve colds.

"Each object has a function," he said. "A chair's function is to seat a person. A desk is to write on. You don't want to use a chair for writing and a desk for sitting. You never want to mix up functions."

A great part of Vaporub's success in India has been its clear and sharp position in the consumer's mind. It is cold relief in a jar, which a mother rubs tenderly on her child's cold at bedtime. As I thought more about balms, I realized that they were quite the opposite. Adults rub balms on themselves for headaches during the day. Vaporub was succeeding precisely because it was not a balm; it was a rub for colds.

Every brand manager since has had to learn that same lesson. It is of the utmost importance to know who you are and not be led astray by others. Tap into your roots when you are unsure. You cannot be all things to all people.

This did not prevent us from building a successful business with adults, but as my boss used to say, "Adult colds, that is an armchair. But it is still a chair and not a desk."

When I took over the brand we were spending most of our advertising rupees in the winter, a strategy that worked in North America and other countries. However, my monthly volume data stubbornly suggested that we were shipping a lot of Vaporub between July and September, the hot monsoon season. "People must be catching lots of colds in the monsoon," I told my boss, and I got his agreement to bring forward a good chunk of our media to the warm monsoon months. Sure enough, we were rewarded with an immediate gain in sales.

I followed this up by getting our agency to make a cinema commercial (we had no television at that time) showing a child playing in the rain and catching cold. We coined a new ailment, "wet monsoon colds," and soon the summer monsoon season became as important as the winter in terms of sales.

Another factor in our success was the introduction of a small 5-gram tin, which still costs 10 cents and accounts for 40% of our volume. At first it was not successful, so we had to price it so that it was cheaper to buy four 5-gram tins than a 19-gram jar. The trade thought we were crazy. They said henceforth no one would buy the profitable jar; they would trade down to the tin. But that didn't happen. Why? Because we had positioned the tin for the working class. We were right in believing that middle-class consumers would stay loyal to the middle-class size.

Moves like these made us hugely successful and placed us first in the Indian market share by far. But instead of celebrating, my boss seemed depressed. He called me into his office, and he asked me how much the market was growing.

"Seven percent," I said.

"Is that good?"

"No," I replied, "But *we* are growing 20%, and that's why we're now number one in India."

"I don't give a damn that we are number one in a small pond. That pond has to become a lake, and then an ocean. We have to grow the market. Only then will we become number one in the world."

Thus I acquired another important mind-set: when you are number one, you must not grow complacent. Your job is to grow the market. You always must benchmark yourself against the best in the world, not just against the local competition. In the Third World this is an especially valuable idea, because markets there are so much less competitive.

Being receptive to regional variations, tapping the opportunity that the monsoon offered, introducing a size for the rural and urban poor, and learning to resist complacency and grow the market—all are variations on the theme of local thinking, of tapping into the roots of pluralism and diversity.

On Not Reinventing the Wheel

We could not have succeeded in building the Vicks business in India without the support of the native traders who took our products deep into the hinterland, to every nook and corner of a very large country. Many times we faced the temptation to set up an alternative Western-style distribution network. Fortunately, we never gave in to it. Instead, we chose each time to continue relying on the native system.

Following the practice of British companies in India, we appointed the largest wholesaler in each major town to become our exclusive stock point and direct customer. We called this wholesaler our stockist. Once a month our salesman visited the stockist, and together they went from shop to shop redistributing our products to the retailers and wholesalers of the town. The largest stockist in each state also became our Carrying-and-Forwarding Agent (in other words, our depot) for reshipping our goods to stockists in smaller towns. Over time, our stockists expanded their functions. They now work exclusively on P&G business under the supervision of our salesmen; they hire local salesmen who provide interim coverage of the market between the visits of our salesmen; they run vans to cover satellite villages and help us penetrate the interior; they conduct local promotions and advertising campaigns; and they are P&G's ambassadors and lifeline in the local community. The stockists perform all these services for a 5% commission, and our receivables are down to six days outstanding.

In our own backyard, we found and adopted an efficient low-cost distribution system perfected by Indian traders over hundreds of years. Thank God we chose to build on it rather than reinvent the wheel.

On Taking Ancient Medicine

We learned our most important lesson about diversity and tapping into roots shortly after I became head of the company in the early 1980s. We found ourselves against a wall. The chemists and pharmacists had united nationwide and decided to target our company and boycott our products in their fight for higher margins from the entire industry. At the same time, productivity at our plant was falling, while wages kept rising. As a result, our profitability had plummeted to two percent of sales.

Beset by a hostile environment, we turned inward. The answer to our problems came as a flash of insight about our roots, for we suddenly realized that Vicks Vaporub and other Vicks products were all-natural, herbal formulas. All their ingredients were found in thousand-year-old Sanskrit texts. What was more, this ancient *Ayurvedic* system of medicine enjoyed the special patronage of the government. If we could change our government registration from Western medicine to Indian medicine, we could expand our distribution to food shops, general stores, and street kiosks and thus reduce dependence on the pharmacists. By making our products more accessible, we would enhance consumer satisfaction and build competitive advantage. What was more, a new registration would also allow us to set up a new plant for Vicks in a tax-advantaged "backward area," where we could raise productivity dramatically by means of improved technology, better work practices, and lower labor costs.

I first tested the waters with our lawyers, who thought our solution to the problem quite wonderful. We then went to the government in Delhi, which was deeply impressed to discover all the elements of Vaporub's formula in the ancient texts. They advised to check with the local FDA in Bombay. The regulators at the FDA couldn't find a single fault with our case and, to our surprise and delight, promptly gave us a new registration.

Lo and behold, all the obstacles were gone! Our sales force heroically and rapidly expanded the distribution of our products to the nondrug trade, tripling the outlets which carried Vicks to roughly 750,000 stores. Consumers were happy that they could buy our products at every street corner. At the same time we quickly built a new plant near Hyderabad, where productivity was four times what it was in our Bombay plant. Our after-tax profits rose from 2% to 12% of sales, and we became a blue chip on the Bombay Stock Exchange.

Finally, we decided to return the compliment to the Indian system of medicine. We persuaded our headquarters to let us establish an R&D Center to investigate additional all-natural, Ayurvedic therapies for coughs and colds. When I first mooted this idea, my bosses at the head office in the United States practically fell off their chairs. Slowly, however, the idea of all-natural, safe, and effective remedies for a self-limiting ailment sold around the world under the Vicks name grew on them.

We set up labs in Bombay under the leadership of a fine Indian scientist who had studied in the United States. They began by creating a computerized data bank of herbs and formulas from the ancient texts; they invented a "finger-printing" process to standardize herbal raw materials with the help of computers; and they organized clinical trials in Bombay hospitals to confirm the safety and efficacy of the new products. We now have two products being successfully sold in the Indian market—Vicks Vaposyrup, an all-natural cough liquid, and Vicks Hot-sip, a hot drink for coughs and colds. The lab today is part of P&G's global health-care research effort and has 40 scientists and technicians working with state-of-the-art equipment.

Of Local Passions and Golden Ghettos

The story of Vicks in India brings up a mistaken notion about how multinationals build global brands. The popular conception is that you start with a powerful brand name, add standardized product, packaging, and advertising, push a button, and bingo—you are on the way to capturing global markets. Marlboro, Coke, Sony Walkman, and Levis are cited as examples of this strategy.

But if it's all so easy, why have so many powerful brands floundered? Without going into the standardization versus adaptation debate, the Vicks story demonstrates at least one key ingredient for global market success: *the importance of local passion.* If local managers believe a product is theirs, then local consumers will believe it too. Indeed, a survey of Indian consumers a few years ago showed that 70% believed Vicks was an Indian brand.

What is the universal idea behind Vicks Vaporub's success in India? What is it that made it sell? Was it "rubbing it on the child with tender, loving care?" Could that idea be revived in the United States? Some people argue that the United States has become such a rushed society that mothers no longer have time to use a bedtime rub on their children when they've got a cold. Others feel that Vaporub could make its marketing more meaningful by striking a more contemporary note.

The Vicks story shows that a focus on the particular brings business rewards. But there are also psychic rewards for the manager who invests in the local. Going back to my roots reinvigorated me as a person and brought a certain fullness to my life. Not only was it pleasant to see familiar brown faces on the street, it also was enormously satisfying to be a part of the intense social life of the neighborhood, to experience the joys and sorrows of politics, and to share in the common fate of the nation. But at another level I also began to think of my work as a part of nation building, especially training and developing the next generation of young managers who would run the company and the country. It discharged a debt to my tutor at Harvard and a responsibility that we all have to the future.

Equally, it seems to me, there are powerful though less obvious psychic rewards for an international manager on transfer overseas who chooses to get involved in the local community. When such people approach the new country with an open mind, learn the local language, and make friends with colleagues and neighbors, they gain access to the wealth of a new culture. Not only will they be more effective as managers, they also will live fuller, richer lives.

Unfortunately, my experience in Mexico indicates that many expatriate managers live in "golden ghettos" of ease with little genuine contact with locals other than servants. Is it any surprise that they become isolated and complain of rootlessness and alienation in their new environment? The lesson for global companies is to give each international manager a local "mentor" who will open doors to the community. Ultimately, however, it is the responsibility of individual managers to open their minds, plunge into their local communities, and try to make them their own.

On Global Thinking

It would be wrong to conclude from the Vicks story that managing a global brand is purely a local affair. On the contrary, the winners in the new borderless economy will be the brands and companies that make best use of the richness of experience they get from their geographical diversity. Multinational companies have a natural advantage over local companies because they have talented people solving similar problems for identical brands in different parts of the world, and these brand managers can learn from each other's successes and failures. If a good idea emerges in Egypt, a smart brand manager in Malaysia or Venezuela will at least give it a test.

The Surat lady's teakettle became the basis of a national campaign in India. "One-pointedness" emerged from a hole-in-the-wall in Bombay, but it became the fulcrum on which we built a world-class business over a generation. Advertising for colds during the hot monsoon months seems highly parochial, but it taught us the importance of advertising year round in other places. The stockist system found applicability in Indonesia and China.

Even the strange Ayurvedic system of medicine might plausibly be reapplied in the form of efficacious herbal remedies for common ailments in Western countries.

Business truths are invariably local in origin, but they are often expressions of fundamental human needs that are the same worldwide. Local insights with a universal character thus can become quickly global—though only in the hands of flexible, open-minded managers who can translate such ideas into new circumstances with sensitivity and understanding. My admonition to think local is only half the answer. Managers also must remember to think global. The insights we glean from each microcosm are ultimately universal.

Organizational specialists often express a fear that companies will demotivate their local managers by asking them to execute standardized global marketing packages. If they impose these standardized marketing solutions too rigidly, then this fear may be justified. However, this does not happen in successful companies. In fact, the more common disease in a global company is the "not invented here" syndrome, which especially afflicts subsidiaries and managers whose local triumphs have left them arrogant and unwilling to learn from successes in other parts of the world.

We in India were no different. But slowly and painfully we learned that useful lessons can emerge anywhere. For all our efforts to tap into the roots of Indian pluralism, we were dealing with a global brand. The product itself, the positioning, and the packaging were basically the same everywhere. Global brands are not free-for-alls, with each subsidiary doing its own thing. It took us six months, for example, to persuade our marketing people to try a new advertising idea for Vaporub that came from Mexico. It asked the consumer to use Vaporub on three parts of the body to obtain three types of relief. When we finally tried "Three-by-Three" in our advertising, it worked brilliantly.

It is deeply wrong to believe that going global is a one-stop, packaged decision. Local managers can add enormous value as they tap into local roots for insights. But it is equally wrong to neglect the integrity of the brand's core elements. Smart global managers nourish each blade of grass without neglecting the garden as a whole.

On Karma

Although the principles of managing a business in the Third World are the same as in the West, there are still big differences between the two. For me, the greatest of these is the pervasive reality of poverty.

I have lost the towering confidence of my youth, when I believed that socialism could wipe away poverty. The problem of socialism is one of performance, not vision. If it worked, we would all be socialists. Ironically, the legacy of the collectivist bias in Indian thinking has been the perpetuation of poverty. We created an over-regulated private sector and an inefficient public sector. We did not allow the economy to grow and produce the surplus that might have paid for direct poverty programs. We created an exploitative bureaucracy that fed on itself. Today, happily, we are righting the balance by liberalizing the economy, reducing state control, and restoring legitimacy to the market. I am confident that these changes will foster the entrepreneurialism and eco-nomic vitality India needs to create prosperity and eliminate the destitution of so many of its people.

Despite the problems, I find managers in India and other poor countries more optimistic than their counterparts in rich nations. The reason is that we believe our children will be better off than our parents were, and this idea is a great source of strength. We see our managerial work as nation building. We are the benign harbingers of technology and modernity. As we learn to manage complex enterprises, we empower people with the confidence they need to become responsible, innovative, and self-reliant.

It seems to come down to commitment. In committing to our work we commit to a here and now, to a particular place and time. The meaning in our lives comes from nourishing a particular blade of grass. It comes from absorbing ourselves so deeply in the microcosm of our work that we forget ourselves, especially our egos. The difference between subject and object disappears. The Sanskrit phrase *nishkama karma* describes this state of utter absorption, in which people act for the sake of the action, not for the sake of the reward from the action. This is also the meaning of happiness.

Reading 7-2   Subsidiary Initiative to Develop New Markets

Julian Birkinshaw and Nick Fry

In 1980, NCR's Scottish subsidiary in Dundee was on the verge of closure. The operation had been

▌ The authors wish to thank Gunnar Hedlund, Bruce Kogut, and seminar participants at the Institute of International Business for their helpful comments on earlier drafts. The research on which this paper is based has been reported in two academic journal articles: "Entrepreneurship in Multinational Corporations: The Characteristics of Subsidiary Initiatives," *Strategic Management Journal*, 1997; and "How Subsidiary Mandates and Gained and Lost," *Journal of International Business Studies*, 1996.
▌ Julian Birkinshaw, Assistant Professor, Institute of International Business, Stockholm School of Economics; and Nick Fry, Professor, Richard Ivey School of Business, University of Western Ontario, October 1997.

established as a second-source manufacturer of NCR products, but a combination of technological changes in the marketplace and internal problems had seen it shrink from 6,500 employees in 1969 to just 770 in 1980. Dundee's most promising product, the automatic teller machine (ATM), was struggling in the British marketplace because of serious quality problems.

Jim Adamson, the newly-appointed general manager, had a mandate to turn the operation around or close it. At an operational level, Adamson worked on improving manufacturing quality and restoring the confidence of major customers. At a more strategic level, he began to develop a vision for Dundee as NCR's strategic centre for the ATM business. Product development responsibility officially lay with HQ in Dayton, but Adamson began directing resources towards upgrading and renewing the Dundee product line to meet the emerging demands of the big British banks, Dundee's key customers. Faced with active resistance from the development group in Dayton, Adamson pursued a delicate strategy of co-operating with them while continuing privately to sponsor Dundee's independent research program.

A successful product upgrade in 1982 was followed 18 months later by a next-generation ATM that set new standards in functionality, reliability and serviceability. Dundee's global market share reached 20% in 1984. The following year, responsibility for the global ATM business was officially transferred from Dayton to Dundee. Adamson had secured his vision of a self-sufficient ATM business; and by 1986, Dundee had secured 35% of world-wide shipments, a clear lead over competitors IBM and Diebold.

Apart from being an exemplary story of turnaround management and strong leadership, the NCR Dundee case provides insight into the changing relationship between headquarters and subsidiaries in large multinational corporations (MNCs). NCR Dundee developed over a period of five years from being a second-source manufacturer, entirely reliant on Dayton for product specifications, to a self-sufficient operation with leading-edge expertise in ATM development. More importantly, this turnaround went far beyond what corporate management had requested: indeed, Adamson's shift into product development was actively resisted by many people at headquarters who saw Dayton as the global centre for ATM development. Ultimately, it was Adamson's deliberately unconventional and somewhat subversive approach that provided the impetus for Dundee's resurgence, and led to NCR's world-leading position in the ATM industry.[1]

The NCR Dundee case is typical of what we call *subsidiary initiative:* the proactive and deliberate pursuit of a new business opportunity by a subsidiary company, undertaken with a view to expand the subsidiary's scope of responsibility in a manner consistent with the strategic goals of the MNC. Subsidiary initiative is important for two reasons. It is the principal means by which multinational corporations tap into new opportunities in markets around the world; and it enhances operational efficiency through internal competition between units. But at the same time, subsidiary initiative is an elusive beast. Many of the corporations we studied actively discouraged entrepreneurial efforts in their subsidiaries around the world, while others agreed to the concept in principle but hindered its development in practise. Subsidiary managers, it appears, need to have a lot of tactical savvy, persistence, and luck if they are to be effective in their pursuit of initiatives. In the words of one subsidiary manager, there is a "corporate immune system"[2] lurking in most large organizations, whose role is to kill off all intruding initiatives for fear that they might infect the rest of the organism.

In this paper we report on a four-year research study of subsidiary initiative in five countries (see appendix for details of methodology). Our study examined the strategies used by subsidiary managers to get through the corporate immune system in their parent companies, and the types of resistance they faced. The research also revealed a subtle shift in the locus of responsibility between headquarters and subsidiary. Initiative shows that subsidiary managers are beginning to take responsibility for the destiny of their operations, which in turn suggests a more central role for subsidiary units in the implementation of corporate strategy than previously recognized. It also suggests a lot of management issues for parent company managers

---

[1]The NCR Dundee story is taken from personal interviews; research undertaken by Graeme Martin at Dundee Business School; and Kotter, J., *A Force for Change* (New York: Free Press, 1990).

[2]We are indebted to Gerhard Schmidt of HP who first suggested this concept of the corporate immune system. The theoretical underpinnings of the concept are developed more fully in a separate paper, Birkinshaw, J.M. and J. Ridderstråle, "Fighting the Corporate Immune System: A Process Study of Peripheral Initiatives in Large Multinational Corporations," *International Business Review,* 1999: 149–180.

Figure 1   The External Initiative Process

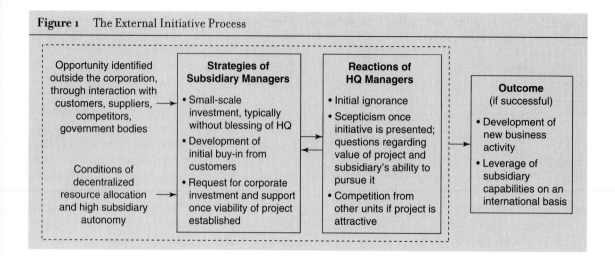

as they re-appraise their innate suspicion of maverick subsidiary managers and learn how to exploit, rather than stifle, the latent entrepreneurship in far-flung operations.

Subsidiary Initiative—Two Distinct Forms   It became clear to us early on this research that subsidiary initiative took two distinct forms.[3] One form—which the NCR Dundee case typifies—was *externally focused*. It involved the identification of new or enhanced business opportunities through interaction with customers, suppliers and government bodies in the subsidiary's marketplace. The other form was *internally focused*. It involved the identification of new business opportunities that the subsidiary could take on *within the existing boundaries of the corporation*. For example, we identified cases of subsidiaries bidding internally for planned global-scale investments, and cases of subsidiaries identifying poorly-performing HQ-based activities that they could take over responsibility for.

The common theme to external and internal initiatives was the entrepreneurial component: the need for proactive, pushy, and sometimes machi-

avellian tactics by subsidiary managers as they sought to gain currency for their projects in headquarters; and the sceptical reaction of HQ managers for whom subsidiary initiative was something of an oxymoron. In many respects, however, the two forms of initiative were very different. They were pursued with distinctly different tactics, they faced different forms of resistance, and they had significantly different impacts on the management of the MNC as a whole.

External Initiatives   External initiatives were typically built on the un-met demands of customers in the local marketplace. In the NCR Dundee case, Barclays and the other major British banks were investing heavily in ATMs, so the Dundee development group worked with the banks in order to incorporate their product needs into the next generation of ATMs (Figure 1). There were several variants on this theme:

- At GE Canada, the business development manager responded in 1991 to a government-sponsored program looking for energy-efficient lighting in federal buildings by starting up an entirely new business called GE Energy Management.[4]

---

[3]Four types of initiative were identified in the Canadian study, reported in the Birkinshaw, J. "Entrepreneurship in Multinational Corporations: The Characteristics of Subsidiary Initiatives," *Strategic Management Journal*, 1997. However, the subsequent research in Scotland and Sweden has indicated that a coarser distinction into just two types is more generalizable.

[4]This example is drawn from a teaching case "The GE Energy Management Initiative," page 711 of this volume.

- Pharma's British subsidiary established a joint venture with a small U.K. company in 1992 to develop a new technology for transmitting drugs through the skin.[5]
- Hewlett-Packard's Panacom subsidiary based in Waterloo, Canada, identified an emerging market for the "X terminal," a RISC-chip based workstation, through international industry contacts.

No less critical than the identification of an interesting business opportunity was the need for a relatively high degree of autonomy in the subsidiary. Faced with the strong likelihood of rejection if the project had been presented to HQ management in its embryonic form, subsidiary managers preferred to do the initial development work with their own funds. Hewlett-Packard (Canada), for example, had access to development funds for country-specific projects during the 1980s, which facilitated the X-terminal development as well as several other projects. On the other hand, many subsidiaries did not have this level of autonomy. Some were able to assemble "skunkworks" groups working in their own time to demonstrate the viability of their ideas. Others could not gain access to development funds with the result that their promising ideas languished.

The initiative champion always emerged in the early stages of the initiative. He or she was typically the individual who identified the business opportunity in the first place, though sometimes the subsidiary general manager took ownership of the project because of its importance to the subsidiary. A surprisingly consistent strategy was adopted by initiative champions. First, the idea was tested in a small way, using subsidiary resources and without the knowledge of HQ. As the project took shape, the initiative champion sought out allies: typically local customers who were interested in buying the product or service, but sometimes also personal contacts or mentors at HQ. Finally, once the viability of the project had been demonstrated, the champion made

a formal representation to HQ management and requested their investment and support. This basic model was seen in a variety of guises:

- At NCR Dundee, Jim Adamson's initial product development efforts were undertaken against the will of the R&D group in Dayton, but once the market-success of Dundee's second generation product was self-apparent, HQ management bowed to the inevitable and transferred official responsibility for ATM development to Dundee.
- Hewlett-Packard (Canada)'s former president Malcolm Gissing funded a small Calgary development group in 1985 to develop an oil-well data management system. For seven years the group existed as an "orphan" business without a line of reporting through one of HP's business groups. In 1992 the group finally achieved corporate legitimacy when it became a business unit within the Test and Measurement division.
- In 1987 a small group of engineers in Honeywell Canada bootlegged a PC-interface for Honeywell's TDC3000 process control system. The system, known as PCNM, quickly gained support with a number of Canadian customers. The development group subsequently gained permission from HQ management in Phoenix to build PCNM as a world standard product.

As suggested by these vignettes, other parts of the corporation were almost universally opposed to the subsidiary's initiative. We termed this collective resistance the corporate immune system, to illustrate its apparent intention to kill off the intruding initiative. We observed a wide variety of ways in which resistance to initiative was manifested:

- Pharma's British subsidiary encountered outright opposition from the HQ development group whose toes they were treading on. The HQ development group eventually vetoed the project, though fortunately for the British development group it was possible to arrange alternative funding through the marketing arm of the company.
- Two HP Canada initiatives, the X terminal and the Calgary development group, were challenged by U.S.-based divisions that were under-

---

[5]Pharma is the disguised name of a European pharmaceuticals corporation.

taking development work in similar areas. In both cases, the U.S. division argued that the development in question fell within their charter, and that the Canadian operation should be closed down.

- GE Canada's energy management business was almost closed down when its parent division in the US, GE Supply, rationalized its operations in 1994. The problem was not that the Energy Management business was performing badly: it was simply too small, and too far from GE Supply's core business area, to survive the rationalization.

The combination of outright opposition, internal competition and passive indifference represented a challenging set of obstacles for the initiative champions. Just over half of the external initiatives we studied survived this process, but this success rate is probably overstated because it represents only those stories that subsidiary managers were willing to share with us. Our sense is that the research focused on the latter parts of a long and mostly invisible process. Many other initiatives fell at the first hurdle or never got out of the starting blocks.

But for those initiatives that survived, the rewards for the subsidiary were impressive. NCR Dundee became a $1 billion operation; HP Canada's X terminal business reached sales levels of $120 million four years after its inception; and for GE Canada a market-leading position was

established in the emerging energy efficiency industry. For the corporation as a whole, the rewards were multi-faceted. Most obviously, NCR, HP, GE and others gained new and vibrant businesses in emerging areas. More subtly, they also benefited from the development and maturation of one of their foreign subsidiaries. Some might argue that this is a mixed blessing, but if we see business becoming ever more global, then the nurturing of new and valuable capabilities in outlying parts of the multinational network can only heighten the MNC's global reach.

Internal Initiatives   Internal initiatives were built on opportunities identified within the boundaries of the corporation. Subsidiary managers in the study were very conscious of their own unit's strengths and weaknesses, and were frequently on the lookout for new activities they could take on that dovetailed with their capabilities (Figure 2). The following examples illustrate the scope of ideas pursued:

- IBM began manufacturing PCs in Greenock, Scotland in 1982. Towards the end of the 1980s, plant management began looking for ways to extend the scope of their operations. In 1991 they identified a small monitor development group near London as a logical complement to their manufacturing, and succeeded in getting it relocated to Greenock. Subsequently, they iden-

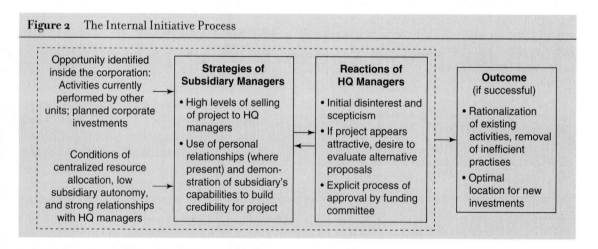

Figure 2   The Internal Initiative Process

| Opportunity identified inside the corporation: Activities currently performed by other units; planned corporate investments

Conditions of centralized resource allocation, low subsidiary autonomy, and strong relationships with HQ managers | Strategies of Subsidiary Managers

• High levels of selling of project to HQ managers
• Use of personal relationships (where present) and demonstration of subsidiary's capabilities to build credibility for project | Reactions of HQ Managers

• Initial disinterest and scepticism
• If project appears attractive, desire to evaluate alternative proposals
• Explicit process of approval by funding committee | Outcome (if successful)

• Rationalization of existing activities, removal of inefficient practises
• Optimal location for new investments |

tified the order fulfilment and help centre functions as Europe-wide activities that could potentially be centralized in Greenock. Both initiatives were successful.

- Back in 1972, a factory manager in Honeywell Canada was touring the plant of a sister subsidiary in the U.S. making a control switch, and saw a great opportunity. He proposed to HQ that the Canadian plant take over responsibility for the manufacture of the control switch on a North American basis.

- Monsanto Canada's top management identified an interesting proposal in the corporation's long range plan in 1991. Monsanto was developing a new formulation for its best-selling agrochemical product, with the intention of bringing it to market around 1996. Canadian management saw a great opportunity to argue for the investment to be made in Canada because of the country's strong agricultural industry.

Two conditions facilitated the development of internal initiatives. First, and in marked contrast to external initiatives, internal initiatives needed a relatively tight level of integration into the corporate system. Subsidiary managers emphasized that it was important for them to be tied in to the corporate network so that they became aware of investment opportunities at the earliest possible time: As one manager observed, "the best way to win a competitive investment is to write the specifications." One 3M Canada manager accidentally heard about an embryonic investment plan on a routine visit to St Paul, which subsequently led to a $20 million investment in Canada.

Second, the subsidiary had to have, or be prepared to work hard for, a reputation as a trustworthy and reliable operation. Subsidiary managers were typically confronted with a simple implicit challenge: Why would we risk investing in a foreign country when we can stick with tried-and-tested solutions closer to home? The response in many cases was to mitigate the risk by capitalizing on personal contacts at HQ. In other cases, such as IBM Scotland, initiative success was built on the

back of many years of manufacturing excellence. In the absence of either contacts or reputation, however, the subsidiary's prospects were very limited.

Unlike external initiatives, that typically avoided confrontation with HQ managers in the early stages, internal initiatives had to pursue a more orthodox line of attack through the formal lines of authority. Monsanto Canada's initiative, described above, led to the establishment of a group whose role was to assess four possible locations for the new agrochemical investment. Similarly, 3M Canada pursued several initiatives aimed at winning new manufacturing investments in Canada, each of which had to pass through two operating committees in the U.S. The process was methodical and incremental, with subsidiary management gradually moving up through the corporate hierarchy building support and commitment from all the key individuals. Often this process took up to a year. In one case, the initiative was put on hold for two years until the arrival of a new manufacturing director in the U.S. who was more amenable to the proposal.

Two additional tactics were observed in internal initiatives. One was a two-pronged approach. The initiative champion made a formal proposal through the official lines of authority. At the same time, the subsidiary president utilized his personal contacts at a much higher level in HQ to build legitimacy for the proposal and smooth its course through the system. The second was the use of a *quid pro quo,* some sort of concession by the subsidiary to compensate the losing party. The best example of this was Honeywell's Canada's proposal in 1986 that it become the sole north American manufacturer of zone valves and "fan and limit" devices. The proposal encountered strong resistance from the plant in Minnesota that was currently making these products for the U.S. However, a deal was negotiated whereby the Toronto plant would swap its other manufacturing responsibilities for the exclusive production of zone valves and fan and limit devices. Both plants ended up shedding a few jobs, but both emerged with higher volumes and more efficient operations.

Internal initiatives were, as a matter of course, competitive. Either the subsidiary was challenging other units for a new investment, or it was proposing a transfer that would leave the previous incumbent short. Resistance from the corporate immune systems was therefore inevitable, and it took a variety of forms.

- The first line of defence was passive disinterest: If we ignore it, maybe it will go away. Honeywell Canada's initial proposal for a manufacturing rationalization came back with "superficial comments." As one manager noted, it was seen as a "strategic plan for the top shelf, not something to incite quantum change."
- The second line of defence was scepticism about the subsidiary's abilities, and a suggestion that other options be considered. Monsanto Canada initially faced this reaction when it proposed locating the new agrochemical investment in Canada, but through an innovative design they were able to demonstrate a superior expected rate of return over the competing location in the U.S.
- The third line of defence was outright resistance. In one case, the magnitude of the loss that the U.S. operation faced provoked very strong feelings that the initiative should be halted. As one manager recalled, "There was extreme amount of local resistance, marketing, engineering, everybody. How could you ship your son the foster child, how could you do that? Look at all the things that could go wrong! We've earned the right to continue."

Resistance of various forms is, of course, only to be expected. HQ managers were confronted with possible changes that could cause them to lose out; they were naturally cautious when it came to sanctioning proposals from subsidiary managers with whom they were not personally familiar; and in some cases there was an element of ethnocentrism that made it hard to accept that important activities would be transferred from the home country to a foreign subsidiary. This last point should not be overstated, because top management in Honeywell, Monsanto and several of the other companies in the study were vocal supporters of the need to globalize their operations. Nevertheless, ethnocentric attitudes still endured in various parts of the organization, as many of the subsidiary managers interviewed in this research discovered.

At first glance, the outcome from internal initiatives was less spectacular than that observed in external initiatives. For IBM Scotland, the result was an "extended value chain" from development through to market support; for 3M Canada, it was a robust, export-oriented manufacturing operation. For Monsanto Canada, it was a significant greenfield investment in the heart of the company's large prairie market. But in each case the net impact for the corporation as a whole appeared small. There were no new products, and no immediate new customers. The cake was simply split in a different way, with the subsidiary getting a larger slice.

However, a simple analysis of the configuration of activities before and after the initiative does not tell the whole story. As Gordon Brown, the controller of IBM's Greenock plant commented, "by extending the value chain and linking various activities together in one location, millions of dollars were saved, customer satisfaction improved, and market share increased." In essence, the process itself created a new vitality in the initiative-taking subsidiary, and the subsequent improvements in performance were often spectacular.

But the enduring value of internal initiatives was rather more subtle. We saw the subsidiary managers as entrepreneurs, looking for inefficient practises within the multinational system and proposing solutions to make them more efficient. Many internal sourcing relationships, for example, are retained because they have always been organized in a certain way. But guaranteed sales can make a plant lazy, and soon the internal customer is putting up with a sub-standard product or an inflated price from its supplier. Internal initiatives offer a mechanism for inefficient sourcing relationships to be changed. And their threat fosters a more challenging environment that keeps manufacturing operations on their toes. The same principle applies to other value-adding activities. We saw several cases

Figure 3   Two Subsidiary Roles

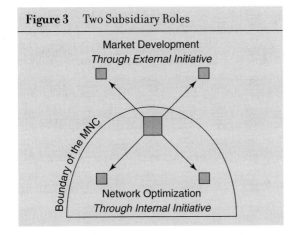

Market Development
Through External Initiative

Boundary of the MNC

Network Optimization
Through Internal Initiative

of product management jobs being shifted from the US to Canada, for example, because a strong business case could be made that the jobs would be undertaken more efficiently in Canada.

Towards a Model of Internal Competition   Our study suggests two potentially important roles for foreign subsidiaries (Figure 3). The first role is driven by external initiative and can be stylized as one of *market development*. This role is well-documented in the literature.[6] It sees the subsidiary both identifying and acting on new business opportunities in its local market. The second role is less well understood. We will refer to it *network optimization* because it envisions the subsidiary seeking out and eliminating inefficient activities within the multinational network. The process of network optimization, of course, is driven by internal initiative. Our suggestion is that some subsidiaries, by virtue of their history, their local environment, or their management, will pursue market development roles, while others, for equally circumstantial reasons, will pursue network optimization roles. A

third group are likely to fulfil neither role, but our belief is that many of these could move towards one or other of the first two roles. Figure 3 illustrates this perspective.

The network optimization model has some far-reaching implications. First, it suggests that many of the value-adding activities being undertaken within the boundaries of the MNC are "contestable," that is they could potentially be performed by a number of different units. Of course, a great many activities are firmly embedded in their local environment, or they are so large and asset-specific that they could not in practical terms be moved. But in the course of this study we saw examples of manufacturing, development, logistics, marketing, and business management activities changing locations. Much of what is done inside the MNC appears to be neutral with regard to its physical location. And increasingly there are subsidiaries looking to "win" some of the more mobile activities that are not locked in to a single location. The trend, therefore, is towards internal competition, as a mechanism through which activities are allocated and re-allocated within the MNC.

We must be careful not to overstate this point, because we are very aware of the inertia that inhibits a high level of fluidity within the corporate network, as well as the need for collaborative relationships between units. But there are a number of trends that will push MNCs more and more towards an organization model based on internal competition. One is the increasing globalization of business that reduces the cost of product and capital flows across borders. The second is the increasing use of internal benchmarking as a means of highlighting the relative efficiency levels of different units within the MNC. This trend is particularly critical in Europe where many MNCs are still going through the painful process of rationalizing their manufacturing networks. And the third is the growing level of initiative shown by subsidiary managers *and* inward investment agencies in their pursuit of "mobile" investment.

Faced with the changes described here, many of the subsidiary managers interviewed during this

---

[6]For example, Bartlett and Ghoshal refer to contributor and strategic leader subsidiaries, while many Canadian academics have used the concept of "world mandate" subsidiaries (see: Bartlett, C.A. and S. Ghoshal, "Tap Your Subsidiaries for Global Reach," *Harvard Business Review,* 1986; Etemad, H. and L.S. Dulude, *Managing the Multinational Subsidiary* (London: Croom Helm, 1986)).

study were thinking very hard about their future. Increasingly they were asking themselves: "What is the unique value added of this unit to this corporation? What do we do better than anyone else?" They were looking for what we might call their *sustainable* competitive advantage vis-à-vis their internal competitors. Two examples will clarify this idea:

- Motorola's East Kilbride operations was one of 16 around the world that fabricated silicon wafers for semiconductors. All the key performance measures such as cost, service and quality were easily compared, so new investments were (obviously) made in the top performing sites, of which East Kilbride was one. East Kilbride's management therefore had a clear goal, namely to stay ahead of their internal competitors on the key performance metrics. If this was achieved, the operation would be the recipient of new investment when times were good, and avoid closure when times are tough.

- Honeywell's Scottish subsidiary in Newhouse manufactured a range of control valves and related items for the European market. During the seventies and early eighties control valves were mechanical devices, but the general manager of Newhouse became aware of the impending shift towards electronic devices and he invested discretionary funds in the development of an electronic manufacturing capability. When, in 1991, corporate management decided to invest in a global-scale facility for electronic fan-coils, Newhouse was the obvious location because all the necessary capabilities were already in place.

East Kilbride's strategy was to be the lowest-cost/highest quality source for silicon wafers; Newhouse chose to differentiate itself from its sister plants around the world by investing in a new technology.[7] Both strategies appeared to create sustainable positions for the subsidiaries in question. More

importantly, they both offered clearly-defined benefits to their corporate parents.

Initiative, viewed in this way, offers a win-win solution through which subsidiary growth is achieved in a manner that also contributes to the MNC's competitive advantage. However, it is not always the case that HQ and subsidiary management's views are in harmony. In the last part of this paper we will examine some of the perceptions, mostly held by HQ managers, that engendered a certain uneasiness whenever we discussed subsidiary initiative, and that lay behind the resistance we observed in our case studies.

Two Contrarian Views: The Dangers Inherent in Initiative   In the course of our research we observed many instances where there were no signs of subsidiary initiative, and we heard many arguments in opposition to our view that subsidiary initiative should be encouraged. These opposing arguments took two basic forms.

The first opposing perspective saw subsidiary initiative as acceptable under certain conditions. It is widely accepted that different subsidiaries have different roles—some are strategic centres, some have contributory roles, others are just implementers of corporate strategy. Using this approach, some people argued that only those subsidiaries at the more "evolved" end of the spectrum should be taking initiative. This group, they argued, had the capabilities on which further development could be based, and the management expertise necessary to drive initiatives to completion. The rest were better suited to focusing on their implementational roles.

We found considerable evidence to support this perspective. Just under half of the subsidiaries we surveyed claimed to have pursued some form of initiative in the last five years; the rest saw themselves as implementers. When asked why they had not pursued initiatives, the latter group typically responded with comments such as "We are exclusively focused on meeting the needs of our local customers," "It is not appropriate for us at this stage" or "It is very difficult because of the level of centralization in the corporation." Clearly there are fundamental

---

[7]It should be clear that this distinction parallels Michael Porter's generic strategies as the basis for sustainable advantage vis-à-vis industry competitors. See Porter, M.E., *Competitive Strategy* (New York: Free Press, 1980).

differences between the two groups that are at least in part based on level of subsidiary development.

But a difficult question remains: How does a passive subsidiary transform itself into an initiative-taking one? There is evidently a development process that subsidiaries go through over time, which sees them gradually build up resources, take on more and more responsibilities, and build their credibility within the corporation. Our evidence suggests that initiative is an important step in the development process. However, it may also be one that HQ management will actively resist. Initiative, after all, is easy to view as insubordination, which is galling for a corporate parent that is accustomed to a more docile and obedient subsidiary.

The "growing pains" experienced by Pharma's UK subsidiary were typical in this regard. This subsidiary saw itself providing strategic leadership in one area of drug development, while managers at HQ saw it taking a much more modest marketing and drug-testing role. As a result the two sides clashed repeatedly over a five year period. The subsidiary proposed a series of initiatives, and business unit managers at HQ stalled, challenged, or rejected them all. The process was "exhausting and frustrating" for both sides, and after five years no clear progress had been made towards a more harmonious relationship. 3M Canada's experience was more constructive. In this case, management started small, taking on small manufacturing operations that plants in the US did not even want. Gradually 3M Canada built up their manufacturing capabilities which led to some measure of credibility south of the border. Eventually this gave them the self-confidence and legitimacy to pursue more significant initiatives.

There is one other problem with an approach to subsidiary management that sees some as initiative-takers and others as passive implementers. If the objective of initiative is to identify and pursue new opportunities, how can corporate management know in advance where those opportunities will arise? If the Japanese, German and British subsidiaries are charged with market development and network optimization responsibilities, what happens to the great new business opportunity spotted by the Italian general manager? Our belief is that *every* subsidiary needs to have a latent entrepreneurial role, so that opportunities can be pursued wherever they arise. This does not mean letting every subsidiary wander off to pursue its own pet projects, but it does require that the corporate systems make it possible for long-shots to find their way through the corporate immune system.

We should dwell on this point a little longer, just because it is typically the least clearly understood part of our argument. Taken to extremes, an organizational system that simply encouraged initiative would quickly lead to anarchy. Initiatives would spring up in areas that lay far beyond the espoused business domain of the corporation; and head office managers would be inundated with proposals from subsidiary units that made little or no strategic sense. Our approach is more measured. Control systems are clearly needed to constrain the number of ill-thought-out initiatives, but increasingly these systems should be based on the development of a shared understanding of the corporation's strategic priorities, rather than on direct intervention into the affairs of the subsidiary. The concept is similar to that of employee empowerment. Subsidiary managers are given the tools they need to manage their operation effectively, and a clear indication of the boundaries of their responsibilities. Within those limits they are then given a free rein to pursue opportunities as they see fit, on the assumption that they understand their operation, and the local marketplace, better than the corporate managers sitting in a distant head office. New roles and responsibilities are therefore *assumed* by the subsidiary, rather than *assigned* from above, an important distinction.[8] Again, control systems are needed to make it work, but the philosophy of empowerment underlying this model shifts the headquarters-subsidiary

---

[8]This distinction was originally made by Hagström, P., *The Wired MNC* (Institute of International Business, Stockholm School of Economics, 1993). It should be pointed out that one of the key differences between the current work and the work of Bartlett, Ghoshal, and Nohria on the "differentiated network" is the suggestion that roles can be assumed by subsidiary units rather than assigned by the parent company.

relationship from mutual suspicion and interference towards one of trust and shared destiny.

The second opposing view on initiative was even less accommodating. These managers simply felt that subsidiary initiative was more trouble than it was worth. One HQ manager recounted an unfortunate episode during which a subsidiary manager within his business area had undertaken a series of investments that he insisted were needed to build market presence, but which had led to spiralling costs and slow decision-making. For the HQ manager in question, subsidiary initiative meant opportunism and "empire building." He had since shifted towards a system of fairly tight control over subsidiary expenditure to ensure that such problems were not encountered again.

This position is difficult to argue against, because there are—as with this case—occasional cases of empire building where the subsidiary manager's initiative is not consistent with the best interests of the corporation. A priori, it is impossible to be sure whether the subsidiary managers is acting entrepreneurially or opportunistically. How the act is interpreted therefore comes down to whether there is a strong level of trust between the individuals in question. Unfortunately, one bad experience can jaundice the HQ manager's attitude forever.

We do not, therefore, propose that all subsidiary initiatives are put forward in good faith. While most probably are, it is the responsibility of managers in HQ to carefully scrutinize all initiatives, and to do their best to separate the wheat from the chaff. However, we do think there are compelling reasons for believing that initiative has a critical role in the transferral of information about the dispersed sources of expertise throughout the MNC. The discussions we had with one Scottish subsidiary manager—we will call him John Bryant—make this point most graphically. Bryant was in charge of a large Scottish assembly operation, a long way from the head office in Boston, Massachusetts. He saw the dedication with which the employees work, and he observed the high quality output that left the plant every day. Bryant knew that corporate management had a global network of plants to manage,

that they could not know in detail how each worked, but he believed his operation was one of the best. As the leader of 500 people, he was also personally concerned about their livelihood.

We asked him about initiative. Did he actively seek new investments for his plant? Bryant did not hesitate. "It is my *obligation* to seek out new investment" he responded. "No-one else is going to stand up for these workers at head office. They are doing a great job, and I owe it to them to build up this operation. I get very angry with some of my counterparts in other parts of the country, who just toe the party line. They have followed their orders to the letter, but when I visit their plants I see unfulfilled potential everywhere."

Concluding Comments   Before subsidiary initiative becomes a legitimate and pervasive phenomenon in large MNCs, there will have to be some significant, though quite subtle, shifts in the roles of subsidiary and parent company managers. For subsidiary managers, we see an emerging role that is fundamentally more entrepreneurial than has been historically recognized. As one manager in this research pointed out, "No-one in head office wakes up in the morning thinking about what they can do in Canada today." That responsibility lies with the subsidiary manager. He or she has to be prepared to identify opportunities and then build support for them in head office. But the process is difficult, and the manager runs the risk of wasting his or her efforts if the initiative is not well selected. The following points should be borne in mind:

- The magnitude of the initiative should be proportional to the reputation of the subsidiary in head office. One subsidiary management team in our study spent a decade pursuing a "big hit" investment to no avail. Now they are pursuing a host of smaller projects with considerable success.
- Management must understand the reasons why resistance is being encountered, and look for ways to mitigate it. If the initiative threatens to put some people out of a job, they should look for some form of compromise that can be inter-

preted as a win-win. If none of the HQ managers know them personally, they should try to involve someone with whom they have already developed a relationship.

- Nationalistic arguments should not be emphasized. As one manager put it "if I go down there wrapped in my Canadian flag, I provoke all sorts of unnecessary challenges." Rather, the imperative is to focus on the technical or economic arguments why the location (which just happens to be in Canada) makes sense.
- It is important to recognize that initiatives can be both externally- and internally-focused, and that most subsidiaries are good at only one type.

The emerging role for HQ managers is no less demanding. We envision a subtle shift through which managers become more open to new and challenging ideas from the peripheral parts of the organization. This does not mean abandoning the tried-and-tested systems by which new proposals are evaluated, but it does require a change in attitude that will encourage more subsidiary managers to bring their initiatives forward for consideration. Again, a few points to consider:

- Systems can be instituted that encourage the flow of initiatives in a controlled manner. Some corporations send out request-for-proposal invitations whenever major capital investments are planned; others have instituted "challenge" mechanisms for changing internal sourcing relationships.
- Other systems can be put in place with the simple objective of breaking down cross-national prejudices. Several corporations we studied used global business teams, secondments and transfers of senior managers, or they made a point of managing business units outside the home country. These approaches foster an environment in which subsidiary initiative is more welcome.
- It is important for HQ management to be clear on the difference between challenging and resisting an initiative. A challenge is a means of seeking additional information, looking at alternatives, and coming to a decision about the initiative's merits. Resistance uses many of the same techniques, but it is fundamentally prejudiced so it attaches greater importance to negative evidence.

Our purpose with this paper was to explore the strategies used by subsidiary managers in pursuit of initiative, understand the forms of resistance typically encountered, and to assess the implications of initiative for the management of the MNC. Our underlying premise should by now be clear: we believe strongly in the value of subsidiary initiative as a means of developing new markets and as a mechanism for improving the internal allocation of activities in the multinational. Nonetheless, there are also strong arguments against subsidiary initiative, and we have done our best to put these forward. We have collected some outstanding success stories during this research study, and our belief is that the potential exists for yet more. But subsidiary initiative remains a little-understood and risky proposition in most peoples' minds. Our hope is that this paper provides some clarification of the mechanisms, the possible benefits, and the potential costs of subsidiary initiative; and that it encourages managers to consider ways of fostering the appropriate shifts in behaviour that are needed for initiative to thrive.

Appendix: Research Methodology

The research study on which this paper is based consisted of two phases. In the first phase, we undertook intensive case-study interviews at both the subsidiary and corporate headquarters levels. 132 interviews were conducted in twenty subsidiaries and their parent companies, in the United States, Canada, Great Britain, Sweden and Belgium. During this interview phase we focused on specific initiatives that the subsidiaries had undertaken, in order to understand the process through which they came about, the resistance they faced, and their impact on the strategies of the parent companies.

The second phase was a large-sample questionnaire study of 260 subsidiary companies in three countries (Great Britain, Canada, Sweden). This study sought to empirically test the hypotheses developed in the first phase, and most critically the role played by subsidiary initiative as the mechanism through which subsidiaries gained international management responsibilities such as "centres of excellence" and "world product mandates."

CHAPTER 8

Preparing for the Future:
Evolution of the Transnational

In the 10 years since the first edition of this book was published, we have repeatedly been asked both by managers and by our students "what's next?" The model of the transnational company we have described in this book was drawn from the experiences of companies in the 1980s. How has leading-edge practice evolved since then? How must the transnational model evolve to respond to the needs of the future?

The question has been given an added urgency by the turmoil experienced by many of the world's largest MNCs over the last decade. Highly publicized problems in companies like Ford, Boeing, and Kodak—as well as the scandals that destroyed Enron and Worldcom—have led many to question the fundamental viability of companies as large, as diversified, and as geographically dispersed as these corporate behemoths. And it is not just in the United States where such problems have been emerging. In Europe, once revered names like ABB, Olivetti, and Philips have been making headlines more as problem cases than as role models. Even much admired Japanese companies such as Mazda, Yamaha, Toshiba, and the Industrial Bank of Japan have lost their lustre as deteriorating performance has led to layoffs and top-management changes.

Some critics have interpreted such turmoil in some of the largest and most visible MNCs as a sign that the era of the large worldwide companies may be over. Though many still survive and even dominate various geographic and business areas, these critics would have us believe that these are the last generation of dinosaurs still roaming the earth completely unaware of their inevitable and impending fate. The meteoric impact of simultaneous market and technological revolutions of the 1990s, they believe, will lead to the extinction of the entire population, to be replaced by more agile small companies or by a completely new genetically engineered species of "virtual corporations."[1]

Based on our own ongoing work in a number of companies, we believe that this news of the MNC's death is exaggerated. Indeed, our own research has indicated that it is precisely because of their experience in the international operating environment that such companies develop the best chance of surviving. Most obviously, this is due to their access to a wider scope of markets and resources and their ability to secure competitive positions and competencies unobtainable by purely domestic companies. But even more important, it is because the management in such companies gains invaluable experience in routinely dealing with the fast-changing, multidimensional

[1]For one example of this line of thinking, see T.W. Malone and R.J. Laubacher, "The Dawn of the E-lance Economy," *Harvard Business Review,* September–October 1998, pp. 145–52.

demands and opportunities that are part of the global business environment. Through this experience, they develop an organizational capability that is increasingly valuable in today's complex and dynamic operating context.

In many ways, therefore, the transnational organizational and management issues we have described represent perhaps one of the most advanced forms of the modern corporation. The core management challenge in all companies is to embrace rather than to deny or minimize environmental complexity and uncertainty, and the demanding context of the transnational organization provides the ideal laboratory in which to develop such skills. In short, the challenge of managing across borders is the ideal way to develop the skills required for managing across boundaries of all kinds in the modern corporation.

In this concluding chapter, we examine a number of the organizational transformations currently underway in MNCs, and we describe what we see as their emerging management model—which is one possible answer to the "what's next" question. In this process, we also suggest a new way of thinking about large companies. Instead of defining a large company in terms of a formal structure by which the overall company is divided into a series of business, geographic, and functional units, we describe it in terms of three core processes that characterize this new management approach. The entrepreneurial process drives the opportunity-seeking, externally focused ability of the organization to open new markets and create new businesses. The integration process allows it to link and leverage its dispersed worldwide resources and capabilities to build a successful company. The renewal process maintains its ability to challenge its own beliefs and practices and to continuously revitalize itself so as to develop an enduring institution. Effective management of these three processes also calls for some very different roles and tasks of frontline, middle, and top-level managers. We illustrate these organizational processes and management roles on the basis of the experiences of a number of different American, European, and Japanese companies.

The Entrepreneurial Process: Supporting and Aligning Initiatives

The traditional cross-border organization was built in a highly structured manner that allowed those at the top to coordinate and control the multifunctional, multibusiness, multinational operations. But this increasingly complex structure looks very different from the top than from the bottom (see Figure 8-1). From the top, the CEO sees order, symmetry, and uniformity—a neat instrument for step-by-step decomposition of the company's tasks and priorities. From the bottom, hapless frontline managers see a cloud of faceless controllers—a formless sponge that soaks up all their energy and time. The result, as described so colorfully by GE's Jack Welch, is "an organization that has its face toward the CEO and its backside toward the customer." The key assumption in these companies is that the entrepreneurial tasks would be carried out by the top management, while frontline managers would be primarily responsible for the operational implementation of top-down strategies. Such a management approach had not been a major constraint in the benevolent, high-growth environment that most companies enjoyed in the 1960s and 1970s. Throughout that period of rapid international market expansion, the

Figure 8-1   Top-Down versus Bottom-Up View of the Organization

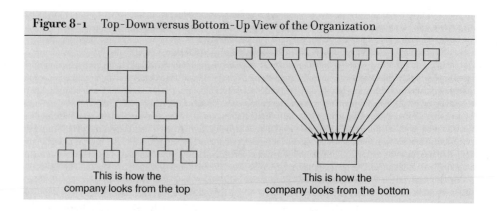

This is how the company looks from the top

This is how the company looks from the bottom

opportunities for growth were enormous and the key management challenge was to allocate a company's financial resources among competing opportunities.

But in recent years market growth has slowed and, as we pointed out in the first chapter of this book, the motivation for companies expanding abroad has shifted from one focused primarily on securing new markets or low-cost productive inputs, to a worldwide search for vital intelligence or scarce competencies not readily obtainable in the home market. As knowledge and specialized skills have gradually replaced capital as the scarcest and most important source of competitive advantage, managers have become increasingly aware that, unlike money, expertise cannot be accumulated at and allocated from the top. The critical task now is to use the knowledge and insight of widely dispersed frontline managers to identify and exploit fast-moving opportunities in a rich and complex global environment. In short, the entrepreneurial function must now be focused not at the top of the hierarchy but at the bottom.

The challenge of rebuilding the initiative, creativity, and drive of those on the front lines of worldwide operations does not, however, mean that a company must now become a society of geographically spread, independent entrepreneurs held together by a top management acting as a combination of a bank and a venture fund. Instead, companies will be required to build an organization in which a well-linked entrepreneurial process will drive the company's opportunity-seeking, externally focused ability to create and exploit avenues for profitable growth wherever they may arise. It is this integrated entrepreneurial process that will bring the worldwide company advantages to the local frontline entrepreneurs and save the entrepreneurial transnational corporation from the myths of internal venturing and "intrapreneurship" that have already proven so flawed in practice. The entrepreneurial transnational corporation will not be a hierarchical organization with fewer layers of management and a few scattered skunk works or genius awards: It will be a company built around a core entrepreneurial process that will drive everybody, and everything the company does.

The entrepreneurial process will require a close interplay among three key management roles. The frontline entrepreneurs will be the spearheads of the company, and their responsibility will be to create and pursue new growth opportunities. The coaches in senior-management positions will play a pivotal role in reviewing, developing, and

Figure 8-2 The Entrepreneurial Process: Management Roles and Tasks

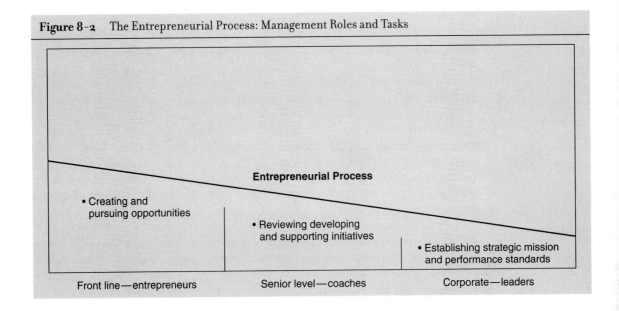

supporting the frontline initiatives. Corporate leaders at the top of the organization will establish the overall strategic mission of the company that will define the boundary within which the entrepreneurial initiatives must be contained; they will also set the highly demanding performance standards that these initiatives must meet (see Figure 8-2). Just as the structural units of corporate, divisional, and operating-unit management groups were the fundamental building blocks of the hierarchical division-alized company, the three management roles of entrepreneurs, coaches, and leaders and their interrelationships will be the core building blocks of the new entrepreneurial transnational corporation. The recent reorganization of a large American computer company provides an example of how such a management process can be structured.

Confronted with the challenge of rapidly changing customer demands and the constraints of a traditional matrix organization that impeded the company's ability to marshal its own formidable technological resources to help its customers, the company decided to restructure itself to create "a network of entrepreneurs in a global corporation." As described by top management, the objective was to create a management approach "which starts with opportunity and capitalizes upon the innovation, creativity, and excellence of people to secure the future of the company." This objective was enshrined in the vision statement: to build "a global IT service company based on people who are enthusiastic about coming to work every day knowing that they are highly valued, encouraged to grow and increase their knowledge and are individually motivated to make a positive difference."

To achieve this vision, the company restructured itself into a large number of relatively small units, each unit being headed by a person formally designated as an entrepreneur. There were different kinds of entrepreneurial units, corresponding to different tasks such as product creation, field sales and support, or industry marketing. All shared a common mandate, however, "to think and act as heads of companies in a networked holding." Pursuit of opportunities was defined as their key challenge. Each entrepreneur was assured significant support and the top management collectively declared that "everyone in the company works for the entrepreneurs." At the same time, it was emphasized that no one could afford to own or control all the expertise, resources, or services necessary for achieving his or her objectives.

Pursuant to the reorganization, senior regional, divisional, and functional managers were relieved of their normal consolidation and control tasks and were instead regrouped as a pool of coaches. The label of coach highlighted that they should not play in the actual game. Yet the metaphor was that of a football coach who bore overall responsibility for the team's success, had the expertise to improve the players' skills, possessed the experience to guide the team's strategy, and had the authority to change players when the need arose.

In operational terms, each entrepreneur had an allotted coach to support him or her, but also a separate "board" that has formal responsibility to "review and question the validity of the entrepreneur's strategy and plan, provide feedback, monitor performance, encourage, stimulate, support, and, via the chairperson, propose rewards or change of the entrepreneur" (see Figure 8-3).

The coach's main task was to help the entrepreneur succeed both through personal guidance and support and also by acting as a link between the entrepreneur and all others in the company whose resources the entrepreneur might need to succeed. The board, of which the assigned coach was often the chairperson, acted in a manner not dissimilar from regular corporate boards. The chairperson was nominated by the top management and other members were selected by the entrepreneur, in consultation with the chairperson, from the company's pool of coaches. In selecting her board members, the entrepreneur looked for specific expertise and, if the desired skills are not available within the

Figure 8-3   The Operational Structure

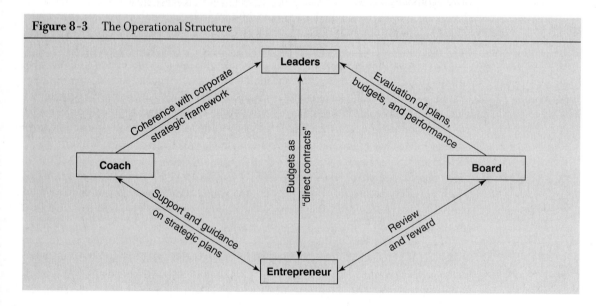

company, she could appoint outsiders such as customers, university professors, or even one of the employees from her unit.

The board was the company's key instrument for maintaining rigorous financial control. Its key tasks were to challenge the entrepreneur's plans, review her budget proposals, monitor performance against budgets, and to continuously advise top management on resource allocation decisions. Budgets were seen as sacrosanct: Once the budget was proposed and approved, the entrepreneur must achieve it, taking personal responsibility for initiating any changes that might become necessary because of unforeseen developments. But on the other side of the commitment, no one in the company could tamper with an approved budget except in response to the entrepreneur's demonstrated inability to fulfill to the contract.

Although the uniform financial control system provided rigor and discipline to the exercise of bottom-up initiative, top management of the company also recognized the need for a clear statement of strategic mission to provide direction and coherence to the entrepreneurial process. In contrast to the company's historical focus on proprietary products, the mission statement described the need for refocusing on customer service and on providing and integrating multivendor products and services. The simple yet unambiguous statement was explained and debated throughout the company over a six-month period to ensure not only intellectual understanding but also emotional commitment on the part of all employees.

Just the statement and its elaboration was, however, not enough. The process of discussion and debate revealed the need for establishing some clear performance standards and norms to link the mission with specific projects and plans. In response, top management articulated five key performance parameters—each clearly linked to the mission statement—and set specific overall goals against each parameter. For example, "increase market share faster than competition" or "profit above local competitors" was translated into tangible but differentiated objectives for the different entrepreneurial units, and approval of plans was linked to these objectives.

Whereas this is only one example of the transformation a company can go through to build the entrepreneurial process, it illustrates four key attributes that appear to be common to companies that are able to capture the creative energy of their people to develop new business opportunities.

First, they build their organizations around relatively small units. Matsushita, as we described in the case in Chapter 4 has proliferated the world with its National, Panasonic, Quasar, Technic, and other branded consumer electronic products on the strength of its "one product–one division" concept: As soon as an existing division comes out with a successful new product, it is split up as a separate division. Leading pharmaceutical company GSK (formerly Glaxo Smith Kline) has pulled apart its enormous R&D organization to create seven "centers of excellence for drug discovery"—stand-alone units of up to 400 scientists that compete with each other for research funds. One can observe the same practice in companies as diverse as Johnson and Johnson, 3M, and Bertelsmann: To maintain the entrepreneurial spirit each unit must be restricted in size so that every member of the unit can personally know all others.

To build such small units, these companies have abandoned the notion of functionally complete "strategic business units," which own all key resources so as to be in full control over their performance. Instead, they have structured incomplete "performance units" that are interdependent and must use each other's resources to achieve their own goals. The product divisions in Matsushita or Canon do not control the sales units, which are structured as separate companies, as are often the technology units. And, in contrast to the arbitrary and conflict-generating distinctions among cost centers, revenue centers, and profit centers, the performance centers are not differentiated on the basis of their activities. Whether they sell to customers, or produce for internal customers, or work to build new technologies, all performance centers are treated similarly in the planning, budgeting, and control systems.

Second, they create a multistage resource allocation process instead of up-front commitment to a clearly articulated long-term plan. Any employee can propose to start a new business at 3M and "a single coherent sentence can often suffice as starting plan." But, at each stage of developing the proposal, from the initial idea to product development, prototyping, technical and market testing, and commercialization, the entrepreneur must propose a specific budget and clearly quantified mileposts; all approvals are subject to satisfactory performance against the earlier commitments. As 3M managers grudgingly admit, "We spend all our time preparing budgets, but it seems to help."

Third, they tend to adopt a highly structured and rigorously implemented financial control system. At 3M, for example, such financial discipline is maintained through a standardized management reporting system that is applied uniformly to all operating units, who are forbidden by a central directive from creating their own systems. At the level of product families, 3,900 monthly P&L statements are generated centrally, and these are made available online to all the units within 10 days of every financial closing. Similarly, at Matsushita, a new division receives start-up capital from the corporate headquarters and loans, when justified under normal commercial conditions; it pays interest on the loans to the corporate "bank" at regular market rates, together with 60 percent of pretax profits as dividend. Performance expectations are uniform across all divisions, regardless of the maturity of the market or the company's competitive position. If a division's operating profits fall below 4 percent of sales for two successive years, the divisional manager is replaced.

An essential corollary of such rigorous financial control is the sanctity of the budget of each entrepreneurial unit. In traditional divisionalized companies, budgets are cascaded down across each layer of the hierarchy and managers at each level are expected to achieve the aggregate budget at their level. Such an aggregation process essentially translates into sudden changes of approved budgets for certain units in response to unanticipated problems faced by other units within the administrative control of a common manager. In contrast, in companies with a firm commitment to bottom-up initiative, the budgets of the small entrepreneurial units are not changed except in response to variances in the unit's own performance. There is neither a cascading down of budget approvals nor an aggregation up of budget achievements: The budget of each unit is approved separately and its performance is monitored individually right up to top management.

And finally, all these companies have a clearly articulated and widely understood and shared definition of the "opportunity horizon" that provides a lightning rod to channel organizational aspirations and energy into cohesive corporate development. The boundaries of the opportunity horizon tend to be precise enough to clearly rule out activities that do not support the company's strategic mission, and yet broad enough to prevent undue constraints on the creativity and opportunism of frontline managers. Without such a clearly defined strategic mission, frontline managers have no basis for selecting among the diverse opportunities they might confront and bottom-up entrepreneurship soon degenerates into a frustrating guessing game. The actual definition of the boundaries may be stated in very different terms—a strong technology focus in Canon or 3M or specific customer groups in SAS or Cartier, for example—but it provides a basis for strategic choice among different initiatives and serves as a guideline for the entrepreneurs themselves to focus their own creative energy.

The Integration Process: Linking and Leveraging Competencies

In this world of converging technologies, category management, and global competition, the entrepreneurial process alone is not sufficient. Tomorrow's successful transnational companies will also have a strong integration process to link their diverse assets and resources into corporate competencies, and to leverage these competencies in their pursuit of new opportunities. (This was at the core of the worldwide learning process discussed in Chapter 5.) In the absence of such an integration process, decentralized entrepreneurship may lead to some temporary performance improvement as existing slack is harnessed, but long-term development of new capabilities or businesses will be seriously impeded. Many highly decentralized companies including Matsushita have recently experienced this problem. In describing the transnational organization, we have suggested how worldwide integration can coexist with entrepreneurship at the national level, but the challenge of managing the symbiosis between entrepreneurship and integration extends beyond managing across geographic boundaries to those between the different businesses and functions of a company. The following example will illustrate how such a broader integration process can be built and managed.

Nikkei Business recently ranked Kao as the third in its list of Japan's most creative companies—well ahead of other local superstars including NEC, Toyota, Seibu, and Canon. The company had earned this distinction because of its outstanding record of introducing innovative, high-quality products to beat back not only domestic rivals such as Lion but also its giant global competitors such as Procter & Gamble (P&G) and Unilever. Technological and design innovations in Merries, Kao's brand of disposable diapers, reduced P&G's market share in Japan from nearly 90 percent to less than 10. Similarly, the introduction of Attack, Kao's condensed laundry detergent, resulted in the company's domestic market share surge from 33 to 48 percent, while that of Lion declined from 31 to 23 percent. In the 1980s, this innovative capability allowed this traditional soap company to expand successfully into personal care products where it established Sofina as the largest selling cosmetics brand in Japan, and into floppy disks in which it grew to be the second largest player in North America.

A powerful entrepreneurial process lies at the heart of Kao's innovative ability. It practices all the elements of the entrepreneurial process we have described: small functionally incomplete units driven by aggressive targets, rigorous financial discipline, a structured new product creation process, and a clear definition of its strategic mission in terms of utilizing its technological strengths to develop products with superior functionality.

However, the wellspring behind this entrepreneurial process has been what Dr. Yoshio Maruta, the chairman of Kao, describes as "biological self-control." As the body reacts to pain by sending help from all quarters, "if anything goes wrong in one part of the company, all other parts should know automatically and help without having to be asked." A companywide integration process has allowed Kao to link and leverage its core competencies in research, manufacturing, and marketing not only to solve problems but also to create and exploit new opportunities. And this integration process in Kao, like the entrepreneurial process, is built on some well-defined roles, tasks, and value-added on the part of the frontline entrepreneurs, the senior-level coaches, and the corporate leaders (see Figure 8-4).

The small and relatively autonomous work units of the entrepreneurial corporation—each responsible for specific customer groups or product lines or functional competencies—create an enormous centrifugal force, which, in the absence of a countervailing centripetal force, can overwhelm the company with inconsistencies, conflicts, and fragmentation. The first task in integration, therefore, is to create a glue to hold the different parts together and to align their initiatives. A set of clear and motivating organizational values provides the basis for such normative integration, and developing, nurturing, and embedding these values become a key task of the management group we have described as corporate leaders.

The organizational processes of Kao are designed to foster the spirit of harmony and social integration based on the principle of absolute equality of human beings, individual initiative, and the rejection of authoritarianism. Free access of everyone to all information "serves as the core value and the guiding principle of what Dr. Maruta describes as Kao's "paperweight organization": a flat structure, with a small handle of a few senior people in the middle, in which all information is shared horizontally and not filtered

Figure 8-4   The Integration Process: Management Roles and Tasks

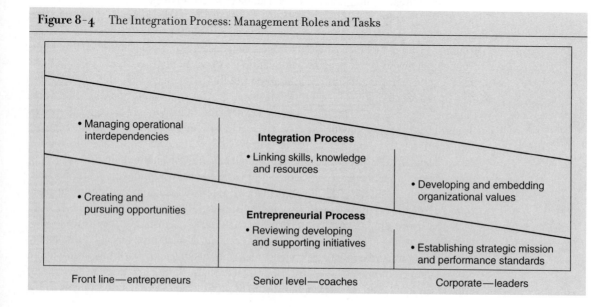

vertically. "In today's business world, information is the only source of competitive advantage," said Dr. Maruta. "This makes it necessary to share all information. If someone has special and crucial information that others don't have, that is against human equality, and will deprive us and the organization of real creativity and learning." These core values of human equality and free sharing of all information are embedded throughout the organization not only through continuous articulation and emphasis by Dr. Maruta and other members of the top-management team but also through their own behaviors and through a set of institutionalized practices.

For example, Dr. Maruta and his top-management colleagues share the 10th floor of Kao's head office building, together with a pool of secretaries. A large part of this floor is open space, with conference tables, overhead projectors, and lounging chairs spread around. This is known as "decision space," where all discussions with and among the top management take place. Anyone passing, including the chairman, can sit down and join in any discussion, on any topic, and they frequently do. The executive vice president in charge of a particular business or a specific territory can, therefore, be engaged in a debate on a topic that he has no formal responsibility for. The same layout and norm are duplicated in the other floors, in the laboratories, and in workshops. Workplaces look like large rooms: There are no partitions, only tables and chairs for spontaneous or planned discussions in which everyone has free access and can contribute as equals.

A biweekly Kao newspaper keeps every employee informed about competitors' moves, new product launches, overseas developments, and key meetings. Open computer-based access to company information ensures that all employees can, if they wish, retrieve data on sales records of any product from any of Kao's numerous outlets, or product development anywhere in the company. The latest findings from each of Kao's research laboratories are available for all to see, as are the details of the previous days' production and inventory at every Kao plant. "They can even," says Dr. Maruta, "check up on the president's expense account." The benefits from this open sharing of data outweigh the risk of leaks, the company believes, because, in an environment of flux, "leaked information instantly becomes obsolete."

Even though the corporate leaders carry the principal responsibility for developing and embedding the corporate values that provide the context for integration, it is the frontline entrepreneurs who must integrate the day-to-day activities of the company by managing the operational interdependencies across the different product, functional, and geographic units. This requires certain attitudes and some specific skills, but also some facilitating infrastructures and processes.

In Kao, information technology is a key element of the infrastructure and its own extensive value-added networks (Kao VANs) provide the anchors for operational integration. Fully integrated information systems control the flows of materials, products, and ideas from the stage of new product development, to production planning involving over 1,500 types of raw materials, to distribution of over 550 types of final products to about 300,000 retail stores.

Kao's logistics information system (LIS) links the corporate headquarters, all the factories, the independent wholesalers, and the logistics centers through a network that includes a sales planning system, an inventory control system, and an online supply system. Using LIS, each salesperson at Kao's 30 wholesalers projects sales plans on the basis of a head office campaign plan, an advertising plan, and past market trends. These are corrected and adjusted at the corporate level and provide the basis for the daily production schedules of each factory. A separate computerized ordering system, built on point-of-sales terminals installed in the retail stores and connected to LIS, allows automatic replenishment of store inventory based on the previous day's sales data.

Kao's marketing intelligence system (MIS) tracks sales by product, region, and market segment, and develops new approaches to advertising and media planning, sales promotion, market research, and statistical analysis. Another sophisticated computerized system, ECHO, codes all telephone queries and complaints about Kao's products online. Linked to MIS, ECHO is an invaluable "window on the customer's mind" that allows the company to fine-tune formulations, labeling, and packaging and also to develop new product ideas.

These extensive IT networks provide the tools for the frontline managers in Kao to carry much of the burden of day-to-day operational coordination and integration, which, in most companies, are the key tasks of middle and senior management. But these IT networks are not seen as a replacement for face-to-face meetings. Indeed the company has one of the most extensive systems of intrafunctional, interfunctional, and interbusiness meetings to facilitate exchange of ideas and joint development of new initiatives and projects. Top management, marketers, and research scientists meet at regular conferences. "Open space" meetings are offered every week by different units, and people from any part of the organization can participate in such meetings.

Within the R&D organization, the wellspring of Kao's innovations, monthly conferences are hosted, in turn, by different laboratories to bring junior researchers together. Researchers can nominate themselves to attend any of these meetings; similarly, any researcher in the host laboratory is free to invite anyone he or she wishes to meet from any of Kao's several laboratories spread around the world. It is through the collaborative work triggered by such meetings that Kao developed many of its breakthrough innovations, such as a special emulsifier developed jointly by three different laboratories, which later proved to be crucial for Sofina's success. Similar processes are in place in most of the other businesses and functions, and these meetings—perhaps even more than the IT linkages—provide the means for Kao's frontline entrepreneurs to build and leverage their own lateral networks within the company.

But whereas the leaders create the context of integration and the frontline managers link and align operational activities, it is the group of coaches in senior management who serve as the engine for linking the diverse skills, expertise, and resources in different research, manufacturing, and marketing units to launch the strategic thrusts of Kao and maintain their momentum over time. If the entrepreneurs are the linchpins for the entrepreneurial process, the coaches are the pivots for the integration process.

A companywide "total creative revolution"(TCR) project serves as the main vehicle for the senior managers in Kao to pull together teams from different parts of the company to find creative responses to emerging problems or new opportunities. TCR is the fourth phase in a two-decade-long program that started its life as an organizationwide computerization initiative (the CCR movement) and evolved into a total quality control (TQC) program, then a total cost reduction (TCR) effort. Total creative revolution—the second TCR project—was aimed at making "innovation through collaborative learning" the centerpiece of Kao's strategic thrust through the 1990s.

According to Dr. Maruta, "Kao must be like an educational institution—a company that has learnt how to learn." And senior managers are formally expected to be "the priests"—the teachers who must facilitate this process of shared learning. Thus, when a small and distant foreign subsidiary faced a problem, it was one of these constantly traveling senior managers who helped the local management team identify the appropriate expert in Japan and sponsored a task force to find a creative solution. Similarly, when some factory employees were made redundant following the installation of new equipment, one of these coaches sponsored five of them to form a team to support a factory in the United States to install and commission a plant imported from Japan. Over time, this group became a highly valued flying squad available to help new production units get over their teething troubles.

The success of Sofina was the result of a very similar process, albeit on a much larger scale. Sensing an opportunity to create a high-quality, reasonably priced range of cosmetics that would leverage Kao's technological strengths and emphasize the functionality of "skin care" rather than "image," the top management of Kao presented it as a corporate challenge. To create such a product and to market it successfully, Kao would need to integrate its capabilities both within specific functions, such as diverse technologies in emulsifiers, moisturizers, and skin diagnosis lodged in different laboratories, and across functions including R&D, corporate marketing and sales, production, and market research.

Instead of trying to create one gigantic team, a few senior managers including the head of the Tokyo Research Laboratory, the director of marketing research, and a director of marketing formed themselves into a small team to coordinate the project. They created small task forces, as required, to address specific problems—such as developing a new emulsifier—but kept the lateral coordination tasks among the operating managers at the simplest possible level. When the new emulsifier created some problems of skin irritation, a different group was established to develop a moisturizer and a chemical to reduce irritation. Similarly, when the Sofina foundation cream was found to be sticky on application, they set it up as a challenge for a marketing team, who responded by positioning the product as "the longest lasting foundation that does not disappear with perspiration," converting the stickiness into a strength. This group of senior managers continued to play this integrating and coordinating role for over a decade, as the project evolved from its initial vision to a nationwide success.

◼ The Renewal Process: Managing Rationalization and Revitalization

The historical management processes in large MNCs have been premised on the assumption that environmental changes will be relatively linear and incremental. The accounting, budgeting, planning, and control systems have been designed to provide order and efficiency to an essentially vertical process of managing information. The frontline units provide data. This data is analyzed by middle-level managers to create useful information. Information obtained from several different sources is combined to generate knowledge within the organization. Finally, top management absorbs and institutionalizes this knowledge to build wisdom that becomes a part of the accepted perspectives and norms within the company. In an environment of relative stability, the order and efficiency of such a linear process have allowed these companies to continuously refine their operational processes through incremental accumulation and exploitation of knowledge.

In an environment of often turbulent and unpredictable change, however, incremental operational refinement is not enough; companies now also need the ability to manage strategic renewal. They must create mechanisms in which established ways of thinking and working are continuously challenged. If the integration process links and leverages existing capabilities to defend and advance current strategies, the renewal process continuously questions those strategies and the assumptions underlying them and inspires the creation of new competencies to prepare the ground for the very different competitive battles the company is likely to confront in the future.

The renewal process is built on two symbiotic components. It consists, on the one hand, of an ongoing pressure for rationalization and restructuring of existing businesses to achieve continuous improvement of operational performance. This rationalization component aims to refine existing operations incrementally to achieve ever-improving current results. Rigorous benchmarking against best-in-class competitors provides the scorecard on concrete operational measures such as value-added per employee, contributions per unit of fixed and working capital, time to market for new products, and customer satisfaction. This process pinpoints performance gaps and focuses organizational energy on closing those gaps.

The other part of renewal is revitalization—the creation of new competencies and new businesses, the challenging and changing of existing rules of the game, and the leapfrogging of competition through quantum leaps. Driven by dreams and the power of ideas, it focuses on "business not as usual" to create breakthroughs that would take the company to the next stages of its ambition. Revitalization may involve fast-paced, small bets to take the company into new business domains—as Canon is trying in the field of semiconductors—or big "bet the company" moves to transform industries—as Nokia did throughout the 1990s as it led the twin technology and marketing revolutions that defined the emergence of the mobile phone industry.

As with entrepreneurship and integration, rationalization and revitalization are also often viewed in mutually exclusive terms. Managers complain of the insatiable appetite of the stock market for short-term results, which forces them to focus on rationalization rather than revitalization. Some justify poor operating results as the evidence of long-term investments. The renewal process, in contrast, emphasizes the essential symbiosis between the present and the future: There is no long-term success without short-term performance just as short-term results mean little unless they contribute to building the long-term ambition. Rationalization provides the resources needed for revitalization—not just money and people, but also legitimacy and credibility—whereas revitalization creates the hope and the energy needed for rationalization.

Amid the general bloodbath that has characterized the semiconductor business, Intel has been among the few players that have achieved steady growth together with satisfactory financial returns. While its fortunes have turned with the tide—from spectacular successes in the 1970s when it introduced, in quick succession, the 1130 DRAM, the 1702 EPROM, and the 8086 microprocessor, to heavy losses in the mid-1980s when the company was forced to exit the DRAM and SRAM businesses and cut 30 percent of its workforce, to phenomenal success again with the 80386 32-bit microprocessor in the late 1980s and the Pentium in the 1990s—Intel has so far taken most of the correct turns as it hit the forks in the road, avoiding hitting the dividers, as many of its competitors have done.

In this process, the company has continuously renewed itself, changing its products and strategies and adopting its organization and culture, to respond to the dramatic changes in its business environment. From the "self-evident truth" that Intel was a "jellybean" memory company, it changed itself into a logic devices company—selling boards—and then to a systems house—providing solutions in boxes. From a heritage of manufacturing inefficiency that was almost celebrated as the evidence of creativity in product development, Intel has now become cost competitive vis-à-vis its Japanese rivals. Its marketing focus has evolved too, from selling product features to OEM customers in the early 1970s, to positioning-oriented marketing in the 1980s (emphasizing compatibility with end-user standards), to full-fledged end-user marketing in the 1990s in direct partnership with the final customers of the company's microprocessors. To support these changes, Intel has also transformed its culture. From an organization of "bright, talkative, opinionated, rude, arrogant, impatient, and very informal macho men interested only in results and not in niceties," the company has evolved into a better balance between task focus and friendly work environment in which "people don't have to be Milky the milk biscuit to get their work done, but then, they don't have to be Attila the Hun either," as CEO Andy Grove colorfully put it.

Intel's ability to stay one step ahead of competition—which is all that separates the winners from the losers in the semiconductor business—has been built on some demanding roles and contributions of managers at all levels of the company (see Figure 8-5). But, if the frontline entrepreneurs drive the entrepreneurial process and the senior-level coaches anchor the integration process, it is the corporate-level leaders who inspire and energize the renewal process. It is they who create and manage the tensions between short-term performance and long-term ambition, challenging the organization continuously to higher levels of operational and strategic performance.

Until the demise of Noyce in 1990, Intel had been led by the trio of Gordon Moore as chairman, Robert Noyce as vice chairman, and Andy Grove as president, who collectively formed the company's executive committee. Of these, whereas Noyce looked after external relations, it was Moore and Grove who guided the company internally: Moore in the role of the technology genius and architect of long-term strategy, and Grove as the detail-oriented resident pragmatist. Moore was the quiet, long-term-oriented, philosophical champion of revitalization. Grove, on the other hand, served as the vocal, aggressive, and demanding driver of rationalization.

When Motorola's competitive microprocessor gained momentum at the cost of Intel's 16-bit 8086 chip, it was Grove who initiated "operation crush"—an "all out combat" plan, complete with war rooms and SWAT teams, to make 8086 the industry standard. But it was Moore who built the company's long-range planning process and provided the

Figure 8-5   The Renewal Process: Management Roles and Tasks

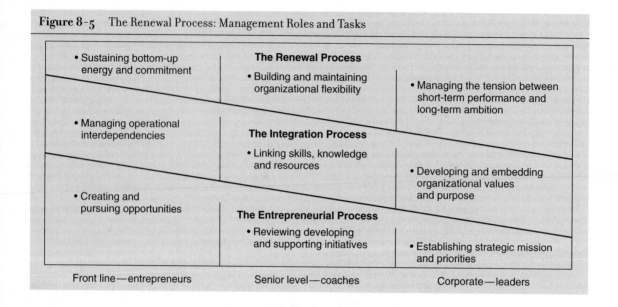

blueprint for technological evolution—what has since come to be known as "Moore's law." In essence, the two divided the rationalization and revitalization components of the renewal responsibility between them in a way that was originally serendipitous but has since been institutionalized within the company as an unusual management concept: two-in-a-box. It has become normal in Intel for two executives with complementary skills to share the responsibilities of one role.

Whether through a combination of more than one person, as in the case of Andy Grove and Gordon Moore at Intel or Sochiro Honda and Takeo Fujisawa at Honda Motors, or single-handedly, as Jack Welch did so masterfully at GE, creating and managing this tension between the short term and the long term, between current performance and future ambition, between restructuring and revitalization, is a key part of the corporate leader's role in the entrepreneurial corporation. In this role, the leader is the challenger—the one who is constantly upping the ante, and creating the energy and the enthusiasm necessary for the organization to accept the perpetual stretch that such challenging implies.

Personal credibility within and outside the organization is a prerequisite for the corporate leader to play this role, but it is not enough. Charisma sustains momentum for short periods but fatigue ultimately overtakes the organization that depends on individual charisma alone for its energy. To inspire self-renewal, companies must develop an inspiring corporate ambition—a shared dream about the future and the company's role in that future—and must imbed that ambition throughout the organization. Whether the ambition focuses on something as tangible as size, as in Canon's expressed desire to be a company as big as IBM and Matsushita combined, or something less tangible, such as Intel's desire to be the best in the world, what matters is the emotional commitment the leader can build around the dream. Ultimately, it is this emotional commitment that unleashes the human energy required to sustain the organization's ability to continuously renew itself. And developing, marshaling, and leveraging this energy is key to simultaneous rationalization and revitalization, and will perhaps be the single most important challenge for the corporate leaders of the transnational companies of the future.[2]

Although the leaders must provide the challenge and the stretch necessary for organizational self-renewal, it is the coaches who must mediate the complex trade-offs that simultaneous restructuring and revitalization imply. It is they who must manage the tension between building new capabilities and stretching existing resources, and the conflict inherent in the high and unrelenting performance demands of the company. This requires enormous flexibility and an environment of mutual trust and tolerance, and creating such processes and attitudes is a key element of the coach's role.

As described by Andy Grove, in the semiconductor business "there are the quick, and there are the dead." In a highly volatile technological and market environment, the company has developed the ability to be very flexible in moving human resources as needs change. Levels change up or down at Intel all the time—people move in every direction, upward, sideways, or downward. Careers advance not by moving up the organization, but by individuals filling corporate needs. Official rank, decision-making authority, and remuneration—highly correlated in most companies—are treated separately at Intel and this separation among different kinds of rewards lies at the core of Intel's organizational flexibility. But such a system is also susceptible to gaming, and needs a high level of openness and transparency in decision-making processes and mutual trust and tolerance among people to be effective. Flexibility requires not only that the organization act fairly but also that it be seen to be acting fairly; creating and protecting such fairness— necessary in any winning team—is again a key task for the coaches.

Although Intel's action-oriented and direct management style, if somewhat confrontative, has evolved in Grove's mold of aggressive brilliance, it is the senior-management group heading different operating divisions and corporate functions that has embedded the norms of transparency and openness at all levels of the company. Key decisions at Intel are typically made in open meetings, all of which have preannounced agendas, and inevitably close with action plans and deadlines. During a meeting, participants are encouraged to debate the pros and cons of a subject aggressively through what is described as "constructive confrontation." But once something has been decided on, Intel has the philosophy of "agree or disagree, but commit." As a result, everyone has the opportunity to influence key decisions relevant to himself and to openly advocate their perspectives and views and is party to the final decisions, even though the decisions may not always conform to their personal preferences. The opportunity for such active participation on an equal basis in open and transparent decision processes, coupled with the norm of disciplined and fast implementation once a decision has been taken, creates the environment of trust, which, in turn, is key to the operational and strategic flexibility of the company.

The effectiveness of the renewal process ultimately depends on the ability of frontline managers to generate and maintain the energy and commitment of people

---

[2] For an elaboration of the importance of individual energy and focus in driving the renewal process, see S. Ghoshal and H. Bruch, "Beware the Busy Manager," *Harvard Business Review,* February 2002, pp. 63–69.

within their units. The battles for efficiency and integration, for rationalization and revitalization, are ultimately fought at the level of the salesperson in the field, the operator in the plant, and the individual research scientist or engineer in the laboratory. While the energizing ambition personified by the top management and the open and transparent decision-making processes orchestrated by the senior managers provide the anchors for the grassroots-level commitment at Intel, two other elements of its organizational philosophy and practices also contribute a great deal in maintaining the enthusiasm of its frontline teams.

First, at Intel, there is not only fairness in management processes but there is also fairness in organizational outcomes. In contrast to companies that cut frontline jobs at the first sight of performance problems, Intel adopted the "125 percent solution" to deal with the industrywide recession in the early 1980s: Instead of retrenching people, all salaried workers—including the chairman—were required to work an additional 10 hours per week without additional compensation. When the recession continued in 1982, still unwilling to lay off large numbers of people, the company proposed a 10 percent pay cut on top of the 125 percent solution. As the economy pulled out of the recession, returning the company to profitability, the pay cuts were first restored in June 1983 and, by November 1983, the employees who had accepted pay cuts received special bonuses. Several years later, when the memory product bloodbath finally forced the company to reduce its workforce by 30 percent, the cuts were distributed across all levels of the company, instead of being concentrated at the lowest ranks.

Second, at Intel, it is legitimate to own up to one's personal mistakes and to change one's mind. Gordon Moore regretfully but openly acknowledges his personal role in missing the engineering workstation revolution, even though the company was among the pioneers for this opportunity. Andy Grove, the symbol of the company's confrontative, task-oriented culture, had long insisted on not having any recreation facilities in the company. "This is not a country club. You come here to work," he would say to all employees. But as the organization grew, and the need for supplementing the task focus with concern for a friendly work environment became manifest, he gave in and made a celebration of being beaten down. At the dedication of the new facilities, he appeared in his bathing suit and took a shower under a big banner that read, "'There will never be any showers at Intel'—Andy Grove." Such open acknowledgment of errors and goodhearted acceptance of alternatives one has personally opposed creates an environment in which failures are tolerated and changes in strategy do not automatically create winners and losers. It is this overall environment that, in turn, co-opts the frontline managers into the corporate ambition and allows them to sustain energy and commitment at the lowest levels of the organization.

■ A Model for the Future

Over the last decade, many observers of large corporations have highlighted some of the vulnerabilities of the traditional company's strategy and organization described in this chapter. The specific prescriptions of needing to build entrepreneurship, integration, and renewal capabilities are also not new. Academics, consultants, and managers themselves have long recognized these needs to respond to a variety of changing environmental demands. Typically, however, these changing external demands and the consequent need for new internal capabilities have been studied in a piecemeal fashion, triggering ad hoc responses.

Facing slowing economic growth and increasingly sophisticated customer demands, companies have attempted to decentralize resources and authority to capture the creative energy and entrepreneurship of frontline managers. But prescriptions of creating and managing chaos have ignored the need for clarity of strategy and the discipline of centralized financial control to channel bottom-up energy into a coherent corporate direction. Companies that have attempted such radical decentralization without a centrally managed strategic framework have soon lost their focus and their ability to leverage resources effectively and have been forced to retreat to the known devil of their old ways.

Observing the ever-increasing pace of globalization of markets and the rising cost, complexity, and convergence of technologies, managers have recognized the need to consolidate and integrate their diverse organizational capabilities. But presented typically with examples of high-tech and highly centralized Japanese companies, they have confused capabilities with technologies, and integration with centralization. Similarly, faced with the rapid enhancement of the skills and resources of once-distant competitors and the changing norms and expectations in the many societies in which they operate, companies have realized the limits of incremental improvements and the need for dramatic change. Yet guided by prescriptions of creating dreamlike, long-term ambitions, they have allowed short-term performance to slip, thereby abandoning the long term too because of increasing resource scarcity.

In contrast to these fragmented and often contradictory prescriptions, we have presented a broad model encompassing the key capabilities we believe companies must develop to respond to the environmental demands of the 2000s. Nothing needs a theory more than practice, and the lack of an integrated theory of the new organization, we believe, has prevented companies from abandoning the old divisional model even though they have long recognized its constraints. The model of the future organization we have presented here is aimed to provide such a theory for practice.

The real challenge in building this new organization lies in the changes in management roles we have described. The metamorphosis of frontline managers—those who drive the operations in subsidiaries worldwide, for example—from being operational implementers to becoming aggressive entrepreneurs, will require some very new skills and capabilities. Similarly, the transformation of the middle-management role—global product or business managers, for instance—from that of administrative controller to that of inspiring coach will represent a traumatic change. But the management group that will be most severely challenged in the new organization will be the one currently at the top of the hierarchy—the CEO and other top-level executives. Not only will they have to change their role from that of resource allocator and political arbitrator to that of institutional leader, they will also have to create the infrastructures and the contexts necessary for the others to play the new roles demanded of them. The managers who can build the attitudes and skills appropriate for these new roles and the companies that can develop and retain such managers are likely to emerge as the future winners in the game of global competition.

Case 8-1   The Transformation of BP

The Transformation of BP

On June 25th 1992 the Board of BP, the UK's largest industrial enterprise, cut its dividend and removed its Chief Executive Robert Horton. The move came as the company sought to overcome a series of interlinked challenges—the transition to private sector ownership which had coincided with the stock market collapse in 1987; the fall in oil prices after the Gulf War; rising debts and increasing unit costs.

Within a decade the company was leading the restructuring of the sector, had reduced costs and debt and was earning after-tax income of over $1 billion a month. By 2001 BP was generating annual revenues of $120 billion, employing 100,000 people in over 100 countries, and had taken its place as one of the three supermajors in the oil industry (see financials in Exhibit 1).

Within the oil industry and beyond, BP had become a model of both financial performance and corporate social responsibility, breaking ranks by accepting that the risks of climate change were too dangerous to ignore and by refusing to accept the long entrenched trade off between environmental protection and increased energy consumption which many had come to take for granted.

This study looks at how that transformation was achieved, and in particular at the way in which changes in the management of the company influenced both performance and reputation.

▌ This case was written by Michelle Rogan, PhD student, together with Lynda Gratton and Sumantra Ghoshal, both members of the faculty, at the London Business School.

London Business School

© London Business School, March 03.

▌ Sussex Place, Regent's Park, London NW1 4SA, United Kingdom.

Building the Platform for Superior Performance

In retrospect it is possible to see that a number of the changes necessary to achieve the transformation of BP had begun before 1992.

As Chairman and Chief Executive, Horton had begun a process of "cultural change" shaking up BP's entrenched bureaucracies and reducing staff numbers. John Browne, Chief Executive of BP Exploration from 1989 to 1995 and subsequently Chief Executive of BP as a whole had initiated radical steps in 1989 to focus exploration spending on a limited number of the best prospects around and to reduce costs.

The real impact of such developments only became apparent however after 1992 under the leadership of Horton's successor David Simon (later to become a Minister in Tony Blair's first Government as Lord Simon of Highbury). Simon stabilized the company increasing revenues and reducing costs and laid the foundation for the process of transformation which can be dated from 1995 when Browne, backed by his deputy Rodney Chase, took over the reins of the business.

Nick Butler, policy advisor to Browne and his top team throughout the period, described what followed as "Act 1, taking the steps to create a high-grade business portfolio and human capital. Creating the base for something interesting."

Ralph Alexander one of BP's Group Vice Presidents recalled:

> When Browne stepped in as CEO in 1995, we knew we had to create something different. We looked at the ROACE; we were all operating within a limited space. We realised that to break out we had to redefine ourselves. It was not about beating Exxon, but how to

Exhibit 1 Balance Sheet and Income Statement

BP Amoco Statement of Financial Position (1991 to 1999)

	Dec91	Dec92	Dec93	Dec94	Dec95	Dec96	Dec97	Dec98	Dec99
Assets									
Cash & equivalents	1,340.79	377.50	310.28	293.28	616.20	258.57	275.56	875.00	1,551.00
Receivables—total (net)	7,954.98	6,979.22	5,245.13	6,639.36	7,141.68	8,740.68	7,005.20	6,835.00	10,488.00
Inventories—total	5,596.91	5,102.29	3,941.97	4,302.48	4,389.84	5,085.21	4,284.46	3,642.00	5,124.00
Prepaid expenses	2,141.15	1,901.09	1,613.43	1,703.52	2,031.12	2,540.07	2,704.14	3,508.00	4,230.00
Current assets—other	1,568.93	1,550.77	1,168.70	940.68	1,020.24	1,546.35	1,822.68	2,366.00	2,084.00
Current assets—total	18,602.76	15,910.87	12,279.50	13,879.32	15,199.08	18,170.88	16,092.04	17,226.00	23,477.00
Plant, property & equip (gross)	64,571.10	61,390.56	59,623.04	63,034.92	66,856.92	69,587.44	71,811.60	120,820.00	121,925.00
Accumulated depreciation	27,642.34	28,320.05	29,149.60	31,749.12	35,160.84	36,343.45	37,482.80	63,469.00	66,242.00
Plant, property & equip (net)	36,928.76	33,070.51	30,473.44	31,285.80	31,696.08	33,243.99	34,328.80	57,351.00	55,683.00
Investments at equity	2,131.80	2,429.59	2,433.44	2,669.16	3,263.52	3,302.26	3,570.66	4,162.00	4,334.00
Investments and advances—other	1,335.18	747.45	484.62	525.72	157.56	157.17	117.86	5,121.00	5,319.00
Intangibles	452.54	374.48	156.62	137.28	152.88	157.17	147.74	151.00	292.00
Deferred charges	0.00	0.00	0.00	0.00	0.00	0.00	0.00	0.00	0.00
Assets—other	0.00	0.00	0.00	0.00	0.00	15.21	318.72	489.00	456.00
Total assets	**59,451.04**	**52,532.90**	**45,827.62**	**48,497.28**	**50,469.12**	**55,046.68**	**54,575.82**	**84,500.00**	**89,561.00**
Liabilities									
Accounts payable	5,873.67	5,278.96	4,476.83	5,959.20	6,809.40	7,843.29	6,407.60	5,450.00	8,680.00
Notes payable	2,008.38	2,450.73	1,009.13	787.80	965.64	1,235.39	1,093.94	1,659.00	3,809.00
Accrued expenses	3,857.81	3,405.05	2,309.33	2,375.88	2,717.52	2,638.09	2,631.10	2,897.00	4,041.00
Taxes payable	1,277.21	1,254.81	1,155.41	1,054.56	1,725.36	2,055.04	2,353.88	2,395.00	2,558.00
Debt (long-term) Due in one year	1,071.51	1,221.59	817.06	837.72	185.64	552.63	793.48	1,178.00	1,091.00
Other current liabilities	3,683.90	3,178.55	2,579.72	2,383.68	2,730.00	3,618.29	3,514.22	4,587.00	3,096.00
Total current liabilities	17,772.48	16,789.69	12,347.47	13,398.84	15,133.56	17,942.73	16,794.22	18,166.00	23,275.00
Long-term debt	12,168.09	11,667.77	10,555.26	8,899.80	7,425.60	5,871.06	5,330.26	10,918.00	9,644.00

(*continued*)

Exhibit 1 *(concluded)*

BP Amoco Statement of Financial Position (1991 to 1999)

	Dec91	Dec92	Dec93	Dec94	Dec95	Dec96	Dec97	Dec98	Dec99
Deferred taxes (balance sheet)	755.48	619.10	366.42	444.60	586.56	684.45	647.40	1,632.00	1,783.00
Investment tax credit	0.00	0.00	0.00	0.00	0.00	0.00	0.00	0.00	0.00
Minority interest	561.00	385.05	147.75	170.04	168.48	184.21	92.96	1,072.00	1,061.00
Liabilities—other	8,271.01	8,003.00	8,008.05	8,335.08	8,725.08	8,740.68	8,285.06	10,926.00	10,517.00
Total liabilities	**39,528.06**	**37,464.61**	**31,424.95**	**31,248.36**	**32,039.28**	**33,423.13**	**31,149.90**	**42,714.00**	**46,280.00**
Shareholders' Equity									
Preferred stock	22.44	18.12	17.73	18.72	18.72	20.28	19.92	21.00	21.00
Common stock	2,520.76	2,046.05	2,013.83	2,146.56	2,174.64	2,387.97	2,392.06	4,842.00	4,871.00
Capital surplus	3,925.13	3,251.03	2,968.30	3,244.80	3,347.76	3,733.21	3,776.50	3,056.00	3,684.00
Retained earnings (net other)	13,454.65	9,753.09	9,402.81	11,838.84	12,888.72	15,482.09	17,237.44	33,867.00	34,705.00
Less: treasury stock	0.00	0.00	0.00	0.00	0.00	0.00	0.00	0.00	0.00
Total shareholders' equity	**19,922.98**	**15,068.29**	**14,402.67**	**17,248.92**	**18,429.84**	**21,623.55**	**23,425.92**	**41,786.00**	**43,281.00**
Total liabilities & equity	59,451.04	52,532.90	45,827.62	48,497.28	50,469.12	55,046.68	54,575.82	84,500.00	89,561.00
BP Amoco Income Statement (1991 to 1999)									
Sales (net)	57,725.01	58,852.50	51,638.63	50,667.48	57,047.48	69,780.36	71,274.40	68,304.00	83,566.00
Cost of goods sold	43,140.21	45,612.90	39,116.81	39,076.20	43,950.86	55,305.12	56,424.20	53,059.00	65,995.00
Gross profit	14,584.80	13,239.60	12,521.81	11,591.28	13,096.62	14,475.24	14,850.20	15,245.00	17,571.00
Selling, general, & admin expenses	6,637.50	6,984.42	5,664.74	4,680.27	5,389.38	5,277.48	5,546.48	5,609.00	5,541.00
Operating income before depreciation	7,947.30	6,255.18	6,857.08	6,911.01	7,707.24	9,197.76	9,303.72	9,636.00	12,030.00
Depreciation, depletion, & amortiz	4,403.76	3,927.63	3,856.28	3,333.87	3,220.04	3,463.20	3,047.12	5,255.00	4,708.00
Operating income after depreciation	3,543.54	2,327.55	3,000.80	3,577.14	4,487.20	5,734.56	6,256.60	4,381.00	7,322.00
Interest expense	1,407.15	1,355.82	1,085.96	872.10	837.40	700.44	577.28	1,172.00	1,359.00
Non-operating income/expense	(7.08)	985.89	363.47	729.81	954.32	1,491.36	401.80	784.00	3,343.00

Special items	0.00	(1,759.38)	(354.60)	55.08	(1,529.44)	(804.96)	(101.68)	850.00	(2,280.00)
Pretax income	2,129.31	198.24	1,923.71	3,489.93	3,074.68	5,720.52	5,979.44	4,843.00	7,026.00
Income taxes—total	1,451.40	1,000.05	1,012.09	1,058.76	1,309.82	1,726.92	1,915.52	1,520.00	1,880.00
Minority interest	(56.64)	8.85	2.96	18.36	(7.90)	12.48	13.12	63.00	138.00
Income before extraordinary items & discontinued operations (EI&DO)	732.78	(812.43)	907.19	2,411.28	1,771.18	3,979.56	4,049.16	3,258.35	5,006.00
Extraordinary items	0.00	0.00	0.00	0.00	0.00	0.00	0.00	0.00	0.00
Discontinued operations	0.00	0.00	0.00	0.00	0.00	0.00	0.00	0.00	0.00
Net income (loss)	734.55	(810.66)	908.66	2,412.81	1,772.76	3,981.12	4,050.80	3,260.00	5,008.00
Income before EI&DO	732.78	(812.43)	907.19	2,411.28	1,771.18	3,979.56	4,049.16	3,258.35	5,006.00
Preferred dividends	1.77	1.77	1.48	1.53	1.58	1.56	1.64	1.65	2.00
Available for common before EI&DO	732.78	(812.43)	907.19	2,411.28	1,771.18	3,979.56	4,049.16	3,258.35	5,006.00
Common stk equivalents—savings	0.00	0.00	0.00	0.00	0.00	0.00	0.00	0.00	0.00
Adjusted available for common	732.78	(812.43)	907.19	2,411.28	1,771.18	3,979.56	4,049.16	3,258.35	5,006.00
Earnings per Share									
Primary—excluding EI&DO	1.68	(1.80)	2.00	5.29	3.83	8.52	4.26	2.04	1.55
Primary—including EI&DO	1.68	(1.80)	2.00	5.29	3.83	8.52	4.26	2.04	1.55
Fully diluted—excluding EI&DO	1.68	(1.80)	2.00	5.29	3.83	8.52	4.26	2.04	1.54
Fully diluted—including EI&DO	1.68	(1.80)	2.00	5.29	3.83	8.52	4.26	2.04	1.54
Common Shares									
For primary EPS calculation	448.25	450.42	452.92	456.17	461.50	467.75	950.30	1,606.33	3,231.00
For fully diluted EPS calculation	—	—	—	—	—	—	—	1,606.33	3,249.50
Outstanding at fiscal year end	449.41	451.55	454.26	458.55	464.61	470.85	960.43	1,613.84	3,247.34

Source: Compustat, accessed February 14, 2001.

beat the ROACE of Microsoft. We wanted to create a company with sufficient scale to take regional shocks and with enough reach to thrive in almost any circumstances.

Thus began a series of mergers and acquisitions that would put BP in the superweight category. Browne led BP through two critical and successful mergers totalling $120 billion, first with Amoco in 1998 and then with ARCO in 1999. BP had become the third largest company in the oil industry, trailing behind only Royal Dutch Shell and Exxon-Mobil. With its acquisition of Burmah Castrol in July 2000, BP had become a combined group with a market value of more than $200 billion. BP's goals moving forward from the three mergers were to lop $4 billion off its annual costs worldwide, to sell assets of $10 billion and to boost capital spending to a total of $26 billion over the three years to the end of 2001.

While achieving scale, these mergers also created a large, fragmented company. By 2000, the company consisted of three camps, divided by their very different heritages: approximately 60,000 from BP, 40,000 from Amoco and 20,000 from ARCO. BP's management had to decide how to bring together the diverse strengths of the three different heritage companies into a single new business. Though unifying the company would be a challenge, management believed a single global brand supported by an integrated global organization was the best way forward.

Sir John Browne explained the core premises on which the management of BP based its responses to this challenge:

The organization that we evolved from 1995 onwards was founded on several simple concepts. Number one was our observation that people work better in smaller units, because the closer you can identify people to objectives and targets, the better things happen. So we started off with what we came to call the "Atomic Structure," so that the big, long-term targets of the company could be divided up and deployed into smaller units that could take full ownership of these targets . . .

. . . The second premise was contradictory to that, and that was our observation that any organization of

scale could create proprietary knowledge through learning . . . so the question was how could you get independent atomic units to work together to share information, to learn and to retain that learning . . .

. . . The third theme we observed was the very different interaction between people of equal standing, if you will, when they reviewed each other's work, than there was when a superior reviewed the work of a subordinate. We concluded that the way to get the best answers would be to get peers to challenge and support each other, than to have a hierarchical challenge process.

. . . The fourth organizational element was very much oriented towards the strategic and operating foundation of the company, in a pure business sense. You could have strategic aims for each business segment, and it could all be translated into targets, but there had to be more to it. That more had to do with the company, as a whole, so we focused on something called reputation.

Creating Performance Leaders: The Atomic Organization

A cornerstone of Act I was an increasing emphasis on leadership development and deployment. To quote Nick Butler:

10 or 12 years ago, BP was a collection of fiefdoms. These fiefdoms were extremely separate: they lived in separate buildings, had separate management systems and different philosophies. The fiefdoms did not mix and the people barely came together at the top. John's fundamental philosophy was that to succeed, these disparate parts had to be brought together as one company with a coherent overall strategic direction, one share price and one set of metrics. That was the only way to extract the benefits of the synergies and to make the whole something more than the parts.

At the centre of this integration were the 400 men and women who collectively led the enterprise. Leading this group were the six Managing Directors, who had total, collective responsibility for the policy of the enterprise. This group formally met in weekly meetings to review and gather experiences. They also used these meetings as an opportunity to discuss the movement of people within the top 300. A separate committee met as needed to allocate capital. The team met in away days twice a year—once with the full main board, including the non-exec's—to consider longer-term strategy. Informal dialogue within the team was high. As Nick Butler explained,

> Initially the different businesses were located in separate buildings and only met at formal meetings, The first step was to move into the same building. At first they were on separate floors in the same building, but they were still not really meeting. So the process took another step forward. The whole management team was integrated; they were located on the same floor in the same building. That produced real change—real cooperation and a close association across the boundary lines.

This close association was further bonded through their respective chiefs of staff who met to discuss agendas and schedules, and make sure that all the links were working.

Browne and his team believed the primary task of the top management was to focus on strategic issues: about reputation, economic shifts, societal shifts, and strategic issue based governance. To achieve this, the board rarely used any operational reports. As Chase commented, "If you preoccupy your management with operational not strategic issues, you never get to this position. We have chosen a form of organisation that has given almost the entirety of operational delivery to some very young men and women of fantastic talent around the world. We preoccupy ourselves strategically."

Next came the 40 Group Vice Presidents, who oversaw large pieces of the business. Until the reorganization of 2001, this group did not have individual accountability for specific business areas, but shared collective responsibility for the total operation. Their primary roles were to coach the Business Unit leaders, to manage the succession process and to make sure that each BU head had a performance contract which was both achievable and a stretch.

This group of Vice Presidents was also the primary feed for top management succession. In Browne's words: "this is the group from which the top 6 (the Managing Directors of the future) will be identified. It means that at any one time there are about 15 who could be my successor, and that in turn means that we have a sufficient pool of talent both to manage a company of this size and to ensure that there is no complacency."

At the base, and core, of BP's organization, below the level of the Group VPs, lay a relatively simple architecture of 150 Business Units, each led by its own Business Unit leader. While the top team managed the external relations of the firm, particularly with the governments, engaged in debate regarding long-term strategic meaning and purpose, the Business Unit leaders focused on the delivery of operating performance.

Chase described the Business Unit structure of BP as "an extraordinarily flat, dispersed, decentralised process of delivery." A Business Unit could be an oil field, a gas field, a refinery, a chemical pant, or a regional marketing area. As Chase explained, "The reason we selected 150 was that each had to be potentially material to the rest of the group. If there wasn't potential to build a billion-dollar business, we would not make it a business unit." The dismantling of the hierarchical, functionally based company had begun in 1990 when CEO Robert Horton launched Project 1990 which included a large scale restructuring of BP and the removal of many management layers. David Simon, who assumed the role of CEO in 1992, continued this decomposition by further breaking down the functional walls and restructuring the company into 90 different Business Units. Browne and his team continued this process and by 2000 the company consisted of 150 separate Business Units held together by strong performance management processes.

Horizontally, the 150 Business Units were further organised into 15 Peer Groups. The Peer Groups consisted of a network of related Business Units within a particular business stream—essentially those in a similar business, facing similar challenges.

Setting the Targets: The Performance Contract

Driving down vertically through the business was the Performance Contract process designed to create a clear "line of sight" for individual Business Unit leaders and the collective corporate business goals (see Exhibit 2). As Chase described, "We run our businesses with very tightly defined key performance indicators. Some are financial. Others relate to our commitment to be a force for good. We use exactly the same process—define the goal,

Exhibit 2   Performance Management Process

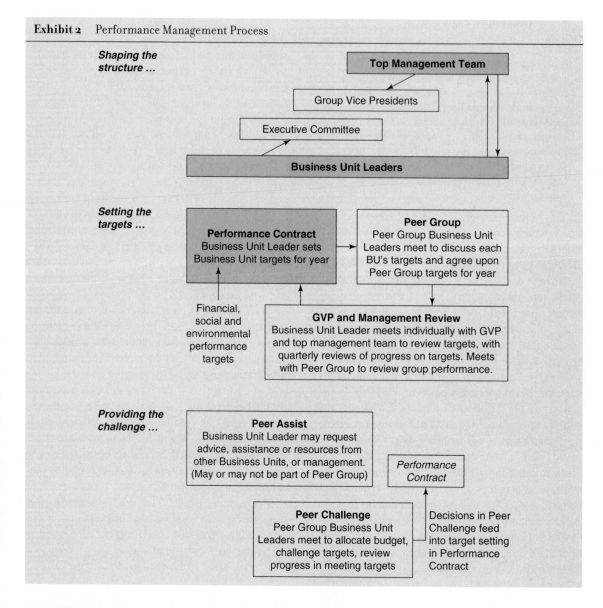

define the input to achieve the goal and then start monitoring."

David Watson, Group Vice President, Business Information, described the performance management process as a "structure for having conversations." The Performance Contract was the product of a series of such conversations—within the Business Unit, within the Peer Group and with the top management team. In an annual process, Busi-ness Unit leaders worked with their teams to identify their unit's goals for the year—financial, social and environmental—and documented them in the Performance Contract. Next they met with their Business Unit peer group to align each unit's targets with those of the collective peer group. The final conversation was with the top management team (see Exhibit 3 for an example of a performance contract).

Exhibit 3   Performance Contract

1999 BU Performance Contract

Financial	1998 Baseline	1998 Actual	1999 Contract	1999 Stretch
Net income				
Income improvement[1]				
Net cash flow				
Prize delivery[2]				
Net investment				

Creating a Safety Culture

Develop and implement Poland Safety Contract to Employees and Contractors.
Implement employee near-miss program achieving 300 near miss reports in 1999.

People Basics

100% BP Staff employees receive appraisals for their 1998 performance.
100% BP Staff employees engage in a career development discussion with their Team Leader.
100% BP Team Leaders receive upward feedback.

Other

Establish Poland as a business unit
Establish comprehensive safety programme—2Q.

- Institute assurance programme—3Q (planned for September 15th).

Establish Management information processes to ensure reliable and timely reporting—3Q.
   Manage lobby plan with values tied to each category and 100% deliverables with 1999 key contacts plan.

Manage volume growth and protect market share

- Balance growth, market share and profitability. Considering this balance, ensure operational processes are in place to achieve 1999 volume increases of xx in LPG and xx in retail.

Rebase costs for current environment
Identify levers to re-base costs to achieve 10% ROACE by 2002—1Q.

Improve capital efficiency and decapitalise as suitable
Deliver 30% capital efficiency improvement in new builds and complete **full cost** builds for xx million per site.
Develop decapitalisation options & landbank strategy—2Q.
Develop Retail strategy to support consideration for further investment with Financial Memorandum to CAC in 2Q.

Leading Indicators of Progress

Prize/Key Activity Set	1Q	2Q	3Q	4Q	Yr
New build start-ups					
Specific divestments ($6 million)					
Additional divestments ($4 million)					
LPG Slawkow terminal on-line					
Management Information improved processes and streamline transaction accounting					

(continued)

Exhibit 3   *(concluded)*

KPI's	1998 Actual	1999 Plan	1999 Latest Estim.	1999 Stretch	PG5 Range	PG3 CoCo Avg.
Fuel margin (cpl)						
Retail volume growth						
Retail MSC like-for-like growth						
MSC/onsite costs (incl. depr)						
CoCo onsite costs ($k/site)						
Offsite costs ($million)						
Onsite costs/GP						
Offsite costs/SOC						
SOC/$ invested (CoCo)						

	1998 Actual	1999 Plan	1999 Latest Estim.	1999 Stretch	PG5 BM	LPG PG Avg.
LPG volume						
LPG bulk installations (#)						
LPG unit margin ($/tonne)						
LPG debtor days (end-year)						
LPG fixed cost cover						
S&D retail added value (cpl)						
Supply LPG added value ($/tonne)						
Filling plants ($million)						
Transport cylinder ($/tonne)						
Transport bulk ($/tonne)						

[1]'99 Income (including prize) less delta margin less delta forex less delta tax rate less 98 income.
[2]No prize delivery until income improvement = target improvement − prize.

"The actual contract is relatively simple," said Chase. "A few financial goals—profit before tax, cash flow, investment, return on invested capital—I have never seen more than four. Then there are two or three high-level non-financial targets. Once the contract is decided, people are free to achieve them in whatever way they find appropriate."

Quarterly, the top team met with the Business Unit leaders to review progress towards the goals. Failure to meet the terms of the contract was a serious matter and at times meant reassignment of the Business Unit leader. "There is an understanding here . . . that this is a performance culture and

either you deliver or you don't," explained Richard Newton, Group Vice President. Chase commented, "You deliver what you promise—that is our performance mantra. If you do not believe you can deliver, do not make the promise." What if someone does not deliver? "We start from the assumption that if you can't cut it in a particular job you might be able to somewhere else. You are given one or two options to perform somewhere else."

Providing the Stretch: The Peer Challenge   Performance Contracts set the unit's targets, but Peer Groups provided the challenge and stretch to each unit. The peer group played three roles in the challenge. First, business goals were discussed within the Peer Groups prior to the finalisation of the Performance Contract. Second, Peer Groups were a key mechanism for determining resource allocation. Finally, they were the primary means of knowledge sharing. One executive described Peer Groups as "the forum in which Business Units must fight their corner, justify their promises to their closest colleagues and prove they deserve the resources they seek in competition with other Business Units."

"The Peer Challenge," Polly Flinn, Business Unit Head and Vice President Retail Marketing, explained, "was about convincing people in similar positions to support your investment proposal knowing they could invest that same capital [elsewhere] and going eyeball to eyeball with them—and then having to reaffirm whether you have made it or not over the coming months or quarters."

The key for the Peer Group process to reach its full potential was an obligation for every high performing Business Unit to assist and improve the under-performing units. Chase summarized the reasons why the peer group structure worked for BP:

> One of the things we find when we talk to other companies is that they disbelieve us when we say that our performance units have a high capacity and bias to improve one another. The point is they have to do that or they can't meet their goals, because they have performance outputs for the whole peer group. Today the top three Business Units in the Peer Group are responsible for the improvement of the bottom three. That's how they work in a structural sense. They are measured for it.

The performance measurement associated with the peer group processes forced the Business Unit leaders to "grab good ideas from one another and to impose their good ideas on one another," added Chase. This motivation was built into the bonus structure. 50% of a Business Unit leader's bonus was based on peer group performance and 50% on Business Unit performance.

Integration through Collective Learning   If performance management was the foundation of Act I

then relentless collective learning was the leverage point.

"In order to generate extraordinary value for shareholders, a company has to learn better than its competitors and apply that knowledge throughout its business faster and more widely than they do," said Sir John Browne. "Any organisation that thinks it does everything the best and that it need not learn from others is incredibly arrogant and foolish." This commitment to knowledge and insight was deeply ingrained in BP. John Manzoni, Head of BP's Gas, Renewables and Power business, explained,

> I always say to people, your seat at the table inside BP depends on your level of insight, it does not depend on the position where you sit in the organisation. And you find all over the place that people get to sit at important tables and have important conversations and the reason that they are there is because they bring insight.

Four factors converged to help BP become a learning organisation: the intellectual curiosity of the top management team, the firm-wide attention to relentlessly building human capital, the Peer Assist processes and the depth and quality of conversations. Together they ensured that insights were leveraged across the company.

Intellectual Curiosity at the Top   Balancing the competitive nature of the performance-driven side of BP's culture was the intellectual curiosity and openness to knowledge sharing of the people in the company, especially evident in the top team. Browne and his colleagues were described by a *Financial Times* journalist as "an unusually active and well-financed university faculty—earnest, morally engaged and careful of other's sensibilities."[1] Strategic thinking and deep questioning of business purpose were the normal way of operating. In Sir John Browne's words,

> This company is founded on a deep belief in intellectual rigour. In my experience, unless you can lay out rational arguments as the foundation of what you do,

---

[1]Lloyd, John, "Company Law," *The Business Financial Times Weekend Magazine,* September 9, 2000.

nothing happens. Rigour implies that you understand the assumptions you have made . . . assumptions about the state of the world, of what you can do, and how your competitors will interact with it, and how the policy of the world will or will not allow you to do something.

While Browne's appetite for knowledge was insatiable, he himself was a creator of knowledge— a sort of theory builder. As theory builder he relentlessly engaged his top team in discussions around ideas. The resulting intellectual, strategic focus of the team was extraordinary. Asked about the genesis of the strategic nature of the senior team, Chase had this to say,

> We are a deeply questioning team; we constantly inspect what we do to find out whether it is in fact the exercise of laziness or prejudice. We do it in every area; we do it behaviourally, in business process terms, and in operational delivery. . . . It helps if your CEO is a very strategic thinker. John is not only a strategic thinker by predisposition but by intellectual learning and a constant search for strategic improvement. He is a continuous researcher for new ideas. He is an unusual CEO; he constantly surrounds himself with strategic stimuli.

Asked to describe some of the strategic issues discussed in the top management team, John Browne elaborated,

> . . . We look at economic history, the rate of change in capital intensive industries and we ask ourselves how we think the oil industry will change as a result of transportation changes . . . based on what happened, for instance, when canals were put in the UK in the late 18th century. We think about these long-term trends, and what are the consequences of doing the business we are doing, and how we can manage these consequences. Those consequences matter. Environmental questions related to burning oil and gas influence supply and demand parameters of oil and gas because if people worry about that, then they inevitably change their attitude about how they get their energy. . . . We test our assumptions. . . . What is really going to happen. Could the price of oil drop below $10 a barrel over the medium term? Unlikely, but what happens if it does? We think about how technological substitution in the short term will work . . . the main point is that all these things we keep interrogating and asking

ourselves how dependent are we on one or the other of these factors.

This openness to questioning and learning extended beyond the boundaries of the enterprise. The members of the top team had also established networks of talking partners across industry. Sir John Browne's membership of the boards of Intel and Goldman Sachs provided added insights into industry models. As Nick Butler explained,

> Membership of the board of Intel has been critical to him. About 18 months ago people thought that established businesses like BP would be destroyed by IT, there would be no need for intermediaries. What he had seen at Intel convinced him that this was not the case, there was some potential in B2B, but very little in B2C. The insights from Intel averted risks of over investment even though we looked old fashioned at the time.

The team were also involved with Cambridge University, having set up a multidisciplinary institute on fluid flow analysis which brought together chemists, engineers, physicists, and academic staff. Members of the top team visited the institute four or five times per year and maintained contacts with numerous faculties not just in Cambridge but also at Stanford, Yale, and a wide range of other very high quality academic institutions around the world. As Nick Butler, who held many of these links on behalf of Browne explained, "the process keeps us in touch with people who know more than we do. It is a daily reminder that we are only one relatively small part of a complex world. It is a reminder of all things we do not know."

Relentlessly Building Human Capital   The intellectual curiosity of the top team provided a model for the company. Seeking those within the company who had the insight necessary to run the business was an obsession. The focus on the development of individual talent began from the top with the profound obligation the top team felt to the long-term intellectual health of BP. Much of their time on a day-to-day basis was spent coaching the talented men and women in the organisation. Each member typically coached and mentored cohorts of seven to ten Group Vice Presidents. Chase described how he saw this role,

I gossip with them about what is really going on within the inner cabinet, I share confidences, I tell them about my discussions with John Browne. I build trust with them. I agree with them what their weaknesses are, and agree to work with them. You have to take the time to engage them with examples that will make them broader and wiser. To develop their sense of responsibility for the firm; who are they developing. The greatest pleasure I get is from this development of talent.

In turn, the Group Vice Presidents coached the Business Unit Heads. A subgroup also sat on the Learning and Development Committee. The committee met monthly to discuss the long-term development of key talent. As David Watson, a member of the committee explained, "We are experimenting with a new learning model based on reflection. Each committee meeting is two days of deep, meaningful dialogue." Watson continued, "The whole way we are thinking about learning and development is starting with the brand values: the possibility that actually what we should be developing for future leadership is people with the brand values deeply embedded, not just people who know how to run a part of the business."

BP's management also created forums for the development and expression of its collective intellect through university based education programs for executives. In a special programme developed at Cambridge University, BP executives debated issues such as the social impact of business, the future of international society, valuing nature and ethics. At Stanford and Harvard they used case studies to hone their knowledge of globalisation and sources of competitive advantage, and their skills in country risk analysis. The themes of all the programs had a common thread summed up in the name of the Cambridge program, "Thinking into the Future—Learning from the Past." The programs represented a new orientation of the company towards society, its customers and its employees.

Through formal processes, high potential individuals had the option to enter the Group Development Program (GDP). This program was a combination of skill assessment, training and development and career progression. A subset of those individuals in the GDP was selected to serve as "turtles" or personal assistant.[2] As a turtle, the executive would become a shadow to Chase, Browne, or another top team member and be involved in all conversations, all meetings, and all discussions of the top management. "They come with us around the world. They sit in all our executive meetings," explained Chase, "It is a 15 hour a day job and they do it for about 12 months. But in return they see everything."

Turtles and the GDP were examples of the "stretch" that was part of a career at BP. Manzoni, who was the first personal assistant to Browne even before the word "turtle" was used, explained, "I have had tremendous opportunities for learning because I have had no bloody idea how to do the job that I have been put into almost every single time." Those that succeeded were rewarded with rapid advancement in their careers at BP.

But this relentless building of human capital was not simply limited to those on the Group Development Program or the "turtles." From the end of 1999 onwards the company had put substantial resources behind stitching together the 275 human resource Intranet systems it had developed and inherited. As Dave Latin, who managed the project commented, "Following the mergers we saw this as an opportunity to simplify. What got the board excited was the aspiration that e-hr could touch each of the 100,000 employees and cause a shift in behaviour." Over the following two years an ever increasing portfolio of Intranet based developmental tools was rolled out across the world.

"Competencies Online" enabled individuals to assess their current skills and development needs by seeking e-enabled feedback from their peers and colleagues; individuals profiled and communicated their competencies and job aspirations on myProfile, whilst myAgent continuously scouted and reported back job and project vacancies with similar competency needs. Managers who posted the competency profiles of the job and project

[2]Derived from Teenage Mutant Ninja Turtles, adventure cartoon characters popular in the 1980s, the term "turtle" was used to describe a person who is able to do "high-energy, surprising things and appear to be normal," explained Lee Edwards, former turtle to CEO Sir John Browne.

vacancies in their team using myJobMarket automatically received matched information from the many thousands of on-line resumes. Within a year BP had created a vibrant and transparent internal labour market, with over 17,000 logging in every week to the myCareer portal. The goal was to get to a situation, by the end of 2001, when all BP employees would use the portal to profile their skills, find job matches, identify their development needs and access learning and development opportunities.

Leveraging through Peer Assist   Performance Contracts and Peer Challenge were the backbone of the performance management process. However the heart of the collective intellectual and social capital of the organization was most evident in Peer Assists. Business Unit leaders regularly provided help to one another—to help identify the best strategy, to learn more about a new area of work, or to give validation to a decision—in the form of advice or actual resources through a Peer Assist. Peer Assists spanned peer group boundaries, often requiring the involvement of people in multiple divisions of the company.

Polly Flinn, former Amoco employee and Vice President of Retail Marketing, learned quickly at BP that federal behaviour was the norm. While serving as the retail Business Unit lead in Poland in 1999, Flinn asked for assistance from four leaders at BP who came together in a Peer Assist team to look at the Poland strategy and give Flinn their advice. After Flinn implemented the advice from the Peer Assist, the retail marketing business in Poland became profitable for the first time. In 1998, the Business Unit lost $20 million; in 2000 it earned $6 million. "This was BP at its best," recalled Flinn. When Flinn was faced with the near impossible task of masterminding the development and rollout of BP's new retail offering, BP Connect, she called on the Peer Assist process once again, but this time on a much grander scale. "The BP Connect Peer Assist was Poland times 30," recalled Flinn. "Of the 300 people involved, only 10% actually had Performance Contract goals related to BP Connect, yet because of their desire to share their skills and their expectations of federal behaviour, people contributed."

Leaders at BP viewed participation in a Peer Assist as having mutual benefits for both parties. "First, the team that has asked for the Peer Assist obtains strategic and operational insight from the most respected experts in BP," explained Flinn. "Secondly it is a development opportunity for the people who participate. People want to do it." Top management also participated in Peer Assists, especially regarding strategic issues. Chase, deputy CEO, visited the prototype BP Connect in Atlanta and "became in effect the brand champion for this offer in terms of explaining it to other businesses in BP. He helped to build support for the retail network" said Flinn.

Creating Purposeful Conversations   People learn and share learning through conversations. At BP, management explicitly focused on enhancing the depth, breadth and quality of conversations at all levels, as a means to supporting organization-wide learning. As Rodney Chase described,

> One of the most pressing reasons to create a dialogue . . . has been the rise of connectivity within the space in which BP operates. There are people who by dint of communications, flexibility and immediacy have the capacity to find things out and transmit the information instantaneously. . . . It is palpable, it is very real and it is expressed with great frequency. It is on my screen now everyday.

"There's no point in just changing a process," explained Watson. "It has to start with changing the fabric—the information. If it is the same information, we'll get the same conversations, so we have to provide different information for different conversations." The source of the information that fuelled the conversations had shifted—no longer were communications primarily a top down process. There was a growing recognition that the information for dialogue and conversation came from many sources including families and young employees.

"This organisation does not work as a series of instructions—it works by conversations and consensus. It takes longer to get there but once you do, the whole organisation moves," Manzoni explained.

Beyond enhancing the richness and diversity of information, the company made an effort to improve and sharpen the quality of conversations through two means: linking conversations to purpose, and legitimizing dissent and challenge.

According to John Browne, "people do not learn, at least in a corporate environment, without a target. You can implore people to learn, and they will to some extent. But if you say 'look the learning is necessary in order to cut the cost of drilling a well by 10%', then they will learn with a purpose." This philosophy was built into BP by linking as many conversation processes as possible to tangible and concrete goals. Peer assists and peer reviews, performance contracts—they were all primarily aimed at developing intense, purposeful conversations, driven by concrete goals and targets.

The other basis of enhancing the learning value of conversations was to legitimize dissent and challenge. Again in the words of John Browne,

People are challenged the whole time. "Just run that by me one more time" is the mildish challenge. "I don't understand it" to "surely you've got this wrong" to "no, that is far too conventional and we have to think of a different way"—the discussions, debates and challenges happen everywhere. I participate in it; everyone participates in it. If you were sitting in the management committee, sometimes it gets very hot indeed. "No it doesn't make sense"—"well make it make sense!" The questions are continuously around . . . for example Rodney and I have worked together since 1984, and we have worked close up through the ranks and it is a very close relationship. You would think we would be so familiar with each other that we would know the way each other thinks, but it is actually the reverse. We challenge each other very hard, in a very appropriate way, but it is the purpose of the relationship to get a better result, and we do that. And that, in turn, encourages others to do that.

Deep inside the organization, conversations and dialogue occurred in forums such as Performance Contract discussions or message boards on the intranet. Use of the intranet was not limited to young hires. Rodney Chase, a thirty year veteran of BP, checked the message boards daily and was actively engaged in the communication. Chase saw dialogue with employees and stakeholders as essential to operating as a business in society.

For a global institution we are very nimble. When we want something to happen around the world, we can get all the swallows in our worldwide organization to flip like that. They can go in this direction, they can go in that direction. How does it happen? I have no idea. It is some combination of informal word of mouth, networks, which are encouraged, informal networks based on career friendships or based on professional groupings, or based on clubs on the Intranet. If you've got an important message that needs to get out in the firm it will happen in 24 hours. And you can be certain that every thinker in the organization will have heard about it and will be thinking about it. It means that the forces for inertia have been largely swept away.

Aligning Organizational and Individual Values
When John Browne and Rodney Chase joined what was then British Petroleum as young graduates, they were joining one of the United Kingdom's most prestigious branded companies. But over time the relationship between the oil industry and society had become increasingly tense. While society demanded the products of energy—heat, light and mobility—it also demanded that the production of these things be done harmlessly. When accidents occurred, public outrage was the result. In 1989, the Exxon Valdez oil spill in Alaska was one such accident. Later in 1995, the Shell Brentspar incident was another.[3] The two major points of tension were the societal impact of the extraction of oil and the environmental impact of emissions during refining and consumption of fuel.

This tension came to a head for BP in 1997 when an NGO, Amnesty International, accused BP of funding private armies in Colombia. A team of BP engineers had discovered what they soon realised to be the largest oil reservoir in the western hemisphere. The oil find had attracted merchants and

---

[3]Shell in 1995 planned to dispose of an offshore loading buoy by scuttling it in deep water off the northwestern coast of Britain. Environmentalists were outraged and a consumer boycott ensued. Shell stations were vandalised, some of them firebombed, or shot upon with automatic weapons. Finally Shell brought the buoy to a Norwegian port and eventually dismantled it.

investors, labourers and contractors, the army, and the guerrillas who wanted to extract their own political rent from the process. The team was in the middle of a region of underdeveloped infrastructure, complex social problems, and a government fighting a 35-year civil war. Upon setting up exploration operations, BP was accused by Amnesty International of providing lethal training to the Colombian security forces through the services of a British-owned private security firm. The Amnesty International news release asserted that these "Colombian security forces have been responsible for widespread extrajudicial executions, torture and 'disappearances' of civilians." BP's reputation was badly tarnished. Though BP denied the accusation, the management realized that a change in the way that BP worked with local communities needed to occur.

Awakening of a Force for Good   The question "What is your personal Colombia?" echoed in the minds of all BP's executives. Memories of the incident affected every decision made by an executive and shaped a new outlook regarding BP's role as a business. Edwards explained, "When we talked to the outside world, the oil industry was seen as big, powerful, dirty, secretive, grey—and we didn't want that. We didn't want to be an unknown player in a big sector not known for goodness or as a force for goodness." Chase described the formation of the concept of force for good,

> We now have a century of dealing with nations with the fundamental task of the search for and extraction of energy raw materials. It is very much out of that history that the commitment to becoming a force for good was born. . . . It's not enough for us simply to find the resources and create for the host nations the wealth extraction from the release of those resources. It is not seen either by them or us as a sufficient force for good. We have to recognise and plan more specifically other goals which are not so obviously the role of the commercial enterprise.

John Browne personally saw the company's efforts at being a force of good more in terms of building reputation—the last of the core premises of organizational design he had enumerated. "There is, I believe, no conflict between investing in reputation and creating long-term shareholder value," he said. The primary benefit of reputation, however, lay in building the emotional strength of the organization. As he described,

> The interesting thing about the behaviour of this firm is that we always start with the foundation of rationality but we recognize that that in itself will not take you far. What you have to apply on top of it is an emotional state. . . .
>
> It is easy to detach the employees from a company. A company is pretty impersonal and artificial, and it produces continuous contradictions which have to be resolved. We have the contradiction that we produce oil and gas, and we want to reduce the impact of that on the environment. The question to us is how do you genuinely allow people to transform all their individuality into the company because if they can do that then people will begin to think and behave in a way that is aligned to the goals of the company.
>
> To build the reputation, we picked four areas. First, safety: when you invite someone to come and work, you should send them home in the same shape as when they arrived—that is a minimum requirement for respect of a person, and you have to take that terribly seriously. Second, you have to take care of the natural environment. It is important because people do not want companies to make a mess and leave them behind. Third, everyone wants a place in the ideal which is free of all discrimination; it doesn't matter what you stand for in terms of your race, gender, sexual orientation or religious beliefs. All that matters is merit. Fourth, the company has to invest in the community from which the people have come, so as to narrow the gap between life within the company and life outside the company.

In a show of commitment to these goals, Browne took an unusual and risky stand in a speech regarding climate change at Stanford University. He admitted that global climate change was a problem that BP could no longer ignore and outlined BP's plans for addressing the problem.

> The time to consider the policy dimensions of climate change is not when the link between greenhouse gases and climate change is conclusively proven but when the possibility cannot be discounted and is taken seriously by the society of which we are part. We in BP have reached that point. . . . To be absolutely clear— we must now focus on what can and what should be

done, not because we can be certain climate change is happening, but because the possibility can't be ignored. If we are all to take responsibility for the future of our planet, then it falls to us to begin to take precautionary action now.[4]

The steps Browne outlined were to control BP's emissions, to fund continuing scientific research, to take initiatives for joint implementation, to develop alternative fuels for the long term, and to contribute to the public policy debate in search of the wider global answers to the problem. In an industry characterized by an old boys network spanning the major oil companies, this move was met with surprise and hostility. "Some of the sceptics and the press said, 'He has left the church. He is no longer with the industry,'" recalled Edwards, "But as soon as [Browne] made this speech, the internal feedback was unbelievable—from children of employees, spouses." BP officially removed itself from the Global Climate Coalition, a lobbying and public relations organisation based in Washington, D.C. which opposed government intervention with regard to the climate. Browne was, in fact, responding to internal pressures to leave the coalition. BP's employees felt that what the coalition was arguing for was "intellectually unjustifiable" because credible scientists were finding the opposite—that gas emissions were contributing to global warming.

A year later, in April 1998, BP began to receive recognition for its bold moves. *Oil & Gas Journal* highlighted BP in a review of financial strategies of the top oil and gas companies.

> Within the top 10, there is one striking example of a company being driven by a different vision. BP has designated corporate citizenship and being "forward-thinking about the environment, human rights, and dealing with people and ethics" as "the new fulcrum of competition between oil companies in the late 1990s." Several of the other leading companies have adopted parts of this approach, with Shell probably going the furthest. But none has been as explicit or committed as BP.[5]

[4]Sir John Browne in a speech at Stanford University, California, May 19, 1997.

[5]Common financial strategies found among top 10 oil and gas firms. *Oil & Gas Journal*, Tulsa, April 20, 1998, Anonymous.

The stand that Browne took placed BP in a distinctive position in its industry. As an example, following the Stanford speech, BP struck up an agreement with the Environmental Defense Fund to design a system for trading greenhouse gas emissions within BP. In this system, revenues and costs of carbon trades were treated like actual cash flows, which allowed BP to measure environmental performance as financial performance. These actions were part of the company's increasing concern with being progressive and green—in other words being a force for good. Being a force for good was about having "goals that are worth pursuing for everyone; that have to do with making society better as a result of our participation than if we had not been there," remarked Chase.

From Act I to Act II: The Challenges and Questions   In July 2000, after a wide ranging exercise involving staff throughout the company as well as external specialists, BP launched a new corporate branding designed to project both the changes which had taken place and the company's aspirations for the future.

The company would be known simply as "bp," with the familiar BP shield and Amoco torch replaced by a fresh, new symbol depicting a vibrant sunburst of green, white and yellow. Named the Helios mark after the sun god of ancient Greece, the new logo was intended to exemplify dynamic energy—in all its forms, from oil and gas to solar—that the company delivered to its ten million daily customers around the world. The attributes of the brand—progressive, green, innovative and performance-driven—were the values that would shape BP's future.

At a press conference, the launch of the new brand, under the provocative slogan "beyond petroleum" was described by one analyst as "a sun rise brand for a sun set company." Though the company had made great progress on many fronts, BP clearly needed to produce a final proof point, that it could achieve long term growth with short-term returns.

BP's financial situation, relative to that of the other super majors, Exxon Mobil and Royal Dutch

Exhibit 4   BP, Royal Dutch Shell (RD), Exxon Mobil (XOM), and S&P 500 Index Share Price Comparison

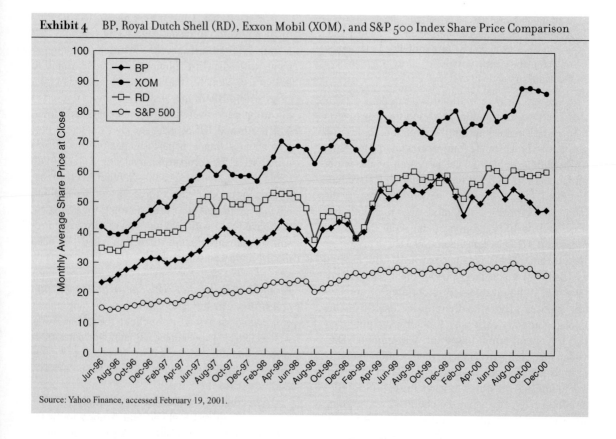

Source: Yahoo Finance, accessed February 19, 2001.

Shell, added to the challenge of achieving long term growth. Over 90% of BP's 500,000 shareholders were individual investors. As of the end of the third quarter of 2000, its net debt-to-capital ratio was 25%, increased from 19% in the previous quarter and well above Exxon Mobil's 9.5% and Royal Dutch's 1.7%.[6] Although BP's ROCE, at 19.7%, was the highest of the international majors in 2000,[7] its stock was trading at a discount to Exxon Mobil (see Exhibit 4 for comparison).[8] Alexander, as the voice of concern of BP's management, explained the challenge the company faced, "We cannot deliver what our brand means unless we can grow ROCE and the top line at the same time. We

have built ROCE [by cost cutting], but we have not grown the top line."

Those on the outside were sceptical of BP's growth strategy. A financial analyst expressed doubt of BP's possible success.

BP is coming to the end of its restructuring and acquisition phase. It is now signalling a return to an organic growth oriented strategy. . . . We are sceptical that BP can sustain its target of 10% annual earnings growth. . . . Our view is supported by history, which shows that few companies are able to grow capital employed organically and cut costs at the same time. If BP does manage to deliver underlying earnings growth of over 10% annually it will be a major achievement.[9]

▌ [6]Salomon Smith Barney Equity Research Report, November 13, 2000.
▌ [7]Ibid.
▌ [8]UBS Warburg Global Equity Research Report, November 9, 2000.

▌ [9]Commerzbank Securities Research Report, September 22, 2000.

But beyond these issues was a broader question of the role of public and private sector companies in the energy field. As Nick Butler reflected:

I believe that over the last century the world has been artificially divided into the public and the private sectors. The private sector has been seen as exploitative, narrow and self-interested. The public world has been seen as representing the interests of the whole community. This dichotomy has been established and underpins the political debate. This was not always the case in economic history . . . the two used to run together and to work for common purpose. It is interesting now to see if the moment is coming when the two sectors can once again work in harmony. The possibility is very interesting for a company such as BP.

Sir John Browne echoed the same issue:

However big Shell, Exxon-Mobil and BP are, together they control only 9% of the world's oil production. This is not exactly market dominance. The rest is controlled by different versions of state-owned organizations. We are looking at how the interface is changing, and as you see what is happening in China and in Saudi Arabia, you recognize that that interface is changing. Who will get to do what? Will states do things themselves or will there be some new partnership?

To respond to these questions and challenges, Browne once again reorganized BP in 2001. At the heart of the reorganization was the desire to grow organically, and to respond to the opportunities for growth that would largely lie in the hands of different markets, and the respective governments. In the words of Sir John, "As we set up the targets, it was clear that the organization structure would need to change in order to be right for the next phase of the company—that of organic growth."

The Reorganization of 2001   One change was to consolidate the business units, thus reducing their total number. "We had created too many components," said Browne "and with growing scale, that had led to too much complexity, too many interactions. We had to balance complexity against ownership."

For example, the company consolidated its four business units in Alaska into one. They shared drilling capacity, operated in a single taxation environment, and single reputational environment. While consolidating the units, decentralization was maintained, perhaps enhanced, by delegating accountability down from the business unit leaders to the next level of managers.

The role and deployment of the Group Vice Presidents were also changed. Instead of being jointly and severely responsible for performance, they were made personally accountable for the performance of the sum of their business units. Previously, in order to integrate the leadership cadre, they had all been located in London. "That worked," said Sir John, "but actually in a decentralized model, the senior managers of the company should be out there with the business units to build relationships." So, he distributed the Group VP's around the world—as Presidents or Regional Directors in the U.S., in Asia, in Latin America, and so on. "Now they have both business and regional accountability," he said. "They have a specific remit, and they are the face of the company."

At the heart of this change was an acknowledgement of the regional role as an enabler of organic growth. "It is not completely clear to me," said Sir John, in a marvelous example of British understatement, "that the business goals of the corporate and the goals of the government are automatically aligned without a lot of effort. . . . You can say to them you want them to work five times harder and they will say why? So that you can bring in imported equipment and take out the money?"

"Take the case of Trinidad," he said. "I have heard this time and again from Prime Ministers and Presidents there. They used to be a big producer of sugar, and they couldn't afford to buy the boiled sweets that were made in the U.K. . . . We have a gigantic amount of gas in Trinidad, and we have to think and we have to do several things. We have to work with the government to build capacity. Our role is very much recruitment and training of people—we are less good at doing what governments should be doing such as building roads. Number two, we need to work with them to expand the number of small and medium enterprises in the country . . . build things with other people who will use some of that gas. . . . We are going to be a part of all that investment, not exclusively, but our reputation and the fact that we will be there and making sure the project works will allow other people to come in and invest. This is good news for us, because they will use the gas, and it is good news for the government. We have to build this mutuality."

To build this mutuality, BP needed strong local relationships. "It would be extraordinarily unwise to continuously go to a government, flying in from London, saying I need the following things. You need someone who can set it in the context and say the company is doing this, and this is where the mutual advantage is." This was the enhanced role for the Group VP's—thereby opening doors for the business units so that they could effectively do their work to grow the business.

The third element of the 2001 reorganization was a consolidation and strengthening of the functional competencies of BP. "We believed that greater emphasis was needed for enhancing our marketing skills, and understanding the differences between marketing and sales. That difference is now put in real organizational terms, so for the first time in the company's history, we have a marketing director and she is in charge of the strategic side." Similarly, the technology group was given full accountability for the strategic goals and targets in the areas of technology development, and for deployment of people. "We have to focus heavily not only on how we retain and deploy people in this area, but how we continuously renew the quality of people because this is a very fundamental part of our functional capability," said Sir John.

Similarly, the highly fragmented internal supply and trading organization was consolidated into one entity, with the goal of stopping internal transactions and to leverage scale. In the words of Sir John,

"It is certainly true that returns to supply and trading increase with scale—they just do, and you can prove it—and we have reached such a scale that we had to consider that benefit. But, equally, your reputation is highly dependent on how you use that scale, especially in unregulated markets, and that worries us a lot. In unregulated markets, these decisions of judgment are critical to the reputation of the firm, and that is something that has to be done in one place."

While describing these organizational changes, John Browne emphasized BP's fundamental philosophy about organizing:

> The thing about organization is nothing is ever fixed, at least in BP, and we renew ourselves by learning what is good about the past and changing all things that are not so good. They are behaviour dependent. Grouping the Group Vice Presidents in London to make them into a team so that they knew each other, and could interact among themselves in a way that made the peer groups effective—that worked. I believe that investment will endure, and now we can send them outside London. In three or five years time, we may have to change again because it might become silo-like, and we might think that the best way would be to bring them all back to London or New York, or try something completely different.

Was this reorganization enough, or even right, as a response to the challenges and questions? Sir John was slightly philosophical in his reply:

> Some of our competitors do not have a good reputation. Yet they trade at a higher multiple than BP. Does reputation matter? If you are from Mars, would you not say that those with worse reputations are valued more highly? . . . This debate which still goes on is about deep-seated values. Recruitment, motivation, great place to work . . . these should all in theory be expressed in market value at the end, but in practice may take more than one period to do so. But, in the end, I firmly believe that the more a company reflects the values of the society from which its people are drawn, the better the company is.

Case 8-2   GE's Two-Decade Transformation: Jack Welch's Leadership

Jack Welch glowed with pride at General Electric's Annual Meeting in March 1999. For the first time, GE's revenues exceeded $100 billion, operating margins were at an all-time high of 16.7%, and earnings per share had increased 14% over 1997's record level. In recognition of this outstanding performance and the company's transformation over the previous two decades, the *Fortune* poll of U.S. corporate executives had voted GE the country's "Most Admired Company" for the second year running, and the *Financial Times* had named it the "Most Respected Company in the World."

While the mood at the annual meeting was clearly upbeat, some shareholders worried about Welch's intention to retire at the end of 2000. The company he would hand over to his successor was radically different from the GE he took over in 1981. The question on many minds was whether anyone could sustain the blistering pace of change and growth characteristic of the Welch era. It would be a tough act to follow. (See Exhibit 1 for financial summary of Welch's era at GE.)

The GE Heritage

Founded in 1878 by Thomas Edison, General Electric grew from its early focus on the generation, distribution, and use of electric power to become, a hundred years later, one of the world's leading diversified industrial companies. In addition to its core businesses in power generation, household appliances, and lighting, by 1978 the company was also engaged in businesses as diverse as aircraft engines, medical systems, and diesel locomotives.

▌ Research Associate Meg Wozny prepared this case under the supervision of Professor Christopher A. Bartlett. HBS cases are developed solely as the basis for class discussion. Cases are not intended to serve as endorsements, sources of primary data, or illustrations of effective or ineffective management.
▌ Copyright © 1999 President and Fellows of Harvard College. Harvard Business School case 399-150.

Long regarded as a bellwether of American management practices, GE was constantly undergoing change. In the 1930s, it was a model of the era's highly centralized, tightly controlled corporate form. By the 1950s, GE had delegated responsibility to hundreds of department managers, leading a trend towards greater decentralization. But a subsequent period of "profitless growth" in the 1960s caused the company to strengthen its corporate staffs and develop sophisticated strategic planning systems. Again, GE found itself at the leading edge of management practice.

When Reg Jones, Welch's predecessor, became CEO in 1973, he inherited the company that had just completed a major reorganization. Overlaying its 10 groups, 46 divisions, and 190 departments were 43 strategic business units designed to support the strategic planning that was so central to GE's management process. Jones raised strategic planning to an art form, and GE again became the benchmark for hundreds of companies that imitated its SBU-based structure and its sophisticated planning processes. Soon, however, Jones was unable to keep up with reviewing and approving the massive volumes of information generated by 43 strategic plans. Explaining that "the review burden had to be carried on more shoulders," in 1977 he capped GE's departments, divisions, groups, and SBUs with a new organizational layer of "sectors," representing macrobusiness agglomerations such as consumer products, power systems, or technical products.

In addition to his focus on strategic planning, Jones spent a great deal of time on government relations, becoming the country's leading business statesman. During the 1970s, he was voted CEO of the Year three times by his peers, with one leading business journal dubbing him CEO of the Decade in 1979. When he retired in 1981, *The Wall Street Journal* proclaimed Jones a "management legend,"

Exhibit 1 Selected Financial Data ($ millions)

General Electric Company and Consolidated Affiliates

	1998	1997	1996	1995	1994	1993	1992	1991	1990	1986	1981
Revenues	$100,469	$90,840	$79,179	$70,028	$60,109	$55,701	$53,051	$51,283	$49,696	$36,725	$27,240
Earnings from continuing operations	9,296	8,203	7,280	6,573	5,915	4,184	4,137	3,943	3,920	3,689	N/A
Loss from discontinued operations	—	—	—	—	-1,189	993	588	492	383	N/A	N/A
Net earnings	9,296	8,203	7,280	6,573	4,726	4,315	4,725	2,636	4,303	2,492	1,652
Dividends declared	4,081	3,535	3,138	2,838	2,546	2,229	1,985	1,808	1,696	1,081	715
Earned on average share owners' equity	25.7%	25.0%	24.0%	23.5%	18.1%	17.5%	20.9%	12.2%	20.2%	17.3%	19.1%
Per share											
Net earnings	2.84	2.50	2.20	1.95	1.38	3.03	2.75	2.55	2.42	2.73	N/A
Net earnings—diluted	2.80	2.46	2.16	1.93	1.37	2.52	2.75	1.51	2.42	N/A	N/A
Dividends declared	1.25	1.08	0.95	0.845	0.745	1.31	1.16	1.04	0.96	1.18	N/A
Stock price range (1)	103.9–69	76.6–47.9	53.1–34.7	36.6–24	27.4–22.5	26.7–20.2	87.5–72.7	78.1–53	75.5–50	44.4–33.2	69.9–51.1
Total assets of continuing operations	355,935	304,012	272,402	228,035	185,871	251,506	192,876	166,508	152,000	84,818	20,942
Long-term borrowings	59,663	46,603	49,246	51,027	36,979	28,194	25,298	22,602	20,886	100,001	1,059
Shares outstanding—average (in thousands)	3,268,998	3,274,692	3,307,394	3,367,624	3,417,476	1,707,979	1,714,396	1,737,863	1,775,104	912,594	227,528
Employees at year end											
United States	163,000	165,000	155,000	150,000	156,000	157,000	168,000	173,000	183,000	302,000	N/A
Other countries	130,000	111,000	84,000	72,000	60,000	59,000	58,000	62,000	62,000	71,000	N/A
Discontinued operations (primarily U.S.)	—	—	—	—	5,000	6,000	42,000	49,000	53,000	N/A	N/A
Total employees	293,000	276,000	239,000	222,000	221,000	222,000	268,000	284,000	298,000	373,000	404,000

(1) Price unadjusted for four 2-for-1 stock splits during the period.

adding that by handing the reins to Welch, GE had "replaced a legend with a live wire."

Welch's Early Priorities: GE's Restructuring

When the 45-year-old Welch became CEO in April 1981, the U.S. economy was in a recession. High interest rates and a strong dollar exacerbated the problem, resulting in the country's highest unemployment rates since the Depression. To leverage performance in GE's diverse portfolio of businesses, the new CEO challenged each to be "better than the best" and set in motion a series of changes that were to radically restructure the company over the next five years.

#1 or #2: Fix, Sell, or Close   Soon after taking charge, Welch set the standard for each business to become the #1 or #2 competitor in its industry— or to disengage. Asked whether this simple notion represented GE's strategy, Welch responded, "You can't set an overall theme or a single strategy for a corporation as broad as GE." By 1983, however, Welch had elaborated this general "#1 or #2" objective into a "three circle concept" of his vision for GE. (See Exhibit 2.) Businesses were categorized as core (with the priority of "reinvesting in productivity and quality"), high-technology (challenged to "stay on the leading edge" by investing in R&D), and services (required to "add outstanding people and make contiguous acquisitions"). To a question about what he hoped to build at GE, Welch replied:

> A decade from now, I would like General Electric to be perceived as a unique, high-spirited, entrepreneurial enterprise . . . the most profitable, highly diversified company on earth, with world quality leadership in every one of its product lines.[i]

But as GE managers struggled to build #1 or #2 positions in a recessionary environment and under attack from global—often Japanese—competitors, Welch's admonition to "fix, sell, or close" uncompetitive businesses frequently led to the latter options. Scores of businesses were sold, including central air-conditioning, housewares, coal mining, and, eventually, even GE's well-known consumer electronics business. Between 1981 and 1990, GE freed up over $11 billion of capital by selling off more than 200 businesses, which had accounted for 25% of 1980 sales. In that same time frame, the company made over 370 acquisitions, investing more than $21 billion in such major purchases

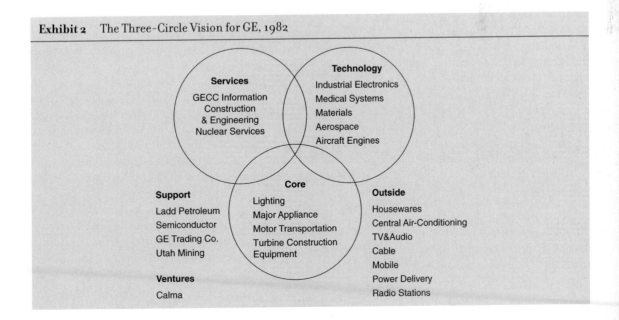

Exhibit 2   The Three-Circle Vision for GE, 1982

Services
GECC Information
Construction
& Engineering
Nuclear Services

Technology
Industrial Electronics
Medical Systems
Materials
Aerospace
Aircraft Engines

Support
Ladd Petroleum
Semiconductor
GE Trading Co.
Utah Mining

Core
Lighting
Major Appliance
Motor Transportation
Turbine Construction
Equipment

Outside
Housewares
Central Air-Conditioning
TV&Audio
Cable
Mobile
Power Delivery
Radio Stations

Ventures
Calma

Exhibit 3   Changes in the GE Business Portfolio

Major Acquisitions ($21 billion total)	Major Divestitures ($11 billion total)
• Calma (CAD/CAM equipment) • Intersil (semiconductors) • Employers Reinsurance Corp. • Decimus (computer leasing) • RCA (NBC Television, aerospace, electronics) • Kidder, Peabody (investment banking) • Polaris (aircraft leasing) • Genstar (container leasing) • Thomson/CGR (medical equipment) • Gelco (portable building leasing) • Borg-Warner Chemicals (plastics) • Montgomery Ward Credit (credit cards) • Roper (appliances) • Penske Leasing (truck leasing) • Financial Guaranty Insurance Co. • Tungsram (light bulbs) • Burton Group Financial Services • Travelers Mortgage (mortgage services) • Thorn Lighting (light bulbs) • Financial News Network (cable network) • Chase Manhattan Leasing • Itel Containers (container leasing) • Harrods/House of Fraser Credit Cards	• Central Air Conditioning • Pathfinder Mines • Broadcasting Properties (non-RCA TV & radio stations) • Utah International (mining) • Housewares (small appliances) • Family Financial Services • RCA Records • Nacolah Life Insurance (RCA's) • Coronet Carpets (RCA's) • Consumer Electronics (TV sets) • Carboloy (industrial cutting tools) • NBC Radio Networks • Roper Outdoor Lawn Equipment • GE Solid State (semiconductors) • Calma (CAD/CAM equipment) • RCA Globcomm international telex) • Ladd Petroleum (oil exploration & refining) • RCA Columbia Home Video • Auto Auctions (auctions of used cars)

Source: The Business Engine.

as Westinghouse's lighting business, Employers Reinsurance, RCA, Kidder Peabody, and Thomson/CGR, the French medical imaging company. (See Exhibit 3.)

Internally, Welch's insistence that GE become more "lean and agile" resulted in a highly disciplined destaffing process aimed at all large headquarters groups, including a highly symbolic 50% reduction in the 200-person strategic planning staff. Welch described his motivation:

> We don't need the questioners and checkers, the nit-pickers who bog down the process. . . . Today, each staff person has to ask, "How do I add value? How do I make people on the line more effective and competitive?"[ii]

As he continued to chip away at bureaucracy, Welch next scrapped GE's laborious strategic plan-

ning system—and with it, the remaining corporate planning staff. He replaced it with "real time planning" built around a five-page strategy playbook, which Welch and his 14 key business heads discussed in shirtsleeves sessions "unencumbered by staff." Each business's playbook provided simple one-page answers to five questions concerning current market dynamics, the competitors' key recent activities, the GE business response, the greatest competitive threat over the next three years, and the GE business's planned response.

The budgeting process was equally radically redefined. Rather than documenting internally focused comparisons with past performance, results were now evaluated against external competitively based criteria: Do sales show increases in market share, for example? Do margins indicate a cost advantage compared with competition?

In 1985, Welch eliminated the sector level, previously the powerful center of strategic control. (See Exhibits 4a and 4b.) By reducing the number of hierarchical levels from nine to as few as four, Welch ensured that all businesses reported directly to him. He said:

> We used to have department managers, sector managers, subsector managers, unit managers, supervisors. We're driving those titles out. . . . We used to go from the CEO to sectors to groups to businesses. Now we go from the CEO to businesses. There is nothing else. Zero.[iii]

Through downsizing, destaffing, and delayering, GE eliminated 59,290 salaried and 64,160 hourly positions between 1981 and 1988; divestiture eliminated an additional 122,700. Even when offset by the acquisitions, the number of employees at GE declined from 404,000 in 1980 to 330,000 by 1984 and 292,000 by 1989. Between 1981 and 1985, revenues increased modestly from $27.2 billion to $29.2 billion, but operating profits rose dramatically from $1.6 billion to $2.4 billion. This set the base for strong increases in both sales and earnings in the second half of the decade (see Exhibit 5).

This drastic restructuring in the early- and mid-1980s earned Welch the nickname "Neutron Jack," a term that gained currency even among GE managers when the CEO replaced 12 of his 14 business heads in August 1986. Welch's new "varsity team" consisted of managers with a strong commitment to the new management values, a willingness to break with the old GE culture, and most of all, an ability to take charge and bring about change. Despite his great dislike for a nickname he felt he did not deserve, Welch kept pushing the organization for more change. The further into the restructuring he got, the more convinced he became of the need for bold action:

> For me, the idea is to shun the incremental and go for the leap. . . . How does an institution know when the pace is about right? I hope you won't think I'm being melodramatic if I say that the institution ought to stretch itself, ought to reach, to the point where it almost comes unglued. . . . Remember the theory that a manager should have no more than 6 or 7 direct reports? I say the right number is closer to 10 or 15.[iv]

The Late 1980s: Second Stage of the Rocket

By the late 1980s, most of GE's business restructuring was complete, but the organization was still reeling from culture shock and management exhaustion. Welch was as eager as anyone in GE to move past the "Neutron-Jack" stage and begin rebuilding the company on its more solid foundations.

The "Software" Initiatives: Work-Out and Best Practices   Years after launching GE's massive restructuring effort, Welch concluded, "By mid-1988 the hardware was basically in place. We liked our businesses. Now it was time to focus on the organization's software." He also acknowledged that his priorities were shifting: "A company can boost productivity by restructuring, removing bureaucracy and downsizing, but it cannot sustain high productivity without cultural change."

In 1989, Welch articulated the management style he hoped to make GE's norm—an approach based on openness, candor, and facing reality. Simultaneously, he refined the core elements of the organizational culture he wanted to create—one characterized by speed, simplicity, and self-confidence.[1] Over the next few years, he launched two closely linked initiatives—dubbed Work-Out and Best Practices—aimed at creating the desired culture and management approach.

Work-Out   In late 1988, during one of Welch's regular visits to teach in the company's Management Development Institute, he engaged a group of GE managers in a particularly outspoken session about the difficulty they were having implementing change back at their operations. In a subsequent discussion with James Baughman, GE's director of

---

[1] Interestingly, Welch's first attempts at articulating and communicating GE's new cultural values were awkward. For example, in 1986 he defined 10 desirable cultural "attitudes and policies" which few in GE could remember, let alone practice. Furthermore, he communicated his new organizational model as the GE Business Engine, a concept that many found depersonalizing since it seemed to depict people as inputs into a financial machine. Gradually, Welch became more comfortable articulating cultural values which he continued to refine into what he termed "GE's social architecture." Eventually his concept of The Business Engine evolved to become The Human Engine.

Corporate Executive Office

John F. Welch, Jr.
Chairman

Edward E. Hood, Jr., Executive Officer | John F. Burlingame
Vice Chairman of the Board, Executive Officer | Vice Chairman of the Board, Executive Officer

Corporate Staff

Corporate Finance Staff
Brian H. Rowe
Senior Vice President
Finance

Office of General Counsel & Secretary
Walter A. Schlotterbeck
Senior Vice President
General Counsel & Secretary

Corporate Technology Staff
Arthur M. Bueche
Senior Vice President

Corporate Production & Operating Services
Leonard C. Maier, Jr.
Senior Vice President

Corporate Planning & Development Staff
Daniel J. Fox
Senior Vice President

Corporate Relations Staff
Frank P. Doyle
Senior Vice President

Corporate Productivity & Quality Staff
Walter A. Schlotterbeck
Senior Vice President
General Counsel & Secretary

Executive Manpower Staff
Thedore P. LeVino
Senior Vice President

Sectors

Consumer Products Sector
Paul W. Van Orden
Executive Vice President
& Sector Executive

Services & Materials Sector
Lawrence A. Bossoy
Executive Vice President
and Sector Executive

Aircraft Engine Business Group
Brian H. Rowe
Senior Vice President—
& Group Executive

Technical System Sector
James A. Baker
Executive Vice President
& Sector Executive

*Utah International Inc.
Alexander M. Wilson
Chairman of the Board
& Chief Executive Officer

Industrial Products Sector
Louis V. Tomasetti
Executive Vice President
& Sector Executive

Power Systems Sector
Herman R. Hill
Executive Vice President
& Sector Executive

International Sector
Robert R. Fredrick
Executive Vice President
& Sector Executive

Businesses

Lighting Business Group

Major Appliance Business Group

Air Conditioning Business Division

Housewares and Audio Business Division

Television Business Division

General Electric

Broadcasting Company, Inc.

General Electric Cablevision Corporation

Engineering Materials Group

Plastics Business Operations

Battery Business Department

Electromaterials Business Department

Information Services Business Division

General Electric Credit Corporation

Aerospace Business Group

Industrial Electronics Business Group

Medical Systems Business Operations

Advanced Microelectronics Operations

Mobile Communications Business Development

International Trading Operations

General Electric Espanola, S.A. Latin American

General Electric do Brasil, S.A.

Canadian General Electric Company Limited

Tribune Construction and Engineering

Nuclear Energy

Large Transformer

Ladd Petroleum Corp.

798

Exhibit 4b GE Organization in 1992

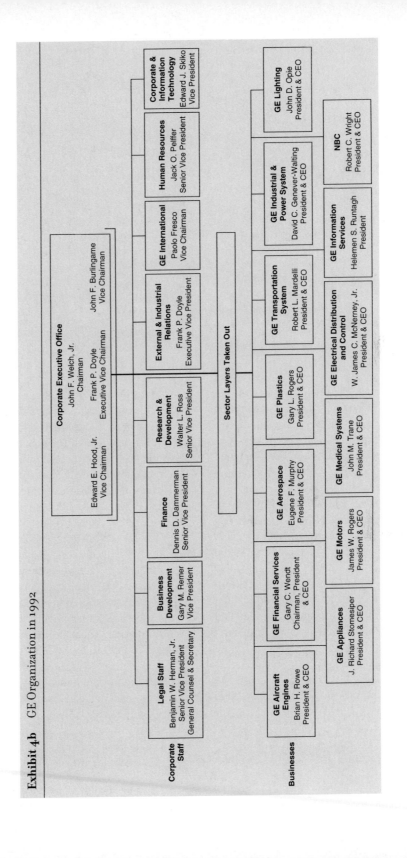

Exhibit 5   General Electric's Performance in Three Eras (millions of dollars)

	Borch		Jones		Welch		
	1961	1970	1971	1980	1981	1990	1998
Sales	4,666.6	8,726.7	9,557.0	24,950.0	27,240.0	52,619.0	100,469.0
Operating profit	431.8	548.9	737.0	2,243.0	2,447.0	6,616.0	13,477.0
Net earnings	238.4	328.5	510.0	1,514.0	1,652.0	4,303.0	9,296.0
ROS	5.1%	3.8%	5.3%	6.1%	6.1%	8.2%	10.8%
ROE	14.8%	12.6%	17.2%	19.5%	18.1%	19.8%	25.4%
Stock market capitalization	6,283.7	7,026.7	10,870.5	12,173.4	13,073.4	50,344.9	334,236.9
S&P 500 Stock Price Index—composite	65.7	83.0	97.9	119.4	126.4	330.2	1,095.4
Employees	279,547	396,583	402,000	366,000	404,000	298,000	293,000
U.S GNP ($ billion)	523.0	982.0	1,063.0	2,626.0	2,708.0	5,524.5	8,508.9

Source: GE Annual Reports, Survey of Current Business, Datastream.

management development, Welch wondered how to replicate this type of honest, energetic interaction throughout the company. His objective was to create the culture of a small company—a place where all felt engaged and everyone had voice. Together, they developed the idea of a forum where employees could not only speak their minds about how their business might be run more effectively, but also get immediate responses to their ideas and proposals. By the time their helicopter touched down at GE's headquarters, Welch and Baughman had sketched out a major change initiative they called "Work-Out"—a process designed to get unnecessary bureaucratic work out of the system while providing a forum in which employees and their bosses could work out new ways of dealing with each other.

At Welch's request, Baughman formed a small implementation team and, with the help of two dozen outside consultants, led the company-wide program rollout. Assigned to one of GE's businesses, each consultant facilitated a series of off-site meetings patterned after the open-forum style of New England town meetings. Groups of 40 to 100 employees were invited to share views about their business and how it might be improved. The three-day sessions usually began with a talk by the unit

boss, who presented a challenge and a broad agenda. Then, the boss was asked to leave, allowing employees aided by facilitators to list their problems, debate solutions, and prepare presentations. On the final day, the bosses returned and were asked to listen to their employees' analyses and recommendations. The rules of the process required managers to make instant, on-the-spot decisions about each proposal, in front of everyone. About 80% of proposals got immediate yes-or-no decisions; if the manager needed more information, he or she had to charter a team to get it by an agreed-upon decision date.

Armand Lauzon, a manager at a GE Aircraft Engine factory, described to *Fortune* how he felt as his employees presented him with their suggestions in a room where they had carefully arranged the seating so his boss was behind him. "I was wringing wet within half an hour," he said. "They had 108 proposals; I had about a minute to say yes or no to each one. And I couldn't make eye contact with my boss without turning around, which would show everyone in the room I was chickenshit." In total, Lauzon supported all but eight of the 108 proposals.

By mid-1992, over 200,000 GE employees—well over two-thirds of the workforce—had participated in Work-Out, although the exact number was hard to determine, since Welch insisted that none of the meetings be documented. "You're just going to end up with more bureaucracy," he said. What was clear, however, was that productivity increases, which had been growing at an average annual rate of 2% between 1981 and 1987, doubled to a 4% annual rate between 1988 and 1992.[2]

Best Practices   As Work-Out was getting started, Welch's relentless pursuit of ideas to increase productivity resulted in the birth of a related movement called Best Practices. In the summer of 1988, Welch gave Michael Frazier of GE's Business Development department a simple challenge: How can we learn from other companies that are achieving higher productivity growth than GE? Frazier selected nine companies, including Ford, Hewlett Packard, Xerox, and Toshiba, with different best practices to study. In addition to specific tools and practices, Frazier's team also identified several characteristics common to the successful companies: they focused more on developing effective processes than controlling individual activities; customer satisfaction was their main gauge of performance; they treated their suppliers as partners; and they emphasized the need for a constant stream of high-quality new products designed for efficient manufacturing.

On reviewing Frazier's report, Welch became an instant convert and committed to a major new training program to introduce Best Practices thinking throughout the organization, integrating it into the ongoing agenda of Work-Out teams. As a result of the Best Practices program, many GE managers began to realize they were managing and measuring the wrong things. (Said one, "We should have focused more on *how* things get done than on just *what* got done.") Subsequently, several units began radically revising their whole work approach. For example, the head of the corporate audit staff explained: "When I started 10 years ago, the first thing I did was count the $5,000 in the petty cash box. Today, we look at the $5 million in inventory

on the floor, searching for process improvements that will bring it down."

Going Global   During the early- and mid-1980s, internationalization had remained a back-burner issue at GE, but strong advocates of globalization such as Paolo Fresco, the Italian-born president of GE Europe, understood why Welch had to concentrate his early efforts on the rationalization of the U.S. operations. "It's very difficult to jump into the world arena if you don't have a solid base at home," said Fresco, "but once the solid base was created, we really took the jump."

The first rumblings of the emerging globalization priority came in Welch's challenges to his Corporate Executive Council meetings during 1986. Reflecting his own early experience in GE Plastics, he did not try to impose a corporate globalization strategy, preferring to let each business take responsibility for implementing a plan appropriate to its particular needs:

> When I was 29 years old I bought land in Holland and built the plants there. That was "my land" for "my business." I was never interested in the global GE, just the global Plastics business. The idea of a company being global is nonsense. Businesses are global, not companies.[v]

This did not mean, however, that Welch was uninvolved in his business managers' globalization plans. In 1987, he focused their attention by raising the bar on GE's well-known performance standard: from now on, "#1 or #2" was to be evaluated on *world* market position. As if to underline his seriousness, a few months later he announced a major deal with Thomson S.A., in which GE agreed to exchange its struggling consumer electronics business for the large French electronics company's medical imaging business, a business in which GE had a leading global position.

To provide continuing momentum to the internationalization effort, in 1989 Welch appointed Paolo Fresco as head of International Operations and in 1992 made him a vice-chairman and member of his four-man corporate executive office. Fresco, a key negotiator on the Thomson swap, continued to broker numerous international deals: a joint venture

---

[2]In GE, productivity was defined by the following calculation:
Productivity = Real Revenue (net of price increases)/Real Costs (net of inflationary increases).

with German-based Robert Bosch, a partnership with Toshiba, and the acquisition of Sovac, the French consumer credit company. As Eastern Europe opened, he initiated a major thrust into the former Communist bloc, spearheaded by the purchase of a majority share in the Hungarian lighting company, Tungsram. Fresco became the locator and champion of new opportunities. "I fill vacuums," he said. "All these assignments are temporary—once they are complete, I get out of the way."

Like subsequent strategic initiatives, globalization was not a one-time effort, but an ongoing theme that Welch doggedly pursued over the years. Taking advantage of Europe's economic downturn, GE invested $17.5 billion in the region between 1989 and 1995, half on new plants and facilities and half to finance 50 or so acquisitions. Then, in 1995, after the Mexican peso collapsed, the company again saw the economic uncertainty as a great buying opportunity. Within six months GE had acquired 16 companies, positioning it to participate in the country's surprisingly rapid recovery. And as

Asia slipped into crisis in 1997–1998, Welch urged his managers to view it as a buying opportunity rather than a problem. In Japan alone the company spent $15 billion on acquisitions in six months.

By 1998, international revenues were $42.8 billion, almost double the level just five years earlier. The company expected to do almost half its business outside the United States by 2000, compared with only 20% in 1985, the year before the first international push. More important, global revenues were growing at almost three times the rate of domestic sales. (See Exhibit 6).

Developing Leaders   While the global thrust and the new cultural initiatives were being implemented, Welch was also focusing on the huge task of re-aligning the skill sets—and, more important, the mindsets—of the company's 290,000 employees with GE's new strategic and organizational imperatives. Amidst the grumbling of those who felt over-worked in the new demanding environment and the residual distrust left over from the layoffs of the

Exhibit 6   Growth through Globalization

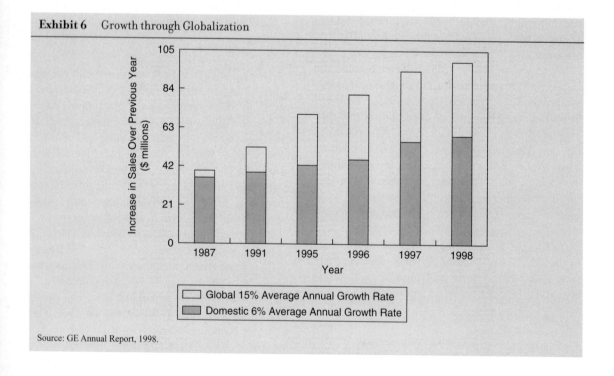

Source: GE Annual Report, 1998.

1980s, he recognized his challenge was nothing short of redefining the implicit contract that GE had with its employees:

> Like many other large companies in the U.S., Europe and Japan, GE has had an implicit psychological contract based on perceived lifetime employment. This produced a paternal, feudal, fuzzy kind of loyalty. That kind of loyalty tends to focus people inward. But in today's environment, people's emotional energy must be focused outward on a competitive world. . . . The new psychological contract, if there is such a thing, is that jobs at GE are the best in the world for people willing to compete. We have the best training and development resources and an environment committed to providing opportunities for personal and professional growth.[vi]

Like all GE managers, Welch grew up in an organization deeply committed to developing its people. He wanted to harness that tradition and use it to translate his broad cultural changes down to the individual level. This would mean adapting GE's well-established human resource systems to his goals. For example, for as long as he could remember, the company's top executives had committed substantial amounts of time to the rigorous management appraisal, development, and succession planning reviews known as Session C. He began using this process to help achieve his objectives, predictably adding his own intense personal style to its implementation.

Starting in April and lasting through May each year, Welch and three of his senior executives visited each of his businesses to review the progress of the company's top 3,000 executives. Welch kept particularly close tabs on the upper 500, all of whom had been appointed with his personal approval. In these multi-day meetings, Welch wanted to be exposed to high-potential managers presenting results on major projects. In an exhaustive 10- to 12-hour review in each business, Welch asked the top executive to identify the future leaders, outline planned training and development plans, and detail succession plans for all key jobs. The exercise reflected his strong belief that good people were GE's key assets and had to be managed as a company resource.

"I own the people," he told his business heads. "You just rent them."

As these reviews rolled out through GE, all professional-level employees expected honest feedback about where they were professionally, reasonable expectations about future positions they could hold, and the specific skills required to get there. Managers at every level used these discussions as the basis for coaching and developing their staff. (As a role model, Welch estimated he spent at least 70% of his time on people issues, most of that teaching and developing others.)

A strong believer in incentives, Welch also radically overhauled GE's compensation package. From a system driven by narrow-range increases in base salary supplemented by bonuses based on one's business performance, he implemented a model in which stock options became the primary component of management compensation. He expanded the number of options recipients from 300 to 30,000 and began making much more aggressive bonus awards and options allocations strongly tied to the individual's performance on the current program priority (globalization, for example, or best practices initiatives).

Through all of these human resource tools and processes, Welch's major effort was increasingly focused on creating an environment in which people could be their best. Entering the 1990s, he described his objective for GE in these terms:

> Ten years from now, we want magazines to write about GE as a place where people have the freedom to be creative, a place that brings out the best in everybody. An open, fair place where people have a sense that what they do matters, and where that sense of accomplishment is rewarded in the pocketbook and the soul. That will be our report card.

A key institution that Welch harnessed to bring about this cultural change was GE's Crotonville management development facility. Welch wanted to convert Crotonville from its management training focus and its role as a reward or a consolation prize for those who missed out on a promotion to a powerful engine of change in his transformation effort.

Exhibit 7   Welch at GE's Crotonville Center

A typical note Welch sent to 30 participants to prepare for his session of GE's Executive Development Course (EDC):

Dear EDC Participants,

I'm looking forward to an exciting time with you tomorrow. I've included here a few thoughts for you to think about prior to our session:

As a group—

Situation: Tomorrow you are appointed CEO of GE.

- What would you do in first 30 days?
- Do you have a current "vision" of what to do?
- How would you go about developing one?
- Present your best shot at a vision.
- How would you go about "selling" the vision?
- What foundations would you build on?
- What current practices would you jettison?

Individually—

1. Please be prepared to describe a leadership dilemma that you have faced in the past 12 months, i.e., plant closing, work transfer, HR, buy or sell a business, etc.
2. Think about what you would recommend to accelerate the Quality drive across the company.
3. I'll be talking about "A, B & C" players. What are your thoughts on just what makes up such a player?
4. I'll also be talking about energy/energizing/edge as key characteristics of today's leaders. Do you agree? Would you broaden this? How?

I'm looking forward to a fun time, and I know I'll leave a lot smarter than when I arrived.

—Jack

Source: *The Leadership Engine.*

In the mid-1980s, when he was cutting costs almost everywhere else, he spent $45 million on new buildings and improvements at Crotonville. He also hired some experienced academics—Jim Baughman from Harvard and Noel Tichy from Michigan—to revolutionize Crotonville's activities.

Under Welch's direct control and with his personal involvement, Crotonville's priority became to develop a generation of leaders aligned to GE's new vision and cultural norms. Increasingly, it evolved from a training center to a place where teams of managers worked together on real priority issues and decided on results-oriented action. And this led to the gradual replacement of outside faculty by GE insiders acting as discussion leaders. Leading the change was Welch, who twice a month traveled to Crotonville to teach and interact with GE employees. ("Haven't missed a session yet," he boasted in the late 1990s.) (See Exhibit 7.) It was during one of these sessions that the idea for Work-Out emerged, and it was at Crotonville that many of the Best Practices sessions were held.

Despite all the individual development and the corporate initiatives, not all managers were able to achieve Welch's ideal leadership profile. (See Exhibit 8.) Of greatest concern to the CEO were those who seemed unwilling or unable to embrace the open, participative values he was espousing. In

Exhibit 8   GE Leadership Capabilities

- Create a clear, simple, reality-based, customer-focused vision and are able to communicate it straightforwardly to all constituencies.

- Understand accountability and commitment and are decisive . . . set and meet aggressive targets . . . always with unyielding integrity.

- Have the self-confidence to empower others and behave in a boundaryless fashion . . . believe in and are committed to Work-Out as a means of empowerment . . . be open to ideas from anywhere.

- Have a passion for excellence . . . hate bureaucracy and all the nonsense that comes with it.

- Have, or have the capacity to develop global brains and global sensitivity and are comfortable building diverse global teams.

- Stimulate and relish change . . . are not frightened or paralyzed by it. See change as opportunity, not just a threat.

- Have enormous energy and the ability to energize and invigorate others. Understand speed as a competitive advantage and see the total organizational benefits that can be derived from a focus on speed.

Source: 1992 Annual Report.

1991, he addressed the problem and the seriousness of its consequences:

> In our view, leaders, whether on the shop floor or at the top of our businesses, can be characterized in at least four ways. The first is one who delivers on commitments—financial or otherwise—and shares the values of our company. His or her future is an easy call. Onward and upward. The second type of leader is one who does not meet commitments and does not share our values. Not as pleasant a call, but equally easy. The third is one who misses commitments but shares the values. He or she usually get a second chance, preferably in a different environment.
>
> Then there's the fourth type—the most difficult for many of us to deal with. That leader delivers on commitments, makes all the numbers, but doesn't share the values we must have. This is the individual who typically forces performance out of people rather than inspires it: the autocrat, the big shot, the tyrant. Too

often all of us have looked the other way and tolerated these "Type 4" managers because "they always deliver"—at least in the short term.[vii]

To reinforce his intention to identify and weed out Type 4 managers, Welch began rating GE top-level managers not only on their performance against quantifiable targets but also on the extent to which they "lived" GE values. Subsequently, many of GE's 500 officers started using a similar two-dimensional grid to evaluate and coach their own direct reports. And when coaching failed, Welch was prepared to take action on the type 4s. "People are removed for having the wrong values," he insisted. "We don't even talk about the numbers."

To back up this commitment to the new leadership criteria, a few years later GE introduced a 360° feedback process. Every employee was graded by his or her manager, peers and all subordinates on a 1 to 5 scale in areas such as teambuilding, quality focus, and vision. Welch described it as a powerful tool for detecting and changing those who "smile up and kick down." Tied into the evaluation process and linked to the Session C human resource planning exercise, the 360° feedback became the means for identifying training needs, coaching opportunities, and, eventually, career planning—whether that be up, sideways, or out.

Into the 1990s: The Third Wave

Entering the 1990s, Welch felt that GE's new foundation had been laid. Despite the slowdown in the industrial sector in the first few years of the new decade, he was committed to the task of rebuilding the company at an even more urgent pace. The new initiatives rolled on.

Boundaryless Behavior   Moving beyond the earlier initiatives aimed at strengthening GE's individual businesses, Welch began to focus on creating what he called "integrated diversity." He articulated his vision for GE in the 1990s as a "boundaryless" company, one characterized by an "open, anti-parochial environment, friendly toward the seeking and sharing of new ideas, regardless of their origins"—in many ways an institutionalization of the openness "Work-Out" had initiated and "best practices" transfers had reinforced. Describing his barrier-free vision for GE, Welch wrote:

> The boundaryless company we envision will remove the barriers among engineering, manufacturing, marketing, sales, and customer service; it will recognize no distinctions between domestic and foreign operations—we'll be as comfortable doing business in Budapest and Seoul as we are in Louisville and Schenectady. A boundaryless organization will ignore or erase group labels such as "management," "salaried" or "hourly," which get in the way of people working together.[viii]

One of Welch's most repeated stories of how best practices could be leveraged by boundaryless behavior described how managers from Canadian GE identified a small New Zealand appliance maker, Fisher & Paykel, producing a broad range of products very efficiently in its small, low-volume plant. When the Canadians used the flexible job-shop techniques to increase productivity in their high-volume factory, the U.S. appliance business became interested. More than 200 managers and employees from the Louisville plant went to Montreal to study the accomplishments, and soon a Quick Response program had cut the U.S. production cycle in half and reduced inventory costs by 20%. Not surprisingly, GE's Appliance Park in Louisville became a "must see" destination for many other businesses, and within a year, the program had been adapted for businesses as diverse as locomotives and jet engines.

The CEO gave the abstract concept of boundarylessness teeth not only by repeating such success stories but also by emphasizing that there was no place at GE for the adherents of the old culture: "We take people who aren't boundaryless out of jobs. . . . If you're turf-oriented, self-centered, don't share with people and aren't searching for ideas, you don't belong here," he said. He also changed the criteria for bonuses and options awards to reward idea-seeking and sharing, not just idea creation. Five years later, Welch had a list of boundarylessness success stories:

> We quickly began to learn from each other: productivity solutions from Lighting; "quick response" asset

management from Appliances; transaction effectiveness from GE Capital; cost-reduction techniques from Aircraft Engines; and global account management from Plastics.[ix]

One of the most impressive examples of the way ideas and expertise spread throughout GE was the company's "integration model." Developed on the lessons drawn from literally hundreds of post-acquisition reviews, the model guided the actions of managers in any part of the company responsible for integrating a newly acquired operation: from taking control of the accounts to realigning the organization, and from identifying and removing "blockers" to implementing GE tools and programs. By the late 1990s, GE's integration programs were completed in about 100 days.

Stretch: Achieving the Impossible   To reinforce his rising managerial expectations, in the early 1990s Welch made a new assault on GE's cultural norms. He introduced the notion of "stretch" to set performance targets and described it as "using dreams to set business targets, with no real idea of how to get there."[x] His objective was to change the way targets were set and performance was measured by creating an atmosphere that asked of everyone, "How good can you be?"

Stretch targets did not replace traditional forecasting and objective-setting processes. Managers still had to hit basic targets—adjusted to recognize the world as it turned out to be, not some rigid plan negotiated a year earlier. But during the budget cycle they were also required to set higher, "stretch" goals for their businesses. While managers were not held accountable for these goals, those who achieved them were rewarded with substantial bonuses or stock options. Said Welch: "Rigorous budgeting alone is nonsense. I think in terms of . . . what is the best you can do. You soon begin to see what comes out of a trusting, open environment."

Within a year of introducing the concept of stretch, Welch was reporting progress:

> We used to timidly nudge the peanut along, setting goals of moving from, say, 4.73 in inventory turns to 4.91, or from 8.53% operating margin to 8.92%; and

then indulge in time-consuming high-level, bureaucratic negotiations to move the number a few hundredths one way or the other. . . . We don't do that anymore. In a boundaryless organization with a bias for speed, decimal points are a bore. They inspire or challenge no one, capture no imaginations. We're aiming at 10 inventory turns, at 15% operating margins.[xi]

By the mid-1990s, stretch goals were an established part of GE's culture. A senior executive explained: "People like problem solving. They want to go to that next level. That's becoming a bigger driver for the company than Work-Out." But the introduction of stretch targets did not come without implementation difficulties. According to Steve Kerr, the head of Crotonville, "You absolutely have to honor the don't-punish-failure concept; stretch targets become a disaster without that." Unless properly managed, he explained, stretch could easily degenerate into a justification for forcing people to work 60-hour weeks to achieve impossible goals. "It's not the number per se, especially because it's a made-up number. It's the process you're trying to stimulate. You're trying to get people to think of fundamentally better ways of performing their work."[xii]

In early 1996, Welch acknowledged that GE did not meet two of its four-year corporate stretch targets: to increase operating margins from their 1991 level of 10% to 15% by 1995, and inventory turns from 5 to 10 times. However, after decades of single-digit operating margins and inventory turns of 4 or 5, GE did achieve an operating margin of 14.4% and inventory turns of almost 7 in 1995. "In stretching for these 'impossible' targets," said Welch, "we learned to do things faster than we would have going after 'doable' goals, and we have enough confidence now to set new stretch targets of at least 16% operating margin and more than 10 turns by 1998."[xiii]

Service Businesses   In 1994, Welch launched a new strategic initiative designed to reinforce one of his earliest goals: to reduce GE's dependence on its traditional industrial products. In the early 1980s, he had initiated the initial tilt towards service businesses through the acquisition of financial service companies such as Employers Reinsurance and Kidder, Peabody. "Nearly 60% of GE's profits now comes from services," said Welch in 1995. "Up from 16.4% in 1980. I wish it were 80%."[xiv]

To fulfill that wish, Welch began moving to the next stage—a push for product services. During his annual strategic reviews with senior managers, Welch began to challenge his managers "to participate in more of the food chain." While customers would always need high-quality hardware, Welch argued that GE's future challenge would be to offset slowing growth for its products by supplementing them with added-value services. Describing it as one of "the biggest growth opportunities in [GE's] history," he named a cadre of rising executives to focus on the issue. At the same time, he asked Vice Chairman Paolo Fresco to set up a Services Council through which top managers could exchange ideas.

Soon, all GE's businesses were exploring new service-based growth opportunities. The medical business, for example, developed a concept called "In Site." This involved placing diagnostic sensors and communications capability into their installed base of CT scanners, MRI equipment, and other GE medical devices. The system linked the equipment directly to GE's on-line service center, continuously diagnosing its operating condition in real time. Soon, GE was offering its remote diagnostics and other services to all medical equipment—including non-GE products.

Like other internal "best practice" service examples, the "In Site" story was shared in the Services Council, and soon online diagnostic technology was being transferred to other GE businesses. In Aircraft Engines, critical operating parameters of GE jet engines were monitored by GE Service experts while the engines were in flight, providing the company with a major value-added benefit for its customers. The same-real time diagnostic concepts were also applied in GE's power systems business, and other businesses had plans to develop remote diagnostic capability as well.

According to Welch, the opportunity for growth in product services was unlimited. With an advantage unique in the world—an installed base of some

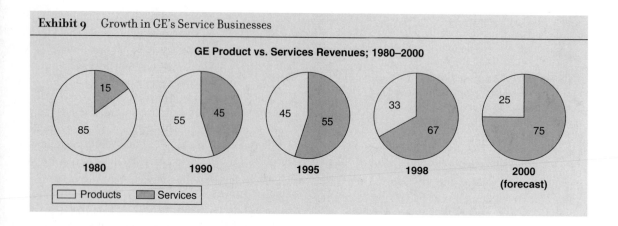

Exhibit 9   Growth in GE's Service Businesses

GE Product vs. Services Revenues; 1980–2000

1980: Products 85, Services 15
1990: Products 55, Services 45
1995: Products 45, Services 55
1998: Products 33, Services 67
2000 (forecast): Products 25, Services 75

Products   Services

9,000 GE commercial jet engines, 10,000 turbines, 13,000 locomotives, and 84,000 major pieces of medical diagnostic imaging equipment—he felt GE had an incredibly strong platform on which to build. Commented Lewis Edelheit, GE's senior VP for Corporate Research and Development:

> A few years ago, businesses were seen as a pyramid, with the base as the product and the other elements—services, manufacturing processes and information—resting on that base. We are now looking at turning the pyramid upside down. The product will become just one piece of the picture—the tip of that inverted pyramid. The biggest growth opportunities may come from providing services to the customer: providing the customer with ways to become more productive—and with information so valuable the customer will pay for it.[xv]

By 1996, GE had built an $8 billion equipment services business, which was growing much faster than the underlying product businesses. Equally important, in Welch's view, it was changing internal mindsets from selling products to "helping our customers to win." GE's product services were to be aimed at making customers' existing assets—power plants, locomotives, airplanes, factories, hospital equipment and the like—more productive. Yet while GE was helping its customers reduce their capital outlays, its managers were also shifting demand from low-margin products to their newer

high-profit services with margins almost twice the company average.

This initiative led to a new round of acquisitions. In 1997 alone, GE made 20 service-related acquisitions and joint ventures, including a $1.5 billion acquisition of a jet engine service business and the $600 million purchase of a global power generation equipment service company. GE's radical business shift over two decades led Welch to claim, "We have changed the very nature of what we do for a living. Today, services account for two-thirds of our revenues." (See Exhibit 9.)

Closing Out the Decade: Welch's Final Chapter

As he entered the last half of the decade, Welch was aware that he would reach GE's mandatory retirement age in 2001. Yet his commitment to keep building GE was undiminished, despite critics who continued to question if the company could keep adding value to such a highly diversified business portfolio. In the 1995 Annual Report, he tackled the issue head on:

> The hottest trend in business is the rush toward breaking up multi-business companies. The obvious question to GE, the world's largest multi-business company, was, "When are you going to do it?" The short answer is that we're not. . . . We are a company intent

on getting bigger, not smaller. Our only answer to the trendy question "What do you intend to spin off?" is "Cash—and lots of it."

Despite hospitalization for triple bypass surgery in 1995, he showed no signs of slowing down. Indeed, many felt he gained new energy in his post-operative state as the pressure for performance and new initiatives continued.

Six Sigma Quality Initiative   When a 1995 company survey showed that GE employees were dissatisfied with the quality of its products and processes, Welch met with Lawrence Bossidy, an old friend who had left GE in 1991 to become CEO of AlliedSignal Inc. Welch learned how the Six Sigma quality program Bossidy had borrowed from Motorola Inc. had helped AlliedSignal dramatically improve quality, lower costs, and increase productivity. Immediately, he invited Bossidy to GE's next Corporate Executive Council meeting. His presentation of the AlliedSignal program won universal rave reviews.

After the meeting, Welch asked Gary Reiner, vice president for Business Development, to lead a quality initiative for GE. Reiner undertook a detailed study of the impact of quality programs at companies like Motorola and AlliedSignal. His analysis concluded that GE was operating at error rates ten thousand times the Six Sigma quality level of 3.4 defects per million operations. Furthermore, he estimated that the gap was costing the company between $8 billion and $12 billion a year in inefficiencies and lost productivity. On the basis of Reiner's findings, at GE's 1996 annual gathering of its 500 top managers in Boca Raton, Welch announced a goal of reaching Six Sigma quality levels company-wide by the year 2000, describing the program as "the biggest opportunity for growth, increased profitability, and individual employee satisfaction in the history of our company."

Like all initiatives announced in Boca (services, globalization, etc.), Six Sigma quality was more than a slogan: it was a well-developed program, with a detailed plan for its implementation. Fur-

thermore, it would be monitored throughout the year in a carefully linked series of management meetings that Welch started to refer to as GE's "operating system"—the series of planning, resource allocation, review, and communication meetings that were at the heart of its management process. The Boca initiative announcement was followed up by a first progress report at the two-day March CEC meeting; then in the April Session C reviews, Welch would check how key human resources had been deployed against the target; the July strategic review sessions would review the impact of the initiative on each business's three-year outlook; October's Officers Meeting tracked progress and showcased best practice; and the November operating plan reviews would fold the impact into the following year's forecasts. (See Exhibit 10.) Said Welch, "We are relentless."

Six Sigma participation was not optional, and Welch tied 40% of bonus to an individual's Six Sigma objectives. To provide managers the skills, Reiner designed a massive training of thousands of managers to create a cadre of "Green Belts," "Black Belts," and "Master Black Belts" in Six Sigma quality. "Green Belt" training took about four weeks, followed by implementation of a five-month project aimed at improving quality. Black Belts required six weeks of instruction in statistics, data analysis, and other Six Sigma tools which prepared the candidate to undertake three major quality projects that resulted in measurable performance increases. Master Black Belts—full-time Six Sigma instructors—mentored the Black Belt candidates through the two-year process.

At the January 1998 Boca Raton meeting, speakers from across the company and around the world presented Six Sigma best practice and achievements. Managers from Medical Systems described how Six Sigma designs produced a tenfold increase in the life of CT scanner x-ray tubes; the railcar leasing business described a 62% reduction in turnaround time at its repair shops, making it two to three times faster than its nearest rival; and a team from the plastics business described how the Six Sigma process added 300 million pounds of

Exhibit 10   The GE Management System

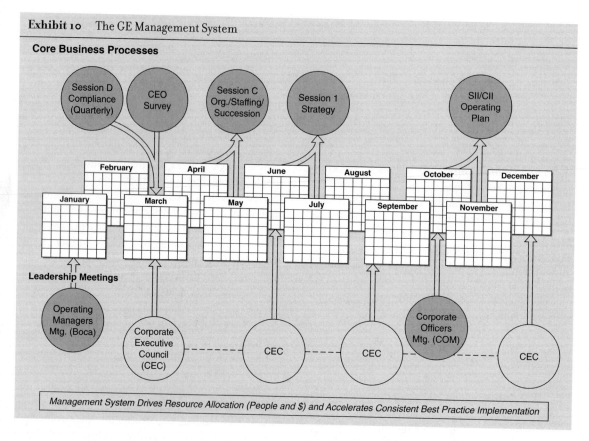

new capacity, equivalent to a "free plant." In all, 30,000 Six Sigma projects had been initiated in the prior year.

At the April 1999 Annual Meeting, Welch announced that in the first two years of Six Sigma, GE had invested $500 million to train the entire professional workforce of 85,000. In addition, 5,000 managers had been appointed to work on the program full-time as Black Belts and Master Black Belts, leading Welch to claim "they have begun to change the DNA of GE to one whose central strand is quality." Returns of $750 million over the investment exceeded expectations, and the company was forecasting additional returns of $1.5 billion in 1999 (Exhibit 11). Clearly delighted by the program, Welch stated, "In nearly four decades with GE, I have never seen a company initiative move so willingly and so rapidly in pursuit of a big idea."

"A Players" with "Four E's"   The closer he got to his planned retirement date, the more Welch seemed to focus on the quality of the organization he would leave to his successor. While he felt he had assembled a first-class team of leaders at the top of the company, he wanted to continue upgrading quality deep in the organization. This implied not only raising the bar on new hires but also weeding out those who did not meet GE's high standards. Modifying his earlier language of four management types, he began describing GE as a company that wanted only "A Players"—individuals with vision, leadership, energy, and courage. He described what he was trying to achieve:

The GE leader sees this company for what it truly is: the largest petri dish of business innovation in the world. We have roughly 350 business segments. We see them as 350 laboratories whose ideas are there to be shared, learned, and spread as fast as we can. The

Exhibit 11   Costs and Benefits of GE's Six Sigma Program

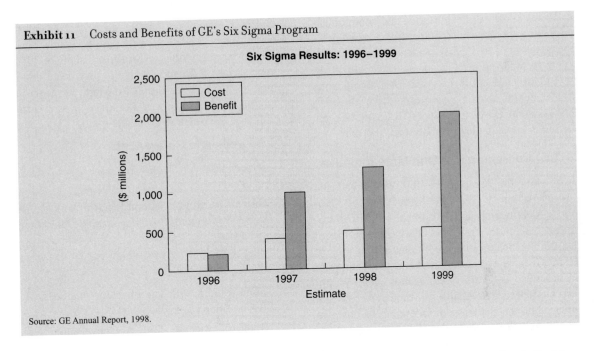

Source: GE Annual Report, 1998.

leader sees that sharing and spreading near the top of his or her responsibilities.

"A Players" were characterized by what Welch described as the 4E's—energy ("excited by ideas and attracted to turbulence because of the opportunity it brings"), ability to energize others ("infecting every-one with their enthusiasm for an idea and having everyone dreaming the same big dreams"), edge ("the ability to make tough calls") and execution ("the consistent ability to turn vision into results").

To meet the company's need for exceptional lead-ership talent, Welch insisted that GE move to phase three of its globalization initiative. Beyond focusing on global markets and global sources—the earlier two phases of globalization—he urged his managers to expand their efforts in "globalizing the intellect of the company." At the same time, he urged his top management group to take strong action to upgrade the quality of their existing employees:

> We're an A-plus company. We want only A players. We can get anyone we want. Shame on any of you who aren't facing into your less-than-the-best. Take care of your best. Reward them. Promote them. Pay them well. Give them a lot of [stock] options and don't spend all

that time trying to work plans to get Cs to be Bs. Move them on out early. It's a contribution.[xvi]

To help clarify those decisions, the company im-plemented a performance appraisal system that re-quired every manager to rank his or her employees into five categories—the "top" 10% as 1s, the "strong" 15% as 2s, the "highly valued" 50% as 3s, the "borderline" 15% as 4s, and the "least effec-tive" 10% as 5s.[3] Every group, even a 10-person team, had to be ranked on this so-called "vitality curve." All 1s and most 2s received stock options but anyone rated a 5 had to go. Welch elaborated on the need to weed out poor performers: "With the 5s it's clear as a bell. I think they know it, and you know it. It's better for everyone. They go on to a new place, a new life, a new start." At the other end of the scale, Welch expected managers to take ac-tion on their top performers to develop them: "You send your top 10 on and see how many of them get into the top 10 of the whole business."

---

[3]Eventually, the five categories were reduced to three—the top 20%, the high-performance 70%, and the bottom 10%. The practice of counseling out the bottom 10% continued.

Welch knew that the nurturing and continuously upgrading the quality of management was one of the main keys to GE's success. He felt that the talent he amassed over 18 years—especially at the senior management levels—was of a significantly higher quality than in past years. "I've got all A players in the Corporate Council. It wasn't like that before. I'm really pleased about that," he said.

Toward Retirement: One More Initiative

Just when the organization felt Welch had put his final stamp on GE, at the 1999 Operating Managers' Meeting in Boca, the 64-year-old CEO introduced his fourth strategic initiative—e-business.[4] Describing the impact of the Internet as "the biggest change I have ever seen," he launched a program he described as *"destroyyourbusiness .com."* Within two months each unit had a full-time *dyb.com* team focused on the challenge of redefining its business model before someone else did. "Change means opportunity," he told them. "And this is our greatest opportunity yet."

Yet Welch also knew that GE was late to the Internet party. As he acknowledged in his address to shareholders three months after the Boca meeting, "Big companies like us were frightened by the unfamiliarity of the technology. We thought this was mysterious, Nobel Prize stuff, the province of the wild-eyed and purple haired." But the more he explored the Internet and talked to people about it, the more Welch came to believe that, through processes like Six Sigma, GE had done the really hard work of building the assets needed to support e-business—like strong brands, top ranked product reliability, great fulfillment capability, and excellent service quality. "It's much harder for a dot com startup to challenge us when they don't have the fundamentals down," he said. "They're popcorn stands without a real business or operating capabilities."

As the organization cranked up to push the new initiative through the monthly schedule of reviews that GE operating system required, Welch was impressed by early results from the *dyb.com* teams. "Digitizing the company and developing e-business

models is easier—not harder—than we ever imagined," he said. But others were more sanguine. Said David Mark, a partner at McKinsey and Co., "It's going to take a decade for this to play out. I don't think it's a simple transition." If Mark was correct, building GE's e-business would be a long-term challenge for Welch's successor.

Sources and References

Byrne, John A., "Jack," *Business Week,* June 8, 1998.

Cosco, Joseph P., "General Electric Works It All Out," *Journal of Business Strategy,* May–June 1994.

Filipczak, Bob, "CEOs Who Train," *Training,* June 1996.

Grant, Linda, "GE: The Envelope, Please," *Fortune,* June 26, 1995.

Hodgetts, Richard M., "A Conversation with Steve Kerr, GE's Chief Learning Officer," *Organizational Dynamics,* March 22, 1996.

Kandebo, Stanley, "Engine Services Critical to GE Strategy," *Aviation Week,* February 23, 1998.

Koenig, Peter, "If Europe's Dead, Why Is GE Investing Billions There?" *Fortune,* September 9, 1996.

Lorenz, Christopher, "The Alliance-Maker," *Financial Times,* April 14, 1989.

Norman, James R., "A Very Nimble Elephant," *Forbes,* October 10, 1994.

Rifkin, Glenn, "GE: Bringing Good Leaders to Life," *Forbes,* April 8, 1996.

Tichy, M. Noel and Eli Cohen, *The Leadership Engine: How Winning Companies Build Leaders at Every Level* (HarperBusiness, New York, 1997).

Tichy, M. Noel and Eli Cohen, "The Teaching Organization," *Training & Development,* July 1998.

Tichy, M. Noel and Stratford Sherman, *Control Your Destiny or Someone Else Will* (HarperBusiness, New York, 1994).

---

[4]The three earlier ones were globalization, services, and Six Sigma.

Tichy, M. Noel and Stratford Sherman, "Walking the Talk at GE," *Training & Development,* June 1996.

Slater, Robert, *Get Better or Get Beaten!* (New York: McGraw-Hill, 1996).

Smart, Tim, "GE's Brave New World," *Business Week,* November 8, 1993.

Stewart, Thomas A., "GE Keeps Those Ideas Coming," *Fortune,* August 12, 1991.

▎Endnotes

[i]"General Electric: 1984" (HBS Case No. 385-315), by Professor Francis J. Aguilar and Richard G. Hamermesh and RA Caroline Brainard. © 1985 by the President and Fellows of Harvard College.

[ii]Noel Tichy and Ram Charan, "Speed, Simplicity, Self-Confidence: An Interview with Jack Welch," *Harvard Business Review,* September–October 1989.

[iii]Anon, "GE Chief Hopes to Shape Agile Giant," *Los Angeles Times,* June 1, 1988.

[iv]Tichy and Charan, op. cit., p. 112.

[v]Robert Slater, *Jack Welch and the GE Way: Management Insights and Leadership Secrets of the Legendary CEO* (New York: McGraw-Hill, 1998), p. 195.

[vi]Tichy and Charan, op. cit., p. 120.

[vii]GE Annual Report, 1991.

[viii]GE Annual Report, 1989.

[ix]GE Annual Report, 1995.

[x]GE Annual Report, 1993.

[xi]GE Annual Report, 1993.

[xii]"Stretch Goals: The Dark Side of Asking for Miracles," Interview excerpts with Steve Kerr, GE's Vice President of Leadership Development. *Fortune,* November 13, 1995.

[xiii]GE Annual Report, 1995.

[xiv]Tim Smart, "Jack Welch's Encore," *Fortune,* October 28, 1996.

[xv]Lewis Edelheit, "GE's R&D Strategy: Be Vital," *Research Technology Management,* March–April, 1998.

[xvi]Slater, op. cit., p. 39.

Reading 8-1   The Myth of the Generic Manager: New Personal Competencies for New Management Roles

Christopher A. Bartlett
Sumantra Ghoshal

Over the years, the Boston Celtics have won more National Basketball Association championships than any other team in the league. They have achieved that record through the effectiveness of their organization—the exceptional leadership ability of their general managers, as epitomized by the legendary Red Auerbach, the strong team development skills of coaches such as Tom Heinson, and the outstanding on-court talent of players like Larry Bird. But it is clear to everyone in the Celtics organization that the capable general manager, the savvy coach, and the star player all add value in very different ways. While Auerbach's career demonstrates that a good player can occasionally evolve into a great coach, and even go on to become an exceptional general manager, the instances of such a progression are extremely rare. Success in one role is not a good predictor of performance in another. Heinson made the transition from player to coach with ease, yet was not seen to have general management potential; and despite the fact he was one of the game's greatest players ever, few expect Larry Bird to become as successful a coach as Heinson, let alone a general manager of Auerbach's standing.

When it comes to management of companies, both our theory and our practice are very different. In theory, we believe in a generic role called "the manager," who is expected to add value to the company in a generic way, carrying out a generic set of tasks and possessing some generic capabilities. This assumption is manifest in the scores of books and articles on "the manager's job"[1] and in generic distinctions such as those between management and leadership.[2] It is also embedded in the currently burgeoning literature on management competencies.[3] With some important exceptions,[4] our theory of management is that at each organizational level, managers play similar roles and have similar responsibilities, only for a different size and scope of activities. The metaphor is that of the Russian doll: at each level of the hierarchy, the manager is similar but bigger than the manager a level below.

Practice, however, has always been very different from this theory. The Russian doll model of management is firmly rooted in a hierarchical model of organizations. But, in reality, a hierarchy sharply differentiates roles vertically. In hierarchical organizations, top-level managers set direction by formulating strategy and controlling resources; middle-level managers mediate the vertical information processing and resource allocation processes by assuming the role of administrative controllers; and, swamped by direction and control from above, front-line managers find themselves in the role of operational implementers. Despite their differences, however, theory and practice have actually reinforced each other: the theory has made the hierarchy legitimate while the practice has made it operational.

Over the last decade, top-level managers around the world have recognized the limitations of the classic hierarchy. Alarmed by the loss of efficiency, speed, and flexibility, they have delayered and destaffed their organizations, reengineered their operations, and have invested significant amounts of money and management time to spread the message of "empowerment" throughout their companies.[5] However, in most cases all they have bought is a little breathing time. How their companies function has not changed because the behaviors and relationships of their people have not changed.

The reason for this failure is simple. The problems of the hierarchy cannot be overcome without explicitly challenging both the Russian doll theory

[1]Henry Mintzberg's book *The Nature of Managerial Work* (New York, NY: Harper and Row, 1973) is one of the most celebrated pieces of work on this topic. In his analysis, Mintzberg compares the work patterns of managers in very different kinds of managerial jobs in some very different kinds of organizations (such as companies, schools, and public hospitals), treating them as a sample from a population of "managers." The concept of a generic management role is inherent in the study design. The same assumption is also manifest in Peter Drucker's *The Practice of Management* (London: Heinemann, 1955) and John Kotter's *The General Managers* (New York, NY: The Free Press, 1982), although the focus of these authors is clearly on the role of corporate top management. There are some exceptions to this rule, however (see Note 4).

[2]See John Kotter, *A Force of Change: How Leadership Differs from Management* (New York, NY: The Free Press, 1990).

[3]For a recent and comprehensive review of this literature, see Elena P. Antonacopoulou and Louise FitzGerald, "Reframing Competency in Management Development," *Human Resource Management Journal*, 6/1 (1996): 27–48.

[4]Joseph L. Bower's book *Managing the Resource Allocation Process: A Study of Corporate Planning and Investment* (Boston, MA: Division of Research, Graduate School of Business Administration, Harvard University, 1970) is a good example of such exceptions. Based on this study of the resource allocation process, Bower develops a model in which front-line, middle, and top-level managers play clearly differentiated roles. Rosabeth Kanter's article "The Middle Manager as Innovator" [*Harvard Business Review*, 60/4 (1982): 95–105] also highlights such differences in management roles by suggesting the special role that middle managers can play in facilitating innovations.

[5]While these trends are well-known and have been widely documented in the business press, Nitin Nohria's research on the changes in strategy, organization, culture, and governance of the 100 largest U.S.-based companies over the 1978–1994 period provides clear and systematic evidence of these developments. A brief report of this study is available in Nitin Nohria, "From the M-form to the N-form: Taking Stock of Changes in the Large Industrial Corporation," Working Paper no. 16/1996, the Strategic Leadership Research Programme, London Business School, 1996.

and the pecking-order practice of management. The reality is that large, diversified companies have and need a CEO or a leadership team, just as much as they have and need managers to run individual units and others to provide intermediate-level coordination and integration. Unless their activities and expected contributions are explicitly defined, these managers will tend to slip into the comfortable and familiar role structure of grand strategists, administrative controllers, and operational implementers. The only way to prevent this hierarchical relationship is to define the distinct value added of each of the management groups in terms of the different roles they need to play.

This is a key lesson from our recent research in twenty large European, American, and Asian companies.[6] Based on our analysis of the experiences of these companies, we have developed a model of the roles that front-line, senior, and top-level managers need to play for companies to achieve the organizational capabilities they are seeking.[7] These changes in management roles and personal capabilities are part of a fundamental change in organizational philosophy that is redefining the modern corporation.

[6] The twenty companies we studied were: Intel, 3M, AT&T, Corning, Beckton Dickensen, and Andersen Consulting in the United States; Asea Brown Boveri (ABB), Ikea, International Service Systems (ISS), Richardson Sheifield, Cartier, Royal Dutch Shell, Lufthansa, and Philips in Europe: and the LG Group (erstwhile Lucky Goldstar), Canon, Kao Corporation, Komatsu, Toyota, and Reliance Industries in Asia. In each of these companies, we conducted extensive interviews with managers (over 400, in total) at different levels, both in their corporate headquarters and in their different divisions and national subsidiaries. We also collected additional data from a variety of internal and external documents. Except for Toyota, we have written and published detailed case studies on all these companies, which are available either through the Harvard case clearing system or from the International Case Clearing House (ICCH). Our overall findings and conclusions from this study are available in Sumantra Ghoshal and Christopher A. Bartlett, *The Individualized Corporation* (New York, NY: HarperCollins, 1997).

[7] We have described these managerial roles in Christopher A. Bartlett and Sumantra Ghoshal, "Beyond the M-form: Toward a Managerial Theory of the Firm," *Strategic Management Journal*, 14 (Special Issue, Winter 1993): 23–46. In that article, written primarily for our academic colleagues, we have compared and contrasted our descriptions of these roles vis-à-vis those that are implied in some of the key strands of the related literature. In the present article, written primarily for a practitioner audience, we do not refer to this academic literature, but those interested in such references can find them in the 1993 article.

New Organization Model: New Management Roles

To understand the new management roles, one must first recognize the major elements of the emerging organizational framework that is shaping them. Despite the considerable differences in businesses, national origin, and corporate history in companies as diverse as GE, Komatsu, ABB, and Corning, we found that they were converging on a similar post-transformational organization model that represented a major change from their traditional authority-based hierarchies. Other companies we studied—such as 3M, ISS, and Kao—already shared many of these emerging organizational characteristics and therefore had avoided the worst aspects of the classic authority-based hierarchy. In many ways, this latter group provided both the inspiration and the example for other companies undergoing major organizational transformations.

The clearest and most widespread trend we observed was that companies were rethinking their old approach of dividing the organization from the top down into groups, sectors, and divisions. Instead, they were building from the bottom up on a foundation of small front-line operating units. For example, the $35 billion Swiss-based electro-technical giant, ABB, divided its operations into 1,300 local operating companies, each of which operates as a separate legal entity with its own balance sheet and P&L responsibilities. In 3M, the company's $15 billion dollars of sales generated by a portfolio of over 60,000 products are managed by 3,900 profit centers that are at the heart of the company's entrepreneurial process. ISS, the Denmark-based cleaning services organization, attributes its growth into a $2 billion multinational corporation to its policy of forming not one national subsidiary, but four or five small autonomous businesses in each of the 17 countries it has expanded into, allowing each of them to grow by serving a particular client group.

The second common characteristic in the emerging organizational model is the portfolio of cross-unit integrative processes. These processes are designed to break down the insulated vertically oriented relationships that have dominated the classic authority-based hierarchy. In ABB, the tensions embodied in the company's global matrix were resolved through a proliferation of business boards, functional councils, and project teams designed to play a primary role in ABB's management process at every level of the organization. At 3M, the R&D community's carefully developed network of communication channels and decision-making forums became the model for similar relationships to link the company's marketing and manufacturing resources across its portfolio of innovative front-line units. ISS made extensive use both of training and development and of cross-unit meetings and committees to ensure that knowledge and expertise developed in one part of the company were rapidly transferred system-wide.

Finally, in the emerging organization, these changes to the old structure and processes were supported by a strong commitment to genuine empowerment, a philosophy that represented a formidable challenge to the authority-based culture in most classic hierarchies. In ABB, CEO Percy Barnevik based the company's management practice on the twin principles of radically decentralized responsibility and tightly held individual accountability. 3M was known for its core principles that espoused a commitment to entrepreneurship and a belief in the individual. The company had long worked to translate those beliefs into a culture that "stimulates ordinary people to produce extraordinary performance." In his 30 years as the CEO of ISS, Poul Andreassen had developed a set of guiding principles, central to which was a genuine respect for his workers and a delegation of responsibility as close to the individual cleaning contract as possible.

This radically decentralized yet horizontally linked organizational model with a strong culture of empowerment required companies to break with the old hierarchy of nested roles that was implicit in the Russian doll model of management. In these and other companies we studied, operating-level managers had to evolve from their traditional role as front-line implementers to become innovative entrepreneurs; senior-level managers had to rede-

fine their primary role from administrative controllers to developmental coaches; and top-level executives were forced to see themselves less as their company's strategic architects and more as their organizational leaders. The implications of such role changes on the distribution of key tasks and responsibilities are profound.

The Operating-Level Entrepreneurial Role   In identifying the new roles and responsibilities of those running business units, national subsidiaries, or other such front-line units, we studied the activities of scores of operating-level managers as they struggled to adjust to the demands of the new corporate model. We focus here on a select group of managers at ABB, 3M, and ISS not as definitive role models, but as illustrations of the framework of management tasks we have developed.

Don Jans headed the relays business unit that was part of Westinghouse's troubled power transmission and distribution business that was sold to ABB in 1989. Westinghouse had long regarded relays as a mature business, and Jans and his team had been encouraged to milk their slowly declining, modestly profitable operation. Yet, when exposed to ABB's decentralized entrepreneurial environment, the same management group turned their mature business into one with the performance profile of a young growth company. Within three years of the ownership change, export sales skyrocketed, new products were introduced, and operating profits doubled. Equally important, the revitalized U.S. relays unit began developing an electronic capability to supplement its traditional electro-mechanical expertise, thus laying the foundation for long-term expansion into a major new growth area.

At 3M, we saw a similar example of front-line entrepreneurship. In 1989, Andy Wong became the leader of a project team that had been struggling for over a decade to commercialize a portfolio of the company's optical technologies that had never found market applications. Over the next four years, Wong redeployed the unit's resources, refocused its energy and attention, protected the operations from several threats to shut them down, and remotivated the discouraged team. By 1994, Wong's unit had become a showcase within 3M by introducing two new products, both of which proved to be highly successful in the marketplace.

At ISS, we observed Theo Buitendijk take over the firm's small Dutch commercial cleaning business and double revenues within two years. He took the company into the specialized higher margin segment of slaughterhouse cleaning, eventually becoming the company's center of expertise in this sector and supporting its expansion throughout Europe. Like Jans, Buitendijk had previously been a traditional line manager in a classic authoritarian hierarchy (in his case, Exxon), but found that the different organizational context in ISS not only allowed, but encouraged him to redefine his role and change his behavior.

In each of these companies, a similar framework of organizational structure, processes, and culture supported the entrepreneurial activities of front-line managers like Jans, Wong, and Buitendijk as they took the initiative to drive the performance and enhance the capabilities of their units. Among their many tasks and responsibilities, we identified three that were central to their role as entrepreneurs rather than just implementers (see Table 1).

The most striking set of activities and achievements common to the operating-level entrepreneurs we studied were those related to their taking the initiative to create and pursue new business opportunities. In contrast to the role they played in their previous situations (as implementers of programs and priorities pushed down from above), managers such as Jans and Buitendijk found that

Table 1   Transformation of Management Roles and Tasks

	Operating-Level Managers	Senior-Level Manager	Top-Level Managers
Changing role	• From operational implementers to aggressive entrepreneurs	• From administrative controllers to supportive coaches	• From resource allocators to institutional leaders
Primary value added	• Driving business performance by focusing on productivity, innovation and growth within front-line units	• Providing the support and coordination to bring large company advantage to the independent front-line units	• Creating and embedding a sense of direction, commitment, and challenge to people throughout the organization
Key activities and tasks	• Creating and pursuing new growth opportunities for the business	• Developing individuals and supporting their activities	• Challenging embedded assumptions while establishing a stretching opportunity horizon and performance standards
	• Attracting and developing resources and competencies	• Linking dispersed knowledge, skills, and best practices across units	• Institutionalizing a set of norms and values to support cooperation and trust
	• Managing continuous performance improvement within the unit	• Managing the tension between short-term performance and long-term ambition	• Creating an overarching corporate purpose and ambition

they were not only free to initiate new activities, they were expected to do so. Jans rose to the challenge by expanding into export markets in Mexico, Canada, and the Far East and by committing to the development of microprocessor-based relays (despite the substantial up-front investment involved). Buitendijk's move into abattoir cleaning initially caused a sharp drop in his company's profitability but then proved to be a much more attractive segment than the company's highly competitive core business of office cleaning.

Beyond developing new products and markets, these front-line entrepreneurs had all expanded the assets, resources, and capabilities of their operating units. Rather than playing the more traditional passive-dependent role defined by corporate processes such as head count authorization, capital budget allocation, and management development procedures, these individuals saw it as their responsibility to develop the limited resources they had and, as one of them described it, "do more with less." Andy Wong's actions in upgrading his unit's existing technological and manufacturing resources were impressive enough, but his creation of an entirely new marketing capability in a resource-constrained operation was truly entrepreneurial. Through persistent negotiations with senior management, creative internal resource reallocations, and persuasive recruiting within the company, he was able to reinforce his small struggling unit with an experienced marketing manager. He then backed this manager with the distribution support of two other 3M divisions that agreed to help bring his unproven product to market. Don Jans' ability to develop a microprocessor-based product line exhibited the same commitment to build on and leverage existing capabilities. He became recognized as a "giver" rather than a "receiver," as ABB terminology referred to managers who became net developers rather than consumers of the organization's scarce resources.

The third basic responsibility of front-line managers was the one with which they were most familiar: to ensure continuous performance improvement in their operating units. In the new organizational context, however, they were given considerably more freedom, incentive, and support to find ways to do so. Although Don Jans had long been working to maximize operating performance in Westinghouse, within the ABB organization he was able to achieve substantial additional expense cuts, inventory and receivables reductions, and operating efficiency improvements largely because he was given what Barnevik described as "maximum degrees of freedom to execute."

Andy Wong knew that by leveraging his unit's existing assets and resources he could build the credibility and confidence he would need to obtain additional investment and support. It was for this reason that Wong initially invested a large part of his energy in focusing development attention on only two technologies and reducing manufacturing costs by 50%. It was only after gaining organizational confidence in his operating effectiveness that he won both the freedom to engage in the resource development and the time to implement his unit's entrepreneurial new product launch.

These three cases show the untapped potential for performance improvement available to most companies. The dramatically changed management behavior of Jans and Buitendijk along with Wong's rapid transition from engineer to project team leader suggests that inside every hierarchy, even the most authoritarian, there are entrepreneurial hostages waiting to be unleashed. But the new entrepreneurial tasks can only be accomplished after the historical structures, processes, and cultural norms are replaced by a new organizational framework that requires front-line managers to abandon their old implementation role.

The Senior-Level Developmental Role   The risk of redefining the role of operating-level managers as entrepreneurs rather than implementers is that it will fragment the company's resources and capabilities and lead to the kind of undisciplined, localized expansion that conglomerates experienced in the 1960s. To prevent this, the senior-level managers—those between the front-line units and the corporate-level management—must redefine their role from the historic preoccupation with authority-based control to a focus on support-based management and organization development.

Traditionally, senior managers' power came from their pivotal position in large and complex hierarchies (where they typically were responsible for the organization's divisions, regions, or key functions). They played a vital intermediary role, disaggregating corporate objectives into business unit targets and aggregating business unit plans for corporate review. They were the linchpins in the resource allocation process due to corporate management's reliance on their input in capital budgeting and personnel appointment decisions. They stood at the crossroads of internal communication, interpreting and broadcasting management's priorities, then channeling and translating front-line feedback.

These classic senior management tasks have been challenged by the creation of small independent front-line units, the radical decentralization of assets and resources to support them, and the empowerment of the operating managers in charge. They have been further undermined by the delayering of middle levels of the organization and the impact of new information technologies on internal communication. Left to fulfill their traditional role, senior managers find themselves increasingly frustrated by the irrelevance and powerlessness of their position. Unless there is a radical realignment of their role, this group can become the silent subverters of change whose invisible, yet persistent resistance can derail even the most carefully planned transformation program.

Some companies have successfully redesigned the senior management role by making it a key part of supporting the front-line units, both by coordinating their activities and by coaching their operating-level entrepreneurs. Ulf Gundemark, Don Jan's boss and the head of ABB's worldwide relays business area, played a central role in managing the tension inherent in the company's ambition "to be global and local, big and small, radically decentralized with central reporting and control." Similarly, Paul Guehler, vice president of 3M's Safety and Security Systems Division to which Andy Wong's unit belonged, challenged Wong to define the focus and priorities in his business, while simultaneously helping him build the support and obtain the resources necessary to make it succeed. At ISS, Waldemar Schmidt, head of the European region, supported Theo Buitendijk's new business initiative despite its short-term profit impact, and he led the effort to leverage the expertise his unit developed into a European business capability.

In none of these cases did these managers see their roles in the traditional terms of administrative controllers and information relays. Instead of dominating their front-line managers, usurping their authority, or compromising their sense of responsibility for their operations, this new generation of senior managers added value to that activity through three core tasks. First, they become a vital source of support and guidance for the front-line entrepreneurs; second, they took primary responsibility for linking and leveraging the resources and competencies developed in the front-line units; and third, they played a key role in ensuring resolution of the numerous tensions and conflicts built into the management process (see Table 1).

When a company decides to change its dominant management model from one driven by authority to one built on empowerment, the basic orientation of the senior manager's task is changed from direction and control to development and support. ABB not only reflected this change in its cultural norms, it institutionalized it in the way key senior-level jobs were structured. For example, although Ulf Gundemark was the relays business area head, he had a staff of only four to help him run the $250 million worldwide business. As a result, he routinely asked managers in operating units to take on broader responsibilities, stretching their abilities and developing their contacts and support as they did so. To develop the worldwide relays strategy, he assembled a nine-person team of managers drawn from the front lines of his operating companies. To guide the ongoing business operations, he created a business area board that included his staff members and four key company presidents, including Don Jans. As Jans put it, "I'm a much broader manager today than I was at Westinghouse. . . . We feel we are rediscovering management."

Paul Guehler described his primary job as "to help develop the people to develop the business." He worked intensively with Wong and his team, challenging them to refine their plans, forcing them to commit them to paper, and, most important, encouraging them to communicate and defend them in multiple forums in order to build up their struggling unit's thin support within 3M. At ISS, Waldemar Schmidt had a similar philosophy about his role, stating that "the most important thing I can do is to show an interest, to show that I care about them and their performance." He backed his words with actions, developing a strongly supportive relationship with his front-line managers that manifested itself in frequent telephone calls to say "Well done!" or "How can I help?"

The second element of this role focuses more on the level of organization development, as senior-level managers take on the task of linking the knowledge and expertise developed in their front-line units and embedding them as organizational capabilities to be leveraged company-wide. Gundemark's actions in forcing his front-line relays companies to rationalize and specialize in overlapping structures and responsibilities was a first step in integrating the portfolio of independent relays operations. He then appointed key specialists in each of the companies to functional councils whose primary purpose was to identify best practice and capture other benefits of coordination in R&D, quality, and purchasing. Waldemar Schmidt achieved similar cross-unit linkages through his regular meetings specifically devoted to leveraging the expertise of particular country units. When Theo Buitendijk's unit in Holland was shown to have superior performance in customer retention, for example, Schmidt gave him a day at his next European presidents conference to discuss his approach.

Beyond these important developmental tasks, however, those in senior management positions still must accept responsibility for the performance of the front-line units they supervise. The common

bottom-line contribution of the three managers we described is that they all played the pivotal role in ensuring that those reporting to them kept the strategic objectives and operating priorities in balance. In ABB, this task was framed by a global matrix that was designed to legitimize rather than minimize the tensions and paradoxes inherent in most management decisions. To manage the conflict resolution vital to the organization's smooth operation, senior-level managers such as Ulf Gundemark developed and managed a portfolio of supplemental communications' channels and decision forums such as the worldwide business board and the functional councils we described. These and other forums (such as the steering committees that act as local boards for each of the front-line companies) not only serve a development and integration role, but they also become the place where differences are aired and resolution obtained on the conflicting perspectives and interests created by the matrix.

In 3M, this critical balancing role is so ingrained in the culture that senior-level managers such as Paul Guehler have integrated it into their ongoing management approach. For example, in what he terms his "give-and-take management style," Guehler tightened the screws on Wong's operations by requiring them to make the cuts necessary to meet their financial objectives, while behind the scenes he was defending against attempts to close the unit down and was lining up resources and support to back their proposed development initiatives.

Senior-level managers are often the forgotten and forsaken group in the organizational transformation process. Amid rounds of delayering, destaffing, and downsizing, many corporate executives have overlooked the fact that the success of small, empowered front-line units depends on a company's ability to bring large company benefits to those units. Organizations that dismantle their vertical integration mechanisms without simultaneously creating the horizontal coordination processes quickly lose potential scale economies. Even more important, they lose the benefits that come from leveraging each unit's assets, knowledge, and capabilities company-wide. At the same time, such intense horizontal flows can also paralyze the organization by distracting or overburdening front-line managers. It is the managers in the middle who can make "inverting the pyramid" operational, not only by developing and supporting the front-line entrepreneurs, but also by absorbing most of the demands of the cross-business, cross-functional, and cross-geographic integration needs. In this way, they can prevent those at the operating level from becoming overwhelmed by the ambiguity, complexity, and potential conflicts that often accompany such horizontal networked organizations and allow them instead to focus on their vital entrepreneurial tasks.

The Top Management Leadership Role   Those at the apex of many of today's large, complex organizations find themselves playing out a role that they have inherited from their corporate forbears: to be the formulators of strategy, the builders of structure, and the controllers of systems. As these three tools became increasingly sophisticated, there was a growing assumption that they could allow organizations to drive purposefully towards their clearly defined goals, largely free from the idiosyncrasies of individual employees and the occasional eccentricities and pathologies of their behavior. To some extent, the objective was achieved. Under the strategy, structure, and systems doctrine of management, most large companies eventually became highly standardized and efficient operations, with individual employees being managed as inputs in the predicable but depersonalized system.

To free these entrepreneurial hostages requires a rollback of this dehumanizing management paradigm and thus a rethinking of top management's role. The role has to change from one grounded in the old doctrine of strategy, structure, and systems to one based on a new philosophy focusing on purpose, process, and people. Those at the top of most of the entrepreneurial companies in our study had evolved from being the formulators of corporate strategy to becoming the shapers of a broader corporate purpose with which individual employees could identify and feel a sense of personal commitment. Instead of focusing on formal structures that

gave them control over the firm's financial resources, they devoted much of their efforts to building processes that added value by having the organization work more effectively together. Rather than becoming overly dependent on the management systems that isolated them from the organization and treated employees as factors of production, they created a challenging organizational context that put them back in touch with people and focused them on affecting individual inputs rather than just monitoring collective outputs.

In this radically redefined view of their role, those at the top first had to create a work environment that fostered entrepreneurial initiative rather than compliant implementation. Poul Andreassen was not someone who readily accepted the status quo. Like many of the CEOs we observed, he was constantly questioning the past and challenging his organization to achieve more. To overcome the constrained potential of continuing to operate ISS as a Danish office cleaning business, Andreassen began to conceive of the company as a more broadly defined professional service organization. His explicit objective was to create a world-class company, "to make ISS and service as synonymous as Xerox and photocopying." By broadening the opportunity horizon, he legitimized the entrepreneurial initiatives of his management team as they expanded into new markets and unexplored business segments. The challenging environment that he developed continued to support the entrepreneurial initiatives of operating-level managers such as Theo Buitendijk (as he developed the abattoirs cleaning business in Holland) and the ISS manager in Germany who saw an opportunity to expand into the former East Germany to start a business in the removal of building rubble.

The second key task common to the top managers we studied was to shape the organizational context necessary to support the radically decentralized structure and the management philosophy of empowerment. To ensure that the organization did not fragment its efforts or dissipate its scarce resources in this more decentralized form, traditional control-based values had to be replaced with norms of trust and support. Over the years, 3M's top managers have created an organization with such values, allowing resources and expertise to move freely across its 3,900 profit centers located in 47 divisions and 57 country operations. From the earliest days, they developed clear integrating norms such as the recognition that while products belong to the division, technologies belong to the company. They reinforced such beliefs by carefully developing a framework for collaboration and support. For example, the strong mutually supportive relationships within 3M's scientific community were formed and reinforced through institutionalized grassroots forums, internal technology fairs, and cross-unit transfer practices. Overarching all of this was a sense of trust embedded in the respect those at the top had for individuals and their ideas. As current CEO Livio "Desi" DeSimone reminds his managers, they must listen carefully to subordinates and continually ask, "What do you see that I am missing?" It was this respectful, supportive, and trusting environment that allowed entrepreneurs like Andy Wong to take risks and that encouraged senior managers like Paul Guehler to back them.

Finally, the top-level managers we observed also played the vital role of providing the organization with a stabilizing and motivating sense of purpose. As chief executive of ABB, Percy Barnevik believed that he had to develop more than just a clear strategy for his newly merged worldwide entity. He felt that he had to create an organizational environment that made people proud to belong and motivated to work for the company. He articulated ABB's overall mission not in terms of its market share, competitive position, or profit objectives, but in terms of the ways in which ABB could contribute to sustainable economic growth and world development. He emphasized a sensitivity to environmental protection and a commitment to improving living standards worldwide, reflecting those beliefs not only in the company's formal mission statement, but also in the major strategic decisions he took. The company's pioneering investments in Eastern Europe, its transfer of technology to China and India, and its innovations in environmentally sensi-

tive processes gave substance to its articulated purpose. These efforts also made ABB's employees feel that they were contributing to changing the world for the better. As corporate executive VP Goran Lindahl explained, "In the end, managers are loyal not to a particular boss or even to a company, but to a set of values they believe in and find satisfying."

The approach taken by Barnevik and Lindahl (and their counterparts in companies such as 3M and ISS) reflected the simple belief that their job as the top-level leaders was not simply to manage an economic entity whose activities could be directed through strategic plans, resource allocation processes, and management control systems. Equally important was their role as the principal architects of a social institution able to capture the energy, commitment, and creativity of those within it by treating them as valued organizational members, not just contracted company employees. In addition to managing the strategy and structure, they took the time to develop a corporate purpose and shape the integrating organizational processes. Rather than simply monitoring the performance of divisions or subsidiaries through abstract systems, they focused their attention on the people within the organizations— those whose motivations and actions would drive the company's performance.

New Management Roles, New Personal Competencies

Over the past few years, companies as diverse as AT&T, British Airways, BP, Siemens, and The World Bank have invested enormous amounts of management time and effort to define the ideal profile of their future corporate leaders. Siemens, for example, has defined 22 desirable management characteristics under five basic competencies of understanding, drive, trust, social competence, and what they call a "sixth sense." The World Bank's ideal profile identifies 20 attributes and groups them into seven quite different categories of intellectual leadership, team leadership, staff development, work program management, communication, interpersonal impact, and client orientation. Pepsico's desired competency profile for its executives of the future has 18 key dimensions defining how individuals see the world, how they think, and the way they act.

This focus on personal characteristics is understandable given the widespread problems that so many individuals have had adjusting to the transformed organizational environment and performing the redefined management tasks. Indeed, this emerging interest in individual competencies has created a cottage industry among consultants eager to promote their expertise in identifying, measuring, and developing the desired personal capabilities to lead in the new corporate environment. Yet, despite prodigious efforts in designing questionnaires, conducting interviews, and running seminars to define the profile of leadership competencies, few of these programs have won the kind of credibility and support necessary for widespread adoption and application.

One problem is that the profiles that have been generated often include an inventory of personality traits, individual beliefs, acquired skills, and other personal attributes and behaviors assembled on the basis of unclear selection criteria and with little logical linkage to bind them. Furthermore, these profiles are often developed based on surveys of current managers or analysis of the most successful individual performers in the existing context. As such, they risk defining future leadership needs in terms of the historical organizational roles and capabilities that were required to succeed in the old organizational forms.

The most important limitation of these management competency exercises is that they are almost always defined as a single ideal profile. While such an assumption may not have been entirely irrational in the more symmetrical roles typical of the traditional authority-based hierarchy, this extension of the Russian doll model is not viable in the emerging delayered organization with its differentiated set of management roles and tasks.

As part of our research into post-transformation organizations, we studied the adaptation of managers to their redefined responsibilities. Instead of asking managers to describe the personal characteristics they felt were most important, we observed those who had demonstrated their effectiveness in performing the key tasks of the redefined management roles. Rather than trying to develop a list of generic competencies with universal application, we were able to differentiate the profiles of managers who succeeded in adding value in very different ways at each level of the organization.

Despite the fact that we were developing more differentiated profiles based on performance rather than opinion, the notion of individual competencies still seemed too vague and unfocused to be of great practical value. To be more useful to managers, the concept had to be more sharply defined and more clearly applicable to human resource discussions and activities. This led us to develop a simple classification model that helped us allocate the broadly defined competencies into three categories. In the first, we listed deeply embedded personal characteristics like attitudes, traits, and values that were intrinsic parts of the individual's character and personality. The second category included attributes such as knowledge, experience, and understanding that generally could be acquired through training and career path development. The third category was composed of specialized skills and abilities that were directly linked to the job's specific task requirements and were built on the individual's intrinsic capabilities and acquired knowledge (see Table 2).

By categorizing management competencies in this way, we not only gave the concept a sharper definition, but were also able to identify much more clearly how managers could focus attention on different attributes of the profile in various important human resource decisions. In particular, our observations led us to develop some propositions about the role different attributes play in the vital management responsibilities for selecting, developing, and supporting people in their particular job responsibilities.

Selecting for Embedded Traits   There is a high rate of failure among managers attempting to adapt from their historic roles in traditional companies

Table 2   Management Competencies for New Roles

Role/Task	Attitude/Traits	Knowledge/Experience	Skills/Abilities
Operating-Level Entrepreneurs	**Results-Oriented Competitor**	**Detailed Operating Knowledge**	**Focuses Energy on Opportunities**
• Creating and pursuing opportunities	• Creative, intuitive	• Knowledge of the business's technical, competitive, and customer characteristics	• Ability to recognize potential and make commitments
• Attracting and utilizing scarce skills and resources	• Persuasive, engaging	• Knowledge of internal and external resources	• Ability to motivate and drive people
• Managing continuous performance improvement	• Competitive, persistent	• Detailed understanding of the business operations	• Ability to sustain organizational energy around demanding objectives
Senior-Management Developers	**People-Oriented Integrator**	**Broad Organizational Experience**	**Develops People and Relationships**
• Reviewing, developing, supporting individuals and their initiates	• Supportive, patient	• Knowledge of people as individuals and understanding how to influence them	• Ability to delegate, develop, empower
• Linking dispersed knowledge, skills, and practices	• Integrative, flexible	• Understanding of the interpersonal dynamics among diverse groups	• Ability to develop relationships and build teams.
• Managing the short-term and long-term pressures	• Perceptive, demanding	• Understanding the means-ends relationships linking short-term priorities and long-term goals	• Ability to reconcile differences while maintaining tension
Top-Level Leaders	**Institution-Minded Visionary**	**Understanding Company in Its Context**	**Balances Alignment and Challenge**
• Challenging embedded assumptions while setting stretching opportunity horizons and performance standards	• Challenging, stretching	• Grounded understanding of the company, its businesses and operations	• Ability to create an exciting, demanding work environment
• Building a context of cooperation and trust	• Open-minded, fair	• Understanding of the organization as a system of structures, processes, and cultures	• Ability to inspire confidence and belief in the institution and its management
• Creating an overarching sense of corporate purpose and ambition	• Insightful, inspiring	• Broad knowledge of different companies, industries and societies	• Ability to combine conceptual insight with motivational challenges

to their newly defined tasks in transformed and reengineered organizations. This underscores the importance of identifying selection criteria that can help product success in radically redefined roles. For example, when ABB was created in 1988 through merger, 300 top and senior management positions were filled. Despite the careful selection of those appointed to these positions, over 40% of them were no longer with the company six years later. As the company's leadership recognized at the time, the central problem was to identify the candidates who had already developed the personal traits that were needed to succeed in the radically different organizational and managerial context that Percy Barnevik had defined for ABB.

When faced with such a situation, most companies we observed tended to select primarily on the basis of an individual's accumulated knowledge and job experience. These were, after all, the most visible and stable qualifications in an otherwise tumultuous situation. Furthermore, selecting on this basis was a decision that could be made by default, simply by requiring existing managers to take on totally redefined job responsibilities.

In such situations, however, past experience did not prove to be a good predictor of future success. The most obvious problem was that much of the acquired organizational expertise was likely to reflect old management models and behavioral norms. Equally problematic were the personal characteristics of those who had succeeded in the old organizational environment. As many companies discovered, the highly task-oriented senior managers who were both comfortable and successful in the well-structured work environment of their traditional company often found great personal difficulty in adjusting to the coaching and integrating roles that became an important part of their redefined responsibilities.

As a result, many companies are coming to believe that it is much more difficult to convince an authoritarian industry expert to adopt a more people-sensitive style than to develop industry expertise in a strong people manager. It is a recognition that is leading them to conclude that innate personal characteristics should dominate acquired experience as the key selection criteria. Equally importantly, they are recognizing that because the management roles and tasks differ widely at each level of the organization, so too will the attitudes, traits, and values of those most likely to succeed in each position. Recruitment and succession planning in such an environment becomes a much more sophisticated exercise of identifying the very different kinds of individuals who can succeed as operating-level entrepreneurs, senior-level developers, and top management leaders.

In ISS, for example, the company had long recognized the vital importance of recruiting individuals who were result-oriented competitors to run their front-line operating units. Although the front-line manager's job at ISS could be regarded as a low-status position managing supervisors in the mature and menial office cleaning business, ISS knew that by structuring the role to give managers status and autonomy, they could attract the kind of energetic, independent, and creative individuals they wanted. Like many of ISS's operating-level entrepreneurs, Theo Buitendijk had spent his early career in a traditional hierarchical company, but he had been frustrated by the constraints, controls, and lack of independence he felt. Status elements like the "managing director" title and the prestige company car signaled the importance ISS attached to this position, but entrepreneurial individuals like Buitendijk were even more attracted by the independence offered by operating their own business behind what ISS managers called "Chinese walls" to prevent unwanted interference. By creating an environment that motivated self-starters would find stimulating, ISS had little difficulty in training them in industry knowledge and helping them develop the specific job skills they required to succeed.

The personal profile required to move to the next level of management was quite different, however, and few of the operating-level entrepreneurs were expected or indeed had an ambition to move up to the divisional management level. One who did was Waldemar Schmidt, an operating-level entrepreneur who had turned around the company's Brazilian business before being appointed head of the European division. Despite his relatively limited knowledge of the European market, Schmidt impressed Poul Andreassen as a people-oriented individual who had a genuine interest in developing and supporting others. Indeed, the company's Five Star training program had originated in Brazil as part of Schmidt's commitment to continually upgrade his employees. Furthermore, he was recognized as being a very balanced individual who tended to operate by influence more than authority, yet was demanding of himself and others. These were qualities that Andreassen regarded as vital in his senior managers and felt they far outweighed Schmidt's more limited European knowledge or experience.

At the top level of the organization, another set of personal qualities was felt to be important. When Poul Andreassen became the president of ISS in 1962, he too was selected primarily on the basis of his personal traits rather than his experience in the company or his proven leadership skills. As a young engineer in his mid-30s, he was frustrated in his job with a traditional large company and was looking for the opportunity to build a very different kind of organization. Despite his lack of industry background of ISS-specific management skills, he was attractive because he was much less interested in running an ongoing company than he was in building a more ambitious organization. His most appealing characteristic was his willingness to question and challenge everything, and even after thirty years in the job, he still felt that his best days were when he could go into the field and confront his division or business unit managers so as to help "stir up new things."

Like Red Auerbach of the Boston Celtics, there will be a few individuals who have the breadth of personal traits and the temperamental range to adapt to the very different roles and tasks demanded of them at different organizational levels. At ISS, Waldemar Schmidt progressed from successful operating-level entrepreneur to effective senior management developer, and, after Poul Andreassen's retirement, was asked to succeed him as top-level corporate leader. One of management's most important challenges is to identify the personal characteristics that will allow an individual to succeed in a new and often quite different role and, equally important, to recognize when someone who is successful at one level lacks the individual traits to succeed at the next. For those with the perceived potential, however, the next key challenge is to develop the knowledge and expertise that can support and leverage their embedded personal traits.

Developing for Knowledge Acquisition   While training and development activities are rarely very effective in changing the deeply embedded personal traits, attitudes, and values, they are extremely appropriate means of developing the kind of knowledge and experience that allows an individual to build on and apply those embedded individual attributes. For example, as a person who is naturally creative, engaging, and competitive learns more about a particular business, its customers, and technologies, he or she becomes a much more effective and focused operating-level entrepreneur. Poul Andreassen understood this well and made training and development one of the few functions that he controlled directly from ISS's small corporate office. Under the ISS philosophy of ensuring that all employees had the opportunity to use their abilities to the fullest, the Five Star development program defined five levels of training that allowed front-line supervisors with the appropriate profile to gain the knowledge and experience they would need in a broader management job.

Because of its strong promote-from-within culture, 3M also had a long-standing commitment to develop its people to their potential. Soon after a new employee enters the company (within six months for a clerical employee or three years for a laboratory scientist) a formal Early Career Assessment process is initiated both to ensure that the individual is a proper fit with the company and to define a program to prepare them for their next career opportunity. For example, a promising accounting clerk might be set the personal education goal of becoming a Certified Public Accountant within three years, while at the same time being given an internal development assignment to provide experience in preparing financial statements and participating in audits. This process continues (albeit in a somewhat less structured format) throughout an individual's career in 3M, with the company providing internal business courses and technical seminars as well as supporting participation in external education programs.

On-the-job training is still the primary emphasis, and those with the will and the perceived personal potential are given every opportunity to develop that promise. For example, Andy Wong, who turned the struggling Optical Systems (OS) project into a showcase of entrepreneurial success, was carefully prepared for that role over five years. This quiet engineer first caught the eye of Ron Mitsch, a senior R&D executive who was impressed by the young man's tenacious, self-motivated competitiveness—personal qualities that 3M looked for in its front-line entrepreneurs. Wanting to give him the opportunity to prove that potential, the mentor told Wong about an opportunity to lead a small technical development team in the OS unit. While demonstrating his energy and persuasive persistence, Wong began to expand his knowledge about the unit's optical technologies, as he struggled to develop the understanding he needed to focus his team's rather fragmented efforts. After a couple of years in the OS laboratory, Wong was asked to take on the additional responsibility for the unit's inefficient manufacturing operations. Although he had no prior production or logistics experience, his initiatives in rationalizing the complex sourcing arrangements, simplifying the manufacturing process, and consolidating production in a single plant resulted in a 50% cost reduction and simultaneous improvement in product quality. It was through these experiences that Wong was able to broaden his knowledge of the business beyond his focused understanding of the technology and expand his familiarity with the organization's re-

sources beyond his scientific contacts. Through careful career path development, he developed the kind of knowledge and experience he needed to allow him to use his naturally competitive traits effectively as the newly appointed project team leader for optical systems.

While the developmental path for operating-level entrepreneurs focused on enhancing knowledge and expertise in a particular business, market, or function, the track to the next level of management usually required a much richer understanding of the organization and how it operated. Wong's boss Paul Guehler also began his 3M career in the R&D laboratory and was also identified as someone who looked beyond the technologies he was developing to the businesses they represented. It was this budding entrepreneurial attitude that led to his transfer to 3M's New Business Ventures Division. In this position, his natural curiosity and intuitiveness were leveraged by focusing him on the task of exploring market opportunities and business applications for high potential ideas and innovations. After a decade in this division, Guehler was transferred to the Occupational Health and Safety Products Division. In this position, his experience as an R&D manager gave him the opportunity to broaden his understanding of the mainstream organizational processes and how to manage them. A subsequent move to the Disposable Products Division helped him build on that experience, particularly when he was appointed Business Director for disposable products in Europe. This responsibility for a highly competitive product in a fast-changing market greatly expanded his experience in assessing the capabilities and limitations of a diverse group of individuals and organizational units and further expanded his understanding of the organizational dynamics and strategic tensions of having them work together. By the time he was appointed as general manager and later vice president of the Safety and Security Systems Division of which Wong's OS unit was a part, he brought not only hard-headed business knowledge, but some sensitive organizational insights into his new role. As his diagnosis of the OS unit's situation indicates:

> You have to have people in these positions who recognize other people's talents and support their ideals for building a business. My job is to create an environment where people come forward with ideas and are supported to succeed. . . . So while the OS group probably thought I was being too tough, my objective was to get them to recognize their opportunities, to hold them accountable for their actions, to help them build their credibility, and ultimately to support them so they could succeed. . . . One of my most important roles is not only to develop business, but to develop the people who can develop the business.

At the top level of 3M management, the need for a breadth of knowledge and experience was even greater. In 1991, when the company was planning the transition to a new chief executive, board member and ex-CEO Lou Lehr said that the successful candidate was likely to be a career 3M executive five to ten years from retirement (for no other reason than it usually took 30 to 35 years to accumulate the breadth of experience to be effective in the top job in this diversified company).

Desi DeSimone, the CEO elected in 1991, was described in one news account as "a textbook example of the quintessential 3M CEO." He had moved up through technical, engineering, and manufacturing management positions to assume general management roles as managing director of the Brazilian subsidiary and eventually area vice president of 3M's Latin American operations. He was recognized as a senior manager with top management potential. "There were always people taking an interest in my development," DeSimone said on assuming the CEO job. In classic 3M fashion, he was brought back to corporate headquarters where he could be given experiences that would provide him with the background and knowledge to help him succeed in top-level positions.

Through the 1980s, he was assigned to head up each of 3M's three business sectors in succession, to broaden his knowledge of their markets and technologies as well as to refine the skills necessary to have an impact on their performance. After spending most of his career focused on the company's far-flung units in Canada, Australia, and Latin America, it was important for him to get a better sense of the organization's core structure, processes, and culture. By immersing him in corporate-level activities for more than a decade, 3M's top management and the board's appraisal committee wanted to ensure that he had the organizational understanding that was vital for any leader. Finally, DeSimone's promotion to the board in 1986 was important not only in bringing his expertise to board-level decisions, but also in broadening him as an executive by exposing him to the perspectives and experiences of top-level executives from other companies in different industries.

In companies like 3M where an understanding of the strongly held organizational values and cultural norms are central to the source of competitive advantage, the importance of a career-long development process must not be underestimated. Sometimes, however, a manager's strong links to the company's existing policies and practices become disadvantageous, particularly when the embedded beliefs have deteriorated into blind assumptions or outmoded conventional wisdom. In such cases, selection of an outsider with the desired personal characteristics can break the pathological cycle of inwardly focused indoctrination. But it does so at the risk of stranding the new leader without the relevant knowledge required to develop the appropriate top management skills for the company. The risks are particularly high were knowledge and experience accumulated in prior work is of limited relevance in the new situation. So while Larry Bossidy was able to make a relatively smooth transition from his top management job at GE to the leadership of Allied, another traditionally structured diversified industrial goods company, John Sculley's move from Pepsico to Apple became problematic due to his lack of computer industry background and his inexperience in managing the more informal network culture of Silicon Valley. Such problems underscore the important linkage between personal traits and acquired knowledge, on the one hand, and the development of the skills and abilities required to perform a job effectively, on the other.

Coaching for Skills Mastery   Of all the elements in the competencies profile, the particular skills and abilities an individual develops are probably the best indicators of job success, since they are the most directly linked to a position's key roles and tasks. Not everyone becomes effective in these highly specific yet critical personal skills, and the challenge for management is to identify those who can succeed and to help them develop these skills. The reason is that most of these skills rely heavily on tacit knowledge and capabilities that often grow out of the interaction between an individual's embedded traits and accumulated experience. So, for example, the critical entrepreneurial ability to recognize potential in people and situations is not an easily trainable skill, but one that often develops naturally in individuals who are curious and intuitive by nature and who have developed a richly textured understanding of their particular business and organizational environment.

Thus while some broader skills can be selected for and other simpler ones can be trained for, most of the critical skills are largely self-developed through on-the-job experience as individuals apply their natural talents and accumulated experience to the particular challenges of the job. In this process, the most effective role management can play is to coach and support those they have selected and prepared for the job by providing the resources, reinforcement, and guidance to encourage the self-development process.

ABB executive vice president Goran Lindahl clearly articulated the notion that an individual's natural characteristics should be the dominant factor in selection: "I will always pick a person with tenacity over one with just experience." Lindahl also spent a substantial amount of his time planning developmental job experiences for the individuals he selected. However, he considered his principal and most difficult management role to be acting as a teacher and a coach to help those in the organization leverage their experiences and fulfill their natural potential. It was this commitment "to help engineers become managers, and managers grow into leaders" that was vital to the development of the skills required to meet the demanding new job requirements.

Don Jans was surprised when he was asked to continue to head the relays company that ABB took over as part of the acquired Westinghouse power transmission and distribution business. "The prevailing view was that we had lost the war," he said, "and that the occupying troops would just move in." Yet Lindahl and Ulf Gundemark (his worldwide relays business manager) were impressed that Jans, like most of the Westinghouse managers, was a very capable individual with long industry experience. They felt that, with proper coaching, his natural energy, persistence, and competitiveness could be channeled towards the new skills he would need to manage in a very different way within ABB.

Jans met their expectations and—with his bosses' encouragement, support, and coaching—was able to develop a whole range of new skills that helped him turn around his relays company. By redefining Jans's company as part of an interdependent global network, ABB's senior-level management was able to refocus his attention on export markets, thereby helping him reignite his latent ability to identify and exploit opportunities. Through their own highly motivating and inspiring management approach, Barnevik, Lindhal, Gundemark, and others provided Jans with role models that encouraged him to tap into his own engaging personality and develop a more motivating approach to drive his people to higher levels of performance. ABB's cultural norm of high interest and involvement in the operations (what Lindahl called the "fingers in the pie" approach) led Jans to expand on his natural results-orientated competitiveness and develop a skill for creating and sustaining energy around the demanding objectives he set for his organization.

Meanwhile, Lindahl was helping support a very different set of new skills in the select few operating-level entrepreneurs that had been identified to take on senior-level business or regional responsibilities. One such individual was Ulf Gundemark, the young manager who was running the Swedish relays company and who had twelve years of experience in various parts of the organization. Lindahl promoted him to worldwide relays manager because he demonstrated the vital personality characteristics that Lindahl described as "generous, flexible, and statesmanlike." Driven by his boss's urging to become a "giver" rather than a "receiver" of management resources and constrained by his lack of division-level staff, Gundemark leveraged his naturally supportive disposition into a sophisticated skill of developing the operating-level managers reporting to him by delegating responsibilities and empowering them to make decisions. Lindahl also encouraged Gundemark to establish formal and informal management forums at all levels of his organization. By applying his flexible and integrative personality to his growing understanding of the organizational dynamics, Gundemark gradually acquired a strong ability to develop interpersonal relationships and team behavior. Finally, largely by following the example of his boss, Gundemark developed the vital senior management skill of maintaining the pressure for both long- and short-term objectives while helping the organization to deal with the conflicts that were implied. Although many were unwilling or unable to manage the very different task requirements of a senior manager's job (indeed, Lindahl estimated that even after careful selection, half the candidates for these positions either stepped aside or were moved out of the role), managers like Gundemark—who were able to develop their people skills and relationship-building skills—usually succeeded in these roles.

At the top levels of management, an even more subtle and sophisticated set of skills and abilities was necessary. More than just driving the company's ongoing operations or developing its resources and capabilities, these individuals had to be able to lead the company to becoming what Lindahl

described as "a self-driven, self-renewing organization." The most fundamental skill was one that CEO Percy Barnevik had encouraged in all his top team—to create an exciting and demanding work environment. Harnessing his own innate restlessness, Lindahl focused his naturally striving and questioning personal style on his broad knowledge of the company and its businesses to develop a finely honed ability to challenge managers' assumptions while stretching them to reach for new objectives. His bi-monthly business meetings were far from traditional review sessions. Lindahl led his senior managers through scenario exercises that forced them to think beyond straight-line projections and consider how they could respond to new trade barriers, political realignments, or environmental legislation. He also recognized that it was top management's role to develop the organization's values. "In the end," he said "managers are not really loyal to a particular boss or even to a company, but to the values they represent." One of the most vital was to create an environment of mutual cooperation and trust. By consistently applying his own natural forthright and open personal approach to a sophisticated understanding of the organization, he was able to create a belief in the institution and in the fairness of its management processes that was a prior condition for both entrepreneurial risk taking and shared organizational learning.

Finally, Lindahl's sharp mind and inspiring personal manner were able to articulate messages that provided the organization with conceptual insight about the business while simultaneously providing them with concrete motivational challenges. He routinely demonstrated this ability in his far-sighted views about ABB's role in helping develop the industrial infrastructure in a realigned global political economy. Furthermore, he translated those insights into challenges for his management. As a result of his skills and abilities, the company was able to radically rebalance its own value chain from the developed world to the emerging giants such as China, India, and Eastern Europe.

The reason this set of top management skills is so difficult to develop is that it both reflects and reinforces the conflicts, dilemmas, and paradoxes framed by the post-transformational organization. Unlike the classic top management task that focused on managing "alignment" and ensuring "fit," the role we have described involves at least as much energy being devoted to questioning, challenging and even defying the company's traditional strategic assumptions and embedded organizational practices. The required competencies involve an even greater level of subtlety and sophistication to maintain a balance between challenging embedded beliefs and creating a unifying sense of purpose and ambition. Not surprisingly, only a handful of people have the potential to develop these scarce leadership skills, and perhaps the most critical task of top management is to identify these individuals and provide them with the necessary development opportunities and coaching support to allow them to fulfill that potential.

From Organization Man to Individualized Corporation

The dramatic changes in management roles and the individual competencies required to implement them are part of a broader redefinition of the relationship between the corporation and its employees in the post-transformational organization. In earlier decades, when capital was the scarce resource, top management's primary role was to use its control over investments to determine strategy as well as to create structures and systems to shape employee behavior in ways that would support those capital allocation decisions. The strategy-structure-systems doctrine of management led to the development of what William Whyte termed "the organization man"—the employee whose behavior was molded to suit the needs of the corporation and to support its strategic investments.

As the industrial era evolves into the information age, however, the scarce resource is shifting from capital to knowledge. But because the organization's vital knowledge, expertise, and strategic information exist at the operating levels rather than at the top, the whole authoritarian hierarchy has had to be dismantled and the roles and tasks of each management level radically redefined. Far from wanting to subjugate individual differences by requiring conformity to a standardized organizational model, companies are recognizing that in a knowledge-based environment, diversity of employee perspectives, experience, and capabilities can be an important organizational asset.

This realization implies a fundamental reconceptualization of the underlying management philosophy. Instead of forcing the individual to conform to the company's policies and practices, the overall objective is to capture and leverage the knowledge and expertise that each organizational member brings to the company. Thus the notion of "the organization man" and the Russian Doll model of nested roles that it reflected and supported are giving way to a concept we call "the individualized corporation"— one that capitalizes on the idiosyncrasies and even the eccentricities of exceptional people by recognizing, developing, and applying their unique capabilities.

This change in organizational philosophy has important implications for management practice. One of the most basic needs is to change the multitude of personnel practices aimed at recruiting, developing, and promoting people on the basis of a single corporate model—an approach most recently exemplified by the unrealistic competency lists of personal characteristics, many of which seem to resemble the idealized profile of the Boy Scout Law (trustworthy, loyal, helpful, friendly, and so on). Equally important, however, is the need for employees to accept that their career paths may not lead inexorably up the hierarchy, but will more likely take them where they best fit and therefore where they can add the most value for the organization. Together these changes are exposing the myth of the generic manager and are redefining the basic relationship between companies and their employees in a way that recognizes and capitalizes on diversity rather than trying to minimize and suppress it.

Reading 8-2   The New Global Game: How Your Company Can Win in the Knowledge Economy

Y. Doz, J. Santos, and P. J. Williamson

The global game has changed. Yesterday, competing in for a share of the global economy meant building an efficient network of production, sales, and service subsidiaries capable of *penetrating markets around the world*. But the demands of the new knowledge economy are turning this strategy on its head. Today the challenge is to innovate by *learning from the world*. Whether you aspire to be a successful global company or a national champion, your company will have to differentiate itself by searching out and mobilizing untapped pockets of technology and market intelligence that are scattered across the globe and using that knowledge as the raw material to fuel innovation.

In this article we explore why this new kind of global competitive game is emerging, what it means for the way companies will compete in the future, and how companies need to respond to improve their chances of winning.

The Changing Global Game

Fifty years ago winning the global competitive game was about *selling* internationally—opening up export markets—because back then few companies had the capabilities, information and knowledge to sell outside their home markets. Twenty five years ago the game was about *investing* internationally—to create an efficient network of production, sales and distribution operations through foreign direct investment. Again, at a time when only leading multinationals

knew how to efficiently set up, manage, and adapt their products and processes in a foreign environment, they could rely on these capabilities to underpin higher profits than their purely domestic rivals. More recently, companies have sought competitive advantage in their capability at international sourcing, not only of raw materials and components, but of services and information as well. This kind of sourcing expertise used to be a scarce skill.

The Curse of Mobility   But as the global mobility of products, investment, and information has improved, companies have found themselves in a vicious cycle of declining competitive advantage. Today's markets are so efficient that anything that is mobile: capital, goods, and information is now quite readily accessible by all the competitors that count. As a result, it's harder and harder for companies to rely on even the best worldwide sourcing of materials, components, or information to gain advantage, because their competitors can do the same. Nor will having a network of subsidiaries capable of manufacturing and selling products around the world going to set them apart—too many competitors can now perform that trick as well. In this sense, the increased mobility of investment, physical products and information that can be expressed as bits and bytes has become the curse of traditional ways of gaining competitive advantage.

But there is one thing that still sets some companies apart from their competitors: the depth and diversity of complex knowledge they have been able to accumulate and exploit. Complex knowledge such as:

- A detailed understanding emerging needs among lead customers

▌ This article is based on the authors' book: *From Global to Metanational: How Companies Win in the Knowledge Economy,* published by Harvard Business School Press in November 2001. For more on this subject see the website www.metanational.net

- A grasp of how competition is evolving in bell-whether markets
- Mastery of complex, new technologies that cannot easily be codified and spurted across the Internet

There are reasons why this kind of complex knowledge differentiates leading companies, and helps keep them ahead of competition are three-fold. First, its forward-looking, so its helps them innovate to stay ahead of the competitive game. Second, its "messy"—in the sense that its difficult to codify and make explicit. Third, its "sticky"—in that its hard to disentangle from its existing context and use somewhere else. These last two characteristics that make this kind of complex knowledge difficult for competitors to learn and apply. Rivals therefore find it difficult to imitate competitive advantages that rely on this kind of knowledge.

The Global Knowledge Game   If it is the quality and extent of your company's stock of complex knowledge base that ultimately matters in creating competitive advantage in today's high-mobility world, then who has the edge in this new game of knowledge stakes? Consider some examples:

A money-losing semiconductor firm in Southern Europe became a world leader by combining knowledge drawn from customers in places as diverse as San Jose, California; Tokyo; and Helsinki with pockets of technical expertise scattered from Grenoble to Milan, Noida (in Uttar Pradesh, India), Ang Mo Kio (in Singapore), and Carrolton (in Texas). With this unique combination of specialist knowledge, the firm was able to achieve something that eluded its competitors: It created tailored solutions for customer applications by incorporating dozens of specialized circuits on a single silicon chip. This breakthrough capability provided ST Microelectronics with the foundation for a semiconductor business that has created more than $50 billion in shareholder value and employs more than 40,000 people around the world.

A record company built an organization capable of identifying future global "hit artists" from local talent in the bars and clubs of cities like Sao Paolo, Reykjavik, Naples, Paris, Athens, and Hong Kong. By connecting this new talent with its own detailed knowledge of the international music markets and its global capabilities in creating, promoting, and distributing new albums, the company was able to sell millions of recordings by these new stars. This capability proved critical to building what was to become the world's largest record company: Polygram netted its owners a sale price of more than $10 billion in 1998.

A start-up flat-panel display company successfully entered an industry in which competitors have invested hundreds of millions of dollars to establish themselves. It did so by accessing capabilities it found inside institutions and companies including LETI (France), Motorola (USA), Raytheon (USA), Futaba (Japan), Rhône Poulenc (France), SAES-Getters (Italy), Unipac (Taiwan), and Sumitomo (Japan) to create a new type of flat-panel display. This unorthodox strategy allowed PixTech to achieve the advantages of global scale overnight.

Certainly each of these companies innovated using complex knowledge that their competitors would have found it hard either to buy or to innovate. But they went one better: all three innovated by combining complex knowledge drawn from different sources scattered around the world. The kind of innovations they came up with were therefore very hard for competitors to copy. To have a chance of matching ST Microelectronics, Polygram or Pixtech, competitors were not only faced with the problem of mastering complex knowledge, they also had to overcome the challenges of identifying and accessing knowledge from multiple locations scattered across the globe, and then of moving and combining this knowledge in ways that would allow them to innovate.

Five years of detailed research into how these an other companies have turned the curse of mobility to their advantage has led us to a simple, but far-reaching conclusion: *The winners in the global knowledge economy will be those companies with a superior capability to access, mobilise and leverage untapped pockets of knowledge scattered around the world.*

The question for senior management is this: How well is your company equipped to win this new, knowledge game?

▮ Fishing in the Global Knowledge Pool

To win in the new global knowledge game a company first needs to be able to gather more distinctive knowledge than its competitors, and do it faster. But where are most companies fishing for this kind of knowledge?

In most cases the answer is in a limited, local pond in their home country, around the headquarters or a handful of R&D sites. Consider a simple statistic: For US-owned firms, a recent study found that just under 9% of their patents came from research conducted abroad. But does any of these companies really believe that 91% of all new technical knowledge relevant to their business is being produced in their home country? Or does historical inertia cause them to fish for new knowledge in their local pool? This myopia about where to fish for new knowledge isn't confined to US companies either. A survey of 144 of the world's largest industrial firms about the role of their different geographic units in building competitive advantage concluded: "the sample firms perceived that their domestic operations and/or indigenous resources and capabilities of their home countries continued to provide the main source of competitiveness—especially in terms of technological capacity and skilled professional manpower."[1]

There are may reasons companies tend to fish for new knowledge around their birthplace: for most of them it has historically been the fount of innovation, it is probably where they have the greatest concentration of qualified people, it is a familiar context that makes it easy to internalise the knowledge they acquire.

But ask Motorola is if fishing almost exclusively in the US knowledge pool was sufficient to keep it globally competitive in the mobile telecommunications business? Knowledge from the Nordic countries that was used by Nokia and Ericsson turned out to be critical in the global competitive race. Ask

the Finns or the Swedes if they were paying enough attention to what was happening in Japan before NTT DoCoMo's "i-mode" stole a march as the first mobile broad-band success?

Mobile telephony is not a quirky exception. In industry after industry we studied, the knowledge companies need to keep up in the innovation race was becoming more and more dispersed around the world.

The Increasing Dispersion of Knowledge You Need   Eight fundamental forces are driving this trend toward greater global dispersion of the knowledge that companies need to win globally. We group them into two categories: those driving the dispersion of technological knowledge and those driving dispersion of market knowledge.

Forces Driving Dispersion of Technological Knowledge

- *Industry Convergence.* As industries converge, different streams of technology converge, and companies will need to master a more diverse range of technologies. But these industries and technologies have tended to grow up in different locations around the world. To access the new technologies, companies must therefore draw from a wider range of locations. For example, because the pharmaceutical and biotechnology industries developed in different places, the convergence of these industries means pharmaceutical companies can no longer rely on their home base as the source of innovation. They need to draw technology from a broader set of locations. Or witness the way in which the convergence of publishing, broadcasting, and the Internet has increased the range of technologies (and hence the geographic sources) that companies such as AOL Time Warner or Bertelsmann need to reach consumers in the electronic age.
- *Technology Transfer.* As multinationals transplant competencies to new locations through their subsidiaries, new pools of competencies will develop. As a result, the pools of specialist

---

[1] John H. Dunning, "The Geographical Sources of Competitiveness of Firms: Some Results from a New Survey," *Transnational Corporations* 5, no. 3 (1996).

knowledge a company could usefully access for innovation becomes more dispersed. When Hewlett-Packard moved its process engineering skills from the United States to Singapore to manufacture calculators, for example, it set off a chain of events in which the engineers there began to alter the calculator designs, gradually building a design competence that was then applied to keyboards and eventually to the complete design of inkjet printers, so that a new competency pool emerged on the other side of the world.

- *Offshore Sourcing.* As companies use contract manufacturing located outside traditional clusters, the sources of new knowledge that flow from manufacturing process improvements will also become more dispersed. Today, for example, Taiwan has an almost 70 percent share of the world manufacturing of scanners and a more than 60 percent share of the world manufacturing of computer keyboards and mice. Although the core technologies may have originated in California, it is inevitable that new knowledge about the manufacture and design of these components will be generated in Taiwan. Again, this drives increased dispersion of the knowledge that companies need.

- *Technological Complexity.* As products become more complex, the relevant sources of knowledge needed to design, market, and deliver them to customers become more dispersed. Most of the knowledge required to produce a simple, standard product may be found in a single location. But consider what knowledge is required today to develop and build a new aircraft. Hundreds of specialized technologies from materials science to advanced avionics and artificial intelligence must be brought together, along with a detailed understanding of the different economics of individual airlines' route structures and service aspirations. As Boeing discovered when it set out to develop its 777 aircraft, the plethora of knowledge and capabilities required simply didn't exist in the United States, let alone Seattle, despite the city's long history of airframe design and manufacture.

- *"Random" Breakthroughs.* New technological breakthroughs still have a large element of serendipity. Random events don't always occur in the strongest existing clusters or locations with the most resources devoted to a particular problem. For instance, the creation of the "www" (World Wide Web) and "http" occurred in Geneva, Switzerland, at the European High-Energy Particle Physics Lab, CERN (around 1990), as a tool to enable collaboration between physicists and other researchers. A couple of years later it was picked up by a few students at the University of Illinois, and Mosaic (the precursor of Netscape) was born. In early 1997, the world was amazed by Dolly, a lamb cloned from the DNA of an adult sheep mammary. Dolly was "created" by researchers in Edinburgh, Scotland—not the most obvious source of a breakthrough in genetic engineering.

Forces Driving Dispersion of Market Knowledge

- *New Customer Interactions.* As products and services are introduced into new, formerly peripheral markets, new knowledge about potential customer applications or tastes will emerge from fragmented locations. In adapting its product to the Buenos Aires market for ice cream, for example, Haagen-Daz developed its "dulce de leche" flavor, named after the popular Argentine caramelized milk dessert. Within a year, the new Argentine flavor was introduced throughout the United States and Europe, where it sold more than all but vanilla in the stores carrying it.

- *Globalization of Customers.* As corporate customers, distributors, and retailers themselves become more global, the relevant knowledge they have accumulated will become more dispersed in small pockets across their own organizations. In seeking the knowledge of hard disk drives it needed from Seagate, for example, ST Microelectronics discovered that the information was dispersed throughout Seagate's operations in the United States and Asia.

- *Solution Selling.* As more and more companies sell "solutions" rather than separate products or services, they will need to bring together dispersed knowledge, as the know-how that underpins all of the pieces of a complex solution is unlikely to be found in a single location. As IBM has moved away from selling hardware alone and toward selling solutions, for example, it has found an increasing need to bring together knowledge of the customer with hardware, software, and systems-integration expertise from sources both inside and outside IBM in different locations spread around the world.

These eight forces are combining to drive ever-greater dispersion in the knowledge sets that companies need to win in the new global economy. A survey we conducted among European and U.S. multinationals in 1998 underscores the trend. On average, respondents expected that over the next five years almost half of the breakthrough technologies in their industry would come from outside their home continent. Likewise, they anticipated that 42 percent of the most innovative products would emerge outside their home continent.

Building Your Company's "Sensing" Network

In order to rise to the challenge of increased knowledge dispersion, a company needs to extend its capabilities in identifying new sources of relevant technologies, competencies, and understanding about leading-edge customers. This means learning how to sense and process this complex knowledge into a form that the corporation can use efficiently. But identifying and accessing knowledge that rivals have already mastered will only bring competitive parity. Building new sources of competitive advantage requires a *sensing network* that can identify innovative technologies or emerging customer needs that competitors have overlooked—a network that pre-empts global sources of new knowledge. The prevailing logic of sensing is *discovery and reconnaissance*.

Sensing involves the following:

- The capacity to identify a *sensing need*. A goal, even if broadly defined, is essential to move

from aimless exploration to purposeful reconnaissance work.
- The capability to *prospect* the world for sources of relevant knowledge, unearthing new pockets of knowledge ahead of competitors.
- The capacity to *access* new knowledge once its location is identified—not a trivial task when the required knowledge is complex or when it needs to be pried loose from a tight-knit local club.

Your sensing network may be comprised of:

- Alliances with lead customers, suppliers, other partners, or even competitors who can provide access to new market or technical knowledge.
- Targeted acquisitions to access specialist know-how.
- Links with venture capital funds to intercept promising new technologies or ideas at an early stage.
- Cooperation with universities or research institutes in various parts of the world.
- "Roving reporters" charged with identifying and assessing out pockets of emerging technologies or new customer applications.
- Existing subsidiaries and sites as they generate new knowledge in the course of adapting your products and services to local markets.

Mobilising Dispersed and Fragmented Knowledge

It is clearly not enough for a company to amass a rich hoard of knowledge from around the world. Stopping there risks becoming exceptionally well informed, but impotent. The winners in the knowledge economy will be those companies that can not only access this dispersed knowledge, but also mobilise it to create innovative products, services, processes and business models and then leverage these innovations across the world's markets through an large-scale, efficient network of operations.

This requires building a set of structures (which may be virtual, temporary, or both) to translate new knowledge into innovative products or specific market opportunities. These new structures (the evidence suggests that existing operating units and systems will seldom do the job) need to mobilize knowledge that is scattered in pockets around the corporation and use it to pioneer new products and services, sometimes with the help of lead customers. Polygram created such a structure—the international repertoire network—for unlocking the potential appeal of unknown global artists. This new structure enabled Polygram to connect and mobilize a complex bundle of dispersed knowledge about new acts, international markets, and local capabilities to create international hits.

We call these structures "magnets." They may take the form of a project to develop a new solution for a lead customer, to design a global product or service platform, or units such as Polygram's International Repertoire Centres staffed by people dedicated to mobilising and leveraging knowledge that is scattered around the world. Whatever their organisational form, these magnets attract dispersed, potentially relevant knowledge and use it to create innovative products, services, or processes, and they then facilitate the transfer of these innovations into the network of day-to-day operations. The battle here will be to design and operate a better set of magnets than your competitors—activities where the driving forces here are *entrepreneurship* and *mobilization.*

Leveraging Innovations

Once a new product, service, or business model has been pioneered, its profit potential must be realized. This means scaling up the supply chain, improving efficiencies, making incremental improvements, and engineering local adaptations. Most multinationals are already proficient in this arena where the logic is *efficiency, flexibility,* and *financial discipline.*

Just as in the industrial economy, therefore, the ability to produce, market, distribute and sell products and services around the globe will be critical. But the ability to reap the benefits of global leverage and local adaptation will be given taken for granted among premier league companies. What will distinguish the leaders from the followers will

be the capability to access, mobilise and leverage the global knowledge pool to come up with innovations that open up "clear blue water" between them and their competitors.

Three Paths to Success in the Knowledge Economy

For every company, winning in the knowledge economy means building the capabilities to access, mobilise and leverage knowledge more effectively and faster than the competition. Few companies will be able to win this game fishing in a restricted, local knowledge pond. The success stories of the future will excel in sensing specialist knowledge about new technologies and emerging market needs that are scattered anywhere around the globe. They will mobilize this dispersed knowledge to create new products, services, processes and business models. They will harvest value from those innovations by leveraging them across their chosen markets.

What it takes to address this challenge depends on your corporate starting point. There are three main paths to success in the knowledge economy.

National Champions Need to Begin "Learning from the World"   National champions who have historically located their key knowledge activities in their own back yard need to build their capability to "learn from the world" by:

- Building a "sensing" organisation capable of prospecting for and accessing new pockets of knowledge scattered around the world
- Fostering a corporate culture that transcends the home culture
- Building a cosmopolitan management team

A practical place to start is to select a potential innovation project—a new business area, a new product or service—where the relevant knowledge does not all lie on home turf. Set it up to act as a magnet for knowledge dispersed around the world. The goal is to demonstrate the worth of innovation based on learning from distant and unfamiliar locations. In implementing this first pilot a number of guidelines are helpful to bear in mind:

- *Pick a pilot project of strategic importance that is largely outside the realm of existing operational experience.* By choosing such a project, the need to find and access knowledge from places and areas of expertise where the company is not currently strong will become obvious to all.
- *Use the pilot project to get people involved in prospecting and sensing.* A good pilot project will create, and clearly demonstrate, the need to look outside the company and the home base for new knowledge. This reinforces the value of sensing activities.
- *Set up a magnet around a lead customer, a new product or service platform, or new activity.* A good magnet will encourage magnet will require moving and melding knowledge from many different locations.
- *Include a set of people with diverse backgrounds in the magnet team.* Err on the side of excessive interaction and communications among members until your company gains experience in moving and melding complex knowledge from different sources.
- *As the innovation takes shape, forge a direct link between the magnet and the day-to-day operating network.* When the innovation has an unknown pedigree, there are likely to be severe problems in getting the day-to-day operations to adopt it. It is therefore important to forge a direct link between the magnet team and a receptive part of your operation that must leverage it.

Visible success in a few pilot projects will be far more effective than rhetoric or coercion in convincing your company of the benefits from "learning from the world."

Multinationals Need to Unlock the Knowledge Locally Imprisoned in Their Subsidiaries

A geographically fragmented knowledge base is the enemy of companies with a strong network of proud and semi-independent national subsidiaries. Above all else, they must take initiatives to fight fragmentation by mobilising knowledge imprisoned in their own local subsidiaries. Specific initiatives include:

- Setting up an innovation project that depends on connecting knowledge from a number of locations—for example, a project that leverages off the convergence of two technologies developed in subsidiaries or sites in different parts of the world.
- Break the assumption that "voice equals weight"—i.e, that large and profitable subsidiaries dominate the innovation agenda. Break the traditional assumption that small or peripheral subsidiaries should have little "voice" in the innovation process
- Emphasise the opportunities wasted by the failure to leverage past innovations across the globe

Select a lead customer, a global platform, or a global activity to act as a magnet for an innovation that is only possible by mobilizing knowledge scattered around the organization. To be effective, this magnet must transcend the boundaries of national subsidiaries. It must demonstrate the importance of magnets in unlocking global value from knowledge that is imprisoned in local subsidiaries or their environments. It must also persuade sceptical country managers that they can benefit by making use of innovations that are the product of mobilising knowledge from different parts of the world. However, it is important to avoid the trap of trying to transform an existing multinational operations network into something that can undertake the sensing or magnet functions as well. Sensing, mobilizing, and leveraging need to remain distinct and differentiated roles. The existing operations should remain focused on leveraging innovations. New structures need to be put in place to act as sensing units and innovation magnets.

Startups and New Globalizers Need to Leapfrog Existing Competitors

Today's budding multinationals and new economy companies it means leapfrogging their older cousins to build "Metanational" companies designed to win the new global game, rather than emulating the internationalisation strategies of the past.[2] This means:

- Don't create a senior management ghetto in a single location.
- Seek out and leverage global diversity—recruit people from multiple nationalities and backgrounds from the start; look for unity in a common corporate culture and value system, rather than shared nationality or business experience.
- Assess each international foray according to the ratio of learning over investment.
- Leverage partners to make yourself an "instantly global."

The goal is to create a new type of Metanational company that will be tuned to harness and exploit this hidden potential of knowledge scattered around the globe by building new structures, teams, and processes around global lead customers, global platforms, and global activities. These structures will form a new sub-organization dedicated to entrepreneurship and innovation, with a unique set of roles, responsibilities, culture, and incentives. A flexible, efficient operating network, augmented by the capabilities of suppliers, subcontractors, and alliance partners, will turn these metanational innovations into global profits and shareholder value.

Conclusion

Winning in the global knowledge economy is not about choosing between innovation and operating efficiency, or between exploitation and entrepreneurship. It is about winning a global tournament played at three different levels: It is a race to identify and access new technologies and market trends ahead of the competition, a race to turn this dispersed knowledge into innovative products and services, and a race to scale and exploit these innovations in markets around the world.

The knowledge economy is now with us. Whether you are a national champion, a multinational or a budding globaliser the question is the same: Do you have what it takes to win?

---

[2]We use the prefix *meta*—from the Greek term for "beyond"—to emphasize a key point: Metanational companies do not draw their competitive advantage from their home country, nor even from a set of national subsidiaries. Metanationals view the world as a global canvas dotted with pockets of technology, market intelligence, and capabilities. They see untapped potential in these pockets of specialist knowledge scattered around the world. By sensing and mobilising this scattered knowledge, they are able to innovate more effectively than their rivals.

Index

N

O

P